Y0-ABO-517

Customer Support Information

Plunkett's Green Technology Industry Almanac 2012

Please register your book immediately...

if you did not purchase it directly from Plunkett Research, Ltd. This will enable us to fulfill your requests for assistance. Also, it will enable us to notify you of future editions.

Your purchase includes access to Book Data and Exports online

As a book purchaser, you can register for free, 1-year, 1-seat online access to the latest data for your book's industry trends, statistics and company profiles. This includes tools to export company data. Simply send us this registration form, and we will send you a user name and password. In this manner, you will have access to our continual updates during the year. Certain restrictions apply.

_____ YES, please register me as a purchaser of the book.
I did not buy it directly from Plunkett Research, Ltd.

_____ YES, please register me for free online access. I am the actual, original purchaser. (Proof of purchase may be required.)

Customer Name _____

Title_____

Organization _____

Address _____

City_____State_____Zip_____

Country (if other than USA) _____

Phone_____Fax _____

E-mail _____

Return to: **Plunkett Research®, Ltd.**

Attn: Registration
P.O. Drawer 541737, Houston, TX 77254-1737 USA
713.932.0000 · Fax 713.932.7080 · www.plunkettresearch.com
customersupport@plunkettresearch.com

* Purchasers of used books are not eligible to register. Use of online access is subject to the terms of the end user license agreement.

PLUNKETT'S GREEN TECHNOLOGY INDUSTRY ALMANAC 2012

The only comprehensive guide to green companies & trends

Jack W. Plunkett

Published by:
Plunkett Research®, Ltd., Houston, Texas
www.plunkettresearch.com

PLUNKETT'S GREEN TECHNOLOGY INDUSTRY ALMANAC 2012

Editor and Publisher:
Jack W. Plunkett

Executive Editor and Database Manager:
Martha Burgher Plunkett

Senior Editor and Researcher:
Jill Steinberg

Editors, Researchers and Assistants:
Keith Beeman, III
Kalonji Bobb
Elizabeth Braddock
Xiaowen Chen
Jamey Crane
Jeremy Faulk
Larissa Matin
Isaac Snider
Suzanne Zarosky

Enterprise Accounts Managers:
Emily Hurley
Kelly Burke

Information Technology Manager:
Wenping Guo

Information Technology Intern:
Danil K. Safin

Video & Graphics Manager:
Geoffrey Trudeau

Special Thanks to:
Ernst & Young
International Energy Agency
International Service for the Acquisition of Agri-biotech Applications
Organization for Economic Cooperation & Development
Roland Berger
The Economist
U.S. Bureau of Labor Statistics
U.S. Census Bureau
U.S. Department of Energy
U.S. Energy Information Administration
United Nations
Waterfootprint.org

Plunkett Research®, Ltd.
P. O. Drawer 541737, Houston, Texas 77254 USA
Phone: 713.932.0000   Fax: 713.932.7080
www.plunkettresearch.com

Published by:
Plunkett Research®, Ltd.
P. O. Drawer 541737
Houston, Texas 77254-1737

Phone: 713.932.0000
Fax: 713.932.7080
Internet: www.plunkettresearch.com

ISBN13 # 978-1-60879-672-4
(eBook Edition # 978-1-60879-934-3)

PLUNKETT'S GREEN TECHNOLOGY INDUSTRY ALMANAC 2012

CONTENTS

Continued on next page

A Short Green Technology Industry Glossary

10-K: An annual report filed by publicly held companies. It provides a comprehensive overview of the company's business and its finances. By law, it must contain specific information and follow a given form, the "Annual Report on Form 10-K." The U.S. Securities and Exchange Commission requires that it be filed within 90 days after fiscal year end. However, these reports are often filed late due to extenuating circumstances. Variations of a 10-K are often filed to indicate amendments and changes. Most publicly held companies also publish an "annual report" that is not on Form 10-K. These annual reports are more informal and are frequently used by a company to enhance its image with customers, investors and industry peers.

Agricultural Biotechnology (AgriBio): The application of biotechnology methods to enhance agricultural plants and animals.

Alternative Fuel: Includes methanol, denatured ethanol and other alcohols, separately or in mixtures of 85% by volume or more with gasoline or other fuels, CNG, LNG, LPG, hydrogen, coal derived liquid fuels, fuels other than alcohols derived from biological materials, electricity, neat biodiesel, or any other fuel determined to be substantially not petroleum and yielding substantial energy security benefits and substantial environmental benefits. It is defined pursuant to the EPACT (Energy Policy Act of 1992), alternative fuels.

Alternative Fuels Data Center (AFDC): A program sponsored by the Department of Energy to collect emissions, operational and maintenance data on all types of alternative fuel vehicles across the country.

Alternative Fuels Utilization Program (AFUP): A program managed by Department of Energy with the goals of improving national energy security by displacing imported oil; improving air quality through the development and widespread use of alternative fuels for transportation and increasing the production of alternative fuel vehicles.

Alternative Motor Fuels Act of 1988 (AMFA): Public Law 100-494. Encourages the development, production and demonstration of alternative motor fuels and alternative fuel vehicles.

Alternative-Fuel Provider: A fuel provider (or any affiliate or business unit under its control) is an alternative-fuel provider if its principal business is producing, storing, refining, processing, transporting, distributing, importing or selling (at wholesale or retail) any alternative fuel (other than electricity); or generating, transmitting, importing or selling (at wholesale or retail) electricity; or if that fuel provider produces, imports, or produces and imports (in combination) an average of 50,000 barrels per day of petroleum, and 30% (a substantial portion) or more of its gross annual revenues are derived from producing alternative fuels.

APAC: Asia Pacific Advisory Committee. A multi-country committee representing the Asia and Pacific region.

Applied Research: The application of compounds, processes, materials or other items discovered during basic research to practical uses. The goal is to move discoveries along to the final development phase.

Baby Boomer: Generally refers to people born from 1946 to 1964. In the U.S., the initial number of Baby Boomers totaled about 78 million. The term evolved to describe the children of soldiers and war industry workers who were involved in World War II and who began forming families after the war's end. In 2011, the oldest Baby Boomers began reaching the traditional retirement age of 65.

Basic Research: Attempts to discover compounds, materials, processes or other items that may be largely or entirely new and/or unique. Basic research may start with a theoretical concept that has yet to be proven. The goal is to create discoveries that can be moved along to applied research. Basic research is sometimes referred to as "blue sky" research.

Bi-Fuel Vehicle: A vehicle with two separate fuel systems designed to run either on an alternative fuel, or on gasoline or diesel, using only one fuel at a time. Bi-fuel vehicles are referred to as "dual-fuel" vehicles in the CAA and EPACT.

Binary Cycle Generation: A method of geothermal electricity generation where lower-temperature geothermal sources are tapped. The geothermal steam source is used to heat another liquid that has a lower boiling point, which then drives the turbine. Also see "Flash Steam Generation."

Biochemical Conversion: The use of enzymes and catalysts to change biological substances chemically to produce energy products. The digestion of organic wastes or sewage by microorganisms to produce methane is an example of biochemical conversion.

Biochemicals: Chemicals that either naturally occur or are identical to naturally occurring substances. Examples include hormones, pheromones and enzymes. Biochemicals function as pesticides through non-toxic, non-lethal modes of action, disrupting insect mating patterns, regulating growth or acting as repellants. They tend to be environmentally desirable, and may be produced by industry from organic sources such as plant waste (biomass). Biochemicals also may be referred to as bio-based chemicals, green chemicals or plant-based chemicals.

Biodiesel: A fuel derived when glycerin is separated from vegetable oils or animal fats. The resulting byproducts are methyl esters (the chemical name for biodiesel) and glycerin which can be used in soaps and cleaning products. It has lower emissions than petroleum diesel and is currently used as an additive to that fuel since it helps with lubricity.

Bioenergy: Useful, renewable energy produced from organic matter, which may either be used directly as a fuel or processed into liquids and gases. See "Biomass."

Bioethanol: A fuel produced by the fermentation of plant matter such as corn. Fermentation is enhanced through the use of enzymes that are created through biotechnology. Also, see "Ethanol."

Biomass: Organic, non-fossil material of biological origin constituting a renewable energy source. The biomass can be burnt as fuel in a system that creates steam to turn a turbine, generating electricity. For example, biomass can include wood chips and agricultural crops.

Biorefinery: A refinery that produces fuels from biomass. These fuels may include bioethanol (produced from corn or other plant matter) or biodiesel (produced from plant or animal matter).

Biotechnology: A set of powerful tools that employ living organisms (or parts of organisms) to make or modify products, improve plants or animals (including humans) or develop microorganisms for specific uses. Biotechnology is most commonly thought of to include the development of human medical therapies and processes using recombinant DNA, cell fusion, other genetic techniques and bioremediation.

B-to-B, or B2B: See "Business-to-Business."

B-to-C, or B2C: See "Business-to-Consumer."

Business-to-Business: An organization focused on selling products, services or data to commercial customers rather than individual consumers. Also known as B2B.

Business-to-Consumer: An organization focused on selling products, services or data to individual consumers rather than commercial customers. Also known as B2C.

California Air Resources Board (CARB): The state agency that regulates the air quality in California. Air quality regulations established by CARB are often stricter than those set by the federal government.

California Low-Emission Vehicle Program: A state requirement for automakers to produce vehicles with fewer emissions than current EPA standards. The five categories of California Low-Emission Vehicle Program standards, from least to most stringent, are TLEV, LEV, ULEV, SULEV and ZEV.

Cap and Trade: A system in which governments attempt to reduce carbon emissions by major industry. First, an overall "cap" is placed, by government regulation, on total carbon emissions for particular companies and/or their industries. The "trade" part of cap and trade allows companies that operate efficiently on a carbon basis, and thereby emit a lower amount of carbon than law allows, to sell or trade the unused part of their carbon allowances to firms that are less efficient.

Capacity Factor: The ratio of the electrical energy produced by a generating unit for a certain period of time to the electrical energy that could have been produced at continuous full-power operation during the same period.

Capex: Capital expenditures.

Capital Expenditures: Expenditures to acquire or add to capital assets that will yield benefits over several years.

Carbon Air Capture: The use of technology to capture carbon dioxide directly from the air. The intent is to reduce the harmful effects of carbon in the atmosphere while capturing and storing carbon dioxide for safe use in industrial and energy applications.

Carbon Capture and Storage: See "Carbon Sequestration (CCS)."

Carbon Dioxide (CO2): A product of combustion that has become an environmental concern in recent years. CO2 does not directly impair human health but is a "greenhouse gas" that traps the earth's heat and contributes to the potential for global warming.

Carbon Intensity: The amount of carbon dioxide that a nation emits, on average, in order to create a unit of GDP (gross domestic product, a measure of economic output).

Carbon Monoxide (CO): A colorless, odorless gas produced by the incomplete combustion of fuels with a limited oxygen supply, as in automobile engines.

Carbon Sequestration (CCS): The absorption and storage of CO2 from the atmosphere by the roots and leaves of plants; the carbon builds up as organic matter in the soil. In the energy industry, carbon sequestration refers to the process of isolating and storing carbon dioxide (a so-called greenhouse gas). One use is to avoid releasing carbon dioxide into the air when burning coal at a coal-fired power plant. Instead, the carbon dioxide is stored in the ground or otherwise stored in a permanent or semi-permanent fashion. Other uses include the return to the ground of carbon dioxide that is produced at natural gas wells, and the introduction of carbon dioxide into oil wells in order to increase internal pressure and production. This process is also known as carbon capture and storage (CCS).

Catalyst: A substance that initiates a chemical reaction or causes it to proceed more rapidly.

CCS: See "Carbon Sequestration (CCS)."

Cellulosic Ethanol: See "Ethanol."

Clean Air Act (CAA): A law setting emissions standards for stationary sources (e.g., factories and power plants). The original Clean Air Act was signed in 1963, and has been amended several times, most recently in 1990 (P.L. 101-549). The amendments of 1970 introduced motor vehicle emission standards (e.g., automobiles and trucks). Criteria pollutants included lead, ozone, CO, SO2, NOx and PM, as well as air toxics. In 1990, reformulated gasoline (RFG) and oxygenated gasoline provisions were added. The RFG provision requires use of RFG all year in certain areas. The oxygenated gasoline provision requires the use of oxygenated gasoline during certain months, when CO and ozone pollution are most serious. The regulations also require certain fleet operators to use clean fuel vehicles in 22 cities.

Clean Fuel Vehicle (CFV): Any vehicle certified by the Environmental Protection Agency as meeting certain federal emissions standards. The three categories of federal CFV standards, from least to most stringent, are LEV, ULEV and ZEV. The ILEV standard is voluntary and does not need to be adopted by states as part of the Clean-Fuel Fleet Program. CFVs are eligible for two federal programs, the California Pilot Program and the Clean-Fuel Fleet Program. CFV exhaust emissions standards for light-duty vehicles and light-duty trucks are numerically similar to those of CARB's California Low-Emission Vehicle Program.

Climate Change (Greenhouse Effect): A theory that assumes an increasing mean global surface temperature of the Earth caused by gases (sometimes referred to as greenhouse gases) in the atmosphere (including carbon dioxide, methane, nitrous oxide, ozone and chlorofluorocarbons). The greenhouse effect allows solar radiation to penetrate the Earth's atmosphere but absorbs the infrared radiation returning to space.

Coalbed Methane (CBM): A natural methane gas that is found in coal seams, while traditional natural gas deposits are trapped in porous rock formations. A small amount of CBM is already produced successfully in the Rocky Mountain region of the U.S.

Cogeneration: See "Combined Heat and Power (CHP) Plant."

Combined Cycle: An electric generating technology in which electricity is produced from waste heat that would otherwise be lost when exiting from one or more gas (combustion) turbines. The exiting heat is routed to a conventional boiler or to a heat recovery steam generator for utilization by a steam turbine in the production of electricity. Such designs increase the efficiency of the electric generating unit. This process is also known as cogeneration or "combined heat and power" (CHP). One novel approach, know as ISCC or integrated solar combined cycle, adds the use of concentrated solar power (CSP) from mirrors, focused on a tower in order to generate additional steam, which is fed into the system. (See "Concentrated Solar Power (CSP).")

Combined Heat and Power (CHP) Plant: A facility that generates power via combined cycle technology. See "Combined Cycle."

Compact Fluorescent Lamp (CFL): A type of light bulb that provides considerable energy savings over traditional incandescent light bulbs.

Compressed Air Energy Storage (CAES): A storage system that directs surplus electricity to a compressor, which pumps air deep into layers of porous sandstone underneath dense, almost impermeable shale. The sandstone expands, trapping the air, which is later released. As the air rushes upward, it fires a turbine on the surface, thereby producing energy.

Compressed Natural Gas (CNG): Natural gas that has been compressed under high pressures, typically between 2000 and 3600 psi, held in a container. The gas expands when released for use as a fuel.

Concentrated Photovoltaic (CPV): A technology in which the use of mirrors, lenses or other items concentrate and thus vastly increase the intensity of sunlight during the photovoltaic process.

Concentrating Photovoltaic Power (CPV): An enhanced solar energy generating plant that relies on photovoltaic technology, but uses an advanced optical system to focus a large area of sunlight onto each cell for maximum efficiency. CPV panels are mounted on trackers (heliostats) to keep the focal point on the cell as the sun moves across the sky.

Concentrating Solar Power (CSP): The use of solar thermal collectors to absorb solar heat and then heat water, oil or other substances with that energy. CSP technologies include the use of large numbers of

mirrors that reflect and concentrate sunlight upon "solar towers." As heat accumulates in the solar towers, it produces steam that is used to drive turbines and generate electricity. In the latest systems, CSP utilizes heliostats, or motor-driven mirrors, to track the sun through the sky during the day. (See "Heliostat.")

Contract Manufacturing: A business arrangement whereby a company manufactures products that will be sold under the brand names of its client companies. For example, a large number of consumer electronics, such as laptop computers, are manufactured by contract manufacturers for leading brand-name computer companies such as Dell and Apple. Many other types of products, such as shoes and apparel, are made under contract manufacturing. Also see "Original Equipment Manufacturer (OEM)" and "Original Design Manufacturer (ODM)."

CPV: See "Concentrating Photovoltaic Power (CPV)."

CRM: See "Customer Relationship Management (CRM)."

CSP: See "Concentrating Solar Power (CSP)."

Customer Relationship Management (CRM): Refers to the automation, via sophisticated software, of business processes involving existing and prospective customers. CRM may cover aspects such as sales (contact management and contact history), marketing (campaign management and telemarketing) and customer service (call center history and field service history). Well known providers of CRM software include Salesforce, which delivers via a Software as a Service model (see "Software as a Service (Saas)"), Microsoft and Oracle.

Dendrimer: A type of molecule that can be used with small molecules to give them certain desirable characteristics. Dendrimers are utilized in technologies for electronic displays. See "Organic LED (OLED)."

Development: The phase of research and development (R&D) in which researchers attempt to create new products from the results of discoveries and applications created during basic and applied research.

Distributed Power Generation: A method of generating electricity at or near the site where it will be consumed, such as the use of small, local generators or fuel cells to power individual buildings, homes or neighborhoods. Distributed power is thought by many analysts to offer distinct advantages. For example, electricity generated in this manner is not reliant upon the grid for distribution to the end user.

Echo Boomers: See "Generation Y."

ECM: Electronic Contract Manufacturing. See "Contract Manufacturing."

EMEA: The region comprised of Europe, the Middle East and Africa.

Emission: The release or discharge of a substance into the environment. Generally refers to the release of gases or particulates into the air.

EMS: Electronics Manufacturing Services. See "Contract Manufacturing."

Energy Intensity: The amount of energy needed for a nation to produce a unit of GDP (gross domestic product, a measure of economic output).

Energy Policy Act of 1992 (EPACT): (P.L. 102-486) A broad-ranging act signed into law on October 24, 1992. Titles III, IV, V, XV and XIX of EPACT deal with alternative transportation fuels. EPACT accelerates the purchase requirements for alternative fuel vehicles (AFVs) by the federal fleet, proposes eliminating the cap on CAFE credits that manufacturers can earn by producing dual- and flexible-fuel vehicles and requires fleets in large urban areas to purchase AFVs. EPACT also establishes tax incentives for purchasing AFVs, converting conventional gasoline vehicles to operate on alternative fuels and installing refueling or recharging facilities by the private sector.

Enzyme: A protein that acts as a catalyst, affecting the chemical reactions in cells.

Ethanol: A clear, colorless, flammable, oxygenated hydrocarbon, also called ethyl alcohol. In the U.S., it is used as a gasoline octane enhancer and oxygenate in a 10% blend called E10. Ethanol can be used in higher concentrations (such as an 85% blend called E85) in vehicles designed for its use. It is typically produced chemically from ethylene or biologically from fermentation of various sugars from carbohydrates found in agricultural crops and cellulose residues from crops or wood. Grain ethanol production is typically based on corn or sugarcane. Cellulosic ethanol production is based on agricultural waste, such as wheat stalks, that has been treated with enzymes to break the waste down into component sugars.

EU: See "European Union (EU)."

EU Competence: The jurisdiction in which the European Union (EU) can take legal action.

European Community (EC): See "European Union (EU)."

European Union (EU): A consolidation of European countries (member states) functioning as one body to facilitate trade. Previously known as the European Community (EC), the EU expanded to include much of Eastern Europe in 2004, raising the total number of member states to 25. In 2002, the EU launched a unified currency, the Euro. See europa.eu.int.

FASB: See "Financial Accounting Standards Board (FASB)."

FD&C Act: See "Federal Food Drug and Cosmetic Act (FD&C Act)."

Federal Food, Drug and Cosmetic Act (FD&C Act): A set of laws passed by the U.S. Congress, which controls, among other things, residues in food and feed.

Feed-in Tariff (FIT): Guaranteed prices for output from electric generation, typically offered in long-term contracts to firms that operate renewable electric generating plants based on solar, wind or wave technology. The prices are typically much higher than those paid for electricity from conventional power plants, because most renewable sources operate at lower efficiency and higher cost per KWH. The intent is to encourage investment in renewable plants by guaranteeing a price for output that will create a positive return on investment.

Feedstock: Any material converted to another form of fuel or energy product. For example, corn starch can be used as a feedstock for ethanol production.

Financial Accounting Standards Board (FASB): An independent organization that establishes the Generally Accepted Accounting Principles (GAAP).

Flash Steam Generation: The most common type of hydroelectric power generation technique. Flash steam describes a system where a high temperature geothermal steam source can be used to directly drive a turbine. Also see "Binary Cycle Generation."

Flexible-Fuel Vehicles (FFVs): Vehicles with a common fuel tank designed to run on varying blends of unleaded gasoline with either ethanol or methanol.

Flow Cell Battery: A massive electricity storage device based on a series of modules. Each module contains a large number of fuel cells. The flow cell battery technology receives electricity from a generating or transmission source, conditions it into appropriate format via transformers and stores it in the fuel cell modules using sophisticated technology. On a large scale, a flow cell battery has the ability to store enough electricity to power a small city.

Food and Drug Administration (FDA): The U.S. government agency responsible for the enforcement of the Federal Food, Drug and Cosmetic Act, ensuring industry compliance with laws regulating products in commerce. The FDA's mission is to protect the public from harm and encourage technological advances that hold the promise of benefiting society. www.fda.gov

Fuel Cell: An environmentally friendly electrochemical engine that generates electricity using hydrogen and oxygen as fuel, emitting only heat and water as byproducts.

GAAP: See "Generally Accepted Accounting Principles (GAAP)."

GDP: See "Gross Domestic Product (GDP)."

Generally Accepted Accounting Principles (GAAP): A set of accounting standards administered by the Financial Accounting Standards Board (FASB) and enforced by the U.S. Security and Exchange Commission (SEC). GAAP is primarily used in the U.S.

Generation M: A very loosely defined term that is sometimes used to refer to young people who have grown up in the digital age. "M" may refer to any or all of media-saturated, mobile or multi-tasking. The term was most notably used in a Kaiser Family Foundation report published in 2005, "Generation M: Media in the Lives of 8-18 year olds." Also, see "Generation Y" and "Generation Z."

Generation X: A loosely-defined and variously-used term that describes people born between approximately 1965 and 1980, but other time frames are recited. Generation X is often referred to as a group influential in defining tastes in consumer goods, entertainment and/or political and social matters.

Generation Y: Refers to people born between approximately 1982 and 2002. In the U.S., they number more than 90 million, making them the largest generation segment in the nation's history. They are also known as Echo Boomers, Millenials or the Millenial Generation. These are children of the Baby Boom generation who will be filling the work force as Baby Boomers retire.

Generation Z: Some people refer to Generation Z as people born after 1991. Others use the beginning date of 2001, or refer to the era of 1994 to 2004. Members of Generation Z are considered to be natural and rapid adopters of the latest technologies.

Geoengineering: The attempt to modify the Earth's environment through artificial means in order to counteract undesirable changes in weather, water or other natural systems.

Geological Information System (GIS): A computer software system which captures, stores, updates, manipulates, analyzes, and displays all forms of geographically referenced information.

Geosynthetic: A synthetic material used for such construction purposes as strengthening a roadway base or embankment, erosion control and drainage liners, geosynthetics (sometimes referred to as geotextiles) are typically made of polymers. They may reduce costs, enhance the useful life of a project, save weight or increase strength.

Geotextile: See "Geosynthetic."

Geothermal Electric Power Generation: Electricity derived from heat found under the earth's surface. Also see "Flash Steam Generation," "Binary Cycle

Generation" and "Hot Dry Rock Geothermal Energy Technology (HDR)."

Geothermal Plant: A plant in which the prime mover is a steam turbine. The turbine is driven either by steam produced from hot water or by natural steam that derives its energy from heat found in rocks or fluids at various depths beneath the surface of the earth. The energy is extracted by drilling and/or pumping.

GHG: See "Greenhouse Gas (GHG)."

Global Warming: An increase in the near-surface temperature of the Earth. Global warming has occurred in the distant past as the result of natural influences, but the term is most often used to refer to a theory that warming occurs as a result of increased use of hydrocarbon fuels by man. See "Climate Change (Greenhouse Effect)."

Green Building: A building that has energy conservation and renewable energy features designed to reduce energy consumption.

Green Pricing: In the case of renewable electricity, green pricing represents a market solution to the various problems associated with regulatory valuation of the non-market benefits of renewables. Green pricing programs allow electricity customers to express their willingness to pay for renewable energy development through direct payments on their monthly utility bills.

Greenhouse Gas (GHG): See "Climate Change (Greenhouse Effect)."

Grid (The): In the U.S., the networks of local electric lines that businesses and consumers depend on every day are connected with and interdependent upon a national series of major lines collectively called "the grid." The grid is divided into three major regions: the East, West and Texas regions. The regions are also known as "interconnects." In total, the grid consists of about 200,000 miles of high-voltage backbone lines and millions of miles of smaller local lines.

Gross Domestic Product (GDP): The total value of a nation's output, income and expenditures produced with a nation's physical borders.

Heat Pump: A year-round heating and air-conditioning system employing a refrigeration cycle.

Heliostat: A motor-driven mirror which is used in concentrating solar power and in concentrating photovoltaic power. The mirror is engineered so that it tracks the sun's movement through the sky during the day, thus capturing the maximum amount of solar output. (See "Concentrating Solar Power (CSP)" and "Concentrating Photovoltaic Power (CPV).")

High-Temperature Collector: A solar thermal collector designed to operate at a temperature of 180 degrees Fahrenheit or higher.

Hot Dry Rock Geothermal Energy Technology (HDR): A technique that drills holes into the ground until rock of a suitably high temperature is reached. Pipes are then installed in a closed loop. Water is pumped down one pipe, where it is heated to extraordinarily high temperatures, and then is pumped up the other pipes as steam. The resulting steam shoots up to the surface, which drives a turbine to power an electric generating plant. As the steam cools, it returns to a liquid state which is then is pumped back into the ground. The technology was developed by the Los Alamos National labs in New Mexico.

Hybrid-Electric Vehicle (HEV): A vehicle that is powered by two or more energy sources, one of which is electricity. HEVs may combine the engine and fuel system of a conventional vehicle with the batteries and electric motor of an electric vehicle in a single drive train.

Hydrocarbons: Organic compounds of hydrogen and carbon. Mixtures including various hydrocarbons include crude oil, natural gas, natural gas condensate and methane.

Hydroelectric Energy: The production of electricity from kinetic energy in flowing water.

Hydroelectric Plant: An electric generating plant in which the turbine generators are driven by falling water, typically located at a dam or major waterfall.

Hydroelectric Power Generation: Electricity generated by an electric power plant whose turbines are driven by falling water. It includes electric utility and industrial generation of hydroelectricity, unless otherwise specified. Generation is reported on a net basis, i.e., on the amount of electric energy generated after deducting the energy consumed by station auxiliaries and the losses in the transformers that are considered integral parts of the station.

IEEE: See "Institute of Electrical and Electronic Engineers (IEEE)."

IFRS: See "International Financials Reporting Standards (IFRS)."

Independent Power Producer: A corporation, person, agency, authority or other legal entity or instrumentality that owns electric generating capacity and is a wholesale electric producer without a designated franchised service area.

Industrial Biotechnology: The application of biotechnology to serve industrial needs. This is a rapidly growing field on a global basis. The current focus on industrial biotechnology is primarily on enzymes and other substances for renewable energy such as biofuels; chemicals such as pharmaceuticals, food additives, solvents and colorants; and bioplastics. Industrial biotech attempts to create synergies between biochemistry, genetics and microbiology in order to develop exciting new substances.

Industry Code: A descriptive code assigned to any company in order to group it with firms that operate in similar businesses. Common industry codes include the NAICS (North American Industrial Classification System) and the SIC (Standard Industrial Classification), both of which are standards widely used in America, as well as the International Standard Industrial Classification of all Economic Activities (ISIC), the Standard International Trade Classification established by the United Nations (SITC) and the General Industrial Classification of Economic Activities within the European Communities (NACE).

Infrastructure: 1) The equipment that comprises a system. 2) Public-use assets such as roads, bridges, water systems, sewers and other assets necessary for public accommodation and utilities. 3) The underlying base of a system or network. 4) Transportation and shipping support systems such as ports, airports and railways.

Initial Public Offering (IPO): A company's first effort to sell its stock to investors (the public).

Investors in an up-trending market eagerly seek stocks offered in many IPOs because the stocks of newly public companies that seem to have great promise may appreciate very rapidly in price, reaping great profits for those who were able to get the stock at the first offering. In the United States, IPOs are regulated by the SEC (U.S. Securities Exchange Commission) and by the state-level regulatory agencies of the states in which the IPO shares are offered.

Institute of Electrical and Electronic Engineers (IEEE): An organization that sets global technical standards and acts as an authority in technical areas including computer engineering, biomedical technology, telecommunications, electric power, aerospace and consumer electronics, among others. www.ieee.org.

Integrated Solar Combined Cycle (ISCC): See "Combined Cycle."

Intellectual Property (IP): The exclusive ownership of original concepts, ideas, designs, engineering plans or other assets that are protected by law. Examples include items covered by trademarks, copyrights and patents. Items such as software, engineering plans, fashion designs and architectural designs, as well as games, books, songs and other entertainment items are among the many things that may be considered to be intellectual property. (Also, see "Patent.")

Intelligent Transportation Systems (ITS): ITS includes a broad number of information technologies that can provide an electronic communications link to cars and trucks, enabling drivers to be alerted to road hazards, delays, construction and accidents. At the same time, ITS can transmit driving directions and a wealth of additional driving-related information. ITS enables automated drive-through toll collection and truck pre-clearance along highways and at bridge and tunnel crossings. ITS technologies are likewise in use at border stations, points of entry and customs checkpoints, especially in the NAFTA zone. ITS also includes vehicle-to-vehicle communications for improved safety and collision avoidance.

International Financials Reporting Standards (IFRS): A set of accounting standards established by the International Accounting Standards Board (IASB) for the preparation of public financial statements. IFRS has been adopted by much of the world, including the European Union, Russia and Singapore.

IP: See "Intellectual Property (IP)."

ISO 9000, 9001, 9002, 9003: Standards set by the International Organization for Standardization. ISO 9000, 9001, 9002 and 9003 are the highest quality certifications awarded to organizations that meet exacting standards in their operating practices and procedures.

LDCs: See "Least Developed Countries (LDCs)."

Least Developed Countries (LDCs): Nations determined by the U.N. Economic and Social Council to be the poorest and weakest members of the international community. There are currently 50 LDCs, of which 34 are in Africa, 15 are in Asia Pacific and the remaining one (Haiti) is in Latin America. The top 10 on the LDC list, in descending order from top to 10th, are Afghanistan, Angola, Bangladesh, Benin, Bhutan, Burkina Faso, Burundi, Cambodia, Cape Verde and the Central African Republic. Sixteen of the LDCs are also Landlocked Least Developed Countries (LLDCs) which present them with additional difficulties often due to the high cost of transporting trade goods. Eleven of the LDCs are Small Island Developing States (SIDS), which are often at risk of extreme weather phenomenon (hurricanes, typhoons, Tsunami); have fragile ecosystems; are often dependent on foreign energy sources; can have high disease rates for HIV/AIDS and malaria; and can have poor market access and trade terms.

Light Emitting Diode (LED): A small tube containing material that emits light when exposed to electricity. The color of the light depends upon the type of material. The LED was first developed in 1962 at the University of Illinois at Urbana-Champaign. LEDs are important to a wide variety of industries, from wireless telephone handsets to signage to displays for medical equipment, because they provide a very high quality of light with very low power requirements. They also have a very long useful life and produce very low heat output when. All of these characteristics are great improvements over a conventional incandescent bulb. Several advancements have been made in LED technology. See "Organic LED (OLED)," "Polymer Light Emitting Diode (PLED)," "Small Molecule Organic Light Emitting Diode (SMOLED)" and "Dendrimer."

Liquefied Natural Gas (LNG): Natural gas that is liquefied by reducing its temperature to -260 degrees Fahrenheit at atmospheric pressure. The volume of the LNG is 1/600 that of the gas in its vapor state. LNG requires special processing and transportation. First, the natural gas must be chilled in order for it to change into a liquid state. Next, the LNG is put on specially designed ships where extensive insulation and refrigeration maintain the cold temperature. Finally, it is offloaded at special receiving facilities where it is converted, via regasification, into a state suitable for distribution via pipelines.

LNG: See "Liquefied Natural Gas (LNG)."

LOHAS: Lifestyles of Health and Sustainability. A marketing term that refers to consumers who choose to purchase and/or live with items that are natural, organic, less polluting, etc. Such consumers may also prefer products powered by alternative energy, such as hybrid cars.

Low-E: A coating for windows that can prevent warmth from escaping from the inside of a building during the winter, while preventing solar heat from entering the building during the summer. Significant savings in energy usage can result.

Low-Emission Vehicle (LEV): Describes a vehicle meeting either the EPA's CFV LEV standards or CARB's California Low-Emission Vehicle Program LEV standards.

Low-Temperature Collectors: Metallic or nonmetallic solar thermal collectors that generally operate at temperatures below 110 degrees Fahrenheit and use pumped liquid or air as the heat-transfer medium. They usually contain no glazing and no insulation, and they are often made of plastic or rubber, although some are made of metal.

M2M: See "Machine-to-Machine (M2M)."

Machine-to-Machine (M2M): Refers to the transmission of data from one device to another, typically through wireless means such as Wi-Fi or cellular. For example, a Wi-Fi network might be employed to control several machines in a household from a central computer. Such machines might include air conditioning and entertainment systems. Wireless sensor networks (WSNs) will be a major growth factor in M2M communications, in everything from factory automation to agriculture and transportation. In logistics and retailing, M2M can refer to the use of RFID tags to transmit information. See "Radio Frequency Identification (RFID)."

Materials Science: The study of the structure, properties and performance of such materials as metals, ceramics, polymers and composites.

Medium-Temperature Collectors: Solar thermal collectors designed to operate in the temperature range of 140 degrees to 180 degrees Fahrenheit, but that can also operate at a temperature as low as 110 degrees Fahrenheit. The collector typically consists of a metal frame, metal absorption panels with integral flow channels (attached tubing for liquid collectors or integral ducting for air collectors) and glazing and insulation on the sides and back.

Megawatt (MW): One million watts.

Methane: A colorless, odorless, flammable hydrocarbon gas (CH_4); the major component of natural gas. It is also an important source of hydrogen in various industrial processes. Also, see "Coalbed Methane (CBN)."

Methanol: A light, volatile alcohol (CH_3OH) eligible for motor gasoline blending. It is also used as a feedstock for synthetic textiles, plastics, paints, adhesives, foam, medicines and more.

Millenials: See "Generation Y."

NAFTA: See "North American Free Trade Agreement (NAFTA)."

NAICS: North American Industrial Classification System. See "Industry Code."

Nanotechnology: The science of designing, building or utilizing unique structures that are smaller than 100 nanometers (a nanometer is one billionth of a meter). This involves microscopic structures that are no larger than the width of some cell membranes.

New Urbanism: A relatively new term that refers to neighborhood developments that feature shorter blocks, more sidewalks and pedestrian ways, access to convenient mass transit, bicycle paths and conveniently placed open spaces. The intent is to promote walking and social interaction while decreasing automobile traffic. The concept may also include close proximity to stores and offices that may be reached by walking rather than driving.

North American Free Trade Agreement (NAFTA): A trade agreement signed in December 1992 by U.S. President George H. W. Bush, Canadian Prime Minister Brian Mulroney and Mexican President Carlos Salinas de Gortari. The agreement eliminates tariffs on most goods originating in and traveling between the three member countries. It was approved by the legislatures of the three countries and had entered into force by January 1994. When it was created, NAFTA formed one of the largest free-trade areas of its kind in the world.

ODM: See "Original Design Manufacturer (ODM)."

OECD: See "Organisation for Economic Co-operation and Development (OECD)."

OEM: See "Original Equipment Manufacturer (OEM)."

Oil Shale: Sedimentary rock that contains kerogen, a solid, waxy mixture of hydrocarbon compounds. Heating the rock to very high temperatures will convert the kerogen to a vapor, which can then be condensed to form a slow flowing heavy oil that can later be refined or used for commercial purposes. The United States contains vast amounts of oil shale deposits, but so far it has been considered not economically feasible to produce from them on a large scale. (Not to be confused with crude oil that is produced from shale formulations.)

OLED: See "Organic LED (OLED)."

Organic LED (OLED): A type of electronic display based on the use of organic materials that produce light when stimulated by electricity. Also see "Polymer," "Polymer Light Emitting Diode (PLED)," "Small Molecule Organic Light Emitting Diode (SMOLED)" and "Dendrimer."

Organic Polymer: See "Polymer."

Organisation for Economic Co-operation and Development (OECD): A group of more than 30 nations that are strongly committed to the market economy and democracy. Some of the OECD members include Japan, the U.S., Spain, Germany, Australia, Korea, the U.K., Canada and Mexico. Although not members, Estonia, Israel and Russia are invited to member talks; and Brazil, China, India, Indonesia and South Africa have enhanced engagement policies with the OECD. The Organisation provides statistics, as well as social and economic data; and researches social changes, including patterns in evolving fiscal policy, agriculture, technology, trade, the environment and other areas. It publishes over 250 titles annually; publishes a corporate magazine, the OECD Observer; has radio and TV studios; and has centers in Tokyo, Washington, D.C., Berlin and Mexico City that distributed the Organisation's work and organizes events.

Original Design Manufacturer (ODM): A contract manufacturer that offers complete, end-to-end design, engineering and manufacturing services. ODMs design and build products, such as consumer electronics, that client companies can then brand and sell as their own. For example, a large percentage of laptop computers, cell phones and PDAs are made by ODMs. Also see "Original Equipment Manufacturer (OEM)" and "Contract Manufacturing."

Original Equipment Manufacturer (OEM): A company that manufactures a product or component for sale to a customer that will integrate the component into a final product or assembly. The OEM's customer will distribute the end product or resell it to an end user. For example, a personal computer made under a brand name by a given company may contain various components, such as hard drives, graphics cards or speakers, manufactured by several different OEM "vendors," but the firm doing the final assembly/manufacturing process is the final manufacturer. Also see "Original Design Manufacturer (ODM)" and "Contract Manufacturing."

Ozone: A molecule made up of three atoms of oxygen. It occurs naturally in the stratosphere and provides a protective layer shielding the Earth from harmful ultraviolet radiation. In the troposphere, it is a chemical oxidant, a greenhouse gas and a major component of photochemical smog.

Ozone-Depleting Substances: Gases containing chlorine that are being controlled because they deplete ozone. They are thought to have some indeterminate impact on greenhouse gases.

Passive Solar: A system in which solar energy (heat from sunlight) alone is used for the transfer of thermal energy. Heat transfer devices that depend on energy other than solar are not used. A good example is a passive solar water heater on the roof of a building.

Patent: An intellectual property right granted by a national government to an inventor to exclude others from making, using, offering for sale, or selling the invention throughout that nation or importing the invention into the nation for a limited time in exchange for public disclosure of the invention when the patent is granted. In addition to national patenting agencies, such as the United States Patent and Trademark Office, and regional organizations such as the European Patent Office, there is a cooperative international patent organization, the World Intellectual Property Organization, or WIPO, established by the United Nations.

Pathogen: Any microorganism (e.g., fungus, virus, bacteria or parasite) that causes a disease.

Peak Watt: A manufacturer's unit indicating the amount of power a photovoltaic cell or module will produce at standard test conditions (normally 1,000 watts per square meter and 25 degrees Celsius).

Peer Review: The process used by the scientific community, whereby review of a paper, project or report is obtained through comments of independent colleagues in the same field.

Photovoltaic (PV) Cell: An electronic device consisting of layers of semiconductor materials fabricated to form a junction (adjacent layers of materials with different electronic characteristics) and electrical contacts, capable of converting incident light directly into electricity (direct current). Photovoltaic technology works by harnessing the movement of electrons between the layers of a solar cell when the sun strikes the material.

Photovoltaic (PV) Module: An integrated assembly of interconnected photovoltaic cells designed to deliver a selected level of working voltage and current at its output terminals, packaged for protection against environment degradation and suited for incorporation in photovoltaic power systems.

PLED: See "Polymer Light Emitting Diode (PLED)."

Plug-in Hybrid Electric Vehicles (PHEV): A PHEV is an automobile that features an extra high-capacity battery bank that gives the vehicle a longer electric-only range than standard hybrids. These cars are designed so that they can be plugged into a standard electric outlet for recharging. The intent is to minimize or eliminate the need to use the car's gasoline engine and rely on the electric engine instead.

P-OLED: See "Polymer Light Emitting Diode (PLED)."

Polyethylene Terephthalate (PET): A plastic resin of the polyester family and one of the most common thermoformed plastics. Plastic soda bottles are a common use of PET. PET is also fully recyclable.

Polymer: An organic or inorganic substance of many parts. Most common polymers, such as polyethylene and polypropylene, are organic. Organic polymers consist of molecules from organic sources (carbon compounds). Polymer means many parts. Generally, a polymer is constructed of many structural units (smaller, simpler molecules) that are joined together by a chemical bond. Some polymers are natural. For example, rubber is a natural polymer. Scientists have developed ways to manufacture synthetic polymers from organic materials. Plastic is a synthetic polymer.

Polymer Light Emitting Diode (PLED): An advanced technology that utilizes plastics (polymers) for the creation of electronic displays (screens). It is based on the use of organic polymers which emit light when stimulated with electricity. They are solution processable, which means they can be applied to substrates via ink jet printing. Also referred to as P-OLEDs.

Product Lifecycle (Product Life Cycle): The prediction of the life of a product or brand. Stages are described as Introduction, Growth, Maturity and finally Sales Decline. These stages track a product from its initial introduction to the market through to the end of its usefulness as a commercially viable product. The goal of Product Lifecycle Management is to maximize production efficiency, consumer acceptance and profits. Consequently, critical processes around the product need to be adjusted during its lifecycle, including pricing, advertising, promotion, distribution and packaging.

Pumped-Storage Hydroelectric Plant: A plant that usually generates electric energy during peak load periods by using water previously pumped into an elevated storage reservoir during off-peak periods, when excess generating capacity is available to do so. When additional generating capacity is needed, the water can be released from the reservoir through a conduit to turbine generators located in a power plant at a lower level.

PV: See "Photovoltaic (PV) Cell."

R&D: Research and development. Also see "Applied Research" and "Basic Research."

Radio Frequency Identification (RFID): A technology that applies a special microchip-enabled tag to an individual item or piece of merchandise or inventory. RFID technology enables wireless, computerized tracking of that inventory item as it moves through the supply chain from factory to transport to warehouse to retail store or end user. Also known as radio tags.

Rate Base: The value of property upon which a utility is permitted to earn a specified rate of return as established by a regulatory authority. The rate base generally represents the value of property used by the utility in providing service.

Refuse-Derived Fuel (RDF): Fuel processed from municipal solid waste that can be in shredded, fluff or dense pellet forms.

Renewable Energy Resources: Energy resources that are naturally replenishing but flow-limited. They are virtually inexhaustible in duration but limited in the amount of energy that is available per unit of time. Renewable energy resources include biomass, hydro, geothermal, solar, wind, ocean thermal, wave action and tidal action.

Return on Investment (ROI): A measure used to determine the efficiency of an investment. It is the (total gain from an investment, minus the cost of that investment), divided by the cost of the investment. ROI may also be adjusted to reflect the average yearly return on an investment.

RoHS Compliant: A directive that restricts the total amount of certain dangerous substances that may be incorporated in electronic equipment, including consumer electronics. Any RoHS compliant component is tested for the presence of Lead, Cadmium, Mercury, Hexavalent chromium, Polybrominated biphenyls and Polybrominated diphenyl ethers. For Cadmium and Hexavalent chromium, there must be less than 0.01% of the substance by weight at raw homogeneous materials level. For Lead, PBB, and PBDE, there must be no more than 0.1% of the material, when calculated by weight at raw homogeneous materials. Any RoHS compliant component must have 100 ppm or less of mercury and the mercury must not have been intentionally added to the component. Certain items of military and medical equipment are exempt from RoHS compliance.

R-Value (R Value): A method of measuring the effectiveness of building materials such as insulation. Technically, it is the resistance that a material has to heat flow. The higher the R-Value, the better the insulation provided. It is the inverse of U-Value. See "U-Value (U Value)."

SIC: Standard Industrial Classification. See "Industry Code."

Six Sigma: A quality enhancement strategy designed to reduce the number of products coming from a manufacturing plant that do not conform to specifications. Six Sigma states that no more than 3.4 defects per million parts is the goal of high-quality output. Motorola invented the system in the 1980s in order to enhance its competitive position against Japanese electronics manufacturers.

Small Molecule Organic Light Emitting Diode (SMOLED): A type of organic LED that relies on expensive manufacturing methods. Newer technologies are more promising. See "Polymer" and "Polymer Light Emitting Diode (PLED)."

Small Power Producer: A producer that generates electricity by using renewable energy (wood, waste, conventional hydroelectric, wind, solar or geothermal) as a primary energy source. Fossil fuels can be used, but renewable resources must provide at least 75% of the total energy input. It is part of the Public Utility Regulatory Policies Act, a small power producer.

Smart Buildings: Buildings or homes that have been designed with interconnected electronic sensors and electrical systems which can be controlled by computers. Advantages include the ability to turn appliances and systems on or off remotely or on a set schedule, leading to greatly enhanced energy efficiency.

Smart Grid: The use of computers to monitor and improve the efficiency of distribution systems for electricity. Components may include remote sensors, automated controls and integrated communications between various parties on the grid. The intent is to eliminate brown outs and better anticipate and deliver power.

Smart Meter: High-tech electric meters that relay information to electricity providers on a continual basis, showing the amount of power being used by a consumer or business. The intent is to better inform consumers about their usage, while enabling electricity providers to charge higher fees during times of the day when usage is higher across its entire distribution network. The theory is that higher fees during peak times and better informed consumers will lead to lower peak loads.

SMOLED: See "Small Molecule Organic Light Emitting Diode (SMOLED)."

Software as a Service (SaaS): Refers to the practice of providing users with software applications that are hosted on remote servers and accessed via the Internet. Excellent examples include the CRM (Customer Relationship Management) software provided in SaaS format by Salesforce. An earlier technology that operated in a similar, but less sophisticated, manner was called ASP or Application Service Provider.

Solar Energy: Energy produced from the sun's radiation for the purposes of heating or electric generation. Also, see "Photovoltaic (PV) Cell," "Concentrated Solar Power (CSP)" and "Passive Solar."

Solar Radiation Management: The attempt to use technology to deflect solar rays from the Earth's atmosphere. (Also, see "Geoengineering.")

Solar Thermal Collector: A device designed to receive solar radiation and convert it into thermal energy. Normally, a solar thermal collector includes a frame, glazing and an absorber, together with the appropriate insulation. The heat collected by the solar thermal collector may be used immediately or stored for later use. Typical use is in solar hot water heating systems. Also, see "Passive Solar" and "Concentrated Solar Power (CSP)."

Solar Tower: See "Concentrated Solar Power (CSP)."

Solar Updraft Tower: A renewable energy power plant that heats air in a large greenhouse, thereby creating convection that causes air to rise and escape through a tall, specially-designed tower. The upward moving air drives electricity-producing turbines.

Subsidiary, Wholly-Owned: A company that is wholly controlled by another company through stock ownership.

Superconductivity: The ability of a material to act as a conductor for electricity without the gradual loss of electricity over distance (due to resistance) that is normally associated with electric transmission. There are two types of superconductivity. "Low-temperature" superconductivity (LTS) requires that transmission cable be cooled to -418 degrees Fahrenheit. Newer technologies are creating a so-called "high-temperature" superconductivity (HTS) that requires cooling to a much warmer -351 degrees Fahrenheit.

Supply Chain: The complete set of suppliers of goods and services required for a company to operate its business. For example, a manufacturer's supply chain may include providers of raw materials, components, custom-made parts and packaging materials.

Sustainable Development: Development that ensures that the use of resources and the environment today does not impair their availability to be used by future generations.

Tidal Energy: A source of power derived from the movement of waves. Tidal energy traditionally involves erecting a dam across the opening to a tidal basin. The dam includes a sluice that is opened to allow the tide to flow into the basin; the sluice is then closed, and as the sea level drops, traditional hydropower technologies can be used to generate electricity from the elevated water in the basin.

U-Value (U Value): A measure of the amount of heat that is transferred into or out of a building. The lower the U-Value, the higher the insulating value of a window or other building material being rated. It is the reciprocal of an R-Value. See "R-Value (R Value)."

Value Added Tax (VAT): A tax that imposes a levy on businesses at every stage of manufacturing based on the value it adds to a product. Each business in the supply chain pays its own VAT and is subsequently repaid by the next link down the chain; hence, a VAT is ultimately paid by the consumer, being the last link in the supply chain, making it comparable to a sales tax. Generally, VAT only applies to goods bought for consumption within a given country; export goods are exempt from VAT, and purchasers from other countries taking goods back home may apply for a VAT refund.

Waste Energy (Waste-to-Energy): The use of garbage, biogases, industrial steam, sewerage gas or industrial, agricultural and urban refuse ("biomass") as a fuel or power source used in turning turbines to generate electricity or as a method of providing heat.

Wind Energy: Energy present in wind motion that can be converted to mechanical energy for driving pumps, mills and electric power generators. Wind pushes against sails, vanes or blades radiating from a central rotating shaft.

Wind Turbine: A system in which blades (windmills) collect wind power to propel a turbine that generates electricity.

World Trade Organization (WTO): One of the only globally active international organizations dealing with the trade rules between nations. Its goal is to assist the free flow of trade goods, ensuring a smooth, predictable supply of goods to help raise the quality of life of member citizens. Members form consensus decisions that are then ratified by their respective parliaments. The WTO's conflict resolution process generally emphasizes interpreting existing commitments and agreements, and discovers how to ensure trade policies to conform to those agreements, with the ultimate aim of avoiding military or political conflict.

WTO: See "World Trade Organization (WTO)."

Zero-Emission Vehicle (ZEV): Describes a vehicle meeting either the EPA's CFV ZEV standards or CARB's California Low-Emission Vehicle Program ZEV standards. ZEV standards, usually met with electric vehicles, require zero vehicle emissions.

INTRODUCTION

PLUNKETT'S GREEN TECHNOLOGY INDUSTRY ALMANAC, the first edition of our guide to the green technology field, is designed as a general source for researchers of all types.

For purposes of this book, we define green technology as the application of advanced systems and services to a wide variety of industry sectors in order to improve sustainability. The data and areas of interest covered are intentionally broad, ranging from the various aspects of the green technology industry, to emerging technology, to an in-depth look at the major firms (which we call "THE GREEN TECHNOLOGY 325") within the many segments that make up the green technology industry (sometimes referred to as "greentech," "clean technology" or "cleantech).

This reference book is designed to be a general source for researchers. It is especially intended to assist with market research, strategic planning, employment searches, contact or prospect list creation and financial research, and as a data resource for executives and students of all types.

PLUNKETT'S GREEN TECHNOLOGY INDUSTRY ALMANAC takes a rounded approach for the general reader. This book presents a complete overview of the green technology field (see "How To Use This Book"). For example, the changes in

packaging, building materials, lighting, transportation and other fields are covered in exacting detail, along with easy-to-use tables on all facets of green technology in general: from growth in renewable energy consumption worldwide to U.S. federal funding for green technology research and development.

THE GREEN TECHNOLOGY 325 is our unique grouping of the most noteworthy corporations in all segments of the green technology industry. Tens of thousands of pieces of information, gathered from a wide variety of sources, have been researched and are presented in a unique form that can be easily understood. This section includes thorough indexes to THE GREEN TECHNOLOGY 325, by geography, industry, sales, brand names, subsidiary names and many other topics. (See Chapter 4.)

Especially helpful is the way in which PLUNKETT'S GREEN TECHNOLOGY INDUSTRY ALMANAC enables readers who have no business background to readily compare the financial records and growth plans of green technology companies and major industry groups. You'll see the mid-term financial record of each firm, along with the impact of earnings, sales and strategic plans on each company's potential to fuel growth, to serve new markets and to provide investment and employment opportunities.

No other source provides this book's easy-to-understand comparisons of growth, expenditures, technologies, corporations and many other items of great importance to people of all types who may be studying this, one of the most exciting industries in the world today.

By scanning the data groups and the unique indexes, you can find the best information to fit your personal research needs. The major companies in green technology are profiled and then ranked using several different groups of specific criteria. Which firms are the biggest employers? Which companies earn the most profits? These things and much more are easy to find.

In addition to individual company profiles, an overview of green technology and its trends is provided. This book's job is to help you sort through easy-to-understand summaries of today's trends in a quick and effective manner.

Whatever your purpose for researching the green technology field, you'll find this book to be a valuable guide. Nonetheless, as is true with all resources, this volume has limitations that the reader should be aware of:

- Financial data and other corporate information can change quickly. A book of this type can be no more current than the data that was available as of the time of editing. Consequently, the financial picture, management and ownership of the firm(s) you are studying may have changed since the date of this book. For example, this almanac includes the most up-to-date sales figures and profits available to the editors as of early 2012. That means that we have typically used corporate financial data as of mid-2011.

- Corporate mergers, acquisitions and downsizing are occurring at a very rapid rate. Such events may have created significant change, subsequent to the publishing of this book, within a company you are studying.

- Some of the companies in THE GREEN TECHNOLOGY 325 are so large in scope and in variety of business endeavors conducted within a parent organization, that we have been unable to completely list all subsidiaries, affiliations, divisions and activities within a firm's corporate structure.

- This volume is intended to be a general guide to a vast industry. That means that researchers should look to this book for an overview and, when conducting in-depth research, should contact the specific corporations or industry associations in question for the very latest changes and data. Where possible, we have listed contact names, toll-free telephone numbers and Internet site addresses for the companies, government agencies and industry associations involved so that the reader may get further details without unnecessary delay.

- Tables of industry data and statistics used in this book include the latest numbers available at the time of printing, generally through mid-2011. In a few cases, the only complete data available was for earlier years.

- We have used exhaustive efforts to locate and fairly present accurate and complete data. However, when using this book or any other source for business and industry information, the reader should use caution and diligence by conducting further research where it seems appropriate. We wish you success in your endeavors, and we trust that your experience with this book will be both satisfactory and productive.

Jack W. Plunkett
Houston, Texas
February 2012

HOW TO USE THIS BOOK

The two primary sections of this book are devoted first to the green technology industry as a whole and then to the "Individual Data Listings" for THE GREEN TECHNOLOGY 325. If time permits, you should begin your research in the front chapters of this book. Also, you will find lengthy indexes in Chapter 4 and in the back of the book.

📹 Video Tip
For our brief video introduction to the green technology industry, see www.plunkettresearch.com/video/greentech.

THE GREEN TECHNOLOGY INDUSTRY

Glossary: A short list of green technology industry terms.

Chapter 1: Major Trends Affecting the Green Technology Industry.
This chapter presents an encapsulated view of the major trends that are creating rapid changes in the green technology industry today.

Chapter 2: Green Technology Industry Statistics.
This chapter presents in-depth statistics ranging from an industry overview to the consumption of renewable fuels, investment in greentech research, size of the greentech workforce, market size and much more.

Chapter 3: Important Green Technology Industry Contacts – Addresses, Telephone Numbers and Internet Sites.
This chapter covers contacts for important government agencies, green technology organizations and trade groups. Included are numerous important Internet sites.

THE GREEN TECHNOLOGY 325

Chapter 4: THE GREEN TECHNOLOGY 325: Who They Are and How They Were Chosen.
The companies compared in this book (the actual count is 329) were carefully selected from the green technology industry, largely in the United States. 143 of the firms are based outside the U.S. For a complete description, see THE GREEN TECHNOLOGY 325 indexes in this chapter.

Individual Data Listings:
Look at one of the companies in THE GREEN TECHNOLOGY 325's Individual Data Listings. You'll find the following information fields:

Company Name:

The company profiles are in alphabetical order by company name. If you don't find the company you are seeking, it may be a subsidiary or division of one of the firms covered in this book. Try looking it up in the Index by Subsidiaries, Brand Names and Selected Affiliations in the back of the book.

Industry Code:

Industry Group Code: An NAIC code used to group companies within like segments. (See Chapter 4 for a list of codes.)

Business Activities:

A grid arranged into six major industry categories and several sub-categories. A "Y" indicates that the firm operates within the sub-category. A complete Index by Industry is included in the beginning of Chapter 4.

Types of Business:

A listing of the primary types of business specialties conducted by the firm.

Brands/Divisions/Affiliations:

Major brand names, operating divisions or subsidiaries of the firm, as well as major corporate affiliations—such as another firm that owns a significant portion of the company's stock. A complete Index by Subsidiaries, Brand Names and Selected Affiliations is in the back of the book.

Contacts:

The names and titles up to 27 top officers of the company are listed, including human resources contacts.

Address:

The firm's full headquarters address, the headquarters telephone, plus toll-free and fax numbers where available. Also provided is the World Wide Web site address.

Financials:

Annual Sales (2011 or the latest fiscal year available to the editors, plus up to four previous years): These are stated in thousands of dollars (add three zeros if you want the full number). This figure represents consolidated worldwide sales from all operations. These numbers may be estimates.

Annual Profits (2011 or the latest fiscal year available to the editors, plus up to four previous years): These are stated in thousands of dollars (add three zeros if you want the full number). This figure represents consolidated, after-tax net profit from all operations. These numbers may be estimates.

Stock Ticker, International Exchange, Parent Company: When available, the unique stock market symbol used to identify this firm's common stock for trading and tracking purposes is indicated. Where appropriate, this field may contain "private" or "subsidiary" rather than a ticker symbol. If the firm is a publicly-held company headquartered outside of the U.S., its international ticker and exchange are given. If the firm is a subsidiary, its parent company is listed.

Total Number of Employees: The approximate total number of employees, worldwide, as of the end of 2011 (or the latest data available to the editors).

Apparent Salaries/Benefits:

(The following descriptions generally apply to U.S. employers only.)

A "Y" in appropriate fields indicates "Yes."

Due to wide variations in the manner in which corporations report benefits to the U.S. Government's regulatory bodies, not all plans will have been uncovered or correctly evaluated during our effort to research this data. Also, the availability to employees of such plans will vary according to the qualifications that employees must meet to become eligible. For example, some benefit plans may be available only to salaried workers—others only to employees who work more than 1,000 hours yearly. Benefits that are available to employees of the main or parent company may not be available to employees of the subsidiaries. In addition, employers frequently alter the nature and terms of plans offered.

NOTE: Generally, employees covered by wealth-building benefit plans do not *fully* own ("vest in") funds contributed on their behalf by the employer until as many as five years of service with that employer have passed. All pension plans are voluntary—that is, employers are not obligated to offer pensions.

Pension Plan: The firm offers a pension plan to qualified employees. In this case, in order for a "Y" to appear, the editors believe that the employer offers a defined benefit or cash balance pension plan (see discussions below).The type and generosity of these plans vary widely from firm to firm. Caution: Some employers refer to plans as "pension" or "retirement" plans when they are actually 401(k) savings plans that require a contribution by the employee.

- Defined Benefit Pension Plans: Pension plans that do not require a contribution from the employee are infrequently offered. However, a few companies, particularly larger employers in high-profit-margin industries, offer defined benefit pension plans where the employee is guaranteed to receive a set pension benefit upon retirement. The amount of the benefit is determined by the years of service with the company and the employee's salary during the later years of employment. The longer a person works for the employer, the higher the retirement benefit. These defined benefit plans are funded entirely by the employer. The benefits, up to a reasonable limit, are guaranteed by the Federal Government's Pension Benefit Guaranty Corporation. These plans are not portable—if you leave the company, you cannot transfer your benefits into a different plan. Instead, upon retirement you will receive the benefits that vested during your service with the company. If your employer offers a pension plan, it must give you a summary plan description within 90 days of the date you join the plan. You can also request a summary annual report of the plan, and once every 12 months you may request an individual benefit statement accounting of your interest in the plan.

- Defined Contribution Plans: These are quite different. They do not guarantee a certain amount of pension benefit. Instead, they set out circumstances under which the employer will make a contribution to a plan on your behalf. The most common example is the 401(k) savings plan. Pension benefits are not guaranteed under these plans.
- Cash Balance Pension Plans: These plans were recently invented. These are hybrid plans—part defined benefit and part defined contribution. Many employers have converted their older defined benefit plans into cash balance plans. The employer makes deposits (or credits a given amount of money) on the employee's behalf, usually based on a percentage of pay. Employee accounts grow based on a predetermined interest benchmark, such as the interest rate on Treasury Bonds. There are some advantages to these plans, particularly for younger workers: a) The benefits, up to a reasonable limit, are guaranteed by the Pension Benefit Guaranty Corporation. b) Benefits are portable—they can be moved to another plan when the employee changes companies. c) Younger workers and those who spend a shorter number of years with an employer may receive higher benefits than they would under a traditional defined benefit plan.

ESOP Stock Plan (Employees' Stock Ownership Plan): This type of plan is in wide use. Typically, the plan borrows money from a bank and uses those funds to purchase a large block of the corporation's stock. The corporation makes contributions to the plan over a period of time, and the stock purchase loan is eventually paid off. The value of the plan grows significantly as long as the market price of the stock holds up. Qualified employees are allocated a share of the plan based on their length of service and their level of salary. Under federal regulations, participants in ESOPs are allowed to diversify their account holdings in set percentages that rise as the employee ages and gains years of service with the company. In this manner, not all of the employee's assets are tied up in the employer's stock.

Savings Plan, 401(k): Under this type of plan, employees make a tax-deferred deposit into an account. In the best plans, the company makes annual matching donations to the employees' accounts, typically in some proportion to deposits made by the employees themselves. A good plan will match one-half of employee deposits of up to 6% of wages. For example, an employee earning $30,000 yearly might deposit $1,800 (6%) into the plan. The company will match one-half of the employee's deposit, or $900. The plan grows on a tax-deferred basis, similar to an IRA. A very generous plan will match 100% of employee deposits. However, some plans do not call for the employer to make a matching deposit at all. Other plans call for a matching contribution to be made at the discretion of the firm's board of directors. Actual terms of these plans vary widely from firm to firm. Generally, these savings plans allow employees to deposit as much as 15% of salary into the plan on a tax-deferred basis. However, the portion that the company uses to calculate its matching deposit is generally limited to a maximum of 6%. Employees should take care to diversify the holdings in their 401(k) accounts, and most people should seek professional guidance or investment management for their accounts.

Stock Purchase Plan: Qualified employees may purchase the company's common stock at a price below its market value under a specific plan. Typically, the employee is limited to investing a small percentage of wages in this plan. The discount may range from 5 to 15%. Some of these plans allow for deposits to be made through regular monthly payroll deductions. However, new accounting rules for corporations, along with other factors, are leading many companies to curtail these plans—dropping the discount allowed, cutting the maximum yearly stock purchase or otherwise making the plans less generous or appealing.

Profit Sharing: Qualified employees are awarded an annual amount equal to some portion of a company's profits. In a very generous plan, the pool of money awarded to employees would be 15% of profits. Typically, this money is deposited into a long-term retirement account. Caution: Some employers refer to plans as "profit sharing" when they are actually 401(k) savings plans. True profit sharing plans are rarely offered.

Highest Executive Salary: The highest executive salary paid, typically a 2010 amount (or the latest year available to the editors) and typically paid to the Chief Executive Officer.

Highest Executive Bonus: The apparent bonus, if any, paid to the above person.

Second Highest Executive Salary: The next-highest executive salary paid, typically a 2010 amount (or the latest year available to the editors) and typically paid to the President or Chief Operating Officer.

Second Highest Executive Bonus: The apparent bonus, if any, paid to the above person.

Other Thoughts:

Apparent Women Officers or Directors: It is difficult to obtain this information on an exact basis, and employers generally do not disclose the data in a public way. However, we have indicated what our best efforts reveal to be the apparent number of women who either are in the posts of corporate officers or sit on the board of directors. There is a wide variance from company to company.

Hot Spot for Advancement for Women/Minorities: A "Y" in appropriate fields indicates "Yes." These are firms that appear either to have posted a substantial number of women and/or minorities to high posts or that appear to have a good record of going out of their way to recruit, train, promote and retain women or minorities. (See the Index of Hot Spots For Women and Minorities in the back of the book.) This information may change frequently and can be difficult to obtain and verify. Consequently, the reader should use caution and conduct further investigation where appropriate.

Growth Plans/ Special Features:

Listed here are observations regarding the firm's strategy, hiring plans, plans for growth and product development, along with general information regarding a company's business and prospects.

Locations:

A "Y" in the appropriate field indicates "Yes."

Primary locations outside of the headquarters, categorized by regions of the United States and by international locations. A complete index by locations is also in the front of this chapter.

Chapter 1

MAJOR TRENDS AND TECHNOLOGIES AFFECTING THE GREEN TECHNOLOGY INDUSTRY

Major Trends and Technologies Affecting the Green Technology Industry:

1) Green Technology Industry Introduction
2) Demand for Green Technologies and Conservation Practices Evolves, Fueling Investment and New Product Development
3) The Developed World Shows Dramatic Improvements in Carbon Dioxide (CO_2) Emissions Rates/China Sets Ambitious Carbon Goals
4) Water Conservation Technologies to Enjoy Tremendous Growth/China Targets Desalination
5) Lighting Technologies, LEDs and CFLs Conserve Power and Offer New Product Development Potential
6) Packaging and Consumer Products Forge Ahead/Wal-Mart and Coca-Cola Improve Packaging Sustainability
7) Energy Intensity is a Prime Focus in China/U.S. Achieves Dramatic Energy Intensity Results
8) Interest in Geoengineering Grows
9) Environmentalists Campaign for Chemical Industry Reform
10) Homes and Commercial Buildings Seek Green Certification
11) Wireless Sensor Networks (WSNs) Ready to Spread/Nanotechnology Applications
12) Clean Diesel Technology Gains Acceptance

13) Major Research in Advanced Lithium Batteries
14) Nanotechnology Sees Applications in Fuel Cells and Solar Power/Micro Fuel Cells
15) Fuel Cell and Hydrogen Power Research Continues
16) Fuel Efficiency Becomes a Key Selling Element/Stiff Emissions Standards Adopted in the U.S. and Abroad
17) Car and Bike Sharing Programs Proliferate
18) Electric Cars and Plug-in Hybrids (PHEVs) Enter Market in Low Numbers
19) Proposals for U.S. Electricity Grid Enhancements include a "Smart Grid," Regional Transmission Organizations (RTOs) and Technologies such as Flow Cell Batteries
20) Superconductivity Comes of Age
21) Clean Coal and Coal Gasification Technologies Advance/Carbon Capture Proves Costly
22) Bio-plastics Become a Reality/Plastic Packaging Made from Corn and Soy
23) New Display Technologies with PLEDs

1)   Introduction to the Green Technology Industry

The phrase "Green Technologies" implies the application of advanced systems and services to a wide variety of industry sectors in order to improve sustainability. That means that the goals could include: reduction of waste, spoilage and shrinkage; improvement of energy efficiency and energy conservation; creation of systems that are energy self-sustaining; the reduction carbon emissions; a reduction in the production of toxic waste and the emission of toxic gasses such as volatile organic compounds (VOCs); creation of products that are biodegradable; enhancement of water conservation and water quality; and promotion of the reuse and recycling of materials of all types.

The application of such technologies, systems and practices need not be especially high tech in nature. For example, better design and engineering is creating packaging for a wide range of products that is lighter in weight, more recyclable and less reliant on petrochemicals. This improved engineering is also leading to both products and their related packaging that have a smaller footprint—thus more units can be shipped in one shipping container, cutting down on the total amount of energy used in transporting a large volume of units.

The global consumer class (the "middle class" segment of the population—those with at least enough income to make a modest amount of discretionary purchases) is booming. The middle class grew from about 1.1 billion in 1980 to 2.0 billion by 2011, and is expected by to soar to 5 billion by 2030. This rapid expansion will put tremendous pressure on resources of all types, including energy, water, food, construction materials and industrial materials. Moreover, this soaring demand will put powerful upward pressure on prices, which, in turn, will make the cost of greener conservation and efficiency technologies increasingly easier to justify.

In general, the technologies and related services in the "green" sector can be grouped into the following categories:

Energy
- Renewable and alternative energy production
- Energy conservation
- Energy storage

Water
- Water conservation
- Water recycling
- Production of water from alternative sources, such as desalination

Environmental and Pollution Devices and Services

- Waste management, disposal and recycling
- Toxic waste elimination, remediation
- Emission control
- Inspection, engineering, testing and consulting
- Product and systems design and re-engineering

Other Resources
- Recycling and conservation of metals, woods, paper, chemicals and plastics
- Conservation of land, waterways and wildlife habitat

Primary industry sectors targeted for the application of green technologies include:

- Agriculture
- Food processing and distribution
- Energy
- Manufacturing
- Transportation and Shipping
- Construction, building operation and building maintenance
- Power generation and distribution
- Water systems

The broad field of energy will be focused on conservation and efficiency as well as the development of new energy sources. In fact, throughout the green technology sector, conservation is where the low-hanging fruit lies. The easiest green solutions will be in better insulation in buildings; lighter materials in cars, trucks and airplanes; reduction of today's massive leaks in municipal water systems; and better storage, in the emerging world, of agricultural products in order to reduce spoilage.

Simply making efficiency in material and energy use a consideration in engineering and design of all types is already having a dramatic effect on sustainability. For example, Wal-Mart, the world's largest retailer by far, recently set a goal for its suppliers to reduce packaging on average by 5% from 2008 to 2013. At first glance, this may not sound like much, but the fact is that the amount of packaged products that flow through Wal-Mart in a given year, with its $400 billion+ in annual revenues, is so massive that 5% will add up to a tremendous amount.

As part of this process, the company has created a sustainable packaging scorecard for more than 627,000 items that are sold in its stores and Sam's Clubs. The scorecard evaluates environmental attributes of packaging, and enables its suppliers to measure how their packaging reduces energy consumption, cuts waste and fuels sustainability. The company even has an annual "Sustainable Packaging Expo" where its suppliers can meet with leading packaging manufacturers and designers to learn about the latest technologies and innovations. Long term, Wal-Mart has set a goal of being packaging-neutral by 2025, that is, recycling packaging and waste to the extent that it uses no more packaging materials than it creates.

Over the longer term, more advanced technologies and solutions will be developed and applied. Future answers to green challenges will be found in areas as diverse as highly efficient automobiles that virtually drive themselves, lighter aircraft bodies and changes in building materials. Convergence of multiple technologies (including nanotechnology, biotechnology and information technologies such as artificial intelligence and predictive analytics), along with the continuing advance of miniaturization, will guide these efforts.

The electric utilities industry has told us for decades that it is a lot easier and cheaper to conserve electricity through the use of efficient industrial systems, buildings and appliances than it is to build more capacity to generate additional power. However, conservation is not an immediate fix; instead, it is a long-term evolution. For example, a few decades ago, one of the major expenders of energy in a typical American home was the gas pilot light, burning 24/7 on furnaces, cooking stoves and water heaters. Today's appliances don't have pilot lights; they have on-demand electric igniters, so that no gas is burned while the appliance is idle. Likewise, today's refrigerators use about 75% less electricity than the refrigerators of 1975, while holding 20% more capacity, because they feature better insulation and more efficient cooling systems. Otis, a world leader in elevator design and manufacture, recently introduced its Gen2 elevator, which uses up to 75% less electricity than previous models. These are good examples of simple, extremely cost-effective reductions in energy usage, but such changes take time—we didn't see old-technology refrigerators tossed out of all homes in America at once.

Ever since the dawn of the Industrial Revolution, factories have been burning such fuels as coal and natural gas to make steam, flame their furnaces and turn their engines, but historically they let the resulting excess heat escape through stacks. Now, with the concept of co-generation (or CHP, "combined heat and power"), this is less and less likely to be the case. In manufacturing plants, co-generation is being widely applied as a simple, relatively low tech method to capture and reuse factory heat that is generated by industrial processes. That salvaged heat may be used in any of several ways to power a turbine that creates electricity. The electricity can then be used by the factory, sold to the grid, or both.

Oil and gas fields are becoming much more efficient. For decades oil fields flared off excess gas in brilliant, multi-story towers of flame, even in Alaska, relatively close to the lower 48 states' gas-hungry consumers. Today, except in the remotest fields, that is less likely to happen, as investments have been made in gathering systems and pipelines to bring the gas to market. Meanwhile, advanced technologies and practices are enabling older fields to be productive for much longer periods of time, greatly increasing the total amount of oil and gas that each well will produce over a lifetime.

Throughout the energy arena, the list of potential applications for nanotech to enhance production, storage and conservation continues to grow. For example, a lot of time and money is being invested in research using nanotube technology to create highly efficient energy storage devices—essentially giant batteries. Success could bring a significant breakthrough for the solar and wind energy industries, where storage solutions are vital to making alternative power generation more viable. Cost-effective ways to store electricity would mean that wind power could be captured when the wind is blowing and utilized later, and solar power could likewise be banked.

Nanotech will bring forth revolutionary new processes in the entire energy sector. A global oil industry conference on nanotechnology was held in November 2009. Discussion at the conference included the application of nanotech to such areas as improved drilling (for instance, the ability to withstand harsh environments, high temperatures and the high pressures of deep wells), drilling fluids, "smart" drill bits, enhanced methods for downhole measurement and monitoring, long-lasting coatings and improved post-drilling water filtration.

Tremendous strides in green technology are also being made throughout the transportation services and transport equipment industries. Lee Schipper, a Senior Engineer at the Precourt Energy Efficiency Center at Stanford University, points out that air transportation in developed countries today uses 50% to 60% less energy per passenger-kilometer travelled than it did in the early 1970s, and trucking uses 10% to 25% less fuel per ton-kilometer. Additional developments in transportation include the use of natural gas to fuel public transportation and the development of energy-efficient light rail.

2) Demand for Green Technologies and Conservation Practices Evolves, Fueling Investment and New Product Development

In recent years, an emphasis on and support for green technologies has come from three distinct directions: citizens and their non-profit organizations, governments and the corporate and investment sector. In many cases, concerned citizens and their non profit organizations have been the earliest supporters of sustainability and green practices. This category includes people concerned about sustainability, the environment and similar issues. Frequently, once organizations were established, lobbying ensued along with organized funding of selected green projects. Examples of green initiatives that evolved in this manner include recent bans on plastic grocery bags in many communities.

Next, mandates and funding emerged from government agencies. Through the years, as citizens became more interested in seeing green technologies developed and adopted, they influenced government at various levels. This occurred both at massive scale on the national government level (such as the Clean Air Act in the United States) and on state and local level (such as state mandates that electric utilities generate a certain amount of their power via renewable sources). Eventually, government began providing substantial economic incentives through tax credits, loan guarantees, subsidies and funding for research and development related to green technologies. A good example would be hybrid and fully electric vehicles.

In the United States, federal and some state governments have offered substantial tax credits, rebates and other payments to people who chose to purchase electric or hybrid vehicles, while offering financial support for research and development as well as manufacturing in related sectors such as advanced automobile batteries and electric propulsion. U.S. federal government support for green technology was allocated in the 2009 economic stimulus bill and later government actions. This support included broad authority for the Department of Energy to guarantee loans for renewable energy related companies, including the infamous $535 million loan guarantee for Solyndra, a failed solar technology firm. Government support for new solar and wind installations (considering loan guarantees,

various incentives and mandates that utilities buy a certain percentage of their electric power from renewable means) was so generous in 2010-2011 that companies investing in new projects on a large scale faced little to no risk—government support was virtually guaranteeing them a profit. Investment banks had a field day arranging financing packages for such projects, and many billions of dollars were involved.

As government mandates for green technologies were issued, the venture capital community entered the fray in a big way. Venture capital investments in the U.S. in green tech grew by 73% in the third quarter of 2011 compared to the same period in 2010, according to Ernst & Young, to a new total of $1.1 billion invested in 76 companies. Energy generation, efficiency and storage technology firms topped the list.

Tax credits from government and donations from non-profits cannot establish a viable, long-term green industry by themselves. The true, long-term support for green technologies will eventually have to come from actual consumers of goods and services. To put it another way, sustainability eventually must become self-sustaining on a financial basis. This will become particularly true in today's economic climate, where taxpayers worldwide are demanding more effective and efficient government programs and better management of government debt and expenditures (thus putting pressure on government to reduce grants, tax credits and other types of funding that might otherwise be used to foster green technology). There is growing evidence that this consumer-driven market for green tech is slowly taking shape. Today, giant corporations, among the biggest end-users of raw materials, products and services that might be more efficiently consumed through the application of green technologies, are likely to have their own sustainability departments or special executives in this area. For example, global software giant SAP AG has a "Chief Sustainability Officer." Likewise, leading investment banks are developing experts in green tech. Goldman Sachs operates a "Clean Technology and Renewables Group."

As the return on investment from adopting green tech increases, such as the return on retrofitting older buildings so that they use considerably less energy in day-to-day operation, then businesses and households will see the logic in making investments in such technologies. As green technologies advance, and they are doing so at considerable speed in many sectors, and economies of scale kick in thanks to high-volume manufacturing, then it will become easier and easier for consumers to change their buying and capital investment habits to support green technologies. Put another way, high-efficiency light bulbs at $30 each are not very appealing to consumers, but bulbs at $6 that have considerably longer life and burn much less power than traditional bulbs would be relatively easy to sell, despite the fact that they would be four times as expensive as traditional bulbs.

Many manufacturers and services firms, both large and small, see great profit potential in positioning at least a part of their offerings around sustainability. General Electric, one of the world's largest industrial companies, famously launched its "Ecomagination" branding of a vast array of its products in 2005, all aimed at better energy conservation or better green footprint. GE's products in the Ecomagination line range from more efficient air conditioning systems to high efficiency lighting, advanced water treatment and desalination systems, and highly evolved energy management and control systems. In addition, GE is offering a growing line of medical equipment that uses less power, such as CT scanners, X-Ray systems and ultrasound devices. In transportation, its eco-friendlier products include efficient railroad locomotives. The firm publishes an annual report covering its Ecomagination initiative, and maintains a high level officer who is the VP of Ecomagination. GE states that it generated $85 billion in revenues from these products from 2005 through 2010.

Internet Research Tip:
For a fun look at GE's view of sustainability in action, see: www.ecomagination.com.

---

3) **The Developed World Shows Dramatic Improvements in Carbon Dioxide (CO2) Emissions/China Sets Ambitious Carbon Goals**

Concern about carbon dioxide (CO_2) emissions and air quality are global. China's rapid industrialization has led to massive air quality problems in its cities (and to water quality problems in many parts of the nation.) Other emerging nations continue to face similar challenges as they attempt to balance rapid expansion and sustainable development goals. Air quality can be so poor in New Delhi, India at times that it is difficult to see and challenging for airplanes to land. The looming industrialization of the continent of Africa will pose the same types of challenges. In late 2011, The International Energy

Agency (IEA) published a global report on CO2 emissions, those that result from fuel combustion. Since one of the IEA's primary functions is to track global usage of such energy sources as oil and coal, it is reasonable for them to estimate the carbon output from those fuels.

The good news was from developed nations such as America. In 2009, emissions in the developed world fell by 6.5% from the previous year. The fact that many developed nations, including the U.S., were still suffering from a slow economy in 2009 may be responsible for some part of this decrease. However, the long-term news was also excellent: emissions had declined over time to the extent that they were down by 6.4% from 1990 levels. This decrease was in spite of higher populations, higher economic activity and greater numbers of cars, trucks and aircraft. America is making very significant progress in this regard thanks to the rapidly growing adoption of natural gas as an alternative to coal—a direct result of the discoveries of massive amounts of gas in shale fields. Green technologies and the increasing use of natural gas improved the world's emissions to the point that emissions declined slightly for the world as a whole during 2009. In the United States, despite a growing population, emissions peaked in the early 2000s, and declined by 13.7% from 2000 to 2009.

The emerging world, including China, is a different story. As emerging nations enjoy high economic growth rates, they tend to greatly increase their use of fossil fuels and their output of carbon emissions and other types of pollution. Thanks to rapid growth of industrial output and electricity usage, as well as high growth in the use of cars and other transportation, emissions increased by 5.0% in China in 2009, 5.5% in all of Asia and 3.6% in the Middle East. In its five-year plan for the period 2011-2015, China set goals to improve energy efficiency while cutting pollution and greenhouse gas emissions. Further details were approved "in principle" by Chinese government leaders in July 2011. One important measure of carbon emissions is "carbon intensity," that is carbon emissions per unit of GDP. The Chinese plan is to improve energy efficiency by 16% by 2015, while improving carbon intensity by 17%. Over the much longer term, China's ability to lower the amount of CO2 it generates will be enhanced through its plans to dramatically increase its use of nuclear energy, thus reducing the amount of coal needed for generation of electricity during future economic growth. By 2020, the nation hopes to improve its carbon intensity by 40% to 45%.

The world's challenge is to enhance the global adoption of clean technologies and energy efficiency to the extent that emissions are brought under control, but to do so in a manner that does not stifle the global economy. Coming developments in technologies for energy conservation, cleaner transport, more efficient buildings and factories, along with clean alternatives to the traditional burning of coal for electric generation all offer tremendous promise. Global carbon emissions from fuel usage totaled about 29 billion tons in 2009. About 40% was from the production of electricity and heat, 20% from manufacturing and construction activities, 22% from transportation and 16% from other uses. Adjusted for inflation, the world's carbon intensity dropped an impressive 27% from 1980 to 2009.

4)   Water Conservation Technologies to Enjoy Tremendous Growth/China Targets Desalination

Water may offer the biggest single sustainability challenge of the near future, while water technologies will be one of the green tech areas offering the biggest business opportunities. Not surprisingly, China is already targeting this sector aggressively, and over the mid term we are likely to see China develop a high-value, low-price product advantage in this area, in the same way that they have recently done in solar PV cells. Israel, a highly competitive nation in software and computer fields, is also pursuing water technologies. The devastating drought suffered by Texas and other Southwestern states in 2011 was a dramatic reminder of the looming demand for water technologies and conservation. The potential growth for demand looks very intense when you factor in global population growth, from 7 billion in 2011 to 9 billion by 2050, and the continuing rapid rise in global industrialization and the middle class.

Agriculture is the biggest user of water by far (by some estimates accounting for more than 70% of all water use), and much of the future of water technology lies in tools that will enable farmers to continue to allow their crops to flourish while reducing the total amount of water that they use. One of the most useful green technologies in this area will be advanced drip irrigation systems, delivering water exactly where it is needed in exactly the quantities required for healthy plants. Over the mid term, remote wireless sensors will be in the most advanced farms, gathering soil moisture and nutritional content

data, and alerting monitoring systems as to when and where to send irrigation. Irrigation equipment was already something in the neighborhood of a $10 billion global market by 2011, and it will grow very rapidly as the demand for and cost of water rise. The UN estimates that global food output will have to increase by 70% by 2050 thanks to the next two billion people who will be added to the planet's population and to rising household incomes that will increase discretionary food purchases. While advanced agricultural technology, such as "precision agriculture" and genetically modified seeds (that produce much more crop output per acre) offer the promise of filling this need, water efficiency absolutely has to be enhanced or such increased crop production will be impossible.

Industrial water (estimated to account for at least 15% of global water use) is also a critical issue, and a very promising field for water conservation and recycling technologies. As the price of water inevitably increases and strong demand ensues, business and industry will begin to place a strong focus on water conservation, in the same way that they have been placing a growing emphasis on energy conservation over the past several years. Also, municipal water systems, thanks to aging, leaking systems, are among the world's biggest water wasters. Technologies for the detection and repair of city water system leaks will be in high demand.

Not surprisingly, the biggest challenges from increased water use and restricted supply will arise in the world's two most populous nations: India and China. In China, much of the answer will come from desalination of sea water. In fact, analysts at SBI Energy forecast that the global desalination technology market will soar to $50 billion per year by 2020. China has already set a goal of increasing its capacity for desalination by a factor of more than four from 2010 through 2020, from 680,000 cubic meters daily to 3 million cubic meters. China, seeing not only its own intensifying need for fresh water but also a growing global market, is likely to utilize the same tactics in the desalination sector that it did in solar cells. That is, China may provide support to manufacturers of desalination equipment via low cost loans, low cost land, investment by both local and national government, export subsidies and official research and development efforts from universities and government-sponsored institutes. China's investment in this industry by 2020 is likely to run into tens of billions of dollars.

As with other industries, most of the technology for China's desalination is initially coming from other nations, such as Israel. Eventually, however, China will rely on domestic manufacturing for its desalination needs. Meanwhile, China is investing regionally in water conservation and other technologies. In the manufacturing center of Tianjin, for example, nearly 90% of industrial water is recycled, while more than 50% of farm irrigation is based on water-conserving technologies such as drip irrigation.

5) Lighting Technologies, LEDs and CFLs Conserve Energy and Offer New Product Development Potential

One of the easiest targets for green technology advancement is in lightning. It is universal, it is essential and it burns a lot of electricity. LED (light emitting diode) lights can be vastly more power efficient that traditional bulbs (incandescent bulbs and fluorescent tubes). CFLs (compact fluorescent lights) are also much more energy efficient. However, it is worth noting that many consumers have complained about the color of the light, which has improved in recent years, and that these bulbs contain a trace of highly toxic mercury, creating an environmental hazard when not disposed of properly.

Lighting is found in everything from residential and commercial buildings to roadways, signs, medical equipment and automobiles, burning as much as 25% of the world's electric output. Residential lighting is the largest use. Unfortunately, traditional bulbs give off a lot of heat that is often unwanted, in addition to burning a lot of power. Analysts at McKinsey, the global management consulting firm, estimate that LEDs had only a 10% share of general lighting (by dollar value) as of 2010, but will grow to 59% by 2020, soaring to a $94 billion annual business.

Lighting is selected by consumers based on multiple factors, including light intensity, color or quality of light and other aesthetic effects. Energy efficiency and life of the bulb are also factors. The challenge for the light bulb industry is to ramp up enough economy of scale in manufacturing to bring LED prices to levels where consumers will find it generally acceptable to pay somewhat more for bulbs that last longer and use less power. Quality of light will remain a critical factor, especially among Baby Boomers who require better light in order to read and see well as their eyes age. As of 2011, traditional light bulbs could be purchased for less than $1 each—a compelling price for high quality light, despite their high electric usage. Advanced LED replacements were in the $30 to $40 range. Some

observers expect those prices to drop by as much as 90% over ten years, bringing LED lights into a reasonable price range for consumers in developed nations—those who burn the most electricity with their lighting.

Significant competition in the LED field will ensue since this is such a vast and potentially lucrative global market. Watch for major consumer electronic firms such as Korea's Samsung and LG, along with Japan's Toshiba and Panasonic to be potentially strong competitors. This may create challenges for current industry bulb leaders, including GE, Philips and Sylvania. In the not too distant future, OLEDs (organic light emitting diodes) will offer significant promise as highly efficient lighting sources. However, at present, expense is a challenge.

Meanwhile, the U.S. and some other nations have set regulations requiring a gradual increase in the efficiency of bulbs. Less efficient bulbs will eventually be outlawed. For example, controversial regulations in the U.S. may soon require that 100-watt bulbs must use about 30% less electricity than traditional bulbs. Other categories of bulb wattage may be forced to meet similar requirements over a period of a few years. In response, manufacturers are beginning to offer incandescent bulbs that are based on halogen technology and shaped like normal bulbs. They are more energy efficient, have an expected lifespan similar to traditional bulbs, and are only slightly more expensive to purchase. However, they put out a lot of heat. Also, manufacturers are offering an ever-growing line of CFLs and LEDs that are slowly coming down in price. Switching the entire world to such lighting over a few years could produce a dramatic reduction in the amount of electricity burned in a typical household.

Firms seeking to offer innovative products for the lighting marketplace have many avenues to pursue other than bulbs. New products that turn lights on and off when people enter or leave a room, new types of fixtures that make the most of the output of advanced bulbs such as LEDs and similar items will enter the marketplace.

Light Bulb Comparison:

Traditional 60-watt incandescent bulb
- Uses 60 watts of electricity.
- Creates unwanted heat.
- Lasts about 1,000 hours.
- Costs less than $1.00
- Creates high quality light.

LED (Light Emitting Diode)
- Uses 10 to 12 watts of electricity.
- Burns in a cooler manner.
- Lasts up to 25,000 hours—extremely cost-effective over the long term.
- Costs about $10.00 to $40.00, but prices will drop quickly.
- Creates high quality light.

CFL (Compact Fluorescent Light)
- Uses 14 watts of electricity.
- Burns in a cool manner.
- Lasts 6,000 hours.
- Costs approximately $3.00 to $10.00
- Creates light that consumers do not like, but quality may be improving.

Halogen Bulb
- Uses about 45 watts of electricity.
- Creates high heat.
- Lasts about 1,000 hours.
- Costs less than $2.00.
- Creates high quality light.

6) Packaging and Consumer Products Forge Ahead for Sustainability/Wal-Mart and Coca-Cola Improve Packaging Sustainability

There are several very significant reasons why industry sectors of all types are focusing on improvements to packaging as a path to sustainability. To begin with, in the U.S., packaging accounts for about one-fourth of all material sent to landfills. Packaging often is both bulky and heavy. If packaging can be reduced in weight, then it saves in total shipping costs. Better still, if it can be reduced in both weight and dimensional size, then more items can be packed in one container, and the total shipping cost can be reduced dramatically. Once the item arrives in the warehouse or retail store, smaller size means that more items can be stored per shelf—yet another efficiency.

Finally, packaging can be expensive, and it often represents a fairly high percentage of the total cost of manufacturing and distributing an item. Packaging may involve plastics, aluminum or paper, all of which are subject to fluctuations in basic commodity costs. Simply put, reducing the amount of packaging used saves costs and increases sustainability.

The Coca-Cola Company, owners of one of the world's most recognized brands and a global leader in the beverages business with more than $35 billion in annual revenues, recently published a report titled "Creating Sustainable Packaging." The report describes their efforts to reduce waste in packaging. When you consider the millions of glass bottles, plastic bottles and aluminum cans involved in delivering Coca-Cola drinks to customers worldwide, not to mention the related cardboard and plastic packages that go with them, the numbers involved can be extremely significant—24.4 billion unit cases of beverages in one year. Also, a reduction in such waste could have a dramatic effect on the firm's bottom line.

According to Coca-Cola, "Systemwide packaging efficiency efforts in 2009 avoided the use of approximately 85,000 metric tons of primary packaging, resulting in an estimated cost savings of more than $100 million." Part of the firm's effort has been focused on plastics, as more than 50% of its beverage volume is shipped in PET (polyethylene teraphthalate) plastic bottles. In 2009, Coca-Cola introduced what it calls the "PlantBottle" PET package, which is a recyclable drink bottle made partly (about 30% as of 2011) from plant-based ethanol instead of oil-based PET. While much of the food industry's packaging of this type has been based on the use of ethanol from food-crop plants such as sugarcane, in the future they may be able to utilize agricultural waste instead.

In 2010 alone, the firm was able to eliminate the use of the equivalent of 79,000 barrels of oil through this new technology. By 2020, the company plans for all of its plastic containers to meet its 30% plant-based content goal. Competitor PepsiCo is also very active in this regard. Nonetheless, the companies may not be able to distribute carbonated drinks in bottles made of 100% plant-based plastic for many, many years, if ever. However, the types of plastic bottles used to package fruit drinks such as Coca-Cola's Odwalla brand can be made of 100% plant material today. Companies active in using plant material to make beverage containers include Virent, a Wisconsin-based firm owned partly by Cargill, Shell and Honda, as well as Gevo and Avantium.

Wal-Mart has been a world leader in recognizing the potential good that can be done by reducing packaging, and it is working closely with suppliers for innovative solutions to packaging challenges. As the world's largest retailer, progress made at Wal-Mart makes a significant difference, while setting a standard that is often adopted across an entire industry or product category. Wal-Mart, with more than $400 billion in annual revenues, has nearly irresistible power as a purchaser because of the sheer volume of merchandise that it buys each year. Consequently, when the firm tells its supplier base of 100,000 firms that it wants to boost sustainability, things happen on a scale that can't be topped by any other for-profit organization. For example, when Wal-Mart told suppliers it wanted to promote CFL energy-efficient light bulbs starting in 2007, the manufacturers it deals with ramped up production, achieved economies of scale and dropped prices. By 2010, Wal-Mart had sold more than 350 million CFL bulbs.

Sometimes the most obvious, and easiest to implement, green tech and sustainability projects can have the biggest effect. Wal-Mart's determination to change the way that laundry detergent is packaged is a perfect example. Liquid laundry detergent has long been extremely popular among consumers. For years, it was sold in giant plastic bottles in watered-down form. When using it, the consumer poured a large cupful into the washing machine, not realizing that much of what was in that cup was water. These laundry bottles were bulky, awkward and heavy. Nonetheless, that was the industry standard. Selling concentrated detergent instead, eliminating much of the water from the bottle, was of such obvious potential benefit that it had been tried occasionally by the detergent industry. However, consumers shunned the smaller bottles—since they were smaller but priced the same as large bottles, consumers assumed they represented bad value. Concentrated detergents always flopped.

Then Wal-Mart came along, with its unbeatable ability to change the way both manufacturers and consumers act. Once Wal-Mart decided to push the smaller laundry bottles, it gave the new products prime end-cap shelf space. Methods were developed to emphasize the product benefits to customers. Unilever, a leading detergent maker working closely with Wal-Mart, printed graphics on detergent labels showing how the new small bottles equaled the same number of wash loads as the detergent contained in the old bottles. Television talk shows were enlisted to help spread the word. By 2008, Wal-Mart sold only concentrated versions of liquid detergent in its stores. The company had changed an entire industry with one idea, as concentrated detergent was quickly on sale throughout the retail world. Consumers understood, benefitted from and accepted the change. Sustainability was boosted significantly. Smaller, lighter bottles times thousands of Wal-Mart stores meant immense savings in packaging, cardboard cases to hold the bottles, and freight. Over a three-year period, Wal-Mart estimated that the changes

saved 125 million pounds of cardboard cartons, 95 million pounds of plastic resin and 400 million gallons of water, along with 500,000 gallons of diesel fuel that would have been used in the shipping process.

The new detergent coincided with the rapid adoption of a new, front-loading design in washing machines. These front loaders, very popular with consumers, work best with concentrated liquid detergents designated "HE" (high efficiency) that produce fewer suds during the wash. The HE detergents are also formulated to work perfectly in cold water. In the past, the primary energy usage during the operation of a clothes washing machine was for the heating of water. By working well in cold water, HE detergents enable a dramatic reduction in the use of energy for washing a family's laundry.

A lot of money will be made over the mid term by companies that create innovative solutions to packaging needs. This will range from shipping pallets made of plastic or treated paper instead of today's wooden slats, to packaging that incorporates nanotechnology to make it especially effective, strong or light. New packaging shapes, boxes and bottles that are easier and cheaper to manufacture, and the ease of recycling will then prevail as well. The packaging industry will work very closely with product manufacturers as always, but they will also begin to work more closely with shipping and third-party logistics services firms to provide comprehensive, systemic solutions and innovations.

7) Energy Intensity is a Prime Focus in China/U.S. Achieves Dramatic Energy Intensity Results

In a global sense, energy efficiency may advance at the creeping pace of a turtle, but over the years the compounding results are exceptional. "Energy intensity" refers to the amount of energy required for a nation to produce a unit of GDP (gross domestic product—a basic measure of economic output). A nation's goal should be to make intensity as low as possible. In constant dollars (adjusted for inflation and expressed as year 2005 dollars), the U.S. economy grew from $1.84 trillion in GDP in 1949 to $13.3 trillion in 2008—an increase of 623%. During the same period, America's annual energy consumption rose from 31.98 quadrillion BTU to 99.4 quadrillion BTU—an increase of only 210%. Energy consumption per dollar of GDP (on the same constant, year 2005 dollar basis) dropped from 17.34 thousand BTU to 7.47 thousand BTU.

In other words, after removing any distortion caused by inflation, America required only 43.5% as much energy to create a dollar of economic output in 2008 as it required shortly after the close of World War II, while America's energy intensity improved by a factor of 2.29 times. A table of this progress, as published by the U.S. Energy Information Administration (EIA), shows steady improvements in energy intensity, year by year, for the past 60 years. This fall in energy used per unit of economic output is not limited to America by any means, but is more of a global phenomenon. China, the world's largest consumer of energy and a major concern in terms of pollution and emissions, is showing steady improvement, cutting its energy intensity by about 50% from 1980 through 2004. Its latest five-year plan includes a goal for a further dramatic improvement.

In recent years, annual growth in energy usage has slowed in developed nations such as those in the EU, along with Canada, Australia, The U.S. and others, while efficiency has soared. The challenge is to make efficient technologies inexpensive, widespread and readily adoptable in emerging nations. This is especially important in light of the fact that there will be big increases in the total demand for energy as the world's middle classes grow and emerging nations become more industrial. The EIA projects global demand for energy to balloon from 508 quadrillion BTU in 2008 to 678 quadrillion BTU in 2030. This is a 33% increase, a mere fraction of the expected increase in global economic activity. Most of the increased energy use will occur in emerging nations, particularly India and China. Accelerating improvements in energy and conservation technologies will be at work to an increasing degree, reducing total demand, lessening the impact of emissions and greatly boosting efficiency. This is a massive market opportunity for innovative firms that develop significant technologies and services in this regard.

8)   Interest in Geoengineering Grows

Geoengineering may sound like science fiction to some, but it is attracting brilliant minds and serious money. For example, a firm called Intellectual Ventures, co-founded by Microsoft's Bill Gates, is sponsoring geoengineering research. This unique branch of technology is generally focused on using man's ingenuity to improve, on a grand scale, the climate in general, specific weather conditions or air quality. To a large degree, such research is focused on using new practices to reduce the amount of carbon dioxide (CO_2) in the atmosphere.

Over recent years, scientists and engineers have proposed several potential methods for reducing the greenhouse gas effect, cooling the Earth's temperature, increasing rainfall, decreasing hurricanes or otherwise reengineering the planet. For example, many methods of deflecting solar rays from the Earth, and thus reducing the Earth's temperature, have been proposed. Suggested methods include sending light-reflecting particles of various types or a vast mist of seawater into the upper atmosphere, reflecting sunlight away before it has an opportunity to cause heat on the ground below.

Much of today's well-funded research is focused on capturing CO_2 from the air, regardless of whether that CO_2 was the result of industrial processes, electric power generation, or transportation. This is serious business for many reasons. To begin with, the U.S. Department of Energy (DOE) recently announced $2.3 billion in funding for research and technology in capturing carbon from the air. Next, CO_2 has real value of its own, as it is commonly used in a wide variety of industrial and energy applications. For example, injecting CO_2 into an oil well is a widely accepted method for enhancing recovery of oil reserves. Recently, several startups have been founded that focus on feeding CO_2 to algae as a nutrient. The algae produce a natural oil in abundance that can be refined into fuel for transportation. CO_2 is also used to make sodas ("carbonated drinks") bubble.

One of the leading firms in this effort is a Canadian company, Carbon Engineering (CE). Its focus is on cost effective, industrial scale, air-capture technologies, including in-house engineering, laboratory work, and pilot research in tandem with outsourced design and testing performed by engineering firms and vendors.

CE has an in-house group of full-time engineers, chemists, and physicists. The team is boosted by a handful of part-time senior engineers with expertise in areas of particular importance to CE who are retained on long-term consulting contracts. All of CE's R&D activities are undertaken in partnership with leading engineering firms and equipment vendors, and with industrial or academic consultants. Incorporated in 2009 and privately owned, CE is funded by angel investors including Bill Gates and N. Murray Edwards, a wealthy oil and gas man. CE grew from academic work conducted on carbon management technologies by Professor David Keith's research groups at the University of Calgary and Carnegie Mellon University.

Today's pioneers in carbon air capture are relying on various uses of sorbents that naturally absorb CO2. Their goal is to repurpose that CO2 as something useful and hopefully lucrative. For some technologies, such as those offered by Global Thermostat, a carbon air capture facility might be located near a coal-burning electric generating plant. Other technologies are less location-dependent for the capture process. However, all of the competing technologies would be most efficient if they were near some sort of facility with high demand for CO2. In other words, they might best be sited in an older oil field where injection of huge amounts of CO2 into wells would increase production. Likewise, they would do well sited near one of the algae-to-fuel plants that depend on CO2 to feed the algae. A leading pioneer in this oil-growing algae field is a firm called Synthetic Genomics, founded by biotech innovator J. Craig Venter, and backed with hundreds of millions of dollars from ExxonMobil.

Companies Active in Geoengineering for CO$_2$ Capture:

Carbon Engineering, www.carbonengineering.com, is based in Calgary, Canada.

Kilimanjaro Energy, www.kilimanjaroenergy.com, is based in New York City and has additional operations in San Francisco. It was formerly known as Global Research Technologies.

Global Thermostat, www.globalthermostat.com , is also based in New York City.

---

9) Environmentalists Campaign for Chemical Industry Reform

Concern for the environment is nothing new, yet decisions affecting the chemical sector are making headlines. Microsoft curtailed its use of polyvinyl chloride (PVC), also known as vinyl, for computer packaging products. Other companies cutting their use of PVC include Hewlett Packard, Wal-Mart Stores and Kaiser Permanente. Another potentially harmful chemical is bisphenol-a, or BPA. Some animal studies have linked BPA to hormonal changes. The Canadian government was the first to declare it toxic. A number of Canada's retailers, including Wal-Mart Canada, had previously banned food-related containers such as baby bottles, sipping cups and other plastic holders made with the plastic.

Environmentalists and health advocates claim that PVC is dangerous because it releases dioxins, which potentially cause cancer. Elements in PVC

called phthalates are also suspected of causing reproductive disorders. This is a blow to the vinyl producers in the world, which make 16 billion pounds of the plastic per year amounting to more than $6 billion in sales, according to the Vinyl Institute.

Concerns are also increasing about plastic waste in such products as bottled water. In response, bottlers such as PepsiCo are using less plastic in their packaging. PepsiCo's Aquafina brand as of 2009 is being sold in bottles that are about 20% less in weight. The U.S. division of Nestlé SA first lightened its plastic bottles as early as 2007, while Coca-Cola continues to produce lighter and lighter bottles for its Dasani brand.

In the European Union, a proposal known as REACH (Registration, Evaluation and Authorization of Chemicals) requires chemical producers to test their products for hazardous substances and submit test results to a central EU chemicals agency in Finland. REACH became a reality on June 1, 2007 with the establishment of the European Chemicals Agency (ECHA). Supporters hope to curb the production and importation of hazardous chemicals in Europe, while detractors voice concerns about the burden placed on businesses to carry out the testing. Countries outside the EU (which include the U.S., Australia, Brazil, India and Japan among others) are wary of the initiative as it may hinder trade, and call for the alignment of REACH requirements with test guidelines issued by the Organisation for Economic Co-operation and Development (OECD), a group of 30 member countries that produces internationally agreed instruments decisions and recommendations on economic and social issues.

In early 2009, environmentalists won a rare skirmish against the chemicals industry in China. The site for a proposed $3.6 billion plant outside Zhangzhou was moved 60 miles to spare the 1.5 million residents of the nearby port city of Xiamen from toxic fumes generated by the production of paraxylene, a petrochemical used in making polyester and cleaning agents.

By 2011, packaging companies were working with manufacturers to design packages that used fewer materials, were lower in weight, were easier to recycle and generally have a lower impact on the environment. The net result also means lower total shipment weights and thereby lower shipping costs; and in some cases, lower packaging costs as well. For example, concentrated laundry detergents marketed under the high efficiency (HE) label are a way for consumers to use less detergent per load of laundry. Since the detergent is concentrated, there is less water in the product and packaging is therefore smaller and lighter in weight.

10) Homes and Commercial Buildings Seek Green Certification

In a growing trend, many homebuilders across the U.S. are constructing homes in accordance with the National Association of Home Builders' (NAHB) "green" specifications. These specifications require resource-efficient design, construction and operation, focusing on environmentally friendly materials. Today's much higher energy costs are spurring this trend. In addition, local building codes in many cities, such as Houston, are requiring that greater energy efficiency be incorporated in plans before a building permit can be issued.

There are several advantages to building along eco-sensitive lines. Lower operating costs are incurred because buildings built with highly energy-efficient components have superior insulation and require less heating and/or cooling. These practices include using oriented strand board instead of plywood; vinyl and fiber-cement sidings instead of wood products; and insulated foundations, windows and doors. Low-maintenance landscaping demands less water and weeding. Heating and cooling equipment with greater efficiency is being installed, as well as dishwashers, refrigerators and washing machines that use between 40% and 70% less energy than their 1970s counterparts. Wastewater heat recovery systems use hot wastewater to heat incoming water. Even toilets are more efficient than before. Current models use a mere 1.28 gallons of water per flush, as opposed to four gallons in the 70s.

The main disadvantage is that this kind of building is often more expensive than traditional construction methods. Added building costs often reach 10% to 15% and more per home; however, some homebuyers are willing to pay the increased price for future savings on utilities and maintenance. As energy prices increased over the last decade, builders became more amenable to constructing homes with energy-savings measures. In addition, some consumers are inclined to spend more when they feel they are buying environmentally friendly products, including homes. (Marketing analysts refer to this segment as "LOHAS," a term that stands for "Lifestyles of Health and Sustainability." It refers to consumers who choose to purchase items that are natural, organic, less polluting and so forth. Such consumers may also prefer products powered by alternative energy, such as hybrid cars.)

The U.S. government and all 50 states offer tax incentives in varying amounts to builders using solar technology. A handful of "zero-energy homes" that produce as much electricity as they use are being built (see www.zeroenergy.com.) By installing photovoltaic panels or other renewable sources to generate electricity, and using improved insulation and energy-efficient appliances and lighting, the zero-energy goal may be achieved, at least in sunny climates such as those in the American West and Southwest.

In the commercial sector, businesses may have several reasons to build greener, more energy-efficient buildings. To begin with, long-term operating costs will be lower, which will likely more than offset higher construction costs. Next, many companies see great public relations benefit in the ability to state that their new factory or headquarters building is environmentally friendly. Many office buildings, both public and private, are featuring alternative energy systems, ultra-high-efficiency heating and cooling, or high-efficiency lighting. In California, many public structures are incorporating solar power generation.

Even building maintenance is getting involved— building owners are finding that they can save huge amounts of money by scheduling janitorial service during the day, instead of the usual after-hours, after-dark schedule. In this manner, there is no need to leave lighting, heating or cooling running late at night for the cleaning crews.

An exemplary green office building is Bank of America Tower (formerly One Bryant Park), a 54-story skyscraper on the Avenue of the Americas in New York City. Completed in 2009, the $1.2-billion project is constructed largely of recycled and recyclable materials. Rainwater and wastewater is collected and reused, and a lighting and dimming system reduces electrical light levels when daylight is available. The building supplies about 70% of its own energy needs with an on-site natural gas burning power plant. It was the first skyscraper to rate platinum certification by adhering to the Leadership in Energy and Environmental Design (LEED) standards, set by the U.S. Green Building Council in 2000 (see www.usgbc.org).

The Pearl River Tower, a 71-story skyscraper set to open in 2011 in Guangzhou, China, may be the first major zero-energy building, or may at least come close. Designed by Chicago architecture firm SOM, the tower is planned to be 58% more energy efficient than traditional skyscrapers by using solar roof panels, novel wind turbines embedded in four openings spaced throughout the tower and walls with eight-inch air gaps that trap heat which then rises to power heat exchangers for use in cooling systems. The building encompasses about 2.3 million square feet of floor space.

A growing number of buildings are being retrofitted to use energy more efficiently. One example is the initiative underway at Citigroup, Inc. The banking firm is turning off lobby escalators, incorporating more natural light and using recycled materials in dozens of its properties around the world. Citigroup says it can save as much as $1 per square foot per year by making its offices more efficient. Elsewhere, Google, Inc. installed a solar rooftop at its California headquarters as early as 2007, and retail chains such as Wal-Mart and Kohl's are installing solar panels on their California stores. In Wal-Mart's case, it had 31 solar installations in California and Hawaii by mid-2010, and had an additional 20 to 30 sites in California and Arizona planned.

The Environmental Protection Agency (EPA) sponsored a contest in 2010, challenging commercial buildings to cut energy use over a 12-month period. The winner was the Morrison Residence Hall at the University of North Carolina-Chapel Hill. The hall cut its energy consumption by approximately 36% and saved more than $250,000 on its energy bills. Green initiatives during the year included expanding a solar-powered hot water system, upgrading lighting and convincing students to cut down on hot water use.

Sports stadiums are also going green in a big way. Lincoln National Field, the home of the Philadelphia Eagles, announced in late 2010 plans to install 2,500 solar panels, 80 wind turbines (each measuring 20 feet high) and a natural gas and biodiesel-burning generator. The field is contracting with Florida-based Solar Blue, which will spend $30 million to install the equipment. In return, the Eagles will pay Solar Blue fixed amounts for energy with increases of 3% per year for a period of 20 years. Solar Blue is free to sell excess energy created in the stadium to the local utility. Staples Center in Los Angeles and New Meadowlands Stadium in New York also have significant green initiatives underway.

LEED standards have been adopted by companies such as Ford, Pfizer, Nestlé and Toyota, which have all built LEED-certified structures in the U.S. In addition, the standards have been adopted by 25 states and 48 cities for government-funded projects, including New York, Los Angeles and Chicago. Industry analysts estimate the value of

government-financed construction projects at $200 billion per year. One of the world's largest green complexes is the campus of King Abdullah University of Science and Technology (KAUST) in Saudi Arabia. The campus spans more than 118 million square feet of classrooms, laboratories and a coral reef ecosystem, and features more than 13,500 square feet of solar thermal panels and upwards of 54,300 square feet of photovoltaic arrays.

LEED is not without competition. Another green verification program called Green Globes is backed by the Green Building Initiative in the U.S. Green Building Initiative is a group led by a former timber company executive and funded by several timber and wood products firms. Several U.S. states have adopted Green Globes guidelines instead of those supported by LEED for government-subsidized building projects. In Canada, a version of Green Globes for existing buildings is overseen by the Building Owners and Managers Association of Canada (BOMA Canada) under the brand "BOMA Best." Green Globes is more wood friendly than LEED, which is not surprising considering the involvement of the timber industry. It promotes the use of wood and wood products in construction with fewer restrictions than LEED, which approves of wood if it comes from timber grown under sustainable forestry practices approved by the Forest Stewardship Council, an international accrediting group.

In a similar vein, the Environmental Protection Agency (EPA) established WaterSense, a voluntary public-private partnership program to promote water-efficient products and services; and EnergyStar, a program that promotes energy efficiency. WaterSense certifies low-flow toilets that use a mere 1.28 gallons per flush, creates standards for bathroom-sink faucets that flow at no more than 1.5 gallons per minute and offers a certification program for irrigation companies that use water-efficient practices. EnergyStar homes are at least 15% more efficient than homes built to the 2004 U.S. residential code.

Retail giant Wal-Mart has been pursuing an aggressive policy to reduce energy use in its stores. The company is investing $500 million to reduce greenhouse gas emissions from its stores and distribution centers by 20% through 2012. The firm also pledged to increase the fuel efficiency of its trucking fleet by 25% by the year 2008, and up to 50% by 2015.

Dow Chemical has invested $100 million (plus a $10 million grant from the Department of Energy) in researching new plastic photovoltaic roof panels using thin-film solar cells. Prototypes of the product, called Powerhouse, were tested in early 2010 with a goal of commercial release of the product sometime in 2011. Dow has not published pricing, but observers estimate that Powerhouse (or products like it) would cost a homeowner about $10,000 after subsidies and tax rebates for approximately 1,000 square feet of roofing material. This compares to about $5,000 for traditional asphalt shingles. Dow projects the value of the solar shingles market could reach $5 billion by 2015.

Internet Research Tip: Green Buildings

For a look at government-sponsored projects in green commercial buildings, see:

1) Rebuilding America, www.energyfuturecoalition.org/What-Were-Doing/Energy-Efficiency/Rebuilding-America

2) U.S. Green Building Council, www.usgbc.org

In Europe, the EU has mandated that member states revisit building codes every five years and create standards of energy efficiency. Buildings are also required to submit an energy certificate that can be shown to prospective buyers and renters. Elsewhere, nations such as Japan that are focused on becoming much more energy-efficient are emphasizing the use of green methods in new construction.

11) Wireless Sensor Networks (WSNs) Ready to Spread/Nanotechnology Applications

A Wireless Sensor Network (WSN) consists of a grouping of remote sensors (which may include RFID-equipped sensors) that transmit data wirelessly to a receiver that is collecting information into a database. Special controls may alert the network's manager to changes in the environment, traffic or hazardous conditions within the vicinity of the sensors. Long-term collection of data from remote sensors can be used to establish patterns and make predictions, as well as to manage surveillance in real time.

Intel and other firms are working on convergence of MEMS, RFID (wireless radio frequency identification devices) and tiny computer processors (microprocessors embedded with software). In a small but powerful package, such remote sensors can monitor and transmit the stress level or metal fatigue in a highway bridge or an aircraft wing, or monitor manufacturing processes and product quality in a

factory. In our age of growing focus on environmental quality, they can be designed to analyze surrounding air for chemicals, pollutants or particles, using lab on a chip technology that already largely exists. Some observers have referred to these wireless sensors as "smart dust," expecting vast quantities of them to be scattered about the Earth as the sensors become smaller and less expensive over the near future. Energy efficiency is going to benefit greatly, particularly in newly-built offices and factories. An important use of advanced sensors will be to monitor and control energy efficiency on a room-by-room, or even square meter-by-square meter, basis in large buildings.

In an almost infinite variety of possible, efficiency-enhancing applications, artificial intelligence (AI) software can use data gathered from smart dust to forecast needed changes, and robotics or microswitches can then act upon that data, making adjustments in processes automatically. For example, such a system of sensors and controls could make adjustments to the amount of an ingredient being added to the assembly line in a paint factory or food processing plant; increase fresh air flow to a factory room; or adjust air conditioning output in one room while leaving a nearby hallway as is. The ability to monitor conditions such as these 24/7, and provide instant analysis and reporting to engineers, means that potential problems can be deterred, manufacturing defects can be avoided and energy efficiency can be enhanced dramatically. Virtually all industry sectors and processes will benefit.

Intel and other firms have developed methods that enable such remote sensors to bypass the need for internal batteries. Instead, they can run on "power harvesting circuits" that are able to reap power from nearby television signals, FM radio signals, WiFi networks or RFID readers.

HP Labs, part of Hewlett-Packard, has proposed an ambitious and far-reaching project called the Central Nervous System for the Earth (CeNSE). Peter Hartwell, a researcher at HP Labs, envisions 1 trillion nanoscale sensors and actuators embedded in the environment and connected to networks of computers, software and services to exchange and act upon information. While HP acknowledges significant challenges in terms of getting the cost for such sensors down to a miniscule amount, they see significant potential benefits. According to HP, Hartwell envisions the use of sensing nodes about the size of a pushpin. These nodes would incorporate the ultimate in wireless sensor technologies, including MEMS accelerometers that can detect even the slightest amount of motion. In vast quantities, they could be stuck to bridges and buildings to warn of structural strains or weather conditions, and scattered along roadsides to monitor traffic, weather and road conditions. Embedded in everyday electronics, CeNSE nodes might track hospital equipment, sniff out pesticides and pathogens in food, or even "recognize" the person using them and adapt to personal needs. Hartwell is working on a motion and vibration detector sensitive enough to "feel" a heartbeat. The source of that sensitivity is a 5mm-square, three-layer silicon chip that can detect a change in the position of its center chip of less than 1-billionth the width of a human hair. It is about 1,000 times more sensitive than accelerometers used in a Wii game machine today, according to HP. There is the potential to add sensors for such things as light, temperature, barometric pressure, airflow and humidity. Eventually, such sensing units might be added to mobile phones for broad consumer use. For example, with a wave over food, a sensor might report the presence of salmonella. As of 2010, HP Labs was collaborating with Royal Dutch Shell to develop a new sensor for deployment in the first real-world application of CeNSE. The sensor would be used in seismic imaging.

Electricity metering is an ideal area for the use of remote wireless sensors. In the U.S., the economic stimulus package devised by the Obama administration included $4.5 billion in funds for smartgrid development. As of early 2011, millions of smart meters had been installed by utility companies throughout the U.S. Utilities in California and Texas are spending $6 billion on advanced digital meters and other related systems.

Internet Research Tip: Wireless Network Systems (WNS)

For more information on wireless network systems and remote sensors, see:

UCLA Center for Embedded Networked Sensing, http://research.cens.ucla.edu

Dust Networks, Inc., www.dust-inc.com

Crossbow Technology, www.xbow.com

---

12) Clean Diesel Technology Gains Acceptance

During the early 1980s, when U.S. drivers were still reeling from Arab oil embargos and fuel rationing, diesel-powered cars were particularly popular in the U.S. Mercedes-Benz made a very high-quality line of diesels at that time, and about 75% of its cars sold in the U.S. were diesel-powered.

Diesel cars unfortunately proved to be noisy, polluting and, in some cases, unreliable. American consumers drifted away from diesel for many years, particularly during the 1990s when gasoline was readily available at reasonable prices. However, new, advanced diesel engines appear to be making a comeback in the U.S.

In Europe, extremely fuel-efficient diesels, ranging from Volkswagens to BMWs, achieving from 40 to 71 mpg, account for about 55% of all cars sold. Diesels of this type tend to be small and very inexpensive to operate. This is important in Europe, where parking places are hard to find and fuel is quite expensive. European diesel fuel historically had lower sulfur content that that sold in the U.S., which makes the European engines cleaner. Today, in both the U.S. and Europe, new technologies such as Daimler's BlueTec are in place that reduce nitrogen-oxide emissions.

U.S. environmental regulators, particularly in California, are beginning to make encouraging comments about diesel technology. In late 2006, the U.S. government began requiring oil refineries to produce low-sulfur diesel. That, combined with cleaner emissions provided by new engines and much better mileage than conventional gasoline engines, is making diesel powered cars an attractive commodity in the U.S. The fact is that diesel vehicles can be very efficient, and the diesel option can add less cost per vehicle than a hybrid option. A diesel engine creates more power than a gasoline engine from a similar amount of fuel. Volkswagen, BMW, Mercedes-Benz, Honda and Kia, among others, are selling diesel models in the U.S.

However, two things may put a damper on sales of diesel cars in the U.S. First, diesel prices are sometimes much higher per gallon than gasoline. Adding insult to injury is the additional refining cost of transitioning to low-sulfur diesel fuel and a higher federal excise tax (24.4 cents per gallon or 6 cents higher than on regular gasoline).

The second factor that may slow the sale of diesel cars in America is that nation's focus on boosting hybrid and electric vehicles. Tax rebates and other financial incentives, combined with the promise of using very little liquid fuel, if any, will draw consumers to electric cars who otherwise might have considered diesel.

Volkswagen already offers a diesel engine option to U.S. consumers for its New Beetle, Jetta, Passat and Touareg models. Jeep, a Chrysler vehicle, offers a diesel version of its small Liberty SUV as well as its larger Grand Cherokee. Ford sells a popular F150

Diesel while Dodge has a diesel version of its Ram 1500 pickup.

Internet Research Tip:
Volkswagen does a terrific job of explaining the virtues of its diesel-powered cars and its TDI turbocharged direct injection technology at http://tdi.vw.com.

Honda is getting into the diesel act as well. Honda's 2.2 CTDi diesel-powered Civic is already sold in the U.K. and the firm will offer an advanced diesel engine in CR-V models in England and in Accords for the European market. The mileage of these diesel models is substantially better than their gasoline-powered siblings. Clearly, since the cars cost only a small amount more than gasoline-powered models, the diesels offer true advantages.

Mercedes, a Daimler subsidiary, sells diesel options in its E, M, GL and R-Class models, and plans to offer a diesel option in its popular C-Class and S-Class sedans in 2012. "CDI" stands for common-rail direct injection, a technology that also makes diesels allowable in the U.S. regulatory environment. It uses precise, electronic fuel injection that enables the engine to put out more power and less pollution while achieving better fuel economy. In Europe, Mercedes offers the GL350 BlueTec. In addition to the diesel engine, Mercedes uses low resistance tires and a seven-speed automatic transmission to boost fuel economy.

Meanwhile, ultra-low-sulfur diesel fuel was introduced at retail pumps in America in October 2006. New EPA emissions rules took effect across America in 2009 requiring that diesel engines meet exacting standards for low air pollution. The newer clean diesel fuel eliminates 97% of sulfur emissions. While it was previously impossible for automakers to sell diesel-powered cars in several U.S. states, due to tough state-level emissions regulations, new technologies combined with the new clean diesel fuels now make diesels legal in all 50 states.

The advent of biodiesel, a fuel derived when glycerin is separated from vegetable oils or animal fats, is altering the landscape in a small way. The resulting byproducts are methyl esters (the chemical name for biodiesel) and glycerin, which can be used in soaps and cleaning products. It has lower emissions than petroleum diesel and is currently used as an additive to that fuel since it helps with lubricity. A small number of public filling stations are offering biodiesel, and it is also available from some petroleum distributors. However, refiners of biodiesel have consistently failed to earn a profit, and many have taken bankruptcy.

13) Major Research in Advanced Lithium Batteries

There are many obstacles to all-electric vehicles. The biggest potential problems are battery capacity and battery cost. Lithium-ion batteries are becoming more powerful, safe and efficient thanks to technological breakthroughs like those of startup manufacturer A123Systems (www.a123systems.com). Lithium-ion batteries pose multiple technical challenges. In the past, the batteries have shown a tendency to overheat, catch fire or explode. However, A123Systems is building batteries made of nanoparticles of lithium iron phosphate modified with trace metals instead of cobalt oxide. The result is a more stable power source with twice as much energy as nickel-metal hydride batteries. A123Systems was selected in August 2009 for a $249 million grant from the U.S. Department of Energy to build advanced battery manufacturing plants in the U.S. This is in addition to $100 million in refundable tax credits awarded from the Michigan Economic Development Corporation earlier in the year. As of early 2011, A123 had opened a 291,000-square-foot facility in Livonia, Michigan, as part of its U.S. expansion. (The company also maintains manufacturing facilities in China and Korea.) The firm is engaged in developing energy storage technology for power grids and batteries for commercial applications in addition to those for use in electric vehicles.

Nissan and GM are powering their PHEVs with lithium-ion batteries that are based on manganese rather than the cobalt oxide technology traditionally used in batteries for laptop computers. The manganese technology provides more stability and is a big leap ahead in battery manufacturing overall.

Despite all of the battery technology investment in the U.S. and Europe, the early leaders in advanced batteries were in Asia, particularly Japan, Korea and China. This is logical when you consider the fact that Asian firms have long been world leaders in advanced batteries for mobile consumer electronics such as cellphones. Without their advances in smaller, longer-lasting batteries, today's tiny mobile phones and iPods would not have been possible.

U.S.-based companies actively trying to become leaders in advanced batteries for electric vehicles also include Quantum Technologies, Altair Nanotechnologies and ActaCell. However, one of A123's top American competitors may be Ener1, www.ener1.com, which owns an advanced lithium-ion electric vehicle battery unit called EnerDel. EnerDel has two cutting-edge manufacturing plants in Indiana.

A joint venture comprised of U.S.-based Johnson Controls (a leader in automotive systems and a major manufacturer of traditional car batteries) and France-based Saft (a leader in battery technology) plans to convert a former Johnson Controls automobile parts factory in Michigan into an advanced lithium-ion battery plant. The factory will make batteries for Ford's planned plug-in hybrid as early as 2012.

In the U.S. the 2009 American Recovery and Reinvestment Act provided $2.4 billion for investment in lithium-ion batteries. By late 2010, 17 new battery plants in Michigan were in production, under construction or in the planning stages according to the state Department of Energy, Labor and Economic Growth.

Nissan is investing several billion dollars in the construction of manufacturing plants for advanced batteries and retooling existing assembly plants to result in the production of up to 500,000 vehicles per year on three continents. The lithium manganese battery technology was developed in a joint venture between Nissan and NEC. In Tennessee Nissan is spending $1.6 billion in loans backed by the U.S. Department of Energy on a lithium-ion battery plant and an electric vehicle assembly line.

Nissan made a significant breakthrough in lithium-ion technology with the development of its laminated battery. Its shape and flexibility allow it to be used in a variety of models and they have two times the capacity and power of traditional batteries of the same weight (but at half the size). Nissan's Leaf runs on a 24-kilowatt-hour laminated battery made of 192 lithium-manganese cells capable of generating enough current to power an AC motor to 107 horsepower.

Over the long-term, watch for further advances in battery technology that may fuel vehicles for up to 400 miles per charge. That will make a tremendous difference in consumer interest. The expensive Tesla roadster already claims a relatively long range of more than 240 miles.

IBM, along with automotive companies such as Toyota, is working on a radical new lithium battery that could be far lighter than current lithium batteries and have a range of as much as 500 miles. The Battery 500 Project is researching a "lithium-air" battery that, instead of shuttling ions back and forth between two metal electrodes, moves them between one metal electrode and air. The concept is similar to zinc-air batteries used to power hearing aids. The problem there is that zinc-air batteries are not rechargeable and limited to a very small size. If all goes well, IBM hopes to have a prototype of the battery in the laboratory by 2012 and a full-size demo battery by 2015. Spurring the project along is a bill introduced in the U.S. Senate in mid-2010 that offers a $10 million prize to the developer of a commercial electric car battery with a 500 mile range per charge.

Yet another new battery concept on the horizon is a liquid battery developed by David Bradwell when he was a graduate student at MIT in 2007. The technology uses electrodes and an electrolyte that liquefy during operation, enabling the battery to handle high currents without fracturing. It is hoped that such a battery could be used to store enormous amounts of solar or wind power for use at night or when the wind is not blowing. Even better, Bradwell believes that the system could ultimately cost less than $100 per kilowatt-hour for a new installation.

The plethora of companies investing in and developing new battery technologies is likely to cause a glut on the market as early as 2014 and on into 2015, according to analysts at PRTM Management Consulting, a unit of Pricewater-houseCoopers. PRTM forecasts the global electric vehicle industry will reach $300 billion by 2020, which includes a potential $50 billion for battery manufacturers.

The estimated cost of a 24 kilowatt-hour lithium-ion battery pack in late 2010 was $15,600. Other analysts are concerned that prices for lithium batteries will remain high over the mid-term. Although the U.S. Department of Energy set a goal of reducing car battery costs by 70% by 2014, many experts agree that the goal is too aggressive. This is due to the fact that costs for components and materials (such as nickel, manganese and cobalt) are likely to remain high in response to increased demand.

Companies to Watch in Advanced Battery Technology:
A123 Systems, Inc.
ActaCell
Altair Nanotechnologies
Better Place
BYD
EnerDel division of Ener1
Johnson Controls-Saft joint venture
NEC
Nissan
Panasonic
Quantum Technologies
Sharp
Tesla
Source: Plunkett Research, Ltd.

14) Nanotechnology Sees Applications in Fuel Cells and Solar Power/Micro Fuel Cells

Potential methods of generating energy with nanotechnology are nearly boundless, and some applications are creating synergies between plastics and nanotech. However, the most immediately promising possibilities are for solar power and fuel cell power. Michael Graetzel, a Swiss scientist, invented a new kind of solar cell that uses dye molecules and titanium dioxide. This enables manufacturers to place highly efficient and versatile solar cells in flexible plastic sheets, rather than the traditional glass and silicon cells. Konarka Technologies, Inc., with U.S. offices in Lowell, Massachusetts (www.konarka.com), has a portfolio of more than 350 global patents and patent applications for its technology. Its solar cells, based on Graetzel's work, are literally printed out on long sheets of plastic that can be cut into virtually any shape or size, making them ideal for a variety of applications, including large architectural installations and in the field with portable electronics or in places where there are no power lines.

Another player in the solar power arena is Nanosolar, Inc. www.nanosolar.com, a Palo Alto, California-based company. The firm has an advanced technology that prints nanodots onto thin-film solar cells. In late 2010, Nanosolar completed a 1.1 megawatt solar power plant in Luckenwalde, Germany with Beck Energy.

A new development in nanosolar technology is multi-junction solar cells, which were exhibited by researchers from the Imperial College, London at the Royal Society Summer Science Exhibition in 2009 in the U.K. These cells layer on top of each other, with

each layer capturing energy from a particular color in the spectrum of sunlight. Converting energy from the entire spectrum may result in the ability to turn as much as 50% of the energy in sunlight into electricity compared to the 20% or so that is gleaned using conventional solar cells. As of late 2010, efficiencies of 42.3% efficiency in laboratory testing had been achieved by Spire Semiconductor.

Another way that nanotechnology may impact solar cells is the use of quantum dots instead of silicon. Quantum dots, which are nanoscale semiconductor crystals, could significantly lower the cost of photovoltaic cells. In 2006, Victor Klimov of Los Alamos National Laboratory in New Mexico demonstrated that quantum dots have the capability to react to light and store energy more efficiently than silicon. Although scientists are years away from actually manufacturing usable quantum dot solar cells on a commercial scale, the technology has been established.

Meanwhile carbon nanohorns, a variation of carbon nanotubes, are being used in fuel cells to make them lighter, cheaper and more efficient. SFC Energy AG (www.sfc.com), formerly Smart Fuel Cell AG, based in Germany; NEC, the giant Japanese electronics firm; and several other companies are creating such fuel cells for use in mobile phones and laptops, as well as traffic signals, remote sensors and metering systems. As these fuel cells become more compact, powerful and longer lasting, many other applications will become available for both mobile and set devices. Toshiba released the first commercial fuel cell for mobile equipment, the Dynario. A direct-methanol fuel cell (DMFC), the Dynario, uses a combination of methanol and ambient oxygen to create electricity. On one methanol cartridge (which takes about 20 seconds to load into the unit), the Dynario can charge two mobile phones or devices such as MP3 players. The product was available in limited release (only 3,000 units) in Japan, and retailed for about $325.

As of late 2010, scientists at MIT were working on a lithium-ion battery with a positive electrode made of carbon nanotubes. The technology has the potential to deliver 10 times as much power as conventional batteries and store five times as much energy as a conventional ultracapacitor. The MIT researchers are working on improved techniques to speed the process of creating the nanotubes.

15) Fuel Cell and Hydrogen Power Research Continues

The fuel cell is nothing new, despite the excitement it is now generating. It has been around since 1839, when Welsh physics professor William Grove created an operating model based on platinum and zinc components. Much later, the U.S. Apollo space program used fuel cells for certain power needs in the Apollo space vehicles that traveled from the Earth to the Moon.

In basic terms, a fuel cell consists of quantities of hydrogen and oxygen separated by a catalyst. Inside the cell, a chemical reaction within the catalyst generates electricity. Byproducts of this reaction include heat and water. Several enhancements to basic fuel cell technology are under research and development at various firms worldwide. These include fuel cell membranes manufactured with advanced nanotechnologies and "solid oxide" technologies that could prove efficient enough to use on aircraft. Another option for fuel cell membranes are those made of hydrocarbon, which cost about one-half a much as membranes using fluorine compounds.

Fuel cells require a steady supply of hydrogen. Therein lies the biggest problem in promoting the widespread use of fuel cells: how to create, transport and store the hydrogen. At present, no one has been able to put a viable plan in place that would create a network of hydrogen fueling stations substantial enough to meet the needs of everyday motorists in the U.S. or anywhere else.

Many currently operating fuel cells burn hydrogen extracted from such sources as gasoline, natural gas or methanol. Each source has its advantages and disadvantages. Unfortunately, burning hydrocarbons such as oil, natural gas or coal to generate the energy necessary to create hydrogen results in unwanted emissions. Ideally, hydrogen would be created using renewable, non-polluting means, such as solar power or wind power. Also, nuclear or renewable sources could be used to generate electricity that would be used to extract hydrogen molecules from water.

The potential market for fuel cells encompasses diverse uses in fixed applications (such as providing an electric generating plant for a home or a neighborhood), portable systems (such as portable generators for construction sites) or completely mobile uses (powering anything from small hand-held devices to automobiles). The potential advantages of fuel cells as clean, efficient energy sources are enormous. The fuel cell itself is a proven technology—fuel cells are already in use, powering a U.S. Post Office in Alaska, for example. (This project, in Chugach, Alaska, is the result of a joint venture between the local electric association and the U.S. Postal Service to install a one-megawatt fuel cell facility.) Tiny fuel cells are also on the market for use in powering cellular phones and laptop computers.

Shipments of fuel cell-equipped mobile devices could grow very rapidly if they can eliminate the need for frequent recharging of current battery-powered models. The "Medis 24/7 Power Pack" is a portable, disposable power source for small electronic devices such as cell phones and MP3 players. Manufactured by Medis Technologies, it is based on Direct Liquid Fuel cell technology, and may be of particular utility in military applications. Elsewhere, MTI MicroFuel Cells manufactures a power pack for portable electronics that is based on direct methanol fuel cell technology that it calls Mobion.

Internet Research Tip: Micro Fuel Cells
For more information on research involving fuel cells for small applications, visit:
MTI MicroFuel Cells www.mtimicrofuelcells.com
Tekion Solutions, Inc. www.tekion.com

Electric Vehicles vs. Fuel Cells
Nearly all of the major automobile makers had significant fuel cell research initiatives at one time. While the potential for fuel cell-powered vehicles seemed extremely promising, the automobile industry has made a profound and long-lasting shift toward plug-in electric hybrids and all-electric vehicles as the new technology base of choice. This is due to several reasons, including:

1) The tremendous success and wide consumer acceptance of Toyota's Prius hybrid car. This success gave Toyota early dominance in the electric car field while other makers were still dreaming about fuel cells. An important feature of the Prius is its very affordable price—something that might never be accomplished in a fuel cell vehicle.

2) The technical hurdles of distributing, storing and transporting hydrogen as a fuel have proven extremely difficult to overcome.

3) The costs of building a fuel cell platform for automobiles remains vastly more expensive than building an electric or hybrid vehicle.

4) Consumers, bureaucrats, investors and legislators already understand and trust the safety and ease of use of electricity, whether fixed or portable. This cannot be said for hydrogen.

Now, Nissan and other leading automobile firms have ambitious plans for electric-drive vehicles (as opposed to today's hybrid electric cars which run on electricity only part of the time, relying on a gasoline engine the rest of the time). Given the financial constraints that automakers are working under today, these car manufacturers have downgraded or abandoned their focus on fuel cells. In particular, technical breakthroughs in advanced batteries for electric vehicles are occurring quickly. This will spur the electric car market while lessening the near-term interest in fuel cells.

Source: Plunkett Research, Ltd.

GM invested $1 billion in fuel cell vehicle research. The company leased 100 fuel cell-equipped Equinox crossover vehicles to customers as a test, starting in early 2008. The Equinox will go about 200 miles on a hydrogen fill up. Initially, the vehicles were provided to government officials, celebrities, journalists and business leaders in New York City, Washington D.C. and Los Angeles. GM has long had aggressive goals for commercializing and producing fuel cell vehicles. However, the financial and technical hurdles would be high, and GM assigned itself a daunting task. It may never happen, unless GM can see its way to real profits from fuel cells. Nonetheless, in January 2008, the firm unveiled a fuel cell concept car, the Cadillac Provoq, at the Consumer Electronics Show, which is held in Las Vegas each year. One of GM's thoughts for eventual commercial development is a wide variety of car and truck bodies that would mount onto a single, radical "skateboard" chassis design, which integrates the engine directly into the chassis. The skateboard stores fuel cell stacks and hydrogen supplies as well as circuitry that manages the flow of electric power through the various systems necessary to stop, start and maneuver the vehicle. The chassis would include a docking port that links the body above to the electronic control systems. However, the firm's deep financial problems of 2008-09 that led to bankruptcy and a government bailout, along with its intense focus on the Chevy Volt electric car (with a booster gasoline engine) have combined to move GM's fuel cell project to the back burner, perhaps forever.

GM is not the only manufacturer with significant investments in fuel cells. Honda is currently leasing

test models of its FCX Clarity fuel cell-powered car to small numbers of customers in the U.S. and Japan. Toyota began making a small number of fuel cell-powered cars available on 30-month leases in July 2006. In late 2007, a prototype Highlander hydrogen-hybrid fuel cell vehicle traveled 2,300 miles from Alaska to Vancouver, Canada, getting more than 300 miles per tank of hydrogen. In September 2010, Toyota stated that it hoped to have a fuel-cell vehicle on the market in limited quantities in 2015, but only in a few regions where hydrogen fueling stations would be available.

The former DaimlerChrysler invested about $1 billion in its own fuel cell initiative. In 2008 Chrysler featured its ecoVoyager concept car at the Detroit Auto Show. Nonetheless, Chrysler's bankruptcy of 2009 made risky ventures such as fuel cell research much less feasible. As of 2007, Ford had 30 fuel cell-powered Focus compact cars in customer trials, but decided in 2009 to divert hydrogen fuel cell research funds to focus on electric vehicles.

British startup manufacturer developed a fuel cell-powered prototype in 2009 that is about the size of a golf cart. Though small, the vehicle is tough thanks to a body made of carbon composites. There is an electric motor for each of the car's wheels, and ultracapacitors capture and store energy when the brakes are engaged. Riversimple's car has a range of about 199 miles per tank and a top speed of about 50 mph. The company hopes to build hydrogen filling stations in British cities.

Mercedes-Benz also has a hydrogen vehicle, the B-Class F-Cell. The B-Class F-Cell has a range of 249 miles and a top speed of 109 mph. As of early 2011, the vehicle was available to Americans only in Los Angeles, California, because southern California is currently the only region in the country with more than one hydrogen fueling station. There were five stations in early 2011, with another 13 planned for completion by the end of 2012.

Meanwhile, BMW unveiled a hybrid of sorts in 2006 that allows drivers to use either hydrogen or gasoline at the flick of a switch. (The hydrogen is not used in a fuel cell. Instead, it is burned as a fuel in an internal-combustion engine that ordinarily would burn gasoline.) The car uses a V-12 engine that can be powered by either fuel. BMW put 100 of its Hydrogen 7 cars on loan to celebrities in California and Germany in 2007. In 2010, BMW was testing a hydrogen-electric drivetrain hybrid that might be used in next-generation Minis and front-wheel-drive BMWs, according to Britain's Autocar web site. Since more hydrogen than gasoline is required to run an engine the same number of miles, the prototype has a hydrogen tank that utilizes space usually reserved for luggage or passengers. The use of hydrogen offers multiple technical challenges.

After the initial enthusiasm over fuel cells, during which many governments planned to introduce large numbers of fuel cell power plants and vehicles, energy agencies have scaled back their goals. The difficulties surrounding the technology are proving much more stubborn than they initially appeared to be. For example, Japan, one of the largest proponents of fuel cell technology, initially wanted 50,000 fuel cell vehicles on the road by 2010, a goal that couldn't be met.

Unfortunately, fuel cells remain grossly expensive due to their limited production and the industry's current low-technology base. Moreover, hydrogen is not readily available to drivers. GM's head of strategic planning projected that 12,000 stations in the largest cities across the U.S. would put 70% of the population within two miles of a hydrogen filling station. The cost would be about $1 million per station. Numerous solutions have been proposed through the years. Honda promoted a Home Energy Station in Southern California that it hoped would convert natural gas into enough hydrogen to power fuel cells that could run a family's vehicle, as well as supply electricity and hot water for the family home.

Another problem is that many people still have concerns about the safety of hydrogen. Naturally gaseous at room temperature, storing hydrogen involves using pressurized tanks that can leak and, if punctured, could cause explosions. It is also difficult to store enough hydrogen in a vehicle to take it the 300+ miles that drivers are used to getting on a tank of gasoline. To do so, hydrogen must be compressed to 10,000 pounds per square inch and stored on board in bulky pressure tanks.

One idea for storage is cooling the hydrogen to a liquid state and storing it in a cooled tank, but this requires constant refrigeration. A mid-term solution to the problem of creation and storage of hydrogen is to use existing fuels, such as methane, gasoline and diesel. These fuels could be broken down in the car, on-demand, to produce hydrogen, which would then power the fuel cell. Although this would relieve the hydrogen storage problems, it would not remove the need for fossil fuels and it would still produce emissions such as carbon dioxide, though in reduced quantities.

The Bush administration launched a "Hydrogen Fuel Initiative" in 2003, and Congress provided over $1 billion for research. In May 2008, the EU's government funded 470 million Euros for fuel cell and hydrogen research, and Germany has promised as much as 500 million Euros. In 2010, U.S. President Obama signed a Nationwide Hydrogen Highway Initiative into law that requires the Federal Transit Administration and the Department of Energy to build up to 200,000 hydrogen fueling stations not more than five miles apart in more regions of the country. Will this be enough to bring fuel cells to the mass market? Maybe not. It remains to be seen whether such stations will be constructed, despite the possibility of up to $2.1 million in subsidies for each new hydrogen filling station, and up to $300,000 for the addition of a hydrogen pump to an existing filling station. In addition, there are still massive challenges to solve in designing and marketing vehicles that can store and burn hydrogen fuel. A U.S. Department of Energy study determined that it would take public funding of $45 billion to get 10 million fuel cell cars on the road by 2025, assuming that mass production would create a dramatic reduction in the cost of manufacturing fuel cells, and that public funding would encourage the development of a network of fueling stations. Meanwhile, electric cars are clearly the next wave.

16) Fuel Efficiency Becomes a Key Selling Element/Stiff Emissions Standards Adopted in the U.S. and Abroad

By mid-2009, the price per gallon of gasoline in the U.S. averaged around $2.50, which continued more or less into 2010. This was followed by rapidly rising prices in 2011, reaching as high as $3.74 per gallon through September. The fluctuating market for gasoline has many consumers reconsidering the vehicles they are willing to drive. Light trucks, usually defined as minivans, pickups and sport utility vehicles (SUVs), have gradually lost market share to smaller, more fuel-efficient vehicles. This was very bad news indeed for the Big Three (General Motors, Ford and Chrysler). U.S. carmakers in the 1990s and early 2000s saw 60% or more of their unit sales in America to be in light trucks, which earned very high profit margins. In contrast, Asian car manufacturers such as Honda, Kia, Hyundai and Nissan offer product lines comprised of more than 50% sedans or smaller vehicles.

This is not to say that light trucks no longer sell in America. In fact, they remain a very large market, although smaller than in the past. Consumers are now more likely to buy a more fuel efficient vehicle, unless they really need a truck, SUV or minivan in order to carry their typical loads. Light trucks are still needed by certain consumers and by many types of businesses, regardless of the fact that the cost of filling them with fuel has soared. To put this in perspective: In 2004, "truck" sales (primarily pickups, vans and SUVs) hit their peak in the U.S., selling 9.6 million units or about 55.5% of car/truck sales combined. For 2010, the number of trucks sold was up to 5.9 million compared to 2009's 5.0 million, comprising a surprising 50.4% of new vehicle sales in the U.S. For the manufacturers, gross profits per light truck unit are many times higher than the profits made from small cars.

CAFE (corporate average fuel economy) standards were first issued by U.S. federal regulators in the 1970s as a method of setting average fuel economy standards for carmakers. In December 2007, the U.S. federal government signed a fuel efficiency bill into law that requires automakers to raise their average combined gas mileage fleet-wide to 35 miles per gallon (mpg) by 2020 for all cars and light trucks. The government then established a further requirement of 31.6 mpg for all cars and trucks by 2015. In 2009, the Obama Administration substantially raised those requirements to an average of 35.5 mpg by 2016. During 2011, the Obama Administration planned to raise the bar considerably to 54.5 mpg by 2025.

In order to reach such high levels of efficiency, higher manufacturing costs will impact sticker prices. Some auto industry observers believe that these tough mileage requirements will add much higher manufacturing costs than those estimated by the government.

When considering the effect of CAFE rules, bear in mind that they are a sort of average (a "harmonic mean") for a manufacturer's entire line of cars and light trucks, and that number is arrived at by a circuitous calculation, with separate considerations for a company's domestic cars, imported cars and light trucks. The more that a car maker offers ultra efficient cars, such as electrics and hybrids, the closer it comes to meeting the rules. As with all federal regulations, the CAFE update (at 700 pages written in 2011) is immense and intricate. For example, firms can earn various "credits" that enable them to temporarily avoid penalties if they do not meet the standards.

In general, meeting such high average fuel efficiency will require a combination of several things. To begin with, manufacturers will be forced to build much lighter vehicles. This means that in some cases they will go so far as to eliminate the spare tire and wheel in order to save 100 to 150 pounds. At the same time, they will engineer lighter engines, use plastic where possible as a replacement for metals, and look for weight savings in everything from seats to bumpers. For example, Ford is designing a new Ecoboost three-cylinder engine. Utilizing turbocharging, this much lighter powerhouse will produce 118 horsepower per liter, compared to about 70 horsepower for current four-cylinder models. Fuel efficiency will be greatly enhanced. The first use of the engine was planned for the 2012 Ford Focus.

According to the U.S. Environmental Protection Agency, the most fuel-efficient 2011 car models included the Toyota Prius hybrid, Ford Fusion hybrid, Honda Civic hybrid, Honda CR-Z hybrid and Lexus HS250h hybrid. Not surprisingly, lightweight, advanced diesel models rank highly for mileage, including the Volkswagen Golf TDI, Jetta TDI and Beetle TDI.

In Europe, where extremely high fuel taxes combined with small parking spaces and roads that are frequently narrow encourage consumers to purchase lightweight, high efficiency vehicles (about one-half of all new passenger vehicles sold are diesel-powered). Meanwhile, in 2008 the EU made a formal proposal for Euro VI emission standards to take effect starting in 2013. The proposal requires an 80% reduction of nitrogen oxide (NOx) and a 66% reduction of the particulate matter (PM) emission limit.

Environmental groups lobbying for lower emissions levels in America and elsewhere claim that these reductions can be accomplished by updating air conditioning refrigerants, designing more efficient transmissions, and making exterior designs more aerodynamic, while utilizing such things as turbochargers and cylinder deactivators in smaller, more efficient engines. Some groups project that these changes could be made at a cost of $1,960 per vehicle, and that the costs will be recouped by savings at the gas pump. Other observers claim that many of the proposed changes are not feasible, and if they were, they would cost upwards of $4,360 per vehicle.

A study by the National Academy of Sciences projected that improvements of as much as 40% in gasoline-powered automobile fuel economy could be achieved within 10 to 15 years through the use of enhanced technologies. For example, advanced transmissions and fuel-injection systems could minimize fuel usage and curtail unwanted power loss. While the manufacture of lighter vehicles could improve mileage, weight is not the single overriding factor. Technologies are available that could do wonders for fuel efficiency, although they would take considerable time, money and effort to fully deploy.

A study, prepared in part by John DeCicco at Environmental Defense, declared that the adoption of current and emerging technologies could drive the average efficiency of U.S. cars to 46 mpg and SUVs to 40 mpg. The study was co-authored by Feng An of the Argonne National Laboratory and Marc Ross, a physicist and automobile expert at the University of Michigan. They propose that two-thirds of the improvement would come from powertrain technology, while one-third would come from cutting three important factors: vehicle weight, air resistance and rolling resistance. Hyundai is focusing on technologies such as gasoline direct injection, dual continuously variable valve timing and eight-speed automatic transmissions in order to dramatically enhance mileage.

A proven gas-saving measure is an inexpensive shift to a six-speed automatic transmission. The cost for the addition is a mere $400, but the measure can add one to two miles per gallon in efficiency. This kind of transmission was already being used in many new vehicles as of 2008. The 2011 Ford Mustang proves that drivers can enjoy fast acceleration as well as excellent fuel efficiency, since the V-6 model delivers 305 horsepower and 31 mpg on the highway. The car has a six-speed transmission, in addition to lower-rolling resistance tires and an electric (as opposed to a hydraulic) power steering system which reduces engine strain. Ford plans to use this electric steering system on all its models by 2012.

GM claims that an improvement of between 6% and 12% in fuel economy can be achieved through cylinder deactivation technology. In these systems, one-half of an engine's cylinders stop firing once a steady cruising speed is reached. Other small changes, such as those incorporated in the 2013 Chevrolet Malibu sedan, can add up. For example, the hood is made of aluminum instead of steel and rounded front corners reduce drag (saving 0.4 mpg on the highway); active shutters behind the grill open and close as needed to cool the engine (savings of 0.3 mpg); and the car has no spare tire but includes an inflator kit for temporary tire fixes (savings of 0.4 mpg). GM already launched the 2012 $19,000 Chevy Cruze Eco, which is equipped with all of the above and promises to deliver 42 mpg.

Trucks can also be made more fuel efficient. The 2011 Ford F-150 has a power-steering system that draws power from the battery instead of requiring an additional hydraulic power-steering system, increasing fuel efficiency by about 4%.

A bright spot on the fuel efficiency horizon is a new hydraulic-hybrid system that is being tested on large service vehicles such as garbage trucks and UPS delivery vans. The EPA's National Vehicle and Fuel Emissions Laboratory in Ann Arbor, Michigan has designed a hybrid garbage truck that uses a diesel engine, assisted by a hydraulic pump and storage tank system, that replaces the drivetrain and transmission. The pump and tanks makes it possible to store and reuse energy normally lost when brakes are applied, thereby increasing fuel efficiency as much as 60% and reducing carbon monoxide emissions by more than 40%. UPS placed an order with hydraulic manufacturer Eaton Corporation and truck builder Navistar for 200 hybrid electric vehicles which hit the streets in cities across the U.S. in 2010. The EPA projects that the cost per vehicle to add the hybrid components is less than $7,000, while fuel savings over a 20-year lifespan could exceed $50,000.

Internet Research Tip: Hybrid Commercial Trucks:
Hybrid trucks and buses will soon be in high demand by major truck fleet operators such as UPS. For the latest information on pilot projects, technologies and fleet purchases, see Calstart's website at www.calstart.org.

Another new technology of note is an artificial neural network. The network, which is composed of models of neurons embedded on standard silicon chips, detects cylinder misfires and controls idle speeds, thus increasing fuel efficiency. These networks are already in use in large-engine vehicles such as Aston-Martin's 12-cylinder DB9 and Ford's E-Series full-size van. GM and Audi are also working on implementing the technology for use in issues relating to variable valve timing and engine performance improvements. Serious measures such as these will have to be taken across the board by automakers in their vehicle designs in order to meet future emissions and efficiency stipulations.

SPOTLIGHT: Motor Scooters

Don't be surprised to see more and more of your neighbors zipping around on stylish motor scooters. The motor scooter dates back to post-war Europe, where Piaggio made the first Vespa in 1946. While scooters have long been extremely popular in densely-populated cities outside the U.S., such as Rome and Bangkok, Americans have rarely been scooter buyers, turning instead to cars, light trucks and powerful motorcycles.

However, extremely high gasoline prices, the difficulty of parking in some U.S. cities and attractive new scooter models are lighting a fire under U.S. consumers. For example, the Vespa has extremely peppy new models that have room for two people and perhaps a shopping bag, get more than 60 mpg and cost about $4,400. Honda and Yamaha have jumped into the market with scooters that feature storage compartments for groceries or helmets along with engines that are powerful enough for highway cruising. Lighter, new scooters with small engines that get up to 120 mpg are offered by other makers for about $3,000.

Another trend is the restoration of classic, Italian-made Lambretta and Vespa scooters. For example, less than $3,000 will get you a fully restored, classic Vespa from the 1960s. In addition to snappy new scooters, sales of full size motorcycles have grown.

Meanwhile, motorbikes are a massive market in India, where, in a typical year, motorbikes outsell cars and trucks by a factor of seven. Indian manufacturer Hero Honda Motors is India's leading seller, and it saw its net income for 2009 rise by 6% to $273.4 million.

17) Car and Bike Sharing Programs Proliferate

A car sharing business called Zipcar (www.zipcar.com) is popping up in growing numbers of U.S. cities that offers drivers inexpensive alternatives to owning their own cars. For an annual fee of about $60 (and a $25 application fee), plus hourly rates starting at $8 and daily rates starting at $69, Zipcar members are issued smart cards that allow them to unlock Zipcar vehicles with a wave of the card over the windshield. The cars are equipped with pre-paid cards for use at gas stations and insurance coverage; and drivers are allowed 180 miles of driving per day. As of early 2011, there were 530,000 members driving 8,000 Zipcars available in the U.S., Canada and in the U.K. Business boomed as gas prices escalated to dizzying heights and then again at the onset of the global economic crisis. Zipcar has spawned a number of similar offerings from competitors including rental car firm Hertz Corp.'s Connect by Hertz (which is available in the U.K., Spain, Germany, France and Canada) and Enterprise Rent-A-Car's WeCar.

Meanwhile, General Motors-sponsored researchers at the Massachusetts Institute of Technology (MIT) are creating a prototype called the CityCar that operates very much like luggage carts found at airports and train stations. CityCars are two-seated, bubble-shaped vehicles with motorized electric wheels that work together to reach speeds of up to 55 miles per hour. When parked, the cars fold to about half their size and stack together, with four stacked cars capable of fitting into a single parking space. Drivers would swipe a credit card in a reader to release a stacked car and restack it at another rack near the driver's destination. The projected cost for using the cars is about $1 per mile.

BMW worked on a similar concept that utilizes collapsible motor scooters that have many safety features typically found on cars such as airbags and seatbelts. The C1 scooter was released in 2001, but sold only 33,700 units before the concept was abandoned.

A new initiative in Paris is Autolib, a car sharing program that plans to put 3,000 electric vehicles on Paris streets by the end of 2011. Along with commissioning the vehicles (designed by CEO Vincent Bolloré), Autolib is building 1,120 electric charging stations for parking and recharging. Station construction began in the summer of 2011, with a launch anticipated by December.

Meanwhile, BMW announced plans to allow drivers in Germany to rent its vehicles by the hour in late 2010. A 12-month pilot program, called "BMW on Demand," offers vehicles from its 1-series of compacts (at about $22.29 per hour) up to its luxury 7 series (about $43.57 per hour). Cars can be picked up and dropped of at the BMW Welt, the company's exhibition and event center next to its headquarters in Munich. BMW is betting that the trend of younger urban drivers choosing not to own vehicles will continue. The project is similar to other European initiatives, including Peugeot's Mu and Daimler's Car2go.

Advertising firm JCDecaux in Paris launched a bicycle-sharing program in 2007. Sturdy, comfortable gray bikes called Vélibs are currently available at 1,639 rental stations throughout the city. Riders can rent bikes by the day or the week, but there are also annual subscriptions that allow unlimited 30-minute maximum rides for about $46 per year. Members create an account using their credit cards which includes permission for the company to charge about $240 if a bike is not returned. JCDecaux turns rider fees over to the city of Paris, but generates additional income through advertising via more than 1,600 billboards throughout Paris. Initially the program was a success with approximately 42 million rentals in the first 18 months, but by early 2009, about half of the 15,000 Vélibs in the original fleet had been stolen and even more had been vandalized. JCDecaux negotiated with city officials, who agreed to pay $500 per bicycle needing replacement, which will cost up to $2 million per year. Despite the difficulties, bike sharing is catching on and spreading in small ways to cities including London, San Francisco and Singapore. Mexico City has a bike rental service called Ecobici with 85 docking stations. During its first three months of operation in 2010, Ecobici attracted 7,000 riders who took more than 200,000 trips.

18) Electric Cars and Plug-in Hybrids (PHEVs) Enter Market in Low Numbers

For the near term, electric cars will range from 100% electric power vehicles that have relatively short ranges and are plugged-in at home overnight to recharge—to cars like the Chevrolet Volt which runs primarily on an electric motor only, but includes a small gasoline-powered generator engine that will recharge the batteries when needed and give an occasional boost to the drivetrain as well. The Volt is designed to go up to 40 miles without recharging, and has the capability to be recharged by plug-in at home. Early sales, especially in the U.S. have been slow. The Chevy Volt and the Nissan Leaf, for example, had sold 928 and 173 units respectively through the end of February 2011. Many challenges face 100% electric cars. GM hopes to boost Volt sales to about 50,000 units yearly in the near term, and Nissan hopes to boost production of the Leaf to 500,000 yearly. It remains to be seen whether consumer demand will rise to these levels. On an encouraging note, the Chevy Volt was named the North American Car of the Year at the influential Detroit Auto Show in 2011. Ford plans to offer an all-electric Focus in 2012 that will feature smartphone apps that tell the driver where the nearest charging station is.

Nissan is taking a different tack with the debut of the Leaf, a fully electric vehicle released in December 2010. With a range of up to 100 miles, the five-seat Leaf sedan is powered by a 480-pound lithium-ion battery that can be recharged overnight on household current. The official retail price is about $32,780, less up to $7,500 federal tax credit in the U.S. The first vehicles are being assembled in Japan, but the firm is investing as much as $2 billion to retool its Smyrna, Tennessee plant to begin manufacturing Leafs and lithium-ion batteries. Nissan got the jump on GM by committing R&D funding to lithium-ion batteries as early as 1990. The company has a next generation battery in the pipeline that promises a range of up to 186 miles per charge. Nissan had developed much of its electric vehicle technology in partnership with Renault.

In addition to adequate battery life, engineers working on electric vehicles are wrestling with the fact that conveniences such as air conditioning, heating and stereos drain a lot of electricity. Technical advances in these accessories may be necessary, since consumers will not buy such cars in volume without them.

Battery maker Johnson Controls, Inc. is expanding its Power Solutions divisions with two new manufacturing plants. However, recent research performed by the company revealed that only 3% of American drivers are financially suited to all-electric vehicles (meaning they travel many miles per year by primarily making short trips). J.D. Power & Associates estimates that by 2020, hybrid vehicles will make up 5.5% of the U.S. car market and battery-powered electric vehicles 1.9%.

Despite the $5 billion in U.S. federal subsidies for battery manufacturing plants and research and development plus the $7,500 tax credit per vehicle for the first 200,000 units per manufacturer, most drivers are finding electric cars too expensive, taking too long to recharge and coming up short when it comes to driving range per charge. The Nissan Leaf, for example (the battery alone is estimated to cost $15,600) requires a 240-volt charger that customers must install for $2,200. Each charge takes about eight hours for a range of about 100 miles, depending on weather conditions.

A little history is in order: An all-electric car has long sounded logical to many people. GM launched the EV1, an all-electric vehicle, in 1996. Unfortunately, the car was a complete flop, and the $1-billion project was abandoned in 1999. In 2002, Ford announced that it would give up on the Think, an electric car model in which it had invested $123 million. These efforts were an attempt to satisfy government demands, not an attempt to fill early consumer needs. Today's electric cars and hybrids are intended to be major product lines for automakers.

Plug-in hybrids (PHEVs) are similar to standard hybrids, but they enable the owner the option of plugging-in at home overnight to recharge the battery. This will eliminate the need to run the car's gasoline engine, using only battery power as long as the relatively short range isn't exceeded. (Standard hybrids recharge only by running the gasoline-powered side of the car, and by drawing on the drag produced by using the brakes.) Toyota made 500 PHEV versions of its Prius available for testing by selected consumers during 2010 (150 of them in the U.S.).

All-electric cars and advanced hybrids will make a steady push into global auto markets due to:

1) Potential technical breakthroughs in batteries, making them lighter, less expensive and longer-lasting. Nanotechnology may be applied to solve battery challenges.
2) An electric car research, development and investment focus at major car manufacturers.
3) Toyota quickly proved global consumer acceptance (and technological superiority) by selling millions of hybrid vehicles worldwide after the 1997 debut of the Prius. Eventually, Toyota hopes to be selling 1 million hybrid vehicles each year.
4) Electricity is user-friendly and easy to understand. Electric utility companies are generally in favor of the electric car trend. Governments are largely enthusiastic and supportive (including financial support to manufacturers and incentives for consumers).
5) Innovative entrepreneurs are focusing on the electric vehicle.
6) In California, the largest auto market in the U.S., the California Air Resources Board (CARB) requires at least 7,500 vehicles with no tailpipe emissions be sold between 2012 and 2014.
7) Last, but not at all least, in the proper package and at an affordable price, consumers see electric cars as green (low- to no-emissions), highly desirable modes of transportation.
Source: Plunkett Research, Ltd.

Irvine, California startup Fisker claimed in 2010 to have orders for about 1,600 of its $87,900 Karma. By 2011, it was making deliveries to customers. Another high-end electric vehicle is the Tango T600, made by Commuter Cars Corporation. For $108,000, drivers can take the two-seater (one seat behind the other) from zero to 60 miles per hour in about four seconds, and reach a top speed of more than 130 mph (there is also a $150,000 model which uses more powerful lithium batteries).

Mitsubishi offers a tiny plug-in vehicle, the MiEV, at a price of more than $40,000. The MiEV can travel up to 100 miles on a charge. Mitsubishi sold approximately 4,000 of the pricey cars in Japan during fiscal 2010.

Chinese auto manufacturer BYD Co. hoped to begin test marketing and all-electric vehicle, the e6, in the U.S. in 2011. The company is also in negotiations to supply the city of Los Angeles with electric buses, a deal which could result in a manufacturing facility in California.

However, the big news in electric cars is at Tesla. The $109,000 Tesla Roadster, which can go up to 125 miles per hour and run 244 miles per charge, can also accelerate from zero to 60 mph in about 4 seconds!

Tesla, www.teslamotors.com, is a serious business startup, with substantial amounts of venture capital raised, and another $465 million in federal loans set in 2009. By early 2011, the firm had delivered 1,500 Tesla Roadsters. Another Tesla model, the Model S family sedan capable of carrying seven people, was unveiled in 2009, with commercial production hoped to start as early as 2012. The Model S is to have a base price of less than $60,000. Tesla has taken a simple route to solve the problem of batteries: the Tesla Roadster has 6,831 lithium-ion, laptop computer batteries linked together in the trunk.

In May 2010, the Toyota Motor Corporation purchased a $50 million stake in Tesla. As part of the deal, Tesla is taking over a large car manufacturing plant in Freemont, California that was formerly operated as a joint venture of Toyota and GM. The new funds and manufacturing facility affords Tesla significant expansion capability.

Toyota and Tesla will jointly develop an electric version of Toyota's compact RAV4 SUV. Toyota also plans to manufacture a compact electric car designed for short urban trips.

On the lowest end of the electric-powered spectrum are small vehicles that began several years ago as glorified golf carts. Recent technological advances, such as the use of lightweight, long-lasting lithium-ion batteries (the type used in cellular phones and laptop computers) have helped the vehicles evolve into marketable alternatives for short-trip driving. The ZAP Xebra, a three-wheel, four-door vehicle with a sticker price of $11,700, can reach speeds of up to 40 mph and have a range of 40 miles per charge. ZAP stands for "zero air pollution."

Chrysler's Global Electric Motorcars LLC subsidiary offers several models, including vehicles with options such as heated seats, steel bumpers and cup holders. Prices start at about $7,395, but buyers may be eligible for a tax credit.

Ford is using $5.9 billion in U.S. Energy Department loans to develop 13 fuel efficient models, including the manufacture of 5,000 to 10,000 electric vehicles as early as 2011-2012. The funds will be used partly to retool manufacturing plants in Illinois, Kentucky, Michigan, Missouri and Ohio.

GM is collaborating with utility companies in nearly 40 states to work out issues relating to power grids and the added demand that electric vehicles pose. Nissan has similar alliances to promote plug-in stations (it also designated a supplier of home charging stations using a 220-volt plug similar to those used for clothes dryers that promised to recharge batteries in less than eight hours). GM and other manufacturers are working on computer chips and software to imbed in electric vehicles that will communicate with utility systems regarding the best times to recharge for the best prices. Recharging on a summer afternoon, for example, would put a strain on grids already powering air conditioners while off-peak charging would not only be cheaper but more efficient since power plants typically have excess electrical capacity at night.

Many observers believe that two kinds of chargers are necessary, one for home use and another for use in commercial parking spaces. This need opens the door for as much as $12 billion in infrastructure costs. A number of companies are hoping to cash in on PHEV charging needs, including Coulomb Technologies, a California firm which plans to install thousands of public chargers in U.S. cities (each station costs between $2,000 and $5,000). ECOtality, a manufacturer based in Arizona, won a $100 million U.S. federal grant to develop its chargers. The company, in collaboration with Nissan, hopes to install 11,000 chargers in five U.S. states by 2013.

The U.S. government will likely be an early buyer of PHEVs for its fleets. However, the most successful market for electric cars may be Europe rather than the U.S. European drivers are generally accepting of small vehicles. More importantly, gasoline prices in Europe are extremely expensive, often $7 per gallon or more due to high taxes, providing much greater incentive for plug-in cars. Moreover, European drivers are generally accustomed to taking shorter trips than consumers

who drive the wide open spaces of the U.S. and Canada.

Meanwhile, governments in Japan and China are pushing electric vehicles in a big way. Japan offers a consumer subsidy of about $9,000 per vehicle and the Tokyo Electric Power Company (TEPCO) recently formed a consortium to develop a technology standard for rapid battery charging. In China, the government is planning to spend $17 billion on electric vehicle technology through 2020 with the goal of getting 5 million electric cars (global bank HSBC estimates that to be 35% of global electric vehicle market) on Chinese roads. Chinese manufacturer Chery Automobile Company completed a $500 million R&D center in the city of Wuhu that is largely dedicated to electric vehicles.

FedEx Corp., Staples, Inc. and the Frito-Lay division of PepsiCo are purchasing 20-foot electric trucks built by American truck manufacturer Navistar International Corp. and British battery manufacturer Modec, and also trucks built by Smith Electric Vehicles. Each truck costs about $150,000 and has a range of between 60 and 100 miles per charge. Since typical delivery routes are fairly short and usually completed by nightfall, electric trucks seem ideal for the delivery market. Limited range poses few problems and the trucks can be recharged at night during off-peak hours. Staples estimates it will save about $6,500 per year in fuel costs per electric vehicle. Another plus in electric trucks is the braking system. The batteries in electric vehicles are recharged when braking, which has a side benefit of putting less wear and tear on breaks than heavy diesel engines. Brakes for electric trucks last four or five years compared to diesel trucks' one to two.

China-based BYD Company Limited entered the car manufacturing business in 2003 by acquiring a small, floundering firm that was owned by the Chinese government. Under BYD, its inexpensive F3 sedan became a popular in China. More importantly, BYD has begun selling a plug-in hybrid in China, the F3DM. At about $22,000, the F3DM can go about 63 miles in electric-only mode, and can recharge quickly from its backup gasoline engine or from a plug-in feature. Watch for a continuing stream of breakthroughs from this extremely innovative company. Thanks to its long term expertise in battery powered products, it could easily grow to be a significant force in electric cars, and its new E6 plug-in electric car may be a strong competitor. However, its auto sales in 2010 were far below projections. A subsidiary of America-based

Berkshire Hathaway, led by famed investor Warren Buffett, purchased a 10% stake in BYD in 2008.

Among the biggest problems facing consumer adoption of electric cars is the cost of the batteries, which can run thousands of dollars per vehicle, depending on the type of batteries and the place of manufacture. Factoring this into the initial purchase price of the car makes electric vehicles expensive. Thus, among the big ideas in electric cars is a radical concept spearheaded by Shai Agassi, formerly of enterprise software giant SAP. Agassi's startup, called Better Place (www.betterplace.com), is promoting a business model where drivers would swap depleted batteries for charged batteries, or plug into convenient power stations, paying for their choice of plans: unlimited miles, a monthly maximum or pay as they go. Under one potential business model, electric cars would be purchased by consumers without the battery costs built-in. Instead, the batteries would be owned by Better Place and leased to the car owners. The company would provide swappable, charged batteries as a service at a cost-per-mile driven, or cost-per-battery swapped. The initial price of the car would then be comparable to that of a gasoline-powered vehicle, and the consumer would pay for the battery as used, rather than up-front.

Making consumers comfortable that they can have charged batteries when needed is key to this plan. Better Place would provide convenient, closely-spaced charging stations in places like parking garages and shopping centers. A trial project was underway in Tokyo in 2010, and the firm hopes to develop a long-term relationship with China's Chery Automobile Company. In January 2010, Better Place raised an additional $350 million in venture capital. In early 2011, BetterPlace began installing 10 recharging stations in Honolulu, Hawaii.

Those charging stations will be useful for drivers who have time to wait for a charge between trips to and from work or the grocery store. But what about drivers whose batteries are nearly depleted, or who are on longer non-stop trips? This is where the swappable batteries and swapping stations come in. In early 2009, Better Place demonstrated the first such swapping station, in Tel Aviv, Israel. There, robotic arms can remove a car's battery, clean it of road dirt and install a fully-charged battery. In about the same amount of time it takes to pump a small tank full of gasoline, the driver is back on the road. Such swapping stations are estimated to cost about $500,000 each.

Better Place calls its grid the Electric Recharge Grid Operator (ERGO). Its job is to not only supply the electricity, it would also monitor the electricity needs of the cars on the road and their locations, supply directions to drivers for the nearest power supply (using special software and in-car GPS) and negotiate with the local electricity utility with regard to the power supply and bulk electricity pricing. Hopefully, much of the power will come from solar and wind generation. That may be particularly true in initial markets like Denmark.

Better Place has negotiated with the Israeli government to alter its tax code to make electric vehicles attractive to consumers. The tax proposal calls for a 10% tax on zero-emission vehicles and a 72% tax on traditional vehicles that run on gasoline. Better Place hopes to have recharge points throughout Israel, and has similar plans for Denmark and Portugal. Meanwhile, Agassi signed an agreement with Carlos Ghosn, CEO of Nissan and Renault, to make the cars.

The savings to drivers promise to be substantial. Better Place figures a driver getting 20 mpg in a traditional car and clocking 15,000 miles per year at $4 per gallon would spend about $3,000 for fuel. Better Place's fuel costs for the same 15,000 miles are projected to be approximately $1,050.

Internet Research Tip: Electric Cars

For the latest on electric car manufacturers see:
Better Place, www.betterplace.com
Coda Automotive, www.codaautomotive.com
Commuter Cars Corporation,
www.commutercars.com
Electric Drive Transportation Association,
www.electricdrive.org
Global Electric Motorcars, www.gemcar.com
Tesla Motors, www.teslamotors.com
Wrightspeed, www.wrightspeed.com
ZAP, www.zapworld.com

---

19) Proposals for U.S. Electricity Grid Enhancements include a "Smart Grid," Regional Transmission Organizations (RTOs) and Technologies such as Flow Cell Batteries

Proposed solutions to the U.S. electricity grid's problems range from reorganization to massive investments in advanced computerization to barely proven technologies. Some engineers promote the use of immense, high-capacity batteries called "flow cell batteries" to store enough excess electricity to make the grid much more flexible and reliable. The use of large-scale storage systems scattered around the grid would mean that generating companies could create excess power during periods of slow demand, store that electricity and then sell it through the grid a few hours later when demand picks up. It would also mean that spikes in demand, such as the demand caused by air conditioners turned on during an extremely hot summer afternoon, could be served quickly by drawing on stored power. A few of these large battery energy storage systems are already in place in Japan, Australia, Alaska and Utah. Others are being tested in several locations worldwide.

Battery systems such as these not only add reliability to an electricity grid system, they also lower costs and improve efficiency. For example, wholesale power can be purchased at night, when demand and energy prices are low, and then sold the next day during peak hours for a premium.

New technology may eventually enable batteries to store the high current necessary for utility-scale storage. MIT has developed liquid metal batteries that use a liquid electrolyte made from metals and heated to 700 degrees Celsius (1,292 degrees Fahrenheit) to maintain a molten state. Meanwhile, start-up Seeo is making a solid state battery of a polymer electrolyte material that would last longer than other batteries and store more energy.

SPOTLIGHT: Battery Energy Storage Systems

For more information on battery energy storage systems, check the following company web sites:
ABB www.abb.com
Prudent Energy www.pdenergy.com
Telepower Australia www.telepower.com.au
A123 Systems www.a123systems.com

Other super-capacity storage technologies include flywheels, pumped hydro storage and compressed air energy storage. (A lack of efficient, large-scale storage systems has also been one of the factors holding back the development of solar power.) For additional thoughts along these lines, visit the Electricity Storage Association at www.electricitystorage.org.

Superconductive wires also hold promise over the long-term. (See "Superconductivity Comes of Age.") Meanwhile, shorter-term solutions to the grid's inadequacies are needed. Multiple changes could vastly increase the reliability and efficiency of the grid. Currently, the grid is something of a free-for-all. Thousands of utility companies utilize it, but there is little communication among those companies regarding their real-time operating status. At the same time, regulation of the grid desperately needs to be revamped. Companies that transmit via the grid and that might be interested in investing in grid infrastructure currently must deal with a quagmire of competing interests. The grid's three interconnects are broken down into about 120 control areas, but operators of those control areas have very little authority beyond making requests (but not demands) of utilities participating within those areas.

U.S. state and federal agencies are making efforts to increase the grid's efficiency and enforce compliance to regulatory standards. After the massive blackout of August 2003, a joint U.S.-Canadian taskforce was created that stipulated 46 recommendations for improvement to the monitoring of transmission lines and for use of the grid. Each recommendation has since been implemented. These recommendations included the establishment of Independent System Operators (ISOs), which are independent, nonprofit organizations. ISOs ensure that electric generating companies have equal access to the power grid. They may be replaced by larger Regional Transmission Organizations (RTOs), which would each cover a major area of the U.S. The North American Electric Reliability Corporation (NERC), www.nerc.com, is now responsible for enforcing mandatory reliability standards on utilities. NERC fines are levied when performance falls below those standards.

The utilities industry is pushing its own vision of the grid's future, via the respected Electric Power Research Institute (EPRI, www.epri.com), an organization of members representing more than 90% of the electricity generated and delivered in the U.S. EPRI envisions creating an environment in which utilities are encouraged to invest heavily in new transmission technologies. Part of its plan is aimed at developing constant communication among the systems pushing power to, and pulling power from, the grid. EPRI hopes the grid will become a self-repairing, intelligent, digital electricity delivery system. As a result, a systems breakdown in one area might be compensated for by users or producers elsewhere, aborting potential blackout situations. The total investment required would be more than $100 billion.

Another part of its technology platform is based on making the grid "smarter," by using state of the art digital switches and sensors to monitor and manage the grid—a vast improvement over today's equipment. This smart grid would incorporate sensors throughout the entire delivery system, employ instant communications and computing power and use solid-state power electronics to sense and, where needed, control power flows and resolve disturbances instantly. The upgraded system would have the ability to read and diagnose problems. It would be self-repairing, by automatically isolating affected areas and re-routing power to keep the rest of the system running. Another advantage of this smart grid is that it would be able to seamlessly integrate an array of locally installed, distributed power sources, such as fuel cells and solar power, with traditional central-station power generation.

Internet Research Tip:

For the latest in research regarding generation and distribution of power by electric utility companies, see the Palo Alto, California-based **Electric Power Research Institute** (EPRI) at my.epri.com.

Also, the GridWise Alliance, www.gridwise.org, is a consortium of public and private utility and energy companies that supports a stronger electricity grid. Members include General Electric (GE), IBM, the Tennessee Valley Authority and Honeywell International.

In 2009, a new transmission "interconnect" was proposed that would connect the Eastern, Western and Texas grids. Called the Tres Amigas superstation, the project will be located in Clovis, New Mexico, and will use superconducting cable to convert different kinds of current from each region into a common direct current for transmission. (Superconductivity is created by cooling transmission cable to as low as minus 418 degrees Fahrenheit, thus enabling the system to transmit electricity with almost none of the power loss associated with standard cables.) The current would be converted again to the necessary type to match the destination grid. The interconnect theory behind the project means that electricity can be seamlessly moved from one grid to the next as needed in a more efficient and cost-effective manner.

Tres Amigas is spearheaded by Tres Amigas LLC, run by Phil Harris, the former CEO of PJM Interconnection LLC, a major grid-operations concern. American Superconductor Corporation will provide planning services as well as the superconducting cable. The Clovis location is less than 100 miles from substations in each of the existing grids, and would be especially useful in transmitting power generated from the massive wind power farms in West Texas. The greater connectivity afforded by the superstation could promote the development of new energy sources. Despite the $1 billion cost for the venture, Tres Amigas had moved ahead with construction planning and had been granted approval from the Federal Energy Regulatory Commission (FERC) to offer transmission services at negotiated rates, with operation to begin as early as 2014.

An additional technology advantage to the Tres Amigas project is that it will run on DC (direct current) rather than traditional AC (alternative current), which is much more efficient and will result in less electricity being lost during transmission. Furthermore, Tres Amigas plans to utilize compressed air energy storage technology. This means that wind farms could produce power even when there is low demand, and that power could be stored for later use as needed.

New smart utility meters are beginning to be installed at consumers' locations in major U.S. markets that transmit usage data to utilities, display price fluctuations and alert utilities to service interruptions instantaneously. The meters save utilities the cost of employing meter readers and promote conservation since homeowners can plan activities such as washing clothes or charging plug-in devices at night when prices are lower. Homes with solar panels can use the smart meters to measure and sell excess power back to the utility. There's even the ability, for homeowners willing to participate, for utilities to remotely adjust air conditioning and heating systems to cheaper settings when demand is high. Homeowners might adjust settings remotely as well. The use of smart meters can have dramatic benefits for electric utilities in two ways. First, such meters can promote conservation, thus delaying the need to invest in expensive new generating capacity. Second, the utilities can use a dynamic pricing method that enables them to charge considerably higher rates during times of peak demand.

Internet Research Tip: Smart Meters

For an excellent explanation of smart meters, how they work and how they save energy, see CenterPoint Energy's Energy InSight web page: www.centerpointenergy.com/services/electricity/resi dential/smartmeters

---

In October 2009, U.S. President Obama announced grants totaling $3.4 billion (part of the $862 billion economic stimulus package) to be provided to 100 companies including utilities, manufacturers, cities and other agencies in 49 states. The funds, which are being matched by grant money from private sources totaling an additional $4.7 billion, would be used to pay for approximately 18 million smart meters, 700 automated substations and 200,000 smart transformers. Working together, they are intended to result in higher efficiency, reliability and sustainability. (China has invested substantially in this sector, pumping $7.32 billion into grid projects in 2010 according to market research firm Zpyrme.)

Since state regulators must okay new initiatives undertaken by utilities, a number of roadblocks have slowed the process, in some cases leaving utilities with precious little time to lock in funds promised by the government. For example, Baltimore Gas & Electric, a subsidiary of Constellation Energy Group, was rejected by the Maryland Public Service Commission when it proposed smart grid improvements in June 2010. The DOE responded by extending its deadline for state approval which was eventually granted.

San Francisco, California and Dallas, Texas are two examples of metro areas where smart meters are being installed. In San Francisco, Pacific Gas & Electric (PG&E) plans to install as many as 10 million advanced electric and gas meters by 2012. In Dallas, Oncor Electric Delivery Co. plans to install 3 million meters. The San Francisco project is budgeted at about $2.3 billion. On a national basis, 27.3 million smart meters had been installed by mid-2011, compared to 15.6 million a year earlier, according to FERC.

Proponents of smart meters claim that their efficiencies will offset the high installation costs. PG&E estimated that about 70% of its initial investment will be recouped due to savings in maintenance crew costs. Widespread use of the meters creates a smarter network, as their powerful technology allows communication to flow from utilities to consumers and back again.

The meters also have detractors. Power companies have received complaints from customers claiming that their bills are vastly higher due to the meters showing falsely high readings. In several states, class action lawsuits have been filed. In some cases, manufacturers are blaming a lack of consumer education with regard to reading and using the meters. In others, a fast rollout of the new meters caused problems when old billing systems incurred erroneous charges when interfacing with the new equipment.

Technology firms are hoping to cash in on the federal funds-supported smart meter initiative. According to research firm IDC Energy Insights, North American utilities were projected to spend $17.5 billion on computer software, hardware and communications services related to intelligent grid technology between 2010 and 2013. Companies including ABB, Cisco Systems, Ambient Corp., IBM and Microsoft are all promoting new products that support smart grid needs. ABB, for example, specializes in high-voltage direct current links (HVDC) that are ideally suited for transmitting power over long distances. Likewise, appliance manufacturers such as General Electric, Whirlpool and LG are developing new, smart products that turn themselves off when electricity demand is high (and most expensive) and back on when demand falls.

SPOTLIGHT: Ray Bell's Smart Meter

Silicon Valley entrepreneur Ray Bell has a serious entry in the smart meter market with his advanced technology concept. In addition to measuring power usage, the Bell meter acts as an Internet router, monitoring energy usage remotely and noting problems instantaneously. Better yet, the meters communicate via WiMAX for extra-long range wireless transmission. Bell signed a deal with General Electric to license his wireless interface and network software, which GE uses in manufacturing the meters and marketing them to utilities. Intel Capital (the capital arm of Intel, which is a manufacturer of WiMAX chip sets) is another investor in Bell's startup company, Grid Net, www.grid-net.com. The global market opportunity is vast. New smart units cost between $125 and $300 each. Bell and GE face competition from Washington state-based Itron, among others, but Grid Net's GE and Intel-backed credentials place it in the forefront of the smart meter market.

---

20) Superconductivity Comes of Age

Superconductivity is based on the concept of using super-cooled cable to distribute electricity over distance, with little of the significant loss of electric power incurred during traditional transmission over copper wires. It is one of the most promising technologies for upgrading the ailing electricity grid.

Superconductivity dates back to 1911, when a Dutch physicist determined that the element mercury, when cooled to minus 452 degrees Fahrenheit, has virtually no electrical resistance. That is, it lost zero electric power when used as a means to distribute electricity from one spot to another. Two decades later, in 1933, a German physicist named Walther Meissner discovered that superconductors have no interior magnetic field. This property enabled superconductivity to be put to commercial use by 1984, when magnetic resonance imaging machines (MRIs) were commercialized for medical imaging.

In 1986, IBM researchers K. Alex Muller and Georg Bednorz paved the path to superconductivity at slightly higher temperatures using a ceramic alloy as a medium. Shortly thereafter, a team led by University of Houston physicist Paul Chu created a ceramic capable of superconductivity at temperatures high enough to encourage true commercialization.

In May 2001, the Danish city of Copenhagen established a first when it implemented a 30-meter-long "high temperature" superconductivity (HTS) cable in its own energy grids. Other small but successful implementations have occurred in the U.S.

Internet Research Tip:

For an easy-to-understand overview of superconductivity and its many current and future applications, visit the Superconductivity Technology Center of the Los Alamos National Labs: www.lanl.gov/orgs/mpa/mpastc.shtml

---

Today, the Holy Grail for researchers is a quest for materials that will permit superconductivity at temperatures above the freezing point, even at room temperature. There are two types of super-conductivity: "low-temperature" superconductivity (LTS), which requires temperatures lower than minus 328 degrees Fahrenheit; and "high-temperature" superconductivity (HTS), which operates at any temperature higher than that. The former type requires the use of liquid helium to maintain these excessively cold temperatures, while the latter type can reach the required temperatures with much cheaper liquid nitrogen. Liquid nitrogen is pumped through HTS cable assemblies, chilling thin strands of ceramic material that can carry electricity with no loss of power as it travels through the super-cooled cable. HTS wires are capable of carrying more than 130 times the electrical current of conventional copper wire of the same dimension. Consequently, the weight of such cable assemblies can be one-tenth the weight of old-fashioned copper wire.

While cable for superconductivity is both exotic and expensive, the cost is plummeting as production ramps up, and the advantages can be exceptional. Increasing production to commercial levels at an economic cost, as well as producing lengths suitable for transmission purposes remain among the largest

hurdles for the superconductor industry. Applications that are currently being implemented include use in electric transmission bottlenecks and in expensive engine systems such as those found in submarines.

Another major player in HTS components is Sumitomo Electric Industries, the largest cable and wire manufacturer in Japan. The firm has begun commercial production of HTS wire at a facility in Osaka. In addition, Sumitomo has developed electric motors based on HTS coil. The superconducting motors are much smaller and lighter than conventional electric motors, at about 90% less volume and 80% less weight.

Another leading firm, AMSC, formerly American Superconductor (www.amsc.com), sells technology to wind turbine makers, enabling them to design full 10 megawatt class superconductor wind turbines that will operate with higher efficiency than traditional models. It is also participating in advanced-technology electric transmission projects. For example, in collaboration of LS Cable in Korea, it is supplying technology for over 30 miles of superconducting cable systems for the Korean electric grid, starting in late 2010.

Advanced-generation HTS cable has been developed at American Superconductor, utilizing multiple coatings on top of a 100-millimeter substrate, a significant improvement over its earlier 40-millimeter technology. The goal is to achieve the highest level of alignment of the atoms in the superconductor material resulting in higher electrical current transmission capacity. This will increase manufacturing output while increasing efficiency. This is a convergence of nanotechnology with superconductivity, since it deals with materials at the atomic level. The company is well set up to increase production as demand increases.

Leading Firms in Superconductivity Technology:
Sumitomo Electric Industries, http://global-sei.com
AMSC, www.amsc.com
Nexans, www.nexans.com
SuperPower, Inc., www.superpower-inc.com

---

21) Clean Coal and Coal Gasification Technologies Advance/Carbon Capture Proves Costly

In 2010, global production of coal was 3.73 billion tons of oil equivalent, up from 3.41 billion tons in 2009, according to BP plc. While coal is an abundant resource in many parts of the world, it is generally burned in a manner that creates significant amounts of air pollution. On a global scale, the burning of coal produces more carbon dioxide than any other fossil fuel source. "Clean coal" technologies have been developed, but such technologies are enormously expensive.

In the U.S., coal comes from several different regions. The Northern Appalachian area of the Eastern U.S. and the Illinois Basin in the Midwest produce coal that is high in sulfur, which emits more pollutants. In contrast are the enormous stores of coal in Wyoming and Montana, which burn at lower temperatures and produce less energy than high-sulfur coal, but create less pollution. In existing mines, the U.S. has about 250 billion tons of recoverable coal. Combined with coal seams outside of mines, the U.S. has 500 billion tons of recoverable coal.

According to BP, coal accounted for 29.6% of global energy consumption in 2010, compared to 25.6% in 2000. China used 48.2% of the global supply and made up almost two-thirds of global consumption growth. Meanwhile, use of coal in the OECD nations rose by 5.2% (the largest year over year rise since 1979). Production was up sharply in the U.S. and Asia, but slowed in the EU in 2010.

As of 2010, a number of U.S. utilities were turning away from coal in favor of less polluting fuels such as natural gas. This is due partly to stricter emissions regulations now placed on coal-burning plants. Texas-based Calpine acquired 19 power plants from Pepco Holdings, Inc. for $1.63 billion. The bulk of the plants burn natural gas, and Calpine is planning to convert its coal burning concerns in New Jersey and Delaware to gas also. North Carolina utility Progress Energy plans to close 11 coal burning plants by 2017.

In 2011, the Environmental Protection Agency (EPA) established the Cross-State Air Pollution Rule, which affected about 1,000 power plants in 27 U.S. states. The plants must cut emissions of sulfur dioxide by 73% and nitrogen oxide by 54%, from 2005 levels, by 2012. The requirements were estimated to cost businesses and their customers $2.4 billion per year to implement.

The Rule created an immediate uproar. A number of analysts stated major concerns about its impact on the reliability and stability of the U.S. power grid. Others consider the total costs to the economy to be much too high, particularly while the economy is struggling to recover from the Great Recession of 2007-09. The Federal Energy Regulatory Commission (FERC) announced in August 2011 that 81 gigawatts of generating capacity

is likely to be lost by 2018 as coal plants are restricted or closed. That amounts to approximately 8% of all U.S. generating capacity, which could easily result in blackouts and rolling brownouts in addition to substantial raises in electricity rates.

The EPA subsequently softened the requirements with a proposal in October 2011 to offer 10 U.S. states more flexibility in meeting the rule and all 27 states now have until 2014 to comply instead of 2012. Even after these changes, this is still a daunting regulation with the potential for massive economic consequences.

High-sulfur coal is now easier to sell in some markets, since advanced filtering units called scrubbers are in use by a growing number of electric generating companies. Scrubbers are multistory facilities that are built adjacent to smokestacks. They capture sulfur as the coal exhaust billows through the smokestack and sequester it for storage before it can be cleaned. Unfortunately, scrubbers are extremely expensive. Costs of $400 million for a single scrubber are common. For example, Progress Energy budgeted $1 billion on the technology for three of its newer coal-burning plants, which generate enough revenue to justify the expense.

Multiple clean coal technologies are in development. Scientists at the University of Texas are developing a new technology that blasts sound waves into the flue ducts of coal-fired power plants. The noise, which registers at more than 150 decibels (about as loud as a jet engine at takeoff) causes tiny ash particles in the emission stream to vibrate and stick to larger ones, thereby making larger particles that are easier to capture by pollution control equipment like scrubbers.

Yet another technology to reduce emissions is the use of photosynthesis to capture exhaust gases, such as CO_2 from power plants. A company called GS CleanTech (now a part of GreenShift Corporation, www.greenshift.com) developed a CO_2 Bioreactor that converts a concentrated supply of carbon dioxide into oxygen and biomass in the form of algae, which can then be converted into fuel. Competitor GreenFuel Technologies (www.greenfuelonline.com) uses a different method of recycling carbon dioxide from flue gases, achieving the same end result: algae. An early test of GreenFuel's reactor at the Massachusetts Institute of Technology promised the removal of 75% of the carbon dioxide in the exhaust sampled. The biggest company in this field is Synthetic Genomics, www.syntheticgenomics.com, which received a massive investment from ExxonMobil.

Coal-gasification plants could become a trend for electric generation plant construction over the long term. However, costs remain a significant obstacle. Such plants use a process that first converts coal into a synthetic gas, later burning that gas to power the electric generators. The steam produced in the process is further used to generate electricity. The process is called Integrated Gasification Combined Cycle (IGCC). While these plants are much more expensive to construct than traditional coal-burning plants, they produce much less pollution. Since the coal isn't actually burnt, these plants can use lower-cost coal that is high in sulfur. In addition, such plants reduce the amount of mercury emitted from the use of coal by as much as 95%. Two existing "demonstration" plants use IGCC technology, built and operated with federal subsidies. They are located in Mulbery, Florida and West Terre Haute, Indiana. Japan has constructed a demonstration plant, the Nakoso Power Station at Iwaki City.

American Electric Power (AEP), a Columbus, Ohio electric utility, shelved plans to build an IGCC carbon-capture plant in West Virginia due to the company's concerns that state regulators would not allow it to be reimbursed for $668 million cost above through raises in customer utility rates. Without substantial government support on the federal and state levels, power companies are unlikely to be able to afford IGCC efforts.

An additional step that can be added to IGCC plants is the capture or "sequestration" of carbon dioxide. The technology to do so already exists. For example, Norway's Statoil has used it for years at its natural-gas wells in the North Sea. The sequestered carbon dioxide can be pumped underground. Fortunately, carbon dioxide can be used in oil and gas wells to enhance recovery in a process known as CO_2 flooding. These floods sit near large, natural reservoirs of CO_2. The DOE estimated that U.S. oil production using CO_2 flooding could multiply fourfold by 2020.

Internet Research Tip: Carbon Capture and Sequestration (CCS)

For an excellent discussion of carbon capture and sequestration technologies, research and demonstration projects, see the U.S. Department of Energy's web site for the NETL (National Energy Technology Laboratory) www.netl.doe.gov/technologies/carbon_seq/index.html.

South African fuel company Sasol Ltd. has had success in making liquid fuel from coal that powers gasoline, diesel and jet engines. Germany first used the technology, which is called Fischer-Tropsch after the scientists who developed it, during World War II. In the decades since then, the technology has been refined and improved to the point that Sasol provides a significant portion of South Africa's fuel needs and is expanding with gas-to-liquids plants in Qatar and Nigeria.

In the U.S., recent federal stimulus funding includes money for carbon capture and sequestration research and demonstration. FutureGen Alliance, www.futuregenalliance.org, a project involving a utilities consortium funded by subsidies from the U.S. government, hopes to build a plant in Mattoon, Illinois to test cutting-edge techniques for converting coal to gas, capturing and storing pollutants and burning gas for power. By late 2010, FutureGen Alliance signed an agreement with the DOE to build the FutureGen 2.0 CO_2 pipeline network and CO_2 storage site to be built in Morgan County, Illinois.

Carbon capture and storage is a global effort, especially in Europe where $10.5 billion in government funding has been promised for new projects, according to Bloomberg new Energy Finance (BNEF). Funding is far less in other countries: $5.1 billion in the U.S.; $4.9 billion in Canada; and $2.5 billion in Australia.

22) Bio-plastics Become a Reality/Plastic Packaging Made from Corn and Soy

The next big thing in plastics is the use of corn sugar, sugarcane or soybeans as opposed to petrochemicals to make packaging that is biodegradable. The hope is also that bio-plastics may be cheaper to produce than their traditional, petrochemical-based counterparts, and that they may be more environmentally acceptable. Bio-refiner Cargill, Inc. is vastly increasing its production of soybeans and corn derivatives to make plastics for use in carpets, disposable plates and cups, candles, lipsticks and body panels for automobiles and construction equipment. Metabolix, a Massachusetts-based bioscience company, makes a polyester called polyhydroxy-alkanoate (PHA) that is among the first 100% bioplastics. It is durable, can withstand extreme heat and is biodegradable. Metabolix, in a joint venture with Archer Daniels Midland called Telles, is producing and marketing "Mirel" branded PHA pellets from its corn mill in Clinton, Iowa that generates 110 million pounds of PHA each year. Mirel is to be used by Newell Rubbermaid to make a biodegradable Paper Mate brand pen that will sell for $1.25, only slightly more than non-biodegradable plastic pens.

Plastic packaging made from corn sugars is rapidly gaining favor over oil-based plastics with retailers such as Wal-Mart, Wild Oats Market and food suppliers including Del Monte and Newman's Own, especially in light of fluctuating oil prices. The corn-based plastics are manufactured by NatureWorks, a subsidiary of Cargill, Inc., which in 2010 doubled its production capacity to 140,000 metric tons a year of Ingeo, a bioplastic used in fresh food containers and textiles. This can be considered a part of a broader movement towards the use of renewables by major corporations. For example, at General Electric (GE), a landmark "ecomagination" program of dozens of products including wind power, more efficient jet engines or new high-efficiency power generators that meet government standards for energy efficiency. Revenues from these products reached $18 billion in 2009, while the company surpassed $5 billion in ecomagination research and development investment in 2009, one year ahead of schedule. The company is committed to invest another $10 billion by 2015, despite the fact that 2010 revenues from these products remained flat at $18 billion. Industry analysts see these developments as part of the growth of an environmental technology sector.

In 2009, BASF launched Ecovio and Ecoflex, new biodegradable and compostable plastics used for coating paper and manufacturing shrink films. Both products contain higher percentages (75% and 66% respectively) of bio-based materials such as corn, making them faster to break down in landfills. In 2010, BASF announced it would terminate its business regarding the additive Envirocare to focus on its two biodegradable and compostable products.

Massachusetts-based Novomer is developing technology that combines traditional chemical feedstocks with carbon dioxide and carbon monoxide that would otherwise be released into the air. The resulting combination is material that can be used in plastics and coatings. Novomer is partnering with Praxair to supply carbon dioxide and Kodak Specialty Chemicals to support the process development. The company hopes to have products such as plastic packaging on the market by 2012.

Brazil is the world leader in cost-efficient ethanol production. In July 2011, industrial giant Mitsui & Co., Ltd., of Japan and The Dow Chemical Company of the U.S. announced an exciting joint venture in bioplastics from sugarcane in Brazil. Dow has already operated in Brazil for decades. Mitsui will buy a 50% stake in Dow's Brazilian sugarcane business. Mitsui has a significant long term interest in "green" chemicals. Together, Dow and Mitsui will produce biopolymers in Brazil in large quantities.

23) New Display Technologies with PLEDs

State of the art LEDs (light emitting diodes) have the potential to greatly reduce energy usage while providing very high quality lighting and displays. In addition, solar power is now being combined with the latest LEDs to create fully-renewable energy light sources.

The LED was first developed in 1962 at the University of Illinois at Urbana-Champaign. LEDs are important to a wide variety of industries, from wireless telephone handsets to signage to displays for medical equipment, because they provide a very high quality of light with very low power requirements. They also have an extremely long useful life and produce little heat output. All of these characteristics are great improvements over a conventional incandescent bulb or the LCD (liquid crystal display).

On a groundbreaking day in 1989 at Cambridge University, researchers discovered that organic LEDs (OLEDs) could be manufactured using polymers. The plastic substance known as PPV (polyphenylenevinylene) emits light when layered between electrodes. The resulting product is referred to as a PLED (polymer light emitting diode). Soon, many industries realized the advantages of PLEDs as display devices that emit their own light. In contrast, the older LCD (liquid crystal display) technology works on a system whereby a separate light source has to be filtered in several stages to create the desired image. PLED is more direct, more efficient and much higher quality. PLED is also an excellent system for the manufacture of extremely thin displays that can work at very low voltage. The useful life of a PLED can be 40,000 hours. Advanced displays utilizing PLED can be viewed at angles approaching 180 degrees, and they can produce quality images in flat panels, even at very low temperatures.

Cambridge Display Technology (CDT, www.cdtltd.co.uk), a subsidiary of Sumitomo Chemical Group, points out several exciting uses for these polymer LEDs that may develop over the mid-term. For example, the low energy requirements of PLEDs could be used to create packaging for consumer or business goods that have a display incorporated into the front of the package. This display could provide a changing, entertaining and highly informative description of the product to be

found within the package. Since PLEDs can be
incorporated into flexible substrates, displays for
advertising or information purposes can be built in
the shape of curves. The possibilities are nearly
endless. Most likely, new uses will develop as larger
and larger numbers of PLEDs are manufactured and
higher volume leads to lower prices.

For example, Canadian technology firm
Carmanah Technologies Corp. (www.carmanah.com)
combined LEDs with solar panels for use in marine
buoys. It has expanded further into lighting products
for airfields, railways and general outdoor lighting,
providing lights that are easy to install as well as
powered entirely by renewable solar energy.

Chapter 2

GREEN TECHNOLOGY INDUSTRY STATISTICS

Contents:

GreenTech Industry Overview

Global Green Technology Industry Annual Revenue	2.05	Tril. $US	2010	RB
Projected	8.33	Tril. $US	2020	RB
Global Middle Class Population	2.0	Billion	2011	OECD
Projected	4.9	Billion	2030	OECD
Venture Capital Investment in GreenTech, U.S.	3.98	Bil. $US	2010	EY
First 3 Quarters 2011	3.30	Bil. $US	2011[1]	EY
Energy Intensity: World	6.8	MBtus/$US GDP	2015	DOE
U.S.	6.7	MBtus/$US GDP	2015	DOE
U.S. Renewable Energy Consumption by Transportation	1,098	Tril. Btu	2010	DOE
Total U.S. Energy Consumption by Transportation	27,507	Tril. Btu	2010	DOE
U.S. Renewable Energy Consumption by Industry	2,249	Tril. Btu	2010	DOE
Total U.S.Energy Consumption by Industry	30,139	Tril. Btu	2010	DOE
U.S. Renewable Energy Production	8,064	Tril. Btu	2010	DOE
Total U.S. Energy Production	75,031	Tril. Btu	2010	DOE
Number of US GreenTech Businesses	2,154,700		2009	BLS
Estimated Food Production Increase Required by 2050	70	%	2011	UN
Land Area Employing Biotech Crops: Global	148.0	Mil. Ha	2010	ISAAA
Land Area in 2010	44.2	Mil. Ha	2000	ISAAA
Global Waste Water Revenues	170	Bil. $US	2010	Fortune
Daily US water usage, per capita	2,057	gals./day	2010	WFP
Agricultural Water Usage, as % of Total: US	41	%	2011	Economist
China	70	%	2011	Economist
India	90	%	2011	Economist
Global Decline in Carbon Emissions since 1990	15.4	%	2009	IEA
Decline in Carbon Emissions from the Developed World	6.5	%	2009	IEA
Decline in U.S. Carbon Emissions since 1990	33.6	%	2009	IEA
Increase in Carbon Emissions from the Previous Year: Asia	5.5	%	2009	IEA
China	5.0	%	2009	IEA
Middle East	3.6	%	2009	IEA
Global Carbon Emissions from Fuel	29.0	Bil. Tons	2009	IEA
Carbon Intensity of Energy Use: World	58.3	M/Ts/Bil. Btus	2015	DOE
U.S.	55.7	M/Ts/Bil. Btus	2015	DOE
Number of Alternative Fuel Vehicles In Use, U.S. [3]	826,318	Vehicles	2009	EIA
Hybrid Electric Vehicle Sales, U.S.	274,200	Vehicles	2010	EIA
Estimated Share of Global General Lighting using LED Bulbs	10.0	%	2010	McKinsey
Projected Share of Global General Lighting using LED Bulbs	59.0	%	2020	McKinsey
Projected Global LED Annual Revenue	94.0	Bil. $US	2020	McKinsey

[1] As of Q3 2011. [2] Reserves that can be commercially recovered. [3] An alternative fuel vehicle must have the input fuel as an alternative to gasoline or diesel. For this reason gasoline-electric and diesel-electric hybrids are excluded.

BLS = Bureau of Labor Statistics; Census = U.S. Census Bureau; DOE = U.S. Dept. of Energy; EIA = U.S. Energy Information Administration; EY = Ernst & Young; IEA = International Energy Agency; ISAAA = International Service for the Acquisition of Agri-biotech Applications; OECD = Organization for Economic Co-operation & Development; RB = Roland Berger; UN = United Nations; WFP = waterfootprint.org

Source: Plunkett Research, Ltd. Copyright© 2012, All Rights Reserved

www.plunkettresearch.com

Global Alternative Energy Industry Overview

	Number	Unit	Year	Source
Global Wind Power				
Cumulative Installed Wind Turbine Capacity, End of Year (2015 figure is a projection.)	459,000	MW	2015	GWEC
	197,039	MW	2010	GWEC
	158,908	MW	2009	GWEC
	120,291	MW	2008	GWEC
	93,820	MW	2007	GWEC
	74,052	MW	2006	GWEC
Global Geothermal Power				
Cumulative Installed Geothermal Power Capacity, End of Year (2015 figure is a projection.)	11,600	MW	2015	PRE
	10,900	MW	2010	BP/IGA
	10,710	MW	2009	BP/IGA
	10,313	MW	2008	BP/IGA
	9,922	MW	2007	BP/IGA
	9,485	MW	2006	BP/IGA
Global Fuel Ethanol Production				
Production	43,500	TTOE	2010	BP
	38,418	TTOE	2009	BP
	35,627	TTOE	2008	BP
	26,955	TTOE	2007	BP
	21,048	TTOE	2006	BP
Global Hydroelectric Power Consumption				
Consumption*	775.6	MTOE	2010	BP
	736.3	MTOE	2009	BP
	724.7	MTOE	2008	BP
	696.5	MTOE	2007	BP
	684.4	MTOE	2006	BP
Global Nuclear Power Consumption				
Consumption*	626.2	MTOE	2010	BP
	614.0	MTOE	2009	BP
	619.2	MTOE	2008	BP
	622.1	MTOE	2007	BP
	635.4	MTOE	2006	BP
Global Solar Power				
Cumulative Installed Photovoltaic (PV) Power (IEA Photovoltaic Power Systems Program Member Countries)	40,000	MW	2010	BP/IEA
	22,929	MW	2009	BP/IEA
	15,599	MW	2008	BP/IEA
	9,173	MW	2007	BP/IEA
	6,775	MW	2006	BP/IEA

* Based on gross generation and not accounting for cross-border electricity supply. Converted on the basis of thermal equivalence assuming 38% conversion efficiency in a modern thermal power station.

MW = Megawatts
TTOE = Thousand Tonnes Oil Equivalent
MTOE = Million Tonnes Oil Equivalent
IEA = International Energy Agency
IGA = International Geothermal Association

GWEC = Global Wind Energy Council
BP = British Petroleum
BTM Consult = BTM Consulting APS
PRE = Plunkett Research Estimate

Source: Plunkett Research, Ltd. Copyright© 2010, All Rights Reserved
www.plunkettresearch.com

Number and Percent Distribution of GreenTech Establishments, by Industry Sector, U.S. 2009

Industry sector	Total Number of U.S. GreenTech Establishments	Percent distribution of all GreenTech Establishments
Construction	820,700	38.1
Professional and business services	779,100	36.2
Other services (Repair and maintenance services, Professional organizations)	183,300	8.5
Natural resources and mining	88,700	4.1
Information	77,000	3.6
Manufacturing	77,700	3.6
Trade, transportation, and utilities	49,300	2.3
Public administration	42,100	2
Education and health services	26,400	1.2
All other sectors	10,400	0.5
Total	2,154,700	100

Source: U.S. Bureau of Labor Statistics

Plunkett Research, LTD

www.plunkettresearch.com

Energy Production by Renewable Energy, U.S.:
Selected Years, 1950-2010

(In Billions of Btus; Latest Year Available)

Year	Conventional Hydroelectric Power	Renewable Energy				Total Renewable	Total, Renewable & Non-Renewable
		Geothermal	Solar/PV	Wind	Biomass		
1950	1,415,411	NA	NA	NA	1,562,307	2,977,718	35,540,384
1955	1,359,844	NA	NA	NA	1,424,143	2,783,987	40,147,667
1960	1,607,975	359	NA	NA	1,319,870	2,928,204	42,803,347
1965	2,059,077	1,978	NA	NA	1,334,761	3,395,816	50,673,882
1970	2,633,547	5,511	NA	NA	1,430,962	4,070,021	63,495,439
1975	3,154,607	33,780	NA	NA	1,498,734	4,687,120	61,320,192
1980	2,900,144	52,699	NA	NA	2,475,500	5,428,343	67,175,384
1985	2,970,192	97,421	111	60	3,016,233	6,084,017	67,698,304
1990	3,046,391	170,747	59,420	29,007	2,735,110	6,040,675	70,704,627
1991	3,015,943	177,626	62,354	30,796	2,781,798	6,068,516	70,362,376
1992	2,617,436	178,699	63,520	29,863	2,931,678	5,821,196	69,955,461
1993	2,891,613	185,673	66,060	30,987	2,908,446	6,082,779	68,315,363
1994	2,683,457	173,464	68,102	35,560	3,027,535	5,988,118	70,725,632
1995	3,205,307	152,057	69,347	32,630	3,099,082	6,558,423	71,173,992
1996	3,589,656	163,359	70,245	33,440	3,155,301	7,012,000	72,485,899
1997	3,640,458	166,698	69,586	33,581	3,107,908	7,018,230	72,471,857
1998	3,297,054	168,450	69,053	30,853	2,928,929	6,494,338	72,876,215
1999	3,267,575	170,921	67,937	45,894	2,965,132	6,517,460	71,742,198
2000	2,811,116	164,364	65,421	57,057	3,005,661	6,103,620	71,331,982
2001	2,241,858	164,461	64,267	69,617	2,624,160	5,164,363	71,734,563
2002	2,689,017	171,164	63,006	105,334	2,705,408	5,733,929	70,772,921
2003	2,824,533	175,119	62,010	114,571	2,805,435	5,981,667	70,039,769
2004	2,690,078	178,236	62,533	141,749	2,997,605	6,070,201	70,187,541
2005	2,702,942	180,703	63,446	178,088	3,103,664	6,228,843	69,427,313
2006	2,869,035	181,200	68,441	263,738	3,225,769	6,608,183	70,791,751
2007	2,446,389	185,774	75,657	340,503	3,488,962	6,537,285	71,439,733
2008	2,511,108	192,433	88,548	545,548	3,867,220	7,204,857	73,114,303
2009	2,668,824	200,185	97,766	721,129	3,915,188	7,603,091	72,602,973
2010	2,508,824	212,404	109,404	923,753	4,309,675	8,064,060	75,031,467

NA = Not available

Note: Most data are estimates. Totals may not equal sum of components due to independent rounding.

Source: U.S. Department of Energy, Energy Information Administration

Plunkett Research, Ltd.

www.plunkettresearch.com

Total Renewable Electricity Generation by Energy Source and State, 2009

(Thousands of Kilowatt hours; Latest Year Available)

State	Hydroelectric	NonHydroelectric						Total
		Biomass		Geo-thermal	Solar Thermal / PV	Wind	Total	
		Waste	Wood & Derived Fuels[2]					
Alabama	12,535,373	14482	3,035,375	NA	NA	NA	3,049,857	15,585,230
Alaska	1,323,744	6511	NA	NA	NA	7,027	13,538	1,337,283
Arizona	6,427,345	21,990	136,641	NA	14,145	29,545	202,321	6,629,666
Arkansas	4,192,706	57,050	1,528,501	NA	NA	NA	1,585,550	5,778,256
California	27,888,036	2,467,661	3,732,016	12,852,783	647,390	5,839,813	25,539,662	53,427,698
Colorado	1,885,724	56,164	388	NA	25,585	3,163,836	3,245,973	5,131,697
Connecticut	509,546	758,108	622	NA	NA	NA	758,730	1,268,276
Delaware	NA	125,611	NA	NA	NA	NA	125,611	125,611
Florida	208,202	2,376,737	1,954,125	NA	9,470	NA	4,340,332	4,548,534
Georgia	3,259,683	79,600	2,745,569	NA	NA	NA	2,825,170	6,084,853
Hawaii	112,649	284,426	NA	167,591	1,390	251,427	704,835	817,483
Idaho	10,434,264	NA	477,948	75,950	NA	313,418	867,316	11,301,580
Illinois	136,380	709,743	461	NA	16	2,819,532	3,529,752	3,666,132
Indiana	503,470	302,644	NA	NA	NA	1,403,192	1,705,836	2,209,306
Iowa	971,165	167,888	194	NA	NA	7,420,520	7,588,601	8,559,766
Kansas	12,798	NA	NA	NA	NA	2,863,267	2,863,267	2,876,065
Kentucky	3,317,641	100,874	262,660	NA	NA	NA	363,534	3,681,175
Louisiana	1,236,351	67186	2,296,773	NA	NA	NA	2,363,959	3,600,310
Maine	4,211,679	272,872	3,366,750	NA	NA	298,623	3,938,244	8,149,923
Maryland	1,888,769	375,722	175,057	NA	NA	NA	550,780	2,439,549
Massachusetts	1,201,076	1,107,875	115,384	NA	43	5,956	1,229,257	2,430,334
Michigan	1,371,926	834,011	1,489,001	NA	NA	300,172	2,623,184	3,995,110
Minnesota	809,088	887,304	796,331	NA	NA	5,053,022	6,736,657	7,545,745
Mississippi	NA	6960	1,417,319	NA	NA	NA	1,424,279	1,424,279
Missouri	1,816,693	73,338	2,090	NA	NA	499,377	574,805	2,391,498
Montana	9,505,940	NA	94,642	NA	NA	820,924	915,566	10,421,506
Nebraska	433,690	66,195	NA	NA	NA	382,634	448,829	882,519
Nevada	2,460,595	NA	890	1,633,213	174,309	NA	1,808,412	4,269,007
New Hampshire	1,680,492	151,278	984,181	NA	NA	62,477	1,197,936	2,878,428
New Jersey	32,081	928,206	NA	NA	10,707	20,918	959,831	991,912
New Mexico	270,963	33664	NA	NA	NA	1,546,718	1,580,382	1,851,345
New York	27,615,106	1,664,816	535,853	NA	NA	2,266,339	4,467,008	32,082,114
North Carolina	5,171,257	131,491	1,757,350	NA	4,563	NA	1,893,404	7,064,660
North Dakota	1,475,251	11572	NA	NA	NA	2,997,530	3,009,102	4,484,353
Ohio	527,746	209,611	409,685	NA	NA	14,114	633,410	1,161,156
Oklahoma	3,552,573	163010	68,064	NA	NA	2,698,199	2,929,273	6,481,846
Oregon	33,033,513	128,332	674,381	NA	NA	3,469,714	4,272,427	37,305,940

(Continued on next page)

Total Renewable Electricity Generation by Energy Source and State, 2009 (cont.)

(Thousands of Kilowatt hours; Latest Year Available)

State	Hydroelectric	NonHydroelectric						Total
		Biomass		Geo-thermal	Solar Thermal / PV	Wind	Total	
		Waste	Wood & Derived Fuels[2]					
Pennsylvania	2,682,866	1,579,336	694,242	NA	3,562	1,074,788	3,351,928	6,034,794
Rhode Island	4,736	144,600	NA	NA	NA	NA	144,600	149,336
South Carolina	2,332,005	137,254	1,610,717	NA	NA	NA	1,747,971	4,079,977
South Dakota	4,432,451	5775	NA	NA	NA	420,981	426,756	4,859,207
Tennessee	10,211,962	36,300	862,421	NA	NA	51,747	950,468	11,162,430
Texas	1,028,657	429,075	649,298	NA	NA	20,026,103	21,104,476	22,133,134
Utah	835,257	47,878	NA	279,121	NA	159,537	486,536	1,321,793
Vermont	1,485,825	24,190	393,266	NA	NA	11,589	429,045	1,914,871
Virginia	1,478,630	709,203	1,708,316	NA	NA	NA	2,417,519	3,896,149
Washington	72,932,704	167,022	1,305,162	NA	NA	3,572,486	5,044,670	77,977,375
West Virginia	1,645,927	NA149	NA689	NA	NA	742,439	741,602	2,387,529
Wisconsin	1,393,988	519,174	769,156	NA	NA	1,051,965	2,340,295	3,734,284
Wyoming	966,572	NA	NA	NA	NA	2,226,205	2,226,205	3,192,777
U.S. Total	273,445,094	18,442,595	36,050,138	15,008,658	891,179	73,886,132	144,278,703	417,723,797

[1] Includes landfill gas and MSW biogenic (paper and paper board, wood, food, leather, textiles and yard trimmings), agriculture byproducts/crops, sludge waste, and other biomass solids, liquids and gases.

[2] Black liquor, and wood/wood waste solids and liquids.

MSW = Municipal Solid Waste.

PV = Photovoltaic.

NA = No data reported.
Note: Totals may not equal sum of components due to independent rounding.

Source: U.S. Energy Information Administration, Form EIANA923, "Power Plant Operations Report."

Source: U.S. Energy Information Administration

Plunkett Research, Ltd.

www.plunkettreasearch.com

Renewable Energy Consumption by Energy Source, 2006 vs. 2010

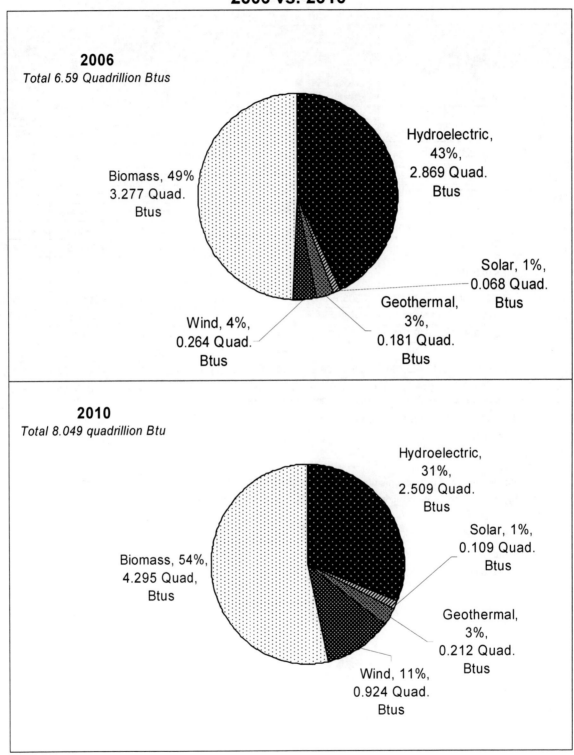

2006
Total 6.59 Quadrillion Btus

Hydroelectric, 43%, 2.869 Quad. Btus

Biomass, 49% 3.277 Quad. Btus

Solar, 1%, 0.068 Quad. Btus

Geothermal, 3%, 0.181 Quad. Btus

Wind, 4%, 0.264 Quad. Btus

2010
Total 8.049 quadrillion Btu

Hydroelectric, 31%, 2.509 Quad. Btus

Solar, 1%, 0.109 Quad. Btus

Biomass, 54%, 4.295 Quad, Btus

Geothermal, 3%, 0.212 Quad. Btus

Wind, 11%, 0.924 Quad. Btus

Source: U.S. Energy Information Administration

Plunkett Research, Ltd.

www.plunkettreasearch.com

Renewable Energy Consumption by Source, U.S.: Selected Years, 1950-2010

(In Billions of Btus; Latest Year Available)

Year	Hydroelectric Power[1]	Biomass[2]	Geothermal[3]	Solar[4]	Wind[5]	Total
1950	1,415,411	1,562,307	NA	NA	NA	2,977,718
1960	1,607,975	1,319,870	359	NA	NA	2,928,204
1970	2,633,547	1,430,962	5,511	NA	NA	4,070,021
1980	2,900,144	2,475,500	52,699	NA	NA	5,428,343
1990	3,046,391	2,735,110	170,747	59,420	29,007	6,040,675
1995	3,205,307	3,101,142	152,057	69,347	32,630	6,560,483
1996	3,589,656	3,156,806	163,359	70,245	33,440	7,013,506
1997	3,640,458	3,105,220	166,698	69,586	33,581	7,015,542
1998	3,297,054	2,927,489	168,450	69,053	30,853	6,492,898
1999	3,267,575	2,963,291	170,921	67,937	45,894	6,515,618
2000	2,811,116	3,008,228	164,364	65,421	57,057	6,106,186
2001	2,241,858	2,622,347	164,461	64,267	69,617	5,162,550
2002	2,689,017	2,700,598	171,164	63,006	105,334	5,729,119
2003	2,824,533	2,807,132	175,119	62,010	114,571	5,983,364
2004	2,690,078	3,009,666	178,236	62,533	141,749	6,082,261
2005	2,702,942	3,116,408	180,703	63,446	178,088	6,241,587
2006	2,869,035	3,276,351	181,200	68,441	263,738	6,658,765
2007	2,446,389	3,502,273	185,774	75,657	340,503	6,550,596
2008	2,511,108	3,851,924	192,433	88,548	545,548	7,189,561
2009	2,668,824	3,899,122	200,185	97,766	721,129	7,587,025
2010	2,508,824	4,294,929	212,404	109,404	923,753	8,049,313

[1] Conventional hydroelectric net generation (converted to Btu using the fossil-fueled plants heat rate).

[2] Includes energy from wood and wood-derived fuels; municipal solid waste from biogenic sources, landfill gas, sludge waste, agricultural byproducts and other biomass (through 2000, also includes non-renewable waste such as municipal solid waste from non-

[3] Geothermal electricity net generation (converted to Btu using the geothermal energy plants heat rate), and geothermal heat pump and direct use energy.

[4] Solar thermal and photovoltaic electricity net generation (converted to Btu using the fossil-fueled plants heat-rate), and solar thermal direct use energy.

[5] Wind electricity net generation (converted to Btu using the fossil-fueled plants heat rate).

Source: U.S. Department of Energy, Energy Information Administration

Plunkett Research, Ltd.

www.plunkettresearch.com

Renewable Energy Consumption by Energy Use Sector and Energy Source, 2006-2010

(Quadrillion Btu; Latest Year Available)

Sector and Source	2006	2007	2008	2009	2010[p]
Total	6.659	6.551	7.191	7.587	8.049
Biomass	3.277	3.503	3.852	3.899	4.295
Biofuels	0.771	0.991	1.372	1.567	1.855
Biodiesel[1]	0.033	0.046	0.040	0.040	0.028
Ethanol[2]	0.453	0.569	0.800	0.910	1.088
Losses and Coproducts	0.285	0.377	0.532	0.617	0.738
Biodiesel Feedstock[3]	*	0.001	0.001	0.001	0.001
Ethanol Feedstock[4]	0.285	0.376	0.531	0.616	0.738
Waste	0.397	0.413	0.436	0.452	0.454
Landfill Gas	0.157	0.173	0.187	0.204	0.213
MSW Biogenic[5]	0.171	0.165	0.169	0.168	0.164
Other Biomass[6]	0.069	0.075	0.079	0.079	0.076
Wood and Derived Fuels[7]	2.109	2.098	2.044	1.881	1.986
Geothermal	0.181	0.186	0.192	0.200	0.212
Hydroelectric Conventional	2.869	2.446	2.512	2.669	2.509
Solar Thermal/PV	0.068	0.076	0.089	0.098	0.109
Wind	0.264	0.341	0.546	0.721	0.924
Residential	0.472	0.522	0.556	0.552	0.554
Biomass	0.390	0.430	0.450	0.430	0.420
Wood and Derived Fuels[8]	0.390	0.430	0.450	0.430	0.420
Geothermal	0.018	0.022	0.026	0.033	0.037
Solar Thermal/PV[9]	0.063	0.070	0.080	0.089	0.097
Commercial	0.117	0.118	0.125	0.129	0.127
Biomass	0.102	0.102	0.109	0.112	0.108
Biofuels	0.001	0.002	0.002	0.003	0.003
Ethanol[2]	0.001	0.002	0.002	0.003	0.003
Waste	0.036	0.031	0.034	0.036	0.034
Landfill Gas	0.004	0.003	0.003	0.003	0.003
MSW Biogenic[5]	0.026	0.021	0.026	0.028	0.026
Other Biomass[6]	0.007	0.007	0.005	0.005	0.005
Wood and Derived Fuels[7]	0.065	0.069	0.073	0.072	0.070
Geothermal	0.014	0.014	0.015	0.017	0.019
Hydroelectric Conventional	0.001	0.001	0.001	0.001	0.001
Solar Thermal/PV	N/A	N/A	*	N/A	*
Wind	N/A	N/A	N/A	*	*
Transportation	0.475	0.603	0.827	0.934	1.098
Biomass	0.475	0.603	0.827	0.934	1.098
Biofuels	0.475	0.603	0.827	0.934	1.098
Biodiesel[1]	0.033	0.046	0.040	0.040	0.028
Ethanol[2]	0.442	0.557	0.786	0.894	1.070

(Continued on next page)

Renewable Energy Consumption by Energy Use Sector and Energy Source, 2006 - 2010 (cont.)

(Quadrillion Btu; Latest Year Available)

Sector and Source	2006	2007	2008	2009	2010[p]
Industrial	1.930	1.964	2.053	2.005	2.249
Biomass	1.897	1.944	2.031	1.982	2.229
Biofuels	0.295	0.387	0.544	0.630	0.754
Ethanol[2]	0.010	0.010	0.012	0.013	0.016
Losses and Coproducts	0.285	0.377	0.532	0.617	0.738
Biodiesel Feedstock[3]	*	0.001	0.001	0.001	0.001
Ethanol Feedstock[4]	0.285	0.376	0.531	0.616	0.738
Waste	0.130	0.144	0.144	0.154	0.168
Landfill Gas	0.081	0.093	0.093	0.104	0.118
MSW Biogenic[5]	0.006	0.006	0.003	0.004	0.004
Other Biomass[6]	0.043	0.046	0.048	0.047	0.046
Wood and Derived Fuels[7]	1.472	1.413	1.344	1.198	1.307
Geothermal	0.004	0.005	0.005	0.004	0.004
Hydroelectric Conventional	0.029	0.016	0.017	0.018	0.016
Solar Thermal/PV	N/A	N/A	N/A	N/A	*
Wind	N/A	N/A	N/A	N/A	N/A
Electric Power[10]	3.665	3.345	3.630	3.967	4.022
Biomass	0.412	0.423	0.435	0.441	0.440
Waste	0.231	0.237	0.258	0.261	0.252
Landfill Gas	0.073	0.077	0.092	0.097	0.092
MSW Biogenic[5]	0.139	0.138	0.141	0.137	0.135
Other Biomass[6]	0.019	0.022	0.026	0.027	0.025
Wood and Derived Fuels[7]	0.182	0.186	0.177	0.180	0.189
Geothermal	0.145	0.145	0.146	0.146	0.153
Hydroelectric Conventional	2.839	2.430	2.495	2.650	2.492
Solar Thermal/PV	0.005	0.006	0.009	0.009	0.013
Wind	0.264	0.341	0.546	0.721	0.924

[1]Biodiesel primarily derived from soybean oil. [2]Ethanol primarily derived from corn minus denaturant. [3]Losses and co-products from the production of biodiesel. Does not include natural gas, electricity, and other non-biomass energy used in the production of biodiesel.

[4]Losses and co-products from the production of fuel ethanol. Does not include natural gas, electricity, and other non-biomass energy used in the production of fuel ethanol.

[5]Includes paper and paper board, wood, food, leather, textiles and yard trimmings.

[6]Agriculture byproducts/crops, sludge waste, and other biomass solids, liquids and gases.

[7]Black liquor, and wood/wood waste solids and liquids. [8]Wood and wood pellet fuels.

[9]Includes small amounts of distributed solar thermal and photovoltaic energy used in the commercial, industrial and electric power sectors.

[10]The electric power sector comprises electricity-only and combined-heat-power (CHP) plants within North American Classification System (NAICS) 22 category whose primary business is to sell electricity, or electricity and heat, to the public.

* = Less than 500 billion Btu; p = preliminary data; PV = Photovoltaic; MSW = Municipal Solid Waste.

Notes: Totals may not equal sum of components due to independent rounding.

Energy consumption for the noncombustible renewable energy sources (geothermal, hydroelectric conventional, solar thermal, PV and wind) used in electricity generation is determined by mulitiplying generation times the fossil fuel equivalent heat rate.

Source: U.S. Energy Information Administration

Plunkett Research, Ltd.   www.plunkettreasearch.com

Renewable Energy Consumption in the Residential, Commercial & Industrial Sectors, U.S.: 2004-2010

(In Billions of Btus; Latest Year Available)

	2004	2005	2006	2007	2008	2009	2010
Residential Sector							
Biomass (Wood[1])	410,000	430,000	390,000	430,000	450,000	430,000	420,000
Geothermal[2]	14,000	15,900	18,300	22,000	26,400	32,800	36,800
Solar[3]	56,769	57,943	63,405	69,610	80,031	89,068	96,724
Total	480,769	503,843	471,705	521,610	556,431	551,868	553,524
Commercial Sector[4]							
Hydroelectric[5]	1,052	860	927	764	591	692	902
Biomass	105,319	104,777	102,289	102,354	109,327	111,624	107,758
Wood[1]	70,327	69,649	64,729	69,428	72,983	72,440	70,282
Waste[6]	34,237	34,249	36,309	30,960	34,214	36,355	34,091
Fuel Ethanol[7]	755	879	1,251	1,966	2,130	2,829	3,385
Geothermal[2]	12,000	13,600	14,000	14,400	14,800	16,700	18,500
Total	118,371	119,237	117,216	117,518	124,719	129,018	127,182
Industrial Sector							
Hydroelectric[5]	32,556	31,951	28,756	15,715	16,514	18,235	15,924
Biomass	1,816,561	1,836,920	1,896,628	1,943,982	2,031,185	1,982,241	2,228,743
Wood[1]	1,475,735	1,451,729	1,472,379	1,413,086	1,343,874	1,198,023	1,306,965
Waste[6]	131,930	148,248	129,562	144,363	143,624	154,406	167,959
Fuel Ethanol[7]	6,283	6,843	9,668	9,840	11,645	12,968	15,518
Geothermal[2]	3,800	4,300	4,400	4,700	5,000	4,200	4,200
Total	1,852,917	1,873,172	1,929,784	1,964,397	2,052,699	2,004,676	2,248,889

Notes: All values are estimated, except for commercial sector hydroelectric power and waste. Totals may not equal sum of components due to independent rounding.

[1] Wood and wood-derived fuels.

[2] Geothermal heat pump and direct use energy.

[3] Solar thermal direct use energy and photovoltaic electricity net generation (converted to Btu using the fossil-fueled plants heat rate). Includes a small amount of commercial sector use.

[4] Including commercial/industrial combined-heat-and-power (CHP) and commercial/industrial electricity-only plants.

[5] Conventional hydroelectricity net generation (converted to BTU using the fossil-fueled plants heat rate).

[6] Municipal solid waste from biogenic sources, landfill gas, sludge waste, agricultural byproducts, and other biomass. Through 2000, also includes non-renewable waste (municipal solid waste from non-biogenic sources, and tire-derived fuels).

[7] The fuel ethanol (minus denaturant) portion of motor fuels, such as E10, consumer by these sectors.

Source: U.S. Department of Energy, Energy Information Administration

Plunkett Research, Ltd.

www.plunkettresearch.com

Renewable Energy Consumption in the Transportation & Electric Power Sectors, U.S.: 2004-2010

(In Billions of Btus; Latest Year Available)

	2004	2005	2006	2007	2008	2009	2010
Transportation Sector							
Fuel Ethanol[1]	286,290	327,426	441,702	556,791	785,844	893,863	1,069,657
Biodiesel[2]	3,429	11,589	33,249	45,699	40,294	40,390	28,336
Total	289,720	339,015	474,951	602,490	826,138	934,253	1,097,993
Electric Power Sector[3]							
Hydroelectric[4]	2,656,470	2,670,131	2,839,353	2,429,909	2,494,003	2,649,898	2,491,999
Biomass	388,066	405,695	412,482	423,447	435,274	441,011	440,440
Wood[5]	165,189	184,973	181,815	185,956	177,348	180,046	188,688
Waste[6]	222,877	220,722	230,667	237,492	257,926	260,966	251,752
Geothermal[7]	148,436	146,903	144,500	144,674	146,233	146,485	152,904
Solar[8]	5,764	5,502	5,036	6,047	8,516	8,697	12,643
Wind[9]	141,749	178,088	263,738	340,503	545,548	721,127	923,746
Total	3,340,484	3,406,319	3,665,109	3,344,581	3,629,575	3,967,218	4,021,732

[1] The ethanol portion of motor fuels (such as E10 and E85) consumed by the transportation sector.

[2] Either a diesel fuel substitute or diesel fuel additive or extender.

[3] The electric power sector comprises electricity only and combined heat and power (CHP) plants within the NAICS 22 category whose primary business is to sell electricity, or electricity and heat, to the public.

[4] Conventional hydroelectricity net generation (converted to Btu using the fossil-fueled plants heat rate).

[5] Wood and wood-derived fuels.

[6] Municipal solid waste from biogenic sources, landfill gas, sludge waste, agricultural byproducts, and other biomass. Through 2000, also includes non-renewable waste (municipal solid waste from non-biogenic sources, and tire-derived fuels).

[7] Geothermal electricity net generation (converted to Btu using the geothermal energy plants heat rate).

[8] Solar thermal and photovoltaic electricity net generation (converted to Btu using the fossil-fueled plants heat rate).

[9] Wind electricity net generation (converted to Btu using the fossil-fueled plants heat rate).

Source: U.S. Department of Energy, Energy Information Administration

Plunkett Research, Ltd.

www.plunkettresearch.com

U.S. Fuel Ethanol Production and Consumption, 1981-2011

Year	Fuel Ethanol Production (Million Gallons)	Fuel Ethanol Production (Trillion Btu)	Fuel Ethanol Net Imports (Thousand Barrels)	Fuel Ethanol Stocks (Thousand Barrels)	Fuel Ethanol Consumption (Million Gallons)	Fuel Ethanol Consumption (Trillion Btu)	Fuel Ethanol, Excluding Denaturant, Consumption (Trillion Btu)
1981	83.074	7.047	N/A	N/A	83.074	7.047	6.86
1982	225.487	19.129	N/A	N/A	225.487	19.129	18.62
1983	415.372	35.237	N/A	N/A	415.372	35.237	34.3
1984	510.314	43.292	N/A	N/A	510.314	43.292	42.14
1985	617.123	52.353	N/A	N/A	617.123	52.353	50.96
1986	712.066	60.407	N/A	N/A	712.066	60.407	58.8
1987	818.875	69.468	N/A	N/A	818.875	69.468	67.62
1988	830.743	70.475	N/A	N/A	830.743	70.475	68.6
1989	842.611	71.481	N/A	N/A	842.611	71.481	69.58
1990	747.669	63.427	N/A	N/A	747.669	63.427	61.74
1991	866.346	73.495	N/A	N/A	866.346	73.495	71.54
1992	985.024	83.563	N/A	1791	985.024	83.563	81.34
1993	1154.328	97.925	244	2114	1151.01	97.644	95.047
1994	1288.938	109.345	279	2393	1288.938	109.345	106.436
1995	1357.65	115.174	387	2186	1382.598	117.29	114.17
1996	973.476	82.583	313	2065	991.704	84.13	81.892
1997	1288.308	109.291	85	2925	1255.758	106.53	103.696
1998	1405.026	119.193	66	3406	1387.596	117.714	114.583
1999	1465.002	124.281	87	4024	1442.7	122.389	119.133
2000	1622.334	137.628	116	3400	1653.414	140.265	136.533
2001	1765.176	149.746	315	4298	1740.69	147.669	143.74
2002	2140.152	181.556	306	6200	2073.12	175.87	171.191
2003	2804.424	237.909	292	5978	2826.012	239.74	233.363
2004	3404.436	288.81	3542	6002	3552.192	301.344	293.328
2005	3904.362	331.22	3234	5563	4058.628	344.307	335.148
2006	4884.348	414.356	17408	8760	5481.21	464.989	452.62
2007	6521.046	553.202	10457	10535	6885.69	584.136	568.597
2008	9308.754	789.693	12610	14226	9683.352	821.471	799.619
2009	10937.808	927.891	4720	16594	11036.592	936.271	909.66
2010	13297.914	1127.473	-9115.315	17941	12858.497	1090.217	1061.225
2011*	10328.136	875.679	-16268.365	177985	9623.991	815.977	794.756

* January to September 2011

Source: U.S. Energy Information Administration

Plunkett Research, Ltd.

www.plunkettresearch.com

Biodiesel Consumption and Production, U.S. 2001-2011

Year	Biodiesel Production (Million Gallons)	Biodiesel Production (Trillion Btu)	Biodiesel Imports (Thousand Barrels)	Biodiesel Exports (Thousand Barrels)	Biodiesel Net Imports (Thousand Barrels)	Biodiesel Stocks (Thousand Barrels)	Biodiesel Consumption (Million Gallons)	Biodiesel Consumption (Trillion Btu)
2001	8.58	1.09	78.28	39.32	38.96	N/A	10.21	1.30
2002	10.48	1.34	190.89	55.55	135.34	N/A	16.17	2.06
2003	14.21	1.81	93.64	109.76	-16.12	N/A	13.53	1.73
2004	27.98	3.57	97.26	123.54	-26.29	N/A	26.88	3.43
2005	90.79	11.58	206.71	205.76	0.95	N/A	90.83	11.59
2006	250.44	31.96	1,069.19	827.66	241.54	N/A	260.58	33.25
2007	489.83	62.50	3,342.06	6,477.03	-3,134.97	N/A	358.16	45.70
2008	678.11	86.52	7,501.60	16,128.03	-8,626.44	N/A	315.80	40.29
2009	506.28	64.60	1,843.59	6,332.17	-4,488.57	711.00	316.55	40.39
2010	309.36	39.47	545.53	2,503.39	-1,957.87	672.00	228.77	29.19
2011[*]	548.59	70.00	479.21	1,438.63	-959.42	10,052.00	485.65	61.97

* January to September 2011

Source: U.S. Energy Information Administration

Plunkett Research, Ltd.

www.plunkettresearch.com

Light Bulb Comparison

	Traditional 60-watt Incandescent Bulb	LED (Light Emitting Diode)	CFL (Compact Flourescent Light)	Halogen Bulb
Wattage	60	12	14.0	45
Heat emission	Radiates unnecessary heat	Radiates little or no heat	Radiates little heat	Radiates high heat
Average lifetime	1,000 hours	25,000 hours	6,000 hours	1,000 hours
Cost	<$1.00	$10.00-40.00[1]	$3.00-$10.00	<$2.00
Light Quality	High	High	Low[2]	High

[1] Despite these figures, costs are expected to fall sharply in the near-term.

[2] Consumers have indicated dissatisfaction with the light quality, but improvements are possible.

Source: Plunkett Research © 2012

Plunkett Research, Ltd.

www.plunkettresearch.com

Global Area of Biotech Crops by Country: 2010

(In Millions of Hectares; Latest Year Available)

Rank	Country	Area	Biotech Crops
1*	USA	66.8	Maize, soybean, cotton, canola, sugarbeet, alfalfa, papaya, squash
2*	Brazil	25.4	Soybean, maise, cotton
3*	Argentina	22.9	Soybean, maize, cotton
4*	India	9.4	Cotton
5*	Canada	8.8	Canola, maize, soybean, sugarbeet
6*	China	3.5	Cotton, papaya, poplar, tomato, sweet pepper
7*	Paraguay	2.6	Soybean
8*	Pakistan	2.4	Cotton
9*	South Africa	2.2	Maize, soybean, cotton
10*	Uruguay	1.1	Soybean, maize
11*	Bolivia	0.9	Soybean
12*	Australia	0.7	Cotton, canola
13*	Phillippines	0.5	Maize
14*	Myanmar	0.3	Cotton
15*	Burkino Faso	0.3	Cotton
16*	Spain	0.1	Maize
17*	Mexico	0.1	Cotton, soybean
18	Colombia	<0.1	Cotton
19	Chile	<0.1	Maize, soybean, canola
20	Honduras	<0.1	Maize
21	Portugal	<0.1	Maize
22	Czech Republic	<0.1	Maize, potato
22	Poland	<0.1	Maize
24	Egypt	<0.1	Maize
25	Slovakia	<0.1	Maize
26	Costa Rica	<0.1	Cotton, soybean
27	Romania	<0.1	Maize
28	Sweden	<0.1	Potato
29	Germany	<0.1	Potato
	Total	**148**	

* 17 biotech mega-countries growing 50,000 hectares or more of biotech crops.

Source: Clive James, ISAAA

Plunkett Research, Ltd.

www.plunkettresearch.com

National R&D Expenditures & R&D as a Percentage of GDP, by Country: 1985-2007

(In Billions of Constant 2000 US$[1]; Latest Year Available)

Year	U.S.	Japan[2]	China	Germany[3]	France	South Korea	U.K.	Russian Federation	Canada	Italy
1985	164.5	58.4	NA	35.3	23.3	NA	22.5	NA	8.1	11.7
1990	186.7	80.5	NA	41.6	29.2	NA	25.3	35.6	9.9	15.6
1995	199.9	83.7	10.9	42.2	30.5	14.8	24.9	8.8	12.1	12.9
1996	210.8	89.2	11.8	42.7	30.6	16.2	24.6	9.6	12.0	13.2
1997	222.9	92.6	14.8	44.4	30.2	17.3	24.5	10.5	12.5	14.0
1998	235.2	95.0	16.3	46.0	30.6	15.2	25.1	9.1	13.8	14.5
1999	250.9	95.3	20.5	49.4	31.8	16.0	26.9	10.1	14.9	14.4
2000	268.1	98.8	27.0	52.3	32.9	18.5	27.8	11.7	16.7	15.2
2001	271.7	101.6	30.9	53.1	34.3	20.8	28.1	13.8	18.5	16.1
2002	265.9	103.2	37.7	53.7	35.2	21.7	28.7	15.3	18.7	16.8
2003	272.3	105.8	43.5	54.2	34.6	23.3	28.8	16.9	19.0	16.5
2004	275.8	107.6	52.0	54.1	35.1	26.4	28.5	16.2	20.0	16.6
2005	286.5	115.1	60.7	54.5	34.9	28.8	29.9	16.0	20.3	16.6
2006	298.8	120.3	70.2	57.3	35.7	32.7	31.2	17.3	20.2	17.6
2007	307.8	124.6	87.1	58.5	36.1	37.0	32.9	19.6	19.7	NA

Expenditure as Percentage of GDP

Year	U.S.	Japan[2]	China	Germany[3]	France	South Korea	U.K.	Russian Federation	Canada	Italy
1985	2.75	2.58	NA	2.60	2.17	NA	2.24	NA	1.42	1.10
1990	2.65	2.81	NA	2.61	2.32	NA	2.14	2.03	1.51	1.25
1995	2.51	2.71	0.57	2.19	2.29	2.37	1.94	0.85	1.70	0.97
1996	2.55	2.81	0.57	2.19	2.27	2.42	1.86	0.97	1.65	0.99
1997	2.58	2.87	0.64	2.24	2.19	2.48	1.80	1.04	1.66	1.03
1998	2.61	3.00	0.65	2.27	2.14	2.34	1.79	0.95	1.76	1.05
1999	2.66	3.02	0.76	2.40	2.16	2.25	1.86	1.00	1.80	1.02
2000	2.75	3.04	0.90	2.45	2.15	2.39	1.85	1.05	1.91	1.05
2001	2.76	3.12	0.95	2.46	2.20	2.59	1.82	1.18	2.09	1.09
2002	2.66	3.17	1.07	2.49	2.23	2.53	1.82	1.25	2.04	1.13
2003	2.66	3.20	1.13	2.52	2.17	2.63	1.75	1.28	2.04	1.11
2004	2.59	3.17	1.23	2.49	2.15	2.85	1.69	1.15	2.08	1.10
2005	2.62	3.32	1.33	2.48	2.10	2.98	1.73	1.07	2.05	1.09
2006	2.66	3.40	1.42	2.54	2.10	3.22	1.76	1.07	1.98	1.13
2007	2.68	3.44	1.49	2.54	2.08	3.47	1.79	1.12	1.88	NA

NA = Not available. GDP = Gross Domestic Product. OECD = Organization for Economic Co-operation and Development.

[1] Conversions of foreign currencies to U.S. dollars are calculated with each country's GDP implicit price deflator and OECD purchasing power parity exchange rates.

[2] Data on Japanese research and development in 1996 and later years may not be consistent with data in earlier years because of changes in methodology.

[3] Data for 1985 and 1990 are for West Germany.

Source: U.S. National Science Foundation

Plunkett Research, Ltd.

www.plunkettresearch.com

Federal Funding for R&D by Character of Work, U.S.:
Fiscal Years 1975-2010

(In Millions of Current US$; Latest Year Available)

Fiscal Year	Total R&D and R&D Plant	Total R&D	Basic Research	Applied Research	Development	R&D Plant
1975	19,860	19,039	2,588	4,141	12,309	821
1976	21,616	20,780	2,767	4,852	13,160	837
1977	24,818	23,450	3,259	5,255	14,936	1,367
1978	27,141	25,845	3,699	5,908	16,238	1,296
1979	29,621	28,145	4,193	6,342	17,610	1,475
1980	31,386	29,830	4,674	6,923	18,233	1,556
1981	34,590	33,104	5,041	7,171	20,891	1,486
1982	37,822	36,433	5,482	7,541	23,410	1,390
1983	40,009	38,712	6,260	7,993	24,458	1,297
1984	44,012	42,225	7,067	7,911	27,246	1,787
1985	50,180	48,360	7,819	8,315	32,226	1,821
1986	52,951	51,412	8,153	8,349	34,910	1,539
1987	57,100	55,254	8,942	8,998	37,313	1,846
1988	58,827	56,769	9,474	9,177	38,119	2,057
1989	63,572	61,406	10,602	10,164	40,641	2,165
1990	65,831	63,559	11,286	10,337	41,937	2,272
1991	64,148	61,295	12,171	11,798	37,327	2,853
1992	68,577	65,593	12,490	12,001	41,102	2,985
1993	70,415	67,314	13,399	13,491	40,424	3,101
1994	69,451	67,235	13,523	13,888	39,824	2,215
1995	70,443	68,187	13,877	14,557	39,752	2,256
1996	69,399	67,653	14,464	13,796	39,393	1,746
1997	71,753	69,827	14,942	14,423	40,461	1,927
1998	73,914	72,101	15,613	15,309	41,178	1,813
1999	77,386	75,341	17,444	16,084	41,813	2,046
2000	77,356	72,863	19,570	18,901	34,393	4,493
2001	84,003	79,933	21,958	22,756	35,219	4,070
2002	90,158	85,853	23,668	24,338	37,846	4,305
2003	97,928	93,661	24,751	26,320	42,589	4,267
2004	105,371	101,377	26,121	27,237	48,019	3,994
2005	112,995	109,224	27,140	26,598	55,485	3,771
2006	112,271	110,146	26,585	26,951	56,610	2,125
2007	115,923	113,754	26,866	27,228	59,661	2,168
2008	116,476	114,625	27,559	27,538	59,528	1,851
2009[1]	116,569	114,454	28,536	26,265	59,653	2,115
2010[2]	188,559	58,356	29,848	28,507	57,920	2,285

1 = Preliminary. 2 = Projected
Note: In FY 2000 the National Institutes of Health (NIH) reclassified as research the activities that it had previously classified as development. Also in FY 2000, the National Aeronautics and Space Administration (NASA) reclassified and transferred funding for Space Station and Space Station Research from R&D to R&D plant. NIH and NASA data for FY 2000 and forward reflect these changes. In FY 2006 NASA began reporting funding for Space Operations, the Hubble Space Telescope, Stratospheric Observatory for Infrared Astronomy, and the James Webb Space Telescope as operational costs; previously these had been reported as R&D plant.
Source: U.S. National Science Foundation
Plunkett Research, Ltd.
www.plunkettresearch.com

U.S. Department of Energy
Funding for Scientific Research: 2010-2012

(In Thousands of US$)

Area of Scientific Research	FY 2010 Current Appropriation	FY 2011 Congressional Request	FY 2011 Annualized CR	FY 2012 Congressional Request
Energy Programs	**10,340,250**	**11,353,690**	**10,309,351**	**12,007,391**
Energy Efficiency & Renewable Energy	**2,216,392**	**2,355,473**	**2,242,500**	**3,200,053**
Hydrogen and Fuel Cell Technologies	170,297	137,000	-	100,450
Biomass & Biorefinery Systems R&D	216,225	220,000	-	340,500
Solar Energy	243,396	302,398	-	457,000
Wind Energy	79,011	122,500	-	126,859
Geothermal Technology	43,120	55,000	-	101,535
Water Power	48,669	40,488	-	38,500
Vehicle Technologies	304,223	325,302	-	588,003
Building Technologies	219,046	230,698	-	470,700
Industrial Technologies	94,270	100,000	-	319,784
Federal Energy Management Program	32,000	42,272	-	33,072
Electricity Delivery & Energy Reliability	168,484	185,930	171,982	237,717
Nuclear Energy	774,578	824,052	786,637	754,028
Fuel Cycle Research & Development	131,938	201,000	-	155,010
Fossil Energy Programs	**938,520**	**760,358**	**951,133**	**520,707**
Fossil Energy Research & Development	659,770	586,583	672,383	452,975
Coal	393,485	403,850	-	291,358
Fuels & Power Systems	393,485	403,850	-	0
Innovations for existing plants	50,630	65,000	-	0
Combined cycle	61,341	55,000	-	0
Advanced turbines	31,158	31,000	-	0
Carbon sequestration	149,944	143,000	-	0
Fuels	24,341	12,000	-	0
Fuel cells	48,683	50,000	-	0
Advanced research	27,388	47,850	-	0
Naval Petroleum & Oil Shale Reserves	23,627	23,614	23,627	14,909
Strategic Petroleum Reserve	243,823	138,861	243,823	121,704
Northeast Home Heating Oil Reserve	11,300	11,300	11,300	10,119
Science	**4,963,887**	**5,121,437**	**4,903,710**	**5,416,114**
High Energy Physics	790,811	829,000	-	797,200
Proton accelerator-based physics	438,369	439,262	-	411,207
Electron accelerator-based physics	30,212	24,707	-	22,319
Non-accelerator physics	97,469	88,539	-	81,852
Theoretical physics	68,414	69,524	-	68,914
Advanced technology R&D	156,347	189,968	-	171,908
Nuclear Physics	522,460	562,000	-	605,300
Biological & Environmental Research	588,031	626,900	-	717,900
Basic Energy Sciences	1,598,968	1,835,000	-	1,985,000
Other				
Uranium Enrichment D&D Fund	573,850	730,498	573,850	504,169
Energy Information Administration	110,595	128,833	110,595	123,957
Non-Defense Environmental Cleanup	254,673	225,163	244,673	219,121

Source: U.S. Department of Energy, Office of Science

Plunkett Research, Ltd.

www.plunkettresearch.com

Federal R&D & R&D Plant Funding for Energy, U.S.: Fiscal Years 2009-2011

(In Millions of US$; Latest Year Available)

Funding Category and Agency	2009 Actual	2009 ARRA*	2010 Prelim.	2011 Proposed	% Change (2010-11)
Total	2,234	1,560	2,392	2,549	6.6
Department of Energy	2,095	1,560	2,266	2,421	6.8
Energy programs	2,095	1,175	2,266	2,148	-5.2
Energy efficiency and renewable energy	850	1,116	996	1,031	3.5
Electricity delivery and energy reliability	75	10	122	144	18.0
Fossil energy	540	49	511	458	-10.4
Nuclear energy	630	0	637	515	-19.2
ARPA-E	0	385	0	273	-
Nuclear Regulatory Commission	101	0	81	78	-3.7
Tennessee Valley Authority	18	0	17	20	17.6
National Inst. of Food & Agriculture-Biomass R&D (USDA)	20	0	28	30	7.1

* Represents funds appropriated through the American Recovery and Reinvestment Act of 2009.

ARPA-E = Advanced Research Projects Agency-Energy

Notes: Detail may not add to total because of rounding. Percentage change calculated on unrounded data.

Source: U.S. National Science Foundation

Plunkett Research, Ltd.

www.plunkettresearch.com

Federal R&D & R&D Plant Funding for General Science & Basic Research, U.S.: Fiscal Years 2009-2011

(In Millions of US$; Latest Year Available)

Funding Category and Agency	2009 Actual	2009 ARRA[1]	2010 Prelim.	2011 Proposed	% Change (2010-11)
Total	9,941	4,187	10,395	11,055	6.3
Department of Energy, Office of Science	4,372	1,407	4,470	4,642	3.8
Department of Homeland Security	802	0	857	866	1.1
National Science Foundation (NSF)	4,767	2,780	5,068	5,547	9.4
Biological sciences	657	260	715	768	7.5
Computer and information science and engineering	575	235	619	685	10.6
Education and human resources	846	100	873	892	2.2
Engineering	665	265	744	826	11.0
Geosciences	809	347	890	955	7.4
Integrative activities	242	550	275	296	7.6
Major research equipment and facilities	170	400	117	165	40.8
Mathematical and physical sciences	1,244	490	1,352	1,410	4.3
Office of cyberinfrastructure	199	80	214	228	6.4
Social, behavioral and economic sciences	241	85	255	269	5.3
U.S. polar research programs	474	174	451	528	17.0
Budget authority adjustment[2]	-1,351	-206	-1,436	-1,474	2.6

Notes: Detail may not add to total because of rounding. Percent change derived from unrounded data. Not all federally sponsored basic research is categorized in subfunction 251 (the category covered in this table). Data derived from agencies' submissions to Office of Management and Budget per MAX Schedule C, agencies' budget justification documents, and supplemental data obtained from agencies' budget offices.

[1] Represents funds appropriated through the American Recovery and Reinvestment Act of 2009.

[2] Budget authority adjustment subtracts costs for research facilities, major equipment support, and other non-R&D from total NSF budget authority.

Source: U.S. National Science Foundation

Plunkett Research, Ltd.

www.plunkettresearch.com

Federal R&D & R&D Plant Funding for Transportation, U.S.:
Fiscal Years 2009-2011

(In Millions of US$; Latest Year Available)

Funding Category & Agency	2009 Actual	2009 ARRA[1]	2010 Prelim.	2011 Proposed	% Change (2010-11)
Total	1,357	104	1,448	2,071	43.1
Air transportation	745	104	810	1,433	77.0
Federal Aviation Administration (DOT)	331	0	375	358	-4.3
National Aeronautics & Space Administration, aeronautics	414	104	435	1,075	-
Aeronautics Research	414	104	435	503	15.6
Space Technology	0	0	0	572	-
Ground transportation (DOT)	554	0	575	591	2.7
Federal Highway Administration	432	0	442	442	0.0
Federal Motor Carrier Safety Administration	7	0	7	6	-7.6
Federal Railroad Administration	37	0	42	45	7.7
Federal Transit Administration	15	0	14	33	131.1
National Highway Traffic Safety Administration	63	0	71	65	-8.5
Water transportation	18	0	24	20	-16.7
U.S. Coast Guard (DHS)	18	0	24	20	-16.7
Other transportation[2] (DOT)	40	0	39	27	-31.1

Notes: Detail may not add to total because of rounding. Percent change calculated on unrounded data. Data derived from agencies' submissions to Office of Management and Budget per MAX Schedule C, agencies' budget justification documents, and supplemental data obtained from agencies' budget offices.

DOT = U.S. Department of Transportation; DHS = U.S. Department of Homeland Security.

[1] Represents funds appropriated through the American Recovery and Reinvestment Act of 2009.

[2] Includes Office of the Secretary, Pipeline and Hazardous Materials Safety Administration, and the Research and Innovative Technology Administration.

Source: U.S. National Science Foundation

Plunkett Research, Ltd.

www.plunkettresearch.com

Federal R&D & R&D Plant Funding for Natural Resources & Environment, U.S.: Fiscal Years 2009-2011

(In Millions of US$; Latest Year Available)

Funding Agency	2009 Actual	2009 ARRA[1]	2010 Prelim.	2011 Proposed	% Change (2010-11)
Total	2,371	244	2,498	2,684	7.4
Conservation and land management	384	0	415	403	-2.9
Department of the Interior[2]	44	0	50	51	2.0
Forest Service (USDA)	340	0	365	352	-3.6
Pollution control and abatement	565	0	597	608	1.8
Environmental Protection Agency	563	0	595	606	1.9
Leaking underground storage tanks	1	0	0	0	33.3
Oil spill response research	1	0	1	1	0.0
Science and technology	535	0	567	580	2.3
Superfund	26	0	27	25	-8.2
U.S. Coast Guard (DHS)	2	0	2	2	0.0
Recreational resources	25	0	27	28	3.7
National Park Service (DOI)	25	0	27	28	3.7
Water resources	29	0	29	25	-13.8
Army Corps of Engineers (DOD)	11	0	11	11	0.0
Bureau of Reclamation (DOI)	18	0	18	14	-22.2
Other natural resources	1,368	244	1,430	1,620	13.3
National Oceanic and Atmospheric Administration (DOC)	754	170	770	941	22.2
National environmental satellite, data and information service	119	0	95	253	166.1
National marine fisheries service	9	0	62	61	-1.6
National ocean service	74	0	68	81	18.6
National weather service	33	0	37	27	-26.0
Office of oceanic and atmospheric research	406	170	412	430	4.5
Office of marine and aviation operations	113	0	97	89	-7.8
U.S. Geological Survey	615	74	661	679	2.8
Biological research	185	0	205	201	-1.8
Enterprise information	5	15	1	1	-9.4
Facilities	0	0	0	0	-
Geographic research	42	0	47	54	13.8
Geologic hazards, resources and processes	216	45	222	227	2.3
Global change	41	0	58	72	23.9
Water resources investigations	126	15	127	124	-2.6

DHS = Department of Homeland Security; DOC = Department of Commerce; DOD = Department of Defense; DOI = Department of the Interior; USDA = U.S. Department of Agriculture.

Notes: Detail may not add to total because of rounding. Percent change derived from unrounded data. Data derived from agencies' submissions to Office of Management and Budget per MAX Schedule C, agencies' budget justification documents, and supplemental data obtained from agencies' budget offices.

[1] Represents funds appropriated through the American Recovery and Reinvestment Act of 2009.

[2] Includes Bureau of Land Management, Office of Surface Mining and Reclamation, and Minerals Management Service.

Source: U.S. National Science Foundation

Plunkett Research, Ltd.

www.plunkettresearch.com

Federal R&D & R&D Plant Funding for Agriculture, U.S.:
Fiscal Years 2009-2011

(In Millions of US$; Latest Year Available)

Funding Category and Agency	2009 Actual	2009 ARRA*	2010 Prelim.	2011 Proposed	% Chg. (2010-11)
Total	2,073	176	2,189	2,054	-6.2
Department of Agriculture (USDA)					
Agricultural Marketing Service	2	0	2	3	50.0
Agricultural Research Service	1,214	176	1,275	1,148	-10.0
Animal & Plant Health Inspection Service	30	0	30	30	0.0
Economic Research Service	80	0	81	87	7.4
Federal Grain Inspection Service	7	0	7	8	14.3
Foreign Agricultural Service	1	0	1	1	0.0
National Agricultural Statistics Service	7	0	7	7	0.0
National Institute of Food and Agriculture[1]	732	0	786	770	-2.0
Agriculture and Food Research Initiative[2]	201	0	262	429	63.7
McEntire-Stennis Cooperative Forestry	28	0	29	29	0.0
Payments to 1890 Colleges & Tuskegee Institute	46	0	49	49	0.0
Payments under the Hatch Act	207	0	215	215	0.0
Special research grants	124	0	136	41	-69.9
Other research programs	126	0	95	7	-92.6

* Represents funds appropriated through the American Recovery and Reinvestment Act of 2009.

[1] Created by the Food, Conservation, and Energy Act of 2008 (P.L. 110-234) to replace the Cooperative State Research, Education, and Extension Service.

[2] Created by the Food, Conservation, and Energy Act of 2008 (P.L. 110-234) to replace the National Research Initiative.

Notes: Detail may not add to total because of rounding. Percent change derived from unrounded data. Source data from USDA submission to Office of Management and Budget per MAX Schedule C, USDA budget justification documents, and supplemental data obtained from USDA budget office.

Source: U.S. National Science Foundation

Plunkett Research, Ltd.

www.plunkettresearch.com

Federal Funding for Research, by Agency & Field of Science & Engineering, U.S.: Fiscal Year 2009

(In Millions of Current US$; Latest Year Available)

Field	All	HHS	DOD	DOE	NSF	USDA	NASA	Other
Total research, all fields	54,801	29,524	6,128	6,466	4,742	1,880	1,931	4,130
Environmental sciences	3,352	392	371	336	814	10	470	959
Life sciences	29,299	24,862	611	338	725	1,535	105	1,123
Mathematics & computer sciences	3,333	191	1,085	926	955	9	30	137
Physical sciences	5,593	329	745	2,565	942	90	581	341
Psychology	1,853	1,708	54	0	7	0	6	78
Social sciences	1,123	270	23	0	192	191	0.4	447
Other sciences, nec	1,341	649	87	2	253	0	111	239
Engineering	8,907	1,123	3,152	2,299	855	43	629	806

Notes: FY 2009 data in this table are estimates of administration budget proposals. Detail may not sum to total due to rounding.

DOD = Department of Defense; DOE = Department of Energy; HHS = Department of Health and Human Services; NASA = National Aeronautics and Space Administration; NSF = National Science Foundation; USDA = Department of Agriculture.

nec = Not Elsewhere Classified.

Source: U.S. National Science Foundation

Plunkett Research, Ltd.

www.plunkettresearch.com

Major Patenting U.S. Universities: 2010

(By Utility Patents Granted; Latest Year Available)

U.S. University	Patents
University of California	349
Massachusetts Institute of Technology	174
Stanford University	155
Wisconsin Alumni Research Foundation	136
California Institute of Technology	134
University of Texas	122
University of Illinois	85
University of South Florida	83
Columbia University	82
University of Michigan	78
University of Pennsylvania	77
University of Washington	74
Cornell Research Foundation Inc.	74
John Hopkins University	71
Georgia Tech Research Corp.	67
Research Foundation of State University of New York	61
University of Central Florida	60
University of Southern California	60
New York University	59
Northwestern University	58
University of Maryland	52
Purdue Research Foundation	51
University of Massachusetts	50
University of Utah Research Foundation	47
Harvard College, President & Fellows	47
Duke University	42
University of Florida Research Foundation, Inc.	42

Notes: Only those universities with 40 or more patents are listed. Utility Patents (representing 90% of total U.S. patents) are issued "for the invention of a new and useful process, machine, manufacture, or composition of matter, or a new and useful improvement thereof," according to USPTO definitions. Additional categories include Design Patents (issued for a new original, and ornamental design for an article of manufacture); Plant Patents (for new or invented asexually reproduced plants and seedlings); and Reissue Patents (issued to correct errors in previously issued patents).

Source: U.S. Patent and Trademark Office (USPTO)

Plunkett Research, Ltd.   www.plunkettresearch.com

Chapter 3

IMPORTANT GREEN TECHNOLOGY INDUSTRY CONTACTS

Addresses, Telephone Numbers and Internet Sites

XLVI.	Packaging Industry Associations
XLVII.	Packaging Industry Resources
XLVIII.	Plastics Industry Associations
XLIX.	Plastics Industry Resources
L.	Ratings for Sustainability
LI.	Recycling & Waste Industry Associations
LII.	Research & Development, Laboratories
LIII.	Robotics Associations
LIV.	Science & Technology Resources
LV.	Smart Meter Industry Associations
LVI.	Soap & Cleansers Industry Associations
LVII.	Stocks & Financial Markets Data
LVIII.	Technology Transfer Associations
LIX.	Trade Associations-General
LX.	Trade Associations-Global
LXI.	Trade Resources
LXII.	U.S. Government Agencies
LXIII.	Water Technologies & Resources

I.   Agriculture Industry Associations

Brazilian Sugarcane Industry Association
Av. Brigadeiro Faria Lima, 2179, Fl. 9
Sao Paulo, SP 01452-000 Brazil
Phone: 55-11-3093-4949
Fax: 55-11-3812-1416
Web Address: unica.com.br
The Brazilian Sugarcane Industry Association (Uniao da Industria de Cana-de-Acucar, or UNICA), created in 1997, is the country's largest trade association representing producers of sugar, ethanol and bioelectricity. Its member companies are responsible for approximately 50% of Brazil's ethanol production and 60% of the country's sugar production. UNICA maintains a number of international offices, including one in Washington D.C.

II.   Alternative Energy-Biomass

Biofuels Association of Australia (BAA)
28 Elaroo St.
Morningside, QLD 4170 Australia
Phone: 0437-932-949
E-mail Address: *info@biofuelsassociation.com.au*
Web Address: www.biofuelsassociation.com.au
The Biodiesel Association of Australia (BAA) is an organization that works to represent the interests of

the biofuels industry. In February 2007, the group merged with Renewable Fuels Australia and incorporated.

Biomass Research and Development (BR&D)
E-mail Address: *sarah.lynch@ee.doe.gov*
Web Address: www.usbiomassboard.gov
Biomass Research & Development (BRD) is a multi-agency effort to coordinate and accelerate all federal bio-based products and bioenergy research and development.

Centre for the Development of Renewable Energy Sources (CEDER)
Autovia de Navarra A15
Salida 56
Lubia, 42290 Spain
Phone: 34-975-281-013
Fax: 34-975-281-051
E-mail Address: *ceder@ciemat.es*
Web Address: www.ceder.es
The Centre for the Development of Renewable Energy Sources (CEDER) is a unit of Spain's CIEMAT (Research Centre for Energy, Environment and Technology). CEDER focuses on biomass energy, wind energy and energy efficiency.

EERE Biomass Program
1000 Independence Ave. SW
EE-2E, 5H-021
Washington, DC 20585 US
Phone: 202-586-5188
Toll Free: 877-337-3463
E-mail Address: *eere_biomass@ee.doe.gov*
Web Address: www1.eere.energy.gov/biomass/
The Biomass Program of the Office of Energy Efficiency and Renewable Energy (EERE), a division of the U.S. Department of Energy, provides information on biomass and biodiesel technology.

National Biodiesel Board (NBB)
605 Clark Ave.
Jefferson City, MO 65101 US
Phone: 573-635-3893
Fax: 573-635-7913
Toll Free: 800-929-3437
E-mail Address: *info@biodiesel.org*
Web Address: www.biodiesel.org
The National Biodiesel Board (NBB) is a national trade association that promotes the biodiesel industry.

Northeast Regional Biomass Program (NRBP)
400 N. Capitol St. NW, Ste. 382

Washington, DC 20001 US
Phone: 202-624-8464
Fax: 202-624-8463
Web Address: www.nrbp.org
The Northeast Regional Biomass Program (NRBP) is one of five Regional Biomass Energy Programs established and funded by the U.S. Department of Energy. The Northeast region consists of 11 states: Connecticut, Delaware, Maine, Maryland, Massachusetts, New Hampshire, New Jersey, New York, Pennsylvania, Rhode Island and Vermont. The NRBP is administered by the CONEG Policy Research Center, Inc.

Western Regional Biomass Energy Program (WRBEP)
1600 Broadway, Ste. 1700
Denver, CO 80202 US
Phone: 303-623-9378
Fax: 303-534-7309
E-mail Address: *awalker@westgov.org*
Web Address: www.westgov.org/bioenergy
The Western Regional Biomass Energy Program (WRBEP) is one of five Regional Biomass Energy Programs established and funded by the U.S. Department of Energy. Thirteen states participate in the WRBEP including Arizona, California, Colorado, Kansas, Nebraska, Nevada, New Mexico, North Dakota, Oklahoma, South Dakota, Texas, Utah and Wyoming.

III. Alternative Energy-Clean Coal

Center for Energy and Economic Development (CEED)
333 John Carlyle St., Ste. 530
Alexandria, VA 22314 US
Phone: 703-684-6292
E-mail Address: *info@cleancoalusa.org*
Web Address: www.ceednet.org
The Center for Energy and Economic Development (CEED) is a nonprofit organization that promotes clean coal electricity generation.

Department of Energy Clean Coal Program
1000 Independence Ave. SW
Office of Fossil Energy (FE-22)
Washington, DC 20585 US
Phone: 301-903-4130
Fax: 202-586-4403
Toll Free: 800-342-5363
E-mail Address: *The.Secretary@hq.doe.gov*

Web Address:
www.fossil.energy.gov/programs/powersystems/cleancoal
The Department of Energy's Clean Coal Program provides information about new technologies and policies to reduce air emissions and other pollutants from coal-burning power plants.

European Clean Coal Commission
Attn: Dr. Ing. Pierre Dechamps
Rue de la Loi 200
Brussels, B-1049 Belgium
Phone: 32-2-295-66-23
Fax: 32-2-296-42-88
E-mail Address: *info@euro-cleancoal.net*
Web Address: www.euro-cleancoal.net
The European Clean Coal Commission provides information and research for the clean coal industry.

Gladstone Centre for Clean Coal (GC3)
Faculty of Engineering and Physical Systems
Central Queensland University
Rockhampton, QLD 4702 Australia
Phone: 61-7-4930-9895
Fax: 61-7-4930-6703
E-mail Address: *c.greensill@cqu.edu.au*
Web Address: www.gc3.cqu.edu.au
The Gladstone Centre for Clean Coal (GC3) promotes the research and use of clean coal technology in Australia.

International Energy Agency (IEA) Clean Coal Centre
10-18 Putney Hill
Gemini House
London, SW15 6AA UK
Phone: 44-0-20-8780-2111
Fax: 44-0-20-8780-1746
E-mail Address: *mail@iea-coal.org.uk*
Web Address: www.iea-coal.org.uk
The International Energy Agency (IEA) Clean Coal Centre was established to promote clean coal in its 24 member countries.

IV. Alternative Energy-Clean Transportation

ACEEE's Green Book Online
529 14th St. NW
Washington, DC 20045 US
Phone: 202-507-4000
Fax: 202-429-2248
E-mail Address: *greenercars@aceee.org*

Web Address: www.greenercars.org
Green Book Online is the official web site for the
American Council for an Energy-Efficient Economy
(ACEEE)'s Green Book publication, which rates cars
on how they impact the environment.

Clean Cities Program
3610 Collins Ferry Rd.
U.S. Department of Energy - NETL
Morgantown, WV 26507-0880 US
Phone: 304-285-4535
Toll Free: 877-337-3463
E-mail Address: *Kay.Kelly@netl.doe.gov*
Web Address: www.eere.energy.gov/cleancities
The Clean Cities Program, sponsored by the U.S.
Department of Energy, is a federal program to
promote the use of alternative transportation fuels in
U.S. cities.

WestStart-CALSTART
48 S. Chester Ave.
Pasadena, CA 91106 US
Phone: 626-744-5600
Fax: 626-744-5610
E-mail Address: *calstart@calstart.org*
Web Address: www.calstart.org
WestStart-CALSTART is a nonprofit organization
that works to help in the development of advanced
transportation technologies and to foster companies
that will help clean the air, lessen dependence on
foreign oil, reduce global warming and create jobs.

V.	Alternative Energy-Ethanol

American Coalition for Ethanol (ACE)
5000 S. Broadband Ln., Ste. 224
Sioux Falls, SD 57108 US
Phone: 605-334-3381
Fax: 605-334-3389
E-mail Address: *bjennings@ethanol.org*
Web Address: www.ethanol.org
The American Coalition for Ethanol (ACE) is a
nonprofit organization representing farmers,
commodity organizations, ethanol producers and
other businesses in the ethanol industry.

Canadian Renewable Fuels Association (CRFA)
350 Sparks St., Ste. 1005
Ottawa, ON K1R 7S8 Canada
Phone: 613-594-5528
Fax: 613-594-3076
E-mail Address: *R.Speer@greenfuels.org*
Web Address: www.greenfuels.org

The Canadian Renewable Fuels Association (CRFA)
is a nonprofit organization whose mission is to
promote renewable fuels for automotive
transportation through consumer awareness and
government liaison activities.

Ethanol India
E-mail Address: *info@ethanolindia.net*
Web Address: www.ethanolindia.net
Ethanol India provides information and links to the
ethanol industry in India and abroad.

Ethanol Producers and Consumers (EPAC)
172 Ball Rd.
Nashua, MT 59248 US
Phone: 406-785-3722
Fax: 406-785-2252
E-mail Address: *epac@ethanolmt.org*
Web Address: www.ethanolmt.org
Ethanol Producers and Consumers (EPAC) is a
nonprofit organization that promotes the ethanol
industry.

Governors' Ethanol Coalition (GEC)
1111 O St., Ste. 223
Lincoln, NE 68509 US
Phone: 402-471-2867
Fax: 402-471-3064
Web Address: www.ethanol-gec.org
The Governors' Ethanol Coalition (GEC) is a group
of governors from 33 states in the United States and
six foreign that work together to promote the ethanol
industry.

National Ethanol Vehicle Coalition (NEVC)
3216 Emerald Ln., Ste. C
Jefferson City, MO 65109 US
Phone: 573-635-8445
Fax: 573-635-5466
Toll Free: 877-485-8535
E-mail Address: *info@e85fuel.com*
Web Address: www.e85fuel.com
The National Ethanol Vehicle Coalition (NEVC),
established in 1996, is a nonprofit organization that is
one of the leading advocates in the U.S. for
expanding the use of 85% (E85) ethanol motor fuel.
It also advocates the production of so-called flexible
fuel vehicles, which can run on higher than
conventional 10% ethanol fuels.

Renewable Fuels Association (RFA)
425 3rd St. SW, Ste. 1150
Washington, DC 20024 US

Phone: 202-289-3835
Fax: 202-289-7519
Web Address: www.ethanolrfa.org
The Renewable Fuels Association (RFA) is a trade
organization representing the ethanol industry. It
publishes a wealth of useful information, including a
listing of biorefineries and monthly U.S. fuel ethanol
production and demand.

VI.   Alternative Energy-Fuel Cells

California Fuel Cell Partnership (CaFCP)
3300 Industrial Blvd., Ste. 1000
West Sacramento, CA 95691 US
Phone: 916-371-2870
Fax: 916-375-2008
E-mail Address: *info@cafcp.org*
Web Address: www.fuelcellpartnership.org
The California Fuel Cell Partnership (CaFCP) is a
collaboration of 32 organizations that are committed
to promoting commercialized hydrogen fuel cells for
automotive applications.

Canadian Hydrogen and Fuel Cell Association (CHFCA)
4250 Wesbrook Mall
Vancouver, BC V6T 1W5 Canada
Phone: 604-822-9178
Fax: 604-822-8106
E-mail Address: *info@chfca.ca*
Web Address: www.chfca.ca
The Canadian Hydrogen and Fuel Cell Association
(CHFCA) is a nonprofit organization that provides
information relating to hydrogen and fuel cell
technology and seeks to raise awareness of the
positive impact of these technologies. It was formed
following the merger of the Canadian Hydrogen
Association (CHA) and Hydrogen & Fuel Cells
Canada (H2FCC).

DoD Fuel Cell
E-mail Address: *FuelCell@erdc.usace.army.mil*
Web Address: dodfuelcell.cecer.army.mil
DoD Fuel Cell provides information about the
Department of Defense's fuel cell program, which is
sponsored by the Army Corps of Engineers.

EERE Hydrogen, Fuel Cells & Infrastructure Technologies Program
1000 Independence Ave. SW
Mail Stop EE-1
Washington, DC 20585 US
Phone: 202-586-2336

Toll Free: 877-337-3463
E-mail Address: *Sunita.Satyapal@ee.doe.gov*
Web Address:
www1.eere.energy.gov/hydrogenandfuelcells
The Hydrogen, Fuel Cells & Infrastructure
Technologies Program of the Energy Efficiency and
Renewable Energy (EERE), a division of the U.S.
Department of Energy (DOE), works to develop and
successfully introduce fuel cell technologies to the
global market.

Eye for Fuel Cells
45 Whitechapel Rd.
Black Lion House
London, E1 1DU UK
Phone: 44-0-2073-75-75-00
Fax: 44-0-2073-75-75-11
E-mail Address: *jburnham@eyeforfuelcells.com*
Web Address: www.eyeforfuelcells.com
Eye for Fuel Cells provides extensive news and
information about recent developments in the fuel
cell industry.

Fuel Cell and Hydrogen Energy Association (FCHEA)
1133 19th St. NW, Ste. 947
Washington, DC 20036 US
Phone: 202-736-5738
E-mail Address: *rcox@fchea.org*
Web Address: www.fchea.org
The Fuel Cell and Hydrogen Energy Association
(FCHEA) is an industry association dedicated to
fostering the commercialization of fuel cells and
hydrogen energy technologies in the U.S.

Fuel Cell Europe
44 rue des Palais, Bte. 71
Brussels, 1030 Belgium
Phone: 32-2211-3411
E-mail Address: *secretariat@fuelcelleurope.org*
Web Address: www.fuelcelleurope.org
Fuel Cell Europe is a nonprofit association of
European universities and research institutes, fuel cell
manufacturers and suppliers intended to promote the
commercialization of fuel cell technology.

Fuel Cell Markets
Thorney Weir House
Iver, SL0 9AQ UK
Phone: 44-0-1895-442-269
Fax: 44-0-1895-431-880
Web Address: www.fuelcellmarkets.com

Fuel Cell Markets provides news and information about the fuel cell and hydrogen industries.

Fuel Cell Today
Gate 2, Orchard Rd.
Royston, SG8 5HE UK
E-mail Address: *info@fuelcelltoday.com*
Web Address: www.fuelcelltoday.com
Fuel Cell Today is an Internet portal that provides news, commentary and information on the fuel cell industry.

Fuel Cells 2000
1100 H St. NW, Ste. 800
Washington, DC 20005 US
Phone: 202-785-4222
Fax: 202-785-4313
E-mail Address: *jennifer@fuelcells.org*
Web Address: www.fuelcells.org
Fuel Cells 2000, run by the Breakthrough Technologies Institute (BTI), is a site devoted to preparing and disseminating information on fuel cells and the fuel cell industry.

National Fuel Cell Research Center (NFCRC)
University of California-Irvine
Irvine, CA 92697-3550 US
Phone: 949-824-1999 x212
Fax: 949-824-7423
E-mail Address: *gss@nfcrc.uci.edu*
Web Address: www.nfcrc.uci.edu
The National Fuel Cell Research Center (NFCRC) promotes the development of efficient fuel cells and partnerships to advance fuel cell technology.

Ohio Fuel Cell Coalition (OFCC)
737 Bolivar Rd., Ste. 1000
Cleveland, OH 44115 US
Phone: 216-363-6890
Fax: 216-363-6893
E-mail Address: *pat.valente@fuelcellcorridor.com*
Web Address: www.fuelcellcorridor.com
The Ohio Fuel Cell Coalition (OFCC) is a group of industry, academic and government leaders from throughout the State of Ohio who are dedicated to developing a forward-looking plan to advance the fuel cell industry in Ohio.

VII. Alternative Energy-General

Alliance to Save Energy (ASE)
1850 M St. NW, Ste. 600
Washington, DC 20036 US

Phone: 202-857-0666
Fax: 202-331-9588
E-mail Address: *info@ase.org*
Web Address: www.ase.org
The Alliance to Save Energy (ASE) promotes energy-efficiency worldwide to achieve a healthier economy, a cleaner environment and energy security.

American Council for an Energy-Efficient Economy (ACEEE)
529 14th St. NW, Ste. 600
Washington, DC 20045-1000 US
Phone: 202-507-4000
Fax: 202-429-2248
E-mail Address: *info@aceee.org*
Web Address: www.aceee.org
The American Council for an Energy-Efficient Economy (ACEEE) is a nonprofit organization dedicated to advancing energy-efficiency as a means of promoting both economic prosperity and environmental protection.

American Council on Renewable Energy (ACORE)
1600 K St., Ste. 700
Washington, DC 20006 US
Phone: 202-393-0001
Fax: 202-393-0606
E-mail Address: *info@acore.org*
Web Address: www.acore.org
The American Council On Renewable Energy (ACORE) is a nonprofit organization focused on accelerating the adoption of renewable energy technologies into the mainstream of American society. With an interest in trade, finance and policy, ACORE promotes all renewable energy options for the production of electricity, hydrogen, fuels and end-use energy.

Bloomberg New Energy Finance
Phone: 212-617-4050
Web Address: www.bnef.com
This unit of media giant Bloomberg LP publishes white papers and podcasts, produces conferences and presentations, and provides in-depth coverage of alternative energy projects and investments.

Business Council for Sustainable Energy (BCSE)
1629 I St. NW, Ste. 501
Washington, DC 20002 US
Phone: 202-785-0507
Fax: 202-785-0514
E-mail Address: *bcse@bcse.org*

Web Address: www.bcse.org
The Business Council for Sustainable Energy (BCSE) strives to realize goals for the nation's economic, environmental and national security. The Council focuses on the promotion of clean energy technologies as solutions to certain environmental challenges.

Center for Energy Efficiency and Renewable Technologies (CEERT)
1100 11th St., Ste. 311
Sacramento, CA 95814 US
Phone: 916-442-7785
Fax: 916-447-2940
Toll Free: 877-758-4462
E-mail Address: info@ceert.org
Web Address: www.ceert.org
The Center for Energy Efficiency and Renewable Technologies (CEERT) provides technical support to environmental advocates and clean technology developers.

Chinese Renewable Energy Industries Association (CREIA)
Xicheng District
A4 Chegongzhuang St., Wuhua Plz., Ste. A2106
Beijing, 100044 China
Phone: 86-10-68002617-18
Fax: 86-10-68002674
E-mail Address: creia@creia.net
Web Address: www.creia.net
The Chinese Renewable Energy Industries Association (CREIA) was established in 2000 under official government sanction to promote the use of renewable energy sources within China.

Clean Energy Council
18 Kavanagh St., Ste. 201
Southbank, VIC 3006 Australia
Phone: 61-3-9929-4100
Fax: 61-3-9929-4101
E-mail Address: info@cleanenergycouncil.org.au
Web Address: www.cleanenergycouncil.org.au
The Clean Energy Council is an amalgamation of the Australian Wind Energy Industry Association (Auswind) and the Australian Business Council for Sustainable Energy (BCSE). It includes over 400 businesses covering a quarter of Australia's total electricity production including gas, wind, hydro and bioenergy; and in the spectrum of business in the low-emission energy and energy efficiency sectors including solar PV, solar hot water, biomass, geothermal and cogeneration.

Coalition for Affordable and Reliable Energy (CARE)
101 Constitution Ave. NW, Ste. 500 E
Washington, DC 20001 US
Phone: 202-463-2600
Fax: 202-463-2666
E-mail Address: contact@careenergy.com
Web Address: www.careenergy.com
The Coalition for Affordable and Reliable Energy (CARE) promotes the development of alternative energy.

European Renewable Energy Council
63-67 Rue d'Arlon
Brussels, B-1040 Belgium
Phone: 32-2-546-1933
Fax: 32-2-546-1934
E-mail Address: erec@erec.org
Web Address: www.erec.org
The European Renewable Energy Council (EREC), which is formed of eight nonprofit organizations, represents the industrial and research communities in the following sectors of renewable energy: solar electricity, small hydropower, solar thermal, biomass, wind and geothermal.

EUROSOLAR (European Association for Renewable Energy)
Kaiser-Friedrich-Straße 11
Bonn, 53113 Germany
Phone: 49-228-362373
Fax: 49-228-361279
E-mail Address: info@eurosolar.org
Web Address: www.eurosolar.de
EUROSOLAR (the European Association for Renewable Energy) was founded in 1988. It is a registered non-profit making organization that conducts its work independently of political parties, institutions, commercial enterprises and interest groups. It states that it is dedicated to the cause of completely substituting for nuclear and fossil energy through renewable energy.

Fresh Energy
408 St. Peter St., Ste. 220
St. Paul, MN 55102 US
Phone: 651-225-0878
Fax: 651-225-0870
E-mail Address: info@fresh-energy.org
Web Address: www.fresh-energy.org
Fresh Energy is a nonprofit organization that works to promote clean electricity, energy efficiency,

transportation policy, global warming solutions and energy justice.

Interstate Renewable Energy Council
P.O. Box 1156
Latham, NY 12110 US
Phone: 518-458-6059
E-mail Address: *info@irecusa.org*
Web Address: www.irecusa.org
Interstate Renewable Energy Council (IREC), formed in 1982 as a nonprofit organization, supports market-oriented services promoting renewable energy, aimed at education, coordination, procurement, the adoption and implementation of uniform guidelines and standards, workforce development, and consumer protection.

Ministry of New and Renewable Energy-Gov. of India
Lodhi Rd.
Block-14, CGO Complex
New Delhi, 110 003 India
Phone: 91-11-24361298
Fax: 91-11-24361830
E-mail Address: *asfa.moca@nic.in*
Web Address: www.mnes.nic.in
The Ministry of New and Renewable Energy is the website for the Government of India's sustainable energy programs. The website provides recent developments and public information regarding various renewable energy issues.

National Energy Foundation (NEF)
Davy Ave.
Knowlhill
Milton Keynes, MK5 8NG UK
Phone: 01-908-665-555
Fax: 01-908-665-577
E-mail Address: *info@nef.org.uk*
Web Address: www.nef.org.uk
The National Energy Foundation (NEF) aims to help people and businesses throughout the UK reduce their carbon emissions through the use of energy efficiency measures and renewable energy sources.

REN21 (Renewable Energy Policy Network for the 21st Century)
15 rue de Milan
Paris, Cedex 9 75441 France
Phone: 33-1-44-3750-90
Fax: 33-1-44-3750-95
E-mail Address: *secretariat@ren21.net*
Web Address: www.ren21.net

REN21 is a global organization that promotes the development of renewable energy. The goal of REN21 is the promotion of policies that will increase the wise use of renewable energy worldwide. In order to achieve this objective, REN21 encourages action in three areas: policy, advocacy and knowledge exchange. REN21 convenes and engages key leaders and stakeholders in national legislation and international processes. REN21 and its participants encourage the inclusion of renewable energy matters in the deliberations of appropriate meetings and venues, and target relevant political processes.

Renewable Energy & Energy Efficiency Partnership (REEEP)
Vienna International Ctr.
Rm. D1732, Wagramerstrasse 5
Vienna, A-100 Austria
Phone: 43 1 26026-3425
Fax: 43 1 21346-3425
E-mail Address: *info@reeep.org*
Web Address: www.reeep.org
The Renewable Energy and Energy Efficiency Partnership (REEEP) is a global, public-private partnership that structures policy and regulatory initiatives for clean energy, and facilitates financing for energy projects. Backed by more than 200 national governments, businesses, development banks and NGOs, REEEP hopes to contribute to international, national and regional policy dialogues. Its aim is to accelerate the integration of renewables into the energy mix and to advocate energy efficiency as a path to improved energy security and reduced carbon emissions, ensuring socio-economic benefits.

Renewable Energy Policy Project (REPP)
1612 K St. NW, Ste. 202
Washington, DC 20006 US
Phone: 202-293-2898
Fax: 202-293-5857
E-mail Address: *gsterzinger@repp.org*
Web Address: www.crest.org
The Renewable Energy Policy Project (REPP) is devoted to creating policy tools and disseminating information on public policy about alternative energy.

RenewableUK
Greencoat House
Francis St.
London, SW1P 10H UK
Phone: 020-7901-3000
Fax: 202-7901-3001

E-mail Address: *info@renewable-uk.com*
Web Address: www.bwea.com
RenewableUK (formerly the British Wind Energy
Association, or BWEA) is the leading trade and
professional body representing the UK's wind, wave
and tidal power generation industry.

**Sustainable Energy Association of Singapore
(SEAS)**
2 Bukit Merah Central
18-02 SPRING Bldg.
159835 Singapore
Phone: 65-6338-8578
Fax: 65-276-4257
Web Address: www.seas.com
The Sustainable Energy Association of Singapore
(SEAS) represents the interests of companies in
renewable energy, carbon trading, energy efficiency,
clean development mechanism projects and their
financial institutions.

VIII.   Alternative Energy-Geothermal

EERE Geothermal Technologies Program
1000 Independence Ave. SW, Mail Stop EE-1
Office of Efficiency & Renewable Energy-
Geothermal
Washington, DC 20585 US
Phone: 202-586-5463
Toll Free: 877-337-3463
Web Address: www1.eere.energy.gov/geothermal
The Geothermal Technologies Program of the Office
of Energy Efficiency and Renewable Energy (EERE),
a division of the U.S. Department of Energy, works
with U.S. industries to develop geothermal energy
into an economically competitive contributor to the
U.S. energy supply.

Geothermal Education Office
664 Hilary Dr.
Tiburon, CA 94920 US
Phone: 415-435-4574
Fax: 415-435-7737
E-mail Address: *geo@marin.org*
Web Address: www.geothermal.marin.org
The Geothermal Education Office works to promote
public understanding of geothermal resources.

Geothermal Energy Association
209 Pennsylvania Ave. SE
Washington, DC 20003 US
Phone: 202-454-5261
Fax: 202-454-5265

E-mail Address: *kathy@geo-energy.org*
Web Address: www.geo-energy.org
The Geothermal Energy Association is a trade
association of U.S. companies involved in the
geothermal industry.

Geothermal Resources Council (GRC)
2001 2nd St., Ste. 5
Davis, CA 95617 US
Phone: 530-758-2360
Fax: 530-758-2839
E-mail Address: *crobinson@geothermal.org*
Web Address: www.geothermal.org
The Geothermal Resources Council (GRC) is an
association that encourages the development of
geothermal resources and provides information on
geothermal energy.

International Geothermal Association
Sudurlandsbraut 48
Reykjavik, 108 Iceland
Phone: 354-588-4437
Fax: 354-588-4431
E-mail Address: *iga@samorka.is*
Web Address: iga.igg.cnr.it/index.php
The International Geothermal Association (IGA) is a
scientific, educational and cultural organization that
has more than 2000 members in 65 countries. The
IGA is a nonprofit, non-governmental organization in
within the Economic and Social Council of the
United Nations.

**International Ground Source Heat Pump
Association (IGSHPA)**
374 Cordell S.
Stillwater, OK 74078 US
Phone: 405-744-5175
Fax: 405-744-5283
E-mail Address: *igshpa@okstate.edu*
Web Address: www.igshpa.okstate.edu
The International Ground Source Heat Pump
Association (IGSHPA), which is affiliated with
Oklahoma State University, promotes geothermal
energy technology on the local, state, national and
global levels.

IX.   Alternative Energy-Hydroelectric

National Hydropower Association (NHA)
1 Massachusetts Ave. NW, Ste. 850
Washington, DC 20001 US
Phone: 202-682-1700
Fax: 202-682-9478

E-mail Address: *help@hydro.org*
Web Address: www.hydro.org
The National Hydropower Association (NHA) is the only national trade association dedicated exclusively to representing the interests of the hydropower industry. Its members span the breadth of the industry and all related fields.

X.	Alternative Energy-Solar

American Solar Energy Society (ASES)
4760 Walnut St., Ste. 106
Boulder, CO 80301 US
Phone: 303-443-3130
Fax: 303-443-3212
E-mail Address: *ases@ases.org*
Web Address: www.ases.org
The American Solar Energy Society (ASES) is a nonprofit association committed to advancing the use of solar energy to benefit citizens and the global environment, promoting widespread solar energy use in the near future and long-term.

California Solar Center
E-mail Address:
webmaster@californiasolarcenter.org
Web Address: www.californiasolarcenter.org
California Solar Center provides news and information on California's solar industry. It is a project of the Rahus Institute, which is focused on the implementation of renewable resource technologies.

California Solar Energy Industry Association
P.O. Box 782
Rio Vista, CA 94571 US
Phone: 916-747-6987
E-mail Address: *info@calseia.org*
Web Address: www.calseia.org
The California Solar Energy Industry Association promotes the use of solar thermal and photovoltaic systems in California.

Canadian Solar Industries Association (CanSIA)
150 Isabella St., Ste. 605
Ottawa, Ontario K1S 1V7 Canada
Phone: 613-736-9077
Fax: 613-736-8938
Toll Free: 866-522-6742
E-mail Address: *info@cansia.ca*
Web Address: www.cansia.ca
The Canadian Solar Industries Association (CanSIA) is the national organization representing professional companies involved in the design, sale and

installation of solar electric, solar thermal and passive solar technologies.

CPV Consortium
980 9th St., Ste, 2000
Sacramento, CA 95814 US
Phone: 916-716-9775
E-mail Address: *cvanzuiden@cpvconsortium.org*
Web Address: www.cpvconsortium.org
The CPV Consortium is a global industry organization that supports the development of the Concentrator Photovoltaics (CPV) industry. Its members include designers and manufacturers of CPV panels, CPV cell suppliers, and tracker suppliers. The membership also includes a large base of companies working on the deployment, test, materials, and other parts of the industry infrastructure.

EERE Solar Energy Technologies Program
1000 Independence Ave. SW, EE-2A
Washington, DC 20585 US
Phone: 202-287-1862
Toll Free: 877-337-3463
E-mail Address: *solar@ee.doe.gov*
Web Address: www1.eere.energy.gov/solar
The Solar Energy Technologies Program of the Office of Energy Efficiency and Renewable Energy (EERE), a division of the U.S. Department of Energy, works with industry participants, universities, federal and state government, and other non-governmental agencies to develop economically competitive photovoltaic materials.

European Solar Thermal Electricity Association (ESTELA)
Renewable Energy House
Rue d'Arlon 63-67
Brussels, B-1040 Belgium
Phone: 32 0(2) 400 10 90
Fax: 32 0(2) 400 10 91
E-mail Address: *estela@estelasolar.eu*
Web Address: www.estelasolar.eu
ESTELA was created in 2007 to promote solar thermal electricity (STE) in Europe and worldwide. ESTELA supports its members by fostering market penetration of solar thermal power.

IEA Photovoltaic Power Systems Programme (PVPS)
Waldweg 8
St. Ursen, CH 1717 Switzerland
Phone: 41-26-494-0030

Fax: 41-26-494-0034
E-mail Address: *mary.brunisholz@netenergy.ch*
Web Address: www.iea-pvps.org
The Photovoltaic Power Systems Programme (PVPS) is a collaborative R&D agreement, established within the International Energy Agency (IEA), that conducts projects regarding solar photovoltaic electricity. IEA PVPS operates worldwide via a network of national teams in member countries. Its website provides information about the results of the IEA PVPS program including publications and other project results.

Institute of Solar Energy (IES)
Ciudad Universitaria
la Avenida de la Complutense
Madrid, 28040 Spain
Phone: 34-91-544-10-60
Fax: 34-91-544-63-41
Web Address: www.ies.upm.es
The IES is a unit of Spain's Polytechnic University of Madrid that focuses on the development of photovoltaic solar energy.

International Solar Energy Society (ISES)
Wiesentalstr. 50
Villa Tannheim
Freiburg, 79115 Germany
Phone: 49-761-459-060
Fax: 49-761-459-0699
E-mail Address: *hq@ises.org*
Web Address: www.ises.org
The International Solar Energy Society (ISES) is an international nonprofit group promoting the advancement of renewable energy technology, implementation and education worldwide. ISES maintains a presence in over 50 countries worldwide.

Solar Electric Power Association (SEPA)
1220 19th St. NW, Ste. 800
Washington, DC 20036 US
Phone: 202-857-0898
Fax: 202-559-2035
E-mail Address: *info@solarelectricpower.org*
Web Address: www.solarelectricpower.org
The Solar Electric Power Association (SEPA) is a nonprofit organization consisting of more than 100 companies and associations in eight countries. It aims to help energy utilities add solar energy to their generation portfolios.

Solar Energy Industries Association (SEIA)
575 7th St. NW, Ste. 400

Washington, DC 20004 US
Phone: 202-682-0556
Fax: 202-682-7779
E-mail Address: *info@seia.org*
Web Address: www.seia.org
Established in 1974, the Solar Energy Industries Association is the American trade association of the solar energy industry. Among its operations is a web site that provides news for the solar energy industry, links to related products and companies and solar energy statistics.

Spanish Photovoltaic Industry Association (ASIF)
14 Avenida del Doctor Arce
Madrid, ES-28002 Spain
Phone: 34-915-900-300
Fax: 34-915-612-987
E-mail Address: *info@asif.org*
Web Address: www.asif.org
The Spanish Photovoltaic Industry Association, known as Asociación de la Industria Fotovoltaica (ASIF), represents manufacturers and users of photovoltaic energy in Spain.

XI.	Alternative Energy-Storage

EERE Energy Storage
1000 Independence Ave. SW, OE-10
Washington, DC 20585 US
Phone: 202-586-9729
Toll Free: 877-337-3463
E-mail Address: *geraldine.harper@ee.doe.gov*
Web Address:
www.eere.energy.gov/de/cs_energy_storage.html
The Distributed Energy Program of the Office of Energy Efficiency and Renewable Energy (EERE), a division of the U.S. Department of Energy, provides a web page with information on energy storage technologies, such as batteries, superconducting magnetic energy storage, flywheels, supercapacitors, compressed air energy storage and pumped hydropower storage.

Electricity Storage Association
830 Claremont Dr.
Morgan Hill, CA 95037 US
Phone: 614-716-1269
E-mail Address: *info@electricitystorage.org*
Web Address: www.electricitystorage.org
The Electricity Storage Association promotes the development and commercialization of improved energy storage delivery systems for use by electricity suppliers and their customers. Its web site provides

information on advanced storage technologies such as flywheels, pumped hydro storage, flow cell batteries and compressed air energy storage.

Energy Storage Council (ESC)
3963 Flora Pl., Fl. 2
St. Louis, MO 63110 US
Phone: 314-363-4545
E-mail Address: *info@energystoragecouncil.org*
Web Address: www.energystoragecouncil.org
The Energy Storage Council (ESC) promotes the research, development and deployment of energy storage technologies, such as large-scale pumped-hydro storage, compressed air energy storage, flywheels, electrochemical capacitors and batteries.

XII.　　Alternative Energy-Wind

American Wind Energy Association (AWEA)
1501 M St. NW, Ste. 1000
Washington, DC 20005 US
Phone: 202-383-2500
Fax: 202-383-2505
E-mail Address: *windmail@awea.org*
Web Address: www.awea.org
The American Wind Energy Association (AWEA) promotes wind energy as a clean source of electricity worldwide. Its website provides excellent resources for research, including an online library, discussions of legislation, and descriptions of wind technologies.

Canadian Wind Energy Association (CanWEA)
170 Laurier Ave. W, Ste. 810
Ottawa, ON K1P 5V5 Canada
Phone: 613-234-8716
Fax: 613-234-5642
Toll Free: 800-922-6932
E-mail Address: *info@canwea.ca*
Web Address: www.canwea.ca
The Canadian Wind Energy Association (CanWEA) is a nonprofit trade association that promotes the development of wind energy.

Danish Wind Industry Association (DWIA)
Rosenorns Alle 9, 5. sal
Frederiksberg C, DK-1970 Denmark
Phone: 45-3373-0330
Fax: 45-3373-0333
E-mail Address: *danish@windpower.org*
Web Address: www.windpower.org
The Danish Wind Industry Association (DWIA) is a nonprofit association whose purpose is to promote wind energy.

EERE Wind & Hydropower Technologies Program
1000 Independence Ave. SW
Washington, DC 20585 US
Phone: 202-586-5348
Toll Free: 877-337-3463
Web Address: www1.eere.energy.gov/windandhydro
The Wind & Hydropower Technologies Program of the Office of Energy Efficiency and Renewable Energy (EERE), a division of the U.S. Department of Energy, works with the U.S wind industry to develop clean, domestic wind energy technologies that can compete with traditional sources. The program also works with the hydropower industry to develop more environment friendly technologies.

European Wind Energy Association (EWEA)
63-65 Rue d'Arlon
Brussels, B-1040 Belgium
Phone: 32-2-546-1940
Fax: 32-2-546-1944
E-mail Address: *ewea@ewea.org*
Web Address: www.ewea.org
The European Wind Energy Association (EWEA) co-ordinates international policy, communications, research and analysis from its headquarters in Brussels. EWEA manages European programs, hosts events and supports the needs of its members.

German WindEnergy Association (BWE)
Marienstr. 19/20
Berlin, 10117 Germany
Phone: 49 (0)30 28 48 21 06
Fax: 49 (0)30 28 48 21 07
E-mail Address: *bwe-berlin@wind-energie.de*
Web Address: www.wind-energie.de/en/
The German WindEnergy Association (BWE) is one of the largest renewable energy associations in the world, with over 19,000 members. Its members include wind turbine manufacturers, operators and their shareholders, planning offices, financiers, scientists, engineers, technicians and lawyers, as well as early conservationists and students. BWE pools expertise and experience from the entire industry. One of BWE's goals is to be an important contact for politicians, business, science and the media.

Global Wind Energy Council (GWEC)
Rue d'Arlon 63-65
Brussels, 1040 Belgium
Phone: 32-2-400-1029
Fax: 32-2-546-1944
E-mail Address: *info@gwec.net*

Web Address: www.gwec.net
The Global Wind Energy Council (GWEC) was
established in early 2005 to provide a credible and
representative forum for the entire wind energy sector
at an international level. GWEC's mission is to
ensure that wind power establishes itself as one of the
world 's leading energy sources, providing
substantial environmental and economic benefits.

Indian Wind Energy Association
Opp. Asian Games Village, August Kranti Marg
PHD House, 3rd Fl.
New Delhi, 110 016 India
Phone: 91-11-26523042
E-mail Address: *manish@inwea.org*
Web Address: www.inwea.org
The Indian Wind Energy Association was organized
to promote and develop wind power in India.

Japanese Wind Energy Association (JWEA)
Chiyoda-ku Kita 2-1
Tokyo, 102-0091 Japan
E-mail Address: *jwea@jsf.or.jp*
Web Address: ppd.jsf.or.jp/jwea
The Japanese Wind Energy Association (JWEA) is
an organization of Japanese energy companies that
research, design and promote wind energy
technology.

XIII. Automotive Industry Resources

Automotive Center
1800 Crooks Rd.
Troy, MI 48084 US
Phone: 248-244-8920
Fax: 248-244-8925
Web Address: www.plastics-car.com
The Automotive Center, sponsored by the American
Chemistry Council's Plastics Division, strives to
provide the automobile designer, stylist or engineer
with up-to-the-minute research and information on
plastics applications in cars.

XIV. Brazilian Government Agencies-Scientific

**National Council for Scientific & Technological
Development**
SHIS QI 1 Conjunto B - Blocos A, B, C & D
Edifício Santos Dumont
Brasilia, DF 71605-001 Brazil
Phone: 55-61-3211-9000

Fax: 55-61-3211-9394
E-mail Address: *presidencia@cnpq.br*
Web Address: www.cnpq.br
The National Council for Scientific & Technological
Development (Conselho Nacional de
Desenvolvimento Cientifico e Tecnologico, or
CNPq) is a Brazilian government agency affiliated
with the country's Ministry of Science and
Technology. CNPq works to promote scientific and
technological research in Brazil through grants and
other support services. The organization also seeks to
encourage the development of Brazilian scientists
and researchers through the awarding of scholarships
and fellowships to students in the sciences.

XV. Canadian Government Agencies-Scientific

**Institute for Chemical Process and Environmental
Technology (ICPET)**
1200 Montreal Rd., Bldg. M-58
NRC Communications & Corporate Relations
Ottawa, ON K1A 0R6 Canada
Phone: 613-949-7673
E-mail Address: *info.icpet@nrc-cnrc.gc.ca*
Web Address: www.nrc-
cnrc.gc.ca/eng/ibp/icpet.html
The Institute for Chemical Process and
Environmental Technology (ICPET) focuses its
research and development activities on chemical
science and engineering. It is a branch of Canada's
National Research Council (NRC).

XVI. Careers-First Time Jobs/New Grads

Black Collegian Online (The)
140 Carondelet St.
New Orleans, LA 70130 US
Phone: 504-523-0154
Web Address: www.blackcollegian.com
The Black Collegian Online features listings for job
and internship opportunities, as well as other tools for
students of color; it is the web site of The Black
Collegian Magazine, published by IMDiversity, Inc.
The site includes a list of the top 100 minority
corporate employers and an assessment of job
opportunities.

CollegeGrad.com, Inc.
234 E. College Ave., Ste. 200
State College, PA 16801 US
Phone: 262-375-6700

Toll Free: 1-800-991-4642
Web Address: www.collegegrad.com
CollegeGrad.com, Inc. offers in-depth resources for
college students and recent grads seeking entry-level
jobs.

Job Web
62 Highland Ave.
Bethlehem, PA 18017-9085 US
Phone: 610-868-1421
Fax: 610-868-0208
Toll Free: 800-544-5272
E-mail Address: callen@naceweb.org
Web Address: www.jobweb.com
Job Web, owned and sponsored by National
Association of Colleges and Employers (NACE),
displays job openings and employer descriptions for
college students and recent graduates. The site also
offers a database of career fairs, searchable by state
or keyword; sample resumes; and other career related
information.

MBAjobs.net
Web Address: www.mbajobs.net
MBAjobs.net is an international service for MBA
students and graduates, employers, recruiters and
business schools. It aims to match MBA graduates
with employers and provides links to online MBA
programs.

MonsterCollege
799 Market St., Ste. 500
San Francisco, CA 94103 US
Toll Free: 800-999-8725
E-mail Address: info@college.monster.com
Web Address: www.college.monster.com
MonsterCollege provides information about
internships and entry-level jobs, as well as career
advice and resume tips, to recent college graduates.

National Association of Colleges and Employers (NACE)
62 Highland Ave.
Bethlehem, PA 18017-9085 US
Phone: 610-868-1421
Fax: 610-868-0208
Toll Free: 800-544-5272
E-mail Address: mcollins@naceweb.org
Web Address: www.naceweb.org
The National Association of Colleges and Employers
(NACE) is a premier U.S. organization representing
college placement offices and corporate recruiters
who focus on hiring new grads.

XVII. Careers-General Job Listings

Career Exposure, Inc.
3934 SW Corbett Ave.
Portland, OR 97239 US
Phone: 503-221-7779
Fax: 503-221-7780
E-mail Address: pr@careerexposure.com
Web Address: www.careerexposure.com
Career Exposure, Inc. is an online career center and
job placement service, with resources for employers,
recruiters and job seekers.

CareerBuilder, Inc.
200 N. LaSalle St., Ste. 1100
Chicago, IL 60601 US
Phone: 773-527-3600
Toll Free: 800-638-4212
Web Address: www.careerbuilder.com
CareerBuilder, Inc. focuses on the needs of
companies and also provides a database of job
openings. The site has over 1 million jobs posted by
300,000 employers, and receives an average 23
million unique visitors monthly. The company also
operates online career centers for 140 newspapers
and 9,000 online partners. Resumes are sent directly
to the company, and applicants can set up a special e-
mail account for job-seeking purposes.
CareerBuilder is primarily a joint venture between
three newspaper giants: The McClatchy Company,
Gannett Co., Inc. and Tribune Company.

CareerOneStop
Toll Free: 877-348-0502
E-mail Address: info@careeronestop.org
Web Address: www.careeronestop.org
CareerOneStop is operated by the employment
commissions of various state agencies. It contains
job listings in both the private and government
sectors, as well as a wide variety of useful career
resources and workforce information.
CareerOneStop is sponsored by the U.S. Department
of Labor.

JobCentral
9002 N. Purdue Rd., Ste. 100
Indianapolis, IN 46268 US
Phone: 317-874-9000
Fax: 317-874-9100
Toll Free: 866-268-6206
Web Address: www.jobcentral.com
JobCentral, operated by the nonprofit
DirectEmployers Association, Inc., links users

directly to job opportunities posted on the sites of participating employers, thus bypassing the usual job search sites. This saves employers money and allows job seekers to access many more job opportunities.

LaborMarketInfo (LMI)
P.O. Box 826880, MIC 57
c/o Employment Dev. Dept., Labor Market Info. Div.
Sacramento, CA 94280-0001 US
Phone: 916-262-2162
Fax: 916-262-2352
Toll Free: 800-480-3287
Web Address: www.labormarketinfo.edd.ca.gov
LaborMarketInfo (LMI) provides job seekers and employers a wide range of resources, namely the ability to find, access and use labor market information and services. It provides statistics for employment demographics on both a local and regional level, as well as career searching tools for California residents. The web site is sponsored by California's Employment Development Office.

Recruiters Online Network
3599 E. Normandy Park Dr.
Medina, OH 44256 US
E-mail Address: *recruitersonline@earthlink.net*
Web Address: www.recruitersonline.com
The Recruiters Online Network provides job postings from thousands of recruiters, Careers Online Magazine, a resume database, as well as other career resources.

True Careers, Inc.
Web Address: www.truecareers.com
True Careers, Inc. offers job listings and provides an array of career resources. It is partnered with CareerBuilder.com, which powers its career information and resume posting functions.

USAJOBS
1900 E St. NW
Washington, DC 20415 US
Phone: 202-606-1800
Web Address: usajobs.opm.gov
USAJOBS, a program of the U.S. Office of Personnel Management, is the official job site for the U.S. Federal Government. It provides a comprehensive list of U.S. government jobs, allowing users to search for employment by location; agency; type of work; or by senior executive positions. It also has special employment sections for individuals with disabilities, veterans and recent college graduates; an information center, offering resume and interview tips and other

information; and allows users to create a profile and post a resume.

XVIII. Careers-Job Reference Tools

NewsVoyager
Web Address: www.newsvoyager.com
NewsVoyager, a service of the Newspaper Association of America (NAA), links individuals to local, national and international newspapers, allowing job seekers to search through thousands of classified sections.

Vault.com, Inc.
75 Varick St., Fl. 8
New York, NY 10013 US
Phone: 212-366-4212
Fax: 212-366-6117
Web Address: www.vault.com
Vault.com, Inc. is a comprehensive career web site for employers and employees, with job postings and valuable information on a wide variety of industries. Its features and content are largely geared toward MBA degree holders.

XIX. Careers-Science

Chem Jobs
730 E. Cypress Ave.
Monrovia, CA 91016 US
Phone: 626-930-0808
Fax: 626-930-0102
E-mail Address: *info@chemindustry.com*
Web Address: www.chemjobs.net
Chem Jobs is a leading Internet site for job seekers in chemistry and related fields, with a particular focus on chemists, biochemists, pharmaceutical scientists and chemical engineers. The web site is powered by Chemindustry.com.

Science Jobs
E-mail Address: *webmaster@science-jobs.org*
Web Address: www.science-jobs.org
Science Jobs is a web site that contains many useful categories of links, including employment newsgroups, scientific journals and placement agencies. It also links to sites containing information regarding internship and fellowship opportunities for high school students and undergrads.

XX. Chemicals Industry Associations

American Chemical Society (ACS)
1155 16th St. NW
Washington, DC 20036 US
Phone: 202-872-4600
Toll Free: 800-227-5558
E-mail Address: *executivedirector@acs.org*
Web Address: www.acs.org
The American Chemical Society (ACS) is a nonprofit
organization aimed at promoting the understanding of
chemistry and chemical sciences. It represents a wide
range of disciplines including chemistry, chemical
engineering and other technical fields.

American Chemistry Council (ACC)
700 2nd St. NE
Washington, DC 20002 US
Phone: 202-249-7000
Fax: 202-249-6100
E-mail Address:
Anne_Kolton@AmericanChemistry.com
Web Address: www.americanchemistry.com
The American Chemistry Council (ACC) represents
leading companies in the chemistry sector and works
to protect public health and the environment. It
includes several substantial business groups,
including the Solvents Industry Group and Plastics
Division.

Brazilian Chemical Industry Association
Av. Chedid Jafet, 222, Bloco C, Fl. 4
Sao Paulo, SP 04551-065 Brazil
Phone: 55-11-2148-4700
Fax: 55-11-2148-4760
E-mail Address: *abiquim@abiquim.com.br*
Web Address: www.abiquim.org.br
The Brazilian Chemical Industry Association
(Associacao Brasileira da Industria Quimica,
ABIQUIM) represents Brazilian manufacturers of
chemical products and assists with a variety of issues
related to the industry, including product quality;
environmental and safety issues; human resource
development; product advocacy; tariff negotiations;
and trade agreements. ABIQUIM runs a 24-hour
hotline for chemical transportation safety issues, and
is also involved with plastics recycling efforts.

ChemAlliance
1850 M St. NW, Ste. 700
Washington, DC 20036-5810 US
Phone: 202-721-4100
Fax: 202-296-8120

Web Address: www.chemalliance.org
ChemAlliance, operated by the Society of Chemical
Manufacturers and Affiliates (SOCMA), provides up-
to-date information concerning the environmental
regulations affecting the chemical industry.

Chemical Industries Association (CIA)
Kings Bldg.
16 Smith Sq.
London, SW1P 3JJ UK
Phone: 44-20-7834-3399
Fax: 44-20-7834-4469
E-mail Address: *enquiries@cia.org.uk*
Web Address: www.cia.org.uk
The Chemical Industries Association (CIA) is the
UK's leading trade association for the chemical and
chemistry-related industries, representing members
both nationally and internationally.

Chemistry Industry Association of Canada
350 Sparks St., Ste. 805
Ottawa, ON K1R 7S8 Canada
Phone: 613-237-6215
Fax: 613-237-4061
Web Address: www.canadianchemistry.ca
The Chemistry Industry Association of Canada,
formerly Canada's Chemical Producers' Association
(CCPA), is a trade association that represents over 50
companies active in Canada's chemistry sector.

Council for Chemical Research (CCR)
1550 M St. NW, Ste. 300
Washington, DC 20005 US
Phone: 202-429-3971
Fax: 202-429-3976
E-mail Address: *pmendez@ccrhq.org*
Web Address: www.ccrhq.org
The Council for Chemical Research (CCR)
represents industry, academia and government
members involved in the chemical sciences and
engineering.

**International Council of Chemical Associations
(ICCA)**
Ave. E. Van Nieuwenhuyse 4, Box 1
Brussels, B-1160 Belgium
Phone: 32-2-676-74-15
E-mail Address: *rba@cefic.be*
Web Address: www.icca-chem.org
The International Council of Chemical Associations
(ICCA) represents chemical manufacturers and
producers all over the world.

International Union of Pure and Applied Chemistry (IUPAC)
104 T.W. Alexander Dr., Bldg. 19
Research Triangle Park, NC 27709 US
Phone: 919-485-8700
Fax: 919-485-8706
E-mail Address: *secretariat@iupac.org*
Web Address: www.iupac.org
The International Union of Pure and Applied Chemistry (IUPAC) is a world authority on chemical nomenclature, terminology, standardized methods for measurement, atomic weights and other critically evaluated data.

Society of Chemical Industry (SCI)
14/15 Belgrave Sq.
London, SW1X 8PS UK
Phone: 44-20-7598-1500
Fax: 44-20-7598-1545
E-mail Address: *secretariat@soci.org*
Web Address: www.soci.org
The Society of Chemical Industry (SCI) is a professional association for networking and problem solving in the international chemical industry. Established in 1881, SCI has members in over 70 countries. Its international headquarters are in London, with additional offices in the U.S., Canada, Continental Europe, India and Australia.

UIC (Union des Industries Chimiques)
Le Diamant A
14 Rue de la Republique
Paris, 92909 France
Phone: 33-1-46-53-11-00
Web Address: www.uic.fr
UIC, the Union des Industries Chimiques (Union of French Chemical Industries), represents chemicals manufacturers in France, including basic, fine, specialty and pharmaceuticals. It provides support to its members in six areas: technical, economic, social, innovation, communication and legal.

| XXI.   Chemicals Industry Resources |

Chemical Cluster Singapore
Phone: 65-6872-0865
Fax: 65-6872-5655
E-mail Address: *support@chemindustry.org.sg*
Web Address: www.chemindustry.org.sg
The Singapore Chemical Industry Council (SCIC) hosts the Chemical Cluster Singapore web site, which provides press releases; environment and safety

information; directories; and links to tenders, buyers and sellers.

Chemical Week
140 E. 45th St.
2 Grand Central Tower, Fl. 40
New York, NY 10017 US
Phone: 212-884-9528
Fax: 212-884-9514
Toll Free: 866-501-7540
E-mail Address: *lyn.tattum@ihs.com*
Web Address: www.chemweek.com
Chemical Week provides chemical makers and processors with news and information pertaining to the international chemicals industry. The site is owned by HIS, Inc.

Chemical-Industry-India.com
c/o Weblink Peripherals (I) Pvt. Ltd.
33 & 33A Rama Rd., Industrial Area
New Delhi, 110 015 India
Phone: 91-11-4142-8131
Fax: 91-11-4142-7820
E-mail Address: *info@chemical-industry-india.com*
Web Address: www.chemical-industry-india.com
The Chemical Industry India portal includes a database of assorted information relating to the chemical industry in India.

ChemWeb.com
730 E. Cypress Ave.
Monrovia, CA 91016 US
Phone: 626-930-0808
Fax: 626-930-0102
Web Address: www.chemweb.com
ChemWeb.com offers members access to numerous chemicals industry journals and databases from a variety of publishers, as well as an online magazine, The Alchemist. It is operated and owned by ChemIndustry.com.

| XXII.   Clean Transportation |

International Council on Clean Transportation (ICCT)
1225 I St. NW, Ste. 900
Washington, DC 20005 US
Phone: 202-534-1600
Web Address: www.theicct.org
By assembling a small group of about 30 top government officials and policymakers from the 10 largest motor vehicle markets—which together account for 85% of the world's new car and truck

sales—and providing them and other interested parties with accurate information about research, best practices, and technical resources for improving the efficiency and environmental performance of cars, trucks and other vehicles, the ICCT hopes to support sustainable transportation.

XXIII. Coatings Industry Associations

American Coatings Association
1500 Rhode Island Ave. NW
Washington, DC 20005 US
Phone: 202-462-6272
Fax: 202-462-8549
E-mail Address: *aca@paint.org*
Web Address: www.paint.org
The American Coatings Association is a nonprofit organization with members involved in the formulation, testing, manufacture and sale of coatings. The organization was formed from the merger of the Federation of Societies for Coatings Technology (FSCT) and the National Paint & Coatings Association (NPCA).

Chemical Coaters Association International (CCAI)
5040 Old Taylor Mill Rd., PMB 13
Taylor Mill, KY 41015 US
Phone: 859-356-1030
Fax: 859-356-0908
E-mail Address: *aygoyer@one.net*
Web Address: www.ccaiweb.com
The Chemical Coaters Association International (CCAI) offers training and information on surface coating technologies. Industry news, job listings and networking are available through the association's web site.

XXIV. Coatings Industry Resources

Coatings Group
Westgate House
120/130 Station Rd.
Redhill, Surrey, RH1 1ET UK
Phone: 44 (0) 1737 855000
Fax: 44 (0) 1737 855358
E-mail Address: *info@quartzltd.com*
Web Address: www.coatings-group.com
The Coatings Group, owned by Quartz Business Media Ltd, organizes a number of coatings events around the world and publishes Polymers Paint

Colour Journal (PPCJ) and Asia Pacific Coatings Journal (APCJ).

Coatings World
70 Hilltop Rd., Fl. 3
Ramsey, NJ 07446 US
Phone: 201-825-2552
Fax: 201-825-0553
E-mail Address: *twright@rodpub.com*
Web Address: www.coatingsworld.com
Coatings World provides information about new coatings technologies, as well as the production and marketing aspects of the worldwide paint and coatings industry. The site is maintained by Rodman Publishing Corp.

Paints & Coatings Industry (PCI)
2401 W. Big Beaver Rd., Ste. 700
Troy, MI 48084 US
Phone: 248-641-0592
Fax: 248-641-8932
E-mail Address: *johanssonk@bnpmedia.com*
Web Address: www.pcimag.com
Paints & Coatings Industry (PCI) magazine surveys the paint and coatings industry, delivering news to coatings manufacturers and formulators. Its web site offers industry news, industry articles, links and classifieds.

XXV. Computer & Electronics Industry Associations

Hong Kong Green Manufacturing Alliance (HKGMA)
8 Cheung Yue St.
31/F Billion Plz.
Kowloon, Hong Kong, China
Phone: 852-2732-3101
Fax: 852-2721-3494
E-mail Address: *hkgma@fhki.org.hk*
Web Address: www.gma.org.hk
The Hong Kong Green Manufacturing Alliance (HKGMA) promotes and assists members in meeting compliance standards with EU and other national legislation regarding the collection and treatment of end-of-life electrical and electronic products and other related hazardous substances.

XXVI. Construction Resources-Energy Efficient Buildings

Building Green
122 Birge St., Ste. 30
Brattleboro, VT 05301 US
Phone: 802-257-7300
Fax: 802-257-7304
E-mail Address: *info@buildinggreen.com*
Web Address: www.buildinggreen.com
Building Green provides research and information on energy-efficient buildings.

EERE Rebuild America
1000 Independence Ave. SW
Mail Stop EE-1
Washington, DC 20585 US
Phone: 202-586-5463
Toll Free: 877-337-3463
Web Address:
www.eere.energy.gov/buildings/program_areas/rebui ld.html
The Building Technologies Program of the Office of Energy Efficiency and Renewable Energy (EERE), a division of the U.S. Department of Energy, operates Rebuild America, which is a network of hundreds of community-based partnerships that are focused on increasing the number of energy-efficient buildings in the nation.

Energy Efficiency Programme Office (E2PO)
140 Hill St.
5th Storey, MICA Bldg.
Singapore, 179369 Singapore
Fax: 65-6235-2611
Toll Free: 800-225-5632
E-mail Address: *contact_NEA@nea.gov.sg*
Web Address: www.e2singapore.gov.sg
To drive energy efficiency improvement in Singapore, the Energy Efficiency Programme Office (E2PO) has been established. The website includes information about energy programs, publications, incentives and development opportunities for power generation, industry, transport, green buildings and the public sector of Singapore.

Green Building Initiative (GBI)
2104 SE Morrison
Portland, OR 97214 US
Fax: 503-961-8991
Toll Free: 877-424-4241
E-mail Address: *info@thegbi.org*
Web Address: www.thegbi.org

The Green Building Initiative (GBI) is a nonprofit network of building industry leaders committed to bringing green to mainstream residential and commercial construction. The GBI believes in building approaches that are environmentally progressive, but also practical and affordable for builders to implement.

GreenSource
2 Penn Plz.
New York, NY 10121-2298 US
Phone: 717-399-8900
Toll Free: 800-360-5549
E-mail Address: *greensourcemag@mcgraw-hill.com*
Web Address: www.greensource.construction.com
GreenSource is McGraw-Hill Construction's on-line directory of information on sustainable design, practice and products. It includes information from GreenSource, Architectural Record and Engineering News-Record magazines for architects, engineers, contractors and consumers. It also offers Internet-only exclusives.

International Self-Powered Building Council (ISPBC)
Web Address: www.ispbc.org
ISPBC (International Self-Powered Building Council) is a non-profit organization based in Washington, D.C. with worldwide chapters comprised of developers, architects, builders, property owners, renewable energy companies, engineers, designers, green building material manufacturers and suppliers. ISPBC is dedicated to the global deployment of Self-Powered-Building (SPB), a power generating, energy-efficient and economically superior Building 2.0 with a sophisticated approach to urban design. ISPBC seeks to achieve this by combining the most advanced photovoltaic (PV) and other renewable energy technologies with cutting edge design to provide stylish and seamlessly integrated modern buildings.

Sustainable Buildings Industry Council (SBIC)
1112 16th St. NW, Ste. 240
Washington, DC 20036 US
Phone: 202-628-7400
Fax: 202-393-5043
E-mail Address: *sbic@sbicouncil.com*
Web Address: www.sbicouncil.org
The Sustainable Buildings Industry Council (SBIC) is an independent, nonprofit organization that concentrates on providing information on energy conservation in regard to building construction.

U.S. Green Building Council (USGBC)
1800 Massachusetts Ave. NW, Ste. 300
Washington, DC 20036 US
Phone: 202-742-3792
Fax: 202-828-5110
Toll Free: 800-795-1747
E-mail Address: *info@usgbc.org*
Web Address: www.usgbc.org
The U.S. Green Building Council (USGBC) is a
coalition of building industry leaders working to
promote environmentally responsible commercial
and residential structures.

XXVII. Corporate Information Resources

bizjournals.com
120 W. Morehead St.
Ste. 400
Charlotte, NC 28202 US
Web Address: www.bizjournals.com
Bizjournals.com is the online media division of
American City Business Journals, the publisher of
dozens of leading city business journals nationwide.
It provides access to research into the latest news
regarding companies both small and large. The
organization maintains 42 websites and 64 print
publications and sponsors over 700 annual industry
events.

Business Wire
44 Montgomery St., Fl. 39
San Francisco, CA 94104 US
Phone: 415-986-4422
Fax: 415-788-5335
Toll Free: 800-227-0845
Web Address: www.businesswire.com
Business Wire offers news releases, industry- and
company-specific news, top headlines, conference
calls, IPOs on the Internet, media services and access
to tradeshownews.com and BW Connect On-line
through its informative and continuously updated
web site.

Edgar Online, Inc.
11200 Rockville Pike, Ste. 310
Rockville, MD 20852 US
Phone: 301-287-0300
Fax: 301-287-0390
Toll Free: 888-870-2316
Web Address: www.edgar-online.com
Edgar Online, Inc. is a gateway and search tool for
viewing corporate documents, such as annual reports

on Form 10-K, filed with the U.S. Securities and
Exchange Commission.

PR Newswire Association LLC
350 Hudson St., Ste. 300
New York, NY 10014 US
Fax: 800-793-9313
Toll Free: 800-776-8090
E-mail Address: *information@prnewswire.com*
Web Address: www.prnewswire.com
PR Newswire Association LLC provides
comprehensive communications services for public
relations and investor relations professionals, ranging
from information distribution and market intelligence
to the creation of online multimedia content and
investor relations web sites. Users can also view
recent corporate press releases from companies
across the globe. The Association is owned by
United Business Media plc.

Silicon Investor
100 W. Main
P.O. Box 29
Freeman, MO 64746 US
E-mail Address: *bobz@talkzilla.com*
Web Address: siliconinvestor.advfn.com
Silicon Investor is focused on providing information
about technology companies. Its web site serves as a
financial discussion forum and offers quotes, profiles
and charts.

XXVIII. Design & Architectural Associations

Center for Universal Design (The) (CUD)
College of Design, North Carolina State University
Campus Box 8613
Raleigh, NC 27695-8613 US
Phone: 919-515-3082
Fax: 919-515-8951
Toll Free: 800-647-6777
E-mail Address: *cud@ncsu.edu*
Web Address: www.design.ncsu.edu/cud
The Center for Universal Design (CUD) is a national
information, technical assistance and research center
that evaluates, develops and promotes products and
environments so that they can be used by all people,
regardless of physical or mental limitations.

XXIX.   Economic Data & Research

Centre for European Economic Research (The, ZEW)
P.O. Box 103443
Mannheim, D-68034 Germany
Phone: 49-621-1235-01
Fax: 49-621-1235-224
E-mail Address: *info@zew.de*
Web Address: www.zew.de/en
Zentrum fur Europaische Wirtschaftsforschung, The Centre for European Economic Research (ZEW), distinguishes itself in the analysis of internationally comparative data in a European context and in the creation of databases that serve as a basis for scientific research. The institute maintains a special library relevant to economic research and provides external parties with selected data for the purpose of scientific research. ZEW also offers public events and seminars concentrating on banking, business and other economic-political topics.

Economic and Social Research Council (ESRC)
Polaris House
North Star Ave.
Swindon, SN2 1UJ UK
Phone: 01793 413000
Fax: 01793 413001
E-mail Address: *comms@esrc.ac.uk*
Web Address: www.esrc.ac.uk
The Economic and Social Research Council (ESRC) funds research and training in social and economic issues. It is an independent organization, established by Royal Charter. Current research areas include the global economy; social diversity; environment and energy; human behavior; and health and well-being.

Eurostat
5 Rue Alphonse Weicker
Joseph Bech Bldg.
Luxembourg, L-2721 Luxembourg
Phone: 44-20-300-63103
Web Address: www.epp.eurostat.ec.europa.eu
Eurostat is the European Union's service that publishes a wide variety of comprehensive statistics on European industries, populations, trade, agriculture, technology, environment and other matters.

Federal Statistical Office of Germany
Wiesbaden, D-65180 Germany
Phone: 49-0-611-75-3444
Fax: 49-0-611-75-3976

Web Address: www.destatis.de
This office publishes a wide variety of nation and regional economic data of interest to anyone who is studying Germany, one of the world's leading economies. Data available includes population, consumer prices, labor markets, health care, industries and output.

India Brand Equity Foundation (IBEF)
249-F Sector 18
Udyog Vihar Phase IV
Gurgaon, Haryana 122015 India
Phone: 91-124-401-4060
Fax: 91-124-401-3873
E-mail Address: *ceo@ibef.org*
Web Address: www.ibef.org
India Brand Equity Foundation (IBEF) is a public-private partnership between the Ministry of Commerce and Industry, the Government of India and the Confederation of Indian Industry. The foundation's primary objective is to build positive economic perceptions of India globally. It aims to effectively present the India business perspective and leverage business partnerships in a globalizing marketplace.

National Bureau of Statistics (China)
57, Yuetan Nanjie, Sanlihe
Xicheng District
Beijing, 100826 China
Phone: 86-10-6852-0066
Fax: 86-10-6878-2000
E-mail Address: *info@stats.gov.cn*
Web Address: www.stats.gov.cn/english
The National Bureau of Statistics of China provides statistics and economic data regarding China's economy and society.

Organization for Economic Co-operation and Development (OECD)
2 rue André Pascal
Cedex 16
Paris, F-75775 France
Phone: 33-145-24-8200
Fax: 33-145-24-8500
Web Address: www.oecd.org
The Organization for Economic Co-operation and Development (OECD) publishes detailed economic, government, population, social and trade statistics on a country-by-country basis for over 30 nations representing the world's largest economies. Sectors covered range from industry, labor, technology and

patents, to health care, environment and globalization.

Statistics Bureau, Director-General for Policy Planning (Japan)
19-1 Wakamatsu-cho
Shinjuku-ku
Tokyo, 162-8668 Japan
Phone: 81-3-5273-2020
E-mail Address: *stat_webmaster@soumu.go.jp*
Web Address: www.stat.go.jp/english
The Statistics Bureau, Director-General for Policy Planning and Statistical Research and Training Institute, a part of the Japanese Ministry of Internal Affairs and Communications, plays the central role of producing and disseminating basic official statistics and coordinating statistical work under the Statistics Act and other legislation.

Statistics Canada
150 Tunney's Pasture Driveway
Ottawa, ON K1A 0T6 Canada
Phone: 613-951-8116
Fax: 613-951-0581
Toll Free: 800-263-1136
E-mail Address: *infostats@statcan.gc.ca*
Web Address: www.statcan.gc.ca
Statistics Canada provides a complete portal to Canadian economic data and statistics. Its conducts Canada's official census every five years, as well as hundreds of surveys covering numerous aspects of Canadian life.

XXX.   Emissions Cap & Trade Associations

International Emissions Trading Association (IETA)
24, Rue Merle d'Aubigne
Geneva, 1207 Switzerland
Phone: 41 22 737 05 00
Fax: 41 22 737 05 08
E-mail Address: *info@ieta.org*
Web Address: www.ieta.org
IETA is a leading association in the carbon emissions cap and trade industry. It sponsors research, publications and conferences on a worldwide basis.

UK Emissions Trading Group (ETG)
8 Duncannon St.
Golden Cross House
London, WC2N 4JF UK
Phone: 020 7484 5274

E-mail Address: *John.Craven@etg.uk.com*
Web Address: www.uketg.com
The business-led UK Emissions Trading Group (ETG) offers a forum for discussion and resolution of all aspects of emissions trading and enables communication to take place between commerce and industry, and the UK Government.

XXXI.   Energy Associations-China, General

China Energy Association (CEA)
7th of Nanlishi St.
Xicheng District
Beijing, 100045 China
Phone: 86-010-68051807
Fax: 86-010-68051799
E-mail Address: *znx18303@126.com*
Web Address: www.zhnx.org.cn
The China Energy Association (CEA) is a membership organization that represents the energy sources sector and energy industry. The organization publishes the Energy Resource World magazine.

XXXII.   Energy Associations-International

International Energy Agency (IEA)
9 rue de la Federation
Paris Cedex 15, 75739 France
Phone: 33-1-40-57-65-00
Fax: 33-1-40-57-65-09
E-mail Address: *info@iea.org*
Web Address: www.iea.org
The International Energy Agency (IEA) is the energy forum for its members' countries and is committed to taking joint measures to meet oil supply emergencies. It shares energy information, coordinates energy policies and helps in the development of national energy programs. The agency publishes a wealth of information each year, including statistics of fuel usage and emissions.

XXXIII.   Energy Industry Resources

BP Statistical Review of World Energy
1 St. James Sq.
London, SW1Y 4PD UK
Phone: 44-20-7496-4000
Fax: 44-20-7496-4630
E-mail Address: *sr@bp.com*
Web Address: www.bp.com/worldenergy

BP Statistical Review of World Energy, a publication of BP p.l.c., is an excellent source of the worlds current and historical energy trends.

XXXIV.   Engineering Indices

Cornell Engineering Library (The)
Engineering Library Cornell University
Carpenter Hall, Fl. 1
Ithaca, NY 14853 US
Phone: 607-255-5933
Fax: 607-255-0278
E-mail Address: *engranswers@cornell.edu*
Web Address: engineering.library.cornell.edu
Cornell University's Engineering Library web site has a number of resources concerning engineering research, as well as links to other engineering industry information sources. Its physical location on Cornell's campus possesses over 400,000 print volumes and more than 2 million micro-forms.

XXXV.   Engineering, Research & Scientific Associations

American Association for the Advancement of Science (AAAS)
1200 New York Ave. NW
Washington, DC 20005 US
Phone: 202-326-6400
E-mail Address: *webmaster@aaas.org*
Web Address: www.aaas.org
The American Association for the Advancement of Science (AAAS) is the world's largest scientific society and the publisher of Science magazine. It is an international nonprofit organization dedicated to advancing science around the globe.

American Institute of Chemical Engineers (AIChE)
3 Park Ave.
New York, NY 10016-5991 US
Phone: 203-702-7660
Fax: 203-775-5177
Toll Free: 800-242-4363
E-mail Address: *steps@aiche.org*
Web Address: www.aiche.org
The American Institute of Chemical Engineers (AIChE) provides leadership in advancing the chemical engineering profession. The organization, which is comprised of more than 40,000 members from over 90 countries, provides informational resources to chemical engineers.

American Physical Society (APS)
1 Physics Ellipse
College Park, MD 20740-3844 US
Phone: 301-209-3200
Fax: 301-209-0865
Web Address: www.aps.org
The American Physical Society (APS) develops and implements effective programs in physics education and outreach. APS publishes a number of research journals dedicated to physics research, including Physical Review, Physical Review Letters and Reviews of Modern Physics.

Asia Pacific Confederation of Chemical Engineers (APCChE)
APCChE Secretariat, C/- Engineers
Australia 11 National Circuit
Barton, 2600 Australia
Phone: 61-2-6270-6547
Fax: 61-2-6273-2358
E-mail Address:
cmcauliffe@engineersaustralia.org.au
Web Address: www.apcche.org
The Asia Pacific Confederation of Chemical Engineers (APCChE) was formed to provide a focus for various nonprofit societies, associations and institutions working in the field of chemical engineering in the Asia-Pacific region. APPChE consists of member societies in 13 countries: China, Korea, Japan, New Zealand, Thailand, India, the Philippines, Indonesia, Singapore, Australia, Malaysia, Taiwan and Hong Kong.

ASM International
9639 Kinsman Rd.
Materials Park, OH 44073-0002 US
Phone: 440-338-5151
Fax: 440-336-5152
Toll Free: 800-336-5152
E-mail Address:
memberservicecenter@asminternational.org
Web Address: www.asminternational.org
ASM International is a worldwide network of materials engineers, aimed at advancing industry, technology and applications of metals and materials. It provides materials information, education and training, as well as networking opportunities for professionals within the materials industry.

Association of Consulting Chemists and Chemical Engineers (ACC&CE)
P.O. Box 297
Sparta, NJ 07871 US

Phone: 973-729-6671
E-mail Address: *accce@chemconsult.org*
Web Address: www.chemconsult.org
The Association of Consulting Chemists and
Chemical Engineers (ACC&CE) was established to
advance the practices of consulting chemists and
chemical engineers.

ASTM International
100 Barr Harbor Dr.
P.O. Box C700
West Conshohocken, PA 19428-2959 US
Phone: 610-832-9500
E-mail Address: *jthomas@astm.org*
Web Address: www.astm.org
ASTM International, formerly the American Society
for Testing & Materials, provides and develops
voluntary consensus standards and related technical
information that promote public health and safety. It
also contributes to the reliability of materials for
industries worldwide.

Brazilian Association of Chemical Engineering
R. Libero Badaro, 152, Fl. 11
Sao Paulo, SP 01008-903 Brazil
Phone: 55-11-3107-8747
Fax: 55-11-3104-4649
E-mail Address: *abeq@abeq.org.br*
Web Address: www.abeq.org.br
The Brazilian Association of Chemical Engineering
is a non-profit organization that works to promote the
development of chemical engineering throughout the
country. Among other activities, it sponsors a variety
of industry networking meetings and publishes a
quarterly scientific journal and a technical magazine,
as well as distributing annual scholarships to
undergraduate and graduate students in the sciences.

**Chemical Industry and Engineering Society of
China (CIESC)**
Xiaoguan Jie 53, Anwai
Beijing, 100029 China
Phone: 86-10-6444-1885
Fax: 86-10-6441-1194
E-mail Address: *ciesc@ciesc.cn*
Web Address: www.ciesc.cn/english/
The Chemical Industry and Engineering Society of
China (CIESC) aims to advance chemical
engineering professionals and the chemical industry
through academic and educational development.
CIESC is affiliated with the China Association for
Science and Technology.

China Academy of Building Research (CABR)
30 Bei San Huan Dong Lu
Beijing, 100013 China
Phone: 010-84272233
Fax: 010-84281369
E-mail Address: *office@cabr.com.cn*
Web Address: www.cabr.cn
CABR is responsible for the development and
management of the major engineering construction
and product standards of China and is also the largest
comprehensive research and development institute in
the building industry in China. Some related
institutes include Institute of Earthquake
Engineering, Institute of Building Fire Research,
Institute of Building Environment and Energy
Efficiency (Building Physics), Institute of Foundation
Engineering as well as many others.

**DECHEMA (Society for Chemical Engineering
and Biotechnology)**
Theodor-Heuss-Allee 25
Frankfurt am Main, 60486 Germany
Phone: 49-69-75-64-0
Fax: 49-69-75-64-201
Web Address: dechema.de
The DECHEMA (Society for Chemical Engineering
and Biotechnology) is a nonprofit scientific and
technical society based in Germany. It was founded
in 1926 to promote research and technical advances
in the areas of chemical engineering, biotechnology
and environmental protection.

**Illuminating Engineering Society of North
America (IESNA)**
120 Wall St., Fl. 17
New York, NY 10005 US
Phone: 212-248-5000
Fax: 212-248-5017
E-mail Address: *iesna@iesna.org*
Web Address: www.iesna.org
A recognized authority on lighting in North America,
the Illuminating Engineering Society of North
America (IESNA) establishes scientific lighting
recommendations. Members include engineers,
architects, designers, educators, students,
manufacturers and scientists.

Industrial Research Institute (IRI)
2200 Clarendon Blvd., Ste. 1102
Arlington, VA 22201 US
Phone: 703-647-2580
Fax: 703-647-2581
Web Address: www.iriweb.org

The Industrial Research Institute (IRI) is a nonprofit organization of over 200 leading industrial companies, representing industries such as aerospace, automotive, chemical, computers and electronics, which carry out industrial research efforts in the U.S. manufacturing sector. IRI helps members improve research and development capabilities.

Institute for Research in Construction (IRC)

1200 Montreal Rd., Bldg. M-24
National Research Council of Canada
Ottawa, ON K1A 0R6 Canada
Phone: 613-993-2607
Fax: 613-952-7673
E-mail Address: *irc.client-services@nrc-cnrc.gc.ca*
Web Address: irc.nrc-cnrc.gc.ca
The Institute for Research in Construction (IRC) provides research, building code development and materials evaluation services. The IRC is Canada's construction technology center and a division of the National Research Council.

Materials Research Society (MRS)

506 Keystone Dr.
Warrendale, PA 15086-7573 US
Phone: 724-779-3003
Fax: 724-779-8313
E-mail Address: *info@mrs.org*
Web Address: www.mrs.org
The Materials Research Society (MRS) is dedicated to basic and applied research on materials of technological importance. MRS emphasizes an interdisciplinary approach to materials science and engineering. It is responsible for the publication of the Journal of Materials Science, a peer-reviewed journal focused on printing advanced research in materials science.

Netherlands Organization for Applied Scientific Research (TNO)

Schoemakerstraat 97, Bldg. A
Delft, NL-2628 VK The Netherlands
Phone: 31-88-866-0000
Fax: 31-15-261-2403
E-mail Address: *infodesk@tno.nl*
Web Address: www.tno.nl
The Netherlands Organization for Applied Scientific Research (TNO) is a contract research organization that provides a link between fundamental research and practical application.

Royal Society (The)

6-9 Carlton House Ter.

London, SW1Y 5AG UK
Phone: 44-20-7451-2500
Fax: 44-20-7930-2170
Web Address: www.royalsoc.ac.uk
The Royal Society, originally founded in 1660, is the UK's leading scientific organization and the oldest scientific community in continuous existence. It operates as a national academy of science, supporting scientists, engineers, technologists and researchers. Its web site contains a wealth of data about the research and development initiatives of its fellows and foreign members.

Royal Society of Chemistry (RSC)

Burlington House, Piccadilly
London, W1J 0BA UK
Phone: 44-20-7437-8656
Fax: 44-20-7437-8883
Web Address: www.rsc.org
The Royal Society of Chemistry (RSC) is one of Europe's largest organizations for advancing the chemical sciences.

XXXVI. Environmental Industry Associations

Air & Waste Management Association (A&WMA)

420 Fort Duquesne Blvd., Fl. 3
Pittsburgh, PA 15222 US
Phone: 412-232-3444
Fax: 412-232-3450
Toll Free: 800-270-3444
E-mail Address: *info@awma.org*
Web Address: www.awma.org
The A&WMA is a nonprofit professional organization that provides education and support to more than 8,000 environmental professionals in 65 nations.

Indoor Air Quality Association (IAQA)

12339 Carroll Ave.
Rockville, MD 20852 US
Phone: 301-231-8388
Fax: 301-231-8321
E-mail Address: *info@iaqa.org*
Web Address: www.iaqa.org
The Indoor Air Quality Association (IAQA) was established in 1995 to promote uniform standards, procedures and protocols in the indoor air quality industry. In 2005 IAQA's membership was consolidated with two very similar organizations: The American Council for Accredited Certifications (ACAC) and the Indoor Environmental Standards

Organization (IESO). The group publishes research and holds conferences, among its many other activities.

International Association of Certified Indoor Air Consultants

1750 30 St.
Boulder, CO 80301
E-mail Address: *fastreply@iac2.org*
Web Address: www.iac2.org
IAC2 is the non-profit, certifying body for home and building inspectors who have fulfilled certain educational and testing requirements including those in the area of indoor air quality. Indoor air quality issues include mold, radon, biologicals, carbon monoxide, formaldehyde, pesticides, asbestos and lead.

International Society of Indoor Air Quality and Climate

2548 Empire Grade
Santa Cruz, CA 95060 US
Phone: 831-426-0148
Fax: 831-426-6522
Web Address: www.isiaq.org
ISIAQ is an international, independent, multidisciplinary, scientific, non-profit organization whose purpose is to support the creation of healthy, comfortable and productive indoor environments. We strongly believe this is achievable by advancing the science and technology of indoor air quality and climate as it relates to indoor environmental design, construction, operation and maintenance, air quality measurement and health sciences.

Institute of Clean Air Companies (ICAC)

1220 N. Fillmore St., Ste. 410
Arlington, VA 22201 US
Phone: 703-812-4811
E-mail Address: *icacinfo@icac.com*
Web Address: www.icac.com
The Institute of Clean Air Companies (ICAC) is a U.S. association of companies that supply air pollution monitoring and control systems, equipment, and services for stationary sources. ICAC has promoted the air pollution control industry and encouraged improvement of engineering and technical standards since 1960. Members are leading manufacturers of equipment to monitor and control emissions of particulate, VOC, SO2, NOx, air toxins and greenhouse gases.

XXXVII.   Environmental Organizations

Center for Environmental Systems Research (CESR)

University of Kassel
Kassel, 34109 Germany
Phone: 0561-804-6110
Fax: 0561-804-6116
Web Address: www.usf.uni-kassel.de/cesr/
The CESR is part of the University of Kassel. It operates four research groups, in \"global and regional dynamics\" covering water and land use changes; \"socio-environmental systems;\" \"integrated water management;\" and \"sustainable energy and material flow management.\" The CESR publishes many important papers and boosts education and research.

Environmental Defense Fund (EDF)

1875 Connecticut Ave. NW, Ste. 600
Washington, DC 20009 US
Web Address: www.edf.org
The EDF focuses on many environmental issues, including climate, energy and water. It has offices in many U.S. cities, as well as in La Paz, Mexico and Beijing, China.

Global Footprint Network

312 Clay St., Ste. 300
Oakland, CA 94607-3510 US
Phone: 510-839-8879
Fax: 510-251-2410
E-mail Address: *info@footprintnetwork.org*
Web Address: www.footprintnetwork.org
Global Footprint Network publishes regional studies of human demands on the ecology which it calls an Ecological Footprint. The Footprint takes into consideration human use of land, water and other resources to fill needs for housing, agriculture, energy and more, along with nature's ability to fulfill those demands. The organization's analysis creates a scale by which one nation may compare its footprint against that of others.

Pembina Institute (The)

608 7th St. S.W., Ste. 200
Calgary, AB T2P 1Z2 Canada
Phone: 780-542-6272
Fax: 780-542-6464
Web Address: www.pembina.org
The Pembina Institute is an independent, not-for-profit environmental policy research and education organization. The Pembina Institute's major policy

research and education programs are in the areas of sustainable energy, climate change, environmental governance, ecological fiscal reform, sustainability indicators, and the environmental impacts of the energy industry.

XXXVIII. Environmental Resources

Center for Clean Air Policy (CCAP)
750 First St. NE, Ste. 940
Washington, DC 20002 US
Phone: 202-408-9260
Fax: 202-408-8896
E-mail Address: *communications@ccap.org*
Web Address: www.ccap.org
The Center for Clean Air Policy (CCAP) promotes and applies solutions to key environmental and energy problems.

Clean Air World
444 North Capital St.
ATTN: NACAA, Ste. 307
Washington, DC 20001 US
Phone: 202-624-7864
E-mail Address: *4cleanair@4cleanair.org*
Web Address: www.cleanairworld.org
Clean Air World is the global outreach and information portal of the National Association of Clean Air Agencies (NACAA, formerly STAPPA/ALAPCO). While NACAA concentrates primarily on air quality issues in the United States, Clean Air World has an international focus with regard to air pollution topics. Clean Air World contains world-wide listings of all available state and local air-pollution agency contacts and information on a wide range of environmental topics related to all aspects of air pollution.

Foundation for Clean Air Progress (FCAP)
601 Pennsylvania Ave. NW
N. Bldg., Ste. 540
Washington, DC 20004 US
E-mail Address: *info@cleanairprogress.org*
Web Address: www.cleanairprogress.org
The Foundation for Clean Air Progress (FCAP) is an organization that provides public education and information about air quality progress.

German Federal Environmental Foundation
Deutsche Bundesstiftung Umwelt
An der Bornau 2
Osnabruck, 49090 Germany
Phone: 0541 96330

Fax: 0541 9633190
E-mail Address: *info@dbu.de*
Web Address: www.dbu.de
The German Federal Environmental Foundation's projects and activities concentrate on environmental technology and research, nature conservation, environmental communication and cultural assets. It is an initiative of the German Government.

Pew Center on Global Climate Change
2101 Wilson Blvd., Ste. 550
Arlington, VA 22201 US
Phone: 703-516-4146
Fax: 703-841-1422
Web Address: www.pewclimate.org
The Pew Center on Global Climate Change was established in 1998 as a nonprofit, non-partisan and independent organization. The Center's mission is to provide credible information, straight answers, and innovative solutions in the effort to address global climate change.

XXXIX. Geoengineering

Geoengineer.org
Web Address: www.geoengineer.org
Geoengineer.org promotes the advancement of international geoengineering practice, research and education through the classification and integration of worldwide geoengineering information and the development of tools, resources and professional activities.

Geotechnical Extreme Events Reconnaissance (GEER)
E-mail Address: *jzupan@berkeley.edu*
Web Address: www.geerassociation.org
The GEER Association is working to develop a systematic approach to conducting the National Science Foundation (NSF)-sponsored reconnaissance efforts of the geotechnical effects of extreme events. The project is formalizing the manner in which extreme events reconnaissance efforts are organized by the GeoPrograms of NSF.

International Society for Soil Mechanics and Geotechnical Engineering (ISSMGE)
Geotechnical Engineering Research Centre, City University
Northampton Square
London, EC1V 0HB UK
Phone: 44-20-7040-8832
E-mail Address: *enquiries@issmge.org*

Web Address: www.issmge.org
The ISSMGE is a professional body representing the interests and activities of engineers, academics and contractors all over the world that actively participate in geotechnical engineering. Its activities include conferences and publications.

XL.   Green Technology Resources

Clentech Group LLC
220 Montgomery St., Ste. 1000
San Francisco, CA 94104 US
Phone: 415-684-1020
Web Address: www.cleantech.com
The CleanTech Group publishes market research and conducts global conferences on green technology issues and topics. It provides valuable newsletters and blogs via its website.

XLI.   Hybrid & Electric Vehicles

EERE FreedomCAR & Vehicle Technologies Program (FCVT)
1000 Independence Ave. SW
Mail Stop EE-2G, Rm. 5G-030
Washington, DC 20585 US
Phone: 202-586-8055
Fax: 202-586-7409
Toll Free: 877-337-3463
E-mail Address: *patrick.davis@ee.doe.gov*
Web Address:
www1.eere.energy.gov/vehiclesandfuels
The FreedomCAR & Vehicle Technologies Program (FCVT) of the Office of Energy Efficiency and Renewable Energy (EERE), a division of the U.S. Department of Energy, works with U.S. industries toward the development of emission- and petroleum-free cars and light trucks. The program focuses on high-risk technological research for fuel cells and advanced hybrid propulsion systems.

Electric Drive Transportation Association (EDTA)
1101 Vermont Ave. NW, Ste. 401
Washington, DC 20005 US
Phone: 202-408-0774
E-mail Address: *info@electricdrive.org*
Web Address: www.electricdrive.org
The Electric Drive Transportation Association (EDTA) is an industry association working to advance electric vehicle transportation technologies

and supporting infrastructure through policy, information and market development initiatives.

XLII.   Industry Research/Market Research

Forrester Research
400 Technology Sq.
Cambridge, MA 02139 US
Phone: 617-497-7090
Toll Free: 866-367-7378
Web Address: www.forrester.com
Forrester Research is a publicly traded company that identifies and analyzes emerging trends in technology and their impact on business. Among the firm's specialties are the financial services, retail, health care, entertainment, automotive and information technology industries.

Gartner, Inc.
56 Top Gallant Rd.
Stamford, CT 06904-7700 US
Phone: 203-964-0096
E-mail Address: *andrew.spender@gartner.com*
Web Address: www.gartner.com
Gartner, Inc. is a publicly traded IT company that provides competitive intelligence and strategic consulting and advisory services to numerous clients worldwide.

MarketResearch.com
11200 Rockville Pike, Ste. 504
Rockville, MD 20852 US
Phone: 240-747-3000
Fax: 240-747-3004
Toll Free: 800-298-5699
E-mail Address:
customerservice@marketresearch.com
Web Address: www.marketresearch.com
MarketResearch.com is a leading broker for professional market research and industry analysis. Users are able to search the company's database of research publications including data on global industries, companies, products and trends.

Plunkett Research, Ltd.
P.O. Drawer 541737
Houston, TX 77254-1737 US
Phone: 713-932-0000
Fax: 713-932-7080
E-mail Address:
customersupport@plunkettresearch.com
Web Address: www.plunkettresearch.com

Plunkett Research, Ltd. is a leading provider of market research, industry trends analysis and business statistics. Since 1985, it has served clients worldwide, including corporations, universities, libraries, consultants and government agencies. At the firm's web site, visitors can view product information and pricing and access a large amount of basic market information on industries such as financial services, InfoTech, e-commerce, health care and biotech.

XLIII. Internet Usage Statistics

Pew Internet & American Life Project
1615 L St. NW, Ste. 700
Washington, DC 20036 US
Phone: 202-419-4500
Fax: 202-419-4505
E-mail Address: *data@pewinternet.org*
Web Address: www.pewinternet.org
The Pew Internet & American Life Project, an initiative of the Pew Research Center, produces reports that explore the impact of the Internet on families, communities, work and home, daily life, education, health care and civic and political life.

XLIV. MBA Resources

MBA Depot
Web Address: www.mbadepot.com
MBA Depot is an online community and information portal for MBAs, potential MBA program applicants and business professionals.

XLV. Natural Gas Vehicles

Asia Pacific Natural Gas Vehicles Association (ANGVA)
Level 2, Block A, Lot 3288 and 3289
Off Jalan Ayer Hitam, Kawasan Institutusi Bangi
Kajang, Selangor 43000 Malaysia
Phone: 603-8926-1798
Fax: 603-8926-1834
E-mail Address: *leegs@angva.org*
Web Address: www.angva.org
ANGVA serves the needs of fleet operators, vehicle manufacturers, gas suppliers, equipment suppliers, refueling equipment providers, consultants, government representatives, non governmental organizations (NGO) and others involved with the natural gas vehicles industry by promoting the use of natural gas as the fuel for the transportation sector.

Natural Gas Vehicles for America (NGVAmerica)
400 N. Capitol St. NW
Washington, DC 20001 US
Phone: 202-824-7366
Fax: 202-824-7087
E-mail Address: *rkolodziej@ngvamerica.org*
Web Address: www.ngvc.org
Natural Gas Vehicle for America (NGVAmerica) is a national organization dedicated to the development of a growing, sustainable and profitable market for vehicles powered by natural gas or hydrogen. NGVAmerica represents more than 100 companies interested in the promotion and use of natural gas and hydrogen as transportation fuels, including: engine, vehicle and equipment manufacturers fleet operators and service providers natural gas companies and environmental groups and government organizations.

XLVI. Packaging Industry Associations

Sustainable Packaging Coalition (SPC), c/o GreenBlue
600 E. Water St., Ste. C
Charlottesville, VA 22901 US
Phone: 434-817-1424
E-mail Address: *spcinfo@greenblue.org*
Web Address: www.sustainablepackaging.org
The Sustainable Packaging Coalition (SPC) is an industry working group dedicated to a more robust environmental vision for packaging. Through strong member support, an informed and science-based approach, supply chain collaborations and continuous outreach, we endeavor to build packaging systems that encourage economic prosperity and a sustainable flow of materials. The SPC is a project of GreenBlue®, a nonprofit that equips business with the science and resources to make products more sustainable.

XLVII. Packaging Industry Resources

Sustainable Packaging Alliance
5 Brooklyn Ave.
Dandenong, VIC 3175 Australia
Phone: 61-0-3-9791-5888
Fax: 61-0-3-9706-7700
Web Address: www.sustainablepack.org
SPA is the global distributor of PIQET, a web based business tool used for rapid packaging environmental impact assessments. PIQET is used to optimise packaging system design from a sustainability

perspective in all stages of the product development process.

XLVIII.   Plastics Industry Associations

National Association for PET Container Resources (NAPCOR)
P.O. Box 1327
Sonoma, CA 95476 US
Phone: 707-996-4207
Fax: 707-935-1998
E-mail Address: *information@napcor.com*
Web Address: www.napcor.com
The National Association for PET Container Resources (NAPCOR) is the trade association for the PET plastic industry in the U.S. and Canada.

XLIX.   Plastics Industry Resources

Packaging Today
E-mail Address: *editor@packagingtoday.com*
Web Address: www.packagingtoday.com
Packaging Today provides news on the packaging, paper, oil and gas, plastics and recycling industries.

L.   Ratings for Sustainability

Global Reporting Initiative (GRI)
P. O. Box 10039
Amsterdam, 1001 EA The Netherlands
Phone: 31-0-20-531-0000
Fax: 31-0-531-0031
E-mail Address: *guidelines@globalreporting.org*
Web Address: www.globalreporting.org
The Global Reporting Initiative (GRI) is a network-based organization that produces a comprehensive sustainability reporting framework that is widely used around the world. GRI's core goals include the mainstreaming of disclosure on environmental, social and governance performance. The Reporting Framework sets out the principles and Performance Indicators that organizations can use to measure and report their economic, environmental, and social performance.

LI.   Recycling & Waste Industry Associations

Association of Postconsumer Plastic Recyclers
1001 G St. NW, Ste. 500
Washington, DC 20001 US
Phone: 202-316-3046

Web Address: www.plasticsrecycling.org
The Association of Postconsumer Plastic Recyclers is the national trade association representing companies who acquire, reprocess and sell the output of more than 90 percent of the post-consumer plastic processing capacity in North America. Its membership includes independent recycling companies of all sizes, processing numerous resins. APR strongly advocates the recycling of all post-consumer plastic packaging.

Environmental Services Association (ESA)
154 Buckingham Palace Rd.
London, SW1W 9TR UK
Phone: 020-7824-8882
Fax: 020-7824-8753
E-mail Address: *info@esauk.org*
Web Address: www.esakuk.org
The Environmental Services Association (ESA) works on behalf of our Members to support and promote the waste and resource management industry. We work with governments, parliaments and regulators to bring about a sustainable system of waste and resource management for the UK.

Institute of Scrap Recycling Industries
1615 L St. NW, Ste. 600
Washington, DC 20036
Phone: 202-662-8500
Fax: 202-626-0300
Web Address: www.isri.org
ISRI, a Washington, DC, based trade association, represents nearly 1,600 private and public for-profit companies – ranging from small, family-owned businesses to multi-national corporations -- operating at more than 6,000 facilities in the United States and 30 countries worldwide. Our members are manufacturers and processors, brokers and industrial consumers of scrap commodities, including ferrous and nonferrous metals, paper, electronics, rubber, plastics, glass and textiles. ISRI's associate members include equipment and service providers to the scrap recycling industry.

National Solid Wastes Management Association (NSWMA)
4301 Connecticut Ave. NW, Ste. 300
Washington, DC 20008 US
Phone: 202-244-4700
Fax: 202-966-4824
Toll Free: 800-424-2869
Web Address: www.environmentalistseveryday.org

NSWMA is a trade association representing for-profit companies in North America that provide solid, hazardous and medical waste collection, recycling and disposal services, and companies that provide professional and consulting services to the waste services industry.

LII.   Research & Development, Laboratories

Commonwealth Scientific and Industrial Research Organization (CSRIO)

CSIRO Enquiries
Bag 10
Clayton South, Victoria 3169 Australia
Phone: 61-3-9545-2176
Fax: 61-3-9545-2175
E-mail Address: *enquiries@csiro.au*
Web Address: www.csiro.au
The Commonwealth Scientific and Industrial Research Organization (CSRIO) is Australia's national science agency and a leading international research agency. CSRIO performs research in Australia over a broad range of areas including agriculture, minerals and energy, manufacturing, communications, construction, health and the environment.

Fraunhofer-Gesellschaft (FhG) (The)

Fraunhofer-Gesellschaft zur Forderung der angewandten Forschung e.V.
Postfach 20 07 33
Munich, 80007 Germany
Phone: 49-89-1205-0
Fax: 49-89-1205-7531
Web Address: www.fraunhofer.de
The Fraunhofer-Gesellschaft (FhG) institute focuses on research in health, security, energy, communication, the environment and mobility. FhG includes over 80 research units in Germany. Over 70% of its projects are derived from industry contracts.

Helmholtz Association

Anna-Louisa-Karsch-StraBe 2
Berlin, 10178 Germany
Phone: 49-30-206329-0
Fax: 49-30-206329-65
E-mail Address: *org@helmholtz.de*
Web Address: www.helmholtz.de/en
The Helmholtz Association is a community of 17 scientific-technical and biological-medical research centers. Helmholtz Centers perform top-class research in strategic programs in several core fields: energy, earth and environment, health, key technologies, structure of matter, aeronautics, space and transport.

Idaho National Laboratory (INL)

1765 N. Yellowstone Hwy.
P.O. Box 1625
Idaho Falls, ID 83415 US
Phone: 208-526-0111
Toll Free: 866-495-7440
Web Address: www.inl.gov
Idaho National Laboratory (INL) is a multidisciplinary, multiprogram laboratory that specializes in developing nuclear energy with research concerning the environment, energy, science and national defense.

Indira Gandhi Institute of Development Research

Gen. A. K. Vaidya Marg
Goregaon (E)
Mumbai, 400 065 India
Phone: 022-2840-0919
Fax: 022-2840-2752
E-mail Address: *nachane@igidr.ac.in*
Web Address: www.igidr.ac.in
The Indira Gandhi Institute of Development Research (IGIDR) focuses on research of the economic, technological, social, political and ecological aspects of development and the influence of international trading, financial and economic systems on countries. It also includes an examination of energy, technology and environmental problems in a global setting.

Leibniz Association of German Research Institutes (WGL)

Eduard-Pfluger-Str. 55
Bonn, D-53113 Germany
Phone: 49-228-30815-210
Fax: 49-228-30815-255
E-mail Address: *info@leibniz-gemeinschaft.de*
Web Address: www.leibniz-gemeinschaft.de
The Leibniz Association of German Research Institutes (WGL) is a research organization that comprises over 85 institutes. WGL works on international interdisciplinary research and acts as a bridge between traditional research and customer oriented applications. The association focuses on scientific excellence and social relevance.

Los Alamos National Laboratory (LANL)

Bikini Atoll Rd., SM 30
P.O. Box 1663

Los Alamos, NM 87545 US
Phone: 505-667-5061
Fax: 505-665-4411
Toll Free: 888-841-8256
E-mail Address: *community@lanl.gov*
Web Address: www.lanl.gov
The Los Alamos National Laboratory (LANL), a
national energy lab in New Mexico, was originally
built as a work site for the team that designed the first
atomic bomb during World War II. Currently, it
provides a continual stream of research in physics
and energy matters. Much of that research is put to
use in the commercial sector.

Max Planck Society (MPG)
Hofgartenstr. 8
Munich, 80539 Germany
Phone: 49-(89)-210-80
Fax: 49-(89)-210-811-11
E-mail Address: *post@gv.mpg.de*
Web Address: www.mpg.de
The Max Planck Society (MPG) currently maintains
80 institutes, research units and working groups that
are devoted to basic research in the natural sciences,
life sciences, social sciences, and the humanities.
Max Planck Institutes work largely in an
interdisciplinary setting and in close cooperation with
universities and research institutes in Germany and
abroad.

National Renewable Energy Laboratory (NREL)
1617 Cole Blvd.
Golden, CO 80401-3393 US
Phone: 303-275-3000
E-mail Address: *public_affairs@nrel.gov*
Web Address: www.nrel.gov
The National Renewable Energy Laboratory (NREL)
reduces nuclear danger, transfers applied
environmental technology to government and non-
government entities and forms economic and
industrial alliances.

National Research Council Canada (NRC)
1200 Montreal Rd.
Bldg. M-58
Ottawa, ON K1A 0R6 Canada
Phone: 613-993-9101
Fax: 613-952-9907
Toll Free: 877-672-2672
E-mail Address: *info@nrc-cnrc.gc.ca*
Web Address: www.nrc-cnrc.gc.ca
National Research Council Canada (NRC) is
comprised of 20 government organization, research

institutes and programs that carry out
multidisciplinary research. It maintains partnerships
with industries and sectors key to Canada's economic
development.

Oak Ridge National Laboratory (ORNL)
1 Bethel Valley Rd.
P.O. Box 2008
Oak Ridge, TN 37831 US
Phone: 865-574-4160
Fax: 865-574-0595
E-mail Address: *strohlhf@ornl.gov*
Web Address: www.ornl.gov
The Oak Ridge National Laboratory (ORNL) is a
multiprogram science and technology laboratory
managed for the U.S. Department of Energy by U.T.-
Battelle, LLC. It conducts basic and applied research
and development to create scientific knowledge and
technological solutions.

Sandia National Laboratories
1515 Eubank SE
Albuquerque, NM 87123 US
Phone: 505-845-0011
E-mail Address: *webmaster@sandia.gov*
Web Address: www.sandia.gov
Sandia National Laboratories is a national security
laboratory operated for the U.S. Department of
Energy by the Sandia Corporation. It designs all
nuclear components for the nation's nuclear weapons
and performs a wide variety of energy research and
development projects.

SRI International
333 Ravenswood Ave.
Menlo Park, CA 94025-3493 US
Phone: 650-859-2000
E-mail Address: *customer-service@sri.com*
Web Address: www.sri.com
SRI International is a nonprofit research organization
that offers contract research services to government
agencies, as well as commercial enterprises and other
private sector institutions. It is organized into five
R&D areas: Physical Sciences; Biosciences;
Information and Computing Sciences; Engineering
and Systems; and Policy.

LIII.   Robotics Associations

International Federation of Robotics (IFR)
Lyoner Str. 18
Frankfurt am Main, 60528 Germany
Phone: 49-69-6603-1502

Fax: 49-69-6603-2502
E-mail Address: *gl@ifr.org*
Web Address: www.ifr.org
The IFR promotes the robotics industry worldwide, including the fields of industrial robots for manufacturing and other purposes, service robots and robotics research. Among other things, it is focused on research, development, use and international co-operation in the entire field of robotics, and it seeks to act as a focal point for organizations and governmental representatives in activities related to robotics.

LIV.   Science & Technology Resources

Technology Review
1 Main St., Fl. 13
Cambridge, MA 02142 US
Phone: 617-475-8000
Fax: 617-475-8042
Toll Free: 800-877-5230
Web Address: www.technologyreview.com
Technology Review, an MIT enterprise, publishes tech industry news, covers innovation and writes in-depth articles about research, development and cutting-edge technologies.

LV.   Smart Meter Industry Associations

Smart Meter Manufacturers Association of America (SMMAA)
Web Address: www.smmaa.org
The Smart Meter Manufacturers' Association of America (SMMAA) is a group consisting of smart meter manufacturers, which represent roughly 99% of the installed base of electric meters currently deployed in the U.S.

LVI.   Soap & Cleansers Industry Associations

American Cleaning Institute (ACI)
1331 L St. NW, Ste. 650
Washington, DC 20005 US
Phone: 202-347-2900
Fax: 202-347-4110
E-mail Address: *info@cleaninginstitute.org*
Web Address: www.cleaninginstitute.org
The American Cleaning Institute (ACI), formerly the Soap and Detergent Association, is a non-profit trade association representing manufacturers of household, industrial and institutional cleaning products, their

ingredients and finished packaging; oleochemical producers; and chemical distributors to the cleaning product industry.

LVII.   Stocks & Financial Markets Data

SiliconValley.com
750 Ridder Park Dr.
c/o San Jose Mercury News
San Jose, CA 95190 US
Phone: 408-920-5000
Fax: 408-288-8060
Web Address: www.siliconvalley.com
SiliconValley.com, run by San Jose Mercury News, offers a summary of current financial news and information regarding the field of technology.

LVIII.   Technology Transfer Associations

Association of University Technology Managers (AUTM)
111 Deer Lake Rd., Ste. 100
Deerfield, IL 60015 US
Phone: 847-559-0846
Fax: 847-480-9282
E-mail Address: *jtalley@autm.net*
Web Address: www.autm.net
The Association of University Technology Managers (AUTM) is a nonprofit professional association whose members belong to over 350 research institutions, universities, teaching hospitals, government agencies and corporations from 45 countries. The association's mission is to advance the field of technology transfer and enhance members' ability to bring academic and nonprofit research to people around the world.

Federal Laboratory Consortium for Technology Transfer
950 N. Kings Highway, Ste. 208
Cherry Hill, NJ 08304 US
Phone: 856-667-7727
Fax: 856-667-8009
E-mail Address: *flcmso@federallabs.org*
Web Address: www.federallabs.org
In keeping with the aims of the Federal Technology Transfer Act of 1986 and other related legislation, the Federal Laboratory Consortium (FLC) works to facilitate the sharing of research results and technology developments between federal laboratories and the mainstream U.S. economy. FLC affiliates include federal laboratories, large and small

businesses, academic and research institutions, state and local governments and various federal agencies. The group has regional support offices and local contacts throughout the U.S.

Licensing Executives Society (U.S.A. and Canada), Inc.
1800 Diagonal Rd., Ste. 280
Alexandria, VA 22314 US
Phone: 703-836-3106
Fax: 703-836-3107
E-mail Address: *info@les.org*
Web Address: www.lesusacanada.org
Licensing Executives Society (U.S.A. and Canada), Inc., established in 1965, is a professional association composed of about 5,000 members who work in fields related to the development, use, transfer, manufacture and marketing of intellectual property. Members include executives, lawyers, licensing consultants, engineers, academic researchers, scientists and government officials. The society is part of the larger Licensing Executives Society International, Inc. (same headquarters address), with a worldwide membership of some 12,000 members from approximately 80 countries.

State Science and Technology Institute (SSTI)
5015 Pine Creek Dr.
Westerville, OH 43081 US
Phone: 614-901-1690
Fax: 614-901-1696
Web Address: www.ssti.org
The State Science and Technology Institute (SSTI) is a national nonprofit group that serves as a resource for technology-based economic development. In addition to the information on its web site, the Institute publishes a free weekly digest of news and issues related to technology-based economic development efforts, as well as a members-only publication listing application information, eligibility criteria and submission deadlines for a variety of funding opportunities, federal and otherwise.

LIX.   Trade Associations-General

BUSINESSEUROPE
168 Ave. de Cortenbergh
Brussels, 1000 Belgium
Phone: 32(0)-2-237-65-11
Fax: 32(0)-2-231-14-45
E-mail Address: *main@businesseurope.eu*
Web Address: www.businesseurope.eu

BUSINESSEUROPE is a major European trade federation that operates in a manner similar to a chamber of commerce. Its members are the central national business federations of the 34 countries throughout Europe from which they come. Companies cannot become direct members of BUSINESSEUROPE, though there is a support group which offers the opportunity for firms to encourage BUSINESSEUROPE objectives in various ways.

United States Council for International Business (USCIB)
1212 Ave. of the Americas
New York, NY 10036 US
Phone: 212-354-4480
Fax: 212-575-0327
E-mail Address: *membership@uscib.org*
Web Address: www.uscib.org
The United States Council for International Business (USCIB) promotes an open system of world trade and investment through its global network. Standard USCIB members include corporations, law firms, consulting firms and industry associations. Limited membership options are available for chambers of commerce and sole legal practitioners.

LX.   Trade Associations-Global

World Trade Organization (WTO)
Centre William Rappard
Rue de Lausanne 154
Geneva 21, CH-1211 Switzerland
Phone: 41-22-739-51-11
Fax: 41-22-731-42-06
E-mail Address: *enquiries@wto.og*
Web Address: www.wto.org
The World Trade Organization (WTO) is a global organization dealing with the rules of trade between nations. To become a member, nations must agree to abide by certain guidelines. Membership increases a nation's ability to import and export efficiently.

LXI.   Trade Resources

Made-in-China.com - China Manufacturers Directory
Nanjing New & High Technology Industry Development Zone
8-12/F, Block A, Software Bldg., Xinghuo Rd.
Nanjing, Jiangsu 210061 China
Fax: 86-25-6667-0000
Web Address: www.made-in-china.com

Made-in-China.com - China Manufacturers Directory, one of the largest business to business portals in China, helps to connect Chinese manufacturers, suppliers and traders with international buyers. Made-in-China.com contains additional information on trade shows and important laws and regulations about business with China.

LXII. U.S. Government Agencies

Bureau of Economic Analysis (BEA)
1441 L St. NW
Washington, DC 20230 US
Phone: 202-606-9900
E-mail Address: *customerservice@bea.gov*
Web Address: www.bea.gov
The Bureau of Economic Analysis (BEA), an agency of the U.S. Department of Commerce, is the nation's economic accountant, preparing estimates that illuminate key national, international and regional aspects of the U.S. economy.

Bureau of Labor Statistics (BLS)
2 Massachusetts Ave. NE
Washington, DC 20212-0001 US
Phone: 202-691-5200
Toll Free: 800-877-8339
Web Address: stats.bls.gov
The Bureau of Labor Statistics (BLS) is the principal fact-finding agency for the Federal Government in the field of labor economics and statistics. It is an independent national statistical agency that collects, processes, analyzes and disseminates statistical data to the American public, U.S. Congress, other federal agencies, state and local governments, business and labor. The BLS also serves as a statistical resource to the Department of Labor.

Energy Efficiency and Renewable Energy (EERE)
1000 Independence Ave. SW
Mail Stop EE-1
Washington, DC 20585 US
Phone: 202-586-4403
Toll Free: 877-337-3463
Web Address: www.eere.energy.gov
The Energy Efficiency and Renewable Energy (EERE), an office of the U.S. Department of Energy, provides information on bioenergy, geothermal, hydrogen, hydropower, tidal, hydropower, solar, wind and energy conservation methods. The Office also works with U.S. industries to advance the development of various alternative energy technologies.

Energy Information Administration (EIA)
1000 Independence Ave. SW
Washington, DC 20585 US
Phone: 202-586-8800
E-mail Address: *infoctr@eia.doe.gov*
Web Address: www.eia.doe.gov
The Energy Information Administration (EIA) is a vast source of useful information on every branch of the industry. It is operated by the U.S. Department of Energy (DOE). The site includes links to a number of other helpful energy industry web sites.

National Science Foundation (NSF)
4201 Wilson Blvd.
Arlington, VA 22230 US
Phone: 703-292-5111
Toll Free: 800-877-8339
E-mail Address: *info@nsf.gov*
Web Address: www.nsf.gov
The National Science Foundation (NSF) is an independent U.S. government agency responsible for promoting science and engineering. The foundation provides colleges and universities with grants and funding for research into numerous scientific fields.

Office of Scientific and Technical Information (OSTI)
P.O. Box 62
Oak Ridge, TN 37831 US
Phone: 865-576-1188
Fax: 865-576-2865
Toll Free: 800-553-6847
E-mail Address: *reports@osti.gov*
Web Address: www.osti.gov
The U.S. Department of Energy's Office of Scientific and Technical Information (OSTI) provides access to a wealth of energy, science, and technology research and development information from the Manhattan Project to the present.

U.S. Census Bureau
4600 Silver Hill Rd.
Washington, DC 20233-8800 US
Phone: 301-763-4636
Toll Free: 800-923-8282
E-mail Address: *pio@census.gov*
Web Address: www.census.gov
The U.S. Census Bureau is the official collector of data about the people and economy of the U.S. Founded in 1790, it provides official social, demographic and economic information. In addition to the Population & Housing Census, which it

conducts every 10 years, the U.S. Census Bureau numerous other surveys annually.

U.S. Department of Commerce (DOC)
1401 Constitution Ave. NW
Washington, DC 20230 US
Phone: 202-482-2000
Fax: 202-482-5168
E-mail Address: *kgriffis@doc.gov*
Web Address: www.commerce.gov
The U.S. Department of Commerce (DOC) regulates trade and provides valuable economic analysis of the economy.

U.S. Department of Energy (DOE)
1000 Independence Ave. SW
Washington, DC 20585 US
Phone: 202-586-5000
Fax: 202-586-4403
E-mail Address: *the.secretary@hq.doe.gov*
Web Address: www.energy.gov
U.S. Department of Energy (DOE) web site is the best way to gain information from the U.S. Government regarding its many agencies, bureaus and operations in energy. Through the site, users can gain access to government agencies such as Los Alamos National Laboratory, the strategic oil reserves and the agencies that regulate nuclear, geothermal and other types of power.

U.S. Department of Labor (DOL)
200 Constitution Ave. NW
Frances Perkins Bldg.
Washington, DC 20210 US
Phone: 202-693-4676
Toll Free: 866-487-2365
Web Address: www.dol.gov
The U.S. Department of Labor (DOL) is the government agency responsible for labor regulations.

U.S. Environmental Protection Agency (EPA) On-road Vehicles and Engines
1200 Pennsylvania Ave. NW
Office of Transportation and Air Quality (6401A)
Washington, DC 20460 US
Phone: 202-564-1682
E-mail Address: *otaqpublicweb@epa.gov*
Web Address: www.epa.gov/otaq/hwy.htm
The U.S. Environmental Protection Agency (EPA) On-road Vehicles and Engines site, part of the EPA's Office of Transportation and Air Quality (OTAQ), provides details about the best and worst cars and trucks in terms of exhaust emissions. Its web site

allows people to instantly check the emission rating of any vehicle. The site also contains information about industry emission trends and goals.

U.S. Patent and Trademark Office (PTO)
P.O. Box 1450
Mail Stop External Affairs
Alexandria, VA 22313-1450 US
Phone: 571-272-1000
Toll Free: 800-786-9199
E-mail Address: *usptoinfo@uspto.gov*
Web Address: www.uspto.gov
The U.S. Patent and Trademark Office (PTO) administers patent and trademark laws for the U.S. and enables registration of patents and trademarks.

U.S. Securities and Exchange Commission (SEC)
100 F St. NE
Washington, DC 20549 US
Phone: 202-942-8088
Toll Free: 888-732-6585
E-mail Address: *publicinfo@sec.gov*
Web Address: www.sec.gov
The U.S. Securities and Exchange Commission (SEC) is a nonpartisan, quasi-judicial regulatory agency responsible for administering federal securities laws. These laws are designed to protect investors in securities markets and ensure that they have access to disclosure of all material information concerning publicly traded securities. Visitors to the web site can access the EDGAR database of corporate financial and business information.

LXIII. Water Technologies & Resources

American Water Resources Association (AWRA)
P.O. Box 1626
Middleburg, VA 20118 US
Phone: 540-687-8390
Fax: 540-687-8395
E-mail Address: *info@awra.org*
Web Address: www.awra.org
The American Water Resources Association (AWRA) represents the interests of professionals involved in water resources.

Drinking-water.org
Web Address: www.drinking-water.org
This highly informative website about clean drinking water is a project of the National Academy of Sciences.

Global Water Intelligence (GWI)
Phone: 44-1865-204208
Web Address: www.globalwaterintel.com
GWI publishes data about water and water
technologies. It also sponsors conferences. It is part
of the Oxford, UK based Media Analytics, Ltd.

Japan Water Works Association (JWWA)
4-8-9 Kudan Minami
Chiyoda-ku
Tokyo, 102-0074 Japan
Phone: 03-3262-2244
Fax: 03-3264-2205
E-mail Address: *kokusai@jwwa.or.jp*
Web Address: www.jwwa.or.jp
The JWWA is a nonprofit organization created to
develop and improve water supply systems in Japan.

Pacific Institute
654 13th St.
Preservation Park
Oakland, CA 94612
Phone: 510-251-1600
Fax: 510-251-2203
E-mail Address: *info@pacinst.org*
Web Address: www.pacinst.org
The Pacific Institute's aim is to find solutions to
problems like water shortages, habitat destruction,
global warming, and environmental injustice. Based
in Oakland, California, it conducts research,
publishes reports, among other activities. It has
additional offices in Boulder, Colorado.

Water Footprint Network
c/o Universityh of Twente
P.O. Box 217
Enschede, AE 7500 The Netherlands
Phone: 31-53-489-5377
E-mail Address: *info@waterfootprint.org*
Web Address: www.waterfootprint.org
The mission of the Water Footprint Network is to
promote the transition towards sustainable, fair and
efficient use of fresh water resources worldwide by:
advancing the concept of the 'water footprint', a
spatially and temporally explicit indicator of direct
and indirect water use of consumers and producers;
increasing the water footprint awareness of
communities, government bodies and businesses and
their understanding of how consumption of goods
and services and production chains relate to water use
and impacts on fresh-water systems; and encouraging
forms of water governance that reduce the negative

ecological and social impacts of the water footprints
of communities, countries and businesses.

Chapter 4

THE GREEN TECHNOLOGY 325: WHO THEY ARE AND HOW THEY WERE CHOSEN

Includes Indexes by Company Name, Industry & Location

The companies chosen to be listed in PLUNKETT'S GREEN TECHNOLOGY INDUSTRY ALMANAC comprise a unique list. THE GREEN TECHNOLOGY 325 (the actual count is 329 companies) were chosen specifically for their dominance in the many facets of the green technology industry in which they operate. Complete information about each firm can be found in the "Individual Profiles," beginning at the end of this chapter. These profiles are in alphabetical order by company name.

THE GREEN TECHNOLOGY 325 companies are from all parts of the United States, Canada, Europe, Asia/Pacific and beyond. Essentially, THE GREEN TECHNOLOGY 325 includes companies that are deeply involved in the technologies, services and trends that keep the entire industry forging ahead.

Simply stated, THE GREEN TECHNOLOGY 325 contains 329 of the most successful, fastest growing firms in green technology and related industries in the world. To be included in our list, the firms had to meet the following criteria:

1) Generally, these are corporations based in the U.S., however, the headquarters of 143 firms are located in other nations.

2) Prominence, or a significant presence, in green technology, green technology-based services, equipment and supporting fields. (See the following Industry Codes section for a complete list of types of businesses that are covered).

3) The companies in THE GREEN TECHNOLOGY 325 do not have to be exclusively in the green technology field.

4) Financial data and vital statistics must have been available to the editors of this book, either directly from the company being written about or from outside sources deemed reliable and accurate by the editors. A small number of companies that we would like to have included are not listed because of a lack of sufficient, objective data.

INDUSTRY LIST, WITH CODES

This book refers to the following list of unique industry codes, based on the 2007 NAIC code system (NAIC is used by many analysts as a replacement for older SIC codes because NAIC is more specific to today's industry sectors, see www.census.gov/NAICS). Companies profiled in this book are given a primary NAIC code, reflecting the main line of business of each firm.

Agriculture

Agriculture
11511   Agricultural Crop Production Support, Seeds, Fertilizers
Farming
311613   Rendering & Meat Byproduct Processing

Automotive

Automotive Manufacturing
33611   Automobiles, Manufacturing
3363   Automobile Parts Manufacturing
Toys, Sporting Goods & Miscellaneous Manufacturing
336991   Motorcycle, Bicycle, & Parts Manufacturing
Automotive Services
5321   Automobile, Rental/Leasing

Energy

Fuel Mining & Extraction
211111   Oil & Natural Gas Exploration & Production
Utilities
2211   Utilities-Electric
221113   Utilities-Nuclear Generation
221119   Utilities-Alternative Energy Generation
221121   Utilities-Electric, Wholesale Generation

Petroleum-Refining & Manufacturing
324199   Other Petrochemical & Coal Products Manufacturing
325110   Petrochemicals Manufacturing
Alternative Energy
325193   Ethanol Fuel Manufacturing
Manufacturing, Electrical
33591   Battery Manufacturing
335929   Superconducting Materials & Other Wire

Health Care

Health Products, Manufacturing
325414   Biological Products, Manufacturing
33911   Medical/Dental/Surgical Equipment & Supplies, Manufacturing

InfoTech

Computers & Electronics Manufacturing
33411   Computer Networking & Related Equipment, Manufacturing
334111   Computer Hardware, Manufacturing
334310   Audio & Video Equipment, Consumer Electronics
33441   Semiconductors (Microchips)/Integrated Circuits/Components, Manufacturing
334419   Contract Electronics Manufacturing
3345   Instrument Manufacturing, including Measurement, Control, Test & Navigational
Computers & Electronics, Distribution
423430   Computer & Telecommunications Equipment Distribution
Software
5112   Computer Software
511210A   Computer Software, Supply Chain & Logistics

Manufacturing

Chemicals
325   Chemicals, Manufacturing
325199   Other Basic Organic Chemicals/Biofuels
325510   Paints & Coatings, Manufacturing
Construction
326199   Building Products & Construction Materials in Plastic, Manufacturing
Fabricated Metals
332   Steel & Metals--Fabricated Metals Components, Manufacturing
332311   Prefabricated Metal Building & Component Manufacturing
Machinery & Manufacturing Equipment
333   Machinery, Manufacturing
333295   Semiconductor Manufacturing Equipment
33361   Turbine & Turbine Generator Set Unit Manufacturing

| 334413 | Solar Cells, LEDs & Other Semiconductor Products |
| 335999 | Fuel Cells Manufacturing |

Electrical Equipment, Appliances, Tools

| 335 | Electrical Equipment, Manufacturing |
| 335313 | Electrical Switches, Sensors, Microelectronics, Optomechanicals |

Nanotechnology

Nanotechnology

| 541712N | Nanotechnology-General |

Retailing

Nonstore Retailers

| 454319 | Other Fuel Dealers, Retail |

Services

Construction

| 237130 | Construction, Power & Communication Lines and Structures |
| 238210 | Electric Contractors |

Consulting & Professional Services

541330	Engineering Services
541690	Consulting--Scientific & Technical
541712	Research & Development-Physical, Engineering & Life Sciences

Waste Management

562	Waste Disposal, Waste Management
562920	Recycling, Electronic Waste
924110	Water Treatment Systems and Technology

Telecommunications

Telecommunications Equipment

| 334220 | Radio & Wireless Communication, Manufacturing |

Transportation

Aerospace

| 33641 | Aerospace & Aircraft Related Manufacturing |

Ships

| 483111 | Shipping-Deep Sea |

INDEX OF COMPANIES WITHIN INDUSTRY GROUPS

Company	Industry Code	2010 Sales (U.S. $ thousands)	2010 Profits (U.S. $ thousands)
Aerospace & Aircraft Related Manufacturing			
UNITED TECHNOLOGIES CORPORATION	33641	54,326,000	4,711,000
Agricultural Crop Production Support, Seeds, Fertilizers			
ARCADIA BIOSCIENCES INC	11511		
DUPONT AGRICULTURE & NUTRITION	11511	32,733,000	3,052,000
MONSANTO CO	11511	10,502,000	1,128,000
SYNGENTA AG	11511	11,641,000	1,397,000
Audio & Video Equipment, Consumer Electronics			
PANASONIC CORPORATION	334310	90,202,900	-2,079,360
SAMSUNG ELECTRONICS CO LTD	334310	141,842,000	14,811,600
SANYO ELECTRIC COMPANY LTD	334310	20,327,200	-593,280
SHARP CORPORATION	334310	33,512,300	53,470
Automobile Parts Manufacturing			
ENOVA SYSTEMS INC	3363	8,572	-7,420
QUANTUM FUEL SYSTEMS TECHNOLOGIES WORLDWIDE INC	3363	9,605	-46,294
ROBERT BOSCH GMBH	3363	53,060,000	3,171,046
Automobile, Rental/Leasing			
ZIPCAR INC	5321	186,100	-14,120
Automobiles, Manufacturing			
BETTER PLACE	33611		
BYD COMPANY LIMITED	33611	7,130,720	385,420
CODA AUTOMOTIVE INC	33611		
FISKER AUTOMOTIVE	33611		
GENERAL MOTORS COMPANY (GM)	33611	135,592,000	6,503,000
NISSAN MOTOR CO LTD	33611	91,271,000	514,680
TESLA MOTORS INC	33611	116,744	-154,328
Battery Manufacturing			
24M TECHNOLOGIES INC	33591		
A123SYSTEMS	33591	97,312	-152,937
ACTIVE POWER INC	33591	64,955	-3,925
AMERICAN POWER CONVERSION (APC)	33591		
AMPRIUS	33591		
AUTOMOTIVE ENERGY SUPPLY CORPORATION (AESC)	33591		
BEACON POWER CORP	33591	896	-22,680
BOSTON-POWER	33591		
ENER1 INC	33591	77,406	-68,801
EXIDE TECHNOLOGIES	33591	2,685,808	-11,814
MCPHY ENERGY	33591		
MISSION MOTORS	33591		
PRIMEARTH EV ENERGY CO LTD	33591		
SAKTI3	33591		
SEEO	33591		
SOLICORE INC	33591		

Company	Industry Code	2010 Sales (U.S. $ thousands)	2010 Profits (U.S. $ thousands)
XTREME POWER	33591		
Biological Products, Manufacturing			
NOVOZYMES	325414	1,887,240	313,050
Building Products & Construction Materials in Plastic, Manufacturing			
SERIOUS ENERGY INC	326199		
Chemicals, Manufacturing			
AKZO NOBEL NV	325	21,173,100	1,090,470
BASF SE	325	93,180,980	1,083,466
BAYER AG	325	50,706,000	1,880,090
BAYER CORP	325		
BIOAMBER	325		
CABOT CORPORATION	325	2,893,000	154,000
CELANESE CORPORATION	325	5,918,000	377,000
CLARIANT INTERNATIONAL LTD	325	7,839,770	198,200
COULOMB TECHNOLOGIES	325		
DOW CHEMICAL COMPANY (THE)	325	53,674,000	1,970,000
DOW CORNING CORPORATION	325	5,997,300	723,600
DUPONT (E I DU PONT DE NEMOURS & CO)	325	31,505,000	3,031,000
ELEVANCE RENEWABLE SCIENCES INC	325		
EVONIK INDUSTRIES AG	325	19,184,100	1,058,730
GENOMATICA	325		
HUNTSMAN CORPORATION	325	9,250,000	185,000
LANXESS AG	325	10,285,000	547,470
O-FLEXX TECHNOLOGIES GMBH	325		
SASOL LIMITED	325	17,292,000	2,318,000
SIGMA-ALDRICH CORP	325	2,271,000	384,000
SOLVAY SA	325	9,824,030	2,568,760
TRANSPHORM	325		
Computer & Telecommunications Equipment Distribution			
NEXANT INC	423430		
Computer Hardware, Manufacturing			
HEWLETT-PACKARD CO (HP)	334111	126,033,000	8,761,000
HITACHI LTD	334111	109,058,000	-1,026,200
TOSHIBA CORPORATION	334111	74,288,300	-229,530
Computer Networking & Related Equipment, Manufacturing			
COMVERGE INC	33411	119,389	-31,351
ECHELON CORP	33411	111,037	-31,312
SILVER SPRING NETWORKS	33411	70,224	-148,449
Computer Software			
GREENROAD TECHNOLOGIES	5112		
HARA	5112		
JOULEX	5112		
OPOWER	5112		
SCIENERGY	5112		
TAKADU	5112		
TENDRIL	5112		
TIGO ENERGY	5112		

Company	Industry Code	2010 Sales (U.S. $ thousands)	2010 Profits (U.S. $ thousands)
Computer Software, Supply Chain & Logistics			
HELVETA	511210A		
Construction, Power & Communication Lines and Structures			
NOBAO RENEWABLE ENERGY HOLDINGS LTD	237130		
SKYFUEL INC	237130		
SOLARRESERVE	237130		
Consulting--Scientific & Technical			
AMERESCO INC	541690	618,226	28,726
ENERNOC INC	541690	280,157	9,577
RECYCLED ENERGY DEVELOPMENT LLC	541690		
Contract Electronics Manufacturing			
BAREFOOT POWER	334419		
KYOCERA CORP	334419	13,205,900	493,100
Electric Contractors			
AMMINEX A/S	238210		
Electrical Equipment, Manufacturing			
4ENERGY	335		
ABB LTD	335	31,589,000	2,732,000
ALSTOM SA	335	26,434,800	1,760,090
AMANTYS LTD	335		
BABCOCK & WILCOX COMPANY (THE)	335	2,688,811	153,526
BRIDGELUX INC	335	40,000	
BSST LLC	335		
CLIMATEWELL	335		
COMPACT POWER MOTORS GMBH	335		
DIGITAL LUMENS	335		
EVO ELECTRIC	335		
GE ENERGY INFRASTRUCTURE	335	37,514,000	7,271,000
GENERAL COMPRESSION	335		
IOXUS INC	335		
MITSUBISHI ELECTRIC CORPORATION	335	40,172,200	336,940
SCHNEIDER ELECTRIC SA	335	28,242,400	2,480,950
SIEMENS AG	335	103,974,000	5,566,940
SUSTAINX INC	335		
UQM TECHNOLOGIES INC	335	8,692	-4,141
XYLEM INC	335		
Electrical Switches, Sensors, Microelectronics, Optomechanicals			
CAMBRIDGE DISPLAY TECHNOLOGY INC	335313		
ENOCEAN	335313		
ENPHASE ENERGY	335313		
Engineering Services			
BIOS-BIOENERGIESYSTEME GMBH	541330		
CH2M HILL COMPANIES LTD	541330	5,422,801	93,695
Ethanol Fuel Manufacturing			
AMYRIS BIOTECHNOLOGIES INC	325193	80,311	-82,790
MASCOMA CORP	325193		
QTEROS INC	325193		

Company	Industry Code	2010 Sales (U.S. $ thousands)	2010 Profits (U.S. $ thousands)
Fuel Cells Manufacturing			
BALLARD POWER SYSTEMS INC	335999	65,019	-34,936
BLOOM ENERGY CORPORATION	335999		
ELECTROCHEM INC	335999		
ELTRON RESEARCH & DEVELOPMENT INC	335999		
FUELCELL ENERGY INC	335999	69,777	-56,235
HYDROGENICS CORPORATION	335999	20,930	-8,557
IDATECH LLC	335999		
MANHATTAN SCIENTIFICS INC	335999	1,686	-43
MECHANICAL TECHNOLOGY INC	335999	6,224	-12,504
MTI MICROFUEL CELLS INC	335999		
NUVERA FUEL CELLS INC	335999		
PLUG POWER INC	335999	19,473	-46,959
RELION INC	335999		
SFC ENERGY AG	335999	19,150	-5,920
TEKION INC	335999		
UTC POWER	335999		
Instrument Manufacturing, including Measurement, Control, Test & Navigational			
ADURA TECHNOLOGIES	3345		
BADGER METER INC	3345	276,634	28,662
SYNAPSENSE	3345		
TRILLIANT	3345		
Machinery, Manufacturing			
GEODYNAMICS LTD	333	0	-15,700
MITSUBISHI CORP	333	59,030,300	3,573,000
SOLARGENIX ENERGY LLC	333		
Medical/Dental/Surgical Equipment & Supplies, Manufacturing			
3M COMPANY	33911	26,662,000	4,085,000
Motorcycle, Bicycle, & Parts Manufacturing			
ZAP JONWAY	336991	3,816	-19,018
Nanotechnology-General			
CANATU	541712N		
ENERG2	541712N		
GMZ ENERGY	541712N		
Oil & Natural Gas Exploration & Production			
BG GROUP PLC	211111	17,166,000	3,351,000
BP PLC	211111	297,107,000	-3,324,000
CHEVRON CORPORATION	211111	204,928,000	19,136,000
CONOCOPHILLIPS COMPANY	211111	189,441,000	11,417,000
EXXON MOBIL CORPORATION (EXXONMOBIL)	211111	370,125,000	30,460,000
PETROLEO BRASILEIRO SA (PETROBRAS)	211111	133,831,000	22,081,300
ROYAL DUTCH SHELL PLC	211111	368,056,000	20,127,000
SHELL OIL CO	211111	120,000,000	
SUNCOR ENERGY INC	211111	31,461,000	3,594,000
TOTAL SA	211111	230,233,000	15,622,200
Other Basic Organic Chemicals/Biofuels			
AGILYX	325199		
AMEE	325199		

Company	Industry Code	2010 Sales (U.S. $ thousands)	2010 Profits (U.S. $ thousands)
AVANTIUM	325199		
BIODICO INC	325199		
BRASIL ECODIESEL	325199	228,075	-2,541
CHANGING WORLD TECHNOLOGIES INC	325199		
CHEMREC	325199		
DYNAMOTIVE ENERGY SYSTEMS CORPORATION	325199		
EMEFCY LTD	325199		
GREEN BIOLOGICS LIMITED	325199		
HARVEST POWER	325199		
IMPERIAL WESTERN PRODUCTS INC	325199		
IMPERIUM RENEWABLES INC	325199		
JOULE UNLIMITED TECHNOLOGIES	325199		
KAIIMA AGRO-BIOTECH LTD	325199		
KIOR INC	325199	0	-45,930
LANZATECH LTD	325199		
LS9 INC	325199		
NEXTERRA SYSTEMS CORP	325199		
SAPPHIRE ENERGY	325199		
SEQUENTIAL BIOFUELS LLC	325199		
SOLAZYME	325199	37,970	-16,200
SYNTHETIC GENOMICS INC	325199		
SYNTROLEUM CORPORATION	325199	8,410	-9,536
TOPELL ENERGY	325199		
ZEACHEM INC	325199		
Other Fuel Dealers, Retail			
CLEAN ENERGY FUELS CORP	454319	211,834	-44,568
Other Petrochemical & Coal Products Manufacturing			
EVERGREEN ENERGY INC	324199	403	-24,658
HEADWATERS INC	324199	654,699	-49,482
Paints & Coatings, Manufacturing			
SULZER LTD	325510	3,863,400	364,533
Petrochemicals Manufacturing			
EXXONMOBIL CHEMICAL	325110	25,891,000	4,913,000
MITSUI CHEMICALS INC	325110	14,390,400	-333,750
Prefabricated Metal Building & Component Manufacturing			
PROJECT FROG	332311		
Radio & Wireless Communication, Manufacturing			
NUJIRA LTD	334220		
ON-RAMP WIRELESS	334220		
Recycling, Electronic Waste			
ATTERO RECYCLING	562920		
Rendering & Meat Byproduct Processing			
GRIFFIN INDUSTRIES INC	311613		
Research & Development-Physical, Engineering & Life Sciences			
BASF FUTURE BUSINESS GMBH	541712		
BELL LABS	541712		
CHEVRON TECHNOLOGY VENTURES	541712		
DUPONT CENTRAL RESEARCH & DEVELOPMENT	541712		

Company	Industry Code	2010 Sales (U.S. $ thousands)	2010 Profits (U.S. $ thousands)
FUJITSU LABORATORIES LTD	541712		
GE GLOBAL RESEARCH	541712		
HEWLETT-PACKARD LABORATORIES (HP LABS)	541712		
HEWLETT-PACKARD QUANTUM SCIENCE RESEARCH	541712		
HITACHI HIGH TECHNOLOGIES AMERICA INC	541712		
IBM RESEARCH	541712		
NANOH2O	541712		
NEC LABORATORIES AMERICA INC	541712		
PALO ALTO RESEARCH CENTER (PARC)	541712		
RENEGY HOLDINGS INC	541712		
SIEMENS CORPORATE TECHNOLOGY	541712		
TOSHIBA CORPORATE R&D CENTER	541712		
Semiconductor Manufacturing Equipment			
APPLIED MATERIALS INC	333295	9,548,667	937,866
GT ADVANCED TECHNOLOGIES INC	333295	544,245	87,256
Semiconductors (Microchips)/Integrated Circuits/Components, Manufacturing			
DAYSTAR TECHNOLOGIES	33441	0	-28,082
EMCORE CORP	33441	191,278	-23,694
INTEL CORP	33441	43,623,000	11,464,000
SPIRE CORPORATION	33441	79,842	-408
SUPERCONDUCTOR TECHNOLOGIES INC	33441	8,547	-11,968
Shipping-Deep Sea			
PURFRESH	483111		
Solar Cells, LEDs & Other Semiconductor Products			
1366 TECHNOLOGIES INC	334413		
ALEO SOLAR AG	334413	783,000	44,500
AVANCIS GMBH & CO KG	334413		
BOSCH SOLAR ENERGY AG	334413		
BP SOLAR	334413		
CANADIAN SOLAR INC	334413	1,495,509	50,569
CENTRAL ELECTRONICS LIMITED	334413		
CHINA SUNERGY CO LTD	334413	517,219	51,734
CHINA TECHNOLOGY DEVELOPMENT GROUP CORP	334413	8,149	-5,330
CONERGY AG	334413	1,294,400	-63,300
ENECSYS LIMITED	334413		
ENERGY CONVERSION DEVICES INC	334413	254,416	-456,009
ENTECH SOLAR INC	334413	246	-18,280
E-TON SOLAR TECH CO LTD	334413	681,301	-8,796
EVERGREEN SOLAR INC	334413	338,785	-465,437
FIRST SOLAR INC	334413	2,563,515	664,201
GINTECH ENERGY CORPORATION	334413	982,340	150,830
GLOBAL SOLAR ENERGY	334413		
HANWHA SOLARONE CO LTD	334413	1,142,236	114,930
HELIATEK GMBH	334413		
HELIOVOLT CORP	334413		
ICP SOLAR TECHNOLOGIES	334413		

Company	Industry Code	2010 Sales (U.S. $ thousands)	2010 Profits (U.S. $ thousands)
ISOFOTON	334413		
JA SOLAR HOLDINGS CO LTD	334413	1,812,700	273,610
JINKOSOLAR HOLDING CO LTD	334413	705,281	133,617
KONARKA TECHNOLOGIES INC	334413		
KYOCERA SOLAR CORP	334413		
LATTICEPOWER (JIANGXI) CORP	334413		
LDK SOLAR CO LTD	334413	2,577,378	294,367
LEMNIS LIGHTING BV	334413		
MIASOLE INC	334413		
NANOSOLAR INC	334413		
PHOTOWATT INTERNATIONAL SA	334413		
POWERFILM INC	334413		
Q.CELLS SE	334413	1,924,500	26,900
SCHOTT SOLAR	334413		
SOLARONE SOLUTIONS LLC	334413		
SOLARWORLD AG	334413	1,854,800	124,000
SOLFOCUS INC	334413		
SOLOPOWER	334413		
SOLTECTURE GMBH	334413		
SPECTROLAB INC	334413		
STR HOLDINGS INC	334413	371,829	49,311
SUNIVA INC	334413		
SUNPOWER CORPORATION	334413	2,219,230	178,724
SUNTECH POWER HOLDINGS CO LTD	334413	2,901,899	236,900
SUNWAYS AG	334413	316,600	13,300
TERRA SOLAR GLOBAL INC	334413		
TRINA SOLAR LTD	334413	1,857,689	311,453
UNITED SOLAR OVONIC	334413		
VHF TECHNOLOGIES SA	334413		
WURTH ELEKTRONIK GMBH & CO KG	334413		
YINGLI GREEN ENERGY HOLDING CO LTD	334413	1,896,898	210,446
Steel & Metals--Fabricated Metals Components, Manufacturing			
AROTECH CORPORATION	332	73,741	-917
Superconducting Materials & Other Wire			
AMSC CORPORATION	335929	315,955	16,248
Turbine & Turbine Generator Set Unit Manufacturing			
ABENGOA SOLAR	33361	237,923	40,939
CAPSTONE TURBINE CORP	33361	61,554	-67,241
CLIPPER WINDPOWER LLC	33361		
ENERCON GMBH	33361		
GAMESA CORPORACION TECNOLOGICA SA	33361	3,953,240	72,540
IBERDROLA RENOVABLES SAU	33361	2,567,200	
NORDEX AG	33361	1,372,000	29,500
REPOWER SYSTEMS SE	33361	1,716,921	78,471
SINOVEL WIND GROUP CO LTD	33361	3,184,300	447,400
SUZLON ENERGY LIMITED	33361	4,468,300	-213,000
TALBOTT'S BIOMASS ENERGY SYSTEMS LTD	33361		
VESTAS WIND SYSTEMS A/S	33361	9,981,480	225,010

Company	Industry Code	2010 Sales (U.S. $ thousands)	2010 Profits (U.S. $ thousands)
WINWIND OY	33361		
XINJIANG GOLDWIND SCIENCE & TECHNOLOGY CO LTD	33361	2,712,180	355,314
Utilities-Alternative Energy Generation			
AIRTRICITY	221119		
BP ALTERNATIVE ENERGY	221119		
BRIGHTSOURCE ENERGY INC	221119		
CAITHNESS ENERGY LLC	221119		
COVANTA ENERGY CORPORATION	221119		
ELECTRAWINDS SA	221119		
ENEL GREEN POWER SPA	221119	3,091,724	698,979
ESOLAR INC	221119		
GRUPPO FALCK SPA	221119	263,459	56,346
NACEL ENERGY CORP	221119	1,200	-2,800
NAVITAS ENERGY INC	221119		
NEXTERA ENERGY RESOURCES LLC	221119		
ORMAT TECHNOLOGIES	221119	373,230	37,318
RENEWABLE ENERGY SYSTEMS	221119		
SHELL WINDENERGY BV	221119		
SIEMENS CONCENTRATED SOLAR POWER LTD	221119		
SKYPOWER LIMITED	221119		
SOLAIREDIRECT	221119		
SOLARCITY	221119		
STIRLING DK	221119		
SUNRUN	221119		
WINDLAB SYSTEMS	221119		
Utilities-Electric			
ENEL SPA	2211	95,749,700	5,842,700
IBERDROLA SA	2211	40,848,500	3,853,700
Utilities-Electric, Wholesale Generation			
INTERNATIONAL POWER PLC	221121	8,013,419	865,719
SUNEDISON LLC	221121		
ZORLU ENERJI ELEKTRIK URETIM AS	221121	233,200	-35,500
Utilities-Nuclear Generation			
BRITISH ENERGY GROUP PLC	221113		
Waste Disposal, Waste Management			
ASIA ENVIRONMENT HOLDINGS LTD	562	78,869	-2,076
COMPANHIA DE SANEAMENTO BASICO DO ESTADO DE SAO PAULO (SABESP)	562	5,352,000	945,300
CORY ENVIRONMENTAL	562		
GEOPLASMA LLC	562		
UNITED ENVIROTECH LTD	562	69,000	15,000
VEOLIA ENVIRONNEMENT	562	48,681,000	812,750
WASTE MANAGEMENT INC	562	12,515,000	953,000
Water Treatment Systems and Technology			
APTWATER INC	924110		
AQWISE	924110		
ENERGY RECOVERY INC	924110	45,853	-3,608

Company	Industry Code	2010 Sales (U.S. $ thousands)	2010 Profits (U.S. $ thousands)
FILTERBOXX	924110		
HYDROPOINT DATA SYSTEMS	924110		
HYFLUX LTD	924110	462,610	71,000
OASYS WATER	924110		
OSTARA NUTRIENT RECOVERY TECHNOLOGIES	924110		
PURALYTICS	924110		
VOLTEA	924110		
WATERHEALTH	924110		

ALPHABETICAL INDEX

ENOCEAN
ENOVA SYSTEMS INC
ENPHASE ENERGY
ENTECH SOLAR INC
ESOLAR INC
E-TON SOLAR TECH CO LTD
EVERGREEN ENERGY INC
EVERGREEN SOLAR INC
EVO ELECTRIC
EVONIK INDUSTRIES AG
EXIDE TECHNOLOGIES
EXXON MOBIL CORPORATION (EXXONMOBIL)
EXXONMOBIL CHEMICAL
FILTERBOXX
FIRST SOLAR INC
FISKER AUTOMOTIVE
FUELCELL ENERGY INC
FUJITSU LABORATORIES LTD
GAMESA CORPORACION TECNOLOGICA SA
GE ENERGY INFRASTRUCTURE
GE GLOBAL RESEARCH
GENERAL COMPRESSION
GENERAL MOTORS COMPANY (GM)
GENOMATICA
GEODYNAMICS LTD
GEOPLASMA LLC
GINTECH ENERGY CORPORATION
GLOBAL SOLAR ENERGY
GMZ ENERGY
GREEN BIOLOGICS LIMITED
GREENROAD TECHNOLOGIES
GRIFFIN INDUSTRIES INC
GRUPPO FALCK SPA
GT ADVANCED TECHNOLOGIES INC
HANWHA SOLARONE CO LTD
HARA
HARVEST POWER
HEADWATERS INC
HELIATEK GMBH
HELIOVOLT CORP
HELVETA
HEWLETT-PACKARD CO (HP)
HEWLETT-PACKARD LABORATORIES (HP LABS)
HEWLETT-PACKARD QUANTUM SCIENCE
RESEARCH
HITACHI HIGH TECHNOLOGIES AMERICA INC
HITACHI LTD
HUNTSMAN CORPORATION
HYDROGENICS CORPORATION
HYDROPOINT DATA SYSTEMS
HYFLUX LTD
IBERDROLA RENOVABLES SAU
IBERDROLA SA
IBM RESEARCH
ICP SOLAR TECHNOLOGIES
IDATECH LLC
IMPERIAL WESTERN PRODUCTS INC
IMPERIUM RENEWABLES INC

INTEL CORP
INTERNATIONAL POWER PLC
IOXUS INC
ISOFOTON
JA SOLAR HOLDINGS CO LTD
JINKOSOLAR HOLDING CO LTD
JOULE UNLIMITED TECHNOLOGIES
JOULEX
KAIIMA AGRO-BIOTECH LTD
KIOR INC
KONARKA TECHNOLOGIES INC
KYOCERA CORP
KYOCERA SOLAR CORP
LANXESS AG
LANZATECH LTD
LATTICEPOWER (JIANGXI) CORP
LDK SOLAR CO LTD
LEMNIS LIGHTING BV
LS9 INC
MANHATTAN SCIENTIFICS INC
MASCOMA CORP
MCPHY ENERGY
MECHANICAL TECHNOLOGY INC
MIASOLE INC
MISSION MOTORS
MITSUBISHI CORP
MITSUBISHI ELECTRIC CORPORATION
MITSUI CHEMICALS INC
MONSANTO CO
MTI MICROFUEL CELLS INC
NACEL ENERGY CORP
NANOH2O
NANOMIX INC
NANOSOLAR INC
NAVITAS ENERGY INC
NEC LABORATORIES AMERICA INC
NEXANT INC
NEXTERA ENERGY RESOURCES LLC
NEXTERRA SYSTEMS CORP
NISSAN MOTOR CO LTD
NOBAO RENEWABLE ENERGY HOLDINGS LTD
NORDEX AG
NOVOZYMES
NUJIRA LTD
NUVERA FUEL CELLS INC
OASYS WATER
O-FLEXX TECHNOLOGIES GMBH
ON-RAMP WIRELESS
OPOWER
ORMAT TECHNOLOGIES
OSTARA NUTRIENT RECOVERY TECHNOLOGIES
PALO ALTO RESEARCH CENTER (PARC)
PANASONIC CORPORATION
PETROLEO BRASILEIRO SA (PETROBRAS)
PHOTOWATT INTERNATIONAL SA
PLUG POWER INC
POWERFILM INC
PRIMEARTH EV ENERGY CO LTD

PROJECT FROG
PURALYTICS
PURFRESH
Q.CELLS SE
QTEROS INC
QUANTUM FUEL SYSTEMS TECHNOLOGIES
WORLDWIDE INC
RECYCLED ENERGY DEVELOPMENT LLC
RELION INC
RENEGY HOLDINGS INC
RENEWABLE ENERGY SYSTEMS
REPOWER SYSTEMS SE
ROBERT BOSCH GMBH
ROYAL DUTCH SHELL PLC
SAKTI3
SAMSUNG ELECTRONICS CO LTD
SANYO ELECTRIC COMPANY LTD
SAPPHIRE ENERGY
SASOL LIMITED
SCHNEIDER ELECTRIC SA
SCHOTT SOLAR
SCIENERGY
SEEO
SEQUENTIAL BIOFUELS LLC
SERIOUS ENERGY INC
SFC ENERGY AG
SHARP CORPORATION
SHELL OIL CO
SHELL WINDENERGY BV
SIEMENS AG
SIEMENS CONCENTRATED SOLAR POWER LTD
SIEMENS CORPORATE TECHNOLOGY
SIGMA-ALDRICH CORP
SILVER SPRING NETWORKS
SINOVEL WIND GROUP CO LTD
SKYFUEL INC
SKYPOWER LIMITED
SOLAIREDIRECT
SOLARCITY
SOLARGENIX ENERGY LLC
SOLARONE SOLUTIONS LLC
SOLARRESERVE
SOLARWORLD AG
SOLAZYME
SOLFOCUS INC
SOLICORE INC
SOLOPOWER
SOLTECTURE GMBH
SOLVAY SA
SPECTROLAB INC
SPIRE CORPORATION
STIRLING DK
STR HOLDINGS INC
SULZER LTD
SUNCOR ENERGY INC
SUNEDISON LLC
SUNIVA INC
SUNPOWER CORPORATION

SUNRUN
SUNTECH POWER HOLDINGS CO LTD
SUNWAYS AG
SUPERCONDUCTOR TECHNOLOGIES INC
SUSTAINX INC
SUZLON ENERGY LIMITED
SYNAPSENSE
SYNGENTA AG
SYNTHETIC GENOMICS INC
SYNTROLEUM CORPORATION
TAKADU
TALBOTT'S BIOMASS ENERGY SYSTEMS LTD
TEKION INC
TENDRIL
TERRA SOLAR GLOBAL INC
TESLA MOTORS INC
TIGO ENERGY
TOPELL ENERGY
TOSHIBA CORPORATE R&D CENTER
TOSHIBA CORPORATION
TOTAL SA
TRANSPHORM
TRILLIANT
TRINA SOLAR LTD
UNITED ENVIROTECH LTD
UNITED SOLAR OVONIC
UNITED TECHNOLOGIES CORPORATION
UQM TECHNOLOGIES INC
UTC POWER
VEOLIA ENVIRONNEMENT
VESTAS WIND SYSTEMS A/S
VHF TECHNOLOGIES SA
VOLTEA
WASTE MANAGEMENT INC
WATERHEALTH
WINDLAB SYSTEMS
WINWIND OY
WURTH ELEKTRONIK GMBH & CO KG
XINJIANG GOLDWIND SCIENCE & TECHNOLOGY
CO LTD
XTREME POWER
XYLEM INC
YINGLI GREEN ENERGY HOLDING CO LTD
ZAP JONWAY
ZEACHEM INC
ZIPCAR INC
ZORLU ENERJI ELEKTRIK URETIM AS

INDEX OF HEADQUARTERS LOCATION BY U.S. STATE

To help you locate the firms geographically, the city and state of the headquarters of each company are in the following index.

ARIZONA
FIRST SOLAR INC; Tempe
GLOBAL SOLAR ENERGY; Tucson
KYOCERA SOLAR CORP; Scottsdale
RENEGY HOLDINGS INC; Mesa

CALIFORNIA
ADURA TECHNOLOGIES; San Francisco
AMPRIUS; Menlo Park
AMYRIS BIOTECHNOLOGIES INC; Emeryville
APPLIED MATERIALS INC; Santa Clara
APTWATER INC; Long Beach
ARCADIA BIOSCIENCES INC; Davis
BETTER PLACE; Palo Alto
BIODICO INC; Santa Barbara
BLOOM ENERGY CORPORATION; Sunnyvale
BP SOLAR; San Francisco
BRIDGELUX INC; Livermore
BRIGHTSOURCE ENERGY INC; Oakland
BSST LLC; Irwindale
CAPSTONE TURBINE CORP; Chatsworth
CHEVRON CORPORATION; San Ramon
CLEAN ENERGY FUELS CORP; Seal Beach
CLIPPER WINDPOWER LLC; Carpinteria
CODA AUTOMOTIVE INC; Santa Monica
COULOMB TECHNOLOGIES; Campbell
DAYSTAR TECHNOLOGIES; Milpitas
ECHELON CORP; San Jose
ENERGY RECOVERY INC; San Leandro
ENOVA SYSTEMS INC; Torrance
ENPHASE ENERGY; Petaluma
ESOLAR INC; Burbank
FISKER AUTOMOTIVE; Irvine
GENOMATICA; San Diego
GREENROAD TECHNOLOGIES; Redwood Shores
HARA; San Mateo
HEWLETT-PACKARD CO (HP); Palo Alto
HEWLETT-PACKARD LABORATORIES (HP LABS); Palo Alto
HEWLETT-PACKARD QUANTUM SCIENCE RESEARCH; Palo Alto
HYDROPOINT DATA SYSTEMS; Petaluma
IMPERIAL WESTERN PRODUCTS INC; Coachella
INTEL CORP; Santa Clara
LS9 INC; San Francisco
MIASOLE INC; Santa Clara
MISSION MOTORS; San Francisco
NANOH2O; El Segundo
NANOMIX INC; Emeryville
NANOSOLAR INC; San Jose

NEXANT INC; San Francisco
ON-RAMP WIRELESS; San Diego
PALO ALTO RESEARCH CENTER (PARC); Palo Alto
PROJECT FROG; San Francisco
PURFRESH; Fremont
QUANTUM FUEL SYSTEMS TECHNOLOGIES WORLDWIDE INC; Irvine
SAPPHIRE ENERGY; San Diego
SCIENERGY; San Francisco
SEEO; Hayward
SERIOUS ENERGY INC; Sunnyvale
SILVER SPRING NETWORKS; Redwood City
SOLARCITY; San Mateo
SOLARRESERVE; Santa Monica
SOLAZYME; San Francisco
SOLFOCUS INC; Mountain View
SOLOPOWER; San Jose
SPECTROLAB INC; Sylmar
SUNEDISON LLC; Belmont
SUNPOWER CORPORATION; San Jose
SUNRUN; San Francisco
SUPERCONDUCTOR TECHNOLOGIES INC; Santa Barbara
SYNAPSENSE; Folsom
SYNTHETIC GENOMICS INC; La Jolla
TESLA MOTORS INC; Palo Alto
TIGO ENERGY; Los Gatos
TRANSPHORM; Goleta
TRILLIANT; Redwood City
WATERHEALTH; Irvine
ZAP JONWAY; Santa Rosa

COLORADO
CH2M HILL COMPANIES LTD; Englewood
ELTRON RESEARCH & DEVELOPMENT INC; Boulder
EVERGREEN ENERGY INC; Denver
NACEL ENERGY CORP; Denver
SKYFUEL INC; Arvada
TENDRIL; Boulder
UQM TECHNOLOGIES INC; Longmont
ZEACHEM INC; Lakewood

CONNECTICUT
FUELCELL ENERGY INC; Danbury
STR HOLDINGS INC; Enfield
UNITED TECHNOLOGIES CORPORATION; Hartford
UTC POWER; South Windsor

DELAWARE
DUPONT (E I DU PONT DE NEMOURS & CO); Wilmington
DUPONT AGRICULTURE & NUTRITION; Wilmington
DUPONT CENTRAL RESEARCH & DEVELOPMENT; Wilmington

FLORIDA
NEXTERA ENERGY RESOURCES LLC; Juno Beach
SOLICORE INC; Lakeland

GEORGIA
COMVERGE INC; Norcross
EXIDE TECHNOLOGIES; Milton
GE ENERGY INFRASTRUCTURE; Atlanta
GEOPLASMA LLC; Atlanta
JOULEX; Atlanta
SUNIVA INC; Norcross

ILLINOIS
ELEVANCE RENEWABLE SCIENCES INC; Woodridge
HITACHI HIGH TECHNOLOGIES AMERICA INC; Schaumburg
RECYCLED ENERGY DEVELOPMENT LLC; Westmont

IOWA
POWERFILM INC; Ames

KENTUCKY
GRIFFIN INDUSTRIES INC; Cold Spring

MASSACHUSETTS
1366 TECHNOLOGIES INC; Lexington
24M TECHNOLOGIES INC; Cambridge
A123SYSTEMS; Watertown
AMERESCO INC; Framingham
AMSC CORPORATION; Devens
BEACON POWER CORP; Tyngsboro
BOSTON-POWER; Westborough
CABOT CORPORATION; Boston
DIGITAL LUMENS; Boston
ELECTROCHEM INC; Woburn
ENERNOC INC; Boston
EVERGREEN SOLAR INC; Marlboro
GENERAL COMPRESSION; Newton
GMZ ENERGY; Waltham
HARVEST POWER; Waltham
JOULE UNLIMITED TECHNOLOGIES; Cambridge
KONARKA TECHNOLOGIES INC; Lowell
NUVERA FUEL CELLS INC; Billerica
OASYS WATER; Boston
QTEROS INC; Marlborough
SOLARONE SOLUTIONS LLC; Needham
SPIRE CORPORATION; Bedford
ZIPCAR INC; Cambridge

MICHIGAN
AROTECH CORPORATION; Ann Arbor
DOW CHEMICAL COMPANY (THE); Midland
DOW CORNING CORPORATION; Midland
ENERGY CONVERSION DEVICES INC; Auburn Hills
GENERAL MOTORS COMPANY (GM); Detroit
SAKTI3; Ann Arbor

UNITED SOLAR OVONIC; Auburn Hills

MINNESOTA
3M COMPANY; St. Paul
BIOAMBER; Plymouth
NAVITAS ENERGY INC; Minneapolis

MISSOURI
MONSANTO CO; St. Louis
SIGMA-ALDRICH CORP; St. Louis

NEVADA
ORMAT TECHNOLOGIES; Reno

NEW HAMPSHIRE
GT ADVANCED TECHNOLOGIES INC; Merrimack
MASCOMA CORP; Lebanon
SUSTAINX INC; Seabrook

NEW JERSEY
BELL LABS; Murray Hill
COVANTA ENERGY CORPORATION; Fairfield
NEC LABORATORIES AMERICA INC; Princeton

NEW MEXICO
EMCORE CORP; Albuquerque
SCHOTT SOLAR; Albuquerque

NEW YORK
CAITHNESS ENERGY LLC; New York
CHANGING WORLD TECHNOLOGIES INC; West Hempstead
ENER1 INC; New York
GE GLOBAL RESEARCH; Niskayuna
IBM RESEARCH; Yorktown Heights
IOXUS INC; Oneonta
MANHATTAN SCIENTIFICS INC; New York
MECHANICAL TECHNOLOGY INC; Albany
MTI MICROFUEL CELLS INC; Albany
PLUG POWER INC; Latham
TERRA SOLAR GLOBAL INC; New York
XYLEM INC; White Plains

NORTH CAROLINA
BABCOCK & WILCOX COMPANY (THE); Charlotte
SOLARGENIX ENERGY LLC; Sanford

OKLAHOMA
SYNTROLEUM CORPORATION; Tulsa

OREGON
AGILYX; Beaverton
IDATECH LLC; Bend
PURALYTICS; Beaverton
SEQUENTIAL BIOFUELS LLC; Portland

PENNSYLVANIA
BAYER CORP; Pittsburgh

RHODE ISLAND
AMERICAN POWER CONVERSION (APC); West Kingston

TEXAS
ACTIVE POWER INC; Austin
CELANESE CORPORATION; Dallas
CHEVRON TECHNOLOGY VENTURES; Houston
CONOCOPHILLIPS COMPANY; Houston
ENTECH SOLAR INC; Fort Worth
EXXON MOBIL CORPORATION (EXXONMOBIL); Irving
EXXONMOBIL CHEMICAL; Houston
HELIOVOLT CORP; Austin
KIOR INC; Pasadena
SHELL OIL CO; Houston
WASTE MANAGEMENT INC; Houston
XTREME POWER; Kyle

UTAH
HEADWATERS INC; South Jordan
HUNTSMAN CORPORATION; Salt Lake City

VIRGINIA
OPOWER; Arlington

WASHINGTON
ENERG2; Seattle
IMPERIUM RENEWABLES INC; Seattle
RELION INC; Spokane

WISCONSIN
BADGER METER INC; Milwaukee

INDEX OF NON-U.S. HEADQUARTERS LOCATION BY COUNTRY

AUSTRALIA
BAREFOOT POWER; North Ryde
GEODYNAMICS LTD; Milton
WINDLAB SYSTEMS; Barton

AUSTRIA
BIOS-BIOENERGIESYSTEME GMBH; Graz

BELGIUM
ELECTRAWINDS SA; Oostende
SOLVAY SA; Brussels

BRAZIL
BRASIL ECODIESEL; Sao Paulo
COMPANHIA DE SANEAMENTO BASICO DO ESTADO DE SAO PAULO (SABESP); Sao Paulo
PETROLEO BRASILEIRO SA (PETROBRAS); Rio de Janeiro

CANADA
BALLARD POWER SYSTEMS INC; Burnaby
CANADIAN SOLAR INC; Kitchener
DYNAMOTIVE ENERGY SYSTEMS CORPORATION; Vancouver
FILTERBOXX; Calgary
HYDROGENICS CORPORATION; Mississauga
ICP SOLAR TECHNOLOGIES; Montreal
NEXTERRA SYSTEMS CORP; Vancouver
OSTARA NUTRIENT RECOVERY TECHNOLOGIES; Vancouver
SKYPOWER LIMITED; Toronto
SUNCOR ENERGY INC; Calgary
TEKION INC; Burnby

CHINA
BYD COMPANY LIMITED; Shenzhen
CHINA SUNERGY CO LTD; Nanjing
CHINA TECHNOLOGY DEVELOPMENT GROUP CORP; Hong Kong
HANWHA SOLARONE CO LTD; Jiangsu
JA SOLAR HOLDINGS CO LTD; Shanghai
JINKOSOLAR HOLDING CO LTD; Jiangxi Province
LATTICEPOWER (JIANGXI) CORP; Nanchang
LDK SOLAR CO LTD; Jiangxi
NOBAO RENEWABLE ENERGY HOLDINGS LTD; Shanghai
SINOVEL WIND GROUP CO LTD; Beijing
SUNTECH POWER HOLDINGS CO LTD; Wuxi
TRINA SOLAR LTD; Jiangsu
XINJIANG GOLDWIND SCIENCE & TECHNOLOGY CO LTD; Xinjiang
YINGLI GREEN ENERGY HOLDING CO LTD; Baoding

DENMARK
AMMINEX A/S; Soborg
NOVOZYMES; Bagsvaerd
STIRLING DK; Lyngby
VESTAS WIND SYSTEMS A/S; Randers

FINLAND
CANATU; Helsinki
WINWIND OY; Espoo

FRANCE
ALSTOM SA; Levallois-Perret
MCPHY ENERGY; La Motte-Fanjas
PHOTOWATT INTERNATIONAL SA; Bourgoin-Jallieu
SCHNEIDER ELECTRIC SA; Rueil-Malmaison
SOLAIREDIRECT; Paris
TOTAL SA; Courbevoie
VEOLIA ENVIRONNEMENT; Paris

GERMANY
ALEO SOLAR AG; Prenzlau
AVANCIS GMBH & CO KG; Torgau
BASF FUTURE BUSINESS GMBH; Ludwigshafen
BASF SE; Ludwigshafen
BAYER AG; Leverkusen
BOSCH SOLAR ENERGY AG; Erfurt
COMPACT POWER MOTORS GMBH; Unterfohring
CONERGY AG; Hamburg
ENERCON GMBH; Aurich
ENOCEAN; Oberhaching
EVONIK INDUSTRIES AG; Essen
HELIATEK GMBH; Dresden
LANXESS AG; Leverkusen
NORDEX AG; Hamburg
O-FLEXX TECHNOLOGIES GMBH; Duisburg
Q.CELLS SE; Bitterfeld-Wolfen
REPOWER SYSTEMS SE; Hamburg
ROBERT BOSCH GMBH; Stuttgart
SFC ENERGY AG; Brunntahl-Nord
SIEMENS AG; Munich
SIEMENS CORPORATE TECHNOLOGY; Munich
SOLARWORLD AG; Bonn
SOLTECTURE GMBH; Berlin
SUNWAYS AG; Konstanz
WURTH ELEKTRONIK GMBH & CO KG; Niedernhall

INDIA
ATTERO RECYCLING; Nodia
CENTRAL ELECTRONICS LIMITED; Sahibabad
SUZLON ENERGY LIMITED; Pune

ISRAEL
AQWISE; Herzliya
EMEFCY LTD; Caesarea
KAIIMA AGRO-BIOTECH LTD; Kfar Tavor
SIEMENS CONCENTRATED SOLAR POWER LTD; Beit Shemesh

TAKADU; Yehud

ITALY
ENEL GREEN POWER SPA; Rome
ENEL SPA; Rome
GRUPPO FALCK SPA; Milan

JAPAN
AUTOMOTIVE ENERGY SUPPLY CORPORATION (AESC); Zama-shi
FUJITSU LABORATORIES LTD; Kawasaki-shi
HITACHI LTD; Tokyo
KYOCERA CORP; Kyoto
MITSUBISHI CORP; Tokyo
MITSUBISHI ELECTRIC CORPORATION; Tokyo
MITSUI CHEMICALS INC; Tokyo
NISSAN MOTOR CO LTD; Yokohama-shi
PANASONIC CORPORATION; Osaka
PRIMEARTH EV ENERGY CO LTD; Shizuoka
SANYO ELECTRIC COMPANY LTD; Moriguchi City
SHARP CORPORATION; Osaka
TOSHIBA CORPORATE R&D CENTER; Kawasaki-shi
TOSHIBA CORPORATION; Tokyo

KOREA
SAMSUNG ELECTRONICS CO LTD; Seoul

NEW ZEALAND
LANZATECH LTD; Auckland

SINGAPORE
ASIA ENVIRONMENT HOLDINGS LTD; Singapore
HYFLUX LTD; Singapore
UNITED ENVIROTECH LTD; Singapore

SOUTH AFRICA
SASOL LIMITED; Rosebank

SPAIN
ABENGOA SOLAR; Madrid
GAMESA CORPORACION TECNOLOGICA SA; Vitoria-Gasteiz
IBERDROLA RENOVABLES SAU; Madrid
IBERDROLA SA; Bilbao
ISOFOTON; Madrid

SWEDEN
CHEMREC; Stockholm
CLIMATEWELL; Hägersten

SWITZERLAND
ABB LTD; Zurich
CLARIANT INTERNATIONAL LTD; Muttenz
SULZER LTD; Winterthur
SYNGENTA AG; Basel
VHF TECHNOLOGIES SA; Yverdon-les-Bains

TAIWAN
GINTECH ENERGY CORPORATION; Jhunan

THE NETHERLANDS
AKZO NOBEL NV; Amsterdam
AVANTIUM; Amsterdam
LEMNIS LIGHTING BV; Barneveld
ROYAL DUTCH SHELL PLC; The Hague
SHELL WINDENERGY BV; The Hague
TOPELL ENERGY; The Hague
VOLTEA; Sassenheim

TURKEY
ZORLU ENERJI ELEKTRIK URETIM AS; Istanbul

UNITED KINGDOM
4ENERGY; Keyworth
AIRTRICITY; Dublin
AMANTYS LTD; Cambridge
AMEE; London
BG GROUP PLC; Reading
BP ALTERNATIVE ENERGY; London
BP PLC; London
BRITISH ENERGY GROUP PLC; East Kilbride
CAMBRIDGE DISPLAY TECHNOLOGY INC;
Cambourne
CORY ENVIRONMENTAL; London
ENECSYS LIMITED; Cambridge
EVO ELECTRIC; Woking
GREEN BIOLOGICS LIMITED; Abingdon
HELVETA; Abingdon
INTERNATIONAL POWER PLC; London
NUJIRA LTD; Cambourne
RENEWABLE ENERGY SYSTEMS; Hertfordshire
TALBOTT'S BIOMASS ENERGY SYSTEMS LTD;
Stafford

INDEX BY REGIONS OF THE U.S. WHERE THE FIRMS HAVE LOCATIONS

WEST
3M COMPANY
ABENGOA SOLAR
ADURA TECHNOLOGIES
AGILYX
AMERESCO INC
AMPRIUS
AMYRIS BIOTECHNOLOGIES INC
APPLIED MATERIALS INC
APTWATER INC
ARCADIA BIOSCIENCES INC
AROTECH CORPORATION
BABCOCK & WILCOX COMPANY (THE)
BASF SE
BAYER AG
BAYER CORP
BETTER PLACE
BIODICO INC
BLOOM ENERGY CORPORATION
BOSCH SOLAR ENERGY AG
BP ALTERNATIVE ENERGY
BP PLC
BRIDGELUX INC
BRIGHTSOURCE ENERGY INC
BSST LLC
BYD COMPANY LIMITED
CAITHNESS ENERGY LLC
CAMBRIDGE DISPLAY TECHNOLOGY INC
CANADIAN SOLAR INC
CAPSTONE TURBINE CORP
CH2M HILL COMPANIES LTD
CHEVRON CORPORATION
CHEVRON TECHNOLOGY VENTURES
CHINA SUNERGY CO LTD
CLARIANT INTERNATIONAL LTD
CLEAN ENERGY FUELS CORP
CLIPPER WINDPOWER LLC
CODA AUTOMOTIVE INC
COMVERGE INC
CONERGY AG
CONOCOPHILLIPS COMPANY
COULOMB TECHNOLOGIES
COVANTA ENERGY CORPORATION
DAYSTAR TECHNOLOGIES
DOW CHEMICAL COMPANY (THE)
DOW CORNING CORPORATION
DUPONT (E I DU PONT DE NEMOURS & CO)
DUPONT AGRICULTURE & NUTRITION
ECHELON CORP
ELTRON RESEARCH & DEVELOPMENT INC
EMCORE CORP
ENECSYS LIMITED
ENERG2
ENERGY CONVERSION DEVICES INC

ENERGY RECOVERY INC
ENERNOC INC
ENOCEAN
ENOVA SYSTEMS INC
ENPHASE ENERGY
ESOLAR INC
EVERGREEN ENERGY INC
EXIDE TECHNOLOGIES
EXXON MOBIL CORPORATION (EXXONMOBIL)
FIRST SOLAR INC
FISKER AUTOMOTIVE
FUELCELL ENERGY INC
FUJITSU LABORATORIES LTD
GE ENERGY INFRASTRUCTURE
GENERAL MOTORS COMPANY (GM)
GENOMATICA
GREENROAD TECHNOLOGIES
GT ADVANCED TECHNOLOGIES INC
HANWHA SOLARONE CO LTD
HARA
HARVEST POWER
HEADWATERS INC
HEWLETT-PACKARD CO (HP)
HEWLETT-PACKARD LABORATORIES (HP LABS)
HEWLETT-PACKARD QUANTUM SCIENCE
RESEARCH
HITACHI HIGH TECHNOLOGIES AMERICA INC
HITACHI LTD
HUNTSMAN CORPORATION
HYDROGENICS CORPORATION
HYDROPOINT DATA SYSTEMS
IBERDROLA RENOVABLES SAU
IBM RESEARCH
ICP SOLAR TECHNOLOGIES
IDATECH LLC
IMPERIAL WESTERN PRODUCTS INC
IMPERIUM RENEWABLES INC
INTEL CORP
JA SOLAR HOLDINGS CO LTD
JINKOSOLAR HOLDING CO LTD
KYOCERA CORP
LDK SOLAR CO LTD
LEMNIS LIGHTING BV
LS9 INC
MIASOLE INC
MISSION MOTORS
MITSUBISHI ELECTRIC CORPORATION
MITSUI CHEMICALS INC
MONSANTO CO
NACEL ENERGY CORP
NANOH2O
NANOMIX INC
NANOSOLAR INC
NEC LABORATORIES AMERICA INC
NEXANT INC
NEXTERA ENERGY RESOURCES LLC
NISSAN MOTOR CO LTD
NOVOZYMES

ON-RAMP WIRELESS
OPOWER
ORMAT TECHNOLOGIES
PALO ALTO RESEARCH CENTER (PARC)
PANASONIC CORPORATION
PROJECT FROG
PURALYTICS
PURFRESH
Q.CELLS SE
QUANTUM FUEL SYSTEMS TECHNOLOGIES
WORLDWIDE INC
RELION INC
RENEGY HOLDINGS INC
RENEWABLE ENERGY SYSTEMS
REPOWER SYSTEMS SE
ROBERT BOSCH GMBH
ROYAL DUTCH SHELL PLC
SAMSUNG ELECTRONICS CO LTD
SANYO ELECTRIC COMPANY LTD
SAPPHIRE ENERGY
SASOL LIMITED
SCHOTT SOLAR
SCIENERGY
SEEO
SEQUENTIAL BIOFUELS LLC
SERIOUS ENERGY INC
SHARP CORPORATION
SHELL OIL CO
SIEMENS AG
SIEMENS CONCENTRATED SOLAR POWER LTD
SIEMENS CORPORATE TECHNOLOGY
SIGMA-ALDRICH CORP
SILVER SPRING NETWORKS
SKYFUEL INC
SOLARCITY
SOLARRESERVE
SOLARWORLD AG
SOLAZYME
SOLFOCUS INC
SOLOPOWER
SOLVAY SA
SPECTROLAB INC
SULZER LTD
SUNCOR ENERGY INC
SUNEDISON LLC
SUNPOWER CORPORATION
SUNRUN
SUNTECH POWER HOLDINGS CO LTD
SUPERCONDUCTOR TECHNOLOGIES INC
SYNAPSENSE
SYNGENTA AG
SYNTHETIC GENOMICS INC
TENDRIL
TERRA SOLAR GLOBAL INC
TESLA MOTORS INC
TIGO ENERGY
TOSHIBA CORPORATION
TOTAL SA

TRANSPHORM
TRILLIANT
TRINA SOLAR LTD
UNITED TECHNOLOGIES CORPORATION
UQM TECHNOLOGIES INC
VEOLIA ENVIRONNEMENT
VESTAS WIND SYSTEMS A/S
WASTE MANAGEMENT INC
WATERHEALTH
XTREME POWER
ZEACHEM INC
ZIPCAR INC

SOUTHWEST
3M COMPANY
ABENGOA SOLAR
ACTIVE POWER INC
ALSTOM SA
AMERESCO INC
AMERICAN POWER CONVERSION (APC)
APPLIED MATERIALS INC
BABCOCK & WILCOX COMPANY (THE)
BADGER METER INC
BASF SE
BAYER AG
BAYER CORP
BG GROUP PLC
BIODICO INC
BIOS-BIOENERGIESYSTEME GMBH
BP ALTERNATIVE ENERGY
BP PLC
BRIGHTSOURCE ENERGY INC
CABOT CORPORATION
CAITHNESS ENERGY LLC
CELANESE CORPORATION
CH2M HILL COMPANIES LTD
CHEVRON CORPORATION
CHEVRON TECHNOLOGY VENTURES
CLARIANT INTERNATIONAL LTD
CLEAN ENERGY FUELS CORP
CONOCOPHILLIPS COMPANY
COULOMB TECHNOLOGIES
DOW CHEMICAL COMPANY (THE)
DUPONT (E I DU PONT DE NEMOURS & CO)
DUPONT AGRICULTURE & NUTRITION
EMCORE CORP
ENTECH SOLAR INC
EXIDE TECHNOLOGIES
EXXON MOBIL CORPORATION (EXXONMOBIL)
EXXONMOBIL CHEMICAL
FIRST SOLAR INC
FUJITSU LABORATORIES LTD
GE ENERGY INFRASTRUCTURE
GENERAL MOTORS COMPANY (GM)
GLOBAL SOLAR ENERGY
GRIFFIN INDUSTRIES INC
HEADWATERS INC
HELIOVOLT CORP

HEWLETT-PACKARD CO (HP)
HEWLETT-PACKARD QUANTUM SCIENCE
RESEARCH
HITACHI HIGH TECHNOLOGIES AMERICA INC
HITACHI LTD
HUNTSMAN CORPORATION
IBERDROLA RENOVABLES SAU
IBERDROLA SA
IBM RESEARCH
IMPERIAL WESTERN PRODUCTS INC
INTEL CORP
INTERNATIONAL POWER PLC
JOULE UNLIMITED TECHNOLOGIES
KIOR INC
KYOCERA CORP
KYOCERA SOLAR CORP
LANXESS AG
MANHATTAN SCIENTIFICS INC
MITSUBISHI ELECTRIC CORPORATION
MITSUI CHEMICALS INC
MONSANTO CO
NACEL ENERGY CORP
NEXANT INC
NEXTERA ENERGY RESOURCES LLC
NISSAN MOTOR CO LTD
ORMAT TECHNOLOGIES
PETROLEO BRASILEIRO SA (PETROBRAS)
QUANTUM FUEL SYSTEMS TECHNOLOGIES
WORLDWIDE INC
RENEGY HOLDINGS INC
RENEWABLE ENERGY SYSTEMS
ROBERT BOSCH GMBH
ROYAL DUTCH SHELL PLC
SAMSUNG ELECTRONICS CO LTD
SANYO ELECTRIC COMPANY LTD
SAPPHIRE ENERGY
SASOL LIMITED
SHELL OIL CO
SHELL WINDENERGY BV
SIEMENS AG
SIGMA-ALDRICH CORP
SKYFUEL INC
SOLARCITY
SOLVAY SA
SULZER LTD
SUNRUN
SUPERCONDUCTOR TECHNOLOGIES INC
SYNTROLEUM CORPORATION
TESLA MOTORS INC
TOSHIBA CORPORATION
TOTAL SA
UNITED TECHNOLOGIES CORPORATION
VEOLIA ENVIRONNEMENT
VESTAS WIND SYSTEMS A/S
WASTE MANAGEMENT INC
XTREME POWER

MIDWEST

3M COMPANY
A123SYSTEMS
AKZO NOBEL NV
AMERESCO INC
AMERICAN POWER CONVERSION (APC)
AMSC CORPORATION
AROTECH CORPORATION
BABCOCK & WILCOX COMPANY (THE)
BADGER METER INC
BASF SE
BAYER AG
BAYER CORP
BIOAMBER
BP ALTERNATIVE ENERGY
BP PLC
BYD COMPANY LIMITED
CABOT CORPORATION
CAITHNESS ENERGY LLC
CELANESE CORPORATION
CH2M HILL COMPANIES LTD
CHANGING WORLD TECHNOLOGIES INC
CHEVRON CORPORATION
CLARIANT INTERNATIONAL LTD
CLEAN ENERGY FUELS CORP
CLIPPER WINDPOWER LLC
CONOCOPHILLIPS COMPANY
COULOMB TECHNOLOGIES
COVANTA ENERGY CORPORATION
DOW CHEMICAL COMPANY (THE)
DOW CORNING CORPORATION
DUPONT (E I DU PONT DE NEMOURS & CO)
DUPONT AGRICULTURE & NUTRITION
DUPONT CENTRAL RESEARCH & DEVELOPMENT
ECHELON CORP
ELEVANCE RENEWABLE SCIENCES INC
ENEL GREEN POWER SPA
ENER1 INC
ENERGY CONVERSION DEVICES INC
ENERGY RECOVERY INC
EXIDE TECHNOLOGIES
EXXON MOBIL CORPORATION (EXXONMOBIL)
FIRST SOLAR INC
GE ENERGY INFRASTRUCTURE
GENERAL MOTORS COMPANY (GM)
GREEN BIOLOGICS LIMITED
GRIFFIN INDUSTRIES INC
GT ADVANCED TECHNOLOGIES INC
HARVEST POWER
HEADWATERS INC
HEWLETT-PACKARD CO (HP)
HITACHI HIGH TECHNOLOGIES AMERICA INC
HITACHI LTD
HUNTSMAN CORPORATION
INTEL CORP
INTERNATIONAL POWER PLC
JOULEX
LANZATECH LTD

MITSUBISHI ELECTRIC CORPORATION
MITSUI CHEMICALS INC
MONSANTO CO
NAVITAS ENERGY INC
NEXANT INC
NEXTERA ENERGY RESOURCES LLC
NISSAN MOTOR CO LTD
NORDEX AG
ORMAT TECHNOLOGIES
PANASONIC CORPORATION
POWERFILM INC
QUANTUM FUEL SYSTEMS TECHNOLOGIES
WORLDWIDE INC
RECYCLED ENERGY DEVELOPMENT LLC
RENEWABLE ENERGY SYSTEMS
ROBERT BOSCH GMBH
ROYAL DUTCH SHELL PLC
SAKTI3
SAMSUNG ELECTRONICS CO LTD
SASOL LIMITED
SERIOUS ENERGY INC
SHELL OIL CO
SIEMENS AG
SIGMA-ALDRICH CORP
SOLARGENIX ENERGY LLC
SOLVAY SA
SULZER LTD
SUZLON ENERGY LIMITED
SYNGENTA AG
TEKION INC
UNITED SOLAR OVONIC
UNITED TECHNOLOGIES CORPORATION
VEOLIA ENVIRONNEMENT
WASTE MANAGEMENT INC
WINDLAB SYSTEMS
XINJIANG GOLDWIND SCIENCE & TECHNOLOGY
CO LTD
XTREME POWER
ZIPCAR INC

SOUTHEAST

3M COMPANY
AKZO NOBEL NV
AMERESCO INC
AMERICAN POWER CONVERSION (APC)
AROTECH CORPORATION
BABCOCK & WILCOX COMPANY (THE)
BASF SE
BAYER AG
BAYER CORP
BG GROUP PLC
BP ALTERNATIVE ENERGY
BP PLC
CABOT CORPORATION
CAITHNESS ENERGY LLC
CH2M HILL COMPANIES LTD
CHEVRON CORPORATION
CLARIANT INTERNATIONAL LTD

CLEAN ENERGY FUELS CORP
COMVERGE INC
CONOCOPHILLIPS COMPANY
COULOMB TECHNOLOGIES
COVANTA ENERGY CORPORATION
DOW CHEMICAL COMPANY (THE)
DUPONT (E I DU PONT DE NEMOURS & CO)
DUPONT AGRICULTURE & NUTRITION
DUPONT CENTRAL RESEARCH & DEVELOPMENT
ENER1 INC
EXIDE TECHNOLOGIES
EXXON MOBIL CORPORATION (EXXONMOBIL)
GE ENERGY INFRASTRUCTURE
GENERAL MOTORS COMPANY (GM)
GEOPLASMA LLC
GRIFFIN INDUSTRIES INC
HEADWATERS INC
HEWLETT-PACKARD CO (HP)
HEWLETT-PACKARD QUANTUM SCIENCE
RESEARCH
HITACHI HIGH TECHNOLOGIES AMERICA INC
HITACHI LTD
HUNTSMAN CORPORATION
IMPERIAL WESTERN PRODUCTS INC
INTEL CORP
INTERNATIONAL POWER PLC
KIOR INC
KYOCERA CORP
LANZATECH LTD
MITSUBISHI ELECTRIC CORPORATION
MONSANTO CO
NEXANT INC
NEXTERA ENERGY RESOURCES LLC
NISSAN MOTOR CO LTD
PANASONIC CORPORATION
QUANTUM FUEL SYSTEMS TECHNOLOGIES
WORLDWIDE INC
ROBERT BOSCH GMBH
ROYAL DUTCH SHELL PLC
SAMSUNG ELECTRONICS CO LTD
SANYO ELECTRIC COMPANY LTD
SASOL LIMITED
SCIENERGY
SHELL OIL CO
SIEMENS AG
SIGMA-ALDRICH CORP
SOLARGENIX ENERGY LLC
SOLICORE INC
SOLVAY SA
STR HOLDINGS INC
SULZER LTD
SUNIVA INC
SYNGENTA AG
UNITED TECHNOLOGIES CORPORATION
WASTE MANAGEMENT INC
ZIPCAR INC

NORTHEAST
1366 TECHNOLOGIES INC
24M TECHNOLOGIES INC
3M COMPANY
A123SYSTEMS
ABB LTD
AKZO NOBEL NV
ALSTOM SA
AMERESCO INC
AMERICAN POWER CONVERSION (APC)
AMSC CORPORATION
AROTECH CORPORATION
BABCOCK & WILCOX COMPANY (THE)
BALLARD POWER SYSTEMS INC
BASF FUTURE BUSINESS GMBH
BASF SE
BAYER AG
BAYER CORP
BEACON POWER CORP
BELL LABS
BG GROUP PLC
BOSTON-POWER
BP ALTERNATIVE ENERGY
BP PLC
BP SOLAR
CABOT CORPORATION
CAITHNESS ENERGY LLC
CANADIAN SOLAR INC
CAPSTONE TURBINE CORP
CELANESE CORPORATION
CH2M HILL COMPANIES LTD
CHANGING WORLD TECHNOLOGIES INC
CHEVRON CORPORATION
CLARIANT INTERNATIONAL LTD
CLEAN ENERGY FUELS CORP
CLIPPER WINDPOWER LLC
COMVERGE INC
CONOCOPHILLIPS COMPANY
COULOMB TECHNOLOGIES
COVANTA ENERGY CORPORATION
DIGITAL LUMENS
DOW CHEMICAL COMPANY (THE)
DOW CORNING CORPORATION
DUPONT (E I DU PONT DE NEMOURS & CO)
DUPONT AGRICULTURE & NUTRITION
DUPONT CENTRAL RESEARCH & DEVELOPMENT
DYNAMOTIVE ENERGY SYSTEMS CORPORATION
ELECTROCHEM INC
EMCORE CORP
ENER1 INC
ENERNOC INC
ENOCEAN
EVERGREEN SOLAR INC
EXIDE TECHNOLOGIES
EXXON MOBIL CORPORATION (EXXONMOBIL)
FIRST SOLAR INC
FUELCELL ENERGY INC
GAMESA CORPORACION TECNOLOGICA SA

GE ENERGY INFRASTRUCTURE
GE GLOBAL RESEARCH
GENERAL COMPRESSION
GENERAL MOTORS COMPANY (GM)
GMZ ENERGY
GREEN BIOLOGICS LIMITED
GRIFFIN INDUSTRIES INC
GT ADVANCED TECHNOLOGIES INC
HARVEST POWER
HEADWATERS INC
HEWLETT-PACKARD CO (HP)
HITACHI HIGH TECHNOLOGIES AMERICA INC
HITACHI LTD
HUNTSMAN CORPORATION
IBERDROLA RENOVABLES SAU
IBERDROLA SA
IBM RESEARCH
INTEL CORP
INTERNATIONAL POWER PLC
IOXUS INC
ISOFOTON
JOULE UNLIMITED TECHNOLOGIES
KONARKA TECHNOLOGIES INC
KYOCERA CORP
LANXESS AG
MANHATTAN SCIENTIFICS INC
MASCOMA CORP
MECHANICAL TECHNOLOGY INC
MITSUBISHI CORP
MITSUBISHI ELECTRIC CORPORATION
MITSUI CHEMICALS INC
MONSANTO CO
MTI MICROFUEL CELLS INC
NEC LABORATORIES AMERICA INC
NEXANT INC
NEXTERA ENERGY RESOURCES LLC
NISSAN MOTOR CO LTD
NOVOZYMES
NUVERA FUEL CELLS INC
OASYS WATER
OPOWER
PANASONIC CORPORATION
PETROLEO BRASILEIRO SA (PETROBRAS)
PLUG POWER INC
QTEROS INC
RECYCLED ENERGY DEVELOPMENT LLC
ROBERT BOSCH GMBH
ROYAL DUTCH SHELL PLC
SAMSUNG ELECTRONICS CO LTD
SANYO ELECTRIC COMPANY LTD
SASOL LIMITED
SERIOUS ENERGY INC
SHARP CORPORATION
SHELL OIL CO
SIEMENS AG
SIGMA-ALDRICH CORP
SOLARONE SOLUTIONS LLC
SOLVAY SA

SPIRE CORPORATION
STR HOLDINGS INC
SULZER LTD
SUNEDISON LLC
SUNPOWER CORPORATION
SUNRUN
SUSTAINX INC
SYNGENTA AG
SYNTHETIC GENOMICS INC
TERRA SOLAR GLOBAL INC
TIGO ENERGY
TOSHIBA CORPORATE R&D CENTER
TOSHIBA CORPORATION
UNITED TECHNOLOGIES CORPORATION
UTC POWER
VEOLIA ENVIRONNEMENT
VESTAS WIND SYSTEMS A/S
WASTE MANAGEMENT INC
XTREME POWER
XYLEM INC
ZAP JONWAY
ZIPCAR INC

INDEX OF FIRMS WITH
INTERNATIONAL OPERATIONS

GREEN BIOLOGICS LIMITED
GREENROAD TECHNOLOGIES
GRUPPO FALCK SPA
GT ADVANCED TECHNOLOGIES INC
HANWHA SOLARONE CO LTD
HARA
HARVEST POWER
HEADWATERS INC
HELIATEK GMBH
HELVETA
HEWLETT-PACKARD CO (HP)
HEWLETT-PACKARD LABORATORIES (HP LABS)
HEWLETT-PACKARD QUANTUM SCIENCE
RESEARCH
HITACHI HIGH TECHNOLOGIES AMERICA INC
HITACHI LTD
HUNTSMAN CORPORATION
HYDROGENICS CORPORATION
HYFLUX LTD
IBERDROLA RENOVABLES SAU
IBERDROLA SA
IBM RESEARCH
ICP SOLAR TECHNOLOGIES
IDATECH LLC
INTEL CORP
INTERNATIONAL POWER PLC
ISOFOTON
JA SOLAR HOLDINGS CO LTD
JINKOSOLAR HOLDING CO LTD
JOULEX
KAIIMA AGRO-BIOTECH LTD
KONARKA TECHNOLOGIES INC
KYOCERA CORP
KYOCERA SOLAR CORP
LANXESS AG
LANZATECH LTD
LATTICEPOWER (JIANGXI) CORP
LDK SOLAR CO LTD
LEMNIS LIGHTING BV
LS9 INC
MANHATTAN SCIENTIFICS INC
MCPHY ENERGY
MECHANICAL TECHNOLOGY INC
MITSUBISHI CORP
MITSUBISHI ELECTRIC CORPORATION
MITSUI CHEMICALS INC
MONSANTO CO
MTI MICROFUEL CELLS INC
NANOSOLAR INC
NEXANT INC
NEXTERA ENERGY RESOURCES LLC
NEXTERRA SYSTEMS CORP
NISSAN MOTOR CO LTD
NOBAO RENEWABLE ENERGY HOLDINGS LTD
NORDEX AG
NOVOZYMES
NUJIRA LTD
NUVERA FUEL CELLS INC

O-FLEXX TECHNOLOGIES GMBH
ON-RAMP WIRELESS
OPOWER
ORMAT TECHNOLOGIES
OSTARA NUTRIENT RECOVERY TECHNOLOGIES
PANASONIC CORPORATION
PETROLEO BRASILEIRO SA (PETROBRAS)
PHOTOWATT INTERNATIONAL SA
PLUG POWER INC
PRIMEARTH EV ENERGY CO LTD
Q.CELLS SE
QUANTUM FUEL SYSTEMS TECHNOLOGIES
WORLDWIDE INC
RELION INC
RENEWABLE ENERGY SYSTEMS
REPOWER SYSTEMS SE
ROBERT BOSCH GMBH
ROYAL DUTCH SHELL PLC
SAMSUNG ELECTRONICS CO LTD
SANYO ELECTRIC COMPANY LTD
SASOL LIMITED
SCHNEIDER ELECTRIC SA
SCHOTT SOLAR
SERIOUS ENERGY INC
SFC ENERGY AG
SHARP CORPORATION
SHELL OIL CO
SHELL WINDENERGY BV
SIEMENS AG
SIEMENS CONCENTRATED SOLAR POWER LTD
SIEMENS CORPORATE TECHNOLOGY
SIGMA-ALDRICH CORP
SILVER SPRING NETWORKS
SINOVEL WIND GROUP CO LTD
SKYPOWER LIMITED
SOLAIREDIRECT
SOLARRESERVE
SOLARWORLD AG
SOLFOCUS INC
SOLTECTURE GMBH
SOLVAY SA
SPIRE CORPORATION
STIRLING DK
STR HOLDINGS INC
SULZER LTD
SUNCOR ENERGY INC
SUNEDISON LLC
SUNPOWER CORPORATION
SUNTECH POWER HOLDINGS CO LTD
SUNWAYS AG
SUZLON ENERGY LIMITED
SYNAPSENSE
SYNGENTA AG
TAKADU
TALBOTT'S BIOMASS ENERGY SYSTEMS LTD
TEKION INC
TENDRIL
TERRA SOLAR GLOBAL INC

TESLA MOTORS INC
TIGO ENERGY
TOPELL ENERGY
TOSHIBA CORPORATE R&D CENTER
TOSHIBA CORPORATION
TOTAL SA
TRILLIANT
TRINA SOLAR LTD
UNITED ENVIROTECH LTD
UNITED SOLAR OVONIC
UNITED TECHNOLOGIES CORPORATION
VEOLIA ENVIRONNEMENT
VESTAS WIND SYSTEMS A/S
VHF TECHNOLOGIES SA
VOLTEA
WASTE MANAGEMENT INC
WATERHEALTH
WINDLAB SYSTEMS
WINWIND OY
WURTH ELEKTRONIK GMBH & CO KG
XINJIANG GOLDWIND SCIENCE & TECHNOLOGY
CO LTD
XYLEM INC
YINGLI GREEN ENERGY HOLDING CO LTD
ZAP JONWAY
ZIPCAR INC
ZORLU ENERJI ELEKTRIK URETIM AS

Individual Profiles
On Each Of
THE GREEN TECHNOLOGY 325

1366 TECHNOLOGIES INC

www.1366tech.com

Industry Group Code: 334413

Energy/Fuel:	Other Technologies:	Electrical Products:	Electronics:	Transportation:	Other:
Biofuels:	Irrigation:	Lighting/LEDs:	Computers:	Car Sharing:	Recycling:
Batteries/Storage:	Nanotech:	Waste Heat:	Sensors:	Electric Vehicles:	Engineering:
Solar: Y	Biotech:	Smart Meters:	Software:	Natural Gas Fuel:	Consulting:
Wind:	Water Tech./Treatment:	Machinery:			Investing:
Fuel Cells:	Ceramics:				Chemicals:

TYPES OF BUSINESS:

Photovoltaic Technology

BRANDS/DIVISIONS/AFFILIATES:

Direct Wafer
Self-Aligned Cell

CONTACTS: Note: Officers with more than one job title may be intentionally listed here more than once.

Frank van Mierlo, CEO
Rick Tattersfield, COO
Daniel Matloff, CFO

Phone: 781-861-1611	Fax:
Toll-Free:	
Address: 45 Hartwell Ave., Lexington, MA 02421 US	

GROWTH PLANS/SPECIAL FEATURES:

1366 Technologies, Inc. is a solar energy technology firm, established as a spin-off from MIT. The firm's focus is on engineering and manufacturing advanced silicon solar cells, with the goal of lowering costs and making solar power competitive with traditional carbon power sources such as coal. 1366 Technologies combines innovations in silicon cell architecture with lean manufacturing processes to make cost effective and commercially viable high efficiency multi-crystalline solar cells. Developed by a team of scientists, engineers and entrepreneurs, including MIT professor and photovoltaic industry expert Dr. Emanuel Sachs, the company's novel approach breaks the historic efficiency and cost tradeoff of photovoltaics. Its Direct Wafer technology utilizes 156-mm multi-crystalline wafers directly from molten silicon in a semi-continuous, efficient, high-throughput process that eliminates silicon waste. In addition, the firm pioneered the Self-Aligned Cell, which enables mono-crystalline equivalent cell efficiencies at multi-crystalline cell costs. 1366 Technologies is headquartered in Lexington, Massachusetts. In September 2011, the firm received $150 million in loan guarantees from the U.S. Department of Energy.

FINANCIALS: Sales and profits are in thousands of dollars—add 000 to get the full amount. 2011 Note: Financial information for 2011 was not available for all companies at press time.

2011 Sales: $	2011 Profits: $	**U.S. Stock Ticker:** Private
2010 Sales: $	2010 Profits: $	**Int'l Ticker:**
2009 Sales: $	2009 Profits: $	Int'l Exchange:
2008 Sales: $	2008 Profits: $	Employees: Fiscal Year Ends:
2007 Sales: $	2007 Profits: $	Parent Company:

SALARIES/BENEFITS:

Pension Plan:	ESOP Stock Plan:	Profit Sharing:	Top Exec. Salary: $	Bonus: $
Savings Plan:	Stock Purch. Plan:		Second Exec. Salary: $	Bonus: $

OTHER THOUGHTS:

Apparent Women Officers or Directors:
Hot Spot for Advancement for Women/Minorities:

LOCATIONS: ("Y" = Yes)

West:	Southwest:	Midwest:	Southeast:	Northeast: Y	International:

24M TECHNOLOGIES INC

www.24mtechnologies.com

Industry Group Code: 33591

Energy/Fuel:	Other Technologies:	Electrical Products:	Electronics:	Transportation:	Other:
Biofuels:	Irrigation:	Lighting/LEDs:	Computers:	Car Sharing:	Recycling:
Batteries/Storage: Y	Nanotech:	Waste Heat:	Sensors:	Electric Vehicles:	Engineering:
Solar:	Biotech:	Smart Meters:	Software:	Natural Gas Fuel:	Consulting:
Wind:	Water Tech./Treatment:	Machinery:			Investing:
Fuel Cells:	Ceramics:				Chemicals:

TYPES OF BUSINESS:

Energy Storage Technology

BRANDS/DIVISIONS/AFFILIATES:

A123 Systems
North Bridge Venture Partners
Charles River Ventures

CONTACTS: *Note: Officers with more than one job title may be intentionally listed here more than once.*

Throop Wilder, Pres.
Meg O'Leary, Press Contact
Throop Wilder, Co-Founder
Yet-Ming Chiang, Co-Founder

Phone: 781-791-4565	Fax:
Toll-Free:	
Address: One Kendall Square Ste. B6103, Cambridge, MA 02139 US	

GROWTH PLANS/SPECIAL FEATURES:

24M Technologies, Inc. is a privately held company that develops and designs innovative energy storage products using efficient technologies such as fuel cells, rechargeable batteries and flow batteries for the purpose of large-scale deployments in transportation and grid applications. The firm is a spin off of A123 Systems, an alternative battery company, which maintains an equity stake in 24M. It currently remains in the research and developmental stage of operations. The company manages its operations through venture capitalist investments. North Bridge Venture Partners and Charles River Ventures, two top-tier investment firms, have invested an initial $10 million. The company is currently in the process of perfecting its proprietary energy storage system for distribution, which combines lithium-ion and flow battery technologies. In 2011, 24M received the ARPA-E award from the Department of Energy, endowing them with an additional $2.55 million for the purpose of continuing collaborative efforts with MIT, A123 Systems and Rutgers on an energy-storage project.

FINANCIALS: Sales and profits are in thousands of dollars—add 000 to get the full amount. 2011 Note: Financial information for 2011 was not available for all companies at press time.

2011 Sales: $	2011 Profits: $	**U.S. Stock Ticker: Private**
2010 Sales: $	2010 Profits: $	**Int'l Ticker:**
2009 Sales: $	2009 Profits: $	Int'l Exchange:
2008 Sales: $	2008 Profits: $	Employees: Fiscal Year Ends:
2007 Sales: $	2007 Profits: $	Parent Company:

SALARIES/BENEFITS:

Pension Plan:	ESOP Stock Plan:	Profit Sharing:	Top Exec. Salary: $	Bonus: $
Savings Plan:	Stock Purch. Plan:		Second Exec. Salary: $	Bonus: $

OTHER THOUGHTS:

Apparent Women Officers or Directors:
Hot Spot for Advancement for Women/Minorities:

LOCATIONS: ("Y" = Yes)

West:	Southwest:	Midwest:	Southeast:	Northeast:	International:
				Y	

3M COMPANY

www.3m.com

Industry Group Code: 33911

Energy/Fuel:	Other Technologies:	Electrical Products:	Electronics:	Transportation:	Other:
Biofuels:	Irrigation:	Lighting/LEDs:	Computers:	Car Sharing:	Recycling:
Batteries/Storage:	Nanotech:	Waste Heat:	Sensors:	Electric Vehicles:	Engineering:
Solar:	Biotech:	Smart Meters:	Software: Y	Natural Gas Fuel:	Consulting:
Wind:	Water Tech./Treatment:	Machinery:			Investing:
Fuel Cells: Y	Ceramics:				Chemicals:

TYPES OF BUSINESS:

Health Care Products
Specialty Materials & Textiles
Industrial Products
Safety, Security & Protection Products
Display & Graphics Products
Consumer & Office Products
Electronics & Communications Products
Fuel Cell Technology

BRANDS/DIVISIONS/AFFILIATES:

Nida-Core Corp.
3M Cogent, Inc.
Hybrivet Systems, Inc.
Cogent, Inc.
Attenti Holdings S.A.
Arizant, Inc.

CONTACTS: Note: Officers with more than one job title may be intentionally listed here more than once.

George W. Buckley, CEO
Inge G. Thulin, COO
George W. Buckley, Pres.
Patrick D. Campbell, CFO/Sr. VP
Robert D. MacDonald, Sr. VP-Mktg. & Sales
Angela S. Lalor, Sr. VP-Human Resources
Frederick J. Palensky, Exec. VP-R&D
Frederick J. Palensky, CTO
Marschall I. Smith, General Counsel/Sr. VP-Legal Affairs
Roger H.D. Lacey, Sr. VP-Strategy & Corp. Dev.
David W. Meline, Chief Acct. Officer
Brad T. Sauer, Exec. VP-Health Care Bus.
H.C. Shin, Exec. VP-Industrial & Transportation Bus.
Joaquin Delgado, Exec. VP-Electro & Comm. Bus.
Joe E. Harlan, Exec. VP-Consumer & Office Bus.
George W. Buckley, Chmn.
John K. Woodworth, Sr. VP-Corp. Supply Chain Oper.

Phone: 651-733-1110	**Fax:** 651-733-9973
Toll-Free: 800-364-3577	
Address: 3M Center, St. Paul, MN 55144 US	

GROWTH PLANS/SPECIAL FEATURES:

3M Company is involved in the research, manufacturing and marketing of a variety of products. The firm is organized into six segments: Health Care; Consumer and Office; Display and Graphics; Electro and Communications; Industrial and Transportation; and Safety, Security and Protection. The Health Care segment's products include medical and surgical supplies, skin infection prevention products, drug delivery systems, orthodontic products, health information systems and veterinary products. The Consumer and Office segment includes office supply, stationery, construction, home improvement, protective material and visual systems products. The Display and Graphics segment's products include optical film and lenses for electronic displays; touch screens and monitors; screen filters; reflective sheeting; and commercial graphics systems. The Electro and Communications segment's products include packaging and interconnection devices (used in circuits); fluids used in computer chips; high-temperature and display tapes; pressure-sensitive tapes and resins; and products for telecommunications systems. The Industrial and Transportation segment's products include vinyl, polyester, tapes, a variety of non-woven abrasives, adhesives, specialty materials, supply chain execution software, filtration systems, paint finishing products, engineering fluids and components for catalytic converters. The Safety, Security and Protection services segment provides products for personal protection, safety and security, energy control, commercial cleaning and protection, passports and secure cards. In October 2010, the firm acquired remote people monitor supplier, Attenti Holdings S.A., and developer of patient warming products for the prevention of hypothermia in surgery settings, Arizant, Inc. In December 2010, the company acquired biometric security systems provider, Cogent, Inc., with the latter subsequently becoming a subsidiary of 3M called 3M Cogent, Inc. In January 2011, the firm opened an innovation center in Dubai and acquired fiber-reinforced foam materials manufacturer, Nida-Core Corp. In February 2011, the company acquired Hybrivet Systems, Inc., provider of toxin detection products.

The company offers employees medical and dental insurance; domestic partner benefits; tuition reimbursement; and adoption assistance.

FINANCIALS: Sales and profits are in thousands of dollars—add 000 to get the full amount. 2011 Note: Financial information for 2011 was not available for all companies at press time.

2011 Sales: $	2011 Profits: $	**U.S. Stock Ticker: MMM**
2010 Sales: $26,662,000	2010 Profits: $4,085,000	**Int'l Ticker:**
2009 Sales: $23,123,000	2009 Profits: $3,193,000	Int'l Exchange:
2008 Sales: $25,269,000	2008 Profits: $3,460,000	Employees: 80,057 Fiscal Year Ends: 12/31
2007 Sales: $24,462,000	2007 Profits: $4,096,000	Parent Company:

SALARIES/BENEFITS:

Pension Plan:	ESOP Stock Plan:	Profit Sharing:	Top Exec. Salary: $5,901,401	Bonus: $
Savings Plan: Y	Stock Purch. Plan: Y		Second Exec. Salary: $1,553,068	Bonus: $

OTHER THOUGHTS:

Apparent Women Officers or Directors: 4
Hot Spot for Advancement for Women/Minorities: Y

LOCATIONS: ("Y" = Yes)

West:	Southwest:	Midwest:	Southeast:	Northeast:	International:
Y	Y	Y	Y	Y	Y

4ENERGY

Industry Group Code: 335

www.4energy.co.uk

Energy/Fuel:	Other Technologies:	Electrical Products:		Electronics:	Transportation:	Other:
Biofuels:	Irrigation:	Lighting/LEDs:		Computers:	Car Sharing:	Recycling:
Batteries/Storage:	Nanotech:	Waste Heat:	Y	Sensors:	Electric Vehicles:	Engineering:
Solar:	Biotech:	Smart Meters:		Software:	Natural Gas Fuel:	Consulting:
Wind:	Water Tech./Treatment:	Machinery:				Investing:
Fuel Cells:	Ceramics:					Chemicals:

TYPES OF BUSINESS:

Air Cooling Technology

BRANDS/DIVISIONS/AFFILIATES:

CoolFlow
CoolFilter
CoolFocus
CoolScheme
CoolAir
SmartControl
SmartMonitor
SmartPlan

CONTACTS: *Note: Officers with more than one job title may be intentionally listed here more than once.*

Phone: 44-11-5937-2710	Fax:
Toll-Free:	
Address: Debdale Ln., Industrial Estate, Keyworth, NG125HN UK	

GROWTH PLANS/SPECIAL FEATURES:

4ENERGY is a U.K.-based developer of free air cooling technology and products throughout the world. It manages its operations through its subsidiaries, which are located across seven different countries and three continents. The firm's operations are financially backed by three European clean technology funds: The East Midlands Capital Venture Fund; The Environmental Technology Fund; and The Carbon Trust. The company operates through three divisions: Telecoms and Equipment Rooms, Data Centers and Monitoring and Control Systems. The Telecoms and Equipment Rooms division focuses on developing cooling systems, which reduce air conditioning usage by employing thermally sensitive electronic equipment that is insulated from effects caused by drastic temperatures. This division's products include CoolFlow, a technology that directly removes heat from telecommunication based stations; CoolFilter, a stationary filtration system that removes dirt automatically, creating a continuous flow of cool air with minimal operating costs; and CoolFocus, an external and internal cooling system used to keep specialized pieces of equipment operating at their recommended temperatures. The Data Centers division optimizes air flow through its CoolScheme and CoolAir products. CoolScheme produces data reports that analyze infrastructure and thermal properties, in addition to providing system recommendations to increase flow efficiency. CoolAir delivers free air from outside into data centers while simultaneously monitoring humidity, temperature and quality. The Monitoring and Control System division's products include SmartMonitor, a remote real time management system capable of monitoring environmental conditions through web based platforms; SmartControl, which allows information to be autonomously converted and controlled using rule based decision making software; and SmartPlan, a predictive technology that simulates the effects environmental changes have on equipment layout, power and cooling configurations.

FINANCIALS: Sales and profits are in thousands of dollars—add 000 to get the full amount. 2011 Note: Financial information for 2011 was not available for all companies at press time.

2011 Sales: $	2011 Profits: $	**U.S. Stock Ticker: Private**
2010 Sales: $	2010 Profits: $	**Int'l Ticker:**
2009 Sales: $	2009 Profits: $	Int'l Exchange:
2008 Sales: $	2008 Profits: $	Employees: Fiscal Year Ends:
2007 Sales: $	2007 Profits: $	Parent Company:

SALARIES/BENEFITS:

Pension Plan:	ESOP Stock Plan:	Profit Sharing:	Top Exec. Salary: $	Bonus: $
Savings Plan:	Stock Purch. Plan:		Second Exec. Salary: $	Bonus: $

OTHER THOUGHTS:

Apparent Women Officers or Directors:
Hot Spot for Advancement for Women/Minorities:

LOCATIONS: ("Y" = Yes)

West:	Southwest:	Midwest:	Southeast:	Northeast:	International: Y

A123SYSTEMS

Industry Group Code: 33591

Energy/Fuel:		Other Technologies:		Electrical Products:		Electronics:		Transportation:		Other:	
Biofuels:		Irrigation:		Lighting/LEDs:		Computers:		Car Sharing:		Recycling:	
Batteries/Storage:	Y	Nanotech:		Waste Heat:		Sensors:		Electric Vehicles:		Engineering:	
Solar:		Biotech:		Smart Meters:		Software:		Natural Gas Fuel:		Consulting:	
Wind:		Water Tech./Treatment:		Machinery:						Investing:	
Fuel Cells:		Ceramics:								Chemicals:	

TYPES OF BUSINESS:

Batteries, Design & Manufacture
Lithium-Ion Batteries
Nanotechnology
Batteries for Electric Automobiles
Nanophosphate

BRANDS/DIVISIONS/AFFILIATES:

A123Systems China
Hymotion, Inc.

CONTACTS: Note: Officers with more than one job title may be intentionally listed here more than once.

David Vieau, CEO
David Vieau, Pres.
John Granara, Interim CFO
Andrew Cole, VP-Human Resources & Organizational Dev.
Bart Riley, VP-R&D
Bart Riley, CTO
Eric Pyenson, General Counsel/VP
Louis Golato, VP-Oper.
Dan Borgasano, Public Rel.
John Granara, VP-Finance/Controller
Geoff Taylor, VP-Quality
Robert Johnson, VP-Energy Solutions Group
Jason Forcier, VP-Automotive Solutions Group
Desh Deshpande, Chmn.

Phone: 617-778-5700	Fax: 617-778-5749
Toll-Free:	
Address: 321 Arsenal St., Arsenal on the Charles, Watertown, MA 02472 US	

GROWTH PLANS/SPECIAL FEATURES:

A123Systems is the innovator of a powerful, long-lasting, environmentally safe Lithium-Ion battery derived from nanoscale materials, called Nanophosphate lithium battery technology. Founded in 2001 in Watertown, Massachusetts, the company has gone beyond its MIT-research-based design operations to make use of manufacturing space in the U.S., China, Korea and Germany. The batteries, which currently take the form of cylindrical cells, are presently in mass production after successful testing and customer evaluation. The results indicate that this battery sports numerous features that set it apart from its sister products on the market. For example, it was proven to have discharge rates as high as 100C; a fast charge time; high thermal conductivity; very little sensitivity to environmental temperature; virtually no toxicity; and a long cycle life. The battery design is capable of powering a diverse range of high power rechargeable battery applications, including power tools; hybrid electric vehicles, power cells for which are developed through the firm's Hymotion division; heavy duty vehicle fleets; aviation propulsion systems; specialized military equipment, including directed energy weapons and stealth drive applications; and medical devices.

FINANCIALS: Sales and profits are in thousands of dollars—add 000 to get the full amount. 2011 Note: Financial information for 2011 was not available for all companies at press time.

2011 Sales: $	2011 Profits: $	U.S. Stock Ticker: AONE
2010 Sales: $97,312	2010 Profits: $-152,937	Int'l Ticker:
2009 Sales: $91,049	2009 Profits: $-86,589	Int'l Exchange:
2008 Sales: $68,525	2008 Profits: $-80,431	Employees: 2,032 Fiscal Year Ends: 12/31
2007 Sales: $41,349	2007 Profits: $-30,993	Parent Company:

SALARIES/BENEFITS:

Pension Plan:	ESOP Stock Plan:	Profit Sharing:	Top Exec. Salary: $375,000	Bonus: $174,938
Savings Plan:	Stock Purch. Plan:		Second Exec. Salary: $275,000	Bonus: $78,375

OTHER THOUGHTS:

Apparent Women Officers or Directors:
Hot Spot for Advancement for Women/Minorities:

LOCATIONS: ("Y" = Yes)

West:	Southwest:	Midwest:	Southeast:	Northeast:	International:
		Y		Y	Y

ABB LTD

www.abb.com

Industry Group Code: 335

Energy/Fuel:	Other Technologies:	Electrical Products:	Electronics:	Transportation:	Other:	
Biofuels:	Irrigation:	Lighting/LEDs:	Computers:	Car Sharing:	Recycling:	
Batteries/Storage:	Nanotech:	Waste Heat:	Sensors:	Electric Vehicles:	Engineering:	Y
Solar:	Biotech:	Smart Meters:	Software:	Natural Gas Fuel:	Consulting:	
Wind:	Water Tech./Treatment:	Machinery:			Investing:	
Fuel Cells:	Ceramics:				Chemicals:	

TYPES OF BUSINESS:

Diversified Engineering Services
Power Transmission & Distribution Systems
Control & Automation Technology Products
Industrial Robotics
Energy Trading Software

BRANDS/DIVISIONS/AFFILIATES:

ABB (Thailand) Ltd.
ABB (India) Ltd.
Ventyx, Inc.
Trasfor Group
Lorentzen & Wettre
Epyon B.V.

CONTACTS: Note: Officers with more than one job title may be intentionally listed here more than once.

Joseph Hogan, CEO
Michel Demare, CFO
Brice Koch, Head-Mktg. & Customer Solutions
Gary Steel, Head-Human Resources
Diane de Saint Victor, General Counsel
Thomas Schmidt, Head-Corp. Comm.
Johanna Henttonen, Dir.-Investor Rel.
Ulrich Spiesshofer, Head-Discreet Automation & Motion Div.
Bernhard Jucker, Head-Power Prod. Div.
Veli-Matti Reinikkala, Head-Process Automation Div.
Tarak Mehta, Head-Low Voltage Prod. Div.
Hubertus von Grunberg, Chmn.
Frank Duggan, Head-Global Markets

Phone: 41-43-317-7111	Fax: 41-43-317-4420
Toll-Free:	
Address: Affolternstrasse 44, Zurich, CH-8050 Switzerland	

GROWTH PLANS/SPECIAL FEATURES:

ABB, Ltd. is a global leader in power and automation technologies for utility and industrial companies. The company provides a broad range of products, systems and services that improve power grid reliability, increase industrial productivity and enhance energy efficiency. The firm operates in approximately 100 countries, and divides its business into five divisions: power products; power systems; low voltage products; discrete automation and motion; and process automation. The power products segment manufactures and sells high to medium voltage switchgear and apparatus, circuit breakers for various current and voltage levels and power and distribution transformers. The power systems division's applications include engineering of grid systems, power generation systems, network management and substations. Operations of the low voltage products unit include businesses producing low-voltage electrical equipment sold on the wholesale and original equipment manufacturers markets. The discrete automation and motion segment includes products and systems targeted at discrete manufacturing applications, such as robotics and programmable logic controllers, and providing motion in plants, such as motors and drives. This segment incorporates the former operations of the robotics division. The process automation segment offers plant automation and electrification, energy management, process and asset optimization, analytical measurement and telecommunications for such industries as metals and minerals; pharmaceuticals; oil and gas; pulp and paper; chemicals; and petrochemicals. Subsidiaries of the company include ABB (India) Ltd., ABB (Thailand) Ltd. and Ventyx, Inc., a leading software provider to the global energy, utility and communications industries. In 2011, the firm acquired Trasfor Group, which produces inductors and dry-type transformers; Lorentzen & Wettre, a subsidiary of ASSA ABLOY AB, which creates quality control and test instrumentation products for the pulp and paper industry; and Epyon B.V., a developer of network charger software and direct current fast-charging stations. In January 2012, the company agreed to acquire Thomas & Betts Corp. for $4 billion.

FINANCIALS: Sales and profits are in thousands of dollars—add 000 to get the full amount. 2011 Note: Financial information for 2011 was not available for all companies at press time.

2011 Sales: $	2011 Profits: $	**U.S. Stock Ticker:**	
2010 Sales: $31,589,000	2010 Profits: $2,732,000	**Int'l Ticker: ABBN**	
2009 Sales: $31,795,000	2009 Profits: $2,901,000	Int'l Exchange: Zurich-SWX	
2008 Sales: $34,912,000	2008 Profits: $3,118,000	Employees: 116,500 Fiscal Year Ends: 12/31	
2007 Sales: $29,183,000	2007 Profits: $3,757,000	Parent Company:	

SALARIES/BENEFITS:

Pension Plan:	ESOP Stock Plan:	Profit Sharing:	Top Exec. Salary: $1,981,704	Bonus: $944,280
Savings Plan:	Stock Purch. Plan:		Second Exec. Salary: $1,251,606	Bonus: $1,524,037

OTHER THOUGHTS:

Apparent Women Officers or Directors: 4
Hot Spot for Advancement for Women/Minorities: Y

LOCATIONS: ("Y" = Yes)

West:	Southwest:	Midwest:	Southeast:	Northeast:	International:
				Y	Y

ABENGOA SOLAR

www.abengoasolar.com

Industry Group Code: 33361

Energy/Fuel:		Other Technologies:	Electrical Products:	Electronics:	Transportation:	Other:
Biofuels:		Irrigation:	Lighting/LEDs:	Computers:	Car Sharing:	Recycling:
Batteries/Storage:		Nanotech:	Waste Heat:	Sensors:	Electric Vehicles:	Engineering:
Solar:	Y	Biotech:	Smart Meters:	Software:	Natural Gas Fuel:	Consulting:
Wind:		Water Tech./Treatment:	Machinery:			Investing:
Fuel Cells:		Ceramics:				Chemicals:

TYPES OF BUSINESS:

Solar Power Plants
Solar Technology Components

BRANDS/DIVISIONS/AFFILIATES:

Abengoa Solar US
Abengoa SA
Abengoa Solar New Technologies
Helioenergy 1
Solucar Energia

CONTACTS: *Note: Officers with more than one job title may be intentionally listed here more than once.*

Santiago Seage Medela, CEO
Javier Albarracin Guerrero, CFO
Teodoro Lopez del Cerro, Dir.-Eng.
David Fernandez Fuentes, Dir.-Admin. & Control
Valerio Fernandez, Dir.-Oper., Spain
Michael Geyer, Dir.-Int'l Dev.
Ricardo Abaurre, Dir.-Institutional Rel.
Barbara Zubiria Furest, Investor Rel.
Ken May, Dir.-Abengoa Solar IST Div.
Rafael Osuna, Gen. Mgr.-Abengoa Solar New Technologies
Fernando Celaya, Gen. Mgr.-Photovoltaic Tech.
Santiago Seage, Chmn.
Emiliano Garcia Sanz, Gen. Mgr.-US

Phone: 34-95-493-71-11	Fax:
Toll-Free:	
Address: Paseo de la Castallena 31, Madrid, 28046 Spain	

GROWTH PLANS/SPECIAL FEATURES:

Abengoa Solar, formerly Solucar Energia, is a subsidiary of Abengoa SA, a Spanish technology company that offers products and services geared toward sustainable development. Abengoa Solar is engaged in the promotion, construction and operation of solar energy generating plants and customized commercial and industrial installations around the world. The firm utilizes several different types of technology to generate electricity from the sun. Photovoltaic facilities use photovoltaic panels to create electricity directly from sunlight. The Concentrating Solar Power (CSP) plants focus the sun's energy on a heat transfer medium, such as oil, that is then used to create steam, which drives a turbine and generates electricity. CSP facilities include parabolic trough plants, which use parabolic mirrors to focus solar energy on a pipe carrying the heat transfer medium; power tower plants, which use a field of movable mirrors to focus energy on a central tower containing the heat transfer medium; and integrated solar combined cycle (ISCC) plants, which use solar energy to augment the steam created by a gas turbine and partially substitute for fossil fuels. Affiliate Abengoa Solar New Technologies manages the firm's research and development operations. The firm has facilities in Spain, the U.S., Algeria, Morocco and China. The company operates in the U.S. via subsidiary Abengoa Solar U.S., with facilities in Colorado, California, Arizona and Texas. Abengoa Solar and E.ON Climate & Renewables maintain a partnership to own and operate two 50 megawatt (MW) CSP plants. In July 2011, the firm announced the completion of the financing of two 50 MW concentrating solar power plants in Spain; the plants will begin operations in 2012. In September 2011, Abengona Solar announced that the Spanish solar power station Helioenergy 1, jointly owned with E.On, had begun commercial operations; furthermore, the firm began construction on a 280 MW Mojave Solar Project.

FINANCIALS: Sales and profits are in thousands of dollars—add 000 to get the full amount. 2011 Note: Financial information for 2011 was not available for all companies at press time.

2011 Sales: $	2011 Profits: $	**U.S. Stock Ticker:** Subsidiary
2010 Sales: $237,923	2010 Profits: $40,939	**Int'l Ticker:**
2009 Sales: $164,070	2009 Profits: $-89,106	Int'l Exchange:
2008 Sales: $	2008 Profits: $	Employees: 447 Fiscal Year Ends: 12/31
2007 Sales: $	2007 Profits: $	Parent Company: ABENGOA SA

SALARIES/BENEFITS:

Pension Plan:	ESOP Stock Plan:	Profit Sharing:	Top Exec. Salary: $	Bonus: $
Savings Plan:	Stock Purch. Plan:		Second Exec. Salary: $	Bonus: $

OTHER THOUGHTS:

Apparent Women Officers or Directors: 2
Hot Spot for Advancement for Women/Minorities:

LOCATIONS: ("Y" = Yes)

West:	Southwest:	Midwest:	Southeast:	Northeast:	International:
Y	Y				Y

ACTIVE POWER INC

www.activepower.com

Industry Group Code: 33591

Energy/Fuel:		Other Technologies:	Electrical Products:	Electronics:	Transportation:	Other:
Biofuels:		Irrigation:	Lighting/LEDs:	Computers:	Car Sharing:	Recycling:
Batteries/Storage:	Y	Nanotech:	Waste Heat:	Sensors:	Electric Vehicles:	Engineering:
Solar:		Biotech:	Smart Meters:	Software:	Natural Gas Fuel:	Consulting:
Wind:		Water Tech./Treatment:	Machinery:			Investing:
Fuel Cells:		Ceramics:				Chemicals:

TYPES OF BUSINESS:

Manufacturing-Power Supplies
Battery-Free Backup Power Systems
Flywheel Energy Systems

BRANDS/DIVISIONS/AFFILIATES:

CleanSource
Cat UPS
CleanSource DC
CleanSource UPS
PowerHouse
Caterpillar Inc

CONTACTS: *Note: Officers with more than one job title may be intentionally listed here more than once.*

Jan Lindelow, CEO
Jan Lindelow, Pres.
John Penver, CFO
Lisa Brown, VP-Mktg. & Sales Oper.
Jeff Quade, VP-Human Resources
Uwe Schrader-Hausmann, CTO
Noel Foley, VP-Eng.
Jason Rubin, VP-Mfg.
John Penver, VP-Finance
Martin Olsen, VP-Sales/Gen. Mgr.-Americas
Huan Wang, Dir.-Sales, China
Benjamin L. Scott, Chmn.
Dietmar Papenfort, VP-Sales, EMEA & Asia Pacific

Phone: 512-836-6464	Fax: 512-836-4511
Toll-Free:	
Address: 2128 W. Braker Ln., BK12, Austin, TX 78758 US	

GROWTH PLANS/SPECIAL FEATURES:

Active Power, Inc. designs, manufactures and markets battery-free uninterrupted power solutions (UPS) that provide backup electric power in the event of voltage fluctuations or power disturbances. The firm operates in the U.S., U.K., Germany, Japan and China. The company has over 100 issued patents including its one for its flywheel technology. It focuses on improving system reliability and energy and space efficiency, while lowering the cost of electric power for broad industry users, including data centers, airports and clients in the manufacturing, technology, broadcast and communications, financial, utilities, healthcare and government sectors. It markets its flywheels under the CleanSource name. The firm's CleanSource flywheel generator provides a highly reliable, low-cost and non-toxic replacement for lead-acid batteries. It stores kinetic energy in its constantly spinning flywheel. The flywheel apparatus converts its rotary motion into electricity and powers the critical load during utility disturbances or until a standby generator takes over. Its flywheel products have load capabilities ranging from 130 to 1,500 kilovolt-amperes system formats, with the ability to parallel these products to over 8 megawatts of protection. CleanSource DC can directly replace traditional lead-acid batteries. The CleanSource UPS has a 98% efficiency rating. The company also markets continuous power systems under the PowerHouse brand; these systems incorporate its proprietary UPS systems as well as a generator to provide both short and long-term power disturbance protection. PowerHouse products are available in either 20- or 40-foot-long formats. In a joint venture with Caterpillar, Inc., the firm developed the Cat UPS product line, which features advanced power conditioning and flywheel energy storage that provides voltage regulation and harmonics cancellation. Sales to Caterpillar account for about 19% of Active Power's total revenue. In June 2011, the firm announced the opening of a new operations center in the U.K.

FINANCIALS: Sales and profits are in thousands of dollars—add 000 to get the full amount. 2011 Note: Financial information for 2011 was not available for all companies at press time.

2011 Sales: $	2011 Profits: $	**U.S. Stock Ticker:** ACPW
2010 Sales: $64,955	2010 Profits: $-3,925	**Int'l Ticker:**
2009 Sales: $40,311	2009 Profits: $-11,033	Int'l Exchange:
2008 Sales: $42,985	2008 Profits: $-13,442	Employees: 181 Fiscal Year Ends: 12/31
2007 Sales: $33,601	2007 Profits: $-20,492	Parent Company:

SALARIES/BENEFITS:

Pension Plan:	ESOP Stock Plan:	Profit Sharing:	Top Exec. Salary: $354,187	Bonus: $648,900
Savings Plan:	Stock Purch. Plan:		Second Exec. Salary: $232,054	Bonus: $210,002

OTHER THOUGHTS:

Apparent Women Officers or Directors: 3
Hot Spot for Advancement for Women/Minorities: Y

LOCATIONS: ("Y" = Yes)

West:	Southwest:	Midwest:	Southeast:	Northeast:	International:
	Y				Y

ADURA TECHNOLOGIES

www.aduratech.com

Industry Group Code: 3345

Energy/Fuel:	Other Technologies:	Electrical Products:		Electronics:		Transportation:	Other:	
Biofuels:	Irrigation:	Lighting/LEDs:	Y	Computers:		Car Sharing:	Recycling:	
Batteries/Storage:	Nanotech:	Waste Heat:		Sensors:	Y	Electric Vehicles:	Engineering:	
Solar:	Biotech:	Smart Meters:	Y	Software:	Y	Natural Gas Fuel:	Consulting:	
Wind:	Water Tech./Treatment:	Machinery:					Investing:	
Fuel Cells:	Ceramics:						Chemicals:	

TYPES OF BUSINESS:

Energy Management Systems
Wireless Lighting Controls

BRANDS/DIVISIONS/AFFILIATES:

Claremont Creek Ventures
VantagePoint Capital Partners
NGEN Partners

CONTACTS: *Note: Officers with more than one job title may be intentionally listed here more than once.*

Mark Golan, CEO
Philip Lavee, VP-Mktg. & Sales
Charlie Huizenga, CTO
Simon Swain, VP-Met.
Dale Fong, VP-Software
Michael Corr, VP-Hardware

Phone: 415-547-8100	**Fax:** 415-547-8101
Toll-Free: 888-828-8281	
Address: 22 Fourth St., 10th Fl., San Francisco, CA 94103 US	

GROWTH PLANS/SPECIAL FEATURES:

Adura Technologies, founded in 2005, is a provider of energy management systems and wireless lighting controls for new and retrofitted commercial buildings. The firm's systems have been deployed in over 3 million square feet of space for various uses, including offices and parking garages for major municipalities and companies located in the Silicon Valley. The Adura lighting control system includes The Wireless Light Controller, a cost effective control for individual fixtures or small groups of fixtures that turns on lights to the desired level when needed and off when not needed; Sensor Interface, which integrates occupancy sensors and daylight sensors to offer flexible control zoning and the ability to cost-effectively incorporate multiple control strategies; Wall Control Interface, which replaces conventional wall switches with a smart switch; a wireless gateway, which links part of a wireless network, building or floor with the entire Adura system network over the local Ethernet network; and software applications that are intended to give customers greater management over their lighting options. The company has received roughly $17 million in venture-backed funding from three investors: NGEN Partners, Claremont Creek Ventures and VantagePoint Capital Partners.

The firm offers its employees health insurance, a 401(k) plan, commuter checks and Section 125 benefits.

FINANCIALS: Sales and profits are in thousands of dollars—add 000 to get the full amount. 2011 Note: Financial information for 2011 was not available for all companies at press time.

2011 Sales: $	2011 Profits: $	**U.S. Stock Ticker: Private**
2010 Sales: $	2010 Profits: $	**Int'l Ticker:**
2009 Sales: $	2009 Profits: $	Int'l Exchange:
2008 Sales: $	2008 Profits: $	Employees: Fiscal Year Ends:
2007 Sales: $	2007 Profits: $	Parent Company:

SALARIES/BENEFITS:

Pension Plan:	ESOP Stock Plan:	Profit Sharing:	Top Exec. Salary: $	Bonus: $
Savings Plan:	Stock Purch. Plan:		Second Exec. Salary: $	Bonus: $

OTHER THOUGHTS:

Apparent Women Officers or Directors:
Hot Spot for Advancement for Women/Minorities:

LOCATIONS: ("Y" = Yes)

West:	Southwest:	Midwest:	Southeast:	Northeast:	International:
Y					

AGILYX

www.agilyx.com

Industry Group Code: 325199

Energy/Fuel:		Other Technologies:		Electrical Products:		Electronics:		Transportation:		Other:	
Biofuels:	Y	Irrigation:		Lighting/LEDs:		Computers:		Car Sharing:		Recycling:	Y
Batteries/Storage:		Nanotech:		Waste Heat:		Sensors:		Electric Vehicles:		Engineering:	
Solar:		Biotech:	Y	Smart Meters:		Software:		Natural Gas Fuel:	Y	Consulting:	
Wind:		Water Tech./Treatment:		Machinery:						Investing:	
Fuel Cells:		Ceramics:								Chemicals:	

TYPES OF BUSINESS:

Crude Oil Production

BRANDS/DIVISIONS/AFFILIATES:

Environ Strategy Consultants, Inc
Evergreen Engineering
Green EnviroTech Corp

CONTACTS: Note: Officers with more than one job title may be intentionally listed here more than once.

Chris Ulum, CEO
Bob Schwarz, CFO
Kevin DeWhitt, CTO
Dennis D. Bennett, VP-Eng.
Rita Hansen, VP-Oper. & Svcs.
Brent Bostwick, Chief Commercialization Officer
Vraig Garrison, Dir.-Tech. Oper.
Bill McAtee, Dir-Oper.
Darren Wood, Plant Mgr.
Cade Swail, Dir.-Supply Chain Mgmt.

Phone: 503-217-3160	**Fax:** 503-217-3161
Toll-Free:	
Address: 9600 SW Nimbus Ave., Ste. 260, Beaverton, OR 97008 US	

GROWTH PLANS/SPECIAL FEATURES:

Agilyx is an alternative energy company that uses its proprietary technology to reduce difficult-to-recycle waste plastics into synthetic crude oil. The company strives to address the growing need to find solutions to extending landfill life and finding a cost-effective solution to plastic waste disposal. The firm's patented system consists of four vessels, capable of converting 10 tons of plastic into 2,400 gallons of oil per day. Cartridges are filled with feedstock and placed into a Plastic Reclamation Unit, and are then re-circulated by hot air, converting the feedstock from a solid to a gas. Using negative pressure, the gases are pulled into a central condensing system where they are cooled and condensed into synthetic crude oil. The ultra-sweet, synthetic crude oil produced by the firm's proprietary conversion system is refined either on-site or at neighboring petrochemical processors where it is converted into various petroleum products. The company's primary customers include: producers and recyclers of waste plastic; material recovery facilities; and transfer stations. The firm has several strategic partnership agreements with environmental engineering firms, including Environ Strategy Consultants, Inc.; Evergreen Engineering; and Green EnviroTech Corp. Agilyx has a refinery offtake agreement, and ships its oil from its facility in Tigard, Oregon to a refinery in the U.S Pacific Northwest.

FINANCIALS: Sales and profits are in thousands of dollars—add 000 to get the full amount. 2011 Note: Financial information for 2011 was not available for all companies at press time.

2011 Sales: $	2011 Profits: $	**U.S. Stock Ticker:** Private
2010 Sales: $	2010 Profits: $	**Int'l Ticker:**
2009 Sales: $	2009 Profits: $	Int'l Exchange:
2008 Sales: $	2008 Profits: $	Employees: Fiscal Year Ends:
2007 Sales: $	2007 Profits: $	Parent Company:

SALARIES/BENEFITS:

Pension Plan:	ESOP Stock Plan:	Profit Sharing:	Top Exec. Salary: $	Bonus: $
Savings Plan:	Stock Purch. Plan:		Second Exec. Salary: $	Bonus: $

OTHER THOUGHTS:

Apparent Women Officers or Directors: 1
Hot Spot for Advancement for Women/Minorities:

LOCATIONS: ("Y" = Yes)

West:	Southwest:	Midwest:	Southeast:	Northeast:	International:
Y					

AIRTRICITY
Industry Group Code: 221119

www.airtricity.com

Energy/Fuel:		Other Technologies:		Electrical Products:		Electronics:	Transportation:	Other:	
Biofuels:		Irrigation:		Lighting/LEDs:		Computers:	Car Sharing:	Recycling:	
Batteries/Storage:		Nanotech:		Waste Heat:		Sensors:	Electric Vehicles:	Engineering:	
Solar:		Biotech:		Smart Meters:		Software:	Natural Gas Fuel:	Consulting:	
Wind:	Y	Water Tech./Treatment:		Machinery:				Investing:	
Fuel Cells:		Ceramics:						Chemicals:	

TYPES OF BUSINESS:
Wind Generation
Retail Electricity Sales
Hydropower Purchase & Resale
Electricity & Gas Duel Fuel Plans
Electricity Plans
Gas Plans
Onshore Wind Farms
Offshore Wind Farms

BRANDS/DIVISIONS/AFFILIATES:
Scottish and Southern Energy plc
Greater Gabbard Wind Farm
Clyde Wind Farm
SSE Renewables

CONTACTS: *Note: Officers with more than one job title may be intentionally listed here more than once.*
Kevin Greenhorn, Managing Dir.
Paul Dowling, COO
Steve Cowie, Chief Exec.-Scotland
Mark Ennis, Chief Exec.-Aircity Supply

Phone: 353-1-655 6400	Fax: 353-1-655 6444
Toll-Free:	
Address: Airtricity House, Ravenscourt Office Park, Dublin, Ireland 18 UK	

GROWTH PLANS/SPECIAL FEATURES:
Airtricity is a Dublin-based company which produces and sells wind-generated electricity. Airtricity contracts directly with end user customers and sells at retail prices. The firm supplies electricity to more than 375,000 Irish customers through 32 operational wind farms throughout Europe, which generate over 500 megawatts (MWs) of power. The firm's renewable energy development affiliate company, known as SSE Renewables, maintains marine, biomass, offshore/onshore wind farm, hydro and solar projects in the U.K. and continental Europe. The company is currently developing two of Europe's larger wind farms: Greater Gabbard, a 504 MW offshore wind farm located off the Suffolk coast of England; and Clyde, a 350 MW onshore wind farm located in the Upper Clyde Valley in Scotland. Airtricity is a subsidiary of Scottish and Southern Energy plc, a generator of renewable energy in the UK and Ireland, with a current renewable electricity generation capacity of over 3,400 MW and over 1,400 MW of renewable energy projects under development.

FINANCIALS: Sales and profits are in thousands of dollars—add 000 to get the full amount. 2011 Note: Financial information for 2011 was not available for all companies at press time.

2011 Sales: $	2011 Profits: $	U.S. Stock Ticker: Subsidiary
2010 Sales: $	2010 Profits: $	Int'l Ticker:
2009 Sales: $	2009 Profits: $	Int'l Exchange:
2008 Sales: $	2008 Profits: $	Employees: Fiscal Year Ends: 3/31
2007 Sales: $	2007 Profits: $	Parent Company: SCOTTISH AND SOUTHERN ENERGY PLC

SALARIES/BENEFITS:
Pension Plan:	ESOP Stock Plan:	Profit Sharing:	Top Exec. Salary: $	Bonus: $
Savings Plan:	Stock Purch. Plan:		Second Exec. Salary: $	Bonus: $

OTHER THOUGHTS:
Apparent Women Officers or Directors:
Hot Spot for Advancement for Women/Minorities:

LOCATIONS: ("Y" = Yes)
West:	Southwest:	Midwest:	Southeast:	Northeast:	International: Y

AKZO NOBEL NV

www.akzonobel.com

Industry Group Code: 325

Energy/Fuel:	Other Technologies:	Electrical Products:	Electronics:	Transportation:	Other:	
Biofuels:	Irrigation:	Lighting/LEDs:	Computers:	Car Sharing:	Recycling:	
Batteries/Storage:	Nanotech:	Waste Heat:	Sensors:	Electric Vehicles:	Engineering:	
Solar:	Biotech:	Smart Meters:	Software:	Natural Gas Fuel:	Consulting:	
Wind:	Water Tech./Treatment:	Machinery:			Investing:	
Fuel Cells:	Ceramics:				Chemicals:	Y

TYPES OF BUSINESS:

Specialty Chemicals
Coatings
Decorative Paints

BRANDS/DIVISIONS/AFFILIATES:

Axko Nobel India Limited
Eka Chemicals AB
Ralph Lauren Paint
Glidden
Dulux
Liquid Nails
Lindgens Metal Decorating Coatings and Inks
Changzhou Prime Automotive Paint Co., Ltd.

CONTACTS: Note: Officers with more than one job title may be intentionally listed here more than once.

Hanz Wijers, CEO
Keith Nichols, CFO
Marjan Oudeman, Head-Human Resources
Graeme Armstrong, Head-R&D & Innovation
Sven Dumoulin, General Counsel
Marjan Oudeman, Head-Organizational Dev.
Tim Van der Zanden, Head-Corp. Media Rel.
Huib Wurfbain, Dir.-Investor Rel.
Hans de Vriese, Dir.-Control
Leif Darner, Managing Dir.-Performance Coatings
Rob Frohn, Managing Dir.-Specialty Chemicals
Tex Gunning, Managing Dir.-Decorative Paints
Erik Bouts, Gen. Mgr.-Decorative Paints, US
Karel Vuursteen, Chmn.-Supervisory Board
Waqar Malik, CEO-Chemicals Pakistan
Werner Fuhrmann, Head-Supply Chain

Phone: 31-20-502-7555	Fax: 31-20-502-7666
Toll-Free:	
Address: Strawinskylaan 2555, Amsterdam, 1077 ZZ The Netherlands	

GROWTH PLANS/SPECIAL FEATURES:

Akzo Nobel N.V. is a leading international producer of chemicals and coatings, operating in over 80 countries worldwide. The company is divided into three segments: Decorative Paints, Performance Coatings and Specialty Chemicals. The Decorative Paints division includes paint, lacquer and varnish products, as well as adhesives, floor leveling compounds, mixing machines and training courses. Brands in this division consist of Sikkens, Dulux, Glidden, Martha Stewart Living, Ralph Lauren Paint, Devoe Paint, Mulco, Hammerite and Liquid Nails Adhesive. The segment has offices in the U.K., Continental Europe, the Americas and Asia. Akzo Nobel's Performance Coatings division makes a variety of chemical products including powder, industrial and marine coatings; wood finishes and adhesives; and a line of car refinishes. The Specialty Chemicals division produces pulp and paper chemicals; polymer chemicals such as metal alkyls and suspending agents; surfactants used in hair and skincare products; base chemicals such as salt and chlor-alkali products used in the manufacture of glass and plastics; and functional chemicals used in toothpaste, ice cream and flame retardants. This division operates through several subsidiaries, including Eka Chemicals AB, a provider of colloidal silica products; and Chemicals Pakistan, which operates exclusively in the Pakistani market. In April 2010, the firm renamed its Indian decorative paints business, formerly ICI India, to Azko Nobel India Limited. In June 2010, Azko Nobel completed the acquisition of the powder coatings business of The Dow Chemical Company. In July 2010, it agreed to acquire the Swedish-based company Lindgens Metal Decorating Coatings and Inks. In September 2010, the company announced that Wal-Mart had selected it to be the primary supplier of paints to its U.S. retail locations. In the same month, it agreed to acquire Changzhou Prime Automotive Paint Co., Ltd. In October 2010, it sold its National Starch business to Corn Products International for $1.3 billion.

FINANCIALS: Sales and profits are in thousands of dollars—add 000 to get the full amount. 2011 Note: Financial information for 2011 was not available for all companies at press time.

2011 Sales: $	2011 Profits: $	U.S. Stock Ticker:
2010 Sales: $21,173,100	2010 Profits: $1,090,470	Int'l Ticker: AKZA
2009 Sales: $18,566,600	2009 Profits: $1,162,670	Int'l Exchange: Amsterdam-Euronext
2008 Sales: $20,387,300	2008 Profits: $981,340	Employees: 55,590 Fiscal Year Ends: 12/31
2007 Sales: $18,481,000	2007 Profits: $12,770,600	Parent Company:

SALARIES/BENEFITS:

Pension Plan:	ESOP Stock Plan:	Profit Sharing:	Top Exec. Salary: $	Bonus: $
Savings Plan:	Stock Purch. Plan:		Second Exec. Salary: $	Bonus: $

OTHER THOUGHTS:

Apparent Women Officers or Directors: 1
Hot Spot for Advancement for Women/Minorities:

LOCATIONS: ("Y" = Yes)

West:	Southwest:	Midwest:	Southeast:	Northeast:	International:
		Y	Y	Y	Y

Sales, profits and employees may be estimates. Financial information, benefits and other data can change quickly and may vary from those stated here.

ALEO SOLAR AG

www.aleo-solar.de

Industry Group Code: 334413

Energy/Fuel:		Other Technologies:	Electrical Products:	Electronics:	Transportation:	Other:
Biofuels:		Irrigation:	Lighting/LEDs:	Computers:	Car Sharing:	Recycling:
Batteries/Storage:		Nanotech:	Waste Heat:	Sensors:	Electric Vehicles:	Engineering:
Solar:	Y	Biotech:	Smart Meters:	Software:	Natural Gas Fuel:	Consulting:
Wind:		Water Tech./Treatment:	Machinery:			Investing:
Fuel Cells:		Ceramics:				Chemicals:

TYPES OF BUSINESS:
Solar Panel Manufacturing

BRANDS/DIVISIONS/AFFILIATES:
aleo solar Deutschland GmbH
aleo solar Espana SL
aleo solar Italia srl
avim Solar Production Co. Ltd.
Johanna Solar Technology GmbH

CONTACTS: *Note: Officers with more than one job title may be intentionally listed here more than once.*
York zu Putlitz, CEO
York zu Putlitz, CFO
Norbert Schlesiger, Chief Sales Officer
Jens Sabotke, CTO
Jens Sabotke, Chief Dev. Officer
Herman Iding, Head-Corp. Comm.
Jasmin Michaelis, Head-Investor Rel.

Phone: 49-3984-8328	Fax: 49-3984-8328-115
Toll-Free:	
Address: Gewerbegebiet Nord, Prenzlau, 17291 Germany	

GROWTH PLANS/SPECIAL FEATURES:
Aleo Solar AG is a German firm engaged in the design and manufacture of solar panels sold under the aleo brand name. The products of aleo solar include silicon-based photovoltaic panels and CIGSSe (Copper, Indium, Gallium, Sulfur and Selenium) thin-film solar cells. aleo solar's silicon-based panels are made to a customer's specifications using polycrystalline or monocrystalline four-, five-, six- or eight-inch silicon cells. The firm markets these products via wholly-owned subsidiary aleo solar Deutschland GmbH in Germany, as well as in the international market. aleo solar operates through three additional wholly-owned subsidiaries and a joint venture. aleo solar Espana SL controls the company's production and sales in Spain. aleo solar's Italian sales operations are handled by aleo solar Italia srl. aleo solar North America, Inc. handles the company's North and Central American operations. The firm owns 50% of avim Solar Production Co. Ltd., a Chinese joint venture with Chinese Sunvim Group Co. Ltd. that controls a portion of its manufacturing operations. Johanna Solar Technology GmbH, in which aleo solar owns 9.23%, is a German firm engaged in the manufacture and production of CIGSSe-based solar cells. The firm's total production capacity is approximately 250 megawatts (MWs); however, it plans to increase its production to 390 MW in the near future. Germany accounts for over half of the firm's sales.

FINANCIALS: Sales and profits are in thousands of dollars—add 000 to get the full amount. 2011 Note: Financial information for 2011 was not available for all companies at press time.

2011 Sales: $	2011 Profits: $	**U.S. Stock Ticker:**
2010 Sales: $783,000	2010 Profits: $44,500	**Int'l Ticker: AS1**
2009 Sales: $498,060	2009 Profits: $21,190	Int'l Exchange: Paris-Euronext
2008 Sales: $538,730	2008 Profits: $23,460	Employees: 878 Fiscal Year Ends: 12/31
2007 Sales: $302,600	2007 Profits: $12,200	Parent Company:

SALARIES/BENEFITS:

Pension Plan:	ESOP Stock Plan:	Profit Sharing:	Top Exec. Salary: $	Bonus: $
Savings Plan:	Stock Purch. Plan:		Second Exec. Salary: $	Bonus: $

OTHER THOUGHTS:
Apparent Women Officers or Directors: 1
Hot Spot for Advancement for Women/Minorities:

LOCATIONS: ("Y" = Yes)

West:	Southwest:	Midwest:	Southeast:	Northeast:	International:
					Y

ALSTOM SA

www.alstom.com

Industry Group Code: 335

Energy/Fuel:	Other Technologies:	Electrical Products:		Electronics:		Transportation:	Other:
Biofuels:	Irrigation:	Lighting/LEDs:		Computers:		Car Sharing:	Recycling:
Batteries/Storage:	Nanotech:	Waste Heat:		Sensors:		Electric Vehicles:	Engineering:
Solar:	Biotech:	Smart Meters:		Software:	Y	Natural Gas Fuel:	Consulting:
Wind:	Water Tech./Treatment:	Machinery:	Y				Investing:
Fuel Cells:	Ceramics:						Chemicals:

TYPES OF BUSINESS:

Equipment-Electric Power Distribution
Energy & Transport Infrastructure
Power Plant Machinery
Rail Transport Services
Rail Transport Manufacturing
Technical Consulting & Power Plant Refurbishment

BRANDS/DIVISIONS/AFFILIATES:

Alstom Power
Alstom Transport
Alstom Grid
Areva
Transmashholding
Amstar Surface Technology Ltd.
BrightSource Energy, Inc.
Utility Integration Solutions, Inc.

CONTACTS: Note: Officers with more than one job title may be intentionally listed here more than once.

Patrick Kron, CEO
Nicolas Tissot, CFO
Bruno Guillemet, Sr. VP-Human Resources
Keith Carr, Group General Counsel
Philippe Joubert, Deputy CEO
Philippe Cochet, Exec. VP/Pres., Alstom Thermal Power
Henri Poupart-Lafarge, Exec. VP/Pres., Transport Sector
Patrick Kron, Chmn.

Phone: 33-1-41-49-20-00	Fax: 33-1-41-49-24-85
Toll-Free:	
Address: 3 Ave. Andre Malraux, Levallois-Perret, 75795 France	

GROWTH PLANS/SPECIAL FEATURES:

Alstom S.A. is a world leader in integrated power plant, power production services, air quality control systems and rail transport systems with operations in over 70 countries. The company divides its activities into three sectors: transport, power generation and transmission. Alstom Transport develops and markets a complete range of systems, equipment and services for the railway market. Alstom offers rolling stock for high speed and very high speed trains, regional and commuter trains, locomotives, freight cars, metros, trams and tram-trains. The transport division has contracts to build or has built railway cars and equipment for transit systems across the globe, from Russia, China and India to Brazil, Italy and the U.S., among others. The power generation segment, operating as Alstom Power, designs, manufactures, supplies and services products and systems for the power generation sector. Its products and services include boilers, turbines (gas, hydroelectric and steam), turbogenerators, air quality control systems, product retrofitting and control systems. It also provides refurbishment and maintenance of existing plants as well as turnkey solutions for range of fossil fuel-based and renewable energy power generation facilities. Alstom's transmission business, operating under the moniker Alstom Grid, was acquired in June 2010 from Areva. In March 2011, Alstom acquired Utility Integration Solutions, Inc. (UISOL); which develops and commercializes the software platform DRBizNET. In March 2011, Alstom invested a further $75 million in BrightSource Energy, Inc.; this follows an initial investment of $55 million in May 2010. In April 2011, Alstom and Shanghai Electric Group announced their intent to create a 50/50 joint company, Alstom-Shanghai Electric Boiler Co. In May 2011, the firm purchased a 25% stake in the Russian rail manufacturer Transmashholding. In September 2011, Alstom Grid was awarded an approximately $91 million contract in Iraq to design, manufacture, and install the Mosul East gas-insulated switchgear substation.

FINANCIALS: Sales and profits are in thousands of dollars—add 000 to get the full amount. 2011 Note: Financial information for 2011 was not available for all companies at press time.

2011 Sales: $28,147,300	2011 Profits: $621,500	U.S. Stock Ticker:
2010 Sales: $26,434,800	2010 Profits: $1,760,090	Int'l Ticker: ALSO
2009 Sales: $25,209,200	2009 Profits: $1,647,090	Int'l Exchange: Paris-Euronext
2008 Sales: $22,746,000	2008 Profits: $1,107,600	Employees: 85,225 Fiscal Year Ends: 3/31
2007 Sales: $21,880,300	2007 Profits: $686,800	Parent Company:

SALARIES/BENEFITS:

Pension Plan:	ESOP Stock Plan:	Profit Sharing:	Top Exec. Salary: $1,484,610	Bonus: $1,812,200
Savings Plan:	Stock Purch. Plan:		Second Exec. Salary: $	Bonus: $

OTHER THOUGHTS:

Apparent Women Officers or Directors: 3
Hot Spot for Advancement for Women/Minorities: Y

LOCATIONS: ("Y" = Yes)

West:	Southwest:	Midwest:	Southeast:	Northeast:	International:
	Y			Y	Y

AMANTYS LTD
www.amantys.com

Industry Group Code: 335

Energy/Fuel:	Other Technologies:	Electrical Products:	Electronics:		Transportation:	Other:
Biofuels:	Irrigation:	Lighting/LEDs:	Computers:		Car Sharing:	Recycling:
Batteries/Storage:	Nanotech:	Waste Heat:	Sensors:	Y	Electric Vehicles:	Engineering:
Solar:	Biotech:	Smart Meters:	Software:		Natural Gas Fuel:	Consulting:
Wind:	Water Tech./Treatment:	Machinery:				Investing:
Fuel Cells:	Ceramics:					Chemicals:

TYPES OF BUSINESS:
Intelligent Power Switches

BRANDS/DIVISIONS/AFFILIATES:
Amantys Power Drive

CONTACTS: *Note: Officers with more than one job title may be intentionally listed here more than once.*
Bryn Parry, CEO
Richard Ord, Dir.-Mktg.
Mark Snook, Dir.-Tech.
Andy Matthews, VP-Oper.
Richard Ord, Press Contact
Pete Magowan, Chmn.

Phone: 44-1223-652-450	Fax:
Toll-Free:	
Address: St. John's Innovation Park, Cowley Rd., Cambridge, CB4 OWS UK	

GROWTH PLANS/SPECIAL FEATURES:
Amantys Ltd. is a power electronics company that manufactures and sells intelligent power switches. An intelligent power switch allows for tighter control of switching characteristics through the simplification of power converter design, which is achieved by combining a power switching device with advanced analog and digital controls. Tighter control of switching characteristics means that even over varying conditions an intelligent power switch maintains a more consistent performance. As a result, switching losses can be reduced by up to 50%. Amantys' primary product is the Amantys Power Drive, a drop in replacement for similar gate drive products on the market which, without gate resistor changes, drives a range of insulated gate bipolar transistor (IGBT) modules from manufacturers such as Dynex, Infineon, Toshiba and Mitsubishi. The Amantys Power Drive is most applicable in high voltage DC infrastructures, medium voltage motor drives, locomotive traction and wind turbine inverters. In November 2011, the company began offering its Amantys Power Drive for commercial sale.

FINANCIALS: Sales and profits are in thousands of dollars—add 000 to get the full amount. 2011 Note: Financial information for 2011 was not available for all companies at press time.

2011 Sales: $	2011 Profits: $	**U.S. Stock Ticker:** Private
2010 Sales: $	2010 Profits: $	**Int'l Ticker:**
2009 Sales: $	2009 Profits: $	Int'l Exchange:
2008 Sales: $	2008 Profits: $	Employees: Fiscal Year Ends:
2007 Sales: $	2007 Profits: $	Parent Company:

SALARIES/BENEFITS:

Pension Plan:	ESOP Stock Plan:	Profit Sharing:	Top Exec. Salary: $	Bonus: $
Savings Plan:	Stock Purch. Plan:		Second Exec. Salary: $	Bonus: $

OTHER THOUGHTS:
Apparent Women Officers or Directors: 1
Hot Spot for Advancement for Women/Minorities:

LOCATIONS: ("Y" = Yes)

West:	Southwest:	Midwest:	Southeast:	Northeast:	International: Y

AMEE

www.amee.com

Industry Group Code: 325199

Energy/Fuel:	Other Technologies:	Electrical Products:	Electronics:		Transportation:	Other:	
Biofuels:	Irrigation:	Lighting/LEDs:	Computers:		Car Sharing:	Recycling:	
Batteries/Storage:	Nanotech:	Waste Heat:	Sensors:		Electric Vehicles:	Engineering:	
Solar:	Biotech:	Smart Meters:	Software:	Y	Natural Gas Fuel:	Consulting:	Y
Wind:	Water Tech./Treatment:	Machinery:				Investing:	
Fuel Cells:	Ceramics:					Chemicals:	

TYPES OF BUSINESS:
Database of Environmental and Energy Data
Search Engine for Environmental and Energy Data

BRANDS/DIVISIONS/AFFILIATES:
AMEE Platform
AMEEdiscover
AMEEconnect
AMEEapps

CONTACTS: *Note: Officers with more than one job title may be intentionally listed here more than once.*
Tim Murphy, CEO
Stuart Coleman, VP-Sales
Andrew Conway, Chief Science Officer
Andrew Hill, Head-Eng.
Celine Rich-Darley, Head-Bus. Dev.
Sarah Laville, Head-Finance
Calum Alexander, Sr. Science Officer
Tyler Christie, Head-Partnerships & Mktg.
Patricia Mascari, Deputy Head-Finance
Gavin Starks, Chmn.

Phone: 44-207-253-1499	Fax: 44-207-253-1499
Toll-Free:	
Address: Fl. 4, 70/74 City Rd., London, EC1Y 2BJ UK	

GROWTH PLANS/SPECIAL FEATURES:
AMEE is a U.K.-based company that develops software and platforms that the typical business can use to access environmental and energy information. The company's platform-as-a-service (PaaS), AMEE Platform, takes data from over 300 sources, such as the U.K. Department of Energy and Climate Change and the U.S. EPA, and places it in one, easily searchable location. In connection with the AMEE Platform, the firm offers three distinct products: AMEEdiscover, AMEEconnect and AMEEapps. AMEEdiscover is a search engine for environmental information. AMEEconnect is a PaaS that maintains constant communication between AMME and the client's system, thus insuring that the information concerning environmental standards is the most up to date. AMEEapps is a software-as-a-service (SaaS) that allows access to pre-developed applications developed and maintained on the AMEE Platform. AMEE also offers data and technical services that help clients gather information and integrate the AMEE Platform into their systems.

FINANCIALS: Sales and profits are in thousands of dollars—add 000 to get the full amount. 2011 Note: Financial information for 2011 was not available for all companies at press time.

2011 Sales: $	2011 Profits: $	U.S. Stock Ticker: Private
2010 Sales: $	2010 Profits: $	Int'l Ticker:
2009 Sales: $	2009 Profits: $	Int'l Exchange:
2008 Sales: $	2008 Profits: $	Employees: Fiscal Year Ends:
2007 Sales: $	2007 Profits: $	Parent Company:

SALARIES/BENEFITS:
Pension Plan:	ESOP Stock Plan:	Profit Sharing:	Top Exec. Salary: $	Bonus: $
Savings Plan:	Stock Purch. Plan:		Second Exec. Salary: $	Bonus: $

OTHER THOUGHTS:
Apparent Women Officers or Directors: 4
Hot Spot for Advancement for Women/Minorities: Y

LOCATIONS: ("Y" = Yes)
West:	Southwest:	Midwest:	Southeast:	Northeast:	International: Y

AMERESCO INC

Industry Group Code: 541690

www.ameresco.com

Energy/Fuel:	Other Technologies:	Electrical Products:	Electronics:	Transportation:	Other:	
Biofuels:	Irrigation:	Lighting/LEDs:	Computers:	Car Sharing:	Recycling:	
Batteries/Storage:	Nanotech:	Waste Heat:	Sensors:	Electric Vehicles:	Engineering:	Y
Solar:	Biotech:	Smart Meters:	Software:	Natural Gas Fuel:	Consulting:	Y
Wind:	Water Tech./Treatment:	Machinery:			Investing:	
Fuel Cells:	Ceramics:				Chemicals:	

TYPES OF BUSINESS:

Energy Consulting
Landfill Gas-to-Energy Generation
Solar Power Technology
Cogeneration

BRANDS/DIVISIONS/AFFILIATES:

Ameresco Canada
Ameresco Enertech
AmerescoSolutions
Quantum Engineering and Development, Inc.
Applied Energy Group
APS Energy Services Company, Inc.

CONTACTS: Note: Officers with more than one job title may be intentionally listed here more than once.

George P. Sakellaris, CEO
George P. Sakellaris, Pres.
Andrew B. Spence, CFO/VP
CarolAnn Hibbard, VP-Strategic Mktg.
Kathleen A. Devlin, VP-Human Resources
Joseph P. DeManche, Exec. VP-Eng.
Kathleen A. Devlin, VP-Admin.
David J. Corrsin, General Counsel/Exec. VP/Corp. Sec.
Joseph P. DeManche, Exec. VP-Oper.
David J. Anderson, Exec. VP-Bus. Dev.
CarolAnn Hibbard, VP-Comm.
Michael T. Bakas, Sr. VP-Renewable Energy
Keith A. Derrington, Exec. VP/Gen. Mgr.-Federal Oper.
William J. Cunningham, Sr. VP-Corp. Gov't Rel.
Bruce McLeish, VP-Energy Supply & Risk Mgmt.
George P. Sakellaris, Chmn.
Mario Iusi, Pres., Ameresco Canada

Phone: 508-661-2200	Fax: 508-661-2201
Toll-Free: 866-263-7372	
Address: 111 Speen St., Ste. 410, Framingham, MA 01701 US	

GROWTH PLANS/SPECIAL FEATURES:

Ameresco, Inc. is an independent efficiency consulting company that helps corporations decrease operating expenses, upgrade and maintain facilities and stabilize operating costs. From 56 offices in the U.S. and Canada, the firm works with corporate customers to reduce energy consumption, lower operating costs and realize environmental benefits. The company's services address almost all aspects of purchasing and using energy within a facility, including upgrades to a facility's energy infrastructure and the construction and operation of small-scale renewable energy plants. These small-scale plants are typically located near landfills and use landfill gases (LFG) to generate energy. In addition, the company sells and installs photovoltaic (PV) panels and integrated PV systems. It generally retains ownership of these plants, and then sells the generated power to its clients, or sells the entire facility to the customer. Ameresco primary customers include governmental, educational, utility, healthcare and other institutional, commercial and industrial clients. Subsidiaries of the firm include Ameresco Canada, which serves institutional, commercial and industrial energy users in Canada; AmerescoSolutions, which focuses on federal government clients and has national contracts with the U.S. Departments of Defense and Energy; and Ameresco Enertech, which focuses on primary education, higher education and industrial and commercial facilities within Tennessee and Kentucky. In 2010, the firm acquired Quantum Engineering and Development, Inc., an energy service company active in Oregon and Washington. In July 2011, Ameresco purchased Applied Energy Group. In August 2011, it acquired APS Energy Services Company, Inc.

FINANCIALS: Sales and profits are in thousands of dollars—add 000 to get the full amount. 2011 Note: Financial information for 2011 was not available for all companies at press time.

2011 Sales: $	2011 Profits: $	U.S. Stock Ticker: AMRC
2010 Sales: $618,226	2010 Profits: $28,726	Int'l Ticker:
2009 Sales: $428,517	2009 Profits: $19,907	Int'l Exchange:
2008 Sales: $395,854	2008 Profits: $18,273	Employees: 735 Fiscal Year Ends: 12/31
2007 Sales: $	2007 Profits: $	Parent Company:

SALARIES/BENEFITS:

Pension Plan:	ESOP Stock Plan:	Profit Sharing:	Top Exec. Salary: $500,000	Bonus: $200,000
Savings Plan: Y	Stock Purch. Plan:		Second Exec. Salary: $264,750	Bonus: $80,000

OTHER THOUGHTS:

Apparent Women Officers or Directors: 3
Hot Spot for Advancement for Women/Minorities: Y

LOCATIONS: ("Y" = Yes)

West:	Southwest:	Midwest:	Southeast:	Northeast:	International:
Y	Y	Y	Y	Y	Y

AMERICAN POWER CONVERSION (APC)   www.apcc.com
Industry Group Code: 33591

Energy/Fuel:		Other Technologies:	Electrical Products:	Electronics:	Transportation:	Other:
Biofuels:		Irrigation:	Lighting/LEDs:	Computers:	Car Sharing:	Recycling:
Batteries/Storage:	Y	Nanotech:	Waste Heat:	Sensors:	Electric Vehicles:	Engineering:
Solar:		Biotech:	Smart Meters:	Software:	Natural Gas Fuel:	Consulting:
Wind:		Water Tech./Treatment:	Machinery:			Investing:
Fuel Cells:		Ceramics:				Chemicals:

TYPES OF BUSINESS:
Back-Up Power Supplies
Power Protection & Management Products
Consulting Services
PC Accessories
Power Management Software
Fuel Cell-Based Power Backup

BRANDS/DIVISIONS/AFFILIATES:
Schneider Electric SA
InfraStruXure
Fuel Cell Extended Run (FCXR)

CONTACTS: *Note: Officers with more than one job title may be intentionally listed here more than once.*
Jean-Pascal Tricoire, CEO
Emmanuel Babeau, Exec. VP-Finance

Phone:	Fax:
Toll-Free: 800-788-2208	
Address: 132 Fairgrounds Rd., West Kingston, RI 02892 US	

GROWTH PLANS/SPECIAL FEATURES:

American Power Conversion (APC), a subsidiary of Schneider Electric SA, designs, develops, manufactures and markets power protection and management solutions for computer, communications and electronic applications worldwide. The company's products include uninterruptible power supply products, commonly known as UPS; electrical surge protection devices; power distribution products; precision cooling equipment; power management software and accessories; racks and enclosures; and various desktop and notebook personal computer accessories. These products are primarily used with sensitive electronic devices which rely on electric utility power, such as home electronics, PCs, high-performance computer workstations, servers, networking equipment, communications equipment, Internet equipment, data centers, mainframe computers and facilities. APC's UPS products regulate the flow of utility power to the protected equipment and provide seamless back-up power during power interruptions. Back-up power lasts for enough time to continue computer operations, conduct an orderly shutdown, preserve data, work through short power outages or, in some cases, continue operating for several hours or longer. In addition, the firm's Fuel Cell Extended Run (FCXR) product provides hydrogen-based power backup for the firm's InfraStruXure power, cooling, environmental monitoring and management data center for modular and mobile configurations. The company's security and environmental appliances and accessories protect against environmental or human threats and monitor valuable systems with sensors, cameras and accessories. APC's precision cooling equipment regulates temperature and humidity. Lastly, the company provides power management software, consulting services and notebook and PC accessories. In mid 2010, the company formed a new data center software business. The data center software business team will be responsible for software creation and development; sales; service; and marketing programs.

Employees are offered comprehensive health and dental coverage; short- and long-term disability; flexible spending accounts; life insurance; tuition assistance; a relocation program; leaves of absence; holidays; an employee share plan; and a 401(k) plan.

FINANCIALS: Sales and profits are in thousands of dollars—add 000 to get the full amount. 2011 Note: Financial information for 2011 was not available for all companies at press time.

2011 Sales: $	2011 Profits: $	**U.S. Stock Ticker:** Subsidiary
2010 Sales: $	2010 Profits: $	**Int'l Ticker:**
2009 Sales: $	2009 Profits: $	Int'l Exchange:
2008 Sales: $	2008 Profits: $	Employees: 11,390 Fiscal Year Ends: 12/31
2007 Sales: $	2007 Profits: $	Parent Company: SCHNEIDER ELECTRIC SA

SALARIES/BENEFITS:

Pension Plan:	ESOP Stock Plan:	Profit Sharing:	Top Exec. Salary: $	Bonus: $230,019
Savings Plan: Y	Stock Purch. Plan: Y		Second Exec. Salary: $	Bonus: $

OTHER THOUGHTS:
Apparent Women Officers or Directors: 1
Hot Spot for Advancement for Women/Minorities:

LOCATIONS: ("Y" = Yes)

West:	Southwest:	Midwest:	Southeast:	Northeast:	International:
	Y	Y	Y	Y	Y

AMMINEX A/S

www.amminex.net

Industry Group Code: 238210

Energy/Fuel:		Other Technologies:		Electrical Products:		Electronics:	Transportation:	Other:
Biofuels:		Irrigation:		Lighting/LEDs:		Computers:	Car Sharing:	Recycling:
Batteries/Storage:	Y	Nanotech:		Waste Heat:		Sensors:	Electric Vehicles:	Engineering:
Solar:		Biotech:		Smart Meters:		Software:	Natural Gas Fuel:	Consulting:
Wind:		Water Tech./Treatment:		Machinery:				Investing:
Fuel Cells:	Y	Ceramics:						Chemicals:

TYPES OF BUSINESS:

Automotive Emissions Reduction
Clean Energy Storage

BRANDS/DIVISIONS/AFFILIATES:

Ammonia Storage & Delivery System
AdAmmine
HydrAmmine

CONTACTS: Note: Officers with more than one job title may be intentionally listed here more than once.

Jens E. Hinnerskov, CEO
Eric Tech, Pres.
Tue Johannessen, CTO
Ferdinand Panik, Co-Founder
Jens K. Norskov, Co-Founder
Debasish Chakraborty, Head-Fuel Cells Applications
Morgan Hugo, Chmn.

Phone: 45-45-25-61-56	**Fax:**
Toll-Free:	
Address: Gladsaxevej 363, Soborg, DK-2860 Denmark	

GROWTH PLANS/SPECIAL FEATURES:

Amminex A/S is a Danish clean technology firm working within the automotive and energy storage industries. Founded by researchers at the Technical University of Denmark, the firm's business is based on its Ammonia Storage and Delivery System (ASDS). Amminex has two departments, the automotive department and the energy storage department. The automotive department's focus is to reduce the emission of toxic NOx gas from diesel engines in both cars and trucks. Through the use of its ASDS cartridge incorporating its solid formula AdAmmine, the firm is able to produce a safe, clean source of solid state ammonia to reduce NOx. Amminex produces three sizes of ASDS cartridges for the automotive industry, one for small cars, one for large cars and one for trucks. The energy storage department develops solutions incorporating solid ammonia as an energy carrier for high and low temperature fuels cells. The primary product in this department is the HydrAmmine, a solid ammonia-based energy storage solution. HydrAmmine is marketed as a fuel cell-powered backup for telecom towers, as a reliable source of emergency power and as a source of power for electric cars. Amminex owns an approximately 70,000 square foot production plant in Nyborg, Denmark, which it expects to be fully operational in 2012.

FINANCIALS: Sales and profits are in thousands of dollars—add 000 to get the full amount. 2011 Note: Financial information for 2011 was not available for all companies at press time.

2011 Sales: $	2011 Profits: $	**U.S. Stock Ticker:** Private	
2010 Sales: $	2010 Profits: $	**Int'l Ticker:**	
2009 Sales: $	2009 Profits: $	Int'l Exchange:	
2008 Sales: $	2008 Profits: $	Employees:	Fiscal Year Ends:
2007 Sales: $	2007 Profits: $	Parent Company:	

SALARIES/BENEFITS:

Pension Plan:	ESOP Stock Plan:	Profit Sharing:	Top Exec. Salary: $	Bonus: $
Savings Plan:	Stock Purch. Plan:		Second Exec. Salary: $	Bonus: $

OTHER THOUGHTS:

Apparent Women Officers or Directors:
Hot Spot for Advancement for Women/Minorities:

LOCATIONS: ("Y" = Yes)

West:	Southwest:	Midwest:	Southeast:	Northeast:	International: Y

AMPRIUS

www.amprius.com

Industry Group Code: 33591

Energy/Fuel:		Other Technologies:		Electrical Products:		Electronics:	Transportation:	Other:
Biofuels:		Irrigation:		Lighting/LEDs:		Computers:	Car Sharing:	Recycling:
Batteries/Storage:	Y	Nanotech:	Y	Waste Heat:		Sensors:	Electric Vehicles:	Engineering:
Solar:		Biotech:		Smart Meters:		Software:	Natural Gas Fuel:	Consulting:
Wind:		Water Tech./Treatment:		Machinery:				Investing:
Fuel Cells:		Ceramics:						Chemicals:

TYPES OF BUSINESS:

Lithium-Ion Batteries
Silicon Nanostructures

BRANDS/DIVISIONS/AFFILIATES:

GROWTH PLANS/SPECIAL FEATURES:

Amprius is a startup green technology company developing advanced lithium-ion batteries. The firm utilizes silicon-based nanostructure technology originally developed at Stanford University. This silicon technology enables the company to develop dramatic improvements in the energy density and specific energy of lithium-ion batteries. Some of the world's leading investors back Amprius. These investors include such prominent names as Trident Capital, IPV Capital, Google CEO Dr. Eric Schmidt and Kleiner Perkins Caufield & Byers. In March 2011, Amprius raised $25 million from its various investors towards the commercialization of its batteries.

CONTACTS: *Note: Officers with more than one job title may be intentionally listed here more than once.*

Kang Sun, CEO
Yi Cui, Founder

Phone:	Fax:
Toll-Free: 800-425-8803	
Address: 1430 O'Brien Dr., Ste. C, Menlo Park, CA 94025 US	

FINANCIALS: Sales and profits are in thousands of dollars—add 000 to get the full amount. 2011 Note: Financial information for 2011 was not available for all companies at press time.

2011 Sales: $	2011 Profits: $	**U.S. Stock Ticker:** Private
2010 Sales: $	2010 Profits: $	**Int'l Ticker:**
2009 Sales: $	2009 Profits: $	Int'l Exchange:
2008 Sales: $	2008 Profits: $	Employees: Fiscal Year Ends:
2007 Sales: $	2007 Profits: $	Parent Company:

SALARIES/BENEFITS:

Pension Plan:	ESOP Stock Plan:	Profit Sharing:	Top Exec. Salary: $	Bonus: $
Savings Plan:	Stock Purch. Plan:		Second Exec. Salary: $	Bonus: $

OTHER THOUGHTS:

Apparent Women Officers or Directors:
Hot Spot for Advancement for Women/Minorities:

LOCATIONS: ("Y" = Yes)

West:	Southwest:	Midwest:	Southeast:	Northeast:	International:
Y					

AMSC CORPORATION

www.amsc.com

Industry Group Code: 335929

Energy/Fuel:	Other Technologies:	Electrical Products:	Electronics:	Transportation:	Other:	
Biofuels:	Irrigation:	Lighting/LEDs:	Computers:	Car Sharing:	Recycling:	
Batteries/Storage:	Nanotech:	Waste Heat:	Sensors:	Electric Vehicles:	Engineering:	Y
Solar:	Biotech:	Smart Meters:	Software: Y	Natural Gas Fuel:	Consulting:	Y
Wind:	Water Tech./Treatment:	Machinery: Y			Investing:	
Fuel Cells:	Ceramics:				Chemicals:	

TYPES OF BUSINESS:

Superconductivity Products
Power Electronic Switches
SMES Systems
Electric Motors & Generators
Superconducting Materials
Electric Transmission Cables
Wind Turbine Design

BRANDS/DIVISIONS/AFFILIATES:

American Superconductor Corp.
Windtec
PowerModule
D-VAR
Amperium
AMSC India
AMSC Korea
Switch Engineering Oy (The)

CONTACTS: *Note: Officers with more than one job title may be intentionally listed here more than once.*

Daniel McGahn, CEO
Daniel McGahn, Pres.
David Henry, CFO/Sr. VP
Timothy Poor, Exec. VP-Sales
James Maquire, Sr. VP-Projects, Eng. & Grid Segment
Angelo Santamaria, Sr. VP-Global Mfg. Oper.
Susan Dicecco, Sr. VP-Corp. Admin.
John Powell, General Counsel/VP
Timothy Poor, Exec. VP-Bus. Dev. & Wind Segment
Jason Fredette, Managing Dir.-Corp. Comm.
David Henry, Treas.
Charles W. Stankiewicz, Exec. VP/Gen. Mgr.-AMSC Power Systems
Gregory J. Yurek, Chmn.

Phone: 978-842-3000	**Fax:** 978-842-3024
Toll-Free:	
Address: 64 Jackson Rd., Devens, MA 01434-4020 US	

GROWTH PLANS/SPECIAL FEATURES:

AMSC Corporation, formerly American Superconductor Corp., is an energy technologies company offering programmable power electronic converters and high temperature superconductors (HTS) wires. The firm operates in two segments: Wind and Grid. The Wind segment, operating through the Windtec brand, licenses wind turbine designs, provides advanced power electronics and control systems and offers customer support to wind turbine manufacturers. The Grid segment offers transmission planning services to enable electric utilities and renewable energy project developers to connect, transmit and distribute power efficiently, reliably and affordably. AMSC's PowerModule power converters are based on proprietary software and hardware combinations and are used in a broad array of applications, including D-VAR branded grid interconnection and voltage control systems, as well as wind turbine core electrical components and electrical control systems. Its Amperium wire is laminated to meet the electrical and mechanical performance requirements of widely varying end-use applications, including power cables and fault current limiters for the Grid market and generators for the Wind market. Based in Massachusetts, the company maintains operations in Austria, India, China, Korea and the U.S. and sales and service support centers in Germany, Singapore and Australia. Through AMSC India, it serves the growing Indian wind energy and power grid markets; while AMSC Korea serves similar needs in that country. In March 2011, AMSC entered into a definitive agreement to acquire The Switch Engineering Oy, headquartered in Vantaa, Finland. The Switch designs, manufactures and markets wind power products, including permanent magnet generators and power converter systems, as well as grid products such as commercial and small utility-scale solar inverters.

Employees are offered medical, dental, life and AD&D insurance; long-term care insurance; a 401(k); an employee stock purchase plan; short- and long-term disability coverage; tuition reimbursement; a flexible spending plan; an employee assistance program; and discounted rates on wholesale club memberships.

FINANCIALS: Sales and profits are in thousands of dollars—add 000 to get the full amount. 2011 Note: Financial information for 2011 was not available for all companies at press time.

2011 Sales: $286,603	2011 Profits: $-186,284	**U.S. Stock Ticker:** AMSC
2010 Sales: $315,955	2010 Profits: $16,248	**Int'l Ticker:**
2009 Sales: $182,755	2009 Profits: $-16,635	Int'l Exchange:
2008 Sales: $112,396	2008 Profits: $-25,447	Employees: 848 Fiscal Year Ends: 3/31
2007 Sales: $52,183	2007 Profits: $-36,675	Parent Company:

SALARIES/BENEFITS:

Pension Plan:	ESOP Stock Plan:	Profit Sharing:	Top Exec. Salary: $600,000	Bonus: $
Savings Plan: Y	Stock Purch. Plan: Y		Second Exec. Salary: $330,000	Bonus: $4,976

OTHER THOUGHTS:

Apparent Women Officers or Directors: 1
Hot Spot for Advancement for Women/Minorities:

LOCATIONS: ("Y" = Yes)

West:	Southwest:	Midwest:	Southeast:	Northeast:	International:
		Y		Y	Y

AMYRIS BIOTECHNOLOGIES INC

www.amyrisbiotech.com

Industry Group Code: 325193

Energy/Fuel:		Other Technologies:		Electrical Products:	Electronics:	Transportation:	Other:	
Biofuels:	Y	Irrigation:		Lighting/LEDs:	Computers:	Car Sharing:	Recycling:	
Batteries/Storage:		Nanotech:		Waste Heat:	Sensors:	Electric Vehicles:	Engineering:	
Solar:		Biotech:	Y	Smart Meters:	Software:	Natural Gas Fuel:	Consulting:	
Wind:		Water Tech./Treatment:		Machinery:			Investing:	
Fuel Cells:		Ceramics:					Chemicals:	Y

TYPES OF BUSINESS:

Ethanol Production
Artemisinin
Renewable Fuels
Biodiesel
Biochemicals

BRANDS/DIVISIONS/AFFILIATES:

Amyris Fuels LLC
Amyris Brasil SA
Biofene
No Compromise Fuels
US Venture Inc

CONTACTS: Note: Officers with more than one job title may be intentionally listed here more than once.

John Melo, CEO
Mario Portela, COO
Jeryl L. Hilleman, CFO
Jim Richardson, Sr. VP-Vertical Markets & Sales
Jack D. Newman, Sr. VP-Research
Neil Renninger, CTO
Jeff Lievense, Sr. VP-Process Dev. & Mfg.
Tamara Tompkins, General Counsel/Sr. VP
Joel Cherry, Sr. VP-Research Programs & Oper.
Peter Boynton, Chief Commercial Officer
Paulo Diniz, CEO-Amyris Brasil
Joel Velasco, Sr. VP-External Rel.

Phone: 510-450-0761	Fax: 510-225-2645
Toll-Free:	
Address: 5885 Hollis St., Ste. 100, Emeryville, CA 94608 US	

GROWTH PLANS/SPECIAL FEATURES:

Amyris Biotechnologies, Inc. specializes in developing renewable products for both the healthcare and energy sectors. Founded in 2003, Amyris began with the desire to find and provide a reliable, affordable source of artemisinin, an extract from the Chinese Sweet Wormwood plant used in the treatment of Malaria. Treatment of patients with Artemisinin-based Combination Therapies (ACTs) is currently expensive, due to the difficulty of extracting the compound. Amyris likewise develops renewable, cost-effective chemicals with a wide scope of applicability. The renewable farnesene molecule, Biofene, is the basis for a number of applications including emollients, flavors and fragrances, surfactants, isoprene, industrial and automotive oils and lubricants. The firm also runs a wholly-owned subsidiary, Amyris Fuels, LLC, with the goal of developing and distributing renewable, No Compromise fuels when they become available in the U.S. No Compromise fuels are designed to be drop-in fuels, offering environmental benefits while meeting engine and distribution infrastructure requirements. The company generates revenue to support its development enterprise by selling third-party ethanol to wholesale customers in the southeastern U.S. In addition, Amyris Brasil S.A. is a majority-owned subsidiary investigating renewable applications for Brazilian sugarcane, such as a supplement or replacement for petroleum-based diesel fuel. The firm is also exploring a sustainable alternative to current, petroleum-based jet fuel. In March 2011, the firm and U.S. Venture, Inc. announced plans to create a joint venture for the production, marketing and distribution of finished lubricants for the North American market.

Employee benefits include comprehensive medical, dental and vision insurance; flexible spending account plans; life and AD&D insurance; 401(k) plans; and educational reimbursement. Additional perks include an on-site gym and yoga classes.

FINANCIALS: Sales and profits are in thousands of dollars—add 000 to get the full amount. 2011 Note: Financial information for 2011 was not available for all companies at press time.

2011 Sales: $	2011 Profits: $	**U.S. Stock Ticker: AMRS**
2010 Sales: $80,311	2010 Profits: $-82,790	**Int'l Ticker:**
2009 Sales: $64,608	2009 Profits: $-64,800	Int'l Exchange:
2008 Sales: $13,892	2008 Profits: $-42,336	Employees: 346 Fiscal Year Ends: 12/31
2007 Sales: $	2007 Profits: $	Parent Company:

SALARIES/BENEFITS:

Pension Plan:	ESOP Stock Plan:	Profit Sharing:	Top Exec. Salary: $500,000	Bonus: $424,048
Savings Plan: Y	Stock Purch. Plan: Y		Second Exec. Salary: $360,000	Bonus: $100,000

OTHER THOUGHTS:

Apparent Women Officers or Directors: 3
Hot Spot for Advancement for Women/Minorities: Y

LOCATIONS: ("Y" = Yes)

West:	Southwest:	Midwest:	Southeast:	Northeast:	International:
Y					Y

Sales, profits and employees may be estimates. Financial information, benefits and other data can change quickly and may vary from those stated here.

APPLIED MATERIALS INC

www.appliedmaterials.com

Industry Group Code: 333295

Energy/Fuel:	Other Technologies:		Electrical Products:	Electronics:		Transportation:	Other:	
Biofuels:	Irrigation:		Lighting/LEDs:	Computers:	Y	Car Sharing:	Recycling:	
Batteries/Storage:	Nanotech:	Y	Waste Heat:	Sensors:		Electric Vehicles:	Engineering:	Y
Solar:	Biotech:		Smart Meters:	Software:	Y	Natural Gas Fuel:	Consulting:	
Wind:	Water Tech./Treatment:		Machinery:				Investing:	
Fuel Cells:	Ceramics:						Chemicals:	

TYPES OF BUSINESS:

Semiconductor Manufacturing Equipment
LCD Display Technology Equipment
Automation Software
Energy Generation & Conversion Technologies

BRANDS/DIVISIONS/AFFILIATES:

AKT Inc
Varian Semiconductor Equipment Associates Inc

CONTACTS: Note: Officers with more than one job title may be intentionally listed here more than once.

Michael R. Splinter, CEO
Michael R. Splinter, Pres.
George S. Davis, CFO/Exec. VP
Mary Humiston, Sr. VP-Global Human Resources
Ron Kifer, CIO/VP
Omkaram Nalamasu, CTO
Joseph J. Sweeney, General Counsel/Corp. Sec./Sr. VP
Joseph Flanagan, Sr. VP-Worldwide Oper.
Chris Bowers, VP-Corp. Initiatives
Tom Edman, VP/Gen. Mgr.-Display Bus. Group
Charlie Pappis, VP/Gen. Mgr.-Applied Global Svcs.
Randhio Thakur, Exec. VP/Gen. Mgr.-Silicon Systems
Mark R. Pinto, Exec. VP/Gen. Mgr.-Energy & Environmental
Michael R. Splinter, Chmn.
Joseph Flanagan, Sr. VP-Supply Chain

Phone: 408-727-5555	Fax: 408-748-9943
Toll-Free:	
Address: 3050 Bowers Ave., Santa Clara, CA 95054-3299 US	

GROWTH PLANS/SPECIAL FEATURES:

Applied Materials, Inc. (AMI), a global leader in the semiconductor industry, provides manufacturing equipment, services and software to the global semiconductor, flat panel display, solar photovoltaic (PV) and related industries. AMI operates in four segments: Silicon Systems Group; Applied Global Services; Display; and Energy and Environmental Solutions. The Silicon Systems Group develops, manufactures and sells a range of manufacturing equipment used to fabricate semiconductor chips or integrated circuits. The company offers systems that perform most of the primary processes used in chip fabrication. The Applied Global Services segment provides products and services designed to improve the performance and productivity and reduce environmental impact of the fabrication operations of semiconductor, LCD and solar PV manufacturers. Its services encompass four primary components: fabrication services, automation systems, sub-fabrication systems and abatement control systems. The Display segment, which operates through AKT, Inc., designs, manufactures, sells and services equipment to fabricate thin film transistor LCDs for televisions, computer displays and other consumer-oriented electronic applications. The Energy and Environmental Solutions segment provides manufacturing solutions for the generation and conservation of energy. AMI's products and services utilize nanomanufacturing technology, or the production of ultra-small structures, including the engineering of thin layers of film onto substrates. During 2010, Samsung Electronics Co. and Taiwan Semiconductor Manufacturing Company together accounted for approximately 25% of AMI's revenue. In May 2011, the company sold Rhetech and Semitool Austria GmbH to OEM Group, Inc. In November 2011, the firm acquired Varian Semiconductor Equipment Associates, Inc. for $4.2 billion.

Employees are offered medical insurance; flexible spending accounts; adoption benefits; an employee assistance program; health appraisals; health and fitness education; a 401(k) plan; a stock purchase plan; credit union membership; and tuition reimbursement.

FINANCIALS: Sales and profits are in thousands of dollars—add 000 to get the full amount. 2011 Note: Financial information for 2011 was not available for all companies at press time.

2011 Sales: $10,517,000	2011 Profits: $1,926,000	U.S. Stock Ticker: AMAT
2010 Sales: $9,548,667	2010 Profits: $937,866	Int'l Ticker:
2009 Sales: $5,013,607	2009 Profits: $-305,327	Int'l Exchange:
2008 Sales: $8,129,240	2008 Profits: $960,746	Employees: 12,973 Fiscal Year Ends: 10/31
2007 Sales: $9,734,856	2007 Profits: $1,710,196	Parent Company:

SALARIES/BENEFITS:

Pension Plan:	ESOP Stock Plan:	Profit Sharing:	Top Exec. Salary: $972,462	Bonus: $3,400,000
Savings Plan: Y	Stock Purch. Plan: Y		Second Exec. Salary: $565,961	Bonus: $1,400,000

OTHER THOUGHTS:

Apparent Women Officers or Directors: 2
Hot Spot for Advancement for Women/Minorities: Y

LOCATIONS: ("Y" = Yes)

West:	Southwest:	Midwest:	Southeast:	Northeast:	International:
Y	Y				Y

Sales, profits and employees may be estimates. Financial information, benefits and other data can change quickly and may vary from those stated here.

APTWATER INC

www.aptwater.com

Industry Group Code: 924110

Energy/Fuel:	Other Technologies:		Electrical Products:	Electronics:	Transportation:	Other:
Biofuels:	Irrigation:		Lighting/LEDs:	Computers:	Car Sharing:	Recycling:
Batteries/Storage:	Nanotech:		Waste Heat:	Sensors:	Electric Vehicles:	Engineering:
Solar:	Biotech:		Smart Meters:	Software:	Natural Gas Fuel:	Consulting:
Wind:	Water Tech./Treatment:	Y	Machinery:			Investing:
Fuel Cells:	Ceramics:					Chemicals:

TYPES OF BUSINESS:

Water Treatment

BRANDS/DIVISIONS/AFFILIATES:

HiPOx
PulseOx
Rochem AG

CONTACTS: Note: Officers with more than one job title may be intentionally listed here more than once.

David Stanton, CEO
Peter Bokor, COO
David Stanton, Pres.
Terry Applebury, CTO
Mark Minter, Pres., APTwater Services, LLC

Phone: 562-661-4999	**Fax:**
Toll-Free:	
Address: 111 W. Ocean Blvd., Ste. 1980, Long Beach, CA 90802 US	

GROWTH PLANS/SPECIAL FEATURES:

APTwater, Inc. is a water treatment technologies firm developing and marketing products to allow customers to efficiently treat and reuse water with minimal to no waste by-products created. The firm's proprietary HiPOx technology uses clean chemical reactions to solve a wide array of customer's water treatment concerns, including engineering support, professional management and providing cost-effective project delivery solutions. APTwater primarily addresses water treatment solutions for drinking water, water reuse and remediation. HiPOx offers a cost-effective, waste free solution to color, taste and drinking water odor problems. Additionally, the technology's chemical oxidation process effectively destroys endocrine disrupting chemicals (EDCs) and other compounds, allowing for environmentally friendly water reuse. The firm's HiPOx and PulseOx systems have been installed at over 120 environmental remediation sites worldwide. The systems utilize Advanced Oxidation Process chemistry to kill organic contaminants without creating waste residuals. The company's operations & maintenance teams provide full contract facility management services, including water facility and distribution, wastewater facility and collection and storm water systems operation and maintenance; regulatory compliance; billing and collection; operations policy development and training; QA/QC and lab testing; and asset management. The firm markets its water solutions, either directly or through representatives and key alliance partners, to companies in the municipal, industrial and environmental sectors that are seeking to reduce expenditures and to improve their sustainability. In November 2011, the firm announced its merger with Rochem AG, a European advanced water technology firm.

FINANCIALS: Sales and profits are in thousands of dollars—add 000 to get the full amount. 2011 Note: Financial information for 2011 was not available for all companies at press time.

2011 Sales: $	2011 Profits: $	**U.S. Stock Ticker:** Private
2010 Sales: $	2010 Profits: $	**Int'l Ticker:**
2009 Sales: $	2009 Profits: $	Int'l Exchange:
2008 Sales: $	2008 Profits: $	Employees: Fiscal Year Ends:
2007 Sales: $	2007 Profits: $	Parent Company:

SALARIES/BENEFITS:

Pension Plan:	ESOP Stock Plan:	Profit Sharing:	Top Exec. Salary: $	Bonus: $
Savings Plan:	Stock Purch. Plan:		Second Exec. Salary: $	Bonus: $

OTHER THOUGHTS:

Apparent Women Officers or Directors:
Hot Spot for Advancement for Women/Minorities:

LOCATIONS: ("Y" = Yes)

West:	Southwest:	Midwest:	Southeast:	Northeast:	International:
Y					

AQWISE

Industry Group Code: 924110

www.aqwise.com

Energy/Fuel:	Other Technologies:		Electrical Products:	Electronics:	Transportation:	Other:	
Biofuels:	Irrigation:		Lighting/LEDs:	Computers:	Car Sharing:	Recycling:	
Batteries/Storage:	Nanotech:		Waste Heat:	Sensors:	Electric Vehicles:	Engineering:	
Solar:	Biotech:		Smart Meters:	Software:	Natural Gas Fuel:	Consulting:	Y
Wind:	Water Tech./Treatment:	Y	Machinery:			Investing:	
Fuel Cells:	Ceramics:					Chemicals:	

TYPES OF BUSINESS:

Wastewater Treatment Technologies

BRANDS/DIVISIONS/AFFILIATES:

Attached Growth Airlift Reactor (AGAR)
AGAR MBBR
AGAR IFAS
AGAR MBBR+AS
Aqwise Compact Unit

CONTACTS: *Note: Officers with more than one job title may be intentionally listed here more than once.*

Eytan Levy, CEO
Eytan Levy, Pres.
Ron Shechter, CTO

Phone: 972-9-959-1901	**Fax:** 972-9-959-1903
Toll-Free:	
Address: 8 Hamenofim St., Ofek House, Herzliya, 46733 Israel	

GROWTH PLANS/SPECIAL FEATURES:

Aqwise is an Israeli company that develops and implements wastewater treatment solutions for the municipal and industrial markets. The firms advanced technology for the treatment of wastewater is the Attached Growth Airlift Reactor (AGAR) process. This patented AGAR process, if implemented, can increase treatment capacity and improve nutrient removal capabilities, all without increasing tankage. Aqwise offers four products: the AGAR Moving Bed Bio Reactor (MBBR), the AGAR Integrated Fixed film Activated Sludge (IFAS), the AGAR Moving Bed Bioreactor followed by Activated Sludge treatment (MBBR+AS) and the Aqwise Compact Unit. AGAR MBBR is a treatment that provides organic carbon removal through a bio-film process. AGAR IFAS utilizes both the biomass carrier's bio-film and the biomass suspended in the activated sludge, which creates a nitrifying bio-film that aids in the oxidation of ammonium compounds. The AGAR MBBR+AS combines both fixed film and suspended biomass technologies, treating the wastewater first in the MBBR reactor followed by the conventional activated sludge process. The Aqwise Compact Unit is a complete wastewater treatment plant within a standard freight container. Additional services offered by Aqwise include full and ongoing process support, process design, expert consultation, financing and pilot studies conducted by the research & development (R&D) team.

FINANCIALS: Sales and profits are in thousands of dollars—add 000 to get the full amount. 2011 Note: Financial information for 2011 was not available for all companies at press time.

2011 Sales: $	2011 Profits: $	**U.S. Stock Ticker: Private**
2010 Sales: $	2010 Profits: $	**Int'l Ticker:**
2009 Sales: $	2009 Profits: $	Int'l Exchange:
2008 Sales: $	2008 Profits: $	Employees: Fiscal Year Ends:
2007 Sales: $	2007 Profits: $	Parent Company:

SALARIES/BENEFITS:

Pension Plan:	ESOP Stock Plan:	Profit Sharing:	Top Exec. Salary: $	Bonus: $
Savings Plan:	Stock Purch. Plan:		Second Exec. Salary: $	Bonus: $

OTHER THOUGHTS:

Apparent Women Officers or Directors:
Hot Spot for Advancement for Women/Minorities:

LOCATIONS: ("Y" = Yes)

West:	Southwest:	Midwest:	Southeast:	Northeast:	International:
					Y

ARCADIA BIOSCIENCES INC

www.arcadiabio.com

Industry Group Code: 11511

Energy/Fuel:	Other Technologies:		Electrical Products:	Electronics:	Transportation:	Other:	
Biofuels:	Irrigation:		Lighting/LEDs:	Computers:	Car Sharing:	Recycling:	
Batteries/Storage:	Nanotech:		Waste Heat:	Sensors:	Electric Vehicles:	Engineering:	
Solar:	Biotech:	Y	Smart Meters:	Software:	Natural Gas Fuel:	Consulting:	
Wind:	Water Tech./Treatment:		Machinery:			Investing:	
Fuel Cells:	Ceramics:					Chemicals:	Y

TYPES OF BUSINESS:

Agricultural-Based Technologies
Environment Health Technologies
Human Health Technologies

BRANDS/DIVISIONS/AFFILIATES:

TILLING
SONOVA 400

CONTACTS: Note: Officers with more than one job title may be intentionally listed here more than once.

Eric Rey, CEO
Eric Rey, Pres.
Vic Knauf, Chief Scientific Officer
Steve Brandwein, VP-Admin.
Wendy Neal, Chief Legal Officer/VP
Roger Salameh, VP-Bus. Dev., Agriculture
Jeff Bergau, Media Rel.
Steve Brandwein, VP-Finance
Frank Flider, VP-Bus. Dev., Nutrition
Don Emlay, Dir.-Regulatory Affairs

Phone: 530-756-7077	Fax: 530-756-7027
Toll-Free:	
Address: 202 Cousteau Place, Ste. 200, Davis, CA 95618 US	

GROWTH PLANS/SPECIAL FEATURES:

Arcadia Biosciences, Inc. specializes in developing agricultural technologies to benefit the environment and human health. Through advanced breeding techniques, genetic screening and genetic engineering, it develops plants with greater yield ratios and increased climate tolerance. Its crop portfolio includes Nitrogen Use Efficient (NUE) crops, Water Use Efficient (WUE) crops and salt tolerant plants. Arcadia's NUE project seeks to minimize the amount of nitrogen fertilizer required in crop production by 50% to 60%. WUE plants are being developed to offer increased yield, while requiring lower fresh water levels. Its salt tolerance project is developing plants able to produce normal quality and yields in high saline conditions, with a variety of crop applications including corn, rice, alfalfa, soybeans, turf, wheat and vegetables. The plants are also engineered to bind excess salt into the plant, thus reducing an area's saline levels over time. The company's human health project has two current areas of focus: GLA safflower oil and extended shelf-life produce. The GLA safflower oil project is breeding new varieties of safflower whose seeds will have as much as 40% GLA (gamma linolenic acid), an omega-6 fatty acid believed to have therapeutic benefits, which could be utilized to manufacture supplements, functional foods and nutraceuticals. Its extended shelf-life produce project uses the firm's proprietary TILLING breeding technology to discover new genetic varieties of tomatoes, lettuce, melons and strawberries. Other Arcadia projects include a research partnership with Washington State University focused on the production of reduced gluten wheat for individuals with Celiac disease (an autoimmune disorder triggered by glutens found in wheat). In the recent past, the firm completed the first commercial production of SONOVA 400, a 400 milligram GLA-content Safflower oil.

FINANCIALS: Sales and profits are in thousands of dollars—add 000 to get the full amount. 2011 Note: Financial information for 2011 was not available for all companies at press time.

2011 Sales: $	2011 Profits: $	**U.S. Stock Ticker:** Private	
2010 Sales: $	2010 Profits: $	**Int'l Ticker:**	
2009 Sales: $	2009 Profits: $	Int'l Exchange:	
2008 Sales: $	2008 Profits: $	Employees:	Fiscal Year Ends:
2007 Sales: $	2007 Profits: $	Parent Company:	

SALARIES/BENEFITS:

Pension Plan:	ESOP Stock Plan:	Profit Sharing:	Top Exec. Salary: $	Bonus: $
Savings Plan: Y	Stock Purch. Plan:		Second Exec. Salary: $	Bonus: $

OTHER THOUGHTS:

Apparent Women Officers or Directors: 2
Hot Spot for Advancement for Women/Minorities:

LOCATIONS: ("Y" = Yes)

West:	Southwest:	Midwest:	Southeast:	Northeast:	International:
Y					

AROTECH CORPORATION

www.arotech.com

Industry Group Code: 332

Energy/Fuel:		Other Technologies:		Electrical Products:		Electronics:		Transportation:		Other:	
Biofuels:		Irrigation:		Lighting/LEDs:		Computers:		Car Sharing:		Recycling:	
Batteries/Storage:	Y	Nanotech:		Waste Heat:		Sensors:		Electric Vehicles:		Engineering:	Y
Solar:		Biotech:		Smart Meters:		Software:	Y	Natural Gas Fuel:		Consulting:	Y
Wind:		Water Tech./Treatment:		Machinery:	Y					Investing:	
Fuel Cells:		Ceramics:								Chemicals:	

TYPES OF BUSINESS:

Mobile Electric Power Technology
Zinc-Air Batteries
Armor & Armored Vehicles
Defense & Safety Products
Training & Simulation Products

BRANDS/DIVISIONS/AFFILIATES:

MDT Protective Industries Ltd
MDT Armor Corporation
Armour of America
Realtime Technologies Inc
FAAC Inc
Epsilor Electronic Industries Ltd
Electric Fuel Battery Corporation
Concord Safety Solutions Pvt Ltd

CONTACTS: Note: Officers with more than one job title may be intentionally listed here more than once.

Robert S. Ehrlich, CEO
Steven Esses, COO
Steven Esses, Pres.
Thomas J. Paup, CFO
Jonathan Whartman, Sr. VP-Mktg.
Yaakov Har-Oz, General Counsel/VP/Corp. Sec.
Thomas J. Paup, VP-Finance
William Graham, VP-Gov't Affairs
Robert S. Ehrlich, Chmn.

Phone:	Fax: 734-761-5368
Toll-Free: 800-281-0356	
Address: 1229 Oak Valley Dr., Ann Arbor, MI 48108 US	

GROWTH PLANS/SPECIAL FEATURES:

Arotech Corporation is a defense and security products and services company active in three sectors: high-level armoring; interactive simulation and training; and batteries and charging systems. The company's armoring division specializes in manufacturing military armored combat vehicles based on commercial platforms and up-armoring civilian SUVs, buses and vans through its subsidiaries MDT Protective Industries, Ltd., located in Lod, Israel, and MDT Armor Corporation, located in Auburn, Alabama. It also provides ballistic armor kits for rotary and fixed wing aircraft and marine armor under the Armour of America brand. Additionally, the firm holds a 26% interest in Concord Safety Solutions Pvt. Ltd., an Indian company it jointly established with an Indian vehicle manufacturing company and an Indian armor materials company. Arotech's interactive simulation and training division, operating through FAAC, Inc. and Realtime Technologies, Inc., offers simulators, systems engineering and software products to the U.S. military, government and private enterprises. It also provides specialized use-of-force training for police, security personnel and the military under the trade name IES Interactive Training. Arotech's battery and power systems division manufactures and sells lithium and Zinc-Air batteries for defense and security products as well as other military applications. Through Epsilor Electronic Industries, Ltd., the company develops and sells lithium batteries and chargers to the military and private defense industry in the Middle East, Europe and Asia. Through Electric Fuel Battery Corporation, it produces Zinc-Air batteries, rechargeable batteries and battery chargers for the military. Zinc-Air batteries are lighter in weight and possess higher energy density than lithium-based batteries. Moreover, the company produces water-activated lifejacket lights for commercial aviation and marine applications through Electric Fuel, Ltd. Arotech relies heavily on sales to the U.S. military, which accounted for 42% of the company's revenues during 2010.

FINANCIALS: Sales and profits are in thousands of dollars—add 000 to get the full amount. 2011 Note: Financial information for 2011 was not available for all companies at press time.

2011 Sales: $	2011 Profits: $	**U.S. Stock Ticker: ARTX**	
2010 Sales: $73,741	2010 Profits: $- 917	**Int'l Ticker:**	
2009 Sales: $74,534	2009 Profits: $-3,054	Int'l Exchange:	
2008 Sales: $68,949	2008 Profits: $-3,838	Employees: 418	Fiscal Year Ends: 12/31
2007 Sales: $57,719	2007 Profits: $-3,501	Parent Company:	

SALARIES/BENEFITS:

Pension Plan:	ESOP Stock Plan:	Profit Sharing:	Top Exec. Salary: $400,000	Bonus: $265,000
Savings Plan:	Stock Purch. Plan:		Second Exec. Salary: $179,776	Bonus: $89,900

OTHER THOUGHTS:

Apparent Women Officers or Directors:
Hot Spot for Advancement for Women/Minorities:

LOCATIONS: ("Y" = Yes)

West:	Southwest:	Midwest:	Southeast:	Northeast:	International:
Y		Y	Y	Y	Y

ASIA ENVIRONMENT HOLDINGS LTD

www.asiaenv.com

Industry Group Code: 562

Energy/Fuel:	Other Technologies:		Electrical Products:	Electronics:	Transportation:	Other:	
Biofuels:	Irrigation:		Lighting/LEDs:	Computers:	Car Sharing:	Recycling:	
Batteries/Storage:	Nanotech:		Waste Heat:	Sensors:	Electric Vehicles:	Engineering:	Y
Solar:	Biotech:		Smart Meters:	Software:	Natural Gas Fuel:	Consulting:	Y
Wind:	Water Tech./Treatment:	Y	Machinery:			Investing:	Y
Fuel Cells:	Ceramics:					Chemicals:	

TYPES OF BUSINESS:

Water & Wastewater Treatment

BRANDS/DIVISIONS/AFFILIATES:

Penyao
Quanxi
Yixing P&S
JSPV Design
JSPV Research
JSPV Contract

CONTACTS: Note: Officers with more than one job title may be intentionally listed here more than once.

Wang Chung, CEO
Huang Zhengxin, COO
Chew Kok Liang, Sec.
Yang Yung Kang, Controller
Yao Maohong, Exec. Dir.
Zhou Guoya, Head-Design
Shirley Tan Sey Liy, Sec.
Wang Chung, Chmn.

Phone: 65-6309-7488	**Fax:** 65-6309-7480

Toll-Free:

Address: 65 Chulia St. 39-08 OCBC Center, Singapore, 049513 Singapore

GROWTH PLANS/SPECIAL FEATURES:

Asia Environment Holdings Ltd. is an investment holding company in Singapore focused on integrated water and wastewater treatment. The company operates primarily in China under the names Penyao and Quanxi. Its business is divided into three segments: turnkey projects and services; manufacturing; and build-operate-transfer projects. Turnkey projects and services provides consulting; design; production; construction and engineering; installation; commissioning and after sales services for treatment systems, as well as research and development for wastewater treatment techniques and equipment. The manufacturing segment is involved in the manufacture, sale and installation of equipment for treatment systems. The Build-operate-transfer projects division builds, operates and invests in water and wastewater treatment facilities for a set period of 20-30 years. These operating segments are carried out by four subsidiaries: JSPV Contract, in charge of contracting, building, installing and operating water and wastewater treatment projects; Yixing P&S, which customizes, produces and sells environmental protection equipment; JSPV Design, which designs and develops environmental protection projects and equipment; and JSPV Research, a research and development institution currently involved in creating municipal sewage treatment and recovery technology. In September 2011, the firm announced the sale of its 25% equity stake in Pizhou Water Holdings Pte. Ltd. to Lionguard Investments Limited for $450,000.

FINANCIALS: Sales and profits are in thousands of dollars—add 000 to get the full amount. 2011 Note: Financial information for 2011 was not available for all companies at press time.

2011 Sales: $	2011 Profits: $	**U.S. Stock Ticker:**
2010 Sales: $78,869	2010 Profits: $-2,076	**Int'l Ticker: A58.SI**
2009 Sales: $92,100	2009 Profits: $5,120	Int'l Exchange: Singapore-SIN
2008 Sales: $58,910	2008 Profits: $7,940	Employees: Fiscal Year Ends: 12/31
2007 Sales: $	2007 Profits: $	Parent Company:

SALARIES/BENEFITS:

Pension Plan:	ESOP Stock Plan:	Profit Sharing:	Top Exec. Salary: $	Bonus: $
Savings Plan:	Stock Purch. Plan:		Second Exec. Salary: $	Bonus: $

OTHER THOUGHTS:

Apparent Women Officers or Directors: 1
Hot Spot for Advancement for Women/Minorities:

LOCATIONS: ("Y" = Yes)

West:	Southwest:	Midwest:	Southeast:	Northeast:	International:
					Y

ATTERO RECYCLING

Industry Group Code: 562920

www.attero.in

Energy/Fuel:	Other Technologies:	Electrical Products:	Electronics:	Transportation:	Other:	
Biofuels:	Irrigation:	Lighting/LEDs:	Computers:	Car Sharing:	Recycling:	Y
Batteries/Storage:	Nanotech:	Waste Heat:	Sensors:	Electric Vehicles:	Engineering:	
Solar:	Biotech:	Smart Meters:	Software:	Natural Gas Fuel:	Consulting:	
Wind:	Water Tech./Treatment:	Machinery:			Investing:	
Fuel Cells:	Ceramics:				Chemicals:	

TYPES OF BUSINESS:

Electronic Waste Recycling

BRANDS/DIVISIONS/AFFILIATES:

CONTACTS: *Note: Officers with more than one job title may be intentionally listed here more than once.*

Nitin Gupta, CEO
Saurabh Gupta, CFO
Arijit Das, VP-Mktg. & Sourcing
Praveen Bhargava, Dir.-R&D
Pranamesh Das, Dir.-Tech.
DB Chhetri, Head-Admin. & Security
Lakshmi Pillai Gupta, VP-Supply Chain Solutions
Pawandeep Singh Bawa, Head-Sourcing West
Lloyd Sanford, Pres., Supply Chain Solutions

Phone: 91-120-4087100	Fax: 91-120-4087101
Toll-Free: 800-419-3283	
Address: H-59, Sector 63, Nodia, UP 201301 India	

GROWTH PLANS/SPECIAL FEATURES:

Attero Recycling is an Indian end-to-end recycler of electronic waste (e-waste). E-waste is obsolete electronics, components and accessories that have been discarded. E-waste is a concern because it is a rapidly growing waste stream and could potentially contain toxic materials such as mercury, lead and cadmium. Being an end-to-end recycler, Attero both picks up the e-waste, assuring complete data security, and processes it through its state of the art, zero dumping technology treatment plant in Roorkee, India. At the recycling plant e-waste is dismantled and treated in the metallurgical unit to extract maximum value. To insure the destruction and security of data contained within the e-waste, the entire data destruction process is recorded and can be viewed by the customer. The plant in Roorkee is spread over 100,000 square feet and houses an automated facility designed specifically for e-waste recycling. Additionally, all hazardous materials are disposed of through the Common Hazardous Waste Treatment, Storage & Disposal Facility as authorized by the pollution control board. Attero has offices in Noida, Bengaluru and Mumbai, India.

FINANCIALS: Sales and profits are in thousands of dollars—add 000 to get the full amount. 2011 Note: Financial information for 2011 was not available for all companies at press time.

2011 Sales: $	2011 Profits: $	**U.S. Stock Ticker: Private**
2010 Sales: $	2010 Profits: $	**Int'l Ticker:**
2009 Sales: $	2009 Profits: $	Int'l Exchange:
2008 Sales: $	2008 Profits: $	Employees: Fiscal Year Ends:
2007 Sales: $	2007 Profits: $	Parent Company:

SALARIES/BENEFITS:

Pension Plan:	ESOP Stock Plan:	Profit Sharing:	Top Exec. Salary: $	Bonus: $
Savings Plan:	Stock Purch. Plan:		Second Exec. Salary: $	Bonus: $

OTHER THOUGHTS:

Apparent Women Officers or Directors: 1
Hot Spot for Advancement for Women/Minorities:

LOCATIONS: ("Y" = Yes)

West:	Southwest:	Midwest:	Southeast:	Northeast:	International:
					Y

AUTOMOTIVE ENERGY SUPPLY CORPORATION (AESC)
www.eco-aesc.com
Industry Group Code: 33591

Energy/Fuel:		Other Technologies:		Electrical Products:		Electronics:		Transportation:		Other:	
Biofuels:		Irrigation:		Lighting/LEDs:		Computers:		Car Sharing:		Recycling:	
Batteries/Storage:	Y	Nanotech:		Waste Heat:		Sensors:		Electric Vehicles:		Engineering:	
Solar:		Biotech:		Smart Meters:		Software:		Natural Gas Fuel:		Consulting:	
Wind:		Water Tech./Treatment:		Machinery:						Investing:	
Fuel Cells:		Ceramics:								Chemicals:	

TYPES OF BUSINESS:
Batteries for Electric Automobiles

BRANDS/DIVISIONS/AFFILIATES:
NEC Corporation
Nissan Motor Co Ltd

CONTACTS: *Note: Officers with more than one job title may be intentionally listed here more than once.*
Masahiko Otsuka, Pres.

Phone: 046-252-3211	Fax:
Toll-Free:	
Address: 10-1 Hironodai 2-chome, Zama-shi, 228-8052 Japan	

GROWTH PLANS/SPECIAL FEATURES:
Automotive Energy Supply Corporation (AESC), a joint venture between Nissan Motor Co. Ltd. and NEC Corporation, is a manufacturer of advanced lithium-ion battery technology. AESC's primary operating divisions, development and manufacturing, conduct research and development and produce rechargeable lithium-ion batteries in laminate cells, modules and packs that are distributed to original equipment manufacturers (OEMs) and automotive parts suppliers around the world. The company's products include lithium-ion cells (for battery electric vehicles); high power cell (for hybrid electric vehicles); high energy modules (for battery electric vehicles); high power modules (for hybrid electric vehicles); high energy battery packs (for battery electric vehicles); and high power battery packs (for hybrid electric vehicles). Some recent applications for the firm's products include a battery-powered forklift manufactured by Nissan, as well as several Nissan-branded electric vehicles (EVs), which operate solely on battery power; and hybrid vehicles, which use an electric motor and battery pack to augment a gasoline engine. Nissan has also recently introduced the Nissan Leaf, an all-electric vehicle, and aspires to bring EVs to mass-market production by 2012. The Leaf will rely on batteries designed and manufactured by AESC. Nissan owns 51% of the company and NEC Corporation owns 49%.

FINANCIALS: Sales and profits are in thousands of dollars—add 000 to get the full amount. 2011 Note: Financial information for 2011 was not available for all companies at press time.

2011 Sales: $	2011 Profits: $	**U.S. Stock Ticker: Joint Venture**
2010 Sales: $	2010 Profits: $	**Int'l Ticker:**
2009 Sales: $	2009 Profits: $	Int'l Exchange:
2008 Sales: $	2008 Profits: $	Employees: 80 Fiscal Year Ends:
2007 Sales: $	2007 Profits: $	Parent Company: NISSAN MOTOR CO LTD

SALARIES/BENEFITS:
Pension Plan:	ESOP Stock Plan:	Profit Sharing:	Top Exec. Salary: $	Bonus: $
Savings Plan:	Stock Purch. Plan:		Second Exec. Salary: $	Bonus: $

OTHER THOUGHTS:
Apparent Women Officers or Directors:
Hot Spot for Advancement for Women/Minorities:

LOCATIONS: ("Y" = Yes)
West:	Southwest:	Midwest:	Southeast:	Northeast:	International:
					Y

AVANCIS GMBH & CO KG

Industry Group Code: 334413

www.avancis.de

Energy/Fuel:	Other Technologies:	Electrical Products:	Electronics:	Transportation:	Other:
Biofuels:	Irrigation:	Lighting/LEDs:	Computers:	Car Sharing:	Recycling:
Batteries/Storage:	Nanotech:	Waste Heat:	Sensors:	Electric Vehicles:	Engineering:
Solar: Y	Biotech:	Smart Meters:	Software:	Natural Gas Fuel:	Consulting:
Wind:	Water Tech./Treatment:	Machinery:			Investing:
Fuel Cells:	Ceramics:				Chemicals:

TYPES OF BUSINESS:

Solar Energy Technology
CIS Thin Film Technology

BRANDS/DIVISIONS/AFFILIATES:

Royal Dutch Shell (Shell Group)
Compagnie de Saint-Gobain SA
PowerMax

CONTACTS: *Note: Officers with more than one job title may be intentionally listed here more than once.*

Hartmut Fischer, CEO
Hans Peter Hoheisel, COO
Oliver Just, CFO
Heike Degen, Dir.-Human Resources
Franz Karg, CTO
Tom Clarius, Dir.-Quality, Health, Safety & Environment

Phone: 49-3421-7388-0	Fax: 49-3421-7388-111
Toll-Free:	
Address: Solarstrasse 3, Torgau, 04860 Germany	

GROWTH PLANS/SPECIAL FEATURES:

AVANCIS GmbH & Co. KG, a subsidiary of Compagnie de Saint-Gobain SA, develops, produces and markets solar power modules based on advanced CIS (copper indium diselenide) thin-film technology. AVANCIS utilizes Royal Dutch Shell's CIS technology experience and Saint-Gobain's global glass processing and building materials production experience. CIS production offers 50% shorter energy payback time and a fewer number of production stages. The production process from delivery of the glass to the solar power module takes place on a single production line. The firm's product PowerMax is a CIS thin-film technology optimized for high efficiency and low system costs. Some of the company's projects include Salzburg Congress Hall in Austria; the Optic Centre in Wales; Shell Solar in California; and Traditional Inn in Bavaria. Recently, the firm initiated the operations of two new production lines at its plant in Torgau, Saxony. The manufacturing plant is now achieving its maximum production capacity of 20 megawatts peak (MWp) per year. By 2012, the second plant in Torgau should be finished and producing CIS solar modules with a total capacity of 100 MWp per year.

FINANCIALS: Sales and profits are in thousands of dollars—add 000 to get the full amount. 2011 Note: Financial information for 2011 was not available for all companies at press time.

2011 Sales: $	2011 Profits: $	**U.S. Stock Ticker: Subsidiary**
2010 Sales: $	2010 Profits: $	**Int'l Ticker:**
2009 Sales: $	2009 Profits: $	Int'l Exchange:
2008 Sales: $	2008 Profits: $	Employees: Fiscal Year Ends: 12/31
2007 Sales: $	2007 Profits: $	Parent Company: COMPAGNIE DE SAINT-GOBAIN SA

SALARIES/BENEFITS:

Pension Plan:	ESOP Stock Plan:	Profit Sharing:	Top Exec. Salary: $	Bonus: $
Savings Plan:	Stock Purch. Plan:		Second Exec. Salary: $	Bonus: $

OTHER THOUGHTS:

Apparent Women Officers or Directors: 1
Hot Spot for Advancement for Women/Minorities:

LOCATIONS: ("Y" = Yes)

West:	Southwest:	Midwest:	Southeast:	Northeast:	International: Y

AVANTIUM

Industry Group Code: 325199

www.avantium.com/

Energy/Fuel:		Other Technologies:	Electrical Products:	Electronics:	Transportation:	Other:	
Biofuels:	Y	Irrigation:	Lighting/LEDs:	Computers:	Car Sharing:	Recycling:	
Batteries/Storage:		Nanotech:	Waste Heat:	Sensors:	Electric Vehicles:	Engineering:	
Solar:		Biotech:	Smart Meters:	Software:	Natural Gas Fuel:	Consulting:	
Wind:		Water Tech./Treatment:	Machinery:			Investing:	
Fuel Cells:		Ceramics:				Chemicals:	Y

TYPES OF BUSINESS:

Green Technology Company
Cataylsis Research and Services

BRANDS/DIVISIONS/AFFILIATES:

YXY
Flowrence

CONTACTS: *Note: Officers with more than one job title may be intentionally listed here more than once.*

Tom B. van Aken, CEO
Frank C. H. Roerink, CFO
Jeff Kolstad, Chief Scientist
Gert-Jan Gruter, CTO
Janine Kostermann Dohmen, Head-Media Rel.
Jan van der Eijk, Chmn.

Phone: 31-20-586-8080	**Fax:** 31-20-586-8085
Toll-Free:	
Address: Zekeringstraat 29, Amsterdam, 1014 BV The Netherlands	

GROWTH PLANS/SPECIAL FEATURES:

Avantium is a technology company in the Netherlands that specializes in advanced catalysis (chemical reaction) research and development (R&D) and process development for use in the pharmaceutical, energy and chemicals industries. The company has three operating segments: catalysis research, green materials & fuels and pharma. The catalysis research segment is centered upon the company's Flowrence technology platform, a parallel fixed-based reactor technology platform. Avantium offers contractual services in this segment where it works as an extension of the client's R&D department to develop novel catalytic processes. The green materials & fuels segment revolves around the development and implementation of Avantium's YXY technology. YXY technology converts biomass into green building blocks for fuels and materials called Furanics. Furanics are capable of replacing oil as the raw material for a wide range of plastics, car parts, fuel, clothing, etc. This segment operates a pilot plant in Geleen, Netherlands, which demonstrates to potential investors and clients the feasibility and applicability of YXY technology. The pharma segment of the firm focuses on the sale of crystallization systems. These crystallization services, which include Crystalline and Crystal 16, are owned by the recently spun off company Crystallics and are sold to customers such as Mitsubishi Pharmaceuticals, Pfizer, Taiho, GSK and Boehringer-Ingelheim. In April 2011, Avantium announced that it had spun off its pharmaceutical services and development business into a separate entity called Crystallics. This separation will allow Avantium to focus solely on its cleantech and chemical activities. In December 2011, the firm announced the opening of its pilot plant in Geleen, Netherlands.

FINANCIALS: Sales and profits are in thousands of dollars—add 000 to get the full amount. 2011 Note: Financial information for 2011 was not available for all companies at press time.

2011 Sales: $	2011 Profits: $	**U.S. Stock Ticker: Private**		
2010 Sales: $	2010 Profits: $	**Int'l Ticker:**		
2009 Sales: $	2009 Profits: $	Int'l Exchange:		
2008 Sales: $	2008 Profits: $	Employees:	Fiscal Year Ends:	
2007 Sales: $	2007 Profits: $	Parent Company:		

SALARIES/BENEFITS:

Pension Plan:	ESOP Stock Plan:	Profit Sharing:	Top Exec. Salary: $	Bonus: $
Savings Plan:	Stock Purch. Plan:		Second Exec. Salary: $	Bonus: $

OTHER THOUGHTS:

Apparent Women Officers or Directors: 1
Hot Spot for Advancement for Women/Minorities:

LOCATIONS: ("Y" = Yes)

West:	Southwest:	Midwest:	Southeast:	Northeast:	International: Y

BABCOCK & WILCOX COMPANY (THE)

www.babcock.com

Industry Group Code: 335

Energy/Fuel:	Other Technologies:	Electrical Products:	Electronics:	Transportation:	Other:
Biofuels:	Irrigation:	Lighting/LEDs:	Computers:	Car Sharing:	Recycling:
Batteries/Storage:	Nanotech:	Waste Heat:	Sensors:	Electric Vehicles:	Engineering:
Solar:	Biotech:	Smart Meters:	Software:	Natural Gas Fuel:	Consulting:
Wind:	Water Tech./Treatment:	Machinery: Y			Investing:
Fuel Cells:	Ceramics:				Chemicals:

TYPES OF BUSINESS:

Power Generation Systems
Steam Generators
Environmental Equipment
Engineering & Construction Services
Power Plants
Emissions Reduction Equipment
Waste-to-Energy & Biomass Energy Systems
Boiler Cleaning Equipment

BRANDS/DIVISIONS/AFFILIATES:

Nuclear Fuel Services Inc
Babcock & Wilcox Nuclear Energy Inc
Babcock & Wilcox Power Generation Group Inc
Babcock & Wilcox Technical Services Group Inc
Babcock & Wilcox Nuclear Operations Group Inc
American Centrifuge Manufacturing LLC
Thermax Ltd
Anlagenbau und Fordertechnik Arthur Loibl GmbH

CONTACTS: *Note: Officers with more than one job title may be intentionally listed here more than once.*

Brandon Berthards, CEO
Mary Pat Salomone, COO/Sr. VP
Brandon Berthards, Pres.
Anthony S. Colatrella, CFO/Sr. VP
Vangel Athanas, VP-Human Resources
George Dutch, Pres., B&W Technical Svcs. Group
James D. Canafax, General Counsel/Corp. Sec./Sr. VP
Peyton S. Baker, Pres., Babcock & Wilcox Nuclear Oper. Group
Jud Simmons, Head-Media Rel.
Michael P. Dickerson, Investor Rel. Officer/VP
David S. Black, Chief Accounting Officer/VP
Richard L. Killion, Pres., B&W Power Generation Group, Inc.
Christofer M. Mowry, Pres., B&W Nuclear Energy, Inc.
Jenny L. Apker, VP/Treas.
Beth Colling, Chief Compliance Officer
John A. Fees, Chmn.

Phone: 704-625-4900	Fax:
Toll-Free:	
Address: 13024 Ballantyne Corp. Place, Ste. 700, Charlotte, NC 28277 US	

GROWTH PLANS/SPECIAL FEATURES:

The Babcock & Wilcox Company (B&W) designs, supplies and services power generation systems and associated equipment. The company operates in four business units: Babcock & Wilcox Nuclear Operations Group, Inc. (B&W NOG); Babcock & Wilcox Nuclear Energy, Inc. (B&W NE); Babcock & Wilcox Power Generation Group, Inc. (B&W PGG); and Babcock & Wilcox Technical Services Group, Inc. (B&W TSG). B&W NOG designs and supplies nuclear components for government operations. Through subsidiary Nuclear Fuel Services, Inc., the segment operates a uranium fuel materials production facility to supply the U.S.'s fleet of nuclear-powered submarines and aircraft carriers. B&W NE engineers and produces heavy machinery, such as nuclear heat exchangers and steam generators, for civilian nuclear power plants. B&W PGG manufactures steam generation units for a variety of different fuel requirements and industries. B&W TSG provides support for nuclear and national security operations. Additionally, it upgrades, services and replaces parts for existing power plants, pulp and paper mills and industrial applications. Recently, the firm has positioned itself in the renewable energy market through the introduction of tower-mounted steam generators for solar thermal power plants. In May 2011, B&W TSG and USEC, Inc. announced the formation of American Centrifuge Manufacturing, LLC; additionally, B&W announced that its joint venture between B&W PGG and Thermax Ltd. had broken ground on a boiler manufacturing plant in Pune, India. In December 2011, B&W announced the acquisition of material handling equipment manufacturer Anlagenbau und Fordertechnik Arthur Loibl GmbH; the company will be integrated into B&W PGG.

B&W offers its employees medical, dental and vision coverage; life and AD&D insurance; health and wellness programs; a salaried employee incentive program; a 401(k); tuition reimbursement; and two to four weeks vacation.

FINANCIALS: Sales and profits are in thousands of dollars—add 000 to get the full amount. 2011 Note: Financial information for 2011 was not available for all companies at press time.

2011 Sales: $	2011 Profits: $	**U.S. Stock Ticker:** BWC
2010 Sales: $2,688,811	2010 Profits: $153,526	**Int'l Ticker:**
2009 Sales: $2,854,632	2009 Profits: $147,764	Int'l Exchange:
2008 Sales: $3,398,574	2008 Profits: $323,854	Employees: 12,000 Fiscal Year Ends: 12/31
2007 Sales: $	2007 Profits: $	Parent Company:

SALARIES/BENEFITS:

Pension Plan:	ESOP Stock Plan:	Profit Sharing:	Top Exec. Salary: $665,503	Bonus: $841,500
Savings Plan: Y	Stock Purch. Plan:		Second Exec. Salary: $516,363	Bonus: $654,688

OTHER THOUGHTS:

Apparent Women Officers or Directors: 3
Hot Spot for Advancement for Women/Minorities: Y

LOCATIONS: ("Y" = Yes)

West:	Southwest:	Midwest:	Southeast:	Northeast:	International:
Y	Y	Y	Y	Y	Y

BADGER METER INC

www.badgermeter.com

Industry Group Code: 3345

Energy/Fuel:	Other Technologies:	Electrical Products:		Electronics:		Transportation:	Other:	
Biofuels:	Irrigation:	Lighting/LEDs:		Computers:		Car Sharing:	Recycling:	
Batteries/Storage:	Nanotech:	Waste Heat:		Sensors:		Electric Vehicles:	Engineering:	
Solar:	Biotech:	Smart Meters:	Y	Software:	Y	Natural Gas Fuel:	Consulting:	
Wind:	Water Tech./Treatment:	Machinery:					Investing:	
Fuel Cells:	Ceramics:						Chemicals:	

TYPES OF BUSINESS:

Water Meters & Meter Reading
Specialty Meters

BRANDS/DIVISIONS/AFFILIATES:

Cox Flow Measurement Inc
M-Series
GALAXY
ORION
ITRON
BadgerTouch
RESEARCH CONTROL
Badger Meter Europa GmbH

CONTACTS: *Note: Officers with more than one job title may be intentionally listed here more than once.*

Richard A. Meeusen, CEO
Richard A. Meeusen, Pres.
Richard E. Johnson, CFO/Sr. VP/Treas.
Kimberly K. Stoll, VP-Mktg.
Kristie J. Zahn, VP-Human Resources
Gregory M. Gomez, VP-Eng.
Raymond G. Serdynski, VP-Mfg.
William R. Bergum, General Counsel/Sec./VP
Fred J. Begale, VP-Bus. Dev.
Beverly L. Smiley, Controller/VP
Dennis J. Webb, VP-Sales
Richard A. Meeusen, Chmn.
Horst Gras, VP-Int'l

Phone: 414-371-5702	**Fax:** 414-371-5956
Toll-Free: 800-876-3837	
Address: 4545 W. Brown Deer Rd., Milwaukee, WI 53224 US	

GROWTH PLANS/SPECIAL FEATURES:

Badger Meter, Inc. is a leading manufacturer and marketer of products incorporating liquid flow measurement and control technologies. The firm's products are used in a variety of applications, including water, oil and chemicals. Its product lines fall into two categories: water applications and specialty applications. The water applications category includes the sale of water meters and related technologies and services used by water utilities as the basis for generating water and wastewater revenues. The market for the company's water meter products is North America, primarily the U.S., because the meters are designed and manufactured to conform to standards set by the American Water Works Association. These products are also sold for other water purposes including irrigation, water reclamation and industrial process applications. Specialty applications include the sale of meters and related technologies and services for measuring a wide variety of fluids in industries such as food and beverage; pharmaceutical production; petroleum; heating ventilating and air conditioning (HVAC); and measuring and dispensing automotive fluids. It also includes the sales of technology to natural gas utilities for installation on their gas meters. The company's brands include M-Series, GALAXY, ORION, ITRON, BadgerTouch and RESEARCH CONTROL. The firm has manufacturing facilities in Tulsa, Oklahoma; Milwaukee, Wisconsin; Scottsdale, Arizona; Neuffen, Germany; Nogales, Mexico; Brno, Czech Republic; and Berne, Switzerland. Additionally, the company has international sales and customer service offices in Mexico, Singapore, China and Slovakia.

FINANCIALS: Sales and profits are in thousands of dollars—add 000 to get the full amount. 2011 Note: Financial information for 2011 was not available for all companies at press time.

2011 Sales: $	2011 Profits: $	**U.S. Stock Ticker:** BMI
2010 Sales: $276,634	2010 Profits: $28,662	**Int'l Ticker:**
2009 Sales: $250,337	2009 Profits: $34,170	Int'l Exchange:
2008 Sales: $279,552	2008 Profits: $25,084	Employees: 1,293 Fiscal Year Ends: 12/31
2007 Sales: $	2007 Profits: $	Parent Company:

SALARIES/BENEFITS:

Pension Plan: Y	ESOP Stock Plan:	Profit Sharing:	Top Exec. Salary: $535,000	Bonus: $403,475
Savings Plan:	Stock Purch. Plan:		Second Exec. Salary: $299,484	Bonus: $146,962

OTHER THOUGHTS:

Apparent Women Officers or Directors: 3
Hot Spot for Advancement for Women/Minorities: Y

LOCATIONS: ("Y" = Yes)

West:	Southwest:	Midwest:	Southeast:	Northeast:	International:
	Y	Y			Y

Sales, profits and employees may be estimates. Financial information, benefits and other data can change quickly and may vary from those stated here.

BALLARD POWER SYSTEMS INC

www.ballard.com

Industry Group Code: 335999

Energy/Fuel:	Other Technologies:	Electrical Products:	Electronics:	Transportation:	Other:
Biofuels:	Irrigation:	Lighting/LEDs:	Computers:	Car Sharing:	Recycling:
Batteries/Storage:	Nanotech:	Waste Heat:	Sensors:	Electric Vehicles:	Engineering:
Solar:	Biotech:	Smart Meters:	Software:	Natural Gas Fuel:	Consulting:
Wind:	Water Tech./Treatment:	Machinery:			Investing:
Fuel Cells: Y	Ceramics:				Chemicals:

TYPES OF BUSINESS:

Fuel Cells Manufacturing
Automotive Parts Manufacturing
Carbon Products
Residential Cogeneration Fuel Cells

BRANDS/DIVISIONS/AFFILIATES:

Ballard Material Products Inc
AFCC Automotive Fuel Cell Cooperation Corp
Dantherm Power A/S

CONTACTS: Note: Officers with more than one job title may be intentionally listed here more than once.

John W. Sheridan, CEO
John W. Sheridan, Pres.
Tony Guglielmin, CFO/VP
Christopher Guzy, CTO/VP
Kerry Hillier, Corp. Sec.
Paul Cass, VP-Oper.
Lori Rozali, Dir.-Investor Rel.
William Foulds, Pres., Ballard Material Prod. Div.
Michael Goldstein, Chief Commercial Officer/VP
Ian A. Bourne, Chmn.

Phone: 604-454-0900	Fax: 604-412-4700
Toll-Free:	
Address: 9000 Glenlyon Pkwy., Burnaby, BC V5J 5J8 Canada	

GROWTH PLANS/SPECIAL FEATURES:

Ballard Power Systems, Inc. is a world leader in developing, manufacturing and marketing clean energy hydrogen fuel cells. The company's fuel cells are primarily used in transportation and electricity generation, but are also used for material handling, residential cogeneration, backup power and heavy duty applications. The firm operates in two primary segments: Power Generation, which focuses on fuel cell products and services for materials handling, backup power and residential cogeneration purposes; and Material Products, which, through subsidiary Ballard Material Products, Inc., manufactures carbon fiber products primarily for automotive transmissions and gas diffusion layers (GDLs) for fuel cells. Ballard Power Systems also develops automotive fuel cells on a limited, contractual basis, primarily for Daimler AG and Ford Motor Company, through AFCC Automotive Fuel Cell Cooperation Corp. (AFCC). The firm holds a 19.9% minority interest in AFCC, while Daimler and Ford hold 50.1% and 30%, respectively. The fuel cell combines hydrogen obtained from methanol, natural gas, kerosene or renewable sources and oxygen from the air to generate electricity. The only emission as a result of the hydrogen reaction is pure water. The firm is headquartered in Burnaby, British Columbia, where it operates fuel cell manufacturing, stack development, assembly and testing facilities. It also maintains manufacturing facilities for its Material Products segment in Lowell, Massachusetts. Additionally, Ballard Power Systems has a controlling interest in Dantherm Power A/S, a Denmark-based corporation jointly owned with Danfoss Ventures A/S and Dantherm A/S that develops clean energy backup power systems across Europe.

FINANCIALS: Sales and profits are in thousands of dollars—add 000 to get the full amount. 2011 Note: Financial information for 2011 was not available for all companies at press time.

2011 Sales: $	2011 Profits: $	U.S. Stock Ticker:
2010 Sales: $65,019	2010 Profits: $-34,936	Int'l Ticker: BLD
2009 Sales: $47,000	2009 Profits: $-3,258	Int'l Exchange: Toronto-TSX
2008 Sales: $59,580	2008 Profits: $34,079	Employees: 440 Fiscal Year Ends: 12/31
2007 Sales: $65,532	2007 Profits: $-57,302	Parent Company:

SALARIES/BENEFITS:

Pension Plan:	ESOP Stock Plan:	Profit Sharing:	Top Exec. Salary: $488,872	Bonus: $338,175
Savings Plan:	Stock Purch. Plan:		Second Exec. Salary: $285,945	Bonus: $87,911

OTHER THOUGHTS:

Apparent Women Officers or Directors: 1
Hot Spot for Advancement for Women/Minorities:

LOCATIONS: ("Y" = Yes)

West:	Southwest:	Midwest:	Southeast:	Northeast: Y	International: Y

BAREFOOT POWER

Industry Group Code: 334419

www.barefootpower.com

Energy/Fuel:	Other Technologies:	Electrical Products:		Electronics:	Transportation:	Other:
Biofuels:	Irrigation:	Lighting/LEDs:	Y	Computers:	Car Sharing:	Recycling:
Batteries/Storage: Y	Nanotech:	Waste Heat:		Sensors:	Electric Vehicles:	Engineering:
Solar: Y	Biotech:	Smart Meters:		Software:	Natural Gas Fuel:	Consulting:
Wind:	Water Tech./Treatment:	Machinery:				Investing:
Fuel Cells:	Ceramics:					Chemicals:

TYPES OF BUSINESS:

Solar Powered Lighting Solutions

BRANDS/DIVISIONS/AFFILIATES:

Firefly Light
Firefly Mobile Ultra Torch
Firefly Mobile Family
Firefly Fast Phone Charge
PowaPack Junior Matrix
PowaPack Village Kit 15W
Smart Solar (K) Ltd
Barefoot Power Uganda Ltd

CONTACTS:
Note: Officers with more than one job title may be intentionally listed here more than once.

Rick Hooper, CEO
Joyce DeMucci, Mgr.-Global Mktg.
Joyce DeMucci, Mgr.-Prod. Dev.
Dirk Kam, Managing Dir.-Barefoot Power Uganda
Stewart Craine, Co-Founder/Regional Mgr.-Asia & the Pacific
David Hind, Chmn.
Harry Andrews, Co-Founder/Regional Mgr.-Africa

Phone: 61-4-2479-3485	Fax:
Toll-Free:	
Address: 123 Epping Rd., Avaya House, Level 9, North Ryde, NSW 2113 Australia	

GROWTH PLANS/SPECIAL FEATURES:

Barefoot Power (BFP) is an early-stage firm that specializes in renewable, low-cost, rural electrification systems. The firm's micro-solar products are designed to provide lighting and phone charging capabilities to those that would otherwise be without or have to rely upon dirtier and less efficient sources like kerosene. BFP has two product lines, the Firefly series and the PowaPack series. The Firefly series is the smaller of the two product lines. These products generally include a smaller solar panel, producing 1.5 watts (W); phone recharging docks; and one or two lamps. Items within this line include Firefly Light, Firefly Mobile Ultra Torch, Firefly Mobile Family and Firefly Fast Phone Charge. The PowaPack series is the beefier of the two product lines. These products offer larger solar panels (2.5-15W) and multiple lighting points. Items within this line include PowaPack Junior Matrix, PowaPack 5W and PowaPack Village Kit 15W. BFP's products are estimated to provide lighting to 1.87 million households and 274,000 small businesses. BFP has two subsidiaries: Smart Solar (K) Ltd and Barefoot Power Uganda Ltd, which sells the products of BFP in Uganda.

FINANCIALS:
Sales and profits are in thousands of dollars—add 000 to get the full amount. 2011 Note: Financial information for 2011 was not available for all companies at press time.

2011 Sales: $	2011 Profits: $	U.S. Stock Ticker: Private
2010 Sales: $	2010 Profits: $	Int'l Ticker:
2009 Sales: $	2009 Profits: $	Int'l Exchange:
2008 Sales: $	2008 Profits: $	Employees: Fiscal Year Ends:
2007 Sales: $	2007 Profits: $	Parent Company:

SALARIES/BENEFITS:

Pension Plan:	ESOP Stock Plan:	Profit Sharing:	Top Exec. Salary: $	Bonus: $
Savings Plan:	Stock Purch. Plan:		Second Exec. Salary: $	Bonus: $

OTHER THOUGHTS:

Apparent Women Officers or Directors: 1
Hot Spot for Advancement for Women/Minorities:

LOCATIONS: ("Y" = Yes)

West:	Southwest:	Midwest:	Southeast:	Northeast:	International: Y

BASF FUTURE BUSINESS GMBH
www.basf-fb.de/en
Industry Group Code: 541712

Energy/Fuel:	Other Technologies:	Electrical Products:	Electronics:	Transportation:	Other:	
Biofuels:	Irrigation:	Lighting/LEDs:	Computers:	Car Sharing:	Recycling:	
Batteries/Storage:	Nanotech:	Waste Heat:	Sensors:	Electric Vehicles:	Engineering:	Y
Solar:	Biotech:	Smart Meters:	Software:	Natural Gas Fuel:	Consulting:	
Wind:	Water Tech./Treatment:	Machinery:			Investing:	
Fuel Cells:	Ceramics:				Chemicals:	

TYPES OF BUSINESS:
Chemistry & Materials Research
Organic LED Technology
Organic Photovoltaic Materials
Time Temperature Indicators
Waste Heat Recovery
Probiotics

BRANDS/DIVISIONS/AFFILIATES:
BASF AG
ONVU

CONTACTS: Note: Officers with more than one job title may be intentionally listed here more than once.
Thomas Weber, Managing Dir.
Wolfgang Hormuth, Dir.-Strategy & Scouting
Tilo Habicher, Dir.-Health & Environmental Tech.
Joachim Roesch, Dir.-Energy Mgmt.
Stephan Klotz, Dir.-Organic Electronics
Wolfgang Hormuth, Dir.-Scouting & Strategy

Phone: 49-621-60-76811	Fax: 49-621-60-76818
Toll-Free:	
Address: 4 Gartenweg Z 25, Ludwigshafen, 67063 Germany	

GROWTH PLANS/SPECIAL FEATURES:
BASF Future Business GmbH, a subsidiary of BASF SE, strives to discover new business areas for the BASF group, and focuses on chemicals-related new materials and technologies. It currently runs six projects. The organic electronics project focuses on developing materials for organic electronic applications such as organic light emitting diodes (OLEDs), organic field-effect transistors (OFETs) and organic photovoltaic (OPV) products. The Time Temperature Indicators (TTIs) project involves the company's proprietary ONVU TTIs, which are printed labels that show a history of the elapsed time-temperature of a product in a colored visual display. These labels are designed for refrigerated items such as food products, biological specimens and medicinal items, such as vaccines. The thermoelectrics project works with semiconductor alloys to produce electricity from waste heat left over by power plants and automobiles. The magnetocalorics project involves developing magnetic-based cooling systems that promise to have less ecological impact and consume less energy than conventional refrigerants in air conditioners and refrigerators. The pro-t-action project develops probiotic microorganisms for oral hygiene and personal and skin care products. Lastly, the antimicrobial materials project develops new dental cosmetics products, wound management materials (bandages and gels) and sanitizers for medical devices and equipment.

FINANCIALS: Sales and profits are in thousands of dollars—add 000 to get the full amount. 2011 Note: Financial information for 2011 was not available for all companies at press time.

2011 Sales: $	2011 Profits: $	U.S. Stock Ticker: Subsidiary
2010 Sales: $	2010 Profits: $	Int'l Ticker:
2009 Sales: $	2009 Profits: $	Int'l Exchange:
2008 Sales: $	2008 Profits: $	Employees: Fiscal Year Ends: 12/31
2007 Sales: $	2007 Profits: $	Parent Company: BASF SE

SALARIES/BENEFITS:

Pension Plan:	ESOP Stock Plan:	Profit Sharing:	Top Exec. Salary: $	Bonus: $
Savings Plan:	Stock Purch. Plan:		Second Exec. Salary: $	Bonus: $

OTHER THOUGHTS:
Apparent Women Officers or Directors:
Hot Spot for Advancement for Women/Minorities:

LOCATIONS: ("Y" = Yes)

West:	Southwest:	Midwest:	Southeast:	Northeast:	International:
				Y	Y

Sales, profits and employees may be estimates. Financial information, benefits and other data can change quickly and may vary from those stated here.

BASF SE

www.basf.com

Industry Group Code: 325

Energy/Fuel:	Other Technologies:		Electrical Products:	Electronics:	Transportation:	Other:	
Biofuels:	Irrigation:		Lighting/LEDs:	Computers:	Car Sharing:	Recycling:	
Batteries/Storage:	Nanotech:		Waste Heat:	Sensors:	Electric Vehicles:	Engineering:	
Solar:	Biotech:	Y	Smart Meters:	Software:	Natural Gas Fuel:	Consulting:	
Wind:	Water Tech./Treatment:		Machinery:			Investing:	
Fuel Cells:	Ceramics:					Chemicals:	Y

TYPES OF BUSINESS:

Chemicals Manufacturing
Agricultural Products
Oil & Gas Production
Plastics
Coatings
Nanotechnology Research
Nutritional Products
Agricultural Biotechnology

BRANDS/DIVISIONS/AFFILIATES:

Wintershall AG
BASF Canada
BASF Future Business GmbH
Cognis Deutschland GmbH & Co. KG
BASF Hock Mining Chemical Company Ltd.
BASF AG
Inge Watertechnologies AG

CONTACTS: Note: Officers with more than one job title may be intentionally listed here more than once.

Kurt W. Bock, Chmn.-Exec. Board
Hans-Ulrich Engel, CFO
Margret Suckale, Dir.-Human Resources
Andreas Kreimeyer, Exec. Dir.-Research
Kurt W. Bock, Exec. Dir.-Info. Svcs.
Andreas Kreimeyer, Exec. Dir.-Eng & Chemicals Research
Kurt W. Bock, Dir.-Strategic Planning & Controlling
Stefanie Wettberg, VP-Corp. Comm.
Kurt W. Bock, Head-Investor Rel.
Stefan Marcinowski, Exec. Dir.-Crop Protection
Jurgen Hambrecht, Chmn.
Martin Brudermueller, Exec. Dir.-Asia Pacific Div.
Harald Schwager, Head-Global Procurement & Logistics

Phone: 49-621-60-0	Fax: 49-621-60-42525
Toll-Free:	
Address: 38 Carl-Bosch St., Ludwigshafen, 67056 Germany	

GROWTH PLANS/SPECIAL FEATURES:

BASF SE, formerly BASF AG, is a chemical manufacturing company that serves customers in more than 200 countries. The firm operates in six business segments: chemicals; plastics; performance products; agricultural solutions; functional solutions; and oil and gas. The chemicals segment manufactures inorganic, petrochemical and intermediate chemicals for the pharmaceutical, construction, textile and automotive industries. The plastics segment manufactures polystyrene and performance polymers for the manufacturing and packaging industries. The performance products segment produces pigments, inks, printing supplies, coatings and polymers for the automotive, oil, packaging, textile, detergent, sanitary care, construction and chemical industries. BASF also employs chemical nanotechnology to produce pigments used to color coatings, paints, plastics and sunscreen. The firm's agricultural solutions segment produces genetically engineered plants, nutritional supplements, herbicides, fungicides and insecticides for use in agriculture, public health and pest control. The functional solutions segment develops automotive and industrial catalysts; construction chemicals; and coatings and refinishes for the automotive and construction markets. The oil and gas segment, operated through Wintershall AG, focuses on petroleum and natural gas exploration and production in North America, Asia, Europe, the Middle East and Africa. In January 2011, BASF announced the completion of its acquisition of CRI/Criterion's styrene catalysts business. In August 2011, the firm announced the completion of its acquisition of ultra filtration specialists Inge Watertechnologies AG. In October 2011, BASF and Ji'Ning Hock Mining & Engineering Equipment Company Ltd. received approval for the formation of a joint venture company in China to be called BASF Hock Mining Chemical Company Ltd.; BASF will take a majority stake of 75% in the new venture.

U.S. employees are offered medical, dental and vision insurance; life insurance; disability coverage; an employee savings plan; tuition reimbursement; adoption assistance; and a supplier discount.

FINANCIALS: Sales and profits are in thousands of dollars—add 000 to get the full amount. 2011 Note: Financial information for 2011 was not available for all companies at press time.

2011 Sales: $	2011 Profits: $	U.S. Stock Ticker:
2010 Sales: $93,180,980	2010 Profits: $1,083,466	Int'l Ticker: BAS
2009 Sales: $67,557,500	2009 Profits: $1,879,080	Int'l Exchange: Frankfurt-Euronext
2008 Sales: $83,990,800	2008 Profits: $3,925,610	Employees: 110,289 Fiscal Year Ends: 12/31
2007 Sales: $78,122,600	2007 Profits: $5,479,950	Parent Company:

SALARIES/BENEFITS:

Pension Plan:	ESOP Stock Plan:	Profit Sharing:	Top Exec. Salary: $1,532,893	Bonus: $2,124,987
Savings Plan: Y	Stock Purch. Plan:		Second Exec. Salary: $982,371	Bonus: $1,063,144

OTHER THOUGHTS:

Apparent Women Officers or Directors: 5
Hot Spot for Advancement for Women/Minorities: Y

LOCATIONS: ("Y" = Yes)

West:	Southwest:	Midwest:	Southeast:	Northeast:	International:
Y	Y	Y	Y	Y	Y

BAYER AG

www.bayer.com

Industry Group Code: 325

Energy/Fuel:	Other Technologies:		Electrical Products:	Electronics:	Transportation:	Other:	
Biofuels:	Irrigation:		Lighting/LEDs:	Computers:	Car Sharing:	Recycling:	
Batteries/Storage:	Nanotech:		Waste Heat:	Sensors:	Electric Vehicles:	Engineering:	
Solar:	Biotech:	Y	Smart Meters:	Software:	Natural Gas Fuel:	Consulting:	
Wind:	Water Tech./Treatment:		Machinery:			Investing:	
Fuel Cells:	Ceramics:					Chemicals:	Y

TYPES OF BUSINESS:

Chemicals Manufacturing
Pharmaceuticals
Animal Health Products
Synthetic Materials
Crop Science
Plant Biotechnology
Health Care Products

BRANDS/DIVISIONS/AFFILIATES:

Bayer HealthCare
Bayer CropScience
Bayer MaterialScience
Bayer Technology Services
Bayer Business Services
Currenta GmbH & Co
Hornbeck Seed Company Inc
Pathway Medical Technologies Inc

CONTACTS: Note: Officers with more than one job title may be intentionally listed here more than once.

Marijin Dekkers, Chmn.-Board of Mgmt.
Werner Baumann, CFO
Richard Pott, Dir.-Human Resources
Wolfgang Plischke, Dir.-Innovation
Wolfgang Plischke, Dir.-Tech.
Richard Pott, Dir.-Strategy
Michael Schade, Head-Comm.
Alexander Rosar, Head-Investor Rel.
Peter Muller, Head-Finance
Wolfgang Plischke, Dir.-Environment
Jorg Reinhardt, Chmn.-Bayer HealthCare AG
Sandra E. Peterson, Chmn.-Bayer CropScience AG
Patrick Thomas, Chmn.-Bayer MaterialScience AG
Manfred Schneider, Chmn.-Supervisory Board

Phone: 49-214-30-1	Fax:
Toll-Free: 800-269-2377	
Address: Bayerwerk Gebaeude W11, Leverkusen, D-51368 Germany	

GROWTH PLANS/SPECIAL FEATURES:

Bayer AG is a German holding company encompassing over 300 consolidated subsidiaries on five continents. The company operates six business segments: Bayer HealthCare, Bayer CropScience, Bayer MaterialScience, Bayer Business Services, Bayer Technology Services and Currenta. The Bayer HealthCare segment develops, produces and markets products for the prevention, diagnosis and treatment of human and animal diseases. Bayer CropScience is active in the areas of chemical crop protection and seed treatment; non-agricultural pest and weed control; and plant biotechnology. Bayer MaterialScience develops, manufactures and markets polyurethane, polycarbonate, cellulose derivatives and special metals products. Bayer Business Services offers IT infrastructure and applications, procurement and logistics, human resources and management services. Bayer Technology Services offers process development; process and plant engineering; construction; and optimization services. Currenta GmbH & Co., a joint venture with Lanxess AG, offers utility supply, waste management, infrastructure, safety, security, analytics and vocational training services to the chemical industry. The company's pharmaceutical portfolio includes Alka-Seltzer, Asprin, Levitra, Mirena, Aleve, Yaz and the Breeze 2 blood glucose meter. Recently, the firm has received new drug approval for several of its developmental drugs, including Natazia, Safyral and Beyaz oral contraceptives. In 2011, Bayer acquired the American seed company Hornbeck Seed Company Inc; the American developer of mechanical atherectomy in the field of vascular intervention, Pathway Medical Technologies, Inc.; and access to the Romanian National Agricultural Research and Development's winter wheat germplasm.

In addition to health and well-being packages, employee perks include sports amenities, flexible work schedules and a varied program of cultural events.

FINANCIALS: Sales and profits are in thousands of dollars—add 000 to get the full amount. 2011 Note: Financial information for 2011 was not available for all companies at press time.

2011 Sales: $	2011 Profits: $	**U.S. Stock Ticker:**
2010 Sales: $50,706,000	2010 Profits: $1,880,090	**Int'l Ticker: BAYN**
2009 Sales: $42,346,100	2009 Profits: $1,846,390	Int'l Exchange: Frankfurt-Euronext
2008 Sales: $43,536,000	2008 Profits: $2,273,480	Employees: 111,400 Fiscal Year Ends: 12/31
2007 Sales: $42,831,100	2007 Profits: $6,230,580	Parent Company:

SALARIES/BENEFITS:

Pension Plan:	ESOP Stock Plan:	Profit Sharing:	Top Exec. Salary: $1,700,721	Bonus: $2,985,500
Savings Plan: Y	Stock Purch. Plan:		Second Exec. Salary: $1,147,526	Bonus: $1,851,035

OTHER THOUGHTS:

Apparent Women Officers or Directors: 1
Hot Spot for Advancement for Women/Minorities:

LOCATIONS: ("Y" = Yes)

West:	Southwest:	Midwest:	Southeast:	Northeast:	International:
Y	Y	Y	Y	Y	Y

BAYER CORP

www.bayerus.com

Industry Group Code: 325

Energy/Fuel:	Other Technologies:		Electrical Products:	Electronics:	Transportation:	Other:	
Biofuels:	Irrigation:		Lighting/LEDs:	Computers:	Car Sharing:	Recycling:	
Batteries/Storage:	Nanotech:		Waste Heat:	Sensors:	Electric Vehicles:	Engineering:	
Solar:	Biotech:	Y	Smart Meters:	Software:	Natural Gas Fuel:	Consulting:	
Wind:	Water Tech./Treatment:		Machinery:			Investing:	
Fuel Cells:	Ceramics:					Chemicals:	Y

TYPES OF BUSINESS:

Chemicals Manufacturing
Animal Health Products
Over-the-Counter Drugs
Diagnostic Products
Coatings, Adhesives & Sealants
Polyurethanes & Plastics
Herbicides, Fungicides & Insecticides

BRANDS/DIVISIONS/AFFILIATES:

Bayer AG
Bayer HealthCare AG
Bayer MaterialSciences LLC
Bayer CropScience LP
Aleve
Breeze
BaySystems
Alka-Seltzer Plus

CONTACTS: Note: Officers with more than one job title may be intentionally listed here more than once.

Gregory S. Babe, CEO
Gregory S. Babe, Pres.
Willy Scherf, CFO
Joyce Burgess, Dir.-Human Resources
Claudio Abreu, CIO
Lars Benecke, General Counsel/Company Sec./Compliance Officer
Mark Ryan, Chief Comm. Officer
Tracy Spagnol, Treas./VP
Arthur Higgins, Chmn.-Bayer HealthCare AG
Roland Backes, VP-Mergers & Acquisitions
Paul F. Wright, VP-Tax
Timothy Roseberry, Chief Procurement Officer/VP-Corp. Materials Mgmt.

Phone: 412-777-2000	**Fax:** 412-777-2034
Toll-Free:	
Address: 100 Bayer Rd., Pittsburgh, PA 15205-9741 US	

GROWTH PLANS/SPECIAL FEATURES:

Bayer Corp. is the U.S. subsidiary of chemical and pharmaceutical giant Bayer AG. The company operates through four divisions: Bayer HealthCare; Bayer MaterialScience; Bayer Corporate and Business Services; and Bayer CropScience. Bayer HealthCare operates through four units: Bayer Schering Pharma, consumer care, medical care and animal health. Bayer Schering Pharma sells pharmaceuticals including YAZ, Yasmin, Levitra and Mirena. Its consumer care products include analgesics (Aleve and Bayer); cold and cough treatments (Alka-Seltzer Plus and Talcio); digestive relief products (Alka-Mints and Phillips' Milk of Magnesia); topical skin preparations (Domeboro and Bactine); and vitamins (One-A-Day and Flintstones). The medical care division is a leader in self-test blood glucose diagnostic systems; it offers the Breeze and Contour product families that offers alternate site testing and automatic coding and requires smaller blood samples. Its animal health products include vaccines and other preventative measures for farm and domestic animals. Bayer's MaterialScience segment produces coatings, adhesives and sealant raw materials; polyurethanes; and plastics. Bayer CropScience makes products directed toward crop protection, environmental science and bioscience, which include herbicides, fungicides and insecticides. Bayer Corporate and Business Services provides business services to the aforementioned Bayer subsidiaries, such as administration, technology services, mergers/acquisitions and internal auditing.

The company offers benefits to its employees including life, disability, medical, dental and vision coverage; prescription drug reimbursement; a 401(k); and adoption assistance.

FINANCIALS: Sales and profits are in thousands of dollars—add 000 to get the full amount. 2011 Note: Financial information for 2011 was not available for all companies at press time.

2011 Sales: $	2011 Profits: $	**U.S. Stock Ticker: Subsidiary**
2010 Sales: $	2010 Profits: $	**Int'l Ticker:**
2009 Sales: $	2009 Profits: $	Int'l Exchange:
2008 Sales: $	2008 Profits: $	Employees: Fiscal Year Ends: 12/31
2007 Sales: $	2007 Profits: $	Parent Company: BAYER AG

SALARIES/BENEFITS:

Pension Plan:	ESOP Stock Plan:	Profit Sharing:	Top Exec. Salary: $	Bonus: $
Savings Plan: Y	Stock Purch. Plan:		Second Exec. Salary: $	Bonus: $

OTHER THOUGHTS:

Apparent Women Officers or Directors: 1
Hot Spot for Advancement for Women/Minorities:

LOCATIONS: ("Y" = Yes)

West:	Southwest:	Midwest:	Southeast:	Northeast:	International:
Y	Y	Y	Y	Y	

BEACON POWER CORP

www.beaconpower.com

Industry Group Code: 33591

Energy/Fuel:		Other Technologies:	Electrical Products:	Electronics:	Transportation:	Other:
Biofuels:		Irrigation:	Lighting/LEDs:	Computers:	Car Sharing:	Recycling:
Batteries/Storage:	Y	Nanotech:	Waste Heat:	Sensors:	Electric Vehicles:	Engineering:
Solar:		Biotech:	Smart Meters:	Software:	Natural Gas Fuel:	Consulting:
Wind:		Water Tech./Treatment:	Machinery:			Investing:
Fuel Cells:		Ceramics:				Chemicals:

TYPES OF BUSINESS:

Flywheel Energy Storage Systems

BRANDS/DIVISIONS/AFFILIATES:

Smart Energy
Smart Energy Matrix

CONTACTS: Note: Officers with more than one job title may be intentionally listed here more than once.

F. William Capp, CEO
F. William Capp, Pres.
James M. Spiezio, CFO
Matthew L. Lazarewicz, CTO
Gene Hunt, Dir.-Corp. Comm.
James M. Spiezio, VP-Finance
Judith F. McQueeney, VP-Asset Mgmt. & Market Dev.
Virgil G. Rose, Chmn.

Phone: 978-694-9121	Fax: 978-694-9127
Toll-Free: 888-938-9112	
Address: 65 Middlesex Rd., Tyngsboro, MA 01879 US	

GROWTH PLANS/SPECIAL FEATURES:

Beacon Power Corp. designs, manufactures and operates flywheel-based energy storage systems for grid-scale frequency regulation services and other utility-scale energy storage applications. The firm incorporates its flywheel-based systems into company-owned frequency regulation plants that serve the electricity grid, utilities, distributed generation and renewable energy markets. Using flywheel technology, Beacon has developed a line of kinetic batteries, which provide greater reliability; faster response time; cleaner operation, including zero direct emissions of carbon dioxide, nitrogen oxide, sulfur dioxide and mercury; and require less maintenance than typical acid and chemical-based batteries. A flywheel battery consists of a high-density spinning disc enclosed in a vacuum-sealed compartment and rotating on magnetic bearings, allowing it to spin with virtually no friction. Beacon's system, Smart Energy, draws energy from an outside source and stores it as kinetic energy. When fluctuations in demand require extra energy, a generator converts the kinetic energy back to electricity as needed until backup power generators are activated. The company has expanded this technology into the Smart Energy Matrix, which links several Smart Energy systems together. Beacon plans to build megawatt-scale flywheel-based frequency regulation plants around the U.S. The firm is also exploring the potential application of flywheel technology in systems for wind, diesel or flywheel energy storage hybrid power systems on islands, remote grids and in military applications In January 2011, the company's 20 megawatt (MW) flywheel energy storage plant in Stephentown, New York began commercial operations, with an initial eight MW of storage capacity coming online. In late 2011, Beacon filed for bankruptcy, unable to attract sufficient investment or build strong revenues needed for financial stability. In November 2011, following discussions with the U.S. Department of Energy's Loan Programs Office to recover its $39.1 million loan balance, the firm resolved to sell its Stephentown facility by January 2012.

FINANCIALS: Sales and profits are in thousands of dollars—add 000 to get the full amount. 2011 Note: Financial information for 2011 was not available for all companies at press time.

2011 Sales: $	2011 Profits: $	**U.S. Stock Ticker: BCONQ**
2010 Sales: $ 896	2010 Profits: $-22,680	**Int'l Ticker:**
2009 Sales: $ 968	2009 Profits: $-19,060	Int'l Exchange:
2008 Sales: $ 68	2008 Profits: $-23,568	Employees: 73 Fiscal Year Ends: 12/31
2007 Sales: $1,389	2007 Profits: $-12,918	Parent Company:

SALARIES/BENEFITS:

Pension Plan:	ESOP Stock Plan:	Profit Sharing:	Top Exec. Salary: $330,532	Bonus: $69,063
Savings Plan: Y	Stock Purch. Plan: Y		Second Exec. Salary: $222,294	Bonus: $21,714

OTHER THOUGHTS:

Apparent Women Officers or Directors: 1
Hot Spot for Advancement for Women/Minorities:

LOCATIONS: ("Y" = Yes)

West:	Southwest:	Midwest:	Southeast:	Northeast: Y	International:

BELL LABS

www.bell-labs.com

Industry Group Code: 541712

Energy/Fuel:	Other Technologies:		Electrical Products:	Electronics:		Transportation:	Other:	
Biofuels:	Irrigation:		Lighting/LEDs:	Computers:		Car Sharing:	Recycling:	
Batteries/Storage:	Nanotech:	Y	Waste Heat:	Sensors:		Electric Vehicles:	Engineering:	Y
Solar:	Biotech:		Smart Meters:	Software:	Y	Natural Gas Fuel:	Consulting:	
Wind:	Water Tech./Treatment:		Machinery:				Investing:	
Fuel Cells:	Ceramics:						Chemicals:	

TYPES OF BUSINESS:

Research & Development-Communications
Physical Science
Computer Science & Software
Mathematics Research
Optical & Wireless Networking Technologies
Nanotechnology Research

BRANDS/DIVISIONS/AFFILIATES:

Alcatel-Lucent
IMS Service Enhancement Layer
Base Station Router

CONTACTS: Note: Officers with more than one job title may be intentionally listed here more than once.

Jeong H. Kim, Pres.
Rod C. Alferness, Chief Scientist
Thierry Van Landegem, VP-Oper.
Paul Ross, Dir.-Corp. Comm.

Phone: 908-582-8500	**Fax:** 908-508-2576
Toll-Free:	
Address: 600 Mountain Ave., Murray Hill, NJ 07974-0636 US	

GROWTH PLANS/SPECIAL FEATURES:

Bell Labs is the research and development subsidiary of French telecommunications manufacturer Alcatel-Lucent. Winner of seven Nobel prizes and nine U.S. Medals of Science, it designs products and services at the forefront of communications technology and conducts fundamental research in the following fields: physical technologies; computer science and software; mathematical/algorithmic sciences; optical and wireless networking; security solutions; and government research. The physical technologies department is involved in materials research, optical physics and nanotechnology. Computer science and software includes research on systems networking, service infrastructure and convergence application. Mathematical/Algorithmic research involves fundamental mathematics of networks and systems, statistics/data mining and scientific computing. The wireless networking department is involved in software, mobile and Internet research; economic analysis; network planning; and business modeling. The optical networking research department studies fiber optic broadband networking, optical routers, high frequency electronics and photonic device fabrication. Bell Labs' security solutions provide virus prevention and general infrastructure protection. The government research division focuses on the needs of its government clients, specializing in nanotechnology, network reliability/security and laser communications. Its recent projects have included novel cooling technology, a more environmentally friendly form of liquid cooling; soundless speech technology for public cell phone conversations; advancements in firewall efficiency; and nanotechnology advancements in microphones, sensors, batteries, lenses, quantum computing and government communications. Other products include the IMS Service Enhancement Layer, which simplifies and speeds up delivery services; and Base Station Router, which simplifies 3G mobile networks into a single network. The company has eight facilities located in the U.S., Europe and Asia. The firm has generated over 33,000 patents in its history. In February 2010, Bell Labs agreed to expand its Ireland facility with 70 additional personnel.

FINANCIALS: Sales and profits are in thousands of dollars—add 000 to get the full amount. 2011 Note: Financial information for 2011 was not available for all companies at press time.

2011 Sales: $	2011 Profits: $	**U.S. Stock Ticker: Subsidiary**
2010 Sales: $	2010 Profits: $	**Int'l Ticker:**
2009 Sales: $	2009 Profits: $	Int'l Exchange:
2008 Sales: $	2008 Profits: $	Employees: Fiscal Year Ends: 12/31
2007 Sales: $	2007 Profits: $	Parent Company: ALCATEL-LUCENT

SALARIES/BENEFITS:

Pension Plan:	ESOP Stock Plan:	Profit Sharing:	Top Exec. Salary: $	Bonus: $
Savings Plan:	Stock Purch. Plan:		Second Exec. Salary: $	Bonus: $

OTHER THOUGHTS:

Apparent Women Officers or Directors:
Hot Spot for Advancement for Women/Minorities:

LOCATIONS: ("Y" = Yes)

West:	Southwest:	Midwest:	Southeast:	Northeast:	International:
				Y	Y

Sales, profits and employees may be estimates. Financial information, benefits and other data can change quickly and may vary from those stated here.

BETTER PLACE

www.betterplace.com

Industry Group Code: 33611

Energy/Fuel:		Other Technologies:	Electrical Products:	Electronics:	Transportation:		Other:
Biofuels:		Irrigation:	Lighting/LEDs:	Computers:	Car Sharing:		Recycling:
Batteries/Storage:	Y	Nanotech:	Waste Heat:	Sensors:	Electric Vehicles:	Y	Engineering:
Solar:		Biotech:	Smart Meters:	Software:	Natural Gas Fuel:		Consulting:
Wind:		Water Tech./Treatment:	Machinery:				Investing:
Fuel Cells:		Ceramics:					Chemicals:

TYPES OF BUSINESS:

Electric Automobiles
Electric Automobile Charging Stations

BRANDS/DIVISIONS/AFFILIATES:

Israel Corp.
Ofer Group
VantagePoint Venture Partners
Maniv Energy Capital
Morgan Stanley
Continental
Nissan Motor Company Ltd
Renault SA

CONTACTS: Note: Officers with more than one job title may be intentionally listed here more than once.

Shai Agassi, CEO
Charles Stonehill, CFO
Sigi Eshel, VP-Mktg.
Lior Storfer, VP-R&D
Barak Hershkovitz, CTO
Barak Hershkovitz, VP-Prod. Mgmt.
David Kennedy, General Counsel/Corp. Sec.
Jenny Cohen Derfler, VP-Global Oper.
Dan Cohen, VP-Strategic Initiatives
Joe Paluska, VP-Comm.
Moshe Kaplinsky, CEO-Better Place Israel
Evan Thornley, CEO-Better Place Australia
Sidney Goodman, VP-Automotive Alliances
Tal Agassi, VP-Oper. & Global Infrastructure Deployment
Idan Ofer, Chmn.
Johnny Hansen, CEO-Better Place Denmark

Phone: 650-845-2800	Fax: 650-845-2850
Toll-Free:	
Address: 1070 Arastradero Rd., Ste. 220, Palo Alto, CA 94304 US	

GROWTH PLANS/SPECIAL FEATURES:

Better Place is engaged in the design of electric vehicle support networks (EVs) and the operation of charging stations for EVs. The infrastructure envisioned by the firm includes a widespread network of charging spots for battery top-offs, in combination with switching stations enabling cars to swap depleted batteries for fully-charged ones in a few minutes time, thus enabling electric cars to travel greater distances. The charging stations would be approximately the size of a parking meter, while the battery switching stations would be somewhat similar to gas stations. The customer would pull his or her car into the appropriate bay and an automated process would remove the depleted battery and replace it with a fresh one. The firm plans to charge a monthly membership fee to users of its battery switching stations. Prototypes of Better Places' vehicles use rechargeable lithium ion batteries; however, the company is researching other technologies. The initial battery concept for Better Place was developed by Automotive Energy Supply Corp., a joint partnership of the Renault/Nissan alliance and Japanese manufacturer NEC. The Renault Fluence Z.E., developed by Renault/Nissan, is the first commercially available vehicle compatible with the company's battery switching stations and is set to go on sale initially in Israel and Denmark in late 2011. Discussions or partnerships for the development and installation of Better Place charging systems and EV fleets have also been established in Japan, California and Australia. The firm has raised over $500 million in venture capital. Investors include Morgan Stanley; Israel Corp.; Ofer Group; VantagePoint Venture Partners; and Maniv Energy Capital. In October 2010, Better Place announced plans to bring its electric taxi program, currently deployed in Tokyo, to the San Francisco Bay area. In June 2011, the firm completed the first battery switching station in Denmark, with plans to add 19 more throughout the country.

FINANCIALS: Sales and profits are in thousands of dollars—add 000 to get the full amount. 2011 Note: Financial information for 2011 was not available for all companies at press time.

2011 Sales: $	2011 Profits: $	**U.S. Stock Ticker:** Private
2010 Sales: $	2010 Profits: $	**Int'l Ticker:**
2009 Sales: $	2009 Profits: $	Int'l Exchange:
2008 Sales: $	2008 Profits: $	Employees: Fiscal Year Ends:
2007 Sales: $	2007 Profits: $	Parent Company:

SALARIES/BENEFITS:

Pension Plan:	ESOP Stock Plan:	Profit Sharing:	Top Exec. Salary: $	Bonus: $
Savings Plan:	Stock Purch. Plan:		Second Exec. Salary: $	Bonus: $

OTHER THOUGHTS:

Apparent Women Officers or Directors: 2
Hot Spot for Advancement for Women/Minorities: Y

LOCATIONS: ("Y" = Yes)

West:	Southwest:	Midwest:	Southeast:	Northeast:	International:
Y					Y

BG GROUP PLC

Industry Group Code: 211111

www.bg-group.com

Energy/Fuel:	Other Technologies:	Electrical Products:	Electronics:	Transportation:		Other:
Biofuels:	Irrigation:	Lighting/LEDs:	Computers:	Car Sharing:		Recycling:
Batteries/Storage:	Nanotech:	Waste Heat:	Sensors:	Electric Vehicles:		Engineering:
Solar:	Biotech:	Smart Meters:	Software:	Natural Gas Fuel:	Y	Consulting:
Wind:	Water Tech./Treatment:	Machinery:				Investing:
Fuel Cells:	Ceramics:					Chemicals:

TYPES OF BUSINESS:

Oil & Gas Exploration & Production
Natural Gas Transportation & Distribution
Natural Gas Storage
Power Generation Plants
Gas Marketing

BRANDS/DIVISIONS/AFFILIATES:

Pure Energy Resources Limited
EXCO Resources Inc
Queensland Gas Company, Ltd.
Premier Power Limited
Comgas
Gujarat Gas Company Limited
Mahanagar Gas Limited
MetroGas

CONTACTS: Note: Officers with more than one job title may be intentionally listed here more than once.

Frank Chapman, CEO
Martin Houston, COO
Ashley Almanza, CFO
Robert Booker, Exec. VP-Human Resources
Graham Vinter, General Counsel
Edel McCaffrey, Head-Media Rel.
John Grant, Exec. VP-Policy & Corp. Affairs
Catherine Tanna, Exec VP/Managing Dir.-Australia
Chirs Finlayson, Exec. VP/Managing Dir.-BG Advance
Sami Iskander, Exec. VP/Mgr.-Africa, Middle East & Asia
Robert P. Wilson, Chmn.

Phone: 44-118-935-3222	Fax: 44-118-935-3484
Toll-Free:	
Address: 100 Thames Valley Park Dr., Reading, Berkshire RG6 1PT UK	

GROWTH PLANS/SPECIAL FEATURES:

BG Group plc, headquartered in the UK but operating in 27 countries, is engaged in the exploration, development, production, transmission, distribution and supply of natural gas. The company is divided into four business segments: exploration and production; liquefied natural gas; transmission and distribution; and power generation. The company's exploration and production division develops, produces and markets gas and oil in 12 countries. In 2010, the firm produced nearly 236 million barrels of oil equivalent and increased its reserves and resources to approximately 16.2 billion barrels of oil equivalent. BG Group's liquefied natural gas (LNG) division develops and operates infrastructure for the procurement, transport and sale of LNG, as well as LNG liquefaction and regasification facilities. The company's transmission and distribution division aims to develop new markets, transport gas to them and distribute that gas to power generating, industrial, commercial and residential customers. BG Group owns interests in distribution companies in Brazil (Comgas), India (Gujarat Gas Company Limited and Mahanagar Gas Limited), Argentina and Uruguay (MetroGas) and a pipeline in Kazakhstan. The firm's power generation division manages a portfolio of gas-fired power plants in the UK, Italy, Malaysia and Australia.

FINANCIALS: Sales and profits are in thousands of dollars—add 000 to get the full amount. 2011 Note: Financial information for 2011 was not available for all companies at press time.

2011 Sales: $	2011 Profits: $	**U.S. Stock Ticker:**
2010 Sales: $17,166,000	2010 Profits: $3,351,000	**Int'l Ticker: BG**
2009 Sales: $14,737,200	2009 Profits: $3,128,380	Int'l Exchange: London-LSE
2008 Sales: $18,132,500	2008 Profits: $4,512,200	Employees: 6,041 Fiscal Year Ends: 12/31
2007 Sales: $16,430,000	2007 Profits: $3,460,000	Parent Company:

SALARIES/BENEFITS:

Pension Plan:	ESOP Stock Plan:	Profit Sharing:	Top Exec. Salary: $1,811,409	Bonus: $3,081,232
Savings Plan:	Stock Purch. Plan:		Second Exec. Salary: $1,089,840	Bonus: $1,062,066

OTHER THOUGHTS:

Apparent Women Officers or Directors: 1
Hot Spot for Advancement for Women/Minorities:

LOCATIONS: ("Y" = Yes)

West:	Southwest:	Midwest:	Southeast:	Northeast:	International:
	Y		Y	Y	Y

BIOAMBER

www.bio-amber.com

Industry Group Code: 325

Energy/Fuel:		Other Technologies:	Electrical Products:	Electronics:	Transportation:	Other:	
Biofuels:	Y	Irrigation:	Lighting/LEDs:	Computers:	Car Sharing:	Recycling:	
Batteries/Storage:		Nanotech:	Waste Heat:	Sensors:	Electric Vehicles:	Engineering:	
Solar:		Biotech:	Smart Meters:	Software:	Natural Gas Fuel:	Consulting:	
Wind:		Water Tech./Treatment:	Machinery:			Investing:	
Fuel Cells:		Ceramics:				Chemicals:	Y

TYPES OF BUSINESS:

Next-Generation Chemicals

BRANDS/DIVISIONS/AFFILIATES:

Sinoven Biopolymers
DNP Green Technology

CONTACTS: Note: Officers with more than one job title may be intentionally listed here more than once.

Jean-Francois Huc, CEO
Jean-Francois Huc, Pres.
Andrew Ashworth, CFO
Babette Pettersen, Sr. VP-Mktg. & Sales
Jim Millis, CTO
Dilum Dunuwila, VP-Eng.
Kenneth Wall, Sr. VP-Mfg.
Tom Dries, Sr. VP-Oper. Strategy
Ray Balee, VP-Polymers Bus.
Laurent Bernier, VP-Compliance & Intellectual Property
Mike Hartmann, Exec. VP

Phone: 763-253-4480	Fax:
Toll-Free:	
Address: 3850 Annapolis Ln. N., Ste. 180, Plymouth, MN 55447 US	

GROWTH PLANS/SPECIAL FEATURES:

BioAmber, formerly DNP Green Technology, is a next-generation chemicals company. The firm utilizes its proprietary technologies to convert renewable feedstocks into cost-comparable replacement alternatives to petroleum derived chemicals. This fermentation process improves the carbon footprint by consuming carbon dioxide as opposed to releasing it as a byproduct. While primarily focusing on the production of bio-succinic acid, the company's portfolio of bio-based chemicals additionally includes the bio-succinic acid derivative chemicals: 1,4 butanediol (bdo); plasticizers; polymers; and C6 chemicals. The firm's bio-succinic acid is a 97% biobased, direct substitute for petroleum-based succinic acid. BioAmber's intellectual property for the production and manufacturing of bio-succinic acid includes over 40 families of patents, including the orgranism, the fermentation process, the purification of the succinic acid, the transformation of succinic acid into its derivatives and its eventual uses and applications. The firm's bio-succinic acid facility, located in Pomacle, France, is one of the world's largest bio-based manufacturing fermenters, with a 350,000 liter commercial-scale fermenter. BioAmber markets its chemical components in the polyurethane; cosmetics & personal care; de-icing; resins & coatings; foods & flavors; and lubricant markets. Recent acquisitions include Sinoven Biopolymers, a modified polybutylene succinate (PBS) production firm. The firm has a partnership agreement with Mitsui & Co. to create a manufacturing facility to Sarnai, Ontario as well as facilities in Thailand and either the United States or Brazil.

FINANCIALS: Sales and profits are in thousands of dollars—add 000 to get the full amount. 2011 Note: Financial information for 2011 was not available for all companies at press time.

2011 Sales: $	2011 Profits: $	**U.S. Stock Ticker: Private**
2010 Sales: $	2010 Profits: $	**Int'l Ticker:**
2009 Sales: $	2009 Profits: $	Int'l Exchange:
2008 Sales: $	2008 Profits: $	Employees: Fiscal Year Ends:
2007 Sales: $	2007 Profits: $	Parent Company:

SALARIES/BENEFITS:

Pension Plan:	ESOP Stock Plan:	Profit Sharing:	Top Exec. Salary: $	Bonus: $
Savings Plan:	Stock Purch. Plan:		Second Exec. Salary: $	Bonus: $

OTHER THOUGHTS:

Apparent Women Officers or Directors: 1
Hot Spot for Advancement for Women/Minorities:

LOCATIONS: ("Y" = Yes)

West:	Southwest:	Midwest:	Southeast:	Northeast:	International:
		Y			Y

BIODICO INC
www.biodieselindustries.com

Industry Group Code: 325199

Energy/Fuel:		Other Technologies:		Electrical Products:		Electronics:		Transportation:		Other:	
Biofuels:	Y	Irrigation:		Lighting/LEDs:		Computers:		Car Sharing:		Recycling:	
Batteries/Storage:		Nanotech:		Waste Heat:		Sensors:		Electric Vehicles:		Engineering:	
Solar:		Biotech:	Y	Smart Meters:		Software:		Natural Gas Fuel:		Consulting:	
Wind:		Water Tech./Treatment:		Machinery:						Investing:	
Fuel Cells:		Ceramics:								Chemicals:	

TYPES OF BUSINESS:
Modular Biodiesel Production Equipment
Biodiesel Production

BRANDS/DIVISIONS/AFFILIATES:
ARIES
Biodiesel Industries Inc
Biodiesel Industries of Australia

CONTACTS: Note: Officers with more than one job title may be intentionally listed here more than once.
Russell Teall, CEO
Russell Teall, Pres.
Christy Teall, CFO

Phone: 805-683-8103	Fax: 805-456-2192
Toll-Free:	
Address: 426 Donze Ave., Santa Barbara, CA 93101 US	

GROWTH PLANS/SPECIAL FEATURES:
Biodico, Inc., formerly Biodiesel Industries, Inc., builds, owns and operates facilities for the production of biodiesel, an alternative fuel to petro-diesel, for diesel engines. Biodiesel is a nontoxic, biodegradable replacement for petroleum diesel that is made from multiple feedstocks, including vegetable oil, recycled cooking oil and tallow. The company has a host of full-scale modular production units (MPUs). Biodico has installed MPUs in Texas, California, Nevada, Colorado and Australia. These MPUs are typically established through agreements with joint venture partners, including petroleum distributers, mining and industrial companies, municipalities, propulsion and automation companies. One of its major clients is the U.S. Navy, which has assisted in the production of biodiesel at Naval Base Ventura County in California. The firm operates a fully renewable biodiesel facility in Denton, Texas. The facility is capable of producing 3 million gallons of fuel a year and uses biogas from the city's landfill to provide heating for the biodiesel production process. Its facility in Australia, run through affiliate Biodiesel Industries of Australia, has a 3 million gallon annual capacity, with plans to expand to 6 million gallons annually. The firm also works with Cal State University to grow canola plants in selenium-contaminated lands in the Central Valley. The plants extract selenium, present in toxic levels. Canola seed oil is used as biodiesel feedstock as well, and the residual seed pulp acts as a nutritional selenium supplement when used in cattle feed. Other Biodico projects include the collection of waste fryer oil produced at restaurants and food processing facilities; and research and development of algae and jatropha as biodiesel feedstocks. The firm's newest product, ARIES, which was co-developed with Aerojet, utilizes specifically developed in-line sensors and controls driven by advanced automation technology to enable central facilities to offer global technical support, monitoring and operational control.

FINANCIALS: Sales and profits are in thousands of dollars—add 000 to get the full amount. 2011 Note: Financial information for 2011 was not available for all companies at press time.

2011 Sales: $	2011 Profits: $	**U.S. Stock Ticker: Private**
2010 Sales: $	2010 Profits: $	**Int'l Ticker:**
2009 Sales: $	2009 Profits: $	Int'l Exchange:
2008 Sales: $	2008 Profits: $	Employees: Fiscal Year Ends:
2007 Sales: $	2007 Profits: $	Parent Company:

SALARIES/BENEFITS:
Pension Plan:	ESOP Stock Plan:	Profit Sharing:	Top Exec. Salary: $	Bonus: $
Savings Plan:	Stock Purch. Plan:		Second Exec. Salary: $	Bonus: $

OTHER THOUGHTS:
Apparent Women Officers or Directors: 1
Hot Spot for Advancement for Women/Minorities:

LOCATIONS: ("Y" = Yes)
West:	Southwest:	Midwest:	Southeast:	Northeast:	International:
Y	Y				

Sales, profits and employees may be estimates. Financial information, benefits and other data can change quickly and may vary from those stated here.

BIOS-BIOENERGIESYSTEME GMBH

www.bios-bioenergy.at

Industry Group Code: 541330

Energy/Fuel:	Other Technologies:		Electrical Products:	Electronics:	Transportation:	Other:	
Biofuels:	Irrigation:		Lighting/LEDs:	Computers:	Car Sharing:	Recycling:	
Batteries/Storage:	Nanotech:		Waste Heat:	Sensors:	Electric Vehicles:	Engineering:	Y
Solar:	Biotech:	Y	Smart Meters:	Software:	Natural Gas Fuel:	Consulting:	
Wind:	Water Tech./Treatment:		Machinery:			Investing:	
Fuel Cells:	Ceramics:					Chemicals:	

TYPES OF BUSINESS:

Biomass Plant Design & Development
Research Services
Software Development

BRANDS/DIVISIONS/AFFILIATES:

Bioenergy 2020+ GmbH
BIOSTROM Erzeugungs GmbH

CONTACTS: *Note: Officers with more than one job title may be intentionally listed here more than once.*

Ingwald Obernberger, Managing Dir.
Friedrich Biedermann, Project Mgr.-R&D
Berhard Winter, Dir.-IT
Thomas Barnthaler, Project Eng.
Evanthia Vassi, Dir.-Finance & Acct./Controller
Claudia Benesch, Project Eng.
Harald Hirt, Project Eng.
Gerold Thek, Project Mgr.
Norbert Wildbacher, Project Mgr.

Phone: 43-316-481-300	Fax: 43-316-481-300-4
Toll-Free:	
Address: Inffeldgasse 21B, Graz, A-8010 Austria	

GROWTH PLANS/SPECIAL FEATURES:

BIOS-BIOENERGYSYSTEME GmbH (BIOS) is a German firm engaged in the research, development, design and optimization of processes and plants for heat and power production from biomass fuels. The company has completed or is currently working on projects in Belgium, Germany, the U.K., France, Greece, Ireland, Italy, Croatia, Montenegro, Norway, Russia, Switzerland, Hungary, Belarus, South Africa, Honduras, Canada and the U.S. It provides solutions that cover the entire field of thermal biomass utilization (combustion, gasification and combined heat and power systems). BIOS operates in nine working fields: engineering; QM-biomass heating plants; plant monitoring; analyses and measurements; ash utilization; expertise; research and development; CFD simulations; and software development. The company develops energy master plans and feasibility studies to create detailed plans and the realizations of plants. The firm is an industrial partner of the Austrian Bioenergy Competence Centre (Bioenergy 2020+ GmbH), which conducts energetic biomass utilization R&D projects. The company is also a 10% shareholder in BIOSTROM Erzeugungs GmbH, a biomass co-generation heating plant in Vorarlberg, Austria that burns waste wood and has an electric capacity of 1,100 kilowatts, a thermal capacity of 6.2 megawatts (MW) and a chilling capacity of 2.4 MW.

FINANCIALS: Sales and profits are in thousands of dollars—add 000 to get the full amount. 2011 Note: Financial information for 2011 was not available for all companies at press time.

2011 Sales: $	2011 Profits: $	**U.S. Stock Ticker: Private**
2010 Sales: $	2010 Profits: $	**Int'l Ticker:**
2009 Sales: $	2009 Profits: $	Int'l Exchange:
2008 Sales: $	2008 Profits: $	Employees: Fiscal Year Ends:
2007 Sales: $	2007 Profits: $	Parent Company:

SALARIES/BENEFITS:

Pension Plan:	ESOP Stock Plan:	Profit Sharing:	Top Exec. Salary: $	Bonus: $
Savings Plan:	Stock Purch. Plan:		Second Exec. Salary: $	Bonus: $

OTHER THOUGHTS:

Apparent Women Officers or Directors: 3
Hot Spot for Advancement for Women/Minorities: Y

LOCATIONS: ("Y" = Yes)

West:	Southwest:	Midwest:	Southeast:	Northeast:	International:
	Y				Y

BLOOM ENERGY CORPORATION

www.bloomenergy.com

Industry Group Code: 335999

Energy/Fuel:		Other Technologies:		Electrical Products:		Electronics:	Transportation:	Other:
Biofuels:		Irrigation:		Lighting/LEDs:		Computers:	Car Sharing:	Recycling:
Batteries/Storage:		Nanotech:		Waste Heat:		Sensors:	Electric Vehicles:	Engineering:
Solar:		Biotech:		Smart Meters:		Software:	Natural Gas Fuel:	Consulting:
Wind:		Water Tech./Treatment:		Machinery:				Investing:
Fuel Cells:	Y	Ceramics:						Chemicals:

TYPES OF BUSINESS:

Fuel Cell Manufacturing

BRANDS/DIVISIONS/AFFILIATES:

Energy Server
Bloom Boxes
Bloom Electrons
Bloom Energy International

CONTACTS: Note: Officers with more than one job title may be intentionally listed here more than once.

K.R. Sridhar, CEO
George Nguyen, COO
Bill Kurtz, CFO
Matt Ross, Chief Mktg. Officer
David Barber, VP-Human Resources
John Mufich, CIO
Venkat Venkataraman, CTO
Venkat Venkataraman, Exec. VP-Eng.
Bill Kurtz, Chief Commercial Officer
Jim Cook, Sr. VP-Strategic Materials
Gary Workman, VP-Quality
Bill Thayer, Exec. VP-Sales & Service
Girish Paranjpe, Managing Dir.-Bloom Energy Int'l

Phone: 408-543-1500	Fax: 408-543-1501
Toll-Free:	
Address: 1299 Orleans Dr., Sunnyvale, CA 94089 US	

GROWTH PLANS/SPECIAL FEATURES:

Bloom Energy Corporation is a privately-owned developer and manufacturer of on-site power generation systems powered by solid oxide fuel cell (SOFC) technology. The firm's generators, marketed under the Energy Server brand, use SOFC technology to generate 200 kilowatts (kW) of electricity per generator, each of which is about the size of a standard parking space. These generators, called Bloom Boxes, are composed of multiple fuel cell stacks that can accept a wide range of fuels and are manufactured from a common sand-like powder; unlike traditional fuel cells, the company's cells do not use precious metals, molten materials or corrosive acids. This allows Bloom Energy's generators to provide clean, high-efficiency energy at lower costs than other fuel cells. Bloom Boxes also provide better energy security than a shared grid; are easily and quickly installed; and can reduce carbon dioxide emissions by 40% or more, depending on fuel choice. The company also provides operating and maintenance support programs to users of its generators. Bloom Energy's customers include leading companies such as AT&T, Google, Adobe, Wal-Mart, eBay, Safeway, FedEx, Bank of America and The Coca-Cola Company. In January 2011, the firm introduced a new service, Bloom Electrons, which allows customers to purchase energy from an on-site fuel cell generator without buying the entire system. In April 2011, Bloom Energy expanded its California manufacturing facility to 210,000 square feet and added approximately 1,000 new jobs. In May 2011, it established Bloom Energy International to develop a global market for the company's generators.

FINANCIALS: Sales and profits are in thousands of dollars—add 000 to get the full amount. 2011 Note: Financial information for 2011 was not available for all companies at press time.

2011 Sales: $	2011 Profits: $	**U.S. Stock Ticker: Private**
2010 Sales: $	2010 Profits: $	**Int'l Ticker:**
2009 Sales: $	2009 Profits: $	Int'l Exchange:
2008 Sales: $	2008 Profits: $	Employees: Fiscal Year Ends:
2007 Sales: $	2007 Profits: $	Parent Company:

SALARIES/BENEFITS:

Pension Plan:	ESOP Stock Plan:	Profit Sharing:	Top Exec. Salary: $	Bonus: $
Savings Plan:	Stock Purch. Plan:		Second Exec. Salary: $	Bonus: $

OTHER THOUGHTS:

Apparent Women Officers or Directors:
Hot Spot for Advancement for Women/Minorities:

LOCATIONS: ("Y" = Yes)

West:	Southwest:	Midwest:	Southeast:	Northeast:	International:
Y					Y

Sales, profits and employees may be estimates. Financial information, benefits and other data can change quickly and may vary from those stated here.

BOSCH SOLAR ENERGY AG

www.bosch-solarenergy.de

Industry Group Code: 334413

Energy/Fuel:		Other Technologies:		Electrical Products:		Electronics:		Transportation:		Other:	
Biofuels:		Irrigation:		Lighting/LEDs:		Computers:		Car Sharing:		Recycling:	
Batteries/Storage:		Nanotech:		Waste Heat:		Sensors:		Electric Vehicles:		Engineering:	
Solar:	Y	Biotech:		Smart Meters:		Software:		Natural Gas Fuel:		Consulting:	
Wind:		Water Tech./Treatment:		Machinery:						Investing:	
Fuel Cells:		Ceramics:								Chemicals:	

TYPES OF BUSINESS:

Solar Cells & Modules
Ingots
Wafers
Thin Film Technology
Silicon Supply

BRANDS/DIVISIONS/AFFILIATES:

ErSol Solar Energy
Bosch Solar Wafers GmbH
Bosch Solar Modules GmbH
Bosch Solar Thin Film GmbH
Shanghai Electric Solar Energy Co Ltd
Allianz Climate Solutions GmbH
Robert Bosch GmbH
Silicon Recycling Services Inc

CONTACTS: *Note: Officers with more than one job title may be intentionally listed here more than once.*

Holger von Hebel, CEO
Jurgen Pressl, COO
Holger von Hebel, CFO
Holger von Hebel, Head-Human Resources
Volker Nadenau, Head-R&D
Holger von Hebel, Head-IT
Volker Nadenau, CTO
Peter Schneidewind, Head-Prod. Mgmt.
Jurgen Pressl, Head-Mfg.
Holger von Hebel, Head-Legal Affairs
Holger von Hebel, Head-Corp. Dev.
Heide Traemann, Head-Comm.
Holger von Hebel, Head-Finance & Controlling
Eric Daniels, Pres., Solar Energy North America
Jurgen Pressl, Head-Purchasing & Supply Chain Mgmt.

Phone: 49-361-2195-0	**Fax:** 49-361-2195-1133
Toll-Free:	
Address: Wilhelm-Wolff Strasse 23, Erfurt, 99099 Germany	

GROWTH PLANS/SPECIAL FEATURES:

Bosch Solar Energy AG, formerly ErSol Solar Energy, based in Germany, manufactures and markets photovoltaic products such as polycrystalline and monocrystalline solar cells and solar modules. The company also supplies silicon and produces ingots, wafers and thin film photovoltaic solar cells. The firm operates through four divisions: silicon, wafers, solar cells and modules. The silicon division includes subsidiary Silicon Recycling Services, Inc., based in Camarillo, California, which recycles scrap silicon and renders it re-usable for solar cell manufacture. Subsidiary Bosch Solar Wafers GmbH operates the wafers division and manufactures monocrystalline ingots and thin sliced wafers. The solar cells segment operates several production plants in Erfurt and Arnstadt, Germany, producing solar cells with efficiencies in the range of 17%. The modules segment operates through subsidiaries Bosch Solar Modules GmbH, which distributes modules and other system components and markets crystalline solar modules from company produced solar cells; and Bosch Solar Thin Film GmbH, which produces thin-film solar modules at another production facility in Erfurt. The firm's products include crystals and wafers with special twin structure and dopant impurities; the P-series polycrystalline cells; the M2BB and M3BB monocrystalline cells, with two and three solder contacts, respectively; and various colored polycrystalline solar panels, as well as photovoltaic modules and inverters. The company also maintains a 35% stake in Shanghai Electric Solar Energy Co., Ltd., a Chinese manufacturer of solar modules that purchases solar cells from Bosch Solar Energy. The company maintains a strategic partnership with Allianz Climate Solutions GmbH to focus on the development and construction of turnkey solar power stations. In June 2011, the firm announced the completion of one of the largest solar parks in the U.K. in Trefullock, England; in addition, the company announced plans to build a new manufacturing site for solar energy in Malaysia.

FINANCIALS: Sales and profits are in thousands of dollars—add 000 to get the full amount. 2011 Note: Financial information for 2011 was not available for all companies at press time.

2011 Sales: $	2011 Profits: $	**U.S. Stock Ticker: Subsidiary**	
2010 Sales: $	2010 Profits: $	**Int'l Ticker:**	
2009 Sales: $	2009 Profits: $	Int'l Exchange:	
2008 Sales: $	2008 Profits: $	Employees:	Fiscal Year Ends: 12/31
2007 Sales: $	2007 Profits: $	Parent Company: ROBERT BOSCH GMBH	

SALARIES/BENEFITS:

Pension Plan:	ESOP Stock Plan:	Profit Sharing:	Top Exec. Salary: $	Bonus: $
Savings Plan:	Stock Purch. Plan:		Second Exec. Salary: $	Bonus: $

OTHER THOUGHTS:

Apparent Women Officers or Directors: 1
Hot Spot for Advancement for Women/Minorities:

LOCATIONS: ("Y" = Yes)

West:	Southwest:	Midwest:	Southeast:	Northeast:	International:
Y					Y

Sales, profits and employees may be estimates. Financial information, benefits and other data can change quickly and may vary from those stated here.

BOSTON-POWER

www.boston-power.com

Industry Group Code: 33591

Energy/Fuel:	Other Technologies:	Electrical Products:	Electronics:	Transportation:	Other:
Biofuels:	Irrigation:	Lighting/LEDs:	Computers:	Car Sharing:	Recycling:
Batteries/Storage: Y	Nanotech:	Waste Heat:	Sensors:	Electric Vehicles:	Engineering:
Solar:	Biotech:	Smart Meters:	Software:	Natural Gas Fuel:	Consulting:
Wind:	Water Tech./Treatment:	Machinery:			Investing:
Fuel Cells:	Ceramics:				Chemicals:

TYPES OF BUSINESS:

Lithium-Ion Battery Platform Development

BRANDS/DIVISIONS/AFFILIATES:

Sonata
Swing
Swing Key
Swing Medley
Swing Tempo
Swing RESS
Boston-Power Battery (Taiwan) Company Inc
Boston-Power Battery (Shenzhen) Co Ltd

CONTACTS: *Note: Officers with more than one job title may be intentionally listed here more than once.*

Keith Schmid, CEO
Per Onnerud, CTO
Pete Rumsey, Chief Customer Officer
Sonny Wu, Chmn.
Christina Lampe-Onnerud, Int'l. Chmn.

Phone: 508-366-0885	**Fax:** 508-366-0998
Toll-Free:	
Address: 2200 West Park Dr., Westborough, MA 01581 US	

GROWTH PLANS/SPECIAL FEATURES:

Boston-Power is a technology company focused on the development of lithium-ion battery technology platforms. The firm's products are all based upon the aforementioned technology platform and include cells, battery blocks, battery modules and battery systems. Under the cells product line the firm offers the high energy density, long cycle life Swing and Sonata rechargeable lithium-ion cells. Both cells share a common design and can be arranged into modules, blocks and packs and systems. The battery blocks product line consists of the Swing Key, a high-capacity building block available in a 30.8 ampere-hour (Ah) model or a 35.2Ah model. The battery modules product line offer a high-energy density and long-life solution for military systems, electric vehicles and utilities. The products in this line include the Swing Medley and the various Swing Tempo models. The battery systems product line is composed of the Swing RESS, a large-format, high-performance energy storage system. The Swing RESS is applicable for use in wide range of markets, including the transportation market, within battery electric vehicles and plug-in hybrid electric vehicles, and in energy storage systems, such as solar power telecom base stations and off-grid hybrid equipment. Boston-Power, although headquartered in the U.S., has sales and supply chain operations in Sweden; Taiwan, as Boston-Power Battery (Taiwan) Company, Inc.; and China, as Boston-Power Battery (Shenzhen) Co., Ltd.

FINANCIALS: Sales and profits are in thousands of dollars—add 000 to get the full amount. 2011 Note: Financial information for 2011 was not available for all companies at press time.

2011 Sales: $	2011 Profits: $	**U.S. Stock Ticker: Private**
2010 Sales: $	2010 Profits: $	**Int'l Ticker:**
2009 Sales: $	2009 Profits: $	Int'l Exchange:
2008 Sales: $	2008 Profits: $	Employees: Fiscal Year Ends:
2007 Sales: $	2007 Profits: $	Parent Company:

SALARIES/BENEFITS:

Pension Plan:	ESOP Stock Plan:	Profit Sharing:	Top Exec. Salary: $	Bonus: $
Savings Plan:	Stock Purch. Plan:		Second Exec. Salary: $	Bonus: $

OTHER THOUGHTS:

Apparent Women Officers or Directors: 1
Hot Spot for Advancement for Women/Minorities:

LOCATIONS: ("Y" = Yes)

West:	Southwest:	Midwest:	Southeast:	Northeast:	International:
				Y	Y

BP ALTERNATIVE ENERGY

www.bpalternativenergy.com

Industry Group Code: 221119

Energy/Fuel:	Other Technologies:	Electrical Products:	Electronics:	Transportation:	Other:
Biofuels:	Irrigation:	Lighting/LEDs:	Computers:	Car Sharing:	Recycling:
Batteries/Storage:	Nanotech:	Waste Heat:	Sensors:	Electric Vehicles:	Engineering:
Solar:	Biotech:	Smart Meters:	Software:	Natural Gas Fuel:	Consulting:
Wind: Y	Water Tech./Treatment:	Machinery:			Investing:
Fuel Cells:	Ceramics:				Chemicals:

TYPES OF BUSINESS:

Low-Carbon Power Generation
Wind Power
Hydroelectric Power
Solar Power
Natural Gas-Fired Power
Power Marketing
Emissions Trading
Cellulosic Biofuels

BRANDS/DIVISIONS/AFFILIATES:

BP plc
BP Solar
BP Wind Energy
Hydrogen Energy California
Hydrogen Power Abu Dhabi
BP Biofuels
Tropical BioEngeria SA
Companhia Nacional de Acucar e Alcoo

CONTACTS: *Note: Officers with more than one job title may be intentionally listed here more than once.*

Katrina Landis, CEO
Craig Coburn, CFO
Justin Adams, Head-Emerging Bus. & Ventures
Tom Briggs, VP-Comm. & Policy
Dominic Emery, Investor Rel.
John Graham, Pres., BP Wind Energy
Phil New, CEO-BP Biofuels
Mike Petrucci, CEO-BP Solar

Phone: 44-207-496-4000	Fax: 44-207-496-4630
Toll-Free:	
Address: 1 St. James's Sq., London, SW1Y 4PD UK	

GROWTH PLANS/SPECIAL FEATURES:

BP Alternative Energy (BPAE) is BP plc's low-carbon power generation subsidiary. Through BPAE's solar subsidiary, BP Solar, it has solar power projects installed in almost 160 countries. BP Wind Energy, another BPAE subsidiary, owns wind farms in California, Colorado, Indiana, Kansas, Texas, South Dakota and Idaho, producing more than 1,200 megawatts (MW). In the hydrogen power and carbon capture storage (CCS) business, BPAE operates two major hydrogen power plants through joint ventures Hydrogen Energy California and Hydrogen Power Abu Dhabi. In addition, the firm has interests in eight gas-fired power stations with approximately 6,000 MW of generating capacity, including plants in the U.S., the U.K., South Korea, Vietnam and Spain. Through BP Biofuels, it owns three ethanol producing mills in Brazil located in the states of Goias and Minas Gerais. BPAE also owns the Whiting Clean Energy facility, a 525 MW natural-gas plant in Indiana. In February 2011, the firm announced that it had agreed to the joint ownership of the 32 MW Long Island Solar Farm with MetLife. In March 2011, BPAE acquired 83% of Companhia Nacional de Acucar e Alcool (CNAA), an ethanol and sugar producer, for approximately $680 million. In the same month, it began construction on the Sherbino 2 Wind Farm in Texas. In May 2011, the firm commenced construction on the Trinity Hills Wind Farm, also in Texas. In September 2011, BPAE acquired the remaining shares of Tropical BioEngeria SA for approximately $71 million, giving the company full ownership; moreover, the firm also acquired an additional 3% of CNAA for approximately $25 million.

FINANCIALS: Sales and profits are in thousands of dollars—add 000 to get the full amount. 2011 Note: Financial information for 2011 was not available for all companies at press time.

2011 Sales: $	2011 Profits: $	**U.S. Stock Ticker: Subsidiary**
2010 Sales: $	2010 Profits: $	**Int'l Ticker:**
2009 Sales: $	2009 Profits: $	Int'l Exchange:
2008 Sales: $	2008 Profits: $	Employees: Fiscal Year Ends: 12/31
2007 Sales: $	2007 Profits: $	Parent Company: BP PLC

SALARIES/BENEFITS:

Pension Plan: Y	ESOP Stock Plan:	Profit Sharing:	Top Exec. Salary: $	Bonus: $
Savings Plan: Y	Stock Purch. Plan:		Second Exec. Salary: $	Bonus: $

OTHER THOUGHTS:

Apparent Women Officers or Directors: 1
Hot Spot for Advancement for Women/Minorities: Y

LOCATIONS: ("Y" = Yes)

West:	Southwest:	Midwest:	Southeast:	Northeast:	International:
Y	Y	Y	Y	Y	Y

BP PLC

www.bp.com

Industry Group Code: 211111

Energy/Fuel:	Other Technologies:	Electrical Products:	Electronics:	Transportation:	Other:
Biofuels:	Irrigation:	Lighting/LEDs:	Computers:	Car Sharing:	Recycling:
Batteries/Storage:	Nanotech:	Waste Heat:	Sensors:	Electric Vehicles:	Engineering:
Solar:	Biotech:	Smart Meters:	Software:	Natural Gas Fuel:	Consulting:
Wind:	Water Tech./Treatment:	Machinery:			Investing:
Fuel Cells:	Ceramics:				Chemicals: Y

TYPES OF BUSINESS:

Oil & Gas Exploration & Production
Refining
Renewable & Alternative Energy
Lubricants
Natural Gas
Photovoltaic Modules
Gas Stations & Convenience Stores

BRANDS/DIVISIONS/AFFILIATES:

BP
Aral
am/pm
Companhia Nacional de Acucar e Alcool
Castrol
Wild Bean Café

CONTACTS: *Note: Officers with more than one job title may be intentionally listed here more than once.*

Robert Dudley, CEO
Byron E. Grote, CFO
Iain C. Conn, CEO-Mktg. & Refining
Helmut Schuster, Dir.-Human Resources
Mike Daily, Exec. VP-Exploration
Bob Fryar, Exec. VP-Prod.
Rupert Bondy, Group General Counsel
Bernard Loonet, Exec. VP-Dev.
Lamar McKay, Exec. VP
Steve Westwell, Exec. VP-Strategy & Integration
Carl-Henric Svanberg, Chmn.

Phone: 44-2074-96-4000	Fax: 44-20-7496-4630
Toll-Free:	
Address: 1 St. James's Sq., London, SW1Y 4PD UK	

GROWTH PLANS/SPECIAL FEATURES:

BP plc is one of the world's largest integrated oil companies, with reserves of 18.3 billion barrels of oil and gas equivalent and daily production of about 3.8 million barrels of oil equivalent. Its core brands include BP, Aral, am/pm, Castrol and Wild Bean Cafe. The company operates through three segments: Exploration and Production (E&P); Refining and Marketing (R&M); and Alternative Energy. E&P manages BP's upstream activities, including oil and gas exploration, field development and production; and midstream activities, including the management of crude oil and natural gas pipelines, processing and export terminals and liquefied natural gas (LNG) processing facilities. R&M focuses on refining, marketing and transporting crude oil and petroleum products to wholesale and retail customers. This segment also includes the firm's aromatics and acetyls businesses. Alternative Energy processes and markets biofuels, such as ethanol and biodiesel; manages the company's solar, wind and gas-fired power businesses; and conducts biofuel research. BP operates in over 80 countries worldwide. In 2010, a major deepwater Gulf of Mexico well on which BP is the operator and majority owner blew out, creating a massive oil spill and significant liabilities for the firm. As a result, BP announced a change of CEO and it has been selling assets in order to raise cash. In March 2011, BP sold its 93% interest in the Wattenberg Plant for $575.5 million to a subsidiary of Anadarko Petroleum Corp. and also sold 33 refined products terminals and 992 miles of pipeline to Buckeye Partners L.P. for $225 million. In April 2011, the company announced the sale of ARCO Aluminum, Inc. to a consortium of Japanese companies for $680 million. In September 2011, BP announced that it would acquire 3% of Companhia Nacional de Acucar e Alcool, a Brazilian sugar and ethanol producer.

FINANCIALS: Sales and profits are in thousands of dollars—add 000 to get the full amount. 2011 Note: Financial information for 2011 was not available for all companies at press time.

2011 Sales: $	2011 Profits: $	**U.S. Stock Ticker:**
2010 Sales: $297,107,000	2010 Profits: $-3,324,000	**Int'l Ticker: BP**
2009 Sales: $239,272,000	2009 Profits: $16,759,000	Int'l Exchange: London-LSE
2008 Sales: $361,143,000	2008 Profits: $21,666,000	Employees: 92,000 Fiscal Year Ends: 12/31
2007 Sales: $284,365,000	2007 Profits: $21,169,000	Parent Company:

SALARIES/BENEFITS:

Pension Plan: Y	ESOP Stock Plan:	Profit Sharing:	Top Exec. Salary: $1,842,150	Bonus: $2,394,890
Savings Plan: Y	Stock Purch. Plan:		Second Exec. Salary: $1,372,044	Bonus: $2,056,519

OTHER THOUGHTS:

Apparent Women Officers or Directors: 3
Hot Spot for Advancement for Women/Minorities: Y

LOCATIONS: ("Y" = Yes)

West:	Southwest:	Midwest:	Southeast:	Northeast:	International:
Y	Y	Y	Y	Y	Y

BP SOLAR

www.bpsolar.com

Industry Group Code: 334413

Energy/Fuel:	Other Technologies:	Electrical Products:	Electronics:	Transportation:	Other:
Biofuels:	Irrigation:	Lighting/LEDs:	Computers:	Car Sharing:	Recycling:
Batteries/Storage:	Nanotech:	Waste Heat:	Sensors:	Electric Vehicles:	Engineering:
Solar: Y	Biotech:	Smart Meters:	Software:	Natural Gas Fuel:	Consulting:
Wind:	Water Tech./Treatment:	Machinery:			Investing:
Fuel Cells:	Ceramics:				Chemicals:

TYPES OF BUSINESS:

Solar Power Module Manufacturing
Packaged Solar Power Systems
Solar System Accessories
Custom Solar System Design & Consultation
Solar System Installation
Community Solar Education & Preparation
Project Feasibility Studies
Home Solar Power Modules

BRANDS/DIVISIONS/AFFILIATES:

BP plc
BP Alternative Energy

CONTACTS: *Note: Officers with more than one job title may be intentionally listed here more than once.*

Reyad Fezzani, CEO
Eric Daniels, VP-Global Tech.
Michael Petrucci, VP-Global Oper.
Reyed Fezzani, Chmn.

Phone: 415-284-1900	Fax:
Toll-Free:	
Address: 90 New Montgomery St., Ste. 1500, San Francisco, CA 94105 US	

GROWTH PLANS/SPECIAL FEATURES:

BP Solar designs, manufactures and markets solar electric systems for residential, commercial and industrial applications. The firm is a wholly-owned subsidiary of BP Alternative Energy, which in turn is a subsidiary of BP plc. At one time, BP Solar had 203 megawatts (MWs) of cell production capacity through its four major manufacturing plants in Spain, the U.S. and India. The firm has installed solar panels in more than 160 countries. These panels have offset approximately 15.43 million tons of carbon dioxide. Some of the firm's costumers include Ericsson, Long Island Power Authority, NEC and Telstra. In early 2010, BP Solar and FedEx completed their third joint solar project. Faced with falling market prices for solar panels due to intense competition from Chinese manufacturers, BP Solar made the decision in 2011 to focus on developing solar installations and wind down its manufacturing capability. The firm announced that its Frederick, Maryland plant in the U.S. would be phased out by early 2012. In November 2011, the company completed a 32-MW solar farm in Long Island, New York.

FINANCIALS: Sales and profits are in thousands of dollars—add 000 to get the full amount. 2011 Note: Financial information for 2011 was not available for all companies at press time.

2011 Sales: $	2011 Profits: $	**U.S. Stock Ticker: Subsidiary**
2010 Sales: $	2010 Profits: $	**Int'l Ticker:**
2009 Sales: $	2009 Profits: $	Int'l Exchange:
2008 Sales: $	2008 Profits: $	Employees: Fiscal Year Ends: 12/31
2007 Sales: $	2007 Profits: $	Parent Company: BP PLC

SALARIES/BENEFITS:

Pension Plan:	ESOP Stock Plan:	Profit Sharing:	Top Exec. Salary: $	Bonus: $
Savings Plan:	Stock Purch. Plan:		Second Exec. Salary: $	Bonus: $

OTHER THOUGHTS:

Apparent Women Officers or Directors:
Hot Spot for Advancement for Women/Minorities:

LOCATIONS: ("Y" = Yes)

West:	Southwest:	Midwest:	Southeast:	Northeast:	International:
				Y	Y

BRASIL ECODIESEL

www.brasilecodiesel.com.br

Industry Group Code: 325199

Energy/Fuel:		Other Technologies:		Electrical Products:		Electronics:		Transportation:		Other:	
Biofuels:	Y	Irrigation:		Lighting/LEDs:		Computers:		Car Sharing:		Recycling:	
Batteries/Storage:		Nanotech:		Waste Heat:		Sensors:		Electric Vehicles:		Engineering:	
Solar:		Biotech:	Y	Smart Meters:		Software:		Natural Gas Fuel:		Consulting:	
Wind:		Water Tech./Treatment:		Machinery:						Investing:	
Fuel Cells:		Ceramics:								Chemicals:	

TYPES OF BUSINESS:

Biodiesel Manufacturing

BRANDS/DIVISIONS/AFFILIATES:

Grupo Maeda

GROWTH PLANS/SPECIAL FEATURES:

Brasil Ecodiesel, formally known as Brasil Ecodiesel Industria e Comercio de Biocombustiveis e Oleos Vegetais SA, is one of Brasil's largest producers and distributors of biodiesel. The company has two main product divisions: renewable energy production and food. Its renewable energy products include biodiesel, which is a fuel developed from plants and animal fats, and ethanol, a fuel derived from sugar-based plants. The firm has a 25% stake in Tropical Bioenergy, which has a 2.4 million ton annual grinding capacity. The company's food products include cotton, corn and soy. Cotton products are processed indo biofuels and animal feed, while corn and soy products are used for both food and fuels. Brasil Ecodiesel's total crop area is over 210,000 acres. In 2010, the firm crushed over 71,000 tons of soybean grains for its processes. In December 2010, Brasil Ecodiesel acquired Grupo Maeda and incorporated its operations.

CONTACTS: Note: Officers with more than one job title may be intentionally listed here more than once.

Jorge Carlos Aguilera, CEO
Guilherme Augusto D'Avila Mello Raposo, COO
Eduardo de Come, CFO
Eduardo de Come, Chief Investor Rel. Officer
Jose Mendes Renno, Chmn.

Phone: 55-21-3137-3100	**Fax:** 55-21-3137-3101
Toll-Free:	
Address: Av. Brigadeiro Faria Lima, 1461, 4th Fl, S. Twr., Sao Paulo, 01452-921 Brazil	

FINANCIALS: Sales and profits are in thousands of dollars—add 000 to get the full amount. 2011 Note: Financial information for 2011 was not available for all companies at press time.

2011 Sales: $	2011 Profits: $	**U.S. Stock Ticker:**
2010 Sales: $228,075	2010 Profits: $-2,541	**Int'l Ticker:** ECOD3
2009 Sales: $201,730	2009 Profits: $-51,110	Int'l Exchange: Sao Paulo-SAO
2008 Sales: $202,710	2008 Profits: $-113,830	Employees: 1,764 Fiscal Year Ends: 12/31
2007 Sales: $141,000	2007 Profits: $-15,800	Parent Company:

SALARIES/BENEFITS:

Pension Plan:	ESOP Stock Plan:	Profit Sharing:	Top Exec. Salary: $	Bonus: $
Savings Plan:	Stock Purch. Plan:		Second Exec. Salary: $	Bonus: $

OTHER THOUGHTS:

Apparent Women Officers or Directors:
Hot Spot for Advancement for Women/Minorities:

LOCATIONS: ("Y" = Yes)

West:	Southwest:	Midwest:	Southeast:	Northeast:	International:
					Y

Sales, profits and employees may be estimates. Financial information, benefits and other data can change quickly and may vary from those stated here.

BRIDGELUX INC

Industry Group Code: 335

www.bridgelux.com

Energy/Fuel:	Other Technologies:	Electrical Products:		Electronics:	Transportation:	Other:
Biofuels:	Irrigation:	Lighting/LEDs:	Y	Computers:	Car Sharing:	Recycling:
Batteries/Storage:	Nanotech:	Waste Heat:		Sensors:	Electric Vehicles:	Engineering:
Solar:	Biotech:	Smart Meters:		Software:	Natural Gas Fuel:	Consulting:
Wind:	Water Tech./Treatment:	Machinery:				Investing:
Fuel Cells:	Ceramics:					Chemicals:

TYPES OF BUSINESS:

LED Lighting

BRANDS/DIVISIONS/AFFILIATES:

Bridgelux LS Array Series
Bridgelux ES Array Series
Bridgelux RS Array Series
Helieon Sustainable Light Module
Bridgelux Blue Power Chip Series

CONTACTS: *Note: Officers with more than one job title may be intentionally listed here more than once.*

William D. Watkins, CEO
Karl Chicca, COO
Tim Lester, CFO
David Plumer, Chief Sales & Mktg. Officer
Steve Lester, CTO

Phone: 925-583-8400	Fax: 925-583-8401
Toll-Free:	
Address: 101 Portola Avenue, Livermore, CA 94551 US	

GROWTH PLANS/SPECIAL FEATURES:

Bridgelux, Inc. is a developer and manufacturer of cost effective, energy efficient and high power LED lighting solutions. The firm's products consist of LED Arrays, the Helieon Sustainable Light Module and LED Chips. LED Arrays deliver compact, cost-effective and high performance solid-state lighting solutions comparable to light output levels of many conventional light sources. The products in this line include the Bridgelux LS Array Series, Bridgelux ES Array Series and Bridgelux RS Array Series. The Helieon Sustainable Light Module is a plug-and-play sustainable solid state lighting module available as both a DC constant current solution and a 120 volt AC module. The LED Chips line consists of high-power light emitting diode chips. These chips are the basis for all LED lighting products. The products in this line all fall under the high-power gallium nitride Bridgelux Blue Power Chip Series and range from a 24 mil x 24 mil chip to a 60 mil x 60 mil chip. The firm is one of the few vertically integrated LED manufacturers, with approximately 100 patents granted or filed in the U.S. and roughly 200 patents granted or filed internationally.

FINANCIALS: Sales and profits are in thousands of dollars—add 000 to get the full amount. 2011 Note: Financial information for 2011 was not available for all companies at press time.

2011 Sales: $75,000	2011 Profits: $	**U.S. Stock Ticker: Private**
2010 Sales: $40,000	2010 Profits: $	**Int'l Ticker:**
2009 Sales: $	2009 Profits: $	Int'l Exchange:
2008 Sales: $	2008 Profits: $	Employees: 250 Fiscal Year Ends:
2007 Sales: $	2007 Profits: $	Parent Company:

SALARIES/BENEFITS:

Pension Plan:	ESOP Stock Plan:	Profit Sharing:	Top Exec. Salary: $	Bonus: $
Savings Plan:	Stock Purch. Plan:		Second Exec. Salary: $	Bonus: $

OTHER THOUGHTS:

Apparent Women Officers or Directors:
Hot Spot for Advancement for Women/Minorities:

LOCATIONS: ("Y" = Yes)

West:	Southwest:	Midwest:	Southeast:	Northeast:	International:
Y					

BRIGHTSOURCE ENERGY INC

www.brightsourceenergy.com

Industry Group Code: 221119

Energy/Fuel:	Other Technologies:	Electrical Products:	Electronics:	Transportation:	Other:
Biofuels:	Irrigation:	Lighting/LEDs:	Computers:	Car Sharing:	Recycling:
Batteries/Storage:	Nanotech:	Waste Heat:	Sensors:	Electric Vehicles:	Engineering:
Solar: Y	Biotech:	Smart Meters:	Software:	Natural Gas Fuel:	Consulting:
Wind:	Water Tech./Treatment:	Machinery:			Investing:
Fuel Cells:	Ceramics:				Chemicals:

TYPES OF BUSINESS:

Solar Energy Technology
Solar Towers
Electricity Retail
Concentrated Solar Power (CSP)
Ivanpah Power Plant (California)

BRANDS/DIVISIONS/AFFILIATES:

BrightSource Industries (Israel) Ltd
Luz Power Tower
Ivanpah Solar Power Complex
Southern California Edison Company

CONTACTS: Note: Officers with more than one job title may be intentionally listed here more than once.

John M. Woolard, CEO
John M. Woolard, Pres.
Jack Jenkins-Stark, CFO
Lynda Ward Pierce, Sr. VP-Human Resources
Isreal Kroizer, Exec. VP-R&D
Israel Kroizer, Exec. VP-Eng.
Lynda Ward Pierce, Sr. VP-Admin.
Daniel T. Judge, General Counsel/Cop. Sec.
Joseph Desmond, Sr. VP-Comm.
Stephen Wiley, Sr. VP-U.S. Project Dev.
John E. Bryson, Chmn.
Israel Kroizer, Pres., BrightSource Industries (Israel) Ltd.

Phone: 510-550-8161	**Fax:** 510-550-8165	
Toll-Free:		
Address: 1999 Harrison St., Ste. 2150, Oakland, CA 94612 US		

GROWTH PLANS/SPECIAL FEATURES:

BrightSource Energy, Inc. is an alternative energy company engaged in financing, designing and operating solar-thermal (concentrated solar power or CSP) power plants. The company operates some of the world's largest solar power plants, with operations in the U.S., Israel and Australia. The Ivanpah Solar Power Complex will power approximately 140,000 homes in Southern California upon completion. The Solar Energy Development Center in the Negev region of Israel has a production capacity of 6 MW. The company's total combined output capacity is 2.6 gigawatt (GW) of power, with an additional 4 GW under development in the southwestern U.S. BrightSource generates power through its Luz Power Tower (LPT) system, which is believed to be more efficient than traditional parabolic trough solar power generation methods because its uses steam turbine generators. The company estimates that its tower system costs between 30-40% less to install and operate than traditional systems. This increased efficiency is due in part to its steam production method, which mitigates steam loss through heat collecting pipes concentrated in the tower. The system also reduces water usage up to 90% by using air-cooled, rather than water-cooled, power plants. Engineering, product development and equipment supply services are provided by subsidiary BrightSource Industries (Israel) Ltd. BrightSource has a 20-year contract with Southern California Edison. In late 2010, the firm began construction on a solar generating system at Ivanpah, California that will be one of the world's largest solar generators, at a cost of more than $1.6 billion.

FINANCIALS: Sales and profits are in thousands of dollars—add 000 to get the full amount. 2011 Note: Financial information for 2011 was not available for all companies at press time.

2011 Sales: $	2011 Profits: $	**U.S. Stock Ticker:** Private
2010 Sales: $	2010 Profits: $	**Int'l Ticker:**
2009 Sales: $	2009 Profits: $	Int'l Exchange:
2008 Sales: $	2008 Profits: $	Employees: 350 Fiscal Year Ends:
2007 Sales: $	2007 Profits: $	Parent Company:

SALARIES/BENEFITS:

Pension Plan:	ESOP Stock Plan:	Profit Sharing:	Top Exec. Salary: $	Bonus: $
Savings Plan:	Stock Purch. Plan:		Second Exec. Salary: $	Bonus: $

OTHER THOUGHTS:

Apparent Women Officers or Directors: 3
Hot Spot for Advancement for Women/Minorities: Y

LOCATIONS: ("Y" = Yes)

West:	Southwest:	Midwest:	Southeast:	Northeast:	International:
Y	Y				Y

Sales, profits and employees may be estimates. Financial information, benefits and other data can change quickly and may vary from those stated here.

BRITISH ENERGY GROUP PLC

www.british-energy.com

Industry Group Code: 221113

Energy/Fuel:	Other Technologies:	Electrical Products:	Electronics:	Transportation:	Other:
Biofuels:	Irrigation:	Lighting/LEDs:	Computers:	Car Sharing:	Recycling:
Batteries/Storage:	Nanotech:	Waste Heat:	Sensors:	Electric Vehicles:	Engineering:
Solar:	Biotech:	Smart Meters:	Software:	Natural Gas Fuel:	Consulting:
Wind: Y	Water Tech./Treatment:	Machinery:			Investing:
Fuel Cells:	Ceramics:				Chemicals:

TYPES OF BUSINESS:

Nuclear Power Stations
Wind Energy

BRANDS/DIVISIONS/AFFILIATES:

British Energy Generation
Lewis Wind Power
British Energy Direct
Electricite de France SA (EDF)
District Energy
British Energy Renewables
British Energy Power & Energy Trading

CONTACTS: *Note: Officers with more than one job title may be intentionally listed here more than once.*

Andrew Spurr, Managing Dir.
Thomas Kusterer, CFO
David Akers, Dir.-Human Resources
Stuart Crooks, CTO
Jean McDonald, General Counsel
Alain Peckre, Dir.-Operational Support & Continuous Improvement
Rob Guyler, Dir.-Finance
Mark Gorry, Dir.-Safety & Tech.
Brian Cowell, Chief Nuclear Officer Region I
Matt Sykes, Chief Nuclear Officer Region II
Peter Prozesky, Chief Nuclear Officer Region III

Phone: 44-1355-846000	Fax: 44-1355-846001
Toll-Free:	
Address: GSO Business Park, East Kilbride, G74 5PG UK	

GROWTH PLANS/SPECIAL FEATURES:

British Energy Group plc (BEG), a subsidiary of French energy company Electricite de France S.A. (EDF), is one of the UK's largest generators and suppliers of electricity. The company's generation capacity is supplied by eight nuclear power stations with a combined capacity of 9,000 megawatts (MW), which are owned and operated by the group's subsidiary, British Energy Generation. Seven of these power stations operate as gas-cooled reactors, while the eighth station operates as a pressurized water reactor. The firm's alternative energy portfolio, managed by British Energy Renewables, includes a 50% interest in the Lewis Wind Power project, which is planning to build the world's largest onshore wind farm on Scotland's Isle of Lewis. BEG sells its power to the large industrial and commercial energy market through its direct supply business, British Energy Direct. Subsidiary British Energy Power & Energy Trading manages the firm's energy trading in the U.K. Another subsidiary, District Energy, operates four modern, natural-gas-fueled power plants, which produce 10 MW of energy to help meet peak demands and provide backup power.

British Energy offers employees a benefits package that includes paid vacation, paid subscription fees for professional institutions, a pension plan and relocation assistance.

FINANCIALS: Sales and profits are in thousands of dollars—add 000 to get the full amount. 2011 Note: Financial information for 2011 was not available for all companies at press time.

2011 Sales: $	2011 Profits: $	**U.S. Stock Ticker: Subsidiary**	
2010 Sales: $	2010 Profits: $	**Int'l Ticker:**	
2009 Sales: $	2009 Profits: $	Int'l Exchange:	
2008 Sales: $	2008 Profits: $	Employees: 6,121 Fiscal Year Ends: 3/31	
2007 Sales: $	2007 Profits: $	Parent Company: ELECTRICITE DE FRANCE SA (EDF)	

SALARIES/BENEFITS:

Pension Plan: Y	ESOP Stock Plan:	Profit Sharing:	Top Exec. Salary: $	Bonus: $472,208
Savings Plan:	Stock Purch. Plan:		Second Exec. Salary: $	Bonus: $

OTHER THOUGHTS:

Apparent Women Officers or Directors: 1
Hot Spot for Advancement for Women/Minorities:

LOCATIONS: ("Y" = Yes)

West:	Southwest:	Midwest:	Southeast:	Northeast:	International: Y

BSST LLC

www.bsst.com

Industry Group Code: 335

Energy/Fuel:	Other Technologies:	Electrical Products:		Electronics:	Transportation:	Other:
Biofuels:	Irrigation:	Lighting/LEDs:		Computers:	Car Sharing:	Recycling:
Batteries/Storage:	Nanotech:	Waste Heat:	Y	Sensors:	Electric Vehicles:	Engineering:
Solar:	Biotech:	Smart Meters:		Software:	Natural Gas Fuel:	Consulting:
Wind:	Water Tech./Treatment:	Machinery:				Investing:
Fuel Cells:	Ceramics:					Chemicals:

TYPES OF BUSINESS:

Thermoelectric Systems Manufacturing
Waste Heat Recovery Technology

BRANDS/DIVISIONS/AFFILIATES:

Amerigon, Inc.
ZT Plus

CONTACTS: *Note: Officers with more than one job title may be intentionally listed here more than once.*

Lon E. Bell, CEO
Lon E. Bell, Pres.

Phone: 626-593-4515	Fax: 626-815-7441
Toll-Free:	
Address: 5462 Irwindale Ave., Irwindale, CA 91706 US	

GROWTH PLANS/SPECIAL FEATURES:

BSST LLC is the research and development subsidiary of Amerigon, Inc. The firm develops more efficient, effective and practical thermoelectric systems and products for its parent company and other companies in the automotive, computer, consumer, industrial electronics, medical, military and telecommunications industries. BSST focuses on the following applications: personal microclimate conditioning of individuals; thermal management solutions for electronic components and assemblies in confined spaces; thermal management and stable storage solutions for biomedical temperature-sensitive materials; stand-alone telecommunications installation cooling systems; cooled or heated automobile seats and therapy bed pads; and commercially and militarily viable thermal to electrical energy conversion. The company also develops power generation and waste heat recovery projects for military and commercial customers. ZT Plus was formed as a joint venture with 5N Plus, Inc., with the intention of discovering and testing new materials possessing greater thermoelectric efficiency. BSST holds 16 U.S. patents, 24 foreign patents, 29 pending U.S. patents and 46 pending foreign patents. In 2010, the firm bought the remaining 50% interest in ZT Plus from 5N Plus.

BSST offers its employees health, dental and vision coverage; flexible spending accounts; dependent care reimbursement accounts; disability and life insurance; a 401(k) plan; and tuition reimbursement.

FINANCIALS: Sales and profits are in thousands of dollars—add 000 to get the full amount. 2011 Note: Financial information for 2011 was not available for all companies at press time.

2011 Sales: $	2011 Profits: $	U.S. Stock Ticker: Subsidiary
2010 Sales: $	2010 Profits: $	Int'l Ticker:
2009 Sales: $	2009 Profits: $	Int'l Exchange:
2008 Sales: $	2008 Profits: $	Employees: Fiscal Year Ends:
2007 Sales: $	2007 Profits: $	Parent Company: AMERIGON INC

SALARIES/BENEFITS:

Pension Plan:	ESOP Stock Plan:	Profit Sharing:	Top Exec. Salary: $222,000	Bonus: $78,000
Savings Plan: Y	Stock Purch. Plan:		Second Exec. Salary: $	Bonus: $

OTHER THOUGHTS:

Apparent Women Officers or Directors:
Hot Spot for Advancement for Women/Minorities:

LOCATIONS: ("Y" = Yes)

West:	Southwest:	Midwest:	Southeast:	Northeast:	International:
Y					

BYD COMPANY LIMITED

www.byd.com

Industry Group Code: 33611

Energy/Fuel:	Other Technologies:	Electrical Products:	Electronics:	Transportation:		Other:
Biofuels:	Irrigation:	Lighting/LEDs:	Computers:	Car Sharing:		Recycling:
Batteries/Storage:	Nanotech:	Waste Heat:	Sensors:	Electric Vehicles:	Y	Engineering:
Solar:	Biotech:	Smart Meters:	Software:	Natural Gas Fuel:		Consulting:
Wind:	Water Tech./Treatment:	Machinery:				Investing:
Fuel Cells:	Ceramics:					Chemicals:

TYPES OF BUSINESS:

Automobile Manufacturing
Cellular Telephone Equipment Manufacturing
Battery Manufacturing
Advanced Battery Technologies
Hybrid and Electric Cars
Contract Electronics Manufacturing

BRANDS/DIVISIONS/AFFILIATES:

BYD Auto Company Limited
Shenzhen BYD Auto Company Limited
MidAmerican Energy Holdings Co
Berkshire Hathaway Inc
Shenzhen BYD Daimler New Technology Co., Ltd.

CONTACTS: Note: Officers with more than one job title may be intentionally listed here more than once.

Wang Chuan-fu, CEO
Wang Chuan-fu Wang, Pres.
Jing-Sheng Wu, CFO/VP
Jing-Sheng Wu, Corp. Sec.
Nian-qiang Wang, VP
De-he Mao, VP
Long He, VP
Long-zhong Yang, VP
Wang Chuan-fu, Chmn.

Phone: 86-755-8988-8888	Fax: 86-755-8988-8888-64775
Toll-Free:	
Address: No. 3001, Hengping Rd. Pingshan, Longang, Shenzhen, 518118 China	

GROWTH PLANS/SPECIAL FEATURES:

BYD Company Limited (BYD), based in China, is involved in the design and production of automobiles and contract electronics manufacturing. The company operates in three divisions: automobiles, new energy and IT. The automobile division, operating as BYD Auto Company Limited, manufactures low to high-end vehicles, auto molding, auto parts, DM electric cars and all-electric cars. BYD's plug-in hybrid, the F3DM, can travel about 62 miles in electric-only mode and is able to recharge from its backup gasoline engine, its rooftop solar panel charging system or from a plug-in feature. Other models produced include the F0, a four-door compact; F6, a midsized sedan; S8, a hardtop convertible; and e6, a pure electric, zero-emission crossover utility vehicle capable of a 50% charge in 10 minutes. Through Shenzhen BYD Auto Company Limited, the firm manufactures buses and coaches for the Chinese market. In addition to the development of BYD's electric vehicles, the new energy division has developed energy storage solutions based on its Fe battery technology and solar energy stations. The firm's IT division produces rechargeable batteries, battery chargers, electro acoustic components, connectors, keypads, microelectronics, cell phone accessories and opto-electronics. It is a major manufacturer of cell phone handsets as well as batteries for iPods and iPhones. The firm has nine manufacturing facilities located across China and branch offices in the U.S. (Illinois and California), Europe, Japan, South Korea, India, Taiwan and Hong Kong. MidAmerican Energy Holdings Co., a unit of Berkshire Hathaway Inc., owns a 10% stake in the company. In 2010, BYD produced nearly 520,000 automobiles. In April 2010, the company announced plans to open a U.S. headquarters office in Los Angeles. In May 2010, it established Shenzhen BYD Daimler New Technology Co., Ltd., a joint venture with European automaker Daimler AG, to develop electric vehicles. In December 2010, it partnered with Russian firm TagAZ to assemble cars in Russia.

FINANCIALS: Sales and profits are in thousands of dollars—add 000 to get the full amount. 2011 Note: Financial information for 2011 was not available for all companies at press time.

2011 Sales: $	2011 Profits: $	**U.S. Stock Ticker:**
2010 Sales: $7,130,720	2010 Profits: $385,420	**Int'l Ticker: 1211**
2009 Sales: $5,774,200	2009 Profits: $554,990	Int'l Exchange: Hong Kong-HKEX
2008 Sales: $3,900,000	2008 Profits: $180,000	Employees: 180,000 Fiscal Year Ends: 12/31
2007 Sales: $2,800,000	2007 Profits: $230,000	Parent Company:

SALARIES/BENEFITS:

Pension Plan:	ESOP Stock Plan:	Profit Sharing:	Top Exec. Salary: $	Bonus: $
Savings Plan:	Stock Purch. Plan:		Second Exec. Salary: $	Bonus: $

OTHER THOUGHTS:

Apparent Women Officers or Directors:
Hot Spot for Advancement for Women/Minorities:

LOCATIONS: ("Y" = Yes)

West:	Southwest:	Midwest:	Southeast:	Northeast:	International:
Y		Y			Y

CABOT CORPORATION

www.cabot-corp.com

Industry Group Code: 325

Energy/Fuel:	Other Technologies:	Electrical Products:	Electronics:	Transportation:	Other:	
Biofuels:	Irrigation:	Lighting/LEDs:	Computers:	Car Sharing:	Recycling:	
Batteries/Storage:	Nanotech:	Waste Heat:	Sensors:	Electric Vehicles:	Engineering:	
Solar:	Biotech:	Smart Meters:	Software:	Natural Gas Fuel:	Consulting:	
Wind:	Water Tech./Treatment:	Machinery:			Investing:	
Fuel Cells:	Ceramics:				Chemicals:	Y

TYPES OF BUSINESS:

Chemicals Manufacturing
Specialty Fluids
Performance Materials
Metal Oxides
Carbon Black
Supermetals
Nanotechnology
Composite Materials

BRANDS/DIVISIONS/AFFILIATES:

Cabot Superior MicroPowders
Cabot (China) Ltd.
Oxonica Materials, Inc.
Risun Chemicals Company Ltd.

CONTACTS: Note: Officers with more than one job title may be intentionally listed here more than once.

Patrick M. Prevost, CEO
Patrick M. Prevost, Pres.
Eduardo E. Cordeiro, CFO/Exec. VP
Robby D. Sisco, VP-Human Resources
Yakov Kutsovsky, VP-R&D
Douglas A. Church, CIO/VP
Brian A. Berube, General Counsel/VP
Susannah Robinson, Dir.-Investor Rel.
James P. Kelly, Controller/VP
David A. Miller, Exec. VP-Core Segment/Gen. Mgr.-Americas
Xinsheng Zhang, VP/Gen. Mgr.-Asia Pacific
Jane A. Bell, Sec.
Martin O'Neill, VP-Safety, Health & Environmental Affairs
John F. O'Brien, Chmn.
Nick Cross, VP/Gen. Mgr.-EMEA

Phone: 617-345-0100	Fax: 617-342-6103
Toll-Free:	
Address: 2 Seaport Ln., Ste. 1300, Boston, MA 02210 US	

GROWTH PLANS/SPECIAL FEATURES:

Cabot Corporation is engaged in the manufacturing of chemicals, performance materials and specialty fluids. Cabot operates in locations across the world in North America, South America, Europe and Asia. It focuses on producing and handling nanoparticles, modifying surfaces of nanoparticles to alter product functionality and designing particles to impart specific properties in composite materials. The company is organized into four segments: Core, Performance, New Business and Specialty Fluids. The Core division is divided into the Rubber Blacks Business and Supermetals Business. The Rubber Blacks Business manipulates Carbon Black, a form of elemental carbon, to produce particles and aggregates of varied structures and surface chemistries to impart specific functionalities on automotive, building materials, agricultural, coatings, plastics and electronic products. The Supermetals Business produces tantalum (which accounts for nearly all Supermetal sales), niobium and alloys as applications for the production of electronic devices, superalloys, chemical processing equipment and industrial/aerospace applications. The Performance Sector manufactures and sells specialty grade carbon black, fumed silica, fumed alumina and thermoplastic concentrates. The New Business sector is composed of the business development activities of Cabot Superior Micropowders; its inkjet Colorants business, which caters to the inkjet printer market; and its aerogel Business, which manufactures aerogel insulation for the construction industry. The Specialty Fluids division produces and markets cesium formate, used primarily in high pressure/temperature oil and gas well construction as a drilling and completion fluid. In June 2010, Cabot opened a black masterbatch manufacturing facility in Dubai. In July 2010, it acquired Oxonica Materials, Inc. In February 2011, Cabot closed its masterbatch facility in Grigno, Italy and began construction on a new plant in China. In March 2011, Cabot (China) Ltd., a wholly-owned subsidiary of the company, entered into a joint venture with Risun Chemicals Company Ltd. to construct a carbon black manufacturing facility in Xingtai City.

FINANCIALS: Sales and profits are in thousands of dollars—add 000 to get the full amount. 2011 Note: Financial information for 2011 was not available for all companies at press time.

2011 Sales: $3,102,000	2011 Profits: $236,000	**U.S. Stock Ticker: CBT**
2010 Sales: $2,893,000	2010 Profits: $154,000	**Int'l Ticker:**
2009 Sales: $2,243,000	2009 Profits: $-77,000	Int'l Exchange:
2008 Sales: $3,191,000	2008 Profits: $86,000	Employees: 4,100 Fiscal Year Ends: 9/30
2007 Sales: $2,616,000	2007 Profits: $129,000	Parent Company:

SALARIES/BENEFITS:

Pension Plan: Y	ESOP Stock Plan:	Profit Sharing:	Top Exec. Salary: $837,500	Bonus: $1,600,000
Savings Plan: Y	Stock Purch. Plan: Y		Second Exec. Salary: $387,500	Bonus: $454,000

OTHER THOUGHTS:

Apparent Women Officers or Directors: 3
Hot Spot for Advancement for Women/Minorities: Y

LOCATIONS: ("Y" = Yes)

West:	Southwest:	Midwest:	Southeast:	Northeast:	International:
	Y	Y	Y	Y	Y

CAITHNESS ENERGY LLC

www.caithnessenergy.com

Industry Group Code: 221119

Energy/Fuel:	Other Technologies:	Electrical Products:	Electronics:	Transportation:	Other:
Biofuels:	Irrigation:	Lighting/LEDs:	Computers:	Car Sharing:	Recycling:
Batteries/Storage:	Nanotech:	Waste Heat: Y	Sensors:	Electric Vehicles:	Engineering: Y
Solar: Y	Biotech:	Smart Meters:	Software:	Natural Gas Fuel: Y	Consulting:
Wind: Y	Water Tech./Treatment:	Machinery:			Investing:
Fuel Cells:	Ceramics:				Chemicals:

TYPES OF BUSINESS:

Electric Generation
Geothermal Plants
Wind Plants
Solar Plants
Hydroelectric Plants
Coal Plants
Gas Plants

BRANDS/DIVISIONS/AFFILIATES:

Caithness Development LLC
Caithness Long Island Energy Center
Caithness Shepherds Flat LLC
Mescalero Ridge Wind LLC
Caithness Blythe II LLC

CONTACTS: *Note: Officers with more than one job title may be intentionally listed here more than once.*

James D. Bishop, Sr., CEO
Leslie J. Gelber, COO
Leslie J. Gelber, Pres.
Christopher T. McCallion, CFO/Exec. VP
James D. Bishop, Sr., Chmn.

Phone: 212-921-9099	**Fax:** 212-923-9239
Toll-Free:	
Address: 565 5th Ave., 29th Fl., New York, NY 10017 US	

GROWTH PLANS/SPECIAL FEATURES:

Caithness Energy, LLC and its affiliate company Caithness Development, LLC are independent power producers that specialize in the operation, management, acquisition and development of both renewable (solar, geothermal and wind) and environmentally friendly fossil-fuel projects. The firm and its affiliates have over time successfully developed, owned or operated over 2,000 megawatts (MW) of gas turbine projects, 350 MW of geothermal projects, 60 MW of diesel projects, 440 MW of wind projects and 160 MW of solar projects. The company's current projects, with over 2,000 MW of capacity in the U.S. alone, include: Caithness Long Island Energy Center, a power plant in New York State designed to conserve water and produce 350 MW of power; Caithness Shepherds Flat, LLC, an affiliate company that operates a 32,000 acre wind power generation facility in Oregon with a capacity of 909 MW; Mescalero Ridge Wind, LLC, an affiliate company that operates an 800 MW wind power generation plant in New Mexico; and Caithness Blythe II, LLC, which operates the Blythe Energy Project, Phase II, a 76 acre gas-fired combined cycle power facility in Blythe, California with a capacity of 520 MW. The company's solar projects consist of the Soda Mountain Solar project near Baker California, which will have a generation capacity of 350 MW. In addition to its development activities, the firm offers plant services such as asset management; operations and maintenance; and support services.

FINANCIALS: Sales and profits are in thousands of dollars—add 000 to get the full amount. 2011 Note: Financial information for 2011 was not available for all companies at press time.

2011 Sales: $	2011 Profits: $	**U.S. Stock Ticker: Private**
2010 Sales: $	2010 Profits: $	**Int'l Ticker:**
2009 Sales: $	2009 Profits: $	Int'l Exchange:
2008 Sales: $	2008 Profits: $	Employees: Fiscal Year Ends: 12/31
2007 Sales: $	2007 Profits: $	Parent Company:

SALARIES/BENEFITS:

Pension Plan:	ESOP Stock Plan:	Profit Sharing:	Top Exec. Salary: $	Bonus: $
Savings Plan:	Stock Purch. Plan:		Second Exec. Salary: $	Bonus: $

OTHER THOUGHTS:

Apparent Women Officers or Directors:
Hot Spot for Advancement for Women/Minorities:

LOCATIONS: ("Y" = Yes)

West:	Southwest:	Midwest:	Southeast:	Northeast:	International:
Y	Y	Y	Y	Y	Y

CAMBRIDGE DISPLAY TECHNOLOGY INC

www.cdtltd.co.uk

Industry Group Code: 335313

Energy/Fuel:	Other Technologies:	Electrical Products:		Electronics:	Transportation:	Other:
Biofuels:	Irrigation:	Lighting/LEDs:	Y	Computers:	Car Sharing:	Recycling:
Batteries/Storage:	Nanotech:	Waste Heat:		Sensors:	Electric Vehicles:	Engineering:
Solar:	Biotech:	Smart Meters:		Software:	Natural Gas Fuel:	Consulting:
Wind:	Water Tech./Treatment:	Machinery:				Investing:
Fuel Cells:	Ceramics:					Chemicals:

TYPES OF BUSINESS:

Polymer Organic Light Emitting Diode Research & Development

BRANDS/DIVISIONS/AFFILIATES:

Sumitomo Chemical Co Ltd

CONTACTS: Note: Officers with more than one job title may be intentionally listed here more than once.

Jim Veniger, Gen. Mgr.
Emma Jones, VP-Human Resources
Ilesh Bidd, VP-R&D
Junichi Sekihachi, VP-Tech. Planning & Coordination
Hilary Charles, General Counsel
Emma Jones, VP-Facilities
Kazuhiko Miyata, VP-Gen. Affairs

Phone: 44-1954-713-600	**Fax:** 44-1954-713-620
Toll-Free:	
Address: Cambourne Business Park, Bldg. 2020, Cambourne, CB23 6DW UK	

GROWTH PLANS/SPECIAL FEATURES:

Cambridge Display Technology, Inc. (CDT), a subsidiary of Sumitomo Chemical Company, is a leading developer of technologies based on polymer organic light emitting diodes (P-OLEDs). P-OLEDs consist of electroluminescent conductive polymers that emit light when connected to an external voltage source. The technology emits light as a function of its electrical operation, requiring no backlights or filters. The emissive process is also relatively energy efficient, lending itself to the creation of ultra-thin lighting displays that can operate at lower voltages than existing and traditional display processes. Other benefits include brighter, clearer displays with viewing angles approaching 180 degrees, simpler construction offering the potential for cheaper display modules, and ultra-fast response times. A major strength of P-OLED technology is that the components are solution processable, which enables products to be manufactured using printing techniques such as ink jet printing or relief printing. The total thickness of all the layers in a P-OLED display can total less than 500 nanometers, including the glass substrates forming the top and bottom of the device. Potential applications of the company's technology range from displays to photovoltaic cells to high-efficiency light sources. CDT has formed technology partnerships with firms such as Epson; DuPont; Philips; Delta Optoelectronics Inc.; and lighting systems manufacturer Osram GmbH.

FINANCIALS: Sales and profits are in thousands of dollars—add 000 to get the full amount. 2011 Note: Financial information for 2011 was not available for all companies at press time.

2011 Sales: $	2011 Profits: $	**U.S. Stock Ticker: Subsidiary**
2010 Sales: $	2010 Profits: $	**Int'l Ticker:**
2009 Sales: $	2009 Profits: $	Int'l Exchange:
2008 Sales: $	2008 Profits: $	Employees: Fiscal Year Ends: 12/31
2007 Sales: $	2007 Profits: $	Parent Company: SUMITOMO CHEMICAL CO LTD

SALARIES/BENEFITS:

Pension Plan:	ESOP Stock Plan:	Profit Sharing:	Top Exec. Salary: $	Bonus: $
Savings Plan:	Stock Purch. Plan:		Second Exec. Salary: $	Bonus: $

OTHER THOUGHTS:

Apparent Women Officers or Directors: 2
Hot Spot for Advancement for Women/Minorities: Y

LOCATIONS: ("Y" = Yes)

West:	Southwest:	Midwest:	Southeast:	Northeast:	International:
Y					Y

CANADIAN SOLAR INC

www.canadian-solar.com

Industry Group Code: 334413

Energy/Fuel:	Other Technologies:	Electrical Products:	Electronics:	Transportation:	Other:
Biofuels:	Irrigation:	Lighting/LEDs:	Computers:	Car Sharing:	Recycling:
Batteries/Storage: Y	Nanotech:	Waste Heat:	Sensors:	Electric Vehicles:	Engineering:
Solar: Y	Biotech:	Smart Meters:	Software:	Natural Gas Fuel:	Consulting:
Wind:	Water Tech./Treatment:	Machinery:			Investing:
Fuel Cells:	Ceramics:				Chemicals:

TYPES OF BUSINESS:

Photovoltaic Cell Manufacturing
Custom Engineered Solar Specialty Products
Silicon Reclaiming

BRANDS/DIVISIONS/AFFILIATES:

CSI Solar Manufacture Inc
Canadian Solar Manufacturing (Luoyang) Inc
CSI Cells Co. Ltd
Canadian Solar Manufacturing (Changshu) Inc
Canadian Solar Manufacturing (Ontario) Inc

CONTACTS: *Note: Officers with more than one job title may be intentionally listed here more than once.*

Shawn (Xiaohua) Qu, CEO
Shawn (Xiaohua) Qu, Pres.
Michael G. Potter, CFO/Sr. VP
Yan Zhuang, VP-Mktg. & Sales
Jessica Zhou, General Counsel/Corp. Sec.
Charlotte Xi Klein, VP-Global Oper.
Alex Taylor, Dir.-Investor Rel.
Bencheng Li, VP-Ingot & Wafer Div.
Shawn (Xiaohua) Qu, Chmn.
Gregory Spanoudakis, Pres., European Oper.
Xiaohu Wang, VP-Purchasing & Planning

Phone: 519-954-2057	**Fax:** 519-954-2597
Toll-Free:	
Address: 650 Riverbend Dr., Ste. B, Kitchener, ON N2K 3S2 Canada	

GROWTH PLANS/SPECIAL FEATURES:

Canadian Solar, Inc. is a vertically-integrated manufacturer of photovoltaic (PV) cells, modules and custom-designed PV systems. Though the firm is incorporated in Canada, substantially all of its manufacturing operations are carried out through several wholly-owned manufacturing subsidiaries in China, including CSI Solar Manufacture, Inc.; Canadian Solar Manufacturing (Luoyang), Inc.; CSI Cells Co., Ltd.; and Canadian Solar Manufacturing (Changshu), Inc. Additionally, the firm recently established Canadian Solar Manufacturing (Ontario), Inc. to conduct certain manufacturing operations in Canada. The company has three major product lines: standard PV modules, custom engineered solar specialty products and solar system kits. Canadian Solar's crystalline-based PV modules are powered by 5-6 inch solar cells and are able to handle a variety of applications. The company's non-toxic e-Module products are marketed as both economical and environmentally friendly. Building integrated photovoltaic (BIPV) modules, made with laminated solar cells placed between double low iron tempered glass, are used for roof; skylight; shade; and on-grid and off-grid roofing and glazing applications. Its specialty products division has designed a number of custom products, including a solar charger for automobile batteries, another for GPS systems and solar powered marine and bus stop lighting. In addition to standard PV panels and customized solar application products, the company produces solar products on an original equipment manufacturer (OEM) basis. The company also sells ready-to-install, rooftop solar system kits to the residential and commercial building market. Canadian Solar operates a PV Cell Research Center in Suzhou, China, as well as one of the largest silicon reclaiming centers in the world, focused on purchasing, processing and supplying ingots, pot scraps, tops and tails, side wall pieces, broken wafers, reclaimed wafers and broken cells. In June 2011, Canadian Solar established a joint venture with two Chinese firms to construct a new PV cell production facility in Suzhou, China.

FINANCIALS: Sales and profits are in thousands of dollars—add 000 to get the full amount. 2011 Note: Financial information for 2011 was not available for all companies at press time.

2011 Sales: $	2011 Profits: $	**U.S. Stock Ticker: CSIQ**
2010 Sales: $1,495,509	2010 Profits: $50,569	**Int'l Ticker:**
2009 Sales: $630,961	2009 Profits: $22,778	Int'l Exchange:
2008 Sales: $705,006	2008 Profits: $-9,388	Employees: 8,733 Fiscal Year Ends: 12/31
2007 Sales: $302,798	2007 Profits: $- 210	Parent Company:

SALARIES/BENEFITS:

Pension Plan:	ESOP Stock Plan:	Profit Sharing:	Top Exec. Salary: $	Bonus: $
Savings Plan:	Stock Purch. Plan:		Second Exec. Salary: $	Bonus: $

OTHER THOUGHTS:

Apparent Women Officers or Directors: 2
Hot Spot for Advancement for Women/Minorities:

LOCATIONS: ("Y" = Yes)

West:	Southwest:	Midwest:	Southeast:	Northeast:	International:
Y				Y	Y

CANATU

www.canatu.com

Industry Group Code: 541712N

Energy/Fuel:	Other Technologies:		Electrical Products:	Electronics:	Transportation:	Other:	
Biofuels:	Irrigation:		Lighting/LEDs:	Computers:	Car Sharing:	Recycling:	
Batteries/Storage:	Nanotech:	Y	Waste Heat:	Sensors:	Electric Vehicles:	Engineering:	
Solar:	Biotech:		Smart Meters:	Software:	Natural Gas Fuel:	Consulting:	
Wind:	Water Tech./Treatment:		Machinery:			Investing:	
Fuel Cells:	Ceramics:					Chemicals:	

TYPES OF BUSINESS:
Nanomaterials

BRANDS/DIVISIONS/AFFILIATES:
Direct Dry Printing

CONTACTS: Note: Officers with more than one job title may be intentionally listed here more than once.
Risto Vuohelainen, CEO
Mikko Karkkainen, CFO
Erkki Soininen, VP-Mktg. & Sales
Albert G. Nasibuli, Sr. Scientist, Russia
David P. Brown, CTO
Brad Aitchison, Mgr.-Eng.
David P. Brown, Head-Bus. Dev.
Hua Jing, Sr. Scientist, China
Ari Ahola, Chmn.

Phone: 358-50-344-4204	Fax:
Toll-Free:	
Address: Konalankuja 5, Helsinki, 00390 Finland	

GROWTH PLANS/SPECIAL FEATURES:

Canatu is a technology company whose focus is nanotechnology, primarily carbon nanomaterial based components. The firm's research and business is aimed at providing carbon nanobud and carbon nanotube based devices, components and films for the optics and electronics industries. Carbon nanobuds are efficient field emitters with excellent conductive properties and are created when fullerene molecules are attached to the outside surface of carbon nanotubes. Carbon nanobuds, with the versatile properties of the chemical fullerene and the physical properties of carbon, can be customized to contain the specific features for a given application. Some applications that carbon nanobuds could be applicable in include field emission films in displays, flexible transparent electrodes in touch sensors and electron-hole generators in solar cells. Canatu's carbon nanotubes are tailored to specific industrial applications, including purities, patterns, transparency, electrical conductivity and chemical functionality. Using its synthesis process, the firm is capable of producing carbon nanotubes of very high purity. In addition, the company is developing its Direct Dry Printing technology to further allow industrial scale, low cost printing of carbon nanomaterial components.

FINANCIALS: Sales and profits are in thousands of dollars—add 000 to get the full amount. 2011 Note: Financial information for 2011 was not available for all companies at press time.

2011 Sales: $	2011 Profits: $	**U.S. Stock Ticker: Private**
2010 Sales: $	2010 Profits: $	**Int'l Ticker:**
2009 Sales: $	2009 Profits: $	Int'l Exchange:
2008 Sales: $	2008 Profits: $	Employees: Fiscal Year Ends:
2007 Sales: $	2007 Profits: $	Parent Company:

SALARIES/BENEFITS:

Pension Plan:	ESOP Stock Plan:	Profit Sharing:	Top Exec. Salary: $	Bonus: $
Savings Plan:	Stock Purch. Plan:		Second Exec. Salary: $	Bonus: $

OTHER THOUGHTS:
Apparent Women Officers or Directors:
Hot Spot for Advancement for Women/Minorities:

LOCATIONS: ("Y" = Yes)

West:	Southwest:	Midwest:	Southeast:	Northeast:	International: Y

CAPSTONE TURBINE CORP

www.microturbine.com

Industry Group Code: 33361

Energy/Fuel:	Other Technologies:	Electrical Products:		Electronics:	Transportation:	Other:
Biofuels:	Irrigation:	Lighting/LEDs:		Computers:	Car Sharing:	Recycling:
Batteries/Storage:	Nanotech:	Waste Heat:		Sensors:	Electric Vehicles:	Engineering:
Solar:	Biotech:	Smart Meters:	Y	Software:	Natural Gas Fuel:	Consulting:
Wind:	Water Tech./Treatment:	Machinery:	Y			Investing:
Fuel Cells:	Ceramics:					Chemicals:

TYPES OF BUSINESS:

Microturbines
Turbine & Turbine Generator Set Unit Manufacturing
Turbine Parts & Service

BRANDS/DIVISIONS/AFFILIATES:

CONTACTS: *Note: Officers with more than one job title may be intentionally listed here more than once.*

Darren Jamison, CEO
Darren Jamison, Pres.
Edward Reich, CFO/Exec. VP
James Crouse, Exec. VP-Sales & Mktg.
Larry Colson, Sr. VP-Human Resources
Mark Gilbreth, CTO
Mark Gilbreth, Exec. VP-Oper.
Matt Vuolo, VP-Customer Service
Robert Gleason, Sr. VP-Program Mgmt.
Mike Eggers, Dir.-Oper.

Phone: 818-734-5300	Fax: 818-734-5320
Toll-Free:	
Address: 21211 Nordhoff St., Chatsworth, CA 91311 US	

GROWTH PLANS/SPECIAL FEATURES:

Capstone Turbine Corp. develops, manufactures, markets and services microturbine technology systems for use in stationary distributed power generation applications, including cogeneration, resource recovery and secure power. In addition, Capstone's microturbine units can be used as generators for hybrid electric vehicle applications. Microturbines allow customers to produce power on-site in parallel with the electric grid or stand-alone. They run on many different types of fuel including low or high pressure natural gas, biogas, flare gas, diesel, propane and kerosene. The firm's units incorporate four major design features: advanced combustion technology, patented air-bearing technology, digital power electronics and remote monitoring. For customers who do not have access to the electric utility grid, the company's systems can provide an additional source of continuous duty power, thereby providing additional reliability and in most instances, cost savings. With Capstone's stand-alone feature, its customers can produce their own energy in the event of a power outage and can use microturbines as their primary source of power for extended periods. The company's C30 (30-kilowatt), C65 (65kW) and C200 (200kW) products are designed to produce electricity for commercial and industrial users. These products can also be purchased in 600kw, 800kW and 1 megawatt configurations. The firm sells its microturbines primarily through independent distributors and dealers. To ensure that its systems are installed properly, Capstone provides training and certification programs to personnel at its distributors. In 2010, the company purchased the TA100 microturbine product line from Calnetix Power Solutions, Inc.

FINANCIALS: Sales and profits are in thousands of dollars—add 000 to get the full amount. 2011 Note: Financial information for 2011 was not available for all companies at press time.

2011 Sales: $81,890	2011 Profits: $-38,470	U.S. Stock Ticker: CPST
2010 Sales: $61,554	2010 Profits: $-67,241	Int'l Ticker:
2009 Sales: $43,949	2009 Profits: $-41,717	Int'l Exchange:
2008 Sales: $31,305	2008 Profits: $-36,113	Employees: 195 Fiscal Year Ends: 3/31
2007 Sales: $21,018	2007 Profits: $-36,728	Parent Company:

SALARIES/BENEFITS:

Pension Plan:	ESOP Stock Plan:	Profit Sharing:	Top Exec. Salary: $437,800	Bonus: $320,740
Savings Plan: Y	Stock Purch. Plan: Y		Second Exec. Salary: $281,900	Bonus: $92,936

OTHER THOUGHTS:

Apparent Women Officers or Directors:
Hot Spot for Advancement for Women/Minorities:

LOCATIONS: ("Y" = Yes)

West:	Southwest:	Midwest:	Southeast:	Northeast:	International:
Y				Y	Y

Sales, profits and employees may be estimates. Financial information, benefits and other data can change quickly and may vary from those stated here.

CELANESE CORPORATION

www.celanese.com

Industry Group Code: 325

Energy/Fuel:	Other Technologies:	Electrical Products:	Electronics:	Transportation:	Other:	
Biofuels:	Irrigation:	Lighting/LEDs:	Computers:	Car Sharing:	Recycling:	
Batteries/Storage:	Nanotech:	Waste Heat:	Sensors:	Electric Vehicles:	Engineering:	
Solar:	Biotech:	Smart Meters:	Software:	Natural Gas Fuel:	Consulting:	
Wind:	Water Tech./Treatment:	Machinery:			Investing:	
Fuel Cells:	Ceramics:				Chemicals:	Y

TYPES OF BUSINESS:

Manufacturing-Basic Chemicals
Acetyl Products
Technical & High-Performance Polymers
Sweeteners & Sorbates
Ethanol Production

BRANDS/DIVISIONS/AFFILIATES:

Ticona GmbH
Nutrinova Inc
Sunett
Celanese EVA Performance Polymers Inc

CONTACTS: *Note: Officers with more than one job title may be intentionally listed here more than once.*

David N. Weidman, CEO
Doug Madden, COO
David N. Weidman, Pres.
Steven Sterin, CFO/Sr. VP
Peter Holmes, Chief Mktg. Officer
Jacquelyn H. Wolf, Sr. VP-Human Resources
James S. Alder, Sr. VP-Tech.
Gjon N. Nivica, Jr., General Counsel/Sr. VP/Corp. Sec.
James S. Alder, Sr. VP-Oper.
Jay C. Townsend, Sr. VP-Bus. Dev. & Strategy
Mark Oberle, Sr. VP-Corp. Affairs
Andy Green, VP-Investor Rel.
Christopher W. Jensen, Sr. VP-Finance/Treas.
Michael Stubblefield, Gen. Mgr.-Ticona
David N. Weidman, Chmn.
Phoebe Li, Media Contact-Asia
Jay C. Townsend, Sr. VP-Procurement

Phone: 972-443-4000	Fax: 972-443-8519
Toll-Free:	
Address: 1601 W. LBJ Freeway, Dallas, TX 75234-6034 US	

GROWTH PLANS/SPECIAL FEATURES:

Celanese Corporation produces a line of industrial chemicals and advanced materials. It manufactures acetyl products, which are intermediate chemicals for nearly all major industries; and also produces high-performance engineered polymers. The company operates through four segments: advanced engineered materials, consumer specialties, industrial specialties and acetyl intermediates. The advanced engineered materials segment, which is comprised of the company's Ticona engineering polymers business and certain equity affiliates, develops, produces and supplies high-performance technical polymers for application in automotive and electronics products, as well as other consumer and industrial applications. The primary products of advanced engineered materials are polyacetyl products (POM), ultra-high molecular weight polyethylene (GUR) and liquid crystal polymers (LCP). POM is used in a broad range of products including automotive components, electronics and appliances. GUR is used in battery separators, conveyor belts, filtration equipment, coatings and medical devices. The consumer specialties segment consists of the acetate products business and the Nutrinova business. The acetate products business produces and supplies acetate tow, which is used in the production of filters; and acetate flake. Nutrinova serves the food industry, producing Sunett artificial sweetener, as well as sorbates and sorbic acid food protection ingredients. The industrial specialties segment, which consists of the firm's emulsions and EVA performance polymers businesses, produces volatile organic compounds used in a variety of product applications, including paints, coatings, adhesives, building products, textiles, paper and automotive parts. The acetyl intermediates segment produces and supplies acetyl products, including acetic acid, vinyl acetate monomer (VAM), acetic anhydride and acetate esters. These products are generally used as starting materials for colorants, paints, adhesives, coatings, medicines and other products. In November 2010, the firm announced plans to build an ethanol production facility in China for certain chemical and industrial applications.

FINANCIALS: Sales and profits are in thousands of dollars—add 000 to get the full amount. 2011 Note: Financial information for 2011 was not available for all companies at press time.

2011 Sales: $	2011 Profits: $	**U.S. Stock Ticker: CE**
2010 Sales: $5,918,000	2010 Profits: $377,000	**Int'l Ticker:**
2009 Sales: $5,082,000	2009 Profits: $488,000	Int'l Exchange:
2008 Sales: $6,823,000	2008 Profits: $282,000	Employees: 7,250 Fiscal Year Ends: 12/31
2007 Sales: $6,444,000	2007 Profits: $426,000	Parent Company:

SALARIES/BENEFITS:

Pension Plan: Y	ESOP Stock Plan:	Profit Sharing:	Top Exec. Salary: $900,000	Bonus: $2,325,607
Savings Plan: Y	Stock Purch. Plan:		Second Exec. Salary: $632,692	Bonus: $1,021,475

OTHER THOUGHTS:

Apparent Women Officers or Directors: 1
Hot Spot for Advancement for Women/Minorities: Y

LOCATIONS: ("Y" = Yes)

West:	Southwest:	Midwest:	Southeast:	Northeast:	International:
	Y	Y		Y	Y

Sales, profits and employees may be estimates. Financial information, benefits and other data can change quickly and may vary from those stated here.

CENTRAL ELECTRONICS LIMITED   www.celindia.co.in
Industry Group Code: 334413

Energy/Fuel:	Other Technologies:	Electrical Products:	Electronics:	Transportation:	Other:
Biofuels:	Irrigation:	Lighting/LEDs:	Computers:	Car Sharing:	Recycling:
Batteries/Storage:	Nanotech:	Waste Heat:	Sensors:	Electric Vehicles:	Engineering:
Solar: Y	Biotech:	Smart Meters:	Software:	Natural Gas Fuel:	Consulting:
Wind:	Water Tech./Treatment:	Machinery:			Investing:
Fuel Cells:	Ceramics:				Chemicals:

TYPES OF BUSINESS:
Photovoltaic Cells, Modules & Systems
Electronics Components
Railway Signaling Products
Safety Equipment
Microwave Electronics

BRANDS/DIVISIONS/AFFILIATES:

CONTACTS: *Note: Officers with more than one job title may be intentionally listed here more than once.*
S. K. Kaicker, Managing Dir.
S. K. Kaicker, Chmn.

Phone: 91-120-289-51-55	Fax: 91-120-289-51-42
Toll-Free:	
Address: Saur Urja Marg, 4 Industrial Area, Sahibabad, 201010 India	

GROWTH PLANS/SPECIAL FEATURES:
Central Electronics Limited (CEL) was created in 1974 by India's Ministry of Science and Technology to develop renewable energy systems and next-generation electronic equipment. The firm operates in two primary business groups: the Solar Photovoltaic group; and the Strategic Electronics group, which includes two subdivisions, Railway Electronics and Microwave Electronics. The company's Solar Photovoltaic group is one of the country's largest manufacturers of solar photovoltaic (PV) cells, modules and systems. Using screen-printing technology to manufacture monocrystalline silicon solar cells, the firm has supplied PV systems to India and abroad. Applications for its systems include village home and street lighting, portable solar lanterns, water pumping for drinking and irrigation, solar power packs, warning lights at airports, railway signaling, microwave repeaters, traffic signal lighting and industrial applications. CEL's PV modules were the first such equipment from India to be certified for design and quality by the European Commission-Joint Research Centre. The firm's Railway Electronics division designs and manufactures railway signaling and safety equipment, such as axle counters to detect the presence of a train, axle counter block systems and a train actuated warning device. Over 5,000 of the company's products have been installed on Indian railways. The Microwave Electronics division manufactures ferrite phase shifters used for electronic scanning phased array antenna systems. The firm's other products include automatic electronic cathodic protection systems, which help prevent corrosion in underground oil and gas pipelines; and electronic ceramics, including piezoelectric transducers, high alumina products, di-electric material, square plates and piezoelectric discs. CEL has provided PV and other products to a number of customers internationally, including clients in Afghanistan, China, Nepal, Austria, Germany, Sudan, Sri Lanka, Zambia, Mali, Mongolia, Mozambique and Namibia.

FINANCIALS: Sales and profits are in thousands of dollars—add 000 to get the full amount. 2011 Note: Financial information for 2011 was not available for all companies at press time.

2011 Sales: $	2011 Profits: $	**U.S. Stock Ticker: Private**
2010 Sales: $	2010 Profits: $	**Int'l Ticker:**
2009 Sales: $	2009 Profits: $	Int'l Exchange:
2008 Sales: $	2008 Profits: $	Employees: Fiscal Year Ends: 12/31
2007 Sales: $	2007 Profits: $	Parent Company:

SALARIES/BENEFITS:

Pension Plan:	ESOP Stock Plan:	Profit Sharing:	Top Exec. Salary: $	Bonus: $
Savings Plan:	Stock Purch. Plan:		Second Exec. Salary: $	Bonus: $

OTHER THOUGHTS:
Apparent Women Officers or Directors: 1
Hot Spot for Advancement for Women/Minorities:

LOCATIONS: ("Y" = Yes)

West:	Southwest:	Midwest:	Southeast:	Northeast:	International: Y

CH2M HILL COMPANIES LTD

www.ch2m.com

Industry Group Code: 541330

Energy/Fuel:	Other Technologies:	Electrical Products:	Electronics:	Transportation:	Other:	
Biofuels:	Irrigation:	Lighting/LEDs:	Computers:	Car Sharing:	Recycling:	
Batteries/Storage:	Nanotech:	Waste Heat:	Sensors:	Electric Vehicles:	Engineering:	Y
Solar:	Biotech:	Smart Meters:	Software:	Natural Gas Fuel:	Consulting:	Y
Wind:	Water Tech./Treatment:	Machinery:			Investing:	
Fuel Cells:	Ceramics:				Chemicals:	

TYPES OF BUSINESS:

Engineering Services-Consultation
Environmental Engineering & Consulting
Nuclear Management Services
Water & Electrical Utility Services
Decommissioning & Decontamination
Facilities Design & Construction
Project Financing & Procurement
Nanotechnology Research

BRANDS/DIVISIONS/AFFILIATES:

Operations Management International
CH2M HILL Canada, Ltd.
CH2M HILL Lockwood Greene
Industrial Design and Construction
CH2M-IDC China
Wade & Assoicates, Inc.
Goldston Engineering, Inc.
VECO

CONTACTS: *Note: Officers with more than one job title may be intentionally listed here more than once.*

Lee A. McIntire, CEO
Mike Lucki, CFO/Sr VP
John Madia, VP-Human Resources
Margaret McLean, Chief Legal Officer/Corp. Sec./Sr. VP
JoAnn Shea, Chief Acct. Officer/Controller/VP
Jacqueline C. Rast, Sr. VP/Pres-Facilities & Infrastructure Div.
Michael E McKelvy, Pres., Gov't, Environment & Nuclear Div.
William T. Dehn, VP
Robert G Card, Sr. VP/Pres., Energy & Water Div.
Lee A. McIntire, Chmn.
Fred Brune, Pres., CH2M HILL Int'l

Phone: 303-771-0900	**Fax:** 720-286-9250
Toll-Free: 888-242-6445	
Address: 9191 S. Jamaica St., Englewood, CO 80112 US	

GROWTH PLANS/SPECIAL FEATURES:

CH2M HILL Companies, Ltd. is an employee-owned firm that offers engineering, consulting, design, construction, procurement, operations, maintenance and program and project management services to clients in the public and private sectors. CH2M HILL conducts business in several countries worldwide. The company's environmental services division offers its clients ecological and natural resource damage assessments, environmental consulting for remediation projects and treatment systems for properties that have been contaminated by toxic or radioactive waste. The nuclear services segment manages the decontamination and demolition of weapons production facilities and designs nuclear waste treatment and handling facilities. CH2M HILL's Operations Management International subsidiary provides water, wastewater and electrical utility services to private and public clients. CH2M HILL Canada, Ltd. is the Canadian division of the company. CH2M HILL Lockwood Greene is a major engineering and construction firm focused on national and multinational industrial and power clients worldwide. CH2M HILL Industrial Design and Construction, Inc. (IDC) is a high-technology facilities design, construction, maintenance and operations company serving process-intensive technology clients. IDC also has interests in nanotechnology research and manufacturing. CH2M-IDC China provides full-service solution to manufacturing companies that are building or have plants in China.

FINANCIALS: Sales and profits are in thousands of dollars—add 000 to get the full amount. 2011 Note: Financial information for 2011 was not available for all companies at press time.

2011 Sales: $	2011 Profits: $	**U.S. Stock Ticker:** Private
2010 Sales: $5,422,801	2010 Profits: $93,695	**Int'l Ticker:**
2009 Sales: $5,499,318	2009 Profits: $103,742	Int'l Exchange:
2008 Sales: $5,589,900	2008 Profits: $32,056	Employees: 23,000 Fiscal Year Ends: 12/31
2007 Sales: $4,376,200	2007 Profits: $65,999	Parent Company:

SALARIES/BENEFITS:

Pension Plan:	ESOP Stock Plan:	Profit Sharing:	Top Exec. Salary: $	Bonus: $
Savings Plan:	Stock Purch. Plan:		Second Exec. Salary: $	Bonus: $

OTHER THOUGHTS:

Apparent Women Officers or Directors: 3
Hot Spot for Advancement for Women/Minorities: Y

LOCATIONS: ("Y" = Yes)

West:	Southwest:	Midwest:	Southeast:	Northeast:	International:
Y	Y	Y	Y	Y	Y

CHANGING WORLD TECHNOLOGIES INC

www.changingworldtech.com
Industry Group Code: 325199

Energy/Fuel:		Other Technologies:	Electrical Products:	Electronics:	Transportation:	Other:
Biofuels:	Y	Irrigation:	Lighting/LEDs:	Computers:	Car Sharing:	Recycling:
Batteries/Storage:		Nanotech:	Waste Heat:	Sensors:	Electric Vehicles:	Engineering:
Solar:		Biotech:	Smart Meters:	Software:	Natural Gas Fuel:	Consulting:
Wind:		Water Tech./Treatment:	Machinery:			Investing:
Fuel Cells:		Ceramics:				Chemicals:

TYPES OF BUSINESS:

Waste Conversion Technology

BRANDS/DIVISIONS/AFFILIATES:

Thermal Conversion Process
Thermal Depolymerization Process
Thermo-Depolymerization Process LLC
Renewable Energy Solutions LLC

CONTACTS: *Note: Officers with more than one job title may be intentionally listed here more than once.*

Brian S. Appel, CEO
James H. Freiss, COO
Michael J. McLaughlin, CFO
Brian S. Appel, Chmn.

Phone: 516-486-0100	Fax: 516-486-0460
Toll-Free:	
Address: 460 Hempstead Ave., West Hempstead, NY 11552 US	

GROWTH PLANS/SPECIAL FEATURES:

Changing World Technologies, Inc. (CWT) is the owner and developer of what it calls the Thermal Conversion Process (TCP), which, through a low-emission process, converts various waste products into fatty acids used for biodiesel and minerals used in fertilizers.
TCP heats pressurized waste slurry to its reaction point, separating organic and inorganic waste and solids, volatile gasses, diesel and water. TCP technology can break down biological waste, including fats, feathers, greases and bones as well as agricultural waste; and PVC, PET, HDPE and other mixed plastics, including scrap tires, metal recyclers, shredder residue and electronics components from computers and cell phones. The company is striving to extend TCP technology to process municipal solid waste, including sewage sludge and landfills. CWT believes that, using TCP technology, 4 billion barrels of oil could be extracted from the 6 billion tons of agricultural waste the U.S. produces annually. The firm's subsidiaries and affiliate companies include Thermo-Depolymerization Process, LLC, originally a developing and demonstration facility for Thermo-Depolymerization Process (TDP), which evolved TDP into the current, more directed TCP technology; and Renewable Environmental Solutions LLC (RES), which was formed to develop the processing of agricultural waste and low-value streams throughout the world. In recent years, CWT filed for Chapter 11 bankruptcy protection and is currently reorganizing its operations.

FINANCIALS: Sales and profits are in thousands of dollars—add 000 to get the full amount. 2011 Note: Financial information for 2011 was not available for all companies at press time.

2011 Sales: $	2011 Profits: $	U.S. Stock Ticker: Private
2010 Sales: $	2010 Profits: $	Int'l Ticker:
2009 Sales: $	2009 Profits: $	Int'l Exchange:
2008 Sales: $	2008 Profits: $	Employees: Fiscal Year Ends: 12/31
2007 Sales: $	2007 Profits: $	Parent Company:

SALARIES/BENEFITS:

Pension Plan:	ESOP Stock Plan:	Profit Sharing:	Top Exec. Salary: $	Bonus: $
Savings Plan:	Stock Purch. Plan:		Second Exec. Salary: $	Bonus: $

OTHER THOUGHTS:

Apparent Women Officers or Directors:
Hot Spot for Advancement for Women/Minorities:

LOCATIONS: ("Y" = Yes)

West:	Southwest:	Midwest: Y	Southeast:	Northeast: Y	International:

CHEMREC
www.chemrec.com

Industry Group Code: 325199

Energy/Fuel:		Other Technologies:		Electrical Products:	Electronics:		Transportation:		Other:
Biofuels:	Y	Irrigation:		Lighting/LEDs:	Computers:		Car Sharing:		Recycling:
Batteries/Storage:		Nanotech:		Waste Heat:	Sensors:		Electric Vehicles:		Engineering:
Solar:		Biotech:	Y	Smart Meters:	Software:		Natural Gas Fuel:		Consulting:
Wind:		Water Tech./Treatment:		Machinery:					Investing:
Fuel Cells:		Ceramics:							Chemicals:

TYPES OF BUSINESS:
Biofuel Recovery Technologies

BRANDS/DIVISIONS/AFFILIATES:
A300 Booster
OX450 Booster
P500 Expansion Unit
P2000 Replacement Unit
X2000 Combined Cycle Unit

GROWTH PLANS/SPECIAL FEATURES:
Chemrec is a company that uses its proprietary technologies to convert pulp and paper mills into biorefineries. The company is able to do this through its black liquor gasification technology, which it offers on commercial terms to mills looking to expand their operations into biorefinery. Chemrec's gasifier products include the A300 Booster, a 150-300 tons/day atmospheric air-blown unit; OX450 Booster, a 450tons/day atmospheric oxygen-blown unit; P500 Expansion Unit, a 500-550 tons/day pressurized oxygen-blown unit; P2000 Replacement Unit, a 1000-4000 tons/day pressurized oxygen-blown unit; and the X2000 Combined Cycle Unit, a 1000-4000 tons/day pressurized oxygen-blown unit. These products, to different extents, aid in the recovery of black liquor and produce low-carbon biofuels or high heating value fuel gas. Chemrec's development plant is located in Pitea, Sweden.

CONTACTS:
Note: Officers with more than one job title may be intentionally listed here more than once.
Max Jonsson, CEO
Jonas Rudberg, COO
Patrik Lownertz, VP-Mktg. & Sales
Ingvar Landalv, CTO
Hans Nelving, VP-Eng.
Bernard J. Bulkin, Chmn.

Phone: 46-8-440-4060	**Fax:** 46-8-440-4066
Toll-Free:	
Address: Floragatan 10B, Stockholm, SE-114 31 Sweden	

FINANCIALS:
Sales and profits are in thousands of dollars—add 000 to get the full amount. 2011 Note: Financial information for 2011 was not available for all companies at press time.

2011 Sales: $	2011 Profits: $	**U.S. Stock Ticker:** Private
2010 Sales: $	2010 Profits: $	**Int'l Ticker:**
2009 Sales: $	2009 Profits: $	Int'l Exchange:
2008 Sales: $	2008 Profits: $	Employees: Fiscal Year Ends:
2007 Sales: $	2007 Profits: $	Parent Company:

SALARIES/BENEFITS:
Pension Plan:	ESOP Stock Plan:	Profit Sharing:	Top Exec. Salary: $	Bonus: $
Savings Plan:	Stock Purch. Plan:		Second Exec. Salary: $	Bonus: $

OTHER THOUGHTS:
Apparent Women Officers or Directors:
Hot Spot for Advancement for Women/Minorities:

LOCATIONS: ("Y" = Yes)
West:	Southwest:	Midwest:	Southeast:	Northeast:	International: Y

Sales, profits and employees may be estimates. Financial information, benefits and other data can change quickly and may vary from those stated here.

CHEVRON CORPORATION

Industry Group Code: 211111

www.chevron.com

Energy/Fuel:	Other Technologies:	Electrical Products:	Electronics:	Transportation:	Other:	
Biofuels:	Irrigation:	Lighting/LEDs:	Computers:	Car Sharing:	Recycling:	
Batteries/Storage:	Nanotech:	Waste Heat:	Sensors:	Electric Vehicles:	Engineering:	
Solar:	Biotech:	Smart Meters:	Software:	Natural Gas Fuel:	Consulting:	
Wind:	Water Tech./Treatment:	Machinery:			Investing:	
Fuel Cells:	Ceramics:				Chemicals:	Y

TYPES OF BUSINESS:

Oil & Gas Exploration & Production
Power Generation
Petrochemicals
Gasoline Retailing
Coal Mining
Fuel & Oil Additives
Convenience Stores
Pipelines

BRANDS/DIVISIONS/AFFILIATES:

Texaco
Youngs Creek Mining Company LLC
Chevron Phillips Chemical Company
Caltex
Chevron Technology Ventures
Chevron Limited
Atlas Energy, Inc.

CONTACTS: *Note: Officers with more than one job title may be intentionally listed here more than once.*

John S. Watson, CEO
Patricia E. Yarrington, CFO/VP
Joe W. Laymon, VP-Human Resources
John W. McDonald, CTO/VP
R. Hewitt Pate, General Counsel/VP
Jay R. Pryor, VP-Corp. Bus. Dev.
Stephen W. Green, VP-Policy, Gov't & Public Affairs
Pierre R. Breber, Treas./VP
Michael K. Wirth, Exec. VP-Global Downstream & Chemicals
George L. Kirkland, Exec. VP-Global Upstream & Gas/Vice Chmn.
John D. Gass, VP/Pres., Global Gas
Charles A. Taylor, Exec. VP-Strategic Planning
John S. Watson, Chmn.

Phone: 925-842-1000	**Fax:** 925-842-3530
Toll-Free:	
Address: 6001 Bollinger Canyon Rd., San Ramon, CA 94583-2324 US	

GROWTH PLANS/SPECIAL FEATURES:

Chevron Corporation is an integrated energy company that conducts refining, marketing and transportation operations and, to a lesser degree, chemical operations, mining operations and power generation. Refining operations maintains a refining network capable of processing more than 2 million barrels of crude oil per day. Marketing operations operates primarily under the brands Chevron, Texaco and Caltex. In the U.S., the company markets under the Chevron and Texaco brands. The company supplies directly or through retailers and marketers approximately 8,250 Chevron- and Texaco-branded motor vehicle retail outlets. Outside the U.S., the firm supplies approximately 11,300 branded service stations, including affiliates. Transportation operations maintains the Chevron owned and operated system of crude oil, refined products, chemicals, natural gas liquids and natural gas pipelines in the U.S. The company also has direct or indirect interests in other U.S. and international pipelines. Chemical operations include the manufacturing and marketing of fuel and lubricating oil additives and commodity petrochemicals through Chevron Phillips Chemical Company (CPChem), a joint venture company. CPChem operates manufacturing and research facilities in five countries. Mining operations produces and markets coal and molybdenum. The firm owns three coal mines and controls a 50% interest in Youngs Creek Mining Company LLC. The power generation business develops and operates commercial power projects. The company manages the production of more than 3,100 megawatts (MW) of electricity at 13 facilities it owns through joint ventures. Additionally, Chevron operates gas-fired cogeneration facilities that use waste heat recovery to produce additional electricity or to support industrial thermal hosts. In September 2010, the firm acquired 70% ownership in three deepwater concessions in Liberia; and 50% ownership in a block in the Black Sea. In February 2011, the company acquired Atlas Energy, Inc. for $3.2 billion. In March 2011, Chevron agreed to sell Chevron Limited and the Pembroke Refinery to Valero Energy Corporation.

FINANCIALS: Sales and profits are in thousands of dollars—add 000 to get the full amount. 2011 Note: Financial information for 2011 was not available for all companies at press time.

2011 Sales: $	2011 Profits: $	**U.S. Stock Ticker: CVX**
2010 Sales: $204,928,000	2010 Profits: $19,136,000	**Int'l Ticker:**
2009 Sales: $171,636,000	2009 Profits: $10,483,000	Int'l Exchange:
2008 Sales: $273,005,000	2008 Profits: $23,931,000	Employees: 62,000 Fiscal Year Ends: 12/31
2007 Sales: $220,904,000	2007 Profits: $18,688,000	Parent Company:

SALARIES/BENEFITS:

Pension Plan: Y	ESOP Stock Plan:	Profit Sharing:	Top Exec. Salary: $1,793,750	Bonus: $3,000,000
Savings Plan: Y	Stock Purch. Plan:		Second Exec. Salary: $946,042	Bonus: $1,260,000

OTHER THOUGHTS:

Apparent Women Officers or Directors: 3
Hot Spot for Advancement for Women/Minorities: Y

LOCATIONS: ("Y" = Yes)

West:	Southwest:	Midwest:	Southeast:	Northeast:	International:
Y	Y	Y	Y	Y	Y

CHEVRON TECHNOLOGY VENTURES

www.chevron.com/ctv

Industry Group Code: 541712

Energy/Fuel:	Other Technologies:	Electrical Products:	Electronics:	Transportation:	Other:	
Biofuels:	Irrigation:	Lighting/LEDs:	Computers:	Car Sharing:	Recycling:	
Batteries/Storage:	Nanotech:	Waste Heat:	Sensors:	Electric Vehicles:	Engineering:	
Solar:	Biotech:	Smart Meters:	Software:	Natural Gas Fuel:	Consulting:	
Wind:	Water Tech./Treatment:	Machinery:			Investing:	Y
Fuel Cells:	Ceramics:				Chemicals:	

TYPES OF BUSINESS:

Venture Capital
Power & Energy Investments
Diversified Technology Investments
Venture Capital
Hydrogen Energy Technology
Wind Farming Technology
Nanofilms
Biodiesel

BRANDS/DIVISIONS/AFFILIATES:

Chevron Corporation
Catchlight Energy
Project Brightfield

CONTACTS: *Note: Officers with more than one job title may be intentionally listed here more than once.*

Trond Unneland, Managing Exec.
Mike Brooks, Venture Exec.
John Hanten, Venture Exec.
Don Riley, Venture Exec.
Richard Pardoe, Principal

Phone: 713-954-6803	Fax: 713-954-6016
Toll-Free:	
Address: 3901 Briarpark Rd., Houston, TX 77042 US	

GROWTH PLANS/SPECIAL FEATURES:

Chevron Technology Ventures (CTV) is the branch of Chevron Corp. that invests in and commercializes new technologies through a corporate venture capital model. The firm's investments fall into four main business units: Venture capital (early-stage companies offering valuable technologies); biofuels (developing technologies engaged in large-scale commercial production and distribution of non-food biofuels); hydrogen (which entails five hydrogen demonstration fueling facilities in the U.S. and staying abreast of hydrogen technology developments); and emerging energy (which is focused on reducing the company's carbon footprint and running business operations more cost-effectively through the use and development of renewable energy systems). Investment areas of interest which are represented in each of these business categories are vast, including fuel processing and deepwater production, fuel additives and lubricants, biofuels, solar and wind power, advanced ceramics and polymers, networking infrastructures and nanotechnologies. Chevron is engaged in a number of partnerships and associations in an effort to help bring new energy systems to the market, including California Fuel Cell Partnership, National Hydrogen Association and the World Fuel Cell. It also maintains joint venture Catchlight Energy (with Weyerhaeuser Company), which works to commercialize advanced biofuels created from forest-based biomass. To facilitate innovation within Chevron and to create additional value, the company also invests in internal ventures, such as business models created by employees which may have market potential beyond Chevron. Once development milestones are achieved, the commercialization effort may be spun off as an independent company or maintained internally. In March 2010, the company announced plans to construct a solar test facility outside of Bakersfield, California. Project Brightfield will consist of 7,700 photovoltaic panels from seven different companies; one of the companies will be selected for a possible partnership with Chevron.

FINANCIALS: Sales and profits are in thousands of dollars—add 000 to get the full amount. 2011 Note: Financial information for 2011 was not available for all companies at press time.

2011 Sales: $	2011 Profits: $	**U.S. Stock Ticker: Subsidiary**
2010 Sales: $	2010 Profits: $	**Int'l Ticker:**
2009 Sales: $	2009 Profits: $	Int'l Exchange:
2008 Sales: $	2008 Profits: $	Employees: Fiscal Year Ends: 12/31
2007 Sales: $	2007 Profits: $	Parent Company: CHEVRON CORPORATION

SALARIES/BENEFITS:

Pension Plan:	ESOP Stock Plan:	Profit Sharing:	Top Exec. Salary: $	Bonus: $
Savings Plan:	Stock Purch. Plan:		Second Exec. Salary: $	Bonus: $

OTHER THOUGHTS:

Apparent Women Officers or Directors: 1
Hot Spot for Advancement for Women/Minorities:

LOCATIONS: ("Y" = Yes)

West:	Southwest:	Midwest:	Southeast:	Northeast:	International:
Y	Y				

Sales, profits and employees may be estimates. Financial information, benefits and other data can change quickly and may vary from those stated here.

CHINA SUNERGY CO LTD

www.chinasunergy.com

Industry Group Code: 334413

Energy/Fuel:	Other Technologies:	Electrical Products:	Electronics:	Transportation:	Other:
Biofuels:	Irrigation:	Lighting/LEDs:	Computers:	Car Sharing:	Recycling:
Batteries/Storage:	Nanotech:	Waste Heat:	Sensors:	Electric Vehicles:	Engineering:
Solar: Y	Biotech:	Smart Meters:	Software:	Natural Gas Fuel:	Consulting:
Wind:	Water Tech./Treatment:	Machinery:			Investing:
Fuel Cells:	Ceramics:				Chemicals:

TYPES OF BUSINESS:

Photovoltaics Manufacturing
Solar Cell Distribution & Sales
Solar Module Manufacturing

BRANDS/DIVISIONS/AFFILIATES:

CEEG (Shanghai) Solar Science & Technology Co Ltd
CEEG (Nan Jing) New Energy Co Ltd
China Sunergy (US) Clean Tech Inc
China Sunergy Europe GmbH

CONTACTS: Note: Officers with more than one job title may be intentionally listed here more than once.

Stephen Zhifang Cai, CEO
Yongfei Chen, Acting CFO
Robert A. Rice, Chief Sales & Mktg. Officer/VP
Aihua Wang, VP/Gen. Mgr.-R&D
Jianhua Zhao, CTO/Vice Chmn.
Robert A. Rice, Chief Strategy Officer
Tingxiu Lu, Chmn.
Willis He, CEO-China Sunergy (US) Clean Tech Inc

Phone: 86-25-5276-6681	**Fax:** 86-25-5276-6767
Toll-Free:	
Address: No. 123, Fochengxilu W. Rd., Nanjing, 211100 China	

GROWTH PLANS/SPECIAL FEATURES:

China Sunergy Co., Ltd. is engaged in designing, developing, manufacturing and selling solar cells. The company's products include both monocrystalline and multicrystalline silicon solar cells. Its 13 solar cell manufacturing lines have an aggregate annual production capacity of 404 MW, assuming the use of 156-millimeter monocrystalline silicon wafers. Prior to 2010, the firm marketed its products primarily to module manufacturers and system integrators, who then assembled its cells into solar modules and solar power systems for use in various markets. However, following the acquisition of two solar module manufacturers, CEEG (Shanghai) Solar Science & Technology Co., Ltd. and CEEG (Nan Jing) New Energy Co., Ltd., China Sunergy began supplying its cells directly to its own solar module manufacturing operations. The firm's sales network includes three regional offices, located in Shanghai; Munich, Germany; and California. China Sunergy's most significant market outside of China is Europe, primarily Italy and Germany, where it operates through China Sunergy Europe GmbH. China Sunergy's research and development operations are currently focused on the development of selective emitter cells, a version of the standard p-type solar cells with higher conversion efficiencies. Other technologies under development include passivated emitters and rear cells. In June 2011, the company disclosed plans to increase its annual silicon cell production capacity by co-investing in a 1GW project in Yangzhou City. In July 2011, it established China Sunergy (US) Clean Tech, Inc. in San Francisco to bolster its U.S. market presence.

FINANCIALS: Sales and profits are in thousands of dollars—add 000 to get the full amount. 2011 Note: Financial information for 2011 was not available for all companies at press time.

2011 Sales: $	2011 Profits: $	**U.S. Stock Ticker:** CSUN
2010 Sales: $517,219	2010 Profits: $51,734	**Int'l Ticker:**
2009 Sales: $284,865	2009 Profits: $-10,269	Int'l Exchange:
2008 Sales: $350,920	2008 Profits: $-22,938	Employees: 3,599 Fiscal Year Ends: 12/31
2007 Sales: $234,908	2007 Profits: $-4,855	Parent Company:

SALARIES/BENEFITS:

Pension Plan:	ESOP Stock Plan:	Profit Sharing:	Top Exec. Salary: $	Bonus: $
Savings Plan:	Stock Purch. Plan:		Second Exec. Salary: $	Bonus: $

OTHER THOUGHTS:

Apparent Women Officers or Directors:
Hot Spot for Advancement for Women/Minorities: Y

LOCATIONS: ("Y" = Yes)

West:	Southwest:	Midwest:	Southeast:	Northeast:	International:
Y					Y

CHINA TECHNOLOGY DEVELOPMENT GROUP CORP

www.chinactdc.com
Industry Group Code: 334413

Energy/Fuel:	Other Technologies:	Electrical Products:	Electronics:	Transportation:	Other:
Biofuels:	Irrigation:	Lighting/LEDs:	Computers:	Car Sharing:	Recycling:
Batteries/Storage:	Nanotech:	Waste Heat:	Sensors:	Electric Vehicles:	Engineering:
Solar: Y	Biotech:	Smart Meters:	Software:	Natural Gas Fuel:	Consulting:
Wind:	Water Tech./Treatment:	Machinery:			Investing:
Fuel Cells:	Ceramics:				Chemicals:

TYPES OF BUSINESS:

Solar Cell Manufacturing
Solar System Integration
Solar Plant Development & Installation

BRANDS/DIVISIONS/AFFILIATES:

LSP
Linsun Renewable Energy Corporation Limited
Linsun Power Technology (Quanzhou) Corp
LSP Solar GmbH

CONTACTS: *Note: Officers with more than one job title may be intentionally listed here more than once.*

Alan Li, CEO
Liao Lin-Hsiang, COO
Tairan Guo, Acting CFO
Bruno Diaz Herrera, CTO
Tairan Guo, Chief Bus. Dev. Officer
Weining Zhang, Chief Comm. Officer
Alan Li, Chmn.

Phone: 852-3112-8461	**Fax:** 852-3112-8410
Toll-Free:	
Address: 168-200 Connaught Rd., Shun Tak Centre, Fl. 10, Hong Kong, China	

GROWTH PLANS/SPECIAL FEATURES:

China Technology Development Group Corp. (CTDC) is a provider of solar energy products and solutions in China. The firm is headquartered in Hong Kong, where it operates a 100,000-square-foot R&D center and production facility. Additionally, CTDC has sales offices in Milan and Munich. Founded in 1995, the company was formerly engaged in sanitary wares and ceramic tiles manufacturing; system integration services; network security services and related software development; and manufacturing and marketing of a series of nutraceutical products utilizing bio-active components of bamboo. However, the company transitioned into the solar power industry by manufacturing SnO2 solar base plates, a type of transparent conductive oxide, or TCO, glass. TCO glass is a key component of thin-film solar cells. Now, the firm is primarily engaged in the production of solar modules from monocrystalline and multicrystalline solar cells, which it sells under the brand LSP. Initial production capacity at its module manufacturing facility is 65 MW. It plans to expand its annual production capacity to 300 MW by 2012. The firm is also involved in solar system integration and solar plant development. In November 2010, CTDC acquired Linsun Renewable Energy Corporation Limited, including its wholly-owned subsidiary Linsun Power Technology (Quanzhou) Corp. Ltd., a manufacturer of crystalline photovoltaic modules. In January 2011, CTDC announced the completion of an ecological Building Integrated Photovoltaic project in Xiamen Bay, China. In March 2011, it established LSP Solar GmbH in Munich, Germany to expand its sales network in Europe. In October 2011, the firm announced the completion of the 4.8 megawatt (MW) solar farm in Ravenna, Italy.

FINANCIALS: Sales and profits are in thousands of dollars—add 000 to get the full amount. 2011 Note: Financial information for 2011 was not available for all companies at press time.

2011 Sales: $	2011 Profits: $	**U.S. Stock Ticker:** CTDC
2010 Sales: $8,149	2010 Profits: $-5,330	**Int'l Ticker:**
2009 Sales: $	2009 Profits: $-5,635	Int'l Exchange:
2008 Sales: $	2008 Profits: $	Employees: 233 Fiscal Year Ends: 12/31
2007 Sales: $	2007 Profits: $	Parent Company:

SALARIES/BENEFITS:

Pension Plan:	ESOP Stock Plan:	Profit Sharing:	Top Exec. Salary: $	Bonus: $
Savings Plan:	Stock Purch. Plan:		Second Exec. Salary: $	Bonus: $

OTHER THOUGHTS:

Apparent Women Officers or Directors: 1
Hot Spot for Advancement for Women/Minorities:

LOCATIONS: ("Y" = Yes)

West:	Southwest:	Midwest:	Southeast:	Northeast:	International: Y

CLARIANT INTERNATIONAL LTD
www.clariant.com

Industry Group Code: 325

Energy/Fuel:	Other Technologies:	Electrical Products:	Electronics:	Transportation:	Other:	
Biofuels:	Irrigation:	Lighting/LEDs:	Computers:	Car Sharing:	Recycling:	
Batteries/Storage:	Nanotech:	Waste Heat:	Sensors:	Electric Vehicles:	Engineering:	
Solar:	Biotech:	Smart Meters:	Software:	Natural Gas Fuel:	Consulting:	
Wind:	Water Tech./Treatment:	Machinery:			Investing:	
Fuel Cells:	Ceramics:				Chemicals:	Y

TYPES OF BUSINESS:
Performance & Specialty Chemicals
Chemical Additives
Pigments & Dyes
Color & Additive Concentrates
Textile, Leather & Paper Chemicals

BRANDS/DIVISIONS/AFFILIATES:

CONTACTS: *Note: Officers with more than one job title may be intentionally listed here more than once.*
Hariolf Kottmann, CEO
Patrick Jany, CFO
Jurg Witmer, Chmn.

Phone: 41-61-469-5111	Fax: 41-61-469-5901
Toll-Free:	
Address: Rathausstrasse 61, Muttenz, CH-4132 Switzerland	

GROWTH PLANS/SPECIAL FEATURES:
Clariant International, Ltd. is a leading developer, producer and marketer of specialty chemicals, with over 100 group companies on five continents. The firm's businesses are organized into 10 divisions: additives; detergents and intermediaries; emulsions; industrial and consumer specialties; leather services; masterbatches; oil and mining services; paper specialties; pigments; and textile chemicals. Additives include plastic, coating and printing ink ingredients such as flame retardants, high performance waxes and polymer additives. The detergents and intermediaries division produces raw materials used in detergents and other cleaning products as well as chemical intermediaries for agrochemicals and pharmaceuticals. Emulsions and polymer dispersions are used in paints, coatings, adhesives, construction, sealants, textiles, leather and paper. The industrial and consumer specialties unit provides specialty chemicals for the consumer care and industrial markets. The firm's leather services unit is a leading provider of chemicals and services used in the leather manufacturing process. The masterbatches division offers color and additive concentrates and technical compounds for the plastics industry. Clariant's oil and mining services division offers products and services to the oil, refinery and mining industries. The company's paper specialties unit produces dyes, pigments, fluorochemicals, dye fixatives, resins and other products designed to improve color, whiteness and durability of paper products. The pigments division provides organic pigments, pigment preparations and dyes used in coatings, printing, plastics and other products. Clariant's textile chemicals include chemicals for pretreatment, dyeing, printing and finishing of textiles. In April 2010, the company launched a line of sun care and cosmetic products including SPF boosters and ingredients to improve the viscosity and shelf life of cosmetics.

FINANCIALS: Sales and profits are in thousands of dollars—add 000 to get the full amount. 2011 Note: Financial information for 2011 was not available for all companies at press time.

2011 Sales: $	2011 Profits: $	**U.S. Stock Ticker:**
2010 Sales: $7,839,770	2010 Profits: $198,200	**Int'l Ticker: CLN**
2009 Sales: $6,319,270	2009 Profits: $-185,360	Int'l Exchange: Zurich-SWX
2008 Sales: $6,987,390	2008 Profits: $-32,030	Employees: 16,176 Fiscal Year Ends: 12/31
2007 Sales: $7,387,370	2007 Profits: $4,330	Parent Company:

SALARIES/BENEFITS:

Pension Plan:	ESOP Stock Plan:	Profit Sharing:	Top Exec. Salary: $	Bonus: $
Savings Plan:	Stock Purch. Plan:		Second Exec. Salary: $	Bonus: $

OTHER THOUGHTS:
Apparent Women Officers or Directors:
Hot Spot for Advancement for Women/Minorities:

LOCATIONS: ("Y" = Yes)

West:	Southwest:	Midwest:	Southeast:	Northeast:	International:
Y	Y	Y	Y	Y	Y

CLEAN ENERGY FUELS CORP

www.cleanenergyfuels.com

Industry Group Code: 454319

Energy/Fuel:	Other Technologies:	Electrical Products:	Electronics:	Transportation:		Other:
Biofuels:	Irrigation:	Lighting/LEDs:	Computers:	Car Sharing:		Recycling:
Batteries/Storage:	Nanotech:	Waste Heat:	Sensors:	Electric Vehicles:		Engineering:
Solar:	Biotech:	Smart Meters:	Software:	Natural Gas Fuel:	Y	Consulting:
Wind:	Water Tech./Treatment:	Machinery:				Investing:
Fuel Cells:	Ceramics:					Chemicals:

TYPES OF BUSINESS:

Automotive Natural Gas Retailing
LNG, Liquefied Natural Gas Production & Sales
CNG, Compressed Natural Gas Production & Sales

BRANDS/DIVISIONS/AFFILIATES:

Dallas Clean Energy LLC
BAF Technologies Inc
IMW Industries Ltd
Wyoming Northstar Inc
Southstar LLC
M&S Rental LLC
Clean Energy del Peru

CONTACTS: Note: Officers with more than one job title may be intentionally listed here more than once.

Andrew J. Littlefair, CEO
Mitchell Pratt, COO
Andrew J. Littlefair, Pres.
Richard R. Wheeler, CFO
Peter Grace, Sr. VP-Sales
Dennis C.K. Ding, VP-Eng. & Construction
Nate Jensen, General Counsel/VP
Brian Powers, VP-Oper.
Raymond P. Burke, VP-Bus. Dev., Solid Waste
James L. Hooley, VP-Gov't. Rel.
Peter Grace, Sr. VP-Finance
Barclay F. Corbus, Sr. VP-Strategic Dev.
Harrison Clay, VP-Renewable Fuels
Todd Campbell, VP-Public Policy & Regulatory Affairs

Phone: 562-493-2804	Fax: 562-493-4532
Toll-Free:	
Address: 3020 Old Ranch Pkwy., Ste. 400, Seal Beach, CA 90740 US	

GROWTH PLANS/SPECIAL FEATURES:

Clean Energy Fuels Corp. is a leading supplier of natural gas vehicle fuel, which includes both compressed natural gas (CNG) and liquefied natural gas (LNG). Additionally, the company builds CNG and LNG fueling stations; sells renewable biomethane; converts natural gas vehicles; sells natural gas vehicle compression equipment; and finances vehicle acquisitions by customers. Clean Energy serves fleet vehicle operators in markets, such as public transit, waste transport, airports, taxis, seaports and regional trucking. Clean Energy supplies LNG and CNG to approximately 480 customers, operating over 21,270 vehicles. The firm owns, operates or supplies natural gas to 224 fueling stations throughout the U.S. and Canada. Through a joint venture with Clean Energy del Peru, the firm operates one CNG gas station in Lima, Peru. The firm's first LNG plant, located in Willis, Texas, produces up to 35 million gallons of vehicle-grade LNG per year and is equipped with both loading facilities and a 1 million gallon storage tank. The company's LNG plant located in Boron, California has a 1.8 million gallon storage tank and is built to produce up to 60 million gallons of LNG per year. Substantial contract agreements to build and operate CNG and LNG fueling facilities or to buy the exclusive fuel supplier exist with agencies, such as the Los Angeles International Airport, the Metropolitan Tulsa Transit Authority, UPS and major contract freight carrier Dillon Transport. Clean Energy's subsidiaries include Dallas Clean Energy, LLC; BAF Technologies, Inc.; I.M.W. Industries Ltd.; Wyoming Northstar Inc., Southstar LLC and M&S Rental LLC.

FINANCIALS: Sales and profits are in thousands of dollars—add 000 to get the full amount. 2011 Note: Financial information for 2011 was not available for all companies at press time.

2011 Sales: $	2011 Profits: $	**U.S. Stock Ticker:** CLNE
2010 Sales: $211,834	2010 Profits: $-44,568	**Int'l Ticker:**
2009 Sales: $131,503	2009 Profits: $-33,688	Int'l Exchange:
2008 Sales: $129,473	2008 Profits: $-40,857	Employees: 710 Fiscal Year Ends: 12/31
2007 Sales: $117,716	2007 Profits: $-8,894	Parent Company:

SALARIES/BENEFITS:

Pension Plan:	ESOP Stock Plan:	Profit Sharing:	Top Exec. Salary: $520,000	Bonus: $212,888
Savings Plan:	Stock Purch. Plan:		Second Exec. Salary: $345,000	Bonus: $111,519

OTHER THOUGHTS:

Apparent Women Officers or Directors:
Hot Spot for Advancement for Women/Minorities:

LOCATIONS: ("Y" = Yes)

West:	Southwest:	Midwest:	Southeast:	Northeast:	International:
Y	Y	Y	Y	Y	Y

Sales, profits and employees may be estimates. Financial information, benefits and other data can change quickly and may vary from those stated here.

CLIMATEWELL

www.climatewell.com

Industry Group Code: 335

Energy/Fuel:	Other Technologies:	Electrical Products:	Electronics:	Transportation:	Other:
Biofuels:	Irrigation:	Lighting/LEDs:	Computers:	Car Sharing:	Recycling:
Batteries/Storage:	Nanotech:	Waste Heat: Y	Sensors:	Electric Vehicles:	Engineering:
Solar:	Biotech:	Smart Meters:	Software:	Natural Gas Fuel:	Consulting:
Wind:	Water Tech./Treatment: Y	Machinery:			Investing:
Fuel Cells:	Ceramics:				Chemicals:

TYPES OF BUSINESS:

Heating & Cooling Technology

BRANDS/DIVISIONS/AFFILIATES:

ClimateWell 10
RIO
GSS Intellihomes
Triple-State absorption

CONTACTS: *Note: Officers with more than one job title may be intentionally listed here more than once.*

Per Olofsson, CEO
Helena Haglund, CFO
Goran Bolin, CTO/Exec. VP
Anders Blomgren, Dir.-Prod. Dev.
Jan Tjerngren, Head-Mfg.
Pedro Luis Rodriguez, Mgr. Dir.-ClimateWell Iberica
Ake Sund, Chmn.

Phone: 46-8794-0370	Fax: 46-8744-3070
Toll-Free:	
Address: Instrumentvägen 20, Hägersten, SE-126 53 Sweden	

GROWTH PLANS/SPECIAL FEATURES:

ClimateWell is a heating and cooling technology firm. The firm's proprietary Triple-State absorption is a heat pump which has the ability to store energy and convert hot water to cooling and heating without the use of electricity. This method creates a system that is both cost effective and environmentally sound, reducing an average family's CO2 emissions by up to 15 tons annually. Suitable hot water sources for the firm's solutions include solar thermal collectors, waste heat and district heating from electric generators or co-generation. The company markets its technology to single family homes, housing projects, commercial buildings and industrial outlets. In single family homes, ClimateWell's solutions include using the pool to control the temperature of the indoor system; CimateWell 10, a charging, heating and cooling energy storage unit; tap water tanks, which store warm water for domestic use; a boiler, used for back up heating of the system on cloudy days; and solar thermal collectors, which collect the sun's heat and heat the water in the tap water tanks and the salt in ClimateWell 10. In housing projects, the firm creates climate controlled environments by implementing radiant floors, ducted air or fancoils. In commercial outlets, ClimateWell uses dry coolers to dispatch excess heat, chillers to cool the air to be sent throughout the building and ducted air to carry cool air throughout the facility. In industrial applications, the company is able to take the excess heat given off during product manufacturing and to store and convert it into the heating and cooling power to subsequently run the facilities. In 2011, the firm signed a distribution agreement with RIO to market the firm's products throughout Morocco, and GSS Intellihomes to market the firm's solar cooling products throughout Colombia.

FINANCIALS: Sales and profits are in thousands of dollars—add 000 to get the full amount. 2011 Note: Financial information for 2011 was not available for all companies at press time.

2011 Sales: $	2011 Profits: $	**U.S. Stock Ticker: Private**	
2010 Sales: $	2010 Profits: $	**Int'l Ticker:**	
2009 Sales: $	2009 Profits: $	Int'l Exchange:	
2008 Sales: $	2008 Profits: $	Employees:	Fiscal Year Ends:
2007 Sales: $	2007 Profits: $	Parent Company:	

SALARIES/BENEFITS:

Pension Plan:	ESOP Stock Plan:	Profit Sharing:	Top Exec. Salary: $	Bonus: $
Savings Plan:	Stock Purch. Plan:		Second Exec. Salary: $	Bonus: $

OTHER THOUGHTS:

Apparent Women Officers or Directors: 1
Hot Spot for Advancement for Women/Minorities:

LOCATIONS: ("Y" = Yes)

West:	Southwest:	Midwest:	Southeast:	Northeast:	International:
					Y

CLIPPER WINDPOWER LLC

www.clipperwind.com

Industry Group Code: 33361

Energy/Fuel:	Other Technologies:	Electrical Products:	Electronics:	Transportation:	Other:
Biofuels:	Irrigation:	Lighting/LEDs:	Computers:	Car Sharing:	Recycling:
Batteries/Storage:	Nanotech:	Waste Heat:	Sensors:	Electric Vehicles:	Engineering:
Solar:	Biotech:	Smart Meters:	Software:	Natural Gas Fuel:	Consulting:
Wind: Y	Water Tech./Treatment:	Machinery:			Investing:
Fuel Cells:	Ceramics:				Chemicals:

TYPES OF BUSINESS:

Turbine Manufacturing
Wind Project Development & Maintenance

BRANDS/DIVISIONS/AFFILIATES:

Liberty Wind Turbines
MegaFlux
Quantum Drive
United Technologies Corporation
Clipper Windpower Marine Limited

CONTACTS: Note: Officers with more than one job title may be intentionally listed here more than once.

Jesper Rathje, CFO
Victor De Leon, VP-Global Sales
Amir S. Mikhail, Sr. VP-Advanced Tech.
Craig Christenson, Sr. VP-Eng.
Robert T. Loyd, Plant Mgr.-Cedar Rapids Mfg. Facility
Eric D. Novak, General Counsel
Lawrence D. Willey, VP-Oper.
Jeffery W. Maurer, VP-Project Mgmt. & Fleet Svcs.
Christian Anderson, VP-Tower Center of Excellence
Robert Gates, Chief Commercial Officer
James G.P. Dehlsen, Chmn.
Ian Cluderay, VP-Global Supply Chain Mgmt.

Phone: 805-690-3275	**Fax:** 805-899-1115
Toll-Free:	
Address: 6305 Carpinteria Ave., Ste. 300, Carpinteria, CA 93013 US	

GROWTH PLANS/SPECIAL FEATURES:

Clipper Windpower LLC (formerly Clipper Windpower plc), based in California, is a designer and manufacturer of wind turbines, as well as a developer of wind energy projects. The firm is a subsidiary of United Technologies Corporation. From a 330,000 square foot facility in Iowa, the company manufactures and assembles its 2.5-megawatt (MW) Liberty wind turbine. The Liberty is a variable speed wind turbine, featuring four of Clipper's patented MegaFlux permanent magnet generators and its patented Quantum Drive distributed power train. In addition to manufacturing, the firm is capable of developing a wind project through all of its stages; from wind resource acquisition and management, project design and engineering, to financing, construction and operation and maintenance. Besides its manufacturing facility in Iowa, Clipper maintains offices in Colorado, Texas and the U. K. Additionally, the firm operates subsidiary Clipper Windpower Marine Limited. In late 2010, the firm was acquired by United Technologies Corporation.

FINANCIALS: Sales and profits are in thousands of dollars—add 000 to get the full amount. 2011 Note: Financial information for 2011 was not available for all companies at press time.

2011 Sales: $	2011 Profits: $	**U.S. Stock Ticker: Subsidiary**
2010 Sales: $	2010 Profits: $	**Int'l Ticker:**
2009 Sales: $	2009 Profits: $	Int'l Exchange:
2008 Sales: $	2008 Profits: $	Employees: 750 Fiscal Year Ends: 12/31
2007 Sales: $	2007 Profits: $	Parent Company: UNITED TECHNOLOGIES CORPORATION

SALARIES/BENEFITS:

Pension Plan:	ESOP Stock Plan:	Profit Sharing:	Top Exec. Salary: $	Bonus: $
Savings Plan:	Stock Purch. Plan:		Second Exec. Salary: $	Bonus: $

OTHER THOUGHTS:

Apparent Women Officers or Directors:
Hot Spot for Advancement for Women/Minorities:

LOCATIONS: ("Y" = Yes)

West:	Southwest:	Midwest:	Southeast:	Northeast:	International:
Y		Y		Y	Y

Sales, profits and employees may be estimates. Financial information, benefits and other data can change quickly and may vary from those stated here.

CODA AUTOMOTIVE INC

www.codaautomotive.com

Industry Group Code: 33611

Energy/Fuel:	Other Technologies:	Electrical Products:	Electronics:	Transportation:		Other:
Biofuels:	Irrigation:	Lighting/LEDs:	Computers:	Car Sharing:		Recycling:
Batteries/Storage:	Nanotech:	Waste Heat:	Sensors:	Electric Vehicles:	Y	Engineering:
Solar:	Biotech:	Smart Meters:	Software:	Natural Gas Fuel:		Consulting:
Wind:	Water Tech./Treatment:	Machinery:				Investing:
Fuel Cells:	Ceramics:					Chemicals:

TYPES OF BUSINESS:

Electric Automobile Manufacturing

BRANDS/DIVISIONS/AFFILIATES:

CODA Sedan

CONTACTS: *Note: Officers with more than one job title may be intentionally listed here more than once.*

Phil Murtaugh, CEO
Byron Jones, CFO
Sean Blankenship, VP-Mktg.
Andreea Boier-Jennings, VP-Human Resources
Thomas Fritz, Sr. VP-Eng.
John Callery, VP-Mfg. & Quality
Lino Lauro, General Counsel
Chris Rose, Sr. VP-Corp. Dev.
Larkin Hill, Dir.-Corp. Comm.
Chris Paulson, VP-Corp. Strategy & Bus. Dev.
Phillippe Gow, VP-Battery Systems
Kathy Wang, VP-China Corp. Affairs
K. Forrest Beanum, VP-Gov't Rel.
Steven Heller, Chmn.
Mark Atkeson, Sr. VP-China Oper.
Waqas Sherwani, VP-Supply Chain

Phone: 310-390-4890	Fax: 310-397-8985
Toll-Free: 888-461-1654	
Address: 1601 Wilshire Blvd., Santa Monica, CA 90403 US	

GROWTH PLANS/SPECIAL FEATURES:

CODA Automotive, Inc. designs, develops and, with its joint-venture partners, builds electric vehicles under the CODA Automotive brand name. CODA was launched in 2009 by Miles Rubin, who also founded Miles Electric Vehicles, a manufacturer of low speed electric fleet vehicles. CODA's first car, the CODA Sedan, is assembled in China by Hafei Automobile Group and is based on a Hafei chassis re-engineered by Porsche Engineering. After the chassis is finished in China, it is shipped to the U.S. for installation of electric power-train components. The components for the car are manufactured by American suppliers, including UQM Technologies, which provides the motor; Delphi; BorgWarner; and Nexteer Automotive. The CODA Sedan is powered by a 333V Lithium-Ion battery that can provide 134 horsepower. CODA produces its batteries through a joint venture with Chinese battery cell supplier Tianjin Lishen Power Battery, known as Lio Energy Systems. The Tianjin battery production facility has a capacity of 20,000 battery packs per year. The CODA Sedan has a range of 90-120 miles on a six-hour charge, can accelerate from 0-60 in under 11 seconds and has a maximum speed of 80 miles per hour. The battery pack can be charged at any standard outlet, but charges most efficiently from a 220 volt outlet, such as those used for laundry machines. The CODA Sedan also has a regenerative braking system that stores and reuses the kinetic energy produced when the cars brakes are utilized. The sedan is currently available for pre-sales on the company's web site, where potential customers can also sign up for the priority waiting list. Sales will initially be restricted to California; CODA hopes to sell the sedan nationwide by 2013.

FINANCIALS: Sales and profits are in thousands of dollars—add 000 to get the full amount. 2011 Note: Financial information for 2011 was not available for all companies at press time.

2011 Sales: $	2011 Profits: $	U.S. Stock Ticker: Private
2010 Sales: $	2010 Profits: $	Int'l Ticker:
2009 Sales: $	2009 Profits: $	Int'l Exchange:
2008 Sales: $	2008 Profits: $	Employees: Fiscal Year Ends:
2007 Sales: $	2007 Profits: $	Parent Company:

SALARIES/BENEFITS:

Pension Plan:	ESOP Stock Plan:	Profit Sharing:	Top Exec. Salary: $	Bonus: $
Savings Plan:	Stock Purch. Plan:		Second Exec. Salary: $	Bonus: $

OTHER THOUGHTS:

Apparent Women Officers or Directors: 2
Hot Spot for Advancement for Women/Minorities:

LOCATIONS: ("Y" = Yes)

West: Y	Southwest:	Midwest:	Southeast:	Northeast:	International: Y

COMPACT POWER MOTORS GMBH

www.cpmotors.eu/en

Industry Group Code: 335

Energy/Fuel:		Other Technologies:		Electrical Products:		Electronics:		Transportation:		Other:	
Biofuels:		Irrigation:		Lighting/LEDs:		Computers:		Car Sharing:		Recycling:	
Batteries/Storage:	Y	Nanotech:		Waste Heat:		Sensors:		Electric Vehicles:	Y	Engineering:	
Solar:		Biotech:		Smart Meters:		Software:		Natural Gas Fuel:		Consulting:	
Wind:		Water Tech./Treatment:		Machinery:	Y					Investing:	
Fuel Cells:		Ceramics:								Chemicals:	

TYPES OF BUSINESS:

Compact Electric Drives Development

BRANDS/DIVISIONS/AFFILIATES:

CPM90
CPM90 Twin
CPM90 SmartGear
RFTR

GROWTH PLANS/SPECIAL FEATURES:

Compact Power Motors GmbH (CPM) is a developer, producer and marketer of compact electric drives for automotive and generator applications. The products of the company are marketed as efficient, light and compact and include the CPM90 brushless permanent-magnet synchromotors; the CPM90 Twin power packs, coupling two EC motors allowing for higher performance, the CPM90 SmartGear, a drive train that pairs a motor and controller with a dual-stage transmission for electric bikes; and the RFTR, a larger 10 to 80 kilowatt motor designed for electric vehicles and mobile applications. The company's products are used in small city cars, electric scooters, forklift trucks, golf carts, auxiliary power units and in wind energy. CPM has offices in both Germany and China.

CONTACTS: Note: Officers with more than one job title may be intentionally listed here more than once.

Nico Windecker, Managing Dir.
Thomas Leiber, Managing Dir.

Phone: 49-89-2872468-50	Fax: 49-89-2872468-750
Toll-Free:	
Address: Feringastrasse 11, Unterfohring, 85774 Germany	

FINANCIALS: Sales and profits are in thousands of dollars—add 000 to get the full amount. 2011 Note: Financial information for 2011 was not available for all companies at press time.

2011 Sales: $	2011 Profits: $	U.S. Stock Ticker: Private
2010 Sales: $	2010 Profits: $	Int'l Ticker:
2009 Sales: $	2009 Profits: $	Int'l Exchange:
2008 Sales: $	2008 Profits: $	Employees: Fiscal Year Ends:
2007 Sales: $	2007 Profits: $	Parent Company:

SALARIES/BENEFITS:

Pension Plan:	ESOP Stock Plan:	Profit Sharing:	Top Exec. Salary: $	Bonus: $
Savings Plan:	Stock Purch. Plan:		Second Exec. Salary: $	Bonus: $

OTHER THOUGHTS:

Apparent Women Officers or Directors:
Hot Spot for Advancement for Women/Minorities:

LOCATIONS: ("Y" = Yes)

West:	Southwest:	Midwest:	Southeast:	Northeast:	International:
					Y

Sales, profits and employees may be estimates. Financial information, benefits and other data can change quickly and may vary from those stated here.

COMPANHIA DE SANEAMENTO BASICO DO ESTADO DE SAO PAULO (SABESP)

www.sabesp.com.br

Industry Group Code: 562

Energy/Fuel:	Other Technologies:	Electrical Products:	Electronics:	Transportation:	Other:
Biofuels:	Irrigation:	Lighting/LEDs:	Computers:	Car Sharing:	Recycling:
Batteries/Storage:	Nanotech:	Waste Heat:	Sensors:	Electric Vehicles:	Engineering:
Solar:	Biotech:	Smart Meters:	Software:	Natural Gas Fuel:	Consulting:
Wind:	Water Tech./Treatment: Y	Machinery:			Investing:
Fuel Cells:	Ceramics:				Chemicals:

TYPES OF BUSINESS:

Water Treatment
Sewage Services
Wastewater Systems

BRANDS/DIVISIONS/AFFILIATES:

GROWTH PLANS/SPECIAL FEATURES:

Companhia de Saneamento Basico do Estado de Sao Paulo (SABESP), based in Brazil, plans, executes and operates water, sewage and industrial wastewater systems to 27.2 million residential, commercial, industrial and governmental customers in 364 of the 645 cities in the state of Sao Paulo. SABESP also provides treated water to six other cities that manage their own distribution. The firm provides water and sewage services to about 60% of the population of the state. The company's expansion strategy outlines plans to provide 100% of treated water, 90% of collected sewage and 88% of treated sewage services in its supplied cities. SABESP's major stockholder is the Government of the State of Sao Paulo.

CONTACTS: Note: Officers with more than one job title may be intentionally listed here more than once.

Dilma Seli Pena, CEO
Rui de Britto Alvares Alfonso, CFO
Marcelo S.H. de Freitas, CTO
Rui de Britto Alvares Alfonso, Chief Investor Rel. Officer
Manuelito Pereira Magalhaes, Corp. Mgmt. Officer
Marcelo S.H. de Freitas, Enterprises & Environment Officer
Edson de Oliveira Giriboni, Chmn.

Phone: 55-11-3388-8200	Fax: 55-11-3813-0254
Toll-Free:	
Address: 300 Rua Costa Carvalho Pinheiros, Sao Paulo, 05429-000 Brazil	

FINANCIALS: Sales and profits are in thousands of dollars—add 000 to get the full amount. 2011 Note: Financial information for 2011 was not available for all companies at press time.

2011 Sales: $	2011 Profits: $	U.S. Stock Ticker:
2010 Sales: $5,352,000	2010 Profits: $945,300	Int'l Ticker: SBSP3
2009 Sales: $4,974,200	2009 Profits: $874,200	Int'l Exchange: Sao Paulo-SAO
2008 Sales: $3,713,840	2008 Profits: $37,190	Employees: 15,330 Fiscal Year Ends: 12/31
2007 Sales: $	2007 Profits: $	Parent Company:

SALARIES/BENEFITS:

Pension Plan:	ESOP Stock Plan:	Profit Sharing:	Top Exec. Salary: $	Bonus: $
Savings Plan:	Stock Purch. Plan:		Second Exec. Salary: $	Bonus: $

OTHER THOUGHTS:

Apparent Women Officers or Directors:
Hot Spot for Advancement for Women/Minorities: S

LOCATIONS: ("Y" = Yes)

West:	Southwest:	Midwest:	Southeast:	Northeast:	International: Y

COMVERGE INC   www.comverge.com

Industry Group Code: 33411

Energy/Fuel:	Other Technologies:	Electrical Products:		Electronics:	Transportation:	Other:
Biofuels:	Irrigation:	Lighting/LEDs:		Computers:	Car Sharing:	Recycling:
Batteries/Storage:	Nanotech:	Waste Heat:		Sensors:	Electric Vehicles:	Engineering:
Solar:	Biotech:	Smart Meters:	Y	Software:	Natural Gas Fuel:	Consulting:
Wind:	Water Tech./Treatment:	Machinery:				Investing:
Fuel Cells:	Ceramics:					Chemicals:

TYPES OF BUSINESS:

Smart Grid Technology

BRANDS/DIVISIONS/AFFILIATES:

IntelliSOURCE

CONTACTS: *Note: Officers with more than one job title may be intentionally listed here more than once.*

R. Blake Young, CEO
Steve Moffitt, COO/Exec. VP
R. Blake Young, Pres.
David Mathieson, CFO/Exec. VP
Christopher Camino, Chief Mktg. Officer/Exec. VP-Sales
Teresa Naylor, Sr. VP-Human Resources
Arthur Vos, IV, CTO/Sr. VP-Utility Sales
Matthew H. Smith, General Counsel/Sr. VP/Sec.
Jason Cigarran, VP-Investor Rel.
John A. Waterworth, Controller/VP
George Hunt, Sr. VP-Commercial & Industrial Sales
Jason Cigarran, VP-Mktg.
Alec G. Dreyer, Chmn.
Michael D. Picchi, Pres., Comverge Int'l

Phone:	**Fax:** 770-696-7665
Toll-Free: 888-565-5525	
Address: 5390 Triangle Pkwy., Ste. 300, Norcross, GA 30092 US	

GROWTH PLANS/SPECIAL FEATURES:

Comverge, Inc. is a clean energy company and a leading provider of intelligent energy management (IEM) solutions. Its products are designed to improve the smart grid, a system of multiple suppliers and operators delivering power to consumers with the ability to control and adjust power according to usage and demand for the purpose of cutting costs and saving energy. The company operates in two segments: Residential Business and Commercial & Industrial (C&I). The Residential Business segment offers IEM networks to utility customers for use in programs with residential and small commercial end-use participants. Its solutions include a broad range of hardware products, from basic one-way load control switches to more sophisticated smart thermostats, in-home displays and comprehensive two-way data and control systems; its IntelliSOURCE software and various services such as installation and marketing. The segment offers programs that address both peak and base load demands for residential and small commercial end consumers. Such programs include the Virtual Peaking Capacity (VPC) Program, which provides additional capacity through long-term contracts with utilities. The C&I segment provides IEM solutions to utilities and independent system operators, enabling them to reduce energy use and costs. This segment contracts with utilities to provide available capacity to utility customers through pay-for-performance VPC programs. The C&I segment also performs upgrades and maintenance of power systems.

FINANCIALS: Sales and profits are in thousands of dollars—add 000 to get the full amount. 2011 Note: Financial information for 2011 was not available for all companies at press time.

2011 Sales: $	2011 Profits: $	**U.S. Stock Ticker:** COMV
2010 Sales: $119,389	2010 Profits: $-31,351	**Int'l Ticker:**
2009 Sales: $98,844	2009 Profits: $-31,666	Int'l Exchange:
2008 Sales: $77,238	2008 Profits: $-94,106	Employees: 562 Fiscal Year Ends: 12/31
2007 Sales: $	2007 Profits: $	Parent Company:

SALARIES/BENEFITS:

Pension Plan:	ESOP Stock Plan:	Profit Sharing:	Top Exec. Salary: $372,115	Bonus: $350,000
Savings Plan: Y	Stock Purch. Plan:		Second Exec. Salary: $300,000	Bonus: $146,100

OTHER THOUGHTS:

Apparent Women Officers or Directors: 1
Hot Spot for Advancement for Women/Minorities:

LOCATIONS: ("Y" = Yes)

West:	Southwest:	Midwest:	Southeast:	Northeast:	International:
Y			Y	Y	

CONERGY AG

Industry Group Code: 334413

Energy/Fuel:		Other Technologies:	Electrical Products:	Electronics:	Transportation:	Other:
Biofuels:		Irrigation:	Lighting/LEDs:	Computers:	Car Sharing:	Recycling:
Batteries/Storage:		Nanotech:	Waste Heat:	Sensors:	Electric Vehicles:	Engineering:
Solar:	Y	Biotech:	Smart Meters:	Software:	Natural Gas Fuel:	Consulting:
Wind:		Water Tech./Treatment:	Machinery:			Investing:
Fuel Cells:		Ceramics:				Chemicals:

TYPES OF BUSINESS:

Photovoltaics

BRANDS/DIVISIONS/AFFILIATES:

Conergy
SunTechnics

CONTACTS: Note: Officers with more than one job title may be intentionally listed here more than once.

Sebastian Biedenkopf, Managing Dir.
Alexander Gorski, COO
Antje Stephan, Head-Corp. Comm.
Christoph Marx, Dir.-Investor Rel.
Philip Comberg, Chmn.

Phone: 49-40-2371-020	**Fax:** 49-40-2371-02148
Toll-Free:	
Address: Anckelmannsplatz 1, Hamburg, 20537 Germany	

GROWTH PLANS/SPECIAL FEATURES:

Conergy AG is engaged in the design, manufacture, installation and operation of photovoltaic (PV) systems. The company operates in two segments: Conergy PV and the Components Segment. The Conergy PV segment comprises the sales and marketing of self-produced and purchased PV products systems solutions; while the Components segment comprises the company's manufacturing activities. The firm manufactures wafer, cell and module lines; its products include solar-power installations with PV panels, tracking systems inverters, mounting products and system monitoring tools. Conergy operates three manufacturing facilities in Germany: in Frankfurt (Oder), Rangsdorf and Bad Vilbel. The firm's brands include Conergy and SunTechnics. Conergy PV is also involved in the development, financing and implementation of large-scale PV projects. In January 2011, the firm announced plans to construct five new solar projects in Italy with a combined total capacity of 4.1 MW; additionally, the firm announced the sale of its subsidiary Gustrower Warmepumpen GmbH to SmartHeart Inc. In April 2011, Conergy opened its third solar park in Northern Germany completed in the last 12 months. In the same month, it finished a 12.4 MW facility in Thailand, its third solar park in the country. In May 2011, Conergy announced the completion of its first solar power system in North America, located on the roof top of Fujifilm's branch office in Oahu, Hawaii. In June 2011, the company completed a 1.5 MW solar park in Arta, Greece and a 2 MW solar park in Grevena, Greece. In July 2011, Conergy completed Great Britain's largest solar power plant, at 5 MW. In November 2011, the firm disclosed plans to build an 8.2 MW and a 1.2 MW solar park in Grimmen and Thalham, Germany respectively.

FINANCIALS: Sales and profits are in thousands of dollars—add 000 to get the full amount. 2011 Note: Financial information for 2011 was not available for all companies at press time.

2011 Sales: $	2011 Profits: $	**U.S. Stock Ticker:**
2010 Sales: $1,294,400	2010 Profits: $-63,300	**Int'l Ticker: CGY**
2009 Sales: $795,760	2009 Profits: $-105,810	Int'l Exchange: Paris-Euronext
2008 Sales: $1,503,660	2008 Profits: $-317,560	Employees: 1,574 Fiscal Year Ends: 12/31
2007 Sales: $896,000	2007 Profits: $-314,400	Parent Company:

SALARIES/BENEFITS:

Pension Plan:	ESOP Stock Plan:	Profit Sharing:	Top Exec. Salary: $	Bonus: $
Savings Plan:	Stock Purch. Plan:		Second Exec. Salary: $	Bonus: $

OTHER THOUGHTS:

Apparent Women Officers or Directors: 1
Hot Spot for Advancement for Women/Minorities:

LOCATIONS: ("Y" = Yes)

West:	Southwest:	Midwest:	Southeast:	Northeast:	International:
Y					Y

CONOCOPHILLIPS COMPANY

www.conocophillips.com

Industry Group Code: 211111

Energy/Fuel:	Other Technologies:	Electrical Products:	Electronics:	Transportation:	Other:	
Biofuels:	Irrigation:	Lighting/LEDs:	Computers:	Car Sharing:	Recycling:	
Batteries/Storage:	Nanotech:	Waste Heat:	Sensors:	Electric Vehicles:	Engineering:	
Solar:	Biotech:	Smart Meters:	Software:	Natural Gas Fuel:	Consulting:	
Wind:	Water Tech./Treatment:	Machinery:			Investing:	
Fuel Cells:	Ceramics:				Chemicals:	Y

TYPES OF BUSINESS:

Oil & Gas Exploration & Production
Natural Gas Distribution
Refining
Pipelines
Oil Sands Operations
Chemical Production
Technology Investment
Gasoline Retail

BRANDS/DIVISIONS/AFFILIATES:

Flying J
Conoco
Phillips 66
DCP Midstream LLC
Chevron Phillips Chemical Company LLC
Alaska Gas Pipe
CFJ Properties
Energy Technology Ventures

CONTACTS: *Note: Officers with more than one job title may be intentionally listed here more than once.*

James J. Mulva, CEO
Jeff Sheets, CFO/Sr. VP
W.C.W. Chiang, Sr. VP-Mktg.
Carin S. Knickel, VP-Human Resources
Greg C. Garland, Sr. VP-Exploration & Prod., Americas
Luc J. Messier, Sr. VP-Project Dev.
Gene L. Batchelder, Chief Admin. Officer/Sr. VP
Janet Langford Kelly, General Counsel/Corp. Sec./Sr. VP-Legal
Larry E. Archibald, Sr. VP-Bus. Dev. & Exploration
Red Cavaney, Sr. VP-Gov't Affairs
Jeff Sheets, Sr. VP-Finance
Robert A. Herman, VP-Health, Safety & Environment
Alan J. Hirshberg, Sr. VP-Planning & Strategy
W.C.W Chiang, Sr. VP-Refining & Transportation
Rand Berney, Sr. VP-Corp. Shared Svcs.
James J. Mulva, Chmn.
Ryan M. Lance, Sr. VP-Exploration & Prod., Int'l
Luc J. Messier, Sr. VP-Procurement

Phone: 281-293-1000	**Fax:**
Toll-Free:	
Address: 600 N. Dairy Ashford Rd., Houston, TX 77079 US	

GROWTH PLANS/SPECIAL FEATURES:

ConocoPhillips Company is an integrated global energy company. Its business segments include exploration and production; midstream; refining and marketing; chemicals; and emerging businesses. The exploration and production segment explores for, produces, transports and markets crude oil, natural gas and natural gas liquids worldwide. It also mines oil sands to extract bitumen, which it upgrades into synthetic crude oil. The midstream division gathers, processes and markets natural gas produced by the company and others, and also fractionates and markets natural gas liquids. This segment includes the firm's 50% equity investment in DCP Midstream, LLC. The refining and marketing segment purchases, refines, markets and transports crude oil and petroleum products, mainly in the U.S., Europe and Asia. The chemicals group, including the company's 50% equity investment in Chevron Phillips Chemical Company LLC, manufactures and markets petrochemicals and plastics worldwide. The emerging businesses segment oversees businesses such as technologies related to hydrocarbon recovery (including heavy oil), refining, alternative energy, biofuels and the environment. In June 2010, the company sold its 9.03% stake in Syncrude to Sinopec International Petroleum Exploration and Production Company; and sold its 50% ownership of CFJ Properties -Flying J truck stops to Pilot Travel Centers for roughly $626 million. Between late 2010 and early 2011, the firm sold its entire 20% stake in Lukoil (OAO). In January 2011, ConocoPhillips, NRG Energy, Inc. and GE formed joint venture Energy Technology Ventures to invest in alternative venture- and growth-stage firms. In July of the same year, the firm announced plans to split into two publicly traded companies by separating its refining business and its production business. The split is expected to happen in early 2012.

ConocoPhillips' employees receive life, disability, medical and dental insurance; a retirement plan; a savings plan; a health savings account; spending accounts; a Healthy Lifestyle Coach; and scholarships and tuition reimbursement.

FINANCIALS: Sales and profits are in thousands of dollars—add 000 to get the full amount. 2011 Note: Financial information for 2011 was not available for all companies at press time.

2011 Sales: $	2011 Profits: $	**U.S. Stock Ticker: COP**
2010 Sales: $189,441,000	2010 Profits: $11,417,000	**Int'l Ticker:**
2009 Sales: $149,341,000	2009 Profits: $4,858,000	Int'l Exchange:
2008 Sales: $240,842,000	2008 Profits: $-16,998,000	Employees: 29,900 Fiscal Year Ends: 12/31
2007 Sales: $187,437,000	2007 Profits: $11,891,000	Parent Company:

SALARIES/BENEFITS:

Pension Plan: Y	ESOP Stock Plan: Y	Profit Sharing:	Top Exec. Salary: $1,500,000	Bonus: $1,278,788
Savings Plan: Y	Stock Purch. Plan:		Second Exec. Salary: $1,145,000	Bonus: $1,474,560

OTHER THOUGHTS:

Apparent Women Officers or Directors: 5
Hot Spot for Advancement for Women/Minorities: Y

LOCATIONS: ("Y" = Yes)

West:	Southwest:	Midwest:	Southeast:	Northeast:	International:
Y	Y	Y	Y	Y	Y

CORY ENVIRONMENTAL

www.coryenvironmental.co.uk

Industry Group Code: 562

Energy/Fuel:	Other Technologies:	Electrical Products:	Electronics:	Transportation:	Other:	
Biofuels:	Irrigation:	Lighting/LEDs:	Computers:	Car Sharing:	Recycling:	Y
Batteries/Storage:	Nanotech:	Waste Heat:	Sensors:	Electric Vehicles:	Engineering:	
Solar:	Biotech:	Smart Meters:	Software:	Natural Gas Fuel:	Consulting:	
Wind:	Water Tech./Treatment:	Machinery:			Investing:	
Fuel Cells:	Ceramics:				Chemicals:	

TYPES OF BUSINESS:

Waste Management
Recycling
Landfills & Transfer Stations
Street Cleaning
Electric Generation-Landfill Gas

BRANDS/DIVISIONS/AFFILIATES:

Cory Environmental Municipal Services
Cory Environmental Waste Management
Riverside Resource Recovery
Western Riverside Waste Authority
Western Riverside Recycling Facility

CONTACTS: Note: Officers with more than one job title may be intentionally listed here more than once.

Peter Gerstrom, CEO
Toby Warren, Dir.-Human Resources
Sally Dixon, Legal Counsel/Corp. Sec.
John Boldon, Dir.-Planning
John Boldon, Dir.-Comm.
Richard Milnes-James, Group Dir.-Finance
Bernard Kauhold, Dir.-Dev.
Alistair Holl, Dir.-Resource Mgmt.
Chris Jones, Dir.-Risk Mgmt. & Compliance
Jon Steggles, Dir.-Resource Logistics

Phone: 44-2074-17-52-00	Fax: 44-20-7417-5222
Toll-Free:	
Address: 2 Coldbath Sq., London, EC1R 5HL UK	

GROWTH PLANS/SPECIAL FEATURES:

Cory Environmental, founded in 1896 as William Cory and Son Ltd., is one of England's leading waste management companies. The company operates through two main businesses: Cory Environmental Municipal Services, which provides municipal waste collection, recycling and street cleaning; and Cory Environmental Waste Management, which provides waste transport, transfer and disposal services, transporting waste down the River Thames to Essex for disposal. The company operates landfill sites across the U.K. in areas such as the North West, Midlands, Gloucestershire, Bristol and South East England. The firm also operates numerous transfer stations and recycling centers, cleaning streets and collecting waste from over 720,000 people and thousands of businesses for more than 3.9 million tons of garbage and recyclables managed each year. Cory Environmental generates electricity from landfill gas. In addition, the firm operates in integrated beach cleaning and green waste collection, with additional services including grounds maintenance, septic tank emptying, leaf clearance and public convenience cleaning. The company, along with Western Riverside Waste Authority, operates a Materials Recovery Facility (MRF) with an annual capacity of 84,000 tons of co-mingled recyclables. One of Cory Environmental's largest development projects is the Riverside Resource Recovery (RRR) Energy from Waste Facility, which, when fully operational, will process over 640,000 tons of waste from houses and businesses in the central London area. In March 2011, the company opened the Western Riverside Recycling Facility in London.

FINANCIALS: Sales and profits are in thousands of dollars—add 000 to get the full amount. 2011 Note: Financial information for 2011 was not available for all companies at press time.

2011 Sales: $	2011 Profits: $	**U.S. Stock Ticker: Private**
2010 Sales: $	2010 Profits: $	**Int'l Ticker:**
2009 Sales: $	2009 Profits: $	Int'l Exchange:
2008 Sales: $	2008 Profits: $	Employees: Fiscal Year Ends: 12/31
2007 Sales: $	2007 Profits: $	Parent Company:

SALARIES/BENEFITS:

Pension Plan:	ESOP Stock Plan:	Profit Sharing:	Top Exec. Salary: $	Bonus: $
Savings Plan:	Stock Purch. Plan:		Second Exec. Salary: $	Bonus: $

OTHER THOUGHTS:

Apparent Women Officers or Directors: 1
Hot Spot for Advancement for Women/Minorities:

LOCATIONS: ("Y" = Yes)

West:	Southwest:	Midwest:	Southeast:	Northeast:	International:
					Y

COULOMB TECHNOLOGIES

www.coulombtech.com

Industry Group Code: 325

Energy/Fuel:	Other Technologies:	Electrical Products:	Electronics:	Transportation:		Other:	
Biofuels:	Irrigation:	Lighting/LEDs:	Computers:	Car Sharing:		Recycling:	
Batteries/Storage:	Nanotech:	Waste Heat:	Sensors:	Electric Vehicles:	Y	Engineering:	
Solar:	Biotech:	Smart Meters:	Software:	Natural Gas Fuel:		Consulting:	
Wind:	Water Tech./Treatment:	Machinery:				Investing:	
Fuel Cells:	Ceramics:					Chemicals:	Y

TYPES OF BUSINESS:
Electronic Vehicle Charging Stations

BRANDS/DIVISIONS/AFFILIATES:
ChargePoint Network
ChargePoint

CONTACTS: *Note: Officers with more than one job title may be intentionally listed here more than once.*
Pasquale (Pat) Romano, CEO
Pasquale (Pat) Romano, Pres.
Tony Canova, CFO
James Hanley, VP-Worldwide Sales
Richard Lowenthal, CTO
Milton T. (Tom) Tormey, VP-Prod. Mgmt.
Dave Baxter, VP-Eng., Hardware
James Hanley, VP-Bus. Dev.
Anne Smith, Head-Public Rel.
Harjinder S. Bhade, VP-Eng., Software
Colleen Quinn, VP-Government Rel.

Phone: 408-841-4500	Fax:
Toll-Free: 877-370-3802	
Address: 1692 Dell Ave., Campbell, CA 95008 US	

GROWTH PLANS/SPECIAL FEATURES:

Coulomb Technolgies (CT) is an electric vehicle infrastructure company that manufactures and supplies electronic vehicle charging stations. The firm provides the ChargePoint Network, a network of charging stations that provides electricity to electric cars. ChargePoint stations are independently-owned charging stations that charge more than 26,000 vehicles per month. Over 50% of electronic vehicle drivers have a ChargePoint card. Additionally, CT provides ChargePoint Network service plans and a cloud-based solution that handles all driver billings. The firm provides electric vehicle charging for companies such as McDonalds, SAP, Dell, Google, Walgreens, Kohl's and Adobe. Moreover, CT provides charging in municipal parking in the cities of Orlando, San Jose, Palo Alto, Burbank, San Francisco and Houston. ChargePoint stations are located throughout the U.S., Europe, Australia and New Zealand. In May 2011, CT opened its first networked charging station in Taupo, New Zealand.

FINANCIALS: Sales and profits are in thousands of dollars—add 000 to get the full amount. 2011 Note: Financial information for 2011 was not available for all companies at press time.

2011 Sales: $	2011 Profits: $	**U.S. Stock Ticker:** Private	
2010 Sales: $	2010 Profits: $	**Int'l Ticker:**	
2009 Sales: $	2009 Profits: $	Int'l Exchange:	
2008 Sales: $	2008 Profits: $	Employees:	Fiscal Year Ends:
2007 Sales: $	2007 Profits: $	Parent Company:	

SALARIES/BENEFITS:

Pension Plan:	ESOP Stock Plan:	Profit Sharing:	Top Exec. Salary: $	Bonus: $
Savings Plan:	Stock Purch. Plan:		Second Exec. Salary: $	Bonus: $

OTHER THOUGHTS:
Apparent Women Officers or Directors: 2
Hot Spot for Advancement for Women/Minorities:

LOCATIONS: ("Y" = Yes)

West:	Southwest:	Midwest:	Southeast:	Northeast:	International:
Y	Y	Y	Y	Y	Y

Sales, profits and employees may be estimates. Financial information, benefits and other data can change quickly and may vary from those stated here.

COVANTA ENERGY CORPORATION

www.covantaholding.com

Industry Group Code: 221119

Energy/Fuel:	Other Technologies:	Electrical Products:		Electronics:	Transportation:	Other:
Biofuels:	Irrigation:	Lighting/LEDs:		Computers:	Car Sharing:	Recycling:
Batteries/Storage:	Nanotech:	Waste Heat:	Y	Sensors:	Electric Vehicles:	Engineering:
Solar:	Biotech:	Smart Meters:		Software:	Natural Gas Fuel:	Consulting:
Wind:	Water Tech./Treatment:	Machinery:				Investing:
Fuel Cells:	Ceramics:					Chemicals:

TYPES OF BUSINESS:

Waste-to-Energy Power Generation
Traditional Power Plants
Secure Waste & Document Disposal
Hydroelectric Plants

BRANDS/DIVISIONS/AFFILIATES:

Covanta Holding Corporation

CONTACTS: *Note: Officers with more than one job title may be intentionally listed here more than once.*

Anthony J. Orlando, CEO
John Klett, COO/Exec. VP
Anthony J. Orlando, Pres.
Sanjiv Khattri, CFO/Exec. VP
Michael A. Wright, Chief Human Resources Officer/Sr. VP
Paul Gilman, Chief Sustainability Officer/VP
Timothy J. Simpson, General Counsel/Exec. VP/Corp. Sec.
Thomas E. Bucks, Chief Acct. Officer/VP
Samuel Zell, Chmn.
Seth Myones, Pres., Covanta Americas

Phone: 973-882-9000	**Fax:** 973-882-7234
Toll-Free: 866-268-2682	
Address: 40 Lane Rd., Fairfield, NJ 07004 US	

GROWTH PLANS/SPECIAL FEATURES:

Covanta Energy Corporation, a subsidiary of Covanta Holding Corporation, owns and operates approximately 44 modern waste-to-energy (WTE) facilities worldwide, converting 16 million tons a year of municipal solid waste into energy and creating 10 billion pounds of steam. Covanta's WTE facilities produce 9,000 gigawatts of electricity per year, serve the waste disposal needs of approximately 20 million people throughout the U.S., save the equivalent of 16 million barrels of oil per year and recover and recycle 400,000 tons of metals from waste. The company also owns, operates and maintains power generation facilities worldwide through its independent power business. Together, Coventa's WTE and power generation facilities exceed 2,000 megawatts of electricity. The firm's WTE facilities heat non-hazardous municipal and commercial solid waste to extremely high temperatures, reducing it to an inert ash that is only a small fraction of the waste's original volume. Covanta also offers secure services for the destruction of pharmaceutical and commodity wastes, manufacturing wastes and sensitive and confidential documents. Internationally, the company owns a diverse portfolio of energy assets, including coal, hydroelectric, liquid fuel and natural gas facilities. The firm has facilities in Europe and China. In recent years, the company initiated construction on an Energy-from-Waste facility in Dublin, Ireland. The new facility is expected to be complete in 2012. In late 2010, the firm agreed to partner with Crane & Co. to convert Covanta Energy Corporation's paper-making waste fibers into clean renewable energy. In March 2011, the firm sold its interest in the Quezon coal-fired electric generation facility for $215 million.

Covanta offers its employees a retirement and 401(k) plan; educational assistance; company paid financial planning services; and health and welfare benefits.

FINANCIALS: Sales and profits are in thousands of dollars—add 000 to get the full amount. 2011 Note: Financial information for 2011 was not available for all companies at press time.

2011 Sales: $	2011 Profits: $	**U.S. Stock Ticker:** Subsidiary
2010 Sales: $	2010 Profits: $	**Int'l Ticker:**
2009 Sales: $	2009 Profits: $	Int'l Exchange:
2008 Sales: $	2008 Profits: $	Employees:　　Fiscal Year Ends: 12/31
2007 Sales: $	2007 Profits: $	Parent Company: COVANTA HOLDING CORPORATION

SALARIES/BENEFITS:

Pension Plan: Y	ESOP Stock Plan:	Profit Sharing:	Top Exec. Salary: $	Bonus: $
Savings Plan: Y	Stock Purch. Plan:		Second Exec. Salary: $	Bonus: $

OTHER THOUGHTS:

Apparent Women Officers or Directors: 2
Hot Spot for Advancement for Women/Minorities:

LOCATIONS: ("Y" = Yes)

West:	Southwest:	Midwest:	Southeast:	Northeast:	International:
Y		Y	Y	Y	Y

DAYSTAR TECHNOLOGIES

www.daystartech.com

Industry Group Code: 33441

Energy/Fuel:		Other Technologies:	Electrical Products:	Electronics:	Transportation:	Other:
Biofuels:		Irrigation:	Lighting/LEDs:	Computers:	Car Sharing:	Recycling:
Batteries/Storage:		Nanotech:	Waste Heat:	Sensors:	Electric Vehicles:	Engineering:
Solar:	Y	Biotech:	Smart Meters:	Software:	Natural Gas Fuel:	Consulting:
Wind:		Water Tech./Treatment:	Machinery:			Investing:
Fuel Cells:		Ceramics:				Chemicals:

TYPES OF BUSINESS:

Photovoltaic Technology
Solar Power Cells

BRANDS/DIVISIONS/AFFILIATES:

Blitzstrom GmbH
Juwi Solar GmbH

CONTACTS: Note: Officers with more than one job title may be intentionally listed here more than once.

Peter A. Lacey, Interim CEO
Robert Weiss, CTO
Peter A. Lacey, Chmn.

Phone: 408-582-7100	Fax: 408-907-4637
Toll-Free:	
Address: 1010 S. Milpitas Blvd., Milpitas, CA 95035 US	

GROWTH PLANS/SPECIAL FEATURES:

DayStar Technologies develops, manufactures and markets thin-film photovoltaic (PV) products, which have become increasingly popular due to the supply constraints, high prices and political turmoil surrounding hydrocarbon sources. DayStar systems have been adopted to address rural electrification in remote areas and as supplemental energy sources in grid-connected areas of the world. The company develops thin-film solar cells using a copper-indium-gallium-diselenide (CIGS) semiconductor material system that offers better mechanical flexibility and durability than standard solar cells. Additionally, DayStar's PV cells have an average conversion efficiency of over 15%, versus the industry average of 6% to 10% for thin-film PV modules. The firm utilizes a proprietary deposition process to apply the CIGS material to the substrate, which is then encapsulated with an additional packaging material before external electrical leads and junction boxes are added to the module. When operating at an annual manufacturing capacity of 100 megawatts per year, the firm estimates its total manufacturing costs at less than $1 per watt. The company has two manufacturing facilities in California. Blitzstrom GmbH has agreed to purchase at least 50% of DayStar's production through 2011, and Juwi Solar GmbH has expressed interest in purchasing up to 25% of production through 2011.

FINANCIALS: Sales and profits are in thousands of dollars—add 000 to get the full amount. 2011 Note: Financial information for 2011 was not available for all companies at press time.

2011 Sales: $	2011 Profits: $	U.S. Stock Ticker: DSTI
2010 Sales: $0	2010 Profits: $-28,082	Int'l Ticker:
2009 Sales: $0	2009 Profits: $-25,040	Int'l Exchange:
2008 Sales: $0	2008 Profits: $-26,330	Employees: 4 Fiscal Year Ends: 12/31
2007 Sales: $0	2007 Profits: $-36,143	Parent Company:

SALARIES/BENEFITS:

Pension Plan:	ESOP Stock Plan:	Profit Sharing:	Top Exec. Salary: $283,696	Bonus: $
Savings Plan: Y	Stock Purch. Plan:		Second Exec. Salary: $236,123	Bonus: $

OTHER THOUGHTS:

Apparent Women Officers or Directors:
Hot Spot for Advancement for Women/Minorities:

LOCATIONS: ("Y" = Yes)

West:	Southwest:	Midwest:	Southeast:	Northeast:	International:
Y					

DIGITAL LUMENS

www.digitallumens.com

Industry Group Code: 335

Energy/Fuel:	Other Technologies:	Electrical Products:		Electronics:		Transportation:	Other:	
Biofuels:	Irrigation:	Lighting/LEDs:	Y	Computers:		Car Sharing:	Recycling:	
Batteries/Storage:	Nanotech:	Waste Heat:		Sensors:		Electric Vehicles:	Engineering:	
Solar:	Biotech:	Smart Meters:		Software:	Y	Natural Gas Fuel:	Consulting:	
Wind:	Water Tech./Treatment:	Machinery:					Investing:	
Fuel Cells:	Ceramics:						Chemicals:	

TYPES OF BUSINESS:

LED-based lighting systems

BRANDS/DIVISIONS/AFFILIATES:

10,000-Lumen Intelligent Highbay
15,000-Lumen Intelligent Highbay
18,000-Lumen Intelligent Highbay
26,000-Lumen Intelligent Highbay
Lightrules
Black Coral Capital
Flybridge Capital Partners
Stan Venture Partners

CONTACTS: Note: Officers with more than one job title may be intentionally listed here more than once.

Tom Pincince, CEO
Tom Pincince, Pres.
Mike Rubino, CFO
Michael Feinstein, VP-Mktg. & Sales
Brian Chemel, CTO
Fritz Morgan, Chief Product Officer
Colin Piepgras, VP-Eng.
Ken MacLure, VP-Mfg. Oper.
Allison Parker, Head-Media Rel.
Bo Thurmond, VP-North American Sales

Phone: 617-723-1200	Fax:
Toll-Free:	
Address: 110 Canal St., Fl. 7, Boston, MA 02114 US	

GROWTH PLANS/SPECIAL FEATURES:

Digital Lumens develops and manufactures LED-based lighting systems. The company produces what it calls an Intelligent Lighting System (ILS) that can reduce lighting related expenses by up to 90% for commercial and industrial facilities. The ILS is composed of two parts, the Intelligent Highbay LED Fixtures and Lightrules. The Intelligent Highbay LED Fixtures line include three LED light bars, a built in sensor that assesses ambient light and adjusts light output accordingly and wireless mesh networking. Products in this line are the 10,000-Lumen Intelligent Highbay, 15,000-Lumen Intelligent Highbay, 18,000-Lumen Intelligent Highbay and the 26,000-Lumen Intelligent Highbay. Lightrules is the lighting management software that controls the ILS and manages energy resources, measuring the amount of energy used by lights in a given time period and identifying times of peak activity. Digital Lumens products are sold throughout North America and in Europe. The firm's primary investors are Black Coral Capital, Flybridge Capital Partners and Stan Venture Partners.

Digital Lumens offers its employees health insurance through Blue Cross Blue Shield, dental insurance through Delta Dental and life and disability insurance.

FINANCIALS: Sales and profits are in thousands of dollars—add 000 to get the full amount. 2011 Note: Financial information for 2011 was not available for all companies at press time.

2011 Sales: $	2011 Profits: $	**U.S. Stock Ticker: Private**
2010 Sales: $	2010 Profits: $	**Int'l Ticker:**
2009 Sales: $	2009 Profits: $	Int'l Exchange:
2008 Sales: $	2008 Profits: $	Employees: Fiscal Year Ends:
2007 Sales: $	2007 Profits: $	Parent Company:

SALARIES/BENEFITS:

Pension Plan:	ESOP Stock Plan:	Profit Sharing:	Top Exec. Salary: $	Bonus: $
Savings Plan:	Stock Purch. Plan:		Second Exec. Salary: $	Bonus: $

OTHER THOUGHTS:

Apparent Women Officers or Directors: 1
Hot Spot for Advancement for Women/Minorities:

LOCATIONS: ("Y" = Yes)

West:	Southwest:	Midwest:	Southeast:	Northeast:	International:
				Y	

DOW CHEMICAL COMPANY (THE)   www.dow.com

Industry Group Code: 325

Energy/Fuel:	Other Technologies:	Electrical Products:	Electronics:	Transportation:	Other:	
Biofuels:	Irrigation:	Lighting/LEDs:	Computers:	Car Sharing:	Recycling:	
Batteries/Storage:	Nanotech:	Waste Heat:	Sensors:	Electric Vehicles:	Engineering:	
Solar:	Biotech:	Smart Meters:	Software:	Natural Gas Fuel:	Consulting:	
Wind:	Water Tech./Treatment:	Machinery:			Investing:	
Fuel Cells:	Ceramics:				Chemicals:	Y

TYPES OF BUSINESS:

Chemicals Manufacturer
Basic Chemicals
Plastics
Performance Chemicals
Agrochemicals
Hydrocarbons & Fuels

BRANDS/DIVISIONS/AFFILIATES:

Dow Agrosciences LLC
Union Carbide Corporation
Rohm & Haas Company
Pfenex, Inc.
Clean Filtration Technologies, Inc.
Prairie Brands Seeds
Dow Electronic Materials

CONTACTS: *Note: Officers with more than one job title may be intentionally listed here more than once.*

Andrew N. Liveris, CEO
William H. Weidemann, CFO/Exec. VP
Heinz Haller, Chief Commercial Officer/Exec. VP
Gregory M. Freiwald, Exec. VP-Human Resources & Aviation
David E. Kepler, CIO/Exec. VP-Bus. Svcs.
William F. Banholzer, CTO/Exec. VP
Michael R. Gambrell, Exec. VP-Eng. Oper.
Michael R. Gambrell, Exec. VP-Mfg. Oper.
Charles J. Kalil, General Counsel/Sec./Exec. VP-Law & Gov't Affairs
William F. Banholzer, Exec. VP-Ventures, New Bus. Dev. & Licensing
Gregory M. Freiwald, Exec. VP-Corp. Affairs
Doug May, VP-Investor Rel.
Ron Edmonds, Controller/VP
James D. McIlvenny, Sr. VP-Mega Projects
James R. Fitterling, Exec. VP/Pres., Corp. Dev. & Hydrocarbons
Carol Williams, Sr. VP/Pres., Chemicals & Energy
Jerome A. Peribere, Exec. VP/CEO-Dow Advanced Materials
Andrew N. Liveris, Chmn.
Geoffery E. Merszei, Exec. VP/Pres., EMEA/Chmn.-DOW Europe

Phone: 989-636-1463	Fax: 989-636-1830

Toll-Free: 800-422-8193

Address: 2030 Dow Ctr., Midland, MI 48674 US

GROWTH PLANS/SPECIAL FEATURES:

The Dow Chemical Company is a global chemical and plastics company. It delivers a broad range of products and services to customers in about 160 countries, has 188 manufacturing sites in 35 countries and produces roughly 5,000 products. The company operates in eight segments. The electronic and specialty materials segment manufactures semiconductor, display and filtration technology materials. The coatings and infrastructure segment manufactures architectural and industrial coatings, construction chemicals, adhesives and textiles. The health and agricultural sciences segment produces biotechnology products and pest management solutions. The performance systems segment manufactures automotive, polyurethane and epoxy systems, elastomers and oil and gas exploration products. The performance products segment manufactures polyurethanes, epoxy, amines, oxygenated solvents and emulsion polymers. The basic plastics segment manufactures polyethylene, polypropylene and polystyrene. The basic chemicals segment produces ethylene oxide, chlor-alkali and chlorinated organics. Finally, the hydrocarbons and energy segment procures fuels, natural gas liquids and crude oil-based raw materials, and also supplies monomers, power and steam to Dow's operations. The firm's long-term strategy is to move away from commodity chemicals, which do not earn large profit margins, and focus on specialty chemicals. In early 2010, Dow sold its acrylic acid and esters business; and announced its investment in Clean Filtration Technologies, Inc. Subsidiary Dow Electronic Materials broke ground in December 2010 on a manufacturing facility in eastern China. In June 2010, the company sold Dow Haltermann Custom Processing, and divested its Styron division. In June 2011, subsidiary Dow AgroSciences LLC announced plans to acquire the Prairie Brands Seeds segment of Sansgaard Seed Farms, Inc.

Employees are offered life insurance, disability coverage, business travel insurance and a tuition refund policy.

FINANCIALS: Sales and profits are in thousands of dollars—add 000 to get the full amount. 2011 Note: Financial information for 2011 was not available for all companies at press time.

2011 Sales: $	2011 Profits: $	**U.S. Stock Ticker:** DOW
2010 Sales: $53,674,000	2010 Profits: $1,970,000	**Int'l Ticker:**
2009 Sales: $44,875,000	2009 Profits: $336,000	Int'l Exchange:
2008 Sales: $57,361,000	2008 Profits: $579,000	Employees: 49,505 Fiscal Year Ends: 12/31
2007 Sales: $53,375,000	2007 Profits: $2,887,000	Parent Company:

SALARIES/BENEFITS:

Pension Plan:	ESOP Stock Plan:	Profit Sharing:	Top Exec. Salary: $1,691,667	Bonus: $5,000,000
Savings Plan: Y	Stock Purch. Plan: Y		Second Exec. Salary: $877,116	Bonus: $1,791,139

OTHER THOUGHTS:

Apparent Women Officers or Directors: 5
Hot Spot for Advancement for Women/Minorities: Y

LOCATIONS: ("Y" = Yes)

West:	Southwest:	Midwest:	Southeast:	Northeast:	International:
Y	Y	Y	Y	Y	Y

DOW CORNING CORPORATION

www.dowcorning.com

Industry Group Code: 325

Energy/Fuel:	Other Technologies:	Electrical Products:	Electronics:	Transportation:	Other:	
Biofuels:	Irrigation:	Lighting/LEDs:	Computers:	Car Sharing:	Recycling:	
Batteries/Storage:	Nanotech:	Waste Heat:	Sensors:	Electric Vehicles:	Engineering:	
Solar:	Biotech:	Smart Meters:	Software:	Natural Gas Fuel:	Consulting:	
Wind:	Water Tech./Treatment:	Machinery:			Investing:	
Fuel Cells:	Ceramics:				Chemicals:	Y

TYPES OF BUSINESS:

Silicone Materials
Sealants, Coatings & Lubricants
Adhesives
Insulating Materials
Design, Engineering & Testing Services
Custom Manufacturing & Packaging
Consulting
Nanotechnology Research

BRANDS/DIVISIONS/AFFILIATES:

Dow Chemical Company
Corning, Inc.
Dow Corning
Xiameter
Silicon Biotechnology

CONTACTS: Note: Officers with more than one job title may be intentionally listed here more than once.

Stephanie A. Burns, CEO
Robert D. Hansen, Pres.
Joseph D. Sheets, CFO/Exec. VP
Brian J. Chermside, Chief Mktg. Officer/VP
Dave Soldan, Interim Exec. Dir.-Human Resources
Kristy Folkwein, CIO/VP
Kenneth P. Kaufman, VP-Eng.
Kenneth P. Kaufman, VP-Mfg.
Sue K. McDonnell, General Counsel/Sec./Sr. VP
James R. Whitlock, VP/Exec. Dir.-Global Oper.
Mary Lou Benecke, VP-Corp. Comm. & Public Affairs
James R. Whitlock, Sr. VP/Gen. Mgr.-Core Bus.
Thomas H. Cook, Sr. VP/Gen. Mgr.-Specialty Chemicals
Stephanie A. Burns, Chmn.

Phone: 989-496-4000	Fax: 989-496-4393
Toll-Free:	
Address: 2200 W. Salzburg Rd., Midland, MI 48686-0994 US	

GROWTH PLANS/SPECIAL FEATURES:

Dow Corning Corporation, a joint venture between The Dow Chemical Company and Corning, Inc., has been studying and manufacturing silicone and silicone products since 1943. Currently, the firm serves 26 industries, including the automotive, chemical manufacturing, beauty, oil/gas and plastics industries. The company researches and develops applications of silicone in forms ranging from greases, gels and fluids to rigid materials such as resins. Dow Corning's 7,000 products, sold under the Dow Corning and Xiameter brands, include adhesives, insulating materials, sealants, coatings and lubricants. These products are used in computer chips, cell phones and consumer electronics; automotive coatings, paints and lubricants; laundry detergents; tubing for dialysis, hydrocephalus shunts and pacemaker leads; roofing materials and pavement sealants; and for waterproofing clothing fabric. Dow Corning is researching additional silicon-based technologies including using nanotechnology to toughen silicone resins and to develop new liquid crystal materials; and using room-temperature atmospheric pressure plasma to apply different coatings to various substrates, such as consumer electronics, medical devices, pharmaceuticals, airbags and textiles. It has also formed alliances to develop future products, including an alliance with Genencor to create a proprietary Silicon Biotechnology platform. Besides its silicone-based chemical products, the company also also provides analytical and application testing; package recycling; facilities design and engineering; product development; and environmental consulting. Dow Corning maintains operations internationally, with locations in the Americas, Asia, Europe and Australia.

The firm offers its employees 401(k), pension and employee assistance plans; medical, dental, vision, life and disability coverage; three weeks paid vacation time; adoption assistance; and subsidized dependent care.

FINANCIALS: Sales and profits are in thousands of dollars—add 000 to get the full amount. 2011 Note: Financial information for 2011 was not available for all companies at press time.

2011 Sales: $	2011 Profits: $	**U.S. Stock Ticker: Joint Venture**
2010 Sales: $5,997,300	2010 Profits: $723,600	**Int'l Ticker:**
2009 Sales: $5,092,500	2009 Profits: $563,200	Int'l Exchange:
2008 Sales: $5,450,000	2008 Profits: $738,700	Employees: 9,000 Fiscal Year Ends: 12/31
2007 Sales: $4,943,100	2007 Profits: $690,100	Parent Company:

SALARIES/BENEFITS:

Pension Plan: Y	ESOP Stock Plan:	Profit Sharing:	Top Exec. Salary: $	Bonus: $
Savings Plan: Y	Stock Purch. Plan:		Second Exec. Salary: $	Bonus: $

OTHER THOUGHTS:

Apparent Women Officers or Directors: 4
Hot Spot for Advancement for Women/Minorities: Y

LOCATIONS: ("Y" = Yes)

West:	Southwest:	Midwest:	Southeast:	Northeast:	International:
Y		Y		Y	Y

DUPONT (E I DU PONT DE NEMOURS & CO)   www.dupont.com

Industry Group Code: 325

Energy/Fuel:	Other Technologies:	Electrical Products:	Electronics:	Transportation:	Other:	
Biofuels:	Irrigation:	Lighting/LEDs:	Computers:	Car Sharing:	Recycling:	
Batteries/Storage:	Nanotech:	Waste Heat:	Sensors:	Electric Vehicles:	Engineering:	
Solar:	Biotech:	Smart Meters:	Software:	Natural Gas Fuel:	Consulting:	
Wind:	Water Tech./Treatment:	Machinery:			Investing:	
Fuel Cells:	Ceramics:				Chemicals:	Y

TYPES OF BUSINESS:

Chemicals Manufacturing
Polymers
Performance Coatings
Nutrition & Health Products
Electronics Materials
Agricultural Seeds
Fuel-Cell, Biofuels & Solar Panel Technology
Contract Research & Development

BRANDS/DIVISIONS/AFFILIATES:

Seed Consultants, Inc.,
Teflon
Corian
Kevlar
Tyvek
DuPont Agriculture & Nutrition
MECS
Danisco A/S

CONTACTS: *Note: Officers with more than one job title may be intentionally listed here more than once.*

Ellen J. Kullman, CEO
Nicholas C. Farandakis, CFO/Sr. VP
Scott Coleman, Chief Mktg. & Sales Officer
Benito Cachinero-Sanchez, Sr. VP-Human Resources
Douglas Muzyka, Chief Science Officer/Sr. VP
Phuong Tram, CIO/VP-IT
Douglas Muzyka, CTO
Thomas M. Connelly, Jr., Chief Innovation Officer/Exec. VP
Jeffrey A. Coe, Sr. VP-Eng.
Thomas L. Sager, General Counsel/Sr. VP-Legal
Jeffrey A. Coe, Sr. VP-Integrated Oper.
David G. Bills, Sr. VP-Corp. Strategy
Mark P. Vergnano, Exec. VP-Comm.
Karen A. Fletcher, VP-Investor Rel.
Criag F. Binetti, Sr. VP-DuPont Nutrition & Health
Diane H. Gulyas, Pres., DuPont Performance Polymers
Rik L. Miller, Pres., Crop Protection
Linda J. Fisher, Chief Sustainability Officer/VP
Ellen J. Kullman, Chmn.
Donald D. Wirth, VP-Global Oper.
Donald D. Wirth, VP-Supply Chain

Phone: 302-774-1000	Fax:
Toll-Free: 800-441-7515	
Address: 1007 Market St., Wilmington, DE 19898 US	

GROWTH PLANS/SPECIAL FEATURES:

DuPont (E. I. du Pont de Nemours & Co.), founded in 1802, develops and manufactures products in the biotechnology, electronics, materials science, synthetic fibers and safety and security sectors. DuPont operates in seven segments: Agriculture and Nutrition (A&N); Electronic and Communications (E&C); Performance Coatings; Performance Chemicals; Performance Materials (PM); Safety and Protection (S&P); and Pharmaceuticals. A&N delivers seed products, insecticides, fungicides, herbicides, soy-based food ingredients, food quality diagnostic testing equipment and liquid food packaging systems. Brands include Pioneer seeds and Solae soy proteins. E&C provides a range of advanced materials for the electronics industry, flexographic printing, color communication systems and a range of fluoropolymer and fluorochemical products. The Performance Coatings segment supplies automotive liquid and powder coatings, and general industrial applications such as coatings for heavy equipment, pipes and appliances and electrical insulation. Brands include DuPont, Standox, Spies Hecker and Nason. PM manufactures polymer-based materials, which include engineered polymers, specialized resins and films for use in food packaging, sealants, adhesives, sporting goods and laminated safety glass. The S&P segment provides protective materials and safety consulting services. Significant brands include Teflon fluoropolymers, films, fabric protectors, fibers and dispersions; Corian surfaces; Kevlar high strength material; and Tyvek protective material. The Pharmaceuticals segment involves the worldwide manufacturing and marketing activities of the antihypertensive drugs, Cozaar and Hyzaar. The company has operations in over 90 countries around the world as well as having about 17,600 worldwide patents. Of DuPont's consolidated net sales, about 65% are made to customers outside the U.S. In January 2011, the firm acquired the producer of technology, equipment and services for sulfuric acid producers, MECS as well as the enzyme and special foods company, Danisco.

Employees are offered medical, dental and life insurance; disability coverage; dependent care spending accounts; and adoption assistance.

FINANCIALS: Sales and profits are in thousands of dollars—add 000 to get the full amount. 2011 Note: Financial information for 2011 was not available for all companies at press time.

2011 Sales: $	2011 Profits: $	**U.S. Stock Ticker:** DD
2010 Sales: $31,505,000	2010 Profits: $3,031,000	**Int'l Ticker:**
2009 Sales: $26,109,000	2009 Profits: $1,755,000	Int'l Exchange:
2008 Sales: $30,529,000	2008 Profits: $2,007,000	Employees: 60,000 Fiscal Year Ends: 12/31
2007 Sales: $29,378,000	2007 Profits: $2,988,000	Parent Company:

SALARIES/BENEFITS:

Pension Plan: Y	ESOP Stock Plan:	Profit Sharing:	Top Exec. Salary: $1,300,000	Bonus: $2,846,000
Savings Plan: Y	Stock Purch. Plan:		Second Exec. Salary: $727,750	Bonus: $987,000

OTHER THOUGHTS:

Apparent Women Officers or Directors: 7
Hot Spot for Advancement for Women/Minorities: Y

LOCATIONS: ("Y" = Yes)

West:	Southwest:	Midwest:	Southeast:	Northeast:	International:
Y	Y	Y	Y	Y	Y

DUPONT AGRICULTURE & NUTRITION

www.dupont.com/Our_Company/en_US/business/nutrition_health.html

Industry Group Code: 11511

Energy/Fuel:	Other Technologies:		Electrical Products:	Electronics:	Transportation:	Other:	
Biofuels:	Irrigation:		Lighting/LEDs:	Computers:	Car Sharing:	Recycling:	
Batteries/Storage:	Nanotech:		Waste Heat:	Sensors:	Electric Vehicles:	Engineering:	
Solar:	Biotech:	Y	Smart Meters:	Software:	Natural Gas Fuel:	Consulting:	
Wind:	Water Tech./Treatment:		Machinery:			Investing:	
Fuel Cells:	Ceramics:					Chemicals:	Y

TYPES OF BUSINESS:

Agricultural Biotechnology Products & Chemicals Manufacturing
Insecticides
Herbicides
Fungicides
Genetically Modified Plants
Soy Products
Forage & Grain Additives

BRANDS/DIVISIONS/AFFILIATES:

Pioneer Hi-Bred International
DuPont Crop Protection
DuPont Nutrition and Health
Solae Company (The)
DuPont Qualicon
Nandi Seeds Private Limited
MapShots, Inc.
Farms Technology LLC

CONTACTS: *Note: Officers with more than one job title may be intentionally listed here more than once.*

Craig F. Binetti, Pres., DuPont Nutrition & Health
James C. Collins, Pres., DuPont Crop Protection
Paul E. Schickler, Pres., Pioneer Hi-Bred International Inc.
James R. Weigand, Pres., DuPont Sustainable Solutions

Phone: 302-774-1000	Fax:
Toll-Free:	
Address: 1007 Market St., DuPont Bldg., Wilmington, DE 19898 US	

GROWTH PLANS/SPECIAL FEATURES:

DuPont Agriculture & Nutrition (DPAN) is a business unit of global chemical giant DuPont. The company oversees a number of business units covering many aspects of crop protection, genetics, biotechnology, crop chemistry, nutrition science, food quality and safety and protein formulation. Pioneer Hi-Bred International develops advanced plant genetics for a variety of seeds, including alfalfa, corn, hybrid rice, mustard and soybean. DuPont Crop Protection provides herbicide, fungicide and insecticide products and services. DuPont Nutrition and Health provides soy protein, soy fiber and other ingredients under brand names including The Solae Company, a joint venture with Bunge; and DuPont Qualicon. DPAN's major product groups include corn seeds, soybean seeds, other seeds, food ingredients, fungicides, herbicides and insecticides. DPAN has joint ventures in the U.S. and around the world, with projects such as Nandi Seeds Private Limited, an India cotton seeds acquisition company; MapShots, Inc., an agricultural data management company; Farms Technology LLC; GreenLeaf Genetics LLC; and Beijing Kaituo DNA Biotech Research Center Co., Ltd. Regionally, North America accounts for about 50% of the group's sales; Europe, the Middle East and Africa, 23%; Latin America, 17%; and Asia, 10%. Some of the firm's products which have received approval from the Environmental Protection Agency (EPA), include the cleaning and personal care product Zemea propanediol and the herbicide Herculex.

FINANCIALS: Sales and profits are in thousands of dollars—add 000 to get the full amount. 2011 Note: Financial information for 2011 was not available for all companies at press time.

2011 Sales: $	2011 Profits: $	U.S. Stock Ticker: Subsidiary
2010 Sales: $32,733,000	2010 Profits: $3,052,000	Int'l Ticker:
2009 Sales: $27,328,000	2009 Profits: $1,769,000	Int'l Exchange:
2008 Sales: $31,836,000	2008 Profits: $2,010,000	Employees: 60,000 Fiscal Year Ends: 12/31
2007 Sales: $6,842,000	2007 Profits: $894,000	Parent Company: E I DU PONT DE NEMOURS & CO (DUPONT)

SALARIES/BENEFITS:

Pension Plan:	ESOP Stock Plan:	Profit Sharing:	Top Exec. Salary: $	Bonus: $
Savings Plan:	Stock Purch. Plan:		Second Exec. Salary: $	Bonus: $

OTHER THOUGHTS:

Apparent Women Officers or Directors:
Hot Spot for Advancement for Women/Minorities:

LOCATIONS: ("Y" = Yes)

West:	Southwest:	Midwest:	Southeast:	Northeast:	International:
Y	Y	Y	Y	Y	Y

DUPONT CENTRAL RESEARCH & DEVELOPMENT
www2.dupont.com/Science/en_US/rd/index.html
Industry Group Code: 541712

Energy/Fuel:	Other Technologies:		Electrical Products:	Electronics:	Transportation:	Other:	
Biofuels:	Irrigation:		Lighting/LEDs:	Computers:	Car Sharing:	Recycling:	
Batteries/Storage:	Nanotech:		Waste Heat:	Sensors:	Electric Vehicles:	Engineering:	Y
Solar:	Biotech:	Y	Smart Meters:	Software:	Natural Gas Fuel:	Consulting:	
Wind:	Water Tech./Treatment:		Machinery:			Investing:	
Fuel Cells:	Ceramics:					Chemicals:	

TYPES OF BUSINESS:
Polymers & Materials Science
Biochemical Science & Engineering
Materials Science & Engineering
Chemical Science & Catalysis
Polymer Development & Fabrication
Molecular Biotechnology
Nanotechnology Research

BRANDS/DIVISIONS/AFFILIATES:
Neoprene
Tyvek
Kevlar
Mylar
Corian
Butacite
DUPONT (E I DU PONT DE NEMOURS & CO)
Institute for Soldier Nanotechnologies

CONTACTS: *Note: Officers with more than one job title may be intentionally listed here more than once.*
Douglas Muzyka, Chief Science Officer/Sr. VP-DuPont
Ellen J. Kullman, Chmn./CEO-Ellen J. Kullman
Douglas Muzyka, CTO-DuPont

Phone: 302-774-1000	Fax: 302-773-2631
Toll-Free: 800-441-7515	
Address: 1007 Market St., Wilmington, DE 19898 US	

GROWTH PLANS/SPECIAL FEATURES:

DuPont Central Research & Development (CR&D) group is DuPont's main research division and has been responsible for most of its major product breakthroughs, including Neoprene (the first synthetic rubber), Tyvek, Kevlar fiber, Mylar (polyester film), Corian solid surfaces, Butacite polyvinyl butyral, Suva refrigerants and Nomex fiber. Although DuPont has over 75 research and development facilities across the world, its primary research activities have been undertaken at the Experimental Station, located in Wilmington, Delaware, since 1903. In addition to more general research and technologies, CR&D provides leveraged scientific services for existing businesses within DuPont. Organizations within this leveraged aspect include CorporateCenter for Analytical Science, CorporateCenter for Engineering Research and Leveraged Information Technology and Research Services. CR&D operates under the auspices of the Growth Council, a group of senior DuPont business leaders who evaluate research proposals and manage a long-term portfolio of research projects. Council research is divided into three areas: biochemical science and engineering, material science and engineering and chemical science and engineering. DuPont directs roughly $1.5 billion annually towards research and development. Research and development currently under way at CR&D includes nanotechnology, emerging displays technologies, advanced fuel cell energy sources and biomaterials produced from renewable resources such as corn. Through the DuPont MIT (Massachusetts Institute of Technology) Alliance, originally founded in 2000, the company has supported research at MIT labs aimed at researching materials and biotechnology with approximately $60 million in funding. Due to DuPont's support, MIT, in conjunction with the U.S. Army Research Service, established the Institute for Soldier Nanotechnologies at the MIT campus, devoted to research on nanotech fabrics for use by the military.

FINANCIALS: Sales and profits are in thousands of dollars—add 000 to get the full amount. 2011 Note: Financial information for 2011 was not available for all companies at press time.

2011 Sales: $	2011 Profits: $	U.S. Stock Ticker: Subsidiary
2010 Sales: $	2010 Profits: $	Int'l Ticker:
2009 Sales: $	2009 Profits: $	Int'l Exchange:
2008 Sales: $	2008 Profits: $	Employees: Fiscal Year Ends: 12/31
2007 Sales: $	2007 Profits: $	Parent Company: E I DU PONT DE NEMOURS & CO (DUPONT)

SALARIES/BENEFITS:
Pension Plan: Y	ESOP Stock Plan:	Profit Sharing:	Top Exec. Salary: $	Bonus: $
Savings Plan: Y	Stock Purch. Plan:		Second Exec. Salary: $	Bonus: $

OTHER THOUGHTS:
Apparent Women Officers or Directors:
Hot Spot for Advancement for Women/Minorities:

LOCATIONS: ("Y" = Yes)
West:	Southwest:	Midwest:	Southeast:	Northeast:	International:
		Y	Y	Y	Y

DYNAMOTIVE ENERGY SYSTEMS CORPORATION

www.dynamotive.com
Industry Group Code: 325199

Energy/Fuel:		Other Technologies:		Electrical Products:		Electronics:	Transportation:	Other:
Biofuels:	Y	Irrigation:		Lighting/LEDs:		Computers:	Car Sharing:	Recycling:
Batteries/Storage:		Nanotech:		Waste Heat:		Sensors:	Electric Vehicles:	Engineering:
Solar:		Biotech:	Y	Smart Meters:		Software:	Natural Gas Fuel:	Consulting:
Wind:		Water Tech./Treatment:		Machinery:				Investing:
Fuel Cells:		Ceramics:						Chemicals:

TYPES OF BUSINESS:
Biofuels Production Technology
Waste-to-Energy Technology

BRANDS/DIVISIONS/AFFILIATES:
Fast Pyrolysis
DynaMotive Canada Inc
DynaMotive USA Inc
DynaMotive Latinoamericana SA
First Resources Corporation
BINGO

CONTACTS: Note: Officers with more than one job title may be intentionally listed here more than once.
R. Andrew Kingston, CEO
R. Andrew Kingston, Pres.

Phone: 604-295-6800	Fax: 604-295-6805
Toll-Free: 800-852-0938	
Address: 1040 W. Georgia St., Grosvenor Bldg., Ste. 800, Vancouver, BC V6E 4H1 Canada	

GROWTH PLANS/SPECIAL FEATURES:

DynaMotive Energy Systems Corporation is a biofuel technology development firm headquartered in Vancouver, Canada, with operations in the U.S., Australia and Argentina. Its principal business is the development, commercialization and licensing of technology for biomass-to-liquid fuel conversion using its proprietary process, Fast Pyrolysis. Fast Pyrolysis is a process that rapidly heats biomass in an oxygen-free environment to produce a liquid fuel (BioOil). BioOil is a renewable fuel that can be used in place of fossil fuels to produce power, mechanical energy and heat in certain industrial boilers, fuel gas turbines and other industrial applications. It can also be upgraded to motor fuel grade products, offering an alternative to ethanol and biodiesel fuels. The Fast Pyrolysis process uses raw forest and agricultural biomass residues, such as sawdust, sugar cane bagasse, rice husks and wheat straw, among others, converting them into three fuel types: liquid (BioOil), solid (Biochar) and gas (non-condensable gasses). The non-condensable gasses are used to fuel the pyrolysis process, and Biochar, which is similar to coal, is a reusable fuel and also thought to be an effective soil amendment. The system operates essentially as a closed loop with virtually no emissions or waste by-products. DynaMotive and its partners are also engaged in research and development on a range of derivative products. This includes the continued development of the BINGO upgrading process, which involves hydro-reforming BioOil and hydro-treating it to a commercial fuel grade state. Wholly-owned subsidiaries of the company include DynaMotive Canada, Inc.; DynaMotive USA, Inc.; DynaMotive Latinoamericana S.A.; and First Resources Corporation. In February 2011, the company agreed to establish a joint venture with Renewable Oil Corporation (ROC) to produce BioOil in Australia. In July 2011, it formed a partnership with ROC, Virgin Australia and Future Farm Industries Co-operative Research Centre to develop an aviation biofuel from the Mallee eucalyptus tree.

FINANCIALS: Sales and profits are in thousands of dollars—add 000 to get the full amount. 2011 Note: Financial information for 2011 was not available for all companies at press time.

2011 Sales: $	2011 Profits: $	U.S. Stock Ticker: DYMTF
2010 Sales: $	2010 Profits: $	Int'l Ticker:
2009 Sales: $	2009 Profits: $	Int'l Exchange:
2008 Sales: $	2008 Profits: $	Employees: 25 Fiscal Year Ends: 12/31
2007 Sales: $	2007 Profits: $	Parent Company:

SALARIES/BENEFITS:

Pension Plan:	ESOP Stock Plan:	Profit Sharing:	Top Exec. Salary: $521,430	Bonus: $66,142
Savings Plan:	Stock Purch. Plan:		Second Exec. Salary: $333,381	Bonus: $42,288

OTHER THOUGHTS:
Apparent Women Officers or Directors:
Hot Spot for Advancement for Women/Minorities:

LOCATIONS: ("Y" = Yes)

West:	Southwest:	Midwest:	Southeast:	Northeast:	International:
				Y	Y

ECHELON CORP

www.echelon.com

Industry Group Code: 33411

Energy/Fuel:	Other Technologies:	Electrical Products:	Electronics:		Transportation:	Other:
Biofuels:	Irrigation:	Lighting/LEDs:	Computers:		Car Sharing:	Recycling:
Batteries/Storage:	Nanotech:	Waste Heat:	Sensors:	Y	Electric Vehicles:	Engineering:
Solar:	Biotech:	Smart Meters:	Software:		Natural Gas Fuel:	Consulting:
Wind:	Water Tech./Treatment:	Machinery:				Investing:
Fuel Cells:	Ceramics:					Chemicals:

TYPES OF BUSINESS:

Computer Networking Equipment-Energy Controls
Remote Appliance, Sensor & Equipment Controls
Remote Diagnostics
Municipal Transportation Networks
Automation Systems
Utility Grid Diagnostic Systems

BRANDS/DIVISIONS/AFFILIATES:

LonWorks
Networked Energy Services
i.LON
LonWorks 2.0

CONTACTS: Note: Officers with more than one job title may be intentionally listed here more than once.

Ronald A. Sege, CEO
Ronald A. Sege, Pres.
Bill Slakey, CFO/Exec. VP
Anders Axelsson, Sr. VP-Commercial Sales & Market Dev.
Robert Dolin, CTO/VP
Varun Nagaraj, Sr. VP-Prod. Mgmt. & Prod. Mktg.
Rob Hon, Sr. VP-Eng.
Kathleen Bloch, General Counsel/Sr. VP
Russell Harris, Sr. VP-Oper.
C. Michael Marszewski, Principal Acct. Officer
Michael Anderson, Sr. VP-Utilities Sales & Market Dev.
Ronald A. Sege, Chmn.

Phone: 408-938-5200	**Fax:** 408-790-3800
Toll-Free: 888-324-3566	
Address: 550 Meridian Ave., San Jose, CA 95126 US	

GROWTH PLANS/SPECIAL FEATURES:

Echelon Corp. is a provider of control network technology for automation systems. The company develops, markets and supports products and services that allow device manufacturers, integrators and end users to implement control networks in the building, industrial, transportation, utility, home and other automation markets. Services include building automation systems, system failure prediction, municipal transportation applications, remote diagnostics and home pay-per-use capabilities. Its line of products includes transceivers, concentrator products, control modules, routers, network interfaces, development tools and software tools and toolkits. Echelon devises these technologies for both Internet standards and for its LonWorks 2.0 control networking platform. Each device is also capable of communicating with other devices in its control network and taking actions based on information that it receives from them, as well as allowing the integration of products or subsystems from multiple vendors. In the utility sector, Echelon offers its Networked Energy Services (NES) system, a smart metering system that automatically reports energy use, pinpoints power outages and can reduce stress on the grid. For system integrators serving the street lighting, remote facility monitoring and energy management markets, the firm has developed the i.LON Internet server family of products. The firm's transportation products use LonWorks systems and include products for railcars, light rails, buses, motor coaches, fire trucks, naval vessels and aircraft. In August 2011, the company entered a commercial agreement with Holley Metering Limited to develop advanced smart metering products for the Chinese market.

Echelon offers its employees stock options; medical, dental and vision insurance; life and AD&D insurance; short- and long-term disability insurance; flexible spending accounts; and tuition reimbursement.

FINANCIALS: Sales and profits are in thousands of dollars—add 000 to get the full amount. 2011 Note: Financial information for 2011 was not available for all companies at press time.

2011 Sales: $	2011 Profits: $	**U.S. Stock Ticker:** ELON
2010 Sales: $111,037	2010 Profits: $-31,312	**Int'l Ticker:**
2009 Sales: $103,338	2009 Profits: $-32,034	Int'l Exchange:
2008 Sales: $134,047	2008 Profits: $-25,831	Employees: 318 Fiscal Year Ends: 12/31
2007 Sales: $137,577	2007 Profits: $-14,512	Parent Company:

SALARIES/BENEFITS:

Pension Plan:	ESOP Stock Plan:	Profit Sharing:	Top Exec. Salary: $428,483	Bonus: $
Savings Plan: Y	Stock Purch. Plan: Y		Second Exec. Salary: $342,000	Bonus: $

OTHER THOUGHTS:

Apparent Women Officers or Directors: 1
Hot Spot for Advancement for Women/Minorities: Y

LOCATIONS: ("Y" = Yes)

West:	Southwest:	Midwest:	Southeast:	Northeast:	International:
Y		Y			Y

Sales, profits and employees may be estimates. Financial information, benefits and other data can change quickly and may vary from those stated here.

ELECTRAWINDS SA

www.electrawinds.be

Industry Group Code: 221119

Energy/Fuel:		Other Technologies:		Electrical Products:		Electronics:	Transportation:	Other:
Biofuels:	Y	Irrigation:		Lighting/LEDs:		Computers:	Car Sharing:	Recycling:
Batteries/Storage:		Nanotech:		Waste Heat:		Sensors:	Electric Vehicles:	Engineering:
Solar:	Y	Biotech:	Y	Smart Meters:		Software:	Natural Gas Fuel:	Consulting:
Wind:	Y	Water Tech./Treatment:		Machinery:				Investing:
Fuel Cells:		Ceramics:						Chemicals:

TYPES OF BUSINESS:

Wind & Solar Energy
Biomass Energy

BRANDS/DIVISIONS/AFFILIATES:

CONTACTS: Note: Officers with more than one job title may be intentionally listed here more than once.

Luc Desender, CEO
Eddy Baek, CFO
Andries Teerlynck, Mgr.-Sales
Patrick Meersseman, Mgr-Human Resources
Paul Desender, Mgr.-Legal
Dirk Dewettinck, Mgr.-Oper.
Jan Dewulf, Mgr.-Bus. Dev.
Marleen Vanhecke, Mgr.-Comm. & Public Rel.
Jurgen Ackaert, Controller
Peter Goderis, Mgr.-Project Realizations
Filip Dewulf, Mgr.-Commercial Bus. Dev.
Xavier Costenoble, Mgr.-Innovations & Vertical Integration
Anne Vleminckx, Mgr.-Participations
Paul Vandekerkchove, Chmn.
Herman Van Rompuy, Pres., Europe
Andries Teerlynck, Mgr.-Procurement

Phone: 0032-59-56-97-00	Fax: 0032-59-56-97-01
Toll-Free:	
Address: John Cordierlaan 9, Oostende, 8400 Belgium	

GROWTH PLANS/SPECIAL FEATURES:

Electrawinds SA is an energy company, based in Belgium, that produces green energy via solar farms, biomass power plants and wind farms. The company divides itself into three segments: wind, biomass and solar. The wind division oversees the development, construction and operation of wind farms. This division has operations in throughout Europe, parts of Africa and has three projects on the North Sea. The biomass division oversees the company's three biomass power plants in Belgium while also undertaking the research for developing new projects. The solar division operates the 12 solar farms throughout Europe that Electrawind controls, including the 7,700 panel solar farm in Middelkerke, Belgium. The energy produced by this division is able to supply enough power for about 400 families each year. The company currently has operations in Bulgaria, Romania, Belgium, France, South Africa and Italy; with plans to expand into Poland, Ireland, Serbia and Namibia. In May 2011, Electrawind opened a solar farm in Tuscany. In September 2011, the firm opened offices in Constanta, Romania. In January 2012, Electrawind opened its first wind farm in Bulgaria.

FINANCIALS: Sales and profits are in thousands of dollars—add 000 to get the full amount. 2011 Note: Financial information for 2011 was not available for all companies at press time.

2011 Sales: $	2011 Profits: $	U.S. Stock Ticker: Private
2010 Sales: $	2010 Profits: $	Int'l Ticker:
2009 Sales: $	2009 Profits: $	Int'l Exchange:
2008 Sales: $	2008 Profits: $	Employees: Fiscal Year Ends:
2007 Sales: $	2007 Profits: $	Parent Company:

SALARIES/BENEFITS:

Pension Plan:	ESOP Stock Plan:	Profit Sharing:	Top Exec. Salary: $	Bonus: $
Savings Plan:	Stock Purch. Plan:		Second Exec. Salary: $	Bonus: $

OTHER THOUGHTS:

Apparent Women Officers or Directors: 2
Hot Spot for Advancement for Women/Minorities:

LOCATIONS: ("Y" = Yes)

West:	Southwest:	Midwest:	Southeast:	Northeast:	International: Y

ELECTROCHEM INC

www.electrocheminc.com

Industry Group Code: 335999

Energy/Fuel:	Other Technologies:	Electrical Products:	Electronics:	Transportation:	Other:
Biofuels:	Irrigation:	Lighting/LEDs:	Computers:	Car Sharing:	Recycling:
Batteries/Storage:	Nanotech:	Waste Heat:	Sensors:	Electric Vehicles:	Engineering:
Solar:	Biotech:	Smart Meters:	Software:	Natural Gas Fuel:	Consulting:
Wind:	Water Tech./Treatment:	Machinery:			Investing:
Fuel Cells: Y	Ceramics:				Chemicals:

TYPES OF BUSINESS:

Fuel Cells
Proton Exchange Membrane Technology
Fuel Cell Components & Testing Equipment
Software
Contract Research & Development

BRANDS/DIVISIONS/AFFILIATES:

PowerStation System
FuelCell.com

CONTACTS: *Note: Officers with more than one job title may be intentionally listed here more than once.*

Radha Jalan, CEO
Radha Jalan, Pres.
Michael S. Pien, VP-R&D
Steven A. Lis, Sr. Scientist

Phone: 781-938-5300	**Fax:** 781-935-6966
Toll-Free:	
Address: 400 W. Cummings Pk., Woburn, MA 01801 US	

GROWTH PLANS/SPECIAL FEATURES:

ElectroChem, Inc. specializes in fuel cell technology. The firm researches, develops and manufactures fuel cells, fuel cell testing equipment and fuel cell components for business, academic and government research organizations. It has over 600 customers on five continents. ElectroChem focuses its development work on Solid Polymer, or Proton Exchange Membrane (PEM) fuel cells, which operate at low temperatures, have high power density and can start instantly at full capacity. PEM fuel cells can be used in light-duty vehicles, remote/distributed power generation and for applications, such as replacing rechargeable batteries. The company's fuel cell line includes stacks, single cells and hardware/phosphoric acid fuel cells. ElectroChem's equipment line includes the PowerStation System testing management software, manual test stations, humidifiers and demonstration units. The firm also offers accessories and components such as back pressure regulators, catalysts, chemical solutions, electrodes, gas diffusion layers, gaskets, heaters, mass flow controllers, membranes, membrane electrode assemblies and moisture traps. The company provides its customers with contract research and development services. ElectroChem offers its product lines to its research clients worldwide through its direct manufacturing sector and through other manufacturers and distributors in Turkey, Russia, Japan, Korea, continental Europe, Pakistan and India. It also sells its products directly through its e-commerce subsidiary, FuelCell.com. ElectroChem plans to market its first commercial product to the backup and uninterruptible power markets.

FINANCIALS: Sales and profits are in thousands of dollars—add 000 to get the full amount. 2011 Note: Financial information for 2011 was not available for all companies at press time.

2011 Sales: $	2011 Profits: $	**U.S. Stock Ticker: Private**
2010 Sales: $	2010 Profits: $	**Int'l Ticker:**
2009 Sales: $	2009 Profits: $	Int'l Exchange:
2008 Sales: $	2008 Profits: $	Employees: Fiscal Year Ends: 12/31
2007 Sales: $	2007 Profits: $	Parent Company:

SALARIES/BENEFITS:

Pension Plan:	ESOP Stock Plan:	Profit Sharing:	Top Exec. Salary: $	Bonus: $
Savings Plan:	Stock Purch. Plan:		Second Exec. Salary: $	Bonus: $

OTHER THOUGHTS:

Apparent Women Officers or Directors:
Hot Spot for Advancement for Women/Minorities:

LOCATIONS: ("Y" = Yes)

West:	Southwest:	Midwest:	Southeast:	Northeast: Y	International:

Sales, profits and employees may be estimates. Financial information, benefits and other data can change quickly and may vary from those stated here.

ELEVANCE RENEWABLE SCIENCES INC   www.elevance.com

Industry Group Code: 325

Energy/Fuel:		Other Technologies:		Electrical Products:	Electronics:	Transportation:	Other:	
Biofuels:	Y	Irrigation:		Lighting/LEDs:	Computers:	Car Sharing:	Recycling:	
Batteries/Storage:		Nanotech:		Waste Heat:	Sensors:	Electric Vehicles:	Engineering:	
Solar:		Biotech:	Y	Smart Meters:	Software:	Natural Gas Fuel:	Consulting:	
Wind:		Water Tech./Treatment:		Machinery:			Investing:	
Fuel Cells:		Ceramics:					Chemicals:	Y

TYPES OF BUSINESS:
Plant-Based Oils Transformation

BRANDS/DIVISIONS/AFFILIATES:

CONTACTS: Note: Officers with more than one job title may be intentionally listed here more than once.
K'Lynne Johnson, CEO
Mel Luetkens, COO
David Kelsey, CFO
Andy Shafer, Exec. VP-Mktg. & Sales
LaRae Lafrenz, VP-Human Capital
Kara Lawrence, Treas./Comptroller
Del Craig, Exec. VP-Special Projects
Geoffrey Duyk, Chmn.

Phone:	Fax: 630-633-7295
Toll-Free: 866-625-7103	
Address: 2501 Davey Rd., Woodridge, IL 60517 US	

GROWTH PLANS/SPECIAL FEATURES:

Elevance Renewable Sciences, Inc. is a chemicals firm that specializes in converting natural plant-based oils into high-performance commercial products. The firm utilizes oils such as rapeseed, palm, soybean, corn and algae to create renewable solutions for additives for lubricants and fuel; lubricant base oils for enhanced automobile performance; detergents and cleaners through a partnership with the Stepan Company; naturally derived antimicrobials, which are used to control unwanted bacteria, fungi, mold and other organisms; personal care products, including aesthetics sold to Victoria Secret; paraffin-free performance waxes and candles through a partnership with Tetramer Technologies LLC; and advanced biofuels to replace traditional diesel and jet fuels. Elevance Renewable Sciences has received funding from the following investors: Naxos Capital Partners, TPG, Total Energy Ventures, Materia and Cargill. In 2011, the company filed an initial public offering. In April 2011, the firm agreed to partner with NL Grease LLC to commercialize new environmental high performance grease technology and materials. In June 2011, Elevance Renewable Sciences acquired the Delta BioFuels facility in Mississippi.

The firm offers its employees benefits including life, AD&D, medical, dental, vision and disability insurance; a 401(k); flexible dependent and healthcare spending accounts; wellness programs; personal choice, vacation and holiday time off; and travel and employee assistance plans.

FINANCIALS: Sales and profits are in thousands of dollars—add 000 to get the full amount. 2011 Note: Financial information for 2011 was not available for all companies at press time.

2011 Sales: $	2011 Profits: $	U.S. Stock Ticker: Private
2010 Sales: $	2010 Profits: $	Int'l Ticker:
2009 Sales: $	2009 Profits: $	Int'l Exchange:
2008 Sales: $	2008 Profits: $	Employees: Fiscal Year Ends: 12/31
2007 Sales: $	2007 Profits: $	Parent Company:

SALARIES/BENEFITS:

Pension Plan:	ESOP Stock Plan:	Profit Sharing:	Top Exec. Salary: $	Bonus: $
Savings Plan: Y	Stock Purch. Plan:		Second Exec. Salary: $	Bonus: $

OTHER THOUGHTS:
Apparent Women Officers or Directors: 5
Hot Spot for Advancement for Women/Minorities: Y

LOCATIONS: ("Y" = Yes)

West:	Southwest:	Midwest:	Southeast:	Northeast:	International:
		Y			

ELTRON RESEARCH & DEVELOPMENT INC www.eltronresearch.com

Industry Group Code: 335999

Energy/Fuel:		Other Technologies:	Electrical Products:	Electronics:	Transportation:	Other:
Biofuels:		Irrigation:	Lighting/LEDs:	Computers:	Car Sharing:	Recycling:
Batteries/Storage:		Nanotech:	Waste Heat:	Sensors:	Electric Vehicles:	Engineering:
Solar:		Biotech:	Smart Meters:	Software:	Natural Gas Fuel:	Consulting:
Wind:		Water Tech./Treatment:	Machinery:			Investing:
Fuel Cells:	Y	Ceramics:				Chemicals:

TYPES OF BUSINESS:

Fuel Cell Technology
Catalytic Membrane Reactors
Materials Research
Chemical Sensors
Electrolytic Technology
Machining & Welding
Monopropellant Fuels

BRANDS/DIVISIONS/AFFILIATES:

CONTACTS: Note: Officers with more than one job title may be intentionally listed here more than once.

Paul J. Grimmer, Pres.
Freya L. Olson, Admin.-Human Resources
Jong-Hee M. Park, Sr. Scientist
Douglas S. Jack, VP-Tech.
David H. Anderson, Chief Engineer
James Steven Beck, VP-Admin.
Jay G. Patel, Mgr.-Oper.
Pete M. Birkeland, Mgr.-Bus. Dev.
Mary H. Metzger, Acct.
James H. White, Research Fellow
Richard Mackay, Research Fellow
Carl R. Evenson
Mgr.-Tech., Mgr.-Tech.
Sara L. Rolfe, Sr. Scientist
Tina M. Kuntz, Mgr.-Purch.

Phone: 303-530-0263	Fax: 303-530-0264
Toll-Free:	
Address: 4600 Nautilus Court S., Boulder, CO 80301 US	

GROWTH PLANS/SPECIAL FEATURES:

Eltron Research & Development, Inc. is a provider of various technology solutions. The firm researches and develops energy production, chemical processing, environmental protection and catalysis technology. The company seeks efficient strategies for using energy and chemical resources and provides novel approaches for reducing, controlling and monitoring the environmental impact of these technologies. Its research focuses on a number of subjects, including catalytic membrane reactors, electrolytic systems, catalysis, materials science and chemical sensors. Eltron's proprietary catalytic membrane reactors (CMRs) facilitate the exclusive mediation of selected ions from gases to a desired reaction site, acting as short-circuited electrochemical devices. Their operation requires no thermal or electrical input. Eltron's electrolytic systems research and development includes its hydrogen peroxide generator, capable of producing low concentration hydrogen peroxide directly from air and water to serve as an environmentally-friendly alternative for water treatment. The firm's catalysis research covers a wide range of catalytic reactions, including catalysts for low temperature volatile organic compound destruction in both water and air applications, catalysts for the selective oxidation of carbon monoxide into carbon dioxide and catalysts for the low temperature destruction of chemical warfare agents. Eltron's materials research deals with ceramic processing; thin films; high pressure ceramic seals; reverse osmosis polymers; resin transfer molding composites; composites incorporating single-walled nanotubes; wear resistant and antistatic coatings; and ionic liquids. Eltron's chemical sensor research and development focuses on environmental monitoring, industrial hygiene, occupational safety and process control. The company has developed more than 75 patents and patent applications, over 33% of which have been commercially licensed.

Eltron offers its employees a 401(k) plan, flexible hours and an educational refund policy.

FINANCIALS: Sales and profits are in thousands of dollars—add 000 to get the full amount. 2011 Note: Financial information for 2011 was not available for all companies at press time.

2011 Sales: $	2011 Profits: $	**U.S. Stock Ticker: Private**	
2010 Sales: $	2010 Profits: $	**Int'l Ticker:**	
2009 Sales: $	2009 Profits: $	Int'l Exchange:	
2008 Sales: $	2008 Profits: $	Employees:	Fiscal Year Ends:
2007 Sales: $	2007 Profits: $	Parent Company:	

SALARIES/BENEFITS:

Pension Plan:	ESOP Stock Plan:	Profit Sharing:	Top Exec. Salary: $	Bonus: $
Savings Plan: Y	Stock Purch. Plan:		Second Exec. Salary: $	Bonus: $

OTHER THOUGHTS:

Apparent Women Officers or Directors: 6
Hot Spot for Advancement for Women/Minorities: Y

LOCATIONS: ("Y" = Yes)

West:	Southwest:	Midwest:	Southeast:	Northeast:	International:
Y					

EMCORE CORP

www.emcore.com

Industry Group Code: 33441

Energy/Fuel:	Other Technologies:		Electrical Products:	Electronics:	Transportation:	Other:
Biofuels:	Irrigation:		Lighting/LEDs:	Computers:	Car Sharing:	Recycling:
Batteries/Storage:	Nanotech:	Y	Waste Heat:	Sensors:	Electric Vehicles:	Engineering:
Solar:	Biotech:		Smart Meters:	Software:	Natural Gas Fuel:	Consulting:
Wind:	Water Tech./Treatment:		Machinery:			Investing:
Fuel Cells:	Ceramics:					Chemicals:

TYPES OF BUSINESS:

Nanotechnology-Semiconductors
Telecommunications Equipment Components
Lasers
Photovoltaic (PV) Cells
Fiber Optics
Concentrating Photovoltaics (CPVs)

BRANDS/DIVISIONS/AFFILIATES:

EMCORE Photovoltaics
Suncore Photovoltaics Co Ltd

CONTACTS: *Note: Officers with more than one job title may be intentionally listed here more than once.*

Hong Q. Hou, CEO
Christopher Larocca, COO
Mark Weinswig, CFO
Monica Van Berkel, Chief Admin. Officer
Alfredo Gomez, General Counsel/Corp. Sec.
Reuben F. Richards, Jr., Chmn.
Charlie Wang, Exec. VP/Gen. Mgr.-Emcore China

Phone: 505-332-5000	Fax: 505-332-5038
Toll-Free:	
Address: 10420 Research Rd. SE, Albuquerque, NM 87123 US	

GROWTH PLANS/SPECIAL FEATURES:

EMCORE Corp. is a provider of compound semiconductor-based components and subsystems for the broadband, fiber optic, satellite and terrestrial solar power markets. The company operates in two segments: fiber optics and photovoltaics (PV). The fiber optics segment provides optical components, subsystems and systems that enable the transmission of video, voice and data over high-capacity fiber optic cable for the high-speed data and telecommunications, cable television and fiber-to-the-premises networks. The segment also serves satellite communications networks, storage area networks, video transport and defense and homeland security markets. The PV segment provides solar products for satellite and terrestrial applications. Unlike most other PV manufacturers, the company uses non-silicon-based materials, which are more efficient and less prone to material shortages. For satellite applications, EMCORE offers high-efficiency compound semiconductor-based gallium arsenide (GaAs) solar cells, covered interconnect cells and fully integrated solar panels. These panels are designed to withstand high levels of heat and radiation while adhering to efficiency and size requirements. For terrestrial applications, the company offers its high-efficiency GaAs solar cells for use in solar power concentrator systems. EMCORE supplies both government and private industries, including the NASA Jet Propulsion Laboratory; Lockheed Martin; Northrop Grumman; Boeing; and Dutch Space. The firm has four manufacturing facilities, located in New Mexico, California, Pennsylvania and China. In 2010, the company established Suncore Photovoltaics Co., Ltd., a joint venture with San'an Optoelectronics Co., Ltd. for the development, marketing and distribution of concentrating PV (CPV) receivers and systems for terrestrial solar power applications. In March 2011, EMCORE acquired the assets of Soliant Energy, Inc.'s rooftop solar energy product line.

The company offers its employees medical, dental and vision insurance; life and AD&D insurance; a 401(k); an employee assistance program; tuition reimbursement; flexible spending accounts; prepaid legal services; employee referral bonuses; and an employee stock purchase plan.

FINANCIALS: Sales and profits are in thousands of dollars—add 000 to get the full amount. 2011 Note: Financial information for 2011 was not available for all companies at press time.

2011 Sales: $200,928	2011 Profits: $-34,219	**U.S. Stock Ticker: EMKR**
2010 Sales: $191,278	2010 Profits: $-23,694	**Int'l Ticker:**
2009 Sales: $176,356	2009 Profits: $-136,069	Int'l Exchange:
2008 Sales: $239,303	2008 Profits: $-80,860	Employees: 1,000 Fiscal Year Ends: 9/30
2007 Sales: $169,606	2007 Profits: $-58,722	Parent Company:

SALARIES/BENEFITS:

Pension Plan:	ESOP Stock Plan:	Profit Sharing:	Top Exec. Salary: $434,129	Bonus: $95,000
Savings Plan: Y	Stock Purch. Plan: Y		Second Exec. Salary: $425,167	Bonus: $85,000

OTHER THOUGHTS:

Apparent Women Officers or Directors: 1
Hot Spot for Advancement for Women/Minorities:

LOCATIONS: ("Y" = Yes)

West:	Southwest:	Midwest:	Southeast:	Northeast:	International:
Y	Y			Y	Y

Sales, profits and employees may be estimates. Financial information, benefits and other data can change quickly and may vary from those stated here.

EMEFCY LTD

www.emefcy.com

Industry Group Code: 325199

Energy/Fuel:		Other Technologies:		Electrical Products:		Electronics:		Transportation:		Other:	
Biofuels:	Y	Irrigation:		Lighting/LEDs:		Computers:		Car Sharing:		Recycling:	
Batteries/Storage:		Nanotech:		Waste Heat:		Sensors:		Electric Vehicles:		Engineering:	
Solar:		Biotech:	Y	Smart Meters:		Software:		Natural Gas Fuel:		Consulting:	
Wind:		Water Tech./Treatment:	Y	Machinery:						Investing:	
Fuel Cells:		Ceramics:								Chemicals:	

TYPES OF BUSINESS:

Wastewater Treatment Technologies

BRANDS/DIVISIONS/AFFILIATES:

SABRE
EBR

CONTACTS: *Note: Officers with more than one job title may be intentionally listed here more than once.*

Eytan Levy, CEO
Ely Cohen, VP-Mktg.
Ronen Shechter, CTO
Ely Cohen, VP-Bus. Dev.
Ben-Zion Shemesh, VP-Finance

Phone: 972-4-6277-555	**Fax:** 972-4-6277-556
Toll-Free:	
Address: 7 Ha'eshel St., Caesarea, 30889 Israel	

GROWTH PLANS/SPECIAL FEATURES:

Emefcy Ltd. develops wastewater treatment technologies for industrial and municipal plants. The wastewater treatment technology developed by the firm turns what is typically an energy consuming endeavor into one that produces energy. This reversal of the wastewater/energy relationship occurs within an Electrogenic Bioreactor (EBR), or microbial fuel cell, which uses the degradation of organic matter to produce electricity. Emefcy markets its wastewater treatments under the names SABRE and EBR. The SABRE treatment is designed for low to medium loads that incorporates a passive-aeration treatment process. The result of this process is that energy consumption, in comparison to an active sludge treatment, is reduced dramatically. The EBR treatment, as touched on earlier, uses the microbial fuel cell technology and is based upon three components: anodes, where bacterial oxidation occurs; cathodes, where a reduction reaction occurs; and an external circuit with the external load that connects the two. As the organic matter oxidizes, an electric current is produced, thus converting wastewater into energy. In June 2011, GE, through its Energy Technology Ventures, a joint venture company with NRG Energy and ConocoPhilips, announced that it had invested $10 million in Emefcy.

FINANCIALS: Sales and profits are in thousands of dollars—add 000 to get the full amount. 2011 Note: Financial information for 2011 was not available for all companies at press time.

2011 Sales: $	2011 Profits: $	**U.S. Stock Ticker: Private**
2010 Sales: $	2010 Profits: $	**Int'l Ticker:**
2009 Sales: $	2009 Profits: $	Int'l Exchange:
2008 Sales: $	2008 Profits: $	Employees: Fiscal Year Ends:
2007 Sales: $	2007 Profits: $	Parent Company:

SALARIES/BENEFITS:

Pension Plan:	ESOP Stock Plan:	Profit Sharing:	Top Exec. Salary: $	Bonus: $
Savings Plan:	Stock Purch. Plan:		Second Exec. Salary: $	Bonus: $

OTHER THOUGHTS:

Apparent Women Officers or Directors:
Hot Spot for Advancement for Women/Minorities:

LOCATIONS: ("Y" = Yes)

West:	Southwest:	Midwest:	Southeast:	Northeast:	International:
					Y

ENECSYS LIMITED

www.enecsys.com

Industry Group Code: 334413

Energy/Fuel:	Other Technologies:	Electrical Products:	Electronics:	Transportation:	Other:
Biofuels:	Irrigation:	Lighting/LEDs:	Computers:	Car Sharing:	Recycling:
Batteries/Storage:	Nanotech:	Waste Heat:	Sensors:	Electric Vehicles:	Engineering:
Solar: Y	Biotech:	Smart Meters:	Software:	Natural Gas Fuel:	Consulting:
Wind:	Water Tech./Treatment:	Machinery:			Investing:
Fuel Cells:	Ceramics:				Chemicals:

TYPES OF BUSINESS:

Solar Energy Technology

BRANDS/DIVISIONS/AFFILIATES:

CONTACTS: Note: Officers with more than one job title may be intentionally listed here more than once.

Michael J. Fister, CEO
Louis-Philippe Lalonde, VP-Prod. Mgmt.
Paul Garrity, VP-Eng.
Ronald M. Westhauser, VP-Oper.
Chris Poole, Dir.-Finance
Lesley Chisenga, Chief Architect
Asim Mumtaz, Principal Engineer
Mossadiq S. Umedaly, Chmn.
Peter Mathews, VP-Sale North America

Phone: 44-1223-792-101	Fax: 44-1223-792-103
Toll-Free:	
Address: Harston Mill, Royston Rd, Cambridge, CB22 7GG UK	

GROWTH PLANS/SPECIAL FEATURES:

Enecsys Limited is a technology company that develops, manufactures and markets solar micro inverters and monitoring systems. The company's offerings are micro inverters that mount behind solar modules on the railing system and are designed to match the 25-year service life of most solar modules. Enecsys micro inverters are designed to be rugged and withstand high temperatures while also using an energy storage technique that allows for the use of thin film capacitors instead of electrolytic capacitors, thus improving reliability. The firms monitoring system, unlike string inverters, shows the performance of each module, allowing the user to insure that the solar system is performing at optimal levels. Additionally, the monitoring system displays upon its interface the historic pattern of energy generation and total energy generated along with individual performance. Headquartered in Cambridge, U.K., Enecsys also has operations in Taipei City, Taiwan; Redwood Shores, California; and Bad Homburg, Germany. The company sells its products throughout Europe and North America. The firm's investors include Wellington Partners, NES Partners, Good Energies and Climate Change Capital Private Equity.

FINANCIALS: Sales and profits are in thousands of dollars—add 000 to get the full amount. 2011 Note: Financial information for 2011 was not available for all companies at press time.

2011 Sales: $	2011 Profits: $	**U.S. Stock Ticker: Private**
2010 Sales: $	2010 Profits: $	**Int'l Ticker:**
2009 Sales: $	2009 Profits: $	Int'l Exchange:
2008 Sales: $	2008 Profits: $	Employees: Fiscal Year Ends:
2007 Sales: $	2007 Profits: $	Parent Company:

SALARIES/BENEFITS:

Pension Plan:	ESOP Stock Plan:	Profit Sharing:	Top Exec. Salary: $	Bonus: $
Savings Plan:	Stock Purch. Plan:		Second Exec. Salary: $	Bonus: $

OTHER THOUGHTS:

Apparent Women Officers or Directors:
Hot Spot for Advancement for Women/Minorities:

LOCATIONS: ("Y" = Yes)

West:	Southwest:	Midwest:	Southeast:	Northeast:	International:
Y					Y

ENEL GREEN POWER SPA

www.enelgreenpower.com

Industry Group Code: 221119

Energy/Fuel:		Other Technologies:		Electrical Products:		Electronics:	Transportation:		Other:	
Biofuels:	Y	Irrigation:		Lighting/LEDs:		Computers:	Car Sharing:		Recycling:	
Batteries/Storage:		Nanotech:		Waste Heat:	Y	Sensors:	Electric Vehicles:		Engineering:	
Solar:	Y	Biotech:		Smart Meters:		Software:	Natural Gas Fuel:		Consulting:	
Wind:	Y	Water Tech./Treatment:		Machinery:					Investing:	
Fuel Cells:		Ceramics:							Chemicals:	

TYPES OF BUSINESS:

Alternative Energy Generation
Photovoltaic Cell Production

BRANDS/DIVISIONS/AFFILIATES:

Enel SpA
Enel North America Inc
3Sun Srl
Sharp Corporation
STMicroelectronics

CONTACTS: Note: Officers with more than one job title may be intentionally listed here more than once.

Francesco Starace, CEO
Francisco Javier Querol Vidal, Head-Human Resources & Organization
Massimo Ferriani, Head-IT & Comm. Tech.
Vittorio Vagliasindi, Head-Eng. & Construction
Alberto de Paoli, Head-Admin.
Giulio Fazio, Head-Legal Affairs
Ingmar Wilhelm, Head-Bus. Dev.
Francesca Romana Napolitano, Head-Corp. Affairs
Alberto de Paoli, Head-Finance & Control
Felice Egidi, Head-Regulatory Affairs
Attilio Cherubini, Head-Safety & Environment
Silvia Fiori, Head-Internal Audit
Maurizio Bezzeccheri, Head-Iberia & Latin America
Luigi Ferraris, Chmn.
Francesco Venturini, Head-North America
Dino Marcozzi, Head-Procurement

Phone: 39-06-830-51	Fax: 39-06-830-53659
Toll-Free:	
Address: Viale Regina Margherita 125, Rome, 00198 Italy	

GROWTH PLANS/SPECIAL FEATURES:

Enel Green Power SpA (EGP), based in Italy and a subsidiary of Enel SpA, develops and operates renewable energy generation facilities. With approximately 620 plants in operation around the world and a diverse mix of generation sources, the firm has an installed generation capacity of nearly 6,100 megawatts (MW). Over 60% of EGP's generation capacity is located in Italy, while the remainder is located across Europe, North America and Central and South America. Its energy mix consists of 41.6% hydroelectric, 43.5% wind, 12.7% geothermal and the remaining 2.2% from biomass, solar and co-generation facilities. In 2010, the firm produced a total of 2,485.2 MW of energy from renewable sources. EGP has plans to increase its installed capacity to 9,200 MW by 2014. In mid 2010, EGP established a joint venture with Sharp Corp. and STMicroelectronics named 3Sun S.r.l. to produce thin-film photovoltaic cells and panels. In late 2010, the company acquired the 10 MW wind farm La Bouleste in France from Gamesa.

FINANCIALS: Sales and profits are in thousands of dollars—add 000 to get the full amount. 2011 Note: Financial information for 2011 was not available for all companies at press time.

2011 Sales: $	2011 Profits: $	**U.S. Stock Ticker: Subsidiary**
2010 Sales: $3,091,724	2010 Profits: $698,979	**Int'l Ticker:**
2009 Sales: $2,521,856	2009 Profits: $622,550	Int'l Exchange:
2008 Sales: $	2008 Profits: $	Employees: 2,889 Fiscal Year Ends: 12/31
2007 Sales: $	2007 Profits: $	Parent Company: ENEL SPA

SALARIES/BENEFITS:

Pension Plan:	ESOP Stock Plan:	Profit Sharing:	Top Exec. Salary: $	Bonus: $
Savings Plan:	Stock Purch. Plan:		Second Exec. Salary: $	Bonus: $

OTHER THOUGHTS:

Apparent Women Officers or Directors: 4
Hot Spot for Advancement for Women/Minorities: Y

LOCATIONS: ("Y" = Yes)

West:	Southwest:	Midwest:	Southeast:	Northeast:	International:
		Y			Y

Sales, profits and employees may be estimates. Financial information, benefits and other data can change quickly and may vary from those stated here.

ENEL SPA

www.enel.it

Industry Group Code: 2211

Energy/Fuel:		Other Technologies:		Electrical Products:		Electronics:	Transportation:		Other:	
Biofuels:		Irrigation:		Lighting/LEDs:		Computers:	Car Sharing:		Recycling:	
Batteries/Storage:		Nanotech:		Waste Heat:		Sensors:	Electric Vehicles:		Engineering:	
Solar:		Biotech:		Smart Meters:		Software:	Natural Gas Fuel:	Y	Consulting:	
Wind:	Y	Water Tech./Treatment:	Y	Machinery:					Investing:	
Fuel Cells:		Ceramics:							Chemicals:	

TYPES OF BUSINESS:

Electric Utility
Mini-Hydroelectric Generation
Solar Generation
Wind Power Generation
Geothermal Generation

BRANDS/DIVISIONS/AFFILIATES:

Neftegaztechnologiya
RusEnergoSbyt LLC
Enel Green Power
Enel Green Power
Hydro Energy Ltd Piave
Sociedad Termica Portuguesa SA
Spain Sociedad Wind de Andalucia, SA

CONTACTS: *Note: Officers with more than one job title may be intentionally listed here more than once.*

Fulvio Conti, CEO
Paolo Andrea Colombo, Pres.
Livio Vido, Dir.-Eng. & Innovation
Gianfilippo Mancini, Dir.-Generation & Energy Management
Livio Gallo, Dir.-Infrastructure & Networks Div.
Andrea Brentan, Dir.-Iberia & Latin America
Francesco Starace, Dir.-Renewable Energy/CEO-Enel Green Power
Piero Gnudi, Chmn.
Charles Drum, Dir.-Int'l Div.

Phone: 39-06-8305-2783	Fax: 3906-8305-3659
Toll-Free:	
Address: Viale Regina Margherita 137, Rome, 00198 Italy	

GROWTH PLANS/SPECIAL FEATURES:

Enel SpA is one of Italy's largest power companies, as well as one of the largest in Europe, operating in 40 countries and provides power and gas to approximately 49 million customers. The company is also one of the largest in Italy in terms of shareholders and product market share; Enel provides natural gas to more than 2.6 million customers within Italy. The firm has a total generating capacity of 83,000 MW. In North America, Enel operates through Enel Green Power and has hydroelectric and wind power plants that generate more than 788 MW. The company also has a sizeable renewable and traditional energy presence throughout Latin America, with approximately 16 GW of installed capacity. In Russia, Enel operates through several companies; RusEnergoSbyt and Neftegaztechnologiya are among the most substantial and generate over 8,200 MW of electricity. In April 2011, the firm announced the acquisition of 16.67% of Spain Sociedad Wind de Andalucia, SA, making it the primary shareholder with 63.34%. In May 2011, Enel Green Power announced that construction of its $350 million 200 MW wind farm in Kansas has gotten underway. In June 2011, Enel announced the acquisition of an additional 50% of Sociedad Termica Portuguesa SA, thus becoming the sole share holder; in addition, the firm announced the completion of the sale of Maritza East III Power Holdings BV and Maritza O & M Holding BV Netherland to Contour Global LP for $737 million. In July 2011, the firm and Production En & En signed an agreement to form the joint venture Hydro Energy Ltd Piave, a company whose aim is the development of new hydroelectric projects in the province of Belluno. In October 2011, Enel Green Power announced that construction of its $205 million 150 MW wind farm in Oklahoma City has gotten underway.

FINANCIALS: Sales and profits are in thousands of dollars—add 000 to get the full amount. 2011 Note: Financial information for 2011 was not available for all companies at press time.

2011 Sales: $	2011 Profits: $	**U.S. Stock Ticker:**
2010 Sales: $95,749,700	2010 Profits: $5,842,700	**Int'l Ticker: ENEL**
2009 Sales: $82,128,400	2009 Profits: $6,964,190	Int'l Exchange: Milan-BI
2008 Sales: $78,495,900	2008 Profits: $6,832,520	Employees: 78,313 Fiscal Year Ends: 12/31
2007 Sales: $56,395,100	2007 Profits: $5,055,010	Parent Company:

SALARIES/BENEFITS:

Pension Plan:	ESOP Stock Plan:	Profit Sharing:	Top Exec. Salary: $970,693	Bonus: $
Savings Plan:	Stock Purch. Plan:		Second Exec. Salary: $791,580	Bonus: $

OTHER THOUGHTS:

Apparent Women Officers or Directors:
Hot Spot for Advancement for Women/Minorities:

LOCATIONS: ("Y" = Yes)

West:	Southwest:	Midwest:	Southeast:	Northeast:	International: Y

ENER1 INC

www.ener1.com

Industry Group Code: 33591

Energy/Fuel:		Other Technologies:	Electrical Products:	Electronics:	Transportation:	Other:
Biofuels:		Irrigation:	Lighting/LEDs:	Computers:	Car Sharing:	Recycling:
Batteries/Storage:	Y	Nanotech:	Waste Heat:	Sensors:	Electric Vehicles:	Engineering:
Solar:		Biotech:	Smart Meters:	Software:	Natural Gas Fuel:	Consulting:
Wind:		Water Tech./Treatment:	Machinery:			Investing:
Fuel Cells:		Ceramics:				Chemicals:

TYPES OF BUSINESS:

Battery Development & Manufacturing

BRANDS/DIVISIONS/AFFILIATES:

EnerDel
EnerFuel
NanoEner
Enertech

CONTACTS: *Note: Officers with more than one job title may be intentionally listed here more than once.*

Chris Cowger, Pres.
Eddie Luedke, VP-Human Resources
Naoki Ota, CTO
Nicholas Brunero, General Counsel/VP
Dan Allen, Sr. VP-Oper.
Rachel Carroll, VP-Corp. Comm.
Melissa Debes, Chief Acct. Officer/Sr. VP-Finance
Tae-Hee Yoon, CEO/Chmn.-Ener1 Korea, Inc.
Bruce Curtis, Pres., Grid Energy Storage
Thomas C. Goesch, Pres., Transportation
Charles Gassenheimer, Chmn.
Ulrik Grape, Pres., Ener1 Europe
Dan Allen, Sr. VP-Procurement

Phone: 212-920-3500	Fax:
Toll-Free:	
Address: 1540 Broadway, Ste. 25C, New York, NY 10036 US	

GROWTH PLANS/SPECIAL FEATURES:

Ener1, Inc. is an alternative energy company focused on designing, developing and manufacturing high-performance, rechargeable lithium-ion batteries and other systems for energy storage. It divides its business into three segments; battery, fuel cell and nanotechnology. The battery segment develops and markets lithium-ion batteries. The fuel cell segment develops fuel cells and fuel cell systems for use in the transportation and stationery power industries. Its nanotechnology business develops nanotechnology related manufacturing processes and materials. The company operates through four subsidiaries: EnerDel, EnerFuel, EnerTech and NanoEner. EnerDel, the company's primary subsidiary, is an end-to-end solutions provider that develops and manufactures products from small cells to complete battery packs. The subsidiary develops lithium-ion batteries for automotive, military and other industrial uses. EnerFuel is developing a hydrogen fuel cell range extender for use in EREVs (extended range electric vehicles) and other electric based automobiles and has successfully created a high temperature fuel cell stack. Other planned products are in early stages of development. EnerTech, based in South Korea, manufactures both large and small format battery cells and packs for use in cell phones, GPS systems and other commercial utilities. NanoEner has built prototype equipment that utilizes a proprietary vapor deposition and solidification process for depositing materials onto battery electrodes as part of the battery cell manufacturing process. NanoEner is developing electrodes produced from this process for testing and is still in research and development phases. In January 2011, the firm agreed to form a joint venture with the Chinese auto parts company Wanxiang EV Co., Ltd. that will design, manufacture, sell and service lithium-ion battery cells and lithium-ion battery packs in Asia. As of late 2011 the firm was facing significant financial difficulty and was delisted from the NASDAQ stock exchange. In January 2012, the firm filed for Chapter 11 bankruptcy protection. It plans to reorganize.

FINANCIALS: Sales and profits are in thousands of dollars—add 000 to get the full amount. 2011 Note: Financial information for 2011 was not available for all companies at press time.

2011 Sales: $	2011 Profits: $	**U.S. Stock Ticker:** HEV
2010 Sales: $77,406	2010 Profits: $-68,801	**Int'l Ticker:**
2009 Sales: $34,800	2009 Profits: $-51,004	Int'l Exchange:
2008 Sales: $6,848	2008 Profits: $-52,460	Employees: 769 Fiscal Year Ends: 12/31
2007 Sales: $ 280	2007 Profits: $-63,938	Parent Company:

SALARIES/BENEFITS:

Pension Plan:	ESOP Stock Plan:	Profit Sharing:	Top Exec. Salary: $500,000	Bonus: $250,000
Savings Plan:	Stock Purch. Plan:		Second Exec. Salary: $430,000	Bonus: $

OTHER THOUGHTS:

Apparent Women Officers or Directors: 2
Hot Spot for Advancement for Women/Minorities:

LOCATIONS: ("Y" = Yes)

West:	Southwest:	Midwest:	Southeast:	Northeast:	International:
		Y	Y	Y	Y

ENERCON GMBH

Industry Group Code: 33361

www.enercon.de

Energy/Fuel:		Other Technologies:		Electrical Products:		Electronics:		Transportation:		Other:	
Biofuels:		Irrigation:		Lighting/LEDs:		Computers:		Car Sharing:		Recycling:	
Batteries/Storage:		Nanotech:		Waste Heat:		Sensors:		Electric Vehicles:		Engineering:	
Solar:		Biotech:		Smart Meters:		Software:		Natural Gas Fuel:		Consulting:	
Wind:	Y	Water Tech./Treatment:		Machinery:						Investing:	
Fuel Cells:		Ceramics:								Chemicals:	

TYPES OF BUSINESS:

Wind Turbine Manufacturing

BRANDS/DIVISIONS/AFFILIATES:

CONTACTS: *Note: Officers with more than one job title may be intentionally listed here more than once.*

Aloys Wobben, Managing Dir.
Volker Uphoff, Head-Mktg.
Petra Engelhardt, Dir.-Human Resources
Volker Uphoff, Head-Public Rel.
Stefan Lutkemeyer, Manager-Sales
Aloys Wobben, Chmn.

Phone: 49-49-41-927-0	**Fax:** 49-49-41-927-109
Toll-Free:	
Address: Dreekamp 5, Aurich, D-26605 Germany	

GROWTH PLANS/SPECIAL FEATURES:

ENERCON GmbH, founded in 1984, manufactures and designs wind turbines. To support turbine installation, the firm operates mobile cranes of up to 800 tons; special transporters for blades and towers; and hundreds of service vehicles. The firm's turbines have featured gearless systems since 1992, allowing the turbines to operate with fewer rotating parts, resulting in almost frictionless performance. ENERCON offers turbine configurations rated from 330 kilowatts to 7,500 kilowatts. Generally, all of ENERCON's turbine systems feature independent pitch control for each of the three rotor blades, as well as integrated lighting protection and typically operate at speeds around 12-20 revolutions per minute (rpm), with some capable of operating as slow as six rpm and some as fast as 34 rpm. In order to prevent the shut-downs caused by high winds that other turbines systems may suffer from, the firm has developed ENERCON Storm Control software, which causes the rotor blades to rotate slightly out of sync with the wind, thus preventing damage by reducing the rotation speed rather than ceasing rotation altogether. In order to connect the turbines to a power grid, the firm offers ENERCON SCADA, an upgradable and adaptable monitoring and control interface. Each turbine also comes equipped with a modem to signal a central data transmission facility of any malfunction. The firm's service and support division operates over 160 stations worldwide. ENERCON has three production facilities in Germany, as well as facilities in Canada, India, Brazil, Sweden and Portugal. The company has installed enough towers to produce over 22 gigawatts of energy.

FINANCIALS: Sales and profits are in thousands of dollars—add 000 to get the full amount. 2011 Note: Financial information for 2011 was not available for all companies at press time.

2011 Sales: $	2011 Profits: $	**U.S. Stock Ticker:**
2010 Sales: $	2010 Profits: $	**Int'l Ticker: EWEC**
2009 Sales: $	2009 Profits: $	Int'l Exchange: Brussels-Euronext
2008 Sales: $	2008 Profits: $	Employees: 12,000 Fiscal Year Ends: 12/31
2007 Sales: $	2007 Profits: $	Parent Company:

SALARIES/BENEFITS:

Pension Plan:	ESOP Stock Plan:	Profit Sharing:	Top Exec. Salary: $	Bonus: $
Savings Plan:	Stock Purch. Plan:		Second Exec. Salary: $	Bonus: $

OTHER THOUGHTS:

Apparent Women Officers or Directors:
Hot Spot for Advancement for Women/Minorities:

LOCATIONS: ("Y" = Yes)

West:	Southwest:	Midwest:	Southeast:	Northeast:	International: Y

ENERG2

www.energ2.com

Industry Group Code: 541712N

Energy/Fuel:		Other Technologies:		Electrical Products:		Electronics:		Transportation:		Other:	
Biofuels:		Irrigation:		Lighting/LEDs:		Computers:		Car Sharing:		Recycling:	
Batteries/Storage:	Y	Nanotech:	Y	Waste Heat:		Sensors:		Electric Vehicles:		Engineering:	Y
Solar:		Biotech:		Smart Meters:		Software:		Natural Gas Fuel:		Consulting:	
Wind:		Water Tech./Treatment:		Machinery:						Investing:	
Fuel Cells:		Ceramics:								Chemicals:	

TYPES OF BUSINESS:

Energy Storage

BRANDS/DIVISIONS/AFFILIATES:

Firelake Capital Management
Northwest Energy Angels
WRF Capital
Frontier Angel Fund
OVP Venture Partners
Sustainability Investment Fund (The)
University of Washington
Yaletown Venture Partners

CONTACTS: *Note: Officers with more than one job title may be intentionally listed here more than once.*

Eric Luebbe, CEO
Chris Wheaton, COO
Chris Wheaton, CFO
Henry Costantino, VP-R&D
Aaron Feaver, CTO
Phil Souza, VP-Mfg.
Mark Liffmann, VP-Bus. Dev.

Phone: 206-547-0445	Fax: 425-650-7012
Toll-Free:	
Address: 100 N.E. Northlake Way, Seattle, WA 98105 US	

GROWTH PLANS/SPECIAL FEATURES:

EnerG2 develops advanced nano-structured materials for energy storage breakthroughs. The company is currently focused on customizing electrode materials to enhance energy and power density in ultracapacitor, advanced lead-acid batteries and lithium ion chemistries. Ultracapacitors, also known as electric double layer capacitors, are electrochemical capacitors with very high energy density levels. The firm is also developing advanced storage capabilities for hydrogen and methane molecules. EnerG2 utilizes sol-gel processing, a chemical synthesis that gels colloidal suspensions to form solids through heat and catalysts. EnerG2 focuses much of its efforts and attention on three core carbon material groups: monoliths, nano-composites and powders. Monoliths, which are used in methane and natural gas storage systems, are composed of powders in generally solid forms. Nano-Composites, which are essential to hydrogen storage, are created when carbon materials are mixed with chemical and metal hydrides. The firm uses powders in infinitely variable carbon particle sizes in order to make high-performance electrode materials for ultracapacitors. With regard to batteries, an area EnerG2 began applying its technology to in April 2011, the company hopes to be able to extend the life of lead acid batteries for large scale renewable energy power grid usage and utilize its carbons to create more efficient lithium batteries for hybrid cars. EnerG2's investors include WRF Capital, the University of Washington, Frontier Angel Fund, the Sustainability Investment Fund, Yaletown Venture Partners, Firelake Capital Management, Washington Technology Center, OVP Venture Partners and Northwest Energy Angels. In 2010, the firm began construction on a synthetic high-performance carbon electrode material production facility in Albany, Oregon.

FINANCIALS: Sales and profits are in thousands of dollars—add 000 to get the full amount. 2011 Note: Financial information for 2011 was not available for all companies at press time.

2011 Sales: $	2011 Profits: $	**U.S. Stock Ticker: Private**		
2010 Sales: $	2010 Profits: $	**Int'l Ticker:**		
2009 Sales: $	2009 Profits: $	Int'l Exchange:		
2008 Sales: $	2008 Profits: $	Employees:	Fiscal Year Ends:	
2007 Sales: $	2007 Profits: $	Parent Company:		

SALARIES/BENEFITS:

Pension Plan:	ESOP Stock Plan:	Profit Sharing:	Top Exec. Salary: $	Bonus: $
Savings Plan:	Stock Purch. Plan:		Second Exec. Salary: $	Bonus: $

OTHER THOUGHTS:

Apparent Women Officers or Directors:
Hot Spot for Advancement for Women/Minorities:

LOCATIONS: ("Y" = Yes)

West:	Southwest:	Midwest:	Southeast:	Northeast:	International:
Y					

ENERGY CONVERSION DEVICES INC

www.energyconversiondevices.com

Industry Group Code: 334413

Energy/Fuel:		Other Technologies:		Electrical Products:		Electronics:		Transportation:		Other:	
Biofuels:		Irrigation:		Lighting/LEDs:		Computers:		Car Sharing:		Recycling:	
Batteries/Storage:	Y	Nanotech:		Waste Heat:		Sensors:		Electric Vehicles:		Engineering:	
Solar:	Y	Biotech:		Smart Meters:		Software:		Natural Gas Fuel:		Consulting:	
Wind:		Water Tech./Treatment:		Machinery:						Investing:	
Fuel Cells:		Ceramics:								Chemicals:	

TYPES OF BUSINESS:

Solar Energy Technology
Battery Technology
Fuel Cells
Hydrogen Technology

BRANDS/DIVISIONS/AFFILIATES:

United Solar Ovonic LLC
Uni-Solar
Ovonic Battery Company Inc

CONTACTS: Note: Officers with more than one job title may be intentionally listed here more than once.

Julian Hawkins, CEO
Julian Hawkins, Pres.
William C. Andrews, CFO/Exec. VP
Ted F. Amyuni, Exec. VP-Global Sales
Subhendu Guha, Exec. VP-Photovoltaic Tech.
Joe Conroy, Exec. VP-Oper.
Jay B. Knoll, Chief Restructuring Officer/Exec. VP
Stephen Rabinowitz, Chmn.

Phone: 248-475-0100	Fax:
Toll-Free:	
Address: 3800 Lapeer Rd., Auburn Hills, MI 48326 US	

GROWTH PLANS/SPECIAL FEATURES:

Energy Conversion Devices, Inc. (ECD) commercializes materials, products and production processes for the alternative energy generation, energy storage and IT markets. The company operates in two segments: United Solar Ovonic and Ovonic Materials. The United Solar Ovonic segment, which operates primarily through United Solar Ovonic LLC, designs, develops, manufactures and sells photovoltaic (PV) modules. This business is based principally on the proprietary technology for thin-film amorphous silicon PV modules. The PV modules, which the firm markets under the Uni-Solar brand, are lightweight, thin, flexible and durable and can be integrated directly with roofing materials for a seamless appearance. The Ovonic Materials segment, operating primarily through Ovonic Battery Company, Inc. (OBC), invents, designs and develops materials and products based on the firm's materials science technology, principally amorphous and disordered materials. The division currently commercializes nickel metal hydride (NiMH) batteries and Lithium-Ion cathode materials technologies. It is also pursuing technologies in bioreformation, fuel cell and hydrogen storage. ECD manufactures and sells its products through joint venture companies and licensing arrangements with major companies throughout the world. In total, the firm has over 240 U.S. patents. In May 2011, the company opened a new manufacturing facility for its thin-film solar laminates in Ontario, Canada. In July 2011, ECD disclosed plans to divest its OBC subsidiary in order to focus on its United Solar Ovonic business activities. In November 2011, the firm announced that it would temporarily idle all of its manufacturing operations until its existing inventories are exhausted.

The company offers its employees benefits that include a 401(k) plan; medical, vision and dental insurance; life and AD&D insurance; and disability benefits.

FINANCIALS: Sales and profits are in thousands of dollars—add 000 to get the full amount. 2011 Note: Financial information for 2011 was not available for all companies at press time.

2011 Sales: $232,546	2011 Profits: $-302,745	U.S. Stock Ticker: ENER
2010 Sales: $254,416	2010 Profits: $-456,009	Int'l Ticker:
2009 Sales: $316,293	2009 Profits: $8,547	Int'l Exchange:
2008 Sales: $255,861	2008 Profits: $3,853	Employees: 1,300 Fiscal Year Ends: 6/30
2007 Sales: $113,567	2007 Profits: $-25,231	Parent Company:

SALARIES/BENEFITS:

Pension Plan:	ESOP Stock Plan:	Profit Sharing:	Top Exec. Salary: $436,488	Bonus: $
Savings Plan: Y	Stock Purch. Plan:		Second Exec. Salary: $290,160	Bonus: $

OTHER THOUGHTS:

Apparent Women Officers or Directors:
Hot Spot for Advancement for Women/Minorities:

LOCATIONS: ("Y" = Yes)

West:	Southwest:	Midwest:	Southeast:	Northeast:	International:
Y		Y			Y

ENERGY RECOVERY INC

www.energyrecovery.com

Industry Group Code: 924110

Energy/Fuel:	Other Technologies:	Electrical Products:	Electronics:	Transportation:	Other:
Biofuels:	Irrigation:	Lighting/LEDs:	Computers:	Car Sharing:	Recycling:
Batteries/Storage:	Nanotech:	Waste Heat:	Sensors:	Electric Vehicles:	Engineering:
Solar:	Biotech:	Smart Meters:	Software:	Natural Gas Fuel:	Consulting:
Wind:	Water Tech./Treatment: Y	Machinery:			Investing:
Fuel Cells:	Ceramics:				Chemicals:

TYPES OF BUSINESS:

Seawater Desalination Products
Pumps

BRANDS/DIVISIONS/AFFILIATES:

Pump Engineering LLC
Pressure Exchanger
PX
Quadribaric
ERI AquaBold
ERI AquaSpire

CONTACTS: *Note: Officers with more than one job title may be intentionally listed here more than once.*

Thomas S. Rooney, CEO
Thomas S. Rooney, Pres.
Alexander Buehler, CFO
Borja Blanco, Sr. VP-Global Sales & Mktg.
Pierre Vedel, VP-IT
Tim Dyer, CTO
Ismail Nawaz, VP-Oil & Gas Prod. Dev.
Terry Sandlin, VP-Manufacturing
Carolyn Bostick, General Counsel/VP
William Anderson, VP-Oper., Service & Maintenance
Borja Blanco, Sr. VP-Bus. Dev.
Deno Bokas, Chief Acct. Officer
Rodney Clemente, VP-Tech. Svcs.
Imad Al Sharif, VP-Sales, OEM Group
Baji Gobburi, Dir.-Water Prod. Dev.
Audrey Bold, VP-Mktg.
Hans Peter Michelet, Chmn.

Phone: 510-483-7370	**Fax:** 510-483-7371
Toll-Free:	
Address: 1717 Doolittle Dr., San Leandro, CA 94577 US	

GROWTH PLANS/SPECIAL FEATURES:

Energy Recovery, Inc. (ERI) develops, manufactures and sells high-efficiency energy recovery devices for use in the desalination of seawater. The firm's line of Pressure Exchanger (PX) energy recovery devices are designed for use in desalination plants in areas with freshwater shortages, including parts of India, Australia, North Africa and Spain. Desalination has traditionally been an inefficient and expensive approach to converting seawater into fresh water because of the high energy consumption required. ERI's PX devices are designed to reduce energy consumption by capturing and reusing up to 98% of otherwise lost pressure energy from the seawater that is rejected during the desalination process. This improves the energy efficiency of the seawater reverse osmosis (SWRO) process by up to 60%. The operating conditions of its PX devices can also be adjusted to match seasonal changes in seawater salinity and temperature conditions. The company's 7,000 devices active in the desalination market currently save over 900 megawatts of energy and reduce carbon dioxide emissions by 4.6 million tons a year. These devices produce 1.6 billion gallons of potable water each day, enough drinking water for about 25 million people. ERI markets its products under the ERI, PX, PEI, Pressure Exchanger, PX Pressure Exchanger, Pump Engineering and Quadribaric brands. Subsidiary Pump Engineering LLC manufactures centrifugal energy recovery devices (turbochargers) and high pressure pumps. In February 2011, the firm released its new Aqua line of high-pressure desalination pumps, the ERI AquaBold and ERI AquaSpire. In July 2011, ERI disclosed plans to consolidate its North American manufacturing operations, relocating its Michigan operations to the company's production center in San Leandro, California.

ERI offers its employees medical, dental and vision insurance; flexible spending accounts; life and disability insurance; tuition assistance; a 401(k) plan; and company activities such as monthly catered lunches and a softball team.

FINANCIALS: Sales and profits are in thousands of dollars—add 000 to get the full amount. 2011 Note: Financial information for 2011 was not available for all companies at press time.

2011 Sales: $	2011 Profits: $	**U.S. Stock Ticker:** ERII
2010 Sales: $45,853	2010 Profits: $-3,608	**Int'l Ticker:**
2009 Sales: $47,014	2009 Profits: $3,686	Int'l Exchange:
2008 Sales: $52,119	2008 Profits: $8,663	Employees: 129 Fiscal Year Ends: 12/31
2007 Sales: $	2007 Profits: $	Parent Company:

SALARIES/BENEFITS:

Pension Plan:	ESOP Stock Plan:	Profit Sharing:	Top Exec. Salary: $335,153	Bonus: $
Savings Plan: Y	Stock Purch. Plan:		Second Exec. Salary: $280,000	Bonus: $

OTHER THOUGHTS:

Apparent Women Officers or Directors: 3
Hot Spot for Advancement for Women/Minorities: Y

LOCATIONS: ("Y" = Yes)

West:	Southwest:	Midwest:	Southeast:	Northeast:	International:
Y		Y			Y

Sales, profits and employees may be estimates. Financial information, benefits and other data can change quickly and may vary from those stated here.

ENERNOC INC

Industry Group Code: 541690

www.enernoc.com

Energy/Fuel:	Other Technologies:	Electrical Products:	Electronics:		Transportation:		Other:	
Biofuels:	Irrigation:	Lighting/LEDs:	Computers:		Car Sharing:		Recycling:	
Batteries/Storage:	Nanotech:	Waste Heat:	Sensors:		Electric Vehicles:		Engineering:	
Solar:	Biotech:	Smart Meters:	Software:	Y	Natural Gas Fuel:		Consulting:	Y
Wind:	Water Tech./Treatment:	Machinery:					Investing:	
Fuel Cells:	Ceramics:						Chemicals:	

TYPES OF BUSINESS:

Energy Efficiency Technology & Services

BRANDS/DIVISIONS/AFFILIATES:

M2M Communications Corp
Global Energy Partners LLC
PowerTrak
ENERBLOG
PowerTalk
EnergySMART
SiteSMART
SupplySMART

CONTACTS: *Note: Officers with more than one job title may be intentionally listed here more than once.*

Tim Healy, CEO
David Brewster, Pres.
Timothy Weller, CFO
Gregg Dixon, Sr. VP-Mktg. & Sales
Hugh Scandrett, VP-Eng.
Timothy Weller, Treas.
David Samuels, Exec. VP
Tim Healy, Chmn.

Phone: 617-224-9900	**Fax:** 617-224-9910
Toll-Free:	
Address: 101 Federal St., Ste. 1100, Boston, MA 02110 US	

GROWTH PLANS/SPECIAL FEATURES:

EnerNOC, Inc. is a developer and provider of clean energy solutions. The firm uses its network operations center (NOC) to remotely manage and reduce electricity consumption across a network of commercial, institutional and industrial customer sites to enable a more information-based and responsive electric power grid. Its customers are electric power grid operators and utilities, as well as large end-users of electricity. The company has developed a proprietary suite of technology applications and operational processes that enables the ability to make capacity and energy available to grid operators and utilities on demand and remotely manage electricity consumption at commercial and industrial customer sites. These services offer several benefits including reduced environmental impact, value proposition to grid operators and utilities and energy management solutions for end-use customers. Additionally, the firm provides several technology-enabled energy management services to its customers. Advanced metering applications offer meter data gathering and storage services for advanced meters. Building management and energy analytics offer technology-based energy services designed to optimize the way buildings operate, measure the impact of key energy and environmental decisions and enhance the comfort of occupants. The firm's PowerTrak application integrates data from disparate energy management systems with utility metering to gather data on a customer's overall energy usage. Its analysts then use tools, filters and applications to monitor and review this data and provide distilled information and recommendations for performance optimization; energy and carbon emissions reduction; and maintenance prioritizing. The firm's brands include ENERBLOG, PowerTalk, EnergySMART, SiteSMART, SupplySMART and CarbonTrak. In 2011, the firm acquired M2M Communications, a wireless technology solutions provider; and Global Energy, an energy efficiency and demand response program and technology provider.

FINANCIALS: Sales and profits are in thousands of dollars—add 000 to get the full amount. 2011 Note: Financial information for 2011 was not available for all companies at press time.

2011 Sales: $	2011 Profits: $	**U.S. Stock Ticker:** ENOC
2010 Sales: $280,157	2010 Profits: $9,577	**Int'l Ticker:**
2009 Sales: $190,675	2009 Profits: $-6,829	Int'l Exchange:
2008 Sales: $106,115	2008 Profits: $-36,662	Employees: 484 Fiscal Year Ends: 12/31
2007 Sales: $70,242	2007 Profits: $-23,582	Parent Company:

SALARIES/BENEFITS:

Pension Plan:	ESOP Stock Plan:	Profit Sharing:	Top Exec. Salary: $401,538	Bonus: $440,000
Savings Plan:	Stock Purch. Plan:		Second Exec. Salary: $326,250	Bonus: $275,000

OTHER THOUGHTS:

Apparent Women Officers or Directors:
Hot Spot for Advancement for Women/Minorities:

LOCATIONS: ("Y" = Yes)

West:	Southwest:	Midwest:	Southeast:	Northeast:	International:
Y				Y	Y

ENOCEAN

www.enocean.com

Industry Group Code: 335313

Energy/Fuel:	Other Technologies:	Electrical Products:	Electronics:		Transportation:		Other:	
Biofuels:	Irrigation:	Lighting/LEDs:	Computers:		Car Sharing:		Recycling:	
Batteries/Storage:	Nanotech:	Waste Heat:	Sensors:	Y	Electric Vehicles:		Engineering:	
Solar:	Biotech:	Smart Meters:	Software:		Natural Gas Fuel:		Consulting:	
Wind:	Water Tech./Treatment:	Machinery:					Investing:	
Fuel Cells:	Ceramics:						Chemicals:	

TYPES OF BUSINESS:

Wireless Technology

BRANDS/DIVISIONS/AFFILIATES:

EnOcean Dolphin Modules

CONTACTS: *Note: Officers with more than one job title may be intentionally listed here more than once.*

Laurent Giai-Miniet, CEO
Uwe Thumm, CFO
Andreas Schneider, Chief Mktg. Officer
Frank Schmidt, CTO
Armin Anders, VP-Prod. Mgmt.
Norbert Metzner, Dir.-Eng.
Graham Martin, VP-Strategic Alliance
Jim O'Callaghan, Pres., EnOcean, Inc.
Klaus Weltsch, VP-Quality Mgmt. & Mfg.
Samuel Simonsson, Chmn.

Phone: 49-8967-34689-0	Fax: 49-8967-34689-50
Toll-Free:	
Address: Kolpingring 18a, Oberhaching, D-82041 Germany	

GROWTH PLANS/SPECIAL FEATURES:

EnOcean is a self-powered wireless technology firm that manufactures and markets maintenance-free wireless sensor solutions for use in industrial and commercial building installations. By combining miniaturized energy converters, ultra-low power electronic circuitry and reliable wireless solutions, the firm and its affiliated product partners are capable of producing energy harvesting technology, sensors and radio frequency communication for lighting, industrial, building and home automation, automated meter reading and environmental applications. EnOcean Dolphin Modules are the firm's platform energy harvesting wireless sensor technology. The foundation of the module is the EO30001 Dolphin chip, which maintains an energy converter interface and a complete RF transceiver specially designed to complement EnOcean's proprietary short data telegram wireless communication. The modules are used by more than 100 worldwide manufacturers in over 200,000 buildings. Additionally, each module is outfitted with its own individual 32-bit identification number, which allows for the elimination of the potential of overlap with other wireless switches. The firm implements miniaturized energy converters (i.e. linear motion converters, solar cells and thermal converters) instead of batteries in the creation of wireless signals. These signals utilize 868 megahertz (MHz) and 315 MHz frequency bands, which are capable of being transmitted globally. The firm's wireless sensors carry a range of approximately 300 meters outside and up to 30 meters within a building. In February 2011, the firm announced a distribution agreement with Alpha Micro Components to distribute the firm's energy harvesting wireless sensor modules throughout the UK and Ireland.

FINANCIALS: Sales and profits are in thousands of dollars—add 000 to get the full amount. 2011 Note: Financial information for 2011 was not available for all companies at press time.

2011 Sales: $	2011 Profits: $	U.S. Stock Ticker: Private
2010 Sales: $	2010 Profits: $	Int'l Ticker:
2009 Sales: $	2009 Profits: $	Int'l Exchange:
2008 Sales: $	2008 Profits: $	Employees: Fiscal Year Ends:
2007 Sales: $	2007 Profits: $	Parent Company:

SALARIES/BENEFITS:

Pension Plan:	ESOP Stock Plan:	Profit Sharing:	Top Exec. Salary: $	Bonus: $
Savings Plan:	Stock Purch. Plan:		Second Exec. Salary: $	Bonus: $

OTHER THOUGHTS:

Apparent Women Officers or Directors:
Hot Spot for Advancement for Women/Minorities:

LOCATIONS: ("Y" = Yes)

West:	Southwest:	Midwest:	Southeast:	Northeast:	International:
Y				Y	Y

Sales, profits and employees may be estimates. Financial information, benefits and other data can change quickly and may vary from those stated here.

ENOVA SYSTEMS INC

www.enovasystems.com

Industry Group Code: 3363

Energy/Fuel:	Other Technologies:	Electrical Products:	Electronics:	Transportation:	Other:
Biofuels:	Irrigation:	Lighting/LEDs:	Computers:	Car Sharing:	Recycling:
Batteries/Storage:	Nanotech:	Waste Heat:	Sensors:	Electric Vehicles: Y	Engineering: Y
Solar:	Biotech:	Smart Meters:	Software: Y	Natural Gas Fuel:	Consulting:
Wind:	Water Tech./Treatment:	Machinery: Y			Investing:
Fuel Cells:	Ceramics:				Chemicals:

TYPES OF BUSINESS:

Electric Vehicle Systems
Digital Power Management Systems
Engineering Services
Electric, Hybrid & Fuel-Cell Vehicle Components
Drive Systems
Software

BRANDS/DIVISIONS/AFFILIATES:

CONTACTS: Note: Officers with more than one job title may be intentionally listed here more than once.

Mike Staran, CEO
John Mullins, COO
Mike Staran, Pres.
John Micek, CFO
John Micek, Head-Investor Rel.
John R. Wallace, Chmn.

Phone: 310-527-2800	Fax: 310-527-7888
Toll-Free:	
Address: 1560 W. 190th St., Torrance, CA 90501 US	

GROWTH PLANS/SPECIAL FEATURES:

Enova Systems, Inc. develops and manufactures commercial digital power management systems for transportation vehicles and stationary power generation systems. The company's products focus on digital power conversion, power management and system integration. The firm specializes in drive systems and related components for electric, hybrid-electric and fuel cell powered vehicles. Its power management systems control and monitor electric power in automotive or commercial applications, such as in automobiles or stand-alone power generators. Enova's drive systems are composed of an electric motor, an electronics control unit and a gear unit, which can power electric vehicles ranging from light-duty passenger cars to heavy-duty class 8 trucks. Hybrid systems, which are similar to standard electric drive systems, contain an internal combustion engine in addition to the electric motor, eliminating external recharging of the battery system. A hydrogen fuel-cell-based system is similar to a hybrid system, except a fuel cell is used as the power source instead of an internal combustion engine. The company also develops and produces advanced software, firmware and hardware to support its alternative power products. In May 2011, the firm announced its expansion into both the Chinese and European markets.

FINANCIALS: Sales and profits are in thousands of dollars—add 000 to get the full amount. 2011 Note: Financial information for 2011 was not available for all companies at press time.

2011 Sales: $	2011 Profits: $	**U.S. Stock Ticker: ENA**
2010 Sales: $8,572	2010 Profits: $-7,420	**Int'l Ticker:**
2009 Sales: $5,622	2009 Profits: $-7,045	Int'l Exchange:
2008 Sales: $6,443	2008 Profits: $-12,894	Employees: 59 Fiscal Year Ends: 12/31
2007 Sales: $9,175	2007 Profits: $-9,347	Parent Company:

SALARIES/BENEFITS:

Pension Plan:	ESOP Stock Plan:	Profit Sharing:	Top Exec. Salary: $250,000	Bonus: $140,000
Savings Plan: Y	Stock Purch. Plan:		Second Exec. Salary: $185,050	Bonus: $60,000

OTHER THOUGHTS:

Apparent Women Officers or Directors:
Hot Spot for Advancement for Women/Minorities:

LOCATIONS: ("Y" = Yes)

West:	Southwest:	Midwest:	Southeast:	Northeast:	International:
Y					

ENPHASE ENERGY

www.enphase.com

Industry Group Code: 335313

Energy/Fuel:		Other Technologies:		Electrical Products:		Electronics:		Transportation:		Other:	
Biofuels:		Irrigation:		Lighting/LEDs:		Computers:		Car Sharing:		Recycling:	
Batteries/Storage:		Nanotech:		Waste Heat:		Sensors:	Y	Electric Vehicles:		Engineering:	
Solar:	Y	Biotech:		Smart Meters:		Software:	Y	Natural Gas Fuel:		Consulting:	
Wind:		Water Tech./Treatment:		Machinery:						Investing:	
Fuel Cells:		Ceramics:								Chemicals:	

TYPES OF BUSINESS:

Solar Energy Systems

BRANDS/DIVISIONS/AFFILIATES:

D380
M190 & M210
M215
Enphase Envoy Communication Gateway
Enphase Enlighten
Enphase Environ
Enphase Energy SAS
Enphase Energy srl

CONTACTS: *Note: Officers with more than one job title may be intentionally listed here more than once.*

Paul Nahi, CEO
Paul Nahi, Pres.
Sanjeev Kumar, CFO
Bill Rossi, Chief Marketing Officer
Martin Fornage, CTO
Raghu Belur, VP-Prod.
Dennis Hollenbeck, VP-Eng.
Greg Steele, VP-Oper.
Christine Bennett, Mgr.-Public Rel.
Olivier Jacques, Managing Dir.-France
Jeff Loebbaka, VP-Worldwide Sales
Andrew Nichols, VP-American Sales
France Antelme, Sr. Dir.-Prod. Verification
Roberto Colombo, Managing Dir.-Italy

Phone: 877-797-4743	Fax:
Toll-Free:	
Address: 201 1st Ste., Petaluma, CA 94952 US	

GROWTH PLANS/SPECIAL FEATURES:

Enphase Energy is a technology company that develops and produces solar energy systems. The company has four product lines: microinverters; the Enphase Envoy Communication Gateway, a networking hub connecting a solar array's microinverters and modules to the internet; the Enphase Enlighten, a solar power system monitoring software; and the Enphase Environ, a thermostat devise that integrates with the Enphase Enlighten and allows for simultaneous control of the heating and cooling system as well as the solar system. The microinverters are designed for both residential and commercial use and, unlike conventional central inverter devices, connect to each solar panel individually, allowing for said panel to operate individually, thus leading to improvements in energy production. The products within this line are the D380, comprised of two 190 watt microinverters in a single enclosure; the M190 and M210, equipped with a built-in cable making end-to-end connection simple; and the M215, the company's most efficient microinverter. Together these products form the Enphase System which brings new levels of intelligence and connectivity to a solar array. In addition to its U.S. headquarters, Enphase also has operations in France, under Enphase Energy SAS, and Italy, under Enphase Energy srl.

FINANCIALS: Sales and profits are in thousands of dollars—add 000 to get the full amount. 2011 Note: Financial information for 2011 was not available for all companies at press time.

2011 Sales: $	2011 Profits: $	**U.S. Stock Ticker:** Private	
2010 Sales: $	2010 Profits: $	**Int'l Ticker:**	
2009 Sales: $	2009 Profits: $	Int'l Exchange:	
2008 Sales: $	2008 Profits: $	Employees:	Fiscal Year Ends:
2007 Sales: $	2007 Profits: $	Parent Company:	

SALARIES/BENEFITS:

Pension Plan:	ESOP Stock Plan:	Profit Sharing:	Top Exec. Salary: $	Bonus: $
Savings Plan:	Stock Purch. Plan:		Second Exec. Salary: $	Bonus: $

OTHER THOUGHTS:

Apparent Women Officers or Directors: 1
Hot Spot for Advancement for Women/Minorities:

LOCATIONS: ("Y" = Yes)

West:	Southwest:	Midwest:	Southeast:	Northeast:	International:
Y					Y

ENTECH SOLAR INC

www.entechsolar.com

Industry Group Code: 334413

Energy/Fuel:	Other Technologies:	Electrical Products:	Electronics:	Transportation:	Other:
Biofuels:	Irrigation:	Lighting/LEDs:	Computers:	Car Sharing:	Recycling:
Batteries/Storage:	Nanotech:	Waste Heat:	Sensors:	Electric Vehicles:	Engineering:
Solar: Y	Biotech:	Smart Meters:	Software:	Natural Gas Fuel:	Consulting:
Wind:	Water Tech./Treatment:	Machinery:			Investing:
Fuel Cells:	Ceramics:				Chemicals:

TYPES OF BUSINESS:

Photovoltaic Systems
Concentrating Photovoltaic (CPV) Technology
Daylighting Systems

BRANDS/DIVISIONS/AFFILIATES:

Tubular Skylight
ThermaVolt
SolarVolt

CONTACTS: *Note: Officers with more than one job title may be intentionally listed here more than once.*

David Gelbaum, CEO
A.J. McDanal, COO
Shelley Hollingsworth, CFO
Robert Walters, VP-Mktg.
Mark O'Neill, CTO
Doug Williams, VP-Eng. Svcs.
Clay Stevenson, VP-Oper.
David Gelbaum, Chmn.

Phone: 817-224-3600	Fax: 817-224-3601
Toll-Free:	
Address: 13301 Park Vista Blvd., Ste. 100, Fort Worth, TX 76177 US	

GROWTH PLANS/SPECIAL FEATURES:

Entech Solar, Inc. designs, manufactures and installs solar energy systems that provide electricity and thermal energy in commercial and industrial applications as well as in the public sector. The firm develops solar energy products and services utilizing its concentrating photovoltaic (CPV) technology. Products include the ThermaVolt Module, the SolarVolt System and Tubular Skylight. ThermaVolt products are currently being designed as roof- or ground-mounted modules that produce both electricity and thermal energy. The products are comprised of proprietary modules that concentrate sunlight onto solar cells, with the modules deployed on a dual-axis tracking system. Typical system sizes for the ThermaVolt products are expected to be between 50 kilowatts (kW) and 2 megawatts (MW) of electricity. The SolarVolt System is designed to be a roof- or ground-mounted, electricity producing solar system comprised of the company's proprietary air-cooled modules. It is also designed to be deployed on a dual-axis tracking system. SolarVolt technology uses about 95% less silicon material than conventional photovoltaic energy systems. Typical system sizes for these products are expected to range from 1 MW to 10 MW. Tubular Skylight technology is intended to redirect natural light from the sky to the work area beneath the skylight. The company currently focuses on prospective customers in Texas, California, Arizona, New Mexico, Nevada, Utah and Colorado.

FINANCIALS: Sales and profits are in thousands of dollars—add 000 to get the full amount. 2011 Note: Financial information for 2011 was not available for all companies at press time.

2011 Sales: $	2011 Profits: $	**U.S. Stock Ticker: ENSL.OB**
2010 Sales: $ 246	2010 Profits: $-18,280	**Int'l Ticker:**
2009 Sales: $2,192	2009 Profits: $-35,507	Int'l Exchange:
2008 Sales: $30,843	2008 Profits: $-29,343	Employees: 18 Fiscal Year Ends: 12/31
2007 Sales: $18,467	2007 Profits: $-14,385	Parent Company:

SALARIES/BENEFITS:

Pension Plan:	ESOP Stock Plan:	Profit Sharing:	Top Exec. Salary: $206,050	Bonus: $
Savings Plan:	Stock Purch. Plan:		Second Exec. Salary: $146,585	Bonus: $

OTHER THOUGHTS:

Apparent Women Officers or Directors: 1
Hot Spot for Advancement for Women/Minorities:

LOCATIONS: ("Y" = Yes)

West:	Southwest:	Midwest:	Southeast:	Northeast:	International:
	Y				

ESOLAR INC

Industry Group Code: 221119

www.esolar.com

Energy/Fuel:	Other Technologies:	Electrical Products:	Electronics:	Transportation:	Other:
Biofuels:	Irrigation:	Lighting/LEDs:	Computers:	Car Sharing:	Recycling:
Batteries/Storage:	Nanotech:	Waste Heat:	Sensors:	Electric Vehicles:	Engineering:
Solar: Y	Biotech:	Smart Meters:	Software:	Natural Gas Fuel:	Consulting:
Wind:	Water Tech./Treatment:	Machinery:			Investing:
Fuel Cells:	Ceramics:				Chemicals:

TYPES OF BUSINESS:

Thermal Solar Electricity Generation
Concentrating Solar Power (CSP)

BRANDS/DIVISIONS/AFFILIATES:

Idealab
Sierra SunTower
GE Energy

CONTACTS: *Note: Officers with more than one job title may be intentionally listed here more than once.*

John Van Scoter, CEO
John Van Scoter, Pres.
Megan Opp, VP-Mktg. Comm.
Megan Opp, VP-Human Resources
Quoc Pham, VP-Software Dev.
Huy Phan, VP-Prod. Eng.
Carter Moursund, VP-Eng.
Dale Rogers, Sr. VP-Oper.
Quac Pham, VP-Control Systems
Huy Phan, VP-Quality
Dale Rogers, Sr. VP-Projects

Phone: 818-303-9500	Fax: 818-303-9501
Toll-Free: 877-376-5277	
Address: 3355 W. Empire Ave., Ste. 200, Burbank, CA 91504 US	

GROWTH PLANS/SPECIAL FEATURES:

ESolar, Inc. designs and develops Concentrating Solar Power (CSP) scalable power generation units. The firm was founded by Idealab, a venture capital firm focused on developing and operating cutting-edge technology companies. ESolar's CSP technology utilizes a field of mirrors that track the sun and direct sunlight onto a thermal receiver located on a central tower. This thermal energy is used to boil water and produce steam, which then powers traditional steam turbines for electricity generation. Its CSP projects start at 46 megawatts (MW) generation capacity and are scalable up to a 500 MW capacity. A 46 MW power unit takes up approximately 250 acres. ESolar's leading project is Sierra SunTower, located in Lancaster, California, which supplies 5 MW of energy to 4,000 homes through a power purchase agreement with Southern California Edison. Sierra SunTower began commercial operation in recent years. The project's 5 MW output will reduce carbon dioxide emissions by 7,000 tons annually. In 2011, the firm announced an important agreement whereby GE Energy will invest up to $40 million in eSolar. GE plans to use eSolar's technology in its Integrated Solar Combined Cycle (ISCC) power plants.

FINANCIALS: Sales and profits are in thousands of dollars—add 000 to get the full amount. 2011 Note: Financial information for 2011 was not available for all companies at press time.

2011 Sales: $	2011 Profits: $	**U.S. Stock Ticker: Private**
2010 Sales: $	2010 Profits: $	**Int'l Ticker:**
2009 Sales: $	2009 Profits: $	Int'l Exchange:
2008 Sales: $	2008 Profits: $	Employees: Fiscal Year Ends: 12/31
2007 Sales: $	2007 Profits: $	Parent Company:

SALARIES/BENEFITS:

Pension Plan:	ESOP Stock Plan:	Profit Sharing:	Top Exec. Salary: $	Bonus: $
Savings Plan:	Stock Purch. Plan:		Second Exec. Salary: $	Bonus: $

OTHER THOUGHTS:

Apparent Women Officers or Directors: 1
Hot Spot for Advancement for Women/Minorities:

LOCATIONS: ("Y" = Yes)

West:	Southwest:	Midwest:	Southeast:	Northeast:	International:
Y					

E-TON SOLAR TECH CO LTD

www.e-tonsolar.com

Industry Group Code: 334413

Energy/Fuel:	Other Technologies:	Electrical Products:	Electronics:	Transportation:	Other:
Biofuels:	Irrigation:	Lighting/LEDs:	Computers:	Car Sharing:	Recycling:
Batteries/Storage:	Nanotech:	Waste Heat:	Sensors:	Electric Vehicles:	Engineering:
Solar: Y	Biotech:	Smart Meters:	Software:	Natural Gas Fuel:	Consulting:
Wind:	Water Tech./Treatment:	Machinery:			Investing:
Fuel Cells:	Ceramics:				Chemicals:

TYPES OF BUSINESS:

Solar Cell Manufacturing

BRANDS/DIVISIONS/AFFILIATES:

USE18+ Cell

CONTACTS: *Note: Officers with more than one job title may be intentionally listed here more than once.*

Shizhang Wu, CEO
Jiun-Hua Allen Guo, Pres.
Tongqing Zeng, Gen. Mgr.-R&D
Guoshi Liu, Gen. Mgr.-Oper.
Laihuang Luo, Gen. Mgr.-Finance
Shizhang Wu, Chmn.

Phone: 886-6-384-0777	**Fax:** 886-6-384-0872
Toll-Free:	
Address: No. 498, Sec. 2 Bentian Rd. Annan Dist., Tianan, Taiwan	

GROWTH PLANS/SPECIAL FEATURES:

E-TON Solar Tech Co. Ltd. is a Taiwan-based firm engaged in the design and manufacture of solar panels. The company's products, sold under the E-TON brand name, include silicon-based five- and six-inch monocrystalline photovoltaic panels with efficiency ratings ranging from 17.1% to 18.7%. It also markets six-inch multicrystalline cells with a range of 15.7-17.3% efficiency. In addition, the company also offers the USE18+ Cell, which maintains an average energy conversion efficiency of approximately 18%. The firm markets these products both in Taiwan and internationally. E-TON's products are included in installations across the global, including the Gut Erlasse Solar Park in Spain, which is one of the largest solar power plants in the world; and in a roof-mounted installation at London City Hall.

The company offers employees health insurance; yearly health checkups; grants for marriage, birth and new homes; disability coverage; medical loans; and travel subsidies.

FINANCIALS: Sales and profits are in thousands of dollars—add 000 to get the full amount. 2011 Note: Financial information for 2011 was not available for all companies at press time.

2011 Sales: $	2011 Profits: $	**U.S. Stock Ticker:**
2010 Sales: $681,301	2010 Profits: $-8,796	**Int'l Ticker: 3452.TWO**
2009 Sales: $427,700	2009 Profits: $-76,640	Int'l Exchange: Taipei-TPE
2008 Sales: $512,800	2008 Profits: $37,450	Employees: 2,208 Fiscal Year Ends: 12/31
2007 Sales: $179,200	2007 Profits: $26,800	Parent Company:

SALARIES/BENEFITS:

Pension Plan:	ESOP Stock Plan:	Profit Sharing:	Top Exec. Salary: $	Bonus: $
Savings Plan:	Stock Purch. Plan:		Second Exec. Salary: $	Bonus: $

OTHER THOUGHTS:

Apparent Women Officers or Directors:
Hot Spot for Advancement for Women/Minorities:

LOCATIONS: ("Y" = Yes)

West:	Southwest:	Midwest:	Southeast:	Northeast:	International: Y

EVERGREEN ENERGY INC

www.evgenergy.com

Industry Group Code: 324199

Energy/Fuel:	Other Technologies:	Electrical Products:		Electronics:		Transportation:	Other:	
Biofuels:	Irrigation:	Lighting/LEDs:		Computers:		Car Sharing:	Recycling:	
Batteries/Storage:	Nanotech:	Waste Heat:	Y	Sensors:	Y	Electric Vehicles:	Engineering:	Y
Solar:	Biotech:	Smart Meters:		Software:	Y	Natural Gas Fuel:	Consulting:	
Wind:	Water Tech./Treatment:	Machinery:					Investing:	
Fuel Cells:	Ceramics:						Chemicals:	

TYPES OF BUSINESS:

Clean Coal Technology
Coal Production
Research & Engineering
Software development

BRANDS/DIVISIONS/AFFILIATES:

K-Fuel
GreenCert
C-Lock Technology Inc
Evergreen Energy Asia Pacific Corp
KFx Technology LLC

CONTACTS: *Note: Officers with more than one job title may be intentionally listed here more than once.*

Thomas H. Stoner, Jr., CEO
Miles Mahony, COO
Judith Tanselle, Pres.
Diana L. Kubik, CFO/Exec. VP
Michael J. Gionfriddo, CTO
Patrick Kozak, Prod. Dev. & Industry Solutions
Kevin E. Milliman, VP-Eng.
William G. Laughlin, General Counsel/VP/Corp. Sec.
Michael Brennan, Pres., C-Lock Tech./Head-GreenCert Team

Phone: 303-293-2992	Fax: 303-293-8430
Toll-Free:	
Address: 1225 17th St., Ste. 1300, Denver, CO 80202 US	

GROWTH PLANS/SPECIAL FEATURES:

Evergreen Energy, Inc., headquartered in Denver, Colorado, is a cleaner coal technology, energy production and environmental services company that offers combined energy and environmental and economic technologies to coal-fired power generating facilities and industrial coal users in the U.S. and internationally. Its patented technologies include K-Fuel and GreenCert. The firm's proprietary K-Fuel process uses heat and pressure to physically and chemically transform high moisture, low-Btu coals, such as sub-bituminous coal into a more energy efficient, lower emission fuel. This process removes significant amounts of impurities such as mercury and reduces emissions of carbon dioxide, sulfur dioxide and nitrogen oxide. Some K-Fuel facilities are located at coal-fired power generating plants referred to as K-Direct facilities. The GreenCert software suite, provided by the company's subsidiary C-Lock Technology, allows for the tracking and management of carbon emissions, useful in identifying operational efficiency and in the monitoring of emissions for maintenance of environmental standards. The GreenCert division also includes subsidiaries Evergreen Energy Asia Pacific Corp. and KFx Technology, LLC. In March 2011, Evergreen sold the assets of its subsidiary Landrica Development Co., including the Fort Union plant, to Green Bridge Holdings, Inc. In June 2011, the company completed the formation of a joint venture with WPG Resources to develop and commercialize K-Fuel in Australia.

Employment benefits include medical, dental and vision coverage; employee assistance programs; flexible spending accounts; a 401(k) plan; and free use of public transportation.

FINANCIALS: Sales and profits are in thousands of dollars—add 000 to get the full amount. 2011 Note: Financial information for 2011 was not available for all companies at press time.

2011 Sales: $	2011 Profits: $	**U.S. Stock Ticker:** EVEIQ
2010 Sales: $ 403	2010 Profits: $-24,658	**Int'l Ticker:**
2009 Sales: $ 423	2009 Profits: $-58,537	Int'l Exchange:
2008 Sales: $58,901	2008 Profits: $-66,187	Employees: 23 Fiscal Year Ends: 12/31
2007 Sales: $48,657	2007 Profits: $-204,676	Parent Company:

SALARIES/BENEFITS:

Pension Plan:	ESOP Stock Plan:	Profit Sharing:	Top Exec. Salary: $219,231	Bonus: $
Savings Plan: Y	Stock Purch. Plan:		Second Exec. Salary: $185,192	Bonus: $

OTHER THOUGHTS:

Apparent Women Officers or Directors: 2
Hot Spot for Advancement for Women/Minorities:

LOCATIONS: ("Y" = Yes)

West:	Southwest:	Midwest:	Southeast:	Northeast:	International:
Y					

EVERGREEN SOLAR INC

www.evergreensolar.com

Industry Group Code: 334413

Energy/Fuel:	Other Technologies:	Electrical Products:	Electronics:	Transportation:	Other:
Biofuels:	Irrigation:	Lighting/LEDs:	Computers:	Car Sharing:	Recycling:
Batteries/Storage:	Nanotech:	Waste Heat:	Sensors:	Electric Vehicles:	Engineering:
Solar: Y	Biotech:	Smart Meters:	Software:	Natural Gas Fuel:	Consulting:
Wind:	Water Tech./Treatment:	Machinery:			Investing:
Fuel Cells:	Ceramics:				Chemicals:

TYPES OF BUSINESS:
Solar Energy Technology

BRANDS/DIVISIONS/AFFILIATES:
String Ribbon

CONTACTS: Note: Officers with more than one job title may be intentionally listed here more than once.
Michael El-Hillow, CEO
Michael El-Hillow, Pres.
Donald W. Reilly, CFO
Larry Felton, CTO
Carl Stegerwald, VP-Construction Mgmt. & Facilities Eng.
Henry Ng, VP/Gen. Mgr.-China Mfg.
Christian M. Ehrbar, Corp. Sec.
Richard G. Chleboski, VP-Strategy & Bus. Dev.
Edward C. Grady, Chmn.

Phone: 508-357-2221	Fax: 508-229-0747
Toll-Free:	
Address: 138 Bartlett St., Marlboro, MA 01752-3016 US	

GROWTH PLANS/SPECIAL FEATURES:
Evergreen Solar, Inc. develops, manufactures and markets solar power products to the worldwide solar power market. The firm produces wafers, the primary components of photovoltaic (PV) cells used to produce solar panels. Specifically, Evergreen Solar employs its patented String Ribbon technology, which is designed to use significantly less polysilicon than conventional processes, to market solar modules. The primary applications for its products include on-grid generation, in which supplemental electricity is provided to an electric utility grid. The company sells its solar panels using domestic and international distributors, system integrators, project developers and other resellers, who often incorporate its panels with electronics, structures and wiring systems. In January 2011, Evergreen Solar shut down its Devens plant in Massachusetts, laying off 800 workers in the process. Later, in August 2011, the firm filed for bankruptcy protection. While its technology gave the company a cost advantage at one time, falling polysilicon prices and intense competition from China eroded its position dramatically. The firm hopes to reorganize and focus on its China-based, lower-cost manufacturing. In October 2011, it announced plans to auction off assets at its Midland, Michigan, which formerly employed about 40 workers.

FINANCIALS: Sales and profits are in thousands of dollars—add 000 to get the full amount. 2011 Note: Financial information for 2011 was not available for all companies at press time.

2011 Sales: $	2011 Profits: $	U.S. Stock Ticker: ESLRQ
2010 Sales: $338,785	2010 Profits: $-465,437	Int'l Ticker:
2009 Sales: $271,848	2009 Profits: $-266,220	Int'l Exchange:
2008 Sales: $111,959	2008 Profits: $-266,220	Employees: 1,034 Fiscal Year Ends: 12/31
2007 Sales: $69,866	2007 Profits: $-16,602	Parent Company:

SALARIES/BENEFITS:

Pension Plan:	ESOP Stock Plan:	Profit Sharing:	Top Exec. Salary: $500,000	Bonus: $479,991
Savings Plan:	Stock Purch. Plan:		Second Exec. Salary: $338,000	Bonus: $253,500

OTHER THOUGHTS:
Apparent Women Officers or Directors: 1
Hot Spot for Advancement for Women/Minorities:

LOCATIONS: ("Y" = Yes)

West:	Southwest:	Midwest:	Southeast:	Northeast: Y	International: Y

Sales, profits and employees may be estimates. Financial information, benefits and other data can change quickly and may vary from those stated here.

EVO ELECTRIC

www.evo-electric.com

Industry Group Code: 335

Energy/Fuel:	Other Technologies:	Electrical Products:	Electronics:	Transportation:		Other:	
Biofuels:	Irrigation:	Lighting/LEDs:	Computers:	Car Sharing:		Recycling:	
Batteries/Storage:	Nanotech:	Waste Heat:	Sensors:	Electric Vehicles:	Y	Engineering:	Y
Solar:	Biotech:	Smart Meters:	Software:	Natural Gas Fuel:		Consulting:	Y
Wind:	Water Tech./Treatment:	Machinery:				Investing:	
Fuel Cells:	Ceramics:					Chemicals:	

TYPES OF BUSINESS:

Electric Motors
Engineering and Consultancy Services

BRANDS/DIVISIONS/AFFILIATES:

AF-130
AF-230
AFM-140
AFM-240
AFG-140
AFG-240
GKN EVO eDrive Systems

CONTACTS: *Note: Officers with more than one job title may be intentionally listed here more than once.*

David Latimer, CEO
Chris Wolfe, COO
Ivor Thomas, CFO
Michael Lamperth, CTO
Peter Beynon, Dir.-Planning
Peter Beynon, Dir.-Finance
Malte Jaensch, Mgr.-Dev.
Michael Howell, Chmn.

Phone: 44-1483-745-010	**Fax:** 44-1483-770-506
Toll-Free:	
Address: Woking Business Park, Unit 14, Woking, GU21 5JY UK	

GROWTH PLANS/SPECIAL FEATURES:

EVO Electric is a developer and manufacturer of electric motors, generators and integrated drive trains. The firm's products are sold to manufacturers such as Lotus Cars, Nissan and Jaguar Land Rover. EVO divides its operation into four segments: Electric Motors, Electric Generators, Engineering Services and Custom Products. The Electric Motor segment handles the company's Axial Flux Motors. These motors can be configured to operate on various voltage levels and include the AF-130, the AF-230, the AFM-140 and the AFM-240. The Electric Generator segment handles the company's Axial Flux Generators (AFG). Unlike conventional generators, the AFG can operate at low speeds, thus removing the need for a gearbox. The products in this line include the AFG-140 and AFG-240. EVO's Engineering Services offers consultancy and engineering services, including control system design, 3-D mechanical finite element analysis, electronics design and 3-D computational fluid dynamics. The Custom Products division will design and manufacture a product to the exact specifications that a customer requires. In June 2011, EVO announced the formation of a joint venture with GKN Driveline, known as GKN EVO eDrive Systems, aimed at entering the electric and hybrid vehicle systems market. As part of the deal, GKN will acquire a 25.1% stake in EVO.

FINANCIALS: Sales and profits are in thousands of dollars—add 000 to get the full amount. 2011 Note: Financial information for 2011 was not available for all companies at press time.

2011 Sales: $	2011 Profits: $	**U.S. Stock Ticker:** Private	
2010 Sales: $	2010 Profits: $	**Int'l Ticker:**	
2009 Sales: $	2009 Profits: $	Int'l Exchange:	
2008 Sales: $	2008 Profits: $	Employees:	Fiscal Year Ends:
2007 Sales: $	2007 Profits: $	Parent Company:	

SALARIES/BENEFITS:

Pension Plan:	ESOP Stock Plan:	Profit Sharing:	Top Exec. Salary: $	Bonus: $
Savings Plan:	Stock Purch. Plan:		Second Exec. Salary: $	Bonus: $

OTHER THOUGHTS:

Apparent Women Officers or Directors:
Hot Spot for Advancement for Women/Minorities:

LOCATIONS: ("Y" = Yes)

West:	Southwest:	Midwest:	Southeast:	Northeast:	International:
					Y

EVONIK INDUSTRIES AG

www.evonik.com

Industry Group Code: 325

Energy/Fuel:	Other Technologies:	Electrical Products:	Electronics:	Transportation:	Other:	
Biofuels:	Irrigation:	Lighting/LEDs:	Computers:	Car Sharing:	Recycling:	
Batteries/Storage:	Nanotech:	Waste Heat:	Sensors:	Electric Vehicles:	Engineering:	Y
Solar:	Biotech:	Smart Meters:	Software:	Natural Gas Fuel:	Consulting:	
Wind:	Water Tech./Treatment:	Machinery:			Investing:	
Fuel Cells:	Ceramics:				Chemicals:	Y

TYPES OF BUSINESS:

Chemicals, Manufacturing
Industrial Engineering
Electricity Generation
Real Estate
Renewable Energy-Biomass

BRANDS/DIVISIONS/AFFILIATES:

Evonik Degussa
STEAG GmbH
RAG Immobilien
MADAME
2-EHMA
n-BUMA
i-BUMA
Resomer

CONTACTS: *Note: Officers with more than one job title may be intentionally listed here more than once.*

Klaus Engel, CEO
Wolfgang Colberg, CFO
Ralf Blauth, Chief Human Resources Officer
Wilhelm Bonse-Geuking, Chmn.

Phone: 49-201-177-01	Fax: 49-201-177-3475
Toll-Free:	
Address: Rellinghauser Strasse 1-11, Essen, 45128 Germany	

GROWTH PLANS/SPECIAL FEATURES:

Evonik Industries AG is an international industrial group with activities in more than 100 countries worldwide. The firm operates through three primary business areas: chemicals, energy and real estate. The chemicals segment, operating under subsidiary Evonik Degussa GmbH serves the automobile, plastics and rubbers, pharmaceutical, biotechnology, cosmetics, paint and sealants and adhesives industries. This segment has a strong focus on research and development. The energy segment, operating under subsidiary STEAG GmbH, focuses on coal-fired power generation, with capabilities spanning project development, financing, plant construction and operation. Internationally, this segment has power stations in Turkey, Columbia and the Philippines. This segment also offers Clean Competitive Electricity from Coal (CCEC) technology with 45% increased efficiency that is safer and more environment-friendly than conventional power stations. The energy segment is also engaged in renewable energy sources, including biomass, biogas, geothermal and mine gas, maintaining 10 biomass power plants. The real estate segment, operating under subsidiary RAG Immobilien, maintains housing units in Germany, focusing on the Ruhr region, Aachen and the northern Rhine cities of Düsseldorf, Cologne and Bonn. In March 2010, the firm acquired the Methacrylate Specialty Esters operations of Arkema, including the following monomer products: Dimethylaminoethyl Methacrylate (MADAME), 2-Ethylhexyl Methacrylate (2-EHMA) and n-/i-Butyl Methacrylate (n-BUMA and i-BUMA). In March 2011, the firm acquired the Resomer brand and operations from Boehringer Ingelheim.

FINANCIALS: Sales and profits are in thousands of dollars—add 000 to get the full amount. 2011 Note: Financial information for 2011 was not available for all companies at press time.

2011 Sales: $	2011 Profits: $	U.S. Stock Ticker: Private
2010 Sales: $19,184,100	2010 Profits: $1,058,730	Int'l Ticker:
2009 Sales: $16,030,300	2009 Profits: $294,220	Int'l Exchange:
2008 Sales: $21,002,200	2008 Profits: $377,100	Employees: 34,407 Fiscal Year Ends: 12/31
2007 Sales: $19,603,000	2007 Profits: $1,190,040	Parent Company:

SALARIES/BENEFITS:

Pension Plan:	ESOP Stock Plan:	Profit Sharing:	Top Exec. Salary: $	Bonus: $
Savings Plan:	Stock Purch. Plan:		Second Exec. Salary: $	Bonus: $

OTHER THOUGHTS:

Apparent Women Officers or Directors:
Hot Spot for Advancement for Women/Minorities:

LOCATIONS: ("Y" = Yes)

West:	Southwest:	Midwest:	Southeast:	Northeast:	International:
					Y

Sales, profits and employees may be estimates. Financial information, benefits and other data can change quickly and may vary from those stated here.

EXIDE TECHNOLOGIES

www.exide.com

Industry Group Code: 33591

Energy/Fuel:	Other Technologies:	Electrical Products:	Electronics:	Transportation:	Other:
Biofuels:	Irrigation:	Lighting/LEDs:	Computers:	Car Sharing:	Recycling:
Batteries/Storage: Y	Nanotech:	Waste Heat:	Sensors:	Electric Vehicles:	Engineering:
Solar:	Biotech:	Smart Meters:	Software:	Natural Gas Fuel:	Consulting:
Wind:	Water Tech./Treatment:	Machinery:			Investing:
Fuel Cells:	Ceramics:				Chemicals:

TYPES OF BUSINESS:

Automotive Battery Technology
Rechargeable Battery Technology
Battery Recycling
Backup Power Solutions

BRANDS/DIVISIONS/AFFILIATES:

Centra
DETA
Exide
Exide Extreme
Exide NASCAR Select
Orbital
Fulmen
Tudor

CONTACTS: *Note: Officers with more than one job title may be intentionally listed here more than once.*

James R. Bolch, CEO
James R. Bolch, Pres.
Phillip A. Damaska, CFO/Exec. VP
Edward Tetreault, Exec. VP-Human Resources
Paul Cheeseman, VP-Research
Paul Cheeseman, VP-Global Eng.
Barbara A. Hatcher, General Counsel/Exec. VP
Bruce A. Cole, Exec. VP-Bus. Dev. & Strategy
Nicholas J. Iuanow, Treas./VP
Paul Hirt, Pres., Exide Americas
Michael Ostermann, Pres., Exide Europe
Gary Reinert, VP-Strategic Planning & Bus. Dev.
Dean A. Rossi, VP-Global Environment, Health & Safety
John P. Reilly, Chmn.
Luke Lu, Pres., Asia Pacific

Phone: 678-566-9000	Fax: 678-566-9188
Toll-Free:	
Address: 13000 Deerfield Pkwy., Bldg. 200, Milton, GA 30004 US	

GROWTH PLANS/SPECIAL FEATURES:

Exide Technologies is a global provider of stored electrical energy solutions and a manufacturer, supplier and recycler of lead acid batteries for transportation and industrial applications. The company, which maintains operations in over 80 countries, does business through four geographically-based segments: Transportation Americas; Transportation Europe and Rest of World (ROW); Industrial Energy Americas; and Industrial Energy Europe and ROW. The firm's Transportation segments primarily market ignition and lighting batteries for cars, trucks, off-road vehicles, agricultural and construction vehicles, motorcycles, recreational vehicles, marine and other applications. In addition to standard vehicle batteries, Exide Technologies produces Micro-hybrids and lead-acid batteries used on Full Electrical Vehicles. These products are marketed to the original equipment and aftermarket automotive, heavy-duty truck, agricultural and marine industries. Battery brands include Centra, DETA, Exide, Exide Extreme, Exide NASCAR Select, Orbital, Fulmen and Tudor. In North America, its 80 transportation branches also collect spent batteries, which are recycled at its five recycling centers. The Transportation segments account for approximately 65% of the company's annual sales. The firm's Industrial Energy segments supply both motive power and network power solutions. Motive power batteries are used to power electric forklift trucks, floor cleaning machinery, powered wheelchairs, railroad locomotives, mining and electric road vehicles and other vehicles; network power batteries are used for back-up power applications in telecommunications systems, electric utilities, railroads and photovoltaic and uninterruptible power supplies (UPS). The Industrial Energy segments account for approximately 35% of annual sales.

FINANCIALS: Sales and profits are in thousands of dollars—add 000 to get the full amount. 2011 Note: Financial information for 2011 was not available for all companies at press time.

2011 Sales: $2,887,516	2011 Profits: $26,443	U.S. Stock Ticker: XIDE
2010 Sales: $2,685,808	2010 Profits: $-11,814	Int'l Ticker:
2009 Sales: $3,322,332	2009 Profits: $-69,522	Int'l Exchange:
2008 Sales: $3,696,671	2008 Profits: $32,059	Employees: 10,027 Fiscal Year Ends: 3/31
2007 Sales: $2,939,785	2007 Profits: $-105,879	Parent Company:

SALARIES/BENEFITS:

Pension Plan: Y	ESOP Stock Plan:	Profit Sharing:	Top Exec. Salary: $583,013	Bonus: $3,119,356
Savings Plan:	Stock Purch. Plan:		Second Exec. Salary: $419,279	Bonus: $300,000

OTHER THOUGHTS:

Apparent Women Officers or Directors: 1
Hot Spot for Advancement for Women/Minorities:

LOCATIONS: ("Y" = Yes)

West:	Southwest:	Midwest:	Southeast:	Northeast:	International:
Y	Y	Y	Y	Y	Y

EXXON MOBIL CORPORATION (EXXONMOBIL)

www.exxonmobil.com

Industry Group Code: 211111

Energy/Fuel:		Other Technologies:	Electrical Products:	Electronics:	Transportation:	Other:	
Biofuels:	Y	Irrigation:	Lighting/LEDs:	Computers:	Car Sharing:	Recycling:	
Batteries/Storage:		Nanotech:	Waste Heat:	Sensors:	Electric Vehicles:	Engineering:	
Solar:		Biotech:	Smart Meters:	Software:	Natural Gas Fuel:	Consulting:	
Wind:		Water Tech./Treatment:	Machinery:			Investing:	
Fuel Cells:		Ceramics:				Chemicals:	Y

TYPES OF BUSINESS:

Oil & Gas Exploration & Production
Gas Refining & Supply
Fuel Marketing
Power Generation
Chemicals
Petroleum Products
Convenience Stores

BRANDS/DIVISIONS/AFFILIATES:

ExxonMobil Chemical
XTO Energy Inc
ExxonMobil
Esso
Exxon
Mobil

CONTACTS: Note: Officers with more than one job title may be intentionally listed here more than once.

Rex W. Tillerson, CEO
L.J. Cavanaugh, VP-Human Resources
S. Jack Balagia, General Counsel/VP
W.M. Colton, VP-Corp. Strategic Planning
K.P. Cohen, VP-Public & Gov't Affairs
David S. Rosenthal, VP-Investor Rel./Sec.
Donald D. Humphreys, Treas./Sr. VP
Andrew P. Swiger, Sr. VP
P.T. Mulva, Controller/VP
Mark W. Albers, Sr. VP
Suzanne M/ McCarron, Pres., ExxonMobil Foundation
Rex W. Tillerson, Chmn.

Phone: 972-444-1000	**Fax:** 972-444-1505
Toll-Free: 800-252-1800	
Address: 5959 Las Colinas Blvd., Irving, TX 75039-2298 US	

GROWTH PLANS/SPECIAL FEATURES:

Exxon Mobil Corporation (ExxonMobil) is one of the largest international petroleum and natural gas exploration and production companies in the world. Its principal business is energy, involving exploration for and production of crude oil and natural gas; manufacture of petroleum products; and transportation and sale of crude oil, natural gas and petroleum products. Overall, the firm has 10 global business units organized into three areas: Upstream, Downstream and Chemical. The Upstream business focuses on conventional, heavy oil, shale gas, deepwater, liquefied natural gas (LNG), Arctic and sour gas projects. The Downstream business is concerned with refining crude oil and other feedstocks into fuels, lubricants and other chemicals and delivering it to customers through a global distributor network. The Downstream unit also markets its products through about 26,000 retail service stations and three business-to-business segments, Industrial and Wholesale, Aviation and Marine. The Chemical business is focused on the production of olefins, such as ethylene and propylene, and polyolefins, such as polyethylene and polypropylene. In addition, it manufactures specialty chemicals for use in water treatment, coatings, lubricants and oil drilling fluids. As of late 2010, ExxonMobil had proved reserves of 8.9 billion barrels of liquids (including crude, condensate and natural gas liquids); 2.1 billion barrels of bitumen; 681 million barrels of synthetic oil; 78.8 trillion cubic feet of natural gas; and 24.8 billion barrels of oil-equivalent. The company held 14.8 million net acres, of which 2.2 million net acres were offshore. The company has hundreds of affiliates, many with names that include ExxonMobil, Esso, Exxon or Mobil. In June 2010, ExxonMobil acquired XTO Energy, Inc., a U.S.-based oil and gas producer. In August 2011, the company completed the sale of its 65% stake in Esso Malaysia Berhad (EMB), ExxonMobil Malaysia Sdn Bhd and ExxonMobil Borneo Sdn Bhd to San Miguel Corporation.

FINANCIALS: Sales and profits are in thousands of dollars—add 000 to get the full amount. 2011 Note: Financial information for 2011 was not available for all companies at press time.

2011 Sales: $	2011 Profits: $	**U.S. Stock Ticker: XOM**
2010 Sales: $370,125,000	2010 Profits: $30,460,000	**Int'l Ticker:**
2009 Sales: $301,500,000	2009 Profits: $19,280,000	Int'l Exchange:
2008 Sales: $459,579,000	2008 Profits: $45,220,000	Employees: 83,600 Fiscal Year Ends: 12/31
2007 Sales: $390,328,000	2007 Profits: $40,610,000	Parent Company:

SALARIES/BENEFITS:

Pension Plan:	ESOP Stock Plan:	Profit Sharing:	Top Exec. Salary: $2,207,000	Bonus: $3,360,000
Savings Plan:	Stock Purch. Plan:		Second Exec. Salary: $1,085,000	Bonus: $2,144,000

OTHER THOUGHTS:

Apparent Women Officers or Directors: 2
Hot Spot for Advancement for Women/Minorities: Y

LOCATIONS: ("Y" = Yes)

West:	Southwest:	Midwest:	Southeast:	Northeast:	International:
Y	Y	Y	Y	Y	Y

EXXONMOBIL CHEMICAL

www.exxonmobilchemical.com

Industry Group Code: 325110

Energy/Fuel:	Other Technologies:		Electrical Products:	Electronics:	Transportation:	Other:	
Biofuels:	Irrigation:		Lighting/LEDs:	Computers:	Car Sharing:	Recycling:	
Batteries/Storage:	Nanotech:		Waste Heat:	Sensors:	Electric Vehicles:	Engineering:	
Solar:	Biotech:	Y	Smart Meters:	Software:	Natural Gas Fuel:	Consulting:	
Wind:	Water Tech./Treatment:		Machinery:			Investing:	
Fuel Cells:	Ceramics:					Chemicals:	Y

TYPES OF BUSINESS:

Plastics & Rubber Manufacturing
Petrochemicals
Catalyst Technology
Polypropylene

BRANDS/DIVISIONS/AFFILIATES:

Univation Technologies, LLC
Shaw Group (The)
XyMax
PxMax
Exxon Mobil Corporation (ExxonMobil)
Dow Chemical Company (The)
SpectraSyn Elite

CONTACTS: Note: Officers with more than one job title may be intentionally listed here more than once.

Stephen D. Pryor, Pres.
Robert Davis, VP-Global Tech.
Bruce Macklin, Sr. VP-Global Oper.

Phone: 281-870-6000	Fax: 281-870-6661
Toll-Free:	
Address: 13501 Katy Freeway, Houston, TX 77079-1398 US	

GROWTH PLANS/SPECIAL FEATURES:

ExxonMobil Chemical, a division of Exxon Mobil Corporation, is one of the world's largest petrochemical companies, manufacturing and marketing olefins, aromatics, fluids, synthetic rubber, polyethylene, polypropylene, oriented polypropylene packaging films, plasticizers, synthetic lubricant base-stocks, additives for fuels and lubricants, zeolite catalysts and other petrochemical products. The division has manufacturing locations in roughly 18 countries and markets products in more than 150 countries. ExxonMobil Chemical is one of the only major olefins producer with proprietary pyrolysis-reactor technology, which delivers the highest olefin yields in the industry. The unit's XyMax and PxMax aromatics utilize proprietary zeolite shape-selective catalyst technology. This technology increases conversion and reduces losses versus other technologies in the production of higher olefins. Univation Technologies, LLC, a joint venture company owned by ExxonMobil Chemical and Dow Chemical Co., has developed the UNIPOL PE Process for manufacturing linear low density polyethylene and high density polyethelene. The joint venture also furnishes catalysts for metallocene and bimodal resins. Badger Licensing, LLC, a joint venture with The Shaw Group, licenses alkylation technologies. In 2010, the company and Qatar Petroleum announced plans to build a large petrochemical facility in Ras Laffan Industrial City, Qatar, to take advantage of natural gas resources in the area. In May 2010, ExxonMobil Chemical released a new high-performance, high-viscosity metallocene polyalphaolefin under the brand name SpectraSyn Elite.

FINANCIALS: Sales and profits are in thousands of dollars—add 000 to get the full amount. 2011 Note: Financial information for 2011 was not available for all companies at press time.

2011 Sales: $	2011 Profits: $	U.S. Stock Ticker: Subsidiary
2010 Sales: $25,891,000	2010 Profits: $4,913,000	Int'l Ticker:
2009 Sales: $24,825,000	2009 Profits: $2,309,000	Int'l Exchange:
2008 Sales: $24,982,000	2008 Profits: $2,957,000	Employees: 31,000 Fiscal Year Ends: 12/31
2007 Sales: $27,480,000	2007 Profits: $4,563,000	Parent Company: EXXON MOBIL CORPORATION (EXXONMOBIL)

SALARIES/BENEFITS:

Pension Plan:	ESOP Stock Plan:	Profit Sharing:	Top Exec. Salary: $	Bonus: $
Savings Plan:	Stock Purch. Plan:		Second Exec. Salary: $	Bonus: $

OTHER THOUGHTS:

Apparent Women Officers or Directors:
Hot Spot for Advancement for Women/Minorities:

LOCATIONS: ("Y" = Yes)

West:	Southwest:	Midwest:	Southeast:	Northeast:	International:
	Y				Y

Sales, profits and employees may be estimates. Financial information, benefits and other data can change quickly and may vary from those stated here.

FILTERBOXX

www.filterboxx.com

Industry Group Code: 924110

Energy/Fuel:	Other Technologies:		Electrical Products:	Electronics:	Transportation:	Other:
Biofuels:	Irrigation:		Lighting/LEDs:	Computers:	Car Sharing:	Recycling:
Batteries/Storage:	Nanotech:		Waste Heat:	Sensors:	Electric Vehicles:	Engineering:
Solar:	Biotech:		Smart Meters:	Software:	Natural Gas Fuel:	Consulting:
Wind:	Water Tech./Treatment:	Y	Machinery:			Investing:
Fuel Cells:	Ceramics:					Chemicals:

TYPES OF BUSINESS:

Water & Wastewater Treatment

BRANDS/DIVISIONS/AFFILIATES:

FilterBoxx Packaged Water Solutions Inc
Combo Energy Services
FilterBoxx C Series

CONTACTS: *Note: Officers with more than one job title may be intentionally listed here more than once.*

Bill Jones, COO
Lawrence (Larry) Novachis, Pres.
Dave MacDonell, Dir.-Sales, Western Canada & USA
Bill Jones, VP-Oper.
Keith Davison, Sr. Mgr.-Acct.
Brian Flannigan, VP-Chemical Systems
Roland Lamoca, Dir.-Sales, Eastern Canada & USA
Renee Beaucage, Inside Sales Coordinator
John Coburn, Chmn.

Phone: 403-203-4747	**Fax:** 403-203-4774
Toll-Free: 877-868-4747	
Address: 5716 Burbank Rd. SE, Calgary, Alberta T2H 1Z4 Canada	

GROWTH PLANS/SPECIAL FEATURES:

FilterBoxx is a designer and manufacturer of modular water and wastewater treatment package plant systems. The firm implements its proprietary technologies to provide water treatment solutions to its industrial, municipal, resort and aboriginal customer base. FilterBoxx additionally operates in the niche market of harsh and remote settings. The company's offerings include water treatment for drinking water; wastewater-sewage treatment; produced water, processed water and industrial wastewater; and rental/lease/service operations. Through subsidiary FilterBoxx Packaged Water Solutions Inc., the firm fully designs and builds skid mounted and/or containerized S series and C series portable, packaged water and wastewater facilities that are custom built to the client's specifications. Each design has the added benefits of high loading rates, small carbon footprints, lower building costs and the capability of being fitted for remote monitoring. Subsidiary Combo Energy Services offers customers turnkey installation, rental and operation services for all of the firm's manufactured products. Its base camp and rig rental fleets feature wastewater treatment plants that are capable of servicing anywhere from 20 to 300 people. The proprietary Rig Combo and Camp Combo utility support systems feature a wastewater treatment plant, water distribution, two generators and yard lights. Additionally, the Rig Combo features bathrooms, an industrial washing machine, an eye wash station and a safety shower. In July 2011, the firm launched its new FilterBoxx C Series compact wastewater treatment plant, equipped with advanced reinforced hollow fiber membrane treatment systems. The firm maintains facilities throughout Canada, the United States and in Afghanistan.

FINANCIALS: Sales and profits are in thousands of dollars—add 000 to get the full amount. 2011 Note: Financial information for 2011 was not available for all companies at press time.

2011 Sales: $	2011 Profits: $	**U.S. Stock Ticker: Private**
2010 Sales: $	2010 Profits: $	**Int'l Ticker:**
2009 Sales: $	2009 Profits: $	Int'l Exchange:
2008 Sales: $	2008 Profits: $	Employees: Fiscal Year Ends:
2007 Sales: $	2007 Profits: $	Parent Company:

SALARIES/BENEFITS:

Pension Plan:	ESOP Stock Plan:	Profit Sharing:	Top Exec. Salary: $	Bonus: $
Savings Plan:	Stock Purch. Plan:		Second Exec. Salary: $	Bonus: $

OTHER THOUGHTS:

Apparent Women Officers or Directors: 2
Hot Spot for Advancement for Women/Minorities:

LOCATIONS: ("Y" = Yes)

West:	Southwest:	Midwest:	Southeast:	Northeast:	International: Y

FIRST SOLAR INC

www.firstsolar.com

Industry Group Code: 334413

Energy/Fuel:	Other Technologies:	Electrical Products:	Electronics:	Transportation:	Other:
Biofuels:	Irrigation:	Lighting/LEDs:	Computers:	Car Sharing:	Recycling:
Batteries/Storage:	Nanotech:	Waste Heat:	Sensors:	Electric Vehicles:	Engineering:
Solar: Y	Biotech:	Smart Meters:	Software:	Natural Gas Fuel:	Consulting:
Wind:	Water Tech./Treatment:	Machinery:			Investing:
Fuel Cells:	Ceramics:				Chemicals:

TYPES OF BUSINESS:

Photovoltaic Equipment
Thin-Film Solar Modules
Solar Module Collection & Recycling
Photovoltaic Site Operation & Maintenance
Solar Project Engineering, Procurement & Construction
Project Development & Financing

BRANDS/DIVISIONS/AFFILIATES:

RayTracker Inc

CONTACTS: Note: Officers with more than one job title may be intentionally listed here more than once.

Michael J. Ahearn, Interim CEO
Mark Widmar, CFO
Carol Campbell, Exec. VP-Human Resources
David Eaglesham, CTO
Mary Beth Gustafsson, Exec. VP-General Counsel/Sec.
James G. Brown, Pres., Global Bus. Dev.
Maja Wessels, Exec. VP-Global Public Affairs
James Zhu, Chief Acct. Officer
TK Kallenbach, Pres., Components Bus.
Christopher Burghardt, Head of Sales-Europe
Michael J. Ahearn, Chmn.

Phone: 602-414-9300	Fax: 602-414-9400
Toll-Free:	
Address: 350 W. Washington St., Ste. 600, Tempe, AZ 85281 US	

GROWTH PLANS/SPECIAL FEATURES:

First Solar, Inc. develops and manufactures thin-film solar modules based on its proprietary thin-film semiconductor technology and designs, constructs and sells photovoltaic (PV) solar power systems. The firm has 36 production lines that cumulatively have produced 5 GW, or 66 million solar modules, supplying clean electricity to 2.5 million homes. The firm's single-junction polycrystalline thin-film technology utilizes cadmium telluride as the absorption layer, allowing the company to use about 99% less semiconductor material than traditional crystalline silicon modules. The solar modules have dimensions of approximately two feet by four feet, with an average power rating of around 76 watts. First Solar's PV solar power systems business includes: project development; engineering, procurement and construction services; solar site operation and maintenance activities; and project financing. The firm also maintains a collection and recycling program for used solar modules, maximizing the recovery of valuable materials by being able to retain approximately 90% of the original module. First Solar has manufacturing centers worldwide, including plants in Ohio, Malaysia, France and Germany. The company's projects are primarily focused in the North American, European and Asian markets. In January 2011, FirstSolar acquired RayTracker, Inc, a tracking technology and PV balance-of-systems firm. In the same month, it began collaborating with China Guangdong Nuclear Solar Energy Development Co. to develop a solar PV plant in Ordos, Inner Mongolia. In August 2011, the company sold its 290 MW Agua Caliente solar project to NGR Energy, Inc. In September 2011, FirstSolar sold its 230 MW PV Antelope Valley Solar Ranch One project to Exelon Corp. In October 2011, Solar Chile and FirstSolar established a joint venture to co-develop projects throughout Chile. In December 2011, the firm sold its 550 MW PV Topaz Solar Farm power plant to MidAmerican Energy Holding Co.

FINANCIALS: Sales and profits are in thousands of dollars—add 000 to get the full amount. 2011 Note: Financial information for 2011 was not available for all companies at press time.

2011 Sales: $	2011 Profits: $	U.S. Stock Ticker: FSLR
2010 Sales: $2,563,515	2010 Profits: $664,201	Int'l Ticker:
2009 Sales: $2,066,200	2009 Profits: $640,138	Int'l Exchange:
2008 Sales: $1,246,301	2008 Profits: $348,330	Employees: 6,100 Fiscal Year Ends: 12/31
2007 Sales: $503,976	2007 Profits: $158,354	Parent Company:

SALARIES/BENEFITS:

Pension Plan:	ESOP Stock Plan:	Profit Sharing:	Top Exec. Salary: $850,000	Bonus: $2,510,352
Savings Plan:	Stock Purch. Plan:		Second Exec. Salary: $555,000	Bonus: $10,160

OTHER THOUGHTS:

Apparent Women Officers or Directors: 3
Hot Spot for Advancement for Women/Minorities: Y

LOCATIONS: ("Y" = Yes)

West:	Southwest:	Midwest:	Southeast:	Northeast:	International:
Y	Y	Y		Y	Y

Sales, profits and employees may be estimates. Financial information, benefits and other data can change quickly and may vary from those stated here.

FISKER AUTOMOTIVE

www.fiskerautomotive.com

Industry Group Code: 33611

Energy/Fuel:	Other Technologies:	Electrical Products:	Electronics:	Transportation:		Other:
Biofuels:	Irrigation:	Lighting/LEDs:	Computers:	Car Sharing:		Recycling:
Batteries/Storage:	Nanotech:	Waste Heat:	Sensors:	Electric Vehicles:	Y	Engineering:
Solar:	Biotech:	Smart Meters:	Software:	Natural Gas Fuel:		Consulting:
Wind:	Water Tech./Treatment:	Machinery:				Investing:
Fuel Cells:	Ceramics:					Chemicals:

TYPES OF BUSINESS:

Automobile Manufacturing--Electric
Electric Sports Cars
Plug-in Hybrids (PHEVs)

BRANDS/DIVISIONS/AFFILIATES:

Fisker Coachbuild LLC
Quantum Fuel Systems Technologies Worldwide Inc
Karma

CONTACTS: Note: Officers with more than one job title may be intentionally listed here more than once.

Henrik Fisker, CEO
Bernhard Koehler, COO
Marti Eulberg, VP-Global Mktg. & Sales
Russell Datz, Dir.-Public Rel.

Phone: 714-888-4255	Fax: 949-757-4230
Toll-Free:	
Address: 19 Corporate Park, Irvine, CA 92606 US	

GROWTH PLANS/SPECIAL FEATURES:

Fisker Automotive, a joint venture between Fisker Coachbuild LLC and Quantum Fuel Systems Technologies Worldwide, Inc., is a California-based car company that designs, markets and manufactures premium plug-in hybrid automobiles. The company's flagship vehicle, the Karma sedan, is powered by Quantum Technologies' Q-DRIVE technology, which features an electric engine powered by a battery pack, with a gasoline engine supplying backup power. The Karma features two driving modes: Stealth and Sport. The Stealth Drive mode is optimized for efficiency, and the Sport Drive mode delivers the car's full spectrum of power. The car, while achieving an estimated 100 mpg, has the capability of accelerating from 0-60 mph in six seconds and a top speed of 125 mph. The car features a low center of gravity for optimal sport vehicle driving dynamics and regenerative brakes to recapture braking energy. The Karma will be offered in four door sedan and convertible models with pricing to start at $87,900. The company hopes initial production is to be 15,000 vehicles annually. Thirty-two retailers have agreed to carry the vehicles. The firm's mid-term plan is to introduce a $50,000 automobile by 2014. Fisker outsources all possible manufacturing and design tasks. Manufacturing is contracted out to Valmet Automotive, located in Finland, which is the same plant that assembles Porsche's Boxster and Cayman cars. In recent years, the company received a $528.7 million low-interest loan from the Department of Energy program. The $25 billion program is to fund development of alternative vehicles. The company plans to use $169.3 million to finish the production of its Karma sedan. It also plans to develop its next-generation vehicle that would cost $47,400 and would be built in the U.S. In mid 2010, the firm bought a former GM factory in Wilmington, Delaware. In December 2010, China Grand Automotive Group agreed to distribute, market and service Fisker Automotive vehicles.

FINANCIALS: Sales and profits are in thousands of dollars—add 000 to get the full amount. 2011 Note: Financial information for 2011 was not available for all companies at press time.

2011 Sales: $	2011 Profits: $	**U.S. Stock Ticker: Joint Venture**
2010 Sales: $	2010 Profits: $	**Int'l Ticker:**
2009 Sales: $	2009 Profits: $	Int'l Exchange:
2008 Sales: $	2008 Profits: $	Employees: 150 Fiscal Year Ends:
2007 Sales: $	2007 Profits: $	Parent Company: QUANTUM FUEL SYSTEMS TECHNOLOGIES WORLDWIDE INC

SALARIES/BENEFITS:

Pension Plan:	ESOP Stock Plan:	Profit Sharing:	Top Exec. Salary: $	Bonus: $
Savings Plan:	Stock Purch. Plan:		Second Exec. Salary: $	Bonus: $

OTHER THOUGHTS:

Apparent Women Officers or Directors:
Hot Spot for Advancement for Women/Minorities:

LOCATIONS: ("Y" = Yes)

West:	Southwest:	Midwest:	Southeast:	Northeast:	International:
Y					

FUELCELL ENERGY INC
www.fuelcellenergy.com

Industry Group Code: 335999

Energy/Fuel:	Other Technologies:	Electrical Products:	Electronics:	Transportation:	Other:
Biofuels:	Irrigation:	Lighting/LEDs:	Computers:	Car Sharing:	Recycling:
Batteries/Storage:	Nanotech:	Waste Heat:	Sensors:	Electric Vehicles:	Engineering:
Solar:	Biotech:	Smart Meters:	Software:	Natural Gas Fuel:	Consulting:
Wind:	Water Tech./Treatment:	Machinery:			Investing:
Fuel Cells: Y	Ceramics:				Chemicals:

TYPES OF BUSINESS:
Fuel Cell Technology

BRANDS/DIVISIONS/AFFILIATES:
Direct FuelCell
DFC300
DFC1500
DFC3000
DFC-ERG

CONTACTS: *Note: Officers with more than one job title may be intentionally listed here more than once.*
Chip Bottone, CEO
Anthony F. Rauseo, COO/Sr. VP
Chip Bottone, Pres.
Michael Bishop, CFO/Sr. VP
Michael Bishop, Corp. Sec.
Michael Bishop, Treas.
John A. Rolls, Chmn.

Phone: 203-825-6000 **Fax:**
Toll-Free:
Address: 3 Great Pasture Rd., Danbury, CT 06813 US

GROWTH PLANS/SPECIAL FEATURES:
FuelCell Energy, Inc. develops and manufactures fuel cell power plants for ultra-clean, efficient and reliable electric power generation. Its products have generated over 650 million kWh of electricity and are operating at over 50 locations worldwide. The firm's patented carbonate fuel cells, Direct FuelCell (aka DFC Power Plants), are utilized for stationary power generation. FuelCell also develops both carbonate and planar solid oxide fuel cells. These products offer the advantages of near-zero levels of pollutants, quiet operation and reduced levels of carbon emissions. The company works to meet the power requirements of a diverse mix of customers, including manufacturers, utilities, corrections facilities, hospitals, universities and food processors, among others. The firm has three core power plant models: the DFC300, DFC1500 and DFC3000, rated at 300 kilowatts (kW), 1.4 megawatts (MW) and 2.8 MW, respectively. Its latest product is the DFC-ERG (Energy Recovery Generation) plant. With an electrical efficiency of 65%, it utilizes energy normally lost at pressure transformers in major natural gas lines to generate electricity. Fuelcell has worked on the further development of its fuel cell technology with agencies such as the U.S. Departments of Energy and Defense, the Defense Advance Research Projects Agency, the EPA and NASA. The company's products are in use in South Korea, California, Connecticut and Canada. In May 2011, the company announced a $129 million order for 70 MW of fuel cell kits and other equipment and services to POSCO Power. In December 2011, FuelCell announced a partnership agreement with Abengoa S.A. to develop fuel cell power plants in Europe and Latin America.

FINANCIALS: Sales and profits are in thousands of dollars—add 000 to get the full amount. 2011 Note: Financial information for 2011 was not available for all companies at press time.
2011 Sales: $122,600	2011 Profits: $-45,700	**U.S. Stock Ticker:** FCEL
2010 Sales: $69,777	2010 Profits: $-56,235	**Int'l Ticker:**
2009 Sales: $88,016	2009 Profits: $-68,674	Int'l Exchange:
2008 Sales: $100,735	2008 Profits: $-93,357	Employees: 441 Fiscal Year Ends: 10/31
2007 Sales: $48,234	2007 Profits: $-68,674	Parent Company:

SALARIES/BENEFITS:
Pension Plan:	ESOP Stock Plan:	Profit Sharing:	Top Exec. Salary: $386,005	Bonus: $
Savings Plan:	Stock Purch. Plan:		Second Exec. Salary: $278,493	Bonus: $

OTHER THOUGHTS:
Apparent Women Officers or Directors:
Hot Spot for Advancement for Women/Minorities:

LOCATIONS: ("Y" = Yes)
West:	Southwest:	Midwest:	Southeast:	Northeast:	International:
Y				Y	Y

Sales, profits and employees may be estimates. Financial information, benefits and other data can change quickly and may vary from those stated here.

FUJITSU LABORATORIES LTD

jp.fujitsu.com/group/labs/en

Industry Group Code: 541712

Energy/Fuel:	Other Technologies:	Electrical Products:	Electronics:		Transportation:	Other:	
Biofuels:	Irrigation:	Lighting/LEDs:	Computers:	Y	Car Sharing:	Recycling:	
Batteries/Storage:	Nanotech:	Waste Heat:	Sensors:		Electric Vehicles:	Engineering:	Y
Solar:	Biotech:	Smart Meters:	Software:	Y	Natural Gas Fuel:	Consulting:	
Wind:	Water Tech./Treatment:	Machinery:				Investing:	
Fuel Cells:	Ceramics:					Chemicals:	

TYPES OF BUSINESS:

Research & Development
Computing Research
RFID Technology
Semiconductors
Security & Encryption Technology
Robotics Research
Nanotechnology Research

BRANDS/DIVISIONS/AFFILIATES:

Fujitsu Limited

CONTACTS: *Note: Officers with more than one job title may be intentionally listed here more than once.*

Tatsuo Tomita, Pres.
Kazuo Ishida, Corp. Exec. Sr. VP/Dir.
Masami Fujita, Corp. Sr. Exec. VP/Dir.
Kazuhiko Kato, Corp. Exec. VP/Dir.
Michiyoshi Mazuka, Chmn.

Phone: 81-44-754-2613	**Fax:**
Toll-Free:	
Address: 4-1-1, Kamikodanaka, Nakahara-ku, Kawasaki-shi, 211-8588 Japan	

GROWTH PLANS/SPECIAL FEATURES:

Fujitsu Laboratories, Ltd. is Fujitsu Limited's central research and development unit. Fujitsu Lab's stated goal is to make ubiquitous networking a reality, meaning that communication would be possible anytime, anywhere and with anyone. To this end, the firm divides its research into four target areas. The Enabling a More Comfortable Society area is developing organic computer systems that can link multiple magnetic disk drives, connect servers and storage systems autonomously to allow fast access to large quantities of data, and, in the future, possibly repair themselves. Other research in this area includes grid computing; utility computing; business system optimization; semiconductor technology; high-density data storage; advanced CAD (Computer-Aided Design) and VPS (Virtual Product Simulator) systems for product development; and System-on-a-Chip (SoC) technologies. The Communicating Anytime, Anywhere area is developing wireless data exchange technology and services, such as wireless IC RFID (Radio Frequency Identification) tags, which could display product information while shopping and make payments automatically; optical transmission and photonic networking technologies; high-precision radio positioning technology; and nanotechnology. The Supporting Safe and Secure Lifestyles area is researching cryptography and biometric authentication technology; digital watermarking and steganography (hidden information) to help prevent information leakage; environmentally friendly materials; System-in-Package technology, used to make smaller and more reliable LSI (Large-Scale Integration) devices; and bioinformatics, computer technologies used in health-related fields to obtain, analyze and visualize data. Lastly, the Making Interfaces Effortless area is researching bipedal robots featuring neural networks for domestic chores or security details; natural language processors to allow computers or robots to understand voice commands; data compression technologies; and advanced I/O (input/output) devices, such as electronic paper displays and an ultrasonic handwriting pen that requires no special pad. In May 2010, the firm opened a research facility in Singapore.

FINANCIALS: Sales and profits are in thousands of dollars—add 000 to get the full amount. 2011 Note: Financial information for 2011 was not available for all companies at press time.

2011 Sales: $	2011 Profits: $	**U.S. Stock Ticker: Subsidiary**
2010 Sales: $	2010 Profits: $	**Int'l Ticker:**
2009 Sales: $	2009 Profits: $	Int'l Exchange:
2008 Sales: $	2008 Profits: $	Employees: Fiscal Year Ends: 3/31
2007 Sales: $	2007 Profits: $	Parent Company: FUJITSU LIMITED

SALARIES/BENEFITS:

Pension Plan:	ESOP Stock Plan:	Profit Sharing:	Top Exec. Salary: $	Bonus: $
Savings Plan:	Stock Purch. Plan:		Second Exec. Salary: $	Bonus: $

OTHER THOUGHTS:

Apparent Women Officers or Directors:
Hot Spot for Advancement for Women/Minorities:

LOCATIONS: ("Y" = Yes)

West:	Southwest:	Midwest:	Southeast:	Northeast:	International:
Y	Y				Y

GAMESA CORPORACION TECNOLOGICA SA   www.gamesa.es

Industry Group Code: 33361

Energy/Fuel:	Other Technologies:	Electrical Products:	Electronics:	Transportation:	Other:
Biofuels:	Irrigation:	Lighting/LEDs:	Computers:	Car Sharing:	Recycling:
Batteries/Storage:	Nanotech:	Waste Heat:	Sensors:	Electric Vehicles:	Engineering:
Solar:	Biotech:	Smart Meters:	Software:	Natural Gas Fuel:	Consulting:
Wind: Y	Water Tech./Treatment:	Machinery:			Investing:
Fuel Cells:	Ceramics:				Chemicals:

TYPES OF BUSINESS:

Wind Turbine Manufacturing
Wind Farms
Solar Facilities, Development & Maintenance

BRANDS/DIVISIONS/AFFILIATES:

Gamesa Energia
Gamesa Eolica

CONTACTS: *Note: Officers with more than one job title may be intentionally listed here more than once.*

Inigo Gimenez, COO
Jorge Calvet Spinatsch, Pres.
Juana Maria Fernandez, Managing Dir.-Human Resources
Jose Antonio Malumbres, Managing Dir.-Tech.
Jose Antonio Cortajarena, Sec.
Ricardo Chocarro, Managing Dir.-Oper.
David Mesonero, Dir.-Bus. Dev.
Amalia Blanco, Gen. Mgr.-Comm. & External Rel.
Juan Ramon Inarritu, Managing Dir.-Management Control
Inigo Cisneros, Managing Dir.-Legal Svcs.
Javier Perea, Managing Dir.-Offshore
Jeronimo Camacho, Managing Dir.-Institutional Rel.
Jorge Calvet Spinatsch, Chmn.
Jose Antonio Miranda, CEO-China

Phone: 90-2-73-4949	Fax:
Toll-Free:	
Address: Ramon Y Cajal 7-9, Vitoria-Gasteiz, ALV 01013 Spain	

GROWTH PLANS/SPECIAL FEATURES:

Gamesa Corporacion Tecnologica S.A., based in Spain, manufactures and supplies products, installations and services in the renewable energy sectors. More than 50% of installed wind power capacity in Spain is supplied by Gamesa wind generations. The company has installations of around 23,000 megawatts (MW) spanning 30 countries, which amounts to over 5 million tons of petroleum (TPE) per year and prevents the emission of CO2 into the air annually by 31 million tons. Gamesa Energia is charged with the development, construction, operation and sale of wind farms. Gamesa Eolica is one of the top wind turbine manufacturers in the world. In January 2011, the firm announced the sale of its Piecki wind farm to RWE Innogy and HSE Regenerativ. In March 2011, Gamesa announced that it had begun construction on its new office buildings in Sarriguren, Navarre. In April 2011, the firm announced that it had opened a technology lab for advanced material research in Singapore. In May 2011, Gamesa announced that it had agreed to sale its Pelplin wind farm to PGE Energia Odnawialna (PGE EO). In June 2011, the firm announced the sale of its Catalonia wind farm to Greentech Energy Systems. In July 2011, Gamesa and Iberdrola Ingenieria installed the first wind turbine in Honduras; additionally, Gamesa announced the sale of two Greek wind farms to Enel Green Power. In September 2011, the firm announced the sale of a Polish wind farm to PGE EO. In November 2011, Gamesa announced the sale of its Pennsylvanian wind farm to enXco.

FINANCIALS: Sales and profits are in thousands of dollars—add 000 to get the full amount. 2011 Note: Financial information for 2011 was not available for all companies at press time.

2011 Sales: $	2011 Profits: $	**U.S. Stock Ticker:**
2010 Sales: $3,953,240	2010 Profits: $72,540	**Int'l Ticker: GAM**
2009 Sales: $4,397,020	2009 Profits: $154,810	Int'l Exchange: Madrid-MCE
2008 Sales: $4,857,800	2008 Profits: $429,220	Employees: 6,918 Fiscal Year Ends: 12/31
2007 Sales: $3,819,760	2007 Profits: $297,070	Parent Company:

SALARIES/BENEFITS:

Pension Plan:	ESOP Stock Plan:	Profit Sharing:	Top Exec. Salary: $	Bonus: $
Savings Plan:	Stock Purch. Plan:		Second Exec. Salary: $	Bonus: $

OTHER THOUGHTS:

Apparent Women Officers or Directors: 3
Hot Spot for Advancement for Women/Minorities: Y

LOCATIONS: ("Y" = Yes)

West:	Southwest:	Midwest:	Southeast:	Northeast:	International:
				Y	Y

GE ENERGY INFRASTRUCTURE

www.gepower.com

Industry Group Code: 335

Energy/Fuel:	Other Technologies:	Electrical Products:	Electronics:		Transportation:		Other:	
Biofuels:	Irrigation:	Lighting/LEDs:	Computers:		Car Sharing:		Recycling:	
Batteries/Storage:	Nanotech:	Waste Heat:	Sensors:		Electric Vehicles:		Engineering:	
Solar:	Biotech:	Smart Meters:	Software:	Y	Natural Gas Fuel:		Consulting:	
Wind:	Water Tech./Treatment:	Machinery: Y					Investing:	
Fuel Cells:	Ceramics:						Chemicals:	

TYPES OF BUSINESS:

Generation Equipment-Turbines & Generators
Water Processing Technologies and Products
Generators-Wind, Hydro, Geothermal & Turbo
Nuclear Fuel Systems
Pumps & Pipelines
Metering & Control Systems
Energy Management Systems
Consulting-Energy

BRANDS/DIVISIONS/AFFILIATES:

General Electric Co (GE)
GE Energy Services
GE Power & Water
GE Oil & Gas

CONTACTS: *Note: Officers with more than one job title may be intentionally listed here more than once.*

John Krenicki, Jr., CEO
John Krenicki, Jr., Pres.
Daniel Janki, CFO
James Suciu, Pres., Global Sales & Mktg.
Daniel C. Heintzelman, Pres./CEO-Energy Svcs.
Claudi Santiago, Pres./CEO-Oil & Gas
Kishore Hayaraman, Pres./CEO-India

Phone: 678-844-6000	**Fax:** 678-844-6690
Toll-Free:	
Address: 4200 Wildwood Pkwy., Atlanta, GA 30339 US	

GROWTH PLANS/SPECIAL FEATURES:

GE Energy Infrastructure, a subsidiary of the General Electric Co. (GE), designs and supplies energy technology. The division, which accounts for roughly 25% of GE's total revenues, operates in three segments: Energy Services, Oil & Gas and Power & Water. The Energy Services segment serves power generation, industrial, government and other customers worldwide with products and services related to energy production, distribution and management. The firm is a leading provider of Integrated Gasification Combined Cycle (IGCC) technology design and development. IGCC systems convert coal and other hydrocarbons into synthetic gas that is used as the primary fuel for gas turbines in combined-cycle systems. The segment sells steam turbines and generators to the electric utility industry and to private industrial customers for cogeneration applications. Nuclear reactors, fuel and support services for both new and installed boiling water reactors are offered through joint ventures with Hitachi and Toshiba. The Oil & Gas segment designs and manufactures surface and subsea drilling and production systems; equipment for floating production platforms; compressors; turbines; turboexpanders; high pressure reactors; industrial power generation; and a broad portfolio of ancillary equipment. The segment also provides services relating to installing and maintaining this equipment. The Power & Water division designs and manufactures motors and control systems used in industrial applications primarily for oil and gas extraction and mining. Its renewable energy portfolio offers wind turbines solar technology. In addition, it offers water treatment solutions for industrial and municipal water systems including the supply and related services of specialty chemicals, water purification systems, pumps, valves, filters and fluid handling equipment for improving the performance of water, wastewater and process systems, including mobile treatment systems and desalination processes. The segment also sells aircraft engine derivatives for use as industrial power sources. In March 2011, the firm acquired Lineage Power Holdings, Inc.

FINANCIALS: Sales and profits are in thousands of dollars—add 000 to get the full amount. 2011 Note: Financial information for 2011 was not available for all companies at press time.

2011 Sales: $	2011 Profits: $	**U.S. Stock Ticker: Subsidiary**
2010 Sales: $37,514,000	2010 Profits: $7,271,000	**Int'l Ticker:**
2009 Sales: $37,134,000	2009 Profits: $6,842,000	Int'l Exchange:
2008 Sales: $38,570,000	2008 Profits: $6,080,000	Employees: 82,000 Fiscal Year Ends: 12/31
2007 Sales: $30,698,000	2007 Profits: $4,817,000	Parent Company: GENERAL ELECTRIC CO (GE)

SALARIES/BENEFITS:

Pension Plan:	ESOP Stock Plan:	Profit Sharing:	Top Exec. Salary: $	Bonus: $
Savings Plan: Y	Stock Purch. Plan:		Second Exec. Salary: $	Bonus: $

OTHER THOUGHTS:

Apparent Women Officers or Directors:
Hot Spot for Advancement for Women/Minorities:

LOCATIONS: ("Y" = Yes)

West:	Southwest:	Midwest:	Southeast:	Northeast:	International:
Y	Y	Y	Y	Y	Y

GE GLOBAL RESEARCH

www.ge.com/research

Industry Group Code: 541712

Energy/Fuel:	Other Technologies:	Electrical Products:	Electronics:		Transportation:	Other:	
Biofuels:	Irrigation:	Lighting/LEDs:	Computers:		Car Sharing:	Recycling:	
Batteries/Storage:	Nanotech:	Waste Heat:	Sensors:		Electric Vehicles:	Engineering:	Y
Solar:	Biotech:	Smart Meters:	Software:	Y	Natural Gas Fuel:	Consulting:	
Wind:	Water Tech./Treatment:	Machinery:				Investing:	
Fuel Cells:	Ceramics:					Chemicals:	

TYPES OF BUSINESS:

Research & Development
Nuclear & Fossil Fuel Energy Technology
Wind, Solar, Hydroelectric & Biomass Technology
Fuel Cell & Energy Storage Technology
Nanotechnology
Photonics & Optoelectronics
Engine Technology
Biotechnology

BRANDS/DIVISIONS/AFFILIATES:

General Electric Co (GE)

CONTACTS: Note: Officers with more than one job title may be intentionally listed here more than once.

Todd Alhart, Dir.-Comm. & Public Rel.
Mark M. Little, Sr. VP

Phone: 518-387-5000	Fax: 518-387-6696
Toll-Free:	
Address: 1 Research Cir., Niskayuna, NY 12309 US	

GROWTH PLANS/SPECIAL FEATURES:

GE Global Research (GEGR) is the research and development arm of the General Electric Company. GEGR employs over 2,800 researchers at four multi-disciplinary facilities in the U.S., India, China and Germany. The company has advanced technology programs in energy, nanotechnology, photonics, advanced propulsion, materials and biotechnology. Energy research is devoted to both nuclear and fossil-fueled power and a large variety of alternative generation techniques. Renewable energies currently being investigated include photovoltaic, wind, biomass gasification, hydroelectric and various hydrogen technologies that include fuel cells and storage systems. The firm's core nanotechnologies include nanotubes, nanowires, nanocomposites, nano-structured optoelectronics and biomimetics. In photonics, GE researchers are developing optoelectronic materials, photonic devices, optoelectronic integration and signal management and architecture. GEGR strives to revolutionize the plastics and lighting business through the development of light-emitting polymers, photovoltaic polymers, flexible electronics and low-cost processing. The firm's energy and propulsion division is working to design engines with superior power and speed through pulsed detonation phenomenon; pulsed detonation engine configurations; fuel preparation and delivery; performance and flight mission analysis; and proof-of-concept engines. The company also has materials research centers on ceramic composites, thermal barriers, superalloys and optical and luminescent materials, which are the company's trademark. GEGR's biosciences operations are focused on molecular medicine, clinical diagnostics and therapeutics, pharmaceutical development and bioinformatics. The firm is also researching solutions for port and cargo security using a wireless container security device.

FINANCIALS: Sales and profits are in thousands of dollars—add 000 to get the full amount. 2011 Note: Financial information for 2011 was not available for all companies at press time.

2011 Sales: $	2011 Profits: $	U.S. Stock Ticker: Subsidiary
2010 Sales: $	2010 Profits: $	Int'l Ticker:
2009 Sales: $	2009 Profits: $	Int'l Exchange:
2008 Sales: $	2008 Profits: $	Employees: 2,800 Fiscal Year Ends: 12/31
2007 Sales: $	2007 Profits: $	Parent Company: GENERAL ELECTRIC CO (GE)

SALARIES/BENEFITS:

Pension Plan:	ESOP Stock Plan:	Profit Sharing:	Top Exec. Salary: $	Bonus: $
Savings Plan:	Stock Purch. Plan:		Second Exec. Salary: $	Bonus: $

OTHER THOUGHTS:

Apparent Women Officers or Directors:
Hot Spot for Advancement for Women/Minorities:

LOCATIONS: ("Y" = Yes)

West:	Southwest:	Midwest:	Southeast:	Northeast:	International:
				Y	Y

Sales, profits and employees may be estimates. Financial information, benefits and other data can change quickly and may vary from those stated here.

GENERAL COMPRESSION

www.generalcompression.com

Industry Group Code: 335

Energy/Fuel:		Other Technologies:		Electrical Products:		Electronics:		Transportation:		Other:	
Biofuels:		Irrigation:		Lighting/LEDs:		Computers:		Car Sharing:		Recycling:	
Batteries/Storage:	Y	Nanotech:		Waste Heat:		Sensors:		Electric Vehicles:		Engineering:	
Solar:		Biotech:		Smart Meters:		Software:		Natural Gas Fuel:		Consulting:	
Wind:	Y	Water Tech./Treatment:		Machinery:						Investing:	
Fuel Cells:		Ceramics:								Chemicals:	

TYPES OF BUSINESS:

Wind Energy Storage

GROWTH PLANS/SPECIAL FEATURES:

General Compression is a wind farm development company. The firm builds dispatchable wind farms designed to deliver renewable electricity to customers on demand, addressing the issue of intermittency within the wind power industry. The firm's Advanced Energy Storage system utilizes intermittent electricity from conventional wind turbines and stores it as high-pressure air inside underground geologic formations. Electricity may then be created on demand when air is released from the storage areas. The firm maintains partnerships with major energy firms ConocoPhillips, Duke Energy, U.S. Renewables Group and Northwater. It has received funding from firms including U.S. Renewables Group, Northwater Capital Management, Duke Energy and Serious Change L.P. It has also received backing from the U.S. Department of Energy's Advanced Research Project Agency–Energy (ARPA-E) program.

BRANDS/DIVISIONS/AFFILIATES:

U.S. Renewables Group
Northwater Capital Management
Duke Energy
Serious Change LP
Advanced Research Project Agency-Energy

CONTACTS: Note: Officers with more than one job title may be intentionally listed here more than once.

Eric Ingersoll, CEO
Patrick Moran, COO
David Marcus, Pres.
Michael Marcus, Exec. VP

Phone: 617-559-9999	Fax:
Toll-Free:	
Address: 275 Washington St., Newton, MA 02458 US	

FINANCIALS: Sales and profits are in thousands of dollars—add 000 to get the full amount. 2011 Note: Financial information for 2011 was not available for all companies at press time.

2011 Sales: $	2011 Profits: $	U.S. Stock Ticker: Private
2010 Sales: $	2010 Profits: $	Int'l Ticker:
2009 Sales: $	2009 Profits: $	Int'l Exchange:
2008 Sales: $	2008 Profits: $	Employees: Fiscal Year Ends:
2007 Sales: $	2007 Profits: $	Parent Company:

SALARIES/BENEFITS:

Pension Plan:	ESOP Stock Plan:	Profit Sharing:	Top Exec. Salary: $	Bonus: $
Savings Plan:	Stock Purch. Plan:		Second Exec. Salary: $	Bonus: $

OTHER THOUGHTS:

Apparent Women Officers or Directors:
Hot Spot for Advancement for Women/Minorities:

LOCATIONS: ("Y" = Yes)

West:	Southwest:	Midwest:	Southeast:	Northeast: Y	International:

GENERAL MOTORS COMPANY (GM)   www.gm.com

Industry Group Code: 33611

Energy/Fuel:	Other Technologies:	Electrical Products:	Electronics:	Transportation:		Other:
Biofuels:	Irrigation:	Lighting/LEDs:	Computers:	Car Sharing:		Recycling:
Batteries/Storage:	Nanotech:	Waste Heat:	Sensors:	Electric Vehicles:	Y	Engineering:
Solar:	Biotech:	Smart Meters:	Software:	Natural Gas Fuel:		Consulting:
Wind:	Water Tech./Treatment:	Machinery:				Investing:
Fuel Cells:	Ceramics:					Chemicals:

TYPES OF BUSINESS:

Automobile Manufacturing
Security & Information Services
Automotive Electronics
Financing & Insurance
Parts & Service
Transmissions
Engines
Locomotives

BRANDS/DIVISIONS/AFFILIATES:

Chevrolet
Buick
Cadillac
GMC
Opel
AmeriCredit Corp.
FinanciaLinx Corporation
General Motors Financial Company Inc

CONTACTS: *Note: Officers with more than one job title may be intentionally listed here more than once.*

Daniel F. Akerson, CEO
Daniel Ammann, CFO/Sr. VP
Joel Ewanick, Global Chief Mktg. Officer/VP
Cynthia J. Brinkley, VP-Global Human Resources
Terry Kline, CIO/VP-IT
Thomas G. Stephens, Global CTO/Vice Chmn.
Mary T. Barra, Sr. VP-Global Prod. Dev.
Michael P. Millikin, General Counsel/Sr. VP
Stephen J. Girsky, Vice Chmn.-Bus. Dev. & Corp. Strategy
Selim Bingol, VP-Global Comm.
Nick S. Cyprus, Chief Acct. Officer/Controller/VP
Jaime Ardila, Pres., GM South America
Mark L. Reuss, Pres., North America
David N. Reilly, Pres., GM Europe
Robert E. Ferguson, VP-Global Public Policy
Daniel F. Akerson, Chmn.
Timothy E. Lee, Pres., GM Int'l Oper.
Stephen J. Girsky, Vice Chmn.-Global Purchasing & Supply Chain

Phone: 313- 556-5000	Fax:
Toll-Free:	
Address: 300 Renaissance Ctr., Detroit, MI 48265-3000 US	

GROWTH PLANS/SPECIAL FEATURES:

General Motors Company (GM), formerly General Motors Corp., is engaged in the worldwide development, production and marketing of cars, trucks, automotive systems and locomotives. The firm's major North American brands include Chevrolet, Buick, Cadillac and GMC. Besides its North American brands, GM markets vehicles internationally under the following brands: Opel, Vauxhall, Daewoo, Isuzu and Holden. GM is organized into four geographically-based segments: General Motors North America (GMNA), which generated 31% of 2010 vehicle sales; General Motors International Operations (GMIO), 37% (more than two-thirds of which originated in China); General Motors Europe (GME), 20%; and General Motors South America (GMSA), 12%. Recently, the firm emerged from bankruptcy after shedding $79 billion in existing debt, while receiving $30 billion in additional government funding. The U.S. government controls a 26.5% stake in the company. In 2010, GM sold its Saab division to Spyker Cars NV; and completed the wind down of its Pontiac, Saturn and HUMMER brands. In October 2010, in an effort to return to the auto lending business, the firm acquired loan provider AmeriCredit Corp. for $3.5 billion. Following the acquisition, the company was renamed General Motors Financial Company, Inc. (GM Financial). In November 2010, after undergoing an extensive restructuring, the firm completed an IPO. In January 2011, subsidiary GM Daewoo announced it would change its name to GM Korea and begin selling most of its cars under the Chevrolet brand. In April 2011, GM Financial acquired FinanciaLinx Corporation, a leading independent auto leasing company in Canada. In September 2011, GM completed the construction of a new $200 million dollar diesel engine factory in Thailand.

FINANCIALS: Sales and profits are in thousands of dollars—add 000 to get the full amount. 2011 Note: Financial information for 2011 was not available for all companies at press time.

2011 Sales: $	2011 Profits: $	U.S. Stock Ticker: GM
2010 Sales: $135,592,000	2010 Profits: $6,503,000	Int'l Ticker:
2009 Sales: $104,589,000	2009 Profits: $104,690,000	Int'l Exchange:
2008 Sales: $148,979,000	2008 Profits: $-30,860,000	Employees: 202,000 Fiscal Year Ends: 12/31
2007 Sales: $179,984,000	2007 Profits: $-38,732,000	Parent Company:

SALARIES/BENEFITS:

Pension Plan: Y	ESOP Stock Plan:	Profit Sharing:	Top Exec. Salary: $1,133,333	Bonus: $
Savings Plan: Y	Stock Purch. Plan: Y		Second Exec. Salary: $900,000	Bonus: $

OTHER THOUGHTS:

Apparent Women Officers or Directors: 8
Hot Spot for Advancement for Women/Minorities: Y

LOCATIONS: ("Y" = Yes)

West:	Southwest:	Midwest:	Southeast:	Northeast:	International:
Y	Y	Y	Y	Y	Y

Sales, profits and employees may be estimates. Financial information, benefits and other data can change quickly and may vary from those stated here.

GENOMATICA

www.genomatica.com

Industry Group Code: 325

Energy/Fuel:	Other Technologies:	Electrical Products:	Electronics:	Transportation:	Other:	
Biofuels:	Irrigation:	Lighting/LEDs:	Computers:	Car Sharing:	Recycling:	
Batteries/Storage:	Nanotech:	Waste Heat:	Sensors:	Electric Vehicles:	Engineering:	
Solar:	Biotech:	Smart Meters:	Software:	Natural Gas Fuel:	Consulting:	
Wind:	Water Tech./Treatment:	Machinery:			Investing:	
Fuel Cells:	Ceramics:				Chemicals:	Y

TYPES OF BUSINESS:

Intermediate and Basic Chemicals

BRANDS/DIVISIONS/AFFILIATES:

CONTACTS: *Note: Officers with more than one job title may be intentionally listed here more than once.*

Christophe Schilling, CEO
Michael E. Keane, CFO/Exec. VP
Steve Weiss, Head-Mktg.
Tina Jones, VP-Human Resources
Nelson Barton, VP-R&D
Mark Burk, CTO/Exec. VP
Joseph P. Kuterbach, VP-Oper.
William H. Baum, Chief Business Development Officer
Ilene Adler, Head-Media Contact
Damien A. Perriman, VP-Bus. Dev.
Mary Susan Howard, VP-Intellectual Property
William H. Baum, Chmn.

Phone: 858-824-1771	Fax: 858-824-1772
Toll-Free:	
Address: 10520 Wateridge Circle, San Diego, CA 92121 US	

GROWTH PLANS/SPECIAL FEATURES:

Genomatica is a biotechnology company that develops manufacturing processes that produce intermediate and basic chemicals from renewable feedstock. The firm designs it manufacturing processes to have a smaller environmental footprint than petroleum-based processes and to deliver enhanced economics with better sustainability. Using its proprietary biotechnology platform the firm is able to produce the same chemicals in use today, but from renewable feedstock. Some of the chemicals produced by Genomatica's biotechnology platform are butanediol (BDO), an intermediate chemical used in products like running shoes and automotive applications; and butadiene, a basic chemical used in items as diverse as tire rubber and carpeting. The renewable feedstock that the firm incorporates into its processes includes waste, biomass and sugar. The company plans to have its first commercial-scale BDO plant in production in 2013. In January 2012, Genomatica announced the formation of a joint venture with Novamont SpA in Adria, Italy. Novamont will hold the majority share in the new company.

FINANCIALS: Sales and profits are in thousands of dollars—add 000 to get the full amount. 2011 Note: Financial information for 2011 was not available for all companies at press time.

2011 Sales: $	2011 Profits: $	**U.S. Stock Ticker: Private**
2010 Sales: $	2010 Profits: $	**Int'l Ticker:**
2009 Sales: $	2009 Profits: $	Int'l Exchange:
2008 Sales: $	2008 Profits: $	Employees: Fiscal Year Ends:
2007 Sales: $	2007 Profits: $	Parent Company:

SALARIES/BENEFITS:

Pension Plan:	ESOP Stock Plan:	Profit Sharing:	Top Exec. Salary: $	Bonus: $
Savings Plan:	Stock Purch. Plan:		Second Exec. Salary: $	Bonus: $

OTHER THOUGHTS:

Apparent Women Officers or Directors: 3
Hot Spot for Advancement for Women/Minorities: Y

LOCATIONS: ("Y" = Yes)

West:	Southwest:	Midwest:	Southeast:	Northeast:	International:
Y					Y

GEODYNAMICS LTD

www.geodynamics.com

Industry Group Code: 333

Energy/Fuel:	Other Technologies:	Electrical Products:		Electronics:	Transportation:	Other:	
Biofuels:	Irrigation:	Lighting/LEDs:		Computers:	Car Sharing:	Recycling:	
Batteries/Storage:	Nanotech:	Waste Heat:	Y	Sensors:	Electric Vehicles:	Engineering:	Y
Solar:	Biotech:	Smart Meters:		Software:	Natural Gas Fuel:	Consulting:	
Wind:	Water Tech./Treatment:	Machinery:				Investing:	
Fuel Cells:	Ceramics:					Chemicals:	

TYPES OF BUSINESS:

Geothermal Energy Technology

BRANDS/DIVISIONS/AFFILIATES:

Origin Energy

CONTACTS: Note: Officers with more than one job title may be intentionally listed here more than once.

Geoff Ward, CEO
Tim Pritchard, CFO
Alistair Webb, Mgr.-Commercial
Kevin Coates, Mgr.-People
Doone Wyborn, Chief Scientist
Amy Hodson, Mgr.-Tech.
Amy Hodson, Mgr.-Well Eng.
Paul Frederiks, Sec.
Meredith Bird, Mgr.-Corp. Affairs
Kevin Coates, Mgr.-Safety
Robert Hogarth, Mgr.-Reservoir Dev.
Martin Albrecht, Chmn.

Phone: 61-7-3721-7500	Fax: 61-7-3721-7599
Toll-Free:	
Address: 19 Lang Parade, Level 3, Milton, QLD 4064 Australia	

GROWTH PLANS/SPECIAL FEATURES:

Geodynamics Ltd. is an Australia-based energy company specializing in geothermal power collection. The company generates electricity by circulating water from an artificial reservoir over hot granite rocks, a process known as hot fractured rock (HFR) geothermal energy. In Australia, the HFR granite bodies were formed as a result of a magmatic melt and are mostly found within 2-3 miles below the surface. The rocks are insulated by layers of sedimentary rocks that retain the underground heat. Once the granite reaches the required 200 degree Celsius mark, it can be used for power generation. The company speculates that .24 miles of granite heated to the proper temperature could provide energy equal to roughly 40 million barrels of oil and enough ideal locations exist within Australia to power the country for hundreds of years. Its goal is to generate 50 megawatts (MW) by 2012, increase to 500 MW by 2016 and eventually reach 10,000 MW, a figure equivalent to 10-20 coal-fired plants. The firm also maintains a joint venture with Origin Energy to farm-in and further develop geothermal assets in the Cooper Basin.

FINANCIALS: Sales and profits are in thousands of dollars—add 000 to get the full amount. 2011 Note: Financial information for 2011 was not available for all companies at press time.

2011 Sales: $	2011 Profits: $-144,600	U.S. Stock Ticker:
2010 Sales: $	2010 Profits: $-15,700	Int'l Ticker: GDY
2009 Sales: $	2009 Profits: $-16,300	Int'l Exchange: Sydney-ASX
2008 Sales: $	2008 Profits: $	Employees: 50 Fiscal Year Ends: 6/30
2007 Sales: $	2007 Profits: $	Parent Company:

SALARIES/BENEFITS:

Pension Plan:	ESOP Stock Plan:	Profit Sharing:	Top Exec. Salary: $	Bonus: $
Savings Plan:	Stock Purch. Plan:		Second Exec. Salary: $	Bonus: $

OTHER THOUGHTS:

Apparent Women Officers or Directors: 2
Hot Spot for Advancement for Women/Minorities: Y

LOCATIONS: ("Y" = Yes)

West:	Southwest:	Midwest:	Southeast:	Northeast:	International:
					Y

Sales, profits and employees may be estimates. Financial information, benefits and other data can change quickly and may vary from those stated here.

GEOPLASMA LLC

www.geoplasma.com

Industry Group Code: 562

Energy/Fuel:	Other Technologies:	Electrical Products:		Electronics:	Transportation:	Other:
Biofuels:	Irrigation:	Lighting/LEDs:		Computers:	Car Sharing:	Recycling:
Batteries/Storage:	Nanotech:	Waste Heat:	Y	Sensors:	Electric Vehicles:	Engineering:
Solar:	Biotech:	Smart Meters:		Software:	Natural Gas Fuel:	Consulting:
Wind:	Water Tech./Treatment:	Machinery:				Investing:
Fuel Cells:	Ceramics:					Chemicals:

TYPES OF BUSINESS:

Waste-to-Energy
Plasma Gasification Technology
Biomass & Municipal Waste Generation

BRANDS/DIVISIONS/AFFILIATES:

Jacoby Development Inc
Westinghouse Plasma Corporation
Jacoby Group (The)

CONTACTS: *Note: Officers with more than one job title may be intentionally listed here more than once.*

Hilburn O. Hillestad, Pres.
Jim Jacoby, CEO/Chmn. -Jacoby Energy

Phone: 770-399-9930	Fax:
Toll-Free:	
Address: 171 17th St. NW, Ste. 1550, Atlanta, GA 30363 US	

GROWTH PLANS/SPECIAL FEATURES:

Geoplasma LLC is a wholly-owned waste destruction and energy subsidiary of Jacoby Development, Inc., part of the Jacoby Group of companies. The firm's primary goal is to promote plasma gasification technology as a viable and sustainable waste destruction solution. Plasma gasification, which uses electricity and high pressure air to create plasma with temperatures exceeding 10,000 degrees Fahrenheit, was developed by NASA in the 1960s. The company works extensively with Westinghouse Plasma Corporation, a developer of waste-to-energy processes and metallurgical and chemical processing solutions in Japan, where plasma gasification facilities have been used to destroy municipal solid waste (MSW) for nearly a decade. MSW includes items such as product packaging, grass clippings, furniture, clothing, bottles, food waste, newspapers, appliances, paint and batteries. On average, Geoplasma's application of plasma gasification can recover enough energy from 1,000 tons of MSW to power approximately 25,000 homes for a day.

FINANCIALS: Sales and profits are in thousands of dollars—add 000 to get the full amount. 2011 Note: Financial information for 2011 was not available for all companies at press time.

2011 Sales: $	2011 Profits: $	**U.S. Stock Ticker: Subsidiary**
2010 Sales: $	2010 Profits: $	**Int'l Ticker:**
2009 Sales: $	2009 Profits: $	Int'l Exchange:
2008 Sales: $	2008 Profits: $	Employees: Fiscal Year Ends:
2007 Sales: $	2007 Profits: $	Parent Company: JACOBY DEVELOPMENT INC

SALARIES/BENEFITS:

Pension Plan:	ESOP Stock Plan:	Profit Sharing:	Top Exec. Salary: $	Bonus: $
Savings Plan:	Stock Purch. Plan:		Second Exec. Salary: $	Bonus: $

OTHER THOUGHTS:

Apparent Women Officers or Directors:
Hot Spot for Advancement for Women/Minorities:

LOCATIONS: ("Y" = Yes)

West:	Southwest:	Midwest:	Southeast:	Northeast:	International:
			Y		

GINTECH ENERGY CORPORATION

www.gintechenergy.com

Industry Group Code: 334413

Energy/Fuel:	Other Technologies:	Electrical Products:	Electronics:	Transportation:	Other:
Biofuels:	Irrigation:	Lighting/LEDs:	Computers:	Car Sharing:	Recycling:
Batteries/Storage:	Nanotech:	Waste Heat:	Sensors:	Electric Vehicles:	Engineering:
Solar: Y	Biotech:	Smart Meters:	Software:	Natural Gas Fuel:	Consulting:
Wind:	Water Tech./Treatment:	Machinery:			Investing:
Fuel Cells:	Ceramics:				Chemicals:

TYPES OF BUSINESS:

Solar Cell Manufacturing

BRANDS/DIVISIONS/AFFILIATES:

Utech Solar Corporation
Full Square
Phoenix
Douro

CONTACTS: Note: Officers with more than one job title may be intentionally listed here more than once.

Wen-Yen Pan, CEO
Wen-Whe Pan, COO
Wen-Whe Pan, Pres.
Andrew Shih, CFO
Walt K.W. Huang, CTO
Stone Liu, VP-Prod. Div.
J.M. Lee, VP-Eng. Div.
Sam Yang, Dir.-Mfg. Dept.
David W.S. Liu, VP-Admin.
Wen-Yan Pan, Chmn.
David W.S. Liu, VP-Purchasing

Phone: 886-37-586-198	Fax: 886-37-586-199
Toll-Free:	
Address: No. 21 Kebei 1st Rd., Jhunan, 350 Taiwan	

GROWTH PLANS/SPECIAL FEATURES:

Gintech Energy Corporation, based in Taiwan, manufactures photovoltaic cells. It produces six-inch monocrystalline and multicrystalline silicon solar cells. The company's cells average from 15% to 17% conversion efficiency rates. While most of these cells are blue colored, Gintech offers a line of green, gold, brown, red, silver and gray cells for the building integrated photovoltaic cell (BIPV) market. Gintech's products fall under three brands: Full Square, Phoenix and Douro. Its products have been installed overseas in markets including Korea, Spain and Germany. More than 95% of its products are utilized outside of Taiwan. The firm operates two production facilities in Jhunan, Taiwan and one in Guanyin, Taiwan. Along with CTCI Corp. and Mitsubishi Corp., the company owns interest in Utech Solar Corporation, which operates a wafer production plant that began operating in March 2011. The plant is expected to reach a production capacity of 330 megawatts (MW) by March 2012 and an eventual capacity of 1 gigawatt (GW). Gintech has a total production capacity of 870 MW, which it intends to expand to 1.5 GW.

FINANCIALS: Sales and profits are in thousands of dollars—add 000 to get the full amount. 2011 Note: Financial information for 2011 was not available for all companies at press time.

2011 Sales: $	2011 Profits: $	U.S. Stock Ticker:
2010 Sales: $982,340	2010 Profits: $150,830	Int'l Ticker: 3514
2009 Sales: $514,923	2009 Profits: $2,310	Int'l Exchange: Taipei-TPE
2008 Sales: $492,000	2008 Profits: $59,330	Employees: Fiscal Year Ends: 12/31
2007 Sales: $212,290	2007 Profits: $15,140	Parent Company:

SALARIES/BENEFITS:

Pension Plan:	ESOP Stock Plan:	Profit Sharing:	Top Exec. Salary: $	Bonus: $
Savings Plan:	Stock Purch. Plan:		Second Exec. Salary: $	Bonus: $

OTHER THOUGHTS:

Apparent Women Officers or Directors:
Hot Spot for Advancement for Women/Minorities:

LOCATIONS: ("Y" = Yes)

West:	Southwest:	Midwest:	Southeast:	Northeast:	International: Y

Sales, profits and employees may be estimates. Financial information, benefits and other data can change quickly and may vary from those stated here.

GLOBAL SOLAR ENERGY

www.globalsolar.com

Industry Group Code: 334413

Energy/Fuel:	Other Technologies:	Electrical Products:	Electronics:	Transportation:	Other:
Biofuels:	Irrigation:	Lighting/LEDs:	Computers:	Car Sharing:	Recycling:
Batteries/Storage: Y	Nanotech:	Waste Heat:	Sensors:	Electric Vehicles:	Engineering:
Solar: Y	Biotech:	Smart Meters:	Software:	Natural Gas Fuel:	Consulting:
Wind:	Water Tech./Treatment:	Machinery:			Investing:
Fuel Cells:	Ceramics:				Chemicals:

TYPES OF BUSINESS:

Photovoltaic Technology
Photovoltaic Cells
Solar Plant Design & Installation

BRANDS/DIVISIONS/AFFILIATES:

PowerFLEX
Portable Power Pack (P3)
SUNLINQ
Kennedy & Violich Architecture of Boston

CONTACTS: *Note: Officers with more than one job title may be intentionally listed here more than once.*

Jeffrey S. Britt, CEO
Kirk Shockley, COO
Jeffrey S. Britt, Pres.
Steve Alexander, CFO
Jean-Noel Poirier, VP-Mktg.
Urs Schoop, CTO
Timothy Teich, VP-Oper.
Jean-Noel Poirier, VP-Bus. Dev.
Jens Muhling, Co-Managing Dir.-Global Solar Energy Deutschland
Ronald Erdmann, Co-Managing Dir.-Global Solar Energy Deutschland

Phone: 520-546-6313	Fax: 520-546-6318
Toll-Free:	
Address: 8500 Rita Rd., Tucson, AZ 85747 US	

GROWTH PLANS/SPECIAL FEATURES:

Global Solar Energy produces solar energy systems and products, specializing in lightweight and portable systems with universal applications. The company manufactures its PowerFLEX thin-film cells by applying Copper Indium Gallium DiSelenide (CIGS) to a highly flexible base. These cells are integrated into foldable, flexible, portable solar chargers as well as solar glass modules. Portable Power Packs (P3) are solar generators designed to be folded into a package about the size of a laptop computer. They produce between 15 and 55 watts and can be used for hiking, camping, boating, police, military, agricultural and other applications. The company's SUNLINQ power packs produce between 6.5 and 25 watts. Global Solar's solar glass modules are designed to charge lead-acid batteries, and increase in cell efficiency after outdoor exposure. In recent years, the company, in collaboration with Kennedy & Violich Architecture of Boston, combined solar cells with light emitting diodes (LEDs) and attached them to the surface of fabric. The fabric can be made into bags and carried in the daylight. In the daylight the cells generate electricity that is stored in batteries sewn onto the fabric; in the darkness the batteries power LEDs.

FINANCIALS: Sales and profits are in thousands of dollars—add 000 to get the full amount. 2011 Note: Financial information for 2011 was not available for all companies at press time.

2011 Sales: $	2011 Profits: $	**U.S. Stock Ticker: Private**
2010 Sales: $	2010 Profits: $	**Int'l Ticker:**
2009 Sales: $	2009 Profits: $	Int'l Exchange:
2008 Sales: $	2008 Profits: $	Employees: Fiscal Year Ends: 12/31
2007 Sales: $	2007 Profits: $	Parent Company:

SALARIES/BENEFITS:

Pension Plan:	ESOP Stock Plan:	Profit Sharing:	Top Exec. Salary: $	Bonus: $
Savings Plan:	Stock Purch. Plan:		Second Exec. Salary: $	Bonus: $

OTHER THOUGHTS:

Apparent Women Officers or Directors:
Hot Spot for Advancement for Women/Minorities:

LOCATIONS: ("Y" = Yes)

West:	Southwest:	Midwest:	Southeast:	Northeast:	International:
	Y				

GMZ ENERGY

www.gmzenergy.com

Industry Group Code: 541712N

Energy/Fuel:	Other Technologies:	Electrical Products:		Electronics:	Transportation:	Other:
Biofuels:	Irrigation:	Lighting/LEDs:		Computers:	Car Sharing:	Recycling:
Batteries/Storage:	Nanotech:	Waste Heat:	Y	Sensors:	Electric Vehicles:	Engineering:
Solar:	Biotech:	Smart Meters:		Software:	Natural Gas Fuel:	Consulting:
Wind:	Water Tech./Treatment:	Machinery:				Investing:
Fuel Cells:	Ceramics:					Chemicals:

TYPES OF BUSINESS:

ThermoVoltaics

BRANDS/DIVISIONS/AFFILIATES:

BP Alternative Energy
KPCB
Mitsui Global Investments
12BF
Energy Technology Ventures

GROWTH PLANS/SPECIAL FEATURES:

GMZ Energy is an energy company that produces energy using ThermoVoltaics. ThermoVoltaic technology transforms waste heat into electricity. GMZ's solid-state platform technology, developed at Boston College and MIT, using high-performing thermoelectric material to transform waste heat into electricity. The company's products are designed to utilize an automobile's wasted heat for fuel efficiency gains, to recover waste heat in industrial plants and to produce heat and electricity within the same footprint. In recent years, GMZ has received Series C funding from investors including BP Alternative Energy, KPCB, Mitsui Global Investments, 12BF and Energy Technology Ventures.

CONTACTS: *Note: Officers with more than one job title may be intentionally listed here more than once.*

Aaron A. Bent, CEO
Gang Chen, Co-Founder
Zhifeng Ren, Co-Founder

Phone: 781-996-3036	Fax:
Toll-Free:	
Address: 11 Wall St., Waltham, MA 02453 US	

FINANCIALS: Sales and profits are in thousands of dollars—add 000 to get the full amount. 2011 Note: Financial information for 2011 was not available for all companies at press time.

2011 Sales: $	2011 Profits: $	**U.S. Stock Ticker: Private**
2010 Sales: $	2010 Profits: $	**Int'l Ticker:**
2009 Sales: $	2009 Profits: $	Int'l Exchange:
2008 Sales: $	2008 Profits: $	Employees: Fiscal Year Ends:
2007 Sales: $	2007 Profits: $	Parent Company:

SALARIES/BENEFITS:

Pension Plan:	ESOP Stock Plan:	Profit Sharing:	Top Exec. Salary: $	Bonus: $
Savings Plan:	Stock Purch. Plan:		Second Exec. Salary: $	Bonus: $

OTHER THOUGHTS:

Apparent Women Officers or Directors:
Hot Spot for Advancement for Women/Minorities:

LOCATIONS: ("Y" = Yes)

West:	Southwest:	Midwest:	Southeast:	Northeast:	International:
				Y	

GREEN BIOLOGICS LIMITED

www.butanol.com

Industry Group Code: 325199

Energy/Fuel:		Other Technologies:		Electrical Products:	Electronics:	Transportation:	Other:
Biofuels:	Y	Irrigation:		Lighting/LEDs:	Computers:	Car Sharing:	Recycling:
Batteries/Storage:		Nanotech:		Waste Heat:	Sensors:	Electric Vehicles:	Engineering:
Solar:		Biotech:	Y	Smart Meters:	Software:	Natural Gas Fuel:	Consulting:
Wind:		Water Tech./Treatment:		Machinery:			Investing:
Fuel Cells:		Ceramics:					Chemicals:

TYPES OF BUSINESS:

Production of Biofuels
C4 chemicals

BRANDS/DIVISIONS/AFFILIATES:

butylfuel Inc

CONTACTS: *Note: Officers with more than one job title may be intentionally listed here more than once.*

Sean Sutcliffe, CEO
Patrick Simms, COO
Thomas Grote, CFO
Edward Green, Chief Scientific Officer
Tim Davies, CTO
Joel Stone, Global VP-Eng.
Christina Sweeney, Corp. Sec.
Fergal O'Brien, VP-Commercial Oper.
Timothy Staub, VP-Bus. Dev.
Christina Sweeney, Financial Controller
Andrew Rickman, Chmn.
Joel Stone, Pres., North America

Phone: 441235-435710	Fax:
Toll-Free:	
Address: Milton Park, Unit 45A, Abingdon, OX14 4RU UK	

GROWTH PLANS/SPECIAL FEATURES:

Green Biologics Limited (GB) is a biotechnology company that develops products such as biobutanol and other C4 chemicals, for the biofuels and chemicals markets. Biobutanol-chemical products are the firm's key commercial products and include bio-based butanol, a renewable alternative to chemical-grade petro-based butanol; butyl acetates, used as solvents in vinyl, cellulosic and epoxy coatings; and butyl acrylates, used in the production of items such as paints and lacquers. Biobutanol-fuel products are used as a direct replacement for gasoline. Acetone, as a co-product to biobutanol, is used in the production of chemicals such as MIBC, MIBK and Isophorone, and as a cleaning agent and intermediate in medical and pharmaceutical applications. Butyric acid is used in food ingredients, polymers and as a feedstock in the production of cellulose acetate butyrate, a biopolymer used in the production of high impact plastics. GB's head office is in the U.K., where it runs a 7000 square foot facility that houses its labs and pilot facility. The firms U.S. operations are composed of offices near Richmond, Virginia and a 4000 square foot pilot and laboratory in Columbus, Ohio. The company also has satellite offices in Sao Paulo, Brazil; Jinan, China; and New Delhi, India. In January 2012, GB announced the merger between itself and butylfuel, Inc., a U.S. renewable chemical and biofuels company. The new company will continue to operate under the GB name and be headquartered in the U.K.

FINANCIALS: Sales and profits are in thousands of dollars—add 000 to get the full amount. 2011 Note: Financial information for 2011 was not available for all companies at press time.

2011 Sales: $	2011 Profits: $	U.S. Stock Ticker: Private
2010 Sales: $	2010 Profits: $	Int'l Ticker:
2009 Sales: $	2009 Profits: $	Int'l Exchange:
2008 Sales: $	2008 Profits: $	Employees: Fiscal Year Ends:
2007 Sales: $	2007 Profits: $	Parent Company:

SALARIES/BENEFITS:

Pension Plan:	ESOP Stock Plan:	Profit Sharing:	Top Exec. Salary: $	Bonus: $
Savings Plan:	Stock Purch. Plan:		Second Exec. Salary: $	Bonus: $

OTHER THOUGHTS:

Apparent Women Officers or Directors: 1
Hot Spot for Advancement for Women/Minorities:

LOCATIONS: ("Y" = Yes)

West:	Southwest:	Midwest:	Southeast:	Northeast:	International:
		Y		Y	Y

GREENROAD TECHNOLOGIES

www.greenroad.com

Industry Group Code: 5112

Energy/Fuel:	Other Technologies:	Electrical Products:	Electronics:		Transportation:	Other:
Biofuels:	Irrigation:	Lighting/LEDs:	Computers:	Y	Car Sharing:	Recycling:
Batteries/Storage:	Nanotech:	Waste Heat:	Sensors:		Electric Vehicles:	Engineering:
Solar:	Biotech:	Smart Meters:	Software:	Y	Natural Gas Fuel:	Consulting:
Wind:	Water Tech./Treatment:	Machinery:				Investing:
Fuel Cells:	Ceramics:					Chemicals:

TYPES OF BUSINESS:

Safety Management & Driving Performance Technology

BRANDS/DIVISIONS/AFFILIATES:

GreenRoad Driver Improvement Loop
Zurich Fleet Intelligence

GROWTH PLANS/SPECIAL FEATURES:

Greenroad Technologies is a provider of safety management and driving performance solutions for fleet services and other industries around the world. The firm's GreenRoad Driver Improvement Loop product uses technology-based, customized driver self-improvement solutions to immediately reduce the rate of crashes and the amount of fuel consumed. The company's product has been used by approximately 70,000 drivers throughout the U.S. and internationally. Its customers include drivers representing fleets from all industries. Greenroad Technologies has offices in the U.S., Israel and the U.K. In February 2011, the firm and fleet insurer Zurich agreed to jointly develop Zurich Fleet Intelligence, a fleet risk management product. In September 2011, the company released an open integration platform intended to allow customers to integrate the GreenRoad solution with their own individual program.

CONTACTS: *Note: Officers with more than one job title may be intentionally listed here more than once.*

Jim Heeger, CEO
Jim Heeger, Pres.
Bill Wathen, CFO
Tany Roberts, Sr. VP-Mktg.
Amir Shoval, VP-Prod. Mgmt.
Doron Somer, Sr. VP-Eng.
Doron Somer, Sr. VP-Oper.
David Coleman, Sr. VP-Global Bus. Dev.
Eric Weiss, Sr. VP-Oper.
Amir Oz, VP-Systems Eng. & Oper.
Jim Heeger, Chmn.
Aidan Rowsome, Sr. VP-Sales, Europe

Phone: 650-551-1530	**Fax:** 650-551-1539
Toll-Free: 888-658-4420	
Address: 3 Twin Dolphin Dr., Ste. 300, Redwood Shores, CA 94065 US	

FINANCIALS: Sales and profits are in thousands of dollars—add 000 to get the full amount. 2011 Note: Financial information for 2011 was not available for all companies at press time.

2011 Sales: $	2011 Profits: $	**U.S. Stock Ticker:** Private
2010 Sales: $	2010 Profits: $	**Int'l Ticker:**
2009 Sales: $	2009 Profits: $	Int'l Exchange:
2008 Sales: $	2008 Profits: $	Employees: Fiscal Year Ends: 12/31
2007 Sales: $	2007 Profits: $	Parent Company:

SALARIES/BENEFITS:

Pension Plan:	ESOP Stock Plan:	Profit Sharing:	Top Exec. Salary: $	Bonus: $
Savings Plan:	Stock Purch. Plan:		Second Exec. Salary: $	Bonus: $

OTHER THOUGHTS:

Apparent Women Officers or Directors: 3
Hot Spot for Advancement for Women/Minorities: Y

LOCATIONS: ("Y" = Yes)

West:	Southwest:	Midwest:	Southeast:	Northeast:	International:
Y					Y

GRIFFIN INDUSTRIES INC

www.griffinind.com

Industry Group Code: 311613

Energy/Fuel:		Other Technologies:	Electrical Products:	Electronics:	Transportation:	Other:	
Biofuels:	Y	Irrigation:	Lighting/LEDs:	Computers:	Car Sharing:	Recycling:	Y
Batteries/Storage:		Nanotech:	Waste Heat:	Sensors:	Electric Vehicles:	Engineering:	
Solar:		Biotech:	Smart Meters:	Software:	Natural Gas Fuel:	Consulting:	
Wind:		Water Tech./Treatment:	Machinery:			Investing:	
Fuel Cells:		Ceramics:				Chemicals:	

TYPES OF BUSINESS:

Agricultural Waste Recycling
Rendering & Recycling
Biodiesel
Methyl Esters
Fertilizers
Feed Ingredients
Logistics & Export Services
Rendering Research & Development

BRANDS/DIVISIONS/AFFILIATES:

Bio G-3000 Biodiesel Fuel
Nature Safe
VersaGen
Bakery Feeds
Cookie Meal
Darling International Inc

CONTACTS: *Note: Officers with more than one job title may be intentionally listed here more than once.*

Robert A. Griffin, CEO
Robert A. Griffin, Pres.
Anthony Griffin, CFO
John M. Griffin, Chmn.

Phone: 859-781-2010	Fax: 859-572-2575
Toll-Free:	
Address: 4221 Alexandria Pike, Cold Spring, KY 41076 US	

GROWTH PLANS/SPECIAL FEATURES:

Griffin Industries, Inc., a wholly-owned subsidiary of Darling International, Inc., is an independent rendering company headquartered in Cold Spring, Kentucky. The firm maintains operations in 18 states, including dozens of rendering and recycling plants. It collects and recycles billions of pounds of agricultural waste from slaughterhouses, packing plants, butcher shops, supermarkets, hotels and restaurants. This waste includes meat/poultry byproducts, grocery scraps, used restaurant cooking oil and waste from the bakery industry. The company recycles these byproducts into fats, oils, proteins, leather goods, Bio G-3000 Biodiesel Fuel, Nature Safe organic fertilizers, VersaGen methyl esters (which are used as replacements for d-Limonene, mineral spirits, mineral seal oil and other solvents) and VersaGen crude glycerin (a biodegradable product used in various industrial applications). The fatty acids, proteins, oils and tallow derived from the rendering are used to manufacture soaps, gelatins, cosmetics, paints, varnishes, polishes, water repellents and rubber. The company's Nature Safe division manufactures fertilizers from USDA-approved ingredients containing waste byproduct-free animal proteins such as bone, meat, fish, feather, poultry and blood meals. The division produces an extensive product line of fertilizers for the landscaping, sports turf, lawn care, organic farming, golf course, horticulture and nursery industries. The Bakery Feeds division specializes in the recycling of inedible bakery waste, such as pasta, crackers, cereal, bagels, bread, dough, sweet goods and snack chips. The recycling process transforms these byproducts into Cookie Meal, a high-energy feed ingredient used as a replacement for corn in poultry, swine and dairy diets. Bakery Feeds also recycles waste packaging, preventing tons of waste from entering landfills. Through its own vessels, Griffin provides logistics and export services to its international clients. The company also has an extensive rendered products research and development program. In November 2010, the firm was acquired by Darling International, Inc. for approximately $840 million.

FINANCIALS: Sales and profits are in thousands of dollars—add 000 to get the full amount. 2011 Note: Financial information for 2011 was not available for all companies at press time.

2011 Sales: $	2011 Profits: $	**U.S. Stock Ticker:** Subsidiary
2010 Sales: $	2010 Profits: $	**Int'l Ticker:**
2009 Sales: $	2009 Profits: $	Int'l Exchange:
2008 Sales: $	2008 Profits: $	Employees: Fiscal Year Ends: 12/31
2007 Sales: $	2007 Profits: $	Parent Company: DARLING INTERNATIONAL INC

SALARIES/BENEFITS:

Pension Plan:	ESOP Stock Plan:	Profit Sharing:	Top Exec. Salary: $	Bonus: $
Savings Plan:	Stock Purch. Plan:		Second Exec. Salary: $	Bonus: $

OTHER THOUGHTS:

Apparent Women Officers or Directors:
Hot Spot for Advancement for Women/Minorities:

LOCATIONS: ("Y" = Yes)

West:	Southwest:	Midwest:	Southeast:	Northeast:	International:
	Y	Y	Y	Y	

GRUPPO FALCK SPA

www.falck.it

Industry Group Code: 221119

Energy/Fuel:		Other Technologies:	Electrical Products:	Electronics:	Transportation:	Other:
Biofuels:	Y	Irrigation:	Lighting/LEDs:	Computers:	Car Sharing:	Recycling:
Batteries/Storage:		Nanotech:	Waste Heat:	Sensors:	Electric Vehicles:	Engineering:
Solar:		Biotech:	Smart Meters:	Software:	Natural Gas Fuel:	Consulting:
Wind:		Water Tech./Treatment:	Machinery:			Investing:
Fuel Cells:		Ceramics:				Chemicals:

TYPES OF BUSINESS:

Waste & Biomass Power Generation
Steel Production & Distribution
Wind Farms
Financial Services

BRANDS/DIVISIONS/AFFILIATES:

Falk Renewables SpA
Riesfactoring
Cambrian Wind Energy Ltd
Earlsburn Wind Energy Ltd
Ben Aketil Wind Energy Ltd
Millenium Wind Energy Ltd
Kilbraur Wind Energy Ltd
Boyndie Wind Energy Ltd

CONTACTS: Note: Officers with more than one job title may be intentionally listed here more than once.

Piero Manzoni, CEO
Paolo Rundeddu, CFO
Piero Manzoni, Head-Info.
Piero Manzoni, Head-Comm. Tech.
Marco Cavenaghi, Head-Bus. Dev.
Chiara Valenti, Head-Comm.
William Heller, Dir.-Wind Energy & Solar
Carmelo Tantillo, Dir.-WTE & Biomass
Lucia Giancaspro, Head-Corp. Affairs
Alessandra Ruzzu, Head-Institutional Rel.
Frederico Falck, Chmn.
Marco Cavenaghi, Head-Procurement

Phone: 39-02-24331	Fax: 39-0224-33-37-91
Toll-Free:	
Address: Corso Venezia 16, Milan, 20121 Italy	

GROWTH PLANS/SPECIAL FEATURES:

Gruppo Falck S.p.A., headquartered in Milan, Italy, generates power from waste, photovoltaic, biomass and wind projects. The company offers renewable energy services through its subsidiary, Falk Renewables SpA. Falk Renewables designs, constructs and operates waste and biomass fueled power plants and operates three waste burning plants and a composting facility in Italy. U.K. based Falck Renewables produces wind farms, with projects in the U.K., Spain and Italy. The company also operates U.K. wholly-owned subsidiaries, Cambrian Wind Energy Ltd, Earlsburn Wind Energy Ltd., Ben Aketil Wind Energy Ltd., Millenium Wind Energy Ltd., Kilbraur Wind Energy Ltd. and Boyndie Wind Energy Ltd. The firm also provides financial services to partners and energy plant suppliers through subsidiary Riesfactoring. In April 2011, the firm announced that it had started three photovoltaic plants in Sicily with a combined capacity of 13.1 megawatts (MW). In May 2011, Falck Renewables announced that its 138 MW Budduso and Ala dei Sardi wind farm had entered into commercial operation.

FINANCIALS: Sales and profits are in thousands of dollars—add 000 to get the full amount. 2011 Note: Financial information for 2011 was not available for all companies at press time.

2011 Sales: $	2011 Profits: $	U.S. Stock Ticker: Private
2010 Sales: $263,459	2010 Profits: $56,346	Int'l Ticker:
2009 Sales: $246,600	2009 Profits: $-28,800	Int'l Exchange:
2008 Sales: $238,650	2008 Profits: $-23,740	Employees: 257 Fiscal Year Ends: 12/31
2007 Sales: $188,310	2007 Profits: $8,890	Parent Company:

SALARIES/BENEFITS:

Pension Plan:	ESOP Stock Plan:	Profit Sharing:	Top Exec. Salary: $	Bonus: $
Savings Plan:	Stock Purch. Plan:		Second Exec. Salary: $	Bonus: $

OTHER THOUGHTS:

Apparent Women Officers or Directors: 3
Hot Spot for Advancement for Women/Minorities: Y

LOCATIONS: ("Y" = Yes)

West:	Southwest:	Midwest:	Southeast:	Northeast:	International: Y

Sales, profits and employees may be estimates. Financial information, benefits and other data can change quickly and may vary from those stated here.

GT ADVANCED TECHNOLOGIES INC

www.gtat.com

Industry Group Code: 333295

Energy/Fuel:		Other Technologies:		Electrical Products:		Electronics:		Transportation:		Other:	
Biofuels:		Irrigation:		Lighting/LEDs:		Computers:		Car Sharing:		Recycling:	
Batteries/Storage:		Nanotech:		Waste Heat:		Sensors:	Y	Electric Vehicles:		Engineering:	Y
Solar:	Y	Biotech:		Smart Meters:		Software:		Natural Gas Fuel:		Consulting:	
Wind:		Water Tech./Treatment:		Machinery:	Y					Investing:	
Fuel Cells:		Ceramics:								Chemicals:	

TYPES OF BUSINESS:

Solar Cell Manufacturing Equipment

BRANDS/DIVISIONS/AFFILIATES:

Confluence Solar Inc
GT Solar International Inc

CONTACTS: Note: Officers with more than one job title may be intentionally listed here more than once.

Tom Gutierrez, CEO
Tom Gutierrez, Pres.
Rick Gaynor, CFO/VP
P.S. Raghavan, CTO
Vikram Singh, Gen. Mgr./VP-Eng. & PV Equipment Bus. Unit
Hoil Kim, Chief Admin. Officer
Hoil Kim, General Counsel/VP/Sec.
John Tattersfield, VP-Oper.
David C. Gray, Chief Strategy & New. Bus. Officer
John R. Granara, Chief Acct. Officer/Corp. Controller/VP-Finance
David W. Keck, VP/Gen. Mgr.-Polysilicon Div.
Jeffrey J. Ford, VP/Gen. Mgr.-Photovoltaic & Sapphire Systems
Cheryl Duiguid, Gen Mgr./VP-Sapphire Equipment & Materials

Phone: 603-883-5200	**Fax:** 603-595-6993
Toll-Free:	
Address: 243 Daniel Webster Hwy., Merrimack, NH 03054 US	

GROWTH PLANS/SPECIAL FEATURES:

GT Advanced Technologies, Inc., formerly GT Solar International, Inc., through its subsidiaries, is a leading global provider of polysilicon production technology, crystalline ingot growth systems and related photovoltaic manufacturing services for the LED and solar industry. The company's principal products are directional solidification systems (DSS) units, chemical vapor deposition (CVD) reactors, advanced sapphire furnaces and related services. GT Advanced Technologies operates through three segments: polysilicon business, photovoltaic (PV) business and sapphire business. The polysilicon business segment sells CVD reactors and related equipment that facilitate new companies' entry into the polysilicon industry. The segment also provides technology and engineering services for the commissioning, start-up and optimization of the firm's equipment and technology. The PV business segment manufactures and sells DSS crystallization furnaces and ancillary equipment required in the operation of DSS crystallization furnaces to cast multicrystalline silicon ingots. The segment also offers PV parts and services as well as turnkey integration services. The sapphire business segment focuses on the production of sapphire material for the LED and other specialty markets, and on the marketing and sales of sapphire furnaces for customer use. The company and its subsidiaries have customers in Taiwan, China, Korea, India, Germany, Russia and Spain. These include several of the world's largest solar companies as well as companies in the chemical industry. In August 2011, GT Advanced Technologies acquired Confluence Solar, Inc., a private monocrystalline solar ingot technology provider, for $80 million. In 2011, the company completed a rebranding and name change from GT Solar International.

The company offers employees medical and dental insurance; life insurance; disability coverage; a 401(k) plan; and education assistance.

FINANCIALS: Sales and profits are in thousands of dollars—add 000 to get the full amount. 2011 Note: Financial information for 2011 was not available for all companies at press time.

2011 Sales: $898,984	2011 Profits: $174,755	**U.S. Stock Ticker: GTAT**
2010 Sales: $544,245	2010 Profits: $87,256	**Int'l Ticker:**
2009 Sales: $541,027	2009 Profits: $87,968	Int'l Exchange:
2008 Sales: $244,052	2008 Profits: $36,105	Employees: 622 Fiscal Year Ends: 3/31
2007 Sales: $60,119	2007 Profits: $-18,355	Parent Company:

SALARIES/BENEFITS:

Pension Plan:	ESOP Stock Plan:	Profit Sharing:	Top Exec. Salary: $600,385	Bonus: $1,625,000
Savings Plan: Y	Stock Purch. Plan:		Second Exec. Salary: $340,385	Bonus: $512,325

OTHER THOUGHTS:

Apparent Women Officers or Directors: 2
Hot Spot for Advancement for Women/Minorities:

LOCATIONS: ("Y" = Yes)

West:	Southwest:	Midwest:	Southeast:	Northeast:	International:
Y		Y		Y	Y

HANWHA SOLARONE CO LTD

www.hanwha-solarone.com

Industry Group Code: 334413

Energy/Fuel:		Other Technologies:	Electrical Products:	Electronics:	Transportation:	Other:
Biofuels:		Irrigation:	Lighting/LEDs:	Computers:	Car Sharing:	Recycling:
Batteries/Storage:		Nanotech:	Waste Heat:	Sensors:	Electric Vehicles:	Engineering:
Solar:	Y	Biotech:	Smart Meters:	Software:	Natural Gas Fuel:	Consulting:
Wind:		Water Tech./Treatment:	Machinery:			Investing:
Fuel Cells:		Ceramics:				Chemicals:

TYPES OF BUSINESS:

Solar Panel Manufacturing
Photovoltaic Cell Manufacturing
Silicon Ingot Production

BRANDS/DIVISIONS/AFFILIATES:

Solarfun Power Holdings Co Ltd
Hanwha SolarOne Technology Co
Shanghai Linyang Solar Technology Co
Hanwha Solar Electric Power Engineering Co
Nantong Hanwha Import & Export Co
Hanwha SolarOne Deutschland GmbH
Hanwha SolarOne U.S.A. Inc

CONTACTS: Note: Officers with more than one job title may be intentionally listed here more than once.

Ki-Joon Hong, CEO
Tai Seng Png, COO
Ki-Joon Hong, Pres.
Jung Pyo Seo, CFO
Justin Koo Yung Lee, Chief Commercial Officer
Chris Eberspacher, CTO
Sungsoo Lee, Corp. Sec.
Sungsoo Lee, Chief Strategy Officer
Paul Combs, VP-Investor Rel.
Andreas Liebheit, VP/Managing. Dir.-Hanwha SolarOne EMEA
Mohan Narayanan, VP-Tech.
Ki-Joon Hong, Chmn.
Bruce A. Ludemann, VP/Gen. Mgr.-Hanwha SolarOne North America

Phone: 8621-2602-2833	**Fax:** 8621-2602-2889
Toll-Free:	
Address: 888 Linyang Rd., Qidong, Jiangsu, 226200 China	

GROWTH PLANS/SPECIAL FEATURES:

Hanwha SolarOne Co., Ltd., formerly Solarfun Power Holdings Co., Ltd., is a manufacturer of photovoltaic (PV) cells, silicon ingots and PV modules in China. The company manufactures and sells a variety of PV cells, PV modules and raw materials using advanced manufacturing process technologies. Other operations include PV cell processing and PV module processing services. Hanwha SolarOne's silicon ingot production is operated through wholly-owned subsidiary Hanwha SolarOne Technology Co. Through this subsidiary, the company operates 40 mono-crystalline ingot production furnaces and 52 multi-crystalline ingot production furnaces, with an annual manufacturing capacity of 415 megawatts (MW). The firm conducts its business in China through several additional operating subsidiaries, including Shanghai Linyang Solar Technology Co.; Hanwha Solar Electric Power Engineering Co.; and Nantong Hanwha Import & Export Co. Hanwha SolarOne currently has annual production capacities of 800 MW in ingots and wafers; 1.3 GW in cells; and 1.5 GW in modules. PV modules account for approximately 90% of the firm's revenues; sales of PV cells, processing services and various raw materials account for the remaining 10%. The firm sells its products both directly to system integrators and through third party distributors, mostly to customers in China, Europe, the U.S. and Australia. International sales and marketing activities are conducted in Europe through Hanwha SolarOne Deutschland GmbH and in the U.S. through Hanwha SolarOne U.S.A., Inc. During 2010, Germany was its largest sales market, accounting for over 60% of its revenue. In December 2010, the company changed its name from Solarfun Power Holdings Co., Ltd. to Hanwha SolarOne Co., Ltd.

FINANCIALS: Sales and profits are in thousands of dollars—add 000 to get the full amount. 2011 Note: Financial information for 2011 was not available for all companies at press time.

2011 Sales: $	2011 Profits: $	**U.S. Stock Ticker:** HSOL
2010 Sales: $1,142,236	2010 Profits: $114,930	**Int'l Ticker:**
2009 Sales: $553,527	2009 Profits: $-21,276	Int'l Exchange:
2008 Sales: $725,404	2008 Profits: $-41,113	Employees: 10,241 Fiscal Year Ends: 12/31
2007 Sales: $328,344	2007 Profits: $20,294	Parent Company:

SALARIES/BENEFITS:

Pension Plan:	ESOP Stock Plan:	Profit Sharing:	Top Exec. Salary: $	Bonus: $
Savings Plan:	Stock Purch. Plan:		Second Exec. Salary: $	Bonus: $

OTHER THOUGHTS:

Apparent Women Officers or Directors:
Hot Spot for Advancement for Women/Minorities:

LOCATIONS: ("Y" = Yes)

West:	Southwest:	Midwest:	Southeast:	Northeast:	International:
Y					Y

HARA

www.hara.com

Industry Group Code: 5112

Energy/Fuel:	Other Technologies:	Electrical Products:	Electronics:		Transportation:	Other:
Biofuels:	Irrigation:	Lighting/LEDs:	Computers:		Car Sharing:	Recycling:
Batteries/Storage:	Nanotech:	Waste Heat:	Sensors:		Electric Vehicles:	Engineering:
Solar:	Biotech:	Smart Meters:	Software:	Y	Natural Gas Fuel:	Consulting:
Wind:	Water Tech./Treatment:	Machinery:				Investing:
Fuel Cells:	Ceramics:					Chemicals:

TYPES OF BUSINESS:

Energy Management Software

BRANDS/DIVISIONS/AFFILIATES:

CONTACTS: Note: Officers with more than one job title may be intentionally listed here more than once.

Daniel P. Leff, CEO
Tom Foody, CFO
Michael Mann, Sr. VP-Sales & Mktg.
Udo Waibel, CTO
Amit Singh, VP-Prod. Strategy
Victor Chen, Sr. Corp. Counsel
Prakash Menon, VP-Dev.
Stephanie Hess, VP-Corp. Comm.
Volker Enders, VP-Client Svcs.
Ellen Raynor, VP-Program Mgmt.

Phone: 650-249-6740	Fax:
Toll-Free:	
Address: 2755 Campus Dr., Ste. 300, San Mateo, CA 94403 US	

GROWTH PLANS/SPECIAL FEATURES:

Hara is an energy management technology firm, specializing in the production of energy and sustainability software. The firm's software suite focuses on the areas of modeling, forecasting and budgeting; energy efficiency portfolio planning; energy risk management; enterprise analytics for visibility and insight; and project execution management. The company operates by aiding both public sector organizations and global companies, like Aflac; Aerojet; Bloomberg; the City of Philadelphia; Dell; Ebay; Harvard University; and Hasbro, in visually tracking and maintaining inefficiencies in their energy usage so as to provide them with reduced energy costs, risk mitigation and improved operating profit margins. The firm's software platform allows the customer to clearly view their energy expenditure on a single system of record, allowing corporations the ability to create near-term and long-term sustainability strategies. Hara's strategic partnerships with firms such as HP; Itochu; Fugu; Infosys; URS; and Sympliciti, Inc. allow it to offer customers end-to-end software and service solutions in areas of energy management and sustainability, such as climate change strategy; resource monetization; operational efficiency and cost reduction; environmental infrastructure; delivery and support; and product and service optimization. Companies such as Itochu; Navitas Capital, NRG, ConocoPhillips, GE; and Focus Ventures have invested a total of $45 million in support of Hara's technology suite since its inception in 2008.

FINANCIALS: Sales and profits are in thousands of dollars—add 000 to get the full amount. 2011 Note: Financial information for 2011 was not available for all companies at press time.

2011 Sales: $	2011 Profits: $	**U.S. Stock Ticker: Private**
2010 Sales: $	2010 Profits: $	**Int'l Ticker:**
2009 Sales: $	2009 Profits: $	Int'l Exchange:
2008 Sales: $	2008 Profits: $	Employees: Fiscal Year Ends:
2007 Sales: $	2007 Profits: $	Parent Company:

SALARIES/BENEFITS:

Pension Plan:	ESOP Stock Plan:	Profit Sharing:	Top Exec. Salary: $	Bonus: $
Savings Plan:	Stock Purch. Plan:		Second Exec. Salary: $	Bonus: $

OTHER THOUGHTS:

Apparent Women Officers or Directors: 2
Hot Spot for Advancement for Women/Minorities:

LOCATIONS: ("Y" = Yes)

West:	Southwest:	Midwest:	Southeast:	Northeast:	International:
Y					Y

HARVEST POWER

www.harvestpower.com

Industry Group Code: 325199

Energy/Fuel:		Other Technologies:		Electrical Products:		Electronics:	Transportation:		Other:	
Biofuels:	Y	Irrigation:		Lighting/LEDs:		Computers:	Car Sharing:		Recycling:	Y
Batteries/Storage:		Nanotech:		Waste Heat:		Sensors:	Electric Vehicles:		Engineering:	Y
Solar:		Biotech:	Y	Smart Meters:		Software:	Natural Gas Fuel:	Y	Consulting:	
Wind:		Water Tech./Treatment:		Machinery:					Investing:	
Fuel Cells:		Ceramics:							Chemicals:	

TYPES OF BUSINESS:

Organic Soils, Mulches & Natural Fertilizers
Engineered Fuels

BRANDS/DIVISIONS/AFFILIATES:

Covered Aerated Static
Coastal Supply Company Inc

CONTACTS: *Note: Officers with more than one job title may be intentionally listed here more than once.*

Paul Sellew, CEO
Nathan Gilliland, Pres.
Cynthia Mignogna, CFO
Jeff Knapp, Sr. VP-Human Resources
John Eustermann, General Counsel/Sr. VP

Phone: 781-314-9500	Fax:
Toll-Free:	
Address: 221 Crescent St., Ste. 402, Waltham, MA 02453 US	

GROWTH PLANS/SPECIAL FEATURES:

Harvest Power uses organic material to aid communities in the production of clean, renewable energy, engineered fuels and high-value soils, mulches and natural fertilizers. Through its energy gardens, the company is able to recycle energy and nutrients back into communities, fully optimizing the use of the initial organic materials. The company's technology is based on the concepts of anaerobic digestion and composting. Anaerobic digestion uses naturally occurring microorganisms to aid in the breakdown of materials into biogas. Biogas then can be used to produce renewable electricity, natural gas or compressed natural gas fuel. Harvest Power designs and builds either low solids anaerobic digestion systems, which are better suited for pumpable slurries such as wastewater, pulped food scraps and manure; or high solids anaerobic digestion systems, which are suitable for handling stackable material such as yard debris and food scraps. This technology has potential applications such as helping to divert organic material from ending in landfills and incinerators and displacing chemical fertilizers. The company's proprietary Covered Aerated Static pile compost system has built in odor and process controls that aid in creating high-quality garden-ready composts and bio-fertilizers. The company's engineered fuels include processed engineered fuel (PEF) and hog fuel. PEF is derived from woodwaste materials and is an environmentally conscious alternative to coal. Hog fuel comes from a mixture of chips of bark and wood fiber and can be used to power boiler systems. The firm sells its own line of gardening products in both small and bulk quantities, including wood mulches; soils; stone and sand; and bulk nursery container bark and custom mixed products. The firm maintains facilities in California, the Mid-Atlantic, the Midwest and Northeast States, British Columbia and in Ontario. In September 2011, the firm acquired Coastal Supply Company, Inc., a soil and mulch manufacturer.

FINANCIALS: Sales and profits are in thousands of dollars—add 000 to get the full amount. 2011 Note: Financial information for 2011 was not available for all companies at press time.

2011 Sales: $	2011 Profits: $	U.S. Stock Ticker: Private
2010 Sales: $	2010 Profits: $	Int'l Ticker:
2009 Sales: $	2009 Profits: $	Int'l Exchange:
2008 Sales: $	2008 Profits: $	Employees: Fiscal Year Ends:
2007 Sales: $	2007 Profits: $	Parent Company:

SALARIES/BENEFITS:

Pension Plan:	ESOP Stock Plan:	Profit Sharing:	Top Exec. Salary: $	Bonus: $
Savings Plan:	Stock Purch. Plan:		Second Exec. Salary: $	Bonus: $

OTHER THOUGHTS:

Apparent Women Officers or Directors: 2
Hot Spot for Advancement for Women/Minorities:

LOCATIONS: ("Y" = Yes)

West:	Southwest:	Midwest:	Southeast:	Northeast:	International:
Y		Y		Y	Y

HEADWATERS INC

www.headwaters.com

Industry Group Code: 324199

Energy/Fuel:	Other Technologies:		Electrical Products:		Electronics:	Transportation:	Other:	
Biofuels:	Irrigation:		Lighting/LEDs:		Computers:	Car Sharing:	Recycling:	
Batteries/Storage:	Nanotech:	Y	Waste Heat:		Sensors:	Electric Vehicles:	Engineering:	Y
Solar:	Biotech:		Smart Meters:		Software:	Natural Gas Fuel:	Consulting:	
Wind:	Water Tech./Treatment:		Machinery:	Y			Investing:	
Fuel Cells:	Ceramics:						Chemicals:	Y

TYPES OF BUSINESS:

Clean Coal Derivatives Technologies
Synthetic Fuels & Related Technologies
Nanocatalysts
Reagents & Chemicals, Ash
Post-Combustion Coal Products & Services
Architectural Stone & Siding
Ethanol Production
Alternative Energy

BRANDS/DIVISIONS/AFFILIATES:

Headwaters Energy Services Corp.
Headwaters Resources, Inc.
Headwaters Technology Innovation Group, Inc.
FlexCrete
Tapco
Eldorado Stone

CONTACTS: Note: Officers with more than one job title may be intentionally listed here more than once.

Kirk A. Benson, CEO
Donald P. Newman, CFO
Harlan M. Hatfield, General Counsel/VP/Corp. Sec.
Sharon Madden, VP-Investor Rel.
William H. Gehrmann, III, Pres., Headwaters Resources, Inc.
David Ulmer, Pres., Tapco Int'l
Murphy Lents, Pres., Eldorado Stone
Bob Whisnant, Pres., Southwest Concrete Prod.
Kirk A. Benson, Chmn.

Phone: 801-984-9400	Fax: 801-984-9410
Toll-Free:	
Address: 10653 S. River Front Pkwy., Ste. 300, South Jordan, UT 84095 US	

GROWTH PLANS/SPECIAL FEATURES:

Headwaters, Inc. provides products, technologies and services in the building products, construction materials and energy industries. It operates in three segments: light building products, heavy construction materials and energy technology. In the light building products segment, the company designs, manufactures and sells architectural stone veneer, concrete blocks, siding accessories and other professional tools used in exterior residential construction. These products are offered under brand names FlexCrete, Tapco and Eldorado Stone. The heavy construction materials segment, operating primarily through Headwaters Resources, Inc., manages and markets coal combustion products (CCPs), including fly ash used as a substitute for Portland cement. In the energy technology segment, Headwaters is focused on reducing waste and increasing the value of energy feedstocks, primarily in the areas of low-value coal and oil. In coal, the company owns and operates several coal cleaning facilities that remove rock, dirt and other impurities from waste or other low-value coal. The firm also licenses technology and sells reagents to the coal-based solid alternative fuel industry. Subsidiary, Headwaters Energy Services Corp. uses coal cleaning processes that upgrade low value or waste coal by separating ash from the carbon. In oil, its HCAT heavy oil upgrading process uses a liquid catalyst precursor to generate a highly active molecular catalyst to convert residual oil feedstocks into higher-value distillates that can be refined into gasoline, diesel and other products. Additionally, the company owns 51% of and operates a 50 million gallon per year corn-to-ethanol facility in North Dakota. The firm's research and development subsidiary, Headwaters Technology Innovation Group, Inc., has the capacity to work at molecular levels in aligning, spacing and adhering nano-sized crystals of precious and transition metals onto substrate materials. This process creates an array of custom-designed nanocatalysts for chemical and refining processes.

FINANCIALS: Sales and profits are in thousands of dollars—add 000 to get the full amount. 2011 Note: Financial information for 2011 was not available for all companies at press time.

2011 Sales: $591,954	2011 Profits: $-229,921	**U.S. Stock Ticker:** HW
2010 Sales: $654,699	2010 Profits: $-49,482	**Int'l Ticker:**
2009 Sales: $666,676	2009 Profits: $-415,550	Int'l Exchange:
2008 Sales: $886,404	2008 Profits: $-169,680	Employees: 2,735 Fiscal Year Ends: 9/30
2007 Sales: $1,207,844	2007 Profits: $20,054	Parent Company:

SALARIES/BENEFITS:

Pension Plan:	ESOP Stock Plan:	Profit Sharing:	Top Exec. Salary: $650,000	Bonus: $568,473
Savings Plan: Y	Stock Purch. Plan: Y		Second Exec. Salary: $317,750	Bonus: $220,076

OTHER THOUGHTS:

Apparent Women Officers or Directors: 1
Hot Spot for Advancement for Women/Minorities:

LOCATIONS: ("Y" = Yes)

West:	Southwest:	Midwest:	Southeast:	Northeast:	International:
Y	Y	Y	Y	Y	Y

Sales, profits and employees may be estimates. Financial information, benefits and other data can change quickly and may vary from those stated here.

HELIATEK GMBH

www.heliatek.com

Industry Group Code: 334413

Energy/Fuel:	Other Technologies:	Electrical Products:	Electronics:	Transportation:	Other:
Biofuels:	Irrigation:	Lighting/LEDs:	Computers:	Car Sharing:	Recycling:
Batteries/Storage:	Nanotech:	Waste Heat:	Sensors:	Electric Vehicles:	Engineering:
Solar: Y	Biotech:	Smart Meters:	Software:	Natural Gas Fuel:	Consulting:
Wind:	Water Tech./Treatment:	Machinery:			Investing:
Fuel Cells:	Ceramics:				Chemicals:

TYPES OF BUSINESS:

Organic Photovoltaic Modules

GROWTH PLANS/SPECIAL FEATURES:

HELIATEK GmbH, spun off from Technical University of Dresden and the University of Ulm in 2006, is a technology company that develops organic photovoltaic (OPV) modules based on oligomers, or small molecules. OPV modules are the third generation of solar panels, following crystalline and thin-film solar panels, respectively. OPVs use three different technologies, including: OPV DSSC (dye-sensitized solar cells), OPV polymers and OPV oligomers. The latter is the type of OPV that Heliatek incorporates. The company expects to launch its first products in the second half of 2012.

BRANDS/DIVISIONS/AFFILIATES:

CONTACTS: *Note: Officers with more than one job title may be intentionally listed here more than once.*

Thibaud Le Seguillon, CEO
Steffanie Rohr, Head-Mktg.
Martin Pfeiffer, CTO
Michael U. Mohr, VP-Oper.
Barbara Wandk, VP-Finance

Phone: 49-351-21-303430	**Fax:** 49-351-21-303440
Toll-Free:	
Address: Treidlerstrasse 3, Dresden, 01139 Germany	

FINANCIALS: Sales and profits are in thousands of dollars—add 000 to get the full amount. 2011 Note: Financial information for 2011 was not available for all companies at press time.

2011 Sales: $	2011 Profits: $	**U.S. Stock Ticker:** Private
2010 Sales: $	2010 Profits: $	**Int'l Ticker:**
2009 Sales: $	2009 Profits: $	Int'l Exchange:
2008 Sales: $	2008 Profits: $	Employees: Fiscal Year Ends:
2007 Sales: $	2007 Profits: $	Parent Company:

SALARIES/BENEFITS:

Pension Plan:	ESOP Stock Plan:	Profit Sharing:	Top Exec. Salary: $	Bonus: $
Savings Plan:	Stock Purch. Plan:		Second Exec. Salary: $	Bonus: $

OTHER THOUGHTS:

Apparent Women Officers or Directors: 2
Hot Spot for Advancement for Women/Minorities:

LOCATIONS: ("Y" = Yes)

West:	Southwest:	Midwest:	Southeast:	Northeast:	International: Y

HELIOVOLT CORP

www.heliovolt.net

Industry Group Code: 334413

Energy/Fuel:		Other Technologies:	Electrical Products:	Electronics:	Transportation:	Other:
Biofuels:		Irrigation:	Lighting/LEDs:	Computers:	Car Sharing:	Recycling:
Batteries/Storage:		Nanotech:	Waste Heat:	Sensors:	Electric Vehicles:	Engineering:
Solar:	Y	Biotech:	Smart Meters:	Software:	Natural Gas Fuel:	Consulting:
Wind:		Water Tech./Treatment:	Machinery:			Investing:
Fuel Cells:		Ceramics:				Chemicals:

TYPES OF BUSINESS:

Architectural Solar Cells
Thin-Film Photovoltaic Technology

BRANDS/DIVISIONS/AFFILIATES:

FASST Technology
SK Group

CONTACTS: *Note: Officers with more than one job title may be intentionally listed here more than once.*

Jim Flanary, CEO
Jim Flanary, Pres.
Steve Darnell, CFO
B.J. Stanberry, Chief Strategy Officer
B.J. Stanberry, Chmn.
John Prater, Dir.-Supply Chain

Phone: 512-767-6000	Fax:
Toll-Free:	
Address: 6301-8 E. Stassney Ln., Bldg. 8, Austin, TX 78744-3055 US	

GROWTH PLANS/SPECIAL FEATURES:

Heliovolt Corp. is a producer of high-efficiency thin-film solar energy products, which develops and markets technology for applying thin-film photovoltaic coatings to conventional construction materials. The company's primary solution is its proprietary FASST process, a low-cost, flexible manufacturing process for high-performance solar thin-film photovoltaics that prints copper indium gallium selenide (CIGS), a reliable and high-performing thin film compound, directly onto a variety of substrates, such as glass, steel, metal, composites and some polymers. The firm's products can be adapted for use in architectural modules, such as sunshades, sun louvers and curtains, skylights, curtain walls, spandrels, windows and atria; and can also be used in building-integrated photovoltaic (BIPV) systems by being embedded directly into roofing materials, glass and cladding, sunshades, canopies, skylights and modules. Heliovolt also offers customized printing services for a variety of materials. The firm operates a 122,400 square foot sustainable thin-film factory, located in Austin, Texas. In September 2011, Heliovolt announced that the Korean energy group SK Group had invested $50 million to help develop HelioVolt's global capabilities.

FINANCIALS: Sales and profits are in thousands of dollars—add 000 to get the full amount. 2011 Note: Financial information for 2011 was not available for all companies at press time.

2011 Sales: $	2011 Profits: $	U.S. Stock Ticker: Private
2010 Sales: $	2010 Profits: $	Int'l Ticker:
2009 Sales: $	2009 Profits: $	Int'l Exchange:
2008 Sales: $	2008 Profits: $	Employees: Fiscal Year Ends:
2007 Sales: $	2007 Profits: $	Parent Company:

SALARIES/BENEFITS:

Pension Plan:	ESOP Stock Plan:	Profit Sharing:	Top Exec. Salary: $	Bonus: $
Savings Plan:	Stock Purch. Plan:		Second Exec. Salary: $	Bonus: $

OTHER THOUGHTS:

Apparent Women Officers or Directors:
Hot Spot for Advancement for Women/Minorities:

LOCATIONS: ("Y" = Yes)

West:	Southwest:	Midwest:	Southeast:	Northeast:	International:
	Y				

HELVETA

corporate.helveta.com

Industry Group Code: 511210A

Energy/Fuel:	Other Technologies:	Electrical Products:	Electronics:		Transportation:	Other:
Biofuels:	Irrigation:	Lighting/LEDs:	Computers:		Car Sharing:	Recycling:
Batteries/Storage:	Nanotech:	Waste Heat:	Sensors:		Electric Vehicles:	Engineering:
Solar:	Biotech:	Smart Meters:	Software:	Y	Natural Gas Fuel:	Consulting:
Wind:	Water Tech./Treatment:	Machinery:				Investing:
Fuel Cells:	Ceramics:					Chemicals:

TYPES OF BUSINESS:

Supply Chain Management

BRANDS/DIVISIONS/AFFILIATES:

CI World
CI Server
CI World for Forestry
CI World for Food
CI Earth
TracElite
CI Author
CI Audit

CONTACTS: Note: Officers with more than one job title may be intentionally listed here more than once.

Karim Peer, CEO
Chris Powell, CFO
Martin de la Serna, VP-Mktg. & Sales
Nigel Dore, CTO
Tony Lee, Dir.-Bus. Dev.
Michel Trudelle, Dir.-Bus. Dev., Asia Pacific

Phone: 44-1235-432-100	Fax: 44-1235-835-833
Toll-Free:	
Address: 90 Milton Park, Abingdon, OX14 4RY UK	

GROWTH PLANS/SPECIAL FEATURES:

Helveta is a supply chain management firm that provides asset management software for the global supply chain. The company's primary product line is the control intelligence (CI) software platform called CI World. CI World's integrated modular suite of software manages supply chains and tracks assets such as products and materials while also helping producers meet legal and environmental responsibilities. At the center of CI World is the CI Server, which acts as a complete management information system as it generates business information, delivers reports and sends out alerts based upon customer needs. CI World comes in two distinct forms: CI World for Forestry and CI World for Food. CI World for Forestry monitors the timber supply chain with its individual modules, including CI Earth for Forestry, for mapping the forest; TracElite for Forestry, monitoring the chain of custody; CI Author for Forestry, for the production, storage and management of documents pertaining to CI World; and CI Audit for Forestry, for reconciliation and data validation. CI World for Food tracks and manages food assets and offers the same individual modules as CI World for Forestry, but is geared towards the food supply chain. While the firm is headquartered in the U.K., its products have been deployed in South America, Europe, Asia and Africa.

FINANCIALS: Sales and profits are in thousands of dollars—add 000 to get the full amount. 2011 Note: Financial information for 2011 was not available for all companies at press time.

2011 Sales: $	2011 Profits: $	**U.S. Stock Ticker: Private**
2010 Sales: $	2010 Profits: $	**Int'l Ticker:**
2009 Sales: $	2009 Profits: $	Int'l Exchange:
2008 Sales: $	2008 Profits: $	Employees: Fiscal Year Ends:
2007 Sales: $	2007 Profits: $	Parent Company:

SALARIES/BENEFITS:

Pension Plan:	ESOP Stock Plan:	Profit Sharing:	Top Exec. Salary: $	Bonus: $
Savings Plan:	Stock Purch. Plan:		Second Exec. Salary: $	Bonus: $

OTHER THOUGHTS:

Apparent Women Officers or Directors:
Hot Spot for Advancement for Women/Minorities:

LOCATIONS: ("Y" = Yes)

West:	Southwest:	Midwest:	Southeast:	Northeast:	International: Y

Sales, profits and employees may be estimates. Financial information, benefits and other data can change quickly and may vary from those stated here.

HEWLETT-PACKARD CO (HP)

www.hp.com

Industry Group Code: 334111

Energy/Fuel:	Other Technologies:		Electrical Products:	Electronics:	Transportation:	Other:
Biofuels:	Irrigation:		Lighting/LEDs:	Computers:	Car Sharing:	Recycling:
Batteries/Storage:	Nanotech:	Y	Waste Heat:	Sensors:	Electric Vehicles:	Engineering:
Solar:	Biotech:		Smart Meters:	Software:	Natural Gas Fuel:	Consulting:
Wind:	Water Tech./Treatment:		Machinery:			Investing:
Fuel Cells:	Ceramics:					Chemicals:

TYPES OF BUSINESS:

Computer Hardware-PCs
Computer Software
Printers & Supplies
Scanners
Outsourcing
Servers
Consulting
Managed Print Services

BRANDS/DIVISIONS/AFFILIATES:

HP StorageWorks
HP Labs (Hewlett-Packard Laboratories)
Electronic Data Systems Corp (EDS)
HP Mini
ArcSight Inc
3Com Corp
Palm Inc
3PAR, Inc.

CONTACTS: Note: Officers with more than one job title may be intentionally listed here more than once.

Meg Whitman, CEO
Cathie Lesjak, CFO/Exec. VP
Tom Hogan, Exec. VP-Mktg. & Enterprise Sales
Marcela Perez de Alonso, Exec. VP-Human Resources
Prith Banerjee, Sr. VP-Research/Dir.-HP Labs
Randall D. Mott, CIO/Exec. VP
Shane Robison, CTO/Exec. VP
Pete Bocian, Chief Admin. Officer/Exec. VP
Michael J. Holston, General Counsel/Exec. VP/Sec.
Shane Robison, Chief Strategy Officer
Bill Wohl, Chief Comm. Officer/Sr. VP
Todd Bradley, Exec. VP-Personal Systems Group
Ann M. Livermore, Exec. VP-Enterprise Bus.
Vyomesh Joshi, Exec. VP-Imaging & Printing Group
Francesco Serafini, Exec. VP-Emerging Markets
Ray Lane, Chmn.

Phone: 650-857-1501	Fax: 650-857-5518
Toll-Free:	
Address: 3000 Hanover St., Palo Alto, CA 94304 US	

GROWTH PLANS/SPECIAL FEATURES:

Hewlett-Packard Co. (HP) is a global provider of products, technologies, software and services to customers ranging from individuals to large enterprises. Offerings span personal computing and other access devices; imaging and printing-related products and services; enterprise IT infrastructure; and multi-vendor services. The company operates in seven segments: Enterprise Storage and Servers (ESS); HP Services (HPS); HP Software; the Personal Systems Group (PSG); the Imaging and Printing Group (IPG); HP Financial Services (HPFS); and Corporate Investments. The ESS segment provides storage and server solutions such as HP StorageWorks, offering entry-level, mid-range and high-end arrays; storage area networks; network attached storage; storage management software; and virtualization technologies. The HPS segment provides a portfolio of multi-vendor IT services, including technology services; consulting and integration; and outsourcing services such as computer department outsourcing and managed print services. HPS also encompasses the operations of recently-acquired Electronic Data Systems Corporation (EDS), a technology services provider currently managing more than 1 million applications worldwide on behalf of a range of business and government clients. The HP Software segment provides business technology optimization software that allows customers to manage and automate their IT infrastructure, operations, applications, IT services and business processes. The PSG segment provides PCs, workstations, handheld computing devices, digital entertainment systems, calculators, software and services for the commercial and consumer markets. The IPG segment provides consumer and commercial printer hardware, printing supplies, printing media and scanning devices. The HPFS segment provides a broad range of financial life-cycle management services. The Corporate Investments segment includes the Hewlett-Packard Laboratories and certain business incubation projects. In 2010, the firm acquired 3Com Corp. for $2.7 billion; Palm, Inc. for approximately $1 billion; 3PAR, Inc. for $2.35 billion; security analysis specialist Fortify Software; and security software developer, ArcSight, Inc. for $1.5 billion. In February 2011, HP agreed to acquire analytics company Vertica.

FINANCIALS: Sales and profits are in thousands of dollars—add 000 to get the full amount. 2011 Note: Financial information for 2011 was not available for all companies at press time.

2011 Sales: $127,245,000	2011 Profits: $7,074,000	**U.S. Stock Ticker: HPQ**
2010 Sales: $126,033,000	2010 Profits: $8,761,000	**Int'l Ticker:**
2009 Sales: $114,552,000	2009 Profits: $7,660,000	Int'l Exchange:
2008 Sales: $118,364,000	2008 Profits: $8,329,000	Employees: 349,600 Fiscal Year Ends: 10/31
2007 Sales: $104,286,000	2007 Profits: $7,264,000	Parent Company:

SALARIES/BENEFITS:

Pension Plan: Y	ESOP Stock Plan:	Profit Sharing:	Top Exec. Salary: $1,121,944	Bonus: $
Savings Plan: Y	Stock Purch. Plan: Y		Second Exec. Salary: $748,000	Bonus: $3,522,813

OTHER THOUGHTS:

Apparent Women Officers or Directors: 8
Hot Spot for Advancement for Women/Minorities: Y

LOCATIONS: ("Y" = Yes)

West:	Southwest:	Midwest:	Southeast:	Northeast:	International:
Y	Y	Y	Y	Y	Y

HEWLETT-PACKARD LABORATORIES (HP LABS) www.hpl.hp.com

Industry Group Code: 541712

Energy/Fuel:	Other Technologies:	Electrical Products:	Electronics:	Transportation:	Other:	
Biofuels:	Irrigation:	Lighting/LEDs:	Computers:	Car Sharing:	Recycling:	
Batteries/Storage:	Nanotech:	Waste Heat:	Sensors:	Electric Vehicles:	Engineering:	Y
Solar:	Biotech:	Smart Meters:	Software: Y	Natural Gas Fuel:	Consulting:	
Wind:	Water Tech./Treatment:	Machinery:			Investing:	
Fuel Cells:	Ceramics:				Chemicals:	

TYPES OF BUSINESS:
Electronics Research
Printing & Imaging Technology
Internet & Computing Technology
Cloud Services
Sustainable Technologies

BRANDS/DIVISIONS/AFFILIATES:
Hewlett-Packard Co (HP)
Cirious

CONTACTS: Note: Officers with more than one job title may be intentionally listed here more than once.
Prith Banerjee, Dir.-HP Labs/Sr. VP-Research-HP
Vladimir Polutin, Dir.-HP Labs Russia
Chris Whitney, Dir.-HP Labs Singapore
Min Wang, Dir.-HP Labs China
Doron Shaked, Dir.-HP Labs Israel
Sudhir Dixit, Dir.-HP Labs India

Phone: 650-857-1501	**Fax:** 650-857-5518
Toll-Free: 800-752-0900	
Address: 1501 Page Mill Rd., Palo Alto, CA 94304 US	

GROWTH PLANS/SPECIAL FEATURES:
Hewlett-Packard Laboratories (HP Labs) is the research arm of parent Hewlett-Packard Co. (HP). HP Labs maintains seven labs and four research groups located in Palo Alto, California; Fusionopolis, Singapore; Bangalore, India; Beijing, China; Bristol, U.K.; Haifa, Israel; and St. Petersburg, Russia, with additional research teams in Princeton, New Jersey and in Barcelona, Spain. The company concentrates on eight areas of focus: analytics, content transformation, immersive interaction, intelligent infrastructure, cloud, digital commercial print, information management and sustainability. With regard to analytics, the firm focuses on IT security analytics, business analytics, as well as personalization and customer-intelligence analytics. Content transformation includes working to transition data from analog to digital as well as from digital to physical products. Immersive interaction involves making human interactions easier through and with technologies. HP Labs' intelligent infrastructure operations focus on designing networks, devices and scalable architectures to securely connect business and individuals to content and services. Its cloud group is engaged in the research of cloud computing (where applications and files are stored remotely rather than on a user's computer). This division is focused on two main topics: Enterprise Cloud Software Platform (Cirious) and Social Computing. With regard to digital commercial print, the company handles both printing processes for digital commercial print and commercial print automation. The firm's information management group is involved in projects relating to live business intelligence, data and sequence mining, program analysis and semantic automation. Finally, one lab is involved in the sustainability area, which seeks to lower the carbon footprint of technologies, business models and IT infrastructure.

FINANCIALS: Sales and profits are in thousands of dollars—add 000 to get the full amount. 2011 Note: Financial information for 2011 was not available for all companies at press time.

2011 Sales: $	2011 Profits: $	**U.S. Stock Ticker: Subsidiary**
2010 Sales: $	2010 Profits: $	**Int'l Ticker:**
2009 Sales: $	2009 Profits: $	Int'l Exchange:
2008 Sales: $	2008 Profits: $	Employees: Fiscal Year Ends: 10/31
2007 Sales: $	2007 Profits: $	Parent Company: HEWLETT-PACKARD CO (HP)

SALARIES/BENEFITS:
Pension Plan:	ESOP Stock Plan:	Profit Sharing:	Top Exec. Salary: $	Bonus: $
Savings Plan: Y	Stock Purch. Plan:		Second Exec. Salary: $	Bonus: $

OTHER THOUGHTS:
Apparent Women Officers or Directors:
Hot Spot for Advancement for Women/Minorities:

LOCATIONS: ("Y" = Yes)
West:	Southwest:	Midwest:	Southeast:	Northeast:	International:
Y					Y

HEWLETT-PACKARD QUANTUM SCIENCE RESEARCH

www.hpl.hp.com/research/qsr

Industry Group Code: 541712

Energy/Fuel:	Other Technologies:		Electrical Products:	Electronics:		Transportation:		Other:	
Biofuels:	Irrigation:		Lighting/LEDs:	Computers:	Y	Car Sharing:		Recycling:	
Batteries/Storage:	Nanotech:	Y	Waste Heat:	Sensors:		Electric Vehicles:		Engineering:	Y
Solar:	Biotech:		Smart Meters:	Software:	Y	Natural Gas Fuel:		Consulting:	
Wind:	Water Tech./Treatment:		Machinery:					Investing:	
Fuel Cells:	Ceramics:							Chemicals:	

TYPES OF BUSINESS:

Research & Development-Nanotechnology
Molecular-Scale Electronics Research

BRANDS/DIVISIONS/AFFILIATES:

Hewlett-Packard Co (HP)
Advanced Studies Program
Hewlett-Packard Laboratories
Quantum Key Distribution

CONTACTS: Note: Officers with more than one job title may be intentionally listed here more than once.

Stan Williams, Dir.-Quantum Science Research/Sr. HP Fellow
Rich Friedrich, Dir.-Strategy & Innovation Office
Prith Banerjee, Dir.-HP Labs
Ray Beausoleil, Principal Scientist
Ted Kamins, Principal Scientist
Gun-Young Jung, Research Associate
Sudhir Dixit, Dir.-HP Labs India

Phone: 650-857-1501	Fax: 650-857-5518
Toll-Free:	
Address: 3000 Hanover St., Palo Alto, CA 94304-1185 US	

GROWTH PLANS/SPECIAL FEATURES:

Hewlett-Packard Quantum Science Research (QRS), founded in 1995, conducts research in nanoscale science and the fundamental physics of switching, with an emphasis on molecular-scale electronics. It is a research unit of the Advanced Studies Program of Hewlett-Packard Laboratories, which is itself a subsidiary of Hewlett-Packard Co. (HP). QRS focuses on fabricating, measuring and understanding the properties of nanometer-scale structures. In recent years, QRS devised a method of growing and connecting semiconductor nanowires in place. Potential applications include more effective sensors for detecting toxic gases; chemical and biological substances; interconnecting leads in nanometer-scale electronic circuits; and developing devices within nanowires such as transistors. More recently, the firm has been conducting basic research on a variety of nanoscale classical and quantum optics, including developing quantum key distribution (QKD) applications. QKD aims at using quantum principles for security, such as the fact that simply looking at a quantum system changes it, allowing the recipient of the message to know if it has been intercepted. The quantum key can be encoded into very weak pulses of light or even single photons. Currently, QKD can only be used for messages within 60 miles, which is the maximum the weak light beam may travel through a fiber-optic cable without being amplified or otherwise modified, thus corrupting the original key. However, work is being done to extend this range. Researchers also hope to modify QKD for other applications, such as installing devices into mobile phones that securely transmit a quantum key to an ATM without having to plug in or type anything. The firm is also researching nanoscale optics, including attempting to utilize optical connections within blade servers themselves, essentially replacing the copper wires in the blades' processors, and between different servers, with multispectral tunable laser lights. QRS has overseas research laboratories in Beijing, China, and St. Petersburg, Russia.

FINANCIALS: Sales and profits are in thousands of dollars—add 000 to get the full amount. 2011 Note: Financial information for 2011 was not available for all companies at press time.

2011 Sales: $	2011 Profits: $	U.S. Stock Ticker: Subsidiary
2010 Sales: $	2010 Profits: $	Int'l Ticker:
2009 Sales: $	2009 Profits: $	Int'l Exchange:
2008 Sales: $	2008 Profits: $	Employees: Fiscal Year Ends: 10/31
2007 Sales: $	2007 Profits: $	Parent Company: HEWLETT-PACKARD CO (HP)

SALARIES/BENEFITS:

Pension Plan:	ESOP Stock Plan:	Profit Sharing: Y	Top Exec. Salary: $	Bonus: $
Savings Plan: Y	Stock Purch. Plan:		Second Exec. Salary: $	Bonus: $

OTHER THOUGHTS:

Apparent Women Officers or Directors:
Hot Spot for Advancement for Women/Minorities:

LOCATIONS: ("Y" = Yes)

West:	Southwest:	Midwest:	Southeast:	Northeast:	International:
Y	Y		Y		Y

HITACHI HIGH TECHNOLOGIES AMERICA INC www.hitachi-hta.com

Industry Group Code: 541712

Energy/Fuel:		Other Technologies:		Electrical Products:		Electronics:		Transportation:		Other:	
Biofuels:		Irrigation:		Lighting/LEDs:		Computers:	Y	Car Sharing:		Recycling:	
Batteries/Storage:		Nanotech:	Y	Waste Heat:		Sensors:		Electric Vehicles:		Engineering:	Y
Solar:		Biotech:		Smart Meters:		Software:	Y	Natural Gas Fuel:		Consulting:	
Wind:		Water Tech./Treatment:		Machinery:						Investing:	
Fuel Cells:		Ceramics:								Chemicals:	

TYPES OF BUSINESS:
Research & Development
Semiconductor Manufacturing Equipment
Biotechnology Products
Industrial Equipment
Electronic & Industrial Materials
Electronic Components & Systems
Nanotechnology Research
Chromatography Systems

BRANDS/DIVISIONS/AFFILIATES:
Hitachi Ltd
Life Science Group of HTA, Inc. (The)

CONTACTS: Note: Officers with more than one job title may be intentionally listed here more than once.
Monica Degnan, Contact-Media, Western U.S.
Yasukuni Koga, VP-Investor Rel.
Steve Keough, Contact-Media, Central & Eastern U.S.
Takashi Kawamura, Chmn. Exec. Board-Hitachi Ltd.

Phone: 847-273-4141	Fax: 847-273-4407
Toll-Free:	
Address: 10 N. Martingale Rd., Ste. 500, Schaumburg, IL 60173-2295 US	

GROWTH PLANS/SPECIAL FEATURES:
Hitachi High Technologies America, Inc. (HTA) is a subsidiary of Hitachi, Ltd. of Japan. The company was formed in 2002 from the combination of Nissei Sangyo America, Ltd., a subsidiary of Hitachi High-Technologies Corporation of Tokyo, Japan; the Semiconductor Equipment Group of Hitachi America, Ltd.; and Hitachi Instruments, Inc., a subsidiary of Hitachi America, Ltd. HTA offers imaging and analysis tools for nanotechnology, research, failure analysis and inspection. It manufactures and markets a full line of electron microscopes, X-ray analysis systems and accessories. HTA operates through eight divisions: semiconductor etch equipment; semiconductor metrology equipment; SMT production systems; electron microscopes; life sciences-chemical analysis; electronic products, hard disk manufacturing systems; and advanced materials. The semiconductor etch equipment division manufactures dry plasma etch systems. The firm's semiconductor metrology equipment segment offers wafer inspection, defect review and metrology software. Its SMT production systems division offers dispensers, conveyors, feeders and direct drive mounters for semiconductors and component packaging. The electron microscopes division manufactures advanced microscope systems. The Life Science Group of HTA, Inc., provides instruments and analytical equipment, including industry-leading DNA sequencers and isolation equipment, to the biotechnology, chemical and pharmaceutical industries. The electronic products division controls sales of the company's electronic microscopes related technologies. The hard disk manufacturing systems division offers nano imprint systems, disk surface inspection systems, cleaning machines, measurement testers and disk test systems. HTA's advanced materials division offers products from semiconductor wafers to digital media and television products.

HTA offers its employees health plans, retirement packages, saving plans, tuition reimbursement and bonus incentives.

FINANCIALS: Sales and profits are in thousands of dollars—add 000 to get the full amount. 2011 Note: Financial information for 2011 was not available for all companies at press time.

		U.S. Stock Ticker: Subsidiary
2011 Sales: $	2011 Profits: $	Int'l Ticker:
2010 Sales: $	2010 Profits: $	Int'l Exchange:
2009 Sales: $	2009 Profits: $	Employees: Fiscal Year Ends: 3/31
2008 Sales: $	2008 Profits: $	Parent Company: HITACHI LTD
2007 Sales: $	2007 Profits: $	

SALARIES/BENEFITS:

Pension Plan: Y	ESOP Stock Plan:	Profit Sharing:	Top Exec. Salary: $	Bonus: $
Savings Plan: Y	Stock Purch. Plan:		Second Exec. Salary: $	Bonus: $

OTHER THOUGHTS:
Apparent Women Officers or Directors: 1
Hot Spot for Advancement for Women/Minorities:

LOCATIONS: ("Y" = Yes)

West:	Southwest:	Midwest:	Southeast:	Northeast:	International:
Y	Y	Y	Y	Y	Y

HITACHI LTD

www.hitachi.com

Industry Group Code: 334111

Energy/Fuel:	Other Technologies:		Electrical Products:	Electronics:	Transportation:	Other:
Biofuels:	Irrigation:		Lighting/LEDs:	Computers:	Car Sharing:	Recycling:
Batteries/Storage:	Nanotech:	Y	Waste Heat:	Sensors:	Electric Vehicles:	Engineering:
Solar:	Biotech:		Smart Meters:	Software:	Natural Gas Fuel:	Consulting:
Wind:	Water Tech./Treatment:		Machinery:			Investing:
Fuel Cells:	Ceramics:					Chemicals:

TYPES OF BUSINESS:

Computer Hardware Manufacturing
Consumer Appliances & Electronics
Materials Manufacturing
Financial Services Products
Power & Industrial Systems
Medical & Scientific Equipment
Transportation Systems
Consulting Services

BRANDS/DIVISIONS/AFFILIATES:

Clarion Co Ltd
Hitachi Global Storage Technologies Inc
Hitachi High Technologies America Inc
Hitachi Medical Corporation
Sierra Atlantic
Aptivo Consulting SA
Hitachi Medical Systems America
Hitachi Consulting

CONTACTS:
Note: Officers with more than one job title may be intentionally listed here more than once.

Hiroaki Nakanishi, CEO
Hiroaki Nakanishi, Pres.
Kazuhiro Mori, Sr. Exec. VP
Koji Tanaka, Sr. Exec. VP
Takashi Miyoshi, Sr. Exec. VP
Nobuo Mochida, Sr. Exec. VP
Takashi Kawamura, Chmn.

Phone: 81-3-3258-1111	**Fax:** 81-3-4564-2148
Toll-Free:	
Address: 6-6, Marunouchi 1-chome, Chiyoda-ku, Tokyo, 100-8280 Japan	

GROWTH PLANS/SPECIAL FEATURES:

Hitachi, Ltd. is a Japan-based electronics company. Hitachi divides its products and services into the following 11 segments: Information & Telecommunications Systems, Power Systems, Social Infrastructure & Industrial Systems, Construction Machinery, Electronic Systems & Equipment, High Functional Materials & Components, Automotive Systems, Component & Devices, Digital Media & Consumer products, Financial Services and Other. The firm's Information & Telecommunication Systems segment includes communications infrastructure hardware and storage products, accounting for 16% of revenue. The Power Systems segment, accounting for 8%, offers products and services in support of nuclear, thermal and hydroelectric power systems. The Social Infrastructure & Industrial Systems, 11%, handles railway and urban systems. The Construction Machinery segment, 7%, segment supplies heavy machinery for infrastructure development. The Electronic Systems & Equipment segment, 10%, creates a wide variety of digital devices, selling mainly to power companies. The High Functional Materials & Components segment, 13%, develops such products as specialty steels. The Automotive segment has developed electrical motors, inverters and batteries. The Components & Devices, 8%, includes items such as digital cameras. The Digital Media & Consumer Products, 9%, segment produces flat-panel TVs and home appliances. The Financial Services, 4%, segment works on both corporate and client needs and accounts. In January 2011, Hitachi announced the acquisitions of Sierra Atlantic and Aptivo Consulting, SA. In September 2011, Hitachi announced the acquisition of BlueArc, a leader in scalable, high performance network storage; additionally, Hitachi and SFO Technologies Pvt. Ltd. established a joint venture, Hitachi NeST Control Systems Pvt. Ltd., in the field of advanced control systems for thermal power plants. In October 2011, the firm announced the acquisition of Shoden Dara Systems, a provider of data center technology solutions.

FINANCIALS: Sales and profits are in thousands of dollars—add 000 to get the full amount. 2011 Note: Financial information for 2011 was not available for all companies at press time.

2011 Sales: $110,064,400	2011 Profits: $3,138,700	**U.S. Stock Ticker:**
2010 Sales: $109,058,000	2010 Profits: $-1,026,200	**Int'l Ticker: 6501**
2009 Sales: $103,003,801	2009 Profits: $-8,109,571	Int'l Exchange: Tokyo-TSE
2008 Sales: $113,390,020	2008 Profits: $-587,060	Employees: 361,745 Fiscal Year Ends: 3/31
2007 Sales: $87,107,200	2007 Profits: $-278,800	Parent Company:

SALARIES/BENEFITS:

Pension Plan:	ESOP Stock Plan:	Profit Sharing:	Top Exec. Salary: $	Bonus: $
Savings Plan:	Stock Purch. Plan:		Second Exec. Salary: $	Bonus: $

OTHER THOUGHTS:

Apparent Women Officers or Directors: 1
Hot Spot for Advancement for Women/Minorities:

LOCATIONS: ("Y" = Yes)

West:	Southwest:	Midwest:	Southeast:	Northeast:	International:
Y	Y	Y	Y	Y	Y

HUNTSMAN CORPORATION

www.huntsman.com

Industry Group Code: 325

Energy/Fuel:	Other Technologies:	Electrical Products:	Electronics:	Transportation:	Other:	
Biofuels:	Irrigation:	Lighting/LEDs:	Computers:	Car Sharing:	Recycling:	
Batteries/Storage:	Nanotech:	Waste Heat:	Sensors:	Electric Vehicles:	Engineering:	
Solar:	Biotech:	Smart Meters:	Software:	Natural Gas Fuel:	Consulting:	
Wind:	Water Tech./Treatment:	Machinery:			Investing:	
Fuel Cells:	Ceramics:				Chemicals:	Y

TYPES OF BUSINESS:

Chemicals Manufacturing
Polyurethane Manufacturing
Advanced Materials & Surface Technologies
Performance Chemicals
Pigments

BRANDS/DIVISIONS/AFFILIATES:

Huntsman International
Huntsman Pigments LLC

CONTACTS: *Note: Officers with more than one job title may be intentionally listed here more than once.*

Peter R. Huntsman, CEO
Peter R. Huntsman, Pres.
J. Kimo Esplin, CFO/Exec. VP
R. Wade Rogers, Sr. VP-Global Human Resources
Maria Csiba-Womersly, CIO/VP
James R. Moore, General Counsel/Exec. VP/Corp. Sec.
Sean Douglas, VP-Corp. Dev.
Gary Chapman, Contact-Media
Kurt D. Ogden, VP-Investor Rel.
L. Russell Healy, Controller/VP
Anthony P. Hankins, Pres., Polyurethanes
Paul G. Hulme, Pres., Textile Effects
Simon Turner, Pres., Pigments
Stewart A. Monteith, Pres., Performance Prod.
Jon M. Huntsman, Chmn.
Anthony P. Hankins, CEO-APAC
Brian V. Ridd, Sr. VP-Purchasing

Phone: 801-584-5700	Fax: 801-584-5781
Toll-Free:	
Address: 500 Huntsman Way, Salt Lake City, UT 84108 US	

GROWTH PLANS/SPECIAL FEATURES:

Huntsman Corporation is a global manufacturer of differentiated chemical products and inorganic chemical products. The company operates all of its businesses through wholly-owned subsidiary Huntsman International. The firm operates in five business segments: polyurethanes, advanced materials, textile effects, performance products and pigments. The polyurethanes segment (38% of revenues) produces MDI products, propylene oxide, polyols, propylene glycol, thermoplastic urethane, aniline and methyl tert-butyl ether products. The advanced materials segment (13% of revenues) manufactures epoxy resin compounds and formulations; cross-linking, matting and curing agents; and epoxy, acrylic and polyurethane-based adhesives. The textile effects division (8% of revenues) produces textile chemicals and dyes. The firm's performance products segment (28% of revenues) is organized around three market groups: performance specialties, performance intermediates and maleic anhydride and licensing. It produces amines, carbonates and certain specialty surfactants; consumes internally produced and third-party-sourced base petrochemicals in the manufacture of its surfactants, LAB and ethanolamines products; licenses maleic anhydride manufacturing technology (mainly used in the production of fiberglass reinforced resins) and technology on behalf of other Huntsman businesses; and supplies butane fixed bed catalyst used in the manufacture of maleic anhydrides. Huntsman's pigments segment (13% of revenues) manufactures titanium dioxide, used in paints and coatings, plastics, paper, printing inks, fibers and ceramics. In early 2010, Huntsman formed joint ventures with Jurong Ningwu Chemical Co. Ltd. and Zamil Group Holding Company. In July 2010, the firm agreed to acquire the chemical business of Laffans Petrochemicals, Ltd.

FINANCIALS: Sales and profits are in thousands of dollars—add 000 to get the full amount. 2011 Note: Financial information for 2011 was not available for all companies at press time.

2011 Sales: $	2011 Profits: $	**U.S. Stock Ticker: HUN**
2010 Sales: $9,250,000	2010 Profits: $185,000	**Int'l Ticker:**
2009 Sales: $7,665,000	2009 Profits: $-412,000	Int'l Exchange:
2008 Sales: $10,056,000	2008 Profits: $39,000	Employees: 12,000 Fiscal Year Ends: 12/31
2007 Sales: $9,650,800	2007 Profits: $-21,000	Parent Company:

SALARIES/BENEFITS:

Pension Plan: Y	ESOP Stock Plan:	Profit Sharing:	Top Exec. Salary: $1,008,333	Bonus: $1,800,000
Savings Plan: Y	Stock Purch. Plan:		Second Exec. Salary: $1,464,500	Bonus: $4,464,500

OTHER THOUGHTS:

Apparent Women Officers or Directors: 2
Hot Spot for Advancement for Women/Minorities:

LOCATIONS: ("Y" = Yes)

West:	Southwest:	Midwest:	Southeast:	Northeast:	International:
Y	Y	Y	Y	Y	Y

Sales, profits and employees may be estimates. Financial information, benefits and other data can change quickly and may vary from those stated here.

HYDROGENICS CORPORATION

www.hydrogenics.com

Industry Group Code: 335999

Energy/Fuel:		Other Technologies:	Electrical Products:	Electronics:	Transportation:	Other:
Biofuels:		Irrigation:	Lighting/LEDs:	Computers:	Car Sharing:	Recycling:
Batteries/Storage:		Nanotech:	Waste Heat:	Sensors:	Electric Vehicles:	Engineering:
Solar:		Biotech:	Smart Meters:	Software:	Natural Gas Fuel:	Consulting:
Wind:		Water Tech./Treatment:	Machinery:			Investing:
Fuel Cells:	Y	Ceramics:				Chemicals:

TYPES OF BUSINESS:

Fuel Cell Products
Hydrogen Power Products
Fuel Cell Products & Services

BRANDS/DIVISIONS/AFFILIATES:

HySTAT
HyPM
HyPX

CONTACTS: *Note: Officers with more than one job title may be intentionally listed here more than once.*

Daryl Wilson, CEO
Daryl Wilson, Pres.
Jennifer Barber, CFO
Joseph Cargnelli, CTO
Jennifer Barber, Corp. Sec.
Jennifer Barber, Investor Rel.
Filip Smeets, Gen. Mgr.
Douglas S. Alexander, Chmn.

Phone: 905-361-3660	Fax: 905-361-3626
Toll-Free:	
Address: 220 Admiral Blvd., Mississauga, ON L5T 2N6 Canada	

GROWTH PLANS/SPECIAL FEATURES:

Hydrogenics Corporation develops hydrogen and fuel cell power products and testing equipment. Headquartered in Canada, the firm maintains additional offices in Belgium, Germany, Russia, China and the U.S. It operates in two segments: OnSite Generation and Power Systems. Its OnSite Generation segment, based in Belgium, sells hydrogen infrastructure technology and products, and develops, manufactures and installs onsite hydrogen generation systems for customers in the industrial and energy markets. This segment employs the company's HySTAT Refueling Stations, which provide fuel for hydrogen-powered vehicles or backup power for critical infrastructure. Other HySTAT products connected to these stations include a compression module, storage module and fuel dispenser module. The Power Systems segment sells fuel cell products for backup power and light mobility applications, including forklifts and urban transit buses, to original equipment manufacturers (OEMs) and end users. It offers a line of products that includes the commercially available HyPM fuel cell power module. The modules range in output from 4-65 kilowatts (KW) and are configured for stationary, mobile and auxiliary power applications. The company's HyPX Fuel Cell Power Packs, a related system, includes a standard HyPM Power Module integrated with a hydrogen storage tank, thermal management, controls and ultracapacitors that capture and release regenerative power to provide higher power in short bursts. The segment's projects are geared toward developing engines for commercial vans, transit buses, utility vehicles and forklifts.

FINANCIALS: Sales and profits are in thousands of dollars—add 000 to get the full amount. 2011 Note: Financial information for 2011 was not available for all companies at press time.

2011 Sales: $	2011 Profits: $	**U.S. Stock Ticker:**
2010 Sales: $20,930	2010 Profits: $-8,557	**Int'l Ticker: HYG**
2009 Sales: $18,841	2009 Profits: $-9,375	Int'l Exchange: Toronto-TSX
2008 Sales: $39,340	2008 Profits: $-14,319	Employees: 114 Fiscal Year Ends: 12/31
2007 Sales: $38,000	2007 Profits: $-28,100	Parent Company:

SALARIES/BENEFITS:

Pension Plan:	ESOP Stock Plan:	Profit Sharing:	Top Exec. Salary: $336,978	Bonus: $
Savings Plan:	Stock Purch. Plan:		Second Exec. Salary: $214,100	Bonus: $

OTHER THOUGHTS:

Apparent Women Officers or Directors: 1
Hot Spot for Advancement for Women/Minorities:

LOCATIONS: ("Y" = Yes)

West:	Southwest:	Midwest:	Southeast:	Northeast:	International:
Y					Y

HYDROPOINT DATA SYSTEMS

www.hydropoint.com

Industry Group Code: 924110

Energy/Fuel:	Other Technologies:	Electrical Products:	Electronics:	Transportation:	Other:
Biofuels:	Irrigation:	Lighting/LEDs:	Computers:	Car Sharing:	Recycling:
Batteries/Storage:	Nanotech:	Waste Heat:	Sensors:	Electric Vehicles:	Engineering:
Solar:	Biotech:	Smart Meters:	Software: Y	Natural Gas Fuel:	Consulting: Y
Wind:	Water Tech./Treatment: Y	Machinery:			Investing:
Fuel Cells:	Ceramics:				Chemicals:

TYPES OF BUSINESS:

Water Management Technology

BRANDS/DIVISIONS/AFFILIATES:

WeatherTRAK Smart Water Management
WeatherTRAK ET Everywhere
WeatherTRAK Professional Services

CONTACTS: *Note: Officers with more than one job title may be intentionally listed here more than once.*

Paul Ciandrini, CEO
Paul Ciandrini, Pres.
Dennis J. Reilly, Sr. VP-Sales
Peter Carlson, CTO
Peter Carlson, VP-Prod. Mgmt.
Adam Opoczynski, VP-Eng.
Chris Spain, Chief Strategy Officer
Chris Manchuck, VP-Channel Sales
Ben Slick, VP-Key Accounts & Bus. Dev.
Mardi Diamond, VP-Professional Svcs. & Support
Chris Spain, Chmn.

Phone:	**Fax:** 707-769-9695
Toll-Free: 800-362-8774	
Address: 1720 Corp. Cir., Petaluma, CA 94954 US	

GROWTH PLANS/SPECIAL FEATURES:

HydroPoint Data Systems is a smart water management technology firm. Through its proprietary WeatherTRAK Smart Water Management solution, the company targets the effective management of landscape irrigation, one of the top producers of urban water waste. WeatherTRAK eliminates overwatering and saves four times more water than comparable technologies, while reducing energy demand and protecting water quality. Each system is customized to its operator's desired settings and features the WeatherTRAK ET Everywhere service. Once the operator enters the basic information regarding the landscape, the Everywhere service automatically schedules water irrigation based on the landscapes needs and its local weather conditions. Additionally, the firm offers WeatherTRAK Professional Services. This product offers irrigation consulting and includes site evaluations; landscape contractor training; installation and maintenance planning; deployment and optimization; upgrade planning; and an ongoing support team. Many major companies, such as Coca-Cola, Google, AIMCO, Shea Homes and Kohl's, use the system to help increase the sustainability of their operations. In 2011, HydroPoint customers saved 68 million kilowatt hours, 17 billion gallons of water and 91 million pounds of carbon dioxide.

FINANCIALS: Sales and profits are in thousands of dollars—add 000 to get the full amount. 2011 Note: Financial information for 2011 was not available for all companies at press time.

2011 Sales: $	2011 Profits: $	**U.S. Stock Ticker: Private**
2010 Sales: $	2010 Profits: $	**Int'l Ticker:**
2009 Sales: $	2009 Profits: $	Int'l Exchange:
2008 Sales: $	2008 Profits: $	Employees: Fiscal Year Ends:
2007 Sales: $	2007 Profits: $	Parent Company:

SALARIES/BENEFITS:

Pension Plan:	ESOP Stock Plan:	Profit Sharing:	Top Exec. Salary: $	Bonus: $
Savings Plan:	Stock Purch. Plan:		Second Exec. Salary: $	Bonus: $

OTHER THOUGHTS:

Apparent Women Officers or Directors: 1
Hot Spot for Advancement for Women/Minorities:

LOCATIONS: ("Y" = Yes)

West:	Southwest:	Midwest:	Southeast:	Northeast:	International:
Y					

HYFLUX LTD

Industry Group Code: 924110

www.hyflux.com

Energy/Fuel:	Other Technologies:		Electrical Products:	Electronics:	Transportation:	Other:	
Biofuels:	Irrigation:		Lighting/LEDs:	Computers:	Car Sharing:	Recycling:	
Batteries/Storage:	Nanotech:		Waste Heat:	Sensors:	Electric Vehicles:	Engineering:	
Solar:	Biotech:		Smart Meters:	Software:	Natural Gas Fuel:	Consulting:	
Wind:	Water Tech./Treatment:	Y	Machinery:			Investing:	
Fuel Cells:	Ceramics:					Chemicals:	

TYPES OF BUSINESS:

Water Treatment Products
Industrial Liquids Filtration Products
Polylactic Acid Polymer Production
Filtration Products for Plant-Based & Hydrocarbon-Based Oils

BRANDS/DIVISIONS/AFFILIATES:

Kristal
FerroCep
InoCep
ProCep
Gurgle

CONTACTS: *Note: Officers with more than one job title may be intentionally listed here more than once.*

Olivia Lum, CEO/Managing Dir.
Andrew Ngiam Poh Chye, COO/Exec. VP
Olivia Lum, Pres.
Cho Wee Peng, CFO/Exec. VP
Oon Jin Teik, Exec. VP/CEO-China
Foo Hee Kiang, Exec. VP-Commercial Contracts & Industry Rel.
Winnifred Heap, Exec. VP-Capital Markets
Sam Ong, Exec. VP/Deputy CEO

Phone: 65-6214-0777	**Fax:** 65-6214-1211
Toll-Free:	
Address: 202 Kallang Bahru, Hyflux Building, Singapore, 339339 Singapore	

GROWTH PLANS/SPECIAL FEATURES:

Hyflux Ltd., founded in 1989 as a manufacturer of membranes for water treatment facilities, has since expanded to areas benefited by its liquid filtration expertise, including the energy and industrial sectors. It currently operates in four key business areas: Water, Industrial Manufacturing, Specialty Materials and Energy. The Water business primarily offers products for industrial and municipal clients, including products used for wastewater treatment, drinking water purification, raw water purification, seawater desalination and water recycling. It also offers a small selection of water filtration products for the home or office. The Industrial Manufacturing business offers membranes used to purify, concentrate or separate industrial liquids for customers in the chemicals, petrochemicals, pulp and paper, pharmaceuticals, biotechnology and electronics industries. The Specialty Materials business focuses on membranes utilized to help develop polymers and other materials. Its primary polymer is polylactic acid (PLA) made from lactic acid that it obtains as a natural by-product from the fermentation of organic materials. These polymers are used in a range of applications, from food and cosmetics to textiles, electronics and pharmaceuticals. Lastly, the Energy business develops membranes for use with plant-based or hydrocarbon-based oils, including palm oil clarification, biofuel processing, oil recovery and waste oil recycling. Company brand names include Kristal, FerroCep, InoCep and ProCep industrial and municipal filters; and Gurgle home-use products. In total, Hyflux's membranes have been installed at over 1,000 plants in 400 locations across the globe. In January 2011, Hyflux announced that it had been awarded three concessions to develop three water projects at the Hechuan Industrial Park in Chongping City, China. In February 2011, the firm was awarded a concession to develop a wastewater treatment plant in Zunyi City, China. In March 2011, Hyflux announced that it had been contracted to design, build, own and operate the largest seawater desalination plant in Singapore.

FINANCIALS: Sales and profits are in thousands of dollars—add 000 to get the full amount. 2011 Note: Financial information for 2011 was not available for all companies at press time.

		U.S. Stock Ticker:
2011 Sales: $	2011 Profits: $	**Int'l Ticker:** 600
2010 Sales: $462,610	2010 Profits: $71,000	Int'l Exchange: Singapore-SIN
2009 Sales: $404,060	2009 Profits: $57,020	Employees: 2,300 Fiscal Year Ends: 12/31
2008 Sales: $425,350	2008 Profits: $44,850	Parent Company:
2007 Sales: $	2007 Profits: $	

SALARIES/BENEFITS:

Pension Plan:	ESOP Stock Plan:	Profit Sharing:	Top Exec. Salary: $	Bonus: $
Savings Plan:	Stock Purch. Plan:		Second Exec. Salary: $	Bonus: $

OTHER THOUGHTS:

Apparent Women Officers or Directors: 4
Hot Spot for Advancement for Women/Minorities: Y

LOCATIONS: ("Y" = Yes)

West:	Southwest:	Midwest:	Southeast:	Northeast:	International: Y

IBERDROLA RENOVABLES SAU

www.iberdrolarenovables.es

Industry Group Code: 33361

Energy/Fuel:	Other Technologies:	Electrical Products:	Electronics:	Transportation:	Other:
Biofuels:	Irrigation:	Lighting/LEDs:	Computers:	Car Sharing:	Recycling:
Batteries/Storage:	Nanotech:	Waste Heat:	Sensors:	Electric Vehicles:	Engineering:
Solar:	Biotech:	Smart Meters:	Software:	Natural Gas Fuel:	Consulting:
Wind: Y	Water Tech./Treatment:	Machinery:			Investing:
Fuel Cells: Y	Ceramics:				Chemicals:

TYPES OF BUSINESS:

Power Plant Construction
Wind Power Generation
Hydro Power Generation
Tidal Power Generation
Wave Power Generation
Solar Power Generation
Thermoelectric Power Generation
Biomass Power Generation

BRANDS/DIVISIONS/AFFILIATES:

Iberdrola SA

CONTACTS: Note: Officers with more than one job title may be intentionally listed here more than once.

Jose Ignacio Sanchez Galaln, CEO-Iberdrola SA

Phone: 34-91-577-6565	Fax: 34-91-364-2624
Toll-Free:	
Address: Via de los Poblados, 3, Madrid, 28033 Spain	

GROWTH PLANS/SPECIAL FEATURES:

Iberdrola Renovables SAU is a Spanish firm engaged in the development, construction and operation of renewable energy power plants in 23 countries. Iberdrola Renovables is also engaged in the sale of the electricity produced at the firm's various power facilities. The company's primary operations consist of wind farms of various sizes as well as hydroelectric power plants, which consist of both tidal and wave energy plants. The firm is one of the largest operators of wind-powered energy in the world. The company's portfolio of installed generating capacity is 12,000 megawatts (MW), and the firm has an additional 62,000 MW in its development pipeline. Of the 12,000 MW, 5,199 MW are located in Spain, 4,314 MW are in the U.S. and approximately 909 MW are located in the U.K. and the Republic of Ireland. Other parts of Europe account for 1,186 MW, most notably France, Greece, Poland and Portugal. Iberdrola Renovables' small-scale hydroelectric facilities account for approximately 342 MW of the firm's total installed capacity, while other renewable technologies, including solar power facilities, thermoelectric plants and biomass generating stations, make up roughly 54 MW. The company is affiliated with Iberdrola S.A., one of the largest electric companies in the world, which holds an approximate 80% stake in Iberdrola Renovables. In January 2011, Iberdrola Renovables announced the acquisition of the 26 MW Beii Nee Stipa wind farm in Mexico from Gamesa. In March 2011, parent company Iberdrola SA acquired the remaining 20% of Iberdrola Renovables, bringing its ownership to 100%; additionally, the firm began construction on its 80 MW wind farm in Romania. In July 2011, Iberdrola Renovables announced the acquisition of 32 MW Consea II and 18 MW Savalla wind farms in Catalonia from Gamesa Corporacion Tecnologica SA.

FINANCIALS: Sales and profits are in thousands of dollars—add 000 to get the full amount. 2011 Note: Financial information for 2011 was not available for all companies at press time.

2011 Sales: $	2011 Profits: $	U.S. Stock Ticker:
2010 Sales: $2,567,200	2010 Profits: $	Int'l Ticker: IBR
2009 Sales: $2,624,550	2009 Profits: $484,780	Int'l Exchange: Madrid-MCE
2008 Sales: $2,652,240	2008 Profits: $509,730	Employees: 2,064 Fiscal Year Ends: 12/31
2007 Sales: $1,191,300	2007 Profits: $146,900	Parent Company: IBERDROLA SA

SALARIES/BENEFITS:

Pension Plan:	ESOP Stock Plan:	Profit Sharing:	Top Exec. Salary: $	Bonus: $
Savings Plan:	Stock Purch. Plan:		Second Exec. Salary: $	Bonus: $

OTHER THOUGHTS:

Apparent Women Officers or Directors:
Hot Spot for Advancement for Women/Minorities: Y

LOCATIONS: ("Y" = Yes)

West:	Southwest:	Midwest:	Southeast:	Northeast:	International:
Y	Y			Y	Y

IBERDROLA SA

www.iberdrola.es

Industry Group Code: 2211

Energy/Fuel:	Other Technologies:	Electrical Products:	Electronics:	Transportation:	Other:
Biofuels:	Irrigation:	Lighting/LEDs:	Computers:	Car Sharing:	Recycling:
Batteries/Storage:	Nanotech:	Waste Heat:	Sensors:	Electric Vehicles:	Engineering:
Solar:	Biotech:	Smart Meters:	Software:	Natural Gas Fuel:	Consulting:
Wind: Y	Water Tech./Treatment:	Machinery:			Investing:
Fuel Cells:	Ceramics:				Chemicals:

TYPES OF BUSINESS:

Electricity Generation & Distribution
Wind Generation
Hydroelectric Generation
Engineering & Construction
Telecommunications
Real Estate
Gas & Water Distribution

BRANDS/DIVISIONS/AFFILIATES:

Westec Environmental Solutions
Elektro
Iberdrola Renovables SAU

CONTACTS: Note: Officers with more than one job title may be intentionally listed here more than once.

Jose Ignacio Sanchez Galan, CEO
Jose Sainz Armada, CFO
Julián Martínez-Simancas Sánchez, Sec.
Jose Luis San Pedro Guerenabarrena, Dir.-Oper.
Jose Luis del Valle Doblado, Dir.-Strategy & Studies
Fernando Becker Zuazua, Dir.-Corp. Resources
Jose Luis San Pedro, Head-Iberia & Latin America.
Jose Ignacio Sanchez Galan, Chmn.
Amparo Moraleda, Head-Int'l Bus.

Phone: 34-944-151-411	Fax: 34-944-663-194
Toll-Free:	
Address: 8 Cardenal Gardoqui, Bilbao, 48008 Spain	

GROWTH PLANS/SPECIAL FEATURES:

Iberdrola S.A., a Spanish electric utility, serves over 30 million customers worldwide, generating over 154,000 gigawatts hours (GWh) of electricity and with an installed capacity of 44,991 megawatts (MW) in 2010. Iberdrola is one of the world's leaders in renewable energy with an installed capacity of 12,532 MW and generating 25,405 GWh in 2010. The firm has moved beyond power generation in recent years, due to the deregulation of the Spanish electric industry, and now is involved in engineering and construction, real estate, gas and water distribution and telecommunications. The company operates subsidiaries in the U.K., U.S., Europe, India, South America, Africa, the Middle East and Russia. In January 2011, Iberdrola Renovables SAU announced the acquisition of the Beii Nee Stipa wind farm in Mexico from Gamesa. In March 2011, Iberdrola announced that it will absorb its subsidiary Iberdola Renovables into the parent company. In April 2011, the firm announced the completion of the acquisition of the electricity distributor Elektro from AEI for $2.4 billion. In June 2011, the company announced the acquisition of a 20% holding in Westec Environmental Solutions. In July 2011, Iberdrola Renovables announced the acquisition of the wind farms Conesa II and Savalla from Gamesa.

FINANCIALS: Sales and profits are in thousands of dollars—add 000 to get the full amount. 2011 Note: Financial information for 2011 was not available for all companies at press time.

2011 Sales: $	2011 Profits: $	**U.S. Stock Ticker:**
2010 Sales: $40,848,500	2010 Profits: $3,853,700	**Int'l Ticker: IBE**
2009 Sales: $34,755,500	2009 Profits: $3,791,200	Int'l Exchange: Madrid-MCE
2008 Sales: $33,821,600	2008 Profits: $3,839,900	Employees: 31,340　　Fiscal Year Ends: 12/31
2007 Sales: $25,500,000	2007 Profits: $3,440,000	Parent Company:

SALARIES/BENEFITS:

Pension Plan:	ESOP Stock Plan:	Profit Sharing:	Top Exec. Salary: $	Bonus: $
Savings Plan:	Stock Purch. Plan:		Second Exec. Salary: $	Bonus: $

OTHER THOUGHTS:

Apparent Women Officers or Directors:
Hot Spot for Advancement for Women/Minorities:

LOCATIONS: ("Y" = Yes)

West:	Southwest:	Midwest:	Southeast:	Northeast:	International:
	Y			Y	Y

IBM RESEARCH

www.research.ibm.com

Industry Group Code: 541712

Energy/Fuel:	Other Technologies:		Electrical Products:	Electronics:		Transportation:		Other:	
Biofuels:	Irrigation:		Lighting/LEDs:	Computers:	Y	Car Sharing:		Recycling:	
Batteries/Storage:	Nanotech:	Y	Waste Heat:	Sensors:		Electric Vehicles:		Engineering:	Y
Solar:	Biotech:		Smart Meters:	Software:	Y	Natural Gas Fuel:		Consulting:	
Wind:	Water Tech./Treatment:		Machinery:					Investing:	
Fuel Cells:	Ceramics:							Chemicals:	

TYPES OF BUSINESS:

Research & Development
Computing
Software
Networks, Servers & Embedded Systems
Materials Science
Nanomechanics
Display Technology
Semiconductor & Storage Technology

BRANDS/DIVISIONS/AFFILIATES:

Deep Blue
Blue Gene/L
International Business Machines Corp (IBM)

CONTACTS: *Note: Officers with more than one job title may be intentionally listed here more than once.*

John E. Kelly, III, Dir.-IBM Research/Sr. VP-IBM
T.C. Chen, VP-Science
T.C. Chen, VP-Tech.
Christine Halverson, Dir.-Almaden Lab
Dilip Kandlur, Dir.-Austin Lab
Vibha Singhal Sinha, Dir.-India Lab
Leo Gross, Dir.-Zurich Lab
Sachiko Yoshihama, Dir.-Tokyo Lab

Phone: 914-945-3000	Fax: 914-945-2141
Toll-Free:	
Address: 1101 Kitchawan Rd., Rte. 134, Yorktown Heights, NY 10598 US	

GROWTH PLANS/SPECIAL FEATURES:

IBM Research is the R&D arm of International Business Machines Corp. (IBM). It often works with private customers and academic and government research centers. The firm has eight principal research areas. Chemistry research covers polymers, electronic and optical materials, photochemistry and organic and inorganic chemistry. Computer Science & Engineering research covers artificial intelligence, computational biology and medical informatics, computer architecture, data management, graphics and visualization. Electrical Engineering research covers design automation; electrical interconnect and packaging; nanotechnology and nanoscience; signal processing; verification technology; and Very-Large-Scale Integration (VLSI) design. Materials Science research covers dielectric, electrically active organic, lithographic, magnetic, superconducting and nanostructured materials; and material patterning, theory and computational science. Mathematical Sciences research covers algorithms and theory; knowledge discovery and data mining; operations research; and statistics. Physics research covers information systems, including quantum teleportation; information storage systems; magnetism; theory and computational science; nanoscale phenomena, layered materials; and optical sciences. Services Science, Management & Engineering projects address service business design and strategy; business componetization, modeling, monitoring and management; service delivery, operations and quality; organizational relationship management; and service innovation management. Lastly, Systems projects focus on personal and mobile computing, human computer interface research, information access devices and servers and embedded systems. The company operates through eight major research laboratories: Almaden, based in California; Austin Lab, based in Texas; Watson, with facilities in New York and Massachusetts; and international facilities in Japan, Israel, Switzerland, China and India. IBM Research developed the Deep Blue chess-playing supercomputer, and, more recently, the Blue Gene/L supercomputer, capable of over 280 trillion floating-point calculations per second (flops), developed primarily to help understand how human proteins fold.

FINANCIALS: Sales and profits are in thousands of dollars—add 000 to get the full amount. 2011 Note: Financial information for 2011 was not available for all companies at press time.

2011 Sales: $	2011 Profits: $	**U.S. Stock Ticker: Subsidiary**
2010 Sales: $	2010 Profits: $	**Int'l Ticker:**
2009 Sales: $	2009 Profits: $	Int'l Exchange:
2008 Sales: $	2008 Profits: $	Employees: Fiscal Year Ends: 12/31
2007 Sales: $	2007 Profits: $	Parent Company: INTERNATIONAL BUSINESS MACHINES CORP (IBM)

SALARIES/BENEFITS:

Pension Plan:	ESOP Stock Plan:	Profit Sharing:	Top Exec. Salary: $	Bonus: $
Savings Plan:	Stock Purch. Plan:		Second Exec. Salary: $	Bonus: $

OTHER THOUGHTS:

Apparent Women Officers or Directors: 1
Hot Spot for Advancement for Women/Minorities:

LOCATIONS: ("Y" = Yes)

West:	Southwest:	Midwest:	Southeast:	Northeast:	International:
Y	Y			Y	Y

ICP SOLAR TECHNOLOGIES

www.icpsolar.com

Industry Group Code: 334413

Energy/Fuel:		Other Technologies:	Electrical Products:	Electronics:	Transportation:	Other:
Biofuels:		Irrigation:	Lighting/LEDs:	Computers:	Car Sharing:	Recycling:
Batteries/Storage:		Nanotech:	Waste Heat:	Sensors:	Electric Vehicles:	Engineering:
Solar:	Y	Biotech:	Smart Meters:	Software:	Natural Gas Fuel:	Consulting:
Wind:		Water Tech./Treatment:	Machinery:			Investing:
Fuel Cells:		Ceramics:				Chemicals:

TYPES OF BUSINESS:

Photovoltaic Technology
Photovoltaic Construction Materials

BRANDS/DIVISIONS/AFFILIATES:

Sunsei Solar
Sunsei Industrial
Sunsei Construct
Solar Slates
iSun

CONTACTS: *Note: Officers with more than one job title may be intentionally listed here more than once.*

Michael Matvieshen, CEO
Satpal Sidhu, COO
Michael Matvieshen, Pres.
Michael Matvieshen, Sec.
Michael Matvieshen, Treas.
Michael Matvieshen, Chmn.

Phone: 514-270-5770	**Fax:** 514-270-3677
Toll-Free: 888-427-7652	
Address: 7075 Place Robert-Joncas, Unit 131, Montreal, QC H4M 2Z2 Canada	

GROWTH PLANS/SPECIAL FEATURES:

ICP Solar Technologies (ICP) is a Canadian developer, manufacturer and marketer of solar cells and solar cell based products and building materials. The company combines its manufacturing and marketing expertise, developing solar-powered products and solutions for the military, commercial, consumer and value-added resale markets. Its main product line, the Sunsei Solar line of solar chargers, can supply a wide variety of power needs, with applications for RVs, boats and car batteries. The Sunsei Construct line offers Solar Slates, which are power generating roof tiles, offer a resilient and aesthetically unobtrusive means of integrating solar power modules with roofing materials. Sunsei Industrial offers industrial solar chargers for use in a variety of on-grid and off-grid applications. Industrial chargers feature hail resistant glass and corrosion resistant aluminum frames, and are designed using ICP's proprietary advanced thin film technology. The firm also offers iSun, a line of portable solar chargers for smart phones, mobile music players and GPS devices. As an original equipment manufacturer, ICP provides plain solar cells to the home and garden industry and framed panels to automotive manufacturers. ICP's products are marketed through many retailers worldwide, including Conrad Electronics, West Marine, Wal-Mart, Dick Smith Electronics and Amazon.com.

FINANCIALS: Sales and profits are in thousands of dollars—add 000 to get the full amount. 2011 Note: Financial information for 2011 was not available for all companies at press time.

2011 Sales: $	2011 Profits: $	**U.S. Stock Ticker: Private**
2010 Sales: $	2010 Profits: $	**Int'l Ticker:**
2009 Sales: $5,900	2009 Profits: $-9,300	Int'l Exchange:
2008 Sales: $6,541	2008 Profits: $-4,222	Employees: 12 Fiscal Year Ends: 12/31
2007 Sales: $7,603	2007 Profits: $-2,627	Parent Company:

SALARIES/BENEFITS:

Pension Plan:	ESOP Stock Plan:	Profit Sharing:	Top Exec. Salary: $	Bonus: $
Savings Plan:	Stock Purch. Plan:		Second Exec. Salary: $	Bonus: $

OTHER THOUGHTS:

Apparent Women Officers or Directors:
Hot Spot for Advancement for Women/Minorities:

LOCATIONS: ("Y" = Yes)

West:	Southwest:	Midwest:	Southeast:	Northeast:	International:
Y					Y

IDATECH LLC

www.idatech.com

Industry Group Code: 335999

Energy/Fuel:	Other Technologies:	Electrical Products:	Electronics:	Transportation:	Other:
Biofuels:	Irrigation:	Lighting/LEDs:	Computers:	Car Sharing:	Recycling:
Batteries/Storage:	Nanotech:	Waste Heat:	Sensors:	Electric Vehicles:	Engineering:
Solar:	Biotech:	Smart Meters:	Software:	Natural Gas Fuel:	Consulting:
Wind:	Water Tech./Treatment:	Machinery:			Investing:
Fuel Cells: Y	Ceramics:				Chemicals:

TYPES OF BUSINESS:

Fuel Cell Manufacturing
Fuel Processing

BRANDS/DIVISIONS/AFFILIATES:

ElectraGen ME
iGen
ElectraGen H2-1
Investec Limited
GenSys
GenCore

CONTACTS: *Note: Officers with more than one job title may be intentionally listed here more than once.*

Harol (Hal) Koyama, CEO
Harol (Hal) Koyama, Pres.
James Cooke, CFO
Richard Romer, VP-Mktg. & Sales
Margo Maddux, VP-Human Resources
William Pledger, Chief Engineer
Michael A. Otterbach, VP-Oper.
John Jennings, Chmn.

Phone: 541-383-3390	Fax: 541-383-3439
Toll-Free:	
Address: 63065 NE 18th St., Bend, OR 97701 US	

GROWTH PLANS/SPECIAL FEATURES:

IdaTech LLC, a subsidiary of the U.K.-based international specialist banking group Investec Limited, specializes in the development of fuel processors and integrated proton exchange membrane (PEM) fuel cell systems for portable, critical backup and remote power applications. The company's core technology is its patented fuel processing technology, which is capable of converting a variety of fuels, including methanol, natural gas and bio fuels, into high purity hydrogen, on which the fuel cell solutions operate. The firm's products include the ElectraGen H2-1 System and ElectraGen ME System. The ElectraGen H2-1 system, available in 2.5 kilowatt and 5 kilowatt configurations, uses liquid fuel (methanol-water) and provides extended run backup power for telecommunications applications. IdaTech's ElectraGen ME system, also available in 2.5 kilowatt and 5 kilowatt configurations, uses hydrogen fuel and provides extended run backup power for telecommunications applications. In addition, the company's iGen system is an extended run backup power fuel cell system; it acts as a supplement to photovoltaic panels, batteries and small wind turbines used in grid-connected and off-grid applications as well as hybrid power generation applications. In late 2010, the firm acquired GenSys liquid petroleum gas off grid and GenCore backup power stationary fuel cell product lines from Plug Power, Inc. for approximately $5 million.

Employees of the firm receive long-term disability, life, medical and dental insurance; the IdaTech Cafeteria Plan, allowing employees to pay for unreimbursed medical expenses on a pre-tax basis; a 401(k) plan; and health club membership discounts.

FINANCIALS: Sales and profits are in thousands of dollars—add 000 to get the full amount. 2011 Note: Financial information for 2011 was not available for all companies at press time.

2011 Sales: $	2011 Profits: $	**U.S. Stock Ticker: Subsidiary**
2010 Sales: $	2010 Profits: $	**Int'l Ticker:**
2009 Sales: $	2009 Profits: $	Int'l Exchange:
2008 Sales: $	2008 Profits: $	Employees: Fiscal Year Ends: 12/31
2007 Sales: $	2007 Profits: $	Parent Company: INVESTEC LIMITED

SALARIES/BENEFITS:

Pension Plan:	ESOP Stock Plan:	Profit Sharing:	Top Exec. Salary: $	Bonus: $
Savings Plan: Y	Stock Purch. Plan:		Second Exec. Salary: $	Bonus: $

OTHER THOUGHTS:

Apparent Women Officers or Directors: 1
Hot Spot for Advancement for Women/Minorities:

LOCATIONS: ("Y" = Yes)

West:	Southwest:	Midwest:	Southeast:	Northeast:	International:
Y					Y

IMPERIAL WESTERN PRODUCTS INC

www.imperialwesternproducts.com
Industry Group Code: 325199

Energy/Fuel:		Other Technologies:		Electrical Products:	Electronics:	Transportation:	Other:
Biofuels:	Y	Irrigation:		Lighting/LEDs:	Computers:	Car Sharing:	Recycling:
Batteries/Storage:		Nanotech:		Waste Heat:	Sensors:	Electric Vehicles:	Engineering:
Solar:		Biotech:	Y	Smart Meters:	Software:	Natural Gas Fuel:	Consulting:
Wind:		Water Tech./Treatment:		Machinery:			Investing:
Fuel Cells:		Ceramics:					Chemicals:

TYPES OF BUSINESS:

Livestock Feed
Biodiesel
Industrial Chemicals
Janitorial Supplies
Concrete & Asphalt
Waste Pickup, Transportation & Packaging

BRANDS/DIVISIONS/AFFILIATES:

Enforce
Biotane
Imperial Biotane
Supreme Biotane
Bakery Solutions
Biotane Pumping

CONTACTS: Note: Officers with more than one job title may be intentionally listed here more than once.

Bill Trawick, Pres.
Curtis Wright, Mgr.-Methyl Ester & Glycerin Prod.
Joseph Boyd, Lab Mgr.-Biotane

Phone:	Fax: 760-398-0815
Toll-Free: 800-975-6677	
Address: 86-600 Ave. 54, Coachella, CA 92236 US	

GROWTH PLANS/SPECIAL FEATURES:

Imperial Western Products, Inc. (IWP), based in California, manufactures, warehouses and markets feed commodities, including feeds, oils, soaps, methyl esters and glycerin through its 28 divisions. IWP is one of the largest suppliers of feed ingredients, custom mixes, staple ingredients and high-energy feeds to dairy, cattle and poultry feeders in the southwestern U.S., with distribution hubs in California, Arizona and New Mexico; a manufacturing and sales office in Texas; and storage and transfer sites in California and Florida. The company also operates the only California-approved detoxification facility, producing economical and safe feed ingredients. IWP delivers its feed to customers through a company-owned transportation service. The company's line of Enforce products includes tire products, asphalt products, pipe joint lubricants, concrete products, chemicals and janitorial supplies. Enforce asphalt products and pipe joint lubricants are non-toxic, fully biodegradable and contain no petroleum hydrocarbons. Enforce pipe joint lubricants are designed for underwater, dry and subzero temperature applications. IWP is also active in the biodiesel industry, focusing on developments in production technology and consumer education. Through subsidiary Biotane Fuels, the company manufactures Biotane biodiesel, a clean-burning renewable fuel produced from waste restaurant oils. IWP processes more than 50 million pounds of used cooking oil per year to produce both Imperial Biotane and Supreme Biotane. IWP also provides bakery waste pickup and recycling (through Bakery Solutions); bulk liquid and dry transportation; custom labeling and packaging; custom chemical formulation and compounding; silage covering; kitchen grease pickup (through Biotane Pumping); and grinding and chipping of wood.

FINANCIALS: Sales and profits are in thousands of dollars—add 000 to get the full amount. 2011 Note: Financial information for 2011 was not available for all companies at press time.

2011 Sales: $	2011 Profits: $	U.S. Stock Ticker: Private	
2010 Sales: $	2010 Profits: $	Int'l Ticker:	
2009 Sales: $	2009 Profits: $	Int'l Exchange:	
2008 Sales: $	2008 Profits: $	Employees:	Fiscal Year Ends:
2007 Sales: $	2007 Profits: $	Parent Company:	

SALARIES/BENEFITS:

Pension Plan:	ESOP Stock Plan:	Profit Sharing:	Top Exec. Salary: $	Bonus: $
Savings Plan:	Stock Purch. Plan:		Second Exec. Salary: $	Bonus: $

OTHER THOUGHTS:

Apparent Women Officers or Directors:
Hot Spot for Advancement for Women/Minorities:

LOCATIONS: ("Y" = Yes)

West:	Southwest:	Midwest:	Southeast:	Northeast:	International:
Y	Y		Y		

IMPERIUM RENEWABLES INC

www.imperiumrenewables.com

Industry Group Code: 325199

Energy/Fuel:		Other Technologies:		Electrical Products:	Electronics:	Transportation:	Other:
Biofuels:	Y	Irrigation:		Lighting/LEDs:	Computers:	Car Sharing:	Recycling:
Batteries/Storage:		Nanotech:		Waste Heat:	Sensors:	Electric Vehicles:	Engineering:
Solar:		Biotech:	Y	Smart Meters:	Software:	Natural Gas Fuel:	Consulting:
Wind:		Water Tech./Treatment:		Machinery:			Investing:
Fuel Cells:		Ceramics:					Chemicals:

TYPES OF BUSINESS:

Biodiesel

BRANDS/DIVISIONS/AFFILIATES:

Imperium Grays Harbor

CONTACTS: *Note: Officers with more than one job title may be intentionally listed here more than once.*

John Plaza, CEO
John Plaza, Pres.
Todd Ellis, VP-Sales
Sid Watts, Gen. Mgr.-Plant Oper.
Todd Ellis, VP-Bus. Dev.
Aaron Leatherman, Mgr.-Imperium Grays Harbor
Phil Pickett, Chmn.

Phone: 206-254-0203	**Fax:** 206-254-0204	
Toll-Free:		
Address: 568 1st Ave. S., Ste. 600, Seattle, WA 98104 US		

GROWTH PLANS/SPECIAL FEATURES:

Imperium Renewables, Inc. is involved in the refining of biodiesel fuel. The firm operates Imperium Grays Harbor, one of the largest BQ-9000 certified biodiesel refineries in the U.S., which means that it has passed tests performed by The National Biodiesel Accreditation Program for quality control of biofuel at its production facility. Located in Hoquiam, Washington, the 68,000-square-foot facility has a biodiesel production capacity of 100 million gallons per year. Imperium Renewables' pure, unblended and B100 biodiesel is refined from a variety of oils, including soy, canola and many other crops. B100 diesel is non-toxic, biodegradable and can be used in any diesel engine. According to the U.S. Department of Energy, biodiesel emits about 78% less carbon dioxide than conventional diesel fuel. The firm purchases as many materials as possible from small farmers in the Northwestern U.S. and Canada. The company uses virgin (non-recycled) vegetable oils for its fuel production. Imperium Renewables also sells bulk crude glycerol (also known as glycerin), which is a byproduct of its refining process. The company is focused on expanding into other areas of the bio-distillate industry, such as the production of sustainable jet fuel made from biomass and non-edible feedstock sources.

The firm offers employees medical, dental and vision insurance; flexible benefit plans; and a 401(k).

FINANCIALS: Sales and profits are in thousands of dollars—add 000 to get the full amount. 2011 Note: Financial information for 2011 was not available for all companies at press time.

2011 Sales: $	2011 Profits: $	**U.S. Stock Ticker:** Private
2010 Sales: $	2010 Profits: $	**Int'l Ticker:**
2009 Sales: $	2009 Profits: $	Int'l Exchange:
2008 Sales: $	2008 Profits: $	Employees: Fiscal Year Ends: 12/31
2007 Sales: $	2007 Profits: $	Parent Company:

SALARIES/BENEFITS:

Pension Plan:	ESOP Stock Plan:	Profit Sharing:	Top Exec. Salary: $	Bonus: $
Savings Plan: Y	Stock Purch. Plan:		Second Exec. Salary: $	Bonus: $

OTHER THOUGHTS:

Apparent Women Officers or Directors:
Hot Spot for Advancement for Women/Minorities:

LOCATIONS: ("Y" = Yes)

West:	Southwest:	Midwest:	Southeast:	Northeast:	International:
Y					

Sales, profits and employees may be estimates. Financial information, benefits and other data can change quickly and may vary from those stated here.

INTEL CORP
www.intel.com

Industry Group Code: 33441

Energy/Fuel:	Other Technologies:	Electrical Products:	Electronics:		Transportation:	Other:
Biofuels:	Irrigation:	Lighting/LEDs:	Computers:		Car Sharing:	Recycling:
Batteries/Storage:	Nanotech:	Waste Heat:	Sensors:		Electric Vehicles:	Engineering:
Solar:	Biotech:	Smart Meters:	Software:	Y	Natural Gas Fuel:	Consulting:
Wind:	Water Tech./Treatment:	Machinery:				Investing:
Fuel Cells:	Ceramics:					Chemicals:

TYPES OF BUSINESS:

Microprocessors
Semiconductors
Circuit Boards
Flash Memory Products
Software Development
Home Network Equipment
Digital Imaging Products
Healthcare Products

BRANDS/DIVISIONS/AFFILIATES:

Pentium
Dual Core
Numonyx B.V.
SySDSoft
Intel Mobile Communications
McAfee Inc
Wind River Systems, Inc.
Intel Research Labs

CONTACTS: *Note: Officers with more than one job title may be intentionally listed here more than once.*

Paul S. Otellini, CEO
Paul S. Otellini, Pres.
Stacy J. Smith, CFO/Sr. VP
Thomas M. Kilroy, Sr. VP-Mktg. & Sales
Patricia Murray, Sr. VP/Dir.-Human Resources
Justin R. Rattner, VP/Dir.-Intel Labs
Diane M. Bryant, CIO/VP
Justin R. Rattner, CTO
Robert J. Baker, Sr. VP/Gen. Mgr.-Mfg. & Tech. Group
Andy D. Bryant, Chief Admin. Officer/Exec. VP
A. Douglas Melamed, General Counsel/Sr. VP
Leslie S. Culbertson, VP/Dir.-Finance
Ravi Jacob, VP/Treas.
Arvind Sodhani, Exec. VP/Pres., Intel Capital
William M. Holt, Sr. VP/Gen. Mgr.-Mfg. & Tech. Group
David Perlmutter, Exec. VP/Gen. Mgr.-Intel Architecture Group
Jane E. Shaw, Chmn.
Brain M. Krzanich, VP/Gen. Mgr.-Supply Chain & Mfg.

Phone: 408-765-8080	Fax:
Toll-Free:	
Address: 2200 Mission College Blvd., Santa Clara, CA 95054-1549 US	

GROWTH PLANS/SPECIAL FEATURES:

Intel Corp. is a global semiconductor chip maker that develops advanced integrated digital technology platforms for the computing and communications industries. It operates in nine segments: PC Client Group; Data Center Group; Embedded and Communications Group; Digital Home Group; Ultra-Mobility Group; NAND Solutions Group; Wind River Software Group; Software and Services Group; and Digital Health Group. The PC Client Group (72% of revenues) provides Intel architecture-based products and platforms for notebooks, netbooks and desktops. The Data Center Group (20% of revenues) delivers server, storage and workstation platforms. The Embedded Communications Group's products include solutions for applications through long life-cycle support, platform integration and software and architectural scalability. The Digital Home Group provides products for next-generation consumer electronics with interactive Internet content and traditional broadcast programming. The Ultra-Mobility Group offers energy-efficient Intel Atom processors and related chipsets designed for mobile Internet devices (MIDs) within the handheld market segment. The NAND Solutions Group produces flash memory products used in portable memory storage devices, digital camera memory cards and solid-state drives. The Wind River Software Group develops and licenses device software optimization products, including operating systems, for customers in the embedded and handheld market segments. The Software and Services Group promotes Intel architecture as the platform of choice for software applications and operating systems. Lastly, the Digital Health Group offers technology products for healthcare providers and for use in personal healthcare. The Embedded Communications Group, Digital Home Group and Ultra-Mobility Group together account for 4% of revenues; and NAND Solutions Group, Wind River Software Group, Software and Services Group and Digital Health Group, 4%. In February 2011, the company acquired security-software company McAfee, Inc. for $7.68 billion. In March 2011, Intel Mobile Communications acquired Egyptian firm SySDSoft.

The firm offers its employees life, AD&D, disability, medical and dental coverage; an employee assistance program; and flexible spending accounts.

FINANCIALS: Sales and profits are in thousands of dollars—add 000 to get the full amount. 2011 Note: Financial information for 2011 was not available for all companies at press time.

2011 Sales: $	2011 Profits: $	**U.S. Stock Ticker: INTC**
2010 Sales: $43,623,000	2010 Profits: $11,464,000	**Int'l Ticker:**
2009 Sales: $35,127,000	2009 Profits: $4,369,000	Int'l Exchange:
2008 Sales: $37,586,000	2008 Profits: $5,292,000	Employees: 82,500 Fiscal Year Ends: 12/31
2007 Sales: $38,334,000	2007 Profits: $6,976,000	Parent Company:

SALARIES/BENEFITS:

Pension Plan: Y	ESOP Stock Plan:	Profit Sharing: Y	Top Exec. Salary: $1,000,000	Bonus: $5,251,500
Savings Plan: Y	Stock Purch. Plan: Y		Second Exec. Salary: $500,000	Bonus: $1,857,300

OTHER THOUGHTS:

Apparent Women Officers or Directors: 8
Hot Spot for Advancement for Women/Minorities: Y

LOCATIONS: ("Y" = Yes)

West:	Southwest:	Midwest:	Southeast:	Northeast:	International:
Y	Y	Y	Y	Y	Y

INTERNATIONAL POWER PLC

www.internationalpowerplc.com

Industry Group Code: 221121

Energy/Fuel:	Other Technologies:	Electrical Products:	Electronics:	Transportation:	Other:
Biofuels:	Irrigation:	Lighting/LEDs:	Computers:	Car Sharing:	Recycling:
Batteries/Storage:	Nanotech:	Waste Heat: Y	Sensors:	Electric Vehicles:	Engineering:
Solar:	Biotech:	Smart Meters:	Software:	Natural Gas Fuel: Y	Consulting:
Wind: Y	Water Tech./Treatment: Y	Machinery:			Investing:
Fuel Cells:	Ceramics:				Chemicals:

TYPES OF BUSINESS:

Wholesale Electricity Generation
Renewable Energy Development

BRANDS/DIVISIONS/AFFILIATES:

GDF Suez
Opus
Simply Energy

CONTACTS: *Note: Officers with more than one job title may be intentionally listed here more than once.*

Philip Cox, CEO
Guy Richelle, COO
Francois Graux, General Counsel/Sec.
Philip De Chudde, Exec. VP-Bus. Dev. Oversight
Penny Chalmers, Exec. VP-Comm.
Aarti Singhal, Head-Investor Rel.
Steve Riley, CEO-Europe
Tony Concannon, CEO-Australia
Shankar Krishnamoorthy, CEO-Middle East, Turkey & Africa
Willem Van Twembeke, CEO-Asia
Dirk Beeuwsaert, Chmn.
Zin Smati, CEO-North America

Phone: 44-20-7320-8600	Fax: 44-20-7320-8700
Toll-Free:	
Address: 85 Queen Victoria St., Senator House, London, EC4V 4DP UK	

GROWTH PLANS/SPECIAL FEATURES:

International Power plc is an international wholesale power generator and developer with interests in over 21 countries worldwide. GDF SUEZ holds a 70% interest in the company. The firm maintains interests in more than 45 power plants with a total combined generating capacity of more than 72,000 megawatts (MW) located in Australia, Indonesia, Thailand, Pakistan, Bahrain, Oman, Saudi Arabia, Qatar, UAE, Turkey, Spain, Portugal, Italy, Germany, France, the Netherlands and the U.K., Canada and the U.S. International Power also engages in complementary activities such as mining coal and transporting gas via pipeline in Australia, desalinating water in the Middle East and providing steam for district heating systems in Europe. Additionally, the company has interests in electricity retail businesses in Australia and the U.K. The company's other businesses include Opus, a UK-based independent supplier of commercial and residential electricity; and Simply Energy, an Australian electricity and gas retailer. In May 2011, the firm announced that it sold its 33.3% interest in the T-Power CCGT plant to the Japanese conglomerate Itochu for approximately $62 million. In June 2011, International Power announced the transfer of its Thai National Power assets to Glow Energy Public Company Limited for approximately $55 million. Also in June 2011, the firm, PT Supreme Energy and Marubeni Corporation entered into a joint venture agreement for the development of the Rantau Dedap geothermal project in Indonesia. In August of the same year, International Power announced the construction of the 99 MW wind farm in British Columbia. In November 2011, the firm announced the inauguration of the 150 MW Andina Thermal Power Plant and the 150 MW Hornitos Thermal Power Plant in Chile.

FINANCIALS: Sales and profits are in thousands of dollars—add 000 to get the full amount. 2011 Note: Financial information for 2011 was not available for all companies at press time.

2011 Sales: $	2011 Profits: $	**U.S. Stock Ticker:**
2010 Sales: $8,013,419	2010 Profits: $865,719	**Int'l Ticker: IPR**
2009 Sales: $7,924,230	2009 Profits: $954,058	Int'l Exchange: London-LSE
2008 Sales: $6,290,130	2008 Profits: $1,098,020	Employees: 3,520 Fiscal Year Ends: 12/31
2007 Sales: $2,325,000	2007 Profits: $503,000	Parent Company:

SALARIES/BENEFITS:

Pension Plan:	ESOP Stock Plan:	Profit Sharing:	Top Exec. Salary: $1,150,030	Bonus: $631,366
Savings Plan:	Stock Purch. Plan:		Second Exec. Salary: $705,202	Bonus: $372,347

OTHER THOUGHTS:

Apparent Women Officers or Directors: 2
Hot Spot for Advancement for Women/Minorities:

LOCATIONS: ("Y" = Yes)

West:	Southwest:	Midwest:	Southeast:	Northeast:	International:
	Y	Y	Y	Y	Y

IOXUS INC

www.ioxus.com

Industry Group Code: 335

Energy/Fuel:		Other Technologies:	Electrical Products:	Electronics:	Transportation:	Other:
Biofuels:		Irrigation:	Lighting/LEDs:	Computers:	Car Sharing:	Recycling:
Batteries/Storage:	Y	Nanotech:	Waste Heat:	Sensors:	Electric Vehicles:	Engineering:
Solar:		Biotech:	Smart Meters:	Software:	Natural Gas Fuel:	Consulting:
Wind:		Water Tech./Treatment:	Machinery:			Investing:
Fuel Cells:		Ceramics:				Chemicals:

TYPES OF BUSINESS:

Ultracapacitors

BRANDS/DIVISIONS/AFFILIATES:

iCAP

CONTACTS: Note: Officers with more than one job title may be intentionally listed here more than once.

Mark McGough, CEO
Philip Meek, COO
Mark McGough, Pres.
Robert Jaworski, CFO
Chad Hall, VP-Sales
Brendan Andrews, VP-Sales
Jeff Colton, VP-Sales

Phone: 607-441-3500	Fax: 607-433-9014
Toll-Free: 877-751-4222	
Address: 18 Stadium Circle, Oneonta, NY 13820 US	

GROWTH PLANS/SPECIAL FEATURES:

Ioxus, Inc. designs and produces ultracapacitor devices used in energy storage applications. Ultracapacitors, also referred to as electric double-layer capacitors (EDLCs), are rechargeable energy storage devices that can be used to extend the life of batteries and other energy sources. Using a proprietary electrode design, the firm's ultracapacitors offer a number of benefits when compared to conventional energy storage devices. While not capable of storing as much energy as batteries, EDLCs offer much faster charge/discharge cycles; increased charge/discharge lifecycles (as much as several million, compared to several hundred in batteries); higher power densities; and nearly 100% energy storage efficiency. Ultracapacitors are also capable of functioning in much colder environments, including temperatures down to -40 degrees Celsius. This technology can be used in wind energy applications for wind mill blade pitch control; in hybrid vehicles for stabilizing power output and increasing battery life expectancy; industrial equipment that requires quick starting and charging functions; LED lighting; and medical applications. Because of ultracapacitors quick charge/discharge characteristics, they can also be used to increase the fuel efficiency of internal combustion engines; allowing vehicles to shut off while stopped at traffic lights and immediately return to power when the gas pedal is depressed. The company also produces hybrid ultracapacitors, which combine ultracapacitors with lithium-ion batteries and are capable of storing more than twice the energy of standard EDLCs. Ioxus offers single cell versions of its ultracapacitors, as well multi-cell 16-volt modules. It is also capable of designing custom modules for specific customer installations. In January 2012, the firm introduced the iCAP series of ultracapacitors, a 3,000-Farad line of cells designed for energy storage in renewable energy settings.

FINANCIALS: Sales and profits are in thousands of dollars—add 000 to get the full amount. 2011 Note: Financial information for 2011 was not available for all companies at press time.

2011 Sales: $	2011 Profits: $	**U.S. Stock Ticker:** Private
2010 Sales: $	2010 Profits: $	**Int'l Ticker:**
2009 Sales: $	2009 Profits: $	Int'l Exchange:
2008 Sales: $	2008 Profits: $	Employees: Fiscal Year Ends:
2007 Sales: $	2007 Profits: $	Parent Company:

SALARIES/BENEFITS:

Pension Plan:	ESOP Stock Plan:	Profit Sharing:	Top Exec. Salary: $	Bonus: $
Savings Plan:	Stock Purch. Plan:		Second Exec. Salary: $	Bonus: $

OTHER THOUGHTS:

Apparent Women Officers or Directors:
Hot Spot for Advancement for Women/Minorities:

LOCATIONS: ("Y" = Yes)

West:	Southwest:	Midwest:	Southeast:	Northeast:	International:
				Y	

ISOFOTON

www.isofoton.com

Industry Group Code: 334413

Energy/Fuel:	Other Technologies:	Electrical Products:	Electronics:	Transportation:	Other:
Biofuels:	Irrigation:	Lighting/LEDs:	Computers:	Car Sharing:	Recycling:
Batteries/Storage:	Nanotech:	Waste Heat:	Sensors:	Electric Vehicles:	Engineering:
Solar: Y	Biotech:	Smart Meters:	Software:	Natural Gas Fuel:	Consulting:
Wind:	Water Tech./Treatment:	Machinery:			Investing:
Fuel Cells:	Ceramics:				Chemicals:

TYPES OF BUSINESS:

Photovoltaic Cells
Thermal Collector Manufacturing

BRANDS/DIVISIONS/AFFILIATES:

Isofoton North America Inc
Affirma-Toptec
Affirma Energy Engineering & Technology
TopTec

CONTACTS: Note: Officers with more than one job title may be intentionally listed here more than once.

Ignacio de Colmenares Y Brunet, CEO
Emiliano Perezagua, COO
Jesus Alonso, Dir.-R&D

Phone: 34-9-14-14-78-00	Fax: 34-91-414-79-00
Toll-Free:	
Address: Paseo de la Castellana 259, Madrid, 28014 Spain	

GROWTH PLANS/SPECIAL FEATURES:

Isofoton, based in Spain, is among the top producers of photovoltaic cells in the world, offering photovoltaic and thermal solutions based on solar energy. A leader in European manufacturing and the largest producer of photovoltaic cells in Spain, the company has been recognized for its success in opening up foreign markets for its country's economy. Isofoton has completed projects in more than 60 countries on five continents. It operates in the U.S. solar market through subsidiary Isofoton North America, Inc. The firm has demonstrated a strong commitment to using solar energy to improve conditions in developing countries, with many of its projects designed to provide energy for schools and infrastructure in remote rural locations in Ecuador, Peru, Nepal, Indonesia, Tunisia, Ghana, Gambia, Morocco, Algeria and Senegal. The company aims to provide energy solutions for areas with limited power grid access, allowing them to supplement the energy obtained from conventional sources without harming the environment. Isofoton's total photovoltaic production is 180 megawatts (MW), while its total thermal production is 21 MW. Per year, Isofoton generates approximately 70 million kilowatts of photovoltaic electricity. In addition to stand-alone rural electrification projects, Isofoton also produces grid-connected systems and thermal solar systems used in public lighting, water supply, telecommunications, indoor heating and, in Spain, the heating of swimming pools and spas. In order to facilitate its international operations, the firm also provides financial, legal, technical and training services to its clients. In mid 2010, Isofoton was acquired by Affirma-Toptec, a consortium between Affirma Energy Engineering & Technology and TopTec.

FINANCIALS: Sales and profits are in thousands of dollars—add 000 to get the full amount. 2011 Note: Financial information for 2011 was not available for all companies at press time.

2011 Sales: $	2011 Profits: $	**U.S. Stock Ticker:** Private
2010 Sales: $	2010 Profits: $	**Int'l Ticker:**
2009 Sales: $	2009 Profits: $	Int'l Exchange:
2008 Sales: $	2008 Profits: $	Employees: Fiscal Year Ends: 12/31
2007 Sales: $	2007 Profits: $	Parent Company: AFFIRMA-TOPTEC

SALARIES/BENEFITS:

Pension Plan:	ESOP Stock Plan:	Profit Sharing:	Top Exec. Salary: $	Bonus: $
Savings Plan:	Stock Purch. Plan:		Second Exec. Salary: $	Bonus: $

OTHER THOUGHTS:

Apparent Women Officers or Directors:
Hot Spot for Advancement for Women/Minorities:

LOCATIONS: ("Y" = Yes)

West:	Southwest:	Midwest:	Southeast:	Northeast: Y	International: Y

Sales, profits and employees may be estimates. Financial information, benefits and other data can change quickly and may vary from those stated here.

JA SOLAR HOLDINGS CO LTD

www.jasolar.com

Industry Group Code: 334413

Energy/Fuel:	Other Technologies:	Electrical Products:	Electronics:	Transportation:	Other:
Biofuels:	Irrigation:	Lighting/LEDs:	Computers:	Car Sharing:	Recycling:
Batteries/Storage:	Nanotech:	Waste Heat:	Sensors:	Electric Vehicles:	Engineering:
Solar: Y	Biotech:	Smart Meters:	Software:	Natural Gas Fuel:	Consulting:
Wind:	Water Tech./Treatment:	Machinery:			Investing:
Fuel Cells:	Ceramics:				Chemicals:

TYPES OF BUSINESS:

Solar Cell Manufacturing

BRANDS/DIVISIONS/AFFILIATES:

JA Solar USA Inc
JA Development Co Ltd
JA Solar Hong Kong Ltd
Shanghai Jinglong Solar Technology Co., Ltd.
Silver Age Holdings Ltd

GROWTH PLANS/SPECIAL FEATURES:

JA Solar Holdings Co. Ltd. is one of the leading China-based manufacturers of high-performance solar cells and solar power products.   The firm is engaged in the design, manufacture and market high-performance solar cells, which are made from specially processed silicon wafers.   JA Solar currently produces and sells monocrystalline and monocrystalline solar cells.   The company has established a PV module production facility in Fengxian, Shanghai with an annual capacity of 1.2 GW as of the end of 2011, while its multi-crystalline silicon wafer facility in the Donghai, Jiangsu Province has an annual capacity of 300 MW.   The firm's subsidiaries include JA Development Co. Ltd., JA Solar USA, Inc. and JA Solar Hong Kong Ltd.   In July 2011, JA Solar acquired Silver Age Holdings Ltd., a British Virgin Islands company that owns 100% of Solar Silicon Valley Electronic Science and Technology Co. Ltd., a leading producer of solar wafers based in China, for $180 million.

CONTACTS: *Note: Officers with more than one job title may be intentionally listed here more than once.*

Peng Fang, CEO
Jian Xie, COO
Ming Cao, CFO
Yong Liu, CTO
Ming Yang, VP
Baofang Jin, Chmn.
Jonathan Pickering, VP/Pres., JA Solar, Americas Region

Phone: 86-21-6095-5888	**Fax:** 86-21-6095-5858
Toll-Free:	
Address: No.36, Jiang Chang San Rd., ZhaBei, Shanghai, 200436 China	

FINANCIALS: Sales and profits are in thousands of dollars—add 000 to get the full amount. 2011 Note: Financial information for 2011 was not available for all companies at press time.

2011 Sales: $	2011 Profits: $	**U.S. Stock Ticker:** JASO
2010 Sales: $1,812,700	2010 Profits: $273,610	**Int'l Ticker:**
2009 Sales: $566,479	2009 Profits: $-19,290	Int'l Exchange:
2008 Sales: $818,170	2008 Profits: $71,810	Employees: 10,725 Fiscal Year Ends: 12/31
2007 Sales: $369,300	2007 Profits: $54,900	Parent Company:

SALARIES/BENEFITS:

Pension Plan:	ESOP Stock Plan:	Profit Sharing:	Top Exec. Salary: $	Bonus: $
Savings Plan:	Stock Purch. Plan:		Second Exec. Salary: $	Bonus: $

OTHER THOUGHTS:

Apparent Women Officers or Directors: 1
Hot Spot for Advancement for Women/Minorities:

LOCATIONS: ("Y" = Yes)

West: Y	Southwest:	Midwest:	Southeast:	Northeast:	International: Y

JINKOSOLAR HOLDING CO LTD

www.jinkosolar.com

Industry Group Code: 334413

Energy/Fuel:	Other Technologies:	Electrical Products:	Electronics:	Transportation:	Other:
Biofuels:	Irrigation:	Lighting/LEDs:	Computers:	Car Sharing:	Recycling:
Batteries/Storage:	Nanotech:	Waste Heat:	Sensors:	Electric Vehicles:	Engineering:
Solar: Y	Biotech:	Smart Meters:	Software:	Natural Gas Fuel:	Consulting:
Wind:	Water Tech./Treatment:	Machinery:			Investing:
Fuel Cells:	Ceramics:				Chemicals:

TYPES OF BUSINESS:

Solar Cell Manufacturing
Solar Module Manufacturing

BRANDS/DIVISIONS/AFFILIATES:

JinkoSolar (U.S.) Inc
Jiangxi Photovoltaic Materials Co Ltd
JinkoSolar

CONTACTS: Note: Officers with more than one job title may be intentionally listed here more than once.

Kangping Chen, CEO
Longgen Zhang, CFO
Arturo Herrero, Chief Mktg. Officer
Chaolin Zha, Dir.-R&D Tech.
Zhiqun Xu, VP-Prod. Dept.
Xianhua Li, VP
Musen Yu, VP
Xiande Li, Chmn.

Phone: 86-793-846-9699	**Fax:** 86-793-846-1152
Toll-Free:	

Address: 1 Jingke Rd., Shangrao Economic Development Zone, Jiangxi Province, 334100 China

GROWTH PLANS/SPECIAL FEATURES:

JinkoSolar Holding Co., Ltd. is a vertically-integrated solar photovoltaic (PV) product manufacturer, with two production facilities located in China's Jiangxi and Zhejiang Provinces. Its principal products are solar modules, silicon wafers and solar cells. The firm sells its products in China, as well as major international export markets. JinkoSolar's solar module production, which consists of both mono-crystalline and multi-crystalline modules, is supported by its solar cell and silicon wafer operations. Its integrated annual production capacity for silicon wafers, solar cells and modules is approximately 1.1 GW each, with plans to expand to 1.5 GW by the close of 2011. JinkoSolar sells its modules under the JinkoSolar brand, as well as to original equipment manufacturers (OEMs). All of its modules sold in Europe are CE and TUV certified, and all of its modules sold in the U.S. are UL certified. The company's U.S. sales and marketing activities are handled through JinkoSolar (U.S.), Inc., which is based in San Francisco, California. It also maintains sales offices in Shanghai, China; Munich, Germany; and Bologna, Italy. The firm has an aggregate of approximately 400 customers for its solar modules, solar cells and silicon wafers, primarily in China, Germany, India, Italy and Spain. In December 2010, the company established Jiangxi Photovoltaic Materials Co., Ltd., which produces accessory materials for its solar power products. In June 2011, it opened a new research and development center to focus on increasing solar PV conversion efficiency rates. In July 2011, JinkoSolar commenced production of its Quantum Series Q-1 Solar Modules, which feature pseudo-mono multi-crystalline cells that perform at an 18.3% efficiency level.

FINANCIALS: Sales and profits are in thousands of dollars—add 000 to get the full amount. 2011 Note: Financial information for 2011 was not available for all companies at press time.

2011 Sales: $	2011 Profits: $	**U.S. Stock Ticker:** JKS
2010 Sales: $705,281	2010 Profits: $133,617	**Int'l Ticker:**
2009 Sales: $	2009 Profits: $	Int'l Exchange:
2008 Sales: $	2008 Profits: $	Employees: Fiscal Year Ends: 12/31
2007 Sales: $	2007 Profits: $	Parent Company:

SALARIES/BENEFITS:

Pension Plan:	ESOP Stock Plan:	Profit Sharing:	Top Exec. Salary: $	Bonus: $
Savings Plan:	Stock Purch. Plan:		Second Exec. Salary: $	Bonus: $

OTHER THOUGHTS:

Apparent Women Officers or Directors:
Hot Spot for Advancement for Women/Minorities:

LOCATIONS: ("Y" = Yes)

West: Y	Southwest:	Midwest:	Southeast:	Northeast:	International: Y

JOULE UNLIMITED TECHNOLOGIES

www.jouleunlimited.com

Industry Group Code: 325199

Energy/Fuel:		Other Technologies:		Electrical Products:	Electronics:	Transportation:	Other:
Biofuels:	Y	Irrigation:		Lighting/LEDs:	Computers:	Car Sharing:	Recycling:
Batteries/Storage:		Nanotech:		Waste Heat:	Sensors:	Electric Vehicles:	Engineering:
Solar:		Biotech:	Y	Smart Meters:	Software:	Natural Gas Fuel:	Consulting:
Wind:		Water Tech./Treatment:		Machinery:			Investing:
Fuel Cells:		Ceramics:					Chemicals:

TYPES OF BUSINESS:

Biofuel Research & Development

BRANDS/DIVISIONS/AFFILIATES:

Liquid Fuel from the Sun
SolarConverter
Helioculture

CONTACTS: *Note: Officers with more than one job title may be intentionally listed here more than once.*

William J. Sims, CEO
William J. Sims, Pres.
Eric d'Esparbes, CFO/Sr. VP
John Ward, Sr. VP-Prod.
David St Angelo, VP-Eng.
Mark Solakian, General Counsel/Sr. VP
Troy J. Campione, Sr. VP-Corp. Dev.
Dan Robertson, Sr. VP-Biological Sciences
Kevin Madden, VP-Biology Oper.
Chang B. Hong, Intellectual Property Counsel/VP
Mike Glacken, VP-Bioprocessing

Phone: 617-354-6100	Fax: 617-354-6101
Toll-Free:	
Address: 83 Rogers St., Cambridge, MA 02142 US	

GROWTH PLANS/SPECIAL FEATURES:

Joule Unlimited Technologies is a privately-held company that focuses on the development of solar fuel technology. The firm's production process is known as Liquid Fuel from the Sun. Joule's mechanism for producing fuel involves capturing solar energy and creates fuel as a by-product of photosynthetic metabolism. The firm's SolarConverter device produces hydrocarbon fuels and ethanol in a continuous process designed to eliminate photons. Its Helioculture platform converts sunlight and waste CO_2 into clean diesel fuel. Headquartered in Cambridge, Massachusetts, Joule also has a facility in Leander, Texas that tests the company's microorganisms, processes and related variables for fuel production. The firm has six issued patents with over 70 patents pending. It expects commercial development to begin in 2012 and estimates the ability to deliver around 15,000 gallons of diesel per year, with costs as low as $20 per barrel.

Joule offers employees medical, dental and life insurance as well as a 401(k) plan.

FINANCIALS: Sales and profits are in thousands of dollars—add 000 to get the full amount. 2011 Note: Financial information for 2011 was not available for all companies at press time.

2011 Sales: $	2011 Profits: $	U.S. Stock Ticker: Private
2010 Sales: $	2010 Profits: $	Int'l Ticker:
2009 Sales: $	2009 Profits: $	Int'l Exchange:
2008 Sales: $	2008 Profits: $	Employees: Fiscal Year Ends:
2007 Sales: $	2007 Profits: $	Parent Company:

SALARIES/BENEFITS:

Pension Plan:	ESOP Stock Plan:	Profit Sharing:	Top Exec. Salary: $	Bonus: $
Savings Plan: Y	Stock Purch. Plan:		Second Exec. Salary: $	Bonus: $

OTHER THOUGHTS:

Apparent Women Officers or Directors:
Hot Spot for Advancement for Women/Minorities:

LOCATIONS: ("Y" = Yes)

West:	Southwest:	Midwest:	Southeast:	Northeast:	International:
	Y			Y	

JOULEX

www.joulex.net

Industry Group Code: 5112

Energy/Fuel:	Other Technologies:	Electrical Products:	Electronics:		Transportation:	Other:
Biofuels:	Irrigation:	Lighting/LEDs:	Computers:	Y	Car Sharing:	Recycling:
Batteries/Storage:	Nanotech:	Waste Heat:	Sensors:		Electric Vehicles:	Engineering:
Solar:	Biotech:	Smart Meters:	Software:	Y	Natural Gas Fuel:	Consulting:
Wind:	Water Tech./Treatment:	Machinery:				Investing:
Fuel Cells:	Ceramics:					Chemicals:

TYPES OF BUSINESS:

Energy Management Technology

BRANDS/DIVISIONS/AFFILIATES:

JouleX Energy Manager EnergyWise
JouleX Energy Manager
JouleX Mobile

CONTACTS: *Note: Officers with more than one job title may be intentionally listed here more than once.*

Tom Noonan, CEO
Tom Noonan, Pres.
Jon VerSteeg, CFO
Tim McCormick, VP-Mktg. & Sales
Rene Seeber, CTO/Co-Founder
Josef Brunner, Chief Architect & Co-Founder
Ja Hong Lin, CEO/Pres., JouleX K.K.
Mark Davidson, Sustainability Officer
Ja Hong Lin, VP-Asia Pacific

Phone:	Fax:
Toll-Free: 1-888-568-5396	
Address: 107 West Paces Ferry Rd., 1 JouleX Plz., Atlanta, GA 30305 US	

GROWTH PLANS/SPECIAL FEATURES:

JouleX is an enterprise energy management company that provides its clients with comprehensive solutions to decrease energy costs, using techniques and devices that monitor, analyze and control energy consumption. The company's services extend to a variety of products, including servers, PCs, VoIP phones, peripherals, network routers and switches, printers, HVAC (heating, ventilation and air conditioning) and lighting systems, in addition to other hardware and software agents. JouleX's product portfolio includes JouleX Energy Manager (JEM), an agentless technology; Joulex Mobile, a remote powering device; and JEM EnergyWise, which integrates with Cisco EnergyWise and uses installation wizard tools for automated streamline configuration. JEM monitors, measures and reports the usage and utilization of energy consumption throughout the enterprise. JEM is also capable of providing simulations that analyze different scenarios, allowing companies to evaluate the effects of new equipment, capacity, temperatures and power changes using baseline measurements based on green initiative targets. The firm also offers IT enterprises, distributed office environments, facilities, data centers and corporations energy management solutions using optimization methods such as sustainable procurement; sustainability reporting; energy use measurements; identification and optimization of virtualization and cloud environments; system capacity planning; and load adaptive computing.

FINANCIALS: Sales and profits are in thousands of dollars—add 000 to get the full amount. 2011 Note: Financial information for 2011 was not available for all companies at press time.

2011 Sales: $	2011 Profits: $	**U.S. Stock Ticker:** Private
2010 Sales: $	2010 Profits: $	**Int'l Ticker:**
2009 Sales: $	2009 Profits: $	Int'l Exchange:
2008 Sales: $	2008 Profits: $	Employees: Fiscal Year Ends:
2007 Sales: $	2007 Profits: $	Parent Company:

SALARIES/BENEFITS:

Pension Plan:	ESOP Stock Plan:	Profit Sharing:	Top Exec. Salary: $	Bonus: $
Savings Plan:	Stock Purch. Plan:		Second Exec. Salary: $	Bonus: $

OTHER THOUGHTS:

Apparent Women Officers or Directors:
Hot Spot for Advancement for Women/Minorities:

LOCATIONS: ("Y" = Yes)

West:	Southwest:	Midwest:	Southeast:	Northeast:	International:
		Y			Y

KAIIMA AGRO-BIOTECH LTD

Industry Group Code: 325199

Energy/Fuel:		Other Technologies:		Electrical Products:	Electronics:	Transportation:	Other:	
Biofuels:	Y	Irrigation:		Lighting/LEDs:	Computers:	Car Sharing:	Recycling:	
Batteries/Storage:		Nanotech:		Waste Heat:	Sensors:	Electric Vehicles:	Engineering:	
Solar:		Biotech:	Y	Smart Meters:	Software:	Natural Gas Fuel:	Consulting:	
Wind:		Water Tech./Treatment:		Machinery:			Investing:	
Fuel Cells:		Ceramics:					Chemicals:	

TYPES OF BUSINESS:
Agro-Biotech

BRANDS/DIVISIONS/AFFILIATES:
Enhanced Ploidy
DFJ Tamir Fishman Ventures
Draper Fisher Jurvetson
Kleiner Perkins Caufield & Byers.

GROWTH PLANS/SPECIAL FEATURES:
Kaiima Agro-biotech Ltd. is an agro-biotech company whose platforms seek to increase the productivity of crops. Kaiima's work revolves around developing sustainable sources of energy and food without adversely affecting the well-being of the environment. The company's biotechnological offering is the Enhanced Ploidy platform. This platform, when applied to a plant's genome, enhances the plant's properties and affects small changes to its characteristics, including higher yield potential, better water-use efficiency, adaptability to extreme climates and denser concentration of metabolites. The firm is currently using its platform to produce high yielding castor for the bio-polymer and bio-diesel industries, as well as rapeseed to demonstrate the feasibility of the Enhanced Ploidy platform. Those that have invested in Kaiima include DFJ Tamir Fishman Ventures, Draper Fisher Jurvetson and Kleiner Perkins Caufield & Byers.

CONTACTS: *Note: Officers with more than one job title may be intentionally listed here more than once.*
Doron Gal, CEO
Amit Avidov, CTO
Dror Maayany, VP-Admin.
Remy Bitoun, VP-Bus. Dev.
Dror Maayany, VP-Finance
Zohar Benner, VP-Special Projects
Limor Baruch, Dir.-Analytic Laboratory
Doron Gal, Chmn.

Phone: 972-4-9530148	Fax: 972-4-9534720
Toll-Free:	
Address: 10 Harimonim St., Kfar Tavor, 15241 Israel	

FINANCIALS: Sales and profits are in thousands of dollars—add 000 to get the full amount. 2011 Note: Financial information for 2011 was not available for all companies at press time.
2011 Sales: $	2011 Profits: $	U.S. Stock Ticker: Private
2010 Sales: $	2010 Profits: $	Int'l Ticker:
2009 Sales: $	2009 Profits: $	Int'l Exchange:
2008 Sales: $	2008 Profits: $	Employees: Fiscal Year Ends:
2007 Sales: $	2007 Profits: $	Parent Company:

SALARIES/BENEFITS:
| Pension Plan: | ESOP Stock Plan: | Profit Sharing: | Top Exec. Salary: $ | Bonus: $ |
| Savings Plan: | Stock Purch. Plan: | | Second Exec. Salary: $ | Bonus: $ |

OTHER THOUGHTS:
Apparent Women Officers or Directors:
Hot Spot for Advancement for Women/Minorities:

LOCATIONS: ("Y" = Yes)
West:	Southwest:	Midwest:	Southeast:	Northeast:	International: Y

KIOR INC

www.kior.com

Industry Group Code: 325199

Energy/Fuel:		Other Technologies:		Electrical Products:	Electronics:	Transportation:	Other:
Biofuels:	Y	Irrigation:		Lighting/LEDs:	Computers:	Car Sharing:	Recycling:
Batteries/Storage:		Nanotech:		Waste Heat:	Sensors:	Electric Vehicles:	Engineering:
Solar:		Biotech:	Y	Smart Meters:	Software:	Natural Gas Fuel:	Consulting:
Wind:		Water Tech./Treatment:		Machinery:			Investing:
Fuel Cells:		Ceramics:					Chemicals:

TYPES OF BUSINESS:

Biofuel Technology

BRANDS/DIVISIONS/AFFILIATES:

Re-Crude

CONTACTS: *Note: Officers with more than one job title may be intentionally listed here more than once.*

Fred Cannon, CEO
Fred Cannon, Pres.
John H. Karnes, CFO
John Kasbaum, Sr. VP-Commercial
John Hacskaylo, VP-R&D
Dan Strope, VP-Tech.
Edward J. Smith, VP-Eng. & Construction
Christopher A. Artzer, General Counsel/VP/Sec.
W.R. Lyle, Sr. VP-Oper.
Andre Ditsch, VP-Strategy
Gene Staggs, Controller/Treas.
Michael J. Adams, VP-Process Eng.
Joseph S. Cappello, Pres., Int'l
Michael P. McCollum, VP-Supply

GROWTH PLANS/SPECIAL FEATURES:

KiOR, Inc. is a next-generation renewable fuels company based in Pasadena, Texas. The firm has developed a proprietary technology platform to convert low-cost, abundant and sustainable non-food biomass into hydrocarbon-based oil, which it refers to as Re-Crude. Its platform for converting biomass to fuel involves feeding processed biomass material into a biomass fluid catalytic cracking (BFCC) reactor where it reacts with the firm's proprietary catalyst system to produce renewable crude oil, which can then be refined into fuelstocks using standard refining equipment. Unlike other biofuels, such as ethanol or biodiesel, KiOR produces fungible gasoline and diesel blendstocks compatible with the current transportation infrastructure. The company's proprietary catalyst systems, reactor design and refining processes have achieved yields of renewable fuel products of approximately 67 gallons per bone dry ton of biomass, or BDT, at its current demonstration facility. Given this, the firm believes it can produce gasoline and diesel blendstocks at a per-unit unsubsidized production cost below $1.80 per gallon, if produced in a standard commercial production facility with a processing capacity of 1,500 BDT per day. KiOR's initial-scale production facility, located in Columbus, Mississippi, is scheduled to begin production in the second half of 2012. Once complete, it intends to begin constructing larger standard commercial production facilities, with its first planned facility in Newton, Mississippi. In May 2011, the company signed an agreement with FedEx Corporate Services, Inc. to supply renewable diesel blendstocks once it commences commercial production. In June 2011, KiOR held an initial public offering (IPO) of stock on the NASDAQ stock exchange.

Phone: 281-694-8700	**Fax:** 281-694-8799
Toll-Free:	
Address: 13001 Bay Park Rd., Pasadena, TX 77507 US	

FINANCIALS: Sales and profits are in thousands of dollars—add 000 to get the full amount. 2011 Note: Financial information for 2011 was not available for all companies at press time.

2011 Sales: $	2011 Profits: $	**U.S. Stock Ticker:** KIOR
2010 Sales: $	2010 Profits: $-45,930	**Int'l Ticker:**
2009 Sales: $	2009 Profits: $-14,060	Int'l Exchange:
2008 Sales: $	2008 Profits: $	Employees: 107 Fiscal Year Ends: 12/31
2007 Sales: $	2007 Profits: $	Parent Company:

SALARIES/BENEFITS:

Pension Plan:	ESOP Stock Plan:	Profit Sharing:	Top Exec. Salary: $299,897	Bonus: $118,800
Savings Plan: Y	Stock Purch. Plan:		Second Exec. Salary: $235,686	Bonus: $

OTHER THOUGHTS:

Apparent Women Officers or Directors: 1
Hot Spot for Advancement for Women/Minorities:

LOCATIONS: ("Y" = Yes)

West:	Southwest:	Midwest:	Southeast:	Northeast:	International:
	Y		Y		

KONARKA TECHNOLOGIES INC

www.konarka.com

Industry Group Code: 334413

Energy/Fuel:	Other Technologies:	Electrical Products:	Electronics:	Transportation:	Other:
Biofuels:	Irrigation:	Lighting/LEDs:	Computers:	Car Sharing:	Recycling:
Batteries/Storage:	Nanotech:	Waste Heat:	Sensors:	Electric Vehicles:	Engineering:
Solar: Y	Biotech:	Smart Meters:	Software:	Natural Gas Fuel:	Consulting:
Wind:	Water Tech./Treatment:	Machinery:			Investing:
Fuel Cells:	Ceramics:				Chemicals:

TYPES OF BUSINESS:

Photovoltaic Cells
Nanofilms

BRANDS/DIVISIONS/AFFILIATES:

Power Plastic
Partech International
Chevron Corp
Massachusetts Green Energy Fund
Vanguard Ventures

CONTACTS:
Note: Officers with more than one job title may be intentionally listed here more than once.

Howard Berke, CEO
Russell Gaudiana, VP-Research
Christoph Brabec, CTO
Dan Williams, VP-Prod. Dev.
Stuart Spitzer, VP-Eng.
Larry Weldon, VP-Mfg.
Therese Jordan, VP-Bus. Dev.
Shinji Kawahara, VP-Japanese Bus. Dev.
Eitan C. Zeira, VP-Printed Photovoltaics
Kethinni Chittibabu, Principal Scientist
Alessandro Zedda, VP-Materials Dev.
Howard Berke, Chmn.
Alex Valenzuela, VP-European Bus. Dev.
Kevin McGuire, VP-Supply Chain & Quality

Phone: 978-569-1400	Fax: 978-569-1402
Toll-Free:	
Address: 116 John St., Lowell, MA 01852 US	

GROWTH PLANS/SPECIAL FEATURES:

Konarka Technologies, Inc. develops Power Plastic, a nano-enabled polymer-based photovoltaic product that provides a source of renewable power in a variety of forms for commercial, industrial, government and consumer applications. This technology can employ a wider range of the lighter spectrum than traditional photovoltaic products by utilizing both visible and invisible light sources to generate power. The Power Plastic process first prints a light-absorbing dye onto plastic strips containing countless semi-conducting nanometer-scale titanium oxide crystals covered with a light-absorbing dye. The nano-materials absorb sunlight and indoor light; they then convert the light sources to electrical energy after the light energy travels through electrically active materials and a series of electrodes. The company's photovoltaic materials are lightweight, more affordable and provide greater flexibility than standard photovoltaic materials. Konarka's printing process of photo-reactive materials also permits a nearly infinite amount of color and transparency combinations, which allows the strips to be integrated flawlessly into any environment. In past partnerships, Konarka has worked with the military to develop camouflaged tent-like buildings with surface areas that are continually engaged in the generation of electricity. The light weight properties of the photovoltaic cells make them ideal for use as a portable energy source in power notebook PCs, mobile phones or other personal electronics items. The firm maintains various partnerships and joint ventures with 27 partners, including Nu Energy; Enviromena Power Systems; Siemens Corporate Technology; Konica Minolta Holdings, Inc.; the University of California Santa Barbara; and the U.S. Air Force. Konarka has 11 leading investors, including Partech International, Chevron Corp., Massachusetts Green Energy Fund and Vanguard Ventures. In January 2011, the company formed a research partnership with researchers at the University of Texas.

FINANCIALS:
Sales and profits are in thousands of dollars—add 000 to get the full amount. 2011 Note: Financial information for 2011 was not available for all companies at press time.

2011 Sales: $	2011 Profits: $	**U.S. Stock Ticker: Private**
2010 Sales: $	2010 Profits: $	**Int'l Ticker:**
2009 Sales: $	2009 Profits: $	Int'l Exchange:
2008 Sales: $	2008 Profits: $	Employees: Fiscal Year Ends: 12/31
2007 Sales: $	2007 Profits: $	Parent Company:

SALARIES/BENEFITS:

Pension Plan:	ESOP Stock Plan:	Profit Sharing:	Top Exec. Salary: $	Bonus: $
Savings Plan:	Stock Purch. Plan:		Second Exec. Salary: $	Bonus: $

OTHER THOUGHTS:

Apparent Women Officers or Directors:
Hot Spot for Advancement for Women/Minorities:

LOCATIONS: ("Y" = Yes)

West:	Southwest:	Midwest:	Southeast:	Northeast: Y	International: Y

KYOCERA CORP

global.kyocera.com

Industry Group Code: 334419

Energy/Fuel:	Other Technologies:	Electrical Products:	Electronics:	Transportation:	Other:
Biofuels:	Irrigation:	Lighting/LEDs:	Computers:	Car Sharing:	Recycling:
Batteries/Storage:	Nanotech:	Waste Heat:	Sensors:	Electric Vehicles:	Engineering:
Solar:	Biotech:	Smart Meters:	Software:	Natural Gas Fuel:	Consulting:
Wind:	Water Tech./Treatment:	Machinery:			Investing:
Fuel Cells:	Ceramics:				Chemicals:

TYPES OF BUSINESS:

Ceramic Components Manufacturing
Cell Phone Manufacturing
Semiconductor Components
Optoelectronic Products
Consumer Electronics

BRANDS/DIVISIONS/AFFILIATES:

CONTACTS: *Note: Officers with more than one job title may be intentionally listed here more than once.*

Tetsuo Kuba, Pres.
Tsutomu Yamori, Gen. Mgr.-Human Resources
Keijiro Minami, Sr. Exec. Officer/Gen. Mgr-R&D
Osamu Nomoto, Sr. Exec. Officer/Gen. Mgr.-Legal
Hisao Hisaki, VP/Gen. Mgr.-Corp. Dev.
Shoichi Aoki, Gen. Mgr.-Corp. Finance & Acct. Group
Goro Yamaguchi, Gen. Mgr.-Corp. Semiconductor Components Group
Yoshihito Ohta, Managing Exec. Officer
Tatsumi Maeda, Gen. Mgr.-Corp. Electronic Components Group
Yasuyuki Yamamoto, Gen. Mgr.-Corp. Comm. Equipment Group
Makoto Kawamura, Chmn.
Kazumasa Umemura, Gen. Mgr.-Int'l Div.
Masaki Iida, Gen. Mgr.-Purchasing

Phone: 81-75-604-3500	**Fax:** 81-75-604-3501
Toll-Free:	
Address: 6 Takeda Tobadono-cho, Fushimi-ku, Kyoto, 612-8501 Japan	

GROWTH PLANS/SPECIAL FEATURES:

Kyocera Corp. is engaged in a number of high-tech fields, including fine ceramic components, electronic devices, equipment, services and networks. The company has roughly 173 subsidiaries and four affiliates outside Japan, as well as 29 subsidiaries and six affiliates in Japan. Kyocera operates in seven segments: fine ceramic parts; semiconductor parts; applied ceramic products; electronic devices; telecommunications equipment; information equipment; and other. Kyocera's fine ceramic parts group, generating roughly 5% of revenues, develops, manufactures and sells products made from a variety of ceramic materials, such as silicon carbide, that are used in the computing, telecommunications, automotive and industrial sectors. Through its semiconductor parts group (13.1% of revenues) the company provides inorganic ceramic and organic packages for integrated circuit (IC) and other semiconductor and electronic components. Kyocera's applied ceramic products group (14.6% of revenues) consists of five main product lines: solar energy products; cutting tools; circuit board micro drills; jewelry and applied ceramic related products; and dental implants, artificial bone and joint prostheses. The company's electronic devices group (18.6% of revenues) provides electronic components and devices for the telecommunications and information processing industries, including ceramic capacitors; tantalum capacitors; miniature timing devices such as TCXOs (temperature-compensated crystal oscillators); RF modules; liquid crystal displays (LCDs); and connectors for mobile phone handsets and PCs. Kyocera's telecommunications equipment group 17.6% of revenues) includes code division multiple access (CDMA) mobile phone handsets and PHS (personal handy-phone system) products such as PHS mobile phone handsets and base stations. Major products in the firm's information equipment group (21.6% of revenues) include page printers, digital copying machines and multifunctional systems. Kyocera's other segment (9.5% of revenues) produces electronic component materials, electric insulators and synthetic resin molded parts.

FINANCIALS: Sales and profits are in thousands of dollars—add 000 to get the full amount. 2011 Note: Financial information for 2011 was not available for all companies at press time.

2011 Sales: $16,685,400	2011 Profits: $1,612,600	**U.S. Stock Ticker:**
2010 Sales: $13,205,900	2010 Profits: $493,100	**Int'l Ticker: 6971**
2009 Sales: $11,399,859	2009 Profits: $298,040	Int'l Exchange: Tokyo-TSE
2008 Sales: $12,904,360	2008 Profits: $1,072,440	Employees: 66,608 Fiscal Year Ends: 3/31
2007 Sales: $10,880,483	2007 Profits: $902,576	Parent Company:

SALARIES/BENEFITS:

Pension Plan:	ESOP Stock Plan:	Profit Sharing:	Top Exec. Salary: $	Bonus: $
Savings Plan:	Stock Purch. Plan:		Second Exec. Salary: $	Bonus: $

OTHER THOUGHTS:

Apparent Women Officers or Directors:
Hot Spot for Advancement for Women/Minorities:

LOCATIONS: ("Y" = Yes)

West:	Southwest:	Midwest:	Southeast:	Northeast:	International:
Y	Y		Y	Y	Y

KYOCERA SOLAR CORP

www.kyocerasolar.com

Industry Group Code: 334413

Energy/Fuel:	Other Technologies:	Electrical Products:	Electronics:	Transportation:	Other:
Biofuels:	Irrigation:	Lighting/LEDs:	Computers:	Car Sharing:	Recycling:
Batteries/Storage:	Nanotech:	Waste Heat:	Sensors:	Electric Vehicles:	Engineering:
Solar: Y	Biotech:	Smart Meters:	Software:	Natural Gas Fuel:	Consulting:
Wind:	Water Tech./Treatment:	Machinery:			Investing:
Fuel Cells:	Ceramics:				Chemicals:

TYPES OF BUSINESS:

Photovoltaic Systems
Solar Remote Power Systems
Solar Vehicle Power Systems

BRANDS/DIVISIONS/AFFILIATES:

Kyocera Corp
MyGen
Kyocera KD Modules
Kyocera Solar Europe sro
Kyocera (Tianjin) Solar Energy Co Ltd
Kyocera Solar Inc

CONTACTS:
Note: Officers with more than one job title may be intentionally listed here more than once.

Tetsuo Kuba, Pres., Kyocera Corp.
Tatsumi Maeda, Gen. Mgr.-Solar Energy Group, Kyocera Corp.
Nobuo Kitamura, Deputy Gen. Mgr.-Solar Energy Group, Kyocera Corp.

Phone: 480-948-8003	Fax: 480-483-6431
Toll-Free: 800-223-9580	
Address: 7812 E. Acoma Dr., Scottsdale, AZ 85260 US	

GROWTH PLANS/SPECIAL FEATURES:

Kyocera Solar Corp., a subsidiary of Japan-based Kyocera Corporation, is one of the largest producers and suppliers of solar energy products. The firm develops and sells solar electric systems to power remotely located telecommunications equipment, traffic signals and pipeline monitoring systems. The company also sells solar-powered water pumping systems and solar electric systems for boats and recreational vehicles. Additionally, its solar electric solutions can provide clean, uncontaminated water where sources are unsanitary or hard to access. Working through a network of more than 1,500 authorized distributors and dealers, Kyocera Solar operates in several consumer and industrial markets, including water pumping, RV and marine, communication, oil and gas, railroad, lighting and rural development. Its featured products are Kyocera KD Modules, a UL-approved photovoltaic module line consisting of high efficiency 156mm x 156 solar cells; and the MyGen grid-tie photovoltaic power system, which is a utility interactive system designed for use on residential and small commercial buildings. Mounting, control, conversion and storage systems for solar power installations are also offered individually. The firm operates five solar cell manufacturing plants: one in Kadan, Czech Republic; one in Yasu City, Japan; one in Tianjin City, China; and two in Tijuana, Mexico. Its subsidiaries include Kyocera Solar Europe s.r.o., Kyocera (Tianjin) Solar Energy Co., Ltd. and Kyocera Solar, Inc. In January 2011, Kyocera Solar began construction on a second manufacturing facility in the Czech Republic.

FINANCIALS:
Sales and profits are in thousands of dollars—add 000 to get the full amount. 2011 Note: Financial information for 2011 was not available for all companies at press time.

2011 Sales: $	2011 Profits: $	U.S. Stock Ticker: Subsidiary
2010 Sales: $	2010 Profits: $	Int'l Ticker:
2009 Sales: $	2009 Profits: $	Int'l Exchange:
2008 Sales: $	2008 Profits: $	Employees: Fiscal Year Ends: 3/31
2007 Sales: $	2007 Profits: $	Parent Company: KYOCERA CORP

SALARIES/BENEFITS:

Pension Plan:	ESOP Stock Plan:	Profit Sharing:	Top Exec. Salary: $	Bonus: $
Savings Plan: Y	Stock Purch. Plan: Y		Second Exec. Salary: $	Bonus: $

OTHER THOUGHTS:

Apparent Women Officers or Directors:
Hot Spot for Advancement for Women/Minorities:

LOCATIONS: ("Y" = Yes)

West:	Southwest: Y	Midwest:	Southeast:	Northeast:	International: Y

LANXESS AG

www.lanxess.com

Industry Group Code: 325

Energy/Fuel:	Other Technologies:		Electrical Products:	Electronics:	Transportation:	Other:	
Biofuels:	Irrigation:		Lighting/LEDs:	Computers:	Car Sharing:	Recycling:	
Batteries/Storage:	Nanotech:		Waste Heat:	Sensors:	Electric Vehicles:	Engineering:	
Solar:	Biotech:	Y	Smart Meters:	Software:	Natural Gas Fuel:	Consulting:	
Wind:	Water Tech./Treatment:		Machinery:			Investing:	
Fuel Cells:	Ceramics:					Chemicals:	Y

TYPES OF BUSINESS:

Chemicals
Performance Chemicals
Chemical Intermediates
Engineering Plastics
Performance Rubber

BRANDS/DIVISIONS/AFFILIATES:

Rhein Chemie
DSM Elastomers
Darmex SA

CONTACTS: Note: Officers with more than one job title may be intentionally listed here more than once.

Axel C. Heitmann, CEO
Bernhard Duttmann, CFO
Rainier van Roessel, Dir.-Labor Rel.
Werner Breuers, Head-R&D
Werner Breuers, Dir.-Performance Polymers & Advanced Intermediates
Rainier van Roessel, Managing Dir.
Hubert Fink, Head-Basic Chemicals
Jean-Marc Vesselle, Head-Ion Exchange Resins
Rolf Stomberg, Chmn.
Werner Breuers, Head-Procurement

Phone: 49-214-30-33333	Fax: 49-214-30-50691
Toll-Free:	
Address: Kaiser-Wilhelm-Allee 40, Leverkusen, 51369 Germany	

GROWTH PLANS/SPECIAL FEATURES:

Lanxess AG is an independent chemical manufacturing company with operations in 23 countries, including major manufacturing sites in Germany, Belgium, the U.S. and Canada. The company has over 70 fully consolidated subsidiaries worldwide. Lanxess has a portfolio of approximately 5,000 chemical products, divided into three broad product segments: performance chemicals, advanced intermediates and performance polymers. Performance chemicals include material protection products, like disinfectants, industrial corrosion inhibitors, beverage preservatives; functional chemicals, plastic additives, phosphorus and specialty chemicals, organic and inorganic colorants; leather treatments; rubber chemicals; and ion exchange resins. Subsidiary Rhein Chemie makes additives for the lubricant, rubber, polyurethanes and plastics industries. Advanced intermediates include basic chemicals (industrial chemicals and aromatic compounds) and fine chemicals for the pharmaceutical and agrochemical industries. The performance polymers segment encompasses the production of rubber and plastics, which have applications in the automotive and electrical/electronics industries. Products in this segment include butyl rubber, performance butadiene rubber, technical rubber products and semi-crystalline products. Nearly a quarter of the firm's sales are in Germany, with another third in the rest of Europe. The Americas collectively account for another quarter of sales, with Asia-Pacific representing most of the remainder. In November 2010, the company agreed to acquire two business units from Flexsys, a division of Solutia, Inc. In December 2010, it announced plans to construct a leather chemicals facility in China. Also in December, it agreed to acquire DSM Elastomers from Royal DSM NV. In January 2011, its subsidiary Rhein Chemie acquired Argentina-based Darmex SA. In March 2011, Lanxess acquired the material protection business of Syngenta and broke ground on a compounding facility in North Carolina.

The firm offers its employees support services for elder and childcare; flexible work hours; the opportunity to work from home; and management training courses through the Lanxess Academy.

FINANCIALS: Sales and profits are in thousands of dollars—add 000 to get the full amount. 2011 Note: Financial information for 2011 was not available for all companies at press time.

2011 Sales: $	2011 Profits: $	U.S. Stock Ticker:
2010 Sales: $10,285,000	2010 Profits: $547,470	Int'l Ticker: LXSG
2009 Sales: $6,880,100	2009 Profits: $54,420	Int'l Exchange: Frankfurt-Euronext
2008 Sales: $8,864,970	2008 Profits: $230,520	Employees: 14,648 Fiscal Year Ends: 12/31
2007 Sales: $8,908,110	2007 Profits: $150,990	Parent Company:

SALARIES/BENEFITS:

Pension Plan:	ESOP Stock Plan:	Profit Sharing:	Top Exec. Salary: $	Bonus: $
Savings Plan:	Stock Purch. Plan:		Second Exec. Salary: $	Bonus: $

OTHER THOUGHTS:

Apparent Women Officers or Directors:
Hot Spot for Advancement for Women/Minorities:

LOCATIONS: ("Y" = Yes)

West:	Southwest:	Midwest:	Southeast:	Northeast:	International:
	Y			Y	Y

LANZATECH LTD

www.lanzatech.co.nz

Industry Group Code: 325199

Energy/Fuel:		Other Technologies:		Electrical Products:		Electronics:	Transportation:	Other:
Biofuels:	Y	Irrigation:		Lighting/LEDs:		Computers:	Car Sharing:	Recycling:
Batteries/Storage:		Nanotech:		Waste Heat:		Sensors:	Electric Vehicles:	Engineering:
Solar:		Biotech:	Y	Smart Meters:		Software:	Natural Gas Fuel:	Consulting:
Wind:		Water Tech./Treatment:		Machinery:				Investing:
Fuel Cells:		Ceramics:						Chemicals:

TYPES OF BUSINESS:

Biofuel Production
Waste-to-Energy Technology

BRANDS/DIVISIONS/AFFILIATES:

Freedom Pines Biorefinery
PETRONAS
Khosla Ventures
Qiming Ventures
Softbank China Venture Capital

CONTACTS: *Note: Officers with more than one job title may be intentionally listed here more than once.*

Jennifer Holmgren, CEO
Jennifer McFarlane, CFO
Barbara Koehler, Dir.-Human Resources
Sean Simpson, Chief Scientific Officer/Co-Founder
Simon Trevethick, VP-Eng. & Svcs.
Prabhakar Nair, VP-Bus. Dev., Asia
Will Barker, VP-External Affairs
Laurel Harmon, VP-Gov't Rel.
Michael Schultz, VP-Process Dev.
James Zhang, VP-Bus. Dev., China

Phone: 64-9-304-2110	Fax: 64-9-929-3038
Toll-Free:	
Address: 24 Balfour Rd., Auckland, New Zealand	

GROWTH PLANS/SPECIAL FEATURES:

LanzaTech Ltd., founded in 2005, is a developer of alternative and renewable fuel technologies. With operations spread between Illinois, Shanghai and Auckland, the company has developed a gas fermentation process to produce ethanol from non-food resources, primarily industrial and waste gases. LanzaTech's proprietary technology uses captured carbon monoxide (CO) gas, a by-product of industrial production facilities, and its patented, wholly-owned microbe catalyst to convert CO to ethanol. The company also plans to use this technology to produce various industrial chemicals, including isoprene, MEK (Methyl ethyl ketone) and isopropanol. LanzaTech has achieved annual ethanol production capacity of 15,000 gallons at a pilot plant in Glenbrook, New Zealand. The company has partnered with the U.S. Department of Energy, the Defense Advanced Research Projects Agency (DARPA) and the Federal Aviation Administration to produce jet fuels for commercial and military use. The firm has raised over $85 million in financing from investors such as PETRONAS, Khosla Ventures, Qiming Ventures and Softbank China Venture Capital. In September 2011, the company signed a joint venture agreement with China's Shougang Group to construct a demonstration plant for LanzaTech's process technology at one of Shougang's steel mills in China. In January 2012, the firm acquired its first commercial-scale production facility in the U.S., the Freedom Pines Biorefinery, located in Georgia. LanzaTech plans to use the facility to produce biofuel from regionally sourced waste wood.

FINANCIALS: Sales and profits are in thousands of dollars—add 000 to get the full amount. 2011 Note: Financial information for 2011 was not available for all companies at press time.

2011 Sales: $	2011 Profits: $	**U.S. Stock Ticker:** Private
2010 Sales: $	2010 Profits: $	**Int'l Ticker:**
2009 Sales: $	2009 Profits: $	Int'l Exchange:
2008 Sales: $	2008 Profits: $	Employees: Fiscal Year Ends:
2007 Sales: $	2007 Profits: $	Parent Company:

SALARIES/BENEFITS:

Pension Plan:	ESOP Stock Plan:	Profit Sharing:	Top Exec. Salary: $	Bonus: $
Savings Plan:	Stock Purch. Plan:		Second Exec. Salary: $	Bonus: $

OTHER THOUGHTS:

Apparent Women Officers or Directors: 4
Hot Spot for Advancement for Women/Minorities: Y

LOCATIONS: ("Y" = Yes)

West:	Southwest:	Midwest:	Southeast:	Northeast:	International:
		Y	Y		Y

LATTICEPOWER (JIANGXI) CORP

www.latticepower.com

Industry Group Code: 334413

Energy/Fuel:	Other Technologies:	Electrical Products:		Electronics:	Transportation:	Other:
Biofuels:	Irrigation:	Lighting/LEDs:	Y	Computers:	Car Sharing:	Recycling:
Batteries/Storage:	Nanotech:	Waste Heat:		Sensors:	Electric Vehicles:	Engineering:
Solar:	Biotech:	Smart Meters:		Software:	Natural Gas Fuel:	Consulting:
Wind:	Water Tech./Treatment:	Machinery:				Investing:
Fuel Cells:	Ceramics:					Chemicals:

TYPES OF BUSINESS:

Low-cost LED Manufacturing
Low cost LED EPI manufacturing

BRANDS/DIVISIONS/AFFILIATES:

LP-S108B07B
LP-SI08B03G
LP1000
LP-TS1213B1
LP-TS1023B1
LP-TP2020B

CONTACTS: *Note: Officers with more than one job title may be intentionally listed here more than once.*

Sonny Wu, CEO
Hanmin Zhao, CTO

Phone: 0791-8158299	Fax: 0791-8158359
Toll-Free:	
Address: No. 699 North Aixihu Rd., Nanchang, 330029 China	

GROWTH PLANS/SPECIAL FEATURES:

Lattice Power (JIANGXI) Corp. specializes in the development of light-emitting diode (LED) electrostatic particle ionization power (EPI) technology and products. The company operates in two division technology and applications. The company's LED technology products are designed using gallium nitride (Ga-N) and silicon substrate. These products are primarily used in LCD backlighting, for high brightness purposes; chip products, for commercial and display purposes; in addition to other lighting applications. The company's primary product lines include the TS series, which uses lateral chip technology in conjunction with transparent substrate to achieve high electron stimulated desorption (ESD) yield, robust design and low leakage; and the TF series, which reduces the cost of chip production by offering more expansive thermal properties, such as, the ability to operate under higher current densities though Ga-N-on-Silicon EPI technology and vertical thin film chip configurations. Proprietary products of the TF series include LP-S108B07B; LP-SI08B03G; LP1000; and the TS lines, LP-TS1213B1; LP-TS1023B1; and LP-TP2020B. The firm's applications division is comprised of general lighting, LCD device displays and automotive and modular displays. Lattice Power has over 50 international and Chinese patents in the LED EPI chip processing market. In 2012, the company continued expanding its operations with the opening of a new LED research and development center in Changzhoue, Jiangsu Province.

Employees are offered professional training, employee mentors, corporate development and rotation programs.

FINANCIALS: Sales and profits are in thousands of dollars—add 000 to get the full amount. 2011 Note: Financial information for 2011 was not available for all companies at press time.

2011 Sales: $	2011 Profits: $	U.S. Stock Ticker: Private
2010 Sales: $	2010 Profits: $	Int'l Ticker:
2009 Sales: $	2009 Profits: $	Int'l Exchange:
2008 Sales: $	2008 Profits: $	Employees: Fiscal Year Ends:
2007 Sales: $	2007 Profits: $	Parent Company:

SALARIES/BENEFITS:

Pension Plan:	ESOP Stock Plan:	Profit Sharing:	Top Exec. Salary: $	Bonus: $
Savings Plan:	Stock Purch. Plan:		Second Exec. Salary: $	Bonus: $

OTHER THOUGHTS:

Apparent Women Officers or Directors:
Hot Spot for Advancement for Women/Minorities:

LOCATIONS: ("Y" = Yes)

West:	Southwest:	Midwest:	Southeast:	Northeast:	International: Y

LDK SOLAR CO LTD

Industry Group Code: 334413

www.ldksolar.com

Energy/Fuel:	Other Technologies:	Electrical Products:	Electronics:	Transportation:	Other:
Biofuels:	Irrigation:	Lighting/LEDs:	Computers:	Car Sharing:	Recycling:
Batteries/Storage:	Nanotech:	Waste Heat:	Sensors:	Electric Vehicles:	Engineering:
Solar: Y	Biotech:	Smart Meters:	Software:	Natural Gas Fuel:	Consulting:
Wind:	Water Tech./Treatment:	Machinery:			Investing:
Fuel Cells:	Ceramics:				Chemicals:

TYPES OF BUSINESS:

Photovoltaics
Silane Gas Production

BRANDS/DIVISIONS/AFFILIATES:

Jiangxi LDK Solar
Jiangxi LDK Silicon
Jiangxi LDK Polysilicon
LDK Solar Europe Holding SA
LDK Optronics Technology Co
LDK Solar USA Inc
Solar Power Inc

CONTACTS: Note: Officers with more than one job title may be intentionally listed here more than once.

Xiaofeng Peng, CEO
Xingxue Tong, COO
Xingxue Tong, Pres.
Jack Lai, CFO/Exec. VP
Yuepeng Wan, CTO/Sr. VP
Pietro Rossetto, Chief Eng.
Liangbao Zhu, Exec. VP
Yonggang Shao, Exec. VP
Qiqiang Yao, Sr. VP
Xiaofeng Peng, Chmn.

Phone: 86-790-666-8000	Fax: 86-790-666-9000
Toll-Free:	
Address: LDK Ave.,Economic Dev. Zone, Xinyu City, Jiangxi, 338032 China	

GROWTH PLANS/SPECIAL FEATURES:

LDK Solar Co., Ltd. is a vertically-integrated manufacturer of solar photovoltaic (PV) products. The firm produces both multicrystalline and monocrystalline wafers currently at 180-220 micron thicknesses, and provides wafer processing services to solar cell and module manufacturers. Additionally, LDK sells ingots and other chemicals used to produce polysilicon and solar wafers. The firm manufactures multicrystalline ingots from polysilicon feedstock in its directional solidification system furnaces (DSS furnaces) as an interim step in producing wafers. The company sells its products globally to manufacturers of PV products. The firm's polysilicon production line consists of two plants, with a combined annual installed polysilicon production capacity of 12,000 megatons. LDK has an annual wafer production capacity of approximately 3.5 gigawatts (GW). Recently, the firm has expanded into the production of solar cells and modules, with an annual capacity to produce 570 MW of cells and 1.6 GW of solar modules. The company's primary operating subsidiaries are Jiangxi LDK Solar; Jiangxi LDK Silicon; and Jiangxi LDK Polysilicon. Additional subsidiaries include LDK Optronics Technology Co.; LDK Solar USA, Inc.; LDK Solar Europe Holding S.A. In January 2011, LDK acquired a 70% interest in Solar Power, Inc. for $33 million. In April 2011, the company expanded into the sapphire wafer industry by building a new manufacturing plant in Nanchang City, Jiangxi Province. Additionally, LDK invested $35 million to create a new manufacturing line to produce silane gas. In August 2011, it signed an engineering, procurement and construction agreement with Datang Intl. Power Generation Co., Ltd. to develop a 20 MW solar project in the Qinghai province. In October 2011, the firm signed a similar agreement with Guodian Longyuan Zhangye New Energy Ltd. for a project located in Zhangye City.

FINANCIALS: Sales and profits are in thousands of dollars—add 000 to get the full amount. 2011 Note: Financial information for 2011 was not available for all companies at press time.

2011 Sales: $	2011 Profits: $	**U.S. Stock Ticker: LDK**
2010 Sales: $2,577,378	2010 Profits: $294,367	**Int'l Ticker:**
2009 Sales: $1,103,546	2009 Profits: $-237,568	Int'l Exchange:
2008 Sales: $1,643,495	2008 Profits: $66,408	Employees: 22,400 Fiscal Year Ends: 12/31
2007 Sales: $523,946	2007 Profits: $144,301	Parent Company:

SALARIES/BENEFITS:

Pension Plan:	ESOP Stock Plan:	Profit Sharing:	Top Exec. Salary: $	Bonus: $
Savings Plan:	Stock Purch. Plan:		Second Exec. Salary: $	Bonus: $

OTHER THOUGHTS:

Apparent Women Officers or Directors:
Hot Spot for Advancement for Women/Minorities:

LOCATIONS: ("Y" = Yes)

West:	Southwest:	Midwest:	Southeast:	Northeast:	International:
Y					Y

LEMNIS LIGHTING BV

www.lemnislighting.com

Industry Group Code: 334413

Energy/Fuel:	Other Technologies:	Electrical Products:		Electronics:	Transportation:	Other:
Biofuels:	Irrigation:	Lighting/LEDs:	Y	Computers:	Car Sharing:	Recycling:
Batteries/Storage: Y	Nanotech:	Waste Heat:		Sensors:	Electric Vehicles:	Engineering:
Solar: Y	Biotech:	Smart Meters:		Software:	Natural Gas Fuel:	Consulting:
Wind:	Water Tech./Treatment:	Machinery:				Investing:
Fuel Cells:	Ceramics:					Chemicals:

TYPES OF BUSINESS:

LED Lighting Technology
Solar Power Technology

BRANDS/DIVISIONS/AFFILIATES:

Pharox
Pharox 300
Lumis-led luminaire
Oreon
Pharox Solar

CONTACTS: *Note: Officers with more than one job title may be intentionally listed here more than once.*

Remko Gaastra, CEO
John Rooymans, Head-R&D

Phone: 31-342-760-760	Fax: 31-342-760-761
Toll-Free:	
Address: Gildeweg 18, Barneveld, 3771 NB The Netherlands	

GROWTH PLANS/SPECIAL FEATURES:

Lemnis Lighting BV, owned by private equity firm Tendris Holding, is a technology company that develops and markets sustainable lighting. The firm's sustainable lighting innovation products include LED lamps for both indoor and outdoor applications. Lemnis' Pharox led-lamp is a direct replacement for indoor incandescent bulbs and uses up to 90% less energy yet sacrifices very little in lighting quality and atmosphere. The Pharox 300 is the company's dimmable indoor LED option. The Lumis-led luminaire is Lemnis' public outdoor lighting product. The Lumis-led uses 30-70% less energy than traditional lighting sources and is applicable for most outdoor settings, including residential areas, tunnels, public roads and thoroughfares, parks, rural areas and cycle paths. The Lumis-led has already been incorporated into more than 150 outdoor lighting projects in multiple countries. The Lemnis Oreon is the firm's LED lighting product designed for greenhouses. Since crops only use certain parts of the light spectrum to grow, the Oreon produces only those exact wavelengths. The Oreon is 30-50% more efficient than traditional greenhouse lighting sources. In addition to these LED products, the firm also offers the Pharox Solar, an amalgamation of LED technology with solar power. The Pharox Solar offers lighting and other functionalities, such as charging mobile devices, in those moments when access to traditional electrical sources is either restricted or nonexistent. Lemnis' head office is in the Netherlands, and it also has offices in the U.S., Singapore, Hong Kong and South Africa.

FINANCIALS: Sales and profits are in thousands of dollars—add 000 to get the full amount. 2011 Note: Financial information for 2011 was not available for all companies at press time.

2011 Sales: $	2011 Profits: $	**U.S. Stock Ticker: Private**
2010 Sales: $	2010 Profits: $	**Int'l Ticker:**
2009 Sales: $	2009 Profits: $	Int'l Exchange:
2008 Sales: $	2008 Profits: $	Employees: Fiscal Year Ends:
2007 Sales: $	2007 Profits: $	Parent Company: TENDRIS HOLDING

SALARIES/BENEFITS:

Pension Plan:	ESOP Stock Plan:	Profit Sharing:	Top Exec. Salary: $	Bonus: $
Savings Plan:	Stock Purch. Plan:		Second Exec. Salary: $	Bonus: $

OTHER THOUGHTS:

Apparent Women Officers or Directors:
Hot Spot for Advancement for Women/Minorities:

LOCATIONS: ("Y" = Yes)

West:	Southwest:	Midwest:	Southeast:	Northeast:	International:
Y					Y

LS9 INC

www.ls9.com

Industry Group Code: 325199

Energy/Fuel:		Other Technologies:	Electrical Products:	Electronics:	Transportation:	Other:
Biofuels:	Y	Irrigation:	Lighting/LEDs:	Computers:	Car Sharing:	Recycling:
Batteries/Storage:		Nanotech:	Waste Heat:	Sensors:	Electric Vehicles:	Engineering:
Solar:		Biotech:	Smart Meters:	Software:	Natural Gas Fuel:	Consulting:
Wind:		Water Tech./Treatment:	Machinery:			Investing:
Fuel Cells:		Ceramics:				Chemicals:

TYPES OF BUSINESS:

Biofuel Technologies

BRANDS/DIVISIONS/AFFILIATES:

LS9 One-Step Process
LS9 Brasil Biotechnologia
LS UltraClean Fuel
LS Diesel
LS Jet
LS Kerosene
Tailored Product Design
Feedstock Flexibility

CONTACTS: *Note: Officers with more than one job title may be intentionally listed here more than once.*

Ed Dineen, CEO
Ed Dineen, Pres.
Stacey Delaney, Mgr.-Human Resources
Stephen del Cardayre, VP-R&D
Weu Huang, VP-Eng. & Process Dev.
Greg Rood, VP-Oper.
Bernie Chong, Controller
Linda R. Judge, VP-Intellectual Property
Pablo Otero, Dir.-Capital Projects
Lucila de Avila, Managing Dir.-LS9 Brazil

Phone:	Fax: 650-243-5400
Toll-Free: 650-243-5401	
Address: 600 Gateway Blvd., San Francisco, CA 94080 US	

GROWTH PLANS/SPECIAL FEATURES:

LS9, Inc., a California based company, creates second generation biofuel technologies and products using renewable resources. The firm's chemical and fuels portfolio consists of pipeline products, such as the LS UltraClean Fuel series, which encompasses LS Diesel, LS Jet and LS Kerosene, in addition to the sub-group UltraClean Diesel Fuel, which focuses on the production of fatty acide methyl esters (FAME) and fatty acid ethyl esters (FAEE) biodiesel fuel products. FAME and FAEE biodiesel products target the kerosene and aviation fuel markets. Other chemicals and fuel oils are produced using feedstock carbons from natural non-food substances such as inedible parts of plants. Most of the feedstock carbons used are obtained from cellulose agricultural residues and sugar cane syrup. Products are created using proprietary technologies developed by the firm. These technologies include the LS9 One-Step Process; Synthetic Biology; Biocatalysis; Tailored Product Design; and Feedstock Flexibility. In July 2011, the firm was awarded a $9 million grant from the U.S. Department of Energy to expand its research and development activities. That same month, the company announced the opening of LS9 Brasil Biotechnologia (LS BB), a new office in Sao Paulo, Brazil. In November 2011, LS9 expanded its operations by scaling up its technology and expanding the commercialization of its products with increased production runs on its fermentation vessel at the Okeechobee, Florida facility.

FINANCIALS: Sales and profits are in thousands of dollars—add 000 to get the full amount. 2011 Note: Financial information for 2011 was not available for all companies at press time.

2011 Sales: $	2011 Profits: $	**U.S. Stock Ticker: Private**
2010 Sales: $	2010 Profits: $	**Int'l Ticker:**
2009 Sales: $	2009 Profits: $	Int'l Exchange:
2008 Sales: $	2008 Profits: $	Employees: Fiscal Year Ends:
2007 Sales: $	2007 Profits: $	Parent Company:

SALARIES/BENEFITS:

Pension Plan:	ESOP Stock Plan:	Profit Sharing:	Top Exec. Salary: $	Bonus: $
Savings Plan:	Stock Purch. Plan:		Second Exec. Salary: $	Bonus: $

OTHER THOUGHTS:

Apparent Women Officers or Directors: 3
Hot Spot for Advancement for Women/Minorities: Y

LOCATIONS: ("Y" = Yes)

West:	Southwest:	Midwest:	Southeast:	Northeast:	International:
Y					Y

MANHATTAN SCIENTIFICS INC

www.mhtx.com

Industry Group Code: 335999

Energy/Fuel:	Other Technologies:		Electrical Products:	Electronics:	Transportation:	Other:	
Biofuels:	Irrigation:		Lighting/LEDs:	Computers:	Car Sharing:	Recycling:	
Batteries/Storage:	Nanotech:	Y	Waste Heat:	Sensors:	Electric Vehicles:	Engineering:	
Solar:	Biotech:		Smart Meters:	Software:	Natural Gas Fuel:	Consulting:	
Wind:	Water Tech./Treatment:		Machinery:			Investing:	Y
Fuel Cells: Y	Ceramics:					Chemicals:	

TYPES OF BUSINESS:

Fuel Cell Technology
Computer Technology
Nanotechnology
Nano-medicine

BRANDS/DIVISIONS/AFFILIATES:

MicroFuel Cell
Scientific Nanomedicine Inc
Novint Technologies
Teneo Computing Inc
Novint Falcon
Metallicum Inc
Tamarack Storage Devices Inc
Senior Scientific LLC

CONTACTS: *Note: Officers with more than one job title may be intentionally listed here more than once.*

Emmanuel Tsoupanarias, CEO
Emmanuel Tsoupanarias, Pres.
Leonard Friedman, Corp. Sec.
Marvin Maslow, Dir.-Public Rel.
Marvin Maslow, Dir.-Investor Rel.
Chris Theoharis, Treas.
Emmanuel Tsoupanarias, Chmn.

Phone: 212-551-0577	Fax: 212-752-0077
Toll-Free:	
Address: 405 Lexington Ave., Chrysler Bldg., 32nd Fl., New York, NY 10174 US	

GROWTH PLANS/SPECIAL FEATURES:

Manhattan Scientifics, Inc. seeks to acquire, develop and commercialize life-enhancing technologies in various fields, emphasizing the development of nano-materials. The firm is currently focused on the fields of medical technology and advanced materials. Manhattan Scientifics has three wholly-owned subsidiaries: Metallicum, Inc.; Tamarack Storage Devices, Inc.; and Teneo Computing, Inc. Metallicum, a nanotechnology start-up company, is active in developing and manufacturing nano-structured metals for medical implants and other applications. The other two subsidiaries are currently non-operational. The company's goal is to identify significant technologies, acquire them, support their development, secure intellectual property rights and commercialize them through licensing and sales. Historically, the company was involved in the development of three primary technologies. Its MicroFuel Cells, designed as an efficient, environmentally safe, miniature electricity generator powered by methanol and water, could replace lithium ion batteries in portable electronic devices. This technology, which mimics the cells of animals, can be mass produced like printed circuits and could provide up to one week of talk time in a cell phone, instead of the five hours typical of current batteries. The Mid-Range Fuel Cell, acquired from NovArs Gessellschaft fuer neue Technologien, GmbH, is designed as a hydrogen and air fueled, light-weight, portable power source for high-current, low-voltage appliances, including kitchen appliances, cordless power tools and other home and mobility devices. The firm provided the seed capital for the formation of Novint Technologies, developer of the 3D interactive Novint Falcon mouse, which allows users to empirically sense objects displayed on a computer screen. Manhattan Scientifics operates a research facility in Los Alamos, New Mexico and maintains a close association with the Los Alamos National Laboratory. In June 2011, Manhattan Scientifics acquired Senior Scientific, LLC and its affiliate, Scientific Nanomedicine, Inc.

FINANCIALS: Sales and profits are in thousands of dollars—add 000 to get the full amount. 2011 Note: Financial information for 2011 was not available for all companies at press time.

2011 Sales: $	2011 Profits: $	**U.S. Stock Ticker:** MHTX
2010 Sales: $1,686	2010 Profits: $- 43	**Int'l Ticker:**
2009 Sales: $ 633	2009 Profits: $- 446	Int'l Exchange:
2008 Sales: $2,200	2008 Profits: $-2,100	Employees: 1 Fiscal Year Ends: 12/31
2007 Sales: $ 200	2007 Profits: $-3,000	Parent Company:

SALARIES/BENEFITS:

Pension Plan:	ESOP Stock Plan:	Profit Sharing:	Top Exec. Salary: $100,000	Bonus: $
Savings Plan:	Stock Purch. Plan:		Second Exec. Salary: $	Bonus: $

OTHER THOUGHTS:

Apparent Women Officers or Directors:
Hot Spot for Advancement for Women/Minorities:

LOCATIONS: ("Y" = Yes)

West:	Southwest:	Midwest:	Southeast:	Northeast:	International:
	Y			Y	Y

MASCOMA CORP

www.mascoma.com

Industry Group Code: 325193

Energy/Fuel:		Other Technologies:		Electrical Products:	Electronics:	Transportation:	Other:
Biofuels:	Y	Irrigation:		Lighting/LEDs:	Computers:	Car Sharing:	Recycling:
Batteries/Storage:		Nanotech:		Waste Heat:	Sensors:	Electric Vehicles:	Engineering:
Solar:		Biotech:	Y	Smart Meters:	Software:	Natural Gas Fuel:	Consulting:
Wind:		Water Tech./Treatment:		Machinery:			Investing:
Fuel Cells:		Ceramics:					Chemicals:

TYPES OF BUSINESS:

Cellulosic Ethanol Production

GROWTH PLANS/SPECIAL FEATURES:

Mascoma Corp. is involved in the development of carbon biofuels from cellulosic ethanol. Cellulosic ethanol is obtained from the non-edible portion of plant material; though it is identical in composition and performance to ethanol derived from sugar cane or corn, cellulosic ethanol is more environmentally-friendly, less costly and more sustainable than these sources. Mascoma's proprietary Consolidated Bioprocessing technology uses engineered yeast and bacteria to produce large quantities of the enzymes necessary to break down cellulose and ferment the resulting sugars into ethanol. This combination of enzymatic digestion and fermentation significantly reduces costs by eliminating the need for a separate refinery. The firm expects this technology to eventually be able to create ethanol fuel in a matter of days. The company is owned by 11 investors: Flagship Ventures, Khosla Ventures, Marathon Oil, General Motors, VantagePoint Ventures, Pinnacle Ventures, Blackrock, SunOpta, Inc., Kleiner Perkins Caufield & Byers, General Catalyst Partners and Valero. Mascoma operates out of a research and development facility in New Hampshire and The Rome Demonstration Facility in New York. It also has an office in Canada. Through a joint venture with J.M. Longyear and Valero, the firm is constructing Kinross, which will be the company's first commercial plant in Michigan. The facility, which is expected to be completed in 2012, will derive 40 million gallons of cellulosic ethanol from a woody feedstock product. Mascoma hopes that the facility will eventually produce 80 million gallons of ethanol fuel per year.

BRANDS/DIVISIONS/AFFILIATES:

Consolidated Bioprocessing
SunOpta Inc
Khosla Ventures
Marathon Oil
VantagePoint Ventures
Kleiner Perkins Caufield & Byers
General Catalyst Partners
Valero

CONTACTS: *Note: Officers with more than one job title may be intentionally listed here more than once.*

William J. Brady, CEO
William J. Brady, Pres.
David A. Arkowitz, CFO
Regina M. DeTore, VP-Human Resources
Lee R. Lynd, Chief Science Officer
Michael R. Ladisch, CTO
David A. Arkowitz, Corp. Sec.
Alan H. Belcher, Sr. VP-Oper.
Charles E. Wyman, Chief Dev. Officer
David A. Arkowitz, Treas.
Stephen R. Kennedy
Chief Science Officer, Exec. VP-R&D
Bruce A. Jamerson, Chmn.

Phone: 603-676-3320	**Fax:** 603-676-3321
Toll-Free:	
Address: 67 Etna Rd., Ste. 300, Lebanon, NH 03766 US	

FINANCIALS: Sales and profits are in thousands of dollars—add 000 to get the full amount. 2011 Note: Financial information for 2011 was not available for all companies at press time.

2011 Sales: $	2011 Profits: $	**U.S. Stock Ticker: Private**	
2010 Sales: $	2010 Profits: $	**Int'l Ticker:**	
2009 Sales: $	2009 Profits: $	Int'l Exchange:	
2008 Sales: $	2008 Profits: $	Employees:	Fiscal Year Ends:
2007 Sales: $	2007 Profits: $	Parent Company:	

SALARIES/BENEFITS:

Pension Plan:	ESOP Stock Plan:	Profit Sharing:	Top Exec. Salary: $	Bonus: $
Savings Plan:	Stock Purch. Plan:		Second Exec. Salary: $	Bonus: $

OTHER THOUGHTS:

Apparent Women Officers or Directors: 1
Hot Spot for Advancement for Women/Minorities:

LOCATIONS: ("Y" = Yes)

West:	Southwest:	Midwest:	Southeast:	Northeast:	International:
				Y	

MCPHY ENERGY

www.mcphy.com

Industry Group Code: 33591

Energy/Fuel:		Other Technologies:		Electrical Products:		Electronics:		Transportation:		Other:	
Biofuels:		Irrigation:		Lighting/LEDs:		Computers:		Car Sharing:		Recycling:	
Batteries/Storage:	Y	Nanotech:		Waste Heat:		Sensors:		Electric Vehicles:		Engineering:	
Solar:		Biotech:		Smart Meters:		Software:		Natural Gas Fuel:		Consulting:	
Wind:		Water Tech./Treatment:		Machinery:						Investing:	
Fuel Cells:		Ceramics:								Chemicals:	Y

TYPES OF BUSINESS:

Solid State Hydrogen Storage Technology

BRANDS/DIVISIONS/AFFILIATES:

MCP
MGH

CONTACTS: *Note: Officers with more than one job title may be intentionally listed here more than once.*

Pascal Mauberger, CEO
Michel Jehan, COO
Daniel Fruchart, CTO
Adamo Screnci, Chief Commercial Officer
Bruno Wiriath, Chmn.

Phone: 33-4-75-71-15-05	**Fax:** 33-4-75-71-10-01
Toll-Free:	
Address: Z.A. Quartier Riétière, La Motte-Fanjas, 26190 France	

GROWTH PLANS/SPECIAL FEATURES:

McPhy Energy is a French technology company that develops and produces solid state hydrogen storage technology. As a source of energy, hydrogen has a higher energy density per kilometer than natural gas or other combustible fuels. The problem with hydrogen, as a very light gas, arises during storage and transport. McPhy's hydrogen storage products are based on solid state hydrogen storage. The firm's solid state hydrogen technology revolves around metal hydrides, specifically magnesium hydrides. Metal hydrides are the chemical compounds formed when certain metals react with hydrogen gas and are a more efficient and denser hydrogen storage system than either compressed gas or liquid hydrogen. For its solid state hydrogen storage systems, McPhy offers both the MCP series and the MGH series ISO, or freight, containers. The MCP series are fully autonomous units for those customers that require the heat from hydrogenation stored in order to start the dehydrogenation process. The MGH series differs in that it does not store the heat required for dehydrogenation because the customer, such as a solar power plant, already produces enough heat on its own to begin the process. In addition to its ISO containers, McPhy also sells its magnesium hydrides for either hydrogen storage or for use in chemical reactions.

FINANCIALS: Sales and profits are in thousands of dollars—add 000 to get the full amount. 2011 Note: Financial information for 2011 was not available for all companies at press time.

2011 Sales: $	2011 Profits: $	**U.S. Stock Ticker:** Private
2010 Sales: $	2010 Profits: $	**Int'l Ticker:**
2009 Sales: $	2009 Profits: $	Int'l Exchange:
2008 Sales: $	2008 Profits: $	Employees: Fiscal Year Ends:
2007 Sales: $	2007 Profits: $	Parent Company:

SALARIES/BENEFITS:

Pension Plan:	ESOP Stock Plan:	Profit Sharing:	Top Exec. Salary: $	Bonus: $
Savings Plan:	Stock Purch. Plan:		Second Exec. Salary: $	Bonus: $

OTHER THOUGHTS:

Apparent Women Officers or Directors:
Hot Spot for Advancement for Women/Minorities:

LOCATIONS: ("Y" = Yes)

West:	Southwest:	Midwest:	Southeast:	Northeast:	International:
					Y

MECHANICAL TECHNOLOGY INC   www.mechtech.com

Industry Group Code: 335999

Energy/Fuel:		Other Technologies:	Electrical Products:	Electronics:	Transportation:	Other:
Biofuels:		Irrigation:	Lighting/LEDs:	Computers:	Car Sharing:	Recycling:
Batteries/Storage:		Nanotech:	Waste Heat:	Sensors:	Electric Vehicles:	Engineering:
Solar:		Biotech:	Smart Meters:	Software:	Natural Gas Fuel:	Consulting:
Wind:		Water Tech./Treatment:	Machinery:			Investing:
Fuel Cells:	Y	Ceramics:				Chemicals:

TYPES OF BUSINESS:

Fuel Cells
Instrumentation Systems

BRANDS/DIVISIONS/AFFILIATES:

MTI MicroFuel Cells Inc
MTI Instruments Inc
Mobion

CONTACTS: Note: Officers with more than one job title may be intentionally listed here more than once.

Peng K. Lim, CEO
Frederick W. Jones
Frederick W. Jones, CFO/VP
Federick W. Jones, VP-Finance
Peng K. Lim, Pres./CEO-MTI MicroFuel Cells
Peng K. Lim, Gen. Mgr.-MTI Instruments
Frederick W. Jones, VP-Oper., MTI Instruments
James K. Prueitt, VP-Eng. & Oper., MTI MicroFuel Cells, Inc.
Peng K. Lim, Chmn.

Phone: 518-533-2200	Fax: 518-533-2201
Toll-Free: 800-828-8210	
Address: 431 New Karner Rd., Albany, NY 12205 US	

GROWTH PLANS/SPECIAL FEATURES:

Mechanical Technology, Inc. (MTI) is a worldwide supplier of precision non-contact physical measurement solutions, condition based monitoring systems, portable balancing equipment and semiconductor wafer inspection tools. MTI develops and commercializes rechargeable power sources for portable electronics. The company operates in two segments, the Test and Measurement Instrumentation (MTI Instruments) segment, conducted through MTI Instruments, Inc., and the New Energy Segment, conducted through MTI MicroFuel Cells Inc. (MTI Micro). MTI Instruments designs, manufactures and services high quality precision measurement and testing systems for use in a variety of industries. This segment has developed one of the first engineering prototype fuel cells with a replaceable fuel refill. MTI Instruments' three main product lines are aviation and industrial vibration measurement systems; semiconductor and solar metrology systems; and precision measurement instruments, using fiber optic, laser or capacitive technologies to measure product design and quality control processes. MTI Micro is the developer of Mobion, off-the-grid power solutions for various portable electronic devices. Mobion technology offers power packs featuring cord-free, instant recharging that runs 2-10 times longer than lithium-ion batteries before recharging is needed. This technology is based on direct methanol fuel cell (DMFC) technology developed to replace incumbent power packs used by original equipment manufacturers in rechargeable electronic devices like PDAs and smart phones. One of Mobion's innovations is its ability to move water without the need for pumps or other micro-plumbing, allowing for easier miniaturization. It operates in all humidity levels; and its operative temperature range is 32-104 degrees Fahrenheit, comparable to a typical lithium-ion battery.

FINANCIALS: Sales and profits are in thousands of dollars—add 000 to get the full amount. 2011 Note: Financial information for 2011 was not available for all companies at press time.

2011 Sales: $	2011 Profits: $	U.S. Stock Ticker: MKTY
2010 Sales: $6,224	2010 Profits: $-12,504	Int'l Ticker:
2009 Sales: $6,263	2009 Profits: $-3,099	Int'l Exchange:
2008 Sales: $6,224	2008 Profits: $-12,504	Employees: 51 Fiscal Year Ends: 12/31
2007 Sales: $9,028	2007 Profits: $-9,575	Parent Company:

SALARIES/BENEFITS:

Pension Plan:	ESOP Stock Plan:	Profit Sharing:	Top Exec. Salary: $323,077	Bonus: $175,000
Savings Plan: Y	Stock Purch. Plan:		Second Exec. Salary: $176,712	Bonus: $9,415

OTHER THOUGHTS:

Apparent Women Officers or Directors:
Hot Spot for Advancement for Women/Minorities:

LOCATIONS: ("Y" = Yes)

West:	Southwest:	Midwest:	Southeast:	Northeast:	International:
				Y	Y

Sales, profits and employees may be estimates. Financial information, benefits and other data can change quickly and may vary from those stated here.

MIASOLE INC

www.miasole.com

Industry Group Code: 334413

Energy/Fuel:		Other Technologies:		Electrical Products:		Electronics:		Transportation:		Other:	
Biofuels:		Irrigation:		Lighting/LEDs:		Computers:		Car Sharing:		Recycling:	
Batteries/Storage:		Nanotech:		Waste Heat:		Sensors:		Electric Vehicles:		Engineering:	
Solar:	Y	Biotech:		Smart Meters:		Software:		Natural Gas Fuel:		Consulting:	
Wind:		Water Tech./Treatment:		Machinery:						Investing:	
Fuel Cells:		Ceramics:								Chemicals:	

TYPES OF BUSINESS:

Thin Film Solar Panels

BRANDS/DIVISIONS/AFFILIATES:

CONTACTS: *Note: Officers with more than one job title may be intentionally listed here more than once.*

John E. Carrington, CEO
Bob Baker, Pres.
Merle McClendon, CFO
Rob Deline, VP-Mktg.
Cindy Peterson, Gen. Mgr.-Mfg. Oper.

Phone: 408-919-5700	**Fax:** 408-919-5701
Toll-Free:	
Address: 2590 Walsh Ave., Santa Clara, CA 95051 US	

GROWTH PLANS/SPECIAL FEATURES:

Miasole, Inc. is a company engaged in the manufacture and development of Copper Indium Gallium Selenide (CIGS) thin film solar products. The company's products include CIGS material and thin film CIGS-based solar cells. The firm's materials have achieved laboratory efficiencies of 20.2% and differentiate themselves from conventional photovoltaic materials in that they can be deposited onto low-cost, flexible structures. The firm currently markets these products specifically for large scale rooftop and ground mount installations. The company anticipates future applications to include rolled rooftop products and other flexible substrates. Miasole's products have an estimated life span of over 25 years and have achieved an average operating efficiency of around 13%, all at costs comparable to or significantly below silicon-based photovoltaic panels due to the wide variety of suitable substrates. The company expects to reach an average of 15% efficiency in 2012. Its major customers include Chevron, Phoenix Solar, SolarCity, Juwi and Western Solar.

Employees of the company are offered health benefits as well as a stock ownership plan.

FINANCIALS: Sales and profits are in thousands of dollars—add 000 to get the full amount. 2011 Note: Financial information for 2011 was not available for all companies at press time.

2011 Sales: $	2011 Profits: $	**U.S. Stock Ticker: Private**
2010 Sales: $	2010 Profits: $	**Int'l Ticker:**
2009 Sales: $	2009 Profits: $	Int'l Exchange:
2008 Sales: $	2008 Profits: $	Employees: Fiscal Year Ends:
2007 Sales: $	2007 Profits: $	Parent Company:

SALARIES/BENEFITS:

Pension Plan:	ESOP Stock Plan: Y	Profit Sharing:	Top Exec. Salary: $	Bonus: $
Savings Plan:	Stock Purch. Plan:		Second Exec. Salary: $	Bonus: $

OTHER THOUGHTS:

Apparent Women Officers or Directors: 1
Hot Spot for Advancement for Women/Minorities:

LOCATIONS: ("Y" = Yes)

West:	Southwest:	Midwest:	Southeast:	Northeast:	International:
Y					

MISSION MOTORS

Industry Group Code: 33591

www.ridemission.com

Energy/Fuel:	Other Technologies:	Electrical Products:	Electronics:	Transportation:	Other:
Biofuels:	Irrigation:	Lighting/LEDs:	Computers:	Car Sharing:	Recycling:
Batteries/Storage: Y	Nanotech:	Waste Heat:	Sensors:	Electric Vehicles: Y	Engineering: Y
Solar:	Biotech:	Smart Meters:	Software:	Natural Gas Fuel:	Consulting:
Wind:	Water Tech./Treatment:	Machinery:			Investing:
Fuel Cells:	Ceramics:				Chemicals:

TYPES OF BUSINESS:

Electric Powertrain Components
Electric Powertrain Systems
Electric Powertrain Software

BRANDS/DIVISIONS/AFFILIATES:

Electric Vehicle Technology
Vehicle Management Software
Skyline
Mission R

CONTACTS: Note: Officers with more than one job title may be intentionally listed here more than once.

Jit Bhattacharya, CEO
Christopher Moe, CFO
David Salguero, Mgr.-Mktg.
Mike Rosenzweig, Mgr.-Hiring & Oper.
Colin Sebern, Mgr.-IT & Facilities
Jon Wagner, CTO
Jorah Wyer, VP-Prod. Dev.
Tom Smith, Sr. Electrical Engineer
Ray Shan, VP-Oper.
Erik Salo, VP-Bus. Dev.
Evelyn Lassman, Controller
Mason Cabot, Founder
Edward West, Founder
Forrest North, Founder

Phone: 415-666-2000	**Fax:**
Toll-Free:	
Address: 1177 Harrison St., San Francisco, CA 94103 US	

GROWTH PLANS/SPECIAL FEATURES:

Mission Motors is a supplier of modular, flexible high-performance electric powertrain components, systems and software to the hybrid and electric vehicle manufacturing market. The firm's technology can be used in applications such as scoots, passenger vehicles, buses and high-performance electric motorcycles. The company's proprietary Electric Vehicle Technology (EVT) design was developed originally for high-performance powersports applications. In doing so, the firm was capable of creating products that would not only increase the power performance of electric powertrains of all types, but their efficiency and intelligence as well. EVT offers energy storage, drive systems, software intelligence and system integration. EVT's energy storage system combines the component technologies of battery modules; onboard charge systems; battery management systems; and low-voltage vehicle power. The components are then capable of working either independently as their own separate systems or all together. The drive system technology aids in reducing the weight and volume of the component technologies. The firm's proprietary control software helps to optimize the efficiency of the drive systems. The software intelligence feature allows for both manufacturers and the end-user customer to be able to constantly control their vehicles' reliability, performance and safety. The company's Skyline data communications platform monitors real-time battery, drive system and vehicle data that is then relayed to a central server where it can be monitored at any time. The Vehicle Management Software suite (VMS) links the energy storage system, the drive system and the vehicle operator into a single network. EVT's system integration offerings include engineering support at all phases of the project's development; state of the art testing facilities; and engineering and integration services for adapting the vehicles to Mission's gears. In 2011, the firm launched its Mission R electric superbike, a motorcycle capable of traveling at least 160 miles per hour.

FINANCIALS: Sales and profits are in thousands of dollars—add 000 to get the full amount. 2011 Note: Financial information for 2011 was not available for all companies at press time.

2011 Sales: $	2011 Profits: $	**U.S. Stock Ticker: Private**
2010 Sales: $	2010 Profits: $	**Int'l Ticker:**
2009 Sales: $	2009 Profits: $	Int'l Exchange:
2008 Sales: $	2008 Profits: $	Employees: Fiscal Year Ends:
2007 Sales: $	2007 Profits: $	Parent Company:

SALARIES/BENEFITS:

Pension Plan:	ESOP Stock Plan:	Profit Sharing:	Top Exec. Salary: $	Bonus: $
Savings Plan:	Stock Purch. Plan:		Second Exec. Salary: $	Bonus: $

OTHER THOUGHTS:

Apparent Women Officers or Directors: 5
Hot Spot for Advancement for Women/Minorities: Y

LOCATIONS: ("Y" = Yes)

West:	Southwest:	Midwest:	Southeast:	Northeast:	International:
Y					

MITSUBISHI CORP

www.mitsubishicorp.com

Industry Group Code: 333

Energy/Fuel:	Other Technologies:	Electrical Products:	Electronics:	Transportation:	Other:
Biofuels:	Irrigation:	Lighting/LEDs:	Computers:	Car Sharing:	Recycling:
Batteries/Storage:	Nanotech:	Waste Heat:	Sensors:	Electric Vehicles:	Engineering:
Solar:	Biotech:	Smart Meters:	Software:	Natural Gas Fuel:	Consulting:
Wind:	Water Tech./Treatment:	Machinery: Y			Investing:
Fuel Cells:	Ceramics:				Chemicals:

TYPES OF BUSINESS:

Machinery & Automotive Manufacturing
Power System Manufacture
Metals Mining & Production
Chemicals
Food Products & Commodities
Petroleum Exploration & Production
IT Services & Equipment
Solar Cells & Fuel-Cell Systems

BRANDS/DIVISIONS/AFFILIATES:

Penn West Energy Trust
Minera Escondida Limitade
Mitsubishi Motors (Thailand) Co Ltd
Tomori E&P Limited
Frontier Carbon Corporation
Mitsubishi Electric Corporation
Fullerene International Corporation
Jetstar Japan Co.

CONTACTS: *Note: Officers with more than one job title may be intentionally listed here more than once.*

Ken Kobayashi, CEO
Ken Kobayashi, Pres.
Ryoichi Ueda, CFO
Hideto Nakahara, Exec. VP-Global Strategy & Bus. Dev.
Hideyuki Nabeshima, Sr. Exec. VP-Corp. Comm./Chief Compliance Officer
Eiichi Tanabe, Treas.
Masahide Yano, CEO-Living Essentials Group
Koichi Komatsu, Regional CEO-Americas/Chmn.-Mitsubishi Int'l
Seiji Kato, Exec. VP/CEO-Energy Bus. Group
Yorihiko Kojima, Chmn.
Tsunao Kijima, Pres., Mitsubishi Corp. China Co. Ltd.
Hideshi Takeuchi, CEO-Industrial Finance, Logistics & Dev. Group

Phone: 81-3-3210-2121	Fax: 81-3-3210-8583
Toll-Free:	
Address: 3-1 Marunouchi 2-chome, Chiyoda-ku, Tokyo, 100-8086 Japan	

GROWTH PLANS/SPECIAL FEATURES:

Mitsubishi Corp. is one of Japan's largest general trading companies, operating through 200 locations in 80 countries worldwide, with customers in virtually every industry, including energy, metals, machinery, chemicals, food and general merchandise. The company's 550 consolidated subsidiaries and affiliates fall into six business groups: industrial finance, logistics and development; energy; metals; machinery; chemicals; and living essentials. The industrial finance, logistics and development group consists of three smaller divisions: asset finance and business development; development and construction projects; and logistics. The energy business group's operations include crude oil, petroleum, liquefied natural gas and carbon production and marketing. The metals group is involved in the mining of coal and ferrous and non-ferrous metals, as well as steel production. The machinery group manufactures power and electrical systems, transportation infrastructure, defense systems, aeronautical systems and automotive parts. The chemicals group manufactures raw materials for synthetic resins, chemical fertilizers, inorganic raw materials, industrial salts, plastics, electronics materials and life science products. The living essentials group produces food products, food commodities, textiles, paper and packaging, construction materials and other consumer products, including healthcare products. In March 2010, subsidiaries MC Unimetals and Shoji Light Metal merged. In April 2010, Mitsubishi established the Global Environment Business Development Group, intended to develop alternative forms of energy generation, and the Business Service Group, which integrates information technology and logistics management. In June 2010, the firm acquired a 2.5% ownership interest in Minera Escondida Limitade, a Chilean company which operates the world's largest copper mine. In September 2010, the company acquired 50% of Penn West Energy Trust, a natural gas development project in Canada. In January 2011, the firm acquired Tomori E&P Limited, which owns 20% of the Indonesian Senoro-Toili natural gas field. In February 2011, Mitsubishi acquired a 15% stake in four Concentrated Solar Power generation plants in Spain. In August 2011, the agreed to form a joint venture with Qantas Airways Ltd. and JAL Group called Jetstar Japan Co. The joint venture company will be a low cost air carrier.

FINANCIALS: Sales and profits are in thousands of dollars—add 000 to get the full amount. 2011 Note: Financial information for 2011 was not available for all companies at press time.

2011 Sales: $67,689,300	2011 Profits: $6,021,400	U.S. Stock Ticker:
2010 Sales: $59,030,300	2010 Profits: $3,573,000	Int'l Ticker: 8058
2009 Sales: $80,032,700	2009 Profits: $4,083,990	Int'l Exchange: Tokyo-TSE
2008 Sales: $78,400,500	2008 Profits: $4,627,900	Employees: 58,723 Fiscal Year Ends: 3/31
2007 Sales: $46,297,333	2007 Profits: $3,784,493	Parent Company:

SALARIES/BENEFITS:

Pension Plan:	ESOP Stock Plan:	Profit Sharing:	Top Exec. Salary: $	Bonus: $
Savings Plan:	Stock Purch. Plan:		Second Exec. Salary: $	Bonus: $

OTHER THOUGHTS:

Apparent Women Officers or Directors: 1
Hot Spot for Advancement for Women/Minorities:

LOCATIONS: ("Y" = Yes)

West:	Southwest:	Midwest:	Southeast:	Northeast: Y	International: Y

Sales, profits and employees may be estimates. Financial information, benefits and other data can change quickly and may vary from those stated here.

MITSUBISHI ELECTRIC CORPORATION www.mitsubishielectric.com

Industry Group Code: 335

Energy/Fuel:		Other Technologies:		Electrical Products:		Electronics:		Transportation:		Other:	
Biofuels:		Irrigation:		Lighting/LEDs:		Computers:	Y	Car Sharing:		Recycling:	
Batteries/Storage:	Y	Nanotech:	Y	Waste Heat:		Sensors:	Y	Electric Vehicles:		Engineering:	Y
Solar:	Y	Biotech:		Smart Meters:		Software:	Y	Natural Gas Fuel:		Consulting:	
Wind:	Y	Water Tech./Treatment:		Machinery:	Y					Investing:	
Fuel Cells:	Y	Ceramics:								Chemicals:	

TYPES OF BUSINESS:

Electronic Equipment Manufacturer
Power Plant Manufacturing, Nuclear & Fossil
Wind & Solar Generation Systems
Consumer Electronics
Telecommunications & Computer Equipment
Industrial Automation Systems
Chips & Memory Devices
Semiconductors

BRANDS/DIVISIONS/AFFILIATES:

Mitsubishi Corp
Vincotech Holdings S.a r.l.
Mitsubish Electric GEM Power Device Co Ltd
Mitsubish Electric Corp
GEM Electronics

CONTACTS: Note: Officers with more than one job title may be intentionally listed here more than once.

Kenichiro Yamanishi, CEO
Takashi Sasakawa, Exec. Officer-Oper.
Kenichiro Yamanishi, Pres./Representative Exec. Officer
Hiroki Yoshimatsu, Exec. Officer-Acct. & Finance
Kunio Oguchi, Exec. Officer-Advertising & Domestic Marketing
Noritomo Hashimoto, Exec. Officer-Human Resources
Kazuhiko Tsutsumi, Exec. Officer-R&D
Kenji Kuroda, Exec. Officer-Info. Systems & Network Service
Masahary Moriyaso, Exec. Officer-Total Productivity Mgmt.
Tsuyoshi Nakamura, Exec. Officer-Auditing & Legal Affairs
Masaki Sakuyama, Sr. VP-Corp. Strategic Planning & Oper.
Takashi Sasakawa, Sr. VP-Global Strategic Planning & Mktg.
Noritomo Hashimoto, Exec. Officer- Public Rel. & General Affairs
Hiroki Yoshimatso, Exec. Officer- Acct. & Finance
Hideyaso Nonaka, Sr. VP.-Factory Automation Systems
Masaaki Yasui, Exec. Officer-Electronic Systems
Mitsuo Muneyuki, Exec. VP-Export Control & Building Systems
Kazua Kyuma, Exec. VP-Semiconductor & Device
Setsuhiro Shimomura, Chmn.

Phone: 81-3-3218-2111	Fax: 81-3-3218-2185
Toll-Free:	
Address: Tokyo Bldg. 2-7-3 Marunouchi, Chiyoda-ku, Tokyo, 100-8310 Japan	

GROWTH PLANS/SPECIAL FEATURES:

Mitsubishi Electric Corporation, part of the Mitsubishi group of companies, is a global manufacturer, distributor and marketer of electrical and electronic equipment. This equipment is used in information processing and communications; space development and satellite communications; consumer electronics; industrial technology; energy; transportation; and building equipment. The company has five primary business segments: energy and electric systems; home appliances; information and communication systems; industrial automation systems; and electronic devices. The energy and electric systems segment manufactures nuclear and fossil fuel power generation plants and monitoring systems, as well as wind turbines, solar panels and other electricity generators; turbine generators and hydraulic turbine generators; proton beam radiation treatment systems; elevators; security systems; railway systems; and large scale display systems. This segment accounts for 24.8% of the firm's revenues. The home appliances segment (22.3% of revenues) manufactures home electronics such as air conditioners, flat-screen televisions, DVD players, computers and computer monitors. The industrial automation systems segment (22.3% of revenues) includes the manufacturing of programmable logic controllers, circuit breakers and robotics that are created and customized for multiple industrial uses. The information and communication systems segment (11.7% of revenues) includes mobile phones, satellites, aerospace communication systems, digital closed circuit television systems, enterprise information technology networks and Internet servers. The electronic devices segment (4.2% of revenues) makes power modules, high-frequency devices, optical devices, LCD devices and microcomputers. Other business activities (14.7% of revenues) include procurement, logistics, real estate, advertising and finance. In September 2011, Mitsubishi Electric and GEM Electronics (Shanghai) Co., Ltd., of China agreed to a joint venture to create a new company, Mitsubishi Electric GEM Power Device (Hefei) Co., Ltd., which will assemble and test Mitsubishi manufactured electric power modules. Mitsubishi Electric will own 70%, GEM Electronics will own 20%, and Mitsubishi Electric (China) Co., Ltd., will own 10% of the company.

FINANCIALS: Sales and profits are in thousands of dollars—add 000 to get the full amount. 2011 Note: Financial information for 2011 was not available for all companies at press time.

2011 Sales: $47,899,600	2011 Profits: $1,636,300	**U.S. Stock Ticker: Subsidiary**
2010 Sales: $40,172,200	2010 Profits: $336,940	**Int'l Ticker: 6503**
2009 Sales: $40,461,900	2009 Profits: $134,320	Int'l Exchange: Tokyo-TSE
2008 Sales: $40,498,200	2008 Profits: $1,579,800	Employees: 114,433 Fiscal Year Ends: 3/31
2007 Sales: $34,641,700	2007 Profits: $1,105,100	Parent Company: MITSUBISHI CORP

SALARIES/BENEFITS:

Pension Plan:	ESOP Stock Plan:	Profit Sharing:	Top Exec. Salary: $	Bonus: $
Savings Plan:	Stock Purch. Plan:		Second Exec. Salary: $	Bonus: $

OTHER THOUGHTS:

Apparent Women Officers or Directors:
Hot Spot for Advancement for Women/Minorities:

LOCATIONS: ("Y" = Yes)

West:	Southwest:	Midwest:	Southeast:	Northeast:	International:
Y	Y	Y	Y	Y	Y

Sales, profits and employees may be estimates. Financial information, benefits and other data can change quickly and may vary from those stated here.

MITSUI CHEMICALS INC

www.mitsui-chem.co.jp

Industry Group Code: 325110

Energy/Fuel:		Other Technologies:		Electrical Products:		Electronics:	Transportation:		Other:	
Biofuels:	Y	Irrigation:		Lighting/LEDs:		Computers:	Car Sharing:		Recycling:	
Batteries/Storage:		Nanotech:		Waste Heat:		Sensors:	Electric Vehicles:		Engineering:	
Solar:		Biotech:	Y	Smart Meters:		Software:	Natural Gas Fuel:		Consulting:	
Wind:		Water Tech./Treatment:	Y	Machinery:					Investing:	
Fuel Cells:		Ceramics:							Chemicals:	Y

TYPES OF BUSINESS:

Petrochemical Producer
Agrochemicals
Industrial Products
Pharmaceuticals & Medical
Packaging
Dyes & Pigments
Phenols

BRANDS/DIVISIONS/AFFILIATES:

Prime Polymer Co., Ltd.
Tohcello Co., Ltd.
Mitsui Chemicals Agro, Inc.
Mitsui Chemicals Fabro, Inc.
China Petroleum & Chemical Corp

CONTACTS: *Note: Officers with more than one job title may be intentionally listed here more than once.*

Toshikazu Tanaka, CEO
Toshikazu Tanaka, Pres.
Kiichi Suzuki, Sr. Managing Dir.
Yoshiyuki Funakoshi, Sr. Managing Dir.
Shigeru Iwabuchi, Sr. Managing Dir
Yukio Hara, Managing Dir.
Kenji Fujiyoshi, Chmn.

Phone: 81-3-6253-2100	**Fax:** 81-3-6253-4245
Toll-Free:	
Address: Shiodome, 5-2 Higashi-Shimbashi 1-chome, Minato-ku, Tokyo, 105-7117 Japan	

GROWTH PLANS/SPECIAL FEATURES:

Mitsui Chemicals, Inc. (MCI) is a Japanese chemical manufacturer that specializes in petrochemicals, phenols and specialty polymers. The firm's products have applications in the automotive materials; electronic and IT materials; lifestyle, environment and energy; and packaging materials industries. The company is organized into six business sectors: petrochemicals, basic chemicals, polyurethane, functional polymeric materials, fabricated products and functional chemicals. The petrochemicals business sector encompasses the petrochemical feedstocks division, producing chemicals such as ethylene, propylene and butadiene, and Prime Polymer Co., Ltd., specializing in polyethylene and polypropylene. The basic chemicals sector includes the phenols; PET and PTA; and industrial chemicals divisions. The polyurethane sector is comprised of the polyurethane; coatings and engineering materials; and polyurethane development divisions. The functional polymeric materials sector includes the elastomers, performance compound; performance polymers and functional polymeric materials development divisions. The fabricated products sector encompasses the functional film, spunbonded fabric and fabricated products development divisions as well as subsidiary Tohcello Co., Ltd. The functional chemicals business sector consists of the fine and performance chemicals; health care materials; licensing; and functional chemicals materials development division as well as subsidiary Mitsui Chemicals Agro, Inc. The company has numerous subsidiaries, both in Japan and overseas, with manufacturing and sales sites in the U.S., Mexico, Germany, Scotland, Singapore, China, Taiwan, Indonesia, Thailand, Malaysia, India and South Korea. Mitsui operates eight manufacturing sites and four offices and an R&D center in Japan. In October 2010, the firm and China Petroleum & Chemical Corp. entered into a joint venture to construct an ethylene-propylene-diene terploymer (EPT) plant in Shanghai, China

FINANCIALS: Sales and profits are in thousands of dollars—add 000 to get the full amount. 2011 Note: Financial information for 2011 was not available for all companies at press time.

2011 Sales: $17,883,500	2011 Profits: $319,400	**U.S. Stock Ticker:**
2010 Sales: $14,390,400	2010 Profits: $-333,750	**Int'l Ticker: 4183**
2009 Sales: $16,326,500	2009 Profits: $1,045,220	Int'l Exchange: Tokyo-TSE
2008 Sales: $17,832,917	2008 Profits: $247,840	Employees: 12,782 Fiscal Year Ends: 3/31
2007 Sales: $14,299,551	2007 Profits: $443,007	Parent Company:

SALARIES/BENEFITS:

Pension Plan:	ESOP Stock Plan:	Profit Sharing:	Top Exec. Salary: $	Bonus: $
Savings Plan:	Stock Purch. Plan:		Second Exec. Salary: $	Bonus: $

OTHER THOUGHTS:

Apparent Women Officers or Directors:
Hot Spot for Advancement for Women/Minorities:

LOCATIONS: ("Y" = Yes)

West:	Southwest:	Midwest:	Southeast:	Northeast:	International:
Y	Y	Y		Y	Y

MONSANTO CO

Industry Group Code: 11511

Energy/Fuel:	Other Technologies:		Electrical Products:	Electronics:	Transportation:	Other:	
Biofuels:	Irrigation:		Lighting/LEDs:	Computers:	Car Sharing:	Recycling:	
Batteries/Storage:	Nanotech:		Waste Heat:	Sensors:	Electric Vehicles:	Engineering:	
Solar:	Biotech:	Y	Smart Meters:	Software:	Natural Gas Fuel:	Consulting:	
Wind:	Water Tech./Treatment:		Machinery:			Investing:	
Fuel Cells:	Ceramics:					Chemicals:	Y

TYPES OF BUSINESS:

Agricultural Biotechnology Products & Chemicals Manufacturing
Herbicides
Seeds
Genetic Products
Lawn & Garden Products

BRANDS/DIVISIONS/AFFILIATES:

Asgrow
Roundup Ready
Agroeste Sementes
Divergence Inc
Seminis
YieldGard
Roundup
Beeologics

CONTACTS: *Note: Officers with more than one job title may be intentionally listed here more than once.*

Hugh Grant, CEO
Hugh Grant, Pres.
Pierre Courduroux, CFO/Sr. VP
Brett D. Begemann, Chief Commercial Officer/Exec. VP
Steven C. Mizell, Exec. VP-Human Resources
Robert T. Fraley, CTO/Exec. VP
Janet M. Holloway, Chief of Staff
David F. Snively, General Counsel/Exec. VP/Sec.
Kerry J. Preete, Sr. VP-Global Strategy
Janet M. Holloway, Sr. VP-Comm. Rel./Chief of Staff
Tom D. Hartley, Treas./VP
Nicole M. Ringenberg, VP/Controller
Gerald A. Steiner, Exec. VP-Corp. Affairs & Sustainability
Hugh Grant, Chmn.
Consuelo E. Madere, VP-Global Vegetable & Asia Commercial

Phone: 314-694-1000	Fax: 314-694-8394
Toll-Free:	
Address: 800 N. Lindbergh Blvd., St. Louis, MO 63167 US	

GROWTH PLANS/SPECIAL FEATURES:

Monsanto Co. is a global provider of agricultural products for farmers. The company operates in two principal business segments: Seeds and Genomics; and Agricultural Productivity. The Seeds and Genomics segment is responsible for producing seed brands and patenting genetic traits that enable seeds to resist insects, disease, drought and weeds. Major germplasm brands for row crop seeds produced by Monsanto include DEKALB and Channel Bio corn seeds; Asgrow soybean seeds; and Deltapine cotton seeds. Vegetable seeds such as tomato, pepper, eggplant, melon, cucumber, pumpkin, squash, beans, broccoli, onions and lettuce are sold under the Seminis and De Ruiter brands. The company's genetic trait products include Roundup Ready and Roundup Ready 2 Yield for soybeans; SmartStax, YieldGard, and YieldGardVT for corn; Bollgard and Bollgard II for cotton; and Genuity for multiple products. The segment also focuses on cereal grain seeds and biotech wheat products. Monsanto's Agricultural Productivity segment produces herbicide products. The company's selective herbicide brand is Harness, which is used for corn and cotton. Other products include glyphosate-based herbicides, for weed control in nonselective agricultural, industrial, ornamental and turf applications; and lawn and garden herbicides for weed control in residential applications. Both glyphosate-based and lawn and garden herbicides are available under the Roundup brand. Monsanto market its seeds and commercial herbicides through a variety of channels and directly to farmers. Residential herbicides are marketed through the Scotts Miracle-Gro Company. Subsidiaries include Delta and Pine Land Company, a developer of cotton and soybean seeds; and Agroeste Sementes, a Brazilian corn seed company. In February 2011, Monsanto acquired biotechnology research and development firm Divergence, Inc. In June 2011, the company opened a new corn breeding plant in Washington. In September 2011, the firm acquired pest and disease control product developer Beeologics.

Employees are offered life, disability, medical, dental and vision insurance.

FINANCIALS: Sales and profits are in thousands of dollars—add 000 to get the full amount. 2011 Note: Financial information for 2011 was not available for all companies at press time.

2011 Sales: $11,822,000	2011 Profits: $1,607,000	**U.S. Stock Ticker: MON**
2010 Sales: $10,502,000	2010 Profits: $1,128,000	**Int'l Ticker:**
2009 Sales: $11,724,000	2009 Profits: $2,109,000	Int'l Exchange:
2008 Sales: $11,365,000	2008 Profits: $2,024,000	Employees: 20,600 Fiscal Year Ends: 8/31
2007 Sales: $8,563,000	2007 Profits: $993,000	Parent Company:

SALARIES/BENEFITS:

Pension Plan: Y	ESOP Stock Plan:	Profit Sharing:	Top Exec. Salary: $1,409,179	Bonus: $3,070,769
Savings Plan: Y	Stock Purch. Plan: Y		Second Exec. Salary: $610,062	Bonus: $865,000

OTHER THOUGHTS:

Apparent Women Officers or Directors: 5
Hot Spot for Advancement for Women/Minorities: Y

LOCATIONS: ("Y" = Yes)

West:	Southwest:	Midwest:	Southeast:	Northeast:	International:
Y	Y	Y	Y	Y	Y

Sales, profits and employees may be estimates. Financial information, benefits and other data can change quickly and may vary from those stated here.

MTI MICROFUEL CELLS INC

www.mtimicrofuelcells.com

Industry Group Code: 335999

Energy/Fuel:		Other Technologies:	Electrical Products:	Electronics:	Transportation:	Other:
Biofuels:		Irrigation:	Lighting/LEDs:	Computers:	Car Sharing:	Recycling:
Batteries/Storage:		Nanotech:	Waste Heat:	Sensors:	Electric Vehicles:	Engineering:
Solar:		Biotech:	Smart Meters:	Software:	Natural Gas Fuel:	Consulting:
Wind:		Water Tech./Treatment:	Machinery:			Investing:
Fuel Cells:	Y	Ceramics:				Chemicals:

TYPES OF BUSINESS:

Fuel Cells
Direct Methanol Micro Fuel Cells

BRANDS/DIVISIONS/AFFILIATES:

Mechanical Technology Inc
Mobion

CONTACTS: Note: Officers with more than one job title may be intentionally listed here more than once.

Peng K. Lim, CEO
Peng K. Lim, Chmn.

Phone: 518-533-2222	**Fax:** 518-533-2223
Toll-Free: 800-828-8210	
Address: 431 New Karner Rd., Albany, NY 12205 US	

GROWTH PLANS/SPECIAL FEATURES:

MTI Micro Fuel Cells, Inc., a subsidiary of Mechanical Technology, Inc., develops and manufactures direct methanol micro fuel cells (DMFCs) as cord-free rechargeable power pack technology for portable electronics. DMFC systems are being developed as an alternative to existing lithium-ion batteries for use in both consumer and military applications because of their ability to power a wireless electronic device for long periods of time without recharging or refueling. In addition, DMFCs may be instantly refueled without the need for a power outlet or a lengthy recharge. The company's proprietary DMFC technology is marketed under the brand name Mobion. The Mobion cord-free rechargeable power pack is a DMFC designed for manufacturers of hand-held electronic devices like PDAs and smartphones. The Mobion power pack has a unique method of managing the water produced by the fuel cell's chemical reactions, managing the flow internally rather than employing the micro-plumbing technologies of other DMFCs. The Mobion system is capable of running in a wide environmental range encompassing temperatures from 32 degrees Fahrenheit to 104 degrees Fahrenheit at any humidity level. The company has developed a compact and light weight fuel cell charger, with removable cartridges that provide 25 watt-hours of power per cartridge.

FINANCIALS: Sales and profits are in thousands of dollars—add 000 to get the full amount. 2011 Note: Financial information for 2011 was not available for all companies at press time.

2011 Sales: $	2011 Profits: $	**U.S. Stock Ticker:** Subsidiary
2010 Sales: $	2010 Profits: $	**Int'l Ticker:**
2009 Sales: $	2009 Profits: $	Int'l Exchange:
2008 Sales: $	2008 Profits: $	Employees: Fiscal Year Ends: 12/31
2007 Sales: $	2007 Profits: $	Parent Company: MECHANICAL TECHNOLOGY INC

SALARIES/BENEFITS:

Pension Plan:	ESOP Stock Plan:	Profit Sharing:	Top Exec. Salary: $	Bonus: $
Savings Plan:	Stock Purch. Plan:		Second Exec. Salary: $	Bonus: $

OTHER THOUGHTS:

Apparent Women Officers or Directors:
Hot Spot for Advancement for Women/Minorities:

LOCATIONS: ("Y" = Yes)

West:	Southwest:	Midwest:	Southeast:	Northeast:	International:
				Y	Y

Sales, profits and employees may be estimates. Financial information, benefits and other data can change quickly and may vary from those stated here.

NACEL ENERGY CORP

www.nacelenergy.com

Industry Group Code: 221119

Energy/Fuel:	Other Technologies:	Electrical Products:	Electronics:	Transportation:	Other:	
Biofuels:	Irrigation:	Lighting/LEDs:	Computers:	Car Sharing:	Recycling:	
Batteries/Storage:	Nanotech:	Waste Heat:	Sensors:	Electric Vehicles:	Engineering:	Y
Solar:	Biotech:	Smart Meters:	Software:	Natural Gas Fuel:	Consulting:	
Wind: Y	Water Tech./Treatment:	Machinery:			Investing:	
Fuel Cells:	Ceramics:				Chemicals:	

TYPES OF BUSINESS:

Wind Power Facilities

BRANDS/DIVISIONS/AFFILIATES:

Windvest LLC
Wind Energy Facility LLC
Swisher Wind Energy Facility LLC
Hedley Pointe Wind Energy Facility LLC
Leila lakes Wind Energy Facility LLC
Snowflake Wind Energy Facility LLC

CONTACTS: *Note: Officers with more than one job title may be intentionally listed here more than once.*

Mark Schaftlein, CEO
Terry Pilling, COO
Mark Schaftlein, Pres.
Mark Schaftlein, CFO
Michael Biddick, Dir.-Investor Rel.

Phone:	Fax:
Toll-Free: 888-242-5848	
Address: 600 17th St., Ste. 2800S, Denver, CO 80202 US	

GROWTH PLANS/SPECIAL FEATURES:

Nacel Energy Corp. is a development stage wind power generation company engaged in the business of developing wind power generation facilities from green field (or blank slate) up to and including operation. The firm's development efforts are primarily focused upon creating clean, renewable, utility scale wind energy facilities in the 10-30 megawatt (MW) range. The company has six wind energy projects totaling 185 MW or more of potential power generating capacity located on 8,437 acres of land in the Panhandle area of Texas and northern Arizona. WindVest LLC was established by Nacel Energy as a solution to building joint ventures between landowners and other small wind developers. The firm's projects include Blue Creek Wind Energy Facility LLC, a 40 MW facility located in Moore County, Texas; Channing Flats Wind Energy Facility LLC, a 30 MW facility also located in Moore County, Texas; Swisher Wind Energy Facility LLC, a 40 MW facility located in Swisher County, Texas; Hedley Pointe Wind Energy Facility LLC, a 5 MW facility located in Donley County, Texas; Leila lakes Wind Energy Facility LLC, a 40 MW facility located Donley County, Texas; and Snowflake Wind Energy Facility LLC, a 30 MW facility located in Navajo County, Arizona. The company is currently developing other smaller projects around the U.S. and the Dominican Republic.

FINANCIALS: Sales and profits are in thousands of dollars—add 000 to get the full amount. 2011 Note: Financial information for 2011 was not available for all companies at press time.

2011 Sales: $ 100	2011 Profits: $- 700	**U.S. Stock Ticker: NCEN.OB**
2010 Sales: $1,200	2010 Profits: $-2,800	**Int'l Ticker:**
2009 Sales: $ 700	2009 Profits: $-2,300	Int'l Exchange:
2008 Sales: $	2008 Profits: $- 827	Employees: 3 Fiscal Year Ends: 3/31
2007 Sales: $	2007 Profits: $	Parent Company:

SALARIES/BENEFITS:

Pension Plan:	ESOP Stock Plan:	Profit Sharing:	Top Exec. Salary: $180,000	Bonus: $
Savings Plan:	Stock Purch. Plan:		Second Exec. Salary: $37,000	Bonus: $

OTHER THOUGHTS:

Apparent Women Officers or Directors:
Hot Spot for Advancement for Women/Minorities:

LOCATIONS: ("Y" = Yes)

West:	Southwest:	Midwest:	Southeast:	Northeast:	International:
Y	Y				

NANOH2O

Industry Group Code: 541712

Energy/Fuel:	Other Technologies:	Electrical Products:	Electronics:	Transportation:	Other:	
Biofuels:	Irrigation:	Lighting/LEDs:	Computers:	Car Sharing:	Recycling:	Y
Batteries/Storage:	Nanotech:	Waste Heat:	Sensors:	Electric Vehicles:	Engineering:	
Solar:	Biotech:	Smart Meters:	Software:	Natural Gas Fuel:	Consulting:	
Wind:	Water Tech./Treatment: Y	Machinery:			Investing:	
Fuel Cells:	Ceramics:				Chemicals:	

TYPES OF BUSINESS:

Reverse Osmosis Desalination

BRANDS/DIVISIONS/AFFILIATES:

QuantumFlux Membrane
Q+ Projection Software
Qfx SW 400 ES
Qfx SW 365 ES
Qfx SW 75 ES

GROWTH PLANS/SPECIAL FEATURES:

NanoH2O is a developer, manufacturer and marketer of reverse osmosis membranes. Through the firm's QuantumFlux Membrane technology, a thin-film nanocomposite, the company is able to improve desalination productivity and energy efficiency. The company's products include Qfx SW 400 ES, which features a salt rejection rate of 99.75% and an element diameter of 8-inches; Qfx SW 365 ES, which features an element diameter of 8-inches and a salt rejection rate of 99.75%; and Qfx SW 75 ES, which features an element diameter of 4-inches and a salt rejection rate of 99.75%. NanoH2O maintains 4 patents and approximately 11 patent applications. The company was founded in 2005 and maintains its headquarters, manufacturing and research and development facility in El Segundo, California. In August 2011, the firm introduced Q+Projection Software, which allows the firm's customers to optimize their seawater reverse osmosis system.

CONTACTS: Note: Officers with more than one job title may be intentionally listed here more than once.

Jeff Green, CEO/Founder
John Markovich, CFO
Bob Burk, Chief Scientific Officer/Founder
Freidoon Rastegar, Dir.-Eng.
Barry Fischer, Dir.-Mfg.
Kyle MacDonald, VP-Oper.
Will Kain, Dir.-Strategic Planning
Michael DeMartino, VP-Finance
CJ Kurth, VP-R&D

Phone: 424-218-4000	**Fax:** 424-218-4001
Toll-Free:	
Address: 750 Lairport St., El Segundo, CA 90245 US	

FINANCIALS: Sales and profits are in thousands of dollars—add 000 to get the full amount. 2011 Note: Financial information for 2011 was not available for all companies at press time.

2011 Sales: $	2011 Profits: $	**U.S. Stock Ticker: Private**
2010 Sales: $	2010 Profits: $	**Int'l Ticker:**
2009 Sales: $	2009 Profits: $	Int'l Exchange:
2008 Sales: $	2008 Profits: $	Employees: Fiscal Year Ends:
2007 Sales: $	2007 Profits: $	Parent Company:

SALARIES/BENEFITS:

Pension Plan:	ESOP Stock Plan:	Profit Sharing:	Top Exec. Salary: $	Bonus: $
Savings Plan:	Stock Purch. Plan:		Second Exec. Salary: $	Bonus: $

OTHER THOUGHTS:

Apparent Women Officers or Directors:
Hot Spot for Advancement for Women/Minorities:

LOCATIONS: ("Y" = Yes)

West:	Southwest:	Midwest:	Southeast:	Northeast:	International:
Y					

NANOMIX INC

Industry Group Code: 335991

www.nano.com

Energy/Fuel:	Other Technologies:		Electrical Products:	Electronics:		Transportation:	Other:	
Biofuels:	Irrigation:		Lighting/LEDs:	Computers:		Car Sharing:	Recycling:	
Batteries/Storage:	Nanotech:	Y	Waste Heat:	Sensors:	Y	Electric Vehicles:	Engineering:	
Solar:	Biotech:		Smart Meters:	Software:		Natural Gas Fuel:	Consulting:	
Wind:	Water Tech./Treatment:		Machinery:				Investing:	
Fuel Cells:	Ceramics:						Chemicals:	

TYPES OF BUSINESS:

Nanoelectronic Sensors

BRANDS/DIVISIONS/AFFILIATES:

Sensation
NanoTect Monitors
Nanomix Asthma Management System (The)

CONTACTS: *Note: Officers with more than one job title may be intentionally listed here more than once.*

Garrett Gruener, CEO
Scott Schroeder, CFO
John Burcham, Sr. Dir.-Prod. Mktg.
Ray Radtkey, VP-Prod. Dev. & Quality
John Burcham, Sr. Dir.-Bus. Dev.
Scott Schroeder, VP-Finance
Ying-Lan Chang, VP-Platform Dev.
Garrett Gruener, Exec. Chmn.

Phone: 510-428-5300	Fax: 510-658-0425
Toll-Free: 877-626-6649	
Address: 5980 Horton St., Ste. 600, Emeryville, CA 94608 US	

GROWTH PLANS/SPECIAL FEATURES:

Nanomix, Inc. develops nanoelectronic detection devices, primarily for chemical sensing applications. Nanomix's proprietary sensor architecture, Sensation, integrates carbon nanotube electronics with silicon microstructures in order to bridge chemical activity at the molecular level with electrical properties that can be monitored macroscopically. The company's patented use of single-walled carbon nanotubes provides both high sensitivity and robust reliability. The company is currently using this technology in three product lines: biomolecule devices, respiratory devices and NanoTect environmental monitors. In the biomolecule devices segment, Nanomix integrates proprietary chemistries and carbon nanotube detection elements to develop detection devices capable of specific, multiplexed and ultrasensitive detection of proteins, nucleic acids and metabolite chemistries with one test reaction. The Sensation platform can incorporate multiple assay types from one sample, including the cardiac troponin-I assay. In the respiratory devices segment, Sensation technology has led to the development of a new non-invasive device for monitoring asthma. The Nanomix Asthma Management System assesses airway inflammation by measuring the level of nitric oxide in exhaled breath. The company's NanoTect environmental monitors detect low levels of industrial gas and may be used as alarm systems for leaks or to monitor industrial gas build-up.

FINANCIALS: Sales and profits are in thousands of dollars—add 000 to get the full amount. 2011 Note: Financial information for 2011 was not available for all companies at press time.

2011 Sales: $	2011 Profits: $	U.S. Stock Ticker: Private
2010 Sales: $	2010 Profits: $	Int'l Ticker:
2009 Sales: $	2009 Profits: $	Int'l Exchange:
2008 Sales: $	2008 Profits: $	Employees: Fiscal Year Ends:
2007 Sales: $	2007 Profits: $	Parent Company:

SALARIES/BENEFITS:

Pension Plan:	ESOP Stock Plan:	Profit Sharing:	Top Exec. Salary: $	Bonus: $
Savings Plan:	Stock Purch. Plan:		Second Exec. Salary: $	Bonus: $

OTHER THOUGHTS:

Apparent Women Officers or Directors: 1
Hot Spot for Advancement for Women/Minorities:

LOCATIONS: ("Y" = Yes)

West:	Southwest:	Midwest:	Southeast:	Northeast:	International:
Y					

NANOSOLAR INC

www.nanosolar.com

Industry Group Code: 334413

Energy/Fuel:		Other Technologies:		Electrical Products:		Electronics:	Transportation:	Other:
Biofuels:		Irrigation:		Lighting/LEDs:		Computers:	Car Sharing:	Recycling:
Batteries/Storage:		Nanotech:	Y	Waste Heat:		Sensors:	Electric Vehicles:	Engineering:
Solar:	Y	Biotech:		Smart Meters:		Software:	Natural Gas Fuel:	Consulting:
Wind:		Water Tech./Treatment:		Machinery:				Investing:
Fuel Cells:		Ceramics:						Chemicals:

TYPES OF BUSINESS:

Photovoltaic Technology

BRANDS/DIVISIONS/AFFILIATES:

Nanosolar Utility Panel
Energy Capital Partners
Nanosolar Utiliscale
Nanosolar Cell A-100
Google Inc
Benchmark Capital
US Venture Partners
Conergy

CONTACTS: *Note: Officers with more than one job title may be intentionally listed here more than once.*

Geoff Tate, CEO
John McAdoo, CFO
Brian Stone, VP-Worldwide Mktg. & Sales
Becky Baybrook, VP-Human Resources
Dave Jackrel, VP-R&D
Eugenia Corrales, Exec. VP-Eng.
Craig Factor, General Counsel/VP
Eugenia Corrales, Exec. VP-Oper.
Brian Sager, VP-Corp. Dev.
Stephen Huh, VP-Financial Planning & Analysis
Mirco Boldt, VP-Panel Oper.
Ravi Balaji, VP-Cell Oper.
Geoff Tate, Chmn.
Christian Pho Duc, VP-European Mktg. & Sales
Michael Brassington, VP-Supply Chain & Quality

Phone: 408-365-5960	Fax: 408-365-5965
Toll-Free:	
Address: 5521 Hellyer Ave., San Jose, CA 95138 US	

GROWTH PLANS/SPECIAL FEATURES:

Nanosolar, Inc. is a producer of advanced thin-film solar technologies. The firm's technology has been used in product areas such as nanostructured components, printable semiconductors, solar cell architecture, flexible substrate technology, cell-interconnect technology and roll-to-roll process technology. In particular, Nanosolar's nanostructured components and printable semiconductors enable the utilization of solution-coating processes, or printing, to deposit nanoparticles as the most critical layers of a solar cell. Printing is simpler and more robust than other thin-film deposition techniques and can be applied continuously at high speeds with roll-to-roll production methods. The firm's main product is the Nanosolar Utility Panel, a 200-240 watt solar electricity module designed for utility-scale use. Other products include Cell A-100, the firm's proven thin-film technology; PowerSheet, an A-100 technology delivered in an industry-standard package that ensures premium lifetime and full compatibility with existing mounting and installation practices; and Utiliscale, designed for large-scale ground-mounted plant installations. The firm is based in Palo Alto, California, with European operations in Germany and Switzerland. The company was seed-financed by the founders of Google and was incorporated in 2002. Nanosolar's investors include Benchmark Capital, AES Corporation, Energy Capital Partners, Swiss Re, SAC Capital, GLG Partners, MDV and Stanford University. The firm has a long-term agreement with Conergy to develop large-scale photovoltaic systems with tightly interconnected panel and equipment design innovations. Its other development partners include Belectric, EDF Energies Nouvelles, Enxco, AES Solar Energy and Plain Energy. In late 2011, Nanosolar expanded its solar cell plant in San Jose, California, to a 115 megawatt capacity.

FINANCIALS: Sales and profits are in thousands of dollars—add 000 to get the full amount. 2011 Note: Financial information for 2011 was not available for all companies at press time.

2011 Sales: $	2011 Profits: $	**U.S. Stock Ticker: Private**
2010 Sales: $	2010 Profits: $	**Int'l Ticker:**
2009 Sales: $	2009 Profits: $	Int'l Exchange:
2008 Sales: $	2008 Profits: $	Employees: Fiscal Year Ends: 12/31
2007 Sales: $	2007 Profits: $	Parent Company:

SALARIES/BENEFITS:

Pension Plan:	ESOP Stock Plan:	Profit Sharing:	Top Exec. Salary: $	Bonus: $
Savings Plan:	Stock Purch. Plan:		Second Exec. Salary: $	Bonus: $

OTHER THOUGHTS:

Apparent Women Officers or Directors: 2
Hot Spot for Advancement for Women/Minorities:

LOCATIONS: ("Y" = Yes)

West:	Southwest:	Midwest:	Southeast:	Northeast:	International:
Y					Y

NAVITAS ENERGY INC

www.windpower.com

Industry Group Code: 221119

Energy/Fuel:	Other Technologies:	Electrical Products:	Electronics:	Transportation:	Other:
Biofuels:	Irrigation:	Lighting/LEDs:	Computers:	Car Sharing:	Recycling:
Batteries/Storage:	Nanotech:	Waste Heat:	Sensors:	Electric Vehicles:	Engineering: Y
Solar:	Biotech:	Smart Meters:	Software:	Natural Gas Fuel:	Consulting:
Wind:	Water Tech./Treatment:	Machinery:			Investing:
Fuel Cells:	Ceramics:				Chemicals:

TYPES OF BUSINESS:

Electricity Generation-Wind
Engineering & Advisory Services

BRANDS/DIVISIONS/AFFILIATES:

Mendota Hills Wind Farm
Gamesa Corporacion Tecnologica SA

CONTACTS: *Note: Officers with more than one job title may be intentionally listed here more than once.*

Dirk Matthys, Chmn./CEO-Gamesa North America
Jorge Calvet, Chmn./Pres., Gamesa Corporacion
Teodoro Monzon, Managing Dir.-Wind Farm Dev., Gamesa Corporacion

Phone: 612-370-1061	Fax: 612-370-9005
Toll-Free:	
Address: 3001 Broadway St. NE, Ste. 695, Minneapolis, MN 55413 US	

GROWTH PLANS/SPECIAL FEATURES:

Navitas Energy, Inc. is a commercial wind power developer and wind farm operator. It is 77%-owned by Gamesa Corporacion Tecnologica S.A., a Spanish supplier of renewable energy products and a developer and investor of wind farms. Navitas builds wind farms and sells power to electric utilities, municipalities and co-ops on a long-term contractual basis. It also provides financing, engineering, product selection, construction management and maintenance services. Its operational sites include the 50.4-megawatt (MW) Mendota Hills Wind Farm in Lee County, Illinois, the firm's first completed development. The site's 63 wind turbines, which were manufactured by its parent company, operate at 800 kilowatts (kW) each. Estimated at 125 million kilowatt-hours (kWh) produced annually, the site generates enough energy to power about 15,000 homes. Besides operating wind farms, Navitas provides clients interested in wind resources with various services, including wind resource analysis; advice concerning site selection and permits; information on operation and management; a work force ready for construction contracts worldwide; and relationships with technical and regulatory authorities. The company has completed development on wind farms totaling 1,040 MW in 13 states, and its current development portfolio totals approximately 1,500 MW, including wind projects in 12 states throughout the Midwest.

FINANCIALS: Sales and profits are in thousands of dollars—add 000 to get the full amount. 2011 Note: Financial information for 2011 was not available for all companies at press time.

2011 Sales: $	2011 Profits: $	**U.S. Stock Ticker: Subsidiary**
2010 Sales: $	2010 Profits: $	**Int'l Ticker:**
2009 Sales: $	2009 Profits: $	Int'l Exchange:
2008 Sales: $	2008 Profits: $	Employees: Fiscal Year Ends: 12/31
2007 Sales: $	2007 Profits: $	Parent Company: GAMESA CORPORACION TECNOLOGICA SA

SALARIES/BENEFITS:

Pension Plan:	ESOP Stock Plan:	Profit Sharing:	Top Exec. Salary: $	Bonus: $
Savings Plan:	Stock Purch. Plan:		Second Exec. Salary: $	Bonus: $

OTHER THOUGHTS:

Apparent Women Officers or Directors: 1
Hot Spot for Advancement for Women/Minorities: Y

LOCATIONS: ("Y" = Yes)

West:	Southwest:	Midwest:	Southeast:	Northeast:	International:
		Y			

NEC LABORATORIES AMERICA INC

www.nec-labs.com

Industry Group Code: 541712

Energy/Fuel:	Other Technologies:	Electrical Products:	Electronics:	Transportation:	Other:	
Biofuels:	Irrigation:	Lighting/LEDs:	Computers:	Car Sharing:	Recycling:	
Batteries/Storage:	Nanotech:	Waste Heat:	Sensors:	Electric Vehicles:	Engineering:	Y
Solar:	Biotech:	Smart Meters:	Software: Y	Natural Gas Fuel:	Consulting:	
Wind:	Water Tech./Treatment:	Machinery:			Investing:	
Fuel Cells:	Ceramics:				Chemicals:	

TYPES OF BUSINESS:

Communications Technology
Electronics
Broadband & Mobile Networking
Computing
Software
Storage Technologies
Security Systems
Quantum Computing

BRANDS/DIVISIONS/AFFILIATES:

NEC Corporation

CONTACTS: *Note: Officers with more than one job title may be intentionally listed here more than once.*

Kaoru Yano, Chmn.-NEC Corp.

Phone: 609-520-1555	**Fax:** 609-951-2481
Toll-Free:	
Address: 4 Independence Way, Ste. 200, Princeton, NJ 08540 US	

GROWTH PLANS/SPECIAL FEATURES:

NEC Laboratories America, Inc. (NEC Labs) is the U.S.-based research facility in NEC Corporation's global network of research laboratories. NEC Labs is responsible for the technology research and early market validation for NEC's core business. Operating through two laboratories, located in Princeton, New Jersey and Cupertino, California, the company focuses on work in the areas of information analysis and data management; broadband and mobile networking; machine learning; systems technology; large-scale distributed systems; and quantum IT. NEC Labs' information analysis and data management segment is currently developing sophisticated communications networks and databases that are intent-aware, or able to rapidly detect users' intentions and goals. Its broadband and mobile networking division is developing high-performance metropolitan optical networks; mobility management solutions; overlay networks; self-organizing, ad-hoc wireless networks; grid networking; and optical/wireless integration solutions. NEC Labs' machine learning division develops computers with intelligent capabilities, specifically machines that can observe data, learn from data, change behavior and make decisions. Its system technology segment focuses on advanced systems architecture; low-power, tamper-resistant and secure embedded processing architectures to support mobile commerce, digital rights management and multimedia delivery; and practical software analysis and verification technologies. The firm's large-scale distributed systems division offers autonomic management services such as system data mining and analysis and IP service management; and grid storage research that provides unified scalable storage systems. NEC Labs' quantum IT segment is researching new quantum algorithms, decoherence effects in physical systems, methods to protect quantum systems from noise, quantum communication and new applications of quantum computation.

NEC Labs offers employees medical, dental, vision, life, AD&D and disability insurance; tuition assistance; credit union membership; a 401(k); an employee assistance program; flexible spending accounts; and paid time off.

FINANCIALS: Sales and profits are in thousands of dollars—add 000 to get the full amount. 2011 Note: Financial information for 2011 was not available for all companies at press time.

2011 Sales: $	2011 Profits: $	**U.S. Stock Ticker:** Subsidiary
2010 Sales: $	2010 Profits: $	**Int'l Ticker:**
2009 Sales: $	2009 Profits: $	Int'l Exchange:
2008 Sales: $	2008 Profits: $	Employees: Fiscal Year Ends: 3/31
2007 Sales: $	2007 Profits: $	Parent Company: NEC CORPORATION

SALARIES/BENEFITS:

Pension Plan:	ESOP Stock Plan:	Profit Sharing:	Top Exec. Salary: $	Bonus: $
Savings Plan: Y	Stock Purch. Plan:		Second Exec. Salary: $	Bonus: $

OTHER THOUGHTS:

Apparent Women Officers or Directors:
Hot Spot for Advancement for Women/Minorities:

LOCATIONS: ("Y" = Yes)

West:	Southwest:	Midwest:	Southeast:	Northeast:	International:
Y				Y	

NEXANT INC

Industry Group Code: 423430

www.nexant.com

Energy/Fuel:	Other Technologies:	Electrical Products:	Electronics:		Transportation:		Other:	
Biofuels:	Irrigation:	Lighting/LEDs:	Computers:		Car Sharing:		Recycling:	
Batteries/Storage:	Nanotech:	Waste Heat:	Sensors:		Electric Vehicles:		Engineering:	
Solar:	Biotech:	Smart Meters:	Software:	Y	Natural Gas Fuel:		Consulting:	Y
Wind:	Water Tech./Treatment:	Machinery:					Investing:	
Fuel Cells:	Ceramics:						Chemicals:	

TYPES OF BUSINESS:

Energy Industry Software
Enterprise Risk Management
Energy Consulting Services
Energy Market Analysis
Power System Analysis

BRANDS/DIVISIONS/AFFILIATES:

ChemSystems Online
TrakSmart
GEN-SE
TOPAZ
MODELEX
Excelergy BV
PRYM
EE&CM International

CONTACTS: Note: Officers with more than one job title may be intentionally listed here more than once.

Basem Sarandah, CEO
Basem Sarandah, Pres.
Daniel J. Miller, CFO
Martin Milani, CTO
Deborah Forhan Rimmler, General Counsel/Sr. VP
Bob Burdett, Mgr.-Corp. Comm.
Don Bari, Sr. VP-Energy Resources
Paul R. MacGregor, VP-Clean Energy Markets
Terry Fry, Sr. VP-Energy Efficiency
Andrew Spiers, Sr. VP-Energy & Chemicals Consulting, Asia
Richard Sleep, Sr. VP-Energy & Chemicals Consulting (EMEA)

Phone: 415-369-1000	Fax: 415-369-9700
Toll-Free:	
Address: 101 Second St., Ste. 1000, San Francisco, CA 94105-3651 US	

GROWTH PLANS/SPECIAL FEATURES:

Nexant, Inc. is a software developer that is focused on providing technology systems and consulting services to the global energy industry. In addition to a number of software support programs, extensive consulting expertise is offered in every sector of the energy industry along with decision-support systems, training seminars and onsite advisory services. Clients include international energy producers, petroleum and chemical companies; international development organizations; national and regional government agencies; and energy end-users. Nexant offers a host of products marketed through a number of brands and packages, including ChemSystems Online, GEN-SE, TOPAZ, MODELEX, PRYM and TrakSmart. ChemSystems Online provides data, analysis, forecasts, training and planning tools to support the business planning efforts of industry researchers, market analysts and corporate strategists. GEN-SE identifies bad data, such as bad parameters, and bad telemetry in application software. TOPAZ Network Topology Analysis is a topology-evaluation software tool designed specifically to be used in conjunction with GIS software to identify topographical errors. MODELEX is Nexant's power system network modeling tool, enabling engineers to determine how much of an external system has to be modeled and what external data is essential for real-time security. PRYM is an enterprise-wide portfolio risk and yield management tool that complements existing energy trading and risk management systems. TrakSmart is a web-based tool for program management and administration; workflow management; document management; and project tracking. Subsidiary EE&CM International develops programs for pricing policies and regulations; facilitates cooperation among agencies; training, peer-to-peer networking seminars; development of investments in the energy sector and public relations/outreach campaigns. In November 2010, Nexant opened a new office in Bahrain.

FINANCIALS: Sales and profits are in thousands of dollars—add 000 to get the full amount. 2011 Note: Financial information for 2011 was not available for all companies at press time.

2011 Sales: $	2011 Profits: $	**U.S. Stock Ticker:** Private
2010 Sales: $	2010 Profits: $	**Int'l Ticker:**
2009 Sales: $	2009 Profits: $	Int'l Exchange:
2008 Sales: $	2008 Profits: $	Employees: Fiscal Year Ends: 12/31
2007 Sales: $	2007 Profits: $	Parent Company:

SALARIES/BENEFITS:

Pension Plan:	ESOP Stock Plan:	Profit Sharing:	Top Exec. Salary: $	Bonus: $
Savings Plan:	Stock Purch. Plan:		Second Exec. Salary: $	Bonus: $

OTHER THOUGHTS:

Apparent Women Officers or Directors: 1
Hot Spot for Advancement for Women/Minorities:

LOCATIONS: ("Y" = Yes)

West:	Southwest:	Midwest:	Southeast:	Northeast:	International:
Y	Y	Y	Y	Y	Y

NEXTERA ENERGY RESOURCES LLC www.nexteraenergyresources.com

Industry Group Code: 221119

Energy/Fuel:		Other Technologies:		Electrical Products:		Electronics:		Transportation:		Other:	
Biofuels:		Irrigation:		Lighting/LEDs:		Computers:		Car Sharing:		Recycling:	
Batteries/Storage:	Y	Nanotech:		Waste Heat:		Sensors:		Electric Vehicles:		Engineering:	Y
Solar:	Y	Biotech:		Smart Meters:		Software:		Natural Gas Fuel:	Y	Consulting:	
Wind:	Y	Water Tech./Treatment:	Y	Machinery:						Investing:	
Fuel Cells:	Y	Ceramics:								Chemicals:	

TYPES OF BUSINESS:

Solar Energy Facilities
Clean Energy Generation
Power Plant Construction, Operation & Management
Electricity & Natural Gas Marketing
Construction Management Services

BRANDS/DIVISIONS/AFFILIATES:

NextEra Energy Inc
Gexa Energy
NextEra Energy Power Marketing
WindLogics

CONTACTS: *Note: Officers with more than one job title may be intentionally listed here more than once.*

Armando Pimentel, Jr., CEO
Armando Pimentel, Jr., Pres.
Mark R. Sorensen, CFO
John Ketchum, General Counsel/VP/Sec.
Michael O'Sullivan, Sr. VP-Dev.
Mark R. Sorensen, VP-Finance
Mark Maisto, Pres., Commodities & Retail Markets
Mark Ianni, Pres., Gexa Energy GP, LLC
T.J. Tuscai, Sr. VP-Bus. Mgmt.

Phone: 561-694-4000	**Fax:**
Toll-Free: 877-715-4360	
Address: 700 Universe Blvd., Juno Beach, FL 33408 US	

GROWTH PLANS/SPECIAL FEATURES:

NextEra Energy Resources LLC, a subsidiary of NextEra Energy, Inc., owns, develops, constructs, manages and operates power plants using wind, solar, hydroelectric, natural gas and nuclear power. The company operates facilities in 22 U.S. states and Canada. It has over 16,420 megawatts (MW) of generating capacity, more than 95% of which is generated using clean or renewable fuels. 50% of the firm's energy portfolio is comprised of wind resources; 27% is natural gas; 15% nuclear; 5% oil; 2% hydroelectric; and 1% solar and other resources. NextEra Energy Resources has become one of the world's largest generators of wind power, with 75 wind farms in 17 states and Canada generating roughly 8,298 megawatts (MW) of power. The company also operates through a number of subsidiaries. NextEra Energy Power Marketing provides electricity and gas commodity products and marketing and trading services to electric and gas utilities, municipalities and cooperatives, as well as electric generation facilities; and provides electricity and fuel management for NextEra Energy Resources' fleet. WindLogics provides specialized wind services, such as combining on-site data with archived weather data to assist project developers, utilities and others in identifying, building and operating successful wind plants. Gexa Energy is a retail electricity provider serving residential and commercial customers. NextEra Energy Resources also develops, operates and manages generation plants for third parties, providing construction management; land, materials and equipment procurement; facility design; and operation and maintenance services for completed facilities. In November 2011, the firm sold four natural gas plants in California, South Carolina, Alabama and Virginia to an affiliate of LS Power.

NextEra Energy Resources offers its employees medical, dental and vision plans; flexible spending accounts; health and wellness programs; life insurance; education assistance; and adoption assistance;

FINANCIALS: Sales and profits are in thousands of dollars—add 000 to get the full amount. 2011 Note: Financial information for 2011 was not available for all companies at press time.

2011 Sales: $	2011 Profits: $		**U.S. Stock Ticker:** Subsidiary	
2010 Sales: $	2010 Profits: $		**Int'l Ticker:**	
2009 Sales: $	2009 Profits: $		Int'l Exchange:	
2008 Sales: $	2008 Profits: $		Employees:	Fiscal Year Ends:
2007 Sales: $	2007 Profits: $		Parent Company: NEXTERA ENERGY INC	

SALARIES/BENEFITS:

Pension Plan: Y	ESOP Stock Plan:	Profit Sharing:	Top Exec. Salary: $	Bonus: $
Savings Plan: Y	Stock Purch. Plan:		Second Exec. Salary: $	Bonus: $

OTHER THOUGHTS:

Apparent Women Officers or Directors:
Hot Spot for Advancement for Women/Minorities:

LOCATIONS: ("Y" = Yes)

West:	Southwest:	Midwest:	Southeast:	Northeast:	International:
Y	Y	Y	Y	Y	Y

NEXTERRA SYSTEMS CORP

www.nexterra.ca

Industry Group Code: 325199

Energy/Fuel:		Other Technologies:		Electrical Products:	Electronics:	Transportation:	Other:
Biofuels:	Y	Irrigation:		Lighting/LEDs:	Computers:	Car Sharing:	Recycling:
Batteries/Storage:		Nanotech:		Waste Heat:	Sensors:	Electric Vehicles:	Engineering:
Solar:		Biotech:	Y	Smart Meters:	Software:	Natural Gas Fuel:	Consulting:
Wind:		Water Tech./Treatment:		Machinery:			Investing:
Fuel Cells:		Ceramics:					Chemicals:

TYPES OF BUSINESS:

Biomass Gasification Technology

BRANDS/DIVISIONS/AFFILIATES:

ARC Financial Corp
Tandem Expansion Fund

CONTACTS: Note: Officers with more than one job title may be intentionally listed here more than once.

Mike Scott, CEO
Mike Scott, Pres.
Carl Dunaway, VP-Sales
Dejan Sparica, Chief Engineer
Tim Kukler, VP-Admin.
Darcy Quinn, Mgr.-Bus. Dev.
Tim Kukler, VP-Finance
Philip W. Beat, VP-Strategic Rel.
Goran Sparica, VP-Projects
Olavi Tervo, Regional VP-Sales, Brazil

Phone: 604-637-2501	Fax: 604-637-2506
Toll-Free:	
Address: 1300-650 W. Georgia St., Vancouver, BC BC V6B 4N8 Canada	

GROWTH PLANS/SPECIAL FEATURES:

Nexterra Systems Corp. is a developer and supplier of biomass gasification technologies for industrial and institutional use. The firm's biomass gasification technology uses a fixed bed updraft method of gasification to covert biomass fuels, such as wood waste, into syngas, which is then used to produce power and heat at plant-scale applications. This process allows the user to be more self-sufficient in their energy needs, thus reducing energy costs. Nexterra's biomass gasification technology is applicable to many industrial markets and institutions, including the forest industry, in pulp mills, sawmills and cogeneration plants; universities, as seen at the University of South Carolina and the University of Northern British Colombia; governmental facilities, such as the U.S. Department of Energy; and hospitals. Additionally, the firm's technology can be combined with conventional steam turbine equipment to produce electricity. Nexterra's funding comes primarily from ARC Financial Corp. and Tandem Expansion Fund.

FINANCIALS: Sales and profits are in thousands of dollars—add 000 to get the full amount. 2011 Note: Financial information for 2011 was not available for all companies at press time.

2011 Sales: $	2011 Profits: $	U.S. Stock Ticker: Private
2010 Sales: $	2010 Profits: $	Int'l Ticker:
2009 Sales: $	2009 Profits: $	Int'l Exchange:
2008 Sales: $	2008 Profits: $	Employees: Fiscal Year Ends:
2007 Sales: $	2007 Profits: $	Parent Company:

SALARIES/BENEFITS:

Pension Plan:	ESOP Stock Plan:	Profit Sharing:	Top Exec. Salary: $	Bonus: $
Savings Plan:	Stock Purch. Plan:		Second Exec. Salary: $	Bonus: $

OTHER THOUGHTS:

Apparent Women Officers or Directors: 1
Hot Spot for Advancement for Women/Minorities:

LOCATIONS: ("Y" = Yes)

West:	Southwest:	Midwest:	Southeast:	Northeast:	International: Y

NISSAN MOTOR CO LTD

www.nissan-global.com

Industry Group Code: 33611

Energy/Fuel:	Other Technologies:	Electrical Products:	Electronics:	Transportation:		Other:
Biofuels:	Irrigation:	Lighting/LEDs:	Computers:	Car Sharing:		Recycling:
Batteries/Storage:	Nanotech:	Waste Heat:	Sensors:	Electric Vehicles:	Y	Engineering:
Solar:	Biotech:	Smart Meters:	Software:	Natural Gas Fuel:		Consulting:
Wind:	Water Tech./Treatment:	Machinery:				Investing:
Fuel Cells:	Ceramics:					Chemicals:

TYPES OF BUSINESS:

Automobile Manufacturing
Research & Development
Industrial Machinery
Marine Equipment
Logistics Services
Alternative Fuels Research
Financial Services

BRANDS/DIVISIONS/AFFILIATES:

Rogue
Nissan Fuga Hybrid
Fairlady Z Roadster
Renault-Nissan
Altima
Infinity
LEAF
Pathfinder

CONTACTS: *Note: Officers with more than one job title may be intentionally listed here more than once.*

Carlos Ghosn, CEO
Toshiyuki Shiga, COO
Hiroto Saikawa, Exec. VP
Colin Dodge, Exec. VP
Andy Palmer, Exec. VP
Takao Katagiri, Exec. VP
Carlos Ghosn, Chmn.

Phone: 81-45-523-5523	**Fax:**
Toll-Free:	
Address: 1-1, Takashima 1-chome, Nishi-ku, Yokohama-shi, 220-8686 Japan	

GROWTH PLANS/SPECIAL FEATURES:

Nissan Motor Co., Ltd. develops, manufactures, sells and services automotive products in over 160 countries. The company's products, which are sold both in Japan and overseas (principally in North America and Europe), include passenger cars, busses and trucks, along with related components. Brands include Nissan, Infiniti and Forklift, with model offerings such as Nissan Sentra, Nissan Versa, Nissan Altima, Nissan Leaf, Nissan Rogue and Nissan Pathfinder. The Forklift brand offers material handling equipment, including pallet trucks, tow tractors and lifts. Through Nissan Marine, the firm also produces/sells pleasure boats, operates a marina business and exports outboard engines. The company operates offices and production plants in Japan, Africa, North America, Australia, Europe, Asia and the Middle East. Abroad, Nissan and Renault, a French company, manage an alliance that allows each company to maintain its distinct corporate culture and brand identity, while enduring the challenges of market globalization and the accelerating change of technology. Renault-Nissan ranks as one of the world's leading automotive groups, and the two companies operate a joint venture factory in the eastern Indian city of Chennai. The allied firm promotes intensive research and development in alternative fuel technologies. Nissan has been increasing investments in its research and development operations, and plans to produce additional gasoline-electric vehicles as well as subcompact electric cars powered by firm-developed lithium-ion batteries. In January 2012, the firm and Daimler announced plans to manufacture Mercedes-Benz 4-cylinder gasoline engines together in Decherd, Tennessee.

FINANCIALS: Sales and profits are in thousands of dollars—add 000 to get the full amount. 2011 Note: Financial information for 2011 was not available for all companies at press time.

2011 Sales: $112,471,100	2011 Profits: $4,092,400	**U.S. Stock Ticker:**
2010 Sales: $91,271,000	2010 Profits: $514,680	**Int'l Ticker: 7201**
2009 Sales: $89,102,300	2009 Profits: $-2,469,180	Int'l Exchange: Tokyo-TSE
2008 Sales: $108,242,000	2008 Profits: $4,823,000	Employees: 154,328 Fiscal Year Ends: 3/31
2007 Sales: $88,717,000	2007 Profits: $3,905,000	Parent Company:

SALARIES/BENEFITS:

Pension Plan:	ESOP Stock Plan:	Profit Sharing:	Top Exec. Salary: $	Bonus: $
Savings Plan: Y	Stock Purch. Plan:		Second Exec. Salary: $	Bonus: $

OTHER THOUGHTS:

Apparent Women Officers or Directors:
Hot Spot for Advancement for Women/Minorities:

LOCATIONS: ("Y" = Yes)

West:	Southwest:	Midwest:	Southeast:	Northeast:	International:
Y	Y	Y	Y	Y	Y

NOBAO RENEWABLE ENERGY HOLDINGS LTD

www.nobaogroup.com
Industry Group Code: 237130

Energy/Fuel:	Other Technologies:	Electrical Products:		Electronics:	Transportation:	Other:
Biofuels:	Irrigation:	Lighting/LEDs:		Computers:	Car Sharing:	Recycling:
Batteries/Storage:	Nanotech:	Waste Heat:	Y	Sensors:	Electric Vehicles:	Engineering:
Solar:	Biotech:	Smart Meters:		Software:	Natural Gas Fuel:	Consulting:
Wind:	Water Tech./Treatment:	Machinery:				Investing:
Fuel Cells:	Ceramics:					Chemicals:

TYPES OF BUSINESS:

Green Building Technology
Ground Source Heat Pump (GSHP) Technology

BRANDS/DIVISIONS/AFFILIATES:

Nuoxin Energy Technology (Shanghai) Co Ltd
Jiangxi Nobao Electronics Co Ltd
Nobao Energy (Nantong) Co Ltd

CONTACTS: Note: Officers with more than one job title may be intentionally listed here more than once.

Kwok Ping Sun, CEO
E. (Alec) Xu, CFO
Tao Chen, VP-Sales
Jun Chen, CTO
Jian Xiong, VP-Admin.
Jian Xiong, VP-Oper.
Yaluo Sun, Controller
Jingtan Cui, VP-Global Mktg.
Ping Song, VP-Financing & Investment
Jianping Chen, VP-Project Execution
Kwok Ping Sun, Chmn.

Phone: 86-21-6652-0666	Fax: 86-21-6631-2459
Toll-Free:	
Address: Nobao Bldg., Ln. 4, No.150 Yong He Rd., Shanghai, 200072 China	

GROWTH PLANS/SPECIAL FEATURES:

Nobao Renewable Energy Holdings Ltd. is a leading Chinese provider of energy efficiency technologies. The firm offers a number of clean technology management solutions to customers in China, based primarily on ground source heat pump (GSHP) technologies. GSHP uses heat from under the earth's surface, which remains fairly consistent throughout the summer and winter, to provide heating, cooling and hot water supply systems to various types of buildings, including hotels, offices, shopping malls, public facilities and residential buildings. GSHP systems provide winter heating by drawing heat from underground and transferring it to the surface. During the summer, this process is reversed, extracting heat from buildings and transferring it underground. Its operations are fully-integrated, with Nobao manufacturing the equipment, designing and installing the GSHP systems and providing post-installation energy management services through energy management contracts (EMCs). Nobao claims that its GSHP systems can reduce its customers' total energy consumption by 50-70%. The firm currently has nine projects in operation, with nearly 20 additional projects completed but not yet operational. While the company remains focused on expanding its presence in China, in the long term, it plans to expand into the European and North American markets. Nobao operates through three principal subsidiaries: Nuoxin Energy Technology (Shanghai) Co. Ltd; Jiangxi Nobao Electronics Co. Ltd; and Nobao Energy (Nantong) Co. Ltd.

FINANCIALS: Sales and profits are in thousands of dollars—add 000 to get the full amount. 2011 Note: Financial information for 2011 was not available for all companies at press time.

2011 Sales: $	2011 Profits: $	**U.S. Stock Ticker: Private**
2010 Sales: $	2010 Profits: $	**Int'l Ticker:**
2009 Sales: $	2009 Profits: $	Int'l Exchange:
2008 Sales: $	2008 Profits: $	Employees: 167 Fiscal Year Ends: 12/31
2007 Sales: $	2007 Profits: $	Parent Company:

SALARIES/BENEFITS:

Pension Plan:	ESOP Stock Plan:	Profit Sharing:	Top Exec. Salary: $	Bonus: $
Savings Plan:	Stock Purch. Plan:		Second Exec. Salary: $	Bonus: $

OTHER THOUGHTS:

Apparent Women Officers or Directors: 2
Hot Spot for Advancement for Women/Minorities:

LOCATIONS: ("Y" = Yes)

West:	Southwest:	Midwest:	Southeast:	Northeast:	International: Y

NORDEX AG

www.nordex-online.com

Industry Group Code: 33361

Energy/Fuel:		Other Technologies:	Electrical Products:	Electronics:	Transportation:	Other:
Biofuels:		Irrigation:	Lighting/LEDs:	Computers:	Car Sharing:	Recycling:
Batteries/Storage:		Nanotech:	Waste Heat:	Sensors:	Electric Vehicles:	Engineering:
Solar:		Biotech:	Smart Meters:	Software:	Natural Gas Fuel:	Consulting:
Wind:	Y	Water Tech./Treatment:	Machinery:			Investing:
Fuel Cells:		Ceramics:				Chemicals:

TYPES OF BUSINESS:

Wind Turbine Manufacturing

BRANDS/DIVISIONS/AFFILIATES:

Nordex USA, Inc.
N100
N90
N82
N80
Beebe Community Wind Farm LLC
Way Wind LLC
Nordex Energy GmbH

CONTACTS: *Note: Officers with more than one job title may be intentionally listed here more than once.*

Jurgen Zeschky, CEO
Marc Sielemann, COO
Bernard Schaferbarthold, CFO
Lars Bondo Krogsgaard, Chief Sales Officer
Eberhard Voss, CTO
Ralf Peters, Head-Corp. Comm.
Ralf Peters, Head-Investor Rel.
Uwe Luders, Chmn.
Ralf Sigrist, Pres., Nordex USA, Inc.

Phone: 49-40-30030-1000	Fax: 49-40-30030-1101
Toll-Free:	
Address: Langenhorner Chaussee 600, Hamburg, 22419 Germany	

GROWTH PLANS/SPECIAL FEATURES:

Nordex AG is a German manufacturer of wind energy systems, specializing in wind turbines. The company's wind turbines range from 1.5-2.5 megawatts (MW) and include the N100, a 2.5 MW turbine; the N90, which is available in a 2.5 MW version as well as a 2.5 MW offshore version; the N80, also a 2.5 MW turbine; and the N77 and the N82, which both have 1.5 MW and are available exclusively in the Asia-Pacific region. Nordex offers planning, delivery, installation and commissioning services for all its products. Additionally, the firm offers maintenance, service and financing for its products. The company maintains rotor blade production facilities in Germany and China and currently has a total rated output of over 7,100 MW from more than 4,600 individual wind turbines in 34 countries worldwide. Nordex has offices and subsidiaries in 19 countries. The firm operates two wholly-owned subsidiaries Nordex Energy GmbH and Nordex Energy B.V. In March 2011, Nordex USA entered into a joint venture with Beebe Community Wind Farm LLC for the co-development and construction of a wind farm in Michigan. In April 2011, the firm announced that its largest wind farm in France, with a capacity of 75 MW, is now online. In June 2011, Nordex USA entered into a joint venture with Way Wind LLC for the co-development and construction of a wind farm in Nebraska. In July 2011, Nordex USA announced the completion of the largest project ever undertaken by the Nordex Group. The project consisted of 60 N90/2500 wind turbines in Colorado and will produce 150 MW. In August 2011, the firm announced the expansion of its business in Eastern Europe with its entry into the Romanian market with projects totaling 20 MW.

FINANCIALS: Sales and profits are in thousands of dollars—add 000 to get the full amount. 2011 Note: Financial information for 2011 was not available for all companies at press time.

2011 Sales: $	2011 Profits: $	**U.S. Stock Ticker:**
2010 Sales: $1,372,000	2010 Profits: $29,500	**Int'l Ticker: NDX**
2009 Sales: $1,560,300	2009 Profits: $31,920	Int'l Exchange: Paris-Euronext
2008 Sales: $1,702,070	2008 Profits: $71,340	Employees: 2,504 Fiscal Year Ends: 12/31
2007 Sales: $937,090	2007 Profits: $67,990	Parent Company:

SALARIES/BENEFITS:

Pension Plan:	ESOP Stock Plan:	Profit Sharing:	Top Exec. Salary: $	Bonus: $
Savings Plan:	Stock Purch. Plan:		Second Exec. Salary: $	Bonus: $

OTHER THOUGHTS:

Apparent Women Officers or Directors:
Hot Spot for Advancement for Women/Minorities:

LOCATIONS: ("Y" = Yes)

West:	Southwest:	Midwest:	Southeast:	Northeast:	International:
		Y			Y

Sales, profits and employees may be estimates. Financial information, benefits and other data can change quickly and may vary from those stated here.

NOVOZYMES

www.novozymes.com

Industry Group Code: 325414

Energy/Fuel:		Other Technologies:		Electrical Products:		Electronics:		Transportation:		Other:	
Biofuels:	Y	Irrigation:		Lighting/LEDs:		Computers:		Car Sharing:		Recycling:	
Batteries/Storage:		Nanotech:		Waste Heat:		Sensors:		Electric Vehicles:		Engineering:	
Solar:		Biotech:	Y	Smart Meters:		Software:		Natural Gas Fuel:		Consulting:	
Wind:		Water Tech./Treatment:		Machinery:						Investing:	
Fuel Cells:		Ceramics:								Chemicals:	

TYPES OF BUSINESS:

Industrial Enzyme & Microorganism Production
Biopharmaceuticals
Enzymes
Microbiology

BRANDS/DIVISIONS/AFFILIATES:

Mannaway
Stainzyme Plus
Spirizyme
Sucrozyme
Acrylaway
Saczyme
EMD/Merck Crop Bioscience Inc.
Ronozyme NP

CONTACTS: Note: Officers with more than one job title may be intentionally listed here more than once.

Steen Riisgaard, CEO
Steen Riisgaard, Pres.
Benny Loft, CFO/Exec. VP
Henrik Meyer, VP-Mktg.
Per Falholt, Exec. VP-R&D
Thomas Nagy, Exec. VP-Stakeholder Rel.
Thomas Videbaek, Exec. VP-Bio Bus.
Peder Holk Nielsen, Exec. VP-Enzyme Bus.
Adam Munroe, Regional Pres., North America
Pedro Luis Fernandes, Regional Pres., Brazil
Henrik Gurtler, Chmn.
Michael Fredskov Christiansen, Regional Pres., China

Phone: 45-44-46-00-00	**Fax:** 45-44-46-99-99
Toll-Free:	
Address: Krogshoejvej 36, Bagsvaerd, 2880 Denmark	

GROWTH PLANS/SPECIAL FEATURES:

Novozymes is a biotechnology company that specializes in microbiology and enzymes. The firm currently sells over 700 products in 130 countries worldwide. It splits its business into two main areas: Enzyme Business and BioBusiness. The Enzyme Business, which accounts for almost 95% of sales, is split into detergent, technical, food and feed enzymes. Enzymes are used in detergents, such as Mannaway and Stainzyme Plus, which break down water-insoluble stains into matersoluble molecules that can be rinsed away. Technical enzymes transform starch in sugar for starch and fuel industries and are applied in the textile, leather, forestry and alcohol industries. Technical enzymes include the brand name Spirizyme. The company's food enzymes increase the quality or production efficiency in the production of food products such as bread, wine, juice, beer, noodles, alcohol and pasta. Food enzyme products such as Acrylaway, Saczyme and Viscoferm are designed to improve the quality or production speed of foods such as bread, wine, juice, beer and pasta. Feed enzymes, such as Ronozyme NP, are designed to increase the nutritional value of feed and improve phosphorus absorption in animals. This leads to faster growth of animals, while improving the environment by decreasing the phosphorus released through manure. The firm's BioBusiness includes microorganisms and biopharmaceutical ingredients. Microorganisms have three main applications: wastewater treatment, cleaning products and natural growth enhancements for plants and turf grass. Biopharmaceutical products, such as proteins, are provided by the company as a replacement of human/animal substances, lowering the risk of disease transfer in pharmaceutical products. The company is also developing ways to use microorganisms to produce chemicals from renewable sources. In February 2011, Novozymes acquired EMD/Merck Crop BioScience Inc., a company that develops agricultural biologicals. The subsidiary previously belonged to Merck KGaA.

FINANCIALS: Sales and profits are in thousands of dollars—add 000 to get the full amount. 2011 Note: Financial information for 2011 was not available for all companies at press time.

2011 Sales: $	2011 Profits: $	**U.S. Stock Ticker:**
2010 Sales: $1,887,240	2010 Profits: $313,050	**Int'l Ticker: NZYM**
2009 Sales: $1,544,030	2009 Profits: $218,230	Int'l Exchange: Copenhagen-CSE
2008 Sales: $1,453,610	2008 Profits: $189,510	Employees: 5,114 Fiscal Year Ends: 12/31
2007 Sales: $1,327,270	2007 Profits: $185,940	Parent Company:

SALARIES/BENEFITS:

Pension Plan: Y	ESOP Stock Plan:	Profit Sharing:	Top Exec. Salary: $	Bonus: $
Savings Plan: Y	Stock Purch. Plan:		Second Exec. Salary: $	Bonus: $

OTHER THOUGHTS:

Apparent Women Officers or Directors:
Hot Spot for Advancement for Women/Minorities:

LOCATIONS: ("Y" = Yes)

West:	Southwest:	Midwest:	Southeast:	Northeast:	International:
Y				Y	Y

Sales, profits and employees may be estimates. Financial information, benefits and other data can change quickly and may vary from those stated here.

NUJIRA LTD

Industry Group Code: 334220

Energy/Fuel:	Other Technologies:	Electrical Products:	Electronics:		Transportation:	Other:
Biofuels:	Irrigation:	Lighting/LEDs:	Computers:	Y	Car Sharing:	Recycling:
Batteries/Storage:	Nanotech:	Waste Heat:	Sensors:		Electric Vehicles:	Engineering:
Solar:	Biotech:	Smart Meters:	Software:		Natural Gas Fuel:	Consulting:
Wind:	Water Tech./Treatment:	Machinery:				Investing:
Fuel Cells:	Ceramics:					Chemicals:

TYPES OF BUSINESS:

Dynamic Power Supply Technology

BRANDS/DIVISIONS/AFFILIATES:

Coolteq.L
Coolteq.h

GROWTH PLANS/SPECIAL FEATURES:

Nujira Ltd. is a technology company that develops Envelope Tracking (ET) power supply technology for the cellular and digital broadcast markets. ET improves the energy efficiency of radio frequency power amplifiers by replacing the DC supply voltage with a dynamic supply voltage that more closely tracks the amplitude of the radio frequency (RF) signal being transmitted. Nujira's ET is the patented High Accuracy Tracking (HAT) power supply modulator which combines a Switch Mode Power Supply with a high bandwidth linear Error Amplifier, resulting in high bandwidth, high efficiency and low noise. The firm's products include the Coolteq.L, a HAT ET for Long Term Evolution (LTE) smartphones and modems, and the Coolteq.h, a LTE cellular base station and remote radio head power modulator. These Coolteq ETs are applicable in a wide range of items, including cellular terminals, pico and femtocells, cellular infrastructure and digital broadcast systems.

CONTACTS: Note: Officers with more than one job title may be intentionally listed here more than once.

Tim Haynes, CEO
Bernard Morgan, CFO
Jeremy Hendy, VP-Mktg. & Sales
Martin Wilson, Chief Scientist
Gerard Wimpenny, CTO
Gordon Neish, VP-Eng.
Andrew Creeke, VP-Oper.
Julian Hildersley, VP-Strategy
Patrick McNamee, VP-Silicon Oper.
Mike McTighe, Chmn.

Phone: 44-1223-597900	Fax:
Toll-Free:	
Address: Cambourne Business Park, Bldg. 1010, Cambourne, CB23 6DP UK	

FINANCIALS: Sales and profits are in thousands of dollars—add 000 to get the full amount. 2011 Note: Financial information for 2011 was not available for all companies at press time.

2011 Sales: $	2011 Profits: $	U.S. Stock Ticker: Private
2010 Sales: $	2010 Profits: $	Int'l Ticker:
2009 Sales: $	2009 Profits: $	Int'l Exchange:
2008 Sales: $	2008 Profits: $	Employees: Fiscal Year Ends:
2007 Sales: $	2007 Profits: $	Parent Company:

SALARIES/BENEFITS:

Pension Plan:	ESOP Stock Plan:	Profit Sharing:	Top Exec. Salary: $	Bonus: $
Savings Plan:	Stock Purch. Plan:		Second Exec. Salary: $	Bonus: $

OTHER THOUGHTS:

Apparent Women Officers or Directors:
Hot Spot for Advancement for Women/Minorities:

LOCATIONS: ("Y" = Yes)

West:	Southwest:	Midwest:	Southeast:	Northeast:	International: Y

NUVERA FUEL CELLS INC

www.nuvera.com

Industry Group Code: 335999

Energy/Fuel:	Other Technologies:	Electrical Products:	Electronics:	Transportation:	Other:
Biofuels:	Irrigation:	Lighting/LEDs:	Computers:	Car Sharing:	Recycling:
Batteries/Storage:	Nanotech:	Waste Heat:	Sensors:	Electric Vehicles:	Engineering:
Solar:	Biotech:	Smart Meters:	Software:	Natural Gas Fuel:	Consulting:
Wind:	Water Tech./Treatment:	Machinery:			Investing:
Fuel Cells: Y	Ceramics:				Chemicals:

TYPES OF BUSINESS:

Fuel Cells
Hydrogen Fuel Systems

BRANDS/DIVISIONS/AFFILIATES:

Hess Corporation
Forza
PowerTap
Andromeda
Star
PowerFlow
Total Power Solution

CONTACTS: Note: Officers with more than one job title may be intentionally listed here more than once.

Roberto Cordaro, CEO
Roberto Cordaro, Pres.
Robert Schafer, VP-Mktg. & Sales
Scott Blanchet, Dir.-Tech. Dev.
John Gartner, VP-Prod. Dev.
John Gartner, VP-Met. Oper.
Francesco Fragasso, VP-Admin.
Prabhu K. Rao, VP-Commercial Oper.
Francesco Fragasso, VP-Finance
Tim Briggs, Chief Eng.-PowerTap
Gus Block, Dir.-Mktg., Total Power Solution
Darryl Pollica, Chief Eng.-PowerTap
Sandy Pipitone Davis, VP-Organizational Effectiveness
Giampaolo Sibilia, Dir.-European Oper.

Phone: 617-245-7500	Fax: 617-245-7511
Toll-Free:	
Address: 129 Concord Rd., Bldg. 1, Billerica, MA 01821 US	

GROWTH PLANS/SPECIAL FEATURES:

Nuvera Fuel Cells, Inc., majority-owned by Hess Corporation, is a leading developer of fuel cell technology. By focusing on hydrocarbon-fueled fuel cell systems, the company hopes to act as a bridge to the establishment of a hydrogen fuel infrastructure. Nuvera's product line consists primarily of proton exchange membrane fuel cell stacks and fuel processors for automotive applications, as well as power modules for hydrogen and distributed generation applications. The company's technology can convert virtually any hydrocarbon, biofuel or synthetic fuel into hydrogen and removes contaminant byproducts, such as carbon monoxide and sulfur. The firm's Forza project is an industrial power generation system that has been used in a chlorate plant in Italy and transit rail applications in Japan. Its Andromeda and Star projects are working toward on-board hydrogen generation for automobiles. Among the company's products are PowerFlow, a fully automated fuel cell power module utilized in mining and military applications; PowerTap (with manufacturing partners Kusters Zima and Universal Precision Products, Inc.), a system designed to support material handling applications and consisting of a fuel processor, electric-driven hydrogen compressor, cascade storage system and an indoor or outdoor dispenser; Andromeda, a fuel power system that operates without humidification of the hydrogen or air stream; and Total Power Solution, which converts battery operated forklifts to run on hydrogen-powered fuel cell power modules. Nuvera has roughly 125,000 square feet of facilities in Italy and Massachusetts, which includes a chemical laboratory; pilot production, testing and other laboratory facilities; and fuel cell test and fuel processor stations. The space can accommodate a variety of fuel sizes, from 10 watt single cells to 100 kilowatt stacks. The firm's Star units are being produced in conjunction with the U.S. Department of Energy.

FINANCIALS: Sales and profits are in thousands of dollars—add 000 to get the full amount. 2011 Note: Financial information for 2011 was not available for all companies at press time.

2011 Sales: $	2011 Profits: $	**U.S. Stock Ticker: Private**
2010 Sales: $	2010 Profits: $	**Int'l Ticker:**
2009 Sales: $	2009 Profits: $	Int'l Exchange:
2008 Sales: $	2008 Profits: $	Employees: Fiscal Year Ends: 12/31
2007 Sales: $	2007 Profits: $	Parent Company: HESS CORPORATION

SALARIES/BENEFITS:

Pension Plan:	ESOP Stock Plan:	Profit Sharing:	Top Exec. Salary: $	Bonus: $
Savings Plan:	Stock Purch. Plan:		Second Exec. Salary: $	Bonus: $

OTHER THOUGHTS:

Apparent Women Officers or Directors: 1
Hot Spot for Advancement for Women/Minorities:

LOCATIONS: ("Y" = Yes)

West:	Southwest:	Midwest:	Southeast:	Northeast:	International:
				Y	Y

OASYS WATER
www.oasyswater.com

Industry Group Code: 924110

Energy/Fuel:	Other Technologies:		Electrical Products:		Electronics:		Transportation:	Other:	
Biofuels:	Irrigation:		Lighting/LEDs:		Computers:		Car Sharing:	Recycling:	
Batteries/Storage:	Nanotech:		Waste Heat:		Sensors:		Electric Vehicles:	Engineering:	
Solar:	Biotech:		Smart Meters:		Software:		Natural Gas Fuel:	Consulting:	
Wind:	Water Tech./Treatment:	Y	Machinery:					Investing:	
Fuel Cells:	Ceramics:							Chemicals:	

TYPES OF BUSINESS:
Forward Osmosis Desalination

BRANDS/DIVISIONS/AFFILIATES:
Engineered Osmosis
Flagship Ventures
Advanced Technology Ventures
Draper Fisher Jurvetson

GROWTH PLANS/SPECIAL FEATURES:
Oasys Water is a company focused on the production of clean energy, power and water through sustainable resources. Through the firm's proprietary suite Engineered Osmosis, a forward osmosis desalination platform, Oasys Water is able to produce clean drinking water from sea and wastewater. Because of its technological process, Engineered Osmosis is capable of providing potable water at a far less cost than other current desalination methods. The company's technology was founded by Dr. Menachem Elimelech and Rob McGinnis both of Yale University. The firm maintains headquarters in Boston, Massachusetts. Some of Oasys Water's investors include Flagship Ventures; Advanced Technology Ventures; and Draper Fisher Jurvetson.

CONTACTS: *Note: Officers with more than one job title may be intentionally listed here more than once.*
Bob Muscat, CEO
Rob McGinnis, CTO
Jim Matheson, Chmn.

Phone: 617-401-8735	Fax:
Toll-Free:	
Address: 21 Drydock Ave., 7th Fl., Boston, MA 02210 US	

FINANCIALS: Sales and profits are in thousands of dollars—add 000 to get the full amount. 2011 Note: Financial information for 2011 was not available for all companies at press time.

2011 Sales: $	2011 Profits: $	**U.S. Stock Ticker: Private**
2010 Sales: $	2010 Profits: $	**Int'l Ticker:**
2009 Sales: $	2009 Profits: $	Int'l Exchange:
2008 Sales: $	2008 Profits: $	Employees: Fiscal Year Ends: 12/31
2007 Sales: $	2007 Profits: $	Parent Company:

SALARIES/BENEFITS:
Pension Plan:	ESOP Stock Plan:	Profit Sharing:	Top Exec. Salary: $	Bonus: $
Savings Plan:	Stock Purch. Plan:		Second Exec. Salary: $	Bonus: $

OTHER THOUGHTS:
Apparent Women Officers or Directors:
Hot Spot for Advancement for Women/Minorities:

LOCATIONS: ("Y" = Yes)
West:	Southwest:	Midwest:	Southeast:	Northeast:	International:
				Y	

Sales, profits and employees may be estimates. Financial information, benefits and other data can change quickly and may vary from those stated here.

O-FLEXX TECHNOLOGIES GMBH

www.o-flexx.com

Industry Group Code: 325

Energy/Fuel:	Other Technologies:	Electrical Products:	Electronics:	Transportation:	Other:	
Biofuels:	Irrigation:	Lighting/LEDs:	Computers:	Car Sharing:	Recycling:	
Batteries/Storage:	Nanotech:	Waste Heat:	Sensors:	Electric Vehicles:	Engineering:	
Solar:	Biotech:	Smart Meters:	Software:	Natural Gas Fuel:	Consulting:	
Wind:	Water Tech./Treatment:	Machinery:			Investing:	
Fuel Cells:	Ceramics:				Chemicals:	Y

TYPES OF BUSINESS:

Thermoelectric Energy

BRANDS/DIVISIONS/AFFILIATES:

Seebeck
Peltier

CONTACTS: Note: Officers with more than one job title may be intentionally listed here more than once.

Holger Ulland, CEO
Gerhard Span, CTO
Markus Moor, Chmn.

Phone: 49-2065-900-4470	Fax: 49-265-900-447-22
Toll-Free:	
Address: Dr.-Alfred-Herrhausen-Allee 20, Duisburg, D-47228 Germany	

GROWTH PLANS/SPECIAL FEATURES:

O-Flexx Technologies GmbH is a Germany-based and operated company, which develops products and technologies related to the thermoelectric generator field. The firm's products target eight industries and help them convert excess energy into power using custom solutions. These markets and solutions include automotives and the reduction of CO_2 emissions; transportation and the conversion of excess energy from exhaust gas into electrical power; sensors and the facilitation of autonomous and wireless operations; solar thermal systems and the collection of fluid evaporation from stagnant air; geothermal systems and the utilization of steam as an electrical generator; steel production and the acquisition of thermal energy from furnaces during steel casting; steel processing for the purpose of accumulating wasted heat from downstream processes; and finally, the combined heat and power plants industries (CHPs) for the purpose of recovering exhaust gas during cool down processes. The company assists clients with the collection of residual electrical energy from a variety of numerous sources using either a Seebeck or Peltier process, which identify fluctuations in temperatures and electric currents. The company's portfolio includes renowned universities, industry labs and institutes throughout Europe.

FINANCIALS: Sales and profits are in thousands of dollars—add 000 to get the full amount. 2011 Note: Financial information for 2011 was not available for all companies at press time.

2011 Sales: $	2011 Profits: $	**U.S. Stock Ticker: Private**
2010 Sales: $	2010 Profits: $	**Int'l Ticker:**
2009 Sales: $	2009 Profits: $	Int'l Exchange:
2008 Sales: $	2008 Profits: $	Employees: Fiscal Year Ends:
2007 Sales: $	2007 Profits: $	Parent Company:

SALARIES/BENEFITS:

Pension Plan:	ESOP Stock Plan:	Profit Sharing:	Top Exec. Salary: $	Bonus: $
Savings Plan:	Stock Purch. Plan:		Second Exec. Salary: $	Bonus: $

OTHER THOUGHTS:

Apparent Women Officers or Directors:
Hot Spot for Advancement for Women/Minorities:

LOCATIONS: ("Y" = Yes)

West:	Southwest:	Midwest:	Southeast:	Northeast:	International: Y

ON-RAMP WIRELESS
www.onrampwireless.com

Industry Group Code: 334220

Energy/Fuel:	Other Technologies:	Electrical Products:		Electronics:		Transportation:	Other:	
Biofuels:	Irrigation:	Lighting/LEDs:		Computers:		Car Sharing:	Recycling:	
Batteries/Storage:	Nanotech:	Waste Heat:		Sensors:	Y	Electric Vehicles:	Engineering:	Y
Solar:	Biotech:	Smart Meters:	Y	Software:		Natural Gas Fuel:	Consulting:	
Wind:	Water Tech./Treatment:	Machinery:					Investing:	
Fuel Cells:	Ceramics:						Chemicals:	

TYPES OF BUSINESS:
Wireless Technology

BRANDS/DIVISIONS/AFFILIATES:
Ultra-Link Processing
Remote Monitoring Unit

GROWTH PLANS/SPECIAL FEATURES:
On-Ramp Wireless, through its proprietary Ultra-Link Processing (ULP) wireless technology, supports sensor and device communication. The firm's technology efficiently connects billions of difficultly accessed devices in metro scale and challenging settings. ULP technology uses Direct-Sequence Spread Spectrum (DSSS) modulation to address industry concerns such as water efficiency, industrial condition monitoring and asset tracking, and to enable low-power monitoring and control applications within the Smart Grid. The company's signal processing technology is capable of finding weak signals even in high noise settings, allowing for Onramp to offer its customers a wide coverage area, with the added assurance of immunity to high interference, at a cost-effective rate. In April 2011, the firm launched its Remote Monitoring Unit (RMU), a Smart Grid and infrastructure monitoring device.

CONTACTS: Note: Officers with more than one job title may be intentionally listed here more than once.
Joaquin Silva, CEO
Jake Rasweiler, COO
Joaquin Silva, Pres.
Jonas N Olsen, VP-Mktg.
Ted Myers, CTO
Jason Wilson, VP-Prod. Mgmt.
Robert Boesel, VP-Eng.
Jonas N Olsen, VP-Bus. Dev.
Mike Peterson, VP-Finance & Corp. Strategy
Don Telage, Chmn.

Phone: 858-592-6008	Fax: 858-592-6009
Toll-Free:	
Address: 10920 Via Frontera, Ste. 200, San Diego, CA 92127 US	

FINANCIALS: Sales and profits are in thousands of dollars—add 000 to get the full amount. 2011 Note: Financial information for 2011 was not available for all companies at press time.

2011 Sales: $	2011 Profits: $	U.S. Stock Ticker: Private
2010 Sales: $	2010 Profits: $	Int'l Ticker:
2009 Sales: $	2009 Profits: $	Int'l Exchange:
2008 Sales: $	2008 Profits: $	Employees: Fiscal Year Ends:
2007 Sales: $	2007 Profits: $	Parent Company:

SALARIES/BENEFITS:
Pension Plan:	ESOP Stock Plan:	Profit Sharing:	Top Exec. Salary: $	Bonus: $
Savings Plan:	Stock Purch. Plan:		Second Exec. Salary: $	Bonus: $

OTHER THOUGHTS:
Apparent Women Officers or Directors:
Hot Spot for Advancement for Women/Minorities:

LOCATIONS: ("Y" = Yes)
West:	Southwest:	Midwest:	Southeast:	Northeast:	International:
Y					Y

Sales, profits and employees may be estimates. Financial information, benefits and other data can change quickly and may vary from those stated here.

OPOWER

Industry Group Code: 5112

Energy/Fuel:	Other Technologies:	Electrical Products:	Electronics:	Transportation:	Other:
Biofuels:	Irrigation:	Lighting/LEDs:	Computers:	Car Sharing:	Recycling:
Batteries/Storage:	Nanotech:	Waste Heat:	Sensors:	Electric Vehicles:	Engineering:
Solar:	Biotech:	Smart Meters:	Software: Y	Natural Gas Fuel:	Consulting:
Wind:	Water Tech./Treatment:	Machinery:			Investing:
Fuel Cells:	Ceramics:				Chemicals:

TYPES OF BUSINESS:

Energy Management Software

BRANDS/DIVISIONS/AFFILIATES:

Opower Marketplace
Home Energy Reports

CONTACTS: *Note: Officers with more than one job title may be intentionally listed here more than once.*

Daniel Yates, CEO
Alex Laskey, Pres.
Thomas Kramer, CFO
Roderick Morris, Sr. VP-Mktg.
Ben Foster, VP-Prod.
Michael Sachse, General Counsel/VP-Regulatory Affairs
Roderick Morris, Sr. VP-Oper.
Ogi Kavazovic, VP-Strategy & Mktg.
Jeremy Kirsch, Sr. VP-Client Solutions
Nandini Basuthakur, Mgr. Dir.-EMEA/Sr. VP

Phone: 703-778-4544	**Fax:** 703-778-4547
Toll-Free:	
Address: 1515 N. Courthouse Rd., 8th Fl., Arlington, VA 22201 US	

GROWTH PLANS/SPECIAL FEATURES:

Opower produces a cross-channel customer engagement and energy management software platform. The company serves more than 60 utilities, including PG&E, Gulf Power and MidAmerican Energy, as well as over 11 million households. Utilities partner with Opower in order to improve the value of their energy-efficiency portfolios as well as to encourage their customers to become more involved and aware of their energy consumption and efficiency. The company's platform has a significant value to utilities that have in place an Advanced Metering Infrastructure (AMI). The platform is capable of converting hourly data into measurable energy savings, creating an apparent return on investment (ROI) directly to the consumer. The firm's software creates Home Energy Reports, which offer specific energy data and advice directly relevant to the customer's needs. This software is based on the firm's proprietary patent-pending analytics engine and variable-data printing (VDP) technology, which has been proven to boost customer engagement, customer satisfaction and energy savings. Opower is headquartered in Arlington, Virginia and has additional facilities in both San Francisco and London. Recently, the company launched Opower Marketplace, a new social energy application with the Natural Resources Defense Council (NRDC) and Facebook. Additionally, the firm has partnered with Honeywell to provide web and mobile software for thermostats. In July 2011, the firm formed a partnership agreement with First Utility, expanding into the U.K. market.

Employee benefits include medical, dental, vision, life and long-term disability insurance; a 401(k) plan; parental leave programs; a $100 monthly commuter benefit; the ability to bring your dog to work daily; twice annual Innovation Days; and Cinco de Moustache.

FINANCIALS: Sales and profits are in thousands of dollars—add 000 to get the full amount. 2011 Note: Financial information for 2011 was not available for all companies at press time.

2011 Sales: $	2011 Profits: $	**U.S. Stock Ticker: Private**
2010 Sales: $	2010 Profits: $	**Int'l Ticker:**
2009 Sales: $	2009 Profits: $	Int'l Exchange:
2008 Sales: $	2008 Profits: $	Employees: Fiscal Year Ends:
2007 Sales: $	2007 Profits: $	Parent Company:

SALARIES/BENEFITS:

Pension Plan:	ESOP Stock Plan:	Profit Sharing:	Top Exec. Salary: $	Bonus: $
Savings Plan: Y	Stock Purch. Plan:		Second Exec. Salary: $	Bonus: $

OTHER THOUGHTS:

Apparent Women Officers or Directors: 2
Hot Spot for Advancement for Women/Minorities:

LOCATIONS: ("Y" = Yes)

West:	Southwest:	Midwest:	Southeast:	Northeast:	International:
Y				Y	Y

ORMAT TECHNOLOGIES
www.ormat.com
Industry Group Code: 221119

Energy/Fuel:	Other Technologies:	Electrical Products:	Electronics:	Transportation:	Other:
Biofuels:	Irrigation:	Lighting/LEDs:	Computers:	Car Sharing:	Recycling:
Batteries/Storage:	Nanotech:	Waste Heat: Y	Sensors:	Electric Vehicles:	Engineering: Y
Solar:	Biotech:	Smart Meters:	Software:	Natural Gas Fuel:	Consulting:
Wind:	Water Tech./Treatment:	Machinery: Y			Investing:
Fuel Cells:	Ceramics:				Chemicals:

TYPES OF BUSINESS:
Electricity Generation-Geothermal
Geothermal Plant Design & Construction
Small Electric Generators
Procurement Services
Maintenance Services
Construction Services
Engineering Services
Recovered Energy, Biomass & Solar Plants

BRANDS/DIVISIONS/AFFILIATES:
Ormat Energy Converter
NV Energy

CONTACTS: *Note: Officers with more than one job title may be intentionally listed here more than once.*
Yehudit (Dita) Bronicki, CEO
Yoram Bronicki, COO
Yoram Bronicki, Pres.
Joseph Tenne, CFO
Nir Wolf, Exec. VP-Mktg. & Sales
Lucien Y. Bronicki, CTO
Shimon Hatzir, Sr. VP-Eng.
Etty Rosner, Corp. Sec.
Nadav Amir, Exec. VP-Oper.
Joseph Shiloah, Exec. VP-Bus. Dev.
Zvi Kreiger, Sr. VP-Geothermal Resources
Zvi Reiss, Exec. VP-Project Mgmt.
Etty Rosner, Sr. VP-Contract Mgmt.
Lucien Y. Bronicki, Chmn.

Phone: 775-356-9029	Fax: 775-356-9039
Toll-Free:	
Address: 6225 Neil Rd., Ste. 300, Reno, NV 89511 US	

GROWTH PLANS/SPECIAL FEATURES:
Ormat Technologies is engaged in the geothermal and recovered energy power business. The company designs, builds, owns and operates geothermal and recovered energy plants, using equipment that it designs and manufactures. The firm operates in two segments: electricity (accounting for 22% of 2010 revenues) and products (accounting for 78% of revenues). The electricity segment develops, builds, owns and operates geothermal and recovered energy plants in the U.S. and geothermal plants worldwide and sells the electricity they generate. The product segment designs, manufactures and sells equipment for geothermal and recovered energy-based electricity generation, remote power units and other power generating units. Additionally, the segment provides services relating to the engineering, procurement, construction, operation and maintenance of these power plants. The firm's proprietary Ormat Energy Converter is the basis for the company's recovered energy and geothermal plants. The unit converts low, medium and high temperature heat into electrical energy, allowing for geothermal developers to gain access to geothermal resources, such as low temperature geothermal waters and high-pressure steam in electricity production. Ormat owns (or controls) and operates geothermal power plants and recovery energy plants in the U.S., Guatemala, Kenya, Nicaragua, Costa Rica and New Zealand. In March 2011, the company announced a 20 year purchase agreement with NV Energy to purchase 30 megawatts of clean energy generated from the Dixie Meadows geothermal project, located in Churchill County, Nevada. In August 2011, Ormat opened its second Costa Rican geothermal plant.

FINANCIALS: Sales and profits are in thousands of dollars—add 000 to get the full amount. 2011 Note: Financial information for 2011 was not available for all companies at press time.

2011 Sales: $	2011 Profits: $	U.S. Stock Ticker: ORA
2010 Sales: $373,230	2010 Profits: $37,318	Int'l Ticker:
2009 Sales: $415,244	2009 Profits: $68,851	Int'l Exchange:
2008 Sales: $344,833	2008 Profits: $43,608	Employees: 1,146 Fiscal Year Ends: 12/31
2007 Sales: $295,919	2007 Profits: $27,376	Parent Company:

SALARIES/BENEFITS:
Pension Plan:	ESOP Stock Plan:	Profit Sharing:	Top Exec. Salary: $275,923	Bonus: $17,387
Savings Plan:	Stock Purch. Plan:		Second Exec. Salary: $256,929	Bonus: $87,666

OTHER THOUGHTS:
Apparent Women Officers or Directors: 2
Hot Spot for Advancement for Women/Minorities:

LOCATIONS: ("Y" = Yes)
West:	Southwest:	Midwest:	Southeast:	Northeast:	International:
Y	Y	Y			Y

Sales, profits and employees may be estimates. Financial information, benefits and other data can change quickly and may vary from those stated here.

OSTARA NUTRIENT RECOVERY TECHNOLOGIES www.ostara.com

Industry Group Code: 924110

Energy/Fuel:	Other Technologies:	Electrical Products:	Electronics:	Transportation:	Other:
Biofuels:	Irrigation:	Lighting/LEDs:	Computers:	Car Sharing:	Recycling:
Batteries/Storage:	Nanotech:	Waste Heat:	Sensors:	Electric Vehicles:	Engineering:
Solar:	Biotech:	Smart Meters:	Software:	Natural Gas Fuel:	Consulting:
Wind:	Water Tech./Treatment: Y	Machinery:			Investing:
Fuel Cells:	Ceramics:				Chemicals:

TYPES OF BUSINESS:
Nutrient Management Solutions

BRANDS/DIVISIONS/AFFILIATES:
Pearl Process
Crystal Green

CONTACTS: Note: Officers with more than one job title may be intentionally listed here more than once.
F. Phillip Abrary, CEO
F. Phillip Abrary, Pres.
Myles Degenstein, CFO
Edward Jones, CIO
Ahren T. Britton, CTO
Jim Zablocki, VP-Nutrient Oper.
Don Clark, Sr. VP-Tech.
Matt Kuzma, VP-Nutrient Recovery
Aynul Dharas, VP-Projects
Len Zapalowski, Sr. VP
James W. Hotchkies, Mgr. Dir.-EMEA

Phone: 604-408-6697	Fax: 604-408-4442
Toll-Free:	
Address: 690-1199 W. Pender St., Vancouver, BC V6E 2R1 Canada	

GROWTH PLANS/SPECIAL FEATURES:

Ostara Nutrient Recovery Technologies is a nutrient management solutions firm. The company's business is based around the removal of phosphorus and nitrogen from municipal and industrial wastewaters using the firm's proprietary Pearl Process. The process recovers struvite in the form of crystalline pellets between 1 to 3.5 mm in diameter based on a controlled chemical precipitation process that takes place within the system's fluidized bed reactor. Once removed, Ostara converts the pellets to Crystal Green, the firm's slow-release and environmentally friendly fertilizer product. Crystal Green is a less carbon-intensive fertilizer that reduces runoff and leaching; stimulates stronger root development; grows thick, green and healthy canopy; and is suitable for applications such as turf, nursery and agricultural settings. The company's technology is both helpful in protecting waterways from nutrient overload, as well as in providing a cost-effective solution to struvite issues at water treatment facilities. Benefits to water treatment facilities include a reduced volume of sludge and its associated disposal costs; the elimination of plants' downtime and subsequent maintenance costs associated with cleaning clogged pumps, pipes and equipment; and the overall improvement of their systems reliability by the reduction of nutrient loadings and discharge. In an average municipal wastewater treatment facility, Ostara is capable of removing up to 90% of the phosphorus and 40% of the ammonia from the sludge dewatering liquid. In 2011, the firm announced the construction of a nutrient recovery facility at both Clean Water Services' Rock Creek Advanced Wastewater Treatment Facility in Hillsboro, Oregon and at the H.M. Weir Wastewater Treatment Plant in Saskatoon, British Columbia.

FINANCIALS: Sales and profits are in thousands of dollars—add 000 to get the full amount. 2011 Note: Financial information for 2011 was not available for all companies at press time.

2011 Sales: $	2011 Profits: $	U.S. Stock Ticker: Private
2010 Sales: $	2010 Profits: $	Int'l Ticker:
2009 Sales: $	2009 Profits: $	Int'l Exchange:
2008 Sales: $	2008 Profits: $	Employees: Fiscal Year Ends:
2007 Sales: $	2007 Profits: $	Parent Company:

SALARIES/BENEFITS:

Pension Plan:	ESOP Stock Plan:	Profit Sharing:	Top Exec. Salary: $	Bonus: $
Savings Plan:	Stock Purch. Plan:		Second Exec. Salary: $	Bonus: $

OTHER THOUGHTS:
Apparent Women Officers or Directors:
Hot Spot for Advancement for Women/Minorities:

LOCATIONS: ("Y" = Yes)

West:	Southwest:	Midwest:	Southeast:	Northeast:	International: Y

Sales, profits and employees may be estimates. Financial information, benefits and other data can change quickly and may vary from those stated here.

PALO ALTO RESEARCH CENTER (PARC)

www.parc.com

Industry Group Code: 541712

Energy/Fuel:	Other Technologies:	Electrical Products:	Electronics:	Transportation:	Other:	
Biofuels:	Irrigation:	Lighting/LEDs:	Computers:	Car Sharing:	Recycling:	
Batteries/Storage:	Nanotech:	Waste Heat:	Sensors:	Electric Vehicles:	Engineering:	Y
Solar:	Biotech:	Smart Meters:	Software:	Natural Gas Fuel:	Consulting:	
Wind:	Water Tech./Treatment:	Machinery:			Investing:	
Fuel Cells:	Ceramics:				Chemicals:	

TYPES OF BUSINESS:

Research & Development-Office Technology
Computing
Software
Networks
Materials Science
Renewable Energy Technology
Biomedical Science
Environmental Technologies

BRANDS/DIVISIONS/AFFILIATES:

Xerox Corporation
Office of the Future
Scripps-PARC Institute
Startup@PARC
WikiDashboard

CONTACTS: Note: Officers with more than one job title may be intentionally listed here more than once.

Steve Hoover, CEO
Mark Bernstein, Pres.
John Pauksta, CFO
John Pauksta, VP-Human Resources
Walt Johnson, VP-Intelligent Systems Laboratory
Dana Bloomberg, VP-Oper.
Tamara St. Claire, VP-Global Bus. Dev.
John Pauksta, VP-Finance
Damon C. Matteo, VP-Intellectual Capital Mgmt.
Ross Bringans, VP/Dir.-Electronic Materials & Devices Laboratory
Teresa Lunt, VP/Dir.-Computing Science Laboratory

Phone: 650-812-4000	Fax: 650-812-4028
Toll-Free:	
Address: 3333 Coyote Hill Rd., Palo Alto, CA 94304 US	

GROWTH PLANS/SPECIAL FEATURES:

Palo Alto Research Center (PARC) is a research and development firm owned and operated by the Xerox Corporation. The company's areas of focus in research and innovation include biomedical systems; cleantech; nanotechnology; natural language processing; ethnography; networking; human information interaction; optoelectronics and optical systems; intelligent control and autonomous systems; printing; intelligent image recognition; security and privacy; and large area electronic. The company is divided into four research and development organizations: computing science, electronic materials and devices, hardware systems and intelligent systems. It also runs an intellectual capital management division. Together with the Scripps Research Institute, PARC founded the Scripps-PARC Institute for Advanced Biomedical Science. The institute's research centers on such areas as drug discovery, cancer screening, protein purification and cell monitoring. PARC has been instrumental in the creation of technologies such as laser printing, Ethernet, the graphical user interface and ubiquitous computing. Almost every Xerox product on the market today incorporates or has been influenced by PARC inventions. Since its inception, PARC has spawned several technology companies, licensed its technologies across the world and has made significant contributions in such scientific fields as materials, computing, linguistics and sociology. Entrepreneurs who wish to take advantage of PARC research can access the Startup@PARC program, which creates customized partnerships for selected ventures, providing access to high-end technical expertise and facilities resources such as office-lab space and operational support. The firm also offers WikiDashboard, a tool that helps readers further examine the validity and credibility of information and articles derived from Wikipedia.com. In 2010, the firm entered into a joint product development agreement with Power Assure, Inc. to develop a technology project that will reduce data center power consumption.

FINANCIALS: Sales and profits are in thousands of dollars—add 000 to get the full amount. 2011 Note: Financial information for 2011 was not available for all companies at press time.

2011 Sales: $	2011 Profits: $	U.S. Stock Ticker: Subsidiary
2010 Sales: $	2010 Profits: $	Int'l Ticker:
2009 Sales: $	2009 Profits: $	Int'l Exchange:
2008 Sales: $	2008 Profits: $	Employees: Fiscal Year Ends: 12/31
2007 Sales: $	2007 Profits: $	Parent Company: XEROX CORP

SALARIES/BENEFITS:

Pension Plan:	ESOP Stock Plan:	Profit Sharing:	Top Exec. Salary: $	Bonus: $
Savings Plan: Y	Stock Purch. Plan:		Second Exec. Salary: $	Bonus: $

OTHER THOUGHTS:

Apparent Women Officers or Directors: 3
Hot Spot for Advancement for Women/Minorities: Y

LOCATIONS: ("Y" = Yes)

West:	Southwest:	Midwest:	Southeast:	Northeast:	International:
Y					

PANASONIC CORPORATION

www.panasonic.net

Industry Group Code: 334310

Energy/Fuel:	Other Technologies:		Electrical Products:	Electronics:		Transportation:		Other:	
Biofuels:	Irrigation:		Lighting/LEDs:	Computers:		Car Sharing:		Recycling:	
Batteries/Storage:	Nanotech:	Y	Waste Heat:	Sensors:		Electric Vehicles:		Engineering:	
Solar:	Biotech:		Smart Meters:	Software:	Y	Natural Gas Fuel:		Consulting:	
Wind:	Water Tech./Treatment:		Machinery:					Investing:	
Fuel Cells:	Ceramics:							Chemicals:	

TYPES OF BUSINESS:

Audio & Video Equipment, Manufacturing
Batteries
Home Appliances
Electronic Components
Cellular Phones
Medical Equipment
Photovoltaic Equipment
Telecommunications Equipment

BRANDS/DIVISIONS/AFFILIATES:

PanaHome
Technics
Panasonic Mobile Communications Co Ltd
SANYO Electric Company Ltd.
Panasonic Electronic Devices Co., Ltd.
Panasonic Electric Works Co. Ltd.
Panasonic Factory Solutions Co., Ltd.
Panasonic Welding Systems Co., Ltd.

CONTACTS: Note: Officers with more than one job title may be intentionally listed here more than once.

Fumio Ohtsubo, Pres.
Masayuki Matsushita, Vice Chmn.
Toshihiro Sakamoto, Exec. VP
Takahiro Mori, Exec. VP
Yasuo Katsura, Exec. VP
Kunio Nakamura, Chmn.

Phone: 81-6-6908-1121	Fax:
Toll-Free:	
Address: 1006 Oaza Kadoma, Kadoma City, Osaka, 571-8501 Japan	

GROWTH PLANS/SPECIAL FEATURES:

Panasonic Corporation, formerly Matsushita Electric Industrial Co., Ltd., produces consumer, professional and industrial electronics products under brand names such as Panasonic, Technics and PanaHome. The company operates in six segments: Digital AVC (audio, visual and communications) Networks; Home Appliances; Panasonic Electric Works Co. and PanaHome; Components and Devices; SANYO; and Other. Panasonic's Digital AVC Networks products include consumer electronics such as TVs, DVD recorders, camcorders, computers, digital cameras and personal and home audio equipment; business and professional equipment, including printers and fax machines, security products and digital imaging systems; mobile phones; car AVC equipment; memory cards and other recordable media; and healthcare systems such as medical imaging products. Home appliance products include refrigerators, air conditioners, washing machines and clothes dryers, vacuum cleaners, microwave ovens and other cooking appliances, dish washers, electric fans, electric lamps, compressors and vending machines. The Panasonic Electric Works and PanaHome segment supplies lighting fixtures, wiring devices, personal-care products, modular kitchen systems, interior and exterior furnishing materials, automation controls, detached housing, rental apartment housing, medical and nursing care facilities and home remodeling products. Components and devices include semiconductors; general components, such as capacitors, tuners, circuit boards, power supplies, circuit components, electromechanical components and speakers; electric motors; and batteries. Subsidiary SANYO Electric Co., Ltd. is a leading electronics company. It manufactures and sells products in three categories: energy, including solar cells and rechargeable batteries; ecology, such as commercial equipment, home appliances and car electronics; and electronics devices and digital system devices to support the energy and ecology sector. The firm's Other business includes Panasonic Factory Solutions Co., which supplies automated manufacturing systems that support the production of advanced electronics; and Panasonic Welding Systems Co. In December 2010, it established Panasonic Welding Systems India. In the same month, Panasonic agreed to make SANYO and Panasonic Electric Works Co. wholly-owned subsidiaries through share exchange transactions.

FINANCIALS: Sales and profits are in thousands of dollars—add 000 to get the full amount. 2011 Note: Financial information for 2011 was not available for all companies at press time.

2011 Sales: $114,221,700	2011 Profits: $972,600	**U.S. Stock Ticker:**
2010 Sales: $90,202,900	2010 Profits: $-2,079,360	**Int'l Ticker: 6752**
2009 Sales: $85,729,000	2009 Profits: $-4,183,620	Int'l Exchange: Tokyo-TSE
2008 Sales: $93,428,320	2008 Profits: $2,905,150	Employees: 366,937 Fiscal Year Ends: 3/31
2007 Sales: $81,831,200	2007 Profits: $1,949,650	Parent Company:

SALARIES/BENEFITS:

Pension Plan:	ESOP Stock Plan:	Profit Sharing:	Top Exec. Salary: $	Bonus: $
Savings Plan:	Stock Purch. Plan:		Second Exec. Salary: $	Bonus: $

OTHER THOUGHTS:

Apparent Women Officers or Directors:
Hot Spot for Advancement for Women/Minorities:

LOCATIONS: ("Y" = Yes)

West:	Southwest:	Midwest:	Southeast:	Northeast:	International:
Y		Y	Y	Y	Y

PETROLEO BRASILEIRO SA (PETROBRAS)   www.petrobras.com.br

Industry Group Code: 211111

Energy/Fuel:	Other Technologies:	Electrical Products:	Electronics:	Transportation:	Other:	
Biofuels:	Irrigation:	Lighting/LEDs:	Computers:	Car Sharing:	Recycling:	
Batteries/Storage:	Nanotech:	Waste Heat:	Sensors:	Electric Vehicles:	Engineering:	
Solar:	Biotech:	Smart Meters:	Software:	Natural Gas Fuel:	Consulting:	
Wind:	Water Tech./Treatment:	Machinery:			Investing:	
Fuel Cells:	Ceramics:				Chemicals:	Y

TYPES OF BUSINESS:
Oil & Gas Exploration & Production
Oil Refineries
Service Stations
Transportation & Pipelines
Energy Trading

BRANDS/DIVISIONS/AFFILIATES:
Petrobras
Petrobras Distribuidora SA
BSBIOS Industria e Comercio de Biodiesel
Petrobras Biocombustivel SA

CONTACTS: *Note: Officers with more than one job title may be intentionally listed here more than once.*
Jose S. G. de Azevedo, CEO
Almir G. Barbassa, CFO
Guilherme de O. Estrella, Chief Exploration & Prod. Officer
Almir G. Barbassa, Chief Investor Rel. Officer
Renato de S. Duque, Chief Svcs. Officer
Paulo R. Costa, Chief Downstream Officer
Maria das G.S. Foster, Chief Gas & Energy Officer
Dilma V. Rousseff, Chmn.
Jorge L. Zelada, Chief Int'l Bus. Officer

Phone: 55-21-3224-2040	**Fax:** 55-21-3224-9999

Toll-Free:

Address: 65 Ave. Republica do Chile, Rio de Janeiro, 20031-912 Brazil

GROWTH PLANS/SPECIAL FEATURES:

Petroleo Brasileiro SA, known as Petrobras, is owned primarily by the Brazilian government and is one of the world's largest energy companies. It refines, produces and distributes oil and oil-based products both nationally and internationally. The firm divides company activities into six business sectors: exploration and production; refining, transportation and marketing; distribution; gas and power; international; and corporate. Petrobas' exploration and production unit researches, identifies, develops, produces and incorporates oil and natural gas reserves in Brazil. It currently produces roughly 2.1 million barrels of oil per day. The company's refining, transportation and marketing business includes 16 oil refineries that operate approximately 92% of Brazil's total refining capacity. Petrobras (through subsidiary Petrobras Distribuidora SA) distributes approximately 38.6% of the demand for petroleum byproducts in Brazil through nearly 7,000 service stations. The gas and power segment markets domestic and imported natural gas and implements project with the private sector to guarantee fuel throughout Brazil. This division also develops/invests in alternative energy sources, including wind, solar and biofuel energy. Internationally, Petrobras operates in 25 countries, maintaining international operations including exploration and petroleum procurement. Operations not covered by the other segments are classified under the corporate sector. The firm sells fuels and lubricants for the auto, aviation, marine, railroad and other industries. It has a $224 billion investment budget for the 2010-2014 period for improvements and new fields, concentrating on finds in deep offshore waters, including the new Tupi field, which may contain as many as 8 billion barrels of oil. In July 2011, Petrobras acquired 50% of BSBIOS Industria e Comercio de Biodiesel Sul Brasil S.A. through subsidiary Petrobras Biocombustivel SA for $128.4 million. That same month, the firm announced two new oil and gas finds in the Espirito Basin offshore of Brazil.

FINANCIALS: Sales and profits are in thousands of dollars—add 000 to get the full amount. 2011 Note: Financial information for 2011 was not available for all companies at press time.

2011 Sales: $	2011 Profits: $	**U.S. Stock Ticker:**
2010 Sales: $133,831,000	2010 Profits: $22,081,300	**Int'l Ticker: PETR3**
2009 Sales: $103,523,000	2009 Profits: $16,421,100	Int'l Exchange: Sao Paulo-SAO
2008 Sales: $118,257,000	2008 Profits: $18,879,000	Employees: 80,492 Fiscal Year Ends: 12/31
2007 Sales: $87,735,000	2007 Profits: $13,138,000	Parent Company:

SALARIES/BENEFITS:

Pension Plan:	ESOP Stock Plan:	Profit Sharing:	Top Exec. Salary: $	Bonus: $
Savings Plan:	Stock Purch. Plan:		Second Exec. Salary: $	Bonus: $

OTHER THOUGHTS:
Apparent Women Officers or Directors: 2
Hot Spot for Advancement for Women/Minorities:

LOCATIONS: ("Y" = Yes)

West:	Southwest:	Midwest:	Southeast:	Northeast:	International:
	Y			Y	Y

PHOTOWATT INTERNATIONAL SA   www.photowatt.com

Industry Group Code: 334413

Energy/Fuel:		Other Technologies:		Electrical Products:		Electronics:	Transportation:	Other:
Biofuels:		Irrigation:		Lighting/LEDs:		Computers:	Car Sharing:	Recycling:
Batteries/Storage:	Y	Nanotech:		Waste Heat:		Sensors:	Electric Vehicles:	Engineering:
Solar:	Y	Biotech:		Smart Meters:		Software:	Natural Gas Fuel:	Consulting:
Wind:		Water Tech./Treatment:		Machinery:				Investing:
Fuel Cells:		Ceramics:						Chemicals:

TYPES OF BUSINESS:

Photovoltaic Cells, Manufacturing

BRANDS/DIVISIONS/AFFILIATES:

ATS Automation Tooling Systems Inc
ElectraSun
POLIX
Wattea

CONTACTS: Note: Officers with more than one job title may be intentionally listed here more than once.

Thierry Miremont, CEO
Vincent Bes, CFO
Jean-Louis Dubien, Dir.-Oper.
David McAusland, Chmn.

Phone: 33-4-74-93-80-20	Fax: 33-4-74-93-80-40
Toll-Free:	
Address: 33 Rue Saint-Honore, Z.I. Champfleuri, Bourgoin-Jallieu, 38300 France	

GROWTH PLANS/SPECIAL FEATURES:

Photowatt International SA, a subsidiary of the Canadian firm ATS Automation Tooling Systems, Inc., is a producer of photovoltaic products. Based in France, the company offers modules ranging from 12-210 watts, made from glass/Tedlar or bi-glass and guaranteed to last 25 years. Manufacturing of high-output multicrystalline cells is performed using Photowatt's patented POLIX process, which is a vertically integrated process developed by the company internally. The company primarily sells complete systems, either custom-designed or in kits. Photowatt's ElectraSun solar kit, available in three output capacities, is a complete turnkey system designed for use on flat or pitched roofs, while the firm's Wattea solar kit suits all roof types from residential to commercial. The company also designs generators and develops photovoltaic systems for a wide range of applications. Its products can be used as supplemental energy in grid-connected buildings or in remote areas as a primary source of power for pumping stations, maritime beacons or for other applications. Photowatt has also developed special modules for a number of applications, such as panels designed specifically to operate parking meters, and on the habitation module of a polar expedition. The company utilizes a worldwide network of distributors and partners, as well as an online store where customers can customize their photovoltaic installation.

FINANCIALS: Sales and profits are in thousands of dollars—add 000 to get the full amount. 2011 Note: Financial information for 2011 was not available for all companies at press time.

2011 Sales: $	2011 Profits: $	U.S. Stock Ticker: Subsidiary
2010 Sales: $	2010 Profits: $	Int'l Ticker:
2009 Sales: $	2009 Profits: $	Int'l Exchange:
2008 Sales: $	2008 Profits: $	Employees: Fiscal Year Ends: 3/31
2007 Sales: $	2007 Profits: $	Parent Company: ATS AUTOMATION TOOLING SYSTEMS INC

SALARIES/BENEFITS:

Pension Plan:	ESOP Stock Plan:	Profit Sharing:	Top Exec. Salary: $	Bonus: $
Savings Plan:	Stock Purch. Plan:		Second Exec. Salary: $	Bonus: $

OTHER THOUGHTS:

Apparent Women Officers or Directors:
Hot Spot for Advancement for Women/Minorities:

LOCATIONS: ("Y" = Yes)

West:	Southwest:	Midwest:	Southeast:	Northeast:	International: Y

PLUG POWER INC

www.plugpower.com

Industry Group Code: 335999

Energy/Fuel:	Other Technologies:	Electrical Products:	Electronics:	Transportation:	Other:
Biofuels:	Irrigation:	Lighting/LEDs:	Computers:	Car Sharing:	Recycling:
Batteries/Storage:	Nanotech:	Waste Heat:	Sensors:	Electric Vehicles:	Engineering:
Solar:	Biotech:	Smart Meters:	Software:	Natural Gas Fuel:	Consulting:
Wind:	Water Tech./Treatment:	Machinery:			Investing:
Fuel Cells: Y	Ceramics:				Chemicals:

TYPES OF BUSINESS:

Fuel Cell Technology
Onsite Generation Systems
Proton Exchange Membrane Technology
Back-Up Power Systems

BRANDS/DIVISIONS/AFFILIATES:

GenCore
GenSys On-site Power Systems
GenDrive

CONTACTS: Note: Officers with more than one job title may be intentionally listed here more than once.

Andy Marsh, CEO
Andy Marsh, Pres.
Gerry Anderson, CFO
Reid Hislop, VP-Mktg.
Adrian Corless, CTO
Adrian Corless, VP-Eng.
Gerard Conway, Jr., General Counsel/Corp. Sec.
Gerry Anderson, VP-Oper.
Gerard Conway, Jr., VP-Gov't Affairs
Reid Hislop, VP-Investor Rel.
Mark Sperry, Sr. VP-Continuous Power Div.
Erik Hansen, VP-Sales, Service & Hydrogen
George C. McNamee, Chmn.

Phone: 518-782-7700	Fax: 518-782-9060
Toll-Free:	
Address: 968 Albany-Shaker Rd., Latham, NY 12110 US	

GROWTH PLANS/SPECIAL FEATURES:

Plug Power, Inc. designs, develops and manufactures on-site electrical power generation systems incorporating proton exchange membrane (PEM) fuel cells for stationary applications. The company has established an extended enterprise through strategic relationships with marketing, technology, supply chain and government partners. Its product offerings include: on-site hydrogen generating systems, which provide pure, compressed hydrogen without the necessity of transporting hydrogen gas cylinders; GenDrive, a hydrogen-fueled PEM fuel cell system that provides power to industrial vehicles; GenCore Power Back-up systems, which are used to prevent gaps in electricity flow in industrial plant controls and telecommunications; and Gensys On-site Power Systems, which are designed, often for residential homes, to generate continuous power by converting available fuels into electricity and heat. The firm is also developing technology in support of the automotive fuel cell market under a series of agreements with Honda R&D Co., Ltd. of Japan. The company has a total of 150 issued patents, with 21 U.S. patent applications pending.

Plug Power offers employees medical, dental and vision insurance; life insurance; disability coverage; a 401(k) plan; and an employee stock purchase plan.

FINANCIALS: Sales and profits are in thousands of dollars—add 000 to get the full amount. 2011 Note: Financial information for 2011 was not available for all companies at press time.

2011 Sales: $	2011 Profits: $	U.S. Stock Ticker: PLUG
2010 Sales: $19,473	2010 Profits: $-46,959	Int'l Ticker:
2009 Sales: $12,293	2009 Profits: $-40,709	Int'l Exchange:
2008 Sales: $17,901	2008 Profits: $-121,700	Employees: 149 Fiscal Year Ends: 12/31
2007 Sales: $16,271	2007 Profits: $-60,571	Parent Company:

SALARIES/BENEFITS:

Pension Plan:	ESOP Stock Plan:	Profit Sharing:	Top Exec. Salary: $375,000	Bonus: $
Savings Plan: Y	Stock Purch. Plan: Y		Second Exec. Salary: $258,654	Bonus: $

OTHER THOUGHTS:

Apparent Women Officers or Directors: 1
Hot Spot for Advancement for Women/Minorities:

LOCATIONS: ("Y" = Yes)

West:	Southwest:	Midwest:	Southeast:	Northeast:	International:
				Y	Y

Sales, profits and employees may be estimates. Financial information, benefits and other data can change quickly and may vary from those stated here.

POWERFILM INC

www.iowathinfilm.com

Industry Group Code: 334413

Energy/Fuel:	Other Technologies:	Electrical Products:	Electronics:	Transportation:	Other:
Biofuels:	Irrigation:	Lighting/LEDs:	Computers:	Car Sharing:	Recycling:
Batteries/Storage:	Nanotech:	Waste Heat:	Sensors:	Electric Vehicles:	Engineering:
Solar: Y	Biotech:	Smart Meters:	Software:	Natural Gas Fuel:	Consulting:
Wind:	Water Tech./Treatment:	Machinery:			Investing:
Fuel Cells:	Ceramics:				Chemicals:

TYPES OF BUSINESS:

Photovoltaic Technology
Thin-Film Products
Semiconductors
Photovoltaic Tents

BRANDS/DIVISIONS/AFFILIATES:

Iowa Thin Film Technologies

CONTACTS: *Note: Officers with more than one job title may be intentionally listed here more than once.*

Frank Jeffrey, CEO
Merlin Hanson, Chmn.

Phone: 515-292-7606	Fax: 515-292-1922
Toll-Free: 888-354-7773	
Address: 2337 230th St., Ames, IA 50014 US	

GROWTH PLANS/SPECIAL FEATURES:

PowerFilm, Inc., formerly Iowa Thin Film Technologies, manufactures and develops thin, flexible solar panels based on its proprietary low-cost production process. Founded in 1988, the company focuses on developing thin film solar panel technology and an industrial scale manufacturing process to produce high volumes of low cost solar panels. The company's technology and manufacturing process includes the use of roll-to-roll manufacturing to minimize handling costs; a durable, flexible plastic substrate; printed interconnection to automate the cell connection process; and amorphous silicon to avoid dependence on the silicon wafer market cycle. In addition to its solar panel products, PowerFilm is in the process of leveraging its core roll-to-roll manufacturing competence to develop additional thin film semiconductor devices. The company maintains a technology partnership with Hewlett Packard Corporation, funded by the U.S. Display Consortium, to jointly develop flexible, low cost backplane drivers for next generation flat panel displays. PowerFilm hopes that this project, which is in the research and development phase, will enable the company to play a significant role in the future market of flat panel display technology. The company anticipates that future applications for PowerFilm's thin film semiconductor may include RFID tags and electronic paper.

FINANCIALS: Sales and profits are in thousands of dollars—add 000 to get the full amount. 2011 Note: Financial information for 2011 was not available for all companies at press time.

2011 Sales: $	2011 Profits: $	U.S. Stock Ticker: Private
2010 Sales: $	2010 Profits: $	Int'l Ticker:
2009 Sales: $	2009 Profits: $	Int'l Exchange:
2008 Sales: $	2008 Profits: $	Employees:　　　Fiscal Year Ends:
2007 Sales: $	2007 Profits: $	Parent Company:

SALARIES/BENEFITS:

Pension Plan:	ESOP Stock Plan:	Profit Sharing:	Top Exec. Salary: $	Bonus: $
Savings Plan:	Stock Purch. Plan:		Second Exec. Salary: $	Bonus: $

OTHER THOUGHTS:

Apparent Women Officers or Directors:
Hot Spot for Advancement for Women/Minorities:

LOCATIONS: ("Y" = Yes)

West:	Southwest:	Midwest:	Southeast:	Northeast:	International:
		Y			

PRIMEARTH EV ENERGY CO LTD

www.peve.jp

Industry Group Code: 33591

Energy/Fuel:		Other Technologies:	Electrical Products:	Electronics:	Transportation:	Other:
Biofuels:		Irrigation:	Lighting/LEDs:	Computers:	Car Sharing:	Recycling:
Batteries/Storage:	Y	Nanotech:	Waste Heat:	Sensors:	Electric Vehicles:	Engineering:
Solar:		Biotech:	Smart Meters:	Software:	Natural Gas Fuel:	Consulting:
Wind:		Water Tech./Treatment:	Machinery:			Investing:
Fuel Cells:		Ceramics:				Chemicals:

TYPES OF BUSINESS:

Battery Manufacturing-Hybrid Cars
Battery Management Systems

BRANDS/DIVISIONS/AFFILIATES:

Panasonic Corporation
Toyota Motor Corporation
Battery ECU
Panasonic Automotive Systems of America
Panasonic Corporation of North America
Panasonic EV Energy Co Ltd

CONTACTS: Note: Officers with more than one job title may be intentionally listed here more than once.

Yoshiro Hayashi, Pres.

Phone:	Fax:
Toll-Free: 800-211-7262	
Address: 20 Okasaki, Kosai, Shizuoka, 431-0422 Japan	

GROWTH PLANS/SPECIAL FEATURES:

Primearth EV Energy Co., Ltd., formerly Panasonic EV Energy Co., Ltd., develops manufactures and sells nickel metal-hydride batteries, primarily for hybrid electric vehicles (HEVs). Founded in 1996, it is a joint venture between Panasonic Corporation and Toyota Motor Corporation, with Toyota holding a majority stake of 80.5%. Primearth manufactures two HEV rechargeable batteries, the metal case prismatic and the plastic case prismatic modules, which both take up 14% less volume than conventional HEV batteries. Additionally, the metal case battery has a 40% higher cooling performance, and the plastic case battery is approximately 25% lighter than conventional HEV battery modules. Besides batteries, Primearth offers a battery management system known as Battery ECU, which monitors and controls the battery's functions, such as temperature and voltage. The firm's products are used in several current production model vehicles, including the Lexus LS600h, LS600hL, RX450h and GS450h; Toyota Prius, Crown Hybrid, Kluger Hybrid, Camry Hybrid and Estima Hybrid; Daihatsu Hijet Cargo Hybrid; and the Hino Dutro Hybrid. Although not its primary line of business, the company has historically supplied batteries for pure electric vehicles (PEVs) as well. The firm's U.S. sales group consists of Panasonic Automotive Systems of America, a division of Panasonic Corporation of North America, while its Japanese sales group comprises the Automotive Systems Company of Panasonic Corporation. Primearth maintains two production facilities in Kosai, Japan and one in Taiwa, Japan.

FINANCIALS: Sales and profits are in thousands of dollars—add 000 to get the full amount. 2011 Note: Financial information for 2011 was not available for all companies at press time.

2011 Sales: $	2011 Profits: $		**U.S. Stock Ticker:** Joint Venture		
2010 Sales: $	2010 Profits: $		**Int'l Ticker:**		
2009 Sales: $	2009 Profits: $		Int'l Exchange:		
2008 Sales: $	2008 Profits: $		Employees: 1,800	Fiscal Year Ends: 3/31	
2007 Sales: $	2007 Profits: $		Parent Company: TOYOTA MOTOR CORPORATION		

SALARIES/BENEFITS:

Pension Plan:	ESOP Stock Plan:	Profit Sharing:	Top Exec. Salary: $	Bonus: $
Savings Plan:	Stock Purch. Plan:		Second Exec. Salary: $	Bonus: $

OTHER THOUGHTS:

Apparent Women Officers or Directors:
Hot Spot for Advancement for Women/Minorities:

LOCATIONS: ("Y" = Yes)

West:	Southwest:	Midwest:	Southeast:	Northeast:	International:
					Y

PROJECT FROG

www.projectfrog.com

Industry Group Code: 332311

Energy/Fuel:	Other Technologies:	Electrical Products:	Electronics:	Transportation:	Other:	
Biofuels:	Irrigation:	Lighting/LEDs:	Computers:	Car Sharing:	Recycling:	
Batteries/Storage:	Nanotech:	Waste Heat:	Sensors:	Electric Vehicles:	Engineering:	Y
Solar:	Biotech:	Smart Meters:	Software:	Natural Gas Fuel:	Consulting:	
Wind:	Water Tech./Treatment:	Machinery:			Investing:	
Fuel Cells:	Ceramics:				Chemicals:	

TYPES OF BUSINESS:

Pre-Engineered Building Systems

BRANDS/DIVISIONS/AFFILIATES:

CONTACTS: *Note: Officers with more than one job title may be intentionally listed here more than once.*

Ann Hand, CEO
Adam Tibbs, Pres.
Nikki Tankursley, Dir.-Mktg.
Evan Nakamura, Sr. Dir.-Prod. Dev.
John Jackson, Dir.-Architecture
Margot Biehle, General Counsel
Brian Holte, VP-Bus. Dev.
Brian Schroth, VP-Dev.
Marijke Smit, VP-Program Dev.
Anne Gailliot, Dir.-Strategy & Performance
Dave Demaray, Dir.-Estimating
Chuck McDermott, Chmn.
Ash Notaney, VP-Supply Chain

Phone: 415-814-8500	Fax: 415-814-8501
Toll-Free:	
Address: 222 Vallejo St., Ste. 320, San Francisco, CA 94111 US	

GROWTH PLANS/SPECIAL FEATURES:

Project Frog is a green building firm utilizing environmentally conscious building materials and methods to create healthy, energy efficient spaces that are both faster to build than regular construction methods, but also are also highly cost competitive. By utilizing a number of proprietary products, the firm has created an easy to assemble kit of parts that can be rearranged and utilized in flexible, diversified methods. The firm's products are versatile and capable of being implemented in settings such as early childhood; higher education; K-12; healthcare; retreat; public; retail; and workplace facilities. Project Frog offers a high level of construction precision by systematizing the kit, process and the product's delivery. The firm's pre-engineered building systems allow for an accelerated building construction of less than six months from the initial project contract to its occupancy. Each space provides high fresh air ventilation rates and low to no VOC emissions. The firm's technological innovations primarily focus on the areas of parametric design; precision fabrication; lean manufacturing and logistics processing; multidimensional energy performance prediction; and real time monitoring and continuous commissioning. When looking at a 50-year assessment of a Project Frog building, it was found that the firm's structure caused approximately 87% less fossil fuel use, 85% less climate change, 82% less air pollution and 73% less water pollution than comparable buildings using an average amount of energy. The firm is currently working on a 4,000 square foot LEED Gold facility at GE's John F. Welch Leadership Development Center in Ossining, New York. Future projects include an agriculture administrative headquarters in Kauai, Hawaii and the centerpiece building of the Delta Science Center in Oakley, California. In September 2011, GE Energy Financial Services, Claremont Creek Ventures, Greener Capital Partners and RockPort Capital Partners invested $22 million in Project Frog.

FINANCIALS: Sales and profits are in thousands of dollars—add 000 to get the full amount. 2011 Note: Financial information for 2011 was not available for all companies at press time.

2011 Sales: $	2011 Profits: $	**U.S. Stock Ticker:** Private
2010 Sales: $	2010 Profits: $	**Int'l Ticker:**
2009 Sales: $	2009 Profits: $	Int'l Exchange:
2008 Sales: $	2008 Profits: $	Employees: Fiscal Year Ends:
2007 Sales: $	2007 Profits: $	Parent Company:

SALARIES/BENEFITS:

Pension Plan:	ESOP Stock Plan:	Profit Sharing:	Top Exec. Salary: $	Bonus: $
Savings Plan:	Stock Purch. Plan:		Second Exec. Salary: $	Bonus: $

OTHER THOUGHTS:

Apparent Women Officers or Directors: 10
Hot Spot for Advancement for Women/Minorities: Y

LOCATIONS: ("Y" = Yes)

West:	Southwest:	Midwest:	Southeast:	Northeast:	International:
Y					

PURALYTICS

Industry Group Code: 924110

www.puralytics.com

Energy/Fuel:	Other Technologies:		Electrical Products:	Electronics:	Transportation:	Other:	
Biofuels:	Irrigation:		Lighting/LEDs:	Computers:	Car Sharing:	Recycling:	
Batteries/Storage:	Nanotech:		Waste Heat:	Sensors:	Electric Vehicles:	Engineering:	
Solar:	Biotech:		Smart Meters:	Software:	Natural Gas Fuel:	Consulting:	
Wind:	Water Tech./Treatment:	Y	Machinery:			Investing:	
Fuel Cells:	Ceramics:					Chemicals:	

TYPES OF BUSINESS:

Water Purification Technology

BRANDS/DIVISIONS/AFFILIATES:

SolarBag
Shield

CONTACTS: *Note: Officers with more than one job title may be intentionally listed here more than once.*

Mark Owen, CEO
Tom Hawkins, VP-Eng.
Dave Moser, VP-Bus. Dev.

Phone:	Fax:
Toll-Free: 866-462-0282	
Address: 15250 NW Greenbrier Pkwy., Beaverton, OR 97006 US	

GROWTH PLANS/SPECIAL FEATURES:

Puralytics is a water purification technology firm. Its proprietary technology uses light-activated nanotechnology to destroy rather than capture water contaminants. The process involves five photochemical processes that synergistically work together: photocatalytic oxidation; photocatalytic reduction; photolysis; photoadsorption; and photo disinfection. Photocatalytic reduction and absorption provides advanced heavy metal removal. Additionally, increased UV energy enhances and accelerates the photolysis and disinfection of the pathogens. The technology offers superior hydroxyl radical production without the use of chemical additives. The company effectively reduces, absorbs and oxidizes dichromate, arsenic and lead, as well as oxidizes and disinfects legionella. Puralytics offers two product families: SolarBag and Shield. SolarBag uses solar power to purify water without needing the addition of outside sources of light, electricity or chemicals throughout the process. The product is beneficial for developing countries, emergency preparedness, outdoor recreation and military individual water purifiers. Shield incorporates light emitting diodes (LED), which are excellent for stimulating photocatalytic reactions. The system is used in applications that require between 200-2,000 gallons per day of pure water from each unit. The product can be used in industrial laboratories; well water purification; waste waster polishing; military and remote locations; grey water recycling; and point of entry or point of use purification for commercial facilities.

FINANCIALS: Sales and profits are in thousands of dollars—add 000 to get the full amount. 2011 Note: Financial information for 2011 was not available for all companies at press time.

2011 Sales: $	2011 Profits: $	**U.S. Stock Ticker: Private**
2010 Sales: $	2010 Profits: $	**Int'l Ticker:**
2009 Sales: $	2009 Profits: $	Int'l Exchange:
2008 Sales: $	2008 Profits: $	Employees: Fiscal Year Ends:
2007 Sales: $	2007 Profits: $	Parent Company:

SALARIES/BENEFITS:

Pension Plan:	ESOP Stock Plan:	Profit Sharing:	Top Exec. Salary: $	Bonus: $
Savings Plan:	Stock Purch. Plan:		Second Exec. Salary: $	Bonus: $

OTHER THOUGHTS:

Apparent Women Officers or Directors:
Hot Spot for Advancement for Women/Minorities:

LOCATIONS: ("Y" = Yes)

West:	Southwest:	Midwest:	Southeast:	Northeast:	International:
Y					

PURFRESH

www.purfresh.com

Industry Group Code: 483111

Energy/Fuel:	Other Technologies:	Electrical Products:	Electronics:		Transportation:		Other:	
Biofuels:	Irrigation:	Lighting/LEDs:	Computers:		Car Sharing:		Recycling:	
Batteries/Storage:	Nanotech:	Waste Heat:	Sensors:		Electric Vehicles:		Engineering:	
Solar:	Biotech:	Smart Meters:	Software:	Y	Natural Gas Fuel:		Consulting:	
Wind:	Water Tech./Treatment:	Machinery:					Investing:	
Fuel Cells:	Ceramics:						Chemicals:	

TYPES OF BUSINESS:

Shipping-Deep Sea
Produce Transport

BRANDS/DIVISIONS/AFFILIATES:

Purfresh
Intellipur

CONTACTS: Note: Officers with more than one job title may be intentionally listed here more than once.

Brian Westcott, CEO
Brian Westcott, Pres.
Claude-Nicolas Fiechter, VP-Software Dev.
Robert Hayes, VP-Eng.
Ram Prasad, VP-Oper.
Ram Prasad, VP-Finance
David Bouchard, Gen. Mgr.
John Harnett, Sr. Dir.-Purfresh Transport
Malcolm Dodd, Mgr.-Purfresh Africa
Frederick L. A. Grauer, Chmn.
Joseph Hajost, VP-Global Field Oper.

Phone: 510-580-0700	**Fax:** 510-580-0701
Toll-Free:	
Address: 47211 Bayside Pkwy., Fremont, CA 94538 US	

GROWTH PLANS/SPECIAL FEATURES:

Purfresh is an ocean transport solution firm, utilizing its proprietary cargo protection and advanced technology in the transport of fresh produce around the world. The firm's methods offer its customer's reduced profit losses, expanded market opportunities and the assurance of high-quality produce reaching the market. The company offers services including installation and de-installation of Purfresh transport systems; regional central repair and exchange facilities to perform both preventative maintenance as well as system checks; logistics planning; and around the clock data center monitoring to monitor the container throughout the duration of its trip. The Purfresh method of produce transport includes full trip transparency as well as active atmosphere enhancement. These allow for an increased level of prevention against decay; the ability to control ripening; and the reduction of food-borne pathogens. The firm's chemical free methods are optimal for the shipment of both conventional and organic foodstuffs, including apples, bananas, berries, citrus, mangos, potatoes and tomatoes. The company offers its customers informatics software in the form of its Intellipur subscription informatics services. The system includes features such as operational control; a web-based data historian; diagnostic monitoring application; reporting; and automated alarming. Intellipur allows the customer to readily produce and compile cold chain environment reports for storage and transportation as well as to document evidence of control to present to food safety auditors. Purfresh partners include Del Monte; Dole; Freshco; Evergreen; DHL; Kuehne & Nagel; and Univeg.

FINANCIALS: Sales and profits are in thousands of dollars—add 000 to get the full amount. 2011 Note: Financial information for 2011 was not available for all companies at press time.

2011 Sales: $	2011 Profits: $	**U.S. Stock Ticker: Private**	
2010 Sales: $	2010 Profits: $	**Int'l Ticker:**	
2009 Sales: $	2009 Profits: $	Int'l Exchange:	
2008 Sales: $	2008 Profits: $	Employees:	Fiscal Year Ends:
2007 Sales: $	2007 Profits: $	Parent Company:	

SALARIES/BENEFITS:

Pension Plan:	ESOP Stock Plan:	Profit Sharing:	Top Exec. Salary: $	Bonus: $
Savings Plan:	Stock Purch. Plan:		Second Exec. Salary: $	Bonus: $

OTHER THOUGHTS:

Apparent Women Officers or Directors:
Hot Spot for Advancement for Women/Minorities:

LOCATIONS: ("Y" = Yes)

West:	Southwest:	Midwest:	Southeast:	Northeast:	International:
Y					

Q.CELLS SE

Industry Group Code: 334413

www.q-cells.com

Energy/Fuel:	Other Technologies:		Electrical Products:	Electronics:	Transportation:	Other:
Biofuels:	Irrigation:		Lighting/LEDs:	Computers:	Car Sharing:	Recycling:
Batteries/Storage:	Nanotech:	Y	Waste Heat:	Sensors:	Electric Vehicles:	Engineering:
Solar:	Biotech:		Smart Meters:	Software:	Natural Gas Fuel:	Consulting:
Wind:	Water Tech./Treatment:		Machinery:			Investing:
Fuel Cells:	Ceramics:					Chemicals:

TYPES OF BUSINESS:

Solar Cells Manufacturing
String Ribbon Solar Cell Technology
Crystalline Silicon on Glass Technology
Solar Park Planning & Development

BRANDS/DIVISIONS/AFFILIATES:

Q-Cells International GmbH
Calyxo GmbH
VHF-Technologies SA
SunFilm AG
Solibro GmbH
VHF-Technologies SA

CONTACTS: *Note: Officers with more than one job title may be intentionally listed here more than once.*

Nedim Cen, CEO
Andreas Von Zitzewitz, COO
Clemens Jargon, Head-Mktg. & Sales
Nedim Cen, Head-Human Resources
Andreas Von Zitzewitz, Head-R&D
Nedim Cen, Head-Legal & Compliance
Nedim Cen, Head-Corp. Strategy
Nedim Cen, Head-Corp. Comm.
Florian Holzapfel, CEO-Calyxo GmbH
Franz Vollmann, Managing Dir.-Malaysia
Karlheinz Hornung, Chmn.
Marc Van Gerven, CEO-Q-Cells North America
Andreas Von Zitzewitz, Head-Purchasing & Logistics

Phone: 49-3494-6699-0	Fax: 49-3494-6699-199
Toll-Free:	
Address: Sonnenallee 17-21, Bitterfeld-Wolfen, 06766 Germany	

GROWTH PLANS/SPECIAL FEATURES:

Q-Cells SE is one of the top European manufacturers and marketers of integrated solar systems, producing solar cells, modules and large-scale solar grids. It also works to expand thin-film technologies through its subsidiaries. The firm offers three main photovoltaic (PV) cell products. The Q6LMXP3 is a mono-crystalline cell that offers 10% more power than multi-crystalline formats and has a mean efficiency of 18.8%. The Q6LPT3-G2 is multi-crystalline cell with a raw material structure that is rendered nearly invisible through an acid texturing process, improving light absorption and a nominal efficiency of 15.4%-17.4%. The Q6LTT-G23 is similar to the Q6LPT3-G2, also featuring an acid-textured surface for better light absorption; in addition, this cell features a backside with 3x6 busbar pads. The firm has several subsidiaries, including Q-Cells International GmbH, which develops and operates large solar parks and rooftop arrays; and Solibro GmbH, a producer of thin-film solar modules. Additionally, the firm owns a 93% share in Calyxo GmbH, which produces thin-film modules based on a cadmium-telluride technology for which Q-Cells owns a worldwide license. It holds a 58% share of VHF-Technologies SA, a Switzerland-based company developing a technology for applying silicon on a flexible plastic substrate in order to produce flexible solar modules. Q-Cells also maintains a 50% interest in SunFilm AG, a producer of tandem junction silicon based thin-film solar modules. In March 2011, the firm announced plans to expand into the U.K. market and that it would be opening an office in London. In April 2011, Q-Cells announced its entry into the Japanese residential market with integrated PV solutions, making it the first German company to do so. In July 2011, the firm announced the sale of its Zerbst II power plant to MCG Management Capital Group.

FINANCIALS: Sales and profits are in thousands of dollars—add 000 to get the full amount. 2011 Note: Financial information for 2011 was not available for all companies at press time.

2011 Sales: $	2011 Profits: $	**U.S. Stock Ticker:**
2010 Sales: $1,924,500	2010 Profits: $26,900	**Int'l Ticker: QCE**
2009 Sales: $1,047,150	2009 Profits: $-1,771,640	Int'l Exchange: Frankfurt-Euronext
2008 Sales: $1,634,610	2008 Profits: $248,990	Employees: 2,379 Fiscal Year Ends: 12/31
2007 Sales: $1,116,600	2007 Profits: $192,900	Parent Company:

SALARIES/BENEFITS:

Pension Plan:	ESOP Stock Plan:	Profit Sharing:	Top Exec. Salary: $550,223	Bonus: $566,925
Savings Plan:	Stock Purch. Plan:		Second Exec. Salary: $436,154	Bonus: $449,156

OTHER THOUGHTS:

Apparent Women Officers or Directors:
Hot Spot for Advancement for Women/Minorities:

LOCATIONS: ("Y" = Yes)

West:	Southwest:	Midwest:	Southeast:	Northeast:	International:
Y					Y

QTEROS INC

www.qteros.com

Industry Group Code: 325193

Energy/Fuel:		Other Technologies:		Electrical Products:	Electronics:	Transportation:	Other:
Biofuels:	Y	Irrigation:		Lighting/LEDs:	Computers:	Car Sharing:	Recycling:
Batteries/Storage:		Nanotech:		Waste Heat:	Sensors:	Electric Vehicles:	Engineering:
Solar:		Biotech:	Y	Smart Meters:	Software:	Natural Gas Fuel:	Consulting:
Wind:		Water Tech./Treatment:		Machinery:			Investing:
Fuel Cells:		Ceramics:					Chemicals:

TYPES OF BUSINESS:

Cellulosic Ethanol Technology
Bioethanol Manufacturing

BRANDS/DIVISIONS/AFFILIATES:

Q Microbe
Battery Ventures
Venrock Associates
Soros Fund Management LLC
Valero Energy Corp
Long River Ventures
Camros Capital LLC
BP AE Ventures

CONTACTS: Note: Officers with more than one job title may be intentionally listed here more than once.

Mick Sawka, CEO
Kevin A. Gray, Chief Scientific Officer
Susan T. Hager, VP-Corp. Comm. & Gov't Affairs
Christopher J. Dale, VP-R&D
Steve Goldby, Chmn.

Phone: 508-281-4060	Fax:
Toll-Free:	
Address: 100 Campus Dr., 6th Fl., Marlborough, MA 01752 US	

GROWTH PLANS/SPECIAL FEATURES:

Qteros, Inc. is a developer of biomass-to-ethanol technology. The company's premier technology, Q Microbe, is a microscopic organism that breaks down cellulose and hemicellulosic plant materials into simple sugars. The products of this process can then be fermented by yeast into ethanol. By producing its own enzyme, the Q Microbe can simplify the production process and reduce costs associated with conventional conversion schemes. The firm searches for the best biomass materials by conducting research on feedstock and municipal wastewater to find easily exploitable and efficient resources. The company is working on a $3.2 million pilot plant intended to test and implement the Q Microbe technology in large-scale applications. Qteros is owned by the following investors: Battery Ventures, Venrock Associates, Soros Fund Management, LLC, Valero Energy Corp., Long River Ventures, Camros Capital, LLC and BP AE Ventures. In January 2011, the firm and Praj Industries Limited formed a partnership to increase the speed at which industrial-scale cellulosic ethanol products are marketed.

Qteros offers its employees medical, dental and vision insurance; flexible spending accounts; paid time off and holidays; an employee assistance program; short- and long-term disability; life and AD&D insurance; a 401(k) plan; and an employee referral program.

FINANCIALS: Sales and profits are in thousands of dollars—add 000 to get the full amount. 2011 Note: Financial information for 2011 was not available for all companies at press time.

2011 Sales: $	2011 Profits: $	U.S. Stock Ticker: Private
2010 Sales: $	2010 Profits: $	Int'l Ticker:
2009 Sales: $	2009 Profits: $	Int'l Exchange:
2008 Sales: $	2008 Profits: $	Employees: Fiscal Year Ends:
2007 Sales: $	2007 Profits: $	Parent Company:

SALARIES/BENEFITS:

Pension Plan:	ESOP Stock Plan:	Profit Sharing:	Top Exec. Salary: $	Bonus: $
Savings Plan: Y	Stock Purch. Plan:		Second Exec. Salary: $	Bonus: $

OTHER THOUGHTS:

Apparent Women Officers or Directors: 1
Hot Spot for Advancement for Women/Minorities:

LOCATIONS: ("Y" = Yes)

West:	Southwest:	Midwest:	Southeast:	Northeast:	International:
				Y	

QUANTUM FUEL SYSTEMS TECHNOLOGIES WORLDWIDE INC

www.qtww.com

Industry Group Code: 3363

Energy/Fuel:		Other Technologies:		Electrical Products:		Electronics:		Transportation:		Other:	
Biofuels:		Irrigation:		Lighting/LEDs:		Computers:		Car Sharing:		Recycling:	
Batteries/Storage:	Y	Nanotech:		Waste Heat:		Sensors:		Electric Vehicles:	Y	Engineering:	Y
Solar:		Biotech:		Smart Meters:	Y	Software:		Natural Gas Fuel:	Y	Consulting:	
Wind:		Water Tech./Treatment:		Machinery:	Y					Investing:	
Fuel Cells:	Y	Ceramics:								Chemicals:	

TYPES OF BUSINESS:

Fuel Storage Systems
Design & Testing Services
Fuel Delivery & Control Systems
Hydrogen Refueling Products
Fuel-Cell Vehicle Infrastructure
Lithium Ion & Advanced Battery Control Systems
Systems Integration

BRANDS/DIVISIONS/AFFILIATES:

Schneider Power Inc
Q-Drive
Fisker Automotive Inc
Fisker Karma

CONTACTS: Note: Officers with more than one job title may be intentionally listed here more than once.

Alan P. Niedzwiecki, CEO
David Mazaika, COO
Alan P. Niedzwiecki, Pres.
W. Brian Olson, CFO
Neel Sirosh, CTO
Kenneth R. Lombardo, General Counsel/Corp. Sec.
Bradley J. Timon, Chief Acct. Officer/Corp. Controller
Dale L. Rasmussen, Chmn.

Phone: 949-399-4500	Fax: 949-399-4600
Toll-Free:	
Address: 17872 Cartwright Rd., Irvine, CA 92614 US	

GROWTH PLANS/SPECIAL FEATURES:

Quantum Fuel Systems Technologies Worldwide, Inc. develops and produces advanced propulsion systems, energy storage technologies and alternative fuel vehicles. Its technologies include electronic controls; hybrid electric drive systems; hydrogen and natural gas storage; metering systems; and alternative fuel technologies for low emission hybrid, plug-in electric hybrid, fuel cell and alternative fuel vehicles. The company's business operations consist of three segments: Electric Drive & Fuel Systems, Renewable Energy and Corporate. The Electric Drive & Fuel Systems segment supplies advanced propulsion and fuel systems for alternative fuel vehicles to original equipment manufacturer (OEM) customers for use by consumers and for commercial and government fleets. Since 1997, the company has sold approximately 20,000 fuel systems for alternative vehicles. Most of these sales have been made to General Motors. The Renewable Energy segment consists of the business operations of recently acquired Schneider Power, Inc., a Canadian renewable energy company. Quantum Fuel Systems' Corporate division consists of general and administrative expenses incurred at the corporate level that are not directly attributable to the automotive segment. The company is a co-founder of Fisker Automotive, Inc., an American company that sells luxury sports cars based on plug-in hybrid electric vehicle technology. All Fisker Automotive vehicles will feature Q-Drive, Quantum's plug-in hybrid electric vehicle technology. The first Fisker model, the Fisker Karma, is expected to be produced in the near future.

FINANCIALS: Sales and profits are in thousands of dollars—add 000 to get the full amount. 2011 Note: Financial information for 2011 was not available for all companies at press time.

2011 Sales: $20,274	2011 Profits: $-110,330	**U.S. Stock Ticker:** QTWW
2010 Sales: $9,605	2010 Profits: $-46,294	**Int'l Ticker:**
2009 Sales: $23,258	2009 Profits: $-27,993	Int'l Exchange:
2008 Sales: $26,497	2008 Profits: $-86,800	Employees: 102 Fiscal Year Ends: 4/30
2007 Sales: $17,679	2007 Profits: $-140,530	Parent Company:

SALARIES/BENEFITS:

Pension Plan:	ESOP Stock Plan:	Profit Sharing:	Top Exec. Salary: $725,000	Bonus: $
Savings Plan: Y	Stock Purch. Plan:		Second Exec. Salary: $600,000	Bonus: $

OTHER THOUGHTS:

Apparent Women Officers or Directors:
Hot Spot for Advancement for Women/Minorities:

LOCATIONS: ("Y" = Yes)

West:	Southwest:	Midwest:	Southeast:	Northeast:	International:
Y	Y	Y	Y		Y

RECYCLED ENERGY DEVELOPMENT LLC   www.recycled-energy.com

Industry Group Code: 541690

Energy/Fuel:	Other Technologies:	Electrical Products:	Electronics:	Transportation:	Other:
Biofuels:	Irrigation:	Lighting/LEDs:	Computers:	Car Sharing:	Recycling:
Batteries/Storage:	Nanotech:	Waste Heat: Y	Sensors:	Electric Vehicles:	Engineering:
Solar:	Biotech:	Smart Meters:	Software:	Natural Gas Fuel:	Consulting:
Wind:	Water Tech./Treatment:	Machinery:			Investing:
Fuel Cells:	Ceramics:				Chemicals:

TYPES OF BUSINESS:

Co-Generation Technology
Waste Heat-to-Energy

BRANDS/DIVISIONS/AFFILIATES:

Turbosteam LLC

CONTACTS: Note: Officers with more than one job title may be intentionally listed here more than once.

Sean Casten, CEO
Sean Casten, Pres.
Aaron Walters, CFO
Gary Hoppenrath, VP-Eng. & Construction
Myra Karegianes, General Counsel/Sr. VP
Eric Gottung, VP-Bus. Dev.
Dick Munson, Sr. VP-Public Affairs
Scott Kerrigan, Controller/VP
Andres Pena, Sr. VP-Projects & Construction
Leif Bergquist, VP-Bus. Dev.
John Wilson, VP-Bus. Dev.
John Whitehouse, VP-Bus. Dev.
Thomas R. Casten, Chmn.

Phone: 630-590-6030	Fax: 630-590-6037
Toll-Free:	
Address: 640 Quail Ridge Dr., Westmont, IL 60559 US	

GROWTH PLANS/SPECIAL FEATURES:

Recycled Energy Development, LLC (RED) is a clean energy provider focused on developing combined heat and power (cogeneration) facilities and providing waste heat recovery services to existing power plants. The firm aims to reduce greenhouse-gas emissions, as well as reduce energy costs and increase power generation by using waste heat to produce thermal power and electricity. The company also aims to create increased profits for industrial partners by reducing costs, increasing output and providing the possibility of carbon credits. RED provides all of the necessary equipment, capital and services for the development, installation and long-term operation of recycled energy projects, which include combined heat and power plants (CHP) and waste energy recovery. It builds CHP facilities for industrial operations and other large institutions, allowing them to recycle excess heat emitted in the power generation process and use it to power their own operations and resulting in lower electricity costs. The firm's waste energy recovery operations similarly capture energy that manufacturers emit as waste and recycle it into useful forms of heating and cooling. In exchange for RED supplying the capital and operating the energy equipment, customers generally enter into a long-term power purchase agreement with RED. Turbosteam, the company's wholly-owned subsidiary, is a converter of waste energy into electricity. It has installed more than 180 systems in 32 states and 18 countries, saved customers $200 million and lowered global CO_2 emissions by over 4 million tons. Turbostream's services include detailed site engineering; design optimization; and capital equipment and turnkey installations.

FINANCIALS: Sales and profits are in thousands of dollars—add 000 to get the full amount. 2011 Note: Financial information for 2011 was not available for all companies at press time.

2011 Sales: $	2011 Profits: $	U.S. Stock Ticker: Private
2010 Sales: $	2010 Profits: $	Int'l Ticker:
2009 Sales: $	2009 Profits: $	Int'l Exchange:
2008 Sales: $	2008 Profits: $	Employees: Fiscal Year Ends:
2007 Sales: $	2007 Profits: $	Parent Company:

SALARIES/BENEFITS:

Pension Plan:	ESOP Stock Plan:	Profit Sharing:	Top Exec. Salary: $	Bonus: $
Savings Plan:	Stock Purch. Plan:		Second Exec. Salary: $	Bonus: $

OTHER THOUGHTS:

Apparent Women Officers or Directors: 1
Hot Spot for Advancement for Women/Minorities:

LOCATIONS: ("Y" = Yes)

West:	Southwest:	Midwest:	Southeast:	Northeast:	International:
		Y		Y	

Sales, profits and employees may be estimates. Financial information, benefits and other data can change quickly and may vary from those stated here.

RELION INC

Industry Group Code: 335999

www.relion-inc.com

Energy/Fuel:		Other Technologies:		Electrical Products:		Electronics:	Transportation:	Other:	
Biofuels:		Irrigation:		Lighting/LEDs:		Computers:	Car Sharing:	Recycling:	
Batteries/Storage:	Y	Nanotech:		Waste Heat:		Sensors:	Electric Vehicles:	Engineering:	
Solar:		Biotech:		Smart Meters:		Software:	Natural Gas Fuel:	Consulting:	
Wind:		Water Tech./Treatment:		Machinery:				Investing:	
Fuel Cells:	Y	Ceramics:						Chemicals:	

TYPES OF BUSINESS:

Fuel Cell Technology
Backup Power Systems

BRANDS/DIVISIONS/AFFILIATES:

Modular Cartridge Technology
Avista Corporation
E200
T-1000
T-2000
E-2500

CONTACTS: *Note: Officers with more than one job title may be intentionally listed here more than once.*

Gary Flood, CEO
Joe Blanchard, COO
Gary Flood, Pres.
Jim Baumker, CFO
Bill Stafford, VP-Sales
Christie Allen, Dir.-Human Resources
William Fuglevand, VP-R&D
Mark Grimes, VP-Eng.
Christie Allen, Dir.-Admin.
Christie Allen, Corp. Sec.
Michele Wood, VP-Finance

Phone: 509-228-6500	**Fax:** 509-228-6510
Toll-Free: 877-474-1993	
Address: 15913 E. Euclid Ave., Spokane, WA 99216 US	

GROWTH PLANS/SPECIAL FEATURES:

ReliOn, Inc., a majority-owned subsidiary of Avista Corporation, is a developer and marketer of modular proton exchange membrane (PEM) fuel cell products. The company produces a variety of fuel cell products using its patented Modular Cartridge Technology that has only one movable part, a high-efficiency fan. ReliOn products are available for the home and business as back-up power applications ranging from 100 watts (W) to 12 kilowatts (kW) of energy. The firm's fuel cells are able to run on bottled hydrogen and other substantially pure hydrogen sources and can be exchanged while operating. The company has three main products, which serve the telecommunications, security, transportation, utility and government sectors. The E200, with a power range of less than 200W to 500W, is a hydrogen fueled fuel cell system used for small-scale backup power applications. The E-1100 which is a hydrogen fuel cell that offers 1100W of power in a rack-mountable package. The T-1000, with a power range of 100W to 1,200W, is a fuel cell system created specifically for communications backup power applications. The T-2000 fuel cell system, with a power range of 100W to 6kW, assists in large communications backup power loads. More than 2,100kW of fuel cells have been sold to customers in the U.S., Europe, South America, Africa, Asia and Australia. The firm currently has 33 U.S. patents and 18 foreign patents. The company has a number of distribution partners including, Alpine Power Systems, ARMS Power, Consistel, Relong, Technical Distributors and Sysdyne. Relion has a 29,300 square foot facility in Spokane, Washington for research and development, product development, administration and sales and marketing. The company also operates a main office in Beijing. In March 2011, the firm introduced the E-2500 fuel cell system, a compact system that offers approximately 2,500W of power.

Employees are offered medical, dental, and vision insurance; flexible spending accounts; life and AD&D insurance; short- and long-term disability coverage; a 401(k) plan; and tuition assistance.

FINANCIALS: Sales and profits are in thousands of dollars—add 000 to get the full amount. 2011 Note: Financial information for 2011 was not available for all companies at press time.

2011 Sales: $	2011 Profits: $	**U.S. Stock Ticker:** Subsidiary		
2010 Sales: $	2010 Profits: $	**Int'l Ticker:**		
2009 Sales: $	2009 Profits: $	Int'l Exchange:		
2008 Sales: $	2008 Profits: $	Employees:	Fiscal Year Ends: 12/31	
2007 Sales: $	2007 Profits: $	Parent Company: AVISTA CORPORATION		

SALARIES/BENEFITS:

Pension Plan:	ESOP Stock Plan:	Profit Sharing:	Top Exec. Salary: $	Bonus: $
Savings Plan: Y	Stock Purch. Plan:		Second Exec. Salary: $	Bonus: $

OTHER THOUGHTS:

Apparent Women Officers or Directors: 2
Hot Spot for Advancement for Women/Minorities:

LOCATIONS: ("Y" = Yes)

West:	Southwest:	Midwest:	Southeast:	Northeast:	International:
Y					Y

RENEGY HOLDINGS INC

www.renegy.com

Industry Group Code: 541712

Energy/Fuel:		Other Technologies:		Electrical Products:		Electronics:		Transportation:		Other:	
Biofuels:	Y	Irrigation:		Lighting/LEDs:		Computers:		Car Sharing:		Recycling:	
Batteries/Storage:		Nanotech:		Waste Heat:		Sensors:		Electric Vehicles:		Engineering:	
Solar:		Biotech:	Y	Smart Meters:		Software:		Natural Gas Fuel:		Consulting:	
Wind:		Water Tech./Treatment:		Machinery:						Investing:	
Fuel Cells:		Ceramics:								Chemicals:	

TYPES OF BUSINESS:

Biomass Renewable Energy

BRANDS/DIVISIONS/AFFILIATES:

Catalytica Energy Systems Inc
NZ Legacy LLC
Snowflake White Mountain Power
Arizona Public Services
Salt River Project

CONTACTS: *Note: Officers with more than one job title may be intentionally listed here more than once.*

Robert M. Worsley, CEO
Robert M. Worsley, Chmn.

Phone: 480-556-5555	Fax: 480-556-5500
Toll-Free:	
Address: 3418 N. Val Vista Dr., Mesa, AZ 85213 US	

GROWTH PLANS/SPECIAL FEATURES:

Renegy Holdings, Inc. develops and operates a portfolio of biomass to electricity power generation facilities using wood waste as their primary fuel source. The company was formed through a merger of Catalytica Energy Systems, Inc. and the renewable energy divisions of NZ Legacy LLC. Renegy's flagship project is Snowflake White Mountain Power, a 24-megawatt (MW) biomass plant near Snowflake, Arizona. The facility is fueled by a mix of wood waste material, derived from the surrounding National forests and local green waste sites, and waste recycled paper fibers from a newsprint mill located adjacent to the plant site. Other sources for biomass energy include green waste from landfills; sawmill waste; agricultural crops grown for energy uses and other agricultural waste; woody construction and debris waste; animal and ethanol waste; municipal solid waste, such as sewage sludge; and other industrial waste. The facility has two long-term power purchase agreements in place with Arizona Public Services and Salt River Project, Arizona's two largest electric utility companies. The company also owns a 13 MW biomass plant in Susanville, California, which is currently idle. Renegy has more than 1,000 MW of identified biomass energy projects targeted for its near-term growth. Other business activities include an established fuel aggregation and wood products division, which collects and transports forest thinnings and other woody waste biomass fuel to the company's power plants, and which sells logs, lumber, wood shavings and other high value wood by-products. Snowflake White Mountain Power is currently under Chapter 11 bankruptcy protection.

FINANCIALS: Sales and profits are in thousands of dollars—add 000 to get the full amount. 2011 Note: Financial information for 2011 was not available for all companies at press time.

2011 Sales: $	2011 Profits: $	**U.S. Stock Ticker: Private**
2010 Sales: $	2010 Profits: $	**Int'l Ticker:**
2009 Sales: $	2009 Profits: $	Int'l Exchange:
2008 Sales: $	2008 Profits: $	Employees: Fiscal Year Ends: 12/31
2007 Sales: $	2007 Profits: $	Parent Company:

SALARIES/BENEFITS:

Pension Plan:	ESOP Stock Plan:	Profit Sharing:	Top Exec. Salary: $	Bonus: $
Savings Plan:	Stock Purch. Plan:		Second Exec. Salary: $	Bonus: $

OTHER THOUGHTS:

Apparent Women Officers or Directors:
Hot Spot for Advancement for Women/Minorities:

LOCATIONS: ("Y" = Yes)

West:	Southwest:	Midwest:	Southeast:	Northeast:	International:
Y	Y				

RENEWABLE ENERGY SYSTEMS

www.res-group.com

Industry Group Code: 221119

Energy/Fuel:	Other Technologies:	Electrical Products:	Electronics:	Transportation:	Other:	
Biofuels:	Irrigation:	Lighting/LEDs:	Computers:	Car Sharing:	Recycling:	
Batteries/Storage:	Nanotech:	Waste Heat:	Sensors:	Electric Vehicles:	Engineering:	
Solar:	Biotech:	Smart Meters:	Software:	Natural Gas Fuel:	Consulting:	Y
Wind:	Water Tech./Treatment:	Machinery:			Investing:	
Fuel Cells:	Ceramics:				Chemicals:	

TYPES OF BUSINESS:

Alternative Energy Generation
Sustainability Consultancy

BRANDS/DIVISIONS/AFFILIATES:

RES Group
Future Heating Limited
Inbuilt
RES Americas Inc

CONTACTS: *Note: Officers with more than one job title may be intentionally listed here more than once.*

Ian Mays, CEO
Stephen Balint, Dir.-Strategy & Comm.
Anna Stanford, Head-Corp. Comm.
Stefan Foster, Managing Dir.-Inbuilt
David Strong, CEO-Inbuilt
Thomas Riboud, Dir.-RES Southern Africa
Susan Reilly, CEO-RES Americas

Phone: 44-1923-299-200	Fax: 44-1923-299-299
Toll-Free:	
Address: Beaufort Court, Egg Farm Lane, Kings Langley, Hertfordshire, WD4 8LR UK	

GROWTH PLANS/SPECIAL FEATURES:

Renewable Energy Systems, known as the RES Group, is a U.K.-based developer and operator of renewable energy projects, with a primary focus on wind generation. In addition, the RES Group is an independent power producer, with a portfolio of some 700 megawatts (MW) of wind energy capacity. Since its inception, the firm has constructed almost 93 on- and offshore wind farms with a combined capacity of over 5,000 MW, including 3,600 MW in North America, 500 MW in the U.K. and Ireland, 350 MW in France and the remaining capacity across Europe. The company is in the process of developing wind farms in Scandinavia, the U.S., Australia, Canada, Ireland, France and the U.K. Aside from wind projects, the company offers construction services for solar plants using either photovoltaic power (PV) or concentrated solar power (CSP) and has also begun construction on two biomass facilities in the U.K. Through Inbuilt, the company offers expertise and consulting to businesses seeking to reduce their carbon footprint, offering strategic sustainability, carbon management and renewable energy consultancy. Other subsidiaries include RES Americas, Inc., headquartered in Colorado, which has over 12,500 MW of wind projects in development. In late 2010, the company announced plans to develop a biomass plant within the Port of Liverpool. Also in 2010, RES Group acquired the outstanding shares of Future Heating Limited, a developer of large-scale solar thermal systems. In May 2011, the company sold its Keadby Wind Farm in North Lincolnshire, England to SSE Renewables. In September 2011, the firm agreed to sell its Taralga Wind Farm in New South Wales to AusChina Energy group.

FINANCIALS: Sales and profits are in thousands of dollars—add 000 to get the full amount. 2011 Note: Financial information for 2011 was not available for all companies at press time.

2011 Sales: $	2011 Profits: $	**U.S. Stock Ticker: Private**
2010 Sales: $	2010 Profits: $	**Int'l Ticker:**
2009 Sales: $	2009 Profits: $	Int'l Exchange:
2008 Sales: $	2008 Profits: $	Employees: Fiscal Year Ends:
2007 Sales: $	2007 Profits: $	Parent Company:

SALARIES/BENEFITS:

Pension Plan:	ESOP Stock Plan:	Profit Sharing:	Top Exec. Salary: $	Bonus: $
Savings Plan:	Stock Purch. Plan:		Second Exec. Salary: $	Bonus: $

OTHER THOUGHTS:

Apparent Women Officers or Directors: 2

Hot Spot for Advancement for Women/Minorities:

LOCATIONS: ("Y" = Yes)

West:	Southwest:	Midwest:	Southeast:	Northeast:	International:
Y	Y	Y			Y

REPOWER SYSTEMS SE

www.repower.de

Industry Group Code: 33361

Energy/Fuel:	Other Technologies:	Electrical Products:	Electronics:	Transportation:	Other:
Biofuels:	Irrigation:	Lighting/LEDs:	Computers:	Car Sharing:	Recycling:
Batteries/Storage:	Nanotech:	Waste Heat:	Sensors:	Electric Vehicles:	Engineering:
Solar:	Biotech:	Smart Meters:	Software:	Natural Gas Fuel:	Consulting:
Wind: Y	Water Tech./Treatment:	Machinery:			Investing:
Fuel Cells:	Ceramics:				Chemicals:

TYPES OF BUSINESS:

Wind Turbine Manufacturing
Wind Turbine Design

BRANDS/DIVISIONS/AFFILIATES:

Suzlon Energy Limited
REpower USA Corporation
REpower Systems GmbH
REpower Espana SL
REpower UK Limited
REpower Australia Pty. Limited
REpower Italia Srl

CONTACTS: *Note: Officers with more than one job title may be intentionally listed here more than once.*

Andreas Nauen, CEO
Gregor Gnadig, COO
Derrick Noe, CFO
Per Hornung Perdersen, Chief Mktg. Officer
Tulsi R. Tanti, Chmn.

Phone: 49-40-555-5090-0	**Fax:** 49-40-555-5090-39-99
Toll-Free:	
Address: Uberseering 10, Hamburg, 22297 Germany	

GROWTH PLANS/SPECIAL FEATURES:

REpower Systems SE, a subsidiary of India-based Suzlon Energy Ltd., is a German firm engaged in the design, manufacture and distribution of turbines for wind-powered electric plants. The firm's wind turbines range in output from 1.8 to 6.15 megawatts (MW). REpower's portfolio of products includes the 6M turbine, a 6.15 MW product with a 413-foot rotor diameter; the 5M, a 5 MW product with a 413-foot rotor diameter; the 3.2M114, a 3.2 MW product with a 374-foot rotor diameter; the 3.4M104, a 3.4 MW product with a 341-foot rotor diameter; the MM82, a 2.05 MW turbine with a 270-foot rotor diameter; the MM92, a 2.05 MW turbine with a 303-foot rotor diameter; and the MM100, a 1.8 MW turbine with a 328-foot rotor diameter. The 6M and 5M can be used in onshore and offshore applications, while the rest are solely for onshore applications. In addition to turnkey wind turbine products, the company also provides custom design and manufacturing services and turbine servicing and maintenance. The firm's German subsidiary, PowerBlades GmbH, focuses on the production of rotor blades for offshore wind turbines. The company is represented by a range of sales partners and affiliates in worldwide markets across Europe, Asia and North America. Wholly-owned international subsidiaries include REpower Espana S.L.; REpower S.A.S., in France; REpower UK Limited; REpower USA Corporation; REpower Australia Pty. Limited; and REpower Italia S.r.l. In late 2010, REpower established REpower Systems GmbH, a wholly-owned subsidiary for the German wind energy market. In March 2011, the company sold subsidiary Winenergie Logistik GmbH to Universal Windkraft Logistik GmbH. In September 2011, after acquiring more than 95% of REpower's outstanding shares, Suzlon Energy initiated a squeeze-out transaction of the firm's minority shareholders.

FINANCIALS: Sales and profits are in thousands of dollars—add 000 to get the full amount. 2011 Note: Financial information for 2011 was not available for all companies at press time.

2011 Sales: $	2011 Profits: $	**U.S. Stock Ticker: Subsidiary**
2010 Sales: $1,716,921	2010 Profits: $78,471	**Int'l Ticker: RPW**
2009 Sales: $1,819,680	2009 Profits: $78,160	Int'l Exchange: Paris-Euronext
2008 Sales: $221,850	2008 Profits: $2,070	Employees: 2,456 Fiscal Year Ends: 12/31
2007 Sales: $857,000	2007 Profits: $26,700	Parent Company: SUZLON ENERGY LIMITED

SALARIES/BENEFITS:

Pension Plan:	ESOP Stock Plan:	Profit Sharing:	Top Exec. Salary: $	Bonus: $
Savings Plan:	Stock Purch. Plan:		Second Exec. Salary: $	Bonus: $

OTHER THOUGHTS:

Apparent Women Officers or Directors:
Hot Spot for Advancement for Women/Minorities:

LOCATIONS: ("Y" = Yes)

West: Y	Southwest:	Midwest:	Southeast:	Northeast:	International: Y

ROBERT BOSCH GMBH

www.bosch.com

Industry Group Code: 3363

Energy/Fuel:	Other Technologies:		Electrical Products:		Electronics:	Transportation:	Other:	
Biofuels:	Irrigation:		Lighting/LEDs:		Computers:	Car Sharing:	Recycling:	
Batteries/Storage:	Nanotech:		Waste Heat:		Sensors:	Electric Vehicles:	Engineering:	Y
Solar:	Biotech:	Y	Smart Meters:		Software:	Natural Gas Fuel:	Consulting:	
Wind:	Water Tech./Treatment:		Machinery:	Y			Investing:	
Fuel Cells:	Ceramics:						Chemicals:	

TYPES OF BUSINESS:

Auto Parts Manufacturing
Gasoline Systems
Motor, Control & Motion Products
Chassis Systems
Electronics & Multimedia
Energy & Body Systems
Security Systems
Power Tools

BRANDS/DIVISIONS/AFFILIATES:

Shenzhen Wei Ning Da Industrial Co Ltd
Bosch Emission Systems GmbH & Co. KG
ZF Steering Systems GmbH
Bosch Rexroth
Blaupunkt
Bosch-Siemens Hausgerate
Accu Industries Inc

CONTACTS: Note: Officers with more than one job title may be intentionally listed here more than once.

Franz Fehrenbach, Managing Dir.
Stefan Asenkerschbaumer, Dir.-Finance & Financial Statements
Peter Tyroller, Dir.-Sales & Mktg.
Wolfgang Malchow, Dir.-Human Resources & Social Svcs.
Volkmar Denner, Dir.-Research
Siegfried Dais, Dir.-IT
Volkmar Denner, Prod. Planning
Volkmar Denner, Dir.-Eng.
Peter J. Marks, Dir.-Mfg. Coordination
Stefan Asenkerschbaumer, Dir.-Bus. Admin.
Wolfgang Malchow, Dir.-Legal Svcs., Taxes & Internal Auditing
Franz Fehrenbach, Dir.-Corp. Planning, Real Estate & Facilities
Franz Fehrenbach, Dir.-Corp. Comm.
Peter Tyroller, Dir.-Original Equipment Sales
Peter J. Marks, CEO/Chmn./Pres., North & South America
Franz Fehrenbach, Chmn.
Uwe Raschke, Dir.-Asia Pacific
Rudolf Colm, Dir.-Purchasing, Logistics & Insurance

Phone: 49-711-811-0	**Fax:** 49-711-811-6630
Toll-Free:	
Address: Postfach 106050, Stuttgart, 70049 Germany	

GROWTH PLANS/SPECIAL FEATURES:

Robert Bosch GmbH is one of the world's leading manufacturers of automotive components. It has operations in more than 60 countries through approximately 300 subsidiaries. The company operates in three business sectors: automotive technology; industrial technology; and consumer goods and building technology. Its automotive divisions deal in gasoline systems; diesel systems; chassis systems; energy and body systems; car multimedia; automotive electronics; and automotive aftermarket products. Bosch's products include braking and fuel injection systems, starters and alternators. The segment is also involved in a joint venture with ZH Friedrichshafen AG called ZF Steering Systems GmbH, which develops, produces and sells steering technology for passenger and commercial vehicles. Another joint venture, Bosch Emission Systems GmbH & Co. KG with Eberspacher GmbH & Co. KG, provides diesel exhaust after treatment to the automobile industry. The industrial technology unit includes Bosch Rexroth, which supplies a range of motor, control and motion products, and the packaging technology division. The consumer goods and building technology group deals in power tools, thermotechnology, household appliances, security systems, communications and broadband networks. The firm's Blaupunkt subsidiary is a leader in car audio equipment. The firm also owns 50% of European appliance maker Bosch-Siemens Hausgeraete. Bosch is a leader in antilock brake technology, clean diesel technology and factory automation. Some of the subsidiaries of Bosch include Accu Industries Inc., a vehicle equipment manufacturer, and Shenzhen Wei Ning Da Industrial Co Ltd (Weicon), a Shenzhen, China-based diagnostics equipment specialist. The company generates 75% of sales from outside of Germany.

Employees of Bosch USA are offered benefits including medical, dental and vision coverage; long-term care insurance; life and AD&D insurance; travel accident insurance; paid vacations; short- and long-term disability coverage; and an educational assistance program.

FINANCIALS: Sales and profits are in thousands of dollars—add 000 to get the full amount. 2011 Note: Financial information for 2011 was not available for all companies at press time.

2011 Sales: $	2011 Profits: $	**U.S. Stock Ticker:** Private
2010 Sales: $53,060,000	2010 Profits: $3,171,046	**Int'l Ticker:**
2009 Sales: $50,929,800	2009 Profits: $-1,596,980	Int'l Exchange:
2008 Sales: $60,222,300	2008 Profits: $496,440	Employees: 300,000 Fiscal Year Ends: 12/31
2007 Sales: $61,814,400	2007 Profits: $3,803,350	Parent Company:

SALARIES/BENEFITS:

Pension Plan: Y	ESOP Stock Plan:	Profit Sharing:	Top Exec. Salary: $	Bonus: $
Savings Plan: Y	Stock Purch. Plan:		Second Exec. Salary: $	Bonus: $

OTHER THOUGHTS:

Apparent Women Officers or Directors:

Hot Spot for Advancement for Women/Minorities:

LOCATIONS: ("Y" = Yes)

West:	Southwest:	Midwest:	Southeast:	Northeast:	International:
Y	Y	Y	Y	Y	Y

Sales, profits and employees may be estimates. Financial information, benefits and other data can change quickly and may vary from those stated here.

ROYAL DUTCH SHELL PLC   www.shell.com

Industry Group Code: 211111

Energy/Fuel:	Other Technologies:	Electrical Products:	Electronics:	Transportation:	Other:	
Biofuels:	Irrigation:	Lighting/LEDs:	Computers:	Car Sharing:	Recycling:	
Batteries/Storage:	Nanotech:	Waste Heat:	Sensors:	Electric Vehicles:	Engineering:	
Solar:	Biotech:	Smart Meters:	Software:	Natural Gas Fuel:	Consulting:	
Wind:	Water Tech./Treatment:	Machinery:			Investing:	
Fuel Cells:	Ceramics:				Chemicals:	Y

TYPES OF BUSINESS:

Oil & Gas-Exploration & Production
Gas Stations
Refineries
Solar & Wind Power
Chemicals
Consulting & Technology Services
Hydrogen & Fuel Cell Technology

BRANDS/DIVISIONS/AFFILIATES:

Shell Oil Co
Arrow Energy Ltd

CONTACTS: *Note: Officers with more than one job title may be intentionally listed here more than once.*

Peter Voser, CEO
Simon Henry, CFO
Hugh Mitchell, Chief Human Resources Officer
Matthias Bichsel, Dir.-Projects & Tech.
Peter Rees, Dir.-Legal
Marvin Odum, Dir.-Upstream Americas
Mark Williams, Dir.-Downstream
Jorma Ollila, Chmn.
Malcom Brinded, Exec. Dir.-Upstream Int'l

Phone: 31-70-377-9111	**Fax:** 31-70-377-3115
Toll-Free:	
Address: Carel van Bylandtlaan 16, The Hague, 2596 HR The Netherlands	

GROWTH PLANS/SPECIAL FEATURES:

Royal Dutch Shell plc (Shell) is one of the world's largest oil and gas groups, with operations in over 90 countries. The company's business segments include Upstream International; Upstream Americas; Downstream; and Projects & Technology. The Upstream International segment searches for and recovers crude oil and natural gas, liquefies and transports gas and operates the upstream and midstream infrastructure necessary to deliver oil and gas to market. This segment also manages Shell's global liquefied natural gas business, as well as its European wind energy business. The firm's Upstream Americas segment oversees exploration activities in North and South America, including the extraction of bitumen from oil sands for conversion into synthetic crude oil. This segment also oversees Shell's wind energy business in the U.S. The upstream segments together produce roughly 3.3 million barrels of oil equivalent (BOE) daily. The Downstream segment, representing more than 80% of 2010 revenues, manages Shell's manufacturing, distribution and marketing activities for oil products and chemicals, including the refining, supply and shipping of crude oil. This segment oversees the sale a range of products including fuels, lubricants, bitumen and liquefied petroleum gas for home, transport and industrial use, as well as petrochemicals for industrial customers, including raw materials for plastics, coatings and detergents used in the manufacture of textiles, medical supplies and computers. In addition, the downstream segment trades hydrocarbons and other energy related products, supplies the downstream businesses and provides shipping services, while also overseeing Shell's interests in non-wind alternative energy and carbon dioxide emissions management. Shell's worldwide retail network includes approximately 43,000 gasoline stations. The Projects & Technology segment conducts research and provides technical services to both the upstream and downstream segments. In August 2010, Shell and its partner PetroChina International Investment completed the acquisition of Australia-based Arrow Energy Limited for approximately $3.5 billion.

FINANCIALS: Sales and profits are in thousands of dollars—add 000 to get the full amount. 2011 Note: Financial information for 2011 was not available for all companies at press time.

2011 Sales: $	2011 Profits: $	**U.S. Stock Ticker:**
2010 Sales: $368,056,000	2010 Profits: $20,127,000	**Int'l Ticker: RDSA**
2009 Sales: $278,188,000	2009 Profits: $12,718,000	Int'l Exchange: Amsterdam-Euronext
2008 Sales: $458,361,000	2008 Profits: $26,476,000	Employees: 93,000 Fiscal Year Ends: 12/31
2007 Sales: $355,782,000	2007 Profits: $31,926,000	Parent Company:

SALARIES/BENEFITS:

Pension Plan: Y	ESOP Stock Plan:	Profit Sharing:	Top Exec. Salary: $	Bonus: $
Savings Plan:	Stock Purch. Plan: Y		Second Exec. Salary: $	Bonus: $

OTHER THOUGHTS:

Apparent Women Officers or Directors: 1
Hot Spot for Advancement for Women/Minorities:

LOCATIONS: ("Y" = Yes)

West:	Southwest:	Midwest:	Southeast:	Northeast:	International:
Y	Y	Y	Y	Y	Y

SAKTI3

Industry Group Code: 33591

www.sakti3.com

Energy/Fuel:		Other Technologies:		Electrical Products:	Electronics:	Transportation:	Other:
Biofuels:		Irrigation:		Lighting/LEDs:	Computers:	Car Sharing:	Recycling:
Batteries/Storage:	Y	Nanotech:		Waste Heat:	Sensors:	Electric Vehicles:	Engineering:
Solar:		Biotech:		Smart Meters:	Software:	Natural Gas Fuel:	Consulting:
Wind:		Water Tech./Treatment:		Machinery:			Investing:
Fuel Cells:		Ceramics:					Chemicals:

TYPES OF BUSINESS:

Rechargeable Lithium-Ion Batteries

BRANDS/DIVISIONS/AFFILIATES:

GROWTH PLANS/SPECIAL FEATURES:

Sakti3 is a firm aimed at developing advanced solid-state rechargeable lithium-ion batteries. The company seeks to help in the advancement of electric drivetrain vehicle operation by increasing the vehicle's operation range while maintaining a cost-effective price to the consumer. The firm's goal is to create a vehicle that can sustain over 100 miles per gallon. Sakti3's technology is based around solid state batteries due to their improved safety and energy density when compared to other batteries. The company is headquartered in Ann Arbor, Michigan and maintains partnership alliances with firms such as Khosla Ventures; Michigan Economic Development Corporation; Beringea; GM; and Itochu.

CONTACTS: *Note: Officers with more than one job title may be intentionally listed here more than once.*

Ann Marie Sastry, CEO
Ann Marie Sastry, Pres.

Phone: 734-827-2583	**Fax:** 734-827-2733
Toll-Free:	
Address: 1490 Eisenhower Pl., Bldg. 4, Ann Arbor, MI 48108 US	

FINANCIALS: Sales and profits are in thousands of dollars—add 000 to get the full amount. 2011 Note: Financial information for 2011 was not available for all companies at press time.

2011 Sales: $	2011 Profits: $	**U.S. Stock Ticker: Private**
2010 Sales: $	2010 Profits: $	**Int'l Ticker:**
2009 Sales: $	2009 Profits: $	Int'l Exchange:
2008 Sales: $	2008 Profits: $	Employees: Fiscal Year Ends:
2007 Sales: $	2007 Profits: $	Parent Company:

SALARIES/BENEFITS:

Pension Plan:	ESOP Stock Plan:	Profit Sharing:	Top Exec. Salary: $	Bonus: $
Savings Plan:	Stock Purch. Plan:		Second Exec. Salary: $	Bonus: $

OTHER THOUGHTS:

Apparent Women Officers or Directors: 1
Hot Spot for Advancement for Women/Minorities:

LOCATIONS: ("Y" = Yes)

West:	Southwest:	Midwest:	Southeast:	Northeast:	International:
		Y			

SAMSUNG ELECTRONICS CO LTD   www.samsung.com

Industry Group Code: 334310

Energy/Fuel:	Other Technologies:		Electrical Products:	Electronics:	Transportation:	Other:
Biofuels:	Irrigation:		Lighting/LEDs:	Computers:	Car Sharing:	Recycling:
Batteries/Storage:	Nanotech:	Y	Waste Heat:	Sensors:	Electric Vehicles:	Engineering:
Solar:	Biotech:		Smart Meters:	Software: Y	Natural Gas Fuel:	Consulting:
Wind:	Water Tech./Treatment:		Machinery:			Investing:
Fuel Cells:	Ceramics:					Chemicals:

TYPES OF BUSINESS:

Consumer Electronics
Semiconductors
Cellular Phones
Computers & Accessories
Digital Cameras
Fuel-Cell Technology
LCD Displays
Memory Products

BRANDS/DIVISIONS/AFFILIATES:

Samsung Group
Samsung Electronics America
Samsung Digital Imaging Co., Ltd.

CONTACTS: Note: Officers with more than one job title may be intentionally listed here more than once.

Gee-Sung Choi, CEO
Ju-Hwa Yoon, Pres.
Ju-Hwa Yoon, CFO
Gee-Sung Choi, Pres., Digital Media & Comm. Bus.
Charlie Bae, Pres., Samsung Semiconductor, Inc.
Dale Sohn, Pres., Samsung Telecom America
Kun-Hee Lee, Chmn.
Yangkyu Kim, Pres./CEO-Samsung Electronics America

Phone: 82-2-727-7114	Fax: 82-2-727-7892
Toll-Free:	
Address: 250, 2-ga, Taepyung-ro, Jung-gu, Seoul, 100-742 Korea	

GROWTH PLANS/SPECIAL FEATURES:

Samsung Electronics Co., Ltd., part of The Samsung Group, is a global leader in semiconductor, telecommunications and digital convergence technology. The company is organized into two segments: digital media and communications (DMC) or set business and device solutions (DS) or component business. The DMC segment produces a wide array of specialties from mobile telephones to televisions to telecommunications systems. Samsung is a leading provider of cell phones utilizing its WiMax and High-Speed Downlink Packet Access (HSDPA) technologies to provide 3D and multimedia phones. It is also a leader in the HD Television market with its LED and LCD TV and monitor offerings. Samsung cameras and printers also enjoy a top market position, as do its home appliances. This segment also includes its telecommunication networks business. The DS segment is a global leader in memory and LCD devices. Its operations consist of semiconductors and LCDs. The semiconductor unit includes a memory division, which designs and manufactures ICs and is a leader in dynamic random access memory (DRAM), static random access memory (SRAM), flash memory and solid state drives (SSDs); the LSI division, which designs and manufactures logic and analog IC devices for applications in mobile, home, media and ASIC/foundry services; and the storage systems division, which is a leading manufacturer of hard disk drives for computers, camcorders, MP4 players and other digital devices. The LCD business produces panels for televisions, digital information displays and PCs such as LED backlit LCD panels. In April 2010, Samsung merged with an affiliated company, Samsung Digital Imaging Co., Ltd., to increase its market competitiveness within the digital camera sector. In January 2011, it announced the development of the semiconductor industry's first DDR4 DRAM memory module.

FINANCIALS: Sales and profits are in thousands of dollars—add 000 to get the full amount. 2011 Note: Financial information for 2011 was not available for all companies at press time.

2011 Sales: $	2011 Profits: $	U.S. Stock Ticker:
2010 Sales: $141,842,000	2010 Profits: $14,811,600	Int'l Ticker: 000830
2009 Sales: $123,691,000	2009 Profits: $8,587,090	Int'l Exchange: Seoul-KRX
2008 Sales: $97,035,500	2008 Profits: $4,420,700	Employees: 5,049 Fiscal Year Ends: 12/31
2007 Sales: $92,260,000	2007 Profits: $8,560,000	Parent Company: SAMSUNG GROUP

SALARIES/BENEFITS:

Pension Plan:	ESOP Stock Plan:	Profit Sharing:	Top Exec. Salary: $	Bonus: $
Savings Plan:	Stock Purch. Plan:		Second Exec. Salary: $	Bonus: $

OTHER THOUGHTS:

Apparent Women Officers or Directors:
Hot Spot for Advancement for Women/Minorities:

LOCATIONS: ("Y" = Yes)

West:	Southwest:	Midwest:	Southeast:	Northeast:	International:
Y	Y	Y	Y	Y	Y

SANYO ELECTRIC COMPANY LTD

www.sanyo.com

Industry Group Code: 334310

Energy/Fuel:	Other Technologies:	Electrical Products:	Electronics:	Transportation:	Other:
Biofuels:	Irrigation:	Lighting/LEDs:	Computers:	Car Sharing:	Recycling:
Batteries/Storage:	Nanotech:	Waste Heat:	Sensors:	Electric Vehicles:	Engineering:
Solar:	Biotech:	Smart Meters:	Software: Y	Natural Gas Fuel:	Consulting:
Wind:	Water Tech./Treatment:	Machinery:			Investing:
Fuel Cells: Y	Ceramics:				Chemicals:

TYPES OF BUSINESS:

Consumer Electronics
Fuel-Cell Technology
Communications Equipment
Industrial Equipment
Home Appliances
Batteries & Electronic Components
Photovoltaic Technology
Research & Development

BRANDS/DIVISIONS/AFFILIATES:

Panasonic Corporation
Eneloop
SANYO Total Solution

CONTACTS: *Note: Officers with more than one job title may be intentionally listed here more than once.*

Seiichiro Sano, Pres.
Hiroki Ohsaki, Chief Dir.-Finance
Susumu Koike, Exec. VP
Junji Esaka, Exec. VP
Masato Ita, Sr. VP
Morihro Kubo, Sr. VP

Phone: 81-6-6991-1181	**Fax:** 81-6-6992-0009
Toll-Free:	
Address: 2-5-5 Keihan-Hondori 2-Chome, Moriguchi City, 570-8677 Japan	

GROWTH PLANS/SPECIAL FEATURES:

SANYO Electric Company, Ltd., a subsidiary of Panasonic Corporation, is a worldwide conglomerate with approximately 206 affiliates and subsidiaries that are active in energy and environmental technology, and the manufacture and sale of personal and consumer products. SANYO maintains a focus on energy generation, storage and efficient usage, with products such as photovoltaic (solar) systems, small- to large-scale-use rechargeable batteries and other energy efficient components and products designed to be environmentally friendly. The firm has eight business segments: Visual Products, Audio Products, Home Appliances, Air Conditioners, Food Equipment, Biomedical & Medical Equipment, CCTV Products and Batteries. The company offers customized packages of its products and services, called SANYO Total Solution, designed for comprehensive system outfitting, maintenance and support for airports, hospitals, hotels, shopping malls and convenience stores. SANYO invests heavily in research and development, and is focused on a range of areas including solar cell technology; Eneloop reusable batteries; smart energy systems; electric hybrid batteries; photonics devices; flash memory; system-on-chip integrated circuit technology; secure digital content distribution; character and image recognition technologies; water treatment; biotechnologies; advanced fuel cells; and robotics. In October 2011, the firm agreed to transfer its consumer and commercial washing machine business, consumer refrigerator business and its white goods sales businesses in four Southeast Asia countries to Haier Group, a multinational consumer electric and home appliance company. Throughout 2011, SANYO partnered with a variety of companies including InSpec Group, PV Trackers and Hotel Penaga, in order to provide improved green solar technology, systems and utilities.

FINANCIALS: Sales and profits are in thousands of dollars—add 000 to get the full amount. 2011 Note: Financial information for 2011 was not available for all companies at press time.

2011 Sales: $19,620,991	2011 Profits: $-463,285	**U.S. Stock Ticker:** Subsidiary
2010 Sales: $20,327,200	2010 Profits: $-593,280	**Int'l Ticker: 6764**
2009 Sales: $18,067,918	2009 Profits: $-951,286	Int'l Exchange: Tokyo-TSE
2008 Sales: $20,389,900	2008 Profits: $287,000	Employees: 92,675 Fiscal Year Ends: 3/31
2007 Sales: $19,650,000	2007 Profits: $-390,000	Parent Company: PANASONIC CORPORATION

SALARIES/BENEFITS:

Pension Plan:	ESOP Stock Plan:	Profit Sharing:	Top Exec. Salary: $	Bonus: $
Savings Plan:	Stock Purch. Plan:		Second Exec. Salary: $	Bonus: $

OTHER THOUGHTS:

Apparent Women Officers or Directors:
Hot Spot for Advancement for Women/Minorities:

LOCATIONS: ("Y" = Yes)

West:	Southwest:	Midwest:	Southeast:	Northeast:	International:
Y	Y		Y	Y	Y

SAPPHIRE ENERGY

www.saphireenergy.com

Industry Group Code: 325199

Energy/Fuel:		Other Technologies:		Electrical Products:		Electronics:	Transportation:	Other:
Biofuels:	Y	Irrigation:		Lighting/LEDs:		Computers:	Car Sharing:	Recycling:
Batteries/Storage:		Nanotech:		Waste Heat:		Sensors:	Electric Vehicles:	Engineering:
Solar:		Biotech:	Y	Smart Meters:		Software:	Natural Gas Fuel:	Consulting:
Wind:		Water Tech./Treatment:		Machinery:				Investing:
Fuel Cells:		Ceramics:						Chemicals:

TYPES OF BUSINESS:

Biofuels

BRANDS/DIVISIONS/AFFILIATES:

Green Crude
Wellcome Trust (The)
Venrock
Cascade Investment LLC
ARCH Venture Partners

CONTACTS: *Note: Officers with more than one job title may be intentionally listed here more than once.*

Jason Pyle, CEO
Cynthia J. Warner, Pres.
James Lambright, CFO
Xun Wang, VP-R&D
Dan Sajkowski, Sr. Dir.-Downstream Tech.
Dean Venardos, VP-Oper.
Peter Attia, VP-Bus. Dev.
Tim Zenk, VP-Corp. Affairs
Alex Aravanis, VP-Dev.
Jaime Moreno, VP-Projects
Cynthia J. Warner, Chmn.
James Lambright, Pres., Int'l

Phone: 858-768-4706	Fax:
Toll-Free:	
Address: 3115 Merryfield Row, San Diego, CA 92121 US	

GROWTH PLANS/SPECIAL FEATURES:

Sapphire Energy produces renewable, drop-in replacement fuels for diesel, gasoline and jet fuel. The firm's product, Green Crude, is a renewable crude oil that converts sunlight, carbon dioxide and algae into green oils to be refined into fuel. Sapphire Energy has successfully produced 89 cetane diesel and 91-octane gasoline from algae that fully conforms to ASTM (American Society for Testing and Materials) certification standards; participated in a test flight using algae-based jet fuel in a Boeing 737-800 twin-engine aircraft; and supplied the fuel for the first cross-country tour of a gasoline vehicle with its gas replaced by a fuel containing a mixture of hydrocarbons refined directly from Green Crude. The company is owned by several investors, including ARCH Venture Partners; Cascade Investment, LLC, which is an investment holding firm owned by Bill Gates; The Wellcome Trust, which is a major biomedical research charity; and Venrock, the Rockefeller family's venture capital group. Sapphire Energy maintains four facilities located in California and New Mexico. In 2010, the firm began construction on its Integrated Algal Bio-Refinery in New Mexico. In May 2011, the company and The Linde Group agreed to jointly develop a low-cost carbon dioxide delivery system for open-pond, commercial-scale algae-to-fuel cultivation systems.

FINANCIALS: Sales and profits are in thousands of dollars—add 000 to get the full amount. 2011 Note: Financial information for 2011 was not available for all companies at press time.

			U.S. Stock Ticker: Private
2011 Sales: $	2011 Profits: $		Int'l Ticker:
2010 Sales: $	2010 Profits: $		Int'l Exchange:
2009 Sales: $	2009 Profits: $		Employees: Fiscal Year Ends:
2008 Sales: $	2008 Profits: $		Parent Company:
2007 Sales: $	2007 Profits: $		

SALARIES/BENEFITS:

Pension Plan:	ESOP Stock Plan:	Profit Sharing:	Top Exec. Salary: $	Bonus: $
Savings Plan:	Stock Purch. Plan:		Second Exec. Salary: $	Bonus: $

OTHER THOUGHTS:

Apparent Women Officers or Directors: 2
Hot Spot for Advancement for Women/Minorities:

LOCATIONS: ("Y" = Yes)

West:	Southwest:	Midwest:	Southeast:	Northeast:	International:
Y	Y				

SASOL LIMITED

www.sasol.com

Industry Group Code: 325

Energy/Fuel:		Other Technologies:		Electrical Products:	Electronics:	Transportation:	Other:	
Biofuels:	Y	Irrigation:		Lighting/LEDs:	Computers:	Car Sharing:	Recycling:	
Batteries/Storage:		Nanotech:		Waste Heat:	Sensors:	Electric Vehicles:	Engineering:	
Solar:		Biotech:	Y	Smart Meters:	Software:	Natural Gas Fuel:	Consulting:	
Wind:		Water Tech./Treatment:		Machinery:			Investing:	
Fuel Cells:		Ceramics:					Chemicals:	Y

TYPES OF BUSINESS:

Synthetic Fuels Manufacturing
Crude Oil Refining
Natural Gas Production
Coal Mining
Polymers
Solvents

BRANDS/DIVISIONS/AFFILIATES:

Sasol Mining
Sasol Synfuels
Sasol Oil
Sasol Gas
Sasol Synfuels International
Sasol Petroleum International
Sasol Polymers
Sasol Olefins & Surfactants

CONTACTS: Note: Officers with more than one job title may be intentionally listed here more than once.

Lawrence Patrick Davies, CEO
Andre Marinus de Ruyter, Sr. Exec. Dir.-Oper.
Kandimathie Christine Ramon, CFO
Bernard Ekhard Klingenberg, Exec. Dir.-Human Resources
Christiaan Francois Rademan, Exec. Dir.-Info. Mgmt.
Giullean Johann Strauss, Sr. Exec. Dir.-Tech.
Nereus Louis Joubert, Exec. Dir.-Legal & Assurance
Giullean Johann Strauss, Sr. Exec. Dir.-New Bus. Dev.
Alan Cameron, Managing Dir.-Sasol Oil
Joe Makhoere, Managing Dir.-Sasol Solvents
Wrenelle Stander, Managing Dir.-Sasol Gas
Musa Zwane, Managing Dir.-Sasol Electricity
Thembalihle Hixonia Nyasulu, Chmn.
Christiaan Francois Rademan, Exec. Dir.-Supply Chain

Phone: 27-11-441-3563	Fax: 27-11-788-5092
Toll-Free:	
Address: 1 Sturdee Ave., Rosebank, 2196 South Africa	

GROWTH PLANS/SPECIAL FEATURES:

Sasol Limited, based in South Africa, is a diversified holding company with interests in oil and gas, mining and chemicals. Sasol uses in-house technology for the commercial production of synthetic fuels and chemicals from low-grade coal and manufactures a variety of fuel and chemical products sold in over 90 countries. It operates in three divisions: South African Energy, International Energy and Chemicals. In South Africa, liquid fuels are sold through a network of approximately 418 Sasol retail convenience centers and Exel service stations. Sasol additionally operates coal mines to provide feedstock for its synthetic fuel and chemical plants; manufactures and markets synthetic gas; and operates the only inland crude oil refinery in South Africa. The company supplements its coal mining activities by marketing Mozambican natural gas. Domestic subsidiaries include Sasol Mining, which mines over 40 million tons of saleable coal per year; Sasol Synfuels, operator of the world's only commercial coal-based synthetic fuels manufacturing facility; Sasol Oil, a marketer of petrol, diesel, jet fuel, illuminating paraffin, fuel oils, bitumen and lubricants; and Sasol Gas, a distributor of Mozambican-produced natural gas and Secunda-produced methane-rich gas. Its International Energy operations span Europe, Asia and the Americas. The company's international subsidiaries include Sasol Synfuels International, which develops and implements international joint ventures with Sasol Chevron; and Sasol Petroleum International, which develops and manages upstream interests in oil and gas exploration and production in Mozambique, South Africa, Gabon, Nigeria and the joint development zone between Nigeria and Sao Tome & Principe. The Chemicals division consists of a number of subsidiaries, including Sasol Polymers, Sasol Solvents, Sasol Nitro, Sasol Wax, Sasol Infrachem and Sasol Olefins & Surfactants. Sasol's chemicals portfolio includes monomers, polymers, solvents, olefins, surfactants, surfactant intermediates, comonomers, waxes, phenolics and nitrogenous products.

FINANCIALS: Sales and profits are in thousands of dollars—add 000 to get the full amount. 2011 Note: Financial information for 2011 was not available for all companies at press time.

		U.S. Stock Ticker:
2011 Sales: $17,335,900	2011 Profits: $2,409,100	Int'l Ticker: SOL
2010 Sales: $17,292,000	2010 Profits: $2,318,000	Int'l Exchange: Johannesburg-JSE
2009 Sales: $18,329,000	2009 Profits: $3,281,000	Employees: 33,708 Fiscal Year Ends: 6/30
2008 Sales: $15,618,000	2008 Profits: $2,828,000	Parent Company:
2007 Sales: $13,910,000	2007 Profits: $2,410,000	

SALARIES/BENEFITS:

Pension Plan:	ESOP Stock Plan:	Profit Sharing:	Top Exec. Salary: $544,620	Bonus: $597,209
Savings Plan:	Stock Purch. Plan:		Second Exec. Salary: $515,488	Bonus: $412,390

OTHER THOUGHTS:

Apparent Women Officers or Directors: 5
Hot Spot for Advancement for Women/Minorities: Y

LOCATIONS: ("Y" = Yes)

West:	Southwest:	Midwest:	Southeast:	Northeast:	International:
Y	Y	Y	Y	Y	Y

Sales, profits and employees may be estimates. Financial information, benefits and other data can change quickly and may vary from those stated here.

SCHNEIDER ELECTRIC SA

www.schneider-electric.com

Industry Group Code: 335

Energy/Fuel:	Other Technologies:	Electrical Products:	Electronics:	Transportation:	Other:
Biofuels:	Irrigation:	Lighting/LEDs:	Computers:	Car Sharing:	Recycling:
Batteries/Storage:	Nanotech:	Waste Heat:	Sensors:	Electric Vehicles:	Engineering:
Solar:	Biotech:	Smart Meters:	Software:	Natural Gas Fuel:	Consulting:
Wind:	Water Tech./Treatment:	Machinery: Y			Investing:
Fuel Cells:	Ceramics:				Chemicals:

TYPES OF BUSINESS:

Electrical Distribution Products
Infrastructure Products
Building Automation & Control Products

BRANDS/DIVISIONS/AFFILIATES:

Telemecanique
Areva T&D
Electroshield-TM Samara
Uniflair S.p.A.

CONTACTS: Note: Officers with more than one job title may be intentionally listed here more than once.

Jean-Pascal Tricoire, CEO
Jean-Pascal Tricoire, Pres.
Emmanuel Babeau, CFO
Aaron Davis, Chief Mktg. Officer
Karen Ferguson, Exec. VP-Human Resources
Herve Coureil, CIO
Philippe Delorme, Exec. VP-Strategy & Innovation
Eric Pilaud, Exec. VP-Custom Sensors & Technologies
Clemens Blum, Exec. VP-Industry Bus.
Chris Curtis, Exec. VP-Power, North America & Buildings Bus.
Laurent Vernerey, Exec. VP-IT Bus.
Julio Rodriguez, Exec. VP-Power Global & EMEA Bus.
Hal Grant, Exec. VP-Global Supply Chain

Phone: 33-1-41-29-70-00	**Fax:** 33-1-41-29-71-00
Toll-Free:	
Address: 35 rue Joseph Monier, Rueil-Malmaison, 92500 France	

GROWTH PLANS/SPECIAL FEATURES:

Schneider Electric S.A. manufactures and markets a range of products and services for the energy and infrastructure markets in the residential and industrial sectors. Schneider Electric has operations in nearly 200 countries worldwide, with approximately 15,000 sales outlets; 25 research and development sites; 205 manufacturing facilities; and 60 logistics centers. The company works through five core business segments: Power, Industry, IT, Buildings and CST. The firm's Power segment offers products, equipment and systems covering all phases of transmission and electrical distribution, classified according to their voltage level. Low-voltage products, including circuit breakers, switches, security lighting, prefabricated electrical wiring, modular switchgear and communication products, are used in the building market. Medium-voltage equipment is designed to transform electricity and then deliver it to an end user. The company's Industry segment provides automation & control services, specializing in developing platforms and products for human-machine interaction such as contractors, overload relays, soft starters, speed drives, sensors and operator terminals. This segment includes company Telemecanique, which develops products and systems for automation that include abilities in detection, man-machine dialogue and process supervision. The IT segment covers critical power and cooling services, focusing on solutions for information systems manufacturers and financial services companies. The Buildings segment provides building automation and security management services for customers in four areas: hotels, hospitals, office buildings and retail stores. The CST division is a technological business that serves customers in the automotive, aeronautic and manufacturing industries. In June 2010, the firm, in partnership with Alstom, acquired the transmission and distribution activities (Areva T&D) from Areva Group. Following the transaction, Alstom took over the transmission operations, while Schneider took the distribution activities. In October 2010, it agreed to acquire 50% of Electroshield-TM Samara, a leader in medium voltage products and solutions in Russia. In November 2010, the company acquired Uniflair S.p.A.

FINANCIALS: Sales and profits are in thousands of dollars—add 000 to get the full amount. 2011 Note: Financial information for 2011 was not available for all companies at press time.

2011 Sales: $	2011 Profits: $	**U.S. Stock Ticker:**
2010 Sales: $28,242,400	2010 Profits: $2,480,950	**Int'l Ticker: SU**
2009 Sales: $21,457,000	2009 Profits: $1,157,560	Int'l Exchange: Paris-Euronext
2008 Sales: $24,395,700	2008 Profits: $2,240,930	Employees: 123,482 Fiscal Year Ends: 12/31
2007 Sales: $23,060,800	2007 Profits: $2,109,030	Parent Company:

SALARIES/BENEFITS:

Pension Plan:	ESOP Stock Plan:	Profit Sharing:	Top Exec. Salary: $	Bonus: $
Savings Plan:	Stock Purch. Plan:		Second Exec. Salary: $	Bonus: $

OTHER THOUGHTS:

Apparent Women Officers or Directors: 1
Hot Spot for Advancement for Women/Minorities:

LOCATIONS: ("Y" = Yes)

West:	Southwest:	Midwest:	Southeast:	Northeast:	International: Y

SCHOTT SOLAR

www.us.schottsolar.com

Industry Group Code: 334413

Energy/Fuel:		Other Technologies:		Electrical Products:		Electronics:		Transportation:		Other:	
Biofuels:		Irrigation:		Lighting/LEDs:		Computers:		Car Sharing:		Recycling:	
Batteries/Storage:		Nanotech:		Waste Heat:		Sensors:		Electric Vehicles:		Engineering:	
Solar:	Y	Biotech:		Smart Meters:		Software:		Natural Gas Fuel:		Consulting:	
Wind:		Water Tech./Treatment:		Machinery:						Investing:	
Fuel Cells:		Ceramics:								Chemicals:	

TYPES OF BUSINESS:
Photovoltaic Modules & Systems

BRANDS/DIVISIONS/AFFILIATES:
SCHOTT AG
SCHOTT Poly
Carl-Zeiss-Stiftung
Poly 2xx
SCHOTT POWER POLY 275

CONTACTS: Note: Officers with more than one job title may be intentionally listed here more than once.
Gerald Fine, CEO
Gerald Fine, Co-Pres.
Tom Hecht, Chief Sales Officer
Zane Rakes, Dir.-Oper.
Casey Gutowski, Dir.-Bus. Dev.
Tom Hecht, Co-Pres.

Phone:	Fax: 505-212-8585
Toll-Free: 888-457-6527	
Address: 5201 Hawking Dr. SE, Albuquerque, NM 87106 US	

GROWTH PLANS/SPECIAL FEATURES:

SCHOTT Solar, a subsidiary of SCHOTT AG, which is in turn a subsidiary of Carl-Zeiss-Stiftung, is engaged in the designing, manufacturing and marketing of photovoltaic systems for grid-connected residential and commercial customers, as well as for off-grid rural and industrial applications. SCHOTT Solar maintains facilities in Germany, the Czech Republic and Spain. In addition, the firm operates eight solar power production plants in Germany, Spain, Czech Republic and the U.S. These proprietary systems are designed for businesses, schools, utilities and industrial operations. The company's SCHOTT Poly modules, which are used for both commercial and residential buildings, are complete solar systems, which include the solar module, a support structure, wiring, an inverter, a meter and other equipment. These systems, which have an estimated 25-year design life, can be customized to meet the needs of individual clients. The modules are available in 220, 225, 230 and 235 watt classes. Some of the firm's recent projects include a 1.1-megawatt solar installation at the headquarters of The Bell Group in Albuquerque, New Mexico; a 120-kilowatt (kW) solar installation at the distribution facility of Dayton Daily News in Dayton, Ohio; and a 50 kW solar power installation at Los Lunas High School in Los Lunas, New Mexico. In February 2011, the firm introduced the black Poly 2xx series modules, black anodized aluminum frame polycrystalline photovoltaic modules for residential use. In October 2011, the company introduced the 72-cell SCHOTT POWER POLY 275 a 285W module for commercial and utility projects.

FINANCIALS: Sales and profits are in thousands of dollars—add 000 to get the full amount. 2011 Note: Financial information for 2011 was not available for all companies at press time.

2011 Sales: $	2011 Profits: $	**U.S. Stock Ticker:** Subsidiary	
2010 Sales: $	2010 Profits: $	**Int'l Ticker:**	
2009 Sales: $	2009 Profits: $	Int'l Exchange:	
2008 Sales: $	2008 Profits: $	Employees:	Fiscal Year Ends: 9/30
2007 Sales: $	2007 Profits: $	Parent Company: CARL-ZEISS-STIFTUNG	

SALARIES/BENEFITS:

Pension Plan:	ESOP Stock Plan:	Profit Sharing:	Top Exec. Salary: $	Bonus: $
Savings Plan:	Stock Purch. Plan:		Second Exec. Salary: $	Bonus: $

OTHER THOUGHTS:
Apparent Women Officers or Directors:
Hot Spot for Advancement for Women/Minorities:

LOCATIONS: ("Y" = Yes)

West:	Southwest:	Midwest:	Southeast:	Northeast:	International:
Y					Y

Sales, profits and employees may be estimates. Financial information, benefits and other data can change quickly and may vary from those stated here.

SCIENERGY

scienergy.com

Industry Group Code: 5112

Energy/Fuel:	Other Technologies:	Electrical Products:	Electronics:		Transportation:		Other:	
Biofuels:	Irrigation:	Lighting/LEDs:	Computers:		Car Sharing:		Recycling:	
Batteries/Storage:	Nanotech:	Waste Heat:	Sensors:		Electric Vehicles:		Engineering:	Y
Solar:	Biotech:	Smart Meters:	Software:	Y	Natural Gas Fuel:		Consulting:	Y
Wind:	Water Tech./Treatment:	Machinery:					Investing:	
Fuel Cells:	Ceramics:						Chemicals:	

TYPES OF BUSINESS:

Cloud-Based Energy Management

BRANDS/DIVISIONS/AFFILIATES:

Scientific Conservation
Servidyne
SCIenergy Cloud

CONTACTS: *Note: Officers with more than one job title may be intentionally listed here more than once.*

Russ McMeekin, CEO
Russ McMeekin, Pres.
Jeff Moran, CFO
Dave Weinerth, Exec. VP-Mktg.
Pat Richards, CTO
Barry Abramson, Sr. VP-Eng.
Dana DuFrane, Chief Admin. Officer/Exec. VP
Dana DuFrane, General Counsel
Tom Galanty, Exec. VP-Corp. Oper. & Tech.
Andrew Tang, Exec. VP-Corp. Strategy & Utility Channel
Chris Smith, Chief Data Officer
Todd Jarvis, Exec. VP-Cloud Enablement
Pat Richards, VP-Software Eng.
George Plattenburg, VP-Sales

Phone: 415-625-4500	Fax:
Toll-Free:	
Address: 2 Bryant St., Ste. 210, San Francisco, CA 94105 US	

GROWTH PLANS/SPECIAL FEATURES:

SCIenergy is an international energy management firm. The company seeks to enable building owners and operators to optimize the performance of their buildings through high-touch actionable insights and high-tech software solutions. The firm has also completed energy ratings for more than 500 customer buildings. SCIenergy's team features experts in building automation and controls; energy and facilities management; and cloud-based software development and engineering. The firm's proprietary SCIenergy Cloud is a cloud-based energy management platform that includes software applications that enable the company's building experts to use otherwise invisible energy and systems data to identify and realize cost savings options. In conjunction, SCIenergy offers building operators with software-as-a-service (SaaS) solutions that track and maintain the building's performance and look for additional areas that could be improved. The firm implements various strategies depending on the individual building's controls systems automation and energy performance. SCIenergy was formed through the merger of Scientific Conservation and Servidyne. The firm has been an Environmental Protection Agency Energy Star Partner of the Year on nine occasions.

FINANCIALS: Sales and profits are in thousands of dollars—add 000 to get the full amount. 2011 Note: Financial information for 2011 was not available for all companies at press time.

2011 Sales: $	2011 Profits: $	**U.S. Stock Ticker:** Private
2010 Sales: $	2010 Profits: $	**Int'l Ticker:**
2009 Sales: $	2009 Profits: $	Int'l Exchange:
2008 Sales: $	2008 Profits: $	Employees: Fiscal Year Ends:
2007 Sales: $	2007 Profits: $	Parent Company:

SALARIES/BENEFITS:

Pension Plan:	ESOP Stock Plan:	Profit Sharing:	Top Exec. Salary: $	Bonus: $
Savings Plan:	Stock Purch. Plan:		Second Exec. Salary: $	Bonus: $

OTHER THOUGHTS:

Apparent Women Officers or Directors: 1
Hot Spot for Advancement for Women/Minorities:

LOCATIONS: ("Y" = Yes)

West:	Southwest:	Midwest:	Southeast:	Northeast:	International:
Y			Y		

SEEO

Industry Group Code: 33591

Energy/Fuel:		Other Technologies:	Electrical Products:	Electronics:	Transportation:	Other:	
Biofuels:		Irrigation:	Lighting/LEDs:	Computers:	Car Sharing:	Recycling:	
Batteries/Storage:	Y	Nanotech:	Waste Heat:	Sensors:	Electric Vehicles:	Engineering:	Y
Solar:		Biotech:	Smart Meters:	Software:	Natural Gas Fuel:	Consulting:	
Wind:		Water Tech./Treatment:	Machinery:			Investing:	
Fuel Cells:		Ceramics:				Chemicals:	

TYPES OF BUSINESS:
Rechargeable Lithium Ion Batteries

BRANDS/DIVISIONS/AFFILIATES:

GROWTH PLANS/SPECIAL FEATURES:
Seeo is a creator is high-energy rechargeable lithium ion batteries. Founded in 2007, the firm is headquartered in Hayward, California. The company's batteries are solid state with no explosive or flammable components. Seeo's technology is based around a novel solid polymer electrode material, which is capable of safely transporting lithium ions while maintaining a stable support system for high energy electrode chemistries. Benefits of the firm's technology over standard lithium batteries include an increase in battery energy density as well as best in class product lifetime and safety ratings. The company has over 30 patent applications pending. Seeo investors include Khosla Ventures, Google, GSR Ventures and Presidio Ventures.

CONTACTS: *Note: Officers with more than one job title may be intentionally listed here more than once.*
Steve Liu, CEO
Steve Liu, Pres.
Neilesh Mutyala, Mgr.-Mktg.
Mohit Singh, VP-R&D
Franz Kruger, Sr. Tech. Advisor
Peter Paris, Dir.-Prod. Design
Mohit Singh, VP-Eng.
Ken Damon, Dir.-Mfg.
Neilesh Mutyala, Mgr.-Bus. Dev.
Hany Eitouni, VP-Advanced Materials

Phone: 510-782-7336	Fax:
Toll-Free:	
Address: 3906 Trust Way, Hayward, CA 94545 US	

FINANCIALS: Sales and profits are in thousands of dollars—add 000 to get the full amount. 2011 Note: Financial information for 2011 was not available for all companies at press time.
2011 Sales: $	2011 Profits: $	U.S. Stock Ticker: Private
2010 Sales: $	2010 Profits: $	Int'l Ticker:
2009 Sales: $	2009 Profits: $	Int'l Exchange:
2008 Sales: $	2008 Profits: $	Employees: Fiscal Year Ends:
2007 Sales: $	2007 Profits: $	Parent Company:

SALARIES/BENEFITS:
Pension Plan:	ESOP Stock Plan:	Profit Sharing:	Top Exec. Salary: $	Bonus: $
Savings Plan:	Stock Purch. Plan: Y		Second Exec. Salary: $	Bonus: $

OTHER THOUGHTS:
Apparent Women Officers or Directors:
Hot Spot for Advancement for Women/Minorities:

LOCATIONS: ("Y" = Yes)
West:	Southwest:	Midwest:	Southeast:	Northeast:	International:
Y					

SEQUENTIAL BIOFUELS LLC

www.sqbiofuels.com

Industry Group Code: 325199

Energy/Fuel:		Other Technologies:		Electrical Products:	Electronics:	Transportation:	Other:
Biofuels:	Y	Irrigation:		Lighting/LEDs:	Computers:	Car Sharing:	Recycling:
Batteries/Storage:		Nanotech:		Waste Heat:	Sensors:	Electric Vehicles:	Engineering:
Solar:		Biotech:	Y	Smart Meters:	Software:	Natural Gas Fuel:	Consulting:
Wind:		Water Tech./Treatment:		Machinery:			Investing:
Fuel Cells:		Ceramics:					Chemicals:

TYPES OF BUSINESS:

Biofuels Marketing
Biodiesel

BRANDS/DIVISIONS/AFFILIATES:

Pacific Biodiesel
SeQuential-Pacific Biodiesel LLC
Encore Oils

CONTACTS: Note: Officers with more than one job title may be intentionally listed here more than once.

Ian Hill, CEO
Tyson Keever, Gen. Mgr.-SeQuential Pacific Biodiesel LLC

Phone: 503-954-2154	Fax: 503-296-5797
Toll-Free:	
Address: 10111 NE 6th Dr., Portland, OR 97211 US	

GROWTH PLANS/SPECIAL FEATURES:

SeQuential Biofuels LLC is a biofuels marketing and distribution company based in the Pacific Northwest. The company's production unit is a joint venture between SeQuential and Pacific Biodiesel, called SeQuential-Pacific Biodiesel LLC. It owns and operates a facility in Salem, Oregon, with a biodiesel production capacity of about 17 million gallons of biodiesel per year. Its primary feedstock is used cooking oil and locally-sourced canola oil. Encore Oils, a subsidiary of SeQuential-Pacific Biodiesel, collects waste oil and grease traps from restaurants, as well as individuals who drop off excess frying oil at two locations in Oregon. The company partners with regional fuel distributors to provide commercial biodiesel and biodiesel/petroleum diesel blends directly to customers through its mobile retail pumps. SeQuential's fuel is sold out of 37 retail locations in Oregon and Washington, including a SeQuential-branded retail station in Eugene, Oregon. The SeQuential station features solar array canopies over the pumps, a living roof, a Tesla Roadster electric car charger and a convenience store that sells the products from local vendors. Additionally, the firm sells home heating oil from four locations in Oregon.

FINANCIALS: Sales and profits are in thousands of dollars—add 000 to get the full amount. 2011 Note: Financial information for 2011 was not available for all companies at press time.

2011 Sales: $	2011 Profits: $	U.S. Stock Ticker: Private
2010 Sales: $	2010 Profits: $	Int'l Ticker:
2009 Sales: $	2009 Profits: $	Int'l Exchange:
2008 Sales: $	2008 Profits: $	Employees: Fiscal Year Ends:
2007 Sales: $	2007 Profits: $	Parent Company:

SALARIES/BENEFITS:

Pension Plan:	ESOP Stock Plan:	Profit Sharing:	Top Exec. Salary: $	Bonus: $
Savings Plan:	Stock Purch. Plan:		Second Exec. Salary: $	Bonus: $

OTHER THOUGHTS:

Apparent Women Officers or Directors:
Hot Spot for Advancement for Women/Minorities:

LOCATIONS: ("Y" = Yes)

West:	Southwest:	Midwest:	Southeast:	Northeast:	International:
Y					

SERIOUS ENERGY INC

www.seriousenergy.com

Industry Group Code: 326199

Energy/Fuel:	Other Technologies:	Electrical Products:	Electronics:	Transportation:	Other:
Biofuels:	Irrigation:	Lighting/LEDs:	Computers:	Car Sharing:	Recycling:
Batteries/Storage:	Nanotech:	Waste Heat:	Sensors:	Electric Vehicles:	Engineering:
Solar:	Biotech:	Smart Meters:	Software: Y	Natural Gas Fuel:	Consulting:
Wind:	Water Tech./Treatment:	Machinery:			Investing:
Fuel Cells:	Ceramics:				Chemicals:

TYPES OF BUSINESS:

Energy Efficiency Building Software
Energy Efficiency Building Products

BRANDS/DIVISIONS/AFFILIATES:

SeriousEnergy Manager
iWindow
SeriousWindows
Quiet Rock
SeriousCapital
Energy Control Center
Agilewaves Inc

CONTACTS: *Note: Officers with more than one job title may be intentionally listed here more than once.*

Kevin Surace, CEO
Frank Bishop, VP/Gen. Mgr.-Panels Div.
Ian Sullivan, VP/Gen. Mgr.-SeriousWindows
Claire Broido Johnson, Gen. Mgr.-SeriousCapital
Kevin Surace, Chmn.

Phone:	Fax:
Toll-Free: 800-797-8159	
Address: 1250 Elko Dr., Sunnyvale, CA 94089 US	

GROWTH PLANS/SPECIAL FEATURES:

Serious Energy, Inc. produces products and services to increase the value of buildings to their owners and tenants. In use in over 70,000 projects worldwide, the company uses both material science innovations and real-time connected building analytics to create its suite of energy management programs, including: SeriousEnergy Manager (SEM), iWindow, SeriousWindows and Quiet Rock. SEM is a cloud-based service that monitors, controls and helps optimize the energy operation of building facilities. iWindow and SeriousWindows help increase building comfort while reducing heating and cooling by improving envelope energy performance. QuietRock uses reduced-material patented soundproofing technology in order to both improve building productivity as well as increase its density. Additionally, the firm recently launched SeriousCapital, a new energy efficiency financing solution program. The program identifies, finances and installs energy improvements to the customer's building at no upfront costs, allowing for increased net operating incomes and immediate customer savings. SeriousCapital is targeted to institutional and corporate customers, as well as to schools, hospitals, municipalities and universities. The company is headquartered in Sunnyvale, California, maintains six manufacturing facilities and has a network of distributors throughout the U.S. and Canada. In September 2011, the firm launched its Energy Control Center (ECC), which provides 24/7 building energy monitoring and analysis as well as optional automated control services to Serious' customers. In November 2011, the company acquired Agilewaves, Inc., a building energy management technology firm.

FINANCIALS: Sales and profits are in thousands of dollars—add 000 to get the full amount. 2011 Note: Financial information for 2011 was not available for all companies at press time.

2011 Sales: $	2011 Profits: $	**U.S. Stock Ticker: Private**
2010 Sales: $	2010 Profits: $	**Int'l Ticker:**
2009 Sales: $	2009 Profits: $	Int'l Exchange:
2008 Sales: $	2008 Profits: $	Employees: Fiscal Year Ends:
2007 Sales: $	2007 Profits: $	Parent Company:

SALARIES/BENEFITS:

Pension Plan:	ESOP Stock Plan:	Profit Sharing:	Top Exec. Salary: $	Bonus: $
Savings Plan:	Stock Purch. Plan:		Second Exec. Salary: $	Bonus: $

OTHER THOUGHTS:

Apparent Women Officers or Directors: 1
Hot Spot for Advancement for Women/Minorities:

LOCATIONS: ("Y" = Yes)

West:	Southwest:	Midwest:	Southeast:	Northeast:	International:
Y		Y		Y	Y

SFC ENERGY AG

www.sfc.com

Industry Group Code: 335999

Energy/Fuel:	Other Technologies:	Electrical Products:	Electronics:	Transportation:	Other:
Biofuels:	Irrigation:	Lighting/LEDs:	Computers:	Car Sharing:	Recycling:
Batteries/Storage:	Nanotech:	Waste Heat:	Sensors:	Electric Vehicles:	Engineering:
Solar:	Biotech:	Smart Meters:	Software:	Natural Gas Fuel:	Consulting:
Wind:	Water Tech./Treatment:	Machinery:			Investing:
Fuel Cells: Y	Ceramics:				Chemicals:

TYPES OF BUSINESS:

Fuel Cells

BRANDS/DIVISIONS/AFFILIATES:

EFOY Comfort
COM4EV
EFOY Pro
JENNY
EMILY
EMILYCube 2500
PBF Group BV

CONTACTS: *Note: Officers with more than one job title may be intentionally listed here more than once.*

Peter Podesser, CEO
Jens Muller, COO
Gerhard Inninger, CFO
Rolf Bartke, Chmn.

Phone: 49-89-673-592-0	**Fax:** 49-89-673-592-369
Toll-Free:	
Address: Eugen-Saenger-Ring 7, Brunntahl-Nord, 85649 Germany	

GROWTH PLANS/SPECIAL FEATURES:

SFC Energy AG (formerly Smart Fuel Cell AG) develops, produces and markets direct methanol fuel cells (DMFCs) as a complete product, rather than simply fuel cell systems. The firm's products are maintenance free and available in remote locations. The company's miniaturized DMFCs supply fuel through removable tank cartridges, providing utility grid-independent power sources, a quiet alternative to diesel generators and a weather-independent substitute for alternative energies. The firm has designed its products to serve four markets: leisure, mobility, industry and defense. In the leisure market, the company offers the EFOY Comfort line of fuel cells that can be used in mobile homes, cabins and boats. For the mobility segment, SFC Energy has developed the COM4EV fuel cell system to charge electric vehicles. EFOY Pro fuel cells are used by industry customers to power road weather stations, speed cameras, security and surveillance systems and oil and gas equipment, among other applications. For the defense sector, the firm produces JENNY fuel cells, compact, independent and silent portable fuel cell systems built to withstand rugged applications; EMILY, a vehicle-based line that can power on-board defense systems, such as radio or infrared detectors, without turning on the vehicle's engine; and EMILYCube 2500, a portable 100 watt system. In October 2011, the firm agreed to acquire PBF Group B.V., a power management solutions company.

FINANCIALS: Sales and profits are in thousands of dollars—add 000 to get the full amount. 2011 Note: Financial information for 2011 was not available for all companies at press time.

2011 Sales: $	2011 Profits: $	**U.S. Stock Ticker: Private**
2010 Sales: $19,150	2010 Profits: $-5,920	**Int'l Ticker:**
2009 Sales: $14,330	2009 Profits: $-4,640	Int'l Exchange:
2008 Sales: $19,860	2008 Profits: $-3,210	Employees: 97 Fiscal Year Ends: 12/31
2007 Sales: $19,590	2007 Profits: $-3,440	Parent Company:

SALARIES/BENEFITS:

Pension Plan:	ESOP Stock Plan:	Profit Sharing:	Top Exec. Salary: $	Bonus: $
Savings Plan:	Stock Purch. Plan:		Second Exec. Salary: $	Bonus: $

OTHER THOUGHTS:

Apparent Women Officers or Directors:
Hot Spot for Advancement for Women/Minorities:

LOCATIONS: ("Y" = Yes)

West:	Southwest:	Midwest:	Southeast:	Northeast:	International: Y

SHARP CORPORATION

www.sharp-world.com

Industry Group Code: 334310

Energy/Fuel:	Other Technologies:	Electrical Products:	Electronics:	Transportation:	Other:
Biofuels:	Irrigation:	Lighting/LEDs:	Computers:	Car Sharing:	Recycling:
Batteries/Storage:	Nanotech:	Waste Heat:	Sensors:	Electric Vehicles:	Engineering:
Solar:	Biotech:	Smart Meters:	Software: Y	Natural Gas Fuel:	Consulting:
Wind:	Water Tech./Treatment:	Machinery:			Investing:
Fuel Cells:	Ceramics:				Chemicals:

TYPES OF BUSINESS:

Audiovisual & Communications Equipment
Electronic Components
Solar Cells & Advanced Batteries
Home Appliances
Computers & Information Equipment
Consumer Electronics
LCD Flat Panel TVs, Monitors & Displays
Managed Print Services

BRANDS/DIVISIONS/AFFILIATES:

Sharp Electronics (Vietnam) Company Limited
LB-1085
Recurrent Energy LLC
Enel Green Power
ST Microelectronics
AU Optronics Corp (Taiwan)

CONTACTS: *Note: Officers with more than one job title may be intentionally listed here more than once.*

Kozo Takahashi, CEO/Chrm.
Mikio Katayama, COO
Mikio Katayama, Pres.
Moriyuki Okada, Group Gen. Mgr.-Domestic Sales & Mktg.
Nobuyuki Taniguchi, Group Gen. Mgr.-Human Resources
Shigeaki Mizushima, Group Gen. Mgr.-Corp. R&D
Masami Ohbatake, Gen. Mgr.-Info. Systems
Kenji Ohta, CTO/Group Gen. Mgr.-Tokyo Branch
Keiko Okada, Group Gen. Mgr.-Products & Corp. Design Group
Takashi Okuda, Group Gen. Mgr.- Mfg. Promotion
Takashi Okuda, Group Gen. Mgr.- Admin.
Toshio Adachi, Chief Legal Affairs Officer
Masayuki Mohri, Group Gen. Mgr.- Mgmt. Planning Board
Toshishige Hamana, Chief Bus. Planning Officer
Masami Ohbatake, Group Gen. Mgr.- Comm. Systems Group
Katsuaki Nomura, Group Gen. Mgr.-Corporate Acct. & Control
Kazutaka Ihori, Group Gen. Mgr.-Corp. Sales
Kozo Takahashi, CEO & Chmn. Of the Board- Sharp Electronics Corp.
Hiroshi Morimoto, Group Gen. Mgr.-Solar Systems Dev. Group
Katsuhiko Machida, Chmn.
Takashi Okuda, Group Gen. Mgr.-Global Bus. Group

Phone: 81-6-6621-1221	Fax: 81-6-6625-0918
Toll-Free:	
Address: 22-22 Nagaike-cho, Abeno-ku, Osaka, 545-8522 Japan	

GROWTH PLANS/SPECIAL FEATURES:

Sharp Corporation designs, manufactures and distributes audiovisual and communication equipment, information system products and health and environment equipment. Its audiovisual and communication products include LCD color televisions, projectors, DVD recorders and players, Blu-ray Disc recorders and players, mobile communications handsets, mobile phones and PHS terminals. Sharp information system products include personal computers, electronic dictionaries, calculators, fax machines, telephones, POS systems, electronic cash registers, LCD color monitors, information displays, software and ultrasonic cleaners. The firm's health and environment equipment includes refrigerators, superheated steam ovens, microwave ovens, air conditioners, washing machines, vacuum cleaners, air purifiers, humidifiers, electric heaters, small cooking appliances, Plasmacluster Ion generators, LED lights and solar-powered LED lights. The electronic components business produces such items as CCD/CMOS imagers, LCD modules, microprocessors, flash memory, satellite broadcasting components, RF modules, network components, LEDs, optical sensors, optical communication components and regulators. The firm is also a leading manufacturer of crystalline and thin-film solar cells. Sharp offers managed print services outsourcing, where it can take over the complete operation of a client's desktop printers and copiers with the goal of creating significant savings. In addition, the company is working on high-capacity lithium-ion battery technology. Sharp has 29 sales subsidiaries in 24 countries, 23 manufacturing bases in 14 countries and four research and development bases in three countries. In April 2011, Sharp and Taiwan's AU Optronics Corp. established a patent cross license agreement, where both firms would mutually utilize patents relating to LCD panels and modules owned by each party. In December 2011, Sharp launched its newest Eco-Products and technologies that included LCD monitors, thin-film solar modules, LED lighting for office and home purposes and reusable recycling materials.

FINANCIALS: Sales and profits are in thousands of dollars—add 000 to get the full amount. 2011 Note: Financial information for 2011 was not available for all companies at press time.

2011 Sales: $38,711,500	2011 Profits: $248,500	**U.S. Stock Ticker:**
2010 Sales: $33,512,300	2010 Profits: $53,470	**Int'l Ticker: 6753**
2009 Sales: $31,432,600	2009 Profits: $-1,388,960	Int'l Exchange: Tokyo-TSE
2008 Sales: $34,177,400	2008 Profits: $1,019,200	Employees: 55,580 Fiscal Year Ends: 3/31
2007 Sales: $26,620,000	2007 Profits: $870,000	Parent Company:

SALARIES/BENEFITS:

Pension Plan:	ESOP Stock Plan:	Profit Sharing:	Top Exec. Salary: $	Bonus: $
Savings Plan:	Stock Purch. Plan:		Second Exec. Salary: $	Bonus: $

OTHER THOUGHTS:

Apparent Women Officers or Directors:
Hot Spot for Advancement for Women/Minorities:

LOCATIONS: ("Y" = Yes)

West:	Southwest:	Midwest:	Southeast:	Northeast:	International:
Y				Y	Y

Sales, profits and employees may be estimates. Financial information, benefits and other data can change quickly and may vary from those stated here.

SHELL OIL CO

www.shell.us

Industry Group Code: 211111

Energy/Fuel:		Other Technologies:	Electrical Products:	Electronics:	Transportation:	Other:	
Biofuels:	Y	Irrigation:	Lighting/LEDs:	Computers:	Car Sharing:	Recycling:	
Batteries/Storage:		Nanotech:	Waste Heat:	Sensors:	Electric Vehicles:	Engineering:	
Solar:		Biotech:	Smart Meters:	Software:	Natural Gas Fuel:	Consulting:	
Wind:		Water Tech./Treatment:	Machinery:			Investing:	
Fuel Cells:		Ceramics:				Chemicals:	Y

TYPES OF BUSINESS:

Oil & Gas Exploration & Production
Chemicals
Power Generation
Nanocomposites
Nanocatalysts
Refineries
Pipelines & Shipping
Hydrogen Storage Technology

BRANDS/DIVISIONS/AFFILIATES:

Shell Oil Products US
Shell Chemicals Limited
Shell Gas and Power
Shell Exploration and Production
Royal Dutch Shell (Shell Group)
Motiva Enterprises LLC
Shell Hydrogen
Shell Wind Energy

CONTACTS: *Note: Officers with more than one job title may be intentionally listed here more than once.*

Marvin E. Odum, Pres.
Bill Lowrey, General Counsel/Sr. VP/Corp. Sec.
Curtis R. Frasier, Exec. VP-Americas Shell Gas & Power
Marvin E. Odum, Dir.-Shell-Upstream Americas
Mark Quartermain, Pres., Shell Energy North America (US) LP

Phone: 713-241-6161	Fax: 713-241-4044
Toll-Free:	
Address: 910 Louisiana St., Houston, TX 77002 US	

GROWTH PLANS/SPECIAL FEATURES:

Shell Oil Co., an affiliate of Royal Dutch Shell plc, is a chemical, oil and natural gas producer in the U.S., with operations in all 50 states. Shell Oil has a number of divisions, joint ventures and operations, including Shell Oil Products U.S., Motiva Enterprises, Shell Chemicals, Shell Gas and Power, Shell Exploration and Production (SEPCo) and others. These companies discover, develop, manufacture, transport and market crude oil, natural gas and chemical products. Specifically, Motiva Enterprises has three refineries which produce a total of 740,000 barrels of oil per day, as well as a network of approximately 7,700 Shell-branded stations in the eastern and southern U.S. Shell Chemicals is involved in manufacturing chemicals, including ethylene and propylene, for use in cars, computers, packaging and paints. It manufactures 15 billion pounds of chemicals annually for industrial use through three plants. SEPCo explores and develops natural gas in the U.S, with interests in five states and the Gulf of Mexico. Shell Oil's Gas and Power business is involved in power generation, gas pipeline transmission, receiving terminals, liquefied natural gas (LNG), shipping and coal gasification. Other divisions include Shell Hydrogen, focused on the development of hydrogen and fuel cell technologies from regional bases in Houston and Tokyo; and Shell Wind Energy, with eight wind farms in the U.S. and 11 in total.

Employees are offered medical and vision insurance; flexible spending accounts; disability coverage; group auto and home insurance; a group legal plan; a pension plan; a savings plan; and an employee assistance program.

FINANCIALS: Sales and profits are in thousands of dollars—add 000 to get the full amount. 2011 Note: Financial information for 2011 was not available for all companies at press time.

2011 Sales: $	2011 Profits: $	**U.S. Stock Ticker: Subsidiary**
2010 Sales: $120,000,000	2010 Profits: $	**Int'l Ticker:**
2009 Sales: $100,000,000	2009 Profits: $	Int'l Exchange:
2008 Sales: $100,818,000	2008 Profits: $	Employees: 22,000 Fiscal Year Ends: 12/31
2007 Sales: $87,548,000	2007 Profits: $	Parent Company: ROYAL DUTCH SHELL PLC

SALARIES/BENEFITS:

Pension Plan: Y	ESOP Stock Plan:	Profit Sharing:	Top Exec. Salary: $	Bonus: $
Savings Plan: Y	Stock Purch. Plan: Y		Second Exec. Salary: $	Bonus: $

OTHER THOUGHTS:

Apparent Women Officers or Directors:
Hot Spot for Advancement for Women/Minorities:

LOCATIONS: ("Y" = Yes)

West:	Southwest:	Midwest:	Southeast:	Northeast:	International:
Y	Y	Y	Y	Y	Y

SHELL WINDENERGY BV

www.shell.com/home/content/innovation/people_planet/wind

Industry Group Code: 221119

Energy/Fuel:	Other Technologies:	Electrical Products:	Electronics:	Transportation:	Other:
Biofuels:	Irrigation:	Lighting/LEDs:	Computers:	Car Sharing:	Recycling:
Batteries/Storage:	Nanotech:	Waste Heat:	Sensors:	Electric Vehicles:	Engineering:
Solar:	Biotech:	Smart Meters:	Software:	Natural Gas Fuel:	Consulting:
Wind: Y	Water Tech./Treatment:	Machinery:			Investing:
Fuel Cells:	Ceramics:				Chemicals:

TYPES OF BUSINESS:
Wind Turbine Electricity Generation

BRANDS/DIVISIONS/AFFILIATES:
Royal Dutch Shell plc

GROWTH PLANS/SPECIAL FEATURES:
Shell Windenergy BV is engaged in the development and operation of commercial-scale wind developments. The firm is a subsidiary of Royal Dutch Shell and part of its Shell Gas & Power division. It owns interests in 11 wind projects with a total capacity of around 1,100 megawatts (MW). Of this capacity, nearly 900 MW are located in the U.S. The company's operations in the U.S. include the Rock River facility in Wyoming; the Brazos and White Deer facilities in Texas; the Cabazon, Bear River and Whitewater facilities in California; and the Colorado Green facility in Colorado. European projects include the Harburg facility near Hamburg, Germany; the La Muela project in Spain; and an offshore wind park, Egmond aan Zee, in the Netherlands. The company also holds interest in the La Muela Windpark in Spain with TXU Europe Energy Trading B.V.

CONTACTS: Note: Officers with more than one job title may be intentionally listed here more than once.
Jorma Ollila, Chmn.

Phone: 31-70-377-9111	Fax: 31-70-377-3113
Toll-Free:	
Address: Carel van Bylandtlaan 30, The Hague, 2501 AN The Netherlands	

FINANCIALS: Sales and profits are in thousands of dollars—add 000 to get the full amount. 2011 Note: Financial information for 2011 was not available for all companies at press time.

2011 Sales: $	2011 Profits: $	U.S. Stock Ticker: Subsidiary
2010 Sales: $	2010 Profits: $	Int'l Ticker:
2009 Sales: $	2009 Profits: $	Int'l Exchange:
2008 Sales: $	2008 Profits: $	Employees: Fiscal Year Ends:
2007 Sales: $	2007 Profits: $	Parent Company: ROYAL DUTCH SHELL PLC

SALARIES/BENEFITS:

Pension Plan:	ESOP Stock Plan:	Profit Sharing:	Top Exec. Salary: $	Bonus: $
Savings Plan:	Stock Purch. Plan:		Second Exec. Salary: $	Bonus: $

OTHER THOUGHTS:
Apparent Women Officers or Directors:
Hot Spot for Advancement for Women/Minorities:

LOCATIONS: ("Y" = Yes)

West:	Southwest:	Midwest:	Southeast:	Northeast:	International:
	Y				Y

SIEMENS AG

www.siemens.com

Industry Group Code: 335

Energy/Fuel:	Other Technologies:	Electrical Products:	Electronics:	Transportation:	Other:	
Biofuels:	Irrigation:	Lighting/LEDs:	Computers:	Car Sharing:	Recycling:	
Batteries/Storage:	Nanotech:	Waste Heat:	Sensors:	Electric Vehicles:	Engineering:	
Solar:	Biotech:	Smart Meters:	Software:	Natural Gas Fuel:	Consulting:	Y
Wind:	Water Tech./Treatment:	Machinery: Y			Investing:	
Fuel Cells:	Ceramics:				Chemicals:	

TYPES OF BUSINESS:

Electrical Equipment Manufacturing
Energy & Power Plant Systems & Consulting
Medical & Health Care Services & Equipment
Lighting & Optical Systems
Automation Systems
Transportation & Logistics Systems
Photovoltaic Equipment

BRANDS/DIVISIONS/AFFILIATES:

Siemens IT Solutions & Services
Siemens Financial Services
Siemens Canada
Siemens Corporate Technology
Siemens Energy & Automation Inc
Siemens Energy Services
Siemens Healthcare
Osram

CONTACTS: *Note: Officers with more than one job title may be intentionally listed here more than once.*

Peter H. Loscher, CEO
Peter H. Loscher, Pres.
Joe Kaeser, Head-Finance
Brigitte Ederer, Head-Corp. Human Resources & Labor Director
Joe Kaeser, Head-IT Solutions & Svcs.
Klaus Helmrich, Chief Tech. Officer
Siegfried Russwurm, Corp. Sec.
Joe Kaeser, Head-Corp. Finance & Controlling
Roland Busch, CEO-Infrastructure & Cities Sector
Hermann Requardt, CEO-Healthcare Sector
Peter Y. Solmssen, Head-Corp. Legal & Compliance
Michael Suess, CEO-Energy Sector
Gerhard Cromme, Chmn.
Barbara Kux, Chief Sustainability Officer

Phone: 49-69-797-6660	Fax:
Toll-Free:	
Address: Wittelsbacherplatz 2, Munich, 80333 Germany	

GROWTH PLANS/SPECIAL FEATURES:

Siemens AG is one of the largest electrical engineering and electronics companies in the world, operating in the industry, energy and healthcare sectors. Additionally, Siemens is one of the largest providers of ecofriendly technologies, which generates more than one third of its annual revenue. Based in Germany, the firm sells products and services to approximately 190 countries around the globe. The industry sector's offerings range from industry automation products and services to building, lighting and mobility systems, as well as system integration for plant businesses. Additionally, this sector provides networking technology for transportation systems, including airport logistics, postal automation and railway electrification. The energy sector offers products and services related to the generation, transmission and distribution of power, as well as for the extraction, conversion and transportation of oil and gas. The healthcare sector develops, manufactures and markets diagnostic and therapeutic systems, devices and consumables, as well as information technology systems for clinical and healthcare administration settings. Besides these activities, subsidiaries Siemens IT Solutions & Services (SIS) as well as Siemens Financial Services support their industry activities as business partners, meanwhile continuing to build up their own business with external customers. In March 2011, the company announced plans to spin off Osram, one of the world's largest lighting companies, and to take it public later in the year. In October 2011, Siemens announced its investment of 1 billion Euros in Russia. In November 2011, Siemens announced the expansion of its Commercial Finance operations in India, in order to aid business and public sector customers in more efficient investment and how to maximize growth opportunities.

FINANCIALS: Sales and profits are in thousands of dollars—add 000 to get the full amount. 2011 Note: Financial information for 2011 was not available for all companies at press time.

2011 Sales: $97,931,500	2011 Profits: $8,185,900	**U.S. Stock Ticker:**
2010 Sales: $103,974,000	2010 Profits: $5,566,940	**Int'l Ticker: SIE**
2009 Sales: $113,842,000	2009 Profits: $3,404,080	Int'l Exchange: Frankfurt-Euronext
2008 Sales: $107,580,000	2008 Profits: $8,189,070	Employees: 360,000 Fiscal Year Ends: 9/30
2007 Sales: $115,406,000	2007 Profits: $3,535,760	Parent Company:

SALARIES/BENEFITS:

Pension Plan:	ESOP Stock Plan:	Profit Sharing:	Top Exec. Salary: $4,618,982	Bonus: $
Savings Plan:	Stock Purch. Plan:		Second Exec. Salary: $2,098,621	Bonus: $

OTHER THOUGHTS:

Apparent Women Officers or Directors: 5
Hot Spot for Advancement for Women/Minorities: Y

LOCATIONS: ("Y" = Yes)

West:	Southwest:	Midwest:	Southeast:	Northeast:	International:
Y	Y	Y	Y	Y	Y

SIEMENS CONCENTRATED SOLAR POWER LTD

www.energy.siemens.com/mx/en/power-generation/renewables/solar-power/concentrated-solar-power

Industry Group Code: 221119

Energy/Fuel:	Other Technologies:	Electrical Products:	Electronics:	Transportation:	Other:
Biofuels:	Irrigation:	Lighting/LEDs:	Computers:	Car Sharing:	Recycling:
Batteries/Storage:	Nanotech:	Waste Heat:	Sensors:	Electric Vehicles:	Engineering:
Solar: Y	Biotech:	Smart Meters:	Software:	Natural Gas Fuel:	Consulting:
Wind:	Water Tech./Treatment:	Machinery:			Investing:
Fuel Cells:	Ceramics:				Chemicals:

TYPES OF BUSINESS:

Solar Thermal Power Plants
Power Generation
Industrial Heating and Cooling

BRANDS/DIVISIONS/AFFILIATES:

Siemens AG
SunField LP

CONTACTS: *Note: Officers with more than one job title may be intentionally listed here more than once.*

Rene Umlauft, CEO
Michael Axmann, CFO
Gerhard Cromme, Chmn.

Phone: 972-2-995-0111	**Fax:** 972-2-999-5521
Toll-Free:	
Address: 3 Hac'shara St., Beit Shemesh, 99107 Israel	

GROWTH PLANS/SPECIAL FEATURES:

Siemens Concentrated Solar Power Ltd. (CSP), a subsidiary of Siemens AG, is an Israeli firm engaged in the design, manufacture and installation of solar arrays for large scale power generation. The firm's primary product is the solar thermal power plant, which uses its Siemens solar collector assemblies (SCA), a parabolic trough thermal technology to focus solar energy on thermal receivers containing a heat transfer fluid, which is used to generate superheated steam that powers a turbine and generates electricity. Siemens CSP operates in three divisions: power generation, distributed power and industrial heating and cooling. The power generation segment offers the firm's SunField LP power plant plug-in package, which uses its Universal Vacuum Air Collector (UVAC) 2010 solar receivers and Siemens SCA collectors to offer fully engineered solar field packages. Nine of these systems, with a total peak production capacity of 350 megawatts (MW), have been deployed in California's Mojave Desert. The distributed power segment includes smaller-scale installations for office buildings, resorts, industries and hospitals that can be adapted to provide electricity, hot water and heat. The industrial heating and cooling segment provides solar water heaters for industrial and commercial complexes and solar cooling systems for shopping malls, hospitals, hotels, commercial and industrial complexes, campuses and government facilities.

FINANCIALS: Sales and profits are in thousands of dollars—add 000 to get the full amount. 2011 Note: Financial information for 2011 was not available for all companies at press time.

2011 Sales: $	2011 Profits: $	**U.S. Stock Ticker:** Subsidiary
2010 Sales: $	2010 Profits: $	**Int'l Ticker:**
2009 Sales: $	2009 Profits: $	Int'l Exchange:
2008 Sales: $	2008 Profits: $	Employees: Fiscal Year Ends:
2007 Sales: $	2007 Profits: $	Parent Company: SIEMENS AG

SALARIES/BENEFITS:

Pension Plan:	ESOP Stock Plan:	Profit Sharing:	Top Exec. Salary: $	Bonus: $
Savings Plan:	Stock Purch. Plan:		Second Exec. Salary: $	Bonus: $

OTHER THOUGHTS:

Apparent Women Officers or Directors:
Hot Spot for Advancement for Women/Minorities:

LOCATIONS: ("Y" = Yes)

West:	Southwest:	Midwest:	Southeast:	Northeast:	International:
Y					Y

SIEMENS CORPORATE TECHNOLOGY

www.ct.siemens.com

Industry Group Code: 541712

Energy/Fuel:	Other Technologies:		Electrical Products:	Electronics:		Transportation:	Other:	
Biofuels:	Irrigation:		Lighting/LEDs:	Computers:		Car Sharing:	Recycling:	
Batteries/Storage:	Nanotech:	Y	Waste Heat:	Sensors:		Electric Vehicles:	Engineering:	Y
Solar:	Biotech:		Smart Meters:	Software:	Y	Natural Gas Fuel:	Consulting:	
Wind:	Water Tech./Treatment:		Machinery:				Investing:	
Fuel Cells:	Ceramics:						Chemicals:	

TYPES OF BUSINESS:

Research & Development
Materials
Microsystems
Production Processes
Power & Sensor Systems
Software Products
Communications

BRANDS/DIVISIONS/AFFILIATES:

Siemens Corporate Intellectual Property
Siemens Corporate Research
Siemens Technology-to-Business Center
Siemens Technology Accelerator

CONTACTS: *Note: Officers with more than one job title may be intentionally listed here more than once.*

Herman Requardt, Unit Head
Peter Loscher, Pres./CEO-Siemens AG

Phone: 49-89-636-33520	Fax: 49-89-636-35292
Toll-Free:	
Address: Wittelsbacherplatz 2, Munich, 80333 Germany	

GROWTH PLANS/SPECIAL FEATURES:

Siemens Corporate Technology brings together a worldwide network of research facilities and expert scientists to promote and develop new technologies that will help to achieve the strategic goals of its parent company, Siemens AG. Working in close collaboration with Siemens' core business units, Siemens Corporate Technology analyzes company data to develop blueprints for future developments, while also watching research trends to link scientific advances with potential new business applications. The Corporate Technology unit also works to safeguard new technologies on behalf of the company through its Corporate Intellectual Property subdivision. Research is organized into six broad technology divisions: information and communications; strategic marketing; software and engineering; production processes; power and sensor systems; and materials and Microsystems. Siemens Corporate Technology also works in direct partnership with separately managed research and development bodies in the U.S., Europe and Asia, such as Siemens Corporate Research in Princeton, New Jersey and Roke Manor Research, Ltd. in the U.K. The unit also oversees the operation of two business incubators: Siemens Technology-to-Business Center, with locations in Berkeley, California and Shanghai, China; and Siemens Technology Accelerator, located in Munich, Germany. The Technology-to-Business Centers focus on developing ideas into new Siemens products or subsidiaries, while Siemens Technology Accelerator works to create successful spin-off businesses from technologies that have been developed within Siemens Corporate Technology but are not chosen for further development within the Siemens Group. In 2010, Siemens invested 5.1% of sales, $5.45 billion, in research and development. It has 30,100 researchers and developers, with Corporate Technology employing 5,500 employees worldwide.

FINANCIALS: Sales and profits are in thousands of dollars—add 000 to get the full amount. 2011 Note: Financial information for 2011 was not available for all companies at press time.

2011 Sales: $	2011 Profits: $	**U.S. Stock Ticker: Subsidiary**
2010 Sales: $	2010 Profits: $	**Int'l Ticker:**
2009 Sales: $	2009 Profits: $	Int'l Exchange:
2008 Sales: $	2008 Profits: $	Employees: Fiscal Year Ends: 9/30
2007 Sales: $	2007 Profits: $	Parent Company: SIEMENS AG

SALARIES/BENEFITS:

Pension Plan:	ESOP Stock Plan:	Profit Sharing:	Top Exec. Salary: $	Bonus: $
Savings Plan:	Stock Purch. Plan:		Second Exec. Salary: $	Bonus: $

OTHER THOUGHTS:

Apparent Women Officers or Directors:
Hot Spot for Advancement for Women/Minorities:

LOCATIONS: ("Y" = Yes)

West:	Southwest:	Midwest:	Southeast:	Northeast:	International:
Y					Y

SIGMA-ALDRICH CORP

www.sigmaaldrich.com

Industry Group Code: 325

Energy/Fuel:		Other Technologies:		Electrical Products:		Electronics:		Transportation:		Other:	
Biofuels:	Y	Irrigation:		Lighting/LEDs:		Computers:		Car Sharing:		Recycling:	
Batteries/Storage:		Nanotech:		Waste Heat:		Sensors:		Electric Vehicles:		Engineering:	
Solar:		Biotech:	Y	Smart Meters:		Software:		Natural Gas Fuel:		Consulting:	
Wind:		Water Tech./Treatment:		Machinery:						Investing:	
Fuel Cells:		Ceramics:								Chemicals:	Y

TYPES OF BUSINESS:

Chemicals Manufacturing
Biotechnology Equipment
Pharmaceutical Ingredients
Fine Chemicals
Chromatography Products

BRANDS/DIVISIONS/AFFILIATES:

Research Essentials
Research Specialties
Research Biotech
SAFC
Cerilliant Corp
Resource Technology Corp
Vetec Quimica Fina Ltda

CONTACTS: *Note: Officers with more than one job title may be intentionally listed here more than once.*

Rakesh Sachdev, CEO
Rakesh Sachdev, Pres.
Kirk Richter, Interim CFO/VP
Gerrit van den Dool, VP-Sales
Doug Rau, VP-Human Resources
Magnus Borg, CIO/VP
Rakesh Sachdev, Chief Admin. Officer
George Miller, General Counsel/Sr. VP/Sec.
Karen Miller, VP-Strategy & Corp. Dev.
Kirk Richter, Treas.
Gilles Cottier, Pres., SAFC
Frank Wicks, Pres., Research Specialties & Essentials
David Smoller, Pres., Research Biotech
Steve Walton, VP-Quality & Safety
Barret A. Toan, Chmn.
Joseph Porwoll, Pres., Supply Chain

Phone: 314-771-5765	**Fax:** 314-771-5757
Toll-Free: 800-521-8956	
Address: 3050 Spruce St., St. Louis, MO 63103 US	

GROWTH PLANS/SPECIAL FEATURES:

Sigma-Aldrich Corp. is a life science and technology company that develops, manufactures, purchases and distributes a broad range of biochemicals and organic chemicals. The company offers roughly 147,000 chemicals (including 48,000 chemicals manufactured in-house) and 40,000 equipment products used for scientific and genomic research; biotechnology; pharmaceutical development; disease diagnosis; and pharmaceutical and high technology manufacturing. Sigma-Aldrich is structured into four units: research essentials, research specialties, research biotech and SAFC. The research essentials unit sells biological buffers; cell culture reagents; biochemicals; chemicals; solvents; and other reagents and kits. The research specialties unit provides organic chemicals, biochemicals, analytical reagents, chromatography consumables, reference materials and high-purity products. The research biotech unit supplies immunochemical, molecular biology, cell signaling and neuroscience biochemicals and kits used in biotechnology, genomic, proteomic and other life science research applications. The SAFC (fine chemicals) unit offers large-scale organic chemicals and biochemicals used in development and production by pharmaceutical, biotechnology, industrial and diagnostic companies. The company operates in 40 countries, sells its products in nearly 160 countries and services over 1 million customers. Customers include commercial laboratories; pharmaceutical and industrial companies; universities; diagnostics, chemical and biotechnology companies and hospitals; non-profit organizations; and governmental institutions. In December 2010, Sigma-Aldrich acquired Cerilliant Corp. in Round Rock, Texas, which added about 2,800 products to the company's portfolio. In January 2011, the firm purchased Resource Technology Corp., which specializes in analytical chemistry products. In May 2011, Sigma-Aldrich obtained the Brazil-based Vetec Quimica Fina Ltda., which produces over 3,000 products. In April 2011, the company unveiled its new European headquarters in St. Gallen, Switzerland.

FINANCIALS: Sales and profits are in thousands of dollars—add 000 to get the full amount. 2011 Note: Financial information for 2011 was not available for all companies at press time.

2011 Sales: $	2011 Profits: $	**U.S. Stock Ticker:** SIAL
2010 Sales: $2,271,000	2010 Profits: $384,000	**Int'l Ticker:**
2009 Sales: $2,147,600	2009 Profits: $346,700	Int'l Exchange:
2008 Sales: $2,200,700	2008 Profits: $341,500	Employees: 7,890 Fiscal Year Ends: 12/31
2007 Sales: $2,038,700	2007 Profits: $311,100	Parent Company:

SALARIES/BENEFITS:

Pension Plan: Y	ESOP Stock Plan:	Profit Sharing:	Top Exec. Salary: $809,711	Bonus: $1,052,700
Savings Plan: Y	Stock Purch. Plan:		Second Exec. Salary: $488,846	Bonus: $443,352

OTHER THOUGHTS:

Apparent Women Officers or Directors: 2
Hot Spot for Advancement for Women/Minorities: Y

LOCATIONS: ("Y" = Yes)

West:	Southwest:	Midwest:	Southeast:	Northeast:	International:
Y	Y	Y	Y	Y	Y

Sales, profits and employees may be estimates. Financial information, benefits and other data can change quickly and may vary from those stated here.

SILVER SPRING NETWORKS

www.silverspringnet.com

Industry Group Code: 33411

Energy/Fuel:	Other Technologies:	Electrical Products:		Electronics:	Transportation:	Other:
Biofuels:	Irrigation:	Lighting/LEDs:		Computers:	Car Sharing:	Recycling:
Batteries/Storage:	Nanotech:	Waste Heat:		Sensors:	Electric Vehicles:	Engineering:
Solar:	Biotech:	Smart Meters:	Y	Software:	Natural Gas Fuel:	Consulting:
Wind:	Water Tech./Treatment:	Machinery:				Investing:
Fuel Cells:	Ceramics:					Chemicals:

TYPES OF BUSINESS:

Utility Network Management Systems
Smart Grid Equipment

BRANDS/DIVISIONS/AFFILIATES:

Smart Energy Platform
Access Point
UtilityIQ
CustomerIQ
Demand Response
Silver Spring Relay

CONTACTS: Note: Officers with more than one job title may be intentionally listed here more than once.

Scott Lang, CEO
Warren Jenson, COO
Scott Lang, Pres.
John R. Joyce, CFO
Eric Dresselhuys, Chief Mktg. Officer/Exec. VP
Amy Cappellanti-Wolf, Chief Human Resources Officer
George Flammer, Chief Scientist
Raj Vaswani, CTO
Anil Gadre, Exec. VP-Prod.
Michael A. Dillon, General Counsel
Lisa Magnuson, Contact-Media
Don Reeves, Sr. VP-Smart Grid Svcs.
Scott Lang, Chmn.
Gary Gysin, Exec. VP-Worldwide Sales

Phone: 650-298-4200	Fax: 650-363-5240
Toll-Free: 866-204-0200	
Address: 555 Broadway St., Redwood City, CA 94063 US	

GROWTH PLANS/SPECIAL FEATURES:

Silver Spring Networks is a builder of networks for utility companies. The firm seeks to aid utilities in improving efficiency, reliability and customer service while reducing operating costs. Silver Spring Networks offers several network options, including improved outage management; advanced metering services, which reduce field service and support costs; a secure distribution automation product, a unified infrastructure that allows multiple applications to run on it; credit and collection services, which lessen a utility's number of accounts receivable and bad debt write-offs; electric car metering and communications systems; and Demand Response, a program that allows customers to receive automated current, hour-ahead or day-ahead pricing signals. The firm's software products include the Smart Energy Platform, which allows a utility company to use any IP-enabled device, perform intelligent load shedding, deploy IP-based consumer energy portals and more; The CustomerIQ web portal, which allows utilities to directly communicate pricing, usage and recommendations to consumers; and the UtilityIQ suite of smart energy applications. The company's Access Point device links endpoint devices and mission-critical systems to improve intelligent network control and monitoring. Another device, Silver Spring Relay, links the Access Point and Smart Energy Platform endpoint devices. Silver Spring Networks also offers network interface cards, which communicate with in-home devices and can be applied to gas, water and electrical meters, as well as automate load-control devices. The firm's many technology partners include GE Energy, Oracle, Carrier Corporation, Cisco, Digi International, ClipperCreek, S&C Electric Company and ABB.

The firm offers employee benefits including life, disability, medical, dental and vision insurance; a 401(k); an assistance program; paid time off; onsite dry cleaning and fitness center; and flexible spending accounts.

FINANCIALS: Sales and profits are in thousands of dollars—add 000 to get the full amount. 2011 Note: Financial information for 2011 was not available for all companies at press time.

2011 Sales: $	2011 Profits: $	**U.S. Stock Ticker:** Private
2010 Sales: $70,224	2010 Profits: $-148,449	**Int'l Ticker:**
2009 Sales: $3,300	2009 Profits: $-113,463	Int'l Exchange:
2008 Sales: $ 58	2008 Profits: $-40,391	Employees: 200 Fiscal Year Ends:
2007 Sales: $	2007 Profits: $	Parent Company:

SALARIES/BENEFITS:

Pension Plan:	ESOP Stock Plan:	Profit Sharing:	Top Exec. Salary: $	Bonus: $
Savings Plan: Y	Stock Purch. Plan:		Second Exec. Salary: $	Bonus: $

OTHER THOUGHTS:

Apparent Women Officers or Directors: 3
Hot Spot for Advancement for Women/Minorities: Y

LOCATIONS: ("Y" = Yes)

West:	Southwest:	Midwest:	Southeast:	Northeast:	International:
Y					Y

SINOVEL WIND GROUP CO LTD

www.sinovel.com

Industry Group Code: 33361

Energy/Fuel:	Other Technologies:	Electrical Products:	Electronics:	Transportation:	Other:
Biofuels:	Irrigation:	Lighting/LEDs:	Computers:	Car Sharing:	Recycling:
Batteries/Storage:	Nanotech:	Waste Heat:	Sensors:	Electric Vehicles:	Engineering:
Solar:	Biotech:	Smart Meters:	Software:	Natural Gas Fuel:	Consulting:
Wind: Y	Water Tech./Treatment:	Machinery:			Investing:
Fuel Cells:	Ceramics:				Chemicals:

TYPES OF BUSINESS:

Wind Turbine Manufacturing
Wind Power Equipment R&D
Wind Project Consulting

BRANDS/DIVISIONS/AFFILIATES:

SL1500
SL3000
SL5000
SL6000

GROWTH PLANS/SPECIAL FEATURES:

Sinovel Wind Group Co., Ltd. is one of China's leading designers, manufacturers and marketers of large-scale on- and offshore wind turbines. Headquartered in Beijing, the company has manufacturing facilities in China's Dalian, Jilin, Tianjin, Shandong, Jiangsu and Gansu Provinces, as well as the Inner Mongolia Autonomous Region. In addition to the firm's SL1500, SL3000, SL5000 and SL6000 Series wind turbines, it offers certain pre- and post-project services, including wind resource assessment, technical training and maintenance. Sinovel operates the National Offshore Wind Power Technology and Equipment R&D Center to develop innovative offshore wind power technology. In late 2010, the company began construction on a new manufacturing facility in the Hami District of eastern Xinjiang Autonomous Region.

CONTACTS:
Note: Officers with more than one job title may be intentionally listed here more than once.

Han Junliang, Pres.
Gang Tao, CFO/VP
Danghui Chen, CTO/VP
Liu Zhengqi, VP
Deng Yan, VP
Lecheng Li, VP
Han Junliang, Chmn.

Phone: 86-10-6251-5566	**Fax:** 86-10-8250-0072
Toll-Free:	
Address: 59 Zhongguancun St., Culture Bldg., Beijing, 100872 China	

FINANCIALS:
Sales and profits are in thousands of dollars—add 000 to get the full amount. 2011 Note: Financial information for 2011 was not available for all companies at press time.

2011 Sales: $	2011 Profits: $	**U.S. Stock Ticker:**
2010 Sales: $3,184,300	2010 Profits: $447,400	**Int'l Ticker: 601558**
2009 Sales: $2,151,100	2009 Profits: $296,600	Int'l Exchange: Shanghai-SHE
2008 Sales: $806,200	2008 Profits: $	Employees: 1,196 Fiscal Year Ends: 12/31
2007 Sales: $	2007 Profits: $	Parent Company:

SALARIES/BENEFITS:

Pension Plan:	ESOP Stock Plan:	Profit Sharing:	Top Exec. Salary: $	Bonus: $
Savings Plan:	Stock Purch. Plan:		Second Exec. Salary: $	Bonus: $

OTHER THOUGHTS:

Apparent Women Officers or Directors:
Hot Spot for Advancement for Women/Minorities:

LOCATIONS: ("Y" = Yes)

West:	Southwest:	Midwest:	Southeast:	Northeast:	International: Y

Sales, profits and employees may be estimates. Financial information, benefits and other data can change quickly and may vary from those stated here.

SKYFUEL INC

www.skyfuel.com

Industry Group Code: 237130

Energy/Fuel:	Other Technologies:	Electrical Products:	Electronics:	Transportation:	Other:
Biofuels:	Irrigation:	Lighting/LEDs:	Computers:	Car Sharing:	Recycling:
Batteries/Storage:	Nanotech:	Waste Heat:	Sensors:	Electric Vehicles:	Engineering:
Solar: Y	Biotech:	Smart Meters:	Software:	Natural Gas Fuel:	Consulting:
Wind:	Water Tech./Treatment:	Machinery:			Investing:
Fuel Cells:	Ceramics:				Chemicals:

TYPES OF BUSINESS:

Solar Thermal Power Technology
Reflective Films
Controls and Drives for Solar Power

BRANDS/DIVISIONS/AFFILIATES:

SkyTrough
SkyTrakker
OnSun
G.C. Andersen Partners LLC
ReflecTech Mirror Film
ReflecTech Inc
Leaf Clean Energy Company

CONTACTS: Note: Officers with more than one job title may be intentionally listed here more than once.

Richard J. LeBlanc, CEO
Jim Dixon, Interim CFO
Alison Mason, Dir.-Mktg. Comm.
Randy Gee, CTO
Andrew McMahan, VP-Prod. Mgmt.
David White, Chief Eng. Officer
Kelly Beninga, Chief Commercial Officer
Randy Gee, Pres., ReflecTech, Inc.
Eric John, VP-Projects & Transmission
Richard J. LeBlanc, Chmn.

Phone: 303-330-0276	Fax:
Toll-Free:	
Address: 18300 W. Hwy. 72, Arvada, CO 80007 US	

GROWTH PLANS/SPECIAL FEATURES:

SkyFuel, Inc. is a provider of solar thermal power and services. The firm is a major supplier of utility-scale concentrating solar power (CSP) systems. The company captures and utilizes solar radiation to produce steam for electricity generation and industrial applications. SkyFuel's proprietary product, SkyTrough, is an advanced, glass-free parabolic trough solar thermal collector. Its other products include SkyTrakker, which provides the local electronics that control the movement of SkyTrough; and OnSun, an integrated control and drive system that positions a parabolic trough concentrator to focus solar radiation onto a thermal receiver (jointly manufactured with Helac Corporation). ReflecTech, Inc., the firm's wholly-owned subsidiary, holds an exclusive worldwide license for ReflecTech Mirror Film, a high-reflectance silverized polymer film used as a mirror surface in solar technologies such as the SkyTrough. ReflecTech Mirror Film, jointly developed by ReflecTech and the National Renewable Energy Laboratory, is one of the only high-reflectance mirror films proven for outdoor applications. SkyFuel has received funding from investors Leaf Clean Energy Company and G.C. Andersen Partners, LLC. In March 2011, the firm agreed to build a new solar power facility in China. Also in 2011, the company formed new distribution agreements with Italian firm Termoindustriale and Brazilian company Braxenergy.

FINANCIALS: Sales and profits are in thousands of dollars—add 000 to get the full amount. 2011 Note: Financial information for 2011 was not available for all companies at press time.

2011 Sales: $	2011 Profits: $	U.S. Stock Ticker: Private
2010 Sales: $	2010 Profits: $	Int'l Ticker:
2009 Sales: $	2009 Profits: $	Int'l Exchange:
2008 Sales: $	2008 Profits: $	Employees: Fiscal Year Ends:
2007 Sales: $	2007 Profits: $	Parent Company:

SALARIES/BENEFITS:

Pension Plan:	ESOP Stock Plan:	Profit Sharing:	Top Exec. Salary: $	Bonus: $
Savings Plan:	Stock Purch. Plan:		Second Exec. Salary: $	Bonus: $

OTHER THOUGHTS:

Apparent Women Officers or Directors: 2
Hot Spot for Advancement for Women/Minorities: Y

LOCATIONS: ("Y" = Yes)

West:	Southwest:	Midwest:	Southeast:	Northeast:	International:
Y	Y				

SKYPOWER LIMITED

www.skypower.com

Industry Group Code: 221119

Energy/Fuel:	Other Technologies:	Electrical Products:	Electronics:	Transportation:	Other:
Biofuels:	Irrigation:	Lighting/LEDs:	Computers:	Car Sharing:	Recycling:
Batteries/Storage:	Nanotech:	Waste Heat:	Sensors:	Electric Vehicles:	Engineering:
Solar: Y	Biotech:	Smart Meters:	Software:	Natural Gas Fuel:	Consulting:
Wind:	Water Tech./Treatment:	Machinery:			Investing:
Fuel Cells:	Ceramics:				Chemicals:

TYPES OF BUSINESS:

Solar Power Generation

BRANDS/DIVISIONS/AFFILIATES:

SunEdison LLC
Conergy Inc
CIM Group

CONTACTS: *Note: Officers with more than one job title may be intentionally listed here more than once.*

Kerry Adler, CEO
Kerry Adler, Pres.
Richard Ressler, Chmn.

Phone: 416-979-4625	**Fax:** 416-981-8686
Toll-Free:	
Address: 130 Adelaide St. W, Toronto, ON M5H 3P5 Canada	

GROWTH PLANS/SPECIAL FEATURES:

SkyPower Limited, a subsidiary of CIM Group, is a leading Canadian developer of solar energy projects and is active in the construction and operation of solar power facilities. The company operates through three segments: the Solar Energy Group, which develops utility scale solar projects across North America, primarily in Ontairo and the southwestern U.S.; Solar Projects, which works to build solar parks that can power up to 1,000 homes; and Solar Roof Tops, which offers commercial solar panels for residential and business purposes. The firm has projects in Canada and the U.S. via partnerships with SunEdison LLC and Conergy, Inc. SkyPower created a joint venture with SunEdison to develop, build, own and operate solar photovoltaic (PV) farms across Ontario. The joint venture currently operates roughly 88 MW of solar projects, including one of the largest solar PV energy parks in North America, the 9.1 MW First Light facility in Stone Mills Ontario. The company also has three Class 3 solar facility projects in the planning and development stage: the Little Creek Solar Project in North Frederiksburgh, Ontario; the Glenn Arm Power Project, in Kawartha Lake, Ontario; and the Highlight Solar Power Project in Sudbury, Ontario. In early 2010, the firm began construction on the SunE Sky Solar parks in Norfolk, Ontario, through the SunEdison joint venture. When completed, the parks are expected to generate over 19 million kilowatt hours (kWh) of electricity in their first year of operation and nearly 400 million kWh over 20 years. Also in 2010, SkyPower formed a joint venture with Conergy, Inc. to deploy solar energy solutions on commercial rooftops in Canada. In December 2010, the company began construction on an 8.5 MW project in Thunder Bay, Ontario.

FINANCIALS: Sales and profits are in thousands of dollars—add 000 to get the full amount. 2011 Note: Financial information for 2011 was not available for all companies at press time.

2011 Sales: $	2011 Profits: $	**U.S. Stock Ticker:** Subsidiary
2010 Sales: $	2010 Profits: $	**Int'l Ticker:**
2009 Sales: $	2009 Profits: $	Int'l Exchange:
2008 Sales: $	2008 Profits: $	Employees: Fiscal Year Ends:
2007 Sales: $	2007 Profits: $	Parent Company: CIM GROUP

SALARIES/BENEFITS:

Pension Plan:	ESOP Stock Plan:	Profit Sharing:	Top Exec. Salary: $	Bonus: $
Savings Plan:	Stock Purch. Plan:		Second Exec. Salary: $	Bonus: $

OTHER THOUGHTS:

Apparent Women Officers or Directors:
Hot Spot for Advancement for Women/Minorities:

LOCATIONS: ("Y" = Yes)

West:	Southwest:	Midwest:	Southeast:	Northeast:	International: Y

SOLAIREDIRECT

www.solairedirect.com

Industry Group Code: 221119

Energy/Fuel:		Other Technologies:		Electrical Products:		Electronics:		Transportation:		Other:	
Biofuels:		Irrigation:		Lighting/LEDs:		Computers:		Car Sharing:		Recycling:	
Batteries/Storage:		Nanotech:		Waste Heat:		Sensors:	Y	Electric Vehicles:		Engineering:	Y
Solar:	Y	Biotech:		Smart Meters:		Software:	Y	Natural Gas Fuel:		Consulting:	
Wind:		Water Tech./Treatment:		Machinery:						Investing:	
Fuel Cells:		Ceramics:								Chemicals:	

TYPES OF BUSINESS:

Solar Energy
Photovoltaics

BRANDS/DIVISIONS/AFFILIATES:

CONTACTS: *Note: Officers with more than one job title may be intentionally listed here more than once.*

Thierry Lepercq, CEO
Amaury Kornniloff, Head-Bus. Dev.
Thierry Lepercq, Co-Founder
Stephane Jallat, Managing Dir.
Amaury Kornniloff, Deputy Managing Dir.
Frederik Nilsson, Head-Int'l

Phone: 33-1-40-06-02-20	**Fax:** 33-1-40-06-19-90
Toll-Free: 0-810-423-011	
Address: 52 rue de la Victoire, Paris, 75009 France	

GROWTH PLANS/SPECIAL FEATURES:

Solairedirect is an energy company that is involved in solar power generation. From the production of solar panels to the construction and operation of solar power arrays, the firm is involved in every phase of the process. Solairedirect divides its services into three segments, those it offers to private customers, those it offers to commercial entities and those it offers to much larger entities like city governments. For private customers, the firm's service packages cover every step of solar array installation, from fitting the panels to a houses roof to monitoring performance to insure maximum electricity production. The packages offered to commercial entities are similar to those offered to private customers, in that they are roof top installations, just of a larger scale. For larger entities like local governments, Solairedirect offers solar power plant programs, which handle every aspect of the project and mobilize the appropriate local actors. The company has operations in France, Southern Africa, India, Chile, Morocco and Malaysia.

FINANCIALS: Sales and profits are in thousands of dollars—add 000 to get the full amount. 2011 Note: Financial information for 2011 was not available for all companies at press time.

2011 Sales: $	2011 Profits: $	**U.S. Stock Ticker: Private**	
2010 Sales: $	2010 Profits: $	**Int'l Ticker:**	
2009 Sales: $	2009 Profits: $	Int'l Exchange:	
2008 Sales: $	2008 Profits: $	Employees:	Fiscal Year Ends:
2007 Sales: $	2007 Profits: $	Parent Company:	

SALARIES/BENEFITS:

Pension Plan:	ESOP Stock Plan:	Profit Sharing:	Top Exec. Salary: $	Bonus: $
Savings Plan:	Stock Purch. Plan:		Second Exec. Salary: $	Bonus: $

OTHER THOUGHTS:

Apparent Women Officers or Directors: 2
Hot Spot for Advancement for Women/Minorities:

LOCATIONS: ("Y" = Yes)

West:	Southwest:	Midwest:	Southeast:	Northeast:	International: Y

SOLARCITY

www.solarcity.com

Industry Group Code: 221119

Energy/Fuel:	Other Technologies:	Electrical Products:	Electronics:	Transportation:	Other:
Biofuels:	Irrigation:	Lighting/LEDs:	Computers:	Car Sharing:	Recycling:
Batteries/Storage: Y	Nanotech:	Waste Heat:	Sensors:	Electric Vehicles:	Engineering:
Solar: Y	Biotech:	Smart Meters:	Software:	Natural Gas Fuel:	Consulting:
Wind:	Water Tech./Treatment:	Machinery:			Investing:
Fuel Cells:	Ceramics:				Chemicals:

TYPES OF BUSINESS:

Solar Panel Leasing
Solar Panel Installation
Solar Array Design Services
Solar Array Maintenance & Repair

BRANDS/DIVISIONS/AFFILIATES:

GroSolar
SolarLease

CONTACTS: Note: Officers with more than one job title may be intentionally listed here more than once.

Lyndon Rive, CEO
Peter Rive, COO
Robert Kelly, CFO
Diana Helfrich, VP-Mktg.
Linda Keala, VP-Human Resources
Ben Tarbell, VP-Prod.
Seth Weissman, General Counsel/VP-Legal
Mark Roe, VP-Oper.
Aaron Gillmore, VP-Solar Dev.
John Stanton, VP-Gov't Affairs
Ben Cook, VP-Structured Finance
Tom Leyden, VP-Commercial Sales
Chrysanthe Gussis, VP
Elon Musk, Chmn.

Phone: 650-638-1028	Fax: 650-638-1029
Toll-Free: 888-765-2489	
Address: 3055 Clearview Way, San Mateo, CA 94402 US	

GROWTH PLANS/SPECIAL FEATURES:

SolarCity is a full-service provider of solar power technologies to residential, commercial and government customers. The firm provides initial consultation, design and engineering services; installation, maintenance and monitoring services; and sales and financing of solar panels and solar energy systems. The firm offers several options for consumers. SolarCity's SolarLease product allows participants to install solar systems with no money down, avoiding the initial setup costs generally associated with solar system setup. Customers using the SolarLease then pay SolarCity a set monthly lease payment; in return, SolarCity monitors, maintains and repairs the systems for the entirety of the lease period. When this period expires, customers have the option of upgrading to a new system with the latest solar technology, extending the lease in 5 year increments or having the panels removed for free. SolarCity's PurePower option offers consumers the option of purchasing solar power directly from SolarCity. The firm installs a solar array on the customer's residence or place of business; the customer then purchases the electricity produced by the array from SolarCity at market rates. SolarCity maintains ownership of the solar arrays and is responsible for monitoring, maintenance and repairs. The firm does not manufacture the products it leases; instead, it sources its solar technologies from various solar companies. The company also offers energy efficiency consulting. SolarCity operates in Delaware, Hawaii, Maryland, Massachusetts, New Jersey, New York, Texas, Arizona, California, Oregon, Pennsylvania, Colorado and Washington D.C. In February 2011, SolarCity acquired northeastern U.S. solar panel installer GroSolar. In September 2011, the firm and the U.S. government agreed to a major deal in which SolarCity will install as many as 160,000 rooftop solar installations at the privately run military housing complexes of 124 military bases in 34 states. The deal will roughly double the amount of installed solar panels in the country.

FINANCIALS: Sales and profits are in thousands of dollars—add 000 to get the full amount. 2011 Note: Financial information for 2011 was not available for all companies at press time.

2011 Sales: $	2011 Profits: $	U.S. Stock Ticker: Private
2010 Sales: $	2010 Profits: $	Int'l Ticker:
2009 Sales: $	2009 Profits: $	Int'l Exchange:
2008 Sales: $	2008 Profits: $	Employees: Fiscal Year Ends:
2007 Sales: $	2007 Profits: $	Parent Company:

SALARIES/BENEFITS:

Pension Plan:	ESOP Stock Plan:	Profit Sharing:	Top Exec. Salary: $	Bonus: $
Savings Plan:	Stock Purch. Plan:		Second Exec. Salary: $	Bonus: $

OTHER THOUGHTS:

Apparent Women Officers or Directors: 3
Hot Spot for Advancement for Women/Minorities: Y

LOCATIONS: ("Y" = Yes)

West:	Southwest:	Midwest:	Southeast:	Northeast:	International:
Y	Y				

SOLARGENIX ENERGY LLC

www.solargenix.com

Industry Group Code: 333

Energy/Fuel:		Other Technologies:		Electrical Products:		Electronics:	Transportation:		Other:	
Biofuels:		Irrigation:		Lighting/LEDs:		Computers:	Car Sharing:		Recycling:	
Batteries/Storage:		Nanotech:		Waste Heat:	Y	Sensors:	Electric Vehicles:		Engineering:	Y
Solar:	Y	Biotech:		Smart Meters:		Software:	Natural Gas Fuel:		Consulting:	
Wind:		Water Tech./Treatment:	Y	Machinery:					Investing:	
Fuel Cells:		Ceramics:							Chemicals:	

TYPES OF BUSINESS:

Solar Power Plants
Power Generation
Architecture & Development
Solar Water & Space Heating

BRANDS/DIVISIONS/AFFILIATES:

Power Roof
American South General Contractors
Innovative Design Inc

CONTACTS:
Note: Officers with more than one job title may be intentionally listed here more than once.

John F. Myles, III, CEO
John F. Myles, III, Pres.

Phone: 919-776-2000	**Fax:** 919-775-1915
Toll-Free:	
Address: 1378 McNeill Rd., Sanford, NC 27330 US	

GROWTH PLANS/SPECIAL FEATURES:

Solargenix Energy LLC is a company engaged in the design, manufacture, construction and installation of thermal solar energy systems. The firm's products can be configured to generate electricity, heat water and create steam for residential, industrial, institutional, commercial and utility customers. The company operates in five divisions: power generation; pre-engineered package systems; buildings; solar water and space heating; and franchising and licensing. The power generation segment comprises the firm's various Solar Electric Generation Systems (SEGS) projects around the world. The SEGS can be used as stand-alone power systems or can be combined with other generation technologies, such as combined cycle natural gas, diesel, wind, biomass and landfill gas. The firm has SEGS projects under development with capacities ranging from 1 megawatt (MW) to over 1,000 MW. The pre-engineered packaged systems division is working to commercialize residential combined heating and cooling products for sale to residential and commercial customers. The segment operates in partnership with heat-engine electric generator and air-conditioning companies, such as Yazaki, Carrier and Trane to develop and commercialize its products. Solargenix Energy's building division provides sustainable architectural design and consulting services. The solar water and space heating segment uses the company's solar concentrating technologies to heat water for residential and commercial use. The franchising and licensing segment consolidates Solargenix Energy's patents and intellectual property operations. One of Solargenix Energy's main products is Power Roof, a waterproof building roof structure that is also a high-temperature solar collector; a natural day lighting and insulating system; and a radiant and infiltration barrier. The firm's affiliates include Innovative Design, Inc. and American South General Contractors.

FINANCIALS:
Sales and profits are in thousands of dollars—add 000 to get the full amount. 2011 Note: Financial information for 2011 was not available for all companies at press time.

2011 Sales: $	2011 Profits: $	**U.S. Stock Ticker:** Private	
2010 Sales: $	2010 Profits: $	**Int'l Ticker:**	
2009 Sales: $	2009 Profits: $	Int'l Exchange:	
2008 Sales: $	2008 Profits: $	Employees:	Fiscal Year Ends:
2007 Sales: $	2007 Profits: $	Parent Company:	

SALARIES/BENEFITS:

Pension Plan:	ESOP Stock Plan:	Profit Sharing:	Top Exec. Salary: $	Bonus: $
Savings Plan:	Stock Purch. Plan:		Second Exec. Salary: $	Bonus: $

OTHER THOUGHTS:

Apparent Women Officers or Directors:
Hot Spot for Advancement for Women/Minorities:

LOCATIONS: ("Y" = Yes)

West:	Southwest:	Midwest:	Southeast:	Northeast:	International:
		Y	Y		

SOLARONE SOLUTIONS LLC

www.solarone.net

Industry Group Code: 334413

Energy/Fuel:	Other Technologies:	Electrical Products:		Electronics:	Transportation:	Other:
Biofuels:	Irrigation:	Lighting/LEDs:	Y	Computers:	Car Sharing:	Recycling:
Batteries/Storage:	Nanotech:	Waste Heat:		Sensors:	Electric Vehicles:	Engineering:
Solar: Y	Biotech:	Smart Meters:		Software:	Natural Gas Fuel:	Consulting:
Wind:	Water Tech./Treatment:	Machinery:				Investing:
Fuel Cells:	Ceramics:					Chemicals:

TYPES OF BUSINESS:

Photovoltaic Generators
Photovoltaic Lighting

BRANDS/DIVISIONS/AFFILIATES:

Harvester
Consortium for Solar Lighting
SO-Bright
Essentials
Flare
Basic
Landscape
Shoebox

CONTACTS: Note: Officers with more than one job title may be intentionally listed here more than once.

Moneer H. Azzam, CEO
Moneer H. Azzam, Pres.
Ilze Greene, Dir.-Mktg. & Sales

Phone: 339-225-4530	**Fax:** 339-225-4539
Toll-Free: 877-527-6461	
Address: 330 Reservoir St., Needham, MA 02494 US	

GROWTH PLANS/SPECIAL FEATURES:

SolarOne Solutions LLC is a designer, manufacturer and distributor of small-scale photovoltaic (PV) solutions for lighting and electricity-gathering. The company's products consist of the SolarOne series of PV lighting systems, which includes the Basic series, the Flare series, the Landscape series, the Essentials series, the Shoebox series, the Shelter series, the Canopy series and custom work. All of the firm's lighting products include LED lamps with a 50,000 hour life span, programmable lighting controls, automatic system recalibration for low-energy scenarios and remote control system adjustment. SolarOne's Harvester-branded solar generators can be utilized anywhere off-the-grid power is necessary, providing water purification, lighting, remote power and wireless telecommunication. The firm markets these products through independent dealers to customers including major college campuses, government laboratories and municipalities. The company's SO-Bright technology manufacturing partners include Hadco, Lumec, Gardco, Day-Brite, Duo-Guard and Provincial. In January 2011, SolarOne Solutions received its third patent for its SO-Bright technology. In April 2011, the firm established the Consortium for Solar Lighting, along with companies Inovus Solar, Inc., Sharp Electronics Corporation and Carmanah Technologies Corp.

The firm offers employees benefits including medical insurance.

FINANCIALS: Sales and profits are in thousands of dollars—add 000 to get the full amount. 2011 Note: Financial information for 2011 was not available for all companies at press time.

2011 Sales: $	2011 Profits: $	**U.S. Stock Ticker:** Private
2010 Sales: $	2010 Profits: $	**Int'l Ticker:**
2009 Sales: $	2009 Profits: $	Int'l Exchange:
2008 Sales: $	2008 Profits: $	Employees: Fiscal Year Ends:
2007 Sales: $	2007 Profits: $	Parent Company:

SALARIES/BENEFITS:

Pension Plan:	ESOP Stock Plan:	Profit Sharing:	Top Exec. Salary: $	Bonus: $
Savings Plan:	Stock Purch. Plan:		Second Exec. Salary: $	Bonus: $

OTHER THOUGHTS:

Apparent Women Officers or Directors:
Hot Spot for Advancement for Women/Minorities:

LOCATIONS: ("Y" = Yes)

West:	Southwest:	Midwest:	Southeast:	Northeast: Y	International:

SOLARRESERVE

www.solar-reserve.com

Industry Group Code: 237130

Energy/Fuel:		Other Technologies:	Electrical Products:	Electronics:	Transportation:	Other:
Biofuels:		Irrigation:	Lighting/LEDs:	Computers:	Car Sharing:	Recycling:
Batteries/Storage:		Nanotech:	Waste Heat:	Sensors:	Electric Vehicles:	Engineering:
Solar:	Y	Biotech:	Smart Meters:	Software:	Natural Gas Fuel:	Consulting:
Wind:		Water Tech./Treatment:	Machinery:			Investing:
Fuel Cells:		Ceramics:				Chemicals:

TYPES OF BUSINESS:

Concentrated Solar Power Technology
Energy Storage Technology

BRANDS/DIVISIONS/AFFILIATES:

United Technologies Corp.
US Renewables Group
Rocketdyne
Hamilton Sundstrand
Solar Power Tower
Good Energies
Nazarian Enterprises
Argonaut Private Equity

CONTACTS: Note: Officers with more than one job title may be intentionally listed here more than once.

Kevin Smith, CEO
Michael Whalen, CFO
William R. Gould, Jr., CTO
Tim J. Connor, VP-Eng.
Chris Costanzo, Dir.-Legal
Tom Georgis, VP-Dev.
Chris Gerlach, Dir.-Finance
Matt Held, VP-Project Mgmt. & Construction
Alistair Jessop, VP-Dev.
Tim J. Connor, VP-Tech
Andrew Wang, Dir.-Dev.
Lee Bailey, Chmn.

Phone: 310-315-2200	Fax: 310-315-2201
Toll-Free: 866-622-2778	
Address: 2425 Olympic Blvd., Ste. E. 500, Santa Monica, CA 90404 US	

GROWTH PLANS/SPECIAL FEATURES:

SolarReserve develops solar energy power plants that generate and store electricity using molten salt Solar Power Tower technology. The company's founding partners are United Technologies, a leading advanced technology company, and US Renewables Group, an investment firm dedicated to renewable power and clean fuel ventures. Molten salt technology, originally developed by the Rocketdyne division of Hamilton Sundstrand, a wholly-owned subsidiary of United Technologies Corporation, uses thousands of tracking mirrors (called heliostats) to focus solar energy onto the top of a Power Tower. Within the receiver, the concentrated sunlight heats molten salt, a mixture of sodium and potassium nitrate, to over 1,000 degrees Fahrenheit. Because molten salt maintains 98% thermal efficiency, the energy stored within it can be used 24 hours per day, without needing constant sunlight. No fossil fuels are required to operate the molten salt plants. SolarReserve holds the exclusive worldwide license to build Concentrated Solar Power (CSP) plants using molten salt technology. The company's target regions for CSP development include the Southwest U.S., southern Europe, Australia and Africa. The firm's other partners include Citi's Sustainable Development Investors, Good Energies, Nazarian Enterprises, Argonaut Private Equity, Credit Suisse, and the PCG Clean Energy Fund.

FINANCIALS: Sales and profits are in thousands of dollars—add 000 to get the full amount. 2011 Note: Financial information for 2011 was not available for all companies at press time.

2011 Sales: $	2011 Profits: $	U.S. Stock Ticker: Private
2010 Sales: $	2010 Profits: $	Int'l Ticker:
2009 Sales: $	2009 Profits: $	Int'l Exchange:
2008 Sales: $	2008 Profits: $	Employees: Fiscal Year Ends: 12/31
2007 Sales: $	2007 Profits: $	Parent Company:

SALARIES/BENEFITS:

Pension Plan:	ESOP Stock Plan:	Profit Sharing:	Top Exec. Salary: $	Bonus: $
Savings Plan:	Stock Purch. Plan:		Second Exec. Salary: $	Bonus: $

OTHER THOUGHTS:

Apparent Women Officers or Directors:
Hot Spot for Advancement for Women/Minorities:

LOCATIONS: ("Y" = Yes)

West:	Southwest:	Midwest:	Southeast:	Northeast:	International:
Y					Y

SOLARWORLD AG

www.solarworld.de

Industry Group Code: 334413

Energy/Fuel:	Other Technologies:	Electrical Products:	Electronics:	Transportation:	Other:
Biofuels:	Irrigation:	Lighting/LEDs:	Computers:	Car Sharing:	Recycling:
Batteries/Storage:	Nanotech:	Waste Heat:	Sensors:	Electric Vehicles:	Engineering:
Solar: Y	Biotech:	Smart Meters:	Software:	Natural Gas Fuel:	Consulting:
Wind: Y	Water Tech./Treatment:	Machinery:			Investing:
Fuel Cells:	Ceramics:				Chemicals:

TYPES OF BUSINESS:

Solar Cells
Solar & Wind Energy Parks, Operation & Construction
Renewable Energy Power Stations
Silicon Mining, Processing & Recycling
Silicon Wafers

BRANDS/DIVISIONS/AFFILIATES:

SolarWorld Innovations GmbH
SolarWorld Industries America LP
Sunicon AG
SolarWorld California LLC
SolarWorld Iberica SL
SolarWorld Africa PTY Ltd
SolarWorld Asia Pacific PTE Ltd
Solar Cycle GmbH

CONTACTS: *Note: Officers with more than one job title may be intentionally listed here more than once.*

Frank H. Asbeck, CEO
Boris Klebensberger, COO
Philipp Koecke, CFO
Frank Henn, Chief Sales Officer
Georg Gansen, Deputy Chmn.
Claus Recktenwald, Chmn.

Phone: 49-228-559-20-0	Fax: 49-228-559-20-99
Toll-Free:	
Address: Martin-Luthur-King-St. 24, Bonn, 53175 Germany	

GROWTH PLANS/SPECIAL FEATURES:

SolarWorld AG produces and markets products for various stages of solar power generation. It is also involved in the planning, construction and operation of solar energy power stations. The group has 11 locations worldwide, including production plants, as well as a holding company and joint ventures. Its activities are categorized into five business segments: Wafers, Cells, Modules, Trading and Other. The Wafers segment involves the production of crystalline solar wafers to be later used in solar cell production. Subsidiaries in this segment include Deutsche Solar in Germany and SolarWorld Industries America, L.P. in the U.S. The Cells segment involves the production of silicon-based solar cells for use in solar power modules, and includes subsidiaries Deutsche Cell in Germany and SolarWorld Industries in the U.S. The Modules segment involves the hook-up and framing of solar cells into modules used in power generation, and involves subsidiaries Solar Factory in Germany and SolarWorld Industries in the U.S. The Trading segment involves the international distribution of SolarWorld modules and complete systems. Subsidiaries in this segment include SolarWorld California, LLC; SolarWorld Iberica S.L. in Spain; SolarWorld Africa (PTY.) Ltd.; and SolarWorld Asia Pacific PTE Ltd., located in Singapore. Other subsidiaries of the company include SolarWorld Innovations GmbH, which is in charge of research and development activities; and Sunicon AG, which provides raw materials to the company. Since taking over the solar activities of the Shell Group, SolarWorld has been expanding its presence in North America. In July 2011, the firm and a group of companies including Preiss-Daimler Chemical Park established new joint venture called Solar Cycle GmbH to produce metal products from recycled solar modules. SolarWorld holds a 24% interest in the new company.

FINANCIALS: Sales and profits are in thousands of dollars—add 000 to get the full amount. 2011 Note: Financial information for 2011 was not available for all companies at press time.

2011 Sales: $	2011 Profits: $	**U.S. Stock Ticker:**	
2010 Sales: $1,854,800	2010 Profits: $124,000	**Int'l Ticker: SWV**	
2009 Sales: $1,329,710	2009 Profits: $77,070	Int'l Exchange: Frankfurt-Euronext	
2008 Sales: $1,370,150	2008 Profits: $223,790	Employees: 950 Fiscal Year Ends: 12/31	
2007 Sales: $1,090,400	2007 Profits: $178,900	Parent Company:	

SALARIES/BENEFITS:

Pension Plan:	ESOP Stock Plan:	Profit Sharing:	Top Exec. Salary: $	Bonus: $
Savings Plan:	Stock Purch. Plan:		Second Exec. Salary: $	Bonus: $

OTHER THOUGHTS:

Apparent Women Officers or Directors:
Hot Spot for Advancement for Women/Minorities:

LOCATIONS: ("Y" = Yes)

West:	Southwest:	Midwest:	Southeast:	Northeast:	International:
Y					Y

SOLAZYME

Industry Group Code: 325199

www.solazyme.com

Energy/Fuel:		Other Technologies:		Electrical Products:		Electronics:		Transportation:		Other:	
Biofuels:	Y	Irrigation:		Lighting/LEDs:		Computers:		Car Sharing:		Recycling:	
Batteries/Storage:		Nanotech:		Waste Heat:		Sensors:		Electric Vehicles:		Engineering:	
Solar:		Biotech:	Y	Smart Meters:		Software:		Natural Gas Fuel:		Consulting:	
Wind:		Water Tech./Treatment:		Machinery:						Investing:	
Fuel Cells:		Ceramics:								Chemicals:	

TYPES OF BUSINESS:

Biofuel Research & Development

BRANDS/DIVISIONS/AFFILIATES:

Soladiesel BD
Soladiesel RD
Solazyme Health Sciences
Whole Cell Cosmetics
Golden Chlorella High Protein
Golden Chlorella Omega
Altruest
Solajet

CONTACTS: *Note: Officers with more than one job title may be intentionally listed here more than once.*

Jonathan S. Wolfson, CEO
Jeff Webster, COO
Harrison F. Dillon, Pres.
Tyler W. Painter, CFO
Harrison F. Dillon, CTO
Adrian Galvez, Sr. VP-Eng.
Paul T. Quinlan, General Counsel/Sr. VP
Genet Garamendi, VP-Corp. Comm.
Peter J. Licari, Exec. VP-Tech.
Rogerio Manso, Chief Commercialization Officer-Tailored Oils
Frederic Stoeckel, Sr. VP/Gen. Mgr.-Solazyme Health Sciences
Jerry Fiddler, Chmn.

Phone: 650-780-4777	**Fax:** 650-989-6700
Toll-Free:	
Address: 225 Gateway Blvd., San Francisco, CA 94080 US	

GROWTH PLANS/SPECIAL FEATURES:

Solazyme is a renewable oil and bioproducts firm. The company has developed technology that allows for the large scale production of oil and biomaterials from algae in standard fermentation facilities in an efficient manner. Solazyme's indirect photosynthesis bioproduction process, which reduces carbon dioxide by as much as 95% versus fossil fuel production, utilizes microalgae to convert biomass directly into oil and other biomaterials. In addition to fossil fuels, this technology can be utilized in an array of products, including foods, oleochemicals and cosmetics. The firm has manufactured thousands of gallons of oil and hundreds of tons of biomaterials. The company's products include Soladiesel BD and Soladiesel RD for use in cars and military vehicles; and Solajet, for use as fuel for jets. Through division Solazyme Health Sciences, Solazyme uses its technology to create products such as Alguronic Acid, a unique family of polysaccharides which has been shown to prevent DNA damage and stimulate collagen/elastin production; Golden Chlorella High Protein and Golden Chlorella Omega, nutraceuticals that act as ingredients in consumer products, such as supplements, powder blends, smoothies, juices and health/fitness bars; and Whole Cell Cosmetics, which adds nutrient-rich microalgae to shampoos, conditioners and skin moisturizers. Solazyme Health Sciences also participates in the development of Altruest, a skin care beauty product that has been clinically-proven to reduce the appearance of wrinkles, pore-size and skin roughness. Altruest combines a topical serum containing Alguronic Acid and an oral supplement with ingredients such as algal micronutrients and algal oil. In late 2010, Solazyme formed an exclusive distribution agreement with Sephora International to distribute Algenist in Sephora stores in certain countries in Europe and select countries in Asia and the Middle East. In 2011, the firm formed development agreements with Unilever and Dow.

FINANCIALS: Sales and profits are in thousands of dollars—add 000 to get the full amount. 2011 Note: Financial information for 2011 was not available for all companies at press time.

2011 Sales: $	2011 Profits: $	**U.S. Stock Ticker:** SZYM	
2010 Sales: $37,970	2010 Profits: $-16,200	**Int'l Ticker:**	
2009 Sales: $9,160	2009 Profits: $-16,280	Int'l Exchange:	
2008 Sales: $	2008 Profits: $	Employees: 116	Fiscal Year Ends: 12/31
2007 Sales: $	2007 Profits: $	Parent Company:	

SALARIES/BENEFITS:

Pension Plan:	ESOP Stock Plan:	Profit Sharing:	Top Exec. Salary: $		Bonus: $
Savings Plan:	Stock Purch. Plan:		Second Exec. Salary: $		Bonus: $

OTHER THOUGHTS:

Apparent Women Officers or Directors: 1
Hot Spot for Advancement for Women/Minorities:

LOCATIONS: ("Y" = Yes)

West:	Southwest:	Midwest:	Southeast:	Northeast:	International:
Y					

SOLFOCUS INC   **www.solfocus.com**

Industry Group Code: 334413

Energy/Fuel:	Other Technologies:	Electrical Products:	Electronics:	Transportation:	Other:
Biofuels:	Irrigation:	Lighting/LEDs:	Computers:	Car Sharing:	Recycling:
Batteries/Storage:	Nanotech:	Waste Heat:	Sensors:	Electric Vehicles:	Engineering:
Solar: Y	Biotech:	Smart Meters:	Software:	Natural Gas Fuel:	Consulting:
Wind:	Water Tech./Treatment:	Machinery:			Investing:
Fuel Cells:	Ceramics:				Chemicals:

TYPES OF BUSINESS:

Concentrated Solar Power Technology
CPV

BRANDS/DIVISIONS/AFFILIATES:

CONTACTS: *Note: Officers with more than one job title may be intentionally listed here more than once.*

Mark Crowley, CEO
Robert Legendre, COO
Robert Legendre, Pres.
Bob Raybuck, CFO
Nancy Hartsoch, VP-Mktg.
Steve Horne, CTO
Bob Raybuck, VP-Admin.
Nancy Hartsoch, VP-Bus. Dev.
Bill Heck, VP-Sales
Osvaldo Regalado, VP-Program Mgmt.
Gary D. Conley, Chmn.
Christian Herrero de Egana Y Daucik, Managing Dir.-SolFocus EMEA

Phone: 650-623-7100	**Fax:** 650-623-7101
Toll-Free:	
Address: 510 Logue Ave., Mountain View, CA 94043 US	

GROWTH PLANS/SPECIAL FEATURES:

SolFocus, Inc. is a solar energy company and a supplier of concentrator photovoltaic (CPV) technology. The firm aims to generate solar energy at a cost competitive to traditional fossil fuel sources. The company's CPV technology combines high-efficiency solar cells and advanced optics to offer a solar energy alternative that is capable of delivering clean, renewable and affordable energy. Its units consist of highly reflective power units, durable CPV panels, and dual-axis trackers to follow the sun and maximize energy output. Unlike traditional silicon-based photovoltaics, the firm uses aluminum, glass and steel to create a unit that requires less energy to manufacture and is more durable. Based in Mountain View, California, SolFocus has a manufacturing facility in Mesa, Arizona; maintains European operations in Madrid, Spain; and maintains additional manufacturing partnerships with firms based in India and China. The company has installations located in California, Colorado, Hawaii, Mexico, Spain, Italy, Greece and Australia, including at Palo Alto Water Treatment facility in California; NELHA in Hawaii; APS Star Center in Arizona; and Mesa Water in Arizona.

FINANCIALS: Sales and profits are in thousands of dollars—add 000 to get the full amount. 2011 Note: Financial information for 2011 was not available for all companies at press time.

2011 Sales: $	2011 Profits: $	**U.S. Stock Ticker: Private**
2010 Sales: $	2010 Profits: $	**Int'l Ticker:**
2009 Sales: $	2009 Profits: $	Int'l Exchange:
2008 Sales: $	2008 Profits: $	Employees: 150 Fiscal Year Ends: 12/31
2007 Sales: $	2007 Profits: $	Parent Company:

SALARIES/BENEFITS:

Pension Plan:	ESOP Stock Plan:	Profit Sharing:	Top Exec. Salary: $	Bonus: $
Savings Plan:	Stock Purch. Plan:		Second Exec. Salary: $	Bonus: $

OTHER THOUGHTS:

Apparent Women Officers or Directors: 1
Hot Spot for Advancement for Women/Minorities:

LOCATIONS: ("Y" = Yes)

West:	Southwest:	Midwest:	Southeast:	Northeast:	International:
Y					Y

SOLICORE INC

www.solicore.com

Industry Group Code: 33591

Energy/Fuel:		Other Technologies:	Electrical Products:	Electronics:	Transportation:	Other:
Biofuels:		Irrigation:	Lighting/LEDs:	Computers:	Car Sharing:	Recycling:
Batteries/Storage:	Y	Nanotech:	Waste Heat:	Sensors:	Electric Vehicles:	Engineering:
Solar:		Biotech:	Smart Meters:	Software:	Natural Gas Fuel:	Consulting:
Wind:		Water Tech./Treatment:	Machinery:			Investing:
Fuel Cells:		Ceramics:				Chemicals:

TYPES OF BUSINESS:

Solid State Batteries

BRANDS/DIVISIONS/AFFILIATES:

Flexion
Skylab Technologies Group, Inc.
Leading Edge Technologies, Inc.

CONTACTS: *Note: Officers with more than one job title may be intentionally listed here more than once.*

David B. Corey, CEO
Dan Tillwick, COO
David Eagleson, VP-Sales
Charisse Pacheco, Sr. Dir.-Admin.
David Eagleson, VP-Strategic Accts.
Charisse Pacheco, Sr. Dir.-Finance
William Lese, Chmn.

Phone: 863-603-7640	Fax: 863-616-1341
Toll-Free: 866-884-7735	
Address: 2700 Interstate Dr., Lakeland, FL 33805 US	

GROWTH PLANS/SPECIAL FEATURES:

Solicore, Inc., the result of a merger between Skylab Technologies Group, Inc. and Leading Edge Technologies, Inc., uses patented polyimide polymer matrix electrolyte technology to develop and market next-generation rechargeable batteries. With present models available under the brand name Flexion, the company's solid-state batteries are highly efficient, lightweight, non-toxic and eco-friendly. The batteries feature thin, flexible construction, scalable in size to suit applications from smart cards to hybrid electric vehicles, with obvious potential for use in hand-held and portable communications, electronics, computer and PDA devices. Solicore's battery technology centers around the use of an electrolyte that is a true solid polymer, which avoids the need for any solvents or gelling agents, and ensures safe, non-combustible operation. The company's batteries additionally benefit from high current-carrying capacity and reliable performance across a wide range of temperatures (presently rated as low as -20 degrees Celsius). The absence of both heavy metals and solvent extraction processes further differentiates Solicore's technology from lithium-ion and similar standards, with the advantages of reduced environmental concern about production and disposal of the batteries and the elimination of a costly step in the manufacturing process. The firm's batteries are used in powered cards, which are credit cards that contain microprocessors or memory chips; radio frequency identification devices (RFID); and thin-film medical products to ensure proper dosage control. The firm's partnerships include Blue Chip Engineering; Cardlab; Citala; Gemalto; GSI Technologies; Identita; SiPix Imaging, Inc.; and Techsonic. Investors in the company include Draper Fisher Jurvetson; rho; Ontario Power Generation; CapiTech; Braemer Energy Ventures; Firelake Capital Management; and Air Products.

FINANCIALS: Sales and profits are in thousands of dollars—add 000 to get the full amount. 2011 Note: Financial information for 2011 was not available for all companies at press time.

2011 Sales: $	2011 Profits: $	U.S. Stock Ticker: Private
2010 Sales: $	2010 Profits: $	Int'l Ticker:
2009 Sales: $	2009 Profits: $	Int'l Exchange:
2008 Sales: $	2008 Profits: $	Employees: Fiscal Year Ends:
2007 Sales: $	2007 Profits: $	Parent Company:

SALARIES/BENEFITS:

Pension Plan:	ESOP Stock Plan:	Profit Sharing:	Top Exec. Salary: $	Bonus: $
Savings Plan:	Stock Purch. Plan:		Second Exec. Salary: $	Bonus: $

OTHER THOUGHTS:

Apparent Women Officers or Directors: 1
Hot Spot for Advancement for Women/Minorities:

LOCATIONS: ("Y" = Yes)

West:	Southwest:	Midwest:	Southeast:	Northeast:	International:
			Y		

SOLOPOWER

www.solopower.com

Industry Group Code: 334413

Energy/Fuel:		Other Technologies:	Electrical Products:	Electronics:	Transportation:	Other:
Biofuels:		Irrigation:	Lighting/LEDs:	Computers:	Car Sharing:	Recycling:
Batteries/Storage:		Nanotech:	Waste Heat:	Sensors:	Electric Vehicles:	Engineering:
Solar:	Y	Biotech:	Smart Meters:	Software:	Natural Gas Fuel:	Consulting:
Wind:		Water Tech./Treatment:	Machinery:			Investing:
Fuel Cells:		Ceramics:				Chemicals:

TYPES OF BUSINESS:

Thin-Film Photovoltaic Cell Manufacturing

BRANDS/DIVISIONS/AFFILIATES:

CONTACTS: Note: Officers with more than one job title may be intentionally listed here more than once.

Tim Harris, CEO
Tim Harris, Pres.
Ryan Benton, CFO
Peter Kesser, Sr. VP-Mktg. & Sales
Mustafa Pinarbasi, CTO
Albert J. Boro, Jr., General Counsel/Sec.
Ed Casey, Sr. VP-Oper.
Albert J. Boro, Jr., Sr. VP-Strategic Bus. Dev.
Bruce M. Khouri, Chief Commercial Officer
Lou DiNardo, Chmn.

Phone: 408-281-1582	Fax: 408-281-8342
Toll-Free:	
Address: 5981 Optical Ct., San Jose, CA 95138 US	

GROWTH PLANS/SPECIAL FEATURES:

SoloPower develops thin-film photovoltaic (PV) cells and modules. The firm is in the process of manufacturing and commercializing advanced, high-efficiency, low-cost Copper-Indium-Gallium-Selenide (CIGS) based devices that enable solar electricity generation at costs that are competitive with traditional power generation methods. The company's proprietary electrochemical process provides nearly 100% materials utilization and several other advantages over traditional PV products, including less waste generation; continuous processing with high throughput using low-cost equipment; extremely thin active layers; improved compositional control; high conversion efficiency; and the ability to deposit films on large areas and a variety of shapes/forms. The National Renewable Energy Laboratory (NREL) has measured the efficiency of the firm's flexible CIGS PV module product line at 19.9%, and has measured efficiencies of 15.81-square-inch SoloPower cells as high as 12.2%. SoloPower was founded by Bulent Basol and Homayoun Talieh, who hold 159 patents (as well as more than 60 pending) and have over 50 combined years of experience in the PV and semiconductor industries. In February 2011, the firm agreed to establish a new solar panel manufacturing plant in Wilsonville, Oregon.

FINANCIALS: Sales and profits are in thousands of dollars—add 000 to get the full amount. 2011 Note: Financial information for 2011 was not available for all companies at press time.

2011 Sales: $	2011 Profits: $	**U.S. Stock Ticker: Private**	
2010 Sales: $	2010 Profits: $	**Int'l Ticker:**	
2009 Sales: $	2009 Profits: $	Int'l Exchange:	
2008 Sales: $	2008 Profits: $	Employees:	Fiscal Year Ends:
2007 Sales: $	2007 Profits: $	Parent Company:	

SALARIES/BENEFITS:

Pension Plan:	ESOP Stock Plan:	Profit Sharing:	Top Exec. Salary: $	Bonus: $
Savings Plan:	Stock Purch. Plan:		Second Exec. Salary: $	Bonus: $

OTHER THOUGHTS:

Apparent Women Officers or Directors:
Hot Spot for Advancement for Women/Minorities:

LOCATIONS: ("Y" = Yes)

West:	Southwest:	Midwest:	Southeast:	Northeast:	International:
Y					

SOLTECTURE GMBH

www.sulfurcell.de

Industry Group Code: 334413

Energy/Fuel:	Other Technologies:	Electrical Products:	Electronics:	Transportation:	Other:
Biofuels:	Irrigation:	Lighting/LEDs:	Computers:	Car Sharing:	Recycling:
Batteries/Storage:	Nanotech:	Waste Heat:	Sensors:	Electric Vehicles:	Engineering:
Solar: Y	Biotech:	Smart Meters:	Software:	Natural Gas Fuel:	Consulting:
Wind:	Water Tech./Treatment:	Machinery:			Investing:
Fuel Cells:	Ceramics:				Chemicals:

TYPES OF BUSINESS:

Thin Film Solar Cells

BRANDS/DIVISIONS/AFFILIATES:

Sulfurcell Solartechnik

CONTACTS: *Note: Officers with more than one job title may be intentionally listed here more than once.*

Nikolaus Meyer, CEO
Rudiger Stroh, COO
Martin Beck, CFO
Henrik Krupper, Chief Sales Officer
Kalman Kaufman, Chmn.

Phone: 49-03063-92-3800	**Fax:** 49-03063-92-3801
Toll-Free:	
Address: Barbara Mcclintock St. 11, Berlin, 12489 Germany	

GROWTH PLANS/SPECIAL FEATURES:

Soltecture GmbH (formerly Sulfurcell Solartechnik) is a developer and manufacturer of thin-film solar modules using chalcopyrite-type semiconductors. The company uses copper-indium sulfide (CIS) materials rather than traditional polycrystalline silicon in order to maximize energy absorption and allow for thinner construction. The preassembled modules are weather-resistant and can be built into the external parts of a structure in framed, frameless or roof-integrated configurations. The company's SCG line is made in Germany and rated to output between 50-60 watts. Within the first 10 years, Soltecture guarantees 90% of the electric power collected, and 80% for the 10 years after that. Solar panels tend to collect most power during the summer months (specifically June and July), but integrated drainage holes allow for operation in snowy conditions as well. Soltecture's products can be found across Germany and Europe, and are featured prominently on buildings such as the Ferdinand Braun Institute for High Frequency Technology (Ferdinand-Braun-Institut fur Hochstfrequenztechnik) and the headquarters for Heuchemer GmbH & Co. KG. The modules can also be used in free standing applications. In late 2010, the firm announced the development of a new line of solar modules offering significant increases in efficiency. Rather than using the CIS sulfur-based semiconductors, the new modules will use a CIGSe (copper, indium, gallium and selenide) semiconductor, which will have a peak output capacity of 86.8 watts and offer an efficiency level of 10.7%. In May 2011, the company changed its name to Soltecture GmbH. In December 2011, the firm's German factory achieved a 13.4% efficiency rating for its solar modules.

FINANCIALS: Sales and profits are in thousands of dollars—add 000 to get the full amount. 2011 Note: Financial information for 2011 was not available for all companies at press time.

2011 Sales: $	2011 Profits: $	**U.S. Stock Ticker:** Private
2010 Sales: $	2010 Profits: $	**Int'l Ticker:**
2009 Sales: $	2009 Profits: $	Int'l Exchange:
2008 Sales: $	2008 Profits: $	Employees: Fiscal Year Ends:
2007 Sales: $	2007 Profits: $	Parent Company:

SALARIES/BENEFITS:

Pension Plan:	ESOP Stock Plan:	Profit Sharing:	Top Exec. Salary: $	Bonus: $
Savings Plan:	Stock Purch. Plan:		Second Exec. Salary: $	Bonus: $

OTHER THOUGHTS:

Apparent Women Officers or Directors:
Hot Spot for Advancement for Women/Minorities:

LOCATIONS: ("Y" = Yes)

West:	Southwest:	Midwest:	Southeast:	Northeast:	International: Y

SOLVAY SA

www.solvay.com

Industry Group Code: 325

Energy/Fuel:	Other Technologies:	Electrical Products:	Electronics:	Transportation:	Other:	
Biofuels:	Irrigation:	Lighting/LEDs:	Computers:	Car Sharing:	Recycling:	
Batteries/Storage:	Nanotech:	Waste Heat:	Sensors:	Electric Vehicles:	Engineering:	
Solar:	Biotech:	Smart Meters:	Software:	Natural Gas Fuel:	Consulting:	
Wind:	Water Tech./Treatment:	Machinery:			Investing:	
Fuel Cells:	Ceramics:				Chemicals:	Y

TYPES OF BUSINESS:

Chemicals & Plastics
Pipeline Systems
Detergents
Alternative Energy
Nanotechnology

BRANDS/DIVISIONS/AFFILIATES:

Inergy Automotive Systems
Pipelife
Solvac

CONTACTS: Note: Officers with more than one job title may be intentionally listed here more than once.

Christian Jourquin, CEO
Bernard de Laguiche, CFO
Daniel Broens, Gen. Mgr.-Human Resources
Jean-Michel Mesland, Gen. Mgr.-Research
Jean-Michel Mesland, Gen. Mgr.-Tech.
Dominique Dussard, General Counsel
Erik De Leye, Corp. Press Officer
Patrick Verelst, Head-Investor Rel.
Vincent De Cuyper, Gen. Mgr.-Chemicals
Jacques van Rijckevorsel, Gen. Mgr.-Plastics
Alexis Brouhns, Regional Mgr.-Europe
Roger Kearns, Regional Mgr.-Asia-Pacific
Alois Michielsen, Chmn.
Rene Degreve, Regional Mgr.-North America
Jean-Michel Mesland, Gen. Mgr.-Procurement

Phone: 32-2-509-61-11	**Fax:** 32-2-509-66-17

Toll-Free:

Address: Rue Du Prince Albert, 33, Brussels, B-1050 Belgium

GROWTH PLANS/SPECIAL FEATURES:

Solvay SA, headquartered in Brussels, Belgium, is an international specialty chemicals and plastics company. It manages nearly 400 sales and production facilities in 40 countries. Following a recent restructuring, Solvay operates in three segments: chemicals, plastics and new business development (NBD). The chemicals segment has three operating clusters: minerals, electrochemistry and fluorinated products and oxygen. The minerals cluster focuses on mineral products, such as soda ash and its derivatives, barium strontium carbonates and advanced functional minerals. The electrochemistry and fluorinated products cluster produces halogens, including chlorine and fluorinated gas products. The oxygen cluster produces oxygen products, such as peroxygens, detergent and caprolactones. The plastics segment has two operating clusters: specialties and vinyls. The specialties cluster produces fluorinated coatings, aromatic polyamides, fluorinated fluids, fluoroelastomers and ultra polymers. The vinyls cluster produces PVC alloys, PVC pastes and compounds. Pipelife, a joint venture with Wienerberger of Austria, produces and distributes pipes and fittings systems for water supply, sewage, gas supply, cable protection, irrigation and draining, heating and domestic chimney flues. The NBD segment consists of the firm's research activities in four broad platforms: printable organic electronics, focused on developing organic electroluminescent diodes (OLEDs); renewable energies; nanotechnology; and renewable chemistry. Belgian holding company Solvac owns approximately 30% of Solvay. In February 2010, the company completed the sale of its pharmaceuticals segment to Abbott for $6.98 billion. Additionally, Solvay announced plans to create three Research, Development and Technology (RDT) centers in China, India and Korea. The centers will be completed in 2011. Also in February 2010, the firm announced plans to build a test hydrogen fuel cell to generate 1 megawatt of power in Belgium. In September 2010, it sold its interest in the joint venture Inergy Automotive Systems to Plastic Ominum.

FINANCIALS: Sales and profits are in thousands of dollars—add 000 to get the full amount. 2011 Note: Financial information for 2011 was not available for all companies at press time.

2011 Sales: $	2011 Profits: $	**U.S. Stock Ticker:**
2010 Sales: $9,824,030	2010 Profits: $2,568,760	**Int'l Ticker: SOLB**
2009 Sales: $7,736,100	2009 Profits: $701,060	Int'l Exchange: Brussels-Euronext
2008 Sales: $13,207,000	2008 Profits: $625,000	Employees: 16,800 Fiscal Year Ends: 12/31
2007 Sales: $13,970,000	2007 Profits: $1,140,000	Parent Company:

SALARIES/BENEFITS:

Pension Plan:	ESOP Stock Plan:	Profit Sharing:	Top Exec. Salary: $	Bonus: $
Savings Plan:	Stock Purch. Plan:		Second Exec. Salary: $	Bonus: $

OTHER THOUGHTS:

Apparent Women Officers or Directors:
Hot Spot for Advancement for Women/Minorities:

LOCATIONS: ("Y" = Yes)

West:	Southwest:	Midwest:	Southeast:	Northeast:	International:
Y	Y	Y	Y	Y	Y

SPECTROLAB INC

www.spectrolab.com

Industry Group Code: 334413

Energy/Fuel:	Other Technologies:	Electrical Products:	Electronics:	Transportation:	Other:
Biofuels:	Irrigation:	Lighting/LEDs:	Computers:	Car Sharing:	Recycling:
Batteries/Storage:	Nanotech:	Waste Heat:	Sensors:	Electric Vehicles:	Engineering:
Solar: Y	Biotech:	Smart Meters:	Software:	Natural Gas Fuel:	Consulting:
Wind:	Water Tech./Treatment:	Machinery:			Investing:
Fuel Cells:	Ceramics:				Chemicals:

TYPES OF BUSINESS:

Solar Cells & Panels
Aerospace Components-Solar Cells
Optoelectronic Products
Solar Simulators
Searchlight Systems

BRANDS/DIVISIONS/AFFILIATES:

SX-16 Nightsun
SX-5 Starburst
Boeing Company (The)

CONTACTS: Note: Officers with more than one job title may be intentionally listed here more than once.

David Lillington, Pres.
Nasser H. Karam, Dir.-R&D
Sudharsanan Rengarajan, Dir.-Sensors Prod.

Phone: 818-365-4611	Fax: 818-361-5102
Toll-Free:	
Address: 12500 Gladstone Ave., Sylmar, CA 91342 US	

GROWTH PLANS/SPECIAL FEATURES:

Spectrolab, Inc., a subsidiary of The Boeing Company, is a leading global manufacturer of space solar cells and panels. The company has several products lines, including aerospace products, illumination products, terrestrial products and sensors. Aerospace products include solar cells, panels and larger solar arrays. The firm's solar cells have been used in space since 1958, powering Pioneer 1, NASA's first launched spacecraft; Explorer 6, the satellite that provided the first photograph of the Earth from space; the Apollo 11 mission, which placed the first solar cell panel on the moon; and the Spirit and Opportunity Mars rovers. The company has a production capacity of solar cells totaling roughly 1 megawatt per year. Spectrolab currently offers solar cells with a minimum average efficiency of 28.3% and has developed solar cells with efficiencies as high as 33%. Illumination products include solar simulators and searchlights. The firm's solar simulator products mimic the sun's light in a variety of conditions. These are used to test and calibrate light-sensitive devices and to test optical coatings, thermal coatings and paints. Spectrolab's 30 million candlepower SX-16 Nightsun and SX-5 Starburst searchlights are standard in several dozen countries, where they are installed on more than 30 types of helicopters and maritime patrol aircraft and used in ground, vehicle and shipboard applications. Terrestrial products consist primarily of concentrator solar cells. The company's sensors include Indium Gallium Arsenide (InGaAs), Gallium Arsenide (GaAs) and Germanium (Ge) photodetectors, epitaxial structures and related devices. Spectrolab operates one of the world's largest MOVPE (metalorganic vapor phase-epitaxy) foundries, with a wafer throughput capacity of over 7,000 four-inch wafers per week. The company also operates a packaging laboratory for prototype assembly and testing, providing custom design of photodiodes and laser fiber packages, as well as state-of-the-art modeling tools for performing thermal, mechanical, vibration and optical analysis.

FINANCIALS: Sales and profits are in thousands of dollars—add 000 to get the full amount. 2011 Note: Financial information for 2011 was not available for all companies at press time.

2011 Sales: $	2011 Profits: $	**U.S. Stock Ticker:** Subsidiary
2010 Sales: $	2010 Profits: $	**Int'l Ticker:**
2009 Sales: $	2009 Profits: $	Int'l Exchange:
2008 Sales: $	2008 Profits: $	Employees: Fiscal Year Ends: 12/31
2007 Sales: $	2007 Profits: $	Parent Company: BOEING COMPANY (THE)

SALARIES/BENEFITS:

Pension Plan: Y	ESOP Stock Plan:	Profit Sharing:	Top Exec. Salary: $	Bonus: $
Savings Plan: Y	Stock Purch. Plan:		Second Exec. Salary: $	Bonus: $

OTHER THOUGHTS:

Apparent Women Officers or Directors:
Hot Spot for Advancement for Women/Minorities:

LOCATIONS: ("Y" = Yes)

West: Y	Southwest:	Midwest:	Southeast:	Northeast:	International:

SPIRE CORPORATION

www.spirecorp.com

Industry Group Code: 33441

Energy/Fuel:	Other Technologies:	Electrical Products:	Electronics:	Transportation:	Other:
Biofuels:	Irrigation:	Lighting/LEDs:	Computers:	Car Sharing:	Recycling:
Batteries/Storage:	Nanotech:	Waste Heat:	Sensors:	Electric Vehicles:	Engineering:
Solar: Y	Biotech:	Smart Meters:	Software:	Natural Gas Fuel:	Consulting:
Wind:	Water Tech./Treatment:	Machinery:			Investing:
Fuel Cells:	Ceramics:				Chemicals:

TYPES OF BUSINESS:

Photovoltaic Module Manufacturing
Biomedical Products & Technologies
Electric Utility
Solar Power Generation
Optoelectronics

BRANDS/DIVISIONS/AFFILIATES:

Spire Solar
Spire Solar Systems
Spire Biomedical, Inc.
Spire Semiconductor LLC
Spire Solar India LLC
Spire Taiwan LLC
Spire Solar Technologies Private Limited
Spi-EL Electroluminescence Solar Module Tester

CONTACTS: *Note: Officers with more than one job title may be intentionally listed here more than once.*

Roger G. Little, CEO
Rodger W. LaFavre, COO
Roger G. Little, Pres.
Robert S. Lieberman, CFO
Robert S. Lieberman, Treas.
Stephen J. Hogan, Exec. VP/Gen. Mgr.-Spire Solar
Mark C. Little, CEO-Spire Biomedical
Roger G. Little, Chmn.

Phone: 781-275-6000	**Fax:** 781-275-7470
Toll-Free: 800-510-4815	
Address: 1 Patriots Park, Bedford, MA 01730-2396 US	

GROWTH PLANS/SPECIAL FEATURES:

Spire Corporation develops, manufactures and markets highly engineered products and services in three principal business areas: capital equipment for the PV solar industry; biomedical; and optoelectronics. Spire Solar (84% of revenues), operating in the PV solar area, develops, manufactures and markets specialized equipment for the production of terrestrial photovoltaic modules from solar cells. Its solar production lines include turnkey module, turnkey cell, turnkey thin film and module development lines. Spire's equipment, for which the firm has 26 patents, has been installed in roughly 200 factories in 50 countries. Through Spire Solar Systems, the company provides solar system design and engineering services, offering commercial and federal clients grid-connected distributed photovoltaic systems and custom modules. Spire Biomedical, operating in the biomedical area, provides value-added surface treatments to manufacturers of orthopedic and other medical devices that enhance the durability, antimicrobial or other material characteristics of their products; and performs sponsored research programs into applications of advanced biomedical and biophotonic technologies. Spire Semiconductor, operating in the optoelectronics area, provides custom compound semiconductor foundry and fabrication services on a merchant basis to customers involved in biomedical/biophotonics instruments, telecommunications and defense applications. Services include compound semiconductor wafer growth, other thin film processes and related device processing and fabrication services. This subsidiary also produces gallium arsenide concentrator cells (GaAs). International subsidiaries include Spire Solar India LLC and Spire Taiwan LLC. In February 2011, the firm released new product Spi-EL Electroluminescence Solar Module Tester, an advanced metrology offering. In August 2011, Spire Corporation established new Indian subsidiary Spire Solar Technologies Private Limited.

FINANCIALS: Sales and profits are in thousands of dollars—add 000 to get the full amount. 2011 Note: Financial information for 2011 was not available for all companies at press time.

2011 Sales: $	2011 Profits: $	**U.S. Stock Ticker:** SPIR
2010 Sales: $79,842	2010 Profits: $- 408	**Int'l Ticker:**
2009 Sales: $69,871	2009 Profits: $-5,282	Int'l Exchange:
2008 Sales: $64,964	2008 Profits: $4,775	Employees: 194 Fiscal Year Ends: 12/31
2007 Sales: $37,068	2007 Profits: $-1,933	Parent Company:

SALARIES/BENEFITS:

Pension Plan:	ESOP Stock Plan:	Profit Sharing:	Top Exec. Salary: $515,500	Bonus: $2,480
Savings Plan:	Stock Purch. Plan:		Second Exec. Salary: $190,000	Bonus: $12,000

OTHER THOUGHTS:

Apparent Women Officers or Directors:
Hot Spot for Advancement for Women/Minorities:

LOCATIONS: ("Y" = Yes)

West:	Southwest:	Midwest:	Southeast:	Northeast: Y	International: Y

Sales, profits and employees may be estimates. Financial information, benefits and other data can change quickly and may vary from those stated here.

STIRLING DK

www.stirling.dk

Industry Group Code: 221119

Energy/Fuel:		Other Technologies:		Electrical Products:		Electronics:	Transportation:	Other:
Biofuels:	Y	Irrigation:		Lighting/LEDs:		Computers:	Car Sharing:	Recycling:
Batteries/Storage:		Nanotech:		Waste Heat:		Sensors:	Electric Vehicles:	Engineering:
Solar:		Biotech:	Y	Smart Meters:		Software:	Natural Gas Fuel:	Consulting:
Wind:		Water Tech./Treatment:		Machinery:				Investing:
Fuel Cells:		Ceramics:						Chemicals:

TYPES OF BUSINESS:

Sustainable Energy Technology

BRANDS/DIVISIONS/AFFILIATES:

CONTACTS: *Note: Officers with more than one job title may be intentionally listed here more than once.*

Lars Jagd, CEO
Lotte Glarkrog, CFO
Gerald Marinitsch, Head-R&D
Per Nelson Ottosen, Head-Prod.
Gitte Videcrantz, Head-Project Dept.

Phone: 45-88-1848-00	**Fax:** 45-88-1848-80
Toll-Free:	
Address: Diplomvej Bldg. 373, Lyngby, DK-2800 Denmark	

GROWTH PLANS/SPECIAL FEATURES:

Stirling DK is a leading developer of sustainable energy products and technologies for carbon conscious consumers. The company produces non traditional combustion engine systems that have the ability to generate electricity using high-temperature sources and fuel types other than oil or gas. Possible engine and fuel types include biogas, biological oil and fats, and wood chips. The biogas engine plant comes in a single size and uses direct combustion of bio-liquids of biogas to produce 35 kilowatt (KW) electric and 140 KW thermal. The 1-Engine pyrolysis plant uses untreated waste wood in conjunction with fresh wood chips to product 35 KW electric and 110 KW thermal. The company offers three sizes of engine wood chip plants, including the 1-Engine, which has an output of 35 kilowatts (KW) electric and140 KW of thermal energy; the 2-Engine, which produces 70 KW of electric and 280 KW thermal; and the 4-Engine, which produces 140 KW electric and 560 KW thermal. The firm's customers include heating plants, industries in need of processed heat, municipalities, residential owners and large building real estate administrators such as, nurseries, apartment complexes, hospitals and schools. Stirling's engine systems also have the ability to provide off the grid customers, located in remote areas, with small scale engine applications, enabling them to generate carbon neutral heat and power onsite from local renewable fuel sources. All engine plants can be purchased as stand alones or containerized versions. In December 2011, the firm announced it would be opening 4 engine plant, which will be powered by biomass fuelled from fresh wood chips from around the Tabarz, Thrungia, Germany region, and capable of producing 4,000 Megawatt hours (MWh) of heat and 1,000 MWh of electricity yearly.

FINANCIALS: Sales and profits are in thousands of dollars—add 000 to get the full amount. 2011 Note: Financial information for 2011 was not available for all companies at press time.

2011 Sales: $	2011 Profits: $	**U.S. Stock Ticker: Private**	
2010 Sales: $	2010 Profits: $	**Int'l Ticker:**	
2009 Sales: $	2009 Profits: $	Int'l Exchange:	
2008 Sales: $	2008 Profits: $	Employees:	Fiscal Year Ends:
2007 Sales: $	2007 Profits: $	Parent Company:	

SALARIES/BENEFITS:

Pension Plan:	ESOP Stock Plan:	Profit Sharing:	Top Exec. Salary: $	Bonus: $
Savings Plan:	Stock Purch. Plan:		Second Exec. Salary: $	Bonus: $

OTHER THOUGHTS:

Apparent Women Officers or Directors: 1
Hot Spot for Advancement for Women/Minorities:

LOCATIONS: ("Y" = Yes)

West:	Southwest:	Midwest:	Southeast:	Northeast:	International: Y

STR HOLDINGS INC

www.strholdings.com

Industry Group Code: 334413

Energy/Fuel:	Other Technologies:	Electrical Products:	Electronics:	Transportation:	Other:
Biofuels:	Irrigation:	Lighting/LEDs:	Computers:	Car Sharing:	Recycling:
Batteries/Storage:	Nanotech:	Waste Heat:	Sensors:	Electric Vehicles:	Engineering:
Solar: Y	Biotech:	Smart Meters:	Software:	Natural Gas Fuel:	Consulting:
Wind:	Water Tech./Treatment:	Machinery:			Investing:
Fuel Cells:	Ceramics:				Chemicals:

TYPES OF BUSINESS:

Solar Panel Component Manufacturing

BRANDS/DIVISIONS/AFFILIATES:

PhotoCap

CONTACTS: *Note: Officers with more than one job title may be intentionally listed here more than once.*

Dennis L. Jilot, CEO
Dennis L. Jilot, Pres.
Barry A. Morris, CFO/Exec. VP
Chris F. Holm, VP-Human Resources
Alan N. Forman, General Counsel/VP
Yujia Zhai, Contact-Investor Rel.
Robert S. Yorgensen, Pres., STR Solar
Dennis L. Jilot, Chmn.
Bernardo E. Alvarez, Dir.-Bus. Dev., STR Solar, China

Phone: 860-758-7300	Fax:
Toll-Free:	
Address: 1699 King St., Enfield, CT 06082 US	

GROWTH PLANS/SPECIAL FEATURES:

STR Holdings, Inc. is a leading global provider of components to 80 solar module manufacturers. The firm's solar component manufacturing operations primarily produce encapsulants, which are specialty extruded sheets that protect and preserve the embedded semiconductor circuit. Encapsulants protect solar cells from the elements and bond the multiple layers of a module together. The firm's polymeric PhotoCap products consist primarily of ethylene-vinyl-acetate (EVA), which is modified with additives and put through its proprietary manufacturing process to increase product stability and make the encapsulant suitable for use in extreme, long-term outdoor applications. These products are manufactured at five production facilities in Connecticut, Florida, Spain and Malaysia. STR supplies encapsulants to solar module manufacturers in the U.S., Europe and Asia, including many major manufacturers, such as First Solar, Inc. Sales to First Solar account for nearly 30% of the company's annual sales. The company's encapsulants are used in both crystalline and thin-film solar modules. In December 2010, STR Holdings acquired a 275,000 square-foot building in Connecticut. This facility, which will house a new research and development laboratory, will hold the majority of the company's manufacturing operations. In September 2011, the firm sold its quality assurance segment to Underwriters Laboratories.

FINANCIALS: Sales and profits are in thousands of dollars—add 000 to get the full amount. 2011 Note: Financial information for 2011 was not available for all companies at press time.

2011 Sales: $	2011 Profits: $	**U.S. Stock Ticker:** STRI
2010 Sales: $371,829	2010 Profits: $49,311	**Int'l Ticker:**
2009 Sales: $264,945	2009 Profits: $22,989	Int'l Exchange:
2008 Sales: $288,578	2008 Profits: $28,105	Employees: 2,200 Fiscal Year Ends: 12/31
2007 Sales: $	2007 Profits: $	Parent Company:

SALARIES/BENEFITS:

Pension Plan:	ESOP Stock Plan:	Profit Sharing:	Top Exec. Salary: $500,000	Bonus: $500,000
Savings Plan:	Stock Purch. Plan:		Second Exec. Salary: $261,660	Bonus: $206,000

OTHER THOUGHTS:

Apparent Women Officers or Directors: 1
Hot Spot for Advancement for Women/Minorities:

LOCATIONS: ("Y" = Yes)

West:	Southwest:	Midwest:	Southeast:	Northeast:	International:
			Y	Y	Y

SULZER LTD

www.sulzer.com

Industry Group Code: 325510

Energy/Fuel:	Other Technologies:	Electrical Products:	Electronics:	Transportation:	Other:	
Biofuels:	Irrigation:	Lighting/LEDs:	Computers:	Car Sharing:	Recycling:	
Batteries/Storage:	Nanotech:	Waste Heat:	Sensors:	Electric Vehicles:	Engineering:	Y
Solar:	Biotech:	Smart Meters: Y	Software:	Natural Gas Fuel:	Consulting:	
Wind:	Water Tech./Treatment:	Machinery: Y			Investing:	
Fuel Cells:	Ceramics:				Chemicals:	

TYPES OF BUSINESS:

Machinery & Services
Coatings & Surface Technologies
Pump Products & Services
Turbine Equipment Services
Repair & Maintenance Services

BRANDS/DIVISIONS/AFFILIATES:

Sulzer Metco
Sulzer Turbo Services
Sulzer Pumps
Sulzer Chemtech
Sulzer Innotec
C.L. Engenharia Ltda.
SAB Technical Services
Sulzer India, Ltd.

CONTACTS: Note: Officers with more than one job title may be intentionally listed here more than once.

Ton Buchner, CEO
Jurgen Brandt, CFO
Alfred Gerber, General Counsel/Corp. Sec.
Peter Alexander, Pres., Sulzer Turbo Svcs.
Kim Jackson, Pres., Sulzer Pumps
Cesar Montenegro, Pres., Sulzer Metco
Urs Fankhauser, Pres., Sulzer Chemtech
Jurgen Dormann, Chmn.

Phone: 41-52-262-11-22	Fax: 41-52-262-01-01
Toll-Free:	
Address: Zurcherstrasse 14, Winterthur, 8401 Switzerland	

GROWTH PLANS/SPECIAL FEATURES:

Sulzer, Ltd. is a machinery, equipment and surfacing technology business with over 160 locations worldwide. It consists of five core divisions: Sulzer Metco, which accounts for 20% of sales; Sulzer Turbo Services, 12%; Sulzer Pumps, 50%; Sulzer Chemtech, 18%; and Sulzer Innotec. Sulzer Metco is a global supplier of products, solutions, services and equipment for thin-film, thermal-spray and other functional surface technologies. It also provides specialized machining services. The Sulzer Turbo Services segment offers repair, manufacturing and maintenance services for thermal turbomachinery, generators, motors and other rotating equipment. It also manufactures and markets replacement parts for gas and steam turbines, compressors, generators and motors. Sulzer Pumps develops and sells centrifugal pumps, manufactured through 13 facilities. Sulzer Chemtech is a leader in process technology, separation towers and two-component mixing and dispensing systems. Lastly, Sulzer Innotex offers contract research and special technical services, such as diagnostics and certified testing. It also provides production and engineering services. Sulzer primarily serves companies in the oil and gas, hydrocarbon processing, power generation, automotive, aviation and pulp and paper industries. In recent years, Sulzer Chemtech acquired India-based SAB Technical Services and Germany-based Manfred Preu Kolonnenservice. In June 2010, the firm announced plans to acquire Dowding & Mills, a repair and service provider for motors and generators. In July 2010, the company acquired the diamond-like carbon (DLC) coatings activities of Bekaert. In August 2010, Sulzer divested its Winterthur real estate portfolio and real estate services business to Implenia, Ltd., and Auwiesen Immobilien AG, respectively. In September 2010, the firm delisted subsidiary Sulzer India, Ltd., from the Bombay Stock Exchange. In November 2010, the company expanded its business footprint in China and Russia. In April 2011, Sulzer agreed to acquire the Flow Solutions business of Cardo AB. In June 2011, it acquired C.L. Engenharia Ltda., based in Brazil.

FINANCIALS: Sales and profits are in thousands of dollars—add 000 to get the full amount. 2011 Note: Financial information for 2011 was not available for all companies at press time.

2011 Sales: $	2011 Profits: $	**U.S. Stock Ticker:**
2010 Sales: $3,863,400	2010 Profits: $364,533	**Int'l Ticker: SUL1.DE**
2009 Sales: $3,184,880	2009 Profits: $257,040	Int'l Exchange: Zurich-SWX
2008 Sales: $3,530,040	2008 Profits: $306,950	Employees: 13,740 Fiscal Year Ends: 12/31
2007 Sales: $3,362,260	2007 Profits: $240,070	Parent Company:

SALARIES/BENEFITS:

Pension Plan: Y	ESOP Stock Plan:	Profit Sharing:	Top Exec. Salary: $	Bonus: $
Savings Plan:	Stock Purch. Plan:		Second Exec. Salary: $	Bonus: $

OTHER THOUGHTS:

Apparent Women Officers or Directors: 1
Hot Spot for Advancement for Women/Minorities:

LOCATIONS: ("Y" = Yes)

West:	Southwest:	Midwest:	Southeast:	Northeast:	International:
Y	Y	Y	Y	Y	Y

SUNCOR ENERGY INC

www.suncor.com

Industry Group Code: 211111

Energy/Fuel:	Other Technologies:	Electrical Products:	Electronics:	Transportation:	Other:
Biofuels:	Irrigation:	Lighting/LEDs:	Computers:	Car Sharing:	Recycling:
Batteries/Storage:	Nanotech:	Waste Heat:	Sensors:	Electric Vehicles:	Engineering:
Solar:	Biotech:	Smart Meters:	Software:	Natural Gas Fuel:	Consulting:
Wind: Y	Water Tech./Treatment:	Machinery:			Investing:
Fuel Cells:	Ceramics:				Chemicals:

TYPES OF BUSINESS:

Oil & Gas Exploration & Production
Wind Power
Oil Sands Production
Oil Refining & Transportation
Energy Marketing
Ethanol Production

BRANDS/DIVISIONS/AFFILIATES:

Petro-Canada

CONTACTS: *Note: Officers with more than one job title may be intentionally listed here more than once.*

Rick George, CEO
Steve W. Williams, COO
Rick George, Pres.
Bart Demosky, CFO
Boris J. Jackman, Exec. VP-Mktg. & Refining
Sue Lee, Sr. VP-Human Resources
Janice Odegaard, General Counsel/Sr. VP-Legal
Eric Axford, Sr. VP-Oper. Support
Jay Thornton, Exec. VP-Dev.
Sue Lee, Sr. VP-Comm.
Mike MacSween, Sr. VP-In-Situ
Neil Camarta, Exec. VP-Natural Gas
Kevin Nabholz, Exec. VP-Major Projects
Kirk Bailey, Exec. VP-Oil Sands Ventures
John Ferguson, Chmn.
Mark Little, Sr. VP-Int'l & Offshore
Jay Thornton, Exec. VP-Energy Supply & Trading

Phone: 403-296-8000	Fax: 403-296-3030
Toll-Free:	
Address: 112 4th Ave. SW, Calgary, AB T2P 3E3 Canada	

GROWTH PLANS/SPECIAL FEATURES:

Suncor Energy, Inc. is a Canadian energy company. It explores, acquires, develops, produces and markets crude oil and natural gas; transports and refines crude oil; and markets petroleum and petrochemical products. Once recovered, the firm upgrades it to refinery-ready feedstock and diesel oil. The company's mining and in-situ leases have the potential to produce over 18 billion barrels. The natural gas unit develops and acquires natural gas in western Canada and the U.S. Rocky Mountain region. It also explores long-term supplies in the Mackenzie Delta and Corridor in the Northwest Territories, Alaska and Canada's Arctic Islands. Suncor has projects throughout northern Canada with its two largest assets being in Canada's Arctic Islands. Internationally and offshore, the company operates in the North Sea and the east coast of Canada. It has additional interest in Libya, Syria and Trinidad and Tobago. The refining operations include refineries in Alberta, at 135,000-barrels-per-day; Ontario, at 85,000-barrels-per-day; Quebec, at 130,000-barrels-per-day and Colorado, 93,000-barrels-per-day. The firm's products include bitumen blends, sweet and sour crude oil, diesel, gasoline, jet fuel, asphalt, chemicals, heavy fuel and home heating oils, petroleum coke and sulphur. Suncor's desulphurization plant in Ontario produces gasoline, kerosene and jet and diesel fuels. The company has long term goals to continue investing in renewable resources such as wind power and biofuels. Its four wind power plants currently have a total generating capacity of 147 megawatts. In March 2011, Suncor completed the expansion of its St. Clair Ethanol Plant, resulting in doubled production capacity from 200 million to 400 million liters of ethanol per year.

FINANCIALS: Sales and profits are in thousands of dollars—add 000 to get the full amount. 2011 Note: Financial information for 2011 was not available for all companies at press time.

2011 Sales: $	2011 Profits: $	U.S. Stock Ticker:
2010 Sales: $31,461,000	2010 Profits: $3,594,000	Int'l Ticker: SU
2009 Sales: $24,559,700	2009 Profits: $1,104,610	Int'l Exchange: Toronto-TSX
2008 Sales: $27,680,000	2008 Profits: $2,004,000	Employees: 12,076 Fiscal Year Ends: 12/31
2007 Sales: $18,080,000	2007 Profits: $2,850,000	Parent Company:

SALARIES/BENEFITS:

Pension Plan: Y	ESOP Stock Plan:	Profit Sharing:	Top Exec. Salary: $1,270,406	Bonus: $1,757,421
Savings Plan: Y	Stock Purch. Plan:		Second Exec. Salary: $1,276,529	Bonus: $1,221,159

OTHER THOUGHTS:

Apparent Women Officers or Directors: 3
Hot Spot for Advancement for Women/Minorities: Y

LOCATIONS: ("Y" = Yes)

West:	Southwest:	Midwest:	Southeast:	Northeast:	International:
Y					Y

SUNEDISON LLC

www.sunedison.com

Industry Group Code: 221121

Energy/Fuel:		Other Technologies:		Electrical Products:	Electronics:	Transportation:	Other:
Biofuels:		Irrigation:		Lighting/LEDs:	Computers:	Car Sharing:	Recycling:
Batteries/Storage:		Nanotech:		Waste Heat:	Sensors:	Electric Vehicles:	Engineering:
Solar:	Y	Biotech:		Smart Meters:	Software:	Natural Gas Fuel:	Consulting:
Wind:		Water Tech./Treatment:		Machinery:			Investing:
Fuel Cells:		Ceramics:					Chemicals:

TYPES OF BUSINESS:

Solar Power Generation
Solar Power Facility Installation & Management

BRANDS/DIVISIONS/AFFILIATES:

MEMC Electronic Materials Inc

CONTACTS: Note: Officers with more than one job title may be intentionally listed here more than once.

Carlos Domenech, Pres.
Anthony Rabb, CFO
Attila Toth, Chief Mktg. Officer
Per Lindved Madsen, VP-Global Human Resources
Nelu Mihai, CTO
Kevin Lapidus, Sr. VP-Legal
Vinayak Gupta, Sr. VP-Global Oper.
Isaac Fehrenbach, VP-Bus. Dev. & Strategy
Kevin Lapidus, Sr. VP-Gov't Affairs
Brian Jacolick, Sr. VP-Global Bus. Dev.
Tim Derrick, VP-Global Svcs.
Pashu Gopalan, Gen. Mgr.-India
Charles Chan, Gen. Mgr.-China
Pancho Perez, Gen. Mgr.-Europe, Middle East & North Africa

Phone: 650-453-5600	Fax: 443-909-7150
Toll-Free: 866-786-3347	
Address: 600 Clipper Dr., Belmont, CA 94002 US	

GROWTH PLANS/SPECIAL FEATURES:

SunEdison LLC is a leading solar energy producer, operating primarily in the U.S., Canada, Europe and Asia. The company designs, installs and operates solar power systems for commercial buildings, government facilities and utilities, selling all electricity generated to the site host. The firm owns and maintains all of the equipment in the installation, resulting in significantly reduced up-front costs for customers. SunEdison manages more than 425 megawatts (MW) of solar power at more than 540 operational sites worldwide. Its North American installations include those in Canada and in several U.S. states, including New Mexico, Florida, California, Oregon, Colorado, Hawaii, Connecticut, New Jersey, Rhode Island, Massachusetts, Maryland, North Carolina, Arizona and Wisconsin. The company has partnered with SkyPower Corp. to develop, build, own and operate solar photovoltaic farms across Ontario. Other operations include solar energy technology development. Sun Edison maintains U.S. offices in California, Maryland, Colorado, New Jersey, Oregon and Nevada, along with international offices in Greece, Canada, Spain, India, Korea, Thailand, Japan and Italy. The company is a subsidiary of silicon wafer manufacturing firm MEMC Electronic Material, Inc. In 2010, the company and SkyPower jointly developed two new solar parks in Canada.

FINANCIALS: Sales and profits are in thousands of dollars—add 000 to get the full amount. 2011 Note: Financial information for 2011 was not available for all companies at press time.

2011 Sales: $	2011 Profits: $	U.S. Stock Ticker: Subsidiary
2010 Sales: $	2010 Profits: $	Int'l Ticker:
2009 Sales: $	2009 Profits: $	Int'l Exchange:
2008 Sales: $	2008 Profits: $	Employees: Fiscal Year Ends: 12/31
2007 Sales: $	2007 Profits: $	Parent Company: MEMC ELECTRONIC MATERIALS INC

SALARIES/BENEFITS:

Pension Plan:	ESOP Stock Plan:	Profit Sharing:	Top Exec. Salary: $	Bonus: $
Savings Plan:	Stock Purch. Plan:		Second Exec. Salary: $	Bonus: $

OTHER THOUGHTS:

Apparent Women Officers or Directors:
Hot Spot for Advancement for Women/Minorities:

LOCATIONS: ("Y" = Yes)

West:	Southwest:	Midwest:	Southeast:	Northeast:	International:
Y				Y	Y

SUNIVA INC

www.suniva.com

Industry Group Code: 334413

Energy/Fuel:	Other Technologies:	Electrical Products:	Electronics:	Transportation:	Other:
Biofuels:	Irrigation:	Lighting/LEDs:	Computers:	Car Sharing:	Recycling:
Batteries/Storage: Y	Nanotech:	Waste Heat:	Sensors:	Electric Vehicles:	Engineering:
Solar: Y	Biotech:	Smart Meters:	Software:	Natural Gas Fuel:	Consulting:
Wind:	Water Tech./Treatment:	Machinery:			Investing:
Fuel Cells:	Ceramics:				Chemicals:

TYPES OF BUSINESS:

Solar Panel Technology
PV Cell Production

BRANDS/DIVISIONS/AFFILIATES:

ARTisun
Optimus
New Enterprise Associates
HIG Ventures
Warburg Pincus
Advanced Equities Inc
Cogentrix
Goldman Sachs Group Inc

CONTACTS: Note: Officers with more than one job title may be intentionally listed here more than once.

John W. Baumstark, CEO
James M. Modak, CFO
J. Bryan Ashley, Chief Mktg. Officer
Bruce McPherson, VP-R&D
Ajeet Rohatgi, CTO
Stephen P. Shea, Chief Eng. Officer
Gregory Mihalik, VP-Oper.
J. Bryan Ashley, Chief Commercial Officer
Marc Rogovin, VP-Corp. Svcs.
Daniel L. Meier, Chief Scientist
Matt Card, VP-Sales, Americas
John W. Baumstark, Chmn.

Phone: 404-477-2700	Fax: 404-477-2709

Toll-Free:

Address: 5765 Peachtree Industrial Blvd., Norcross, GA 30092 US

GROWTH PLANS/SPECIAL FEATURES:

Suniva, Inc. is a developer, manufacturer and marketer of high-efficiency silicon photovoltaic (PV) cells. The firm's ARTisun monocrystalline solar cells are made of polysilicon, which is created by refining quartz or sand. This series includes the 3busbar line, which provides a 19% efficiency average. In addition, Suniva's customers and partners use ARTisun cells to make ART245-60-3-1 moncrystalline solar modules, which have achieved as much as 16% efficiency. These partners include SOLON AG, a European solar module manufacturer; NorSun AS, a Norwegian producer of monosilicon ingots and wafers; Titan Energy Systems Ltd., an Indian manufacturer and exporter of solar photovoltaic modules; and GS Battery (USA) Inc., a U.S.-based subsidiary of battery and inverter technologies provider GS Yuasa Group of Japan. The firm owns the exclusive rights to more than 40 granted and pending patents from 20 patent families. The company is owned by the following investors: New Enterprise Associates; H.I.G. Ventures; Warburg Pincus; Advanced Equities, Inc.; Cogentrix; and Goldman Sachs Group, Inc. In June 2011, Suniva introduced its newest solar power module series, Suniva Optimus, which produces 260 watts of power per 60-cell panel (over 16% efficiency rate).

FINANCIALS: Sales and profits are in thousands of dollars—add 000 to get the full amount. 2011 Note: Financial information for 2011 was not available for all companies at press time.

2011 Sales: $	2011 Profits: $	**U.S. Stock Ticker:** Private
2010 Sales: $	2010 Profits: $	**Int'l Ticker:**
2009 Sales: $	2009 Profits: $	Int'l Exchange:
2008 Sales: $	2008 Profits: $	Employees: Fiscal Year Ends:
2007 Sales: $	2007 Profits: $	Parent Company:

SALARIES/BENEFITS:

Pension Plan:	ESOP Stock Plan:	Profit Sharing:	Top Exec. Salary: $	Bonus: $
Savings Plan:	Stock Purch. Plan:		Second Exec. Salary: $	Bonus: $

OTHER THOUGHTS:

Apparent Women Officers or Directors:
Hot Spot for Advancement for Women/Minorities:

LOCATIONS: ("Y" = Yes)

West:	Southwest:	Midwest:	Southeast: Y	Northeast:	International:

Sales, profits and employees may be estimates. Financial information, benefits and other data can change quickly and may vary from those stated here.

SUNPOWER CORPORATION

www.us.sunpowercorp.com

Industry Group Code: 334413

Energy/Fuel:	Other Technologies:	Electrical Products:	Electronics:	Transportation:	Other:
Biofuels:	Irrigation:	Lighting/LEDs:	Computers:	Car Sharing:	Recycling:
Batteries/Storage: Y	Nanotech:	Waste Heat:	Sensors:	Electric Vehicles:	Engineering:
Solar: Y	Biotech:	Smart Meters:	Software:	Natural Gas Fuel:	Consulting:
Wind:	Water Tech./Treatment:	Machinery:			Investing:
Fuel Cells:	Ceramics:				Chemicals:

TYPES OF BUSINESS:

Photovoltaic Solar Cells
Solar Panels & Modules
Power Plant Operations

BRANDS/DIVISIONS/AFFILIATES:

PowerGuard Roof System
SunPower T-10 Commercial Solar Roof Tiles
SunPower Tracker
SunPower T-5 Solar Roof Tile System
SunPower Oasis Power Plant
SunRay
SunPower Signature Black Solar Panels
SunPower AC Solar Panels

CONTACTS: Note: Officers with more than one job title may be intentionally listed here more than once.

Thomas H. Werner, CEO
Marty T. Neese, COO
Thomas H. Werner, Pres.
Dennis V. Arriola, CFO/Exec. VP
David Henry, Chief Mktg. Officer
Richard Swanson, CTO
Jack Peurach, Exec. VP-Prod.
Jorg Heinemann, VP-Eng.
Douglas J. Richards, Exec. VP-Admin.
Christopher Japp, General Counsel
Jorg Heinemann, VP-Customer Oper.
Peter Aschenbrenner, VP-Corp. Strategy
Julie Blunden, Exec. VP-Corp. Comm. & Public Policy
Eric Branderiz, Principal Acct. Officer/VP/Corp. Controller
Howard J. Wenger, Pres., Regions
T.J. Rodgers, Chmn.

Phone: 408-240-5500	Fax:
Toll-Free: 800-786-7693	
Address: 77 Rio Robles, San Jose, CA 95134 US	

GROWTH PLANS/SPECIAL FEATURES:

SunPower Corporation is a solar products and services firm operating in two segments: Utility & Power Plants and Residential & Commercial. The Utility & Power Plants segment oversees all aspects of the solar products and system business, including power plant engineering, construction, development, maintenance and operations. Residential & Commercial segment deals with solar equipment sales to residential and small commercial markets, as well as with services pertaining to rooftop and ground-mounted solar power system construction for new home, commercial and public sector projects. Products produced by the company include solar panels, inverters, roof and ground-mounting products and fully integrated systems. The firm offers two types of solar panels: SunPower Signature Black Solar Panels and SunPower AC Solar Panels. PowerGuard Roof System, T-5 Solar Roof Tile System and T-10 Commercial Solar Roof Tiles are the company's roof-mounting products. SunPower also offers SunPower Tracker Systems to be used with ground-mounting. The SunPower Oasis Power Plant is the company's modular solar power block, a fully integrated system that scales from 1 MW distributed installations to large central station power plants, cost-effectively deploying utility-scale solar power systems. SunPower has over 650 megawatts (MW) of solar power plant systems operating or under contract worldwide. Thousands of SunPower rooftop solar power systems have been installed in residential markets. Subsequent with acquisition of SunRay, SunPower acquired a project pipeline of solar photovoltaic projects throughout Europe. In January 2011, the company completed the sale of its 13 MW Roma Solar Power Plant to Allianz Renewable Energy Partners IV Ltd. In September 2011, SunPower completed the sale of its 250 MW California Valley Solar Ranch project to NRG Energy, Inc. In October 2011, the Hawaii Public Utilities Commission approved the contract for SunPower to sell energy to Hawaiian Electric from a 5 MW solar photovoltaic farm to be built in Western Oahu.

FINANCIALS: Sales and profits are in thousands of dollars—add 000 to get the full amount. 2011 Note: Financial information for 2011 was not available for all companies at press time.

2011 Sales: $	2011 Profits: $	U.S. Stock Ticker: SPWRA
2010 Sales: $2,219,230	2010 Profits: $178,724	Int'l Ticker:
2009 Sales: $1,524,300	2009 Profits: $32,521	Int'l Exchange:
2008 Sales: $1,434,919	2008 Profits: $92,293	Employees: 5,150　　Fiscal Year Ends: 12/31
2007 Sales: $774,790	2007 Profits: $9,202	Parent Company:

SALARIES/BENEFITS:

Pension Plan:	ESOP Stock Plan:	Profit Sharing:	Top Exec. Salary: $436,365	Bonus: $11,169
Savings Plan: Y	Stock Purch. Plan:		Second Exec. Salary: $413,673	Bonus: $12,648

OTHER THOUGHTS:

Apparent Women Officers or Directors: 1
Hot Spot for Advancement for Women/Minorities: Y

LOCATIONS: ("Y" = Yes)

West:	Southwest:	Midwest:	Southeast:	Northeast:	International:
Y				Y	Y

SUNRUN

www.sunrunhome.com

Industry Group Code: 221119

Energy/Fuel:	Other Technologies:	Electrical Products:	Electronics:	Transportation:	Other:
Biofuels:	Irrigation:	Lighting/LEDs:	Computers:	Car Sharing:	Recycling:
Batteries/Storage:	Nanotech:	Waste Heat:	Sensors:	Electric Vehicles:	Engineering:
Solar: Y	Biotech:	Smart Meters:	Software:	Natural Gas Fuel:	Consulting:
Wind:	Water Tech./Treatment:	Machinery:			Investing:
Fuel Cells:	Ceramics:				Chemicals:

TYPES OF BUSINESS:

Solar Power

BRANDS/DIVISIONS/AFFILIATES:

Total Solar

CONTACTS: *Note: Officers with more than one job title may be intentionally listed here more than once.*

Edward Fenster, CEO
Lynn Jurich, Pres.
Bill Schuh, VP-Sales
Beth Steinberg, VP-Human Resources
Bill Owens, VP-Prod.
Miguel Pinilla, VP-Eng.
Ashley Giesler, General Counsel
Matt Eggers, VP-Oper.
Susan Wise, Mgr.-Public Rel.
Ashley Giesler, VP-Transactions
Holly Gordon, VP-Legislative & Regulatory Affairs
Bill Stewart, VP-Mktg.

Phone: 415-982-9000	**Fax:** 415-982-9021
Toll-Free: 855-478-6786	
Address: 45 Fremont St., 32nd Fl., San Francisco, CA 94105 US	

GROWTH PLANS/SPECIAL FEATURES:

SunRun, based in California, is a top residential solar power firm. The company's proprietary product line is known as Total Solar. The firm's solar services operate by allowing the customer to choose between a lease and a power purchase agreement (PPA) plan. In the solar lease plan, homeowners pay a fixed rate each month for solar panel usage, independent of the electricity generated from the panels. In the PPA plan, homeowners pay a fixed monthly rate for the panel usage but only pay for the electricity that the panels generate each month. In both situations, SunRun covers all of the upfront costs for the solar panels, power inverter, permits and installation. Homeowners are fixed into the agreement for 20 years, but have the assurance of no fixed rate fluctuations and no maintenance fees for any necessary repairs of the panels. The firm partners with over 25 local solar installers, including Acro Energy in Arizona; Islandwide Solar in Hawaii; Trinity Solar in New Jersey; and Greenspring Energy in Pennsylvania. In 2011, the firm entered into the Oregon and Maryland markets.

Employee benefits include medical, dental and vision insurance; life and accident insurance; short- and long-term disability coverage; a savings plan; bagel Mondays; free lunch on Fridays; and two days of paid time off to volunteer at charities.

FINANCIALS: Sales and profits are in thousands of dollars—add 000 to get the full amount. 2011 Note: Financial information for 2011 was not available for all companies at press time.

2011 Sales: $	2011 Profits: $	**U.S. Stock Ticker: Private**
2010 Sales: $	2010 Profits: $	**Int'l Ticker:**
2009 Sales: $	2009 Profits: $	Int'l Exchange:
2008 Sales: $	2008 Profits: $	Employees: Fiscal Year Ends:
2007 Sales: $	2007 Profits: $	Parent Company:

SALARIES/BENEFITS:

Pension Plan:	ESOP Stock Plan:	Profit Sharing:	Top Exec. Salary: $	Bonus: $
Savings Plan: Y	Stock Purch. Plan:		Second Exec. Salary: $	Bonus: $

OTHER THOUGHTS:

Apparent Women Officers or Directors: 5
Hot Spot for Advancement for Women/Minorities: Y

LOCATIONS: ("Y" = Yes)

West:	Southwest:	Midwest:	Southeast:	Northeast:	International:
Y	Y			Y	

Sales, profits and employees may be estimates. Financial information, benefits and other data can change quickly and may vary from those stated here.

SUNTECH POWER HOLDINGS CO LTD   www.suntech-power.com

Industry Group Code: 334413

Energy/Fuel:	Other Technologies:	Electrical Products:	Electronics:	Transportation:	Other:
Biofuels:	Irrigation:	Lighting/LEDs:	Computers:	Car Sharing:	Recycling:
Batteries/Storage:	Nanotech:	Waste Heat:	Sensors:	Electric Vehicles:	Engineering:
Solar: Y	Biotech:	Smart Meters:	Software:	Natural Gas Fuel:	Consulting:
Wind:	Water Tech./Treatment:	Machinery:			Investing:
Fuel Cells:	Ceramics:				Chemicals:

TYPES OF BUSINESS:

Photovoltaic Equipment
Power Systems Maintenance

BRANDS/DIVISIONS/AFFILIATES:

Asia Silicon Co., Ltd.
NANOPLAS
Low Caron Concept Museum
Victoria-Suntech Advanced Solar Facility
SunBorne Energy
Solar Hybrid AG

CONTACTS: *Note: Officers with more than one job title may be intentionally listed here more than once.*

Zhengrong Shi, CEO
David Hogg, COO
David King, CFO
Andrew Beebe, Chief Commercial Officer
Hongkuan Jian, Chief Human Resources Officer
Stuart R. Wenham, CTO
John Lefebvre, Pres., Suntech America
Ting Lei, Gen. Mgr.-China Bus. Unit
James Hu, Pres., Suntech AMPEA
Yukata Yamamoto, Pres., Suntech Japan
Zhengrong Shi, Chmn.
Jerry Stokes, Pres., Suntech Europe
Xin Luo, Sr. VP-Global Supply Chain

Phone: 86-510-8531-8888	Fax: 86-510-8534-3321
Toll-Free:	
Address: 9 Xinhua Rd., New District, Wuxi, 214028 China	

GROWTH PLANS/SPECIAL FEATURES:

Suntech Power Holdings Co., Ltd., based in China, specializes in the design, development, manufacture and sale of photovoltaic (PV) cells, modules and systems, including building-integrated photovoltaics (BIPVs), for use in residential, commercial, industrial and public utility applications. It is one of the largest producers and suppliers of solar cells and silicone solar products that includes thin film, polycrstalline and monocrystalline modules in the world. The company sells its products to a worldwide market that includes North America, Asia and Europe, including Spain, Germany, the U.S., China, South Korea, Italy, the Middle East, Australia and Japan. The firm's international customers include EDF Energies Nouvelles S.A.; Gamesa Corporation; IBC Solar AG; and Hyosung Corp. Suntech has offices established in thirteen different countries, with regional headquarters in San Francisco, California, Schaffhausen, Switzerland and Wuxi, China. The company leverages its cost advantages by optimizing the balance between automation and manual operations in manufacturing. The firm has an aggregate PV cell manufacturing capacity of 1.1 gigawatts (GW). In January 2011c Suntech became the lead supplier of photovoltaic modules for the Siemens Energy Sector, for the generation, transmission and distribution of power and for the extraction, conversion and transport of oil and gas. In May 2011, Suntech embarked on two new partnerships with SunBorne Energy and Solar Hybrid AG. Suntech will supply Solar Hybrid AG, a provider of comprehensive technical and financial solutions for solar power plants (photovoltaics), with up to 190 megawatts (MW) of solar panels. Suntech will be its main supplier of 100MW solar panels over the next two years for projects throughout India conducted by SunBorne, a specialist in utility scale solar solutions.

FINANCIALS: Sales and profits are in thousands of dollars—add 000 to get the full amount. 2011 Note: Financial information for 2011 was not available for all companies at press time.

2011 Sales: $	2011 Profits: $	**U.S. Stock Ticker: STP**
2010 Sales: $2,901,899	2010 Profits: $236,900	**Int'l Ticker:**
2009 Sales: $1,693,300	2009 Profits: $85,700	Int'l Exchange:
2008 Sales: $1,923,500	2008 Profits: $31,000	Employees: 20,231 Fiscal Year Ends: 12/31
2007 Sales: $1,348,300	2007 Profits: $171,300	Parent Company:

SALARIES/BENEFITS:

Pension Plan:	ESOP Stock Plan:	Profit Sharing:	Top Exec. Salary: $	Bonus: $
Savings Plan:	Stock Purch. Plan:		Second Exec. Salary: $	Bonus: $

OTHER THOUGHTS:

Apparent Women Officers or Directors: 1
Hot Spot for Advancement for Women/Minorities:

LOCATIONS: ("Y" = Yes)

West:	Southwest:	Midwest:	Southeast:	Northeast:	International:
Y					Y

SUNWAYS AG

www.sunways.eu

Industry Group Code: 334413

Energy/Fuel:		Other Technologies:		Electrical Products:		Electronics:		Transportation:		Other:	
Biofuels:		Irrigation:		Lighting/LEDs:		Computers:		Car Sharing:		Recycling:	
Batteries/Storage:	Y	Nanotech:		Waste Heat:		Sensors:		Electric Vehicles:		Engineering:	
Solar:	Y	Biotech:		Smart Meters:		Software:		Natural Gas Fuel:		Consulting:	Y
Wind:		Water Tech./Treatment:		Machinery:						Investing:	
Fuel Cells:		Ceramics:								Chemicals:	

TYPES OF BUSINESS:

Photovoltaic Cells
Consulting
Photovoltaic System Planning & Implementation
Electrical Appliances Trading

BRANDS/DIVISIONS/AFFILIATES:

Sunways Production GmbH
Eco Line

CONTACTS: Note: Officers with more than one job title may be intentionally listed here more than once.

Michael Wilhelm, CEO
Jorg von Strom, COO
Michael Wilhelm, CFO
Jurgen Frei, Chief Sales & Mktg. Officer
Roland Burkhardt, Head-R&D
Roland Burkhardt, CTO
Michael Wilhelm, Chief Strategy Officer
Harald F. Schaefer, Head-Corp. Comm.
Astrid Forst, Dir.-Investor Rel.
Jorg von Strom, Managing Dir.-Sunways Production GmbH
Otto Mayer, Chmn.

Phone: 49-7531-996-77-0	**Fax:** 49-7531-996-77-10
Toll-Free:	
Address: Macairestrasse 3-5, Konstanz, 78467 Germany	

GROWTH PLANS/SPECIAL FEATURES:

Sunways AG develops and produces silicon-based high-performance solar cells, solar inverters and solar modules for use throughout the photovoltaic industry. The firm also offers consultancy services, planning, implementation and delivery of large and small photovoltaic systems on behalf of architects, planners, designers and investors. Company subsidiaries include Sunways Production GmbH, a wholly-owned subsidiary headquartered in Arnstadt, Germany, which operates a production facility of approximately 11,500 square feet dedicated to the manufacture of mono- and multi-crystalline solar cells. Sunways AG also operates international offices in Barcelona, Spain; Konstanz, Germany; and Bologna, Italy. Sunways AG has an active research and development department, which partners with project sponsors, such as the European Union and the German Federal Ministry for Economic Affairs and Technology, to develop various projects. These include the producing of back-contact and bifacial solar cells, facade systems and demonstration projects using transparent solar cells. In December 2010, the company launched the Eco Line of mono- and multi-crystalline solar modules, which are lightweight and offer improved output efficiency.

FINANCIALS: Sales and profits are in thousands of dollars—add 000 to get the full amount. 2011 Note: Financial information for 2011 was not available for all companies at press time.

2011 Sales: $	2011 Profits: $	**U.S. Stock Ticker:**
2010 Sales: $316,600	2010 Profits: $13,300	**Int'l Ticker: SWW**
2009 Sales: $231,870	2009 Profits: $22,080	Int'l Exchange: Frankfurt-Euronext
2008 Sales: $192,680	2008 Profits: $2,480	Employees: 340 Fiscal Year Ends: 12/31
2007 Sales: $271,100	2007 Profits: $1,600	Parent Company:

SALARIES/BENEFITS:

Pension Plan:	ESOP Stock Plan:	Profit Sharing:	Top Exec. Salary: $	Bonus: $
Savings Plan:	Stock Purch. Plan:		Second Exec. Salary: $	Bonus: $

OTHER THOUGHTS:

Apparent Women Officers or Directors: 1
Hot Spot for Advancement for Women/Minorities:

LOCATIONS: ("Y" = Yes)

West:	Southwest:	Midwest:	Southeast:	Northeast:	International:
					Y

SUPERCONDUCTOR TECHNOLOGIES INC   www.suptech.com

Industry Group Code: 33441

Energy/Fuel:		Other Technologies:	Electrical Products:	Electronics:	Transportation:	Other:
Biofuels:		Irrigation:	Lighting/LEDs:	Computers:	Car Sharing:	Recycling:
Batteries/Storage:		Nanotech:	Waste Heat:	Sensors:	Electric Vehicles:	Engineering:
Solar:	Y	Biotech:	Smart Meters:	Software:	Natural Gas Fuel:	Consulting:
Wind:		Water Tech./Treatment:	Machinery:			Investing:
Fuel Cells:		Ceramics:				Chemicals:

TYPES OF BUSINESS:

Semiconductor Technology
Cryogenics
Wire Technology

BRANDS/DIVISIONS/AFFILIATES:

SuperLink
AmpLink
SuperPlex
Conductus Superconducting Wire

CONTACTS: *Note: Officers with more than one job title may be intentionally listed here more than once.*

Jeff Quiram, CEO
Jeff Quiram, Pres.
Bill Buchanan, CFO/Sr. VP
Adam Shelton, VP-Mktg. & Product Mgmt.
Robert B. Hammond, CTO/Sr. VP
Thomas R. Giunta, VP-Eng.
Robert L. Johnson, Sr. VP-Oper.
Martin A. Kaplan, Chmn.

Phone: 805-690-4500	Fax: 805-967-0342
Toll-Free:	
Address: 460 Ward Dr., Santa Barbara, CA 93111 US	

GROWTH PLANS/SPECIAL FEATURES:

Superconductor Technologies, Inc. (STI) is engaged in the research, development and manufacture of high temperature superconductor (HTS) materials and related technologies. HTS materials have the capability to conduct various signals or energy, such as electrical current or radio frequency (RF) signals, with little or no resistance, which facilitates the reduction of power loss, heat generation and electrical noise in electrical systems. STI has developed patented and proprietary technologies relating to matters such as thin-film deposition manufacturing; cryogenic and non-microwave circuit designs, including designs for RF circuit filters; cryogenic packaging and systems, used to maintain HTS materials at their critical temperatures; and other superconducting technologies. The firm's products are used commercially to enhance the performance of wireless telecommunications networks, with companies such as Alltell, AT&T, Sprint Nextel, T-Mobile and Verizon Wireless accounting for more than 10% of the firm's commercial revenues. STI manufactures 2G HTS wire for use in next-generation power applications, such as wind turbines, motors, generators and MRI machines, offering a viable copper alternative for advanced power systems. The company's products are used additionally in tunable HTS filter systems for military communications, signals intelligence and electronic warfare applications. Its products include SuperLink, a high-temperature superconducting filter; AmpLink, a high-performance, ground-mounted amplifier; and SuperPlex, a high-performance multiplexer. In November 2011, STI introduced Conductus Superconducting Wire, the brand name for the new superconducting wire family. In December 2011, the company announced plans to relocate its corporate headquarters to Austin, Texas.

FINANCIALS: Sales and profits are in thousands of dollars—add 000 to get the full amount. 2011 Note: Financial information for 2011 was not available for all companies at press time.

2011 Sales: $	2011 Profits: $	U.S. Stock Ticker: SCON
2010 Sales: $8,547	2010 Profits: $-11,968	Int'l Ticker:
2009 Sales: $10,816	2009 Profits: $-12,979	Int'l Exchange:
2008 Sales: $11,293	2008 Profits: $-12,701	Employees: 105 Fiscal Year Ends: 12/31
2007 Sales: $	2007 Profits: $	Parent Company:

SALARIES/BENEFITS:

Pension Plan:	ESOP Stock Plan:	Profit Sharing:	Top Exec. Salary: $321,179	Bonus: $102,925
Savings Plan: Y	Stock Purch. Plan:		Second Exec. Salary: $251,162	Bonus: $1,980

OTHER THOUGHTS:

Apparent Women Officers or Directors: 1
Hot Spot for Advancement for Women/Minorities:

LOCATIONS: ("Y" = Yes)

West:	Southwest:	Midwest:	Southeast:	Northeast:	International:
Y	Y				

SUSTAINX INC

www.sustainx.com

Industry Group Code: 335

Energy/Fuel:		Other Technologies:		Electrical Products:		Electronics:	Transportation:	Other:	
Biofuels:		Irrigation:		Lighting/LEDs:		Computers:	Car Sharing:	Recycling:	
Batteries/Storage:	Y	Nanotech:		Waste Heat:		Sensors:	Electric Vehicles:	Engineering:	
Solar:		Biotech:		Smart Meters:		Software:	Natural Gas Fuel:	Consulting:	
Wind:		Water Tech./Treatment:		Machinery:	Y			Investing:	
Fuel Cells:		Ceramics:						Chemicals:	

TYPES OF BUSINESS:

Energy Storage Technology
Isothermal Compressed Air Energy Storage

BRANDS/DIVISIONS/AFFILIATES:

ICAES

CONTACTS: *Note: Officers with more than one job title may be intentionally listed here more than once.*

Thomas M. Zarrella, CEO
Thomas M. Zarrella, Pres.
David Neafus, CFO
David Beatty, VP-Eng.
Richard Brody, VP-Bus. Dev.
Dax Kepshire, VP/Gen. Mgr.
Charles Hutchinson, Chmn.

Phone: 603-601-7800	**Fax:** 603-298-0204
Toll-Free:	
Address: 72 Stard Rd, Seabrook, NH 03874 US	

GROWTH PLANS/SPECIAL FEATURES:

SustainX, Inc. is a developer of renewable energy storage technology. The company was founded in 2007 to commercialize technology developed from research at the Thayer School of Engineering at Dartmouth College. Its patented, zero-emission storage solution, isothermal compressed air energy storage (ICAES), stores generated energy until it is needed by the grid. Traditional compressed air energy storage (CAES) technology, long in use but not widely adopted, stores excess and offpeak electricity as compressed air that can later be expanded and used to drive a turbine that generates electricity. The loss of heat during traditional air compression has remained a barrier to wider adoption of CAES technology, but the isothermal (constant temperature) process allows air to reach high pressures without subsequent heat loss. Because the ICAES power unit removes heat during air compression and adds it during expansion, the need to burn natural gas during expansion is eliminated, thus creating a zero-emission storage system. Where traditional CAES technology has often required large underground caves for storage, the ICAES system is site-flexible, meaning it can be deployed in numerous application settings regardless of the geological environment. SustainX's technology can be used for a number of grid applications, including supporting peaking capacity, capturing waste heat for cogeneration and increasing the cost-effectiveness of renewable energy sources. The firm currently has eight issued U.S. patents relating to its energy compression and expansion technology. Though SustainX has not yet reached commercialization, it is currently preparing a demonstration 1 megawatt (MW) system in collaboration with AES Energy Storage, LLC. The company has received venture funding from Polaris Venture Partners, Rockport Capital, Cadent Energy Partners, General Catalyst Partners and GE Energy Financial Services, as well as the National Science Foundation Small Business Innovation Research Program and the Energy Storage Program at the U.S. Department of Energy.

FINANCIALS: Sales and profits are in thousands of dollars—add 000 to get the full amount. 2011 Note: Financial information for 2011 was not available for all companies at press time.

2011 Sales: $	2011 Profits: $	**U.S. Stock Ticker:** Private	
2010 Sales: $	2010 Profits: $	**Int'l Ticker:**	
2009 Sales: $	2009 Profits: $	Int'l Exchange:	
2008 Sales: $	2008 Profits: $	Employees:	Fiscal Year Ends:
2007 Sales: $	2007 Profits: $	Parent Company:	

SALARIES/BENEFITS:

Pension Plan:	ESOP Stock Plan:	Profit Sharing:	Top Exec. Salary: $	Bonus: $
Savings Plan:	Stock Purch. Plan:		Second Exec. Salary: $	Bonus: $

OTHER THOUGHTS:

Apparent Women Officers or Directors:
Hot Spot for Advancement for Women/Minorities:

LOCATIONS: ("Y" = Yes)

West:	Southwest:	Midwest:	Southeast:	Northeast:	International:
				Y	

SUZLON ENERGY LIMITED

www.suzlon.com

Industry Group Code: 33361

Energy/Fuel:	Other Technologies:	Electrical Products:	Electronics:	Transportation:	Other:
Biofuels:	Irrigation:	Lighting/LEDs:	Computers:	Car Sharing:	Recycling:
Batteries/Storage:	Nanotech:	Waste Heat:	Sensors:	Electric Vehicles:	Engineering:
Solar:	Biotech:	Smart Meters:	Software:	Natural Gas Fuel:	Consulting:
Wind: Y	Water Tech./Treatment:	Machinery:			Investing:
Fuel Cells:	Ceramics:				Chemicals:

TYPES OF BUSINESS:

Wind Turbine Generator Manufacturing

BRANDS/DIVISIONS/AFFILIATES:

REpower Systems AG
Hansen Transmissions International NV
S97
S95
S88
S82
S66
S64

CONTACTS: *Note: Officers with more than one job title may be intentionally listed here more than once.*

Tulsi R. Tanti, Managing Dir.
Robin Banerjee, CFO
John O'Halloran, Pres., Tech.
Dhaval Vakil, Dir.-Investor Rel.
He Yaozu, CEO-China Oper.
Tulsi R. Tanti, Chmn.
Silas Zimu, CEO-South African Oper.

Phone: 91-20-4012-2000	Fax: 91-20-4012-2100
Toll-Free:	
Address: 1 Earth, Opp. Magarpatta City, Hadapsar, Pune, 411028 India	

GROWTH PLANS/SPECIAL FEATURES:

Suzlon Energy Limited is an Indian firm engaged in the manufacture, design, development and marketing of wind energy systems, specializing in wind turbine generators. Suzlon's wind turbine generators range in capacity from 600 kilowatts (kW) to 2.1 megawatts (MW). The firm's product portfolio includes the S97 (2.1 MW), S95 (2.1 MW), S88 (2.1 MW), S82 (1.5 MW), S66 (1.25 MW), S64 (1.25 MW) and S52 (600 kW) wind turbines. The company, which operates in 32 countries, currently has an installed capacity of more than 17,000 MW. Other operations include sale and sub-lease of land, infrastructure development and power generation. The company maintains 11 manufacturing facilities in India, China, Germany and Portugal that produce a range of rotor blades, nacelles and nacelle covers, control panels, tubular towers and generators. In addition, the firm has a sizeable research and development presence in various parts of the world, including India, Germany, the Netherlands and Denmark. Suzlon's research efforts have resulted in the implementation of several technological advances to its turbine manufacturing process, such as new non-destructive blade testing methods and the use of acoustic cameras to study the physics involved in experimental and hybrid composite building materials. Subsidiary Hansen Transmissions International N.V., based in Belgium, manufactures gearboxes for captive electricity harnessing. The firm also owns a 95% stake in REpower Systems AG, a German manufacturer of wind turbines. The Suzlon Foundation serves as the firm's outreach arm, sponsoring educational and public health initiatives in communities near Suzlon operations, primarily in India. In Januray 2011, Suzlon opened a new office in South Korea. In October 2011, the firm sold its 26.06% interest in Hansen Transmissions International NV, a wind gearbox manufacturer, to ZF Friedrichshafen AG.

FINANCIALS: Sales and profits are in thousands of dollars—add 000 to get the full amount. 2011 Note: Financial information for 2011 was not available for all companies at press time.

2011 Sales: $3,611,600	2011 Profits: $-267,400	**U.S. Stock Ticker:**
2010 Sales: $4,468,300	2010 Profits: $-213,000	**Int'l Ticker: 532667**
2009 Sales: $5,651,900	2009 Profits: $51,200	Int'l Exchange: Bombay-BSE
2008 Sales: $2,964,300	2008 Profits: $223,200	Employees: 14,000 Fiscal Year Ends: 3/31
2007 Sales: $1,585,620	2007 Profits: $171,560	Parent Company:

SALARIES/BENEFITS:

Pension Plan:	ESOP Stock Plan: Y	Profit Sharing:	Top Exec. Salary: $294,519	Bonus: $
Savings Plan:	Stock Purch. Plan:		Second Exec. Salary: $121,456	Bonus: $

OTHER THOUGHTS:

Apparent Women Officers or Directors:
Hot Spot for Advancement for Women/Minorities:

LOCATIONS: ("Y" = Yes)

West:	Southwest:	Midwest:	Southeast:	Northeast:	International:
		Y			Y

SYNAPSENSE

www.synapsense.com

Industry Group Code: 3345

Energy/Fuel:	Other Technologies:	Electrical Products:		Electronics:	Transportation:	Other:
Biofuels:	Irrigation:	Lighting/LEDs:		Computers:	Car Sharing:	Recycling:
Batteries/Storage:	Nanotech:	Waste Heat:		Sensors:	Electric Vehicles:	Engineering:
Solar:	Biotech:	Smart Meters:	Y	Software: Y	Natural Gas Fuel:	Consulting:
Wind:	Water Tech./Treatment:	Machinery:				Investing:
Fuel Cells:	Ceramics:					Chemicals:

TYPES OF BUSINESS:

Energy Efficiency Data Infrastructure Management Solutions (DCIM)

BRANDS/DIVISIONS/AFFILIATES:

SynapSense Data Center Optimization Platform
SynapSense Active Control
P3 SmartPlug
SmartLink

CONTACTS: *Note: Officers with more than one job title may be intentionally listed here more than once.*

Peter Van Deventer, CEO
Peter Van Deventer, Pres.
F. Ray Nunez, CFO
Troy Mitchell, VP-Sales & Mktg.
Raju Pandey, CTO
Jeff Boone, Sr. VP-Eng.
Pat Weston, VP-Strategic Planning
Ray Pfeifer, Corp. Exec. VP
Ron Bostic, VP-Professional Svcs.

Phone: 916-294-0110	**Fax:** 916-294-0270
Toll-Free:	
Address: 2365 Iron Point Rd., Ste. 100, Folsom, CA 95630 US	

GROWTH PLANS/SPECIAL FEATURES:

SynapSense is a provider of energy efficiency data infrastructure management solutions (DCIM) to more than 25 vertical market segments, including technology, healthcare, finance, defense, aerospace and utilities. The firm monitors weather patterns, such as air pressure, moisture and heat, in data centers and provides advice on how to effectively reduce power usage so as to optimize the customer's return on their investment. The firm's proprietary SynapSense Data Center Optimization Platform focuses on power and cooling infrastructure and saves customers up to 50% of cooling energy. The platform allows customers to optimize their power consumption while maintaining within their current data center footprint. The SynapSense Active Control program allows for the customer to set a tangible return on investment (ROI) time frame, with usual payback within two years. It does so by aligning the cooling capacity with the changes in the information technology (IT) load. The firm offers a complete turn-key solution for each project, including a complete assessment; overall airflow management, which includes reducing variable frequency drive (VFD) fan speeds and increasing computer room air handlers (CRAH) temperature set points; the deployment of SynapSense Active Control to maintain the environment at optimum performance settings; and resetting the new energy baseline and using the SynapSense metering to support the new baseline verification. The firm is headquartered in Folsom, California. In June 2011, the firm added the energy metering tools P3 SmartPlug and SmartLink to its data center optimization platform. In October 2011, the company expanded into the Asia Pacific market with the construction of a Singapore office.

FINANCIALS: Sales and profits are in thousands of dollars—add 000 to get the full amount. 2011 Note: Financial information for 2011 was not available for all companies at press time.

2011 Sales: $	2011 Profits: $	**U.S. Stock Ticker:** Private
2010 Sales: $	2010 Profits: $	**Int'l Ticker:**
2009 Sales: $	2009 Profits: $	Int'l Exchange:
2008 Sales: $	2008 Profits: $	Employees: Fiscal Year Ends:
2007 Sales: $	2007 Profits: $	Parent Company:

SALARIES/BENEFITS:

Pension Plan:	ESOP Stock Plan:	Profit Sharing:	Top Exec. Salary: $	Bonus: $
Savings Plan:	Stock Purch. Plan:		Second Exec. Salary: $	Bonus: $

OTHER THOUGHTS:

Apparent Women Officers or Directors: 1
Hot Spot for Advancement for Women/Minorities:

LOCATIONS: ("Y" = Yes)

West:	Southwest:	Midwest:	Southeast:	Northeast:	International:
Y					Y

Sales, profits and employees may be estimates. Financial information, benefits and other data can change quickly and may vary from those stated here.

SYNGENTA AG

www.syngenta.com

Industry Group Code: 11511

Energy/Fuel:	Other Technologies:		Electrical Products:	Electronics:	Transportation:	Other:	
Biofuels:	Irrigation:		Lighting/LEDs:	Computers:	Car Sharing:	Recycling:	
Batteries/Storage:	Nanotech:		Waste Heat:	Sensors:	Electric Vehicles:	Engineering:	
Solar:	Biotech:	Y	Smart Meters:	Software:	Natural Gas Fuel:	Consulting:	
Wind:	Water Tech./Treatment:		Machinery:			Investing:	
Fuel Cells:	Ceramics:					Chemicals:	Y

TYPES OF BUSINESS:

Agricultural Biotechnology Products & Chemicals Manufacturing
Crop Protection Products
Seeds

BRANDS/DIVISIONS/AFFILIATES:

Dual Gold
Avistar
Acanto
Score
Touchdown
Cruiser
Maxim
Vibrance

CONTACTS: *Note: Officers with more than one job title may be intentionally listed here more than once.*

Michael Mack, CEO
John Ramsay, CFO
Alejandro Aruffo, Head-R&D
Christoph Mader, Head-Legal & Taxes/Corp. Sec.
Mark Peacock, Head-Global Oper.
Robert Berendes, Head-Bus. Dev.
John Atkin, COO-Crop Protection
Davor Pisk, COO-Syngenta Seeds
Martin Taylor, Chmn.

Phone: 41-61-323-9094	Fax: 41-61-323-2324
Toll-Free:	
Address: Schwarzwaldallee 215, Basel, 4058 Switzerland	

GROWTH PLANS/SPECIAL FEATURES:

Syngenta AG is an international agrochemical companies and a leading worldwide supplier of conventional and bioengineered crop protection and seeds. The firm's products designed for crop protection include seed treatments to control weeds, insects and diseases, herbicides, fungicides and insecticides. Additionally, the firm produces seeds for field crops, vegetables and flowers. Its leading marketed products include the following: Dual Gold, Axial and Fusilade selective herbicides; Touchdown, Reglone and Granoxone non-selective herbicides; Bravo, Score and Amistar fungicides; Proclaim, Match and Actara insecticides; and Dividend, Apron, Maxim and Cruiser seed care treatments. Syngenta has a seed portfolio of over 200 product lines and more than 6,800 proprietary varieties. The seeds that the company markets are for field crops, such as corn, soybeans, sugar beets, sunflowers and oilseed rape (canola); vegetables, including tomatoes, lettuce, melons, squash, cabbages, peppers, beans and radishes; and garden plants such as begonias, violas, petunias and many other seasonal flowers and herbs, some of which can also be purchased as plugs or full-grown plants. The firm spends roughly $960 million annually on research and development at its laboratories in the U.S., Sweden, Chile, China, France, India, Singapore and the Netherlands. Syngenta's research and development division is engaged in collaborations with several companies and universities, including Anhui Rice Research Institute of China, Dow AgroSciences and Chromatin, Inc. The company's gene technology has become so refined that single genes can be isolated from a type of plant material and transferred to the DNA of another. This process allows manipulation of such traits as nutrient composition, appearance, and even the specifics of the taste of a certain crop. In May 2011, the firm introduced Vibrance, a fungicide based seed treatment.

FINANCIALS: Sales and profits are in thousands of dollars—add 000 to get the full amount. 2011 Note: Financial information for 2011 was not available for all companies at press time.

		U.S. Stock Ticker:
2011 Sales: $	2011 Profits: $	Int'l Ticker: SYNN
2010 Sales: $11,641,000	2010 Profits: $1,397,000	Int'l Exchange: Zurich-SWX
2009 Sales: $10,992,000	2009 Profits: $1,374,000	Employees: 26,000 Fiscal Year Ends: 12/31
2008 Sales: $11,624,000	2008 Profits: $1,385,000	Parent Company:
2007 Sales: $9,240,000	2007 Profits: $1,109,000	

SALARIES/BENEFITS:

Pension Plan: Y	ESOP Stock Plan:	Profit Sharing:	Top Exec. Salary: $	Bonus: $
Savings Plan: Y	Stock Purch. Plan: Y		Second Exec. Salary: $	Bonus: $

OTHER THOUGHTS:

Apparent Women Officers or Directors: 1
Hot Spot for Advancement for Women/Minorities:

LOCATIONS: ("Y" = Yes)

West:	Southwest:	Midwest:	Southeast:	Northeast:	International:
Y		Y	Y	Y	Y

SYNTHETIC GENOMICS INC

www.syntheticgenomics.com

Industry Group Code: 325199

Energy/Fuel:		Other Technologies:		Electrical Products:	Electronics:	Transportation:	Other:
Biofuels:	Y	Irrigation:		Lighting/LEDs:	Computers:	Car Sharing:	Recycling:
Batteries/Storage:		Nanotech:		Waste Heat:	Sensors:	Electric Vehicles:	Engineering:
Solar:		Biotech:	Y	Smart Meters:	Software:	Natural Gas Fuel:	Consulting:
Wind:		Water Tech./Treatment:		Machinery:			Investing:
Fuel Cells:		Ceramics:					Chemicals:

TYPES OF BUSINESS:

Biofuels
Genomics-Based Technologies

BRANDS/DIVISIONS/AFFILIATES:

Synthetic Genomics Vaccines Inc
Agradis Inc

CONTACTS: *Note: Officers with more than one job title may be intentionally listed here more than once.*

J. Craig Venter, CEO
Aristides A. N. Patrinos, Pres.
Joseph Mahler, CFO
Hamilton O. Smith, Co-Chief Scientific Officer
Jim Flatt, CTO
Fernanda Gandara, Sr. VP-Bus. Dev.
Aristides A. N. Patrinos, Sr. VP-Corp. Affairs
J. Craig Venter, Co-Chief Scientific Officer
Paul Roessler, VP-Renewable Fuels & Chemicals
Toby Richardson, VP-Bioinformatics
Sammy J. Farah, Pres., Synthetic Genomics Vaccines, Inc.
J. Craig Venter, Chmn.

Phone: 858-754-2900	**Fax:** 858-754-2988
Toll-Free:	
Address: 11149 N. Torrey Pines Rd., La Jolla, CA 92037 US	

GROWTH PLANS/SPECIAL FEATURES:

Synthetic Genomics, Inc. is involved in the commercialization of genomic-driven technologies. Founded in 2005, the firm seeks to develop marketable genomic-driven solutions that address energy and environment challenges. The company is focused on developing new biological solutions to increase production and/or recovery rates of subsurface hydrocarbons in collaboration with BP; harnessing photosynthetic organisms to produce energy directly from sunlight and carbon dioxide through an alliance with ExxonMobil Research and Engineering Company; and designing advanced biofuels with superior properties compared to ethanol and biodiesel and developing high-yielding, economic and more disease-resistant feedstocks in partnership with Asiatic Centre for Genome Technology. Synthetic Genomics' extensive scientific team enables it to pursue research and development in several areas, including genome engineering, microbiology, synthetic biology, plant genomics, biochemistry, environmental genomics, bioinformatics and climate change. The firm is a sponsor of fundamental research at the J. Craig Venter Institute, a non-profit organization, with over 400 scientists and staff, that conducts a variety of genomic research programs. Synthetic Genomics has received funding from several investors, including Draper Fisher Juvetson; Plenus, S.A. de C.V.; Biotechonomy LLC; BP plc; ACGT Sdn Bhd.; and Meteor Group. The firm was founded by Dr. J. Craig Venter and Nobel Laureate Dr. Hamilton O. Smith, both of whom remain Synthetic Genomics executives and research leaders. In 2010, the company and the J. Craig Venter Institute established Synthetic Genomics Vaccines, Inc. to develop new vaccines utilizing genomic technology. In October 2011, Synthetic Geonomics and Plenus established Agradis, Inc., a new company formed to develop and market sustainable agricultural biotechnology products.

The firm offers medical, dental, vision, life and disability insurance; an assistance plan; a 401(k); stock options; paid time off and holidays; flexible spending accounts; professional retirement and investment counseling services; wellness programs; and an employee referral program.

FINANCIALS: Sales and profits are in thousands of dollars—add 000 to get the full amount. 2011 Note: Financial information for 2011 was not available for all companies at press time.

2011 Sales: $	2011 Profits: $	**U.S. Stock Ticker:** Private
2010 Sales: $	2010 Profits: $	**Int'l Ticker:**
2009 Sales: $	2009 Profits: $	Int'l Exchange:
2008 Sales: $	2008 Profits: $	Employees: Fiscal Year Ends:
2007 Sales: $	2007 Profits: $	Parent Company:

SALARIES/BENEFITS:

Pension Plan:	ESOP Stock Plan:	Profit Sharing:	Top Exec. Salary: $	Bonus: $
Savings Plan: Y	Stock Purch. Plan: Y		Second Exec. Salary: $	Bonus: $

OTHER THOUGHTS:

Apparent Women Officers or Directors:
Hot Spot for Advancement for Women/Minorities: Y

LOCATIONS: ("Y" = Yes)

West:	Southwest:	Midwest:	Southeast:	Northeast:	International:
Y				Y	

SYNTROLEUM CORPORATION

www.syntroleum.com

Industry Group Code: 325199

Energy/Fuel:		Other Technologies:		Electrical Products:	Electronics:	Transportation:	Other:
Biofuels:	Y	Irrigation:		Lighting/LEDs:	Computers:	Car Sharing:	Recycling:
Batteries/Storage:		Nanotech:		Waste Heat:	Sensors:	Electric Vehicles:	Engineering:
Solar:		Biotech:	Y	Smart Meters:	Software:	Natural Gas Fuel:	Consulting:
Wind:		Water Tech./Treatment:		Machinery:			Investing:
Fuel Cells:		Ceramics:					Chemicals:

TYPES OF BUSINESS:

Synthetic Fuels
Biomass
Coal Liquefaction

BRANDS/DIVISIONS/AFFILIATES:

Bio-Synfining
Fischer-Tropsch
Dynamic Fuels LLC

CONTACTS: Note: Officers with more than one job title may be intentionally listed here more than once.

Edward G. Roth, CEO
Edward G. Roth, Pres.
Karen L. Gallagher, CFO/Sr. VP
Jeffery M. Bigger, Sr. VP-Bus. Dev.
Ronald E. Stinebaugh, Sr. VP-Finance & Acquisitions
Robert Rosene, Jr., Chmn.

Phone: 918-592-7900	Fax: 918-592-7979
Toll-Free:	
Address: 5416 S. Yale Ave. , Ste. 400, Tulsa, OK 74135 US	

GROWTH PLANS/SPECIAL FEATURES:

Syntroleum Corporation is engaged in the commercialization of technology to produce synthetic liquid hydrocarbons. These synthetic liquid hydrocarbons, which are substantially free of contaminants typically found in conventional hydrocarbon products, are marketed to the renewable fuels, gas-to-liquids (GTL), coal-to-liquids (CTL) and biomass-to-liquids (BTL) industries. The firm's Bio-Synfining and Fischer-Tropsch technologies use various feedstocks, including vegetable oils, fats, fatty acids and greases, to make renewable synthetic fuels, such as kerosene, naphtha, diesel, jet fuel and propane. With 160 patents either issued or pending, he firm has quantified over 100 different types of fats and oils for conversion to synthetic fuels. The company provides its licensees with engineering support services including project management, project design packages, technology design application and more. Dynamic Fuels LLC, Syntroleum's 50-50 joint venture with Tyson Foods, has built synthetic fuels facility that is expected to eventually have a 5,000 gallon per day production capacity. The plant, which became operational in late 2010, combines the company's Bio-Synfining technology with Tyson's agricultural feedstock to create ultra-clean middle distillate fuels. In August 2011, Syntroleum and China Petroleum & Chemical Corporation opened a CTL demonstration facility in China.

FINANCIALS: Sales and profits are in thousands of dollars—add 000 to get the full amount. 2011 Note: Financial information for 2011 was not available for all companies at press time.

2011 Sales: $	2011 Profits: $	**U.S. Stock Ticker: SYNM**
2010 Sales: $8,410	2010 Profits: $-9,536	**Int'l Ticker:**
2009 Sales: $27,432	2009 Profits: $5,038	Int'l Exchange:
2008 Sales: $4,890	2008 Profits: $-4,138	Employees: 19 Fiscal Year Ends: 12/31
2007 Sales: $16,472	2007 Profits: $3,751	Parent Company:

SALARIES/BENEFITS:

Pension Plan:	ESOP Stock Plan:	Profit Sharing:	Top Exec. Salary: $260,000	Bonus: $200,000
Savings Plan:	Stock Purch. Plan:		Second Exec. Salary: $175,000	Bonus: $35,000

OTHER THOUGHTS:

Apparent Women Officers or Directors: 1
Hot Spot for Advancement for Women/Minorities:

LOCATIONS: ("Y" = Yes)

West:	Southwest:	Midwest:	Southeast:	Northeast:	International:
	Y				

TAKADU

www.takadu.com

Industry Group Code: 5112

Energy/Fuel:	Other Technologies:		Electrical Products:		Electronics:		Transportation:		Other:	
Biofuels:	Irrigation:		Lighting/LEDs:		Computers:		Car Sharing:		Recycling:	
Batteries/Storage:	Nanotech:		Waste Heat:		Sensors:		Electric Vehicles:		Engineering:	
Solar:	Biotech:		Smart Meters:		Software:	Y	Natural Gas Fuel:		Consulting:	Y
Wind:	Water Tech./Treatment:	Y	Machinery:						Investing:	
Fuel Cells:	Ceramics:								Chemicals:	

TYPES OF BUSINESS:

Water Networks Technology

BRANDS/DIVISIONS/AFFILIATES:

TaKaDu monitor

CONTACTS: *Note: Officers with more than one job title may be intentionally listed here more than once.*

Amir Peleg, CEO
Einat Zviran, COO
Guy Horowitz, VP-Mktg.
Zvika Diamant, VP-R&D
Haggai Scolnicov, CTO
Shirley Segal, Dir.-Strategic Accounts
Limor Bakal, VP-Channels & Bus. Partners
Zvi Arom, Chmn.

Phone: 972-3-5555100	Fax: 972-3-6323055
Toll-Free:	
Address: 4 Derech HaChoresh, Yehud, 56470 Israel	

GROWTH PLANS/SPECIAL FEATURES:

TaKaDu is an Israeli firm focused on developing advanced water networks technology. Approximately 25% to 30% of the world's water consumption is lost due to aging water networks around the world. TaKaDu seeks to lessen this amount of water lost in production through its patented solution, the TaKaDu monitor, which uses multiple resources for data analytics. This product analyzes complex periodic patterns; pressure-flow relations; graph structure; cross-site and spatial correlation; event behavior over space and time; and several other statistical factors. The firm's raw data sources include network operations data; online sensor data, such as flow and pressure; network structure; and external data, such as weather, scheduled fixes and holidays. TaKaDu sends its data to water utilities worldwide through online alerts. In October 2011, the firm was named the 2011 Global Cleantech 100's Company of the Year-Europe & Israel by research firm Cleantech Group.

FINANCIALS: Sales and profits are in thousands of dollars—add 000 to get the full amount. 2011 Note: Financial information for 2011 was not available for all companies at press time.

2011 Sales: $	2011 Profits: $	U.S. Stock Ticker: Private
2010 Sales: $	2010 Profits: $	Int'l Ticker:
2009 Sales: $	2009 Profits: $	Int'l Exchange:
2008 Sales: $	2008 Profits: $	Employees: Fiscal Year Ends:
2007 Sales: $	2007 Profits: $	Parent Company:

SALARIES/BENEFITS:

Pension Plan:	ESOP Stock Plan:	Profit Sharing:	Top Exec. Salary: $	Bonus: $
Savings Plan:	Stock Purch. Plan:		Second Exec. Salary: $	Bonus: $

OTHER THOUGHTS:

Apparent Women Officers or Directors: 4
Hot Spot for Advancement for Women/Minorities: Y

LOCATIONS: ("Y" = Yes)

West:	Southwest:	Midwest:	Southeast:	Northeast:	International: Y

TALBOTT'S BIOMASS ENERGY SYSTEMS LTD www.talbotts.co.uk
Industry Group Code: 33361

Energy/Fuel:		Other Technologies:	Electrical Products:	Electronics:	Transportation:	Other:
Biofuels:	Y	Irrigation:	Lighting/LEDs:	Computers:	Car Sharing:	Recycling:
Batteries/Storage:		Nanotech:	Waste Heat:	Sensors:	Electric Vehicles:	Engineering:
Solar:		Biotech:	Smart Meters:	Software:	Natural Gas Fuel:	Consulting:
Wind:		Water Tech./Treatment:	Machinery:			Investing:
Fuel Cells:		Ceramics:				Chemicals:

TYPES OF BUSINESS:
Boiler & Heater Manufacturing
Biomass-Fueled Boilers
Biomass-Fueled Electrical Generators
Biofuels Technology

BRANDS/DIVISIONS/AFFILIATES:
C1-C10
Bio Junior
Bio Senior
Eccleshall Biomass

CONTACTS: Note: Officers with more than one job title may be intentionally listed here more than once.
Richard Fielding, Head-Woodworking & Industrial Sales
Amy Fielding, Dir.-Commercial

Phone: 44-01785-213366	Fax: 44-01785-256418
Toll-Free:	
Address: Tollgate Dr., Tollgate Industrial Estate, Stafford, ST16 3HS UK	

GROWTH PLANS/SPECIAL FEATURES:
Talbott's Biomass Energy Systems Ltd. is one of the U.K.'s leading manufacturers of biomass heaters and boilers for the efficient conversion of biomass to electricity, as well as a leading biofuel specialist. The company has over 4,000 working installations in over 20 countries, including the U.S., Japan, Finland and Australia. It offers a complete range of heaters and boilers, available as either hand-fired or automatic systems, which can run on biomass, sawdust, wood shavings, wood refuse, paper, cardboard or packaging waste. Talbott's also provides shredders, silos, hoppers, dischargers and related machinery. The company has developed a biomass generator that is able to convert biomass into small scale electrical energy. The firm developed one of the first commercially available biomass-powered electrical generators in the world. The company offers large scale energy generation through high efficiency steam boilers and turbines; including its C1-C10 Biomass broiler, which is able to cleanly burn wood with a higher moisture content. The company's Bio Junior and Bio Senior biomass boilers are its most economical product, mainly purchased for domestic use. Eccleshall Biomass is a partnership of between Talbott's, BiEcc Ltd. and Raleigh Hall Properties that is attempting to establish biomass power plants fueled by energy crops.

FINANCIALS: Sales and profits are in thousands of dollars—add 000 to get the full amount. 2011 Note: Financial information for 2011 was not available for all companies at press time.

2011 Sales: $	2011 Profits: $	U.S. Stock Ticker: Private
2010 Sales: $	2010 Profits: $	Int'l Ticker:
2009 Sales: $	2009 Profits: $	Int'l Exchange:
2008 Sales: $	2008 Profits: $	Employees: Fiscal Year Ends:
2007 Sales: $	2007 Profits: $	Parent Company:

SALARIES/BENEFITS:
Pension Plan:	ESOP Stock Plan:	Profit Sharing:	Top Exec. Salary: $	Bonus: $
Savings Plan:	Stock Purch. Plan:		Second Exec. Salary: $	Bonus: $

OTHER THOUGHTS:
Apparent Women Officers or Directors: 1
Hot Spot for Advancement for Women/Minorities:

LOCATIONS: ("Y" = Yes)
West:	Southwest:	Midwest:	Southeast:	Northeast:	International: Y

TEKION INC

www.tekion.com

Industry Group Code: 335999

Energy/Fuel:	Other Technologies:	Electrical Products:	Electronics:	Transportation:	Other:
Biofuels:	Irrigation:	Lighting/LEDs:	Computers:	Car Sharing:	Recycling:
Batteries/Storage:	Nanotech:	Waste Heat:	Sensors:	Electric Vehicles:	Engineering:
Solar:	Biotech:	Smart Meters:	Software:	Natural Gas Fuel:	Consulting:
Wind:	Water Tech./Treatment:	Machinery:			Investing:
Fuel Cells: Y	Ceramics:				Chemicals:

TYPES OF BUSINESS:

Fuel Cells

BRANDS/DIVISIONS/AFFILIATES:

Formira
Formira Power Pack
Renew Power
BASF AG

CONTACTS: Note: Officers with more than one job title may be intentionally listed here more than once.

Neil Huff, CEO
Neil Huff, Pres.
Richard Masel, Sr. Tech. Advisor

Phone: 604-656-6610	**Fax:** 604-656-6620
Toll-Free:	
Address: 8602 Commerce Ct., Burnby, BC V5A 4N6 Canada	

GROWTH PLANS/SPECIAL FEATURES:

Tekion, Inc. is an electrochemical power company. The firm's products have power outputs ranging from 5-50 watts, and energy outputs from 10-100 watt-hours. The firm aspires to build an end-to-end electrochemical power technology family that offers a portfolio of fuel cells. Currently in development are products for small military sensors, mobile phones and hand-held devices, including the Formira Power Pack, which incorporates fuel cell technology as an internal recharging mechanism for a lithium ion battery assembly. Formira is the firm's proprietary purified formic acid fuel source used in its fuel cells, replacing the methanol utilized in most fuel cells. By using Formira, the company is able to build less complex fuel cells than those that run on methanol, thereby enhancing its miniaturization process; as a result, Tekion's fuel cell will be one of the first able to fit in a cell phone. It already has a second generation working prototype for an original equipment manufacturer (OEM) application. The Formira fuel cells also perform in lower operating temperatures and utilize cheaper catalysts. Tekion plans to market a Formira fuel cell through subsidiary Renew Power as its first commercial product. The direct formic acid fuel cell will be the first fuel cell able to fit in a mobile phone and will be charged by inserting a snap-in OTG fuel capsule. Other applications for the product include satellite phones, PDAs and notebook PCs. The company has an agreement with BASF AG, one of the world's leading producers of formic acid, to continue to develop and refine Tekion's formic acid-based fuel formulas.

FINANCIALS: Sales and profits are in thousands of dollars—add 000 to get the full amount. 2011 Note: Financial information for 2011 was not available for all companies at press time.

2011 Sales: $	2011 Profits: $	**U.S. Stock Ticker:** Private
2010 Sales: $	2010 Profits: $	**Int'l Ticker:**
2009 Sales: $	2009 Profits: $	Int'l Exchange:
2008 Sales: $	2008 Profits: $	Employees: Fiscal Year Ends: 12/31
2007 Sales: $	2007 Profits: $	Parent Company:

SALARIES/BENEFITS:

Pension Plan:	ESOP Stock Plan:	Profit Sharing:	Top Exec. Salary: $	Bonus: $
Savings Plan:	Stock Purch. Plan:		Second Exec. Salary: $	Bonus: $

OTHER THOUGHTS:

Apparent Women Officers or Directors:
Hot Spot for Advancement for Women/Minorities:

LOCATIONS: ("Y" = Yes)

West:	Southwest:	Midwest:	Southeast:	Northeast:	International:
		Y			Y

TENDRIL

www.tendrilinc.com

Industry Group Code: 5112

Energy/Fuel:	Other Technologies:	Electrical Products:	Electronics:		Transportation:		Other:
Biofuels:	Irrigation:	Lighting/LEDs:	Computers:		Car Sharing:		Recycling:
Batteries/Storage:	Nanotech:	Waste Heat:	Sensors:		Electric Vehicles:		Engineering:
Solar:	Biotech:	Smart Meters:	Software:	Y	Natural Gas Fuel:		Consulting:
Wind:	Water Tech./Treatment:	Machinery:					Investing:
Fuel Cells:	Ceramics:						Chemicals:

TYPES OF BUSINESS:

Energy Management

BRANDS/DIVISIONS/AFFILIATES:

Tendril Connect
Tendril Energize
GroundedPower

CONTACTS: *Note: Officers with more than one job title may be intentionally listed here more than once.*

Adrian Tuck, CEO
Ivo Steklac, COO
David Rayner, CFO
Jim Borri, Sr. VP-Sales
Tim Enwall, CIO
Kent Dickson, CTO
Mark Pougnet, Chief Delivery Officer
Tom McDaniel, Chmn.
Brent Hodges, Gen. Mgr.-Australia

Phone: 720-921-2100	**Fax:** 720-921-2101
Toll-Free:	
Address: 2560 55th St., Boulder, CO 80301 US	

GROWTH PLANS/SPECIAL FEATURES:

Tendril is an energy platform firm, which processes end-to-end consumer engagement applications, products and services using its proprietary Tendril Connect technology suite. The firm's product offerings include software, utility solutions and in-home products and applications. Tendril Connect is a cloud-based energy management platform that is both secure, scalable and open standards-based. The platform allows for easily accessed communication between energy service providers and their customers. The firm's utility solutions include Demand Response and Energy Efficiency. Demand Response offers customers the ability to manage and often reduce their peak load during high cost peak time periods. Energy Efficiency helps the customer manage their energy usage. Additionally, the company produces Tendril Energize, an application suite that incorporates human behavioral data in the creation of Energy Efficiency, Load Control and Demand Response programs, which allow energy service providers to continually connect with their customer base to optimize generation costs and balance loads. The company recently acquired GroundedPower, a consumer engagement firm that emphasizes behavioral science research methods. The firm is a venture sponsored by Siemens Venture Capital, Good Energies, RRE Ventures, VantagePoint Capital Partners and GE. Headquartered in Boulder, Colorado, the firm also operates a facility in Melbourne, Australia.

Employee benefits include medical, dental and vision coverage; life and personal accident insurance; short- and long-term disability; supplemental life insurance; education assistance; an employee assistance program; flexible spending accounts; a savings plan; and 4 weeks of paid time off.

FINANCIALS: Sales and profits are in thousands of dollars—add 000 to get the full amount. 2011 Note: Financial information for 2011 was not available for all companies at press time.

2011 Sales: $	2011 Profits: $	**U.S. Stock Ticker: Private**
2010 Sales: $	2010 Profits: $	**Int'l Ticker:**
2009 Sales: $	2009 Profits: $	Int'l Exchange:
2008 Sales: $	2008 Profits: $	Employees: Fiscal Year Ends:
2007 Sales: $	2007 Profits: $	Parent Company:

SALARIES/BENEFITS:

Pension Plan:	ESOP Stock Plan:	Profit Sharing:	Top Exec. Salary: $	Bonus: $
Savings Plan: Y	Stock Purch. Plan:		Second Exec. Salary: $	Bonus: $

OTHER THOUGHTS:

Apparent Women Officers or Directors: 1
Hot Spot for Advancement for Women/Minorities:

LOCATIONS: ("Y" = Yes)

West:	Southwest:	Midwest:	Southeast:	Northeast:	International:
Y					Y

TERRA SOLAR GLOBAL INC

www.terrasolar.com

Industry Group Code: 334413

Energy/Fuel:	Other Technologies:	Electrical Products:	Electronics:	Transportation:	Other:
Biofuels:	Irrigation:	Lighting/LEDs:	Computers:	Car Sharing:	Recycling:
Batteries/Storage:	Nanotech:	Waste Heat:	Sensors:	Electric Vehicles:	Engineering:
Solar: Y	Biotech:	Smart Meters:	Software:	Natural Gas Fuel:	Consulting:
Wind:	Water Tech./Treatment:	Machinery:			Investing:
Fuel Cells:	Ceramics:				Chemicals:

TYPES OF BUSINESS:

Solar Panels
Photovoltaic Cells
Solar Power Plant Construction & Operation

BRANDS/DIVISIONS/AFFILIATES:

China Solar Holdings Limited

CONTACTS: *Note: Officers with more than one job title may be intentionally listed here more than once.*

Jack Chu, CEO
Jim Spencer, Pres.
Sandor Caplan, CTO
Henry Chang Manayan, Exec. VP
Frank B. Ellis, Sr. Tech. Consultant
Henry J. Behnke, III, Sr. Tech. Advisor
William P. Nesmith, Sr. Advisor
Yuan Lee, Chmn.

Phone: 212-332-1819	Fax: 503-227-2925

Toll-Free:

Address: 45 Rockefeller Plz., Ste. 200092, New York, NY 10111 US

GROWTH PLANS/SPECIAL FEATURES:

Terra Solar Global, Inc. develops, manufactures and markets photovoltaic modules and system components and builds and installs solar-power systems for residential, commercial and industrial use around the world. The company is 51% owned by China Solar Holdings Limited. Terra Solar's products, which include multi-function amorphous silicon (a-Si) photovoltaic modules, one of the lowest-cost solar electric energy technologies being sold, can be used in building-integrated photovoltaic systems and utility-interactive residential systems. The firm has also been involved in the construction, development, financing, installation and operation of 13 thin-film photovoltaic manufacturing plants worldwide. Additionally, Terra Solar offers Manufacturing Integrated Photovoltaic Power Projects (MIPPP) options, through which customers can purchase either a five-year interest in the output of 5 MW a-Si manufacturing facility or the generating facility itself. Terra Solar is vertically integrated so that it both manufactures and installs all of its products. The company has contracts with Native American Photovoltaics (NAPV), a U.S. non-profit organization; and the Merchant Marine Academy in Kings Point, New York. The company is in the process of expanding its product line to include copper indium gallium diselenide (CIGS) photovoltaics.

FINANCIALS: Sales and profits are in thousands of dollars—add 000 to get the full amount. 2011 Note: Financial information for 2011 was not available for all companies at press time.

2011 Sales: $	2011 Profits: $	**U.S. Stock Ticker: Subsidiary**
2010 Sales: $	2010 Profits: $	**Int'l Ticker:**
2009 Sales: $	2009 Profits: $	Int'l Exchange:
2008 Sales: $	2008 Profits: $	Employees: Fiscal Year Ends: 12/31
2007 Sales: $	2007 Profits: $	Parent Company: CHINA SOLAR HOLDINGS LIMITED

SALARIES/BENEFITS:

Pension Plan:	ESOP Stock Plan:	Profit Sharing:	Top Exec. Salary: $	Bonus: $
Savings Plan:	Stock Purch. Plan:		Second Exec. Salary: $	Bonus: $

OTHER THOUGHTS:

Apparent Women Officers or Directors:
Hot Spot for Advancement for Women/Minorities:

LOCATIONS: ("Y" = Yes)

West:	Southwest:	Midwest:	Southeast:	Northeast:	International:
Y				Y	Y

Sales, profits and employees may be estimates. Financial information, benefits and other data can change quickly and may vary from those stated here.

TESLA MOTORS INC

www.teslamotors.com

Industry Group Code: 33611

Energy/Fuel:	Other Technologies:	Electrical Products:	Electronics:	Transportation:		Other:
Biofuels:	Irrigation:	Lighting/LEDs:	Computers:	Car Sharing:		Recycling:
Batteries/Storage:	Nanotech:	Waste Heat:	Sensors:	Electric Vehicles:	Y	Engineering:
Solar:	Biotech:	Smart Meters:	Software:	Natural Gas Fuel:		Consulting:
Wind:	Water Tech./Treatment:	Machinery:				Investing:
Fuel Cells:	Ceramics:					Chemicals:

TYPES OF BUSINESS:

Automobile Manufacturing, All-Electric
Battery Manufacturing
Lithium Ion Battery Storage Technologies

BRANDS/DIVISIONS/AFFILIATES:

Tesla Roadster
Model S
Tesla Energy Group
VantagePoint Venture Partners
Draper Fisher Jervetson
Compass Venture Partners
Technology Partners
Toyota Motor Corporation

CONTACTS: Note: Officers with more than one job title may be intentionally listed here more than once.

Elon Musk, CEO/Prod. Architect
Deepak Ahuja, CFO
George Blankenship, VP-Sales
Arnnon Geshuri, VP-Human Resources
Ravi Simhambhatla, VP-IT
J. B. Straubel, CTO
Peter Rawlinson, Chief Engineer/VP-Vehicle Eng.
Gilbert Passin, VP-Mfg.
Eric Whitaker, General Counsel
Diarmuid O'Connell, VP-Bus. Dev.
Ricardo Reyes, VP-Comm.
Jeff Evanson, VP-Investor Rel.
Mike Taylor, VP-Finance
Franz von Holzhausen, Chief Designer
Jim Dunlay, VP-Powertrain Hardware Eng.
Ravi Simhambhatla, VP-Bus. Applications
Greg Reicow, VP-Powertrain Oper.
Elon Musk, Chmn.
Cristiano Carlutti, VP-European Sales & Oper.
Peter Carlsson, VP-Supply Chain

Phone: 650-681-5000	Fax:
Toll-Free:	
Address: 3500 Deer Creek, Palo Alto, CA 94304 US	

GROWTH PLANS/SPECIAL FEATURES:

Tesla Motors, Inc. manufactures high-performance electric automobiles. Its first model, the two-seat Tesla Roadster, accelerates from 0-60 miles per hour (mph) in 3.9 seconds, has a top speed of 125 mph, runs for approximately 170-244 miles per charge and has a base price of $109,000. The vehicle's power supply consists of 6,831 lithium-ion battery cells linked together in the trunk. It offers regenerative braking, meaning it uses braking friction to charge the battery, and also carries an on-board charging unit that can pull power from standard wall outlets or from optional mobile charge kits. A full charge can take as little as 4 hours. The company's second model, the four-door, seven-passenger sports sedan named Model S will be available in 2012 and sell for around $57,000. The Model S has a 160-300 mile range, will go from 0-60 mph in 5.6 seconds and feature a top speed of 120 mph. Tesla is backed by a number of investors including VantagePoint Venture Partners, Draper Fisher Jervetson, Compass Venture Partners and Technology Partners. In mid 2010, the Toyota Motor Corporation purchased a $50 million stake in the firm. As part of the deal, Tesla will take over a large car manufacturing plant in Freemont, California that was formerly operated as a joint venture of Toyota and GM. The new funds and manufacturing facility will give Tesla significant expansion capability. In October 2010, Tesla and Toyota announced an agreement to begin developing an electric version of a Toyota sport utility vehicle, the RAV4. In June 2011, the company opened a new dealership in Park Meadows, Colorado.

FINANCIALS: Sales and profits are in thousands of dollars—add 000 to get the full amount. 2011 Note: Financial information for 2011 was not available for all companies at press time.

2011 Sales: $	2011 Profits: $	**U.S. Stock Ticker: TSLA**
2010 Sales: $116,744	2010 Profits: $-154,328	**Int'l Ticker:**
2009 Sales: $111,943	2009 Profits: $-55,740	Int'l Exchange:
2008 Sales: $14,700	2008 Profits: $-82,800	Employees: 899 Fiscal Year Ends: 12/31
2007 Sales: $	2007 Profits: $	Parent Company:

SALARIES/BENEFITS:

Pension Plan:	ESOP Stock Plan:	Profit Sharing:	Top Exec. Salary: $310,417	Bonus: $
Savings Plan:	Stock Purch. Plan:		Second Exec. Salary: $220,055	Bonus: $

OTHER THOUGHTS:

Apparent Women Officers or Directors: 1
Hot Spot for Advancement for Women/Minorities:

LOCATIONS: ("Y" = Yes)

West:	Southwest:	Midwest:	Southeast:	Northeast:	International:
Y	Y				Y

TIGO ENERGY

www.tigoenergy.com

Industry Group Code: 5112

Energy/Fuel:	Other Technologies:	Electrical Products:	Electronics:	Transportation:	Other:
Biofuels:	Irrigation:	Lighting/LEDs:	Computers:	Car Sharing:	Recycling:
Batteries/Storage:	Nanotech:	Waste Heat:	Sensors:	Electric Vehicles:	Engineering:
Solar: Y	Biotech:	Smart Meters:	Software:	Natural Gas Fuel:	Consulting:
Wind:	Water Tech./Treatment:	Machinery:			Investing:
Fuel Cells:	Ceramics:				Chemicals:

TYPES OF BUSINESS:

Solar Energy Products

BRANDS/DIVISIONS/AFFILIATES:

Tigo Energy Module Maximizer
Impedence Matching
MM-ES50
MM-ES75

CONTACTS: *Note: Officers with more than one job title may be intentionally listed here more than once.*

Sam Arditi, CEO
Ron Hadar, COO
Ron Hadar, Pres.
John Niedermaier, CFO
Jeffrey Krisa, Sr. VP-Mktg. & Sales
Mordechay Avrutsky, VP-R&D, Power Prod.
Maxym Makhota, VP-Software Dev.

Phone: 408-402-0802	Fax: 408-358-6279
Toll-Free:	
Address: 420 Blossom Hill Rd., Los Gatos, CA 95032 US	

GROWTH PLANS/SPECIAL FEATURES:

Tigo Energy creates solar energy products. The firm develops technology to increase both the affordability and manageability of solar energy. Its products offer active management, increased power and improved safety from commercial, utility and residential solar systems. The company's proprietary Tigo Energy Module Maximizer solution connects to each solar panel as a retrofit or is built directly into the junction box, where it engages the firm's patented Impedence Matching technology to pull the maximum amount of power from each module. The system's MM-ES50 and MM-ES75 models bring up to 20% more energy yield from the modules. The system offers active system management with advanced performance analytics and panel level visibility, and enhanced safety capabilities with system deactivation and arc prevention controls. The technology offers a maximum level of conversion efficiency and reliability, while maintaining a low cost rate. The company is headquartered in Los Gatos, California and maintains facilities in New York, Frankfurt, Milan, Tokyo, Shanghai; Paris, Seoul and Tel Aviv. In December 2011, Bessemer Venture Partners invested $18 million in the firm.

FINANCIALS: Sales and profits are in thousands of dollars—add 000 to get the full amount. 2011 Note: Financial information for 2011 was not available for all companies at press time.

2011 Sales: $	2011 Profits: $	**U.S. Stock Ticker: Private**
2010 Sales: $	2010 Profits: $	**Int'l Ticker:**
2009 Sales: $	2009 Profits: $	Int'l Exchange:
2008 Sales: $	2008 Profits: $	Employees: Fiscal Year Ends:
2007 Sales: $	2007 Profits: $	Parent Company:

SALARIES/BENEFITS:

Pension Plan:	ESOP Stock Plan:	Profit Sharing:	Top Exec. Salary: $	Bonus: $
Savings Plan:	Stock Purch. Plan:		Second Exec. Salary: $	Bonus: $

OTHER THOUGHTS:

Apparent Women Officers or Directors: 1
Hot Spot for Advancement for Women/Minorities:

LOCATIONS: ("Y" = Yes)

West:	Southwest:	Midwest:	Southeast:	Northeast:	International:
Y				Y	Y

TOPELL ENERGY

www.topellenergy.com

Industry Group Code: 325199

Energy/Fuel:		Other Technologies:		Electrical Products:	Electronics:	Transportation:	Other:
Biofuels:	Y	Irrigation:		Lighting/LEDs:	Computers:	Car Sharing:	Recycling:
Batteries/Storage:		Nanotech:		Waste Heat:	Sensors:	Electric Vehicles:	Engineering:
Solar:		Biotech:	Y	Smart Meters:	Software:	Natural Gas Fuel:	Consulting:
Wind:		Water Tech./Treatment:		Machinery:			Investing:
Fuel Cells:		Ceramics:					Chemicals:

TYPES OF BUSINESS:

Biomass-to-Fuel
Biofuel

BRANDS/DIVISIONS/AFFILIATES:

Topell Nederland

CONTACTS: *Note: Officers with more than one job title may be intentionally listed here more than once.*

Ewout Maaskant, CEO/Managing Dir.
Maarten Herrebrugh, COO
Thomas Chopin, CFO
Robin Post van der Burg, Dir.-Bus. Dev.

Phone: 31-70-362-6921	**Fax:** 31-70-362-6972
Toll-Free:	
Address: Fluwelen Burgwal 44, The Hague, 2511 CJ The Netherlands	

GROWTH PLANS/SPECIAL FEATURES:

Topell Energy is a Dutch biofuel company developing torrefaction technology, a process that yields higher-density energy solid biofuel from low grade biomass. The torrefaction process involves rapid heating of biomass to very high temperatures, between 480 and 660 degrees Fahrenheit, in an oxygen free environment, essentially removing any traces of moisture within the specimen. Heterogeneous biomass raw materials, such as wood cuttings, wood chips, nutshells, rice hulls and straw, result in a homogenous biofuel product that exhibits many coal-like characteristics and can be pelleted. Because the resulting product repels water and is free of biological activity, the torrefied biomass (often referred to as bio-coal) can be stored in open-air facilities and is resistant to rotting. Markets for bio-coal include direct use of biomass for large-scale industrial heating and residential heating; co-firing of coal and biomass to produce steel; producing transport fuels; and agricultural fertilizer. The firm has built one commercial-scale torrefied biomass facility in the Netherlands, which has an annual production capacity of 60,000 tons. The facility is owned by Topell Nederland, a joint venture between Topell Energy and RWE Innogy GmbH, a subsidiary of RWE AG.

FINANCIALS: Sales and profits are in thousands of dollars—add 000 to get the full amount. 2011 Note: Financial information for 2011 was not available for all companies at press time.

2011 Sales: $	2011 Profits: $	**U.S. Stock Ticker: Private**
2010 Sales: $	2010 Profits: $	**Int'l Ticker:**
2009 Sales: $	2009 Profits: $	Int'l Exchange:
2008 Sales: $	2008 Profits: $	Employees: Fiscal Year Ends:
2007 Sales: $	2007 Profits: $	Parent Company:

SALARIES/BENEFITS:

Pension Plan:	ESOP Stock Plan:	Profit Sharing:	Top Exec. Salary: $	Bonus: $
Savings Plan:	Stock Purch. Plan:		Second Exec. Salary: $	Bonus: $

OTHER THOUGHTS:

Apparent Women Officers or Directors:
Hot Spot for Advancement for Women/Minorities:

LOCATIONS: ("Y" = Yes)

West:	Southwest:	Midwest:	Southeast:	Northeast:	International: Y

Sales, profits and employees may be estimates. Financial information, benefits and other data can change quickly and may vary from those stated here.

TOSHIBA CORPORATE R&D CENTER www.toshiba.co.jp/rdc/index.htm
Industry Group Code: 541712

Energy/Fuel:	Other Technologies:	Electrical Products:	Electronics:		Transportation:	Other:	
Biofuels:	Irrigation:	Lighting/LEDs:	Computers:	Y	Car Sharing:	Recycling:	
Batteries/Storage:	Nanotech: Y	Waste Heat:	Sensors:		Electric Vehicles:	Engineering:	Y
Solar:	Biotech:	Smart Meters:	Software:	Y	Natural Gas Fuel:	Consulting:	
Wind:	Water Tech./Treatment:	Machinery:				Investing:	
Fuel Cells:	Ceramics:					Chemicals:	

TYPES OF BUSINESS:
Research & Development
Semiconductor Processes
MEMS Applications
Biotechnology Tools
Electronic Devices
Software
Medical Devices
Speech Recognition Technology

BRANDS/DIVISIONS/AFFILIATES:
Toshiba Corp.

CONTACTS: *Note: Officers with more than one job title may be intentionally listed here more than once.*
Akira Sudo, CEO/Sr. VP

Phone: 81-44-549-2056	Fax:
Toll-Free:	
Address: 1 Komukai Toshiba-cho, Saiwai-ku, Kawasaki-shi, 212-8582 Japan	

GROWTH PLANS/SPECIAL FEATURES:
Toshiba Corporate R&D Center (CRDC) manages a global network of research laboratories, test facilities and planning groups that support the ongoing commercialization of products and technologies for Toshiba Corporation, its parent company. Toshiba is a global leader in the manufacture of consumer, industrial, medical and communications electronics. CRDC has focused the bulk of its short-term research and development initiatives on digital products and electronic devices, while its scientists and engineers continue to develop a range of platform technologies, including new nanometric semiconductor processes, innovative microelectromechanical systems (MEMS) applications and chip-based biotech tools. The firm has facilities in Japan, the U.K. and China. Its research and development areas include wireless and networking, which include holding teleconferences with people in remote locations; human interface, such as the firm's Yubi de Komimi Hasander Ontology-Based Technology, which is used for gathering word-of-mouth information from blogs; LSI and Storage, which involves the development of Magnetoresistive Random Access Memory (MRAM), the only nonvolatile memory that has no rewriting limitation; advance materials and devices, which includes, among others, the commercialization of a DNA chip for medical applications; and systems and environment, which includes the development of an Incident and Accident Report System that utilizes a Risk Failure Mode and Effects Analysis, RFMEA, to better deliver medical care in a more timely and efficient manner.

FINANCIALS: Sales and profits are in thousands of dollars—add 000 to get the full amount. 2011 Note: Financial information for 2011 was not available for all companies at press time.
2011 Sales: $	2011 Profits: $	U.S. Stock Ticker: Subsidiary
2010 Sales: $	2010 Profits: $	Int'l Ticker:
2009 Sales: $	2009 Profits: $	Int'l Exchange:
2008 Sales: $	2008 Profits: $	Employees: Fiscal Year Ends: 3/31
2007 Sales: $	2007 Profits: $	Parent Company: TOSHIBA CORPORATION

SALARIES/BENEFITS:
Pension Plan:	ESOP Stock Plan:	Profit Sharing:	Top Exec. Salary: $	Bonus: $
Savings Plan:	Stock Purch. Plan:		Second Exec. Salary: $	Bonus: $

OTHER THOUGHTS:
Apparent Women Officers or Directors:
Hot Spot for Advancement for Women/Minorities:

LOCATIONS: ("Y" = Yes)
West:	Southwest:	Midwest:	Southeast:	Northeast: Y	International: Y

Sales, profits and employees may be estimates. Financial information, benefits and other data can change quickly and may vary from those stated here.

TOSHIBA CORPORATION

www.toshiba.co.jp

Industry Group Code: 334111

Energy/Fuel:	Other Technologies:		Electrical Products:	Electronics:	Transportation:	Other:
Biofuels:	Irrigation:		Lighting/LEDs:	Computers:	Car Sharing:	Recycling:
Batteries/Storage:	Nanotech:	Y	Waste Heat:	Sensors:	Electric Vehicles:	Engineering:
Solar:	Biotech:		Smart Meters:	Software:	Natural Gas Fuel:	Consulting:
Wind:	Water Tech./Treatment:		Machinery:			Investing:
Fuel Cells:	Ceramics:					Chemicals:

TYPES OF BUSINESS:

Electronics Manufacturing
Computers & Accessories
Telecommunications Equipment
Semiconductors
Consumer Electronics
Medical & Industrial Equipment
Power Plants
Internet Services

BRANDS/DIVISIONS/AFFILIATES:

Toshiba Consumer Electronics Holding Corporation
Toshiba Medical Systems Corporation
Toshiba Elevator & Building Systems Corporation
Toshiba Mobile Display Co., Ltd.
Toshiba Storage Device Corporation
Westinghouse Electric Company LLC
Toshiba Thailand Co Ltd
Toshiba Corporate R&D Center

CONTACTS: Note: Officers with more than one job title may be intentionally listed here more than once.

Norio Sasaki, CEO
Norio Sasaki, Pres.
Masashi Muromachi, Sr. Exec. VP
Masao Namiki, Sr. Exec. VP
Yoshihiro Maeda, Sr. Exec. VP
Fumio Muraoka, Sr. Exec. VP
Atsutoshi Nishida, Chmn.

Phone: 81-3-3457-4511	Fax: 81-3-3456-1631
Toll-Free:	
Address: 1-1, Shibaura 1-chome, Minato-ku, Tokyo, 105-8001 Japan	

GROWTH PLANS/SPECIAL FEATURES:

Toshiba Corporation is a diversified technology firm active in four business segments: Digital Products; Electronic Devices and Components; Social Infrastructure Systems; and Home Appliances. Digital Products consists of the Visual Products Company, which develops LCD TVs and DVD recorders, Blu-ray disc recorders and DVD players; the Storage Products Company, which develops hard disk drives and optical disc drives; and the Digital Products & Network Company, which markets notebook PCs, PC servers and business communications systems. The Electronic Devices and Communications segment consists of the Semiconductor Company, which manufactures circuits such as NAND flash memory, small signal devices and power devices; and Toshiba Mobile Display Co., Ltd., which manufactures low-temperature polysilicon TFT technology. The Social Infrastructure Systems segment includes the Power Systems Company, which develops nuclear, hydroelectric, thermal and geothermal power plants and related equipment; the Transmission Distribution & Industrial Systems Company, which provides power transmission and distribution systems and industrial computers; the Social Infrastructure Systems Company, which manufactures road traffic control systems, broadcasting systems and air-traffic control systems; Toshiba Elevator & Building Systems Corporation, which manufactures elevators and escalators; Toshiba Solutions Corporation, which offers IT consultation, design and development services; and Toshiba Medical Systems Corporation, which manufactures x-ray systems, ultrasound systems and MRI systems. The Home Appliances & Other division works with Toshiba Consumer Electronics Holding Corporation, supplying home appliances, air conditioners and lighting fixtures. In October 2010, the firm and Fujitsu Limited merged their mobile phone businesses. In December 2010, Toshiba acquired Fujitsu's share in Toshiba Storage Device Corporation. In March 2011, the company announced that in response to the earthquakes in Japan, it would cut electricity consumption at all of its nonessential production facilities and business locations.

Employees are offered medical and dental insurance; a pension program; life insurance; accident insurance; and a housing loan support program.

FINANCIALS: Sales and profits are in thousands of dollars—add 000 to get the full amount. 2011 Note: Financial information for 2011 was not available for all companies at press time.

2011 Sales: $84,076,400	2011 Profits: $1,811,300	**U.S. Stock Ticker:**
2010 Sales: $74,288,300	2010 Profits: $-229,530	**Int'l Ticker: 6502**
2009 Sales: $72,732,800	2009 Profits: $-3,755,040	Int'l Exchange: Tokyo-TSE
2008 Sales: $76,680,800	2008 Profits: $1,274,100	Employees: 202,638 Fiscal Year Ends: 3/31
2007 Sales: $64,330,700	2007 Profits: $1,242,340	Parent Company:

SALARIES/BENEFITS:

Pension Plan: Y	ESOP Stock Plan:	Profit Sharing:	Top Exec. Salary: $	Bonus: $
Savings Plan:	Stock Purch. Plan:		Second Exec. Salary: $	Bonus: $

OTHER THOUGHTS:

Apparent Women Officers or Directors:
Hot Spot for Advancement for Women/Minorities:

LOCATIONS: ("Y" = Yes)

West:	Southwest:	Midwest:	Southeast:	Northeast:	International:
Y	Y			Y	Y

Sales, profits and employees may be estimates. Financial information, benefits and other data can change quickly and may vary from those stated here.

TOTAL SA

www.total.com

Industry Group Code: 211111

Energy/Fuel:		Other Technologies:		Electrical Products:		Electronics:		Transportation:		Other:	
Biofuels:	Y	Irrigation:		Lighting/LEDs:		Computers:		Car Sharing:		Recycling:	
Batteries/Storage:		Nanotech:		Waste Heat:		Sensors:		Electric Vehicles:		Engineering:	
Solar:		Biotech:		Smart Meters:		Software:		Natural Gas Fuel:		Consulting:	
Wind:		Water Tech./Treatment:		Machinery:						Investing:	
Fuel Cells:		Ceramics:								Chemicals:	Y

TYPES OF BUSINESS:

Oil & Gas Exploration & Production
Petrochemicals
Specialty Chemicals
Hydrocarbons
Service Stations
Photovoltaic Cells

BRANDS/DIVISIONS/AFFILIATES:

Total
Elan
Elf
Bostik Inc
Total Petrochemicals
Total UK Limited
UTS Energy Corp.

CONTACTS: Note: Officers with more than one job title may be intentionally listed here more than once.

Christophe de Margerie, CEO
Patrick de la Chevardiere, CFO
Michel Benezit, Pres., Mktg. & Refining
Francois Viaud, Sr. VP-Human Resources
Yves-Louis Darricarrere, Pres., Exploration & Prod.
Jean-Jacques Guilbaud, Chief Admin. Officer
Peter Herbel, Dir.-Legal Affairs
Jean-Jacques Mosconi, Dir.-Strategy
Francois Cornelis, Pres., Chemicals
Philippe Boisseau, Exec. Dir.-Upstream
Christophe de Margerie, Chmn.
Jacques Marraud des Grottes, Sr. VP-Exploration & Prod., Africa
Sonia Sikorav, Chief Purchasing Officer

Phone: 33-1-47-44-45-46	Fax: 33-1-47-44-58-24
Toll-Free:	
Address: 2 Place Jean Miller, La Defense 6, Courbevoie, 92400 France	

GROWTH PLANS/SPECIAL FEATURES:

Total S.A. is one of the world's largest energy companies, with operations in more than 130 countries. The firm's activities are divided into three segments: Upstream, Downstream and Chemicals. The Upstream sector handles oil and gas exploration, development and production. Total produces 2.28 million barrels of oil (BOE) per day, with proven reserves of 10.5 billion BOE. The company has exploration and production activities in more than forty countries and produces oil or gas in thirty countries. The Downstream segment does trading, shipping, refining and marketing of petroleum and other fuels; it is a leader in Europe and Africa in the refining and service station market. Total has a worldwide network of approximately 16,425 service stations under the Total, Elf and Elan brand names. The Chemicals division prepares petrochemicals and fertilizers for the industrial/commercial markets; it is also involved in rubber processing, resins, adhesives and electroplating. The company is focusing on high-growth zones (such as Africa, the Mediterranean Basin and Asia) as well as specialty products such as liquefied petroleum gas, aviation fuel, lubricants, waxes, bitumens and solvents. Total, Electrabel and IMEC have collaborated to form a company called Photovoltech for the production of photovoltaic cells and modules. In April 2010, Total sold Mapa Spontex, its consumer specialty chemicals business, to U.S.-based Jarden Corporation. In October 2010, the company purchased Canada-based UTS Energy Corp. for $1.42 billion.

FINANCIALS: Sales and profits are in thousands of dollars—add 000 to get the full amount. 2011 Note: Financial information for 2011 was not available for all companies at press time.

2011 Sales: $	2011 Profits: $	U.S. Stock Ticker:
2010 Sales: $230,233,000	2010 Profits: $15,622,200	Int'l Ticker: FP
2009 Sales: $152,376,000	2009 Profits: $11,476,400	Int'l Exchange: Paris-Euronext
2008 Sales: $213,742,000	2008 Profits: $14,117,800	Employees: 92,855 Fiscal Year Ends: 12/31
2007 Sales: $182,404,000	2007 Profits: $17,572,000	Parent Company:

SALARIES/BENEFITS:

Pension Plan:	ESOP Stock Plan:	Profit Sharing:	Top Exec. Salary: $	Bonus: $1,457,656
Savings Plan:	Stock Purch. Plan:		Second Exec. Salary: $	Bonus: $

OTHER THOUGHTS:

Apparent Women Officers or Directors: 3
Hot Spot for Advancement for Women/Minorities: Y

LOCATIONS: ("Y" = Yes)

West:	Southwest:	Midwest:	Southeast:	Northeast:	International:
Y	Y				Y

TRANSPHORM

www.transphormusa.com

Industry Group Code: 325

Energy/Fuel:	Other Technologies:	Electrical Products:		Electronics:		Transportation:	Other:
Biofuels:	Irrigation:	Lighting/LEDs:	Y	Computers:		Car Sharing:	Recycling:
Batteries/Storage:	Nanotech:	Waste Heat:		Sensors:	Y	Electric Vehicles:	Engineering:
Solar:	Biotech:	Smart Meters:		Software:	Y	Natural Gas Fuel:	Consulting:
Wind:	Water Tech./Treatment:	Machinery:					Investing:
Fuel Cells: Y	Ceramics:						Chemicals:

TYPES OF BUSINESS:

Power Conversion Modules

BRANDS/DIVISIONS/AFFILIATES:

EZ GaN
Google Ventures
Kleiner Perkins Caufield & Byers
Lux Capital
Foundation Capital
Quantum Strategic Partners Ltd

CONTACTS: *Note: Officers with more than one job title may be intentionally listed here more than once.*

Umesh Mishra, CEO/Co-Founder
Primit Parikh, Pres./Co-Founder
Carl Blake, VP-Mktg.
Yifeng Wu, VP-Prod. Dev.
Heber Clement, VP-Backend Mfg.
Jim Hartman, VP-Wafer Fab Mfg.
Dan Hauck, VP-Worldwide Sales

Phone: 805-456-1300	**Fax:**
Toll-Free:	
Address: 115 Castilian Dr., Goleta, CA 93117 US	

GROWTH PLANS/SPECIAL FEATURES:

Transphorm offers power conversion modules that operate through rapidly switching circuits. The firm's technology enables the transformation of electricity from one form to another. It utilizes a material called Gallium Nitride (GaN) that switches at significantly higher frequencies than traditional components. Transphorm's technology, for which the company owns 30 patents, is able to be embedded in virtually any electrical system. Its application-specific power modules represent one of the first-ever complete solutions for today's dramatically inefficient systems. The firm has received funding from several investors, including Google Ventures, Kleiner Perkins Caufield & Byers, Lux Capital, Foundation Capital and Quantum Strategic Partners Ltd. In March 2011, Transphorm released its first product, the EZ GaN power diode.

Transphorm offers its employees several benefits, including comprehensive healthplans and stock options.

FINANCIALS: Sales and profits are in thousands of dollars—add 000 to get the full amount. 2011 Note: Financial information for 2011 was not available for all companies at press time.

2011 Sales: $	2011 Profits: $	**U.S. Stock Ticker: Private**
2010 Sales: $	2010 Profits: $	**Int'l Ticker:**
2009 Sales: $	2009 Profits: $	Int'l Exchange:
2008 Sales: $	2008 Profits: $	Employees: Fiscal Year Ends: 12/31
2007 Sales: $	2007 Profits: $	Parent Company:

SALARIES/BENEFITS:

Pension Plan:	ESOP Stock Plan:	Profit Sharing:	Top Exec. Salary: $	Bonus: $
Savings Plan:	Stock Purch. Plan:		Second Exec. Salary: $	Bonus: $

OTHER THOUGHTS:

Apparent Women Officers or Directors:
Hot Spot for Advancement for Women/Minorities:

LOCATIONS: ("Y" = Yes)

West:	Southwest:	Midwest:	Southeast:	Northeast:	International:
Y					

TRILLIANT

www.trilliantinc.com

Industry Group Code: 3345

Energy/Fuel:	Other Technologies:	Electrical Products:	Electronics:		Transportation:	Other:
Biofuels:	Irrigation:	Lighting/LEDs:	Computers:		Car Sharing:	Recycling:
Batteries/Storage:	Nanotech:	Waste Heat:	Sensors:	Y	Electric Vehicles:	Engineering:
Solar:	Biotech:	Smart Meters: Y	Software:	Y	Natural Gas Fuel:	Consulting:
Wind:	Water Tech./Treatment:	Machinery:				Investing:
Fuel Cells:	Ceramics:					Chemicals:

TYPES OF BUSINESS:

Smart Grid Meters

BRANDS/DIVISIONS/AFFILIATES:

SecureMesh WAN (The)
UnitySuite Network Management System
CellReader

CONTACTS: Note: Officers with more than one job title may be intentionally listed here more than once.

Andy White, CEO
Salim Khan, COO
Salim Khan, Pres.
Steve Geiser, CFO
Rob Conant, Chief Mktg. Officer
Tricie Damaso, Sr. VP-Human Resources
Tom Hines, CIO
Tim Miller, Sr. VP-Met.
Juan Otero, General Counsel/Corp. Sec.
Arnie Liepa, Sr. VP-Channel Bus.
Dave Kranzler, Sr. VP-Networks
Walter Lowes, Managing Dir.-The Americas
Jon Parr, Managing Dir.-EMEA & India
Andy White, Chmn.
Juergen Bender, Managing Dir.-Asia Pacific
Tim Miller, Sr. VP-Supply Chain

Phone: 650-204-5050	Fax: 650-508-8096
Toll-Free:	
Address: 1100 Island Dr., Redwood City, CA 94065 US	

GROWTH PLANS/SPECIAL FEATURES:

Trilliant is a smart grid communications firm that supplies utilities with wireless mesh equipment to allow two-way communication networks throughout the electric grid. The firm also provides electric utilities with end-to-end communications networks that span from the head-end operations center to all devices on the grid, including substations and grid devices such as capacitor banks and transformers. Trilliant's solutions help utilities to utilize renewable resources, improve energy efficiency and optimize their grid operations. The company has more than 200 utility clients who have deployed more than 1 million of the firm's smart meters across 350,000 square miles. The firm's products include The SecureMesh WAN, which provides a long-range, high-bandwidth, low-latency wireless mesh network that covers hundreds of square miles; the UnitySuite Network Management System, which offers a unified view of the complete network, troubleshooting options and more; and CellReader, a series of digital cellular products that offer two-way communication to commercial and industrial meters. Trilliant maintains partnerships with several firms, including meter manufacturers such as Landis+Gyr, GE, Itron and Elster; large systems integrators such as CapGemini, Accenture and IBM; an array of in-home device manufacturers; and distribution automation vendors such as ABB, Cooper, and Telvent. The firm has offices in the U.S., the U.K. and Canada.

FINANCIALS: Sales and profits are in thousands of dollars—add 000 to get the full amount. 2011 Note: Financial information for 2011 was not available for all companies at press time.

2011 Sales: $	2011 Profits: $	U.S. Stock Ticker: Private	
2010 Sales: $	2010 Profits: $	Int'l Ticker:	
2009 Sales: $	2009 Profits: $	Int'l Exchange:	
2008 Sales: $	2008 Profits: $	Employees:	Fiscal Year Ends:
2007 Sales: $	2007 Profits: $	Parent Company:	

SALARIES/BENEFITS:

Pension Plan:	ESOP Stock Plan:	Profit Sharing:	Top Exec. Salary: $	Bonus: $
Savings Plan:	Stock Purch. Plan:		Second Exec. Salary: $	Bonus: $

OTHER THOUGHTS:

Apparent Women Officers or Directors: 1
Hot Spot for Advancement for Women/Minorities:

LOCATIONS: ("Y" = Yes)

West:	Southwest:	Midwest:	Southeast:	Northeast:	International:
Y					Y

Sales, profits and employees may be estimates. Financial information, benefits and other data can change quickly and may vary from those stated here.

TRINA SOLAR LTD

www.trinasolar.com

Industry Group Code: 334413

Energy/Fuel:	Other Technologies:	Electrical Products:	Electronics:	Transportation:	Other:
Biofuels:	Irrigation:	Lighting/LEDs:	Computers:	Car Sharing:	Recycling:
Batteries/Storage:	Nanotech:	Waste Heat:	Sensors:	Electric Vehicles:	Engineering:
Solar: Y	Biotech:	Smart Meters:	Software:	Natural Gas Fuel:	Consulting:
Wind:	Water Tech./Treatment:	Machinery:			Investing:
Fuel Cells:	Ceramics:				Chemicals:

TYPES OF BUSINESS:

Solar Panel Manufacturing
Innovation & Technology
monccrystalline solar cells
multicrystalline solar cells

BRANDS/DIVISIONS/AFFILIATES:

MIT
SERIS
Australia National University
Trina Solar (Spain) S.L.U.
Gestamp Asetym Solar, S.L
Trina Solar Australia Pty. Ltd
Origin Energy Australia

CONTACTS: Note: Officers with more than one job title may be intentionally listed here more than once.

Jifan Gao, CEO
Terry Wang, CFO
Mark Kingsley, Chief Commercial Officer
Stephanie Yang Shao, Chief Human Resources Officer
Gary Yu, Sr. VP-Oper.
Jifan Gao, Chmn.

Phone: 86-519-8548-2008	Fax: 86-519-8517-6021
Toll-Free:	
Address: No. 2 Trina Rd., Industrial Park, Changzhou, Jiangsu, 213031 China	

GROWTH PLANS/SPECIAL FEATURES:

Trina Solar Ltd. is an integrated solar-power products manufacturer. The firm is engaged in the manufacturing of ingots, wafers and solar cells for use in its solar module production. The company's solar modules provide electric power for residential, commercial and industrial applications worldwide. Trina Solar produces standard monocrystalline solar modules ranging from 175-210 watts (W) in power output and multicrystalline solar modules ranging from 225-285 W in power output. Trina Solar markets its products to distributors, wholesalers and PV system integrators. By the end of 2010, the company reached a solar module capacity of 1.2 gigawatts (GW). The company's products have average conversion efficiencies of approximately 19.5% for its monocrystalline solar cells and 18% for its multicrystalline solar cells. The firm's manufacturing capabilities are concentrated in Changzhou, China, and it maintains regional headquarters in both San Jose, California and Zurich, Switzerland. The company has liaison programs with both MIT and SERIS (Singapore national institute for applied solar energy research) to further developments in both innovation and efficiency. In November 2011, the company established its Asia Pacific operating headquarters in Singapore.

FINANCIALS: Sales and profits are in thousands of dollars—add 000 to get the full amount. 2011 Note: Financial information for 2011 was not available for all companies at press time.

2011 Sales: $	2011 Profits: $	U.S. Stock Ticker: TSL
2010 Sales: $1,857,689	2010 Profits: $311,453	Int'l Ticker:
2009 Sales: $845,136	2009 Profits: $97,584	Int'l Exchange:
2008 Sales: $831,901	2008 Profits: $61,360	Employees: 12,863 Fiscal Year Ends: 12/31
2007 Sales: $301,819	2007 Profits: $35,730	Parent Company:

SALARIES/BENEFITS:

Pension Plan:	ESOP Stock Plan:	Profit Sharing:	Top Exec. Salary: $	Bonus: $
Savings Plan:	Stock Purch. Plan:		Second Exec. Salary: $	Bonus: $

OTHER THOUGHTS:

Apparent Women Officers or Directors: 1
Hot Spot for Advancement for Women/Minorities:

LOCATIONS: ("Y" = Yes)

West:	Southwest:	Midwest:	Southeast:	Northeast:	International:
Y					Y

UNITED ENVIROTECH LTD

www.unitedenvirotech.com

Industry Group Code: 562

Energy/Fuel:	Other Technologies:	Electrical Products:	Electronics:	Transportation:	Other:	
Biofuels:	Irrigation:	Lighting/LEDs:	Computers:	Car Sharing:	Recycling:	
Batteries/Storage:	Nanotech:	Waste Heat:	Sensors:	Electric Vehicles:	Engineering:	Y
Solar:	Biotech:	Smart Meters:	Software:	Natural Gas Fuel:	Consulting:	
Wind:	Water Tech./Treatment:	Machinery:			Investing:	
Fuel Cells:	Ceramics:				Chemicals:	

TYPES OF BUSINESS:

Engineering & Water Treatment Services

BRANDS/DIVISIONS/AFFILIATES:

NOVO Envirotech (Guangzhou) Co Ltd
NOVO Envirotech (Tianjin) Co Ltd
United Envirotech Water Treatment (Liaoyang) Co
United Envirotech Water Treatment (Xintai) Co Ltd
Guangzhou Lin Hai Envirotech Co Ltd
United Envirotech Water (Hegang) Co Ltd
United Envirotech (Dafeng) Co Ltd

CONTACTS: *Note: Officers with more than one job title may be intentionally listed here more than once.*

Lin YuCheng, CEO
Wang Ning, COO/Exec. Dir.
Lotus Isabella Lim Mei Hua, Co-Sec.
Lee Bee Fong, Co-Sec.
Lin YuCheng, Chmn.

Phone: 65-6774-7298	**Fax:** 65-6774-8920
Toll-Free:	
Address: 10 Science Pk. Rd., #01-01, Singapore, 117684 Singapore	

GROWTH PLANS/SPECIAL FEATURES:

United Envirotech, Ltd. is a provider of environmental solutions related to water and wastewater treatment. The firm utilizes its membrane bioreactor (MBR) and continuous membrane filtration (CMF) processes in microfiltration, ultrafiltration and reverse osmosis. These processes provide engineering services involving the design, fabrication, installation and commissioning of membrane-based water and wastewater treatment systems. The company, which operates in Singapore, Malaysia and China, also acts as an engineering, procurement and construction (EPC) contractor for major Asian petrochemical firms, such as China National Petroleum Corporation. It serves large industrial parks in China, including those in the developing Guangzhou Nansha, Daya Bay Hui Zhou and Tianjin Economic Development Zones. United Envirotech invests in wastewater treatment plants through transfer-operate-transfer and build-operate-transfer agreements. These projects are usually municipal plants backed by the government of China. United Envirotech has recently begun investing in hazardous waste treatment facilities that treat solid and liquid hazardous wastes generated in the industrial parks. The firm operates through several subsidiaries. NOVO Envirotech (Guangzhou) Co., Ltd. and NOVO Envirotech (Tianjin) Co., Ltd. handle the company's engineering operations; United Envirotech Water Treatment (Liaoyang) Co., Ltd. operates the firm's 7.063 million cubic feet per day municipal water treatment plant in Liaoyang, China; United Envirotech Water (Hegang) Co. Ltd. operates a 5.65 million cubic feet per day plant in Northern China; and United Envirotech Water Treatment (Xintai) Co., Ltd. operates the company's 2.825 million cubic feet per day municipal water treatment plant in Xintai, China. United Envirotech Water Treatment (Guangzhou Nansha), a joint venture between United Envirotech and Guangzhou Nansha Assets Operation Co. Ltd., owns and operates an industrial wastewater treatment plant in the Guangzhou Nansha Chemical Industrial Park, which treats 353,147 cubic feet per day. In September 2011, United Envirotech established new subsidiary United Envirotech (Dafeng) Co. Ltd.

FINANCIALS: Sales and profits are in thousands of dollars—add 000 to get the full amount. 2011 Note: Financial information for 2011 was not available for all companies at press time.

2011 Sales: $61,800	2011 Profits: $12,700	**U.S. Stock Ticker:** UEDVF.PK
2010 Sales: $69,000	2010 Profits: $15,000	**Int'l Ticker:** U19
2009 Sales: $43,000	2009 Profits: $4,000	Int'l Exchange: Singapore-SIN
2008 Sales: $51,000	2008 Profits: $	Employees: 80 Fiscal Year Ends: 3/31
2007 Sales: $	2007 Profits: $	Parent Company:

SALARIES/BENEFITS:

Pension Plan:	ESOP Stock Plan:	Profit Sharing:	Top Exec. Salary: $	Bonus: $
Savings Plan:	Stock Purch. Plan:		Second Exec. Salary: $	Bonus: $

OTHER THOUGHTS:

Apparent Women Officers or Directors: 1
Hot Spot for Advancement for Women/Minorities:

LOCATIONS: ("Y" = Yes)

West:	Southwest:	Midwest:	Southeast:	Northeast:	International: Y

Sales, profits and employees may be estimates. Financial information, benefits and other data can change quickly and may vary from those stated here.

UNITED SOLAR OVONIC

www.uni-solar.com

Industry Group Code: 334413

Energy/Fuel:	Other Technologies:	Electrical Products:	Electronics:	Transportation:	Other:
Biofuels:	Irrigation:	Lighting/LEDs:	Computers:	Car Sharing:	Recycling:
Batteries/Storage:	Nanotech:	Waste Heat:	Sensors:	Electric Vehicles:	Engineering:
Solar: Y	Biotech:	Smart Meters:	Software:	Natural Gas Fuel:	Consulting:
Wind:	Water Tech./Treatment:	Machinery:			Investing:
Fuel Cells:	Ceramics:				Chemicals:

TYPES OF BUSINESS:

Photovoltaic Cells
Photovoltaic Shingles
Roofing Products

BRANDS/DIVISIONS/AFFILIATES:

Energy Conversion Devices Inc
UNI-SOLAR
PowerShingle

CONTACTS: Note: Officers with more than one job title may be intentionally listed here more than once.

Jeffrey Yang, Sr. VP-Tech.

Phone: 248-293-0440	**Fax:** 248-364-5678
Toll-Free: 800-528-0617	
Address: 3800 Lapeer Rd., Auburn Hills, MI 48326 US	

GROWTH PLANS/SPECIAL FEATURES:

United Solar Ovonic (UniSolar), a subsidiary of Energy Conversion Devices, Inc., designs, develops and manufactures a variety of thin-film amorphous photovoltaic (PV) cells including continuous web, thin-film and multilayer systems. UniSolar's products are used to create power panels and a line of roofing products, including photovoltaic laminate products, photovoltaic shingles and metal roofing products. The company specializes in building-integrated photovoltaic systems; ground-mounted power systems; remote power applications; and lighting systems for residential and commercial use. PV modules are sold principally for commercial and industrial roofing applications. The majority of the modules are sold directly to commercial roofing materials manufacturers; builders and building contractors; and solar power installers/integrators that integrate the products into their own sales and services and take on all aspects of marketing, sales and service. Additionally, the company markets to the residential consumer with the new product PowerShingle, which is roughly the same size as a normal roof shingle and resistant to major impacts and hurricane-force winds. UniSolar uses a proprietary continuous roll-to-roll process to manufacture the photovoltaic cells, and the firm believes that it has an advantage over similar products because its PV cells are a frameless laminate that is adaptable for seamless integration into various roofing materials. As of 2010, the company had over 400 megawatts (MW) of PV installations in operation. In May 2011, UniSolar opened a new manufacturing facility in Ontario, Canada, with an initial annualized capacity of 15 MW and expected first year project capital of $4 million. In October 2011, UniSolar's partner Marcegaglia opened a new PV manufacturing plant in Taranto, Italy, producing PV laminates from UNI-SOLAR brand cells.

FINANCIALS: Sales and profits are in thousands of dollars—add 000 to get the full amount. 2011 Note: Financial information for 2011 was not available for all companies at press time.

2011 Sales: $	2011 Profits: $	**U.S. Stock Ticker:** Subsidiary
2010 Sales: $	2010 Profits: $	**Int'l Ticker:**
2009 Sales: $	2009 Profits: $	Int'l Exchange:
2008 Sales: $	2008 Profits: $	Employees: Fiscal Year Ends: 6/30
2007 Sales: $	2007 Profits: $	Parent Company: ENERGY CONVERSION DEVICES INC

SALARIES/BENEFITS:

Pension Plan:	ESOP Stock Plan:	Profit Sharing:	Top Exec. Salary: $	Bonus: $
Savings Plan: Y	Stock Purch. Plan:		Second Exec. Salary: $	Bonus: $

OTHER THOUGHTS:

Apparent Women Officers or Directors:
Hot Spot for Advancement for Women/Minorities:

LOCATIONS: ("Y" = Yes)

West:	Southwest:	Midwest: Y	Southeast:	Northeast:	International: Y

UNITED TECHNOLOGIES CORPORATION

www.utc.com

Industry Group Code: 33641

Energy/Fuel:	Other Technologies:	Electrical Products:	Electronics:	Transportation:	Other:
Biofuels:	Irrigation:	Lighting/LEDs:	Computers:	Car Sharing:	Recycling:
Batteries/Storage:	Nanotech:	Waste Heat:	Sensors:	Electric Vehicles:	Engineering:
Solar:	Biotech:	Smart Meters:	Software: Y	Natural Gas Fuel:	Consulting:
Wind:	Water Tech./Treatment:	Machinery: Y			Investing:
Fuel Cells:	Ceramics:				Chemicals:

TYPES OF BUSINESS:

Aerospace Technology
Elevator & Escalator Systems
HVAC Systems
Fuel Cells & Power Generation
Industrial Systems
Aircraft Parts & Maintenance
Flight Systems
Security Products & Services

BRANDS/DIVISIONS/AFFILIATES:

Otis Elevator Company
Carrier Corp
Sikorsky
Pratt & Whitney
Hamilton Sundstrand
UTC Fire & Security
Goodrich Corp

CONTACTS: Note: Officers with more than one job title may be intentionally listed here more than once.

Louis R. Chenevert, CEO
Gregory J. Hayes, CFO/Sr. VP
J. Thomas Bowler, Jr., Sr. VP-Human Resources & Organization
J. Michael McQuade, Sr. VP-Science
Nancy Davis, CIO/VP
J. Michael McQuade, Sr. VP-Tech.
Charles D. Gill, General Counsel/Sr. VP
Eileen Drake, VP-Oper.
Geraud Darnis, CEO/Pres., Climate, Controls & Security Systems
Michael Dumais, Pres., Hamilton Sundstrand
David P. Hess, Pres., Pratt & Whitley
Didier Michaud-Daniel, Pres., Otis Elevator Company
Louis R. Chenevert, Chmn.
Gregg Ward, Sr. VP-Global Gov't Rel.

Phone: 860-728-7000	Fax:
Toll-Free:	
Address: 1 Financial Plz., Hartford, CT 06103 US	

GROWTH PLANS/SPECIAL FEATURES:

United Technologies Corporation (UTC) provides high-technology products and services to the building systems and aerospace industries worldwide. The company operates through six principle segments: Carrier Corp.; Hamilton Sundstrand; Otis Elevator Company; Pratt & Whitney; Sikorsky; and UTC Fire & Security. Carrier manufactures commercial and residential heating, ventilation and air conditioning (HVAC) as well as refrigeration systems. Hamilton Sundstrand serves commercial, military, regional and corporate aviation as well as space and undersea applications. Its products include flight, engine control, environmental control and propeller systems. Otis manufactures, installs and maintains both elevators and escalators. The segment installs both passenger and freight elevators for low, medium and high speed applications. Pratt & Whitney produces and services commercial, general aviation and military aircraft engines. It also handles rocket engine production for commercial and government space applications. Sikorsky is a world leader in helicopter manufacture and design. UTC Fire & Security offers fire and special hazard detection and suppression systems; fire fighting equipment; electronic security; monitoring and rapid response systems; and service and security personnel services. In September 2011, Otis opened a new manufacturing center in Florence, South Carolina. UTC purchased Goodrich Corp. for $18.4 billion.

Employee benefits include health and life insurance plans; education funding; and savings plans.

FINANCIALS: Sales and profits are in thousands of dollars—add 000 to get the full amount. 2011 Note: Financial information for 2011 was not available for all companies at press time.

2011 Sales: $	2011 Profits: $	**U.S. Stock Ticker:** UTX
2010 Sales: $54,326,000	2010 Profits: $4,711,000	**Int'l Ticker:**
2009 Sales: $52,425,000	2009 Profits: $4,179,000	Int'l Exchange:
2008 Sales: $59,757,000	2008 Profits: $5,053,000	Employees: 208,200 Fiscal Year Ends: 12/31
2007 Sales: $55,716,000	2007 Profits: $4,548,000	Parent Company:

SALARIES/BENEFITS:

Pension Plan:	ESOP Stock Plan:	Profit Sharing:	Top Exec. Salary: $1,589,583	Bonus: $4,407,976
Savings Plan: Y	Stock Purch. Plan:		Second Exec. Salary: $840,000	Bonus: $1,295,570

OTHER THOUGHTS:

Apparent Women Officers or Directors: 5
Hot Spot for Advancement for Women/Minorities: Y

LOCATIONS: ("Y" = Yes)

West:	Southwest:	Midwest:	Southeast:	Northeast:	International:
Y	Y	Y	Y	Y	Y

Sales, profits and employees may be estimates. Financial information, benefits and other data can change quickly and may vary from those stated here.

UQM TECHNOLOGIES INC

www.uqm.com

Industry Group Code: 335

Energy/Fuel:	Other Technologies:	Electrical Products:	Electronics:	Transportation:	Other:
Biofuels:	Irrigation:	Lighting/LEDs:	Computers:	Car Sharing:	Recycling:
Batteries/Storage:	Nanotech:	Waste Heat:	Sensors:	Electric Vehicles:	Engineering:
Solar:	Biotech:	Smart Meters:	Software:	Natural Gas Fuel:	Consulting:
Wind:	Water Tech./Treatment:	Machinery: Y			Investing:
Fuel Cells:	Ceramics:				Chemicals:

TYPES OF BUSINESS:

Electric Motors
Research & Development
Electronic Propulsion Systems
Hybrid Engine Technology
Power Generator Control Systems
Software

BRANDS/DIVISIONS/AFFILIATES:

UQM Power Products Inc

CONTACTS: *Note: Officers with more than one job title may be intentionally listed here more than once.*

Eric R. Ridenour, CEO
Eric R. Ridenour, Pres.
Donald A. French, CFO
Adrian Schaffer, VP-Sales
Jon F. Lutz, VP-Eng.
Donald A. French, Sec.
Ronald M. Burton, Exec. VP-Oper.
Adrian Schaffer, VP-Bus. Dev.
Donald A. French, Treas.
William G. Rankin, Chmn.

Phone: 303-682-4900	Fax: 303-682-4901
Toll-Free:	
Address: 4120 Specialty Pl., Longmont, CO 80504 US	

GROWTH PLANS/SPECIAL FEATURES:

UQM Technologies, Inc. (UQM) is a developer and manufacturer of power dense, high efficiency electric motors, generators and power electronic controllers for the automotive, aerospace, military and industrial markets. The company's emphasis is on developing alternative energy technologies including propulsion systems for electric, hybrid electric and fuel cell electric vehicles. The firm operates out of a 129,304-square-foot manufacturing facility in Longmont, Colorado and a 28,000-square-foot manufacturing plant in Frederick, Colorado. The company's revenue is derived from two primary sources: funded contract research and development services performed for strategic partners, customers and the U.S. government; and the manufacture and sale of the products it designs. UQM's technology base includes a number of proprietary technologies and patents relating to brushless permanent magnet motors, generators and power electronic controllers, together with software code to intelligently manage the operation of its systems. The firm also manufactures motors and electronic products. In April 2011, UQM Technologies merged subsidiary UQM Power Products, Inc. into its existing operations.

UQM offers its employees a 401(k) plan and an employee stock purchase plan.

FINANCIALS: Sales and profits are in thousands of dollars—add 000 to get the full amount. 2011 Note: Financial information for 2011 was not available for all companies at press time.

2011 Sales: $9,021	2011 Profits: $-1,992	**U.S. Stock Ticker: UQM**
2010 Sales: $8,692	2010 Profits: $-4,141	**Int'l Ticker:**
2009 Sales: $8,728	2009 Profits: $-4,402	Int'l Exchange:
2008 Sales: $7,508	2008 Profits: $-4,586	Employees: 79 Fiscal Year Ends: 3/31
2007 Sales: $6,653	2007 Profits: $-3,431	Parent Company:

SALARIES/BENEFITS:

Pension Plan:	ESOP Stock Plan:	Profit Sharing:	Top Exec. Salary: $238,765	Bonus: $100,000
Savings Plan: Y	Stock Purch. Plan: Y		Second Exec. Salary: $236,568	Bonus: $270,000

OTHER THOUGHTS:

Apparent Women Officers or Directors:
Hot Spot for Advancement for Women/Minorities:

LOCATIONS: ("Y" = Yes)

West:	Southwest:	Midwest:	Southeast:	Northeast:	International:
Y					

UTC POWER

www.utcpower.com

Industry Group Code: 335999

Energy/Fuel:	Other Technologies:	Electrical Products:	Electronics:	Transportation:	Other:
Biofuels:	Irrigation:	Lighting/LEDs:	Computers:	Car Sharing:	Recycling:
Batteries/Storage:	Nanotech:	Waste Heat:	Sensors:	Electric Vehicles:	Engineering:
Solar:	Biotech:	Smart Meters:	Software:	Natural Gas Fuel:	Consulting:
Wind:	Water Tech./Treatment:	Machinery:			Investing:
Fuel Cells: Y	Ceramics:				Chemicals:

TYPES OF BUSINESS:

Fuel Cell Manufacturing
Fuel Cell Installations
Microturbine Power Plants
Geothermal Power Plants

BRANDS/DIVISIONS/AFFILIATES:

United Technologies Corporation
PureCell
UTC Fuel Cells
PureComfort
PureCycle

CONTACTS: *Note: Officers with more than one job title may be intentionally listed here more than once.*

Joe Triompo, VP/Gen. Mgr
Mari Simmons-Sifo, Mgr.-Human Resources
J. Michael McQuade, Sr. VP-Science
J. Michael McQuade, Sr. VP-Tech.
Ariana Kalian, VP-Eng.
Ariana Kalian, VP-Mfg.
Michael Brown, General Counsel
Rick Milbourn, Dir.-Finance
Dennis Tonioni, Mgr.-Quality
Dana Kaplinski, Mgr.-Transportation Fuel Cell Bus.
Neal Montany, Dir.-Stationary Bus.

Phone: 860-727-2200	**Fax:** 860-727-2319
Toll-Free:	
Address: 195 Governor's Hwy., South Windsor, CT 06074 US	

GROWTH PLANS/SPECIAL FEATURES:

UTC Power (UTCP), a subsidiary of technology research, development and production company United Technologies Corporation, develops fuel cells and other energy solutions. The company develops and produces fuel cells for on-site power, transportation, space and defense applications, and is also a leader in renewable energy solutions and combined cooling, heating and power solutions for the distributed energy market. It has more than 40 years of experience with fuel cell technology. In the late 1960s, former UTC Power division, UTC Fuel Cells, developed an alkaline fuel cell for use in the U.S. space program and an updated version of the product is still used today. UTCP's main product is the PureCell brand of fuel cell generators. PureCell utilizes phosphoric acid as its electrolyte, making it large and heavy and requiring a long warm up time. Thus, it is used mainly in stationary applications. PureCell provides zero-emission electrical power, heat that can also be converted into energy and drinkable water that can be used as a coolant. The various models of PureCell produce up to 400 kilowatts (kW) of electricity and 1,700,000 BTUs of usable heat per hour. The PureComfort energy product, powered by natural gas, runs three, four, five or six 60 kW microturbines to supply combined cooling, heat and power solutions. The PureCycle geothermal power plant can generate up to 280 kW of electricity and operates at temperatures as low as 195 degrees F, well below the 300 degree F mark under which other geothermal operations fail.

UTC Power offers its employees medical, dental and life insurance; retirement and savings plans; and tuition reimbursement.

FINANCIALS: Sales and profits are in thousands of dollars—add 000 to get the full amount. 2011 Note: Financial information for 2011 was not available for all companies at press time.

2011 Sales: $	2011 Profits: $	**U.S. Stock Ticker:** Subsidiary
2010 Sales: $	2010 Profits: $	**Int'l Ticker:**
2009 Sales: $	2009 Profits: $	Int'l Exchange:
2008 Sales: $	2008 Profits: $	Employees: Fiscal Year Ends: 12/31
2007 Sales: $	2007 Profits: $	Parent Company: UNITED TECHNOLOGIES CORPORATION

SALARIES/BENEFITS:

Pension Plan: Y	ESOP Stock Plan: Y	Profit Sharing:	Top Exec. Salary: $	Bonus: $
Savings Plan: Y	Stock Purch. Plan:		Second Exec. Salary: $	Bonus: $

OTHER THOUGHTS:

Apparent Women Officers or Directors: 3
Hot Spot for Advancement for Women/Minorities: Y

LOCATIONS: ("Y" = Yes)

West:	Southwest:	Midwest:	Southeast:	Northeast: Y	International:

VEOLIA ENVIRONNEMENT
www.veolia.com

Industry Group Code: 562

Energy/Fuel:	Other Technologies:	Electrical Products:	Electronics:	Transportation:	Other:
Biofuels:	Irrigation:	Lighting/LEDs:	Computers:	Car Sharing:	Recycling:
Batteries/Storage:	Nanotech:	Waste Heat:	Sensors:	Electric Vehicles:	Engineering:
Solar:	Biotech:	Smart Meters:	Software:	Natural Gas Fuel:	Consulting:
Wind:	Water Tech./Treatment: Y	Machinery:			Investing:
Fuel Cells:	Ceramics:				Chemicals:

TYPES OF BUSINESS:
Water & Sewage Treatment
Water Treatment Plant Engineering & Construction
HVAC Installations Management
Energy Services
Public Transportation Services
Waste Management & Recycling

BRANDS/DIVISIONS/AFFILIATES:
Veolia Eau-Compagnie Generale des Eaux
Veolia Proprete
Dalkia
Veolia Transdev
m2o city

CONTACTS: Note: Officers with more than one job title may be intentionally listed here more than once.
Antoine Frerot, CEO
Denis Gasquet, COO/Sr. Exec. VP
Pierre-Francois Riolacci, CFO/Exec. VP
Jean-Marie Lambert, Sr. VP-Human Resources
Olivier Orsini, Sec./Exec. VP
Nathalie Pinon, Sr. VP-Investor Rel. & Financial Comm.
Jean-Pierre Fremont, Exec. VP-Public Entities & European Affairs
Jerome Gallot, CEO-Veolia Transdev
Jerome Le Conte, Exec. VP-Waste Mgmt. Div.
Jean-Michel Herrewyn, CEO-Veolia Water
Antoine Frerot, Chmn.

Phone: 01133-17175-0126	Fax:
Toll-Free:	
Address: 36/38, Ave. Kleber, Paris, 75116 France	

GROWTH PLANS/SPECIAL FEATURES:
Veolia Environnement is a leading international environmental services company. It provides water, waste management, energy and passenger transportation services to businesses, municipalities and end-users in over 60 countries. Approximately 34.9% of the firm's revenue is derived from water; 26.8% from environmental services; 21.8% from energy; and 16.6% from transportation. Veolia's water division, operating as Veolia Eau-Compagnie Generale des Eaux, offers water and wastewater services to municipal and industrial clients. Its services include drinking water management, water treatment solutions and water and wastewater plant operation. The firm provides drinking water services to 100 million people and treats 257.8 billion cubic feet of wastewater annually. The company's environmental services division, Veolia Proprete, provides waste management and logistical services, including waste collection; waste processing; office and factory cleaning; production equipment maintenance; polluted soil treatment; and industrial waste discharge management. Over 69.6 million tons of waste is treated per year in 31 countries. Veolia's energy management segment, Dalkia, works with its industrial and municipal clients in 42 countries to optimize energy efficiency. Its services relate to heating and cooling networks, decentralized energy production, production equipment installation and maintenance, integrated facilities management and electrical services on public streets. Veolia Transdev, a 50/50 joint venture with Caisse des Depots et Consignations is a leading private European passenger transport operator, serving 2.54 billion travelers per year. The firm specializes in delegated public utility operation in cooperation with over 4,400 local authorities across the globe. Transport's services include managing rail networks and the associated logistics systems. In March 2011, Veolia Eau-Compagnie Generale des Eaux and Orange established new joint venture m2o city, a company formed to remotely gather water meter information and data from environmental sensors.

FINANCIALS: Sales and profits are in thousands of dollars—add 000 to get the full amount. 2011 Note: Financial information for 2011 was not available for all companies at press time.

2011 Sales: $	2011 Profits: $	U.S. Stock Ticker: VE
2010 Sales: $48,681,000	2010 Profits: $812,750	Int'l Ticker: VIE
2009 Sales: $47,012,100	2009 Profits: $793,500	Int'l Exchange: Paris-Euronext
2008 Sales: $53,901,000	2008 Profits: $593,000	Employees: 287,043 Fiscal Year Ends: 12/31
2007 Sales: $37,760,000	2007 Profits: $1,000,000	Parent Company:

SALARIES/BENEFITS:
Pension Plan:	ESOP Stock Plan:	Profit Sharing:	Top Exec. Salary: $	Bonus: $
Savings Plan:	Stock Purch. Plan:		Second Exec. Salary: $	Bonus: $

OTHER THOUGHTS:
Apparent Women Officers or Directors: 1
Hot Spot for Advancement for Women/Minorities:

LOCATIONS: ("Y" = Yes)
West:	Southwest:	Midwest:	Southeast:	Northeast:	International:
Y	Y	Y		Y	Y

Sales, profits and employees may be estimates. Financial information, benefits and other data can change quickly and may vary from those stated here.

VESTAS WIND SYSTEMS A/S

www.vestas.com

Industry Group Code: 33361

Energy/Fuel:	Other Technologies:	Electrical Products:	Electronics:	Transportation:	Other:
Biofuels:	Irrigation:	Lighting/LEDs:	Computers:	Car Sharing:	Recycling:
Batteries/Storage:	Nanotech:	Waste Heat:	Sensors:	Electric Vehicles:	Engineering:
Solar:	Biotech:	Smart Meters:	Software:	Natural Gas Fuel:	Consulting:
Wind: Y	Water Tech./Treatment:	Machinery:			Investing:
Fuel Cells:	Ceramics:				Chemicals:

TYPES OF BUSINESS:

Wind Turbine Manufacturing
Turbine Installation, Repair & Maintenance Services
Online Turbine Operating Systems

BRANDS/DIVISIONS/AFFILIATES:

Vestas Blades
Vestas Control Systems
Vestas Nacelles
Vestas Towers
VestasOnline
Vestas Americas

CONTACTS: *Note: Officers with more than one job title may be intentionally listed here more than once.*

Ditlev Engel, CEO
Ditlev Engel, Pres.
Henrik Norremark, CFO/Exec. VP

Phone: 45-97-30-00-00	**Fax:** 45-97-30-00-01
Toll-Free:	
Address: Alsvej 21, Randers, 8940 Denmark	

GROWTH PLANS/SPECIAL FEATURES:

Vestas Wind Systems A/S is a leading international manufacturer of wind turbines, having installed over 44,000 turbines in 66 countries worldwide, which generate more than 60 million megawatt (MW)-hours of electricity annually. The firm offers site and project studies and develops, manufactures, sells and markets wind turbines, ranging from the V52-850 kilowatt turbine to the V112-3 MW turbine. Vestas offers land and offshore models, as well as installation, repair and maintenance services. The firm's Supervisory Control and Data Acquisition System (SCADA), called VestasOnline, offers a range of monitoring and control functions, which allow plants to be operated in a manner similar to conventional power plants. It allows customers to view performance data, monitor and control turbines remotely and receive alarm messages via e-mail through its SCADA web server. The company has a number of business units, including Vestas Blades, with facilities in Denmark, Germany, Italy, Spain, China and the U.S.; Vestas Control Systems, located in China, Spain and Denmark; Vestas Nacelles, in China, India, Spain, Germany, Denmark, Norway and Sweden; and Vestas Towers, in Denmark and the U.S. The company currently has plans to invest approximately $1 billion to build six new wind turbine factories in Colorado and a research facility in Houston, Texas as part of its goal to increase its presence in the growing North American marketplace. In June 2011, the firm opened a new office in Singapore.

Vestas offers its employees a range of benefits that vary by location. U.S. benefits include medical, dental and vision coverage; a 401(k) plan; and tuition assistance.

FINANCIALS: Sales and profits are in thousands of dollars—add 000 to get the full amount. 2011 Note: Financial information for 2011 was not available for all companies at press time.

		U.S. Stock Ticker:
2011 Sales: $	2011 Profits: $	**Int'l Ticker: VWS**
2010 Sales: $9,981,480	2010 Profits: $225,010	Int'l Exchange: Copenhagen-CSE
2009 Sales: $9,015,940	2009 Profits: $786,650	Employees: 23,252 Fiscal Year Ends: 12/31
2008 Sales: $8,135,660	2008 Profits: $688,870	Parent Company:
2007 Sales: $7,090,000	2007 Profits: $420,000	

SALARIES/BENEFITS:

Pension Plan:	ESOP Stock Plan:	Profit Sharing:	Top Exec. Salary: $	Bonus: $
Savings Plan: Y	Stock Purch. Plan:		Second Exec. Salary: $	Bonus: $

OTHER THOUGHTS:

Apparent Women Officers or Directors:
Hot Spot for Advancement for Women/Minorities: Y

LOCATIONS: ("Y" = Yes)

West:	Southwest:	Midwest:	Southeast:	Northeast:	International:
Y	Y			Y	Y

VHF TECHNOLOGIES SA

www.flexcell.com

Industry Group Code: 334413

Energy/Fuel:	Other Technologies:	Electrical Products:	Electronics:	Transportation:	Other:
Biofuels:	Irrigation:	Lighting/LEDs:	Computers:	Car Sharing:	Recycling:
Batteries/Storage:	Nanotech:	Waste Heat:	Sensors:	Electric Vehicles:	Engineering:
Solar: Y	Biotech:	Smart Meters:	Software:	Natural Gas Fuel:	Consulting:
Wind:	Water Tech./Treatment:	Machinery:			Investing:
Fuel Cells:	Ceramics:				Chemicals:

TYPES OF BUSINESS:

Flexible Solar Cells
Solar Chargers

BRANDS/DIVISIONS/AFFILIATES:

Flexcell
flexcellgaia
flexcellfama
flexcellhelios
Very-High-Frequency
Sunpack
Sunslick
Sunboard

CONTACTS: *Note: Officers with more than one job title may be intentionally listed here more than once.*

Sebastien Dubail, CEO
Frederic Ryser, CFO
Sebastien Dubail, Head-Sales & Mktg.
Diego Fischer, Head-R&D
Diego Fischer, CTO
Frederic Ryser, Head-Legal Affairs
Sebastien Dubail, Head-Bus. Dev. & Strategy
Frederic Ryser, Head-Investor Rel.
Frederic Ryser, Head-Financial Mgmt.

Phone: 41-24-423-08-90	**Fax:** 41-24-423-08-97
Toll-Free:	
Address: Rue Edouard-Verdan 2, Yverdon-les-Bains, CH-1400 Switzerland	

GROWTH PLANS/SPECIAL FEATURES:

VHF Technologies SA produces flexible custom-designed solar cells and modules under the brand name Flexcell, using its proprietary Very-High-Frequency plasma technology to deposit thin, nano-scale layers of amorphous silicon onto flexible plastic substrates. Since its solar cells are constructed from flexible polymers instead of traditional glass substrates, the resulting product is tougher and more durable than conventional PV cells. Another advantage of the Flexcell technology is that it is not dependent upon the supply of mono- or polycrystalline silicon. The firm's consumer products include outdoor and camping equipment, via the Sunpack, a small, rollable, lightweight solar cell that may be attached to a backpack, tent or other piece of camping equipment, and used to power satellite or cell phones as well as digital cameras, PDAs, MP3 players or GPS systems, and features a universal cigarette lighter adapter for easy plug and play access. The Sunpack comes in 7 or 14 watt configurations. VHF produces the Sunslick brand of 7, 14 or 27 watt, waterproof PV cells for marine and yachting applications. The Sunslick mainly functions as a battery charger and may be mounted on a curved surface, such as a hatch cover, boat deck or vehicle roof; or tied to a dinghy, sail cover or canvas awning. Another commercial product is the Sunboard, a semi-ridged battery charger, also available in 7, 14 or 27 watt configurations; and is designed to mount on a greenhouse, trailer roof or other small building. Flexcell is also customizable to fit a variety of OEM applications, such as navigational aids and road signs; wireless electronics; emergency systems; telecommunications; and stand-alone systems. Some of VHF innovations involve integrating its PV cells into building components and fabric, such as awning covers.

FINANCIALS: Sales and profits are in thousands of dollars—add 000 to get the full amount. 2011 Note: Financial information for 2011 was not available for all companies at press time.

2011 Sales: $	2011 Profits: $	**U.S. Stock Ticker:** Private
2010 Sales: $	2010 Profits: $	**Int'l Ticker:**
2009 Sales: $	2009 Profits: $	Int'l Exchange:
2008 Sales: $	2008 Profits: $	Employees: Fiscal Year Ends: 12/31
2007 Sales: $	2007 Profits: $	Parent Company:

SALARIES/BENEFITS:

Pension Plan:	ESOP Stock Plan:	Profit Sharing:	Top Exec. Salary: $	Bonus: $
Savings Plan:	Stock Purch. Plan:		Second Exec. Salary: $	Bonus: $

OTHER THOUGHTS:

Apparent Women Officers or Directors:
Hot Spot for Advancement for Women/Minorities:

LOCATIONS: ("Y" = Yes)

West:	Southwest:	Midwest:	Southeast:	Northeast:	International: Y

VOLTEA

www.voltea.com

Industry Group Code: 924110

Energy/Fuel:	Other Technologies:		Electrical Products:	Electronics:	Transportation:	Other:
Biofuels:	Irrigation:		Lighting/LEDs:	Computers:	Car Sharing:	Recycling:
Batteries/Storage:	Nanotech:		Waste Heat:	Sensors:	Electric Vehicles:	Engineering:
Solar:	Biotech:		Smart Meters:	Software:	Natural Gas Fuel:	Consulting:
Wind:	Water Tech./Treatment:	Y	Machinery:			Investing:
Fuel Cells:	Ceramics:					Chemicals:

TYPES OF BUSINESS:

Water Purification

BRANDS/DIVISIONS/AFFILIATES:

Capacitive Deionization (CapDI) system
CrossCharge

CONTACTS: *Note: Officers with more than one job title may be intentionally listed here more than once.*

Michiel Lensink, CEO
Jonathan Hodes, CFO
Maarten van Raemdonck, Dir.-Sales
Bert van del Wal, Dir.-R&D
Hank Reinhoudt, Dir.-Prod. Dev. & Applications
Sheila Metherell, Dir.-Oper.
Dean Spatz, Chmn.

Phone: 32-252-200-100	Fax:
Toll-Free:	
Address: Wasbeekerlaan 24, Sassenheim, 2171 AE The Netherlands	

GROWTH PLANS/SPECIAL FEATURES:

Voltea, through its proprietary Capacitive Deionization (CapDI) system, provides a low cost and less environmentally taxing method of producing desalinated brackish water. The firm aims to provide people and businesses with access to both clean and drinkable water without producing any additional negative environmental impact. The CapDI system is based on a single technology platform that involves a three step process of purification, regeneration and flushing. The system is scalable and can be implemented in applications varying in size from small scale applications such as residential water softening to large scale applications such as industrial water re-use. CapDI can handle water volumes ranging from several milliliters per minute to thousands of cubic meters per hour. The system recovers nearly 80-90% of the water it treats; is highly energy efficient due to its reuse of the energy stored in the electrodes during the desalination process; and does not use any additional chemicals such as anti-scalants or biocides during the treatment. The firm maintains a joint venture with Pentair, Inc. in the production of CrossCharge technology, which employs the use of capacitive electrodes with no addition of salt in the removal of hardness and in the purification of water. In 2011, the firm began development of a CapDI system specifically targeted for agricultural use.

FINANCIALS: Sales and profits are in thousands of dollars—add 000 to get the full amount. 2011 Note: Financial information for 2011 was not available for all companies at press time.

2011 Sales: $	2011 Profits: $	**U.S. Stock Ticker: Private**	
2010 Sales: $	2010 Profits: $	**Int'l Ticker:**	
2009 Sales: $	2009 Profits: $	Int'l Exchange:	
2008 Sales: $	2008 Profits: $	Employees:	Fiscal Year Ends:
2007 Sales: $	2007 Profits: $	Parent Company:	

SALARIES/BENEFITS:

Pension Plan:	ESOP Stock Plan:	Profit Sharing:	Top Exec. Salary: $	Bonus: $
Savings Plan:	Stock Purch. Plan:		Second Exec. Salary: $	Bonus: $

OTHER THOUGHTS:

Apparent Women Officers or Directors: 2
Hot Spot for Advancement for Women/Minorities:

LOCATIONS: ("Y" = Yes)

West:	Southwest:	Midwest:	Southeast:	Northeast:	International: Y

WASTE MANAGEMENT INC

Industry Group Code: 562

Energy/Fuel:	Other Technologies:	Electrical Products:		Electronics:	Transportation:	Other:	
Biofuels:	Irrigation:	Lighting/LEDs:		Computers:	Car Sharing:	Recycling:	Y
Batteries/Storage:	Nanotech:	Waste Heat:	Y	Sensors:	Electric Vehicles:	Engineering:	
Solar:	Biotech:	Smart Meters:		Software:	Natural Gas Fuel:	Consulting:	
Wind:	Water Tech./Treatment:	Machinery:				Investing:	
Fuel Cells:	Ceramics:					Chemicals:	

TYPES OF BUSINESS:

Waste Disposal
Recycling Services
Landfill Operation
Hazardous Waste Management
Transfer Stations
Recycled Commodity Trading
Waste Methane Generation

BRANDS/DIVISIONS/AFFILIATES:

Think Green
Agnion Energy, Inc.
Peninsula Compost Company, LLC
Wheelbrator Technologies, Inc.
Recycle America Alliance
TOSS
Bio-In-A-Box
BioSite

CONTACTS: Note: Officers with more than one job title may be intentionally listed here more than once.

David P. Steiner, CEO
David P. Steiner, Pres.
Robert G. Simpson, CFO/Sr. VP
David A. Aardsma, Sr. VP-Mktg. & Sales
Jay Romans, Sr. VP-People
Puneet Bhasin, CIO/Sr. VP
Rick L. Wittenbraker, General Counsel/Chief Compliance Officer/Sr. VP
William Caesar, Chief Strategy Officer
Barry H. Caldwell, Sr. VP-Gov't Affairs & Corp. Comm.
Cherie C. Rice, VP-Finance/Treas.
Patrick J. DeRueda, Pres., Waste Management Recycle America
Mark A. Weidman, Pres., Wheelabrator Technologies, Inc.
Carl Rush, VP-Organic Growth
Jeff Harris, Sr. VP-Midwestern Group
John Pope, Chmn.

Phone: 713-512-6200	Fax: 713-512-6299
Toll-Free:	
Address: 1001 Fannin St., Ste. 4000, Houston, TX 77002 US	

GROWTH PLANS/SPECIAL FEATURES:

Waste Management, Inc. provides comprehensive waste management services to municipal, commercial, industrial and residential customers throughout North America. The company utilizes a number of transfer stations when it is not economical to transport solid waste generated from urban markets directly to landfills. Within these transfer stations, waste is consolidated, compacted and loaded onto long-haul trailers for transport to landfills. Waste Management is the nation's largest collector of recyclables from businesses and households, collecting recyclable materials through subsidiary Recycle America Alliance and depositing them at about a hundred local materials recovery facilities. The firm recycles several different materials, including plastics, rubber, electronics and commodities. The company also has a pulp and paper trading group that reduces paper's overall long-term commodity price exposure. Waste Management operates about 271 solid waste landfills and five secure hazardous waste landfills. Its hazardous waste management services include geosynthetic manufacturing, radioactive waste services and landfill liner installation. The company has developed TOSS, Bio-In-A-Box and BioSite, which are bioremediation systems for materials contaminated with petrochemicals, pesticides, explosives or hazardous organics. Through the subsidiary Wheelbrator Technologies, Inc., the company operates 22 waste-to-energy facilities, which produce electricity through burning solid waste at high temperatures. Additionally, Waste Management promotes environmental initiatives such as Keep America Beautiful, Habitat for Humanity, Red Cross/FEMA and Wildlife Habitat Council, as well as its own Think Green. In March 2011, subsidiary Waste Management Recycle America acquired three recycling facilities in Virginia and Maryland from Canusa Hershman Recycling Company. In 2011, Waste Management opened new facilities in Pennsylvania, Illinois, New Jersey and Texas. It also invested in Agnion Energy, Inc. and Peninsula Compost Company, LLC.

Waste Management offers its employees life, AD&D, medical, dental and vision insurance; prescription drug coverage; family assistance programs; flexible spending accounts; adoption assistance; education savings accounts; an employee stock purchase plan; and tuition reimbursement.

FINANCIALS: Sales and profits are in thousands of dollars—add 000 to get the full amount. 2011 Note: Financial information for 2011 was not available for all companies at press time.

2011 Sales: $	2011 Profits: $	**U.S. Stock Ticker: WM**
2010 Sales: $12,515,000	2010 Profits: $953,000	**Int'l Ticker:**
2009 Sales: $11,791,000	2009 Profits: $994,000	Int'l Exchange:
2008 Sales: $13,388,000	2008 Profits: $1,087,000	Employees: 42,800 Fiscal Year Ends: 12/31
2007 Sales: $13,310,000	2007 Profits: $1,163,000	Parent Company:

SALARIES/BENEFITS:

Pension Plan:	ESOP Stock Plan:	Profit Sharing:	Top Exec. Salary: $1,073,077	Bonus: $1,407,514
Savings Plan: Y	Stock Purch. Plan: Y		Second Exec. Salary: $566,298	Bonus: $487,875

OTHER THOUGHTS:

Apparent Women Officers or Directors: 2
Hot Spot for Advancement for Women/Minorities: Y

LOCATIONS: ("Y" = Yes)

West:	Southwest:	Midwest:	Southeast:	Northeast:	International:
Y	Y	Y	Y	Y	Y

WATERHEALTH

www.waterhealth.com

Industry Group Code: 924110

Energy/Fuel:	Other Technologies:	Electrical Products:	Electronics:	Transportation:	Other:	
Biofuels:	Irrigation:	Lighting/LEDs:	Computers:	Car Sharing:	Recycling:	
Batteries/Storage:	Nanotech:	Waste Heat:	Sensors:	Electric Vehicles:	Engineering:	Y
Solar:	Biotech:	Smart Meters:	Software:	Natural Gas Fuel:	Consulting:	
Wind:	Water Tech./Treatment: Y	Machinery:			Investing:	
Fuel Cells:	Ceramics:				Chemicals:	

TYPES OF BUSINESS:
Water Treatment

BRANDS/DIVISIONS/AFFILIATES:
Dr. Water

CONTACTS: *Note: Officers with more than one job title may be intentionally listed here more than once.*
Sanjay Bhatnagar, CEO
F. Henry Habicht, II, Chmn.
Vikas Shah, COO-India

Phone: 949-716-5790	**Fax:** 949-716-5796
Toll-Free:	
Address: 9601 Irvine Ctr. Dr., Irvine, CA 92618 US	

GROWTH PLANS/SPECIAL FEATURES:
WaterHealth is a water micro-utility whose services purify local water resources of underserved communities throughout the world. The company's water solutions are affordable, safe, de-centralized and scalable. WaterHealth provides its services through its WaterHealth Centers, which are modular constructions that can be ready to dispense water to a community within 20 days from site allocation. The firm's brand of water is Dr. Water, which is purified through a reverse osmosis system that also improves the taste of water; additionally, ultrafiltration processes are incorporated, if necessary, to remove iron, manganese, fluoride and arsenic from the water to provide a better tasting, healthier product. WaterHealth Centers also provides a home delivery service and a hygiene education service that teaches the benefits of drinking safe, clean water. While WaterHealth is headquartered in California, the firm also has offices in Andhra Pradesh, India; Pasig City; Philippines; and Accra, Ghana. In the People's Republic of Bangladesh, the A.K. Khan Group and the International Finance Corporation have partnered with WaterHealth to form a joint venture aimed at installing, operating and maintaining WaterHealth Centers across the Bengali countryside. The firm has provided safe, clean drinking water to over 4 million people and aims to serve over 100 million by 2015. In May 2011, WaterHealth, along with The Coca-Cola Africa Foundation, Diageo plc and the International Finance Corporation, announced a strategic partnership aimed at providing sustainable access to safe drinking water in Africa.

FINANCIALS: Sales and profits are in thousands of dollars—add 000 to get the full amount. 2011 Note: Financial information for 2011 was not available for all companies at press time.

2011 Sales: $	2011 Profits: $	**U.S. Stock Ticker:** Private
2010 Sales: $	2010 Profits: $	**Int'l Ticker:**
2009 Sales: $	2009 Profits: $	Int'l Exchange:
2008 Sales: $	2008 Profits: $	Employees: Fiscal Year Ends:
2007 Sales: $	2007 Profits: $	Parent Company:

SALARIES/BENEFITS:
Pension Plan:	ESOP Stock Plan:	Profit Sharing:	Top Exec. Salary: $	Bonus: $
Savings Plan:	Stock Purch. Plan:		Second Exec. Salary: $	Bonus: $

OTHER THOUGHTS:
Apparent Women Officers or Directors:
Hot Spot for Advancement for Women/Minorities:

LOCATIONS: ("Y" = Yes)
West:	Southwest:	Midwest:	Southeast:	Northeast:	International:
Y					Y

WINDLAB SYSTEMS

www.windlab.com

Industry Group Code: 221119

Energy/Fuel:	Other Technologies:	Electrical Products:	Electronics:	Transportation:	Other:
Biofuels:	Irrigation:	Lighting/LEDs:	Computers:	Car Sharing:	Recycling:
Batteries/Storage:	Nanotech:	Waste Heat:	Sensors:	Electric Vehicles:	Engineering:
Solar:	Biotech:	Smart Meters:	Software:	Natural Gas Fuel:	Consulting:
Wind: Y	Water Tech./Treatment:	Machinery:			Investing:
Fuel Cells:	Ceramics:				Chemicals:

TYPES OF BUSINESS:
Wind Energy Development

BRANDS/DIVISIONS/AFFILIATES:
WindScape
Raptor
Innovation Capital
Lend Lease Ventures

GROWTH PLANS/SPECIAL FEATURES:

Windlab Systems is an Australian wind energy firm. The company is in the process of developing eight wind energy sites in Australia, (five), the U.S. (one), Canada (one) and South Africa (one). Windlab has more than 1,500 megawatts (MW) permitted, 273 (MW) in construction and more than 6500 MW in development globally. Once completed, the firm's projects will supply enough power for approximately 2 million homes. The company has also offered consulting services to other developers, emerging nations, investors and operators on more than 800 MW of operating wind projects. Windlab's proprietary wind assessment models include Raptor and WindScape. The firm's major investors include Australian venture capital groups Lend Lease Ventures and Innovation Capital. In November 2011, Windlab was named to the Global Cleantech 100 list and as one of the top 10 Cleantech companies in the Asia Pacific.

CONTACTS: *Note: Officers with more than one job title may be intentionally listed here more than once.*
Roger Price, CEO
Keith Ayotte, CTO
Richard Mackie, Gen. Mgr.-Australia
Richard Mackie, Gen. Mgr.-South Africa

Phone: 61-2-6175-4600	**Fax:**
Toll-Free:	
Address: 55 Blackall St., Boeing Centre, Level 3, Barton, ACT 2600 Australia	

FINANCIALS: Sales and profits are in thousands of dollars—add 000 to get the full amount. 2011 Note: Financial information for 2011 was not available for all companies at press time.

2011 Sales: $	2011 Profits: $	**U.S. Stock Ticker: Private**
2010 Sales: $	2010 Profits: $	**Int'l Ticker:**
2009 Sales: $	2009 Profits: $	Int'l Exchange:
2008 Sales: $	2008 Profits: $	Employees: Fiscal Year Ends:
2007 Sales: $	2007 Profits: $	Parent Company:

SALARIES/BENEFITS:
Pension Plan:	ESOP Stock Plan:	Profit Sharing:	Top Exec. Salary: $	Bonus: $
Savings Plan:	Stock Purch. Plan:		Second Exec. Salary: $	Bonus: $

OTHER THOUGHTS:
Apparent Women Officers or Directors:
Hot Spot for Advancement for Women/Minorities:

LOCATIONS: ("Y" = Yes)
West:	Southwest:	Midwest:	Southeast:	Northeast:	International:
		Y			Y

WINWIND OY

www.winwind.com

Industry Group Code: 33361

Energy/Fuel:		Other Technologies:		Electrical Products:		Electronics:		Transportation:		Other:	
Biofuels:		Irrigation:		Lighting/LEDs:		Computers:		Car Sharing:		Recycling:	
Batteries/Storage:		Nanotech:		Waste Heat:		Sensors:		Electric Vehicles:		Engineering:	Y
Solar:		Biotech:		Smart Meters:		Software:		Natural Gas Fuel:		Consulting:	
Wind:	Y	Water Tech./Treatment:		Machinery:	Y					Investing:	
Fuel Cells:		Ceramics:								Chemicals:	

TYPES OF BUSINESS:

Wind Turbine Manufacturing
Turbine Maintenance

BRANDS/DIVISIONS/AFFILIATES:

Siva Group
Finnish Industry Investment Ltd

CONTACTS: *Note: Officers with more than one job title may be intentionally listed here more than once.*

Guru Vijendran, COO
Guru Vijendran, CFO
Peter Holmgaard, Chief Sales Officer
Krishnamurthy Vembu, VP-Human Resources
Richard Jones, CTO
Narayan Kumar, Bus. Head-India
Ravichandran Narasimman, Bus. Head-Europe
Farhan Mirza, VP-Global Purchasing & Supply Chain Mgmt.

Phone: 358-207-410-160	Fax: 358-207-410-161
Toll-Free:	
Address: Keilaranta 13, Espoo, FI-02150 Finland	

GROWTH PLANS/SPECIAL FEATURES:

WinWinD Oy, which does business as WinWinD Ltd., designs, develops and assembles turbines for wind power plants. It specializes in low-speed 1 and 3 megawatt (MW) turbines, which are generally called WWD-1 and WWD-3, respectively. The company also has the WinWinD 3 upwind wind turbine. This turbine is lighter in weight and suits all three wind classes because of its different rotor sizes. To guarantee high quality, the company provides WinCare Operation and Maintenance services to its customers, including preventive and corrective maintenance. The wind turbines are monitored 24-hours-a-day, seven-days-a-week and up-to-date production information is always available online. The company has manufacturing plants in Hamina, Finland and Vengal, India. Its Indian operations are run by wholly-owned subsidiary, Winwind Power Energy Private Limited. Currently, WinWinD's products have been installed in Portugal, France, the Czech Republic, Estonia and Sweden. Indian private equity firm Siva Group is a majority stakeholder in WinWinD, with the firm's other large investor being the government-owned Finnish Industry Investment Ltd.

FINANCIALS: Sales and profits are in thousands of dollars—add 000 to get the full amount. 2011 Note: Financial information for 2011 was not available for all companies at press time.

2011 Sales: $	2011 Profits: $	**U.S. Stock Ticker: Private**
2010 Sales: $	2010 Profits: $	**Int'l Ticker:**
2009 Sales: $	2009 Profits: $	Int'l Exchange:
2008 Sales: $	2008 Profits: $	Employees: 800 Fiscal Year Ends:
2007 Sales: $	2007 Profits: $	Parent Company: SIVA GROUP

SALARIES/BENEFITS:

Pension Plan:	ESOP Stock Plan:	Profit Sharing:	Top Exec. Salary: $	Bonus: $
Savings Plan:	Stock Purch. Plan:		Second Exec. Salary: $	Bonus: $

OTHER THOUGHTS:

Apparent Women Officers or Directors:
Hot Spot for Advancement for Women/Minorities:

LOCATIONS: ("Y" = Yes)

West:	Southwest:	Midwest:	Southeast:	Northeast:	International:
					Y

WURTH ELEKTRONIK GMBH & CO KG   www.we-online.com

Industry Group Code: 334413

Energy/Fuel:		Other Technologies:		Electrical Products:		Electronics:		Transportation:		Other:	
Biofuels:		Irrigation:		Lighting/LEDs:		Computers:	Y	Car Sharing:		Recycling:	
Batteries/Storage:		Nanotech:	Y	Waste Heat:		Sensors:	Y	Electric Vehicles:		Engineering:	Y
Solar:	Y	Biotech:		Smart Meters:		Software:		Natural Gas Fuel:		Consulting:	
Wind:		Water Tech./Treatment:		Machinery:						Investing:	
Fuel Cells:		Ceramics:								Chemicals:	

TYPES OF BUSINESS:

Circuit Board Printing
Computer Inductors
Electronic Power Elements
Solar Cells
Photovoltaic Modules

BRANDS/DIVISIONS/AFFILIATES:

Wurth Group
Allied Companies
TWINflex
Microvia
FLATcomp
Wurth Elektronik Radialex
Wurth Solar GmbH

CONTACTS: *Note: Officers with more than one job title may be intentionally listed here more than once.*

Jurgen Klohe, Co-Managing Dir.
Jorg Murawski, Co-Managing Dir.

Phone: 49-79-40-946-0	Fax: 49-79-40-946-400
Toll-Free:	
Address: Salzstrasse 21, Niedernhall, D-74676 Germany	

GROWTH PLANS/SPECIAL FEATURES:

Wurth Elektronik GmbH & Co. KG is the holding company for the Wurth Group's Allied Companies electronic businesses. Its products cover six business areas: printed circuit boards, system solutions in press-fit technology, passive components, electromechanics; transformers and custom magnetics (TCM), and photovoltaic systems. The printed circuit boards are sold primarily under the TWINflex brand name, and the firm utilizes its proprietary Microvia and FLATcomp technology to manufacture them. The firm also sells circuit board heat sink products for automotive applications, such as transmission control. The firm has circuit board manufacturing plants in Niedernhall, Pforzheim, Rot am See and Schopfheim, Germany. The firm's system solutions in press-fit technology products include powerboards, keypads, control panels, central electrical distribution units, press-fit circuit boards and power elements. Passive components include transformers, RF components, power inductors, ferrites and filter connectors. Electromechanical products, including WERI connectors and WESURGE varistors (variable resistors), are manufactured by Wurth Elektronik Radialex. The TCM segment, operated by subsidiary Wurth Solar GmbH, produces CIS-solar modules made from a Copper-Indium-Diselenide (CIS) matrix on a glass or glass-composite backing, with standard varieties supplying 5.5, 12, 23, 35, 55, 75 or 80 watts. The photovoltaic segment is one of Europe's leading manufacturers of solar modules and a system supplier for all products relating to photovoltaic systems. Its residential solar solutions include HOMEline, a low-voltage system that works in the protective extra-low voltage range; POWERline, a system for ideal conditions with an output of 40 kilowatts per hour (kWh); and DESINGline, a system constructed of GeneCIS solar modules that replaces traditional roofing altogether. Through Wurth Solar, the firm also offers solar installations for commercial buildings and integrated installations for architectural purposes.

FINANCIALS: Sales and profits are in thousands of dollars—add 000 to get the full amount. 2011 Note: Financial information for 2011 was not available for all companies at press time.

2011 Sales: $	2011 Profits: $	**U.S. Stock Ticker: Private**
2010 Sales: $	2010 Profits: $	**Int'l Ticker:**
2009 Sales: $	2009 Profits: $	Int'l Exchange:
2008 Sales: $	2008 Profits: $	Employees: Fiscal Year Ends: 12/31
2007 Sales: $	2007 Profits: $	Parent Company:

SALARIES/BENEFITS:

Pension Plan:	ESOP Stock Plan:	Profit Sharing:	Top Exec. Salary: $	Bonus: $
Savings Plan:	Stock Purch. Plan:		Second Exec. Salary: $	Bonus: $

OTHER THOUGHTS:

Apparent Women Officers or Directors:
Hot Spot for Advancement for Women/Minorities:

LOCATIONS: ("Y" = Yes)

West:	Southwest:	Midwest:	Southeast:	Northeast:	International: Y

XINJIANG GOLDWIND SCIENCE & TECHNOLOGY CO LTD

www.goldwindglobal.com

Industry Group Code: 33361

Energy/Fuel:	Other Technologies:	Electrical Products:	Electronics:	Transportation:	Other:
Biofuels:	Irrigation:	Lighting/LEDs:	Computers:	Car Sharing:	Recycling:
Batteries/Storage:	Nanotech:	Waste Heat:	Sensors:	Electric Vehicles:	Engineering:
Solar:	Biotech:	Smart Meters:	Software:	Natural Gas Fuel:	Consulting:
Wind: Y	Water Tech./Treatment:	Machinery:			Investing:
Fuel Cells:	Ceramics:				Chemicals:

TYPES OF BUSINESS:

Wind Turbine Manufacturing
Wind Farm Development
Site Selection & Design
Spare Parts
Equipment Maintenance

BRANDS/DIVISIONS/AFFILIATES:

Goldwind USA
Vensys Energy AG

CONTACTS: Note: Officers with more than one job title may be intentionally listed here more than once.

Wu Gang, CEO
Guo Jian, Pres.
Li Yu Zhuo, Exec. VP
John Titchen, Managing Dir.-Australia
Tim Rosenszweig, CEO-Goldwind USA

Phone: 86-991-3767-999	**Fax:** 86-991-3762-039

Toll-Free:

Address: 107 Shanghai Rd., Urumqi, Xinjiang, 830026 China

GROWTH PLANS/SPECIAL FEATURES:

Xinjiang Goldwind Science & Technology Co., Ltd. (Goldwind), based in China, is a leading manufacturer and developer of wind turbines. The company, which has operations in Asia, Australia, Europe and the Americas, holds approximately 8% of the global market for wind turbines, with over 6,000 turbines in service internationally. The firm primarily manufactures 1.5 megawatt (MW) and 2.5 MW turbines that use permanent magnet direct-drive (PMDD) technology, which has high power generating efficiency and can be adapted to function in a variety of climate conditions, including low and high temperatures, high altitude, low wind velocity and coastal areas. Goldwind also provides wind farm development services divided into three categories: development services, including policy research, investment consulting, project financing, wind farm design, site selection, wind measurement and turbine model selection; construction services, including basic structure design, tower construction supervision, logistics and engineering supervision; and operation services, including equipment servicing, wind farm operation and maintenance, spare parts supply, training consulting and project assessment. The firm also invests in, develops and completes wind farm projects in China and internationally that are then transferred to investors or wind farm operators. Goldwind operates in the U.S. through subsidiary Goldwind USA and in Europe through subsidiary Vensys Energy AG.

FINANCIALS: Sales and profits are in thousands of dollars—add 000 to get the full amount. 2011 Note: Financial information for 2011 was not available for all companies at press time.

		U.S. Stock Ticker:
2011 Sales: $	2011 Profits: $	
2010 Sales: $2,712,180	2010 Profits: $355,314	**Int'l Ticker: 002202**
2009 Sales: $1,598,370	2009 Profits: $261,580	Int'l Exchange: Shanghai-SHE
2008 Sales: $961,630	2008 Profits: $135,820	Employees: 3,908 Fiscal Year Ends: 12/31
2007 Sales: $	2007 Profits: $	Parent Company:

SALARIES/BENEFITS:

Pension Plan:	ESOP Stock Plan:	Profit Sharing:	Top Exec. Salary: $	Bonus: $
Savings Plan:	Stock Purch. Plan:		Second Exec. Salary: $	Bonus: $

OTHER THOUGHTS:

Apparent Women Officers or Directors:
Hot Spot for Advancement for Women/Minorities:

LOCATIONS: ("Y" = Yes)

West:	Southwest:	Midwest:	Southeast:	Northeast:	International:
		Y			Y

Sales, profits and employees may be estimates. Financial information, benefits and other data can change quickly and may vary from those stated here.

XTREME POWER

www.xtremepower.com

Industry Group Code: 33591

Energy/Fuel:		Other Technologies:	Electrical Products:	Electronics:	Transportation:	Other:
Biofuels:		Irrigation:	Lighting/LEDs:	Computers:	Car Sharing:	Recycling:
Batteries/Storage:	Y	Nanotech:	Waste Heat:	Sensors:	Electric Vehicles:	Engineering:
Solar:		Biotech:	Smart Meters:	Software:	Natural Gas Fuel:	Consulting:
Wind:		Water Tech./Treatment:	Machinery:			Investing:
Fuel Cells:		Ceramics:				Chemicals:

TYPES OF BUSINESS:

Power Management Systems
Energy Storage Systems

BRANDS/DIVISIONS/AFFILIATES:

PowerCell
Dynamic Power Resources (DPR)

CONTACTS: *Note: Officers with more than one job title may be intentionally listed here more than once.*

Carlos Coe, CEO
Ken Hashman, CFO
Alan J. Gotcher, CTO
Kin Gill, General Counsel/Sec./VP
Jeff Layton, VP-Oper.

Phone: 512-268-8191	Fax:
Toll-Free:	
Address: 1120 Goforth Rd., Kyle, TX 78640 US	

GROWTH PLANS/SPECIAL FEATURES:

Xtreme Power (XP) designs, engineers, manufactures and operates integrated power management and energy storage systems. Through its proprietary Dynamic Power Resources (DPR) program suite, the firm primarily targets transmission and distribution utilities, commercial and industrial end users and independent power producers. DPR uses the firm's PowerCell technology coupled with high-efficiency power electronics and customizable micro-second controls. PowerCell is a 1kWh (kilowatt hour), 12 volt dry cell battery technology with high power retention and the capacity to quickly charge and discharge large amounts of power. The firm integrates all key operating components into DPR according to each individual customer's energy and power needs. By condensing a number of applications into one product, with or without the use of a grid connection, the customer is able to take advantage of multiple revenue streams and see the best return on investment (ROI). Additional benefits of DPR include an approximate 90% round-trip efficiency rate; a flexible size; and the ability to supply and absorb real and reactive power. The firm is headquartered in Kyle, Texas and has additional representation in Austin, Houston, Maui, Chicago and Washington, D.C.

FINANCIALS: Sales and profits are in thousands of dollars—add 000 to get the full amount. 2011 Note: Financial information for 2011 was not available for all companies at press time.

2011 Sales: $	2011 Profits: $	U.S. Stock Ticker: Private
2010 Sales: $	2010 Profits: $	Int'l Ticker:
2009 Sales: $	2009 Profits: $	Int'l Exchange:
2008 Sales: $	2008 Profits: $	Employees: Fiscal Year Ends:
2007 Sales: $	2007 Profits: $	Parent Company:

SALARIES/BENEFITS:

Pension Plan:	ESOP Stock Plan:	Profit Sharing:	Top Exec. Salary: $	Bonus: $
Savings Plan:	Stock Purch. Plan:		Second Exec. Salary: $	Bonus: $

OTHER THOUGHTS:

Apparent Women Officers or Directors:
Hot Spot for Advancement for Women/Minorities:

LOCATIONS: ("Y" = Yes)

West:	Southwest:	Midwest:	Southeast:	Northeast:	International:
Y	Y	Y		Y	

XYLEM INC

www.xyleminc.com

Industry Group Code: 335

Energy/Fuel:	Other Technologies:	Electrical Products:	Electronics:	Transportation:	Other:	
Biofuels:	Irrigation:	Lighting/LEDs:	Computers:	Car Sharing:	Recycling:	
Batteries/Storage:	Nanotech:	Waste Heat:	Sensors:	Electric Vehicles:	Engineering:	Y
Solar:	Biotech:	Smart Meters:	Software:	Natural Gas Fuel:	Consulting:	Y
Wind:	Water Tech./Treatment: Y	Machinery:			Investing:	
Fuel Cells:	Ceramics:				Chemicals:	

TYPES OF BUSINESS:

Water Treatment Technology
Fluid Technologies
Analytical Instruments
Lighting and Ventilation
Pumps

BRANDS/DIVISIONS/AFFILIATES:

ITT Corporation
AADI
Bell & Gossett
AC Fire Pump

CONTACTS: Note: Officers with more than one job title may be intentionally listed here more than once.

Gretchen W. McClain, CEO
Gretchen W. McClain, Pres.
Mike Speetzen, CFO/Sr. VP
Robyn Mingle, Chief Human Resources Officer/Sr. VP
Frank R. Jimenez, General Counsel/Sr. VP/Corp. Sec.
Colin R. Sabol, Chief Strategy & Growth Officer/Sr. VP
Angela A. Buonocore, Chief Comm. Officer/Sr. VP
Phil De Sousa, Investor Contact
Mike Kuchenbrod, Sr. VP/Pres., Water Solutions
Chris McIntire, Sr. VP/Pres., Analytics
Ken Napolitano, Sr. VP/Pres., Residential & Commercial Water
Markos I. Tambakeras, Chmn.
Bob Wolpert, Sr. VP/Pres., Flow Control & China & India

Phone: 914-323-5700	Fax: 914-323-5800
Toll-Free:	
Address: 1133 Westchester Ave., White Plains, NY 10604 US	

GROWTH PLANS/SPECIAL FEATURES:

Xylem, Inc., formerly the water equipment and services businesses of ITT Corporation, is an equipment and service provider for water and wastewater applications. It offers a broad portfolio of products and services addressing the full cycle of water, from collection, distribution and use to the return of water to the environment. Xylem operates in two segments: Water Infrastructure and Applied Water. The Water Infrastructure segment focuses on the transportation, treatment and testing of water, offering a range of products including water and wastewater pumps; treatment and testing equipment; and controls and systems. The Applied Water segment encompasses all the uses of water, focusing on the residential, commercial, industrial and agricultural markets. The segment's major products include pumps, valves, heat exchangers, controls and dispensing equipment. The company has over 35 major brands, including AADI, which manufactures measuring and monitoring sensors, instruments and systems; Bell & Gossett, a manufacturer of valves, pumps and heat exchanges; and AC Fire Pump, custom designed and built fire pump products. While Xylem is headquartered in New York, it currently has operations at 320 locations within 40 different countries. Additionally, the products of the firm are sold in over 150 countries worldwide. In October 2011, ITT Corporation completed the spin-off of Xylem.

FINANCIALS: Sales and profits are in thousands of dollars—add 000 to get the full amount. 2011 Note: Financial information for 2011 was not available for all companies at press time.

2011 Sales: $	2011 Profits: $	**U.S. Stock Ticker: XYL**
2010 Sales: $	2010 Profits: $	**Int'l Ticker:**
2009 Sales: $	2009 Profits: $	Int'l Exchange:
2008 Sales: $	2008 Profits: $	Employees: Fiscal Year Ends:
2007 Sales: $	2007 Profits: $	Parent Company:

SALARIES/BENEFITS:

Pension Plan:	ESOP Stock Plan:	Profit Sharing:	Top Exec. Salary: $	Bonus: $
Savings Plan:	Stock Purch. Plan:		Second Exec. Salary: $	Bonus: $

OTHER THOUGHTS:

Apparent Women Officers or Directors: 6
Hot Spot for Advancement for Women/Minorities: Y

LOCATIONS: ("Y" = Yes)

West:	Southwest:	Midwest:	Southeast:	Northeast: Y	International: Y

YINGLI GREEN ENERGY HOLDING CO LTD   www.yinglisolar.com

Industry Group Code: 334413

Energy/Fuel:	Other Technologies:	Electrical Products:	Electronics:	Transportation:	Other:
Biofuels:	Irrigation:	Lighting/LEDs:	Computers:	Car Sharing:	Recycling:
Batteries/Storage:	Nanotech:	Waste Heat:	Sensors:	Electric Vehicles:	Engineering:
Solar: Y	Biotech:	Smart Meters:	Software:	Natural Gas Fuel:	Consulting:
Wind:	Water Tech./Treatment:	Machinery:			Investing:
Fuel Cells:	Ceramics:				Chemicals:

TYPES OF BUSINESS:
Photovoltaic Cell Manufacturing
Solar Modules
Photovoltaic System Installation
Polysilicon Production

BRANDS/DIVISIONS/AFFILIATES:
Baoding Tianwei Yingli New Energy Resources Co Ltd
Yingli Solar
Yingli Green Energy Americas Inc
Fine Silicon Co Ltd
Yingli

CONTACTS: Note: Officers with more than one job title may be intentionally listed here more than once.
Liansheng Miao, CEO
Zongwei Li, CFO
Dengyuan Song, CTO
Yiyu Wang, Chief Strategy Officer
Qing Miao, Dir.-Investor Rel.
Jingfeng Xiong, VP-Tech.
Zhiheng Zhao, Sr. VP
Xiangdong Wang, VP
Robert Petrina, Managing Dir.-Yingli Green Energy Americas, Inc.
Liansheng Miao, Chmn.
Darren Thompson, Managing Dir.-Yingli Green Energy Europe

Phone: 86-312-8929-700	Fax: 86-312-8929-800
Toll-Free:	
Address: No. 3055 Middle Fuxing Rd., Baoding, 071051 China	

GROWTH PLANS/SPECIAL FEATURES:
Yingli Green Energy Holding Co., Ltd. designs, manufactures, markets and installs photovoltaic (PV) products and systems. Through subsidiary Baoding Tianwei Yingli New Energy Resources Co., Ltd., Yingli Green Energy designs, manufactures and sells PV modules and also designs, assembles, sells and installs PV systems that are connected to electricity transmission grids or that operate on a stand-alone basis. The firm has installed over 2 gigawatts (GW) of solar power worldwide. The company has expanded its production capacity in recent years. With roughly 1.7 GW of total annual production capacity for multicrystalline polysilicon ingots and wafers, PV cells and PV modules, Yingli Green Energy is currently one of the largest manufacturers of PV products in the world. Through subsidiary Fine Silicon Co., Ltd., the firm also has an in-house polysilicon production capacity of 3,307 tons annually. Additionally, Yingli Green Energy is one of the few large-scale PV companies in China to have adopted vertical integration as its business model. Yingli Green Energy sells PV modules under its own brand names, Yingli and Yingli Solar, to PV system integrators and distributors located in various markets around the world, including China, Germany, Spain, Italy, Greece, France, South Korea and the U.S.

FINANCIALS: Sales and profits are in thousands of dollars—add 000 to get the full amount. 2011 Note: Financial information for 2011 was not available for all companies at press time.
2011 Sales: $
2010 Sales: $1,896,898
2009 Sales: $1,062,844
2008 Sales: $1,107,074
2007 Sales: $556,483

2011 Profits: $
2010 Profits: $210,446
2009 Profits: $-77,880
2008 Profits: $97,730
2007 Profits: $53,330

U.S. Stock Ticker: YGE
Int'l Ticker:
Int'l Exchange:
Employees: 11,000   Fiscal Year Ends: 12/31
Parent Company:

SALARIES/BENEFITS:
Pension Plan: ESOP Stock Plan: Profit Sharing: Top Exec. Salary: $ Bonus: $
Savings Plan: Stock Purch. Plan: Second Exec. Salary: $ Bonus: $

OTHER THOUGHTS:
Apparent Women Officers or Directors:
Hot Spot for Advancement for Women/Minorities:

LOCATIONS: ("Y" = Yes)
West:	Southwest:	Midwest:	Southeast:	Northeast:	International: Y

Sales, profits and employees may be estimates. Financial information, benefits and other data can change quickly and may vary from those stated here.

ZAP JONWAY

Industry Group Code: 336991

www.zapworld.com

Energy/Fuel:	Other Technologies:	Electrical Products:	Electronics:	Transportation:		Other:
Biofuels:	Irrigation:	Lighting/LEDs:	Computers:	Car Sharing:		Recycling:
Batteries/Storage:	Nanotech:	Waste Heat:	Sensors:	Electric Vehicles:	Y	Engineering:
Solar:	Biotech:	Smart Meters:	Software:	Natural Gas Fuel:		Consulting:
Wind:	Water Tech./Treatment:	Machinery:				Investing:
Fuel Cells:	Ceramics:					Chemicals:

TYPES OF BUSINESS:

Light Electric Vehicles
Electric Bicycles & Scooters
Electric ATVs
Lithium Batteries
Electric Fleet Vehicle Manufacturing

BRANDS/DIVISIONS/AFFILIATES:

Zhejiang Jonway Automobile Co. Ltd.
A380
ALIAS EV
ZAPPY
Zapino
ZAP Dude
XEBRA
ZAP Manufacturing, Inc.

CONTACTS: Note: Officers with more than one job title may be intentionally listed here more than once.

Steven Schneider, Co-CEO
Gary Dodd, Pres.
Benjamin Zhu, CFO
Wang Gang, Co-CEO
Priscilla M. Lu, Chmn.

Phone: 707-525-8658	**Fax:**
Toll-Free: 800-251-4555	
Address: 501 Fourth St., Santa Rosa, CA 95401 US	

GROWTH PLANS/SPECIAL FEATURES:

ZAP Jonway, formerly ZAP, is a U.S.-China auto manufacturer focused on the development of electric vehicles (EVs). The new company was formed in January 2011, when ZAP acquired a 51% controlling interest in Chinese automaker Zhejiang Jonway Automobile Co. Ltd. (Jonway). The combined company is currently developing an electric version of Jonway's A380 SUV, with its initial target being the fleet and taxi markets. The firm's other development efforts consist of production and commercialization of its ALIAS EV roadster. The ALIAS, which the firm plans to launch commercially in late 2011, is a three-wheel EV with a range of 100 miles and top speeds of 85 mph. Historically, ZAP manufactured various EVs for the consumer and fleet markets, including the zero-emission ZAPPY and Zapino electric scooters; ZAP Dude electric ATVs; the XEBRA 100% electric sedan and utility pick-up truck; the ZAPTRUCK XL utility truck; and the ZAPVAN SHUTTLE. ZAP Jonway has a number of wholly-owned subsidiaries, such as Voltage Vehicles, engaged primarily in the distribution and sale of advanced technology and conventional automobiles; ZAPWorld Stores, Inc., engaged primarily in consumer sales of ZAP products; ZAP Manufacturing, Inc., primarily involved in the distribution of ZAP products; and ZAP Retail Outlet. The company has worked on projects for the taxi fleet market in China; qualified as a supplier for the U.S. General Service Administration; and designed electric vehicles for a proposal for the conversion to an all-electric USPS fleet. In November 2010, it signed a long-term supply and development agreement with Remy Electric Motors, LLC to use Remy's HVH 250 electric motor in its future cars and SUVs. The two firms will also collaborate on the development of a drivetrain for use in future vehicles.

FINANCIALS: Sales and profits are in thousands of dollars—add 000 to get the full amount. 2011 Note: Financial information for 2011 was not available for all companies at press time.

2011 Sales: $	2011 Profits: $	**U.S. Stock Ticker:** ZAAP.OB
2010 Sales: $3,816	2010 Profits: $-19,018	**Int'l Ticker:**
2009 Sales: $4,068	2009 Profits: $-10,687	Int'l Exchange:
2008 Sales: $7,588	2008 Profits: $9,807	Employees: 555 Fiscal Year Ends: 12/31
2007 Sales: $5,712	2007 Profits: $-28,006	Parent Company:

SALARIES/BENEFITS:

Pension Plan:	ESOP Stock Plan:	Profit Sharing:	Top Exec. Salary: $240,000	Bonus: $
Savings Plan:	Stock Purch. Plan:		Second Exec. Salary: $121,448	Bonus: $

OTHER THOUGHTS:

Apparent Women Officers or Directors: 1
Hot Spot for Advancement for Women/Minorities:

LOCATIONS: ("Y" = Yes)

West:	Southwest:	Midwest:	Southeast:	Northeast:	International:
				Y	Y

Sales, profits and employees may be estimates. Financial information, benefits and other data can change quickly and may vary from those stated here.

ZEACHEM INC

www.zeachem.com

Industry Group Code: 325199

Energy/Fuel:		Other Technologies:		Electrical Products:	Electronics:	Transportation:	Other:
Biofuels:	Y	Irrigation:		Lighting/LEDs:	Computers:	Car Sharing:	Recycling:
Batteries/Storage:		Nanotech:		Waste Heat:	Sensors:	Electric Vehicles:	Engineering:
Solar:		Biotech:	Y	Smart Meters:	Software:	Natural Gas Fuel:	Consulting:
Wind:		Water Tech./Treatment:		Machinery:			Investing:
Fuel Cells:		Ceramics:					Chemicals:

TYPES OF BUSINESS:

Biorefining Technology

BRANDS/DIVISIONS/AFFILIATES:

CONTACTS: *Note: Officers with more than one job title may be intentionally listed here more than once.*

Jim Imbler, CEO
Jim Imbler, Pres.
Andy Vietor, CFO
Dan Verser, Exec. VP-R&D
Tim Eggeman, CTO
Angus Connell, Exec. VP-Eng.
Roger Schoonover, VP-Bus. Dev.
Joe Regnery, Sr. VP-Gov't & Regulatory Affairs
Carrie Atiyeh, Dir.-Public Affairs
Bob Walsh, Chief Commercial Officer
Chris Wilcox, Dir.-Bus. Dev.
Nancy Buese, Chmn.

Phone: 303-279-7045	**Fax:** 303-279-9537
Toll-Free:	
Address: 165 S. Union Blvd., Ste. 380, Lakewood, CO 80228 US	

GROWTH PLANS/SPECIAL FEATURES:

ZeaChem, Inc. uses its proprietary cellulose-based biorefinery platform in the production of intermediate chemicals and advanced fuels, while avoiding the yield and carbon dioxide associated issues commonly seen in traditional and cellulosic based methods. The company's method employs a hybrid process of thermochemical and biochemical processing that efficiently extracts as much energy as possible from biomass feedstocks that contain high levels of cellulose. This process cost-effectively increases output loads, while maintaining one of the lowest fossil carbon footprints of the biorefining methods currently on the market. When comparing the firm's product to traditional gasoline, the company's process creates a 94-98% reduction in greenhouse gas emissions. ZeaChem's approach offers a 40% yield advantage when compared to both other cellulosic enthanol firms and corn based ethanol producers. Its average operating costs are less than $1.00, and its average capital cost is less than $4.00 per gallon. The company is headquartered in Lakewood, Colorado, and maintains a research and development facility in Menlo Park, California. In January 2012, the firm completed construction of the core facility of its new integrated demonstration biorefinery in Boardman, Oregon.

FINANCIALS: Sales and profits are in thousands of dollars—add 000 to get the full amount. 2011 Note: Financial information for 2011 was not available for all companies at press time.

2011 Sales: $	2011 Profits: $	**U.S. Stock Ticker:** Private	
2010 Sales: $	2010 Profits: $	**Int'l Ticker:**	
2009 Sales: $	2009 Profits: $	Int'l Exchange:	
2008 Sales: $	2008 Profits: $	Employees:	Fiscal Year Ends:
2007 Sales: $	2007 Profits: $	Parent Company:	

SALARIES/BENEFITS:

Pension Plan:	ESOP Stock Plan:	Profit Sharing:	Top Exec. Salary: $	Bonus: $
Savings Plan:	Stock Purch. Plan:		Second Exec. Salary: $	Bonus: $

OTHER THOUGHTS:

Apparent Women Officers or Directors: 2
Hot Spot for Advancement for Women/Minorities:

LOCATIONS: ("Y" = Yes)

West:	Southwest:	Midwest:	Southeast:	Northeast:	International:
Y					

ZIPCAR INC

www.zipcar.com

Industry Group Code: 5321

Energy/Fuel:	Other Technologies:	Electrical Products:	Electronics:	Transportation:		Other:
Biofuels:	Irrigation:	Lighting/LEDs:	Computers:	Car Sharing:	Y	Recycling:
Batteries/Storage:	Nanotech:	Waste Heat:	Sensors:	Electric Vehicles:		Engineering:
Solar:	Biotech:	Smart Meters:	Software:	Natural Gas Fuel:		Consulting:
Wind:	Water Tech./Treatment:	Machinery:				Investing:
Fuel Cells:	Ceramics:					Chemicals:

TYPES OF BUSINESS:

Car Sharing Service
Car Rental
Fleet Management Software

BRANDS/DIVISIONS/AFFILIATES:

Catalunya Carsharing S.A.
Avancar
Streetcar Ltd.
Zipvan

CONTACTS: *Note: Officers with more than one job title may be intentionally listed here more than once.*

Scott Griffith, CEO
Mark Norman, COO
Mark Norman, Pres.
Ed Goldfinger, CFO
Rob Weisberg, Chief Mktg. Officer
Doug Williams, VP-Eng.
Dean Breda, General Counsel
Jon Zeitler, Exec. VP-Corp. Dev.
Lesley Mottla, VP-Member Experience
Scott Griffith, Chmn.
Frerk-Malte Feller, Pres., Europe

Phone: 617-995-4231	**Fax:** 617-995-4300
Toll-Free: 866-494-7227	
Address: 25 First St., 4th Fl., Cambridge, MA 02141 US	

GROWTH PLANS/SPECIAL FEATURES:

Zipcar, Inc. is a membership-based car sharing company that offers shared access to automobiles and trucks for users in a growing number of urban areas across the U.S., Canada and the U.K. Originating in Boston, Massachusetts in 1999, Zipcar has since established a presence in urban areas such as New York, Philadelphia, San Francisco, Washington D.C., Atlanta, Chicago, Portland and Seattle. Internationally, the company has set up Canadian operations in Toronto and Vancouver, as well as U.K. operations in London. In all, Zipcar has vehicles in over 180 cities across the U.K. and the U.S. Members reserve vehicles ahead of time (either online or by phone), then pay an hourly or daily fee for the use of the vehicle; the rental price includes all gas and insurance costs, as well as 180 free miles. Members can reserve cars for an hour at a time, or for periods of up to four days. The program is marketed to a range of customers, from those who normally use public transportation but occasionally want access to a car, to those who need a car as a primary mode of transportation but wish to avoid the costs associated with car ownership. Zipcar's university program includes cars on over 225 U.S. campuses, including Yale, Stanford, Johns Hopkins, the University of Michigan and Dartmouth. Members use Zipcards, which make use of radio frequency identification (RFID) technology, to unlock cars, while global positioning system (GPS) technology combined with new smart phone software allows members to locate cars nearby and make reservations on-the-go from their mobile phones. Zipcar holds a minority interest in Catalunya Carsharing S.A., known as Avancar, a car sharing service in Spain. In early 2011, the firm had more than 530,000 members and 8,000 vehicles. In November 2011, Zipcar announced the launch of a pilot program in San Francisco which will include the new offering of full size cargo vans through Zipvan.

FINANCIALS: Sales and profits are in thousands of dollars—add 000 to get the full amount. 2011 Note: Financial information for 2011 was not available for all companies at press time.

2011 Sales: $	2011 Profits: $	**U.S. Stock Ticker:** ZIP
2010 Sales: $186,100	2010 Profits: $-14,120	**Int'l Ticker:**
2009 Sales: $131,180	2009 Profits: $-4,640	Int'l Exchange:
2008 Sales: $	2008 Profits: $	Employees: 474 Fiscal Year Ends: 12/31
2007 Sales: $	2007 Profits: $	Parent Company:

SALARIES/BENEFITS:

Pension Plan:	ESOP Stock Plan:	Profit Sharing:	Top Exec. Salary: $	Bonus: $
Savings Plan:	Stock Purch. Plan:		Second Exec. Salary: $	Bonus: $

OTHER THOUGHTS:

Apparent Women Officers or Directors:
Hot Spot for Advancement for Women/Minorities:

LOCATIONS: ("Y" = Yes)

West:	Southwest:	Midwest:	Southeast:	Northeast:	International:
Y		Y	Y	Y	Y

ZORLU ENERJI ELEKTRIK URETIM AS

www.zoren.com.tr

Industry Group Code: 221121

Energy/Fuel:	Other Technologies:	Electrical Products:	Electronics:	Transportation:	Other:
Biofuels:	Irrigation:	Lighting/LEDs:	Computers:	Car Sharing:	Recycling:
Batteries/Storage:	Nanotech:	Waste Heat: Y	Sensors:	Electric Vehicles:	Engineering: Y
Solar:	Biotech:	Smart Meters:	Software:	Natural Gas Fuel: Y	Consulting:
Wind: Y	Water Tech./Treatment: Y	Machinery:			Investing:
Fuel Cells:	Ceramics:				Chemicals:

TYPES OF BUSINESS:

Electricity Generation
Natural Gas Distribution
Turnkey Projects

BRANDS/DIVISIONS/AFFILIATES:

Zorlu Group
Zorlu Energy Electricity Generation Co Inc
Rotor Electricity Generation Inc
ICFS International LLC
Dorad Energy Ltd
Solad Energy Ltd
Zorlu Energy Pakistan Ltd

CONTACTS: *Note: Officers with more than one job title may be intentionally listed here more than once.*

Arif Ozozan, CEO
Tansel Varan, Dir.-Human Resources
Serhak Simsek, Assistant Gen. Mgr.-Production & Trade
Bulent Cilingir, Dir.-Acquisitions
Tansel Varan, Dir.-Corp. Comm.
I. Sinan Ak, Assistant Gen. Mgr.-Finance
Selen Zorlu Melik, Deputy CEO
Gokmen Topuz, Assistant Gen. Mgr.-Investments Dept.
Zeki Zorlu, Chmn.
Bulent Cilingir, Dir.-Logistics

Phone: 90-212-456-2300	**Fax:** 90-212-422-0099
Toll-Free:	
Address: Zorlu Plz., Istanbul, 34310 Turkey	

GROWTH PLANS/SPECIAL FEATURES:

Zorlu Enerji Elektrik Uretim AS, based in Turkey, operates in the energy sector. The company is part of the Zorlu Group, a holding company with activities in the textile, electronics, energy and property markets. The firm has a total generation capacity of 745 megawatts (MW) produced by five natural gas fired power plants with a capacity of 467.2 MW, seven hydroelectric power plants, one geothermal power plant, one wind power plant and one fuel-oil power plant. The company started production at its wind farm in Osmaniye, Turkey, in 2009. When completed, the wind farm will have a generation capacity of 135 MW. Zorlu Enerji also offers search, exploration, drilling and distribution services for natural gas. In addition to energy generation, Zorlu Enerji provides a number of turnkey services relating to energy project construction and power plant maintenance and operation, including turnkey services for foreign power plants in Greece, Kuwait, India, Russia and Israel. The firm operates principally through sixteen group companies, including Zorlu Energy Electricity Generation Co., Inc.; Rotor Electricity Generation, Inc.; ICFS International LLC; Dorad Energy Ltd.; Solad Energy; and Zorlu Energy Pakistan Ltd., among others.

FINANCIALS: Sales and profits are in thousands of dollars—add 000 to get the full amount. 2011 Note: Financial information for 2011 was not available for all companies at press time.

2011 Sales: $	2011 Profits: $	**U.S. Stock Ticker:**
2010 Sales: $233,200	2010 Profits: $-35,500	**Int'l Ticker: ZOREN**
2009 Sales: $261,400	2009 Profits: $48,200	Int'l Exchange: Istanbul-IST
2008 Sales: $285,500	2008 Profits: $-179,100	Employees: 369 Fiscal Year Ends: 12/31
2007 Sales: $317,880	2007 Profits: $-6,970	Parent Company:

SALARIES/BENEFITS:

Pension Plan:	ESOP Stock Plan:	Profit Sharing:	Top Exec. Salary: $	Bonus: $
Savings Plan:	Stock Purch. Plan:		Second Exec. Salary: $	Bonus: $

OTHER THOUGHTS:

Apparent Women Officers or Directors: 2
Hot Spot for Advancement for Women/Minorities:

LOCATIONS: ("Y" = Yes)

West:	Southwest:	Midwest:	Southeast:	Northeast:	International:
					Y

ADDITIONAL INDEXES

Contents:

INDEX OF FIRMS NOTED AS HOT SPOTS FOR ADVANCEMENT FOR WOMEN & MINORITIES

INDEX OF SUBSIDIARIES, BRAND NAMES AND AFFILIATIONS

Brand or subsidiary, followed by the name of the related corporation

INDEX OF SUBSIDIARIES, BRAND NAMES AND AFFILIATIONS, CONT.

INDEX OF SUBSIDIARIES, BRAND NAMES AND AFFILIATIONS, CONT.

INDEX OF SUBSIDIARIES, BRAND NAMES AND AFFILIATIONS, CONT.

INDEX OF SUBSIDIARIES, BRAND NAMES AND AFFILIATIONS, CONT.

INDEX OF SUBSIDIARIES, BRAND NAMES AND AFFILIATIONS, CONT.

INDEX OF SUBSIDIARIES, BRAND NAMES AND AFFILIATIONS, CONT.

INDEX OF SUBSIDIARIES, BRAND NAMES AND AFFILIATIONS, CONT.

ICFS International LLC; **ZORLU ENERJI ELEKTRIK URETIM AS**
Idealab; **ESOLAR INC**
iGen; **IDATECH LLC**
Impedence Matching; **TIGO ENERGY**
Imperial Biotane; **IMPERIAL WESTERN PRODUCTS INC**
Imperium Grays Harbor; **IMPERIUM RENEWABLES INC**
IMS Service Enhancement Layer; **BELL LABS**
IMW Industries Ltd; **CLEAN ENERGY FUELS CORP**
Inbuilt; **RENEWABLE ENERGY SYSTEMS**
Industrial Design and Construction; **CH2M HILL COMPANIES LTD**
Inergy Automotive Systems; **SOLVAY SA**
Infinity; **NISSAN MOTOR CO LTD**
InfraStruXure; **AMERICAN POWER CONVERSION (APC)**
Inge Watertechnologies AG; **BASF SE**
Innovation Capital; **WINDLAB SYSTEMS**
Innovative Design Inc; **SOLARGENIX ENERGY LLC**
InoCep; **HYFLUX LTD**
Institute for Soldier Nanotechnologies; **DUPONT CENTRAL RESEARCH & DEVELOPMENT**
Intel Mobile Communications; **INTEL CORP**
Intel Research Labs; **INTEL CORP**
Intellipur; **PURFRESH**
IntelliSOURCE; **COMVERGE INC**
International Business Machines Corp (IBM); **IBM RESEARCH**
Investec Limited; **IDATECH LLC**
Iowa Thin Film Technologies; **POWERFILM INC**
Isofoton North America Inc; **ISOFOTON**
Israel Corp.; **BETTER PLACE**
iSun; **ICP SOLAR TECHNOLOGIES**
ITRON; **BADGER METER INC**
ITT Corporation; **XYLEM INC**
Ivanpah Solar Power Complex; **BRIGHTSOURCE ENERGY INC**
iWindow; **SERIOUS ENERGY INC**
JA Development Co Ltd; **JA SOLAR HOLDINGS CO LTD**
JA Solar Hong Kong Ltd; **JA SOLAR HOLDINGS CO LTD**
JA Solar USA Inc; **JA SOLAR HOLDINGS CO LTD**
Jacoby Development Inc; **GEOPLASMA LLC**
Jacoby Group (The); **GEOPLASMA LLC**
JENNY; **SFC ENERGY AG**
Jetstar Japan Co.; **MITSUBISHI CORP**
Jiangxi LDK Polysilicon; **LDK SOLAR CO LTD**
Jiangxi LDK Silicon; **LDK SOLAR CO LTD**
Jiangxi LDK Solar; **LDK SOLAR CO LTD**
Jiangxi Nobao Electronics Co Ltd; **NOBAO RENEWABLE ENERGY HOLDINGS LTD**

Jiangxi Photovoltaic Materials Co Ltd; **JINKOSOLAR HOLDING CO LTD**
JinkoSolar; **JINKOSOLAR HOLDING CO LTD**
JinkoSolar (U.S.) Inc; **JINKOSOLAR HOLDING CO LTD**
Johanna Solar Technology GmbH; **ALEO SOLAR AG**
JouleX Energy Manager; **JOULEX**
JouleX Energy Manager EnergyWise; **JOULEX**
JouleX Mobile; **JOULEX**
JSPV Contract; **ASIA ENVIRONMENT HOLDINGS LTD**
JSPV Design; **ASIA ENVIRONMENT HOLDINGS LTD**
JSPV Research; **ASIA ENVIRONMENT HOLDINGS LTD**
Juwi Solar GmbH; **DAYSTAR TECHNOLOGIES**
Karma; **FISKER AUTOMOTIVE**
Kennedy & Violich Architecture of Boston; **GLOBAL SOLAR ENERGY**
Kevlar; **DUPONT CENTRAL RESEARCH & DEVELOPMENT**
Kevlar; **DUPONT (E I DU PONT DE NEMOURS & CO)**
K-Fuel; **EVERGREEN ENERGY INC**
KFx Technology LLC; **EVERGREEN ENERGY INC**
Khosla Ventures; **LANZATECH LTD**
Khosla Ventures; **MASCOMA CORP**
Kilbraur Wind Energy Ltd; **GRUPPO FALCK SPA**
Kleiner Perkins Caufield & Byers; **TRANSPHORM**
Kleiner Perkins Caufield & Byers; **MASCOMA CORP**
Kleiner Perkins Caufield & Byers.; **KAIIMA AGRO-BIOTECH LTD**
KPCB; **GMZ ENERGY**
Kristal; **HYFLUX LTD**
Kyocera (Tianjin) Solar Energy Co Ltd; **KYOCERA SOLAR CORP**
Kyocera Corp; **KYOCERA SOLAR CORP**
Kyocera KD Modules; **KYOCERA SOLAR CORP**
Kyocera Solar Europe sro; **KYOCERA SOLAR CORP**
Kyocera Solar Inc; **KYOCERA SOLAR CORP**
Landscape; **SOLARONE SOLUTIONS LLC**
LB-1085; **SHARP CORPORATION**
LDK Optronics Technology Co; **LDK SOLAR CO LTD**
LDK Solar Europe Holding SA; **LDK SOLAR CO LTD**
LDK Solar USA Inc; **LDK SOLAR CO LTD**
Leading Edge Technologies, Inc.; **SOLICORE INC**
LEAF; **NISSAN MOTOR CO LTD**
Leaf Clean Energy Company; **SKYFUEL INC**
Leila lakes Wind Energy Facility LLC; **NACEL ENERGY CORP**
Lend Lease Ventures; **WINDLAB SYSTEMS**
Lewis Wind Power; **BRITISH ENERGY GROUP PLC**
Liberty Wind Turbines; **CLIPPER WINDPOWER LLC**
Life Science Group of HTA, Inc. (The); **HITACHI HIGH TECHNOLOGIES AMERICA INC**

INDEX OF SUBSIDIARIES, BRAND NAMES AND AFFILIATIONS, CONT.

INDEX OF SUBSIDIARIES, BRAND NAMES AND AFFILIATIONS, CONT.

INDEX OF SUBSIDIARIES, BRAND NAMES AND AFFILIATIONS, CONT.

INDEX OF SUBSIDIARIES, BRAND NAMES AND AFFILIATIONS, CONT.

Renault SA; **BETTER PLACE**
Renault-Nissan; **NISSAN MOTOR CO LTD**
Renew Power; **TEKION INC**
Renewable Energy Solutions LLC; **CHANGING WORLD TECHNOLOGIES INC**
REpower Australia Pty. Limited; **REPOWER SYSTEMS SE**
REpower Espana SL; **REPOWER SYSTEMS SE**
REpower Italia Srl; **REPOWER SYSTEMS SE**
REpower Systems AG; **SUZLON ENERGY LIMITED**
REpower Systems GmbH; **REPOWER SYSTEMS SE**
REpower UK Limited; **REPOWER SYSTEMS SE**
REpower USA Corporation; **REPOWER SYSTEMS SE**
RES Americas Inc; **RENEWABLE ENERGY SYSTEMS**
RES Group; **RENEWABLE ENERGY SYSTEMS**
Research Biotech; **SIGMA-ALDRICH CORP**
RESEARCH CONTROL; **BADGER METER INC**
Research Essentials; **SIGMA-ALDRICH CORP**
Research Specialties; **SIGMA-ALDRICH CORP**
Resomer; **EVONIK INDUSTRIES AG**
Resource Technology Corp; **SIGMA-ALDRICH CORP**
RFTR; **COMPACT POWER MOTORS GMBH**
Rhein Chemie; **LANXESS AG**
Riesfactoring; **GRUPPO FALCK SPA**
RIO; **CLIMATEWELL**
Risun Chemicals Company Ltd.; **CABOT CORPORATION**
Riverside Resource Recovery; **CORY ENVIRONMENTAL**
Robert Bosch GmbH; **BOSCH SOLAR ENERGY AG**
Rochem AG; **APTWATER INC**
Rocketdyne; **SOLARRESERVE**
Rogue; **NISSAN MOTOR CO LTD**
Rohm & Haas Company; **DOW CHEMICAL COMPANY (THE)**
Ronozyme NP; **NOVOZYMES**
Rotor Electricity Generation Inc; **ZORLU ENERJI ELEKTRIK URETIM AS**
Roundup; **MONSANTO CO**
Roundup Ready; **MONSANTO CO**
Royal Dutch Shell (Shell Group); **AVANCIS GMBH & CO KG**
Royal Dutch Shell (Shell Group); **SHELL OIL CO**
Royal Dutch Shell plc; **SHELL WINDENERGY BV**
RusEnergoSbyt LLC; **ENEL SPA**
S64; **SUZLON ENERGY LIMITED**
S66; **SUZLON ENERGY LIMITED**
S82; **SUZLON ENERGY LIMITED**
S88; **SUZLON ENERGY LIMITED**
S95; **SUZLON ENERGY LIMITED**
S97; **SUZLON ENERGY LIMITED**
SAB Technical Services; **SULZER LTD**
SABRE; **EMEFCY LTD**
Saczyme; **NOVOZYMES**

SAFC; **SIGMA-ALDRICH CORP**
Salt River Project; **RENEGY HOLDINGS INC**
Samsung Digital Imaging Co., Ltd.; **SAMSUNG ELECTRONICS CO LTD**
Samsung Electronics America; **SAMSUNG ELECTRONICS CO LTD**
Samsung Group; **SAMSUNG ELECTRONICS CO LTD**
SANYO Electric Company Ltd.; **PANASONIC CORPORATION**
SANYO Total Solution; **SANYO ELECTRIC COMPANY LTD**
Sasol Gas; **SASOL LIMITED**
Sasol Mining; **SASOL LIMITED**
Sasol Oil; **SASOL LIMITED**
Sasol Olefins & Surfactants; **SASOL LIMITED**
Sasol Petroleum International; **SASOL LIMITED**
Sasol Polymers; **SASOL LIMITED**
Sasol Synfuels; **SASOL LIMITED**
Sasol Synfuels International; **SASOL LIMITED**
Schneider Electric SA; **AMERICAN POWER CONVERSION (APC)**
Schneider Power Inc; **QUANTUM FUEL SYSTEMS TECHNOLOGIES WORLDWIDE INC**
SCHOTT AG; **SCHOTT SOLAR**
SCHOTT Poly; **SCHOTT SOLAR**
SCHOTT POWER POLY 275; **SCHOTT SOLAR**
SCIenergy Cloud; **SCIENERGY**
Scientific Conservation; **SCIENERGY**
Scientific Nanomedicine Inc; **MANHATTAN SCIENTIFICS INC**
Score; **SYNGENTA AG**
Scottish and Southern Energy plc; **AIRTRICITY**
Scripps-PARC Institute; **PALO ALTO RESEARCH CENTER (PARC)**
SecureMesh WAN (The); **TRILLIANT**
Seebeck; **O-FLEXX TECHNOLOGIES GMBH**
Seed Consultants, Inc.,; **DUPONT (E I DU PONT DE NEMOURS & CO)**
Self-Aligned Cell; **1366 TECHNOLOGIES INC**
Seminis; **MONSANTO CO**
Senior Scientific LLC; **MANHATTAN SCIENTIFICS INC**
Sensation; **NANOMIX INC**
SeQuential-Pacific Biodiesel LLC; **SEQUENTIAL BIOFUELS LLC**
Serious Change LP; **GENERAL COMPRESSION**
SeriousCapital; **SERIOUS ENERGY INC**
SeriousEnergy Manager; **SERIOUS ENERGY INC**
SeriousWindows; **SERIOUS ENERGY INC**
SERIS; **TRINA SOLAR LTD**
Servidyne; **SCIENERGY**
Shanghai Electric Solar Energy Co Ltd; **BOSCH SOLAR ENERGY AG**
Shanghai Jinglong Solar Technology Co., Ltd.; **JA SOLAR HOLDINGS CO LTD**

INDEX OF SUBSIDIARIES, BRAND NAMES AND AFFILIATIONS, CONT.

INDEX OF SUBSIDIARIES, BRAND NAMES AND AFFILIATIONS, CONT.

INDEX OF SUBSIDIARIES, BRAND NAMES AND AFFILIATIONS, CONT.

INDEX OF SUBSIDIARIES, BRAND NAMES AND AFFILIATIONS, CONT.

INDEX OF SUBSIDIARIES, BRAND NAMES AND AFFILIATIONS, CONT.

CPSIA information can be obtained at www.ICGtesting.com
Printed in the USA
LVOW032201230412

278870LV00004B/2/P